Reference Guide to

WORLD LITERATURE

THIRD EDITION

VOLUME 2

ST. JAMES REFERENCE GUIDES

American Literature

English Literature, 3 vols.

French Literature, 2 vols.

Holocaust Literature

Short Fiction

World Literature, 2 vols.

Reference Guide to

WORLD LITERATURE

THIRD EDITION

Volume 2
WORKS
INDEX

EDITORS
SARA PENDERGAST
and
TOM PENDERGAST

ST. JAMES
PRESS®

Detroit • New York • San Diego • San Francisco • Cleveland • New Haven, Conn. • Waterville, Maine • London • Munich

THOMSON

★ ™

GALE

Reference Guide to World Literature, 3rd edition

Sara and Tom Pendergast

Project Editor
Kristin Hart

Editorial
Erin Bealmear, Joann Cerrito, Jim Craddock,
Stephen Cusack, Miranda H. Ferrara, Peter

M. Gareffa, Margaret Mazurkiewicz, Carol
A. Schwartz, Christine Tomassini, Michael
J. Tyrkus

Manufacturing
Rhonda Williams

LIBRARY OF CONGRESS CATALOG NUMBER

Reference guide to world literature / editors, Sara Pendergast, Tom
Pendergast.— 3rd ed.
    p. cm.
Includes bibliographical references and index.
    ISBN 1-55862-490-2 (hardcover : set) — ISBN 1-55862-491-0 (v. 1) —
ISBN 1-55862-492-9 (v. 2)
    1. Literature—History and criticism. I. Pendergast, Sara. II.
Pendergast, Tom.
PN524.R44 2003
809—dc21

2002015410

ISBN: 1-55862-490-2

CONTENTS

EDITOR'S NOTE

You are holding in your hands the third edition of the *Reference Guide to World Literature*, the second edition of which was published in 1995 and was itself an updated and expanded edition of *Great Foreign Language Writers*, published in 1984. Expanding on the coverage of these earlier works, the present edition contains some 1100 entries, divided nearly evenly between entries on writers and literary works. The scope of the *Reference Guide* spans recorded history and reaches up to the present.

The Reference Guide to World Literature contains two distinct types of entries: those covering the work of an author and those covering a literary work. Each author entry begins with a biographical summary of the subject and includes details (where known) of the author's birth, education and training, military service, family, career, awards, honors, and honorary degrees. Then follows a selected list of publications by the author, and a selected list of bibliographical and critical works about the author. Finally, each author entry contains a signed critical essay which assesses the author's work, reputation, and influence. Each entry on a literary work contains a brief header indicating the author and date of creation and a signed critical essay. In the case that the author of the literary work is unknown, an introductory section provides information about the known circumstances of the work's creation and a brief listing of critical studies about the work.

The publications section of the author entries attempts to account for all separately published books by the author, including translations into English. Broadsheets, single sermons and lectures, minor pamphlets, exhibition catalogs, etc., are omitted. Dates refer to the first publication in book form unless indicated otherwise; we have attempted to list the actual year of publication, which is sometimes different from the date given on the title page. Reprints of works including facsimile editions are generally not listed unless they involve a revision of the title. Titles are given in modern spelling and are often in "short" form. They are always in italic, except for those that are literal (i.e. non-published) translations, which appear in square brackets. The publication list may contain some or all of the following categories:

Collections: This contains a selection of "standard" editions, including the most recent collection of the complete works and of the individual genres (verse, plays, fiction, etc.). For those collections published after the author's death, only those that have some editorial authority are cited.

Fiction: Where it is not made apparent by the title, collections of short fiction are indicated by the inclusion of "stories" in parentheses after the title.

Verse: This includes collections and individual poems that were published in book form, listed chronologically by date of publication.

Plays: This includes original plays, adaptations, and other works for the stage (libretti, ballet scenarios, etc.). Dates for both publication and production are given. Titles are arranged chronologically by date of first performance or date of first publication, whichever is earliest. Published English translations are listed, but not those of individual productions.

Screenplays/Television Plays/Radio Plays: These categories include original works and adaptations for these media, listed by date of release or first broadcast.

Other: This includes publications that do not fit readily into the above categories, principally miscellanies and nonfiction writing, such as journalism, essays, theoretical works, travel writing, memoirs, letters, etc.

A separate section contains selected works about the author. This section may contain one or both of the following categories:

Bibliography: This includes published works relating to primary and secondary literature. General bibliographies of literary periods, genres, or counties, etc., are rarely listed.

Critical Studies: This includes critical works and biographies of the subject, listed in chronological order of publication. This section concentrates on book-length studies in English published after 1945, although in a few cases selected earlier material is cited. Where there is a noticeable scarcity of critical works in English, publications written in the subject's own language are included. On occasion articles, usually written in English, have also been listed.

This book concludes with a Title Index to the publications lists. This contains titles of all works listed in the fiction, verse, and plays sections of each entry including titles in the writer's original language and English translations, as well as selected important works of nonfiction.

ACKNOWLEDGMENTS

A reference work such as this is the product of many hands. Our thanks begin with Steven Serafin, whose guiding hand in selecting advisers and entries and whose expertise with the languages represented in this collection were indispensable. We would like to thank our advisers for their skill and expertise in selecting suitable entrants to include in this edition. Thanks also to the authors of the entries; many of these authors are the acknowledged authorities on their subject, and their expertise and acumen can be clearly seen in their thoughtful introductions to each of the subjects. We would like to thank our copyeditors, Jennifer Wallace and Michael Najjar, as well as our contacts/friends Kristin Hart and Peter Gareffa at St. James Press. Finally, we would like to thank all those at St. James Press whose names we do not know, but who help turn the electronic files that we work with into the reality that you hold today.

INTRODUCTION

In his letters dating from the second century AD, the Roman orator and statesman Pliny the Younger wrote of finding solace in poetry as a means to embrace the uncertainties of life and to accept, albeit reluctantly, the inevitability of death. "Literature," he said, "is both my joy and my comfort: it can add to every happiness and there is no sorrow it cannot console." The poet took refuge in his work and sought to communicate to others the depth of his emotion and the expanse of his intellect. It is through literature that we embrace our potential and acknowledge our limitations, and it was undoubtedly this presence of mind and spirit that forged the first attempts at literary expression and that continues in our own time to define the essence and value of artistic endeavor.

The growth and development of literature is most often viewed as a reflection of history, mapping the evolution of human culture and serving in its earliest renderings as either documentation or eulogy: to record for posterity or to sing praise and exaltation. It was a task assigned to the scribe not the artist, but in time the purpose and practice of literature would evolve in form and meaning to where the telling of the tale became as important as the tale itself. The nature of literature broadened in scope and objective to provide entertainment as well as instruction. As a result, the reader found pleasure in literature as the imagination unfolded in stories of gods and monsters, the death of kings, and the making of legend. If we believe as posited by philosopher Bernard Berenson that literature is "the autobiography of humanity," then we come to better know ourselves by knowing those who came before us and those with whom we share our existence. In effect, literature becomes a means to examine and to understand the differences, as well as the similarities, among peoples, languages, and societies. It serves to engage our expectation, to enrich our sensibilities, and to elevate our perception of self-awareness and identity.

Designed as a complement to the St. James Reference Guides to American and British literatures, the third edition of the *Reference Guide to World Literature* represents a comprehensive and authoritative survey to literatures written in languages other than English from the earliest known manuscripts to the works of present-day writers of international stature. Merging East and West, the ancient with the contemporary, the *Reference Guide* provides a broad spectrum of world literature extending from the anonymous prose and verse of the *Vedas*, the sacred texts of Hinduism, originating in the third millennium BC, to the ancient Sumerian epic of *Gilgamesh*; from the Hebrew texts of the Old Testament to *The Iliad* of Homer; from the Golden Age of Greek drama to the Indian folk epic the *Mahābhārata*; from the *Confessions* of St. Augustine to the classical poetry of the Tang dynasty; from *The Conference of the Birds* by the Persian poet Farid al-Din Attār to *The Divine Comedy* by Dante Alighiera; from *The Praise of Folly* by Desiderius Erasmus to *Don Quixote* by Miguel de Cervantes; from Molière's *Don Juan* to Goethe's *Faust*; from realism and naturalism to the advent of modernism; from existentialism to the theater of the absurd; from postmodernism to the literature of the new millennium.

The present edition provides expanded coverage of literatures in less represented languages, the primary focus being Arabic, Chinese, and Japanese, as well as previously unrepresented languages including Albanian, Estonian, Indonesian, Kurdish, and Thai. Writers from the Arab world added to the edition include the pre-Islamic poet Imru' al-Qays, the poetess al-Khansā', the classical poet al-Mutanabbī, the Andalusian poet Ibn Khafājah, and the Sufi poets Ibn al-Fārid and Ibn al-'Arabī and contemporary authors such as the Iranian novelist and short-story writer Jalal Al-e Ahmad, the Egyptian short-story writer and dramatist Yūsuf Idrīs, and the Syrian-Lebanese poet Adūnīs. Chinese authors include the Ming dynasty dramatist Tang Xianzu, the novelist Ding Ling, and dramatist, novelist, and Nobel laureate Gao Xingjian. Japanese authors include poets Miyazawa Kenji, Hagiwara Sakutaro, and Nishiwaki Junzaburo and novelists Lao She, Shimazaki Toson, Shiga Naoya, Ibuse Masuji, and Abe Kobo.

Authors writing in previously unrepresented languages include the Albanian novelist and poet Ismail Kadaré, the Estonian poet Jaan Kaplinski and the poet and novelist Jaan Kross, the Indonesian novelist Pramoedya Ananta Toer and the poet Chairil Anwar, the Kurdish poet Abdulla Goran, and the Thai novelist Siburapha. Authors from previously underrepresented literatures include East and Central European writers such as the dramatist Václav Havel, the novelist Ivan Klíma, and the novelist Milan Kundera, writing in Czech; the short-story writer and poet Tadeusz Borowski, and the poet and dramatist Tadeusz Różewicz, writing in Polish; francophone and lusophone writers from North, East, and West Africa including the Moroccan novelist and poet Tahar Ben Jelloun and the novelist Abdelkebir Khatibi, the Tunisian novelist Albert Memmi, and the Ivorian novelist Ahmadou Kourouma, writing in French, and Mozambican poet José Craveirinha, writing in Portuguese.

This edition is also noteworthy for its expanded coverage of contemporary women writers, including the Lebanese novelist Evelyne Accad, the Algerian novelist Assia Djebar, and the Canadian poet and novelist Nicole Brossard, writing in French; the Chilean novelist Isabel Allende, the Nicaraguan poet and novelist Gioconda Belli, and the Argentinian novelist Luisa Valenzuela, writing in Spanish; the Polish poet and Nobel laureate Wisława Szymborska; the Indian novelist Qurratulain Hyder, writing in Urdu; the

Italian novelist Francesca Duranti; the Russian novelist Tatyana Tolstaya; the Japanese novelist Tsushima Yuko; and the Chinese short-story writer and novelist Li Ang. Within the context of the social and political transformation from the postwar twentieth century to the present, the increasing representation and contribution of women on an international basis has redefined the scope and dimension of world literature. Other major contemporary authors include the Martinican novelist Patrick Chamoiseau, writing in French; the Hungarian novelist and short-story writer Péter Esterházy, the Danish novelist Peter Høeg; the Chinese poet Bei Dao and the novelists Mo Yan and Su Tong; and the Japanese novelist Murakami Haruki.

Literature in the new millennium is complex as it is convoluted, informed by diverse and elements: postmodernism, multiculturalism, and global diaspora. Yet it is the voice of Pliny the Younger that resonates to remind us of the true essence of literary endeavor: to bring joy and comfort; to provide inspiration and understanding; to justify our being; and to bear witness on the times in which we live. As noted by author Salman Rushdie, ''Literature is where I go to explore the highest and lowest places in human society and in the human spirit, where I hope to find not absolute truth but the truth of the tale, of the imagination and of the heart.''

—Steven R. Serafin
Hunter College of the City University of New York

ADVISERS

Roger Allen
University of Pennsylvania

Alison Bailey
University of London

Christopher Cairns
University College, Wales

Marvin Carlson
CUNY, New York

Ruby Cohn
University of California, Davis

Bogdan Czaykowski
University of British Columbia

James Diggle
Queen's College, Cambridge

David William Foster
Arizona State University

Michael Freeman
University of Leicester

Janet Garton
University of East Anglia, Norwich

Howard Goldblatt
University of Notre Dame

Theo Hermans
University College, London

Hosea Hirata
Tufts University

Peter Hutchinson
Trinity Hall, Cambridge

R.S. McGregor
University of Cambridge

A.B. McMillin
University of London

David O'Connell
Georgia State University

P.A. Odber de Baubeta
University of Birmingham

Jerzy Peterkiewicz
London

Christopher R. Pike
University of Keele

Girdar Rathi
New Delhi

Sven H. Rossel
University of Vienna

Steven Serafin
Hunter College, CUNY, New York

G. Singh
formerly of Queen's
    University, Belfast

Peter Skrine
University of Bristol

Daniel Weissbort
University of Iowa

CONTRIBUTORS

Donald Adamson
Peter F. Ainsworth
Robin Aizlewood
Ahmed Ali
Margrethe Alexandroni
Hans Christian Andersen
J.K. Anderson
D.J. Andrews
Alireza Anushiravani
Brigitte Edith Zapp Archibald
A. James Arnold
William Arrowsmith
B. Ashbrook
Keith Aspley
Stuart Atkins
Howard Atkinson
Harry Aveling
Peter Avery

K.P. Bahadur
Ehrhard Bahr
D.R. Shackleton Bailey
David M. Bain
Barry Baldwin
Aida A. Bamia
Alan F. Bance
Gabrielle Barfoot
John Barsby
Peter I. Barta
Susan Bassnett
Edward Batley
Roderick Beaton
Janine Beichman
David Bell
Ian A. Bell
Thomas G. Bergin
Alan Best
Binghong Lu
Sandra Blane
Elizabeth Bobrick
Joan Booth
Paul W. Borgeson, Jr.
Patrick Brady
Denis Brass
Gerard J. Brault
S.H. Braund
Peter Broome
Michael Brophy
Catherine Savage Brosman
Gordon Brotherston
Jennifer Brown
Penny Brown
Dorothy Bryson
A.W. Bulloch
Alan Bullock
B. Burns

J.M. Buscall

Alessandro Cancian
Francisco Carenas
Steven D. Carter
Anthony J. Cascardi
Remo Catani
Philip Cavendish
Mary Ann Caws
Andrea C. Cervi
C. Chadwick
Roland A. Champagne
Linda H. Chance
Tom Cheeseman
Ying-Ying Chein
Diana Chlebek
Erik C. Christensen
Mirna Cicioni
John R. Clark
Stephen Clark
Shirley Clarke
David Coad
Michael Collie
Desmond J. Conacher
David Constantine
Ray Cooke
Thomas L. Cooksey
Neil Cornwell
C.D.N. Costa
Sally McMullen (Croft)
Carmen Cross
G.P. Cubbin
Jan Čulík
James M. Curtis
G.F. Cushing
Edmund Cusick
Adam Czerniawski
Lóránt Czigány

James N. Davidson
Catherine Davies
Santiago Daydi-Tolson
René de Costa
Alan Deighton
John Dickie
Sheila J. Dickson
C.E.J. Dolamore
Ken Dowden
Sam Driver
John Dunkley
Osman Durrani

Gwynne Edwards
Stanislaw Eile
Sarah Ekdawi
Robert Elsie

Herman Ermolaev
Jo Evans

Michael Falchikov
Nancy Kanach Fehsenfeld
Jane Fenoulhet
Alvaro Fernández-Bravo
Bruno Ferraro
John Fletcher
John L. Flood
A.P. Foulkes
Wallace Fowlie
Frank J. Frost
Barbara P. Fulks
Michael A. Fuller

David Gascoyne
John Gatt-Rutter
Tina Gianoulis
Margaret Gibson
Robert Gibson
Mary E. Giles
Donald Gilman
Nahum N. Glatzer
John Gledson
Gary Godfrey
Ingeborg M. Goesll
Marketa Goetz-Stankiewicz
Janet N. Gold
Sander M. Goldberg
George Gömöri
D.C.R.A. Goonetilleke
Colin Graham
Peter J. Graves
Roger Green
R.P.H. Green
Claire E. Gruzelier
Albert E. Gurganus

Oscar A. Haac
David T. Haberly
Brigid Haines
Igor Hájek
David M. Halperin
P.T. Harries
Nigel Harris
Patricia Harry
John Hart
Thomas R. Hart
E.C. Hawkesworth
Ronald Hayman
Patrick Heenan
John Hibberd
James Higgins
David Hill
Sabine Hillen

Ian Hilton
Hosea Hirata
Keith Hitchins
Leighton Hodson
Th. Emil Homerin
Edward Waters Hood
Louise Hopkins
Thomas K. Hubbard
Lothar Huber
William M. Hutchins
Lois Boe Hyslop

Margaret C. Ives

David Jackson
Tony James
Regina Janes
D.E. Jenkinson
Lewis Jillings
Jeffrey Johnson
D. Mervyn Jones
Roger Jones
W. Glyn Jones

Bożena Karwowska
Brian Keith-Smith
Hanaa Kilany
Rachel Killick
J.H. King
Peter King
Robert Kirsner
W.J.S. Kirton
Charles Klopp
A.V. Knowles
Wulf Koepke
Jack Kolbert
Kathleen L. Komar
Linn Bratteteig Konrad
David Konstan
Myrto Konstantarakos
Charles Kwong

F.J. Lamport
Jordan Lancaster
Pierre J. Lapaire
David H.J. Larmour
Rex W. Last
Dan Latimer
Renate Latimer
John Lee
Mabel Lee
André Lefevere
Harry Levin
Silvano Levy
Virginia L. Lewis
Dian Li
Emanuele Licastro
Sylvia Li-Chun Lin
Maria Manuel Lisboa
Heather Lloyd

Rosemary Lloyd
Ladislaus Löb
Rosa Lombardi
Jacqueline Long
Dagmar C.G. Lorenz
Andrea Loselle
Gregory L. Lucente
David S. Luft
Torborg Lundell
Christopher Lupke

J.F. Marfany
Gaetana Marrone
Heitor Martins
David Maskell
Eve Mason
Haydn Mason
Derek Maus
Gita May
Jane McAdoo
E.A. McCobb
Patrick McCarthy
A. McDermott
David McDuff
Richard J.A. McGregor
Martin L. McLaughlin
Alexander G. McKay
Keith McMahon
Arnold McMillin
Rory McTurk
Gordon McVay
A.J. Meech
Siegfried Mews
Vasa D. Mihailovich
Michael J. Mikós
Gary B. Miles
Paul Allen Miller
Kristina Milnor
Earl Miner
John Douglas Minyard
Masao Miyoshi
Matthew Mizenko
Edward Moran
Nicole Mosher
Warren Motte
Anna Lydia Motto
Vanna Motta
Kenneth Muir
Brian Murdoch
S.M. Murk-Jansen
Brian Murphy
Walter Musolino

William E. Naff
Susan Napier
Frank J. Nisetich
Paul Norlen

R.J. Oakley
Jeanne A. Ojala

Tom O'Neill
Dayna Oscherwitz

Seija Paddon
Cecil Parrott
Alan K.G. Paterson
Georgina Paul
D. Keith Peacock
Noel A. Peacock
Roger Pearson
Janet Pérez
Elli Philokyprou
Donald Peter Alexander Pirie
David Platton
Gordon Pocock
Beth Pollack
Valentina Polukhina
Charles A. Porter
Oralia Preble-Niemi
Michael P. Predmore
Nicole Prunster
Joseph Pucci
Judith Purver
Dušan Puvačić

Olga Ragusa
Ana M. Ranero
Judy Rawson
J.H. Reid
Robert Reid
John H. Reilly
Barbara Reynolds
Hugh Ridley
Norma Rinsler
Colin Riordan
Michael Robinson
Philip E.J. Robinson
David Rock
Eamonn Rodgers
Margaret Rogister
Michele Valerie Ronnick
Hugh Rorrison
Wendy Rosslyn
John Rothenberg
Andrew Rothwell
Donald Roy
Lisa M. Ruch
R.B. Rutherford

William Merritt Sale, III
Thomas Salumets
Jeffrey L. Sammons
N.K. Sandars
L. Natalie Sandomirsky
Gerlinde Ulm Sanford
Hélène N. Sanko
Kumiko Sato
Barbara Saunders
Barry P. Scherr
Gerd K. Schneider

Thomas Schnellbächer
Irene Scobbie
Mary Scott
Edward Seidensticker
Dorothy S. Severin
Sabina Sharkey
Jocelyn Sharlet
Ruth Sharman
Barnett Shaw
David Shaw
Faiza W. Shereen
Emi Shimokawa
Shoichi Saeki
David Sices
Tony Simoes da Silva
John D. Simons
Colin Smethurst
Christopher Smith
Natalie Smith
Sarah Cox Smith
David Smyth
J. Kelly Sowards
Ronald Speirs
James Russell Stamm
Noel Stanley
Roy Starrs
Paul Starkey
C.C. Stathatos
Susan Isabel Stein
Carl Steiner
R.H. Stephenson
Eric Sterling
Mary E. Stewart

Alexander Stillmark
Elisabeth C. Stopp
Ian C. Storey
Matthew Strecher
Sarah Strong
J.R. Stubbs
Arrigo V. Subiotto
Mary Sugar
Henry W. Sullivan
Helena Szépe
Elzbieta Szoka

John E. Tailby
Myron Taylor
Anna-Marie Taylor
Philip Thody
David Thomas
Judith Thurman
Shawkat M. Toorawa
Robert M. Torrance
Tamara Trojanowska
Andrew T. Tsubaki

Sabine Vanacker
Rolf Venner
Hugo J. Verani
Maïr Verthuy
Robert Vilain
Pascale Voilley

Frank W. Walbank
Bruce Walker

Albert H. Wallace
George Walsh
J. Michael Walton
Edward Wasiolek
Bruce Watson
Shawncey J. Webb
David Welsh
Alfred D. White
Sally A. White-Wallis
Kenneth S. Whitton
Juliet Wigmore
Faith Wigzell
Mark Williams
Rhys Williams
Jason Wilson
Jerry Phillips Winfield
Michael Winkler
A.J. Woodman
M.J. Woods
Tim Woods
James B. Woodward
A. Colin Wright
Barbara Wright
Elizabeth Wright

Xiaobin Yang
John D. Yohannan
Howard T. Young
Robin Young

Magdalena J. Zaborowska
G. Zanker
Jeanne Morgan Zarucchi

ALPHABETICAL LIST OF WRITERS AND WORKS

Abe Kōbō
The Woman in the Dunes
Evelyne Accad
Arthur Adamov
Professor Taranne
Adonis
Aeschylus
The Oresteia
The Persians
Prometheus Bound
The Seven Against Thebes
The Suppliant Maidens
S. Y. Agnon
Demetrio Aguilera Malta
Anna Akhmatova
Poem Without a Hero
Requiem
Akutagawa Ryūnosuke
al-Qasim ibn 'Ali Abu Muhammad
al-Basri al-Hariri
al-Khansa'
Ahmad ibn al-Husayn Abu al-Tayyib
al-Ju'fi al-Kindi al-Mutanabbi
Imru' al-Qays
Alain-Fournier
The Wanderer
Rafael Alberti
Jalâl Âl-e Ahmad
Plagued by the West
Vicente Aleixandre
Vittorio Alfieri
Saul
Dante Alighieri
The Divine Comedy
The New Life
Isabel Allende
The House of the Spirits
Jorge Amado
Anacreon
Hans Christian Andersen
"The Emperor's New Clothes"
"The Snow Queen"
Carlos Drummond de Andrade
Mário de Andrade
Ivo Andrić
The Bridge on the Drina
Jerzy Andrzejewski
Ashes and Diamonds
Jean Anouilh
Antigone
Chairil Anwar
Guillaume Apollinaire
"La Chanson du mal-aimé"
"Zone"
Apollonius of Rhodes

Lucius Apuleius
Cupid and Psyche
Louis Aragon
Le Crève-coeur
Paris Peasant
Reinaldo Arenas
Pietro Aretino
La Cortigiana
José María Arguedas
Deep Rivers
Manlio Argueta
Ludovico Ariosto
Orlando Furioso
Aristophanes
The Birds
The Clouds
The Frogs
Lysistrata
Aristotle
Bettina von Arnim
Antonin Artaud
The Theatre and its Double
Miguel Ángel Asturias
The President
Farid al-Din Abu Hamid
Mohammad Attār
The Conference of the Birds
Aucassin and Nicolette
St. Augustine
The City of God
Confessions, Book I
Marcus Aurelius
Meditations
Decimus Magnus Ausonius
The Mosella
Marcel Aymé
Isaak Babel
Red Cavalry
Ingeborg Bachmann
Bai Juyi
Honoré de Balzac
Cousin Bette
Eugenie Grandet
Lost Illusions
Le Père Goriot
Henri Barbusse
Under Fire: The Story of a Squad
Bashō
Giorgio Bassani
Charles Baudelaire
"Spleen"
"To The Reader"
"Windows"
Beaumarchais
The Barber of Seville

Simone de Beauvoir
The Mandarins
The Second Sex
Samuel Beckett
Endgame
Molloy, Malone Dies, The Unnamable
Waiting for Godot
Bei Dao
Gioconda Belli
Andrei Belyi
Petersburg
Pietro Bembo
Tahar Ben Jelloun
Gottfried Benn
"Palau"
Georges Bernanos
Thomas Bernhard
The Lime Works
Ugo Betti
Bhagavadgītā
The Bible
Willem Bilderdijk
Bjørnstjerne Bjørnson
Peasant Tales
Aleksandr Blok
The Twelve
Johannes Bobrowski
Giovanni Boccaccio
"The Ninth Tale of the Fifth Day of *The Decameron*"
Boethius
The Consolation of Philosophy
Nicolas Boileau
The Art Of Poetry
Heinrich Böll
Group Portrait with Lady
The Lost Honor of Katharina Blum
Jorge Luis Borges
"Death and the Compass"
Tadeusz Borowski
Sebastian Brant
The Ship of Fools
Robert Brasillach
Bertolt Brecht
Baal
The Caucasian Chalk Circle
The Good Person of Szechwan
The Life of Galileo
Mother Courage and her Children
The Threepenny Opera
Gerbrand Adriaensz Bredero

CHRONOLOGICAL LIST OF WRITERS

fl. 8th century BC(?)	Homer
fl. c. 700 BC	Hesiod
c. 612 BC– ?	Sappho
c. 570 BC–c. 475 BC	Anacreon
525/524 BC–456 BC	Aeschylus
518/522 BC–438/446 BC	Pindar
c. 496 BC–406 BC	Sophocles
484 BC–420 BC	Herodotus
480/485 BC–c. 406 BC	Euripides
c. 460 BC–c. 399 BC	Thucydides
c. 450 BC–c. 385 BC	Aristophanes
c. 431 BC–c. 354 BC	Xenophon
c. 429 BC–347 BC	Plato
384 BC–322 BC	Aristotle
384 BC–322 BC	Demosthenes
c. 370 BC–c. 287 BC	Theophrastus
c. 342 BC–c. 295 BC	Menander
c. 300 BC– ?	Theocritus
c. 254 BC–c. 184 BC	Plautus
fl. 250 BC	Apollonius
fl. 250 BC	Callimachus
239 BC–169 BC	Ennius
c. 200 BC–c. 118 BC	Polybius
c. 190 BC–159 BC	Terence
106 BC–43 BC	Cicero
c. 100 BC–44 BC	Caesar
c. 99 BC–c. 55 BC	Lucretius
86 BC–35 BC	Sallust
c. 84 BC–c. 54 BC	Catullus
70 BC–19 BC	Virgil
65 BC–8 BC	Horace
64/59 BC–AD 12/17	Livy
c. 57 BC–19/18 BC	Tibullus
57/50 BC–c. 16 BC	Propertius
43 BC–AD 17	Ovid
c. 4 BC–AD 65	Seneca
c. AD 30–c. AD 104	Martial
AD 34–AD 62	Persius
c. AD 35–c. AD 100	Quintilian
AD 39–AD 65	Lucan
c. AD 46–c. AD 120	Plutarch
AD 50–AD 130	Juvenal
c. AD 56–c. AD 116	Tacitus
d. AD 66	Petronius
c. AD 69–AD 160	Suetonius
c. AD 120–after AD 180	Lucian
AD 121–AD 180	Aurelius
c. AD 123–after 163 AD	Apuleius
2nd/3rd century AD	Longus
c. AD 310–c. AD 395	Ausonius
fl. late 4th century AD	Claudian
c. AD 347–AD 420	St. Jerome
AD 348–AD 405	Prudentius
AD 354–AD 430	St. Augustine
AD 365–427	Tao Qian
fl. c. AD 400	Kālidāsa
c. AD 480–AD 524	Boethius
c. 497–545	Imru Al-Qays
c. 575–646	Al-Khansa'
701/705–762	Li Bai
712–770	Du Fu
772–846	Bai Juyi
c. 915–965	Al-Mutanabbi
c. 935–c. 1020	Abu'l Qāsim Ferdowsi
c. 978– ?	Murasaki Shikibu
1037–1101	Su Shi
1048–1131	Omar Khayyam
1054–1122	Al-Hariri
c. 1058–1139	Ibn Khafajah
c. 1118–1190	Saigyo
c. 1130–1220/1231	Farid al-Din Attār
1160–1210/1220	Hartmann von Aue
c. 1165–1240	Ibn Al-'Arabi
fl. c. 1170	Chrétien de Troyes
c. 1170–c. 1230	Walther von der Vogelweide
1179–1241	Snorri Sturluson
c. 1181–1235	Ibn Al-Farid
fl. late 12th century	Marie de France
fl. 1195–1220	Wolfram von Eschenbach
fl. c. 1200	Gottfried von Strassburg
1207–1273	Jalalu'd-Din Rumi
1209–1292	Muslih-al-Din Sa'di
fl. c. 1250	Hadewijch
c. 1255–1300	Guido Cavalcanti
1265–1321	Dante Alighieri
c. 1283–1352	Kenko
c. 1300(?)–1377	Guillaume de Machaut
1304–1374	Petrarch
1313–1375	Giovanni Boccaccio
1325/26–1389/90	Shams al-Din Muhammad Hafiz
c. 1337– ?	Jean Froissart
1363–1443	Zeami
c. 1365–c. 1430	Christine de Pizan
c. 1430– ?	François Villon
1456–1530	Jacopo Sannazaro
1457–1521	Sebastian Brant
c. 1465–c. 1536	Gil Vicente
1467–1536	Desiderius Erasmus
1469–1527	Niccolò Machiavelli
1470–1520	Bernardo Dovizi da Bibbiena
1470–1547	Pietro Bembo
1474–1533	Ludovico Ariosto
1478/c. 1530–1583/1610	Sūrdās
1478–1529	Baldassarre Castiglione
1483–1546	Martin Luther
1483(?)–1553	François Rabelais
1492–1547	Vittoria Colonna
1492–1549	Marguerite de Navarre
1492–1556	Pietro Aretino
1494–1576	Hans Sachs
c. 1495–1542	Ruzzante
1498–1546/47	Mīrā Bāī

d. 1518	Kabīr
1522–1566	Joachim Du Bellay
c. 1524–1554	Gaspara Stampa
1524/25–1580	Luís de Camões
1524–1585	Pierre de Ronsard
1530–1584	Jan Kochanowski
1532–1623	Tulsīdās
1533–1592	Michel de Montaigne
1544–1595	Torquato Tasso
1548–1600	Giordano Bruno
1550–1616	Tang Xianzu
1567(?)–1625	Honoré d'Urfé
1568–1639	Tommaso Campanella
1581–1647	Pieter Corneliszoon Hooft
1585–1618	Gerbrandt Bredero
1587–1679	Joost van den Vondel
1596–1687	Constantijn Huygens
1606–1684	Pierre Corneille
1610–1660	Paul Scarron
1613–1680	François La Rochefoucauld
1616–1664	Andreas Gryphius
1619–1655	Cyrano de Bergerac
1620–1664	Count Miklós Zrínyi
1621–1695	Jean de La Fontaine
1622–1673	Molière
1622–1676	Hans Jakob Christoffel von Grimmelshausen
1623–1662	Blaise Pascal
1628–1703	Charles Perrault
1634–1693	Madame de Lafayette
1636–1711	Nicolas Boileau
1639–1699	Jean Racine
1642–1693	Ihara Saikaku
1644–1694	Bashō
1651–1695	Sor Juana Inés de la Cruz
1653–1725	Chikamatsu Monzaemon
1668–1747	Alain-René Lesage
1684–1754	Ludvig Holberg
1688–1763	Marivaux
1694–1778	Voltaire
1697–1763	Abbé Prévost
1698–1782	Pietro Metastasio
1707–1793	Carlo Goldoni
1712–1778	Jean-Jacques Rousseau
1713–1784	Denis Diderot
1724–1803	Friedrich Gottlieb Klopstock
1729–1781	Gotthold Ephraim Lessing
1732–1799	Beaumarchais
1733–1813	Christoph Martin Wieland
1740–1814	Marquis de Sade
1741–1803	Choderlos de Laclos
1745–1792	Denis Fonvizin
1749–1803	Vittorio Alfieri
1749–1832	Johann Wolfgang von Goethe
1751–1792	Jakob Michael Reinhold Lenz
1756–1831	Willem Bilderdijk
1759–1805	Friedrich von Schiller
1766–1817	Madame de Staël
1767–1845	August Wilhelm von Schlegel
1768–1848	Chateaubriand
1770–1843	Friedrich Hölderlin
1772–1801	Novalis
1772–1829	Friedrich von Schlegel
1773–1853	Ludwig Tieck
1775(?)–1831	Caroline de la Motte Fouqué
1776–1822	E.T.A. Hoffmann
1777–1811	Heinrich von Kleist
1777–1843	Friedrich de la Motte Fouqué
1778–1842	Clemens Brentano
1781–1838	Adelbert von Chamisso
1783–1842	Stendhal
1785–1859	Bettina von Arnim
1785–1863	Jacob Grimm
1785–1873	Alessandro Manzoni
1786–1859	Wilhelm Grimm
1788–1857	Joseph von Eichendorff
1790–1869	Alphonse de Larmartine
1791–1861	Eugène Scribe
1791–1872	Franz Grillparzer
1795–1829	Aleksandr Griboedov
1797–1848	Annette von Droste-Hülshoff
1797–1854	Jeremias Gotthelf
1797–1856	Heinrich Heine
1797–1863	Alfred de Vigny
1797–1869	Asadullāh Khān Ghālib
1798–1837	Giacomo Leopardi
1798–1855	Adam Mickiewicz
1799–1837	Aleksandr Pushkin
1799–1850	Honoré de Balzac
1800–1855	Mihály Vörösmarty
1801–1836	Christian Dietrich Grabbe
1801–1862	Johann Nepomuk Nestroy
1802–1870	Alexandre Dumas *père*
1802–1885	Victor Hugo
1803–1870	Prosper Mérimée
1803–1899	Guido Gezelle
1804–1875	Eduard Mörike
1804–1876	George Sand
1805–1868	Adalbert Stifter
1805–1875	Hans Christian Andersen
1808–1855	Gérard de Nerval
1809–1849	Juliusz Slowacki
1809–1852	Nikolai Gogol'
1810–1857	Alfred de Musset
1811–1872	Théophile Gautier
1812–1859	Zygmunt Krasiński
1812–1891	Ivan Goncharov
1813–1837	Georg Büchner
c. 1813–1855	Søren Kierkegaard
1813–1863	Friedrich Hebbel
1813–1871	Baron Jószef Eötvös
1814–1841	Mikhail Lermontov
1817–1888	Theodor Storm
1818–1883	Ivan Turgenev
1819–1890	Gottfried Keller
1819–1898	Theodor Fontane
1820–1881	Multatuli
1821–1867	Charles Baudelaire
1821–1880	Gustave Flaubert
1821–1881	Fedor Dostoevskii

c. 1821–1883	Cyprian Kamil Norwid
1822–1896	Edmond Goncourt
1823–1849	Sándor Petöfi
1824–1895	Alexandre Dumas *fils*
1825–1898	Conrad Ferdinand Meyer
1828–1905	Jules Verne
1828–1906	Henrik Ibsen
1828–1910	Lev Tolstoi
1830–1870	Jules Goncourt
1832–1910	Bjørnstjerne Bjørnson
1834–1886	José Hernández
1835–1907	Giosuè Carducci
1839–1908	Joaquim Maria Machado de Assis
1840–1902	Émile Zola
1840–1922	Giovanni Verga
1842–1898	Stéphane Mallarmé
1844–1896	Paul Verlaine
1844–1900	Friedrich Nietzsche
1844–1924	Anatole France
1845–1900	José Maria de Eça de Queirós
1846–1870	Comte de Lautréamont
1846–1916	Henryk Sienkiewicz
1847–1912	Bolesław Prus
1848–1907	Joris-Karl Huysmans
1849–1912	August Strindberg
1850–1893	Guy de Maupassant
1853–1995	José Martí
1854–1891	Arthur Rimbaud
1858–1940	Selma Lagerlöf
1859–1943	Kostes Palamas
1859–1952	Knut Hamsun
1860–1887	Jules Laforgue
1860–1904	Anton Chekhov
1861–1928	Italo Svevo
1861–1941	Rabindranath Tagore
1862–1921	Georges Feydeau
1862–1922	Mori Ogai
1862–1931	Arthur Schnitzler
1862–1944	Jean Giraudoux
1862–1946	Gerhart Hauptmann
1862–1949	Maurice Maeterlinck
1863–1923	Louis Couperus
1863–1933	C. P. Cavafy
1863–1938	Gabriele D'Annunzio
1864–1918	Frank Wedekind
1866–1944	Romain Rolland
1867–1902	Masaoka Shiki
1867–1916	Rubén Darío
1867–1916	Natsume Sōseki
1867–1936	Luigi Pirandello
1868–1918	Edmond Rostand
1868–1936	Maksim Gor'kii
1868–1955	Paul Claudel
1869–1907	Stanisław Wyspiański
1869–1951	André Gide
1870–1953	Ivan Bunin
1871–1922	Marcel Proust
1871–1936	Grazia Deledda
1871–1945	Paul Valéry
1871–1950	Heinrich Mann
1872–1943	Shimazaki Toson
1873–1907	Alfred Jarry
1873–1950	Johannes V. Jensen
1873–1935	Henri Barbusse
1873–1954	Colette
1874–1929	Hugo von Hofmannsthal
1875–1926	Rainer Maria Rilke
1875–1955	Thomas Mann
1876–1944	Max Jacob
1877–1962	Hermann Hesse
1878–1942	Carl Sternheim
1878–1942	Yosano Akiko
1878–1945	Georg Kaiser
1878–1952	Ferenc Molnár
1878–1957	Alfred Döblin
1880–1918	Guillaume Apollinaire
1880–1921	Aleksandr Blok
1880–1934	Andrei Belyi
1880–1942	Robert Musil
1881–1936	Lu Xun
1881–1958	Roger Martin du Gard
1882–1949	Sigrid Undset
1883–1923	Jaroslav Hašek
1883–1924	Franz Kafka
1883–1957	Nikos Kazantzakis
1883–1957	Umberto Saba
1883–1971	Shiga Naoya
1884–1937	Evgenii Zamiatin
1884–1951	Angelo Sikelianos
1885–1922	Velimir Khlebnikov
1885–1939	Stanisław Witkiewicz
1885–1962	Isak Dinesen
1885–1970	François Mauriac
1886–1914	Alain-Fournier
1886–1942	Hagiwara Sakutaro
1886–1951	Hermann Broch
1886–1956	Gottfried Benn
1886–1965	Tanizaki Jun'ichiro
1887–1914	Georg Trakl
1887–1961	Blaise Cendrars
1887–1975	Saint-John Perse
1888–1935	Fernando Pessoa
1888–1948	Georges Bernanos
1888–1970	S.Y. Agnon
1888–1970	Giuseppe Ungaretti
1889–1957	Gabriela Mistral
1889–1963	Jean Cocteau
1889–1966	Anna Akhmatova
1889–1984	Henri Michaux
1890–1938	Karel Čapek
1890–1945	Franz Werfel
1890–1960	Boris Pasternak
1891–1938	Osip Mandel'shtam
1891–1940	Mikhail Bulgakov
1891–1950	Ivan Goll
1891–1970	Nelly Sachs
1891–1974	Pär Lagerkvist
1892–1923	Edith Södergran
1892–1927	Akutagawa Ryunosuke
1892–1938	César Vallejo

1892–1941	Marina Tsvetaeva	1902–1998	Halldór Laxness
1892–1942	Bruno Schulz	1903–1923	Raymond Radiguet
1892–1953	Ugo Betti	1903–1976	Raymond Queneau
1892–1975	Ivo Andrić	1903–1987	Marguerite Yourcenar
1893–1930	Vladimir Maiakovskii	1903–1989	Georges Simenon
1893–1939	Ernst Toller	1904–1962	Abdulla Goran
1893–1945	Mario de Andrade	1904–1969	Witold Gombrowicz
1893–1981	Miroslav Krleža	1904–1973	Pablo Neruda
1894–1938	Boris Pil'niak	1904–1980	Alejo Carpentier
1894–1939	Joseph Roth	1905–1974	Siburapha
1894–1941(?)	Isaak Babel	1905–1980	Jean-Paul Sartre
1894–1961	Louis-Ferdinand Céline	1905–1984	Mikhail Sholokhov
1894–1982	Nishiwaki Junzaburo	1905–1994	Elias Canetti
1895–1925	Sergei Esenin	1906–1972	Dino Buzzati
1895–1952	Paul Éluard	1906–1989	Samuel Beckett
1895–1958	Mikhail Mikhailovich Zoshchenko	1907–1968	Ding Ling
1895–1960	Iurii Olesha	1907–1972	Gnter Eich
1895–1970	Jean Giono	1907–1986	Mircea Eliade
1895–1974	Marcel Pagnol	1907–1988	René Char
1895–1989	Maria Kuncewicz	1907–1990	Alberto Moravia
1895–1998	Ernst Jünger	1907–1995	Miguel Torga
1896–1928	Paul van Ostaijen	1908–1950	Cesare Pavese
1896–1933	Miyazawa Kenji	1908–1966	Elio Vittorini
1896–1948	Antonin Artaud	1908–1967	João Guimarães Rosa
1896–1953	Martinus Nijhoff	1908–1970	Arthur Adamov
1896–1957	Giuseppe Tomasi di Lampedusa	1908–1986	Simone de Beauvoir
1896–1966	André Breton	1909–1944	Miklós Radnóti
1896–1966	Heimito von Doderer	1909–1945	Robert Brasillach
1896–1977	Carl Zuckmayer	1909–1948	Dazai Osamu
1896–1981	Eugenio Montale	1909–1981	Demetrio Aguilera Malta
1897–1970	Tarjei Vesaas	1909–1983	Jerzy Andrzejewski
1897–1982	Louis Aragon	1909–1983	Gabrielle Roy
1898–1956	Bertolt Brecht	1909–1990	Yannis Ritsos
1898–1970	Erich Maria Remarque	1909–1994	Eugène Ionesco
1898–1971	Simon Vestdijk	1910–1976	José Lezama Lima
1898–1987	Tawfiq al-Hakim	1910–1986	Jean Genet
1898–1993	Ibuse Masuji	1910–1987	Jean Anhouilh
1899–1966	Lao She	1910–	Rachel de Queiroz
1899–1972	Kawabata Yasunari	1911–1942	Xiao Hong
1899–1974	Miguel Ángel Asturias	1911–1969	José Mariá Arguedas
1899–1986	Jorge Luis Borges	1911–1986	Fritz Hochwälder
1899–1988	Francis Ponge	1911–1991	Max Frisch
1900–1944	Antoine de Saint-Exupéry	1911–1996	Odysseus Elytis
1900–1970	Leopoldo Marechal	1911–	Naguib Mahfouz
1900–1971	George Seferis	1911–	Czesław Miłosz
1900–1977	Jacques Prévert	1912–1980	Nélson Rodrigues
1900–1978	Ignazio Silone	1912–1985	Elsa Morante
1900–1984	Eduardo De Filippo	1912–2001	Jorge Amado
1900–1987	Gilberto Freyre	1913–1960	Albert Camus
1900–1991	William Heinesen	1913–1989	Sándor Weöres
1900–1999	Nathalie Sarraute	1913–1991	Vasco Pratolini
1901–1938	Ödön von Horváth	1914–1984	Julio Cortázar
1901–1968	Salvatore Quasimodo	1914–1996	Marguerite Duras
1901–1976	André Malraux	1914–1998	Octavio Paz
1901–1990	Ivar Lo-Johansson	1915–1997	Claude Roy
1902–1967	Marcel Aymé	1916–1982	Peter Weiss
1902–1975	Carlo Levi	1916–1991	Natalia Ginzburg
1902–1983	Gyula Illyés	1916–2000	Giorgio Bassani
1902–1987	Carlos Drummond de Andrade	1917–1965	Johannes Bobrowski
1902–1989	Nicolás Guillén	1917–1985	Heinrich Böll

1917–1987	Carlo Cassola	1929–	Christa Wolf
1918–1986	Juan Rulfo	1930–	Adonis
1918–	Aleksandr Solzhenitsyn	1931–1989	Thomas Bernhard
1919–1987	Primo Levi	1931–	Ivan Klíma
1920–1959	Boris Vian	1932–1990	Manuel Puig
1920–1970	Paul Celan	1932–	Umberto Eco
1920–1992	Väinö Linna	1933–	Evgenii Evtushenko
1920–	Ishigaki Rin	1933–	Cees Nooteboom
1920–	Jaan Kross	1934–1984	Uwe Johnson
1920–	Albert Memmi	1935–1989	Danilo Kiš
1921–	Tadeusz Różewicz	1935–	Manlio Argueta
1921–1989	Leonardo Sciascia	1935–	Francesca Duranti
1921–1990	Friedrich Dürrenmatt	1935–	Ōe Kenzaburō
1922–1949	Chairil Anwar	1935–	Rendra
1922–1951	Tadeusz Borowski	1936–1982	Georges Perec
1922–1975	Pier Paolo Pasolini	1936–	Assia Djebar
1922–1991	Vasko Popa	1936–	Vaclav Havel
1922–	José Craveirinha	1936–	Ismail Kadare
1922–	Alain Robbe-Grillet	1936–	Mario Vargas Llosa
1923–1969	Jalal Âl-e Ahmad	1936–	A. B. Yehoshua
1923–1985	Italo Calvino	1937–	Juan José Saer
1923–1998	Miroslav Holub	1938–	Abdelkebir Khatibi
1923–1996	Endō Shūsaku	1938–	Luisa Valenzuela
1923–	Wislawa Szymborska	1939–	Huang Chunming
1924–1986	Vasil Bykaw	1939–	Amos Oz
1924–1993	Abe Kōbō	1940–1996	Iosif Brodskii
1925–1970	Mishima Yukio	1940–	Gao Xingjian
1925–1974	Rosario Castellanos	1940–	Antonio Skármeta
1925–1977	Clarice Lispector	1941–	Jaan Kaplinski
1925–1981	Iurii Trifonov	1942–	Isabel Allende
1925–	Ernesto Cardenal	1942–	Dev Virahsawmy
1925–	Pramoedya Ananta Toer	1943–1990	Reinaldo Arenas
1926–1973	Ingeborg Bachmann	1943–	Evelyne Accad
1926–	René Depestre	1943–	Nicole Brossard
1926–	Siegfried Lenz	1943–	Sasha Sokolov
1927–1991	Yusuf Idris	1944–	Tahar Ben Jelloun
1927–	Günter Grass	1947–	Tsushima Yuko
1927–	Qurratulain Hyder	1948–	Gioconda Belli
1927–	Ahmadou Kourouma	1949–	Bei Dao
1928–	Carlos Fuentes	1949–	Murakami Haruki
1928–	Gabriel García Márquez	1950–	Péter Esterházy
1928–	Edouard Glissant	1951–	Tatyana Tolstaya
1928–	Miodrag Pavlović	1952–	Li Ang
1928–	Elie Wiesel	1953–	Patrick Chamoiseau
1929–	Hugo Claus	1957–	Peter Høeg
1929–	Milan Kundera	1963–	Dorothea Rosa Herilany
1929–	Milorad Pavić	1963–	Su Tong

ALPHABETICAL LIST OF WORKS

"L'Abandonné," story by Guy de Maupassant, 1884

"Abdias," story by Adalbert Stifter, 1843

About This, poem by Vladimir Maiakovskii, 1923

The Aeneid, poem by Virgil, 1st century BC

Aetia, poem by Callimachus, 3rd century BC

Against Sainte-Beuve, prose by Marcel Proust, 1954

The Age of Reason, novel by Jean-Paul Sartre, 1945

Ajax, play by Sophocles, before 441 BC(?)

"Alchemy of the Word," poem by Arthur Rimbaud, 1873

All Quiet on the Western Front, novel by Erich Maria Remarque, 1929

Aminta, play by Torquato Tasso, 1573

Andreas, fiction by Hugo von Hofmannsthal, 1930 (written 1912–13)

"L'Angoisse," poem by Paul Verlaine, 1866

Amphitryo, play by Plautus, 2nd century BC

Andorra, play by Max Frisch, 1961

Anna Karenina, novel by Lev Tolstoi, 1875–77

Annals, prose by Tacitus, early 2nd century AD

Antigone, play by Jean Anhouilh, 1944

Antigone, play by Sophocles, c. 441 BC(?)

"Apology for Raymond Sebond," prose by Michel de Montaigne, 1570

"L'Après-midi d'un faune," poem by Stéphane Mallarmé, 1876

Around the World in Eighty Days, novel by Jules Verne, 1873

"Art," poem by Théophile Gautier, 1856

The Art of Love, poem by Ovid, 1st century BC/1st century AD

The Art of Poetry, poem by Nicolas Boileau, 1674

"Art poétique," poem by Paul Verlaine, 1874

"Arte poética," poem by Pablo Neruda, 1935

Ashes and Diamonds, novel by Jerzy Andrzejewski, 1948

L'Assommoir, novel by Émile Zola, 1877

Athalie, play by Jean Racine, 1691

Aucassin and Nicolette (Anon), romance, 13th century

Auto-da-Fé, novel by Elias Canetti, 1936

Auto da Barca do Inferno, Auto da Barca do Purgatorio, Auto da Barca da Gloria, plays by Gil Vicente, 1517, 1518, 1519

Baal, play by Bertolt Brecht, 1922

Bajazet, play by Jean Racine, 1672

The Balcony, play by Jean Genet, 1956

The Bald Prima Donna, play by Eugène Ionesco, 1950

"Ballade des dames du temps jadis," poem by François Villon, 1489 (written c. 1460?)

"Ballade des pendus," poem by François Villon, 1489

The Barber of Seville, play by Beaumarchais, 1775

"Le Bateau ivre," poem by Arthur Rimbaud, 1871

The Bedbug, play by Vladimir Maiakovskii, 1929

Before the Storm, novel by Theodor Fontane, 1878

Berenice, play by Jean Racine, 1670

Berlin Alexanderplatz, novel by Alfred Döblin, 1929

The Betrothed, novel by Alessandro Manzoni, 1827

The Bible, anonymous verse and prose, c. 900 BC onwards

The Birds, play by Aristophanes, 414 BC

The Birth of Tragedy, prose by Friedrich Nietzsche, 1872

Blood Wedding, play by Federico García Lorca, 1933

The Blue Angel, novel by Heinrich Mann, 1905

The Blue Bird, play by Maurice Maeterlinck, 1909

Blue Flowers, novel by Raymond Queneau, 1965

The Book of the City of Ladies, prose by Christine de Pizan, 1405

Brand, play by Henrik Ibsen, 1865

"Bread and Wine," poem by Friedrich Hölderlin, 1806 (written 1800–01)

Bread and Wine, novel by Ignazio Silone, 1937

The Bridge on the Drina, novel by Ivo Andrić, 1945

The Broken Jug, play by Heinrich von Kleist, 1808

The Bronze Horseman, poem by Aleksandr Pushkin, written 1833

"The Broom," poem by Giacomo Leopardi, 1845

The Brothers, play by Terence, 160 BC

The Brothers Karamazov, novel by Fedor Dostoevskii, 1880

The Brothers Menaechmus, play by Plautus, 2nd century BC

Buddenbrooks, novel by Thomas Mann, 1900

Camille, novel by Alexandre Dumas *fils*, 1848

Cancer Ward, novel by Aleksandr Solzhenitsyn, 1968

Candide, novella by Voltaire, 1759

The Castle, novel by Franz Kafka, 1926 (written 1922)

The Caucasian Chalk Circle, play by Bertolt Brecht, 1948

"Le Chanson du mal-aime," poem by Guillaume Apollinaire, 1913

Characters, prose by Theophrastus, c. 319 BC

The Charterhouse of Parma, novel by Stendhal, 1839

Chatterton, play by Alfred de Vigny, 1835

Chéri, novel by Colette, 1920

The Cherry Orchard, play by Anton Chekhov, 1904

The Christ of Velazquez, poem by Miguel de Unamuno, 1920

Christ Stopped at Eboli, novel by Carlo Levi, 1945

The Cid, play by Pierre Corneille, 1636–37

"Le Cimetière marin," poem by Paul Valéry, 1920

The City of God, prose by St Augustine, 5th century

Cloud in Trousers, poem by Vladimir Maiakovskii, 1915

The Cloud Messenger, poem by Kālidāsa, 5th century

The Clouds, play by Aristophanes, 423 BC

The Colloquies, prose by Desiderius Erasmus, 1518

The Comic Theatre, play by Carlo Goldoni, 1750

The Conceited Young Ladies, play by Molière, 1659

The Conference of the Birds, poem by Farid al-Din Attār, c. 1177

The Confessions, prose by Jean-Jacques Rousseau, 1781

Confessions, Book I, prose by St. Augustine, 4th century

Confessions of Felix Krull, Confidence Man, novel by Thomas Mann, 1922 (complete 1954)

Confessions of Zeno, novel by Italo Svevo, 1923

"Considerando en frio," poem by César Vallejo, 1939

The Consolation of Philosophy, prose by Boethius, early 6th century

Conversation in Sicily, novel by Elio Vittorini, 1939

La cortigiana, play by Pietro Aretino, 1534

The Counterfeiters, novel by André Gide, 1926

"Un Coup de dés jamais n'abolira le hasard," poem by Stéphane Mallarmé, 1914 (written 1897)

Cousin Bette, novel by Honoré de Balzac, 1847

Le Crève-coeur, poems by Louis Aragon, 1941

Crime and Punishment, novel by Fedor Dostoevskii, 1867

Cupid and Psyche, story by Apuleius, c. 180

Cuttlefish Bones, poems by Eugenio Montale, 1925

Cyrano de Bergerac, play by Edmond Rostand, 1897

Danton's Death, play by Georg Bchner, 1835 (complete version 1850)

Daphnis and Chloe, poem by Longus, 2nd/3rd century

Dead Souls, novel by Nikolai Gogol', 1842

Tentativa del hombre infinito, poem by Pablo Neruda, 1926
The Test of Virtue, play by Denis Diderot, 1757
The Theatre and Its Double, prose by Antonin Artaud, 1938
The Theatrical Illusion, play by Pierre Corneille, 1635–36
Thérèse, novel by François Mauriac, 1927
The Thousand and One Nights, anonymous stories, 9th century
The Three Musketeers, novel by Alexandre Dumas *père*, 1844
Three Poems: 2, 63, and 76, poems by Catullus, 1st century BC
The Three Sisters, play by Anton Chekhov, 1901
The Threepenny Opera, play by Bertolt Brecht, 1928
Thus Spoke Zarathustra, prose by Friedrich Nietzsche, 1883–85
Thyestes, play by Seneca, c. 48 BC
 Tiger at the Gates, play by Jean Giraudoux, 1935
The Time of Indifference, novel by Alberto Moravia, 1929
The Tin Drum, novel by Günter Grass, 1959
Titurel, poetic fragment by Wolfram von Eschenbach, written
    c. 1212–20
"To Himself," poem by Giacomo Leopardi, 1835
"To the Reader," poem by Charles Baudelaire, 1861
Torquato Tasso, play by Johann Wolfgang von Goethe, 1790
The Tower, play by Hugo von Hofmannsthal, 1925
The Trial, novel by Franz Kafka, 1925 (written 1914–15)
The Trickster of Seville, play by Tirso de Molina, 1625
The Trojan Women, play by Euripides, 415 BC
Tropisms, prose by Nathalie Sarraute, 1939
The Tutor, play by Jakob Michael Reinhold Lenz, 1774
The Twelve, poem by Aleksandr Blok, 1918
Twenty-Six Men and a Girl, story by Maksim Gor'kii, 1899
Ubu Rex, play by Alfred Jarry, 1896
Uncle Vanya, play by Anton Chekhov, 1897
Under Fire, novel by Henri Barbusse, 1916
Upanishads, anonymous prose and verse, c. 800–c. 500 BC
Vedas, anonymous prose and verse, c. 3000–c. 500 BC
The Village Notary, novel by Baron József Eötvös, 1845

The Visit, play by Friedrich Dürrenmatt, 1956
The Voice of Things, poems by Francis Ponge, 1942
Voices in the Evening, novel by Natalia Ginzburg, 1961
Voyages to the Moon and the Sun, novels by Cyrano de
    Bergerac, 1657–62
The Voyeur, novel by Alain Robbe-Grillet, 1955
Waiting for Godot, play by Samuel Beckett, 1952
"Waiting for the Barbarians," poem by Constantine Petrou Cavafy, 1904
Wallenstein, plays by Friedrich von Schiller, 1798–99
The Wanderer, novel by Alain-Fournier, 1913
The Wandering Scholar in Paradise, play by Hans Sachs, written 1550
War and Peace, novel by Lev Tolstoi, 1869
Water Margin, anonymous novel, 14th century
The Waves of Sea and Love, play by Franz Grillparzer, 1831
We, novel by Evgenii Zamiatin, 1924
The Weavers, play by Gerhart Hauptmann, 1892
The White Guard, novel by Mikhail Bulgakov, 1929
The White Horseman, novella by Theodor Storm, 1888
The Wild Duck, play by Henrik Ibsen, 1884
Wilhelm Meister's Apprenticeship, novel by Johann Wolfgang von
    Goethe, 1795–96
Willehalm, unfinished poem by Wolfram von Eschenbach, written
    c. 1210–12
William Tell, play by Friedrich von Schiller, 1804
"Windows," poem by Charles Baudelaire, 1863
Woman in the Dunes, novel by Abe Kōbō, 1962
Women of Trachis, play by Sophocles, c. 430–20 BC
Woyzeck, play by Georg Büchner, 1879 (written 1835–37)
Yerma, play by Federico García Lorca, 1934
"You the Only One," poem by Paul Éluard, 1928
Young Törless, novel by Robert Musil, 1906
Zadig, novella by Voltaire, 1748
Zazie, novel by Raymond Queneau, 1959
"Zone," poem by Guillaume Apollinaire, 1913

CHRONOLOGICAL LIST OF WORKS

Vedas, anonymous prose and verse, c. 3000–c. 500 BC
Epic of Gilgamesh, anonymous poem cycle, early 2nd millennium BC
The Bible, anonymous verse and prose, c. 900 BC onwards
Upanishads, anonymous prose and verse, c. 800–c. 500 BC
The Iliad, poem by Homer, c. 750 BC
The Odyssey, poem by Homer, c. 720 BC
Fragment 1 ["Address to Aphrodite"], poem by Sappho, 7th century BC
Fragment 31 ["Declaration of Love for a Young Girl"], poem by Sappho, 7th century BC
The City of God, prose by St Augustine, 5th century
Olympian One, poem by Pindar, c. 476 BC(?)
The Persians, play by Aeschylus, 472 BC
The Seven Against Thebes, play by Aeschylus, 467 BC
Prometheus Bound, play by Aeschylus, c. 466–59 BC
The Suppliant Maidens, play by Aeschylus, c. 463 BC
Pythian Odes Four and Five, poems by Pindar, c. 462 BC(?)
The Oresteia, play by Aeschylus, 458 BC
Ajax, play by Sophocles, before 441 BC(?)
Antigone, play by Sophocles, c. 441 BC(?)
Medea, play by Euripides, 431 BC
Women of Trachis, play by Sophocles, c. 430–20 BC
Oedipus the King, play by Sophocles, after 430 BC
Hippolytus, play by Euripides, 428 BC
The Clouds, play by Aristophanes, 423 BC
Electra, play by Euripides, c. 422–16 BC
Ion, play by Euripides, c. 421–13 BC
Electra, play by Sophocles, c. 418–10 BC(?)
The Trojan Women, play by Euripides, 415 BC
The Birds, play by Aristophanes, 414 BC
Lysistrata, play by Aristophanes, 411 BC
Philoctetes, play by Sophocles, 409 BC
Orestes, play by Euripides, 408 BC
The Frogs, play by Aristophanes, 405 BC
Oedipus at Colonus, play by Sophocles, 401 BC
Phaedrus, prose by Plato, 5th/4th century BC
The Republic, prose by Plato, 5th/4th century BC
The Symposium, prose by Plato, 4th century BC
On the Crown, prose by Demosthenes, 330 BC
Characters, prose by Theophrastus, c. 319 BC
The Grouch, play by Menander, 316 BC
Aetia, poem by Callimachus, 3rd century BC
Hecale, poem by Callimachus, 3rd century BC
Idyll I, poem by Theocritus, c. 270s BC
Idyll IV, poem by Theocritus, c. 270s BC
Idyll VII, poem by Theocritus, c. 270s BC
Amphitryo, play by Plautus, 2nd century BC
The Brothers Menaechmus, play by Plautus, 2nd century BC
The Pot of Gold, play by Plautus, 2nd century BC
The Eunuch, play by Terence, 161 BC
Phormio, play by Terence, 161 BC
The Brothers, play by Terence, 160 BC
The Aeneid, poem by Virgil, 1st century BC
Epigrams, poems by Martial, 1st century BC
Georgics, poem by Virgil, 1st century BC
Odes Book I, Poem 5, poem by Horace, 1st century BC
Odes Book IV, Poem 7, poem by Horace, 1st century BC

Poem 85, poem by Catullus, 1st century BC
Three Poems: 2, 63, and 76, poems by Catullus, 1st century BC
In Defence of Marcus Caelius Rufus, prose by Cicero, 56 BC
On the Commonwealth, prose by Cicero, c. 51 BC
Oedipus, play by Seneca, c. 48 BC
Thyestes, play by Seneca, c. 48 BC
On Old Age, prose by Cicero, 44 BC
Loves, poem by Ovid, late 1st century BC
The Poetic Art, poem by Horace, late 1st century BC
Mahābhārata, epic poem attributed to Vyāsa, 1st millennium BC/AD
The Art of Love, poem by Ovid, 1st century BC/1st century AD
Metamorphoses, poem by Ovid, 1st century BC/1st century AD
Kalevala, anonymous poem, origins date to early 1st century AD
The Little Clay Cart, anonymous play, 1st century AD(?)
On the Sublime, anonymous poem, late 1st century AD
Rāmāyana, poem attributed to Vālmīki, 1st/2nd century
Lives of Lysander and Sulla, prose by Plutarch, 1st/2nd century AD
Satire 10, poem by Juvenal, 1st/2nd century AD
Annals, prose by Tacitus, early 2nd century AD
Meditations, prose by Aurelius, c. 170
Cupid and Psyche, story by Apuleius, c. 180
Daphnis and Chloe, poem by Longus, 2nd/3rd century
Confessions, Book I, prose by St. Augustine, 4th century
The Mosella, poem by Ausonius, c. 371
The Cloud Messenger, poem by Kālidāsa, 5th century
Śakuntalā, poem by Kālidāsa, 5th century
The Rape of Proserpine, poem by Claudian, c. 400
The Consolation of Philosophy, prose by Boethius, early 6th century
"Hard Is the Road to Shu," poem by Li Bai, c. 744
"Invitation to Wine," poem by Li Bai, 752
The Thousand and One Nights, anonymous stories, 9th century
Journey to the West, anonymous novel, 11/12th century
Ruba'iyat, poems by Omar Khayyam, 11/12th century
The Song of Roland, poem, c. 1100
Erec and Énide, poem by Chrétien de Troyes, written c. 1170
Lancelot, poem by Chrétien de Troyes, written c. 1170
The Conference of the Birds, poem by Farid al-Din Attār, c. 1177
The Tale of the Campaign of Igor, anonymous poem, c. 1185
Guigamor, poem by Marie de France, late 12th century
The Saga of King Óláf the Saint, prose by Snorri Sturluson, 12th/13th century
Aucassin and Nicolette (Anon), romance, 13th century
Egils saga, anonymous prose, 13th century
Njáls saga, anonymous prose, 13th century
The Poetic *Edda*, anonymous poems, 13th century
The Prose *Edda*, prose by Snorri Sturluson, 13th century
Nibelungenlied, poem, c. 1200
Parzival, poem by Wolfram von Eschenbach, written c. 1200–10
Willehalm, unfinished poem by Wolfram von Eschenbach, written c. 1210–12
Titurel, poetic fragment by Wolfram von Eschenbach, written c. 1212–20
The Romance of the Rose (de Lorris and Meung), poem, c. 1225–70
Rose Garden, prose and verse by Sa'di, 1258
The New Life, poems by Dante Alighieri, 1295
Water Margin, anonymous novel, 14th century

The Divine Comedy, poem by Dante Alighieri, 1321 The Ninth Tale of the Fifth Day of *The Decameron*, story by Giovanni Boccaccio, c. 1350

"Sonnet 90," poem by Petrarch, before 1356

The Book of the City of Ladies, prose by Christine de Pizan, 1405

"Ballade des dames du temps jadis," poem by François Villon, 1489 (written c. 1460?)

"Ballade des pendus," poem by François Villon, 1489

The Ship of Fools, poem by Sebastian Brant, 1494

The Praise of Folly, prose by Desiderius Erasmus, 1511

The Prince, prose by Niccolò Machiavelli, 1513

Orlando Furioso, poem by Ludovico Ariosto, 1515

Auto da Barca do Inferno, Auto da Barca do Purgatorio, Auto da Barca da Gloria, plays by Gil Vicente, 1517, 1518, 1519

The Colloquies, prose by Desiderius Erasmus, 1518

Farsa de Inês Pereira, play by Gil Vicente, 1523

The Mandrake, play by Niccolò Machiavelli, 1524

"Ein feste Burg," hymn by Martin Luther, 1531 (written 1528?)

Gargantua and *Pantagruel*, novels by François Rabelais, 1532–34(?)

La cortigiana, play by Pietro Aretino, 1534

The Wandering Scholar in Paradise, play by Hans Sachs, written 1550

"Ode to Michel de l'Hospital," poem by Pierre de Ronsard, 1552

Lazarillo de Tormes, anonymous novel, 1554

"Heureux qui, comme Ulysse, a fait un beau voyage," poem by Joachim Du Bellay, 1558

"Hymn to Autumn," poem by Pierre de Ronsard, 1563

"Apology for Raymond Sebond," prose by Michel de Montaigne, 1570

The Lusiads, poem by Luís de Camões, 1572

Aminta, play by Torquato Tasso, 1573

"Quand vous serez bien vieille . . . ," poem by Pierre de Ronsard, 1578 (written 1572)

Jerusalem Delivered, poem by Torquato Tasso, 1580

"On the Power of the Imagination," prose by Michel de Montaigne, 1588

"On Vanity," prose by Michel de Montaigne, 1588

The Peony Pavilion, novel by Tang Xianzu, 1598

Peribáñez and the Comendador of Ocaña, play by Lope de Vega Carpio, 1608

Don Quixote, novel by Miguel de Cervantes, 1615

Fuenteovejuna, play by Lope de Vega Carpio, 1619

Life Is a Dream, play by Pedro Calderón de la Barca, 1623

The Trickster of Seville, play by Tirso de Molina, 1625

Justice Without Revenge, play by Lope de Vega Carpio, 1632

The Great Stage of the World, play by Pedro Calderón de la Barca, c. 1635

The Theatrical Illusion, play by Pierre Corneille, 1635–36

The Cid, play by Pierre Corneille, 1636–37

Voyages to the Moon and the Sun, novels by Cyrano de Bergerac, 1657–62

The Conceited Young Ladies, play by Molière, 1659

Tartuffe, play by Molière, 1664

Don Juan, play by Molière, 1665

Maxims, prose by La Rouchefoucauld, 1665–78

The Misanthrope, play by Molière, 1666

The Miser, play by Molière, 1668

Berenice, play by Jean Racine, 1670

Bajazet, play by Jean Racine, 1672

The Hypochondriac, play by Molière, 1673

The Art of Poetry, poem by Nicolas Boileau, 1674

Phaedra, play by Jean Racine, 1677

Fables, stories by Jean de La Fontaine, 1688–89

Athalie, play by Jean Racine, 1691

The Game of Love and Chance, play by Marivaux, 1730

Manon Lescaut, novel by Abbé Prévost, 1733

The False Confessions, play by Marivaux, 1737

A Matter of Dispute, play by Marivaux, 1744

Zadig, novella by Voltaire, 1748

The Dream of the Red Chamber, novel by Cao Xueqin, mid-18th century

The Comic Theatre, play by Carlo Goldoni, 1750

The Mistress of the Inn, play by Carlo Goldoni, 1753

Poem on the Disaster of Lisbon, poem by Voltaire, 1756

The Test of Virtue, play by Denis Diderot, 1757

Candide, novella by Voltaire, 1759

Emile, fiction by Jean-Jacques Rousseau, 1762

The Social Contract, prose by Jean-Jacques Rousseau, 1762

The Philosophical Dictionary, prose by Voltaire, 1764

Minna von Barnhelm, play by Gotthold Ephraim Lessing, 1767

Goetz of Berlichingen, play by Johann Wolfgang von Goethe, 1773

The Sufferings of Young Werther, novel by Johann Wolfgang von Goethe, 1774

The Tutor, play by Jakob Michael Reinhold Lenz, 1774

The Barber of Seville, play by Beaumarchais, 1775

Nathan the Wise, play by Gotthold Ephraim Lessing, 1779

The Confessions, prose by Jean-Jacques Rousseau, 1781

Les Liaisons Dangereuses, novel by Choderlos de Laclos, 1782

The Minor, play by Denis Fonvizin, 1782

The Reveries of a Solitary, prose by Jean-Jacques Rousseau, 1782

Saul, play by Vittorio Alfieri, 1782

Ode to Joy, poem by Friedrich von Schiller, written 1785

Don Carlos, play by Friedrich von Schiller, 1787

Torquato Tasso, play by Johann Wolfgang von Goethe, 1790

Justine, novel by Marquis de Sade, 1791

Wilhelm Meister's Apprenticeship, novel by Johann Wolfgang von Goethe, 1795–96

Jacques the Fatalist, novel by Denis Diderot, 1796

Wallenstein, plays by Friedrich von Schiller, 1798–99

Hymns to the Night, poems by Novalis, 1800

Mary Stuart, play by Friedrich von Schiller, 1800

René, prose by Chateaubriand, 1802

William Tell, play by Friedrich von Schiller, 1804

"Bread and Wine," poem by Friedrich Hlderlin, 1806 (written 1800–01)

The Broken Jug, play by Heinrich von Kleist, 1808

Faust, play by Johann Wolfgang von Goethe: part I, 1808; part II, 1832

Elective Affinities, novel by Johann Wolfgang von Goethe, 1809

Michael Kohlhaas, story by Heinrich von Kleist, 1810

"Hansel and Gretel," story by Jacob and Wilhelm Grimm, 1812

Peter Schlemihl, novella by Adelbert von Chamisso, 1814

The Devil's Elixirs, novel by E.T.A. Hoffmann, 1815–16

The Story of Just Caspar and Fair Annie, novella by Clemens Brentano, 1817

"The Infinite," poem by Giacomo Leopardi, 1819

The Prince of Homburg, play by Heinrich von Kleist, 1821

"Homecoming," 20, poem by Heinrich Heine, 1824

Memoirs of a Good-for-Nothing, novella by Joseph von Eichendorff, 1826

"Moses," poem by Alfred de Vigny, 1826 (written 1822)

The Betrothed, novel by Alessandro Manzoni, 1827

Scarlet and Black, novel by Stendhal, 1830

Eugene Onegin, poem by Aleksandr Pushkin, 1831

Death in Venice, novella by Thomas Mann, 1912

The Gods Are Athirst, novel by Anatole France, 1912

Professor Bernhardi, play by Arthur Schnitzler, 1912

"Le Chanson du mal-aime," poem by Guillaume Apollinaire, 1913

The Wanderer, novel by Alain-Fournier, 1913

"Zone," poem by Guillaume Apollinaire, 1913

Remembrance of Things Past, novel by Marcel Proust, 1913–27

"Un Coup de dés jamais n'abolira le hasard," poem by Stéphane Mallarmé, 1914 (written 1897)

Mist, novel by Miguel de Unamuno, 1914

Platero and I, poem by Juan Ramón Jiménez, 1914

Cloud in Trousers, poem by Vladimir Maiakovskii, 1915

The Gentleman from San Francisco, novella by Ivan Bunin, 1915

"Grodek," poem by Georg Trakl, 1915

The Metamorphosis, novella by Franz Kafka, 1915

Petersburg, novel by Andrei Belyi, 1916

Under Fire, novel by Henri Barbusse, 1916

"La Jeune Parque," poem by Paul Valéry, 1917 (written 1912–17)

The Gas Trilogy, plays by Georg Kaiser, 1917–20

The Twelve, poem by Aleksandr Blok, 1918

"The Eternal Dice," poem by César Vallejo, 1919

Chéri, novel by Colette, 1920

The Christ of Velazquez, poem by Miguel de Unamuno, 1920

"Le Cimetière marin," poem by Paul Valéry, 1920

Kristin Lavransdatter, novels by Sigrid Undset, 1920–22

Confessions of Felix Krull, Confidence Man, novel by Thomas Mann, 1922 (complete 1954)

The Difficult Man, play by Hugo von Hofmannsthal, 1921

Henry IV, play by Luigi Pirandello, 1921

The Insect Play, play by Karel Čapek, 1921

Six Characters in Search of an Author, play by Luigi Pirandello, 1921

The Good Soldier Švejk and His Fortunes in the World War, novel by Jaroslav Hašek, 1921–23

Baal, play by Bertolt Brecht, 1922

"Palau," poem by Gottfried Benn, 1922

Siddhartha, novel by Hermann Hesse, 1922

About This, poem by Vladimir Maiakovskii, 1923

Confessions of Zeno, novel by Italo Svevo, 1923

The Devil in the Flesh, novel by Raymond Radiguet, 1923

Seventh Duino Elegy, poem by Rainer Maria Rilke, 1923

Sonnets to Orpheus, poems by Rainer Maria Rilke, 1923

The Magic Mountain, novel by Thomas Mann, 1924

We, novel by Evgenii Zamiatin, 1924

Cuttlefish Bones, poems by Eugenio Montale, 1925

The Tower, play by Hugo von Hofmannsthal, 1925

The Trial, novel by Franz Kafka, 1925 (written 1914–15)

The Castle, novel by Franz Kafka, 1926 (written 1922)

The Counterfeiters, novel by André Gide, 1926

Paris Peasant, prose poem by Louis Aragon, 1926

Red Cavalry, stories by Isaak Babel, 1926

Tentativa del hombre infinito, poem by Pablo Neruda, 1926

Envy, novel by Iurii Olesha, 1927

Steppenwolf, novel by Hermann Hesse, 1927

Thérèse, novel by François Mauriac, 1927

Some Prefer Nettles, novel by Tanizaki Jun'ichiro, 1928

The Threepenny Opera, play by Bertolt Brecht, 1928

"You the Only One," poem by Paul Éluard, 1928

The Satin Slipper, play by Paul Claudel, 1928–29

All Quiet on the Western Front, novel by Erich Maria Remarque, 1929

The Bedbug, play by Vladimir Maiakovskii, 1929

Berlin Alexanderplatz, novel by Alfred Döblin, 1929

The Holy Terrors, novel by Jean Cocteau, 1929

The Time of Indifference, novel by Alberto Moravia, 1929

The White Guard, novel by Mikhail Bulgakov, 1929

Andreas, fiction by Hugo von Hofmannsthal, 1930 (written 1912–13)

Fontamara, novel by Ignazio Silone, 1930

The Man Without Qualities, novel by Robert Musil, 1930–43

Free Union, poem by André Breton, 1931

Night Flight, novel by Antoine de Saint-Exupéry, 1931

Tales from the Vienna Woods, play by Ödön von Horváth, 1931

The Sleepwalkers, novels by Hermann Broch, 1931–32

Journey to the End of the Night, novel by Louis-Ferdinand Céline, 1932

The Radetzky March, novel by Joseph Roth, 1932

Blood Wedding, play by Federico García Lorca, 1933

Man's Fate, novel by André Malraux, 1933

"Sirens," poem by Giuseppe Ungaretti, 1933

The Infernal Machine, play by Jean Cocteau, 1934

Yerma, play by Federico García Lorca, 1934

"Arte poética," poem by Pablo Neruda, 1935

Mythistorima, poem by George Seferis, 1935

"The Sacred Way," poem by Angelos Sikelianos, 1935

Tiger at the Gates, play by Jean Giraudoux, 1935

Auto-da-Fé, novel by Elias Canetti, 1936

Bread and Wine, novel by Ignazio Silone, 1937

Ferdydurke, novel by Witold Gombrowicz, 1937

Mad Love, prose by André Breton, 1937

Rickshaw Boy, novel by Lao She, 1937

Snow Country, novel by Kawabata Yasunari, 1937

Nausea, novel by Jean-Paul Sartre, 1938

The Theatre and Its Double, prose by Antonin Artaud, 1938

"Considerando en frio," poem by César Vallejo, 1939

Conversation in Sicily, novel by Elio Vittorini, 1939

Tropisms, prose by Nathalie Sarraute, 1939

Le Crève-coeur, poems by Louis Aragon, 1941

Mother Courage and Her Children, play by Bertolt Brecht, 1941

"The Storm," poem by Eugenio Montale, 1941

"Death and the Compass," story by Jorge Luis Borges, 1942

The Outsider, novel by Albert Camus, 1942

Pascual Duarte's Family, novel by Camilo Jos´ Cela, 1942

The Voice of Things, poems by Francis Ponge, 1942

The Flies, play by Jean-Paul Sartre, 1943

The Glass Bead Game, novel by Hermann Hesse, 1943

The Good Person of Szechwan, play by Bertolt Brecht, 1943

The Life of Galileo, play by Bertolt Brecht, 1943

Antigone, play by Jean Anhouilh, 1944

No Exit, play by Jean-Paul Sartre, 1944

The Age of Reason, novel by Jean-Paul Sartre, 1945

The Bridge on the Drina, novel by Ivo Andrić, 1945

Christ Stopped at Eboli, novel by Carlo Levi, 1945

The Death of Virgil, novel by Hermann Broch, 1945

The House of Bernarda Alba, play by Federico García Lorca, 1945

The Madwoman of Chaillot, play by Jean Giraudoux, 1945

Filumena Marturano, play by Eduardo De Filippo, 1946

The President, novel by Miguel Ángel Asturias, 1946

Doctor Faustus, novel by Thomas Mann, 1947

The Kingdom of This World, novel by Alejo Carpentier, 1947

The Maids, play by Jean Genet, 1947

Ode to Charles Fourier, poem by André Breton, 1947

The Plague, novel by Albert Camus, 1947

Ashes and Diamonds, novel by Jerzy Andrzejewski, 1948

The Caucasian Chalk Circle, play by Bertolt Brecht, 1948
The Fire Raisers, play by Max Frisch, 1948
House of Liars, novel by Elsa Morante, 1948
The Second Sex, prose by Simone de Beauvoir, 1949
The Bald Prima Donna, play by Eugène Ionesco, 1950
The Fugitive, novel by Pramoedya Ananta Toer, 1950
The Moon and the Bonfires, novel by Cesare Pavese, 1950
Die Strudlhofstiege, novel by Heimito von Doderer, 1951
The Hussar on the Roof, novel by Jean Giono, 1951
Memoirs of Hadrian, novel by Marguerite Yourcenar, 1951
Molloy, Malone Dies, The Unnamable, novels by Samuel Beckett, 1951–53
"Death Fugue," poem by Paul Celan, 1952 (written 1948)
Waiting for Godot, play by Samuel Beckett, 1952
The Lost Steps, novel by Alejo Carpentier, 1953
The Pillar of Salt, novel by Albert Memmi, 1953
Professeur Taranne, play by Arthur Adamov, 1953
Against Sainte-Beuve, prose by Marcel Proust, 1954
I'm Not Stiller, play by Max Frisch, 1954
The Mandarins, novel by Simone de Beauvoir, 1954
The Last Temptation, novel by Nikos Kazantzakis, 1955
The Voyeur, novel by Alain Robbe-Grillet, 1955
The Balcony, play by Jean Genet, 1956
The Fall, novel by Albert Camus, 1956
"A Sentence for Tyranny," poem by Gyula Illyés, 1956
The Visit, play by Friedrich Dürrenmatt, 1956
Doctor Zhivago, novel by Boris Pasternak, 1957
Endgame, play by Samuel Beckett, 1957
Seamarks, poem by Saint-John Perse, 1957
Sun Stone, poem by Octavio Paz, 1957
Deep Rivers, novel by José Mariá Arguedas, 1958
In the Labyrinth, novel by Alain Robbe-Grillet, 1959
Rhinoceros, play by Eugène Ionesco, 1959
The Tin Drum, novel by Günter Grass, 1959

Zazie, novel by Raymond Queneau, 1959
Andorra, play by Max Frisch, 1961
Voices in the Evening, novel by Natalia Ginzburg, 1961
One Day in the Life of Ivan Denisovich, novella by Aleksandr Solzhenitsyn, 1962
The Physicists, play by Friedrich Dürrenmatt, 1962
Plagued by the West, novel by Jalal Âl-e Ahmad, 1962
Woman in the Dunes, novel by Abe Kōbō, 1962
Poem without a Hero, poem by Anna Akhmatova, 1963
Requiem, poem cycle by Anna Akhmatova, 1963
Marat/Sade, play by Peter Weiss, 1964
Blue Flowers, novel by Raymond Queneau, 1965
The Investigation, play by Peter Weiss, 1965
The Master and Margarita, novel by Mikhail Bulgakov, 1966
Silence, novel by Endō Shūsaku, 1966
One Hundred Years of Solitude, novel by Gabriel García Márquez, 1967
Cancer Ward, novel by Aleksandr Solzhenitsyn, 1968
The German Lesson, novel by Seigfried Lenz, 1968
The Lime Works, novel by Thomas Bernhard, 1970
The Ordeal, novel by Vasil Bykaw, 1970
Group Portrait with Lady, novel by Heinrich Böll, 1971
The Lost Honor of Katharina Blum, novel by Heinrich Böll, 1974
The Periodic Table, stories by Primo Levi, 1975
Kiss of the Spider Woman, novel by Manuel Puig, 1976
A School for Fools, novel by Sasha Sokolov, 1976
A Part of Speech, poems by Iosif Brodskii, 1977
Life: A User's Manual, novel by Georges Perece, 1978
If on a Winter's Night a Traveller, novel by Italo Calvino, 1979
Name of the Rose, novel by Umberto Eco, 1980
The House of the Spirits, novel by Isabel Allende, 1982
Fantasia: An Algerian Cavalcade, novel by Assia Djebar, 1985
Love in the Time of Cholera, novel by Gabriel García Márquez, 1985
Mr. Mani, novel by A.B. Yehoshua, 1989
Rice, novel by Su Tong, 1991

Reference Guide to

WORLD LITERATURE

THIRD EDITION

VOLUME 2

A

L'ABANDONNÉ
Story by Guy de Maupassant, 1884

"L'Abandonné" is the twelfth of Guy de Maupassant's nineteen short stories dealing with the twofold theme of illegitimacy and paternal or parental rejection. It bears a strong thematic resemblance to "Un Fils" ("A Son"), the third such story, and to "Duchoux," the seventeenth in the sporadic series. Admired by Henry James, it inspired Gabriele D'Annunzio.

While her husband takes a siesta, Madame de Cadour walks with Monsieur d'Apreval, the man who was once her lover, to a farm at some distance from Fécamp. On this farm lives their illegitimate son, Pierre Bénédict, whom neither has seen since he was a baby 40 years ago. The road is arduous in the heat of the day, and the old lady comes close to abandoning the project on which she has set her heart. But they arrive eventually and are met by a little girl. Then the child's mother appears. It is only with considerable difficulty that she can be persuaded to offer them two glasses of milk. The farmer is out in the fields. The suspense becomes almost unbearable as Mme. de Cadour awaits his return. When he does appear eventually, he curtly orders his wife to draw him some cider and then goes straight into the house. Mme. de Cadour and M. d'Apreval walk back to Fécamp, in deep dejection.

As is true of almost all of Maupassant's short stories, "L'Abandonné" deals with crisis, a single crisis here, as distinct from the dual crisis that he describes in a minority of his works. Looking in this instance into the innermost secrets of his characters' lives, he chooses the unforgettable turning-point. Mme. de Cadour is about to be reunited with her son, whom she last saw when she nursed him in her arms during his first day on earth. Crises of this kind reveal the truth about human character, bringing to the surface normally hidden depths of greed, callousness, or indifference. The device of the glasses of milk is particularly revealing in this context: even when offered payment for the milk, Mme. Bénédict is reluctant to offer it to her weary visitors.

Like "Duchoux," "L'Abandonné" is a variation on Maupassant's habitual theme of crisis, in that the son and his family never realize that a crisis has taken place. It differs, however, from Duchoux in two major respects. In "L'Abandonné" the mother, as well as the father, play an active part in the storyline. Furthermore, between the son and his parents there is no communication whatever. Thus, two people rather than one feel slighted and downcast; their grief and isolation are heightened by the fact that Pierre Bénédict does not address them with a single word, nor does he even appear to notice them.

Unlike most of Maupassant's short stories, "L'Abandonné" is told solely in the third person. Such third-person narratives, though ostensibly the work of an objective narrator, are sometimes ludic to the extent that they tease the reader with partial or mendacious perceptions of the events described. In "L'Abandonné," however, the authorial voice is devoid of mendacity or ambiguity: except in the one long and rather complex flashback, there is no use of free indirect style; and, as is generally the case in these strictly third-person fictions, much of the narrative consists of dialogue.

Maupassant's narrator is "omniscient" in the sense that he can look into his characters' innermost thoughts. Thus, he shows us memories flitting through Mme. de Cadour's mind of summer afternoons 40 years ago: happy days expectant of happiness as she rested in expectation of her child's birth. This plugging into the stream of her consciousness may well have been inspired by the thought-processes of Flaubert's Emma Bovary. At any rate it is not strictly "naturalist," but then Maupassant—differing from the view taken of his work by so many of his critics and admirers—did not in any case consider himself to be a practitioner of Naturalism. As in *Madame Bovary*, however, the mental recalling of past happiness stands in strong counterpoint to events in the present. Thus, to all intents and purposes, the narrator becomes "omniscient" only in the context of romantic dreams of happiness. The drab present has no need of such an omniscient narrator, it merely requires one who is objective and external.

Following in the tradition of Balzac, and reacting against George Sand, Maupassant seldom idealizes his peasantry (though how picturesquely their farmyard is described!): in "L'Abandonné," as so often elsewhere, he contradicts the topos of idyllic country life derived from Romanticism. The Bénédicts are shown to be more hard-hearted than the lower-middle-class son in *Duchoux*. M. d'Apreval and Mme. de Cadour proceed in utter loneliness, sharing their secret together but treated with incomprehension by the outside world. This loneliness is accentuated by Maupassant's use of narrative voice, which penetrates the recesses of Mme. de Cadour's mind only in order to emphasize her present unhappiness and despair.

"L'Abandonné" is one of the best of all Maupassant's stories of rejected or illegitimate children. Several of these—the second "L'Enfant" ("The Child") and the second "Le Père" ("The Father") for example—are surprising variations on this twofold theme. But "L'Abandonné" is considerably more straightforward in its plot and characterization. Like "Duchoux," it is an exclusively third-person narrative. Moreover, like virtually all Maupassant's stories of rejected or illegitimate children, it concerns a son rather than a daughter. Perhaps, at some deep level of the mind, Maupassant senses that he is projecting a trauma with which he all too readily identifies.

—Donald Adamson

ABDIAS
Story by Adalbert Stifter, 1843

"Abdias" was first published in 1843 in an Austrian novella almanac edited by Andreas Schuhmacher. It appeared again in 1847, revised and expanded, in the fourth volume of Adalbert Stifter's *Studien* (stories). The story narrates the life of the Jew Abdias whose existence is shaped by a series of catastrophes. All three chapters of the tale are named after women: Esther, after Abdias's mother, Deborah, after his wife, and Ditha, after his daughter. All hopes for a harmonious family life aroused by these titles come gradually to naught as the tragedy of Abdias's life unfolds.

Abdias grows up in a Jewish village hidden among Greek and Roman ruins in the desert of North Africa. The time of the events might be the beginning of the 19th century. When Abdias is old enough, his wealthy father, Aron, sends him into the world with a camel and a gold coin, advising him not to come back until he can live on his trading profits. Abdias leaves as a gentle adolescent and returns 15 years later as an accomplished businessman, hardened by the realities of the world of trade. He then sets out to win the lovely Deborah for his wife. He succeeds, and Aron then divides his wealth with his son. Abdias showers his new wife with treasures; however, his happiness is shortlived when he contracts smallpox. Pockmarks disfigure the beauty of his features and Deborah is unable to hide her disgust. Having lost Deborah's love, Abdias strives the more for riches, combining trading skills with those of a warrior. His envied successes, however, end when his powerful enemy, Melek, sacks the Jewish village. Abdias's neighbours blame him for the destruction and demand reparations.

In the midst of this misery, Deborah gives birth to a daughter and they name her Ditha. Abdias is deeply moved by the sight of the newborn child, and Deborah finds Abdias handsome once more. Tragically, Deborah, inexperienced and without proper childbirth care, bleeds to death. When Ditha is old enough to travel, Abdias takes her to Europe. He settles in a secluded valley in the narrator's homeland. Ditha, however, is different from other children: she is blind. Upon realizing this misfortune, Abdias starts trading again to secure Ditha's future through financial security.

When Ditha is almost full grown, her eyesight is restored by the shock from a stroke of lightning. Abdias ceases trading; instead, he takes up farming and devotes himself to teaching his daughter. A few years of great happiness follow. Yet, as unexpectedly as they came, good fortune and happiness cease, for when Ditha is 16 and starting to discover love, she is killed by a flash of lightning. Her death leaves Abdias in a daze, but after several years he suddenly recovers and seeks the long-postponed revenge on his enemy, Melek. By now, however, he has become too weak for that revenge. Instead, he sits on the bench in front of his house and is said to have reached more than a hundred years of age.

The brave character of the Jews in "Abdias" might have been influenced by Johann Gottfried von Herder and Goethe, and the imagery by Jean Paul. Finally the description of Jewish family life and customs has numerous parallels with the Old Testament, in particular the Book of Job. At the beginning of the tale, Stifter ponders human existence. He proposes three possibilities: first, the horrifyingly unyielding Fatum of the Greeks is the incomprehensible and unreasonable cause for all events in a human life; secondly, some higher power causes an individual's destiny; and thirdly, all phenomena could, in the end, be explained to be part of a logical chain of sequences if only we were more advanced in reason:

A serene chain of flowers is suspended through the infinity of the universe and sends its shimmering radiance into human hearts—the chain of cause and effect—and into the head of man was cast the loveliest of these flowers, reason, the eye of the soul, to which we can attach the chain, in order to count back along it, flower by flower, link by link, until we reach that

hand in which the end rests. And if at some future time we have counted properly, and if we can survey the whole sequence, then there will be no such thing as chance for us any more, but consequences, no misfortune but simply guilt; for it is the gaps existing now [in this chain of flowers of reason] which produce the unexpected and the misuse [of reason] which produces the unfortunate.

The promise held out to us in these preceding lines is, however, not perpetuated throughout the story of "Abdias." In fact, Stifter seems to have taken pains to avoid a clear answer to the question: is Abdias's life a series of logically connected events caused by merit and guilt, or is Abdias simply the plaything of the "Unvernunft des Seins" (unreason of being)?

Comparing the earlier text of the almanac version with the final version of the *Studien*, it becomes obvious that Stifter deliberately suppressed all statements that could have been read as pointing to Abdias's guilt. It is no surprise, therefore, that the many interpretations cannot solve the contradiction between Stifter's optimistic philosophical introduction and the subsequent depiction of events that pessimistically seem to prove once again the unreason of all being.

—Gerlinde Ulm Sanford

ABOUT THIS (Pro eto)
Poem by Vladimir Maiakovskii, 1923

In a letter written during the creation of *About This*, the last of Vladimir Maiakovskii's great love poems, he described love as the "heart of everything." It is in these poems—and especially in the major trilogy of *Cloud in Trousers*, *Chelovek* [Man], and *About This*—that Maiakovskii explores his myth of man at the deepest level: the poet-hero, in and through love, confronts the world and the oppressive forces of conformity, inertia, and, ultimately, time.

About This was written between 28 December 1922 and 28 February 1923, a period of separation from Lily Brik that was agreed upon as a result of difficulties in their relationship and which was seen by Maiakovskii as a term of imprisonment. The theme had been turning over in Maiakovskii's head (or heart) throughout 1922, but this separation acted as the final catalyst for a poem that in his autobiography *Ia* [Me] he describes as "along personal lines about life in general." Certainly, with the advent of the NEP (New Economic Policy) and the disappointment of his utopian revolutionary fervour, as well as the personal crisis, this was the time for a reappraisal of his whole life and work.

About This is the longest of Maiakovskii's love poems, consisting of nearly 1,000 verse lines. It was during the later stages of work on the poem that he began to employ the "ladder" form of graphic layout. In technical terms, however, the poem is above all a masterpiece of integrated polymetric composition, utilizing a range of metrical themes that are linked to the genre and thematic structure. More generally, the bold hyperbole and imagery of Maiakovskii's early poetry, his loud rhetoric and virtuosity, are still on show, though tempered; his satire is biting and grotesque; and his lyricism is made all the more painful and intense for the self-deprecating irony that accompanies it:

My ballad's about "he" and "she."
That's not terribly novel.
What's terrible is that "he"—is me,
and "she"—is my beloved.

The poem is made up of a prologue and epilogue and two main narrative parts, "The Ballad of Reading Gaol" (the title borrowed, surprisingly, from Oscar Wilde) and "Christmas Eve" (echoing Gogol'). The narrative is based on a series of journeys, with cinematographic shifts in time and place. It begins, in "The Ballad of Reading Gaol," with the poet-hero, located at Maiakovskii's actual address, attempting to contact his beloved by telephone. Her rejection leads to his metamorphosis, through jealousy, into a bear. He is then carried in a dream sequence to meet his earlier persona, the eponymous hero of *Chelovek*, who at the end of that poem had been left in an eternity of unfulfilled love. The "man" accuses him of giving into the routine of everyday life (often symbolized for Maiakovskii by tea-drinking) and commands the poet-hero to find people who, through altruistic love, will come to save him.

This section then leads into "Christmas Eve," in which Maiakovskii the bear sets off around Moscow in search of someone to make the one journey that matters—to come and save the "man." In the course of his wanderings the poet-hero meets not only Moscow life but also, as Maiakovskii confronts his own self with merciless honesty, his various doubles involved in that life—the family man, the social man, and the young *komsomol* member. This last double, who is encountered first of all, commits suicide. When nobody will help, the poet-hero too contemplates death, but then he turns to his one last chance, his beloved. Wilde's theme of "each man kills the thing he loves" comes together here with Dostoevskii's *Crime and Punishment*, for the negative way out, revenge, now vies with the hope of salvation in her love. But it is not put to the test, for at the last moment the "man" makes a journey over time and space to assert that there is no happiness without happiness for everyone, and Maiakovskii's past and present personae fuse in a classical martyr figure: his ideal here is universal love, *eros* founded on *agape*. The narrative now draws to a close: first the action shifts to Paris in the future, where the poet-hero has become a figure of fun and "half-dies" after being beaten up; then he returns to Moscow to confront his enemies and be silenced—at last—in a hail of bullets; finally, the poet ascends to the stars, but, although this is generally interpreted as a victory, the verse is set in the amphibrachic rhythm that was a "whisper" for Maiakovskii.

The epilogue takes us out of the narrative for Maiakovskii to reassert, in the face of the poem's conclusion, his opposition to the stultifying inertia of life. On the basis of this he then appeals to a scientist of the 30th century, asking to be resurrected, to make the journey out of death into life, to catch up on all his unfulfilled loving. The idea of future resurrection derives from the Russian mystical thinker Nikolai Fedorov, and the great linguist Roman Jakobson, who was a friend of Maiakovskii, attested that his appeal was meant quite literally. But the clarity of Maiakovskii's vision of such a future is not constant, and, although the poem ends with a rhetorical expression of the poet's ideal of universal love, the epilogue, like the poem, has an underlying ambivalence.

In fact, the silence imposed on the lyric poet at the end of "Christmas Eve" was maintained, apart from the two short poems inspired by Tat'iana Iakovleva and some unfinished fragments, for the remaining seven years of Maiakovskii's life. On the existential level the poem offers only one resolution near at hand, the negative one of suicide, and, in view of the interrelation of life and art in Maiakovskii's poetics, it is hardly surprising that the poet's own suicide note resembles very closely that of his *komsomol* double in the poem.

—Robin Aizlewood

THE AENEID (Aeneis)
Poem by Virgil, 1st century, BC

The ancient testimony about Virgil's epic is enlightening: "The *Aeneid* when hardly begun aroused such expectations that Sextus Propertius did not hesitate to declare (2, 34, 65f.) 'Give way, you Roman poets, give way, you poets of Greece; a greater work than the *Iliad* is being born'." The compliment, by a contemporary elegist, signalled the great hopes of Augustus, Maecenas, and cultured Romans generally for the national epic in the making. Aelius Donatus' *Life of Vergil* enlarges on the design and nature of the new epic: ". . . The *Aeneid*, a story rich in incident and variety, a counterpart, so to speak, of both *Iliad* and *Odyssey* together, (an epic) in which both Greek and Roman places and characters were mutually involved, and which was designed (and this was his special intention) to embrace an account of the origins both of Rome and of Augustus." Romans had no doubt about its nationalistic character—that it was designed to glorify Rome. The assumption has been in recent times that glorification meant uncritical adulation, but Virgil's view of the Roman achievement was certainly more complex. Its compositional history is debatable. However, the ancient *Life* notes that "The *Aeneid* he first sketched out in prose, and then set about turning it into a poem piece by piece, as his whim determined, not following any set order in the process. Moreover, to avoid retarding the flow of his invention, he left some passages unfinished, and in others inserted trivial verses which would support the narrative temporarily; he humorously used to remark that they were to serve as 'props' to support the fabric of his work until the permanent supports should come to replace them."

There is general acceptance today of the design to rely on material in Homer's *Odyssey* for the first six books (The Wanderings of Aeneas), and in the *Iliad* for the last six books (the Trojan War in Italy). There is also a tripartite design and responsive pattern in the epic: Books I to IV (The Tragedy of Dido); Books V to VIII (The Birth of a Nation); Books IX to XII (The Tragedy of Turnus), with remarkable symmetry in the responses between books in the first and second half of the epic (I and VII, II and VIII, etc.). Although scholars are sometimes chary of the rigidity of the detected design, there is unanimity on the matter of accent and symmetry throughout the epic; on the alternation of mood in the sequence of books, and on the emphatic, memorable character of the even-numbered books. Homer, Apollonius Rhodius, and Callimachus are demonstrably formative influences on the epic, as are Aratus and the Homeric scholiasts, and there are frequent marks of indebtedness to earlier Roman writers, to Ennius, Marcus Terentius Varro, and Lucretius. The impress of Greek (mostly Hellenistic) and Roman philosophical thought and of Roman and native Italic religion is constant and important for an understanding of the national poem. Stoic, Epicurean, and Academic theory sit easily alongside the Augustan attempts to revive Italian religion and to generate a new Palatine Triad (Apollo, Diana, and Latona), which was closely attached to Augustus' career and the new order he sought to establish. Allegorical readings of the epic are generally discounted, but there is evidence that Virgil looked back to Odysseus as Aeneas' paradigm through the prism of Apollonius' Jason; it is highly probable that he saw Augustus shimmering through the figure of Aeneas, and Cleopatra through the figures of Dido, Amata, and Camilla.

The tripartite structure of the epic is reflected in the triadic design of the separate books. For example, Books I–III each contain three parts: I—Prologue and the storm (recalled in Shakespeare's *The Tempest*); the Venus episodes; and the Trojans at Carthage; II—Sinon, Laocoon and the wooden horse; the Fall of Troy and the death of Priam; Aeneas' departure with Anchises and Ascanius-Julus, and the loss of Creusa; III—Aeneas' travels; the compromise of Jupiter and Juno; death of Turnus. Books IV–XII similarly divide into three parts each.

Twentieth-century scholars have been increasingly conscious of pervasive imagery and symbolism in the separate books and throughout the epic. Warfare and the man of war have been primary targets, with emphasis on complexity, the dilemma, and internal heroism. Tensions between public and private voices and worlds have been significantly explored but hardly resolved. Manliness and heroism (*virtus*, without prejudice to gender), *pietas* (fidelity), kingship and concord, peace and tranquillity, and *humanitas* have been weighed against *furor* (frenzy, madness), *ira* (wrath, anger), cruelty in war, discord, and the wastefulness (but generally not the senselessness) of the deaths of young and old, fathers and sons. Pessimism, associated with suffering, alienation, and loss, has competed with optimism in the interpretation of the epic, but with particular emphasis in Book XII. The verdict is far from unanimous regarding the hero, but one scholar, associated unintentionally with the "Harvard pessimists" (Wendell Clausen), has caught the humane sensibility of the man of war: "Touched in his inmost being, Aeneas hesitates . . . an extraordinary moment of humanity; for the epic warrior never hesitates." Aeneas has to make difficult and agonizing choices; he is a hero who is true to life. The ambiguity and the otherness of the epic are its hallmarks of greatness.

—Alexander G. McKay

AETIA
Poem by Callimachus, 3rd century BC

The *Aetia*, which in antiquity was Callimachus' most famous poem, dealt with the mythological origins of customs, cult rites, and names from throughout the Greek world. It has come down to us in a very fragmentary state. We can for the most part, therefore, reconstruct the poem only in broad outline. It was written in elegiacs and consisted of four books, possibly totalling between 4,000 and 6,000 lines, ʌus attaining epic length.

As we have it, the *Aetia* begins with a defence of Callimachus' literary principles, then depicts the poet's transportation in a dream from his native Cyrene to Mount Helicon, where he meets the Muses, just as his model for the encounter, Hesiod, claimed to have done at the beginning of his *Theogonia* (*Theogony*). Books I and II of the poem are thereafter cast in the form of a dialogue, the Heliconian Muses answering in a learned fashion the poet's antiquarian questions. In Books III and IV the dialogue form is dropped, a unity being imposed by two framing references to Queen Berenice, whose husband Ptolemy III Euergetes was crowned King of Egypt in 247 BC. Book III begins with an elegiac celebration of a victory by Berenice's chariot at the Nemean Games, and then proceeds to describe the

origin of the games, which Callimachus ascribes to a command of Athene to Heracles after his victory over the Nemean lion. Book IV closes with the famous "Lock of Berenice" (translated by Catullus), which discovers the origin of the constellation Coma Berenices (Lock of Berenice) in the disappearance from a temple of the strand of hair which the queen had dedicated to secure her husband's safety as he went off to war; its translation to heaven was "identified" by the court astronomer, Conon. Our version of the *Aetia* concludes with an epilogue in which the poet announces that he will now pass on to the "pedestrian pasture of the Muses," evidently referring to his more prosaic *Iambi*.

It is generally agreed that the *Aetia* was originally composed quite early in Callimachus' career and was published only as Books I and II. At some point after 247 BC, Books III and IV were added, together with the Berenice pieces, of which the "Lock" seems at first to have been circulated independently. Given the epilogue's reference to the *Iambi*, it may be that Callimachus brought the two works together in a collected edition at the same time. It seems certain that the polemical prologue, the "Reply to the Telchines" was placed at the head of the *Aetia* at this juncture too, as an attack on Callimachus' detractors and as a defence not only of the *Aetia* itself but of the poet's entire output, now in its final edition.

In the "Reply," Callimachus represents his critics, whom he calls the Telchines (fabled metal-working sorcerers of notorious maliciousness), as protagonists of "one continuous song in many thousands of lines . . . on kings or . . . heroes of old." This makes them traditionalists in poetic taste, and squares with what we know of, in particular, the epic written at this period. Callimachus claims a preference for poetry of shorter compass and expresses an abhorrence of bombast. He says that Apollo told him early in his career as a poet to "keep the sacrificial victim as fat as possible, but keep the Muse slender," and to strike out on untrodden poetic paths. As we have seen, the *Aetia* was of epic length, but it featured a deliberate discontinuity, which Callimachus may well have felt had a forebear in the disjointed poems of Hesiod, whom he allusively "cites" as a model in his story of his dream encounter with the Muses. Moreover, though he did write poetry in praise of "kings" and traditional "heroes," his treatment of them is sharply at variance with the bombastic poetry, especially epic, written on such themes during the period.

His practice is illustrated by his poem on the victory of Berenice. This is, of course, in elegiacs, which in itself must have seemed innovatory, since victory odes were traditionally written in lyric metres. The poem leads into the *aition* describing the origin of the Nemean Games. This devotes considerable space to the story of how Heracles spent the night with the poor but generous Molorchus before he set out against the Nemean lion. In fact, the heroic feat is set in juxtaposition with something rather less elevated, Molorchus' struggle with household mice, and the *aition* on the Nemean Games is set in ironic contrast with another, on the origin of the mousetrap! This is hardly the grand traditional style.

Another fascinating index of the poet's approach is the story of Acontius and Cydippe, again from Book III. The ostensible point of this poem is to give the history of the famous Acontiad family on the island of Ceos, for which Callimachus draws on the writings of the 5th-century chronicler Xenomedes, actually naming him as his source. But the impression of dry erudition is offset by the love interest in the narrative of the young lovers' difficult path to eventual happiness, and, though the romance is set in the heroic past, the accent is on more everyday human experience, and this is clearly the real point of the poem. Literary self-consciousness, learnedness, a preoccupation with vividness in the depiction of everyday and low motifs, and a love of irony and contrast are thus some of the main hallmarks of the *Aetia*.

As a collection of "origins," the *Aetia* may be a response to the feeling that Greek culture was to some extent under threat after the expansion of the Greek world by Alexander the Great and in view of the levelling of the local dialects of the Greek language itself. In this case, the famed learnedness of the *Aetia* need not in every instance be considered a display of erudition for its own sake.

—G. Zanker

AGAINST SAINTE-BEUVE (Contre Sainte-Beuve)
Prose by Marcel Proust, 1954 (written c. 1909)

There is no such thing as a definitive text of *Against Sainte-Beuve*, though Marcel Proust produced a great deal of draft material for the book he was intending to write, taking as his point of departure the critic Charles-Augustin Sainte-Beuve (1804–69) who helped to put the romantics on the map by demonstrating their affinity with Ronsard, and made no attempt to conceal his distaste for contemporary realism.

Temperamentally out of sympathy with the premises from which Sainte-Beuve had been writing, Proust spent a lot of time—before he put pen to paper—mulling over what he wanted to say. In March 1909 he complained that he had "this bulging suitcase of ideas in the middle of my brain, and I must make up my mind whether to leave or unpack it. But I have already forgotten a lot." (Letter to Georges de Lauris, shortly after 6 March 1909.)

But Proust wasn't at all sure of how he wanted to categorize what he was going to write, or even whether it would be categorizable, mixing as it would critical, autobiographical, and fictional strains. He wrote:

> In showing how he erred, in my view, as a writer and as critic, I would perhaps succeed in making some points that have often occurred to me about what criticism ought to be and what art is. In passing, and in connecting with him, I will do what he so often did—use him as a pretext for talking about certain forms of life.

The draft contains a recollection that was to be seminal for Proust's novel *Remembrance of Things Past* because it leads to the notion of unconscious memory. He recalled a moment of dipping toast in a cup of tea and experiencing, when he put into in his mouth, "a disturbance, scents of geranium and orange trees, a feeling of extraordinary light, of happiness." Suddenly he felt as if he had been transported back into the country house where he spent many of his childhood holidays. Then he remembered how his grandfather used to give him a rusk he had just dipped in tea . . . In several later drafts for the episode in the novel, Proust kept the rusk before substituting the madeleine.

Sainte-Beuve was innovative, both in canvassing the view that criticism should be re-creative, not dogmatic, and in carrying the methods of natural history into moral history. But he wrote as if there were no discontinuity between the writer's everyday life and his work. For Proust the writer has two selves. "A book is the product of a different self from the one we manifest in our habits, our social life, and our vices." The act of writing should be a matter of making contact with "the deep self which is rediscovered only by abstracting one-self from other people and the self which knows other people." The deep self is "the only real self, and artists end up by living for this alone, like a god whom they cease to ignore and to whom they have sacrificed a life which serves only to honour him." Writing emerges from an underground stream of deep reflectiveness.

Sainte-Beuve was helpful to Proust negatively. His complacent preoccupation with mundane materiality seemed so repulsive that Proust rebounded towards the alternative way of living through literature, sacrificing his life to the inner self as if it were a god.

Ignoring the inner self, Sainte-Beuve refused to think of literature as distinct or separable from the rest of the man and his nature, maintaining that to understand an author you need answers to certain biographical questions. What were his religious views? How was he affected by natural scenery? How did he behave with women and with money? Was he rich or poor? What was his routine, the style of his daily life? What were his vices, his weaknesses? According to Sainte-Beuve, none of the answers to these questions was irrelevant in judging the author of a book and the book itself.

Proust's hostility to this view was inflamed by his determination to make his unwritten book add up to more than his unsatisfactory life. He'd never had an adequate literary receptacle for the memories, images, and ideas that swirled through his consciousness when he was in bed, but now, blending fiction experimentally with autobiography and criticism in his attack on Sainte-Beuve, he was taking the first steps towards the autobiographical fiction that would resurrect his past while putting his literary principles into practice. His title, *À la recherche du temps perdu*, does not mean "Remembrance of Things Past," but "In Search of Lost Time."

—Ronald Hayman

THE AGE OF REASON (L'Âge de raison)
Novel by Jean-Paul Sartre, 1945

The Age of Reason is the first volume in the series *Paths of Freedom*. Other volumes, *The Reprieve* (*Le Sursis*) and *Iron in the Soul* (*La Mort dans l'âme*), appeared in 1945 and 1949. One fragment of the final unfinished part appeared in *Les Temps Modernes* in 1949; another was published posthumously in *Oeuvres romanesques* (1981). As the collective title suggests, the series deals with the consequences of absolute freedom as examined in Jean-Paul Sartre's *Being and Nothingness* whereby an individual realizes that, in the absence of universal values and human essence, he faces the painful obligation to create his own morality. But to discover ontological freedom, Sartre shows in the novels, one must pass through the struggle for freedom from political oppression, since, although Sartre began the novel from an non-political perspective before 1939, by the end he had become convinced that to see personal freedom without the political and social contexts that condition and restrict it was contradictory.

Involving multiple characters and plots, *The Age of Reason* is divided into chapters each focusing on one or two story lines; subsequent chapters take up others. The result is a sense of simultaneous action among several personae, whose stories are connected but who receive alternately the narrative focus, allowing Sartre to present reality from their point of view, following his phenomenological emphasis upon perspective. History and politics intrude little, although in the background is the Spanish Civil War, prefiguring the European conflict to come, and suggesting an oppressive historical destiny. The somewhat melodramatic plot lines would not indicate a philosophical novel, but each human dilemma is presented from points of view Sartre developed in *Being and Nothingness*. Problems such as freedom, value, consciousness, corporeality, and human relationships are woven into the plot, as they are felt and lived by the characters.

Mathieu Delarue is an unmarried philosophy professor—like Sartre—whose principal wish is to remain free. When his mistress, Marcelle, learns she is pregnant, he immediately looks for funds to pay for an abortion, since marriage and fatherhood would interfere with his personal freedom. Marcelle, who has ambivalent feelings about the embryo within her, apparently agrees with him, but comes to desire the child as a way of justifying her own life, otherwise seemingly pointless. Mathieu is unable to find money, until he resolves to steal 5,000 francs from Lola, a singer who is the mistress of Mathieu's former pupil Boris. By the time Mathieu forces himself to take the money, however, it is no longer wanted; the meaning of his one bold action is taken from him.

Marcelle has long been secretly seeing Daniel, a homosexual friend of Mathieu, whose attentions add charm to her drab existence. As a homosexual, Daniel cannot accept himself, at least without the mediation of others. His response is masochism. First he tries to drown his cats, but cannot bring himself to punish them as self-punishment. He even considers self-mutilation. He both humiliates and gratifies himself by picking up male prostitutes, whose filth and coarseness appal him and who—he half-hopes—might attack him. He forces himself to pay attention to Marcelle, whom he loathes, particularly in her state of pregnancy. Finally, he conceives of two acts of self-punishment: he confesses his pederasty to Mathieu, and he will marry Marcelle, thus robbing Mathieu of his decision and condemning himself to long-term misery.

Boris and his sister Ivich are frequently the focus of attention. Both refuse the models and classifications proposed by society. Boris is obsessed by time; although young, he feels he has no future. Ivich's principal obsession is corporeality; her consciousness tries to deny its bodily extension or facticity, refusing the demands of food and sleep and desire. A telling scene is that where the drunken Ivich, in a nightclub, stabs her hand with a knife, a gesture of fascination with, but rage against, embodiment. Both characters, like Mathieu, who is drawn by Ivich's apparent freedom from the contingency of being, experience great difficulty in dealing with others, since others represent demands and responsibilities. Boris cannot abide the gaze of Lola, whose lovelorn look demands a response he cannot give. Ivich reacts violently to any claim on her, even the barest claim to her friendship by Mathieu.

Contrasted by Boris, Ivich, Daniel, Marcelle, and even Mathieu is Brunet, his communist friend. To Mathieu he appears solid, genuine. According to Sartrean ontology, consciousness always feels empty (since it is not a thing but an intention, projected toward and clinging to what is not itself), so that most of the characters experience an inner nothingness and feel objectified by others. But Mathieu feels particularly inauthentic next to Brunet, who has committed his freedom to a cause that validates it. Another character who has engaged his freedom is Gomez, a painter, who is fighting with the Republicans in Spain. The Jewish wife of Gomez, Sarah, serves to represent a dilemma both political and personal: what does it mean to be a Jew?

What gives interest to *The Age of Reason* is the way in which Sartre concretizes philosophical problems and perceptions. He excels at rendering in language how existence is felt from the inside and outside—a vague emptiness, the sense of being projected forward without reason, the look of flesh, the glutinous sense of desire. His descriptions of the gaze—how and why it makes one uncomfortable—are masterly. That his characters generally make little of their lives fits his ethics, born of wartime: freedom must be actualized in a cause that must itself promote freedom. Those who deny this deny their own freedom and are in bad faith (the Sartrean term for the self-deception that allows one to see oneself as an essence). Save Brunet and Gomez, no one achieves authenticity: Ivich returns to the bourgeois family she loathes. Daniel will persist in his masochistic bad faith, Marcelle in the belief that another being can justify her. Mathieu does understand, however, that his freedom is meaningless; he has reached the age of reason.

—Catharine Savage Brosman

AITAREYA
See UPANISHADS

AJAX
Play by Sophocles, before 441 BC (?)

The earliest of Sophocles' extant tragedies highlights Ajax, formidable defensive hero of the Greeks at Troy, a tower of defence in the field, a match for Hector in combat, but who ultimately lost the decision over who should inherit Achilles' armour to Odysseus. Madness and suicide were the sequel, prompted by Athena's sense of Ajax's personal affront to her power. The *Little Iliad*, part of the epic cycle, described his attempt to murder the Greek commanders. Athens adopted Ajax as a cult hero, protector of one of the ten tribes, and saviour of the Athenian cause at Salamis (480 BC).

The prologue outlines Ajax's intention, foiled by Athena, to kill Agamemnon, Menelaus, and Odysseus. Athena diverted his attack to captured flocks of sheep and cattle. Odysseus, cowardly in his pursuit of the mad Ajax, is also compassionate in his first appearance; Athena, rebuffed by Ajax in battle, is pitiless. The chorus of sailors sides with Ajax. Tecmessa, the captive bride of Ajax, reveals anxiety and compassion for her master. Ajax (whose name is cognate with the Greek cry of grief) is unrepentant; responsive to claims of family and honour, he yearns for death. Tecmessa's response reverberates with elements of Andromache's parting from Hector (Homer, *Iliad*, Book VI), pleading with Ajax to relent out of respect for his parents, his son (Eurysaces), and for her sake. Ajax's reaction to his loss of prestige recalls Achilles' impulse to withdraw from his commitment to the Greek army at Troy after Agamemnon insulted him. Eurysaces receives his father's shield as legacy. After a grief-laden choral interlude, Ajax emerges with Hector's sword in hand and in a reverie characterized by gentleness and philosophical rumination, a celebrated deception speech that introduces a suggestion of ambiguity regarding his suicide or continuing life, he partly dispels the anxiety of his sympathizers. A messenger reports that Teucer, Ajax's half-brother, has arrived. Thereafter the chorus uniquely leaves the stage and the scene changes from the tent of Ajax to an isolated clump of bushes on the seashore. In a celebrated monologue, Ajax addresses prayers to Teucer, Hermes, the Furies, the sun god and Death; he invokes Salamis and Athens and the forces of nature and dies on his sword, an unforgiving and cursing suicide.

Odysseus' tracking of mad Ajax at the outset of the play is repeated in the final search for the corpse of Ajax. Tecmessa finds the body and covers it with her cloak. Teucer, Ajax's half-brother, tries to ensure Eurysaces against harm; his speech deals with their mutual father, Telamon, whose nature portends rejection for Teucer on his return. Menelaus rejects formal burial for Ajax; Spartan politics and military discipline are uppermost in his nature. However, Teucer rejects Menelaus' edict and initiates the funeral and burial of Ajax. The chorus denounces the inventor of war and emphasizes the continuity of strife. Agamemnon challenges Teucer's arrogance (*hubris*) and maintains an authoritarian position of innate superiority even as Teucer argues against him. Finally Odysseus intervenes with determining statesmanship and enlightened humanism and surprisingly induces Agamemnon to agree to the burial of Ajax; a ceremonial procession ensues.

The play is marked by dramatic irony and abundant ambiguity. Themes and imagery range from the sword and shield to hunting and yoking, from daylight and darkness to disease and time. Ajax, heroic but with 5th-century definition, by degrees exasperated, exaggerated, hubristic, and compassionate, "a solitary shame-culture figure thrown up by a literature of guilt" (Jones), on the verge of suicide provides the finest monologue in Greek tragedy. Tecmessa, who recalls Homeric Andromache, is the sympathetic defender of the family and community against his obdurately heroic but selfish design.

—Alexander G. McKay

ALCHIMIE DU VERBE (Alchemy of the Word)
Verse and prose by Arthur Rimbaud, 1873

"Alchimie du verbe" otherwise known as "Delirium II" ("Délires II") is one of the texts of Arthur Rimbaud's *A Season in Hell*, a work that was printed but not published, in the autumn of 1873. It is very different in tone and nature from the confession of "Foolish Virgin" ("Vierge folle") in "Delirium I," but it continues its sister text to the extent that it begins by turning the spotlight on to Rimbaud himself and on to what he regarded, at the time of writing, as one of his follies, a very particular form of the follies of youth.

It evokes the poet's attitudes, beliefs, studies, and experiences in an earlier phase of his life. The inclusion within the text of "Alchimie du verbe" of some of the poems from "Last Poems" ("Derniers vers"), most of them in modified form, suggests that the period that Rimbaud is evoking might correspond at least in part to the date of composition of the poems in question, from May to August 1872, but this is by no means totally conclusive evidence.

The title (or sub-title), "Alchimie du verbe," raises the question of the nature of this verbal alchemy. Jean Richer's *L'Alchimie du verbe de Rimbaud* (1972) relates to the concept, at times in a somewhat fanciful way, to such notions as the pictographic origin of letters of the alphabet, the numerical value of letters, the symbolism of the Tarot cards and of the signs of the zodiac, correspondences between parts of the human body and letters, and the relationship between sound and sense.

However, "alchemy of the word" is undoubtedly the term by which Rimbaud refers to the rejected poetics. In the opening section of the text Rimbaud alludes to his contemptuous dismissal of contemporary literary and artistic celebrities in a manner reminiscent of the content of his famous letter to Paul Demeny of 15 May 1871. He also alludes to the sonnet "Voyelles" [Vowels] from *Poésies*, in which he had presented the vowels in terms of colours. Yet a more interesting revelation is his claim that he regulated the shape and the movement of each consonant, thereby implying that he responded to them in a similar fashion. It was not necessarily a case of colour hearing, perhaps rather an indication of Rimbaud's unquestioned ability to look at language with fresh eyes.

There is at this stage in the "Alchimie du verbe" an enthusiasm in the writing, as he talks of his dreams of crusades, his voyages of discovery, moral revolutions, his belief in all forms of enchantment.

After the first interlude—the revised versions of the poems "Larme" and "Bonne Pensée du matin"—Rimbaud confides that he had grown accustomed to "simple hallucination": seeing a mosque in place of a factory (in other words, a substitution of the spiritual for the material); a drawing-room at the bottom of a lake (a surreal change of context), but then he writes of "the hallucination of words," a phrase which doubtless sheds new light on what he meant by "l'alchimie du verbe."

After the second quotation-interlude Rimbaud incorporates into the main text a puzzling paragraph in inverted commas which appears to be a little poem in prose which presents the sun, the god of fire, as a bombarding general.

As the text continues to unfold, Rimbaud indicates that the verbal alchemy, or the experiences to which he subjected himself in the cause of poetry, began to affect his health. He refers to the kind of madness for which one is locked away, he states that his sanity was threatened and that he was ripe for death. Although it is not always clear whether his words should be interpreted literally or figuratively, the tone is blacker by far than it was at the beginning. Yet suddenly, shortly before the end, images of the Cross and the rainbow—remainders of his Christian upbringing—and a double mention of "Happiness" in some mysterious way seem to bring him back from the brink, so that the experiences evoked earlier in the text can be put behind him and he can claim, somewhat enigmatically, that he now knows how to salute beauty.

If the *Illuminations* were written after *A Season in Hell*, they could be expressions of this "beauty," but the prose of "Delirium II" itself in places possesses not just a haunting quality but also puts out challenges to the reader. The double-edged proclamation, "Happiness was my fate, my remorse, my worm," relies on the traditional triple formula of the rhetorician, but some sentences cannot be so easily presented, if not dismissed: the reader is invited to join with Rimbaud when he exclaims: "I was idle, prey to a deep fever; I would envy the bliss of beasts—caterpillars, who represent the innocence of limbo, moles, the sleep of virginity!" Delirium? Alchemy of the word? It is a poetry that is almost impossible to define, but one that even today is exciting, bold, revolutionary.

—Keith Aspley

ALF LAILA WA-LAILA

See THE THOUSAND AND ONE NIGHTS

ALL MEN ARE BROTHERS

See WATER MARGIN

ALL QUIET ON THE WESTERN FRONT (Im Westen nichts Neues)
Novel by Erich Maria Remarque, 1929

Erich Maria Remarque's first major novel, *All Quiet on the Western Front*, appeared as a serial in a newspaper in 1928 and in slightly fuller book form in 1929. Enormously successful from the start, it is not only one of Germany's best-selling books ever, but it has probably sold more copies in more languages than any other work of German literature. Even the title of the English translation (echoing the song "All Quiet along the Potomac") has become part of the language, although it misses the negative irony of the original, which refers to the death of the central character as being "nothing new" as well as "not newsworthy." The novel's indictment of the pointlessness of World War I, and its portrayal of a betrayed generation in the latter part of the Great War from the standpoint of one young soldier and his associates reflected the experiences of soldiers in all the combatant nations. The rejection of nationalism in the work accounts for its international popularity when written, and its criticism of war has made for a continued relevance.

Its initial publication in Germany led to controversy. The ten years distance from World War I allowed for objective assessment, but attitudes to the lost war had polarized: those who saw it as a bloody warning accepted Remarque's book; those who attributed Germany's defeat to a stab in the back, or viewed the war as a test by fire of German nationhood rejected it. To the latter groups belonged the Nazis, and Remarque's books were burned in 1933 for "betraying the German soldiers."

The vivid and direct realism and immediate first-person narrative style also led to criticism: Remarque was accused of sensationalism and distortion, and his work was also parodied, although it had a direct and positive influence in Germany and elsewhere (on Theodor Plievier, Adrienne Thomas, Evadne Price, and others). The hysterical tone of some of the early criticism reminds us that the work is not a piece of historical documentation from 1917, but a novel written in 1928. Although Remarque has a short preface declaring the work to be a report on the generation destroyed by the war, whether or not they survived, and although the death of the narrator is reported objectively and briefly at the end of the book, the bulk of it portrays the war through the eyes of a sensitive and literary 20-year-old, Paul Bäumer, who joints up straight from school in 1916, bullied into it by the thoughtless nationalism of his teachers. Stolen youth is a recurrent motif. Although there are flashbacks, the novel begins in (and takes place for the most part in the few weeks of) 1917, when the war has reached a stage of stagnation, and the effect on the ordinary soldier is of stultification. Bäumer's company sustains losses, and gradually the small group of men around him, schoolfellows and workers, are killed. The soldiers become automata, trying to avoid death more than actually fighting. Rapid scene-changes take us to the front (sheltering from shell-fire in a cemetery, under gas attack), behind the lines (once with some French girls), on leave to a Germany that cannot conceive of life at the front, into contact with Russian POWs, and to hospital (where the effects of war are clearest). The increasingly condensed

final chapters are set in 1918, and although the German soldiers are not defeated in the field, they will clearly lose in the face of fresh and better-fed allied troops, and Bäumer dies before the actual armistice. His death is not worth reporting.

Description alternates with speculative passages by Bäumer, and there are (inconclusive) discussions on the futility of the whole war. There are no historical details, certainly no heroics, and not even a real enemy except death, although Bäumer is forced to kill an equally terrified Frenchman. The perspective is consistently that of the ordinary soldier, and the principal officer is a drill sergeant who is more hated than the supposed enemy. Through the eyes of the young narrator we see the deaths of his contemporaries, and portraits of other soldiers, ranging from Bäumer's close friend and father-figure, Katczinsky, the resourceful old soldier, and the drill sergeant Himmelstoss, to others who are nameless ciphers, like a major who is more concerned about proper saluting than the hardship of the front. However, the work is non-political (Remarque was criticized for this). But this reflects reality: the soldiers in the trenches did not mutiny or desert.

Bäumer dies with a look almost of content on his face, but in fact he has come to realize that in him there is an obdurate spark of a life that overrides even his personality. This is the positive element in the work, rather than (as sometimes assumed) the idea of comradeship, which is little more than solidarity in the face of adversity. In fact, Remarque showed in the sequel, *The Road Back*, 1931, how quickly the artificial comradeship of the war crumbled in the Weimar Republic, as the ex-soldiers (one of whom, the central figure of the later novel, is virtually identical to Bäumer) struggled and sometimes failed to make their way. The sequel (which begins during the war) is important to the understanding of *All Quiet on the Western Front*, although it did not enjoy the same popular success.

—Brian Murdoch

AMINTA
Play by Torquato Tasso, 1573

Aminta, a pastoral drama in five acts, written, it is said, in two months, was first performed on the island of Belvedere del Po near Ferrara, most probably on 31 July 1573. It is the first masterpiece of Torquato Tasso, now mainly remembered for his monumental *Jerusalem Delivered*. There is a certain amount of debate as to the exact genre of *Aminta*. It contains elements of the pastoral (there is a shepherd, a shepherdess, a satyr), comedy (there is a happy ending), tragedy (we have a near-rape, a reported killing, an attempted suicide) as well as elements of dramatic and lyrical eclogue. In any case, we can say for certain that Tasso wrote *Aminta* with the classical eclogue in mind. (There are echoes of Theocritus, Moschus, Ovid and Virgil.) In Ferrara four other lyric eclogues were produced in the 30 years preceding *Aminta*, the most influential of which was Sannazaro's *Arcadia*, a pastoral novel with 12 eclogues in poetry, printed in 1504.

The plot of *Aminta* is appealing in its simplicity. The eponymous hero suffers from unrequited love for the beautiful shepherdess, Silvia, a chaste huntress and follower of Diana. Instinctive and natural love finds itself thwarted and inhibited by the disdainful indifference of the proud Silvia. The hero and heroine each have an older adviser and companion, more experienced in the ways of the world: Aminta confides in the cynic Tirsi, a portrait of the author himself, and

Silvia's counsellor is Dafne. Central to the play is the fountain episode. Warned that Silvia will be bathing there, Aminta goes to the fountain to find Silvia bound to a tree with her own hair by the lascivious satyr. Having averted any physical harm, Aminta unties the naked Silvia, who, ungratefully, flees. Thinking that Silvia has been eaten by wolves, Aminta attempts suicide by throwing himself over a cliff. Meanwhile, Silvia reappears, intact, repents of her harshness towards her suitor, and finally takes the miraculously saved Aminta as her lover.

After the Prologue pronounced by Cupid, it is hardly surprising to find that the main subject of *Aminta* is love, or rather the triumph of love over all men, high or low. The turning point in the play is the relenting of Silvia, and her acceptance of Aminta's love. It should be noted that the setting of *Aminta* is not a mythic Arcadia, but an ordinary down to earth place that the spectator can easily identify with: Ferrara. Tasso worked at the court of Ferrara under Alfonso d'Este where *Aminta* was first performed. Apart from the allusions to a city, a river and an island (to be identified with Belvedere), several characters and names in the play were directly inspired by actual members of Alfonso's court: the wise shepherd, Elpino, who brings Aminta and Silvia together is Il Pigna (1530–75), a minister and poet of the court, Licori is Lucrezia Bendidio, a former mistress of Tasso, Batto is G.B. Guarini (1538–1612) author of *Pastor fido*. Mopso is a caricature of the critic from Padua, Sperone Speroni (1500–88), disliked by the author of *Aminta*. Tasso thereby addresses his courtly audience directly, and invites a bringing together of lowly, humble folk with the cultivated courtiers, all under the auspices of love. The potential violence of the satyr can symbolise the threat of violent rebellion to the established order in Ferrara.

The dialogue of *Aminta* is mostly in hendecasyllabic metre, especially for the narrative sections, and blank verse of seven syllables for the lyrical moments. There is a refined sensuality, a musicality and sophistication in the language, helped by the use of repetition, word-play, antithesis, enjambment and extended metaphor. Tasso maintains a unity of place and time, and to underline this, he alludes to the usual classical authors and to more recent vernacular authors, Petrarch, Dante, Poliziano, and Ariosto.

An interesting, even if not convincing critical appreciation of *Aminta*, is that of Richard Cody in his *The Landscape of the Mind* (1969). Inspired by Plato, but more especially by the scholarship and method of Edgar Wind's *Pagan Mysteries in the Renaissance* (1958), Cody sees Aminta as an Orphic lover-poet, and posits all sorts of Platonic theologizing in Tasso's play. Not once does Wind mention Tasso in his treatment of paganism and Platonism in the Italian Renaissance. Cody's reading of *Aminta* as Neo-Platonic pastoral myth would seem misplaced given Wind's silence. When, however, he compares the play with Castiglione's *Cortegiano* (both deal with the perfecting of the courtier's life through love), Cody is on safer ground.

There is a curious mixture of the superficial and the profound in *Aminta*. The love-story, melodrama, stock characters, unreality and quaint pastoralism could be seen as frivolous. However there is something modern in Tasso's treatment of the theme of incompleteness, of desire without possession, of absence without fulfilment, of the abyss—literally for Aminta—faced by man. Tasso, however, constantly avoids the tragic (Silvia is *nearly* raped, she is *almost* devoured by wolves, Aminta *nearly* kills himself), he only plays with cruelty (Silvia tied to a tree) and serious misfortune, before ending this idyll in the comic mode, thereby rewarding both protagonists and

spectators: the lover, Aminta (amante/aminta), would have his wood after all.

—David Coad

AMPHITRYO
Play by Plautus, early 2nd century BC

Amphitryo is imperfectly preserved in the manuscripts of Plautus. Despite a long lacuna three-quarters of the way through the play, the scenic sequence is reasonably clear and only a limited amount of supplementation is required to make the play performable.

The date of the first performance is not known, but it has been argued that it must have been a late play because of the extensive and complicated lyrical passages contained within it. This seems unlikely, since another of Plautus' plays, *The Casket Comedy* (*Cistellaria*), also has a considerable lyric content but is known to have been first performed when Rome was still at war with Carthage. The play as we have it, as the prologue makes clear, represents the text of a post-Plautine revival.

Amphitryo is unique in Roman comedy. All the other extant *palliatae* are based on Greek comedies written in the 4th or 3rd centuries BC, and set in Greek communities of that time, their themes taken from bourgeois life. This play, however, treats in comic fashion a theme from heroic legend, the birth of the great hero Hercules. Speculation about Plautus' source has been extensive. Some have seen the play as an adaptation of a native Italian farce, a dramatic genre which sometimes treated tragic themes in a disrespectful manner. It has also been suggested that what lies behind it was a Roman tragedy which Plautus transformed into a comedy. (In the prologue the play is described as a *tragicomoedia*, a Plautine coinage which has given the world "tragi-comedy.") It is more likely, however, since there is no evidence that he ever turned to sources other than Greek comedy, that Plautus, in looking for material, skipped a generation and, instead of choosing a play by Menander or one of his contemporaries, adapted a mythological spoof by one of the poets of the so-called Middle Comedy. The comedy of that period, written directly after the death of Aristophanes, is known to have produced many plays of this nature, travesties of heroic legend which had become the themes of tragedy. Also at this time the theme of mistaken identity and particularly of identical twins first came to the fore. In *Amphitryo* Jupiter adopts the appearance of Atcumena's husband, Amphitryo, and Mercury that of his servant, Sosia.

The plot displays a grave lack of coherence. Two irreconcilable themes are combined. The first, the miraculous birth of Hercules, is the culmination of the play. Hercules is the product of the union of Jupiter and Alcumena, who slept with the god believing him to be her husband. This took place seven months prior to the action of the play. The second theme is that of "the long night." In order to prolong his sexual enjoyment, Jupiter delays the rising of the sun and as a result of this the return from battle of his rival Amphitryo. Logically this event is more suited to the time of Hercules' conception rather than his birth. It is still a matter of dispute whether the combination of these two themes is to be ascribed to Plautus himself or to the unknown author of the lost Greek original. Since we possess no complete plays of the Middle Comedy, the second possibility cannot easily be discounted. After all, Middle Comedy is the direct successor to Aristophanic comedy and there are several Aristophanic plays which contain comparable inconsistencies of plotting and logic. The theme of the long night will have proved irresistible to any comic poet.

Whatever its source, there is no doubt that Plautus' play contains material borrowed from or parodying tragedy. This is to be found in the diction of Alcumena and in the structure of the ending where a report of the miraculous birth is followed in Euripidean fashion by the appearance of the *deus ex machina*, Jupiter.

Amphitryo is one of Plautus' liveliest and most influential plays. As has been remarked already, it is rich in lyric passages, the most notable of which is the extended and exuberant narrative describing Amphitryo's victory over the Teloboi. There is in the play an entertaining mix between low comedy and genuine pathos. The former is to be found in the exchanges between Mercury and his double, Sosia. These are replete with Plautine jokes which are clearly an addition to the original. The latter is exhibited in the demeanour and dignified protestations of the much abused Alcumena.

There have been many subsequent treatments of the theme, the most notable perhaps being that of Molière. Jean Giraudoux's *Amphitryon 38* claims to be the 38th dramatization of the story.

—David M. Bain

ANDORRA
Play by Max Frisch, 1961

Andorra, a burning attack on prejudice in general and antisemitism in particular, was conceived in 1957, based on Max Frisch's prose sketch "Der andorranische Jude" [The Andorran Jew] in his *Tagebuch 1946–1949* (*Sketchbook 1946–1949*). Frisch wrote five versions before releasing the play. The first performance, at the Schauspielhaus, Zurich, on 2 November 1961, was directed by Kurt Hirschfeld, with Peter Brogle as Andri, and sets by Teo Otto. In Germany, it became the most performed modern play of 1962, joining the wave of literary works dealing with the legacy of Nazism, such as Grass's *The Tin Drum*. German reactions to the play concentrated on this topical aspect. (Outside Germany the play had less impact; it was found uninteresting in London and flopped badly in New York.)

Andorra is a "model" play in a Brechtian sense; Frisch has learnt from *Mother Courage and Her Children* and *The Caucasian Chalk Circle*. The small, self-sufficient town-state, the imaginary Andorra of innkeepers and artisans, does not pretend to represent any 20th-century society in detail or show specific components of Nazism, yet the social and psychological patterns of modern life can be shown at work in it, some basic truths about mankind suggested. The play is thus also a parable, enshrining a lesson. Within Frisch's *oeuvre*, it represents—with *Biedermann und die Brandstifter* (*The Fire Raisers*)—a more overtly politically aware phase between the more personal preoccupations of the novels: it transfers Frisch's burning theme of identity to the stage and to a social context.

The plot is simple: Andri, a boy brought up by Can, the teacher in Andorra, as being a Jewish orphan rescued from the neighbouring country of the anti-semitic "Blacks," is forced by prejudice to become a salesman rather than a carpenter as he wishes; and he is not allowed to marry Can's daughter Barblin. It transpires that Andri is really Can's illegitimate son by the *Señora*, a "Black" (Can said Andri was a Jew in order to avoid this scandal); she is killed by a stone thrown at her when she visits Andorra. The "Blacks" invade Andorra; Andri is identified as a Jew and killed.

The Andorrans lack first-hand experience of Jews, yet have an image of the Jew which they impose on Andri. Only when they have labelled him a Jew with supposedly typical characteristics does he become so like a Jew that the "Blacks," when they invade, can single him out as one (in a macabre, grotesque pseudo-scientific procedure: all the Andorrans parade barefoot in front of a "Jew-inspector"). The Andorrans' lack of imagination and empathy puts Andri in a situation which, when the "Blacks" arrive, is fatal to him; and afterwards they have no grasp of what they have done. Thus "ordinary" Germans who would never hurt a fly might be made to feel how it was that they too were guilty in the extermination of Jews. Frisch hopes that the lesson about prejudice applies also to such phenomena as the colour bar or the McCarthy brand of anti-communism, indeed any situation where men judge others as (supposed) members of an alien group, rather than as unique individuals.

Sartre's essay *Anti-Semite and Jew* (*Réflexions sur la question juive*) showed that the Jew becomes an object of prejudice because of what Christian society has, over the centuries, forced the Jews to be or to seem. To make it clear that there can be no objective basis for the Andorrans' attitude, Frisch makes Andri a non-Jew—biologically speaking—and an ordinary, conforming, soccer-playing youth. But he is allotted a social role which he then plays, trying to be true to a Judaism of which he has as little direct knowledge as does anyone around. When finally told he is not a Jew, he cannot believe it.

The Andorrans, cunning but ultimately stupid, accuse the Jew of ambition because their own talents are not sufficient; of lust and avarice in order to draw attention from their own failings. We do not, however, find out what frustrations in Andorran society explain their pressing need to find a person even lower in the pecking order than themselves. Rather Frisch tends to metaphysics: Andri suffers a characteristically Jewish fate, becomes a martyr, and dies burdened with the sins of the Andorrans, postfiguring Jesus in a world so ethically unaware that it does not know what to do with a saviour.

Can is sometimes the author's mouthpiece or commentator, sometimes an inadequate alcoholic unable to rectify the situation he has brought about. Andri's stepmother is a weak figure. The Señora's visit to Andorra is insufficiently motivated. The soldier's off-stage rape, or seduction, of Barblin while Andri unsuspectingly sits outside her door is gripping, but does not fit the motivation and plot. On the other hand, the demonstrations of prejudice are chilling and memorable on the stage. The carpenter tears apart the journeyman's ill-made chair, claiming to believe that it was made by Andri and proves his incompetence (Jews don't have carpentry in the blood!); the soldier always emphasizes the cowardice of the Jews, but is himself the first collaborator of the "Blacks" when they invade. The Jew inspection, with its final consequence in Barblin's madness, provides one of the strongest endings in the modern repertoire. Few plays combine everyday clarity and broad-brushed symbolism as *Andorra* does.

Frisch uses a colloquial, regionally influenced style; Biblical references, used by Andri as he grows into the role of a martyr, underline themes of guilt, violence, betrayal, and (impossible) redemption. Developing Brechtian technique, Frisch destroys tension about the outcome: the characters successively enter a witness-box to give their views of the story of Andri, by now in the past. Thus we gradually learn that he is not a Jew, and that he will be killed. We discover that the Andorrans are incapable of drawing the moral lessons from the events: this is a very black play, even the well-meaning Can producing a monstrous life-lie in his attempt to do the right thing by his son. Frisch appears to accept the ineluctability of Andri's fate. He chronicles the distortion and destruction of the individual by social pressures, but he has no alternative that convinces even himself. Andri's own suggestion, the saving power of individual love, is rebutted by the plot. Frisch cannot share Brecht's Marxist belief in the possibility of understanding and therefore changing the world and human behaviour. He had read Büanchner's *Woyzeck* at the time of working on *Andorra*, and found its bleakness, its portrayal of the individual becoming a mere object to a stupid and uncaring society, more congenial. Can the audience prove the pessimistic author wrong by helping to produce a more tolerant world?

Frisch set himself an impossible task in *Andorra*. Between realism and abstraction, didacticism and resignation, determinism and hope of change, literalness and symbolism, there are many pitfalls. He himself found the play lacking in mystery. But a sparse structure, clearcut conflicts, and Frisch's eye for the stage make it a potentially shattering theatrical experience.

—Alfred D. White

ANDREAS
Fiction by Hugo von Hofmannsthal, 1932 (written 1912–13)

Andreas, a prose fragment of some 60 pages, constitutes probably about a quarter of a planned novel. It was begun in 1907 and written mainly in 1912–13; Hugo von Hofmannsthal returned to it from time to time but failed to complete it. It was published posthumously in *Corona*, 1930; 50 pages of synopsis, sketches, notes, and miscellaneous reflections found in Hofmannsthal's unpublished papers were added in the 1932 edition, but it was not until 1982 that all the author's extensive and labyrinthine notes were published.

Set in 1778, *Andreas* recounts the experiences of the 22-year-old Andreas von Ferschengelder, notably a series of erotic encounters, during a journey to and subsequent sojourn in Venice. Blending realism and fantasy in a manner, as one critic has put it, half-way between Goethe and Kafka, *Andreas* enriches the traditional mainstream German genre of the Bildungsroman which charts an individual's development towards maturity, self-understanding, and a firm sense of identity, with elements of both the older picaresque novel and the more modern form of symbolic fantasy.

In Venice Andreas recalls how he fell in love with the 17-year-old Romana Finazzer, amid the dignity and stability of the farming communities of the Carinthian mountains, living in close contact with nature and deeply rooted in Christianity. In Romana Hofmannsthal embodied an ideal of purity, innocence, and reverence for the sacrament of marriage, combined with vitality, sensuality, and happy domesticity. Her name suggests the Roman Catholicism that was of central importance to the author, as do those of the two characters who figure most prominently in the proposed continuation: the schizophrenic Maria and the mysterious and ambiguous Maltese Knight Sacramozo (who is sometimes called Sagredo), part spiritual mentor, part alter ego.

Andreas is, however, not yet ready for Romana. Entirely without sexual experience, which he both intensely desires and fears as a "murder in the dark," he would like to go straight from the painful confusions of young manhood to the serene happiness of marriage and parenthood. His encounter with Romana transforms him: it is "allomatic," to use Hofmannsthal's favourite ad hoc coinage. Yet it leads not to courtship and marriage, but to an exploration of the complexities of his sexual nature against the bizarre backcloth of Venice, where everything is incongruous, unpredictable, and confusing, and where anything is possible, especially in the erotic sphere.

In Venice Andreas becomes involved with a series of women whose conflicting conceptions of sexuality compel him to confront his confusions: Zustina, the 15-year-old daughter of an impoverished aristocratic family, who coolly offers her virginity as a lottery prize to a selected circle of wealthy sponsors; her elder sister Nina, a *poule de luxe* beyond Andreas's pocket; Maria/Mariquita, whose portrait owes much to Hofmannsthal's reading of Morton Prince's study in schizophrenia *The Dissociation of a Personality* (1906), and whose two warring personalities, one devout and ascetic, the other worldly and sensual, recall a number of somewhat similar pairings in Hofmannsthal's works, e.g. Ariadne and Zerbinetta, Arabella and Zdenka, Elektra and Chrysotemis, Helene and Antoinette.

Hofmannsthal's original proposed title was *Andreas; oder, Die Vereinigten* (*Andreas; or, the United*). The multiple meanings of "united" indicate his central concerns: it signifies lovers united, either physically or spiritually, but also characters who are united in themselves, who have overcome that dissonance between the spiritual and the physical that torments Andreas and is seen in an extreme forms in Maria/Mariquita, and have succeeded in shaping out of the bewildering jumble of a fragmented self, with all its violent and shameful elements, a hard core of ethical conviction and personal and social commitment. This integration requires the acceptance of complexity and imperfection: Andreas has to learn to understand that there is no health without an awareness of sickness, no innocence without an admission of guilt. (In his conception of Andreas's ethical-religious crisis Hofmannsthal was greatly influenced by William James's *The Varieties of Religious Experience* [1902], especially James's account of the "sick soul"). The "united" are also those who are united with the whole of nature (as in Sacramozo's mystical suicide), united with God, and those who are able to grasp the mystery of life by uniting within themselves its surfaces and its depths.

In Hofmannsthal's later notes the conception and scope changed and broadened to encompass the entire intellectual, spiritual, and social development of Andreas's problematic personality. It acquired a new title: *Andreas; oder, Die Verwandelten* [Andreas; or, the Transformed], and Hofmannsthal stressed the importance of the "more profound, mysterious layer hidden beneath Andreas's ostensibly purely private destiny." Much critical writing on *Andreas* has accordingly been devoted to unravelling its deeper symbolic meanings, especially with reference to the posthumously published parts. These were, however, not written for publication and are often tantalizingly cryptic. Generalized abstractions suggest the novel's deeper themes, vivid specific incidents and details confirm Hofmannsthal's narrative skill, but no clear overall conception emerges, and scholars have reached widely differing conclusions as to how Hofmannsthal might have ended the novel. Some notes indicate that Andreas will eventually marry Romana and have children, and indeed grandchildren, others that he will fail to win her. Other notes suggest that Maria/Mariquita will bring him the yearned-for harmonious totality of erotic fulfilment, as "lover, sister, mother, saint, the *whole* woman . . . belonging to God, sinning without sin." Notes from the 1920s show a continuing interest in "M_1 and M_2," with virtually no reference to Romana, but in Hofmannsthal's very last notes, union with Romana reappears as the "goal to be striven for."

Hofmannsthal struggled, as in the prose version of *Die Frau ohne Schatten* [The Woman Without a Shadow], to find an adequate vehicle for his dense and intricate web of ideas, but in *Andreas* his notes and sketches failed to coalesce into a coherent symbolic narrative. But his profound understanding of human behaviour is evident throughout, and his writing, while allusive, symbolic, and often cryptic, has a richness and beauty that have won widespread admiration.

—D.E. Jenkinson

L'ANGOISSE
Poem by Paul Verlaine, 1866

"L'Angoisse" [Anguish] is the last poem in "Melancholia," a group of seven sonnets which forms the first section of Paul Verlaine's first published volume of verse, *Poèmes saturniens*. In a 20-line epigraph, written shortly before publication, Verlaine presents himself as a victim, born under the sign of Saturn and subject to the malign influence of that dark planet of unhappiness, anger, volcanic passion, and irrationality. If there is a hint of self-mockery in these lines, it is not evident in the poems of "Melancholia." They speak of lost ideals, remembered with some amazement, of lost love recalled as an enchanting paradise, of loneliness and dreams of a quasi-maternal figure, a loving woman who will soothe and calm him. Like a child, the poet demands her complete devotion; in one poem, "A une Femme" [To a Woman], he declares that whatever her worries, she cannot possibly suffer as he does. "L'Angoisse" is no less self-absorbed, but it has a harsher tone; the poet no longer believes that he can attain his ideals, and proclaims the hollowness of all his youthful illusions.

All the sonnets in this section are written in alexandrines (lines of 12 syllables) and are set out in the classical French pattern of two quatrains followed by two tercets (though as if he wished to assert his independence from the beginning, the first poem in "Melancholia" reverses that order and places the tercets before the quatrains). "L'Angoisse" has the conventional shape, but begins less conventionally by abruptly rejecting nature, addressed in the familiar second person: "Nature, rien de toi ne m'émeut" ("Nature, nothing in you can move me"). It rapidly becomes clear, however, that it is not so much nature as "Nature" that Verlaine is rejecting, that is to say, a conventional image with a long literary history, nature as earlier poets had presented it (or, more usually, "her"). No names are mentioned, but the allusions are clear enough. He is unmoved by the "fertile fields" that Virgil praises in his *Georgics*, by the "rosy echo" of Sicilian pastoral (Virgil again, in his *Bucolics*) and by both the splendours of dawn and the "mournful solemnity" of sunset; he thus rejects the "pathetic fallacy," in which human feelings are transferred to inanimate things. What Verlaine rejects is nature experienced and described by man.

The second quatrain considers man himself, and man-made things, and spurns both Art (with a capital A) and Man ("l'Homme" with a capital H). Art is represented here by songs, verse, Greek temples, and the towers of cathedrals whose spiralling staircases lead us towards heaven. Thus the poem slides almost imperceptibly from art to religion: these towers reach up towards an "empty heaven," so that Verlaine can end the quatrain with a firm statement of moral indifference: he is equally unmoved by good and by wicked men. That statement glances back at his rejection of "l'Homme," a term that carries with it two aspects of French thought: the rational tradition, which gave to human intelligence the central place in a comprehensible universe; and 19th-century Romantic humanitarian ideals, that

often saw God as absent or uncaring, and sought an outlet for frustrated religious feeling in devotion to "mankind." Verlaine's poem is more radically negative. He rejects the consolations of Art, Nature, God, and Man alike, and with them any semblance of moral belief.

His first tercet begins emphatically: "Je ne crois pas en Dieu" ("I do not believe in God"). As for rational thought, he "abjures" it: a religious term, but then Verlaine is full of such contradictions, not the least of which here being that his rejection of art is expressed in a formal artistic medium. He goes on to face and reject the last great refuge of Romantic yearnings: love ("l'Amour" with a capital A), "that old irony," and politely requests that it be not mentioned again. The tercet thus ends on a note of mingled scorn, regret, and bitterness.

Thus far the poem has offered a defiant anti-Creed, summed up at the beginning of the tercets (often the turning-point of the traditional sonnet) by the parodic "I do not believe in God." In the final tercet, defiance gives way to the anguish that the sonnet's title has promised. It begins rather disconcertingly (and thus arrestingly) with a feminine adjective: "Lasse de vivre. . ." ("Tired of living"), only explained in the last line of the poem, where the subject of this sentence is revealed as "Mon âme" ("My soul," a feminine noun in French). Tired of life, but afraid to die, his soul, he says, is like a doomed vessel at the mercy of the sea, knowing it faces terrible storms on the voyage it is about to make. The poet's anguish here is due not merely to a melancholy sense of loss, but more urgently to a dreadful foreboding. By rejecting every available ideal and every possible consolation, he has left himself with no haven at all and no defences against the future.

Verlaine's later work is more adventurous both in the range of emotions it expresses and in the formal experiments it undertakes (notably his use of "l'impair," lines with odd numbers of syllables—7, 9, and 11 or 13 instead of the traditional 8, 10 and 12). But *Poèmes saturniens* is an engaging collection precisely because it seems (and at times actually is) less assured, less self-conscious, more open and unguarded than his maturer poems. He was to go on to write *La Bonne Chanson*, which contains many poems in praise of domestic virtue and the redeeming love of his wife; and later, *Sagesse*, in which the adoration is transferred to God. Neither passion was to last. But if Verlaine was an emotional weathercock, there is no reason to doubt the sincerity of the anguish in "L'Angoisse," even though at the age of 22, and with moderate literary success already to his credit, it might seem rather premature to be abandoning all hope. His description of himself is accurate: he was quite aware of his own irrational and inconstant emotions, and of the exorbitant demands that he made on others, on God, and on life in general. In this poem irony has not yet come to his rescue: he seems not to notice that his fierce rejection of Romanticism is itself a Romantic gesture. But here as elsewhere he persuades us to suspend our judgement and believe in his anguish.

—Norma Rinsler

ANNA KARENINA
Novel by Lev Tolstoi, 1875–77

Anna Karenina begins the novel as a mother and wife, settled comfortably in society, respected by her friends and family, and richly endowed by nature. She is beautiful, kind, sensitive, and loving. Before long she is the mistress of Count Vronskii, tormented and despairing and unpleasant in nature and motive. In the end she commits suicide. The mystery of the novel lies in the forces that take Anna from happiness to misery and death. When we first meet her, she is on a mission of domestic counselling. Her brother Stiva Oblonskii is having an affair, and his wife Dolly is threatening to leave him. Anna comes to visit them and to bring about a reconciliation. During this trip she meets Count Vronskii, a dashing and wealthy guardsman, and falls in love with him. Vronskii has been paying court to Kitty, Dolly's sister, but breaks off his courtship of her when he is taken by Anna. In the following months Vronskii pursues Anna and eventually seduces her. Anna's husband, Karenin, a highly-placed government official, ignores the affair until Anna brutally brings it out in the open. After almost dying in childbirth, when she is temporarily reconciled with her husband, Anna goes off with Vronskii to live as his mistress. They live in Italy for a while, return to St. Petersburg, and then settle on Vronskii's farm. Anna becomes progressively possessive, jealous, and miserable.

It is generally assumed that Anna deteriorates and commits suicide because she cannot have her lover and her son too, or because she felt unloved by Karenin, or because a highly conventional and restrictive society has punished her for her sexual boldness by ostracization. There is some validity in these motives and in many others, but Lev Tolstoi has so constructed the novel that it is impossible to settle on one single reason. Karenin is incapable of giving Anna the love that she craves, but he does on occasion—the deathbed scene is an example—offer her love and affection. It is true also that Anna loves her son and, at least at the end of the novel, she cannot have both lover and son, especially in the society she lives in. But when Anna is happy with Vronskii, she does not think of her son. That is, Tolstoi is careful to qualify any cause or motive that we might settle on. What drives Anna to misery and death is far deeper and more complex than any specific motive. Matthew Arnold, in a major statement on *Anna Karenina* in 1886, was astonished that someone like Anna, brought up in beneficent circumstances, would suffer herself to be swept away by passion, and especially for someone as insubstantial as Vronskii. But such a choice is part of the mystery of Anna's actions. What is not in dispute is that Anna is perhaps the greatest female creation of world literature and that her fate engages all our emotional and aesthetic responses. Her last day alive is unmatched in emotional intensity. Tolstoi has created the inexplicable and tragic state of the beauty and fullness of life in the grip of destructive forces.

Anna's tale, however, is only one half of the novel. The other half is Levin's story. Levin is a rural aristocrat who, at the beginning of the novel, is in love with Kitty. His proposal is rejected by Kitty and he returns to the country to brood and to reflect on his fate. He works the land, gets to know the peasants, and comes to recognize that both physical and mental health result from contact with the simple and elemental forces of the country. He meets Kitty after her recuperative trip to Europe, proposes again, and is accepted. Levin and Kitty have children, live simply in the country, and develop a mature love. *Anna Karenina*, then, is a contrast of two loves: Anna's unhealthy and destructive love and Levin and Kitty's healthy love. Tolstoi seems to be proposing that life and love are healthy when they are grounded in children, hard work, and the simple needs of self and family, and that love is unhealthy when it is based on sexual pleasure and self-will. Yet part of the mystery of this contrast is that we sympathize more with Anna than with Levin. Anna's unhealthy and destructive fate strikes us as more real than does Levin's healthy love. Anna dies and Levin and Kitty flourish, but we do not quite believe the Levin story, while Anna's is unbearably real. Levin's story reads like a fable,

Anna's like a tragedy. Still, these two characters, who seem to sum up in some mysterious way the alternatives of the universe, strike us with the immensity of their presences—as does Tolstoi. In Levin's tale Tolstoi convinces the reader that love, happiness, and a life of fulfilment are all possible; yet in Anna's tale he reminds the reader that the most beautiful and best of natures can be destroyed by forces within us.

—Edward Wasiolek

ANNALS (Annales)
Prose by Tacitus, early 2nd century AD

Tacitus' *Annals* is generally considered to be the greatest work of Rome's greatest historian. In its original form the work covered the period from the accession of the emperor Tiberius in AD 14 to the death of Nero in AD 68 in 18 (or, less likely, 16) books, of which only nine now survive in full (I–IV, VI, XII–XV): parts of V, XI, and XVI are extant, while VII–X are completely lost. We do not know exactly when Tacitus was writing the work, although a contemporary reference in Book IV (5.2) probably reflects the circumstances of AD 115.

The *Annals*, as its modern (16th-century) title suggests, is a year-by-year account and thus belongs to one of the oldest and most venerable traditions of Roman historiography, of which the monumental work of Livy, whom Tacitus no doubt wished to rival, is the classic earlier example. Tacitus' narrative appears to have been structured in three groups of six books: the first hexad belongs to Tiberius, the second to Gaius Caligula and Claudius, and the third to Nero. Of these the highlight has seemed to many readers to be the account of Tiberius, who fascinated Tacitus and compelled his admiration and revulsion in almost equal measure. The emperor's personality, of which a reported description is provided at the start of Book I and an authorial obituary at the end of Book VI, frames and dominates the intervening narrative. Midway through the hexad there is a narrative break at the start of Book IV, dividing the reign into two "acts" and emphasizing the gulf between Tiberius' briefer but less evil period (AD 14–22), to which Tacitus nevertheless devotes equal space, and his longer and much worse period (AD 23–37). In keeping with this deterioration Tacitus, later in Book IV, appears to claim that his narrative now lacks the characteristic subject matter of traditional historiography, as if the true bleakness of Tiberius' later years could not be accommodated within the normal generic conventions. As the emperor exiles himself to the island of Capri and his henchman Sejanus assumes control, spies and informers proliferate and the reign of terror gets into its stride. "At no other time was the community more suffocating and fearful, behaving most cautiously of all towards its nearest and dearest: meetings, conversations, familiar and unfamiliar ears were avoided; even mute and inanimate objects, a roof and walls, were routinely inspected."

In its unedifying circumstances Tiberius' accession foreshadows that of Nero, just as the army mutinies which accompanied it, and to which Tacitus devotes apparently disproportionate space, foreshadow the role of the legions at the end of Nero's reign, when Italy reverted to civil war. By such means Tacitus suggests that history is a vicious circle from which there is no escape; brief allusions to the brightness of his own age serve only to throw into sharper relief the unremitting darkness of the surrounding narrative, in which cynicism and innuendo are the prevailing modes. Characters rarely act out of principle but have a variety of unseemly motives attributed to them. To describe Nero's own reign, Tacitus adopts at one moment the stance of a paradoxographer, constructing an alien Rome where fantastic practices defy conventional belief, at another moment that of a dramatist, portraying the Pisonian conspirators as amateur actors who, confusing drama with real life, are vanquished by the truly professional actor Nero himself.

Such constant manipulation of his authorial role is symptomatic of the dazzling and difficult nature of the *Annals* as a whole. Tacitus strains the conventions of vocabulary, grammar, syntax, and sentence structure to their utmost, producing a text which disturbs by its seemingly wilful perversity at the same time as it manoeuvres the reader into accepting its point of view. Commonplace expressions for commonplace things are avoided in favour of circumlocutions or archaizing synonyms: Tacitus' is a world where little is taken for granted; where the dignified is employed to intensify the squalid; where everything is subjected to implied examination; and where the modern is implicitly contrasted with a better past. Metaphor is everywhere and strikingly deployed: the mutinous troops are mentally deranged and require the savage attentions of a physician; Tiberius' son Drusus is an overweening naval commander who capsizes; Sejanus is a master puppeteer pulling the strings of his cronies; and Tiberius' minions are waiters who serve the emperor with crimes until he is glutted.

Since Tacitus relishes the suggestion that the practices and conventions of the early Empire were all pretence, words such as *species* (''display''), *imago* (''image''), and *facies* (''appearance'') are deployed liberally in the narrative. The implication is that the author has penetrated beneath the façade to the underlying reality; yet Tacitus himself manipulates language to disguise rather than to disclose. Avoiding entirely the balance and antithesis associated with Cicero's sentences, he relies instead on the artful juxtaposition of unlike phrases or clauses (*variatio*), which characteristically modify or even confound an initial main-verb statement. As has been well said, ''there are many occasions when we have to read him very closely indeed to perceive that he has in fact denied what one thought he had said.'' Indeed, Napoleon claimed that ''his chief quality is obscurity,'' to which the poet Wieland simply replied that in Racine's judgement he was ''the greatest painter of antiquity.''

—A.J. Woodman

ANTIGONE
Play by Jean Anouilh, 1944

In Greek mythology Antigone, Oedipus' daughter, is put to death because she acts against an edict, made by her uncle Creon, forbidding the burial of her brother Polynices. Sophocles' play *Antigone* dramatizes the story, and it is this on which Jean Anouilh's version is based.

The original play begins after Oedipus' two sons, Eteocles and Polynices, have killed each other over the crown of Thebes, and Creon, the new king of the city and brother of Oedipus' mother and wife, has just given Eteocles an honourable funeral while decreeing that Polynices should suffer the dishonour of remaining unburied on account of his treachery. In spite of this prohibition and the death penalty attached to its violation, Antigone, Polynices' sister, dares to perform the ritualistic burial. When she is caught and brought before the king, she defiantly expresses her fidelity to her brother and her resolution to adhere to the laws of the gods rather than those of her uncle. Creon declares that he will not permit her to act against his authority and condemns her to death. At this point Haemon, Creon's son and Antigone's fiancé, begs his father to moderate his severity but succeeds only in angering him. Tiresias, the blind high priest, warns the king that his excessive use of power will be punished by the gods. Creon's eventual decision to release Antigone comes too late: his niece has hanged herself, his son accidentally kills himself in a struggle with him, and his wife, Eurydice, commits suicide.

In rewriting the story, Anouilh omits the character Tiresias and adds that of the nurse to stress the fact that, as opposed to Sophocles' Amazon-like heroine, Antigone is a young girl who needs reassurance and affection. However, in a scene invented by Anouilh in which Antigone renounces her love for Haemon, she is also shown to be courageous. Creon too is changed. Although, like Sophocles' character, he is angry and indignant when he learns that his orders have been disobeyed, he is less of a tyrant and more of a diplomatic statesman. When he discovers who the culprit is, he quickly becomes concerned with avoiding scandal. In a section that owes little to Sophocles, he tries to persuade his niece to give up her stand and offers to hush up the affair. To convince her, he points out that Polynices and Eteocles were both equally villainous and even admits that her brothers were so unrecognizable after their battle that there was no way of knowing which body had been retrieved and given state honours. It is clear that he does not want Antigone to die, and when he does condemn her it is a political decision aimed at reestablishing his authority and preventing anarchy rather than a punishment for the violation of his law. As in the Greek tragedy, Antigone hangs herself and Haemon and Erydice commit suicide.

Anouilh's play is about the revolt of disillusioned but heroic youth against oppression. Antigone would rather die than live without freedom and ideals. Her confrontation with Creon represents the ageless response of adolescence to the adult world of pragmatism and resignation. She is intractably stubborn and refuses any concession or compromise: if she cannot be free to live according to her moral principles and so retain her self-respect, she prefers to die. What makes this point valid is that her loyalty to her brother comes before her duty to the state. However, the tragic nature of the play lies in the fact that Creon's attitude is equally justifiable. Although he is shown to be wrong in assuming that there are no limits to his power, his primary duty as ruler is the assurance of state security and his decision to let Polynices' body rot in the sun is forced upon him by political necessity. Antigone's heroic stance can therefore also be regarded as unrealistic and immature.

Antigone was first produced in occupied Paris in February 1944 and was, at the time, interpreted as symbolizing the struggle between the resistance and the collaborators. Anouilh was criticized for writing an apparently Nazi play in which Creon, taken to represent Laval and Pétain, is treated sympathetically.

—Silvano Levy

ANTIGONE
Play by Sophocles, c. 441 BC (?).

Antigone and *Oedipius the King* are the most famous and influential of Sophocles' plays. The date of the first production of *Antigone* is not known for certain. The number 32 found in the introductory matter in manuscripts of the play might indicate that it was the 32nd surviving Sophoclean play known to the scholars of Alexandria. There also exists a biographical anecdote to the effect that Sophocles was elected general for the campaign against Samos which took place in 440 BC because of the *Antigone*. This perhaps should be treated with a pinch of salt although it does suggest the chronological sequence, victory of the play followed shortly afterwards by Sophocles' election. Both of these not entirely compelling pieces of evidence tend to suggest a relatively early date for the play.

The play dramatizes the last stages of the troubles of the family of Oedipus. The events unfolding in it can be taken as a kind of sequel to those depicted in Aeschylus' *Seven Against Thebes* (*Septem contra Thebas*). That play ended with ritual mourning for the fratricidal brothers, Eteocles and Polynices. Their death ended all conflict at Thebes and was the fulfilment of their father's curse. In *Antigone* Sophocles introduces new sufferings for the survivors of the conflict. The new king of Thebes, Creon, is not prepared to allow the traitor Polynices burial and in the opening scene of the play, a conversation between Antigone and her sister Ismene, we learn of his proclamation forbidding burial on pain of death. Antigone is determined to defy Creon and give her brother a proper burial. She fails to persuade her sister to assist her in the task and, acting alone, succeeds in burying her brother under cover of a sandstorm. She is discovered making a second visit to the body and Creon's guards bring her before Creon. She defends her defiance of the authority of the legitimate ruler of Thebes by appealing to higher, unwritten laws, laws which come from the gods. Creon condemns her to be buried alive and is not swayed by the pleas made on her behalf by his own son Haemon, Antigone's fiancé. Before she is led off to a cave in the Theban countryside she offers an explanation for her actions: she would not have done what she had done for a husband or for any relation other than a brother, since a brother is irreplaceable. Creon's decision proves disastrous. The seer Teiresias appears, announcing omens and prophesying the destruction of Creon's family. Too late. Creon sets off to rescue Antigone. Soon a messenger arrives at the palace and tells Creon's wife, Eurydice, of how Creon and his attendants reached a cave that was already opened to find Haemon embracing the body of Antigone who had hanged herself. Haemon threatened to kill his father but turned his sword upon himself. Eurydice departs in ominous silence, intent upon suicide. News of her death is communicated to Creon as he returns with the bodies of Antigone and Haemon. The play ends with a depiction of the total desolation of Creon and some pious moralizing by the chorus.

Antigone has often been regarded as a play of philosophical conflict where one kind of right is opposed to another, where divine and human law come into conflict and the rights of the individual are opposed to the rights of the state. These potentialities are implicit in the myth and help explain why the subject has exercised such a fascination, particularly in the age of Enlightenment and during the French Revolution. The outcome of Sophocles' play, however, suggests that it would be mistaken to assume that he intended to set two morally equipollent ideas in conflict. Antigone (from the grave) wins. Creon loses calamitously. He is the one shown by events to be mistaken. On the other hand Antigone herself, towering in her nobility, is a terrifying personality who brings about not only her own destruction but that of many others around her. Those made of the stuff of martyrs are not easy company and her nature sets her apart from everyone else in the play. She is on a level with other proud, isolated Sophoclean heroes, on a different plane from the other

characters in the play, the timid, human Ismene and the authoritarian, but unheroic and weak Creon.

The play contains some of Sophocles' finest and best-known lyrics: the chorus on the wondrous nature of man which the chorus produces in reaction to the news that someone has dared to defy Creon's edict, the second stasimon with its reflections on the destiny of the house of Oedipus couched in the dignified and exalted terminology of the archaic Greek religion, and the great ode on the power of Eros which follows Haemon's plea on Antigone's behalf.

—David M. Bain

APOLOGY FOR RAYMOND SEBOND (Apologie de Raimond Sebond)
Prose by Michel de Montaigne, 1580; revised 1588, and in subsequent editions (written 1570s)

The "Apology for Raymond Sebond" (Book II, chapter 12 of the *Essays*) is by far the longest chapter in Michel de Montaigne's work, amounting to almost a sixth of the total. Written probably over a number of years in the 1570s, it is, in the words of Donald Frame in his biography of Montaigne, his "most thorough exploration and statement of the case for doubt." Since doubt—which for Montaigne became not a negative but a positive and liberating factor in life—is at the very heart of his philosophical stance, we must consider this chapter as being at the core of his work. It is here that we find expressed his famous "Que sais-je?" ("What do I know?") which, in about 1576, he had struck as his motto and engraved on a medallion. But this long chapter is also the most controversial and, in some ways, the most disconcerting.

By his own admission, Montaigne was not in the habit of writing at such length. The circumstances surrounding the composition of the "Apology" are also unusual. Raimond Sebond was a Catalan theologian and doctor who had taught at the University of Toulouse in the middle of the 15th century. Montaigne tells us early in the chapter that his father had had in his possession a copy of Sebond's *Theotogia naturalis* and had asked him to translate it into French. Montaigne duly did, and the translation appeared in 1569. Without this translation and the subsequent defence of the author by Montaigne, Sebond would by now be little more than a footnote in histories of philosophy. For reasons which are not entirely clear Montaigne returned to Sebond a few years later (perhaps at the request of Marguerite de Valois) to analyse in greater detail a book with which he was not fully in sympathy and which, indeed, he appears at times to despise.

He opens his "Apology for Raymond Sebond" with a studied but provocative comment on the importance of knowledge, pointing out (as he does elsewhere in the *Essays*) that one must not assume that knowledge (his word is "science") is the "mother of virtue." For this reason, he says, he enjoys the company of learned men but, unlike his father, is not dazzled by them. This, too, is a common theme in the *Essays* and here it will lead us, after some typical meanderings, to the heart of the chapter and the author's demonstration of the limitations of the human intellect and, above all, of human reason. Montaigne is, of course, not philosophizing in a void. Three main sets of thinkers in particular are the targets of his shafts. The Protestants, whom he blames for their intolerance and for causing such civil unrest; the ancient dogmatic philosophers (because of their dogmatism) and, in some ways surprisingly in view of his previous attachment to their views, the Stoics. What Madeleine Lazard has called his ''natural tendency to scepticism'' makes him suspicious of man's pretensions, given that his judgement can be so easily swayed by vanity, habit, and the vagaries of the imagination.

The 1570s were dark days for France—Montaigne refers gloomily to this ''sick age''—and the events he had been forced to witness caused him to concern himself less with Sebond, who had been writing for quite different times, than with human iniquity and man's inability to arrive at rational decisions. In so doing, he turns Sebond's arguments on their head. Sebond believed in reason, Montaigne questioned its validity. He was much influenced at this time by his reading of the Greek philosopher Pyrrho of Elis (c. 300 BC), who held that certainty of knowledge is unattainable. At the same time, his study of the sceptic Sextus Empiricus took him in the same direction. Montaigne's ''Que sais-je?'' is an expression of his scepticism, or Pyrrhonism, and these influences would remain with him for the rest of his life. It is in the ''Apology,'' however, that we see them fully enunciated for the first time. Here, too, the influence of Socrates, whom he admired above all others, comes to the fore.

Montaigne had seen what conviction politics had done to his country and grieved for it. In his view only fools are certain, and sure of themselves. His personal experience of the horrors of war lends a pained and often bitter tone to this chapter. Death and destruction resulting from human intolerance and a sense of certainty make him doubt the value of knowledge and the power of reason. The question of knowledge is central to his enquiry, and he concludes that philosophy can do little to help man in his search for certainty. This brings him to a position (one which is close to St. Augustine's) that man is lost without the help of divine grace. A practising Catholic all his life, Montaigne came to adopt a fideist position. This fideism, which makes a distinction between faith and reason, allowing the latter to attempt to search for truth without questioning the mysteries of the faith, is perhaps an extension of his ''natural'' scepticism. His ''perpetual confession of ignorance'' can thus be seen not as a retreat (too much is made of Montaigne the gentle recluse) but as a positive way forward. To a modern reader it would seem that Montaigne is trying to square the circle, that is to say both to doubt everything and yet to believe in God. The later chapters of the *Essays* suggest that after the ''Apology for Raymond Sebond'' Montaigne felt that he had succeeded.

—Michael Freeman

L'APRÈS-MIDI D'UN FAUNE
Poem by Stéphane Mallarmé, 1876

Stéphane Mallarmé first envisaged his interlude for a faun as a revolutionary work for the stage. His plan, so he claimed, was that the rhythm of the words would be modelled exactly on the actor's gestures. A letter written to his friend Cazalis in June 1865 mentions, with a vibrant enthusiasm rare during his years in the provinces, that the poem contains ''a very lofty and beautiful idea.'' When this

version was rejected by the actor Coquelin, who felt it lacked sufficient dramatic interest, Mallarmé spent much of the following summer revising it, and, nine years later, sent a third rendition, entitled ''Improvisation of a Faun,'' to the three judges of the anthology entitled *Le Troisième Parnasse contemporain* [The Third Contemporary Parnassus]. Although supported by the poet Théodore de Banville, the poem was rejected yet again and it was not until the following year, 1876, that the final version appeared, subtitled ''eclogue,'' and illustrated by Édouard Manet. Of the three scenes initially envisaged—two monologues for the faun, separated by a dialogue between the two nymphs, Iane and Ianthé—only one remained, and the now nameless nymphs appear solely as belonging to the memory or imagination of the faun. This final version retains few traces of Mallarmé's original concept of a work for the stage.

The poem's narrative content is deceptively simple: a faun awakens on a hot summer's afternoon on the slopes of Mount Etna in Sicily, convinced that earlier the same day he had encountered and attempted to ravish two nymphs. All his attempts to find external proof of their existence and his prowess, however, lead only to doubt and renewed desire. As he plays his flute, the faun wonders whether the forms the nymphs assumed were simply inspired in his dreaming mind by the sound of a bubbling spring or the movement of the breeze in his coat. Was the image of their white bodies suggested, banally enough, by a flock of swans? The transformation of these suggestions through the faun's words and his music leads both to a sense that truth always eludes the seeker's grasp, and to an intensification of sexual longing, provoking the fantasy of raping the goddess Venus herself. Such hubris is punished not by any divine thunderbolt, but by the oppression of afternoon heat, which drives the faun back to sleep and the knowledge that he will see the nymphs again in dream, transformed and eternalized by what Baudelaire called ''the queen of faculties'': the imagination. While the poem thus acknowledges that it is impossible to establish external proof of sensation or memory, it also enshrines the ability of art to transform sublimated physical desire into pure and eternal beauty.

Although the poem is written in couplets of the traditional 12-syllable line, Mallarmé's initial attention to a rhythm determined by gesture and his constant search for perfection ensure that what might appear a hackneyed form constantly explores and exploits to the full the alexandrine's rhythmic potential. While sound-patterning provides important suggestions, the poem's visual appearance also offers guidance to the reader. The broken lines and white spaces of the opening intimate a mind slowly groping towards a memory or a truth, shaken by questions and aware of seemingly endless transpositions between what is internal and what is external. Words in small capitals—''Tell'' and ''Memories''—indicate the artistic and artificial nature of the narrative, while passages in italics denote the faun's evocation of what he believes has happened. Subtle symmetries between opening and conclusion imply the possibility of circularity, suggesting that the ''false confusions'' between the beauty of nature and the faun's musical story-telling create a maze from which there is no exit.

The poem is also richly visual in its images, conjuring up a landscape bathed in sparkling light, where passion assumes the form of a pomegranate burst open and covered with murmuring bees. At the centre of the poem Mallarmé places one of his densest and most beautiful images, an evocation of the imagination and of artistic creation:

Ainsi, quand des raisins j'ai sucé la clarté,
Pour bannir un regret par ma feinte écarté,
Rieur, j'élève au ciel d'été la grappe vide
Et, soufflant dans ses peaux lumineuses, avide
D'ivresse, jusqu'au soir je regarde au travers.

(Thus, when I have drained all brightness from the grapes,
To banish all regret, dismissed by my pretence,
I lift with laughter to the summer skies the empty bunch
And blowing taut the luminous skins, eager
For ecstasy, gaze through them, until the fall of dusk.)

Half-man, half-goat, wholly adolescent, Mallarmé's faun embodies his image of the artistic, as one in whom the erotic desire for beauty fuses with a potent awareness of the transience of experience, and is transformed through the sublimating and intensifying power of the imagination.

Mallarmé's poem inspired numerous works of art in a variety of media. Manet, who had contributed to the original publication, added a series of line drawings stressing the faun's sensuality and evoking the "sonorous, vain and monotonous line" of his flute; Debussy created his own musical prelude, suggesting the contrasts between the faun's uncertainty and lethargy, and his mounting and waning desire; Nijinsky, Bakst, and Diaghilev transformed the faun's afternoon into a ballet in 1912; and countless poets and novelists, particularly Valéry and the Australian symbolist, Chris Brennan, have drawn on the metaphysical, sensual, and sonorous possibilities the poem offers.

While less experimental than *Un coup de dés* and less dense than some of the later sonnets, *L'Après-midi d'un faune*, with its sensuous encapsulation of many of his artistic and metaphysical aims, remains one of Mallarmé's finest achievements.

—Rosemary Lloyd

THE ARABIAN NIGHTS

See THE THOUSAND AND ONE NIGHTS

AROUND THE WORLD IN EIGHTY DAYS (Le Tour du monde en quatre-vingt jours)
Novel by Jules Verne, 1873

Around the World in Eighty Days is striking testimony to the heroic age of applied science, civil engineering, and above all, innovation in transport. Railways and steamships seemed to be making the world a far smaller place in those days. The opening of the Suez Canal in 1869, after more than a decade of endeavour, struck the public imagination with particular force, for now the East was far closer than ever before to the West, and the French could take particular pride in the achievement since it had been masterminded by a compatriot, Ferdinand de Lesseps. Dramatic changes like this took place in a period that was still largely untroubled by thoughts of environmental damage, a time when most Europeans abroad had few scruples in their dealings with what they blithely regarded as inferior cultures. The consequence was a great increase in travel in general and the rise of tourism in particular. Jules Verne gave expression of the spirit of the times in a large number of exciting novels in which the central theme is transport, by every conceivable means, from the most old-fashioned to the most advanced, not to say the most improbably futuristic.

Part of the strength of *Around the World in Eighty Days* lies, however, in the author's willingness, on this occasion, to foreswear such beguiling possibilities as space travel, journeys to the centre of the earth, or epic voyages beneath the surface of the sea. Instead he presents the sort of dream that any armchair traveller might have who glanced through *Bradshaw* and similar railway and shipping timetables and fell to calculating what might just be possible if only everything ran dead on time and money were no object. The tale may be a fantasy, but passengers who were still to some degree amazed and delighted by the short time it was taking them to reach their destinations did not find it hard to identify with Verne's characters as they set out on a far longer trip. Younger readers in particular were fascinated.

To give a human side to his tale of a journey around the world in a mere 80 days, Verne invented just a few relatively simple characters. Anything more complex, it could be argued, would take attention away from the central issue of travel. Besides, Mr. Phileas Fogg serves his function well. He is presented as what some French readers of the time were pleased to regard as a typical English gentleman. A wealthy bachelor with no family attachments and unconstrained leisure, he leads a life of the utmost regularity. The domestic arrangements of his London residence follow a precise, unvarying schedule: he goes out, at exactly the same hour each day, to his club. There he is normally content to partake of a substantial meal, peruse the newspapers, and play whist. One day, however, over cards, there is some talk of an estimate made in *The Daily Telegraph* that it would theoretically be possible to travel eastwards around the world by scheduled rail and steamer services and return to London in 80 days. Discussion ensues, and while playing his hand of cards Fogg calmly wagers £20,000 that he will accomplish the feat. He sets out at once, and all the while readers are invited to admire Fogg's cool imperturbability, compared with the nervous tension and irritability that travellers typically display when trains and boats are late.

By giving Fogg a French valet, Passepartout ("Go-Anywhere"), Verne made it easier for his first readers to identify with the tale, and also invites us to dwell on differences between the conventional phlegmatic temperament of the English upper classes and the traditional vivacity of the French lower classes. Additional complications are brought in with a detective, Fix, who pursues Fogg around the globe in the hope of arresting him for bank robbery. There is just a touch of romance too when the beautiful Aouda is saved from suttee in India and then accompanies Fogg back across Japan, the Pacific, and the United States to London.

The long journey, in fact, is often uneventful, which at the period was no doubt remarkable enough in itself, and like many a tourist from England, we are given to understand, Fogg takes scant interest in the places he passes through. There is correspondingly little descriptive writing in the novel. Occasionally, however, Verne inserts a paragraph of detail about either places or conveyances; these introduce a note of sober realism, as well as appealing particularly to boys' notorious enthusiasm for collecting perfectly useless "facts." Excitement grows when, inevitably, Fogg's carefully calculated timetable is upset. Spending money in the best tradition of the free-spending English milords on the 18th-century Grand Tour, he calmly shells out huge sums for elephants and ships when occasion demands. His sangfroid never deserts him, whether he is himself involved in danger or delay or whether Passepartout is in a scrape more suited to his humbler position on the social scale. When at last Fogg arrives back in London apparently just too late to win his wager, this self-possessed Englishman easily masters his emotions at a misfortune that threatens to reduce him to impoverishment. Then a simple, undeniable scientific truth, which we realize we should have noticed for ourselves, saves him in the nick of time.

—Christopher Smith

ART (L'Art)
Poem by Théophile Gautier, 1856

Théophile Gautier was the acknowledged leader and spokesman of the ''L'Art pour l'Art'' (''Art for Art's sake'') movement which formed a major current in French poetry in the middle decades of the 19th century, and ''Art'' is generally regarded as being its most forthright manifesto. The poem, first published in 1856 in *L'Artiste*, the movement's campaigning review, of which Gautier had recently become co-editor, was incorporated in 1858 into the third, augmented edition of his poetry collection *Émaux et Camées*, first published in 1852. Even though each subsequent edition contained new poems, Gautier insisted that ''Art'' should always come at the end, as a summation of the collection's achievements; critical opinion is divided, however, on the extent to which the other poems exemplify the principles laid down in the ''manifesto.''

The ''Art for Art's sake'' movement was a reaction against the utopianism, rationalism, and utilitarianism which had swept through French letters in the wake of the 1830 revolution, winning Romantics such as Lamartine, Vigny, and Hugo to the cause of art, and particularly poetry, as a force for social progress and oral improvement. It has often been said that mannerist art (art preoccupied by style more than content) flourishes at periods when the artist feels alienated from the prevailing values of his society, and this was certainly the case with Gautier and his followers. Much influenced by 18th-century German aesthetic thinking, they were staunchly opposed to the idea that art should have a social or political purpose. Instead, they propounded a semi-religious belief in the cult of pure beauty as the only moral truth, defining beauty in terms of plastic, sensual form, rather than elevated or uplifting subject-matter. ''Nothing that is beautiful is essential for living . . . Only that which has no use can be beautiful; everything useful is ugly . . . ,'' Gautier had written, controversially, in the preface of his novel *Mademoiselle de Maupin*. ''Art,'' composed at a time when the values of ''Art for Art's sake'' had finally gained ascendancy, is a vibrant reassertion of his aesthetic of formal beauty.

The poem was originally written to reply to Théodore de Banville, an ardent and gifted disciple 12 years Gautier's junior, who earlier in the same year had published in *L'Artiste* an ''Odelette'' [''Little Ode''] in homage to his work and poetic leadership. Banville's poem, half the length of Gautier's response, had expressed admiration for his craftsmanship in two apparently contradictory metaphors: the poet as bird-catcher, deftly snaring dreams in the delicate net of his verse, and as metal-working artisan, engraving and chiselling his ideas into the hard bronze of metre, rhyme, and rhythm. Although Gautier does reserve a space at the end for the more spiritual aspect of the poet's ''rêve,'' it is essentially this second idea of poetry as a difficult craft, and French verse as a solid, refractory material whose resistance needs to be overcome by skill, that he takes up and develops in ''Art'' in a series of virtuoso metaphorical variations. Written in the same awkward verse-form as Banville's text (four-line stanzas of six, six, two and six syllables, rhyming *abab*), the poem itself stands as a triumphant example of difficulty overcome. It opens with an affirmative ''Oui,'' as if continuing and amplifying Banville's argument, and the tone throughout is one of injunction (all but four of its 14 stanzas are constructed as grammatical imperatives), as might be expected of a manifesto aiming to convince by argument as well as by example.

In accordance with his enthusiasm for plastic, sensual beauty, Gautier defined the craft of poetry by analogy with that of the sculptor and the painter, assimilating the linguistic and metrical medium in which the poet works to the materials used in the visual arts (in the first stanza, ''poetry'' occurs in the same line as ''marble,'' ''onyx,'' and ''enamel''). Just as the sculptor should work in hard stone (Paros or Carrara marble, agate, onyx, the ''guardians'' of pure line), rather than the much easier clay, and the painter metaphorically fire his bright colours in the enamellist's oven rather than being satisfied with washed-out water colours, so the poet should employ verse-forms which seem initially uncongenial and technically difficult. Only then will the resultant work be ''robust'' and formally perfect enough to survive the ravages of time, like a Roman medallion bearing an emperor's portrait, dug up by a modern farmer. More helpful, metrically-freer forms are likened dismissively to an over-large shoe which any vulgar foot can slip into at will, highlighting a pronounced élitism in Gautier's views, for he and his followers prided themselves on the inaccessibility of their metrical art to the appreciation of the common herd. Such poetry as theirs, Gautier asserts in a final reversal of values, will ultimately outlast bronze statues and outlive even the gods themselves, conferring an element of immortality on its creators.

However, ''Art'' is perhaps best read as a statement of general aesthetic principle rather than as a specifically poetic programme; it certainly does not give a full account of the expressive range of Gautier's own poetry. His stress on discipline and formal mastery was in part a backward-looking reaction against the Romantic notion of art as spontaneous, uncontrolled expression, and it ultimately caused the whole ''Art for Art's sake'' movement to decline into a cold, neoclassical preciosity which would be severely mocked by Rimbaud little more than a decade after ''Art'' was first published. On the other hand, Gautier's insistence on the ''floating dream'' that the poet must seek to encapsulate in the ''resistant block'' of his verse also looks forward to Symbolism, and the complex metrical experiments that he and his followers conducted in their search for formal difficulty did much to prepare the ground for succeeding generations of poets. Much lauded by Baudelaire, the values expressed in ''Art'' directly influenced Verlaine, Mallarmé, and even Flaubert, so that, in his resolute privileging of form over content, Gautier can plausibly be regarded as one of the pioneers of a genuinely modern French sensibility.

—Andrew Rothwell

THE ART OF LOVE (Ars amatoria)
Poem by Ovid, c. 1 BC

According to Ovid, his poem *The Art of Love* was one of the chief reasons for his exile from Rome to the Black Sea by Augustus in AD 8.

It is certainly true that Ovid's poem, full of stratagems for the lover, clashed unfortunately with Augustus' attempts to introduce new laws enforcing a stricter sense of morality in Roman society, especially with regard to adultery. However, a greater mystery remains surrounding the reasons for Ovid's exile: he himself, in his *Tristia* [Sorrows], at the same point in which he blames the poem, notes that an "indiscretion" made inadvertently by him was the main cause of his banishment. What the exact nature of this indiscretion was has been the subject of great intrigue; given the nature of the content of *The Art of Love*, it is not surprising that many investigators of this incident have looked for a sexual misdemeanour on Ovid's part as the explanation. While this line of enquiry has been fruitless (the most likely explanation being that Ovid came to know of a political intrigue which, because it involved his friends, he kept quiet about), Ovid has, in some ways, only himself to blame for such retrospective historical searching into his personal sexual activities. *The Art of Love* sets out with the claim that all its advice on "love" (which in the terms of the poem more truly means sexual conquests by men) comes from the experience of the author: "what I write, believe me, I have practised. / My poem will deal in truth" (translation here and below from Peter Green, *The Erotic Poems*).

Ovid summarizes the intentions of his poem by noting what the lover must do to succeed: firstly find an appropriate "object" for love; secondly "woo and win" the woman; and thirdly ensure that the affair lasts. With these intentions in mind, *The Art of Love* is divided into three books: the first telling men how to choose and "capture" their chosen woman; the second telling men how to keep this woman; and the third directed at women, instructing them how to behave in reaction to the behaviour suggested to men in the first two books. In this sense, *The Art of Love* is a didactic poem; it does have a (relatively) serious intention of sexual instruction. However, for most commentators the poem is "mock-didactic": it takes the form of the didactic poem and subverts it to comic effect. This is true, but what the term "mock-didactic" does not resolve is the question of how much, in subverting the didactic poem, the didacticism is lost or annulled. How seriously should we take Ovid's teaching in *The Art of Love*?

The Art of Love abounds with metaphors for male mastering of the female. Common among these is the military, the most extended example of which is in Book I, lines 177 and following. Here the victorious military campaign is paralleled with, and fades into, the conquest of man's seduction of woman. Also frequently used are metaphors of the domestication of animals, in which man's taming of the beasts is seen as analogous to his sexual relationship with his lover: examples are the breaking of horses and the yoking of oxen. Related to this idea of man's control of the natural world are metaphors of sowing and reaping, hunting and fowling. The latent aggression built up by such a succession of "mastery" images comes disturbingly to the surface at several points in the poem; when Ovid says that women should see in "the audacity of near-rape" "a compliment" (Book I, lines 676–77), it must be asked of those who see the poem as a comic masterpiece just how amused the reader should be at such a statement.

Yet there is a pervasive sense of authorial irony throughout *The Art of Love* which could perhaps be marshalled in Ovid's defence. Ovid takes the opportunity at several points to interrupt the flow of the poem and draw attention to the poem and indeed himself, in a more critical, scrutinizing way. In Book II (lines 493 and following) the god Apollo materializes and speaks to Ovid, telling him that all lovers should go to his shrine and that the advice "know thyself" is the path to loving wisely. Ovid appears to wait patiently until Apollo has finished and then, after the formality of saying "this god speaks to truth," he continues with a curt "Back to my theme then." What is emphasized here is the practical nature of this poem. It does not deal with hypothetical lovers playing out ideal relationships; its advice appears to be, as Ovid said at the beginning of the poem, embedded in experience and what can be expected in the real world. Thus at another point Ovid himself interrupts the flow of the poem when, after giving advice to women on how to keep their men on tenterhooks, he asks himself why he is spending time giving ammunition to the enemy.

The advice Ovid gives to women is very much what would be expected from one who employs such a range of metaphors for male sexuality. All of Ovid's suggestions place women in a position where their primary objective should be to please men. This leads to some interesting revelations. For example, Ovid says that it is not acceptable for a woman to let a man see her making up her face, but brushing her hair can be an erotic stimulant and is therefore advisable. The extent to which this partner-pleasing aspect of a woman's sexuality should reach becomes completely clear when Ovid suggests that if a woman has lost her own sexual sensations she should, to flatter her lover, fake them with all the accompanying "frenzy," "cries and gasping." Yet even in Book III, when Ovid is at his most chauvinistic and patronizing, he is capable of some degree of self-critical humour. He puts forward a case, to women, for poets as the one group of men who are above stratagems and tricks in love. His plea, "So, girls, be generous with poets," is itself finally a stratagem, hoping to win over women by saying that he, as a poet, is without stratagems to win over women.

It is this sense of irony which, despite the lingering didacticism and rampant chauvinism of *The Art of Love*, both provides the humour which at once "mocks" the didactic form and gives the poem a degree of complexity in its commentary on, as well as reflection of, contemporary social and sexual assumptions.

—Colin Graham

THE ART OF POETRY (L'Art poétique)
Poem by Nicolas Boileau, 1674

Nicolas Boileau's long four-part poem, *The Art of Poetry*, was first published in France in 1674, and in its trenchant style and vigorous argument it laid out the terms of neo-classical criticism in the most accessible and influential way. Along with Rapin's *Réflexions sur la Poétique et les Poètes* [Reflections on Poetics and Poets] from the same year, and Le Bossu's *Traité du Poème épique* [Treatise on the Epic] (1675), Boileau's poem disseminated and consolidated a set of aesthetic principles that dominated European writing and critical thinking for at least 50 years. As the name "neo-classical" suggests, Boileau looks back to the writers of Greece and Rome for critical guidance and authority, but he does so in a less deferential and systematic form than Rapin, and his views overall seem less doctrinaire than pragmatic.

In the earlier part of the poem, Boileau reviews the history of French writing up to the present day, wittily cataloguing the continually difficult task of being a poet, and gently pointing out the failings and limitations of his French predecessors, including Malherbe and Villon. The problem, as he formulates it at the beginning, lies in the relationship between form and content, in the conflicts that arise between meaning and technique:

> Quelque sujet qu'on traite, ou plaisant, ou sublime
> Que toujours le bon sens s'accorde avec la rime:
> L'un l'autre vainement ils semblent se hair
> La Rime est une esclave, et ne doit qu'obéir
>
> (Whatever one's subject, be it light or sublime
> Let good sense and rhyme be in accord:
> Although they seem to be at odds,
> Rhyme is but a slave, and must obey.)

The guiding light for any poet must always be "la raison" for reason alone can arbitrate between the competing claims of an over-ornate and an excessively prosaic style. Throughout the opening canto, Boileau offers a number of bits of equally pragmatic advice, hoping to encourage and advise fledgling writers, after the fashion of his eminent predecessor Horace.

The critique of contemporary writing is developed in Canto II through an elaborate and stylized discussion of the various poetic genres. In pastoral, Boileau claims, too many poets err regularly on the side of bombast or mundanity, and lack the requisite knowledge of Virgil and Theocritus that would show them the middle path. In the elegy, Boileau expresses his distaste for those poets whose emotions, over-calculated, come over as frigid. For them, he recommends the study of Tibullus and Ovid, masters of the correct statement. In the ode, the epigram, and the satire (of which Boileau himself was an influential writer), similar failings can be found, and the cure is always the same: study the classics, particularly those recognized as having excelled in particular genres, and learn from them.

Canto III gives more developed consideration of tragedy and the epic, offering the same advice and providing an extended critique of contemporary acting styles. The conclusion remains the same: read Sophocles and Homer, and admire their workmanship as much as their genius:

> Un poème excellent, où tout marche et se suit
> N'est pas de ces travaux gu'un caprice produit:
> Il veut du temps, des soins, et ce pénible ouvrage
> Jamais d'un écolier ne fut l'apprentissage.
>
> (A fine poem, whose every part functions and fits in
> Is not the product of a whim:
> It demands time and careful effort:
> Such a difficult task is not for a tyro.)

The argument thus sees poetry as a craft, reliant not wholly on inspiration, but on skills and learning. Yet Boileau is neither dismissive of "genius" nor wholly deferential to the classical masters. It is most important to see that he recommends imitation of their work not for its own sake, but because they are demonstrably better-equipped to deal with nature, the goal of all writing. And only the contemporary writer of genius knows how to imitate properly.

In the fourth and final canto of the poem, the negotiation between genius and learning continues, and Boileau seeks to enhance the status of poetry by comparing it with other activities. In poetry, there cannot be, as there may in all other arts and crafts, degrees of competence, only absolute success or failure in any of the specialized genres. There follows, as in Alexander Pope's *An Essay on Criticism* (1711), which was influenced heavily by Boileau, a ringing catalogue of maxims, designed to encourage the poet's high-mindedness and the pursuit of excellence. So alongside the recommendation to learn the tools of the poetic trade, Boileau's poem also defends the genius of the great writer. The poem ends with a patriotic call to Boileau's fellow writers to live up to the models of the classical authors, and a reminder that good writers need equally good critics.

The poem quickly became influential, and its less rigorous defence of the classics gave it strong currency. As it advises and recommends rather than commands, it falls into the more relaxed end of neo-classical thinking. It was known throughout Europe within a few years of publication, being first translated into English by Sir William Soames in 1683. Soames's translation was adapted by John Dryden, who described Boileau as "a living Horace and a Juvenal" and Boileau's influence on English writers of the early 18th-century was considerable.

—Ian A. Bell

ART POÉTIQUE (The Art of Poetry)
Poem by Paul Verlaine, 1884 (written 1874)

"De la musique avant toute chose"—"music above all else"—is the peremptory command with which Paul Verlaine's "Art poétique," written in April 1874, begins. And it ends with an equally peremptory dismissal of all poetry that does not possess this musical quality as mere "literature"—"Et tout le reste est littérature." Verlaine thus formulated, in two memorable lines, two of the basic tenets of the Symbolist movement in late 19th-century France—the equation between poetry and music in preference to the equation between poetry and sculpture that had been current in the middle of the century, and the conviction that the function of poetry is to convey feelings, as music does, rather than to describe events or analyse ideas. Yet, paradoxically, it was also Verlaine who, less than ten years before, in the "Epilogue" to his first volume of verse, *Poémes saturniens*, had asked in another memorable line: "Est-elle en marbre, ou non, la Vénus de Milo?," thus expressing his distrust of inspiration and his desire to shape his work as carefully and as patiently as a sculptor working in marble. But at that time, in 1866, he had been an aspiring young poet aged 22, anxious to please the established older generation. Even so, there are many of his early poems, such as "Soleils couchants," and "Chanson d'automne," which by no means obey these injunctions and which reveal his natural bent towards musicality. Furthermore, from September 1871 until July 1873 he had spent almost two years in the company of the rebellious Arthur Rimbaud, who had encouraged him to break with poetic tradition. So by April 1847, when he was 30 years old and had published three volumes of poetry with a fourth one ready for publication, he felt sufficiently self-confident to proclaim his own credo.

After the arresting opening line "Art poétique" goes on to give a series of detailed recommendations about this new concept of the art of writing poetry, all of which have the same basic aim of breaking away from the well-composed, solidly constructed, thoughtfully argued, nicely rounded, evenly balanced kind of verse. In order to achieve this line with the odd number of syllables—the "vers impair"—which creates an unstable rhythm is to be preferred to the line with an even number of syllables; words are to be chosen casually rather than precisely; colour should give way to nuance: wit and irony have no role to play in poetry; eloquence must be discarded; rhyme is an ostentatious decorative effect that must be used more discreetly and more subtly. In short, poetry, if it is to deserve the name, must have an air of freedom and spontaneity, of coming straight from the heart rather than having been worked over in the mind.

In ''Art poétique'' Verlaine deliberately practises some of what he preaches. The poem is in ''vers impairs'' of nine syllables so that the final syllable in each line is left suspended without a partner. There are occasional casual expressions—''c'est des beaux yeux'' is the conversational form of the more grammatically correct ''ce sont des beaux yeux'', and ''prends l'éloquence et tords-lui son cou'' should strictly be ''tords-lui le cou.'' The rhymes are almost all weak, such as ''impair'' and ''l'air,'' ''fou'' and ''sou,'' with only a single rhyming element so that the rhyme scheme is not over-obtrusive. But the poem's content is obviously important too and it clearly cannot aim at evoking a deeply felt emotion as do the best of Verlaine's misty autumn landscapes and pale moonlit scenes with their hesitant questioning note and whispered confidential tone.

Despite its instructional format, ''Art poétique'' is not a manifesto for the future, either for other Symbolist poets or for Verlaine himself. Although all of them shared the aims of suggesting rather than describing and of consequently putting greater emphasis on the musical quality of poetry, each of them did so in his own particular way. So although Baudelaire, Rimbaud, Mallarmé, and Valéry would have agreed with the opening and closing lines of ''Art poétique'' they would not have subscribed to the detailed recommendations that are particularly and peculiarly Verlainian. Moreover, even as far as Verlaine himself is concerned, what he is really doing is not so much laying down a programme for his future writing as summarizing the characteristics of the best of his past poetry. In the very month that he wrote ''Art Poétique'' Verlaine had just published *Romances Without Words*, which, as the title itself suggests, puts into practice the precepts laid down in ''Art poétique.'' Some of the most successful poems of his next volume, *Sagesse*, had also already been written, conveying with an admirable simplicity and directness the deep distress he had felt after his final violent quarrel with Rimbaud in July 1873 and during the first weeks of the 18-month prison sentence that had resulted from it. But over the course of the next few years, as he slowly completed *Sagesse* ready for its publication in 1881, Verlaine gradually deserted his Symbolist principles and practices so that by the time ''Art poétique'' finally found a place in his next volume of verse *Jadis et naguère*, published in 1884, he had long since abandoned its recommendations and was busy turning out, not poetry, but ''literature.''

—C. Chadwick

ARTE POÉTICA (Art of Poetry)
Poem by Pablo Neruda, 1933 (written 1928)

From classical times the *ars poetica* was the poem where the poet outlined his intentions, and what he thought a poem set out to achieve. These poems can be used as keys to read other less self-conscious poems by the same poet. Pablo Neruda had reached astonishing success early in his life as a poet with his *Twenty Love Poems and a Song of Despair*, when he was only 20 years old. In his attempt to forge a style more modern than the imagistic and sentimental one of these poems, nostalgically recalling past loves from his home town of Temunco, he realized that travel abroad, ideally to Paris, or at least Europe, would allow him to confront his lyrical ambitions with the latest avant-garde movements, especially surrealism. But Neruda was without influence, and could only manage a consular post to the Far East, where he lived from 1927 to 1932. His poem ''Arte poética'' was written in Calcutta sometime between November and December 1928. By then Neruda knew that he was breaking new ground as a poet, without adopting surrealist orthodoxies.

The poem in question is undoubtedly obscure. This difficulty arises not from some hermetic meaning that a reader could decode, or from a difficult use of symbolism, but from the more basic problem that Neruda did not know what he was writing about. His poems were approximations, successive attempts to try and trap in words what his enforced introspection made him experience. Living in an alien environment, far from his family and culture, he was forced into himself, against the grain of his natural tendency to be a sensual poet in contact with an objective nature. This poem tries to describe this alienation.

The poem opens with the poet caught between established categories, an outsider: ''Entre sombra y espacio, entre guarniciones y doncellas'' (''Between shadow and space, between garrisons and damsels''); he evokes his literary persona in Romantic terms as:

> dotado de corazón, singular y sueños funestos,
> precipitadamente pálido, marchito en la frente,
> y con luto de viudo furioso por cada día, de vida

> (endowed with a singular heart and sorrowful dreams
> precipitately pallid, withered in the brow
> and with a furious widower's mourning for each day of life)

where the poet is the widower without his woman/muse, cursed by some ill fate, dressed in the poet's Hamlet-like black clothes. Whatever he absorbs from this alienating environment, whether through dreams or through his senses—''y de todo sonido, que acojo temblando'' (''and from every sound that I welcome trembling'')—he feels ''una angustia indirecta'' (''indirect anguish''). This is the key term in this self-analytical poem, and it derives from his inability to attribute his anguish to any cause.

The poem develops this frustration at not being able to name and pinpoint his anguish with a series of five similes. This is a typical Nerudian technique. He cannot find the exact simile, so he throws out a series of similes, hoping that at least one will evoke his anguish. Each simile is preceded by the idea that it is the ego of the poet that is being compared through ''as'' and ''like.''

The first simile is ''como si llegaran ladrones o fantasmas, / y en una cáscara de extensión fija y profunda'' (''as if thieves or ghosts were coming / and in a shell of fixed and profound expanse'') where the sense is that the shell of his self has been invaded by something alien—thieves, ghosts. Being invaded by threatening outside forces is an acute description of anguish. The second simile is ''como un camarero humillado'' (''like a humiliated waiter''), where the poet sees himself as humiliated, like a waiter in a restaurant serving people, watching them eat. The third simile refers to a self-image that cuts across all his writing, the poet as a bell, but here ''como una campana un poco ronca'' (''like a slightly raucous bell''). Neruda is writing a new kind of poetry, more hoarse than lyrical, dealing with an ugly, unaesthetic world, within the mess and chaos of the tropical Far East. The fourth simile is "como un espejo viejo" ("like an old mirror") where the poet cannot see himself reflected.

However, it is the long fifth simile that catches the peculiar nature of one of his anxieties:

> como un olor de casa sola
> en la que los huéspedes entran de noche perdidamente ebrios,
> y hay un olor de ropa tirada al suelo, y una ausencia de flores.
>
> (like the smell of a solitary house
> where the guests come in at night wildly drunk
> and there is a smell of clothes thrown on the floor, and an
>   absence of flowers.)

This simile pinpoints the poet's loneliness, and the absence of a woman in his life. The absence of a woman becomes one of the main themes in the whole collection of *Residence on Earth*. Following this series of approximate similes, the poet is aware of the relative status of words and confesses in complete honesty that he could have written something quite different, less melancholic—"posiblemente de otro modo aún menos melancólico" ("possibly in another even less melancholic way").

The poem ends with his attempt to describe the truth of his situation in the hostile world:

> pero, la verdad, de pronto, el viento que azota mi pecho,
> las noches de substancia infinita caídas en mi dormitorio,
> el ruido de un día que arde con sacrificio. . .
>
> (but the truth is that suddenly the wind that lashes my chest,
> the nights of infinite substance fallen in my bedroom
> the noise of a day that burns with sacrifice. . .)

(translations by Donald D. Walsh)

The alien elements are wind, night, his bedroom, and his sacrificial life as a clerk. That is, his actual experience demands that he continue to try to be the Romantic poet he thought he was. The typeface changes from italics to roman—"me piden lo profético que hay en mí, con melancolia" ("ask me, mournfully, for what prophecy there is in me"). But no prophetic insight emerges from these poems. Here Neruda slowly discovers that he is not a Victor Hugo, for reality does not allow him to interpret it.

The poem ends on a note of total confusion, the poet faced with a world of unrelated fragments and hostile forces, with time passing. The actual syntax of the closing lines in Spanish reflects the breakdown of a meaningful world: "y un golpe de objetos que llaman sin ser respondidos / hay, y un movimiento sin tregua, y un hombre confuso" ("and there is a swarm of objects that call without being answered, / and a ceaseless movement, and a bewildered man"). That "hay" in the Spanish (there is) should open the sentence. Neruda's vision then is of meaningless movement, of time never letting up, and all the poet can do is offer confused words.

—Jason Wilson

ARTHAVA-VEDA

See THE VEDAS

ASHES AND DIAMONDS (Popiół i diament)
Novel by Jerzy Andrzejewski, 1948

Ashes and Diamonds, first published in the literary magazine *Odrodzenie* in 1947 under the title *Zaraz po wojnie* [Just after the War], is one of the most controversial Polish novels written in the post-war period. Set in a provincial capital, Ostrowiec, between 6 and 9 May 1945—that is, during the first days of Polish People's Republic—it portrays circumstances related to the Communist takeover. Its manifold storyline centres upon the assassination of Stefan Szczuka, the local secretary of the Polish Worker's Party, by Maciek Chełmicki, a soldier of the anti-Communist Home Army. The main conflict between the underground forces and those who support the new order is shown in the broader context of post-war society, which embraces not only heroes and villains, but also the confused victims of declined moral standards. Vengeful officers of the Home Army, youthful delinquents turned into criminals, a judge who attempts to get over his disgraceful conduct in a concentration camp and make a fresh start, a mixture of spineless people and cynical careerists—these represent the damage inflicted by the war upon the Polish population.

Jerzy Andrzejewski's resolute support for the new political system and his corresponding condemnation of those who oppose it failed initially to satisfy the most orthodox Marxists. *Ashes and Diamonds*, however, eventually became a classic of the Polish People's Republic, where more than 25 editions of the novel were printed and where it remained on the school syllabus. The international success of Andrzej Wajda's film also contributed to the novel's high reputation. With the emergence of political opposition and post-Communist Poland, however, the novel's seriously biased message has been challenged subsequently.

Ashes and Diamonds, despite its pro-Communist dedication, can hardly be regarded as a typical example of Socialist Realism. Andrzejewski, once a Catholic writer, attempted to adjust his old dichotomy of good and evil to the Marxist understanding of class struggle and progress. Within this frame, he simply related evil to the "forces of the past" and good to those who fought for "the future" and were thus reshaping the existing social order. Following the novel's epigraph, taken from Cyprian Norwid's poem, he asks whether ashes will eventually bring to light a "starlike diamond," hidden under the post-war rubble. The apocalyptic power of physical and moral devastation, caused by recent events, has been distributed, though, according to the political criteria, where those who do not belong to "the forces of history" and their march forwards are sentenced to be astray also in a moral sense. The ethical decadence of Judge Kossecki, who attempted to survive a concentration camp at any cost, is branded as "the bankruptcy of a petit bourgeois" by an upright Party member, Podgórski. By contrast, Maria Szczuka, a Communist, sacrificed herself in support of her fellow prisoners and died with dignity in Ravensbrück. A party in the Monopol Hotel, which has assembled former aristocrats as well as members of the intelligentsia and the political élite, exudes an apocalyptic atmosphere, while a polonaise danced in the reception room apparently symbolizes an ill-matched alliance between the old and the new.

In a similar way Andrzejewski approaches the political struggle between the Home Army and the Communists, where—despite endeavours to avoid black-and-white simplifications—the latter are ultimately represented as wholly in the right. They are portrayed as deserted heroes, in the middle of an unresponsive, immature society, who fight against the odds for a brilliant future. The Home Army, by contrast, represents only hatred and death, as a force that has placed itself on the wrong side of the barricade. By espousing a cause hostile to progress the Home Army is represented as having reduced to absurdity a sense of duty and often authentic patriotism. As a result, the most conscientious soldiers of the Home Army, such as Andrzej Kossecki and Maciek Chełmicki, are afflicted by an internal struggle between the innate human inclination towards love and friendship and the politically motivated inclination towards hatred and murder. Since the idealized Communists do not share such dilemmas, only the members of the Home Army are tormented by half-conscious longings for peace and normal life. Scenes portraying Andrzej Kossecki's streak of sympathy with a Russian soldier as just another human being, or Chełmicki's instinctive solidarity with his prospective victim, Szczuka, a stranger ''unknown but cherished,'' subordinate humanitarian principles to the writer's political end. Maciek and Andrzej, in Andrzejewski's view, belong to the ''lost generation'' degraded by the war and the wrong cause. Hence, their tragedy is authentic but inevitable. Maciek's death, despite its appearance of accidental killing, represents the logical outcome of his life. It is a form of punishment not only for the assassination of Szczuka, but for the wrongly chosen political code as well. In other words, the author tries to demonstrate that Maciek has been trampled upon by the victorious forces of history, as an individual who has tragically forfeited his rights to love (represented by his affair with Krystyna Rozbicka) and family life in a new society.

Ashes and Diamonds is a novel with an unequivocal message. Sympathy for some ''misguided'' soldiers of the anti-Communist underground does not undermine convictions, articulated by Szczuka, that only the Party represents the right path, even if on its way it makes mistakes. Consequently, the narrative form is very traditional, to accommodate this ideological commitment. Andrzejewski leaves no doubt as to who is right and who is wrong. Every dispute seems to envisage its unavoidable conclusion. Well-argued doubts, voiced by a devoted socialist, Kalicki, Szczuka's old friend, are flatly rejected by Szczuka as the pure misunderstanding of historical inevitability. Still, with all its faults, *Ashes and Diamonds* is skilfully narrated and this accounts for its popularity.

—Stanislaw Eile

L'ASSOMMOIR
Novel by Émile Zola, 1877

L'Assommoir, published in 1877, is the seventh novel in the Rougon-Macquart series and arguably the best. It tells how Gervaise Macquart comes to Paris with her lover, Auguste Lantier—father of the Étienne of *Germinal*—and sets up as a laundress. Lantier deserts her and she takes up with Coupeau, a zinc-worker, by whom she has a daughter, Nana, who recurs in the series as a high-class prostitute in the novel which bears her name. But the bad luck that pursues all Émile Zola's characters intervenes when Coupeau is badly injured falling from the roof of one of the high Second-Empire buildings, which he has been covering with plates of zinc. He refuses the offer to teach him to read and write made by the virtuous and hard-working Goujet, who carries a torch for Gervaise, and begins to drink. Lantier returns and both men live on Gervaise's work as a laundress while also sharing her sexual favours. The tendency to alcoholism that she inherits from her father, Antoine Macquart, takes control of Gervaise and her laundry fails. She turns, unsuccessfully, to prostitution, and then begs for bread. But life in 19th-century working-class Paris is hard, and nobody will give her anything. She dies of starvation in a cupboard underneath the stairs.

Gervaise is the most sympathetically observed of all Zola's characters. With slightly better luck, she could have made a good life for herself and kept her inherited tendency to alcoholism under control. All she wants is an ordinary life in which she can love her husband and children and work for a living at a trade she enjoys and in which she is highly skilled. But, like almost all of the women in 19th-century French fiction, she is let down by the men in her life. Lantier is a wastrel, Coupeau too stupid to cope with misfortune, Goujet an insufficiently aggressive admirer. She is also, however, the victim of a society that is totally indifferent to human suffering and makes no provision for those who fall below the poverty line. The enormous copper-plated still from which the alcohol comes and which finally ruins everybody's life except that of the total abstainer, stands like an obscene god in the corner of the gin palace, the only source of even temporary happiness in a society dedicated, as the Second Empire was, entirely to the making of money.

Food and drink dominate the novel. The irony of the fact that Gervaise dies of starvation is underlined by the description of the immense and complicated banquet that she and the other women who work in the laundry prepare to celebrate her name day. But the peas are slightly too salty and the goose catches fire in the frying pan before being put into the oven to simmer. The guests are thus led to drinking too much and, at the end, they all throw up. At the end of the novel, Lantier survives and is reported as living off other women in working-class Paris. Coupeau dies of a splendidly-described attack of *delirium tremens*, a fact that encouraged a Temperance Society to adapt *L'Assommoir* as a play in which Goujet, who is a total abstainer, rescues Gervaise, marries her, and saves Nana from a life of sin. The play was not successful and alcoholism is only part of the problem. For Zola, human beings at every level in society were equally doomed by their inherited tendencies, whatever they were. For his upper-class characters, it was greed, financial dishonesty, and sexual inadequacy. At the working-class level, where he excels, it is the more brutal emotions and basic physical needs that drive his characters to their destruction.

The doctrine of Naturalism, which Zola espoused, differed from the realistic practices developed by his predecessors mainly in its ideological presuppositions. If human experience was unsatisfying for a realist such as Flaubert, this was just the way things were. There were no philosophical implications. For Zola, in contrast, there was a reason why people were so unhappy. It lay in the inescapability of the laws of physiological and social determinism to which they were subjected. Only science could offer a solution to the problem, and Zola's long-term aim in the Rougon-Macquart series was to show that a solution could be found, once human beings learnt to understand their situation and to act accordingly. The predominant image left by his novels is, nevertheless, of a group of human beings who are in thrall to a set of immutable laws as merciless as the gods who sent the Greek heroes to their doom.

—Philip Thody

ATHALIE
Play by Jean Racine, 1691

In spite of having read Sophocles's *Oedipus Rex*, and translated *Hamlet*, Voltaire still described Jean Racine's 1691 tragedy *Athalie* as the "masterpiece of the human spirit." It is not a verdict to which anyone now subscribes, even in France, and productions of Racine's last play are undertaken more in a spirit of reluctant piety than of theatrical enthusiasm. The plot is taken from the Old Testament (2 Chronicles 22–23 and 2 Kings 11) and describes the defeat of the wicked queen Athalie by the virtuous high priest Joad and the infant king Joas. For the eight years preceding the action which, in the tradition of the French theatre of the 17th century, takes place in less than 24 hours, Joas has been kept hidden by Josabeth, wife of the High Priest, and trained to serve God as an altar-boy in the temple, All the other children of the house of David have been slain by Athalie, in revenge for the killing of her son, Ochozias, and Joad is preparing to proclaim Joas as the rightful king of the Jews. Athalie, a worshipper of Baal, would clearly like to prevent this happening and, as queen of Judah, is in a strong position to do so. However, she has been troubled by a dream in which her mother, Jézabel, having warned her that she is about to fall victim to the God of Israel, turns into a mixture of blood and bones as soon as Athalie tries to embrace her. She feels that the key to the mystery lies in the child, Joas, for whom she feels a strange attraction, and comes to see him in the temple. There, an army of Levites secretly trained by Joad emerges to protect Joas, whom Athalie finds seated upon the throne, and as the people outside the temple acknowledge Joas as their true king, Athalie realizes that she has been defeated.

The French 19th-century critic Charles-Augustin Sainte-Beuve saw *Athalie* as a model of classical tragedy and an appreciation of it the proof of good taste. Its first performance took place in private, with the demoiselles de Saint-Cyr, the young ladies of the aristocratic convent school in Paris, providing the chorus. Racine's attempt to give the chorus in the French theatre something of the same role that it had in Euripides has been much admired by French critics and makes the play into an interesting theatrical experience. Since everything ends happily for the virtuous and only the wicked are punished, it is difficult to see *Athalie* as a tragedy. It has none of the qualities that make *King Lear* such an unforgettable experience, and that transform Racine's own earlier, pagan tragedies into such masterpieces of characterization and dramatic construction. It is more of a sacred drama and one which has the disadvantage of presenting the supposedly virtuous characters in a profoundly unattractive light. The eight-year-old Joas is a self-satisfied prig, who finds total satisfaction in helping with the ceremonies conducted at the high altar. He never meets any other children. His protector, Joad, has a confidence in his own righteousness which makes Dr. Arnold of Rugby seem, by contrast, a model of self-effacing agnostic tolerance. Athalie herself is a marvellous creation, but she is not on stage long enough. Whereas the doomed and passionate heroines of Racine's earlier plays (Hermione, Agrippine, Roxane, Phaedra) are given plenty of lines to express their anguish, Athalie does not appear until Act II, is off-stage for Act III and IV, and appears at the end of Act V only to be defeated almost immediately.

Until he stopped writing profane plays, at the age of 38, after a cabal had ensured an unenthusiastic reception for his greatest tragedy, *Phaedra*, in January 1677, Racine had led a life of moderate dissipation. In 1677, he had even been accused of having been involved in an attempt to murder one of his former mistresses, the actress Du Parc. The formal charge was dropped before it reached open court, perhaps a sign of the protection Racine enjoyed in high places. His marriage in June of the same year to Catherine de Romanet, a young lady of ample means who never went to the theatre in her life, coincided with his appointment as historiographer to Louis XIV. Racine became reconciled, in so far as this was politically expedient, with the Jansenists who had educated him. If *Athalie* was a disguised plea in their favour, it was unsuccessful. In 1708, in obedience to the papal bull, Louis XIV abolished the convent of Port-Royal, and in 1710 all its buildings were razed to the ground. The God in whom Joas and Joad trusted made no appearance. The ruthlessness with which He punished Athalie nevertheless recalls the implacable deities who condemned to their doom the heroines and heroes of the earlier tragedies to which Racine owes his reputation as the greatest of all French playwrights and, quite possibly, of all French writers.

According to Boileau's *The Art of Poetry* (*L'Art poétique*), 1674, which codified the rules officially governing classical tragedy in 17th-century France, Christianity did not provide suitable subject matter for profane literature. Since the plot of *Athalie* is taken from the Old Testament, the play does not go against what is very sensible advice. Like Corneille's *Polyeucte*, whose favourable presentation of an early martyr makes a more direct exaltation of the virtues of Christianity, it is nevertheless a reminder of one of the paradoxes of French literature of the classical period. The models most admired by the writers and literary theoreticians of the time were the works of Greek and Roman antiquity. The official ideology of society was, nevertheless, a Christianity whose refusal to tolerate other religions was epitomized by Louis XIV's revocation, in 1685, of the Edict of Nantes. No French writer of the time protested, and the ethical atmosphere of *Athalie* suggests that this was not simply because they were afraid of what might happen to them. None of them had any notion of human rights and especially not the right of dissent. While not entirely "the masterpiece of the human spirit" that Voltaire claimed it to be, *Athalie* is a good example of an apparent paradox: many of the most famous works from the past are the product of societies in which nobody would want to live, and reflect attitudes that only the most eccentric of their admirers would ever endorse.

—Philip Thody

AUCASSIN AND NICOLETTE (Aucassin et Nicolette)

Anonymous 13th-century romance. Written c. 1200 in the form of a chante-fable (narrative comprised of alternate prose and verse passages), probably in the dialect of Picardy; single manuscript found in 1752.

PUBLICATIONS

Aucassin et Nicolette, edited by Hermann Suchier. 1878; also edited by Francis William Bourdillon, 1887, revised 1897, 1919; Mario Roques, 1925, revised 1929; Jean Dufournet, 1973; Modern French translations by La Curne de Sainte-Palaye, 1752, as *Les Amours du bon vieux temps*, 1756; Legrand d'Aussy, in *Fabliaux et contes du XIIe et du XIIIe siècle*, vol. 2, 1779; Claude Fauriel, in *Histoire de la poésie provençale*, vol. 3, 1846; Alfred Delvau, in *Bibliothèque bleue: Collection des romans de chevalerie*, vol. 1, 1859, and in separate volume, 1866; Alexandre Bida, 1878;

Gustave Michaut, 1901, revised 1905; Albert Pauphilet, 1932; Marcel Coulon, 1933; Gustave Cohen, 1954; Maurice Pons, 1960; Jean Dufournet, 1973. translated as *Aucassin and Nicolette*, in *Tales of the 12th and 13th Centuries*, vol. 2, 1786; also translated by A. Rodney Macdonough, 1880; Francis William Bourdillon, 1887; Andrew Lang, 1887; Elias John Wilkinson Gibb, 1887; M.S. Henry and Edward W. Thomson, 1896; Edward Everett Hale, 1899; Laurence Housman, 1903; Eugene Mason, 1910; Harold Child, 1911; Dulcie Lawrence Smith, 1914; Michael West, 1917; Edward Francis Moyer and Carey DeWitt Eldridge, 1937; Norma Lorre Goodrich, 1964; Pauline Matarasso, 1971; Glyn S. Burgess, 1988.

*

Bibliography: *Aucassin et Nicolette: A Critical Bibliography* by Barbara Nelson Sargent-Baur and Robert Francis Cook, 1981.

Critical Studies: *Studies in the History of the Renaissance* by Walter Pater, 1873; *Le Legs du moyen âge* by Albert Pauphilet, 1950; *Étude styto-statistique du vocabulaire des vers et de la prose dams la chantefable "Aucassin et Nicolette"* by Simone Monsonégo, 1966; *Love's Fools: Aucassin, Troilus, Calisto, and the Parody of the Courtly Lover* by June Hall Martin, 1972; *Les Temps du passé dans "Aucassin et Nicolette"* by Lene Schøsler, 1973.

* * *

Aucassin and Nicolette is an anonymous French romance composed during the first half of the 13th century. Termed a *chante-fable*, the form of the narrative comprises alternating prose and heptasyllabic verse passages, thereby recalling the structure of Boethius' *De Consolatione philosophiae* (*On the Consolation of Philosophy*). An engaging story with witty dialogue, unexpected events, and fortunate conclusion, the work resembles a *fabliau* or *conte*. However, it is generally agreed that it was a dramatic recitation presented by one actor for the prose passages and possibly sung by minstrels for the lyrics. The narrative tells of an adventure of two lovers that suggests parallels with Greek Byzantine romances, but extensive undercutting argues for classifying the work as a parody or satire. The difficulties in determining genre extend to language. In employing the dialect of Picardy, the author appears to be northern French. However, references to Beaucaire and Valance situate the story in the south of France, thereby justifying claims that the original but inextant version was written in Provençal.

The narrative of the romance moves from contention to reconciliation and from separation to reunion. Aucassin loves Nicolette, a Saracen slave converted to Christianity. Aucassin's father, Garin de Beaucaire, forbids marriage, imprisons Nicolette, and insists that his son marry a lady of equal station, and that he fight against Bougars de Valence who has ravaged Garin's country. Aucassin refuses. However, his father consents that, in exchange for waging war, Aucassin can see and embrace Nicolette. Aucassin delivers Bougars to his father, but Garin does not honour his pledge. Aucassin is imprisoned. Nicolette escapes, informs Aucassin of her plans, flees to the forest, and requests shepherds to advise Aucassin of her location. Aucassin learns of the shepherds' encounter with Nicolette and, after meeting a herdsman who has lost one of his oxen, he rejoins Nicolette. Because of Garin's threat to execute Nicolette, the lovers seek refuge in Torelore where Aucassin supports the king in war. The Saracens,

though, take the country and abduct the lovers in separate ships. Aucassin's vessel is wrecked near Beaucaire where he hears of his father's death and his subsequent succession as ruler. Nicolette, arriving in Carthage, learns that she is the king's daughter. She leaves for Beaucaire and, disguised as a minstrel, sings her story to Aucassin and discovers the constancy of his love. Returning to her godparents' house, she is restored to her beauty and reveals her identity to Aucassin. The reunited lovers live happily in marriage.

The adventures and eventual consummation of love recall the narratives of 12th-century romances. Arthurian romances as popularized by Chrétien de Troyes recount the superhuman feats of the legendary king and his knights, and were continued into the 13th century by works such as the *Queste del Sainte Graal* (*Quest of the Holy Grail*) and *La Morte le Roi Artu* (*King Arthur's Death*). Whereas Arthurian romance evokes a mysticism that encourages allegorical interpretation, non-Arthurian romance conveys a realism that often avoids direct moral didacticism. Through courage and perseverance, Aucassin and Nicolette display qualities of Arthurian heroes and heroines, and conform to codes of courtly love. However, irony undercuts the seriousness of circumstances and tone, and allusions to the significance of money and law add a realism that argues for the classification of the work as a non-Arthurian romance. Any direct borrowing from Greek Byzantine romances is unlikely. Nevertheless, tales and themes from this tradition were disseminated by returning crusaders and by Latin and Latinized Greek works, and did inform the plots and character portrayals in Gautier d'Arras's *Eracle* (1174), Aimon de Varenne's *Florimont* (1188), and the widely enjoyed anonymous romance, *Floire and Blancheflor* (c. 1175).

A sharp delineation and a subtle development of character complement the themes of unrequited love, war, and familial disputes. Nicolette, despite the precariousness of imprisonment and risks of escape, remains faithful. Aucassin, like Chrétien's courtly-love heroes, matures in depth and breadth. Initially, he thinks only of his passion for Nicolette; but, after fighting against Bougars, he expands his vision, replacing an ox lost by the herdsman, waging war against the Saracens, and becoming a wise ruler of Beaucaire. Realism penetrates illusion and affords unexpected turns in plot and psychological portrayal. Nicolette assumes her rightful noble standing and, at the end, exchanges the mask of darkened face for her own beautiful complexion. Aucassin recognizes the realities of contentions and, although shunning any training in combat, evolves into a fearless warrior and just lord. A resolution to the romantic entanglements, moreover, requires the use of money, an understanding of circumstances, an insight into emotions, and the recognition of legal ramifications (e.g., the shepherds' refusal to betray Garin) that must be respected but overcome.

Irony and inversion create illusions of simplicity and the fantastic. Aucassin, obsessed by love, notes naively that the sole consequence of decapitation is the incapacity to speak with Nicolette. Compared to a fleur-de-lis "sweeter than the grape," Nicolette lives in a hut built with fragrant flowers and fern leaves. The Queen of Torelore replaces her husband in leading a burlesque campaign against the Saracens, waged with apples, eggs, and cheese.

An artistic eclecticism explains, in part, the originality of this work. By reworking plots and images associated with Arthurian and Greek Byzantine romances, the author shapes an engaging, intricate narrative to established structures and themes. Allusions to contemporary concerns, moreover, enhance relevance, but the extensive employment of lyric verse foreshadows the singing and dancing in Adam de la Halle's dramatic *pastourelle, Jeu de Robin et Marion* (*Play of*

Robin and Marion). Finally, the use of irony in characterization, language, and imagery provides a verve and vibrance characteristic of the parodies in later *fabliaux* and *farces*. In deflating the seriousness of Arthurian romances, ambiguity, exaggeration, and wit heighten the charm and entertainment of a narrative conventional in themes but complex in tone and genre.

—Donald Gilman

AUTO DA BARCA DO INFERNO, AUTO DA BARCA DO PURGATÓRIO, AUTO DA BARCA DA GLÓRIA
Plays by Gil Vicente, 1517, 1518, 1519

These social satires were not originally conceived as a trilogy. However, the first *Barca* was so successful that Gil Vicente used the same allegorical framework for two further works, the second of which was written in Castilian. They exemplify the relationship between Vicente's plays and medieval European drama, but also incorporate Renaissance elements. Each play is framed within an allegory that combines the *Processus Satanus* with a variation on the Journey of Life. The structure is processional but continuity is provided by the constant presence on stage of the Devil and Angel, each with his respective ship. One by one the dead appear and try to gain admittance to the ship that is bound for heaven. According to their conduct while alive, they are taken on board by the Angel, claimed by the Devil, or obliged to serve out a period in Purgatory. The three *Barca* plays have much of the medieval morality plays and goliardic satire in general, while the *Barca da Glória* in particular owes much to the Castilian Dance of Death, namely the arrangement of characters by estate and the appearance of Death the Leveller. The rich symbolism of the two boats derives from the Ship of Vices and the Ship of Virtues of medieval sermon tradition, and must have been laden with significance for the seafaring Portuguese. The *Barcas* also constitute one of the first imitations in Portugal of Greek literature, in this case Lucian of Samosata's *Dialogues of the Dead.* Vicente presents criticism of the living through a trial of the dead. Judgement has been passed, but there is still some argument on the quayside, with attempts to strike a bargain or plead for mercy.

The processional structure allows the playwright to present a wide range of social types. Many of the characters bear the symbol of their profession or vice—even the Angel has a ledger with the balance of people's sins—and may be the personification of an abstract quality. However, because of the vigour of the language used, characters take on a life of their own, and emerge as credible personalities rather than one-dimensional figures.

In the *Auto da Barca do Inferno*, arguably the best of the three plays and certainly the most entertaining, the characters are predominantly urban. The Angel is a noble, dignified figure, in contrast to the sardonic and street-wise Devil who refuses to be conned. The nobleman, D. Anrique, has been corrupt in life and displays the sin of pride, symbolized by the chair carried behind him by his page. He believes that his rank confers special privileges, and he is ridiculed for his foolish belief that he is mourned on Earth. The usurer, a stock type of medieval satire, carries a symbolic bag of gold but soon discovers that his wealth will not buy him a place in heaven. João, the fool, is characterized by his coarse language, preoccupation with bodily functions, and affability. Like the traditional literary fool, he serves a comic function: his apparently inane ramblings are pointed criticisms

that deflate the bombast of the professional types and reinforce the criticisms voiced by the Angel and Devil. João is admitted to the Angel's boat because of his essential innocence, contrasted with the corruption of the others who file before us. The cobbler, João Antão, enters carrying his last, the tool of his trade. Despite going to mass and contributing to church funds, he has not made an honest and full confession, and he has robbed the people for the last 30 years: hence he has died excommunicate. The friar is depicted as a courtier who arrives with his mistress Florença and proceeds to give a virtuoso demonstration of his fencing skills. Believing that his tonsure and habit will save him, he approaches the Angel, who does not deign to answer him. Brízida Vaz is another stereotypical character; her moral failings and professional activities are symbolized by her "hand luggage," the paraphernalia of the procuress. She even tries out her sales patter on the Angel, boasting about her services to the clergy, and speaking blasphemously when she compares her suffering to that of a Christian martyr and suggests that she has carried out God's work on earth.

Vicente's treatment of the Jew is more ambivalent. The goat he carries around his shoulders may symbolize the Devil and it is almost certainly the expiatory goat of Leviticus XVI: 21–22, representing the sins of the world. He does not even attempt to approach the Angel, but the Devil will not allow him to bring his goat on board. The fool accuses him of sacrilege, repeating popular myths about Jewish practices. Satire against members of the legal profession is a medieval commonplace, and Vicente does not miss the opportunity to attack the corrupt judge who has accepted bribes. The Devil tells him that he will meet up with his fellows and see how well they are prospering in hell. Next comes the lawyer, who believes that his education will save him. He is not a doctor of law, only a bachelor, and like the judge, he speaks a bastardized Latin that completely fails to impress. The man hanged for theft is also bound for hell, although he has been informed that last-minute repentance will save him. The Four Knights of the Order of Christ go straight to the heavenly boat because they died in God's service in Africa.

The *Auto da Barca do Purgatório* focuses predominantly on rural characters, who are treated with greater sympathy. Their sins are less serious, and the majority are permitted to expiate their sins in Purgatory. First, the farmer, plough on his back, who has extended the boundaries of his lands by shifting the boundary stones, a crime that is mentioned in Mosaic Law (Deuteronomy XIX: 4, XXVII: 17), medieval civil legislation, and in the manuals for confessors. The farmer takes pride in his profession, and believes that he deserves glory because of his hard life on earth (reminding us of the Beatitudes). He knows his prayers and refuses to give in to the Devil. Next comes the market woman, Marta Gil, who has overcharged her customers and watered the oil. Marta argues that she has only done what was needed to survive in hard times. Because she demonstrates genuine Christian faith, she too is allowed to wait in Purgatory. The shepherd's sin is that of attempted seduction, but he knows his prayers, and his faith that the Devil will not take anyone on Christmas Day. The young shepherdess, Policena, is notable for her simplicity; her sin is that she perceived Mass as the occasion for much gossip. The child is immediately accepted by the Angel because of his complete innocence, but there is no doubt whatsoever about the fate which awaits the gambler, whom the Devil greets as a brother and business partner. The *taful* has not just gambled for money, but has uttered the vilest blasphemies. Like his predecessors in sermon *exempla* and in the Marian Lyrics of Alfonso X of Castile and Leon, the gambler is condemned with no hope of salvation.

The *Auto da Barca da Glória* differs from its predecessors in several respects; the intervention on stage of Death, who leads the characters to their judgement on the quayside; the incorporation of extracts from the Office of the Death; the sombre tone; the absence of humour and popular elements, and its strong anti-clericalism. Referring back to the first voyage, the Devil complains that hitherto Death has only sent him the poor and lowly, while in the second work, his boat was temporarily beached. Now he will deal with the most powerful members of society: the count, duke, king, emperor from the temporal hierarchy, and the bishop, archbishop, cardinal, and pope from the spiritual one. Their sins may be summed up quite simply as the failure to carry out the duties and responsibilities incumbent on them because of their high office, or the exploitation of those less privileged in terms of wealth, status, and power. Each believes his position at the top of the hierarchy and his observance of the external rituals of the church will save him. Only the appearance of Christ in a Second Coming can redeem these sinners, so grave is their wrongdoing, and some critics have viewed this ending as the playwright's way of avoiding giving offence to his royal patrons and the officials of the church.

In each play the dramatic tension arises out of the conflict between good and evil. Linguistically, the plays are characterized by Vicente's deft use of rhyme and the choice of register most appropriate to his characters: rapid speech; short lines; word plays; popular sayings and proverbs; topical jokes and allusions to living personalities; rustic expressions; colloquial speech and outright vulgarity when seeking comic effects; Biblical references alongside macaronic Latin; professional jargon used by characters to impress and to justify themselves. We hear the voice of the people as well as of the court. These plays allow Vicente to paint an intensely satirical picture of Portuguese society as he knew it. Few escape his censure, although there are different degrees of satire, depending on the gravity of their offence.

—P.A. Odber de Baubeta

AUTO-DA-FÉ (Die Blendung)
Novel by Elias Canetti, 1936

Elias Canetti wrote his only novel between autumn 1929 and October 1931 in Vienna but it was four years until he found a publisher, with help from Stefan Zweig. Provisionally titled *Kant fängt Feuer* [Kant Catches Fire], it was planned as a first in a series of eight novels. Each protagonist was to represent a specific social type whose dedication to a single ideal or concept had become an all-consuming obsession. This "Human Comedy of Madmen" was to include the man of truth, the visionary who wants to live in outer space, the religious fanatic, the compulsive collector, the spendthrift, the enemy of death, the actor, and the man of books. Their pathologies comprise the spectrum of existential defects and perversions that are endemic to intellectuals in technological mass society. Since many of these personae were included in *Auto-da-Fé*, Canetti abandoned the larger project in favour of a satirical play, *Komödie der Eitelkeit* (*Comedy of Vanity*, completed in January 1934), an (unfinished) novel about the "Tod-Feind" (literally, the enemy of and unto death), and, ultimately, work leading to his monumental study *Masse und Macht* (*Crowds and Power*). In January 1939, shortly after Canetti's escape to London, he resolved to abstain from all fictional and dramatic writing so long as Hitler was in power, a decision that included the stipulation that new translations of his novel should not be published until the end of World War II.

The three parts of *Auto-da-Fé* (A Head Without a World, Headless World, The World in the Head) portray different ways in which intellectualism encounters social reality. The protagonist through whom these confrontations are acted out is a reclusive private scholar, Dr. Peter Kien, aged 40 and the world's foremost sinologist. He lives entirely for and in his library of 25,000 volumes, a misanthropist hermit with a pathological devotion to his learned pursuits. He treats his books as if they are human, even adding them as imaginary acquaintances in his four-room flat on the top floor of 24 Ehrlichstrasse (literally, honest street), whereas "real people," rather than profit from a noble mind, only meet with his derisive scorn and harsh commands. But in the long run he is bested by his primitive housekeeper Therese Krumbholz whom he marries after she wins his confidence by feigning admiration for a particular book. She systematically mistreats him in order to gain control of his bank account and then drives him from his last room where he had barricaded himself behind a wall of books. Helplessly drifting through the city's underworld, Kien befriends a variety of shady characters who conspire to swindle him out of his money. A Jewish midget, the hunchbacked Fischerle, who claims to be the world's greatest chess player, devises the most successful stratagem to fleece his victim: knowing that Kien will redeem, even at inflated prices, all books pawned at the Theresianum and return them to their owners, he organizes a gang of thieves, involving also Therese and a brutally abusive retired policeman, Benedikt Pfaff, from whom Kien buys back his own library. When Kien discovers their scheme, a row ensues that lands him into police custody where, hallucinating that he has locked his wife in the apartment to die of starvation, he accuses himself of her murder. But Pfaff secures his release by having him declared mentally unfit and keeps him in a completely dark basement room, physically debilitated and close to insanity even though his mind is still lucid. At this stage Kien's brother Georges, a prominent psychiatrist from Paris with "the world in his head," comes to straighten out his affairs but, deceived by Peter's mental acuity, fails to diagnose his incurable madness correctly. The demented scholar, fearing another scheme to take from him the treasures of his library and in his final delusion ever more ravingly the "head without a world," sets his books ablaze and with them burns to death, laughing maniacally.

Canetti's plot, while coherent and credible even in its grotesque episodes and in other excesses of the imagination, appears to be secondary to the novel's extraordinary characters. They lack virtually all the elements that usually define the contradictory but coherent diversity of the human psyche, and they have created for themselves a social environment of stunning depravity. The absence of any redeeming features such as are traditionally accorded to even the most despicable villains lays bare a system of elementary impulses and instinctual drives that serve a very limited number of primitive goals. Most prominent among them are the ruthless, even sadistic enjoyment of power and the greedy satisfaction of basic physical pleasures. *Auto-da-Fé* is thus peopled with a set of monstrous cripples whose single-mindedness forestalls the development of narrative tension through moral complications and subtle psychological contrasts. The resultant intense monotony is highlighted by episodes of an ever more bizarre surreality that, while unpredictable, is none the less fully consistent in its own insane logic. A carefully sustained attitude both of intimate familiarity with and satirical remove from his figures allows the narrator to depict a world blinded by its ferocious obsessions in a style that combines precise observation with grim humour.

His own penetrating intellectualism, while loath to provide explanatory comments, has an edge of critical sharpness that shuns the illusions of comforting sentiment and that is never flushed with streaks of warmth or whimsy. Canetti claimed Kafka and Gogol' as his stylistic models; like these congenial spirits and no less radically than Beckett among his contemporaries, his fictional seismogram of the fascist mentality forces his readers to change their habits of aesthetic perception and to re-examine their own social experiences.

—Michael Winkler

B

BAAL
Play by Bertolt Brecht, 1922

Although written from an ideological position very different from the Marxist one on which his later, better-known plays were based, Bertolt Brecht's first full-length play set a pattern to be followed by the playwright throughout the rest of his career inasmuch as it was subject to a process of repeated revision. The first version, written in 1918, was strongly stamped by Brecht's aversion to another play, *The Lonely One*, by the Expressionist (and later National Socialist) dramatist Hanns Johst. Johst's play had depicted, sympathetically, the downfall of the poet, playwright, and misunderstood "genius" Christian Dietrich Grabbe, as a process of self-destruction prompted by spiritual anguish. Brecht's hero, too, is a poet, but one whose self-destruction buys him a life of great intensity, every passing moment of which is savoured to the full. By 1919 Brecht had already revised the play once, by 1920 for a second time and by 1922 it had undergone a third revision. By now it was acceptable to a publisher, although Brecht felt that it had lost much of its vitality in the process of revision. Certainly, the 1919 version provides the fullest exposition of Baal's subjectivity, but it is still influenced excessively by the polemic against Johst, whereas the first published version is more clearly structured and has been cut to a more performable length. In 1922 the play was given a brief and rather unsuccessful first run after the very considerable theatrical success of Brecht's second play, *Drums in the Night* (*Trommeln in der Nacht*).

The year 1926 saw the completion of yet another version of the play, now with a new title, *Biography of the Man Baal*. The curious mention of "man" in the title reflects the fact that the mythical qualities in the original figure (implicit in his name, which is that of a Canaanite fertility god, and highlighted in his own "Chorale of the Great Baal") have been largely eliminated in favour of a sardonic account, in the manner of the modish "Neue Sachlichkeit" or "New Realism" of the mid-1920s, of the increasingly desolate life of a poet-cum-motor-mechanic. When this Baal runs away from civilization, he finds precious little nature to return to, since it is being engulfed by the relentless spread of the great cities. From the beginning of the 1930s onwards, after Brecht had begun to devote his writing to the cause of a Communist revolution, he experimented with yet another approach to his egocentric first creation. The result was just a few, fragmentary scenes for a work to be entitled "Wicked Baal, the Asocial One." Brecht's unrealized intention was to build a *Lehrstück* (teaching play) around this anarchic figure, so that those performing the play could discover for themselves both the destructive and the creative potential inherent in Baal's self-centred quest for pleasure. Although Brecht failed to carry out the project of a *Lehrstück*, this approach to the character bore fruit elsewhere, in that the "Baal type" re-appeared in numerous guises in other plays (Mauler in *Saint Joan of the Stockyards*, Galileo in *The Life of Galileo*, Puntila in *Mr. Puntila and His Man Matti*), where the function of the figure is to illustrate the conflicts of interest between the individual and society that any social revolution must address.

Baal was originally conceived not simply as the life of a poet but as a poetic drama or "scenic ballad," as it is sometimes called. The play unfolds in a loose sequence of scenes that show Baal moving even further away from social existence until he is left to die alone, crawling out of a woodcutter's hut to gain a last glimpse of the stars. The nearest approach to a plot is provided by Baal's relationship with Ekart, a musician who challenges Baal to cut his ties to society, becomes one of his lovers, and is eventually killed by Baal for flirting with a tart in an inn. The play's unity is created on the level of image and symbol rather than through plot. Baal's most important relationship is not with any individual but with Death, who is present wherever Baal looks, goading him with reminders of transience and thus prompting him to live each moment with the utmost intensity. Death is both Baal's enemy and his ally. Thus Baal's poems are all, indirectly, hymns to Death, sensuous, pathetic, funny, and macabre celebrations of that process of decay which is life-in-death. If one follows Brecht's later injunction to look for the specific historical features of cultural products, the concerns and style of the play point to the background of World War I against which it was conceived. Brecht himself contrived to avoid active military service, but many of his schoolfriends were sent to the front and many did not return. One who did survive, Caspar Neher (a gifted artist who was later to design many sets for Brecht), responded to the play in a manner probably typical of that generation: "Your Baal is as good as ten litres of schnapps."

—Ronald Speirs

BAJAZET
Play by Jean Racine, 1672

The action of *Bajazet*, the fourth in order of performance of Jean Racine's seven great tragedies, is set in Turkey. One of the conventions of the French classical theatre was that the action of tragedies could not take place in an environment in which the audience felt at home. Here Racine, arguing in his preface that distance in space could easily replace distance in time, replaced the traditional heroes and heroines of Greek mythology or Roman history by characters taken from an actual incident that had occurred in Constantinople in 1638. The sultan Amurat is absent from his palace and has left his favourite, Roxane, full powers to act as she wishes. Acomat, his grand Vizier, one of the few genuinely adult characters in Racine's theatre, suspects that Amurat is going to dismiss him and plans to strike first. By plotting with Roxane, whom he knows to be in love with Bajazet, Amurat's brother, he intends to overthrow Amurat and place Bajazet on the throne. However, and unfortunately for Acomat, Bajazet is not in love with Roxane. He prefers the gentler Atalide and is only pretending to love Roxane, hoping to use her to escape from his imprisonment in the seraglio, taking Atalide with him. However, he cannot keep up the pretence. When Roxane presents him with the splendidly Racinian alternative between marrying her and being strangled by the mutes, he refuses. Her ''Sortez!'' (''Get out!'') sends him to his death. But she herself has not long to live, since Amurat, suspecting her infidelity, has sent a secret order for her to be killed. On discovering her lover's death, Atalide commits suicide. Acomat is left fighting, hoping to enable the friends who have joined him in his attempted *coup d'état* to escape.

Bajazet, the most bloodstained of Racine's tragedies, follows the one in which virtually nothing happens, *Bérénice*. In what seems almost like an attempt to prove his versatility, Racine went against the claim which he had made in his Preface to *Bérénice* and in which he had stated that neither death nor blood was necessary in a tragedy. Apart from the relative freedom in choice of subject matter, Racine was nevertheless limited in what he could do by two important factors: the general rules governing classical tragedy in 17th-century France; and the make-up of his own imaginative personality. Since no action was allowed on stage, the scene in which Bajazet gives so good an account of himself that he dies surrounded by the bodies of the first mutes who try to strangle him is simply reported to the audience in classical alexandrines, the only medium of expression permitted. Everything had to happen within 24 hours, and there was no possibility of introducing a Shakespearean scene of comic contrast and relief, everything had to happen in one place.

Since Racine's imagination worked best in confined spaces, this was no problem to him. Both Racine's parents died before he was two years old. He was brought up by one of his aunts and educated in the highly charged emotional atmosphere of Port-Royal, the headquarters of the extremely puritanical Jansenist movement. He tried to escape by writing plays, an activity of which the Jansenists strongly disapproved, but he never threw off the guilt feelings created by this defiance of his adopted mother. The seraglio in *Bajazet* is the ideal setting for the recurring situations that make Racine's tragedies so intriguing a hunting ground for the Freudian analyst as well as such a perfect triumph of theatrical organization and passion. The basic situation in which a passionate, predatory woman is in love with a man who is more attracted to a calmer, restful personality occurs in *Andromache*, in the Hermione-Pyrrhus-Andromache triangle, in *Britannicus*, in a modified form, with Agrippine-Néron-Junie, in *Bajazet* with Roxane-Bajazet-Atalide, in *Phaedra* with Phaedra-Hippolytus-Aricia. So, too, does the situation in which this woman causes the death of the man she loves.

Racine rang the changes on it with exquisite skill; but one still wonders whether he was absolutely conscious of what he was doing. Since he was also skilful enough to take the situation at the moment of crisis, he was also able to present events in such a way as to convince his audience that everything could occur within 24 hours. Each of his tragedies is like a spring wound up exactly to a point where it will unwind and cause the maximum disaster in the minimum time. What creates the tension which causes all the disaster are the emotions of the characters. Dominant among these is the need to be loved by the person with whom they have fallen in love themselves. This need is always frustrated. In none of Racine's plays, more dominated by sex than those of any other writer, do the characters ever touch one another physically, let alone go to bed together; but in *Bajazet*, as always, the ebb and flow of hope and the clash of attempted persuasions give rise to strategic crescendos of poetry and pathos.

—Philip Thody

THE BALCONY (Le Balcon)
Play by Jean Genet, 1956

Jean Genet's first full-length play *The Balcony* is impressively free from the defect he diagnosed himself in *The Maids*. If he had ''invented a tone of voice, a gait, style of gesture,'' he said, he hadn't managed to achieve ''a displacement which, allowing a declamatory tone, would make theatre theatrical.'' (Letter to the publisher Jean-Jacques Pauvert printed as preface to the Paris edition of *The Maids*, 1954). This displacement is present in *The Balcony*.

Genet introduces a lot of anti-naturalistic devices—grotesque make-up, cothurni, outsize costumes—but this is not merely to suggest that theatricality permeates life or that role-playing enters into all our relationships. The play suggests a triangular equation between society, the theatre, and the brothel. Not that sexuality is treated directly. The only reference to a bed is in the stage direction that asks for a mirror with an ornate frame to reflect an unmade bed that would appear, disturbingly, to be situated in the front row in the stalls. The brothel is a house of illusions in which clients act out their fantasies with prostitutes playing the supporting roles.

Though it is only minor characters who get killed, death exerts a strong tidal pull on the action, while the only discussion of lovemaking takes place outside the brothel. Chantal, formerly the madame's favourite girl, is in love with Roger, a leader of the revolution that is going on in the streets of the city. Inside the brothel the subjects that provoke the most passionate speeches are death and dressing up. The man who costumes himself as a bishop has no interest in performing a bishop's duties, only in decking himself out in the clothes. Another timid-looking client takes off his bowler hat and his gloves to put on a cocked hat and a general's uniform. ''Man of war and pomp and circumstances,'' he intones, admiring his reflection in the looking glass, ''there I am in my pure appearance. Nothing, I have nothing contingent in tow.'' He daydreams of being ''close to death . . . where I shall be nothing, but reflected *ad infinitum* in these mirrors, merely an image.'' For him, fantasy and illusion are the only compensations for constant frustration.

With its strong tendency to devalue living actuality in favour of the dead image, the play is reminiscent of Symbolist literature. The brothel is a palace of symbols, and when the queen is killed during the insurrection she can be replaced by Irma, the madame, while insignificant clients, who have turned themselves on by dressing up as a bishop, a judge, and a general, need only the help of costumes and photographers to make their debut in public life as bishop, judge, and general. For all four of them the main function is to animate the image. As the Envoy says, ''The beauty on this earth is all due to masks.'' Every living element in the play seems to lust after its own absence, its replacement by an image, a monument, a costume. Carmen, one of the prostitutes, wants to be with her child, but her desire is not strong enough to make her give up the chance of playing St. Teresa in the brothel:

> IRMA: Dead or alive, your daughter is dead. Think of the grave adorned with daisies and artificial wreaths, at the far end of a garden, and think of looking after this garden in your heart. . .
>
> CARMEN: I'd have liked to see her again.
>
> IRMA: . . . Her image in the image of the garden, and the garden in your heart under the burning robe of St. Teresa. And

you hesitate? I offer you the most envied of all deaths and you hesitate? Are you a coward?

Even for a man who has power in the world outside the brothel, the Chief of Police, nothing matters more than to become a hero in other men's fantasies:

> I'm going to make my image detach itself from me, force its way into your studios, multiply itself in reflections. Irma, my function is weighing me down. Here it will bask in the terrible sunshine of pleasure and death.

Nothing tempts him so much as the idea of a vast mausoleum that will preserve his memory; the idea of posterity matters more than sensations, emotions, or any other direct experience.

With *The Balcony* Genet was breaking a seven-year silence. Since publishing *The Thief's Journal* (*Journal du voleur*) in 1949, he had produced nothing of any substance or length. He collaborated with Sartre in the preparation of the massive biography *Saint Genet, Actor and Martyr*, which came out in 1952 (translated 1963), and he could hardly have failed to be influenced by it. But if it was a crisis of self-consciousness that prompted the silence, the long-term consequence was that it killed two overlapping compulsions—to write novels and to write autobiographically. Both the one-act plays, *The Maids* and *Deathwatch* were essentially about Genet; the three subsequent full length plays are not. No longer self-obsessed, he was able to turn his gaze outwards, and *The Balcony* was the first fruit of his new extroversion.

—Ronald Hayman

THE BALD PRIMA DONNA (La Cantatrice chauve)
Play by Eugène Ionesco, 1950

Ever since its creation at the Théâtre des Noctambules, Paris, in 1950, this masterpiece of the theatre of the absurd—at first not welcomed by the critics, though from the outset a great success with the public—has shown its staying power by constant performances, professional and amateur, that have delighted in its triumphant inconsequentiality. It has the ability to entertain by provoking both laughter and reflection. There is a feeling of happy release from all restraint occasioned paradoxically by the strong underlying form which is a counterpoint to the apparent shapelessness presented by the text at first glance.

Eugène Ionesco wanted to provide a parody of the well-made play, hence his description of the work as an "anti-play." He gives us in miniature—in the space of only one hour's traffic on the stage—a condensed send-up of conventional drama, by standing on its head the assumption that a play is logically structured, with an exposition, a series of developments to constitute a middle that leads in turn to a climax and then a denouement where the tangle of events can be decently restored to order. Since it is precisely order and the feeling of cause and effect that constitute the target for all absurdists, Ionesco is reminding us, like Lewis Carroll before him, that the world is a topsy-turvy place in which existence has no proper beginning, middle, and end and is totally lacking in consistent logical explanation for our thoughts and behaviour. In what becomes not only a parody but a critique of the comfortable assumptions underlying the well-made

play, he succeeds in drawing us willy-nilly into a web of irrationality that makes us, even as we laugh, acknowledge the truth behind his observations of banal everyday life. The aesthetic triumph Ionesco brings off is that, while subverting the lives of his characters and all the respectable order they feel to be a necessary part of existence, he has produced through inspired and sustained nonsense a work that is its own ordered world with not a syllable out of place, with every silence making its telling contribution to the pulse of the play and where the rhythms of language move relentlessly on to one of the most hilarious denouements in modern drama.

The decent world Ionesco satirizes is represented by the suburban English middle class, somewhere in the home counties, totally absorbed in the importance of its own petty obsessions. We are given an exposition, but in it Mr. and Mrs. Smith at their fireside maunder endlessly on about trivia. Mrs. Smith, thinking aloud and listing in full detail all the things she has eaten, her shopping chores, and the habits of every member of the family, provides a fine example of an opening soliloquy that gives us no information at all. Mr. Smith's outburst from behind his newspaper contributes further to our sense that language is being presented as a barrier rather than a communication bridge. The brief but brilliant confusion as the Smiths reminisce about their acquaintances, who, regardless of sex or age, are all called Bobby Watson, is a delight not only for its rhythmic nonsensical patterning but because it typifies what lies at the heart of the play, namely, that language itself can be reduced to a set of signifiers which, far from transmitting meaning, opaquely prevent any illumination from coming through. This constitutes, to use Ionesco's own phrase, that *tragédie du langage* which is to be further explored in the play and reminds us also of the supposed inspiration for this critique of language which Ionesco gleaned from learning English according to the Assimil method. He discovered that to repeat is not to deepen words but to empty them.

As the play moves to its parody of a middle development we meet Mary, the maid, who is as linguistically frank with her account of events and her brandishing of the chamber pot she has bought to shock her employers as the Smiths are mummified in their scleroticized opinions. Mary represents the sense of irrational emotion that is to come into its own at the arrival of the Fireman. Before that we meet a second couple, the Martins, who develop further, in their questioning of each other, the use of language as an investigation of the obvious. They discover they sleep in the same bed and are man and wife. The fullest development is kept for the inconsequential and alarming arrival of the Fireman. His insistence on telling anecdotes raises the nonsensical to a new notch of idiocy, and encourages, by its delight in the irrational, a general release of tension and even the discovery of suppressed passions, as Mrs. Smith indulges in being the coy maiden of her dreams and the bland Mr. Smith gives vent to his wildly violent id. When Mary insists on joining in she is snobbishly rejected by the Smiths and Martins but embraced, literally, by the Fireman, who recognizes in her an old flame. Her wild poem in honour of the Fireman and in praise of the transformative power of fire emphasizes the release that inconsequential images and free association can bring. All this prepares us for what would be a tidy ending if this were a play written to reflect ordered reality. Together, Mary and the Fireman have had a catalytic effect on the behaviour of this pair of primly reserved couples. The finale begins as the Smiths and the Martins engage in a polite exchange of clichés that become ever more extravagant until the couples end up not so much exchanging views as verbally assaulting each other to the point that words as such disappear and are replaced by the letters of the alphabet hurled through the air like material objects in a wild and uproariously funny language game. The only way the people can finally get together and establish a relationship is by repeating meaningless phrases in childish imitation of train noises as they run round the respectable three-piece suite puff-puffing like a steam-engine. This would seem to be the denouement but for Ionesco's final touch of genius. A blackout seems to signify the end to the proceedings except that the light comes up to reveal the Martins seated exactly where the Smiths had been, with Mrs. Martin beginning all over again the same punctiliously dreary catalogue of non-events.

There is an exhilaration in the play that derives from the excellent variations in tempo that Ionesco has allowed from scene to scene. From boring calm to wild verbal and physical expression the play carries the audience along on a wave of positive pleasure in spite of the seeming negativeness of the themes and the deliberate absence of characterization. The effect of *The Bald Prima Donna*, for all its satiric edge, is not depressing, rather we can laugh at ourselves as we recognize in it, as in a distorting mirror, our rational longing for civilized behaviour and logic in conflict with the disruptive energies of emotion.

—Leighton Hodson

BALLADE DES DAMES DU TEMPS JADIS (Ballade of the Ladies of Time Past)
Poem by François Villon, c. 1489 (written c. 1460?)

The refrain of the "Ballade des dames du temps jadis" (the title is apposite, although it was not coined by François Villon himself but by Clement Marot some 70 years later), or "Ballade of the Ladies of Time Past," has perhaps become the most famous line in French poetry. "Mais où sont les neiges d'antan?" ("Where are the snows of yesteryear?''; or "Where is the drift of last year's snow?") has been transformed into a poetic cliché, used to express a vague sense of nostalgia and *Angst* at time's passing. Many of those who quote it (at least in its English version) probably imagine that it is a product of 19th-century Romanticism or of that Victorian sentimentality which gave us so many paintings (now often reproduced as Christmas cards) of winter scenes with snowy landscapes and a coach and horses gliding over icy roads. It is certainly true that it first became well known in the English-speaking world thanks to the version by Dante Gabriel Rossetti. Generations of critics have praised the incomparable beauty of the poem, "one of the master-songs of the world" according to D.B. Wyndham Lewis, and spoken of its sweet melancholy and soft soothing tone. The refrain is better known than the poem, then, but what does it mean? Why did the poet choose snow (indeed snows) as the symbol of the passage of time, and how can the power of this image be explained in terms of its poetic function? A look at the context of the ballade within the work as a whole may help answer some questions, but also throw up others. It may well be that the reception of the poem by a modern reader is quite different from that of Villon's original audience.

The Testament is largely a satirical work aimed at ridiculing selected targets in the Paris of the early 1460s. Of its 2,000 lines over half are in this vein and are mostly impenetrable today to a reader without the benefit of a good annotated edition. The rest (roughly the first 800 lines) is for the most part made up of morose self-analysis, pleas for sympathy, and descriptions of life's various ills. The overall melancholy tone is, however, laced with impertinent and often outrageous wit, and a number of ballades are inserted into the general narrative at more or less appropriate points. The "Ballade des dames du temps jadis" is situated squarely in this early section of the poem and indeed forms part of a triptych on the common theme of *ubi sunt?* (where are they now?), which was a typical medieval topos, asking where all past years are. *Ubi sunt?* poems concern themselves with the disappearance of famous men, kings, princes, masters of their destiny tamed by unforgiving death and now no more than names. The second poem in the triptych, the ballade on the *lords* of time past, is on the face of it close to this hackneyed treatment of a well-worn theme. But to ask about the whereabouts of the ladies of the past is altogether different.

For some 100 lines Villon had been musing on his past, on time, on lost youth and wasted opportunity, on the harsh inequalities of life. The *gracieux gallans* (fun-loving revellers) he had frolicked with in his younger days are now dispersed, some gone to their graves, others to the top of the social pile. He at least is still alive, but he cannot hide his feelings of bitterness at his misfortune. Looking around at the unfairness and randomness of fate, he tries to draw some consolation from the fact that death, the great leveller, puts an end to the human comedy in all its forms. However rich and however powerful men may be, death cuts them all down to size *sans exception.* As for women, however fashionable, however feminine, the same fate awaits them, too. Even the most delicate and desirable female body, he points out, cannot escape the humiliating degradation of old age and death. This last thought serves as an introduction to the famous ballade (three eight-line stanzas and a four-line *envoi*) of the ladies of time past. But what a mixed bunch they turn out to be. Beautiful but morally dubious women like Flora, the Roman courtesan, Thais, an Athenian lady engaged in the same profession, the nun Heloise whose love for Abelard was to have such dire consequences, otherwise unknown ladies referred to merely by their Christian names—Beatrice, Alix—and, most tantalizingly of all, Joan of Arc. The one thing all have in common is that they are now no more. Whatever they did or felt or suffered, they are gone. What is more, women's beauty (and the power it confers) also disappears, like last year's snows. There is no defence against time and death. Similarly, the ballade of the Lords of Time Past which follows gives us a job lot of famous men from the past only to show that nothing is left of their power and glory. Even valiant Charlemagne has perished, as the refrain reminds us. Finally, the third ballade in this series of three, written in a deliberately (and comically) archaic style evokes, in its refrain, not the snow but another natural phenomenon, wind, which blows away all mortals' aspirations. The winds blow, the snow melts, everything fades into insignificance. The possessions of the mighty pass into others' hands, and Villon takes some comfort from the fact that poor and ailing though he may be, he is at least still alive. What these three ballades (and one cannot analyse one without the others) are, then, is a variation on the theme of *ubi sunt?* which in Villon's hands has become part of the *Danse Macabre*, that specifically 15th-century reminder to the worldly of death's dominion.

What is perhaps so special about Villon's treatment of this theme is his tone, which is at times jaunty and provocatively tasteless. Abelard's love affair with Heloise, we are told, brought him castration "as its reward," and among the ladies whose passing we are invited to mourn are Big-Footed Bertha (who?) and the totally obscure Arembourgh. And among the great lords, one king (James II of Scotland) deserves a mention solely because his face was famously disfigured by a port-wine stain. It is as if Mikhail Gorbachev were remembered only for this reason. But, then again, *ubi est Gorbachev?* Should we took at the ''Ballade des dames du temps jadis'' entirely in this light and see it as a parody of the genre? Not quite, for in its curiously haunting cocktail of wistfulness and vulgarity it expresses Villon's determination to never-say-die in the face of death.

But what about last year's snows? Could it be to do with the ladies' fair complexions, or the natural succession of the seasons, as the beautiful snowy mantle of winter gives way to thaw and a new year? Or is it, as the Belgian critic Paul Verhuyck recently claimed, a metaphysical question based on a very physical event, the melting of the snowmen and snow-women (this would help to explain the snows) carved out of snow and ice for the amusement of the people of Paris? This intriguing possibility does not detract from the force of the image, but it does show Villion at his most urban and down-to-earth, taking a scene from everyday life and turning it into a tongue-in-cheek yet profound consideration on the frailty of the human condition.

—Michael Freeman

BALLADE DES PENDUS
Poem by François Villon, 1489 (written 1462)

The ''Ballade des Pendus'' [Ballad of the Hanged Men] (called ''L'Epitaphe Villon'' in the earliest manuscripts and printed editions) is perhaps François Villon's best-known poem. Its macabre subject matter has earned it a prominent place in anthologies and especially in pictorial illustration, and bodies hanging by the neck figure prominently in books and editions. It is often claimed that Villon wrote the poem while under sentence of death himself in 1462, but there is no evidence at all for this, and to suggest that the poet could not have written this ballade without such a stimulus is to deny his powers of imagination. In any case, he would have had plenty of opportunities of contemplating—whether in the Place Maubert or at Montfaucon—the grisly spectacle of decaying bodies dangling by a rope from a gallows.

The ballade (35 lines divided into three ten-line stanzas and a five-line *envoi*) opens with an extraordinarily effective device. The reader is invited to imagine that he is a passer-by who finds himself being addressed by one of the bodies on a gallows. It was not uncommon to have, as in the scene Villon has created, half a dozen convicted criminals sharing a gibbet at any one time. The poem's opening line is meant to shock and to cause a shudder on the reader's part, as he finds himself involved in a gruesome tableau vivant, in which all the other characters are in fact dead. The ''pendu'' who has elected himself to be the spokesman of this pathetic group calls on the *Frères humains* who are fortunate enough still to be alive not to close their hearts to them. The use of the word *frères*, ''brothers'' is of course daring, for no self-respecting reader would wish to be associated with executed criminals in this way. *Humains*, which means both human (playing on the notion of human solidarity) and humane or kindly, reinforces the point that this is an appeal. The reader is reminded, rather slyly, that if he feels compassion God will have mercy on him too, when the time comes for him to meet his maker. The first four lines contain, therefore, a strong element of emotional blackmail. This unusual spokesman makes no attempt to excuse these wretches for their crimes. He admits that they lived life to the full, but now as their bodies rot before our eyes they deserve our pity. The point is made quite clear in 1.9: let no man, he says, laugh at our discomfiture. Instead, as the refrain (1.10 and again 11. 20, 30, 35) has it, he calls

upon the reader to pray to God that he will absolve us all. Cleverly and significantly, this absolution extends not only to the dead criminals but also to the fictional passer-by. We are *all* in need of God's grace.

The conspiratorial tone that has developed is continued in the second stanza. Apologies are duly made for daring to address the passers-by/readers as brothers, and the spokesmen for the dead knows they were put to death ''par justice,'' (''lawfully'') but he reminds us that not all men are fortunate enough to be sensible and to be able to lead an honest life. The voice from beyond the noose pleads with us to intercede on their behalf ''with the son of the Virgin Mary'' so that they should not have to suffer in hell, and begs us not to add insult to injury by taunting these corpses of theirs.

The third stanza, which is the most graphic and also the most typical of Villon at his best, describes the fate that has befallen these once healthy bodies now exposed to rain, sun, and wind. Drenched and baked dry by turns, the blackened corpses have become the targets of wild birds who have pecked out their eyes and chewed at their beards and eyebrows. In a marvellous but chilling image he suggests that they can never feel comfortable, blown this way and that as they are by the wind. Do not be, therefore, he tells us, part of our brotherhood (a careful reference back to the word *frère* used in the opening line of the first two stanzas) but pray to God that we are all absolved. The sense of brotherhood is the key to the poem's message. In the *envoi*, there is a direct appeal to Jesus to save them (and us) from hell, and the penultimate line reminds all men—with a clear reference back to the *humains* of the opening line of the ballade—that this is no laughing matter.

This is a poem that would appear to come from the heart. It skilfully mixes, in an original and gripping way, pity, fear, guilt, and humility, and, on the reader's part, a sense of foreboding. It is designed to move the reader and to appeal to his Christian sense of charity, making him less scornful of those who have (for whatever reason) fallen foul of the law. Although (unusually) Villon never mentions himself in this ballade, he is obviously making an appeal here for understanding and sympathy. He plays on his audience's emotions, describing in vivid detail what must have been a sadly familiar scene. His message is clear: worried about his own fate, he warns others not to stray down the same paths as he himself had. The hanged criminals are portrayed almost as victims themselves. He uses the same adjective he often applies to himself: poor. Pity the poor hanged men, pity poor Villon. The ''Ballade des pendus'' is a plea for help, a plea to someone who might save Villon from himself.

—Michael Freeman

THE BARBER OF SEVILLE (Le Barbier de Séville)
Play by Beaumarchais, 1775

This was the first comedy Beaumarchais wrote for the public stage and the first play in the Figaro trilogy—the second and third being *The Marriage of Figaro*, likewise a comedy, and *A Mother's Guilt*, a drama. Its evolution was unusually protracted. It grew initially out of a short farce (an intermède), *Le Sacristain* [The Sacristan] written for the private theatre of Le Normand d'Étoiles and derived from the Spanish *entremeses* (short farcical plays, often with music, performed between the acts of a longer work) with which Beaumarchais had become familiar during his stay in Spain in the mid 1760s. *Le Sacristain* also resembles the indigenous French *parades* in its scabrous tone and its conventional plot whereby Lindor, the young lover, tries to seduce Pauline, wife of the aged and impotent Bartholo.

From the incomplete manuscript of *Le Sacristain* we can see that Beaumarchais revised his text, first changing Pauline to Rosine and Lindor to Le Comte, who, from being a student, was transformed into a philandering husband who neglects his wife. Beaumarchais also introduced yet more indecent allusions into his text. Such material was clearly not intended for public performance. The text's next transformation was into an *opéra comique*, entitled *Le Barbier de Séville* and no longer extant. It was here that the character of Figaro was first introduced, in order that the "ennobled" Lindor should not demean himself by having to cope with all the material paraphernalia involved in the multiple disguises he needed to use in order to gain access to Rosine. But leaving the physical problems to Figaro had the effect, perceptible in *The Barber of Seville* as we know it today, of marginalizing the Count (now turned into a bachelor again) and profiling the factotum. The choice of a barber character was determined by the figure's traditional use, along with the (young and attractive) sacristan, in the *entremeses*.

When this *opéra comique* was offered to the Comédie-Italienne in Paris, it was refused. Beaumarchais then expunged the obscenities and most of the songs from his text and, early in 1773, offered it to the Comédie-Française, where it was accepted for performance and passed by the censor, Marin. It was due to be performed in February 1773, but the opening was postponed when Beaumarchais was imprisoned as a result of the Chaulnes affair. The Goezman affair followed and, having incorporated into his text allusions to his personal difficulties and those responsible for them, Beaumarchais submitted it to a second censor, Arthaud, who reported favourably. The premiere, announced for February 1774, was again postponed, frustrated in part by Madame Du Barry and in part by the author's loss of his civil rights at the close of the Goezman affair. When the play, in five acts and carrying the approval of a third censor, Crébillon *fils*, was finally staged on 23 February 1775, it was a failure. The reasons appear to have been partly that the actress who sang Rosine's songs was nervous and inaudible, partly that the plot is inadequate to fill five acts, but more importantly that the five-act text to which Beaumarchais had gradually added an excess of dubious jokes and uninteresting allusions to his personal life, was not the one which the actors were familiar with (the play had been in rehearsal for two years), and they performed badly. Beaumarchais promptly stripped away the "accretions," so accelerating the action and emphasizing the elliptical wit of the dialogues. Three days later, the four-act version (a very unusual length) was a resounding success.

Beaumarchais's stated aim with this play was to restore to the theatre something of the fun and verve it had lost during the century, especially in the heyday of the moralizing *drame*. Though the *précaution inutile* (fruitless precaution) theme, whereby the old man tries in vain to isolate his young wife or intended wife from other potential lovers, was a hackneyed one in French literature by the 1770s, Beaumarchais infuses it with new life through memorable characters and a brilliantly honed dialogue in which he exploits fully the resources of ellipsis, assonance, pun, etc. The setting is not an accurate portrayal, but a fantasized Spain, evoked by costume (for which Beaumarchais made exact stipulations), and small details, such as guitar-playing, *alguazils*, and Spanish forms of address. Traces of the earliest heroine, Pauline, are still visible in the role of Rosine (it is impossible to categorize her as solely either an innocent or a coquette), and Figaro, though he appears in relatively few scenes, is memorable for his (more apparent than real) air of energetic

omnicompetence. Bartholo, more astute than the *barbons* (aged guardians or tutors) who were his dramatic forbears, in a well-developed character whom Beaumarchais makes at times surprisingly penetrating, while at other times he intervenes artificially to thwart his villain's intentions, which are at base odiously self-indulgent. It is only in the 20th century that Bazile, Bartholo's venal accomplice (who is involved both with the Church and the fringes of the underworld) has assumed a high-profile role, thanks to the interpretation of Édouard de Max at the Comédie-Française (1916–24). His satanic pre-eminence rests largely on two particularly memorable scenes, and especially the "hymn to calumny" of Act II, scene 8. Though Figaro has sometimes been identified with Revolutionary sentiments, this is a forced interpretation, and his remarks about the advantages conferred by the mere fact of being born noble are no more than commonplaces of the period.

—John Dunkley

LE BATEAU IVRE (The Drunken Boat)
Poem by Arthur Rimbaud, 1871

"Le Bateau ivre" was written in early September 1871, when Arthur Rimbaud was still a month short of his 17th birthday and was going through that period of physical and emotional turmoil characteristic of adolescence. After having been an apparently obedient and docile child in a family ruled by his mother with a rod of iron (his father had abandoned his wife and children in 1860) and a brilliant pupil at school in his native town of Charleville in northeastern France, he had suddenly and violently broken out in open rebellion against all authority the previous summer. He had run away from home three or four times in quick succession, to Paris at the end of August 1870, and possibly yet again to Paris at the end of April 1871, to Brussels at the beginning of October, again to Paris at the end of February 1871, although there is some doubt as to whether this fourth episode actually occurred. It was not only in this physical sense that Rimbaud had repeatedly tried to break free from the discipline imposed by his mother and from the increasingly irksome regimentation of school life. He had found another means of escape into the world of his imagination, and some of his early work (he had already written about 40 poems before "Le Bateau ivre") is evocative of the dream world in which he had sought refuge. The last few lines of "Les Poètes de sept ans," written in May 1871, are particularly relevant to "Le Bateau ivre," in that they present a striking picture of Rimbaud alone in an attic room transforming the pieces of coarse linen on which he is lying into the sails of ships setting off for distant seas and exotic lands. A final aspect of Rimbaud's rebellious attitude that is also relevant to a study of "Le Bateau ivre" is his growing impatience with the restrictive conventions of the poetic tradition in France. He had already written his celebrated "Lettre du voyant" complaining that poetry was nothing more than "prose rimée" and proclaiming that the true poet must abandon the world of ordered reality and its consciously controlled presentation and give free play instead to the disordered world of the imagination.

Such were the circumstances that gave rise to "Le Bateau ivre." But although Rimbaud's escapades of the previous autumn and winter form the basis of the poem, he is not concerned with giving a realistic account of what he had seen and done, still less an intellectual analysis of his thoughts and feelings. His purpose is to convey to the reader the intense excitement and almost delirious happiness he had experienced during his brief spells of freedom. To achieve this aim his vivid imagination transforms his journeys to Paris and Brussels into the fantastic voyages of the drunken boat of the title of the poem, plunging rudderless through countless seas, dancing like a cork on the waves, meeting giant serpents and sea-monsters, icebergs and water-spouts, skies torn by lightening, blood-red sunsets, dazzling wastes of snow and phosphorescent seas. But although Rimbaud experienced a sense of exhilaration at leaving the home in which he had lived for 16 years, he nevertheless also felt a paradoxical tinge of regret for the stable and sheltered existence that he had abandoned, for what the boat describes as "l'Europe aux anciens parapets." There can, however, be no going back, and in the concluding stanzas Rimbaud is filled with the bittersweet longing to set off again and to feel once more the excitement of drifting freely along. Only if he were still a child could he accept, with sadness and resignation, the restrictions of life in Charleville; only if the boat were a toy boat could it be content to sail within the narrow confines of a pond. So in the last stanza, Rimbaud affirms that, having tasted the joys of liberty, he can no longer follow in the wake of others, nor pursue a set course marked out for him, nor sail under surveillance. Not surprisingly therefore, just after having written "Le Bateau ivre," he made yet another escape to Paris, this time a successful one that marked his definitive break with the world of childhood.

"Le Bateau ivre" also marks an early stage in Rimbaud's break with the accepted forms of French poetry. This may not be immediately apparent in that the poem is written in 12-syllable rhyming alexandrines, grouped into 25 four-line stanzas. Furthermore it is rigorously ordered into three distinct parts—the first 17 stanzas describing the prodigious voyages of the drunken boat, the next four expressing its astonishment that it should nevertheless feel regret for the stability of the old world that has been left behind, and the last four debating whether to go forward or back and reaching a final conclusion. But within these three component parts, particularly the long first section, there is a marked simplicity of structure and style as Rimbaud piles images one on top of the other in short uncomplicated sentences. There is also some evidence, in the inappropriate or unusual and even invented words that Rimbaud occasionally uses to make up the syllable count or to provide an adequate rhyme, that he felt constrained by the conventions of versification. At this stage he was not ready to break free of these shackles, but during the coming months, in the course of his short and meteoric career, he was to move away from the rigid pattern of the verse poem and towards the more flexible rhythms of the prose poem, better adapted to the free play of the imagination which was increasingly to become the hallmark of his poetry.

—C. Chadwick

THE BEDBUG (Klop)
Play by Vladimir Maiakovskii, 1929

The action of Vladimir Maiakovskii's most famous play falls into two distinct halves, of which the first is straightforward and the second endlessly problematical. The first part (scenes 1–4) offers a ferocious satire on the revival of bourgeois philistinism in contemporary Soviet Russia, focusing on the ludicrously pretentious Prisypkin and his equally fatuous in-laws. The second part (scenes 5–9) leaps 50

years into the future, presenting a potentially disturbing portrait of a sanitized, soulless society, and perhaps inevitably inviting a reassessment of Prisypkin's "humanity" and Maiakovskii's own intentions.

The play opens in provincial Tambov during 1928 and 1929, towards the end of the notorious NEP period. While private pedlars brazenly tout their wares, the hero-villain Ivan Prisypkin urges his mother-in-law-to-be, Rozaliia Renesans ("Renaissance"), to accumulate goods unstintingly for his imminent "Red wedding." Having abandoned his working-class girlfriend Zoia Berezkina, Prisypkin aims to exploit his proletarian origin and union card to gain entry into a rich bourgeois hairdressing family. Young workers in a hostel condemn Prisypkin's vulgar pretensions and his betrayal of the ideals of the 1917 Communist Revolution. Meanwhile, Prisypkin (who now parades under the absurdly Frenchified name "Pierre Skripkin") takes lessons in the fashionable foxtrot and asserts his right to rest after all his revolutionary exertions. News arrives that the jilted Zoia Berezkina has shot herself. The "Red wedding" between Prisypkin and Elzevira Renesans is duly celebrated, rapidly degenerating into raucous revelry and risqué *double entendre*. Amid the universal intoxication a stove is overturned, causing a sudden conflagration. Firemen rush to the scene, but are too late to rescue the drunken guests. One person remains unaccounted for.

Fifty years later, apparently in a worldwide Communist Federation, a mechanized vote is taken to resurrect a frozen body discovered recently in the "former Tambov." The body is solemnly defrosted by a professor and his team of assistants, which includes Zoia Berezkina, now recovered from her suicide-attempt. Thus, to his astonishment, Prisypkin finds himself resurrected in a highly regulated 1979. Upon scratching himself, Prisypkin joyfully recognizes a bedbug that crawls from his collar on to the wall. The local inhabitants, long protected from all emotional excess, instantly succumb to the various "infections" reintroduced by Prisypkin—men begin to drink beer, lovelorn ladies dance the Charleston, read poetry, and sniff imaginary roses, while even the dogs now beg. The director of the zoo captures the escaped bedbug. Zoia feels disgust as the filthy Prisypkin lolls on a clean bed, surrounded by bottles and cigarette-butts. Prisypkin, now confined in a cage together with his bedbug, is exhibited at the zoo as a hideous example of the "philistinus vulgaris" (nourishing his companion, the "bedbugus normalis"). This salutary demonstration is undermined, however, when Prisypkin emerges from his cage and greets the assembled onlookers and the audience: "Citizens! Brothers! My dear ones! ... Why am I alone in the cage? Dear brothers, come and join me! Why am I made to suffer?! Citizens! ...." Amid general confusion, the zoo director orders the crowd to disperse.

In its original conception, *The Bedbug* seems reassuringly unambiguous. Even before 1917 Maiakovskii had been an arch-Futurist and scourge of the bourgeois, while after the October Revolution he willingly became an idiosyncratic mouthpiece of the Bolsheviks. Throughout 1927 and 1928 the newspaper *Komsomolskaia Pravda* (for which Maiakovskii worked) had campaigned against many undesirable manifestations among young Communists—including a burgeoning philistinism in personal relationships, dress, popular music, dancing, and bourgeois aspirations. Apart from writing satirical verse on such subjects, Maiakovskii himself in 1927–28 had devised a film scenario, *Pozabud' pro kamin* (*Forget about the Hearth*), which contains the essential "germs" of *The Bedbug*—satire on *meshchanstvo* (philistinism), the Red wedding, the fire, the discovery of the frozen body and its resurrection (in this instance after 25 years), the bedbug, and the zoo. The film scenario stands like a skeleton for the later play—its 395 terse descriptions offer no character development, no odious figure of Oleg Bayan, and no mention of the names Prisypkin or Renesans.

The Bedbug, with its flamboyantly grotesque characterization and racily topical dialogue, seemed ideally suited to Meyerhold's theatrical experimentation, and the play's premiere duly took place (on 13 February 1929) at the State Meyerhold Theatre in Moscow. An array of talents was assembled—Vsevolod Meyerhold (director), Maiakovskii (assistant director), Dmitrii Shostakovich (composer), the "Kukryniksy" trio of satirical cartoonists (designers for scenes 1–4), and the constructivist Aleksandr Rodchenko (designer for scenes 5–9), with the splendid actor Igor Ilinskii as the moonfaced Prisypkin. Maiakovskii's polemical extravaganza irreverently flouted the conventions of traditional theatre, allowing hawkers to invade the auditorium, firemen to march through the aisles, and Prisypkin to address the audience.

Meyerhold's production enjoyed great popular success. Yet, although Maiakovskii asserted that "50 years from now Prisypkin will be regarded as a wild animal" (speech on 2 February 1929), and denied that the second half depicted "a socialist society" (speech on 30 December 1928), his apparent vision of the future proved a stumbling-block to the play's acceptance in Stalin's Russia. Western critics have frequently interpreted the second half as a nightmarish dystopia, whose portrait of dehumanized regimentation constitutes "one of the most devastating satires of Communist society in contemporary literature" (Patricia Blake, in *Three Soviet Flays*, 1966).

If this predominantly Western analysis is correct, Maiakovskii—consciously or subconsciously—must have lost faith in the revolution shortly before his death in 1930. In that case, the play switches in midstream from topical satire to prophetic warning, and the vodka-swilling, guitar-strumming, foul-mouthed vulgarian Prisypkin suddenly acquires tragic dimensions as an albeit poor representative of humanity in a dehumanized world.

Such an interpretation, although possible and even attractive, somehow lacks total conviction. Admittedly, the potential for tragedy is present, since Maiakovskii took very seriously such themes as love, resurrection, and caged animals. Complacent audiences naturally condone Prisypkin's vulgarity (and their own) as "common humanity." Nevertheless, Valentin Pluchek's inventive production at Moscow's Satire Theatre in 1981 was perhaps justified in depicting the future society lightheartedly, in the manner of a trivial revue. Against such a background, Prisypkin could never attain tragic proportions; at best, he remained a clownish buffoon.

—Gordon McVay

BEFORE THE STORM (Vor dem Sturm)
Novel by Theodor Fontane, 1878

It is almost inevitable in any account of *Before the Storm* to draw attention to the fact that its author was almost 60 years old when it was completed. In addition, Theodor Fontane was already an established writer of many years' standing, so that in his novelistic debut he emerges as a mature and confident writer. *Before the Storm* was in many ways a labour of love, 15 years in the making. Fontane wrote to his publisher that he was resolved to write it "entirely in my own fashion, according to my own predilections and individual personality, not following any particular model."

For a novel of such great length (all his subsequent works were only half the size and some a great deal shorter than that), the plot—such as it is—can be related in a few words. It concerns the key period between December 1812 and May 1813, a turning point in the fortunes of Prussia as it breaks free from French domination, but it relates more to individual fortunes rather than the destiny of kings and princes.

Berndt von Vitzewitz, a widower, is lord of the manor of the fictitious village of Hohen-Vietz in Brandenburg. He has a son, Lewin, and a daughter, Renate. The son loves a Polish cousin, Kathinka, but she elopes with a Polish count. Lewin falls ill, but then recovers and marries Marie, a girl who is not his social equal.

The father, Berndt von Vitzewitz, demonstrates the links which Fontane perceives to exist between individuals and the destiny of nations. He has lived through the time of Prussia's humiliation, defeat, and occupation at the hands of the French, and curiously his own life reached its nadir at that time, with the death of his beloved wife. He is a man of great strength of character, moral conviction, and sense of purpose, who has the courage to reach beyond the conventions of society and express his allegiance to a higher aim. This combination of powerful individuality and deep loyalty is founded upon a sincere religious conviction: "If I raise this hand, I raise it not to avenge a personal injustice, but against the common enemy," he states. There are other characters like him in the novel, which underlines Fontane's conviction that individuals of strong moral purpose can and do affect the course of history, and that their strength is also Prussia's strength. It is a quality which seems to permeate even the buildings. The church of Hohen-Vietz in its continuity of existence despite the changes of the centuries seems to encapsulate Prussian strength of character: "If the outside of the church had remained more or less unchanged, the interior had undergone all the transformations of five hundred years." The place is filled with a sense of history and strength which transforms the dead stones of which it is constructed and inspires and ennobles the lives of the parishioners.

All these references to individual strength as an historical force come as something of a revelation to those who have read only Fontane's subsequent novels, which are peopled by characters like Botho von Rienacker and Baron von Innstetten who act not out of deep conviction but as prisoners of social convention, and whose individual *Glück* (happiness) is at the mercy of society's need for *Ordnung* (order).

In many other respects, however, *Before the Storm* does anticipate the rest of Fontane's work. This can be seen firstly in his avoidance of violence and sensation—the very title of the novel is *before* the storm, not *during* it. The narrative technique of the detached observer who is not averse to intruding on the narrative on occasion is also established here; as, too, is the centrality of dialogue as a means of revealing character and teasing out issues for debate. At the heart of the work is the notion of life as a process, an evolutionary, changing phenomenon set against the backdrop of eternal verities of moral conduct and belief—and this, too, is reflected in his subsequent works.

Some critics have sought to promote *Before the Storm* as a masterpiece, but it is certainly not in the same category as Fontane's greatest novel, *Effi Briest*. It bears too many marks of the author's self-indulgent obsession with his theme, and in its intricate detail constantly loses sight of the whole. *Pace* the apologists, it would be a mistake to defend the novel on the grounds that it matches precisely what the author set out to achieve. In many respects it is a halfway house between his fiction and his earlier travelogue *Wanderungen durch die Mark Brandenburg* [Wanderings Through the March of Brandenburg]. As an artistic achievement it lacks coherence and drive—but within its fragmentation there are moments of conviction and creative power which look forward to the great novels, in particular to *Effi Briest*.

—Rex Last

BÉRÉNICE
Play by Jean Racine, 1670

Bérénice, the eighth of Jean Racine's 14 plays (two of which are lost), was first performed on 21 November 1670, one week before Corneille's play (*Titus and Berenice*) on exactly the same subject opened at a rival theatre in Paris. The controversy aroused by this clash and the relative success of Racine's play helped reinforce Racine's position as the new force in neo-classical 17th-century tragedy.

Drawn from Suetonius' *Lives of the Caesars*, the subject is the painful separation of the Roman emperor Titus from his beloved Bérénice in the first days of his accession to the throne, under the fore of political necessity, despite his promise to marry her. The tradition that Henrietta of England, sister-in-law of Louis XIV, set both dramatists writing on the same subject, unbeknown to each other, has been discredited—Racine is thought to have pirated the subject from Corneille in order to challenge his older rival, although the reverse has also been argued.

Bérénice is possibly the supreme example of Racine's aesthetic canon of a "simple" action, in which external events are reduced to a minimum and dramatic interest is focused on psychological states, inner conflicts, and emotional flux, such an action being, in Racine's view, necessary to ensure plausibility within the constraints of the neo-classical rule of a 24-hour time span. The only "event" in *Bérénice* is the separation of the lovers, and the time-scale is that of the hours leading up to the event. Racine answers critics of such a minimalist view of the action (*Preface to Bérénice*) that the truly gifted dramatist can make "something" out of "nothing," while lesser dramatists (Corneille is being implied) rely on complications of plot to retain audience interest.

The play is only 1,506 lines long (Corneille's is more than 250 lines longer) and has only three major characters plus their confidants (Corneille's has two sets of lovers plus confidants and a much more complex plot). None the less Racine's play is a rich study of the mental conflicts aroused by sexual passion in the context of affairs of state, focusing on two psychological aspects of the problem—Titus' inability to tell Bérénice of the repudiation and Bérénice's incomprehension once the news is broken.

Bérénice, Queen of Palestine has, for five years, been the constant companion of Titus in Rome. Only now that Titus has taken over the rulership of the Empire from his father Vespasian (who died one week previously) does he waken up to the truth he has long ignored—that Rome will not tolerate his marrying a foreign queen. Titus must repudiate the very woman whose love has rescued him from decadence at the court of Nero and has inspired his rise to political eminence. He attempts to make the announcement to the queen (Act II, scene 4) but collapses into incoherence, stammering "Rome . . . the Empire," and exits, leaving Bérénice in confusion. The news is finally broken by Antiochus, the friend of both Titus and Bérénice, himself king of a neighbouring state and secretly in love with

Bérénice. Antiochus, after five years of silence, has confessed his love to an outraged Bérénice (Act I, scene 4). When, filled with renewed hope of being able to win over the queen, Antiochus breaks the news to Bérénice (Act III, scene 3), he is banished for ever from her presence and the queen must wait (Act IV, scene 1) for a meeting with Titus which confirms the awful truth (Act IV, scene 4). Faced with Bérénice's incomprehension and learning of her intention to take her own life under the pretence of seemingly leaving Rome (Act V, scene 5), Titus informs Bérénice of his decision to take the "noble Roman way" of suicide, rather than enforced separation (Act V, scene 6). Only now does Bérénice understand that Titus loves her still. In the presence of Antiochus (who has been summoned as friend and witness by Titus and who confesses his guilty secret to Titus), Bérénice recognizes her error, and finds in Titus' love the strength to consent to a separation which means a living death. All three lovers quit each other's presence to face an eternity of inner emptiness, and undiminishing sense of loss.

Serious criticisms were put forward by contemporaries of Racine such as Chapelle and Villars who considered both Titus and Bérénice to be lacking in tragic stature: Titus' ultimatum to Bérénice in Act V could be seen as blatant moral blackmail—"consent or I'll kill myself"; Bérénice's disregard for Antiochus is considered odious and her accusations against Titus inconsistent with a character supposedly embodying virtue. Voltaire considered the play unworthy of tragedy. However, although by no means Racine's greatest play, *Bérénice* is a moving representation of the inner destruction wrought by the burden of kingship and political necessity. The warnings of Paulin (the voice of Rome) and Titus' evocations of Roman history are part of Racine's careful presentation of Roman law as an inviolable absolute, incompatible with the equally imperious absolute of love. Titus chooses to remain emperor, but inwardly he is ruined. In the confrontation of two mutually exclusive absolutes ("Rome" and "Bérénice") there are no winners. Only suffering remains and Titus knows this: "But living's not the question: I must reign." Bérénice's farewell does not bespeak the victory of will over passion, but is a lucid consent to undiminished pain issuing from a new understanding of Titus' love for her and a capacity to sublimate this love in an act of renunciation:

> Farewell. Let us, all three, exemplify
> The most devoted, tender, ill-starred love
> Whose grievous history time will e'er record.

Racine's *Bérénice* is notable for poetic resonances created by repeated references to time past and time future, all of which maximize the tragic effect, upon the audience, of the lovers' separation, most notably the recurrent evocation of the past "five years," the most recent past "week" (*huit jours*) since the death of Vespasian, and references to the days and months and years of an interminable future:

> How will we pine a month, a year from now,
> When we're divided by a waste of seas,
> When the day dawns and when the day will end,
> With Titus never seeing Bérénice.

(translations by John Cairncross)

Despite the elegiac quality of many of the lines, noted by Sainte-Beuve, the play is far from lacking in dramatic power. The delay in the meeting of the two lovers between Act II and Act IV builds up considerable dramatic tension, as do the fluctuating hopes and agonies of the hapless Antiochus, whose illusions are a vivid parallel to those of the two lovers. Racine creates dramatic, verbal, and situational irony by careful juxtaposition of scenes such as scenes 2 and 3 in Act II where Titus, having steeled his resolve to announce the eternal separation, is greeted by Bérénice requesting innocently that he spend more time with her, since his presence is her sole comfort and greatest treasure.

Critical interest in *Bérénice* in recent decades has been lively as is attested by the diversity of interpretations of Titus' act of repudiation, seen variously as an act of maturity arising from a sense of responsibility to the political order (J.C. Lapp), an act of self-destruction issuing from masochistic Jansenism (Philip Butler), and an act of infidelity in the name of a purely mythical legality (Roland Barthes). Discussion of the tragic stature of the protagonists is well documented by James Supple, who argues convincingly that "the main source of tragic dignity at the end of the play is Bérénice," whose "monumental effort of self control" is both tragic and heroic and creates the profound and majestic sadness that Racine saw as the principal achievement of this play.

—Sandra Blane

BERLIN ALEXANDERPLATZ
Novel by Alfred Döblin, 1929

Berlin Alexanderptatz: The Story of Franz Biberkopf was published in 1929 by the S. Fischer Verlag, Berlin. S. Fischer had insisted on the subtitle since the first part was nothing but the name of a location. However, Alfred Döblin's title proved appropriate and attractive, indicating that, although Franz Biberkopf is the protagonist, the novel deals primarily with the city, and specifically its proletarian areas around the Alexanderplatz, and its underworld.

Berlin Alexanderplatz remains Döblin's one and only popular success. Although he wrote many novels, short stories, essays, and reviews, he was always identified primarily with this book. He was a respected writer, very active in political circles, and a member of the section for literature in the Prussian *Akademie der Künste*. His innovative narrative techniques inspired younger writers including Bertolt Brecht who applied them to the theatre. From the age of 12, Döblin lived in the eastern, working-class part of Berlin. After World War I, he practised medicine there, and was in daily contact with the poorest members of society. *Berlin Alexanderplatz* betrays an intimate knowledge of the language and mentality of the working class in Berlin, as well as the underworld.

The manuscript, which survives, was begun in late 1927. It can be assumed that Döblin had collected a considerable amount of material before that date. Probably early in 1928 Döblin read the German translation of Joyce's *Ulysses* which he reviewed in spring 1928. Joyce's novel inspired and encouraged Döblin to use the full array of modernist techniques, especially inner monologue, montage of authentic materials, such as newspaper clippings, Bible passages, and political and advertising slogans, and imitations of the sounds and rhythm of the big city around the Alexanderplatz where the new subway system was being built.

While the city provides the framework and is presented in an inimitable vividness, the story-line follows the fate of Franz Biberkopf,

which contributed most to the book's popularity. Biberkopf, a physically strong cement and furniture removal worker, has just served a prison sentence for manslaughter: in a sudden rage he strangled his girlfriend. When he returns to his old milieu around the Alexanderplatz he has difficulties getting back on an even keel. He has promised himself to remain a decent, good human being, and not give in to temptation. But time and again he is betrayed by underworld "friends." His main weakness is boasting when he wants to be an accepted part of the group. The first blow, when a friend steals his girlfriend, is easily forgotten. But then he falls in with Reinhold and his "Pums" gang. As they speed away in cars after a robbery, Reinhold, afraid Biberkopf might talk to the police, throws him out of the car. Biberkopf's arm has to be amputated, but still he has not learned his lesson. While living with the prostitute Mieze, his real love, he wants to show her off to Reinhold. At one stage Reinhold takes advantage of Biberkopf's absence and takes Mieze into the woods where he molests and finally strangles her. Biberkopf is accused initially of the murder, and when he is confronted with Reinhold in the court room at Reinhold's trial, he suffers a mental breakdown. He recovers slowly but ends up a new person after his dismissal from the psychiatric ward. Standing at a factory gate where he now works as a gate keeper, he realizes that he needs others, and they need him.

The narrative, which consists mainly of half-conscious monologues or other subjective forms of storytelling, is interspersed with passages from other texts, like reports on the Berlin slaughterhouses; also allusions to Biblical and mythological characters and events, such as Job, Abraham, and Isaac, figures from the Oresteia, and parts of the Revelation. There are also numerous slightly disguised quotes from classical German literature, together with the latest hits and slogans of the time. These new layers of text add to the complexity of the story. *Berlin Alexanderplatz* assumes an apocalyptic tone at times, then descends to the level of street humour. This provocative mixture counterbalances the straightforward underworld story of Biberkopf, which is made more compelling through its elements of love, crime, and violence. Although the book is anything but easy reading, it has remained popular with a large number of readers to this day.

Human crowds, mass transportation, and mass media are part of the world of *Berlin Alexanderplatz*. It was logical that Döblin adapted the text for a radio play first broadcast in Berlin on 30 September 1930. In this simplified, still very sophisticated version, the voice of Biberkopf was rendered by the then famous actor Heinrich George. George also portrayed Biberkopf in the cinema version of 1931, under the direction of Phil Jutzi. Döblin collaborated on the scenario. Translations of the novel began to appear in 1930; the English translation by Eugene Jolas was published in 1931. In the politically charged atmosphere of the beginning economic depression and political crisis of the years 1929–30, the book reviews reflected the full spectrum of attitudes toward a modernistic narrative strategy, and toward Döblin's depiction of the proletariat. The organized socialist parties, especially the communists, rejected the book vehemently.

Berlin Alexanderplatz made Döblin's life financially easier, so that his family moved to the Kurfürstendamm area. It was to be his last novel before his forced exile from Germany in the spring of 1933. The somewhat abrupt ending of the novel suggests plans for a continuation which Döblin never wrote. The popularity of *Berlin Alexanderplatz* survived its disappearance from the book market between 1933 and 1945. The enduring impact on German readers did not translate into a real international success, since too much hinges on specific linguistic and cultural effects that are lost with the transfer to another language and culture. Döblin's "cinematic style" can, however, be translated into images and sounds, as is demonstrated by the monumental film directed by Rainer Werner Fassbinder.

—Wulf Koepke

THE BETROTHED (I promessi sposi)
Novel by Alessandro Manzoni, 1827

Italy's first important novel, Alessandro Manzoni's *The Betrothed*, is also Europe's first essentially sociological novel. Christian faith suffuses and transcends its entire empirical fabric, and divine Providence is the issue which is continually at stake in its chronicle of cruelty and kindness. At the same time, the retrograde feudal Counter-Reformation society of Spanish-ruled 17th-century Lombardy is clearly projected as an historically defined system of beliefs, norms, values, law, economy, and pernicious relations of power and class flaunted under the name of honour. Many major areas of social practice, from dress and eating to modes of transport and the uses of literacy, contribute to the novel's realistic and moral texture, and structure and system of signification. Mass phenomena like famine, war, riot, and plague are presented from the point of view of the oppressed, and Renzo Tramaglino, a rural artisan, holds centre stage. In many ways a revolutionary novel, developing further much of the potential already displayed in the newly established genre of the historical novel by Sir Walter Scott, *The Betrothed* nevertheless pursues profoundly counter-revolutionary perspectives.

Manzoni's opening device is the invention of the anonymous 17th-century chronicler from whose barely legible manuscript and ingeniously flowery style he purports to derive a factual account and many quaintly moralizing comments. Renzo and his intended bride, Lucia, are prevented from marrying by the local tyrant, Don Rodrigo, and forced to flee from their village near Como. Renzo becomes involved in bread-riots in Milan, where he helps to calm the mob, is denounced for his pains as an agitator and flees to Bergamo, in Venetian territory. Meanwhile, Lucia is kidnapped from her refuge in a Monza nunnery and delivered into the hands of the dread Unnamed, most lawless of the barons, who acknowledges no superior authority. Just when the promised spouses seem most irremediably separated, the plot providentially begins to favour their reunion. The ageing Unnamed is wearying of evil and brooding on death, and Lucia's cry "God will forgive so many things, for a single act of mercy!" precipitates his complete change of heart. Releasing Lucia is his first Christian gesture. Still, Renzo remains proscribed, and it is only the plague that will allow him to return to Milan with impunity to retrace Lucia and make her his wife.

This adventurous plot, in which God disposes somewhat too neatly, and narrative ironies abound, carries a great variety of concerns, insights, and artistic energies. Different milieux, life-histories, and intellectual concerns produce much brilliant narrative (even mini-novels within the novel), or turn into almost free-standing essays— for instance, on *laissez-faire* economics or public health. The first draft, *Fermo e Lucia* (1821–23), is more rambling and uncoordinated, its plot more transparently a peg on which the author hangs his enquiry into history, and more open-ended both as narrative and as directly ideological discourse. The key invention in the published version, guaranteeing the narrative an ideological closure lacking in the draft, was to make the conscience of the deeply aggrieved working-class Renzo the focus through which the reader sees violent

revolt as senseless and abhorrent. His nocturnal wandering through the wilderness to salvation across the River Adda is transformed, by the transcendental realism characteristic of the novel, into a spiritual and existential experience.

The vivid presentation of characters has always been seen as one of the strengths of *The Betrothed*. They are arranged in a hierarchy of seriousness. The moral protagonists are Lucia and the Unnamed, the sublime Cardinal Federigo Borromeo, the crusading Father Cristoforo and the sinister Gertrude, forced into a nunnery at an early age by her aristocratic father and drawn into duplicity and crime. The petty scoundrels high and low that keep the exploitive system going are treated with Manzoni's magisterial humour and irony. These range from the Spanish grandee, Gonzalo of Cordova, to Don Rodrigo and his political uncle, to the lawyer, the pedant, and above all, the feckless parish priest, Don Abbondio, a household name in Italy for laughable timorousness and moral obtuseness. Renzo is the pivotal character along this scale. Like other lower-class figures in the novel, he is projected as engagingly wayward, full of spontaneous vitality, and instinctively upright, but is drawn with a lightness of touch that is always close to condescension.

The novel's focus on the individual as the site of moral choice, on salvation as the integrity of the self here on earth as well as in the hereafter, is precariously balanced by the concept of character as a psychological and (in a literary work) aesthetic given, as well as by the sense of well-nigh absolute social conditioning. The delicacy with which these perspectives are made to coincide largely explains the status of *The Betrothed* as a classic which poses many of the key problems of the 19th-century novel.

For Italians, *The Betrothed* has special national significance. Not only was it the first lifelike, lively, and enlivening representation of Italian society of all classes, but, right under the noses of Northern Italy's Austrian rulers in the post-Napoleonic Restoration, Manzoni depicted Italian subjection to foreign rule, by the same House of Habsburg, at a historical remove, and showed it up as a nonsense. The Italy of the Counter-Reformation shown in the novel corresponded closely enough to the Catholic Restoration and Manzoni's work, mediating the rational heritage of the Enlightenment, implicitly pointed to the alternative of liberal-progressive Catholicism as a middle way forward.

The linguistic revision of *The Betrothed* for the 1840–42 edition confirmed its status as a national literary monument. The change from the hybrid language of the first edition to the living idiom of Florence in the second offered Italy the literary model that the movement towards unity seemed to demand, although the emergence of a common spoken language was to take a different path.

—John Gatt-Rutter

BHAGAVADGĪTĀ

Poem of 18 songs and 700 verses, from Book 6 of the Sanskrit epic *Mahābhārata, q.v.*, dating from c. 400–c. 200 BC, and traditionally attributed to Vyāsa (the supposed compiler of the *Vedas, q.v.*).

PUBLICATIONS

Bhagavadgītā. 1808; edited by F.O Schrader (Kashmiri rescension), 1930; also edited by R.N. Narayanaswami (with translation and commentary), 1936, Franklin Edgerton (bilingual edition, including Edward Arnold's translation), 2 vols., 1944, S.K. Belvalker, 1945, revised 1968, H.M. Lamber (with translation by V.G. Pradhān), 1967–69, R.C. Zaehner, 1969, bilingual edition, 1973, K.K. Bhattacharya, 1972, Tulsīrāmaswami, 1977, J.A.B. van Buitenen (bilingual edition), 1981, G.S. Sadhale, 3 vols., 1985, and R. Iyer (with the Utarragita), 1985; as *Bhăgvăt-Gēētā*, translated by Charles Wilkins, 1785, reprinted 1972; as either *Bhagavadgītā* or *Bhagavad Gītā* (sometimes without accents) translated by John Davies, 1882; K.T. Telang, 1882; Mohini M. Chatterji, 1887; Annie Besant, 1895, revised, 5th edition, 1918; Lionel D. Barnett, 1905; Charles Johnston, 1908; Arthur Ryder, 1929; Franklin Edgerton (bilingual edition), 1952, English only, 1972; Swami Nikhilananda, 1944; Swami Prabhavananda and Christopher Isherwood, 1944; Sarvepalli Radhakrishnan, 1948, bilingual edition, 1970; Nataraja Guru (bilingual edition), 1962; Juan Mascaró, 1962; P. Lal, 1965; Eliot Deutsch, 1968; Kees W. Bolle (bilingual edition), 1979; A.C. Bhaktivedanta, 1981; Nikunja Vihari Banerjee, 1984; Eknath Easwaran, 1986; Hasmukh M. Raval with John L. Safford, 1990; D. Prithipaul (bilingual edition), 1993; as *The Song Celestial*, translated by Edwin Arnold, 1885; as *The Song of the Lord* translated by Edward J. Thomas (bilingual edition), 1931; selections translated in *Hindu Scriptures*, translated by R.C. Zaehner, 1966; *The Song of a Thousand Names*, 1976; *Selections*, translated by Francis G. Hutchins, 1980; as *The Bhagavad Gītā: A Verse Translation* by Geoffrey Parrinder, 1996; *Vedi Sacrifice: Challenge and Response* by Israel Selvanayagam, 1996; translated by Swami Gambhirananda, 1998; translated by Jatindra Mohan Chatterjee, 1998; as *Srimad Bhagavad Gita: A Guide to Daily Living*, translated by Baij Nath Bhandari, 2000.

*

Critical Studies: *Age and Origins of the Gita* by J.N. Farquhar, 1904; *Notes and Index to the Bhagavad Gītā* by K. Browning, 1916; *Essays on the Gita* by Sri Aurobindo, 1928; *The Bhagavad Gita* by Douglas P. Hill, 1928; *The Gita: A Critique* by P. Narasimham, 1939; *The Bhagavad-Gītā and Modern Scholarship* by Satis Chandra Roy, 1941; *A Christian Approach to the Bahagavadgita* by P.S. Mathai, 1956; *Talks on the Gita* by A.V. Bhave, 1960; *The Ethics of the Gītā* by G.W. Kaveeshwar, 1971; *Early Buddhism and the Bhagavadgītā* by K.N. Upadhyaya, 1971; *Introduction to the Bhagavad-gītā* by G.A. Feuerstein, 1974; *Bhagavad-Gītā: An Exegetical Commentary* by R.N. Minor, 1982 *Gītā: The Science of Living* by Jayantil S. Jarivalla, 1984; *Bhagavad Gita Reference Guide* by R.D. Singh, 1984; *The Bhagavadgītā and Jīvana Yoga* by R.N. Vyas, 1985; *Modern Indian Interpreters of the Bhagavadgita* edited by Robert N. Minor, 1986; *The Hindu Gītā: Ancient and Classical Interpretations of the Bhagavadgītā* by Arvind Sharma, 1986; *The Universal Gītā Western Images of the Bhagavadgītā: A Bicentenary Survey* by Eric J. Sharpe, 1986; *Influence of Bhagavadgita on Literature Written in English* edited by T.R. Sharma, 1987; *20th-Century Interpretations of Bhagavadgita: Tilak, Gandhi and Aurobindo* by P.M. Thomas, 1987; *The Quest for Wisdom, Thoughts on the Bhagawadgita* by Adya Rangacharya, translation by P.V. Joshi, 1993; *The Social Role of the Gītā: How and Why* by Satya P. Agarwal, 1993; *The Concept of Yoga in the Gita* by Sarat Chandra Panigrahi, 1994; *Gita darshan: Glimpse of Gita* by Hargun Ladharam Khanchandani, 1994; *Krsna, the Man and his Mission: An Enquiry Into the Rational of Inter-relationship*

Between Krsna's Life, Mission, and Philosophy by Sadananda More, 1995; *The Contemporary Essays on the Bhagavad Gītā*, edited by Braj M. Sinha, 1995; *The Ethical Philosophy of the Gita: A Comparative and Critical Study of the Interpretations of Tilak and Ramanuja* by Madan Prasad Singh, 1996; *The Bhagavad Gītā and St. John of the Cross: A Comparative Study of the Dynamism of Spiritual Growth in the Process of God-realisation* by Rudolf V. D'Souza, 1996; *The Essence of Geeta: A Scientific Exposition of the Principles of Life and Physical Existence as Enshrined in Geeta, Interpreted in Terms of Information Theory and Interaction of Vibrations* by H.C. Mathur, 1997; *Quest for the Original Gītā* by Gajanan Shripat Khair, 1997; *Bhagavat Geeta: A Treatise on Managing Critical Decisions in Work Organisation in Society in Family* by Gouranga P. Chattopadhyay, 1997; *The Bhaktivedanta Purports: Perfect Explanation of the Bhagavad-gītā* by Sivarama Swami, 1997; *Bhagavad Gītā: A Literary Elucidation* by Madhusudan Pati, 1997; *Meeting in God-Experience: St. Teresa de Avila and the Bhagavadgītā on Prayer* by Rudolf V. D'Souza, 1999; *Bhagavadgītā: Beyond the Religious* by Radhakamal Mukherjee, 1999; *Bhagavad Gita and Environment* by K.K. Dua, 1999; *Bhagvada Gita, or, Dhammapada of Buddhism: A Comparative Analysis of the Two* by Dinesh S. Anand, 2000; *Nistraigunya Purusottama Yoga of Srimad Bhagavad Gītā: A Mystic Interpretation and Comparative Study* by Bankey Behari, 2000; *The Bhagavad Gita According to Ghandi*, edited by John Strohmeier, 2000.

*   *   *

The *Bhagavadgītā* (*Gītā* for short) is just an episode in Vyāsa's *Mahābhārata*, but it has achieved even more fame than the larger work. Most devout Hindus recite a few lines of it daily in their homes. The *Gītā* is really a dialogue between Arjuna, the Paṇḍava hero, and Krṣṇa, his divine charioteer, to dispel his hesitation and gloom in having to kill his own kinsmen in order to procure an empire.

Krṣṇa tells Arjuna that death is really of no consequence for it means only rebirth in another form. The immortal soul never dies. Even if you do not believe in the soul's immortality and reincarnation, Krṣṇa tells him, "you should still not grieve. For it is certain that death is inevitable and controlled by destiny. So why worry about what *has* to happen, and of which you are merely the instrument?" Krṣṇa goes on to explain how one can achieve emancipation. It can be either by knowledge, by perfect devotion to god, or by altruistic works. Thus the *Gītā* is a kind of philosophical synthesis. It is also a practical guide to human conduct, and favours renunciation. A man should do his own work and not bother about that of another. Work should be done to perfection, for it is a kind of yoga. It is the man at the top who should set the standard in conduct, for the others lower down follow his example. The wise man makes no distinction between a learned person, a cow, an elephant, a pariah, and even a dog: he is kind to them all. All works should be unselfish, and one should act according to conscience without expecting any reward or fearing any punishment. "Your right is to actions alone," Krṣṇa tells Arjuna, "not to their fruit. Nor should you be enamoured of inaction."

Apart from its unrivalled philosophy, the *Gītā* is also a literary work. The Sanskrit of its verses is simpler in structure than that of other Hindu works on philsophy. It has greater fluidity and smoothness. It has a mixed metre, the *upajati*, some lines being in the *indravajra* and others in the *upendravajra* form. Both of these have 11 syllables each. The poet uses language to suit the occasion, as for example in the musical stanzas of Arjuna's prayer to the Lord when he has disclosed his cosmic form. Death is a mere "change of clothes,"

Enjoyments come to a calm man yet leave him undisturbed, as rivers entering the sea. The mind of the yogi is like "a light in a sheltered place." Passion, anger, and greed are "the triple gates of hell." Creation is like the huge spreading Indian fig tree; its roots are the Primal Being, its stems the creator, its leaves the scriptures, and its branches the living creatures with all their frailties. One is tempted to fell this tree with the formidable axe of dispassion.

The keynote of the *Gītā* is renunciation, and it strongly advocates self-control and the relinquishment of all sensual pleasures—even the thought of them. But it is against ascetics who torture their bodies, calling them "fiends." It considers the *Vedas* merely as aids to emancipation, and "like a tank flooded with water" when the goal is achieved. The universality of the *Gītā* lies in its complete freedom from all dogma. After propounding his doctrine, Kṛṣṇa tells Arjuna, "Don't take my word for it. Reflect on what I have told you and do as you like." In fact Kṛṣṇa goes to the extent of saying, "They are also my devotees, who with faith worship other gods." The *Gītā* is undiluted philosophy expressed in layman's language, and effectively holds a high place in the spiritual literature of the world.

—K.P. Bahadur

THE BIBLE

Compilation of Hebrew and Greek texts. Old Testament collects Hebrew prose and verse works dating from c. 900–100 BC: Pentateuch (Genesis, Exodus, Leviticus, Numbers, Deuteronomy) canonized c. 400 BC; the Former Prophets, principally historical works, canonized c. 200 BC; miscellaneous Writings (e.g. Books of Psalms, Proverbs, Job) gradually canonized individually to c. AD 90, when selection for and authorization of the Old Testament was completed. The first Greek translation, known as the Septuagint (containing some additional writings), was made in the 3rd century BC, revised by Aquila c. AD 135. New Testament collects Greek prose writings from c. AD 50–100: letters of Paul, other letters, the three synoptic gospels (Matthew, Mark, Luke), and the Johannine writings; 39th Easter Letter of Athanasius suggests canonical list completed by AD 367. Non-canonical works of both periods are collected into Old and New Testament Apocrypha. First Latin translations of Old and New Testaments, the Vulgate, made by St. Jerome, *q.v*, c. AD 383–405.

PUBLICATIONS

Bible, translated by Wyclif and others. c. 1380; first printed edition of St. Jerome's Vulgate (Gutenberg), 1452–55; Marietti edition (with variants), 1459; first Hebrew edition of Old Testament, 1488; New Testament (Greek and Latin) edited by Erasmus, 1516; Tyndale, 1525–26 (New Testament), 1530 (Pentateuch); Coverdale, 1535; Rheims-Douai version (Roman Catholic): 1582 (New Testament), 1609 (Old Testament); King James Version, 1611; Revised Standard Version, 1946–52; New English Bible, 1961–70; and many others; annotated editions include *The Interpreter's Bible*, edited by George Buttrick and others, 1952–57, *The Oxford Annotated Bible*, edited by Herbert C. May and Bruce M. Metzger, 1962, *The Jerusalem Bible*, 1966, revised edition, as *The New Jerusalem Bible*, edited by Henry Wansborough, 1986, and *Tyndale's New Testament*, 1989, and *Tyndale's Old Testament*, 1992, both edited by David Daniell.

*

Critical Studies: *The Old Testament in Modern Research* by Herbert F. Hahn, 1954, revised bibliographical essay by Horace D. Hummel, 1970; *The New Testament Background: Selected Documents* edited by C.K. Barrett, 1956; *History of the Bible in English* by F.C. Bruce, 1961; revised editions, 1970, 1979; *The Interpreter's Dictionary of the Bible* edited by George Buttrick, 4 vols., 1962, supplementary volume edited by Keith Crim, 1976; *The Cambridge History of the Bible* edited by P.R. Ackroyd, C.F. Evans, G.W.H. Lampe, and S.L. Greenslade, 3 vols., 1963–70, and *Cambridge Bible Commentary* edited by Ackroyd, A.R.C. Leaney, and J.W. Parker, n.d.; *The Old Testament: An Introduction* by Otto Eissfeldt, revised edition, 1965; *Irony in the Old Testament* by Edwin M. Good, 1965; *New Catholic Encyclopedia* 1967, revised edition edited by Berard L. Marthaler, Gregory F. LaNave, Jonathan Y. Tan, and Richard E. McCarron, 2003; *The Art of the Biblical Story*, 1979, and *Narrative Art in the Bible*, 1989, both by Shimon Bar-Efrat; *The Art of Biblical Narrative* by Robert Alter, 1981; *The Great Code: The Bible and Literature*, 1982, and *Words with Power, Being a Second Study of "The Bible and Literature,"* 1990, both by Northrop Frye; *Poetics and Interpretation of Biblical Narrative* by Adele Berlin, 1983; *The Poet and the Historian: Essays in Literature and Historical Biblical Criticism* edited by Richard E. Friedman, 1983; *The Bible: Story and Plot* by Frank Kermode, 1984, and *The Literary Guide to the Bible*, edited by Alter and Kermode, 1987; *The Bible as Literature* by John B. Gabel and Charles B. Wheeler, 1986; *Literary Approaches to Biblical Interpretation* by Tremper Longman, 1987; *The Book and the Text: The Bible and Literary Theory* edited by Regina M. Schwartz, 1990; *The Bible: God's Word of Man's?* by Stephen Prickett and Robert Barnes, 1991 and *Reading the Text: Biblical Criticism and Literary Theory* edited by Prickett, 1991; *The Passion of Interpretation* by W. Dow Edgerton, 1992; *A History of the Bible as Literature: From Antiquity to 1700* and *From 1700 to the Present Day* by David Norton, 2 vols., 1993; *Dialogues of the Word: The Bible as Literature According to Bakhtin* by Walter L. Reed, 1993; *The Oxford Companion to the Bible* edited by Bruce M. Metzger and Michael D. Coogan, 1994.

* * *

The sacred book of Christianity, the Bible, is divided into two parts. The Old Testament is a religious history of the Jews beginning at the creation of the world; the New Testament is a record of the life and teachings of Jesus and his followers. The Old Testament comprises many of the sacred texts of Judaism. In Christianity, Jesus's life is regarded as the ultimate fullfilment of a destiny long promised, and gradually revealed, to the Jewish people.

The gradual process of divine revelation is reflected in the Bible's structure: it is not one book, but a collection of over 60 books, written over centuries. Within these different books are widely different varieties of writing: heroic prose sagas such as those of Samson and David, the explicit sexual love poetry in the Song of Songs, the prophetic visions of Ezekiel and Isaiah. Through all these different kinds of writing moves the idea of God, an idea that undergoes its own gradual evolution. In Genesis, the earliest book, God has physical, anthropomorphic form, walking in the Garden of Eden and wrestling with Jacob. His sons mate with the most beautiful of mortal women, producing a race of mighty heroes. In the final book, Revelations, God is a terrifying cosmic force surrounded by spirits of Death,

Famine, War, and Plague, promising the scourging and cleansing of the earth. The tension this suggests between God as a loving and as a threatening force is writ large throughout the Bible. In Judges, God demands the genocide of women and children in the land of Canaan to provide room for the newly arrived Israelite settlers. In the Psalms, God is seen to lavish his love on the individual soul.

Despite its apparent catholicity, however, the scope of the Bible is far from universal. The New Testament is only a selection of the texts available to those who compiled it. To elevate it to its canonical status some Christian texts had to be preserved, while others were excluded and suppressed. Surviving or recently discovered extracanonical texts such as the Gospel of Thomas offer glimpses of the richness of the Christian scriptures (and the theological concepts) excluded from the religion the Bible has served to define.

In examining the Bible as literature or as a religious text, one must consider its peculiar relationship to language. How can the divine, which is by definition infinite and, ultimately, unknowable, mediate something of its nature through the limited resources of language? At some of its most mystic and allusive moments, the Bible suggests that language is intimately entwined with God's own nature. Christ is "the Word" made flesh. Which word, or the nature of that word, is never revealed. We can only approach this unspoken, unwritten Word through its incarnation in human form. Christ claims the alphabet was one of the symbols of his being, "I am alpha and Omega" (Revelations 22:13). By implication, language itself, all that is or can be written, is an expression of God.

The Bible privileges language as a divine and perfect gift—it is in his perfect state in Paradise that Adam gives the first names to living things. After the Fall, the perfect and universal language is shattered by God at the tower of Babel, to prevent man prying too deeply into His domain. Writing within post-lapsarian language, the Bible is by necessity driven to indirect means of expression, conveying God through riddle, song, and symbol. God manifests Himself not in words but visual images: a pillar or fire, or a burning tree. Those who attempt to capture God in words fail. Jacob wrestles all night with God, and at dawn asks Him for His name. God's only reply is: "Wherefore is it that thou dost ask after my name?" (Genesis 33:29). When Moses sees God in a fiery tree and asks a similar question, God replies "I AM THAT I AM" (Exodus 4:12). Christ too resists any definition of the divine nature, offering instead symbolic utterances which demand an understanding beyond the literal: "I am the vine" (John 15:1), "I am the sheepfold" (John 10:19), "I am the bright and morning star" (Revelations 22:16).

The tension between the Holy Book and the failings of the written word is demonstrated in the structure of the New Testament. It offers not one account of Jesus's life, but four different, and at one time contradictory, accounts side by side. The Gospels give accounts of God in the external world, through quasi-historical records. Revelations shows the manifestation of God in the inner world of the psyche, through the spiritual world of esoteric visionary experience. Here God makes Himself known through a stream of images both awesome and fascinating: a man who holds in his hand the constellation of the Great Bear; a city built of gems; a woman crowned with stars; a whore clad, evocatively, in a scarlet robe and holding a chalice.

Jesus's own teaching is in the form of narrative—parables, or stories, which teach about God by casting Him in simple domestic or agrarian roles. Jesus's moral teachings are most concisely expressed in Matthew, chapters 5, 6, and 7. They urge compassion, generosity, tolerance, and trust in God.

The most important and influential English translation of the Bible has been the "Authorised" or "King James" version of 1611. Its stark, largely monosyllabic Saxon vocabulary in strongly metered, paratactic prose renders the text with directness, simplicity, and strength. The Bible has contributed to Western culture a stock of symbols: the mountain, the garden, the heavenly city, which have echoed through the art and literature of every age. Its central narrative, that of innocence and temptation, fall and redemption, has impressed its pattern on narrative art from Chaucer to the contemporary novel. Its consistent use of literary symbolism to present divine truth has arguably been instrumental in the development of Western symbolism.

—Edmund Cusick

THE BIRDS (Ornithes)
Play by Aristophanes, 414 BC

Aristophanes' *The Birds* ranks as one of the greatest sustained comic fantasies, but the play took only second prize at the Dionysia of 414 BC. It features two Athenians, Peithetairos ("Persuasive Companion") and Euelpides ("Son of Good Hope"), who abandon Athens for a life among the birds. In 5th-century Greek, "to go to the birds" was a way of saying "go to hell." They seek out Tereus, a mythical character with Athenian associations now become a hoopoe, who agrees to introduce them to the birds and to convince the latter to overcome their fear of men.

It is here that the *grande idée* is conceived by Peithetairos, and in place of the usual *agon* (contest) a two-part exposition ensues, in which Peithetairos persuades the birds that birds used to rule the universe and can do so again by building a city in the air to intercept the sacrifices of men to the gods and thus to starve the gods into submission. This city is, of course, the now famous Cloudcuckooland.

The parabasis differs from those in the comedies of the 420s BC in that the chorus does not speak directly for the comedian, but remains in character, outlining a marvellous cosmogony in which birds are the eldest children of Love, creator of the universe, and benefactors of mankind. In the second half the newly created Cloudcuckooland is besieged by intruders (lawseller, priest, poet, town planner). All are driven off by Peithetairos. In a second series of intruders he dismisses first potential undesirables of city life (a parent beater, an informer, the airy-fairy poet Kinesias) and then Iris (Rainbow), the messenger of the gods, who is roughly treated and even sexually threatened. Finally Prometheus, the great friend of humanity, enters under cover to warn Peithetairos that the gods are in deep trouble and that an embassy is on its way to Cloudcuckooland. Peithetairos is to hold out for the hand of Basileia ("Sovereignty") in any terms of treaty. Peithetairos easily outmanoeuvres the ambassadors and wins Basileia. In a glorious finale this man–bird–god takes his new bride and becomes ruler of the universe.

What are we to make of this incredible and unflagging comedy? Critics usually fall into one of two camps, thinking either that the play is just a brilliant piece of comic escapism, or that in his creation of a city in the clouds Aristophanes has in mind certain contemporary events, with more than a hint of ironic criticism. Those of the latter opinion cite the Athenian atrocity at Melos (416–15 BC), the aggressive expedition launched against Sicily (415 BC), or the religious and political scandals of 415 BC that had driven many prominent Athenians into exile and had caused the downfall of the charismatic leader

Alcibiades. Most assume an ironic tone for the comedy, but the overall impression is one not of irony or satire, but of boundless exuberance and high spirits. Aristophanes does attack some of his usual targets, the law courts, demagogues, and charlatans (e.g. Socrates), but on the whole the play is a glorification of the Athenian spirit. Alan Sommerstein makes the excellent point that if the comedy does reflect the atmosphere of 415–14 BC, it does so with optimism and bellicosity. This play harmonizes well with the public mood, as described by Thucydides.

Other critics adopt an approach that generally eschews any serious political relevance, and find in *The Birds* deep and serious levels of meaning, often involving an extended and almost metaphysical symbolism. Thus for Whitman the comedy is an elaborate metaphor of "the anatomy of Nothingness"—the universe is absurdly created by Love from a wind-egg. Kenneth J. Reckford views *The Birds* as an expression of the creative power of Love: comedy, like Love, creates a splendid fantasy out of original chaos. T.K. Hubbard adds a satirical theme, by stressing the confusion between men and gods—Athens' problems in 415 BC are "rooted in the sophistic delusion that Man himself can somehow become God."

Yet one must always be careful in attributing such depths to Aristophanic comedy. His plays were intended to be popular and imaginative fantasies, creations of the moment, often trivial and frivolous. Such art is by nature not receptive to the grandiose and metaphysical interpretations that modern critics have constructed. It is probably safer to read the play as an excellent fantasy based on the absurd concept of men "going to the birds." Political and social ironies as well as grand critical readings are not the natural interpretations one should draw from such a play.

The Birds is a conspicuous example of the utopian theme in Greek literature. Such ideal creations range from the lost Golden Age of Hesiod, to the Islands of the Blest at the end of the world (Homer, *Odyssey* IV; Pindar; Lucian), to the regions of the next world reserved for the virtuous (as in *The Frogs*). Comedy too had its paradises, usually places where work is unknown and food and drink and sex are found in abundance. Thus in the prologue the Athenians come in search of "a soft and woolly place," where the "problems" of life are attending a wedding feast and realizing a homoerotic fantasy with an attractive boy. There is nothing radically new in Aristophanes' utopia, but he has explored brilliantly the concept of such a paradise among the birds, and to that end the lines between bird and man are deliberately and persistently blurred (e.g. the costuming of Tereus, Euelpides, and Peithetairos; the choral description of the advantages for men of having wings; the identification of a dozen contemporary Athenians as birds). That he can maintain this creation for over 1,750 lines (*The Birds* is longer than any extant Greek tragedy or comedy, save only Euripides' *The Phoenician Women* (*Phoenissae*), is testimony to a comedian at the height of his powers.

—Ian C. Storey

THE BIRTH OF TRAGEDY (Die Geburt der Tragödie)
Prose by Friedrich Nietzsche, 1872

Friedrich Nietzsche's energetic first book *The Birth of Tragedy* is also the *Urtext* of modernism. Its presiding deities, Apollo and Dionysus, would later provide the occasion for Freud's simpler opposition between the id and super-ego. Moreover, such themes as the redemption of life through art (sections 1, 5, 7) and the joyful celebration of suffering (sections 1 and 3) furnished Rilke with much of his material. The notion of a culture spiritually exhausted and desiccated by rationality, cut off from the primitive life-giving forces of myth (sections 20 and 23) resonates throughout T.S. Eliot's critique of modern life in *The Waste Land*. The picture of ancient Greece conjured up by Nietzsche generates not only the ultramontane "Snow Scene" of Thomas Mann's *Magic Mountain* but indeed the novel's very title (section 3). The life-enhancing illusion that overcomes resignation and any Buddhist negation of the will has echoes in Ibsen's theme of the "life-lie." It is difficult in fact to exhaust the list of such influences.

Nietzsche's thesis is that the history of all art is generated by the dynamic tension between the Apollonian and the Dionysian principles, just as the procreation of the race is dependent on the mysterious torque of sex, the mutual attraction and repulsion of male and female. As Nietzsche explains it, the Apollonian is a visual impulse, as is appropriate for the god of light, and light gives Apollo his sovereignty over everything that appeals to sight, including dream images, which one might have expected to be subjects of a darker realm. Less surprisingly, Apollo presides over such plastic arts as sculpture and architecture. Indeed, Doric architecture is the "permanent military encampment of the Apollonian." But Apollo has his music, too, even if it is only the "wave beat of rhythm" a tonal Doricism. As befits a god of clarity, Apollo reinforces distinctions, including that between self and other, hence he is the god of individuation as well.

The Dionysian, on the other hand, is the ecstatic collapse of individuation, a self-oblivion, a melting away of distinctions between self and other, and the restoration of vital contact with nature that appears to be the end of alienation in mystical participation, a return to the "heart of nature." Analogies to this state can be found in narcosis or intoxication, and Dionysus, we remember, is the god of wine. He is, in Nietzsche, the god most intimately involved in music: "Transform Beethoven's 'Hymn to Joy' in painting, . . . then you will approach the Dionysian." He is also the deity in whose name Attic tragedy arose. We are to understand this latter connection by the fact that the Greeks, unique in the ancient world, did not collapse into licentiousness and drunkenness under the influence of this orgiastic foreign god, and that they did not precisely because of the restraining, sublimating influence of Apollo, who held up the Gorgon's head to demonic excess. At times, out of a need for self-preservation, the Apollonian made itself even more rigid, in order to withstand the relentless waves of harmony seeking to engulf it, a threat which, to individuation, can inspire terror as easily as joy.

The historically fragile moment of cooperation and equilibrium between these two powerful forces of Apollo and Dionysus is the moment of Attic Old Tragedy. The site of their equilibrium is the stage itself, where we see, on the one hand, Dionysian man following his trajectory of Titanic excess, whether of love (Prometheus) or of wisdom (Oedipus); on the other hand is the Bacchic chorus, the mirror in which the hero observes himself, but the chorus is also the background from which he emerges, just as dialogue emerges from choral parts, just as the invisible ground of all being is the source of those noumenal emanations, known to us as music, which acquire visibility through the control of Apollo to become dramatic art. Nietzsche imagines that it is by means of tragedy's gorgeous images that the Greeks, knowing full well that it is better not to have been born at all, are seduced nevertheless into affirming life. Greek culture at its most clairvoyant demonstrates a joyful pessimism, a celebration of life despite life's ultimate hopelessness. Thus is the world justified by the Greeks as an aesthetic phenomenon.

The enigmatic beauty of Old Tragedy begins to break down for Nietzsche with the advent of Euripides, in whom the critical faculty gains the upper hand over the artistic. Now to be beautiful, art must be intelligible. Dionysus, always the protagonist of Old Tragedy, however masked and disguised by other identities, is replaced with the ordinary Athenian citizen. Realism becomes the style of the day. Civic mediocrity replaces the dark harmonies of Aeschylus and Sophocles. Reasonableness and sophistical discussion proliferate where once there was song. Behind these depredations reigns the spirit of Socrates, optimistic, moralistic, of Cyclopian shallowness. The only art tolerated by Socrates is the Aesopian fable. Socratic hypertrophy of the intellect holds that the mysteries of being are fathomable. No corner of nature or the psyche must be left in shadow. Socrates thus becomes the stalking horse of science, an activity practised by those who believe they know what they are doing, unlike those supposedly unenlightened souls who act from instinct. It is to the bewilderment of such innocents that Socrates perversely devotes himself in Plato's *Dialogues*. But Nietzsche would side with Socratic antagonists like Callicles (in the *Gorgias*) who accuses Socrates of promoting an upside-down life by valorizing *nomos* (rule) over *physis* (nature). For most men, says Nietzsche, instinct is a creative power, the source of affirmative and productive action, while consciousness is a critical and dissuasive faculty. For Socrates, however, the reverse is true. Consciousness is the creative force, while criticism, the Socratic *daimonion*, has been relegated to instinct. The only inkling that Socrates has of his own monstrosity is the dream that comes to him in prison and urges him to practise music.

Nietzsche introduces the hope that science and the Socratic will not keep the tragic view of life at bay forever, that there may be in the offing a rebirth of tragedy, and if so, a music-producing Socrates will be an appropriate sign of the new age. Already here are indications that science has spread to its limits, that shallow optimism is giving way to "tragic resignation and the destitute need for art." Kant and Schopenhauer have now exposed scientific confidence as illusory. Modern-day opera, with its mistaken Euripidean celebration of words over music, seems to be giving way to a mythical revitalization in German opera, largely through the efforts of Richard Wagner, from whose pen flow torrents of Dionysian melody. If such possibilities are realized, the gates of the Hellenic magic mountain, closed even to the importunities of Goethe and Schiller, may now be on the point of opening once more.

—Dan Latimer

BLIND MAN'S BOY

See LAZARILLO DE TORMES

BLOOD WEDDING (Bodas de sangre)
Play by Federico García Lorca, 1933

Blood Wedding was conceived as a musical piece whose theme engenders its counterpoint-response, with the dialogue an interweaving of voices. Federico García Lorca declared (during an interview

about *Blood Wedding*) that his entire work—poetry and theatre—could be traced to the works of J.S. Bach; he particularly admired the mathematical symmetry and precise intellectual structure.

Blood Wedding is the first and most enigmatic of García Lorca's trilogy of rural Andalusian tragedies, combining realism, fantasy, lyricism, and traditional folkloric materials in a radically innovative way. Mythopoeic realism in the first two acts changes to surrealist fantasy in the third, but the result falls generally within the tradition of classical tragedy that García Lorca strove consciously to evoke. Rather than presenting an ancient myth in modern guise, García Lorca re-created the living primitivism of agrarian Andalusia, where the treeless, volcanic desert near the country towns of Lorca and Gaudix (southeast of Granada, province of Almería) contains numerous long-inhabited caves—some quite luxuriously furnished. Like Yeats, Cocteau, Eliot, and others, García Lorca sought mythic dimensions and poetic language, but the settings of the first two acts echo socio-economic realities of the area. Aspects of the plot, artistically re-elaborated, likewise originated in true events, most notably a sensational crime in Níjar in 1928: a rural bride fled her wedding with her cousin, who was shot and killed by an unknown ambusher (subsequently identified as the groom's brother). García Lorca retained the principal triangle of bride, groom, and rival, and the motivating triad of desire, jealousy, and revenge, but added a longstanding blood feud between the families and modified the fatal event so that groom and rival slay each other. Tripartite settings include the farm homes of the groom and Leonardo in Act I, the Bride's cavern in Act II, and the damp, primeval, druidic forest in Act III (the only setting not based on local reality). García Lorca postulated a broken engagement between the Bride and Leonardo (now married, with an infant son). Yet these complications only stoke the smouldering primal passions of the Bride and Leonardo, leading to the explosion of repressed emotions unleashed at the wedding.

Spain's lack of tradition in the tragic theatre (excepting Romantic variants) challenged García Lorca to attempt modern tragedy, incorporating mythic and telluric elements. Following classical precedent, he made his protagonists victims of inscrutable, irresistible forces, not specifically identified with fate, but blind, impersonal instincts capable of annihilating moral scruples and reversing reason. Stark, spare settings, limited time span (events in the present occupy less than a week), and tightly controlled numbers (only four characters have major roles) echo classical antecedents, as does having the violence occur offstage: spectators hear the mortal cries but do not witness the sacrificial bloodshed.

The uninterrupted existence of ancient customs, millennial oral traditions, and folklore, and primitive agrarian lifestyles in rural Andalusia facilitated the linking of prehistoric roots and modern psychology. García Lorca's familiarity with Spanish translations of Freud and his own experimentation with surrealist technique (*Poet in New York*) offered connections between vanguard literary creativity and the unconscious past, neolithic religions, and Dionysian mysteries. An assiduous reader of classical tragedians, especially Sophocles and Euripides, García Lorca conceived Andalusian rural culture as mythic—inherently violent, primitive, and tragic—and linked directly to prehistoric rituals of sacrifice and proto-religious mysteries of birth, fertility (reproduction), and death. Within this context, contemporary crimes of passion and vengeance become sacrificial rituals, their protagonists merely pawns of powers which, despite centuries of history, continue to be mysterious and irresistible.

One interpretation of *Blood Wedding* views it as a drama of the soil, with the Groom representing water and the Bride the arid lands.

Another interpretation, emphasizing socioeconomic factors, postulates an indictment of arranged marriages based on property rather than on mutual attraction. Still another views the work as a re-enactment of mythic patterns described by Sir James Frazer in *The Golden Bough*, the marriage and death cycle repeated endlessly. Finally, the moon's role in the third act (and lunar associations with agriculture, fertility cycles, and death) underlie interpretations of *Blood Wedding* as a demonstration of the continuing power of the White Goddess and humanity's helplessness before cosmic forces and primal urges. García Lorca's tragedies give weight to women's roles and his heroines are much more interesting than their male counterparts; many of his plays can be read as indictments of women's lot in Spain: the Bride's self-defence and her protestation of innocence are not only a dramatic high point, but unprecedented in Spanish theatre.

Although exotic and fantastic for cosmopolitan theatregoers of García Lorca's day, *Blood Wedding* remains within the bounds of contemporary Andalusian reality for the first two acts. Following Lope de Vega, García Lorca reworked popular songs and dances, doing his own musical adaptations of folk ballads and lullabies, and poetically modifying their lyrics to foreshadow the fatal outcome, thereby enhancing the air of inevitability of the ritualistic violence in the last act. Excepting Leonardo, characters are nameless, generic, archetypal, identified by familial roles (Father, Mother, Wife, Mother-in-Law) or function (the neighbours, woodcutters, wedding guests). García Lorca updates the chorus of Greek tragedy, reincarnating its commentator function in groups extraneous to the action (the woodcutters and girls of the third act, for example). Fantastic, supernatural, surrealistic figures (the Moon, Death in the guise of the old beggar) embody primal powers vested by primitive peoples in the lunar deity. In his poetry García Lorca consistently associates the moon with fatality, mystery, and death, and the horse with unbridled sexual passion, connections maintained in *Blood Wedding*. Amalgamating elements drawn from widely varied sources—ancient myth and modern newspapers, classical tragedy and vanguard literary experimentation, primitive ritual and 20th-century psychology, local socio-economic reality and his own imagination—García Lorca created a uniquely personal, distinctive masterpiece.

—Janet Pérez

THE BLUE ANGEL (Professor Unrat; as Der Blaue Engel)
Novel by Heinrich Mann, 1905

The Blue Angel, written in the autumn of 1904 by then 34-year-old Heinrich Mann and published the following year, exemplifies a movement away from the traditional Bildungsroman, which was felt arguably to be obsolete in the Wilhelminian period, towards a realist and socially and politically conscious approach to the novel. With its North German urban setting (containing echoes of Mann's home town of Lübeck) this tale of the love of a 57-year-old philistine schoolmaster at the local gymnasium for a young chanteuse presents, on the wider front, a satirically critical view of contemporary life in Wilhelminian Germany as its author examines aspects of power and self-destruction.

On one level, the novel depicts a generational conflict as the schoolmaster Rant (inevitably nicknamed ''Unrat'') tyrannically regiments his charges. Symbolically, Unrat is seen dissecting, as he

apparently has done with successive classes over the years, *The Maid of Orleans* (*Die Jungfrau von Orleans*), until the spirit of Schiller's masterpiece is lost. But in fact Mann concerns himself only in part with the school experiences from the perspective of the pupils themselves and their maturing processes (in contrast to Thomas Mann's Hanno Buddenbrook and Robert Musil's Törless), concentrating rather on the behaviour of the schoolmaster himself. That he embodies a wider representative role than the one merely within the confines of the school is revealed early on in the novel: ''what transpired in the school constituted for Unrat the seriousness and reality of life itself. Indolence equated to the corruptability of a useless citizen, inattentiveness and laughter were a form of opposition to the power of the State.'' Moreover, ''no banker and no monarch took an interest in power more strongly than Unrat, no one was more keen on the maintenance of the status quo.'' What he desired was a powerful Church and army, the observance of a strict code of obedience and morals. Opposition to Unrat within the school comes primarily from three 17-year-old boys who serve to reflect different strata of society (the school functions as a microcosm of the town itself): Lohmann, the intellectual bourgeoisie; Kieselack, the petite-bourgeoisie; and the Junker von Erztum. Lohmann in particular is employed by Mann here to portray the component of ''Geist'' *vis-á-vis* Unrat's ''Macht'' in the novelist's present depiction of the problematic duality so symptomatic of his work overall. It is Lohmann who detects the potential anarchist in Unrat.

At the personal level, Unrat's downfall commences with his association with the chanteuse at the Blue Angel, Rosa Fröhlich, the epitome of Bohemiam unconventionality and good-naturedness. Eventual criticism of this liaison from school representatives (and hence society at large) serves only to alienate Unrat still further and stoke the fires of his own ''revolution''—politically, when he decides to vote for the socialist cause at an election and ''make common cause with the rabble against the arrogant superior folk, summon the mob to the palace and bury the opposition of some people in general anarchy'' (phraseology that recurs incidentally in the same or similar form on occasion elsewhere in the novel). Personal and socio-political life now clearly overlap. The dividing line between order and disorder, regimentation and anarchy, is but thin, and the tyrannical Unrat is panicked into overstepping this line.

His resentment at people's sneering, hypocritical interference in his private life drives him further into the arms of Rosa Fröhlich—out of defiance—and hence into a state of anarchy: ''Finally out of the tyrant there emerged the anarchist.'' Unrat now deliberately sets about acts of revenge. As tales of orgies at Unrat's villa spread through the town, representatives of society ''unter den feinen Leuten'' (''the best people'') like Consul Breetpoot, the army (Lieutenant von Gierschke), the Church (pastor Quittjens) all demean themselves before Unrat. The decadence of the scheming smalltown tyrant becomes the degeneracy of the town itself as Mann satirically caricatures Wilhelminian society in his fictional anatomy of a small town.

The concluding sentence of chapter 15 and the opening one of the following formally mark the final stage and inevitability of Unrat's downfall. His Achilles heel ever remains Rosa Fröhlich, and the passionate torments of love, hatred, and jealousy (and concomitant violence) continue inexorably to gnaw away deep within Unrat. The return of Lohmann after a two-year absence (during which time he has outgrown the small-town environment and its stifling influence) proves the final straw. In her final conversation with Lohmann, Rosa Fröhlich recalls with a sigh the seemingly uncomplicated days at the

Blue Angel ("perhaps the best thing!"). Seeing the two together, Unrat flies into a murderous rage. Lohmann leaves and responds in the only way he knows by summoning the police in accord with his bourgeois sense of values. On the subsequent arrest of Unrat, and of Rosa (which Lohmann had not foreseen), it is significant that Mann allows Kieselack to have the final word as he observes Unrat's departure. The dousing of Unrat suggests paradoxically the cleansing of the town's corporate sins. The "normality" of Wilhelminian life can now continue undisturbed.

Who has won in the end? Certainly not Unrat, the polar element of "Macht," who believes himself anarchically avenged on society at large and who thinks he has "won" over Rosa, the embodiment of Art (and "Geist") in one form. Even in that sphere Unrat's 30 years of research into Homer lose out ultimately to the popular songs of the chanteuse. Unrat's gesturings are merely the parody of power at both the personal and social level. At the political level, his behaviour reflects the headlong descent of the tyrant into anarchy. Yet Rosa Fröhlich herself can hardly be seen to have won, since she too is arrested along with Unrat. Equally, in tracing the mentality and hypocrisy of Wilhelminian society, Mann is depicting *its* self-destructive urges at the social level.

Though we do not find in *The Blue Angel* the wide-ranging denunciation of the Wilhelminian period that occurs in the *Kaiserreich*-trilogy—*Der Untertan* (*Man of Straw*), *Die Armen*, and *Der Kopf*—nor the depth of feeling present in the critically acclaimed *Henri Quatre* novels of the 1930s, this novel—the product of Mann's early period of writing—proved a bestseller and was translated into many languages. The filming of the work in 1929 under the title *Der Blaue Engel*, with Emil Jannings and Marlene Dietrich in the main roles, ensured the continuing popular success of the novel and of its author's reputation.

—Ian Hilton

THE BLUE BIRD (L'Oiseau bleu)
Play by Maurice Maeterlinck, 1909

The Blue Bird, a fairytale play for thoughtful children, was one of the most successful theatrical works of a period that discovered the world of childhood, and in doing so, found a potential new audience as well as new territory for artistic exploration. Maurice Maeterlinck acknowledged J.M. Barrie's *Peter Pan* (1908) as a precursor of his own fairytale play, though the genre had already made its mark in Germany with Hauptmann's successful *The Sunken Bell* (*Die versunken Glocke*), 1896, and Elsa Bernstein's *Königskinder* (1897). The fairytale plays of the 1890s tended to be pessimistic and escapist; their Edwardian counterparts are characterized by a more optimistic and positive note. *The Blue Bird* is no exception; indeed it marks a pivotal point in Maeterlinck's creative life, for in it he turned away from the perplexed and inconclusive mood of his earlier plays. *The Blue Bird* is a deliberate attempt to demonstrate that the neo-Romantic or Symbolist manner can be used to convey a happier world-view and send audiences away not bewildered and despairing so much as rejuvenated and reconciled with life and death.

The two main child characters, Tyltyl and his little sister Mytyl, are the children of a poor woodcutter and clearly related to Hansel and Gretel in the Grimm brothers' fairytale. But what befalls them distinguishes them from the traditional stereotype. In the first of the

play's 12 tableaux they "awaken" into a dream sequence that will provide them with a profound insight into the meaning of existence and the "soul" of things, but one that is appropriate to their mental and emotional capacities as children. The third tableau, and the most memorable, takes them to the Land of Memory: here they are reunited with their dead grandfather and grandmother, who come to life again exactly as the children remember them because, as Grandmother Tyl explains, "We dead awaken every time you think of us." The theme of death surfaces again in tableau seven, when at midnight the children rouse the dead in a cemetery only to find that their fear is uncalled for: instead of beholding a gruesome phantasmagoria, they watch as it is transformed into a fairy garden inundated with light and joy.

The plot is based on a simple quest pattern. At the start, the fairy Bérylune (is she their elderly neighbour in disguise?) gives the children a magic hat and diamond and sends them off in search of the mythical blue bird that will bring health and happiness to her ailing daughter. On their way through various versions of the other world (such as the Palace of Night or the Garden of the Happinesses) they see many blue birds, but none survives. Yet when, in tableau 12, they reawaken to "real life" in their beds, Tyltyl's own pet bird has started to look magically blue, and in a spontaneous gesture of childish generosity he gives it to the neighbour for her daughter. When the child comes back with it to thank him, the blue bird escapes and flies away, leaving Tyltyl to break the magic of the fiction by addressing the audience directly as the curtain falls: "If any of you can find it, bring it back to us. We shall need it in order to be happy."

This basic storyline is carried by a wealth of imaginative motifs and makes full use of the stagecraft and new production and lighting techniques available to modern theatres of the period. Transformations abound; actors personify the souls of trees in a scene whose "green" preoccupations have grown in relevance; and the children are accompanied on their adventures by Bread, Water, Sugar, Milk, and Light—figures precariously poised on the borderline between allegory and pantomime. Most appealing of all are the treacherous, sinuous cat and the ever-faithful dog whose boisterous antics must have delighted generations of theatre-goers especially at Christmas time. Frequent touches of humour offset the ever-present risk of sentimentality. Because the play is by a great Symbolist writer and is clearly addressing fundamental aspects of existence, the urge to make every detail conform to an overall interpretation is great. Yet Maeterlinck was a past master at the controlled build-up of suspense and wonder, and well aware that paradoxes and contrasts are dramatically effective and give the spectator pause for thought. Highly visual and three-dimensional though his fairy drama is, its essence is as hard to grasp as the blue bird itself. Analogies with symphonic music—such as the development and transformation of themes and the contrasts of tonalities, speeds rhythms, and sound colours—come closer to accounting for the persistent satisfaction *The Blue Bird* provides. Despite its occasional excesses, it remains a bold attempt to lead 20th-century audiences away from the surface of things and to rescue the theatre from the serious concerns of realism without forgetting the darker aspects of existence.

The Blue Bird was first performed at the Moscow Art Theatre in a production by Stanislavsky in 1908. London followed in 1909; the French premiere did not take place until 1911, when it coincided with Maeterlinck being awarded the Nobel prize for literature.

—Peter Skrine

THE BLUE FLOWERS (Les Fleurs bleues)
Novel by Raymond Queneau, 1965

The Blue Flowers is a carefully structured and fast-paced fantasy where Raymond Queneau's Rabelaisian gusto is at its best. Queneau's fascination for mathematics dates back to his early years, as does his preference for well-constructed books that follow elaborate rules and not just the author's whim. From the point of view of structure, he has always quoted the English-language masters, most notably Joyce, Conrad, and Faulkner, as his major source of influence. Better read in modern American fiction than most French novelists before World War II because of his unusually good command of English, he claimed with excessive modesty (and partiality) to have learnt everything about structure from them. However there is no match for his sophisticated use of numerical formulas. For instance his first novel was divided into 91 sections, for the arcane reason that 91=7 multiplied by 13. Both 7 and 13 are lucky numbers, 7 having the added charm of representing a cipher for the name Raymond Queneau, since there are 7 letters in each of these words. The structure of *The Blue Flowers* follows a similarly strict and at first enigmatic principle. The numbers chosen this time are historical dates 175 years apart: 1264, 1439, 1614, 1789, 1964. The novel follows the metamorphoses of the character of the duc d'Auge as he takes part in the momentous events for which these dates are famous in the history of France. Like all his books then, *The Blue Flowers* is both a game in Oulipian sense of an activity where chance plays no part, and a meditation on history. This most original aspect of his work is doubly important to literary history because of its influence on Georges Perec, whose sophisticated onomastic games take Queneau's principles one step further.

The duc d'Auge has a double, Cidrolin, who lives in the 20th century throughout the book. They actually seem to be each other's dream self, as they take centre stage in turn until they finally meet in the 1964 section of the novel. Both characters are widowed, with grown-up daughters, and are looking for a new partner. The dates selected enable Queneau to refer to some of the most significant landmarks of French history (Louis, the two famous meetings of the States-general, etc.), but what really interests him is the problematic status of history as a science. Just one year after *The Blue Flowers* Queneau published *Une histoire modèle* [A Model for the Study of History] which he had actually begun writing during World War II. This book, which reveals preoccupations not unlike Valéry's is essential to an understanding of *The Blue Flowers*. A leitmotif in the novel is the question repeatedly put by the duc d'Auge to the priest he has in his service, Onésiphore Biroton, about universal history in general and general history in particular. In echo to this Queneau places the following reflection in the mouth of Cidrolin's son-in-law Yoland: "Today's news is tomorrow's history."

Many of the truly hilarious touches to be found in *The Blue Flowers* result from this play on time and history. A joyful spirit of anachronism pervades the whole book and helps create fanciful effects: tourists are called nomads, mammoths still roam freely well into the Renaissance, etc.

As always with Queneau the humour also derives largely from puns, phonetic spellings, and other verbal games. Queneau likes to spell "Western" "ouestern" and "sandwich" "sandouiche." He delights in transcribing sentences just as they sound when we speak them, with the result that words run together in delirious fashion: "Stèfstuesténoci" stands for "Stèphe se tut et Sthène aussi." By 1965 Queneau had not yet been led to change his opinion on the evolution of the French language. He still thought that the French spoken in the street or "néo-français" was becoming increasingly different from the standard written French taught in schools. Up to and including *The Blue Flowers*, all his novels were written to show that "néo-français" was a legitimate new medium for serious modern fiction. It is partly because of his erudite passion for linguistics that word-play, a constant feature of his works, is never superficial and tiresome, but on the contrary always relevant and thought-provoking. His was a learned and tongue-in-cheek brand of surrealism. Indeed his attitude towards language, though not unlike Tristan Tzara's, never evinces any of the powerless anger characteristic of Dada. It is closer to the amused and bemused fondness to be found in the works of the other great dissident surrealist Michel Leiris. One of the most endearing qualities of Queneau's manner is that every single text of his is suffused with his unbounded love for words.

—Pascale Voilley

THE BOOK OF THE CITY OF LADIES (Le Livre de la cité des dames)
Prose by Christine de Pizan, 1405

The Book of the City of Ladies was written as a defence of women and is one of several works that Christine de Pizan wrote on this subject. Christine de Pizan states clearly her position on the worth of women and refutes the unfavourable portrayal of women prevalent at the time.

By writing the work and drawing upon many literary sources, Christine de Pizan became, herself, an example of the abilities and worth of her female contemporaries. However, as scholars have attested, she was not interested merely in composing a defence of these women but also in creating a universal history of women, past, present, and future which would evidence the innate talents and qualities of woman.

The work is written in the form of an allegory depicting three ladies, Reason, Justice, and Rectitude (this third lady, called Droiture in French, translated as either Rectitude or Right-thinking, was added by Christine to the usual list of allegorical figures) who visit Christine de Pizan in her study. She introduces her subject matter by describing her despair upon reading in text after text of the little value and many vices attributed to women and of their inferiority of body and mind. She humbly laments her disappointment at discovering that she is such a vile, worthless creature and apologizes to God for being a woman. She next asks God why he created her such rather than making her a man. (The underlying irony is scarcely concealed here, for how could she have read and understood the texts if she were as worthless as they tell her?) Suddenly a light appears and she sees three ladies who have been sent by God to help her see her error in believing the falsehoods she has been reading. These ladies, Reason, Justice, and Rectitude, also have come to assist her in the construction of a city of ladies. By using this motif, Christine de Pizan immediately connects her work to the *City of God* of St. Augustine and to Christianity. Her refutation of misogyny is surrounded by holy approval; woman is to be vindicated of the role in which she has, unjustly, been cast.

Drawing upon a number of sources, especially Boccaccio's *Concerning Famous Women*, Christine de Pizan recounts many examples of brave, virtuous women from both ancient and contemporary times, from pagan and Christian societies. She divides the book into three parts: Part I, The Foundation and the Walls, Part II, The Buildings and Their Dwellers, and Part III, The Towers and the Noble Ladies Chosen to Dwell There. In Part I, Reason answers Christine de Pizan's questions and guides her to the truth. In this section, Christine de Pizan speaks of the intentions and motivations of the slanders of women and cites examples contrary to the accusations made. She also includes examples of women's ability in politics, in science, and in war. In Part II, Christine de Pizan questions Rectitude about the accusations against women, such as lack of loyalty, infidelity, unchasteness, and weakness of character. She also discusses the value of women to society, the benefits of good marriages (based on the Christian concept of perfect union, viewing husband and wife in the same relationship as Christ the Bridegroom and his Bride the Church) and the usefulness of study for women. In this section, the ''High Women of France'' are welcomed into the city. Part III contains Justice's defence of women. More illustrious women, mostly martyrs, are welcomed into the city. This is perhaps the weakest section of the work because of the very long and repetitious accounts of the martyrdom of these women. Christine de Pizan concludes her book by exhorting all women to be virtuous and earn a place in the City of Ladies.

Throughout the text, Christine de Pizan uses the device of appearing to be convinced, although with enormous sadness, of the contrary side of the argument that she is intent upon proving. Her immediate stimulus to writing is her reading of the *Lamentations of Mathéole*, a text that supposedly extols the value of women but in reality slanders them. Puzzled by what she has read in the light of her own experience as a woman, she senses that the texts, Mathéole's as well as others she has read, are wrong, but accepts them, since so many learned men are in agreement. Here, Christine de Pizan attacks blind obedience to majority opinion. The three ladies condemn her acceptance of these ideas and say they have been sent to enlighten her; by enlightening Christine de Pizan they also enlighten the reader.

Within the work, Marina Warner has identified five recurring themes that treat the five areas in which Christine de Pizan feels her society needs enlightenment and in which she hopes to achieve improvement by leading people to right-thinking. They are as follows: lack of access to education for women; the disappointment evidenced by the birth of a girl; the accusation that women encourage and welcome rape; the insistence that women's delight in fine clothes and their own attractiveness is linked to loose morals; and the problem of battered women, primarily married women, and that of drunken and/or spendthrift husbands.

To teach the reader right-thinking on these issues, Christine de Pizan employs examples drawn from familiar sources such as Boccaccio, but she freely reworks the material for her purposes. A case in point is her treatment of Medea. She includes Medea among the woman skilled in sciences and medicine but does not mention her murdering her children. Christine de Pizan also intersperses anecdotes from her own personal experiences and her comments upon the ills of her own time. Christine de Pizan's style, which is patterned after Latin sentence structure, has rendered her work difficult for her readers, but it witnesses her own erudition and interest in literary form and creativity.

In spite of her talent and the richness of *The Book of the City of Ladies*, it is only recently that the work has once again begun to be appreciated. Because its author borrowed so extensively from

Boccaccio, it has often been considered a translation of his *Concerning Famous Women*. However, Boccaccio's work includes only pagan women and deals with infamous as well as admirable women, whereas Christine de Pizan's work includes only praiseworthy women but both pagan and Christian. In addition, Christine de Pizan's purpose in writing was entirely different—the defence of women. Although many feminists find the work too conservative, the text is one of the first major feminist works.

—Shawncey J. Webb

THE BOOK OF THE THOUSAND NIGHTS AND ONE NIGHT

See THE THOUSAND AND ONE NIGHTS

BRAND
Play by Henrik Ibsen, 1866

Henrik Ibsen wrote *Brand* in Arricia and Rome at the beginning of what was to be a 27-year self-imposed exile from his homeland. The play, set in contemporary Norway, contains both an exploration of the consequences of an individual's unswerving allegiance to the dictates of his will and a savage attack upon the expediency and vacillation of the Norwegian establishment. The theme of individual will would appear to owe much to the influence of the Danish philosopher Søren Kierkegaard's emphasis upon the centrality of human willpower and freedom of choice and his view that the individual should commit him- or herself unreservedly to a consciously chosen way of life. The satire was probably ignited by Norway's refusal to support Denmark in its war against Germany over Schleswig-Holstein. In Berlin in May 1864, at the beginning of his journey to Italy and less than four months before commencing *Brand*, Ibsen had been forcibly reminded of Norway's betrayal of Denmark by a victory parade, during which captured Danish canons were spat upon by the crowds which lined the streets.

Brand is a dramatic poem intended for publication rather than performance. Its action includes the crossing of a stormy fjord and Brand's death beneath an avalanche, effects which, although possible to contrive on the late 19th-century stage, would demand elaborate set changes. It was probably in consequence of these that the play's first production in Stockholm in 1885 ran for six and a half hours!

The figure of the priest, Brand, dominates the play. From his introduction in the first scene we watch him unerringly follow his beliefs until his death at the close of the play. The play's other characters are markedly subsidiary and, in a manner reminiscent of the morality play, are included either to reveal those human relationships which Brand is prepared to abandon in his total commitment to what he believes to be his vocation, or to offer a vivid contrast to his character by satirizing those in power in the Church or state who would employ compromise and expediency.

At the beginning of Act One, high in the mountains, Brand is seen to reject, one by one, weakness of resolve represented by the mountain guide who will not risk crossing the mountain in bad weather; a lighthearted view of life represented by the artist Enjar, who dances with Agnes along the edge of a crevasse; and the wild emotionalism represented by the young mad-girl Gerd. Also introduced at this early point in the play is the "heavy weight," "the burden of being tied to another human being" which Brand has inherited from his early home-life and which is to colour his subsequent activity and his view of his relationship with God. During the following four acts we witness Brand's attempts to get closer to God by repeatedly avoiding the "burden" of close personal relationships. To follow this course needs enormous willpower and, in Act Two, Ibsen questions the necessity for such a total commitment to self-will in the words of the anonymous villager who replies to Brand's characteristically forceful assertion that man "cannot deny his calling. / He dares not block the river's course; / It forces its way towards the ocean," with the words, "Yet if it lost itself in marsh or lake, / It would reach the ocean in the end, as dew."

As the play progresses, Brand's commitment to what he believes to be the will of God leads first to the rejection of his mother; then to the sacrifice of his son who dies in consequence of Brand's refusal to leave the unhealthy valley in which he and his family are living; and finally to the death of Agnes, his wife, who, out of love, has constantly submitted herself to his will. Brand's experience is now transferred from the personal to the public world where he becomes involved, along with the mayor, in the construction of a new and grander church building. It is in this section of the play that Ibsen satirizes both the close interrelationship between the Norwegian Church and state and the national tendency to compromise, a feature of the play which angered or delighted contemporary Norwegians. Realizing that in building the new church he has sullied himself by his association with secular politics and has compromised his belief in "all or nothing," Brand inspires the townspeople to climb into the mountains in search of the "church of life" untarnished by secular concerns. The people are, however, incapable of such a rigorous faith. They turn against Brand, stone him, and return to their homes.

In the mountains, now deprived of both private and public human relationships, Brand again meets the young girl Gerd, who taunts him with his own deep-seated pride by calling him the messiah, "the Greatest of all." His hubris has, however, brought Brand to the "ice-church," a fitting image for his cold, loveless view of God's will. At this point Gerd shoots her rifle at her imagined tormenter, the hawk (variously interpreted as uncontrolled emotion or those things in life which we fear), and in so doing engulfs both herself and Brand in an avalanche of snow. Brand's final words are to ask God, "If not by Will, how can man be redeemed?" The reply offers the ultimate negation of his way of life. "He is the God of Love," replies a disembodied voice through the thunder of the avalanche. Redemption, it seems, cannot be found in the cold abstraction of the Will but, as Agnes sought unsuccessfully to teach her husband, only in the warmth of human love.

—D. Keith Peacock

BREAD AND WINE (Brot und Wein)
Poem by Friedrich Hölderlin, 1806 (written 1800–01)

"Bread and Wine" is in the strict formal sense an elegy, written in elegiac distichs or couplets of a hexameter followed by a pentameter. Each of the nine strophes has nine of these distichs, except the seventh, which has only eight. It is an elegy in a less technical sense, too, being a lament for the human condition. The emotions it communicates range between despair at the loss of a civilization viewed as ideal (ancient Greece), and ecstatic hope for escape from a dark and disappointing present into an ideal future. Both poles are a form of longing. Yet far from being straightforwardly escapist, "Bread and Wine" is characterized by a tenacious allegiance to this present and by the recognition that we must in the meantime ("indessen") make do.

The evocation in the first strophe of the coming of night and the stillness of the city seems self-contained (it was published separately in 1807 as "Night"). But it begins already to adumbrate around the idea of memory the tensions that the rest of the poem will articulate, and functions as a prologue or overture. Contained within the becalmed features of the vesperal town are the residues of its daylight activities—and it is not quite sleeping, for the bells chime, fountains continue to play, and lovers, a solitary man with thoughts of his youth, and a watchman are awake to experience night.

Night is "the Stranger," simultaneously "scarcely concerned about us," and unfathomably controlling the aspirations of mankind. Like Friedrich Hölderlin's philhellene friend Heinse, the poem's dedicatee, most of us are more comfortable with daylight, but (Hölderlin argues that the mystery of night, too, is worthy of contemplation. She grants "forgetting and sacred intoxication" and at the same time "sacred remembering," and this contradiction is the impetus for a creative relationship with past and present, and the production of "the forward-rushing word," or poetry.

Being wakeful at night is the condition of visionary enthusiasm, the will to search for "*ein Eigenes*" (something of our own). And this, in the third strophe, is sought in ancient Greece, in specific locations: the Isthmus of Corinth, Parnassus, Olympus, Thebes, all foci of myth. The ecstatic vision overlaps into the next strophe, but after four lines is punctured with the realization of loss. Now, as the poet writes, none of the attributes of Greek life obtain any longer: "But where are the thrones? where are the temples, and the vessels filled with nectar, and where are the songs for the pleasure of the gods?" (lines 59–60).

Here Friedrich Hölderlin's poem manifests for a moment the trembling equipoise of lament and celebration, and sudden grief at the passing of Greek civilization tips over into the re-creative memory of the presence of divinity in Greek life. The loss is real, but the joy at its memory is equally real. Then in the fifth strophe what was specific to that past takes on the characteristics of human life in general: mankind, not only the Ancients, responds with joy to the presence of the divine in his life—"This is man" (line 87). An inevitable and natural component of this response is poetry: "Now words for this must grow, like flowers" (line 90).

The generic returns gradually to the specific in the first eight lines of strophe six, which describe the rise of Greek civilization as the need to honour these present gods—and again, the sense of past glory shifts to a painful sense of present loss. These transitions always obey the natural rhythms of the emotions, not the formal divisions of the strophes. The overall structure of the poem makes use of these overlaps as subtly as the individual lines of verse make use of enjambment, rhythmic variation, and repetition to convey the suppleness and dynamism of the poet's feelings.

Where the feelings require it, however, the breaks between strophes articulate the sense of a close. The end of the sixth strophe announces the advent of the last god, this time in human form, to put an end to the celebrations. This god/man is reminiscent of Christ, but also of the wine-god Dionysus (also born of a divine father and a mortal mother). The isolation of man at this point is expressed temporally and spatially—modern men are late-comers to Greek culture, arriving after the party is over, so to speak; the gods are still there, but stay overhead in their heaven. They are eternal and, like night, seem to care little whether or not we live on (lines 111–12). The situation of the lovers, the solitary and the night-watchmen in the dark (strophe 1) is symbolically the same as that of modern man in a post-Greek world: mindful of a lost past; hopeful of a glorious future; needful of something to cling to in the meantime. That something is simultaneously their memory and their hope:

> Then life consists in dreaming of the gods. But mad wandering helps, like sleep, and deprivation and the night make us strong until enough heroes have grown up in the iron cradle, with hearts full of power to match those on high like before.
>
> (lines 115–18)

This "meantime" is a precarious and confusing state—and the poet is sure neither of what to do nor of what to say, is not even sure of the function of poets in these lean years: "wozu Dichter in dürftiger Zeit?"

This is a low point, when the hope of regeneration is obscured by the difficulties of survival, but like every emotion in "Bread and Wine" it is not final. Hölderlin reflects that poets are the priests of the wine-god Dionysus, and their function is to remind man that Christ-Bacchus left behind gifts of bread and wine which are tokens of the past and continuing existence of divinity. They were left at the end of the day—recalling both the Last Supper and the fading daylight of Greek civilization. David Constantine in *Hölderlin* (1988) most clearly stresses how a fruitful reading will not restrict itself to decoding the religious mythological references, but will focus on the "consoling, reconciling and mediating" function of the god.

The last strophe reaffirms the poet's task of announcing the reconciliation of day with night and heaven with earth, using a mixture of Biblical and mythological images. The hymn of anticipation is tempered at the very end where the soul's joy becomes a smile—only a smile, but a smile all the same. Mankind has not left the confusion of the present, he still lacks the glory of Greece and light, but even if the gates from Hell are not flung open, their guardian Cerberus is dozing and there is hope yet.

—Robert Vilain

BREAD AND WINE (Pane e vino)
Novel by Ignazio Silone, 1937

Bread and Wine, Ignazio Silone's second novel, centres on the crisis of conscience of Pietro Spina, a Communist activist who returns from exile to foment resistance to the Fascist government among the peasants of the Abruzzi. In the background of that (partly autobiographical) crisis are two bleakly emblematic historical moments in 1935: Stalin's purges in the Soviet Union, the debasement of a revolutionary dream; and the invasion of Ethiopia by Italy, the apogee of Benito Mussolini's dictatorship. But Spina's journey of self-questioning is as much ethical and spiritual as political. His return to

the Abruzzi is also an admission of his sense of belonging to his native area, and a coming to terms with the religiosity of his youth. Spina's political and ethical path emerges in relation to that of his old teacher Don Benedetto, a much-loved priest ostracized for his calm recalcitrance towards the regime. Both men met ultimately in a humanistic religion shorn of its judgemental and ritualistic elements, and in a political commitment whose strength is in individual ethics rather than in collective organization.

When we first encounter Spina, he is ill and being sheltered from the authorities in a stable. Don Benedetto, through a doctor who is another of his old pupils, arranges for Spina to be disguised as a priest and taken to the isolated village of Pietrasecca to recuperate. In his vestments, Spina adopts a different name (Paolo Spada) and a different identity which, paradoxically, allows him to rediscover aspects of his own personality. The peasants' expectations of him as priest expose his moral frailty and yet gradually strengthen both his understanding of their lives and his sense of responsibility towards others. Passing through the village of Fossa dei Marsi on his journey to Pietrasecca, Spina offers words of comfort to a girl dying from the after-effects of a self-induced abortion. As we later discover, the girl recovers and her initial adulation of the "priest" matures into mutual trust.

In Pietrasecca, Spina stays at an inn run by Matalena, a widow who regards the priest's presence in her establishment as a blessing and conspires with an old witch to concoct spells to keep him there. Matalena's superstitious version of Christianity is one of many cameos of peasant life in the novel. Spina also develops an intense platonic relationship with Cristina, the daughter of a wealthy family fallen on hard times, who feels the calling to become a nun. The only way in which Spina can fully express his feelings for Cristina is in the imaginary dialogues he writes in his diary, dialogues in which he also analyses the transformation he is undergoing.

Hampered by his disguise, Spina is frustrated in his attempts at political activity in Pietrasecca. He returns to Rome to renew his contacts with the underground communist movement. But in dialogue with Battipaglia, a party functionary, Spina's doubts emerge, notably as regards to the conformist response of the revolutionaries to events in the Soviet Union. A visit to an embittered old comrade, Uliva, further deepens Spina's disenchantment: Uliva has reached the conclusion that all revolutions are destined to end in dictatorship. Later that day, Spina learns that Uliva has killed both himself and his wife by setting off explosives with which he had been intending to carry out an attack. Despite this, Spina still hopes to take an insurgent back to the Abruzzi with him, and goes in search of Murica, a young student from his own village. Spina's final encounter in Rome is with Murica's ex-girlfriend, Annina, who tells the harrowing story of being callously abandoned by Murica after her attempt to protect him from arrest had resulted in her being raped by the police.

Spina returns to Fossa dei Marsi, where he witnesses the celebrations for the outbreak of the Ethiopian war. His disgust is so strong that, during the night, he daubs anti-war graffiti around the village. The resulting public outcry and police investigation are diverted only with the help of false rumours put about by some young people sympathetic to him. Following a relapse in his medical condition, Spina decides to leave the area, but arranges to visit Don Benedetto before he goes. During their brief but emotional reunion, the priest reassures Spina of the importance of what he is doing, and that his distance from the faith is only a "banal misunderstanding." On Spina's return to Pietrasecca, the student Murica visits him on Don

Benedetto's prompting, and relates his own version of his story: he was threatened into collaborating with the police against his comrades. Murica then tells of his return to his native village and to a form of Christianity as the basis for his politics. Spina subsequently learns of Murica's murder by the police. At Pietrasecca, Spina also renews his relationship with Cristina, who has changed her plans to become a nun and in part revised her beliefs following family tragedy. While visiting Murica's family, Spina learns that his disguise has been exposed. Pausing only to deliver his diary to Cristina, he takes to the hills. On learning of Spina's true identity and feelings, Cristina follows him with food, wine, and clothes, only to be brought to exhaustion by the freezing weather and the arduous path. As she says her final prayers, a wolf closes in.

The novel's ending is an attempt to lift Cristina into a dimension of symbolic self-sacrifice, but it arguably only confirms her as a version of certain Christian stereotypes of women as victim, a model of virginal saintliness. *Bread and Wine* has also been criticized for naivety, and impracticality in its rejection of all forms of political organization. The book's effectiveness is largely dependent on certain episodes which the device of a revolutionary disguised as a priest allows Silone to create: Spina's politicized intervention in a game of cards; the bland complicity with the regime of the lawyer Zabaglia, once a socialist oratorical firebrand; Spina's meetings with a mendicant friar and a local priest. The imperviousness of the peasants to the state's propaganda emerges in several telling scenes.

The title *Bread and Wine* summarizes the dominant themes of Spina's journey. Its biblical associations are well known. Bread and wine are also used as images of local belonging. The Italian title of the book's second version, *Vino e pane* (''wine and bread''), in reversing a commonplace, perhaps suggests the prioritization of the communality symbolized by wine over the fulfilment of need symbolized by bread. Under Fascist rule, the simple acts of generosity in which wine is offered acquire a greater human significance.

—John Dickie

BRENNU-NJÁLS SAGA

See NJÁLS SAGA

THE BRIDGE ON THE DRINA (Na Drini ćuprija)
Novel by Ivo Andrić, 1945

The Bridge on the Drina consists of a 400-year chronicle, covering the period from the moment in 1516 when the future bridge is first imagined by the ten-year-old child ultimately responsible for building it, up to the partial destruction of the bridge during World War I. In between the narrator tells of the bridge's construction, of the human dramas that it witnesses, of the historical events that affect the nearby regions most directly, and of the manner in which the bridge itself comes to influence the lives of those who live near it.

Like most of Ivo Andrić's fiction, *The Bridge on the Drina* deals with Bosnia's past. His ''protagonist'' is an actual stone bridge in the city of Višegrad. Much of what is described in the novel follows historical fact closely: there really was a Bosnian peasant's son who

was pressed into the service of the Ottoman court; having risen to become grand vizier, he then ordered the building of this bridge in the land of his origin. Bosnia itself remained under Turkish rule until the late 19th century, though the empire's decline—indirectly but effectively portrayed throughout the novel—caused shifts in power toward the nearby Christian countries. Of central concern to the novel is the religious and ethnic mix of Višegrad—primarily Moslem and Orthodox Christian, but also with a few Jews and, particularly after Austrian influence grew, Roman Catholics as well. Decades of peaceful if at times uneasy co-existence are regularly swept away by the passions arising from distant events. In this sense, the novel turned out to be tragically prescient of the events that would follow the break-up of modern Yugoslavia and the civil war that once again wreaked havoc on this region.

The book therefore reminds its modern readers that the death and suffering of most recent times have their origins in the past. During the bridge's construction Christian peasants are forced to work to the point of exhaustion, and the impalement of one of them, who has tried to sabotage the Moslem-led effort, is described in clinical detail. Later, in the 19th century, the bridge is regularly adorned with the heads of those accused of being involved with a Serbian revolt against the Turks. Much of what the bridge witnesses involves the cruelty and harshness of people toward others.

While wars and natural disasters bring suffering to the inhabitants of Višegrad, the bridge stands seemingly aloof, above and apart from the tragedies of individual lives. It outlasts the humans that come and go, and appears to stand for continuity, for an almost reassuring sameness and durability. These qualities are emphasized again and again by the narrator, who seems more concerned with the course of history than with the lives of the fragile and often undeserving mortals who live near the bridge.

Andrić's achievement is to undercut the outlook of his own third-person narrator and to offer a much more sensitive and profound view of human nature. One of the negative figures is a schoolmaster who himself keeps a chronicle of life in the town, but it remains only a few pages long, since to him virtually no event is of sufficient importance to be included. To Andrić, though, any event, whether small or large, that distinguishes good from evil, or inner strength from moral weakness, is significant. Humans can be and often are cruel, but evil exists in this book as the backdrop against which more noble deeds occur.

Some of the grandest actions are, in keeping with the narrator's view, carried out by historically notable people: the novel judges the decision of Mehmed Pasha to build the bridge positively, despite the hardship that he unwittingly inflicts on many. However, much attention is paid to those more ordinary people who show a capability for change, who turn out to be either better or worse than their past actions would lead others to expect. Of all the young Serbian men who meet on the bridge shortly before World War I it is the least prepossessing of these, a person whose own grandfather (another figure in the novel) had died in a lunatic asylum, who goes off to fight the Austrians. History itself seems to recognize and record good or brave actions and to punish evil. Thus Radisav, the person who had been sabotaging the construction of the bridge, lives on in legend. Meanwhile the man responsible for capturing and executing him goes insane, and the narrator, for all his meticulousness, is able to identify him only as the ''Plevljak,'' the man from Plevlje. His name has been obliterated by history, while Radisav's survives.

The Bridge on the Drina is, then, ultimately concerned with individual lives and individual fates; the story of the bridge provides an opportunity not just for a meditation on historical events but even more for an examination of the moral issues illustrated by the characters who come and go throughout the novel. Not by chance, Andrić devotes the final two-thirds of his novel to the last 35 or so years that it covers. In this way he is able to develop a few characters in greater depth and to draw careful parallels between some of the earlier figures and those with whom he deals toward the end.

The lessons that he thereby presents are perhaps best illustrated by Alihodja Mutevelić, who gradually comes to the fore. A member of the family that for centuries had served as guardians of the bridge, he is nailed to the bridge by his ear for refusing to support the resistance to the Austrian takeover in chapter 9, and in the last chapter, 24, he dies just after a pier of the bridge is blown up in the war. It turns out, despite the narrator's belief in immutability, that nothing is forever. Alihodja, a person who seems to have lived in harmony with life's flow and to have accepted the inevitable changes, views the bridge's missing span. His last thought is that, despite everything, people of exalted soul who would make the world a better place cannot have vanished from the earth, for if they were to do so then the love of God would not exist either. This faith—that good people and the memory of goodness will endure—runs throughout the novel and constitutes perhaps the most salient moral to be drawn from the story of the bridge on the Drina.

—Barry P. Scherr

THE BROKEN JUG (Der zerbrochene Krug)
Play by Heinrich von Kleist, 1808

The Broken Jug (begun in Berne in 1803 and completed in Königsberg in 1806) was the outcome of a literary contest between Heinrich von Kleist and three other young writers now forgotten, Heinrich Zschokke, Ludwig Wieland, and Heinrich Gessner. The four friends had agreed to write, respectively, a comedy, a short story, a verse satire, and a poetic idyll on the topic of an etching entitled *Le juge; ou, la cruche cassée* [The Judge or Broken Jug] by Jean Jacques Le Veau after a late 18th-century painting by Louis Philibert Debucourt which, in its turn, was based on Jean Baptiste Creuze's celebrated rococo painting *La cruche cassée*. It was Kleist who won the prize, giving the German theatre one of its rare comic masterpieces.

Adapting the French model to the style of the Flemish painter David Teniers, Kleist sets his play in a Dutch village at the end of the 17th century. The peasant woman Marthe Rull accuses Ruprecht, a young farmer engaged to her daughter Eve, of breaking the eponymous jug during a nocturnal visit to Eve's bedroom. Supervised by a visiting government inspector, the judge Adam is forced to conduct an investigation which reveals that he himself broke the jug when, caught by Ruprecht in the act of trying to seduce Eve, he escaped through her window, losing his wig and being hit over the head in the process. In due course Adam is sacked and Ruprecht and Eve are united but Marthe, with the jug still broken, is left to appeal to a higher court for any compensation.

The 13 consecutive scenes form a drama of detection which strictly observes the classical unities of time, place, and action as it uncovers, in analytical fashion, the events of the recent past. Kliest depicts contemporary German village life, thinly disguised by the remote setting, through accurately drawn rustic characters and a dialogue

which, though cast in stylized blank verse, is rich in everyday speech rhythms, popular proverbs, colloquialisms, and dialect terms. Parodying Sophocles's *Oedipus Rex* in the manner of Aristophanes, with echoes of Shakespeare's *Measure for Measure* and the Bible, he operates simultaneously at several levels of meaning. He derives broadly farcical comedy from the plight of the corrupt judge who, despite all evasions and subterfuges, is ironically driven to convict himself of the crime under investigation. The comedy element is emphasized by coarse references to bodily functions and beatings; the mock heroic treatment of trivialities and the mock epic breadth of detail within the tightly woven plot; and above all by a dynamic language that conveys his concerns mimetically rather than discursively, turning confusion itself into art by the brilliant acts of original syntactical and onomatopoeic effects, significant puns and quibbles, nagging questions and counter-questions, and extended metaphors that have a habit of assuming an exuberantly autonomous existence of their own. For all the merriment, however, the judge constantly betrays his tragic doubts and fears.

At a social and political level, Adam's abuse of his office embodies, in grotesque distortion, Kleist's critique of Prussian jurisdiction, while the shattered picture on the jug, which showed the Emperor Charles V handing the Netherlands over to his son Phillip II, playfully suggests his distress at the disintegration of the Holy Roman Empire and at the subjugation of fragmented Germany in the Napoleonic era. At a religious level, varying the myth of creation, Kleist associates Eve's purity with the innocence of Paradise, and Adam's villainy with the fall of man and with the devil himself. At a philosophical level the court hearing, which is the most sustained example of Kleist's favourite device of cross-examination, dramatizes the search for knowledge which lies at the heart of all his writings. Eve, in particular, is thrown into a painful dilemma by Ruprecht's suspicions about her fidelity and Adam's threats to send Ruprecht to war if she exposes his advances. Her demand for absolute trust represents Kleist's recurrent plea for the supremacy of intuition over reason and for a belief transcending the evidence of the senses and the conclusions of the intellect, a longing contradicted by grave misgivings since his famous "Kant crisis" of 1801, when he decided that objective truth was inaccessible to the human mind with its inescapably subjective categories of perception. The misunderstandings and errors engulfing all the characters, whether involuntary or deliberately induced, proclaim his despair over what he saw as the inability of thought and language to penetrate an enigmatic universe and to provide genuine communication between its baffled inhabitants. Although in this instance the truth is finally discovered, Kleist's scepticism, underlined by the open ending of Marthe's quest for compensation, persists as a dark background to the laughter.

The first performance in Weimar on 2 March 1808, directed by Goethe, proved a failure. Goethe himself claimed that the play, with its "otherwise witty and humorous subject matter," lacked "a swiftly executed action," while a member of the local aristocracy, Henriette von Knebel, described it as "tasteless," "boring," and suffering from "moral leprosy." The real causes of the failure, however, are more likely to have been Goethe's division of the continuous sequence of episodes into three separate acts, stilted classical acting, and the audience's conventional squeamishness. By the mid-19th century the realistic aspects of the play had begun to be appreciated, and Friedrich Hebbel, for one, described it as "one of those works against which only the audience can fail." More recently, it has been applauded for its expressive language, its sociopolitical implications, and its metaphysical questionings. Obliquely reflecting Kleist's serious preoccupations through its light-hearted surface, *The Broken Jug* is unlikely to lose the secure position it now holds in the German repertoire.

—Ladislaus Löb

THE BRONZE HORSEMAN (Medny vsadnik)
Poem by Aleksandr Pushkin, 1837 (written 1833)

Aleksandr Pushkin's epic poem *The Bronze Horseman* was written at the peak of his creativity in 1833 and ranks as one of his greatest works. Apart from all its literary virtues, it has mythopoeic significance as it produces the archetypal account of the myth of St. Petersburg, which has not lost its vitality today. The poem is named after an equestrian statue of the city's founder, Peter the Great. The statue was commissioned by Catherine the Great and is the work of the French sculptor Falconet. The figure is seated on a mounting horse facing west; it symbolizes the aspiration of Peter and his successors to westernize Russia. The city of St. Petersburg came to be built as a result of this desire causing a rift among Russians. All important dichotomies of the myth of the city and its founder inform the poem: European splendour and Russian poverty; urban civilization and unsuitable climatic conditions; irreparable animosity and conflict of interests between fathers and sons.

Comprised of an epigraph, a prologue, and two parts, *The Bronze Horseman* combines the assuredness of expression and the technical maturity of a classic with the freshness of the beginnings of a literary tradition. In a manner reminiscent of 17th-century and early 18th-century fiction, Pushkin assures his reader in the epigraph that the narrative is "based on truth." Then a many-voiced text follows with both inter- and intra-textual dialogic features, heralding not only classic realism but also the literature of modernity. The author-narrator has two personae in the poem. We hear the first of these in the prologue which acquaints us with Peter, his cause, and his city. The first time he is referred to, the narrator uses the pronoun "he" instead of his name as though he were describing a divine figure. Peter is praised for having Petersburg built. Besides the city's strategic importance in stopping foreign invasion, it also serves as a "window to the west." In the light of the whole poem, this metaphor summarizes the duality of the city: a window allows those inside to see the outside world but also allows the uninvited destructive forces to sneak in. But the narrator, for the time being, sings his panegyric: the impressive city grew out of the barely inhabited landscape in a short time and its beauty puts Moscow—the old capital—to shame.

In the introduction to Part One, the narrator's tone changes suddenly. As he describes a dreadful flood in the city, his enthusiasm disappears completely. His poetic imagery becomes threatening: the river Neva, like an invalid, is restless in her bed; the rain keeps lashing the window angrily. The narrator's focus on Peter's greatness shifts to a new hero, Evgenii. He suggests that he is fond of, and familiar with, the name and thus overtly links *The Bronze Horseman* with Evgenii Onegin. Unlike Onegin, however, Evgenii is poor and undistinguished; his surname is irrelevant since he is presented as a type rather than as an individual. He is the quintessential "little man" who works as a clerk and has the most modest of plans: to marry his beloved Parasha and raise a small family. But the city frustrates his plans. His bride lives with her mother on the islands by the sea, divided from Evgenii by the bridges. These have been lifted: the river is flooding, destroying low-lying areas, basements, and ground floors. The poorer people live here and their possessions and lives are in jeopardy. The Tsar and the wealthy look upon the devastation from their residences upstairs where the rising waters do not reach. As Evgenii sits paralyzed with fear for the well-being of Parasha under a marble lion across from the Bronze Horseman, Peter, with profound indifference, looks at the devastation of the city he founded against the odds of nature. Now the narrator calls him an "idol," suggesting that Peter was self-serving and tyrannical when he ordered the construction of his diabolical city.

Part Two concludes the tragedy of the little man. Parasha's house and the people in it have been washed away by the flood waters. In the meantime, the city is only too quick to forget the disaster of many: it resumes its ordinary ways. Evgenii goes insane, loses his job, and becomes homeless, roaming the streets of the city. The narrator has come full circle from the beginning of the poem: his sympathy is entirely with Evgenii, who threatens the ominous statue of the city's founder. The Bronze Horseman, in turn, chases his unfortunate, mad subject for whose predicament he is responsible, along the empty city streets. Evgenii is found abandoned and dead at the place where his beloved used to live.

Of all Russian literature, perhaps this poem has been the most influential. It generated the powerful themes of the "little man" of the conflict between the westernized bureaucrats and the plebeian citizens of St. Petersburg, of the fantastic city in which human aspirations come to nought. *The Bronze Horseman* already bears many distinguishing features of the Russian psychological realism that produced the greatest 19th-century novels. Following in Pushkin's footsteps, Tolstoi developed the theme of contrasting Moscow and Petersburg; the alienated and victimized character had a great impact on Dostoevskii, and the mysterious elements directly influenced Gogol' and, later, Belyi. The poem's significance transcends the boundaries of its national literature: Pushkin is one of the earliest European writers to look at the impersonal metropolis from the viewpoint of the homeless and dispossessed.

—Peter I. Barta

THE BROOM (La ginestra)
Poem by Giacomo Leopardi, 1845 (written 1836)

Although lacking the melodiousness of many of his shorter lyrics "The Broom, or, The Flower of the Desert," a long poem of 317 lines written at the end of his life, stands as a valid example of fluent philosophical reasoning in which Giacomo Leopardi embraces a grand overview of history and all life, as he argues the case for a moral way of living through humility, perseverance, and unselfconscious honesty at the level of individual consciousness. Published only posthumously in the 1845 edition of his work prepared by his close friend Antonio Ranieri, the poem's placement at the end of the collection was apparently a recognition of its epithetic qualities. It deals with themes, recurrent throughout Leopardi's poetry, such as death, the insignificance of humanity, the power of Nature, history, and the role of the poet in society.

The poem's setting is the volcano of Mount Vesuvius which is seen as symbolizing Nature in all its impassively destructive fury. From the outset, the poet also focuses on his sighting of the scented flower on the volcano's desolate slopes; a flower which, in its turn, symbolizes life in the midst of death. As with many external objects and human figures in Leopardi's poetry, the broom flower transmutes into a more private, emotive symbol for the poet, assuming a consoling significance for a sombre, dejected mind:

> I meet you here once more, O you the lover
> Of all sad places and deserted worlds,
> The constant comrade of afflicted fortune.

(translated by John Heath-Stubbs)

By the end of the poem the plant is emblematized, becoming more than a mere scent or vision, provoking more than a sentimental response as it comes to evoke the most perfect existential attitude, as the poet sees it; a dignified resignation in the face of life's constant adversity (seen in the impending menace of the live volcano that will eventually destroy the broom's fragile beauty):

> And you, O gentle broom,
> Who with your fragrant thickets
> Make beautiful this spoiled and wasted land,
> You, too, must shortly fall beneath the cruel
> Force of the subterranean fire, returning
> To this, its wonted place,
> Which soon shall stretch its greedy fringe above
> Your tender shrubs. You then
> Will bend your harmless head, not obstinate
> Beneath the rod of fate. . .

(translated by John Heath-Stubbs)

For Leopardi, a passionately idealistic poet with an equally pessimistic outlook, this singular affirmation of enduring life—the image of the broom—represented a significant progress in the development of his philosophy. In other poems, Leopardi often swung between extremes, exalting life's virtuous offerings like youth, love, and peace but then denouncing its deceptions in which the promise of youth could be cut down by an early death, or love could be shown as an illusion through rejection. In ''The Broom,'' a process of reasoning leads the poet to formulate a balanced attitude to survive the extremes. It is a mature conclusion that, not surprisingly, made the broom an enduring symbol of Leopardi's own dedication to the poetical task.

This maturity extends to Leopardi's view of humanity which was promulgated in opposition to the politics and religious ideologies of his time. His view of a materialistic universe was obviously a rejection of Restoration values in which a Catholic perspective dominated, with its emphasis on the transcendental significance of life. But his was also, and even more so, a criticism of the liberal-moderate position which denied the importance of transcendent value systems such as those proposed by conventional religion, but still advanced its own humanistic credo which emphasized the exclusiveness of man. Leopardi saw this as an arrogant assertion whose irrational fervour misrepresented the truth of things. The sarcasm with which he decried liberalism's blind belief in the ''magnificent / Progressive destiny of Humankind'' (John Heath-Stubbs), despite the evidence of the relentless destruction of civilizations through history (and Leopardi offers the example of Pompeii in the poem), is a

measure of how strong was Leopardi's sense of disassociation from his time.

The Leopardian poet stands alone with his sense of ''deep contempt'' while accepting the ''oblivion'' his age may sentence him too for his non-conformity. In his own lifetime Leopardi was, however, recognized as one of the great literary figures of his age. In this attitude we may see both Leopardi's passion and, ironically, a certain ingenuous arrogance of his own. Still, in confirmation of his relevance, of his modernism, Leopardi's view of humanity's place in the scheme of things accords closely with our own which is induced by a new, more moral and expansive scientific culture than the mechanistic and reductionist one that existed in the 19th century; one which affirms now not man's centrality but humankind's precious smallness in the mystery which is Space.

Leopardi illustrates his position perhaps most graphically through the image of the apple casually falling on the ants' carefully constructed nest, thereby destroying it. Human beings, Leopardi says, are like the ants, Nature showing ''no more care / Or value for man's need / Than for the ants.''

In the final analysis, Leopardi indirectly and metaphorically suggests a humble role for the poet as well, which is consistent with his humbling definition of humanity. It is encapsulated in one of his descriptions of the broom flower:

> . . . O courteous flower,
> As if in pity of the doom of others,
> And cast a pleasant fragrance to the skies,
> Making the desert glad.

Poetry such as Leopardi's, struggling its way to a sympathetic but still honest assessment of life, could be seen to parallel in its significance for the reader the assuaging effects of the scent and vision of the broom seen on the dark, barren slopes of a volcano by the observer. One of Leopardi's merits was an ability to see reason and meaning in his own nihilism, and so to survive it and triumph over it.

—Walter Musolino

THE BROTHERS (Adelphoe)
Play by Terence, 160 BC

The Brothers (the Latin title *Adelphoe* is a transliteration of the Greek word for brothers), Terence's final and most famous play, was first produced in Rome at the funeral games of Lucius Aemilius Paullus in 160 BC. It is a version of a lost Greek play, Menander's *Second Adelphoi* which takes its title from two contrasting pairs of brothers from successive generations in the same family.

At the start of the play one of the elder pair of brothers, Micio, sets the scene and explains the underlying situation. Micio, an urban and urbane Athenian, is the brother of Demea, a hard-working, strict, puritanical countryman. Demea fathered two sons and because of poverty handed over the elder one, Aeschinus, to be brought up in town by his bachelor brother, while himself bringing up in the country the younger son, Ctesipho. Micio tells us of his own ideas on how to bring up a son and of how they contrast with those of his brother. He believes that sons should be won over by kindness, not cowed by terror. As Aeschinus has grown up and reached young manhood Micio has turned a blind eye to his misdemeanours while encouraging him to confide in him and to treat him as a friend. Demea, on the other hand, cannot abide what he sees as Micio's indulgence and is a much stricter father to Ctesipho.

Presently Micio has the first of several confrontations with Demea who arrives bringing the bad news that Aeschinus is in trouble again for stealing a girl from a whoremonger. It is the talk of the town. Micio remains calm but once he is alone admits to some anxiety. He believed Aeschinus had given up this sort of thing, and had even mentioned marriage. We soon discover, however, that the girl has not been abducted for Aeschinus' personal pleasure, but on behalf of the lovesick Ctesipho. Aeschinus has amatory problems of his own. Nine months earlier, when drunk, he raped Pamphila, the daughter of their next-door neighbour Sostrata, and the girl is expecting a child. Despite Micio's parental leniency, this is a matter he could not bring himself to reveal to his adoptive father.

The action of the play consists of the resolution of the problems regarding these amatory affairs. After some misunderstandings all ends well with Aeschinus doing the right thing by Pamphila, and the baby born during the course of the play having the prospect of being brought up as a legitimate Athenian. It is Micio who takes charge when he finds out about Aeschinus' affairs from Sostrata's spokesman Hegio, and sees to it that the marriage will take place. Demea spends most of the play in a fog of misapprehension, hearing of and imparting bad news and being sent on fool's errands. His blind confidence in Ctesipho's virtue makes him putty in the hands of the clever household slave Syrus. The play ends with Aeschinus' marriage in progress and with the assurance that Ctesipho can live with his girlfriend on Demea's farm.

How close the Latin play is to the Greek is, as always in the discussion of Latin drama, a matter of controversy. Terence himself, through his prologue speaker, admits that he has incorporated into the Menander play a scene from another play by another dramatist: *The Suicide Pact* by Diphilus. This slapstick scene, which occurred at the beginning of Diphilus' play, follows the opening confrontation between Demea and Micio. In it the girl is brought to Micio's house by Aeschinus and the slave Parmeno. The whoremonger, Sannio, attempts to claim her back and receives a beating for his pains. In performance, perhaps, the scene is accommodated to its context and does not trouble the spectator. The reader, however, will find it strange that an incident which took place the previous night and is already the talk of the town should be prolonged into the morning. It is easier to imagine it as the immediate aftermath of the break-in taking place outside the pimp's house.

The most controversial feature of the play is its ending and here too there is evidence that Terence has altered what was in his original. Totally defeated in the battle for his sons' affections, Demea in a monologue reflects on how his stern moral attitudes and strict conduct have brought about the situation: his brother's amiability has meant that he has complete control over the sons. Demea tells the audience that he will change his ways and imitate his brother, that *he* will now be genial and generous. He becomes affable to those he had treated brusquely before. His acts of generosity, however, turn out to be at Micio's expense. In order to prevent any delay to the wedding Demea gives instructions for the wall dividing the two houses to be broken down and the households united. He ensures that Syrus and Hegio are rewarded. The culmination of this generosity is the forcing of Micio to take as his wife the 60-year-old Sostrata. In a volte-face at the very

end of the play Demea announces that he has been acting as he has to show up the shallowness of Micio's conduct. Micio has won his sons' affection by indulgence. If the boys want someone to advise them and keep them on the right track, Demea will always be there. Aeschinus appears to accept this.

This ending has shocked and, indeed, repelled many critics. How can it be that the ineffective, unsympathetic, and foolish Demea should turn the tables on Micio? Many have seen this as a sop to a Roman audience which would have found unacceptable an ending which endorsed liberal Greek values. The ancient commentator Donatus does indeed provide evidence for Terentian activity at the end of the play. He tells us that in the Greek play, Micio did not resist Demea's suggestion that he should marry Sostrata. There is also internal evidence to take into account. It is very hard to believe that Menander would have introduced the contradiction between Demea's monologue and his concluding speech. If Demea's activities in the last act were really designed to show up Micio, this would have been made clear in the monologue. What exactly happened in the Menander play is and will remain a matter for dispute. An attractive hypothesis is that Micio simply takes everything in his stride, accepting with equanimity all that Demea suggests. Demea's final speech does not ensure his triumph, but makes him look even more ridiculous. When Aeschinus agrees with what he says he is laughing at him. Micio's victory does not mean that he should be regarded as a kind of saint or a model moral educator. The play is not a philosophical tract about education. Neither father is entirely successful in dealing with his son; Micio merely displays more common sense.

Terence's changes hardly improve the play; however, his achievements do not lie in dramatic construction. His strengths rather are his command of the Latin language and mastery of dramatic dialogue. These enable him to keep faith with the subtlety and pathos of his original. The scene between Micio and Aeschinus is exquisitely rendered. In it Micio, fully aware that Aeschinus is involved with the girl and has been ashamed to reveal to him what he has done, after teasing him by inventing a fictitious legal dispute and an adjudication on the part of Micio which would mean that the girl would have to marry another, eventually reveals all and offers a gentle reproof. The scene is a considerable achievement for an author working in a literature that had only been in existence for 80 years.

—David M. Bain

THE BROTHERS KARAMAZOV (Brat'ia Karamazovy)
Novel by Fedor Dostoevskii, 1880

The Brothers Karamazov was Fedor Dostoevskii's last great novel, bringing to culmination many of the themes of his earlier fiction, such as the debate between religion and atheism, the battle between good and evil in the hearts of "broad" Russian characters, clashes of incompatible rival women, the ever-fascinating legal process, and, above all, Dostoevskii's longstanding attempts to create a "positively good man" capable of leading Russia's spiritual regeneration. Moreover, the three brothers seem to reflect the three main stages of the author's life: Dmitrii, his youthful Romantic period; Ivan, his attachment to atheistic socialist circles; and Alesha, his spiritually reborn post-Siberian period.

The longest of the novels, *The Brothers Karamazov* is also one of the most tightly constructed, topographically exact (the town of

Skotoprigonevsk is closely modelled on Staraia Russa where Dostoevskii spent his last years), and chronologically compact: the main action of the book takes place over a period of only three days, but with much interleaving of narration as we follow the lives of the three brothers in long, intercalated sections with a constant feeling of acceleration driving the action on. Each brother in turn, with the aid of significant dreams (and, in Ivan's case, delirium), learns important facts about himself and, for all the narration's pace, the reader shares a strong sense of epiphanic development.

The novel's main theme is the nature of fatherhood. On the one hand we have the saintly elder Zosima, a spiritual father to Alesha, the youngest brother; on the other the irresponsible, scheming, lecherous Fedor Karamazov, a father in the biological sense alone, whose possible murder is a topic of discussion from early in the book. This crime, once committed, provides a source of guilt for all of his sons: Alesha, the novice sent out into the world by Zosima, who for all his Christian goodness cannot avert the parricide; Dmitrii, cheated by his father and a rival for the favours of the amoral Grushenka; and Ivan, the haughty intellectual, spiritual descendant of Raskol'nikov, whose formula ''if God does not exist, then all is permitted'' falls onto the receptive ears of his bastard half-brother, the lackey Smerdiakov who, in fact, proves to be the actual perpetrator of the crime.

As a detective story this chronicle of small-town life is handled in masterly fashion with concatenations of circumstances and fatally coincidental sums of money all seeming to impugn the passionate Dmitrii, who is eventually tried and condemned. Rarely, if ever, has the tension of mounting circumstantial evidence been portrayed in such a gripping manner (Dostoevskii was inspired by a comparable real-life case). His response to the new legal system in Russia adds particular vividness to the description of the trial, in which not only Dmitrii, or even the Karamazov family, but effectively the whole of Russia is judged before the world.

The Brothers Karamazov was Dostoevskii's last attempt to create a ''positively good man.'' Father Zosima, though charismatic, is, perhaps, too pale and other-worldly for this role, but Alesha, through counselling distressed adults and children, gains authority as the novel progresses, and it is with him that the book ends. More memorable, however, is his brother Ivan's exposition of the reasons for rejecting God's world: the examples he adduces of gross cruelty to innocent children make his ''returning of the ticket'' to God very persuasive. His principal thought is expressed in the ''Legend of the Grand Inquisitor,'' a profound and disturbing meditation on Christianity, free will, and happiness, at the end of which Alesha kisses his brother, just as Christ had responded to the Inquisitor with a silent kiss. Subsequently Ivan's brilliant Euclidian mind proves unable to resist a mocking petty bourgeois devil and he falls into insanity. In the world of Dostoevskii's novels Christianity and the intellectual have a purely negative relationship.

Dmitrii, aware that his nature contains elements of both the Madonna and Sodom, shares his father's impulsive, passionate character but none of his cynicism or buffoonery. Dmitrii's romance with Grushenka, who also alternates between satanic pride and self-abasement, voluptuousness and spiritual sublimation, makes this one of the great love stories in all literature. Also fascinating are all three brothers' relations with two other mentally troubled women, Katerina Ivanovna and Liza Khokhlakova, revealing a disturbingly dark side of passion first seen in Igrok (The Gambler) but also encountered in ensuing novels, particularly The Idiot and The Devils. The depiction of these women's behaviour together with the parricide itself strongly attracted the professional interest of Sigmund Freud.

The Brothers Karamazov is a rich and fascinating text containing crime, passion, psychology, religion, and philosophy. It is indeed one of the great novels of the world.

—Arnold McMillin

THE BROTHERS MENAECHMUS (Menaechmi)
Play by Plautus, early 2nd century BC

Plautus' The Brothers Menaechmus is a classic exploitation of the old folktale motif of two twins being mistaken for each other. It is the only surviving play of Greek and Roman comedy which exploits this motif, although there will have been others now lost. The nearest surviving parallel is Plautus' Amphitryo, where Jupiter and Mercury take on the appearance of their human counterparts and similar confusions result. Menaechmi was one of the most popular plays of the Renaissance period, both in Latin and in vernacular versions, and it continued to be imitated by European dramatists down to the 18th century. In more recent times it has been successfully turned into a musical, The Boys from Syracuse. Its attraction lies partly in the neatness of its plot, partly in the comic possibilities to which Plautus puts the mistaken identities, and partly in its sheer inconsequentiality.

The plot is as follows. The Menaechmus brothers originate from Syracuse. The elder Menaechmus, who was kidnapped as a boy, grew up in Epidamnus and is now established there with a wife and household. Impatient of the demands of his dowried wife, he is having an affair with the courtesan next door, Erotium, and has stolen one of his wife's gowns to present to her. The younger, whose name has been changed from Sosicles to Menaechmus in memory of his lost brother, comes to Epidamnus to search for his twin with Messenio, a slave. He is taken for the elder Menaechmus, first by Erotium's cook Cylindrus, secondly by Erotium herself, who invites him in for lunch and postprandial sex and gives him the gown to take to the embroiderer's for alterations; next by Menaechmus' hangeron Peniculus, who is peeved at being excluded from the lunch; and finally by the wife and her father, who conclude from his denials that he has become insane and summon a doctor. Meanwhile the real Menaechmus has fallen foul not only of Peniculus and his wife but also of Erotium, to whom he denies having received the gown back for alterations. He finds himself questioned by the doctor, and is about to be hauled away for treatment when he is rescued by Messenio, who takes him for Sosicles. Finally Sosicles returns and the recognition is effected; the two brothers decide to go back together to Syracuse, leaving the wife behind.

The play is neatly constructed on the principles that the twins shall not meet until the final act; that they shall appear alternately; and that they shall interact with the same group of minor characters to the puzzlement of all. Closely analysed, the plot reveals an intricate symmetrical series of repetitions, inversions, and reversals, and throughout all the gown acts as a linking device, passing from the wife to Menaechmus to Erotium to Sosicles and (potentially at least) back to the wife at the end. The possession of the gown also serves to distinguish the two brothers visually, which would otherwise have been difficult if we assume identical masks and costumes. The audience has to use its wits, but other clues of identification are skilfully built into the structure: Menaechmus' offstage entrances are always from the town (conventionally audience's right) and Sosicles' from the harbour (audience's left); Menaechmus tends to enter with sung or recited monologues, whereas Sosicles enters in ordinary conversation. In a play of this kind, the confusion of identities by the on-stage characters and the superior knowledge of the spectators are everything. It scarcely matters that the brothers are kept apart solely by chance, and even the more serious improbability that Sosicles, mistaken by everybody for someone else, does not perceive that this someone is his long-lost twin is readily overlooked.

The Menaechmi has much in common with the typical farce, although that word does not do justice to its comparative refinement. There are two splendid scenes of broad visual comedy: one when Sosicles, accused of insanity by the wife and father, pretends to be insane, mounting an imaginary charger under the inspiration of Bacchus and Apollo and uttering suitably paratragic language; the other when Messenio and Menaechmus use fisticuffs and eye-gouging to beat off the pack of slaves trying to drag the latter away for treatment. The essence of the humour remains the dramatic irony of mistaken identity. On the other hand, there is no real characterization beyond the traditional stereotypes, and although some have tried to find one, no real theme or moral. Neither the infidelity of Menaechmus nor the opportunism of Sosicles is condemned, and the potential symbolic implications of the search for the lost twin and his final restoration to his family are overshadowed by the comic aspects of the treatment. It can be argued that the play centres on the opposition between duty and pleasure, represented for Menaechmus by his wife and Erotium but, since in the end he is rejected by (and rejects) both, it is not clear what the moral of this would be. Rather, the play reflects the holiday atmosphere of the festival at which it was performed, when questions of morality could be laid aside for the moment, and in this lies its charm.

Although the Greek original of *Menaechmi* cannot now be identified, certain elements of the play can be recognized as Plautine, notably the extended role of Peniculus and the setpiece "songs" which in some sense replace the choral interludes of the Greek. The comparison of *Menaechmi* with its most famous imitation, Shakespeare's *Comedy of Errors*, is also instructive. Shakespeare has toned down the immorality and opportunism of the two brothers, made the wife a much more sympathetic character, and given the play a romantic frame by introducing the father of the twins at the beginning and uniting him with his long-lost wife at the end. He has also, taking a hint from Plautus' *Amphitryo*, added to the confusion by introducing a pair of twin servants to accompany the twin brothers. Shakespeare's play is thus both more complicated and more varied in tone; Plautus' aims were more limited, but, on its own terms, *Menaechmi* can be considered a very successful play.

—John Barsby

BRUHADĀRANUYAKA

See UPANISHADS

BUDDENBROOKS: THE DECLINE OF A FAMILY
(Buddenbrooks: Verfall einer Familie)
Novel by Thomas Mann, 1900

Buddenbrooks, Thomas Mann's first novel, was published in 1900. Its setting is the distinctive social and commercial life of Lübeck, a city rich in the traditions of the Hanseatic League and lying close to the north Baltic coast of Germany. The novel relates the history of four generations of a bourgeois family, the Buddenbrooks, who are prominent in the city during the middle 50 years of the 19th century. Its subtitle, "The Decline of a Family," makes evident the descending line of the fortunes of the Buddenbrook family, a theme typical of the European naturalist novel of the time. Yet the causes of the decline are not to be found in economic misfortune or mismanagement, nor indeed in that kind of moral degeneration which so interested writer of the period, but rather in their intellectual and emotional refinement, an increasing sensitivity which makes it difficult for the successive generations of the family to face up to the rigours of economic activity successfully (or, in the case of the final generation, at all). The decreasing ability of the family to defend its interests shows itself in its increasing interest in reflection and in art, notably music. These alternative poles of activity are clearly identified with the philosophy of Arthur Schopenhauer and the music of Richard Wagner.

Buddenbrooks is based on many aspects of the author's own life and that of his family. In writing the novel, Mann not only included significant experiences from his early years but worked his way through his own family history and built the structure of his plot around it. The close parallels between Mann's family and the Buddenbrooks and the resultant exposure of family skeletons worried various members of the family, notably his uncle Friedrich Mann, who felt bitter at his portrayal in the figure of the decadent *roué*, Christian Buddenbrook. At the same time, the portrait of his family's history led Mann to an understanding of the history of an entire class and culture in the mid-19th century, and the novel stands as a monument to a way of life long since overtaken by events. Mann was also interested to explore how it was that he and his brother Heinrich Mann should emerge in the family as writers, at the end of a long line of merchants with no particular interest in art or literature. As a result of this diversity, the novel amounts to a source book for the themes of the first 20 years of Mann's writing, and contains first statements of many of Mann's subsequent themes. It also offers a by no means uncritical exploration of the values and attitudes of the German middle-classes. Mann was struck by the similarity between aspects of his novel and the pioneering work by the sociologist Max Weber into the relationship between *The Protestant Ethic and the Spirit of Capitalism*, the title of Weber's famous study, published in 1905.

The literary classification of *Buddenbrooks* has never been easy. It has its origins in elements of the German novel tradition, and draws some important elements from the distinctive culture of the whole Baltic region and the Hanseatic League, to which the Scandinavian family novels of the Norwegian writers Alexander Kielland and Jonas Lie also contributed. At the same time, there are clear indications that elements of the European tradition in the realist novel have been integrated into the novel. The influence of the Goncourt brothers (notably *Renée Mauperin*, 1864) has often been discussed, as has that of Tolstoi. Mann's description of his work as "the first and only Naturalist novel in Germany" should not be taken as an indication of its closeness to the style and techniques of Émile Zola, although the device of the recurring symbol, the so-called leitmotif, is often traced back both to Wagner and to Zola. Certainly Gerhart Hauptmann's naturalism, with its focus on the lower classes in society and on explicitly "scientific" approaches to social problems such as alcoholism and heredity, finds few echoes in Mann's work. Theodor Fontane offers perhaps a closer model. It might be most useful to think of the novel, as a reviewer suggested in 1907, as "Naturalism on the way to becoming Symbolism."

The novel has enjoyed enormous popularity both in Germany, before and after the Third Reich, and in the rest of the world. It has clearly proved possible to read the novel as a German version of family chronicles such as John Galsworthy's *The Forsyte Saga*, but such readings fail to do justice to at least two aspects of the novel. The novel clearly uses the narrative modes of realism, but is concerned to transcend them and to problematize the relationship between author and reality in a way which anticipates features of the modern novel. Clearly, too, the work contains a density of philosophical reflection brilliantly integrated into the handling of more or less everyday themes. In the tension between a commitment to reality and the abstraction from (sometimes even devaluing of) the everyday through philosophical and artistic distance—an ambiguity which Mann would increasingly characterize as irony—lies the unique appeal of the novel, offering an explanation of its importance both to the general and to the specialist reader.

—Hugh Ridley

C

CAMILLE (La Dame aux camélias)
Novel and play by Alexandre Dumas *fils*, 1848 and 1852

Alexandre Dumas *fils*'s *Camille* is actually two separate works: a novel, and the play the author drew from it. The two tell a similar story, based loosely on Dumas's youthful personal experiences with a well-known Parisian courtesan, Marie (*née* Alphonsine) Duplessis. Written in 1848, the novel, which uses events that had taken place between 1844, when Dumas was 20, and 1847, when Marie died, had such considerable success that the young author decided to transform it into a play for the Paris stage. He did so the following year, but political events and problems with the censors kept it from being produced until 1852, at which time it enjoyed spectacular popularity.

The novel is of course more detailed and intricate than the play; it is also a more original and complex literary work. It, too, uses "true" facts of Dumas's life as a point of departure for its plot, whose story is told in the first person by three narrators: an unnamed young man, the frame narrator, who represents the author as his ideal friend; a youthful protagonist, Armand Duval, who also reflects the author's character, as well as his personal experience; and the heroine, here named Marguerite Gautier, whose life following the departure of Armand is recounted posthumously in her diary, given to her lover after her death.

The frame narrator tells of attending an auction at which society ladies bid for the worldly possessions of a recently-deceased courtesan, Marguerite Gautier, which are being sold off to pay her debts. Moved by sentiments he does not fathom, he pays an extravagant sum for a copy of *Manon Lescaut* bearing the cryptic inscription: "Manon to Marguerite. Humility." A mysterious young man who comes to his home—Armand Duval—offers to buy the volume back from him. When the narrator returns it to him as a gift, Armand shows him a remarkable letter written by the book's recipient on her deathbed. The narrator later helps Armand to effect the transfer of Marguerite's body to a perpetual concession in the Montmartre cemetery, and nurses him back to health following his collapse upon the opening of his mistress's coffin. During Armand's convalescence, he recounts the story of his love to his new friend: how he fell in love at first sight with Marguerite, met her again at the theatre and made a fool of himself, calling assiduously but anonymously at her home throughout her lengthy illness, arranged to be introduced into her elegant house, and at last became her lover. Tormented by jealousy, to distance her from the corruptions of Parisian life and a wealthy lover, and to repair her fragile health (the heroine established consumption as the 19th century's literary illness of choice), Armand takes Marguerite to the country, where the two lovers lead an idyllic life troubled only by another contemporary problem, money. A letter from Armand's father, however, puts an end to this existence: while his son is trying to see him in Paris, Duval senior persuades Marguerite to sacrifice herself and give up her love for the sake of Armand's liaison. Armand, whose jealousy had already been felt, thinks she has returned to her earlier life of pleasure. He abuses his former mistress both psychologically and physically, unaware of his father's visit and the real motive for her departure, which she has vowed to conceal. After a final night of love that she grants him at his request, he insults her with a scornful letter containing money for her favours, then leaves for Egypt. It is only upon his return to Paris that he learns the truth from his father and from Marguerite's diary, which posthumously reveals her sacrifice. Armand is left with his remorse, and the narrator concludes: "I am not the apostle of vice, but I would gladly be the echo of noble sorrow wherever I hear its voice in prayer . . . ."

Dumas's play follows the same general outline, changing some of the characters in accordance with stage practice and permitting Armand to see his mistress just before she dies, thus somewhat alleviating the bleakness of the novel's ending. It is in the traditional five acts of serious French drama, the first taking place in Marguerite's boudoir, the second in her dressing-room, the third in the country (Auteuil here, at present a part of urban Paris, rather than the novel's Bougival, now in its suburbs), the fourth in the salon of another brilliant courtesan, Olympe, and the final one in Marguerite's bedroom. The character of Gaston, Armand's and Marguerite's friend, is elaborated, particularly in the first and last acts, perhaps to compensate for the frame narrator's necessary disappearance from the dramatic genre; so is that of Marguerite's wealthy lover, who here becomes two characters: Count de Giray and Arthur de Varville, again perhaps in compensation for the disappearance of another of the novel's characters, Marguerite's elderly protector.

New and shocking in content, although banal in form, this play inaugurated Dumas *fils*'s career as one of the principal dramatists of his time. Although it is characteristic in its examination of the seamier side of Parisian society, it is more personal and "romantic" than his later dramatic works, such as *The Outer Edge of Society, Les Idées de Madame Aubray*, and *Le Fils naturel*, generally cited as models of the social "thesis-play." It was more successful and influential finally than the novel, gaining fame as the source for opera, *La Traviata* (Verdi saw the play in Paris during a visit), as an international melodramatic vehicle for actresses like Bernhardt, Duse, Ethel Barrymore, and Lillian Gish, and as a starring cinematic role for, among others, Alia Nazimova (with Rudolph Valentino as Armand), Norma Talmadge (with Gilbert Roland), and, most unforgettably, Greta Garbo (with Robert Taylor).

—David Sices

CANCER WARD (Rakovyi korpus)
Novel by Aleksandr Solzhenitsyn, 1968

One of Aleksandr Solzhenitsyn's two large-scale novels written in the Soviet Union, *Cancer Ward* was submitted for publication in the leading literary journal *Novyi mir* [New World], but its rejection after initial acceptance and its subsequent publication abroad let to Solzhenitsyn's disgrace and eventual expatriation. Sharp as some of the political points may be, however, the novel is most powerful as a moral testimony, for all the characters are confronted with questions of life and death, of truth and falsehood. Not for nothing does discussion of Tolstoi's story "What Do Men Live For?" form a central point in the novel's moral structure. Solzhenitsyn's cosmos, like that of Tolstoi, is built on moral categories.

The doctors, nurses, and, particularly, patients in *Cancer Ward* are drawn from a wide range of Soviet society—young, old, innocent, corrupt, idealistic, cynical—all brought together, like the political prisoners elsewhere in Solzhenitsyn's fiction, by a specific form of isolation and deprivation of freedom. The central character and catalyst, Oleg Kostoglotov, arrives at the hospital from the camps, much as the author himself had done in 1954. In many ways he resembles his creator, though Solzhenitsyn has warned against making such an association. Like Kostoglotov, Soviet society as a whole was in transition at this time, and most of the characters in the novel reassess their lives in the light of political changes as well as in face of death or, at least, cancer treatment that can emasculate and cripple. Only Rusanov, the Stalinist party boss, is not prepared to reconsider his life and conscience: "There are questions," he says defensively, "on which a definite opinion has been established, and they are no longer open to discussion." From his dreams, however, we see that even his world has been shaken by the changes going on outside the ward and he eventually attempts to justify himself as "not the only one." His daughter Avieta, recommending books with titles like *It's Morning Already* and *Light over the Earth*, may seem like a parody, but such book titles were far from uncommon in Communist literature of the time, and reflect the artificial world in which Rusanov and his ilk were cocooned while others suffered and died. It is notable that, unlike Tolstoi in his novella *Smert' Ivana Il'icha* (*The Death of Ivan Ilyich*)—often associated with *Cancer Ward*—Solzhenitsyn metes out no retribution for Rusanov's sins.

Solzhenitsyn is one of the great 20th-century realists, steeped in the tradition of Tolstoi and Dostoevskii, drawing from the former the moral inspiration and breadth of vision without Tolstoi's quietism, and from Dostoevskii a desire to narrate polyphonically, although—for all the characters' individual voices and viewpoints—we never lose sight of Solzhenitsyn's beliefs and opinions. An example of the strength of the novel's narrative realism may be found in the way the sensation of love is depicted, right down to the precise part of the body where it is first felt, its description in many ways echoing the way cancer is described and located. The nature of X-ray treatment is conveyed no less graphically, Solzhenitsyn sharing with Thomas Mann an aversion to chemical or mechanical treatment (*Cancer Ward* has more than once been compared to *The Magic Mountain*) and, like him, believing that the best therapy for all ailments lies in the psyche and the spirit. Further examples of strong realism may be seen in the new openness about sexual attraction (between Kostoglotov and two of the carers, for example). Alongside his bold thematic innovations, however, and in some ways no less important, stands Solzhenitsyn's magnificent service in freeing the Russian language from the greyness of Sovietization, and particularly in the rediscovery of its historical roots.

Symbolism exists in *Cancer Ward* at various levels. In Solzhenitsyn's view all Europe was sick with wars and death camps, but his dominant concern was and is Russia: the most Russo-centred of all modern writers, who once said, "my main character is all of Russia," Solzhenitsyn fills his novel with references to 19th-century Russian culture. Europe apart, he was, most obviously, concerned in this novel with Soviet society's sickness from the cancer of Stalinism, a disease for which the only cure would be a new, specifically Russian, morality. Nor is it likely to be coincidental that Podduev the informer has cancer of the tongue or that the promiscuous Ania suffers from breast cancer.

Like Dostoevskii, Solzhenitsyn advances his ideas through the conversations and arguments of his characters. In this way the author,

continuing his pathology of Russia, constructs an ideological (or anti-ideological) structure which, apart from its great human interest and absorbing realism, may be seen as a prologue to his main work, *Gulag Archipelago*. *Cancer Ward* shows as clearly as any other of his fictional works the literary achievement of Solzhenitsyn, a writer indebted to Tolstoi who felt more akin to Dostoevskii, before he finally abandoned fiction in order to undertake his awesome major task of rewriting the history of the origins of Soviet Russia in *The Red Wheel*.

—Arnold McMillin

CANDIDE
Novella by Voltaire, 1759

The most devastating and corrosive of Voltaire's ironic works, *Candide; or, Optimism*, anatomizes the world's potential for disaster and examines the corresponding human capacity for optimism. Deeply influenced by the shattering earthquakes in Lima in 1746 and in Lisbon in 1755, which caused terrible and indiscriminate suffering, Voltaire was eager to put to the test the optimistic and benevolist philosophy associated with Leibniz, Bolingbroke, and Shaftesbury, epitomized by the phrase in Pope's *Essay on Man* (1733–34), "Whatever is, is right"—words which, according to Voltaire, "only insult us in our present misery." As he said in his preface to his *Poem on the Disaster of Lisbon*, "all things are doubtless arranged and set in order by Providence, but it has long been too evident that its superintending power has not disposed them in such a manner as to promote our eternal happiness." From such a sceptical perspective, any optimistic attitude will inevitably seem vapid, but Voltaire went beyond the confines of philosophical argument, and violently caricatured the system of belief he sought to oppose. Allied to venerable stoical traditions of acceptance and consolation, the optimistic philosophy of Leibniz in particular saw the presence of evil in the word as part of God's plan. After all, without evil, how could individuals exercise free choice? Without being tested, how could their faith have meaning? The "optimist" argument then, was complex and sophisticated, but like all ironists Voltaire chose to simplify it to the extent that it seemed complacent and absurd, and he went on to cast doubt on our chances of ever securing "eternal happiness."

The literary form he chose for his examination was the philosophical tale, a stylized narrative designed to test certain propositions, using simplified characters and sketchy, exotic descriptions. Voltaire had previously exploited this form in the oriental tale *Zadig*, and a similar inquiry into similar issues had recently motivated Samuel Johnson's *Rasselas* (1759), But what becomes apparent in *Candide* is the enormous wit and vigour of the inquiry, animated by a genuinely savage indignation at what he saw as the failure of compassion and the insensitivity of the "optimists." The two central figures in the tale, Candide and Dr. Pangloss, interact to show the world as an arena of suffering and misery, constantly beset by catastrophe largely caused by human vice and folly. But they also convey a wonderful sense of human resilience comically holding on to an absurd optimism in the most depressing of circumstances.

The hapless Candide represents the traditional figure of the innocent abroad. Unjustly expelled from the baronial hall of his mistress, Lady Cunégonde, he is press-ganged into the Bulgar army, flogged 4,000 times, involved in a meaningless war in which many thousands die and more are cruelly maimed and left without homes, and reduced finally to begging for bread. At this point he is reunited with his tutor, Dr. Pangloss, a teacher of "metaphysico-theologo-cosmolonigology," now even worse off than he is, but none the less still holding on to his belief that "it is impossible for things not to be where they are, because everything is for the best." The twin heroes then suffer the natural catastrophes of tempest, shipwreck, and earthquake, and witness the man-made cruelties of an *auto-da-fé*, Candide is flogged again and Pangloss is hanged.

The narrative then reunites Candide with his beloved Cunégonde, who has a harrowing tale of mistreatment of her own to recount, and the two lovers spend the rest of the book travelling extensively throughout Europe and the New World, sometimes together, sometimes apart, witnessing a cornucopia of human folly and cruelty, much of it based on recognizable examples from recent years. The characters undergo an appalling series of humiliations, disappointments, and reversals, but, in Voltaire's ironic vision, hope springs eternal in the human breast, absurd and groundless though it might seem. Indeed, the main characters are even reunited with a revived Pangloss, who managed to recover from his hanging, survived a subsequent dissection, and is maintaining an optimistic demeanour despite suffering the most miserable life as a Turkish galley-slave—in the face of everything he is able to say "I still hold my original views."

Like Swift and Dr. Johnson, Voltaire sardonically seeks to discover if there is any reliable source of happiness for mankind. With its many twists and surprises, the book seems to strip away the comforts of reason or wealth or high office, and shows the impossibility of a just society. The normal circumstances of human life in this narrative are suffering, humiliation and fear. But the characters never seem to fall into despair, and by the end Candide has come to learn the harsh lesson that Voltaire is putting forward—"that the goodness of Providence is the only asylum in which man can take refuge in the darkness of reason, and in the calamities to which his weak and frail nature is exposed" (Preface to *Poem on the Disaster of Lisbon*). At the conclusion of *Candide* the characters have suffered disasters enough, but remain victims of envy, spleen, physical infirmity, and boredom, and they find as much comfort as the world offers in retreat, working together with as little disagreement as possible, tending a small garden.

Candide is thus one of the most playful and at the same time most serious of works, in which the ironies of human life are unveiled, intensified by the constant reminders of recent history, and in which a deeply equivocal resignation is reached. It is deliberately disorientating to read, switching its ironic perspectives around, but its eventual effect is of a gleeful carnival rather than a sombre procession.

—Ian A. Bell

THE CASTLE (Das Schloss)
Novel by Franz Kafka, 1926 (written 1922)

The protagonist of *The Castle*, called simply K., arrives late one evening in a village and finds shelter in an inn. He is awakened by an official and told that he needs permission from the castle to stay there. K.'s response is: "What village is this I have wandered into? Is there a castle here?" But he then asserts that he is a land surveyor who has been appointed by the castle. When the official calls the castle he is informed that no such appointment has been made, but almost

immediately a call back from the castle reverses this and appears to confirm K.'s claim. K.'s reaction is surprising: "That was unpropitious for him, on the one hand, for it meant that the castle was well informed about him . . . and was taking up the challenge with a smile."

This opening establishes a fundamental ambiguity in the relationship between K. and the castle. It is never clear whether K. has really been summoned by the castle or whether he invents the story to try to justify his presence. In either case his purpose is to penetrate into the castle and to obtain absolute confirmation of the position he claims for himself.

The image of the castle dominates the novel. The actual building is ramshackle and dilapidated and is frequently shrouded in darkness. It houses a vast hierarchy of officials who are constantly engaged in frenetic bureaucratic activity, all to no apparent purpose. They are obscene and immoral, regarding the women of the village as their rightful prey while the village sees it as the highest honour for a woman to be the mistress of an official. The castle has absolute dominion over the village. The villagers treat it with awe, devotion, and obedience. To them it is omnipotent and infallible. It seems to assume the qualities which they project onto it.

So, too, it is with K. For him it has a dual aspect: it is both an enemy with which he enters into a desperate struggle and a goal which contains the certainty for which he yearns. K. is brash, arrogant, and aggressive, totally confident of achieving his aim. On his first day he sets out to reach the castle on foot but although it is visible, he can find no road that leads to it. Finally, he gives up in exhaustion. The rest of the novel consists of a series of unsuccessful manoeuvres by K. to make contact with the castle. He focuses his attention on the official Klamm who has special responsibility for village affairs. Klamm embodies a peculiar quality of the castle itself; everyone who sees him has a different version of his appearance. Like the castle he seems to reflect back people's assumptions about him. K. now identifies Klamm as the means of reaching the castle but he tries in vain to see him. Eventually he lies in wait for him in the inn yard, but a servant comes out to tell him that Klamm will not emerge as long as K. is there. K. feels that this is a kind of victory he has won over Klamm, but he is simultaneously aware that it is an entirely futile victory.

From this point K.'s attitude gradually changes. It is significantly affected by the story of the Barnabas family which occupies a key place in the text. He hears the story from Barnabas's sister Olga who describes how their sister Amalia had one night received a peremptory summons from a castle official demanding that she come to him in the inn. Amalia had torn up the message and thrown it in the messenger's face. Thereafter they have been shunned by the village and their business has collapsed. Amalia has withdrawn into herself and devoted her time caring for their ailing parents. Yet Olga insists that there is no direct evidence that the castle is responsible for their plight; rather their condition is a consequence of their own assumption of guilt because of Amalia's disobedience. Olga tells K. that she would have obeyed such a summons and argues that, despite appearances, the official might well have been in love with her sister. To placate the castle Olga now prostitutes herself with the castle servants to atone for the supposed insult to the messenger while, for the same reason, Barnabas has waited in the castle for years to offer his own services as a messenger. The first message he has been given is a cryptic one to K. which, it transpires, might never have been meant for K. at all. K. sees Barnabas as another possible lead to the castle, while Barnabas tries to interpret his service to K. as a sign of favour from the castle. There is a cruel irony in their relationship. They mirror each other's hopes, but there is no sign that either can provide the other with what he desires. Olga's tale nevertheless contributes to a shift in K.'s outlook. At first he sympathizes with Amalia and condemns the castle, but by the end he is much closer to sharing Olga's attitude. His earlier suspicion of the castle starts to give way to an acceptance of its potential benevolence.

K. grows ever more weary but pursues his quest until he stumbles by chance into the bedroom of yet another official who tells K. that, if an official is taken unawares in the night, he will answer all the intruder's questions and give him all the assistance he requests. This is precisely the situation in which K. now finds himself. In a moment of unforeseen revelation, the way to his goal stands open and he falls asleep. This episode encapsulates the central ambiguity of the narrative. K. may be so worn out by his struggle that he is incapable of seizing his opportunity when it presents itself. Alternatively, he may have overcome his arrogance and recognized his human limitations. Both these interpretations are permitted by the text.

Soon afterwards the manuscript breaks off. We have the testimony of Max Brod, Franz Kafka's friend and literary executor, that Kafka had told him that K., on his death-bed, was to receive word from the castle: "that though K.'s legal claim to live in the village was not valid... he was to be permitted to live and work there." The fact that Kafka never wrote this ending is entirely appropriate. Far from being inconclusive the novel's open-endedness precisely expresses a quintessential quality of Kafka's work. The castle contains an unfathomable bureaucratic authority but, at the same time, the text repeatedly insinuates that it is the seat of some transcendental principle. However, the nature of this principle is not spelled out. It might equally well be argued that it is the principle of divine truth or the principle of evil and negation. The ultimate mystery at the heart of the castle remains a mystery; neither K., nor the reader, can ever know the unknowable.

—B. Ashbrook

THE CAUCASIAN CHALK CIRCLE (Der kaukasische Kreidekreis)
Play by Bertolt Brecht, 1948

The notion of a play based on the Chinese parable dramatized by Li Hsing Too probably occurred to Bertolt Brecht in the early 1920s. He suggested the theme to Klabund (1890–1928), whose *Chalk Circle* (*Der Kreidekreis*) was produced in Berlin in 1925 by Max Reinhardt, under whom Brecht studied stage craft. In Danish exile Brecht returned to the motif and framed a story that he completed in Finland in 1940, setting the action in his hometown at the end of the Thirty Years War. The protagonist of "The Augsburg Chalk Circle" is Anna, servant to a wealthy Protestant named Zingli. When the household is sacked by Catholic troops, Frau Zingli abandons her young son and flees. Anna spirits the boy out of the city, enters into an unhappy marriage of convenience, and raises him as her own, only to see him reclaimed by Frau Zingli after the peace in an attempt to regain her, by then, late husband's property. Anna appeals to the earthy Judge Dollinger, who awards her custody after subjecting both "mothers" to the chalk circle test reminiscent of King Solomon's sword.

In 1943 in Los Angeles Brecht began recasting the story for a Broadway debut and enlisted Ruth Berlau as collaborator. A draft of *The Caucasian Chalk Circle* was finished in June 1944 with a revision in September, but the Broadway production never materialized before

Brecht was subpoenaed to testify in the congressional hearing on "communist infiltration of the motion picture industry." He left the United States the day after his testimony. The play was first produced in English by the Carleton College Players on 4 May 1948 at the Nourse Little Theatre in Northfield, Minnesota. The German premiere, with music by Paul Dessau, was staged by Brecht's own Berliner Ensemble on 7 October 1954 at the Theater am Schiffbauerdamm. Of the three dozen or so plays Brecht wrote, *The Caucasian Chalk Circle* is considered—together with *The Life of Galileo, Mother Courage and Her Children, The Good Person of Szechwan*, and *Mr. Puntila and His Man Matti*—as one of his five great works.

Between story and play the setting of the main action shifted from Augsburg to Grusinia during one of the myriad Persian wars. This "parable-like play," as Brecht styled it, is in six acts, the first serving as a prologue. A tribute to Soviet Marxism, the prologue opens in Georgia, after Hitler's defeat. Members of two communes, the Rosa Luxemburg fruit growers and the Galinsk goat breeders, convene to resolve their dispute over a valley. The goat breeders, who were relocated during the war, want to use the valley as pasture, but the fruit growers' plan to irrigate it for orchards and vineyards. The fruit growers' project is by common agreement the more productive. To conclude the meeting, the fruit growers present a play directed by the singer Arkadi Cheidze for the entertainment of their comrades. The singer functions as chorus, both narrating and interpreting the action.

"In olden times, in bloody times" Grusinian governor Georgi Abashvili is deposed and executed by order of Prince Kazbeki, one of a clique of disaffected princelings. While escaping from the palace the governor's wife leaves behind her infant son Michael. The child is saved by Grusha, an unmarried kitchen maid. Pursued by hostile soldiers in search of the heir, Grusha makes her way over the mountains to her brother's farm. In transit she once abandons the child herself—exemplary of Brecht's *Verfremdungseffekt* (alienation effect), calculated here to prevent the audience from sympathizing too strongly with the heroine and thus relinquishing critical judgement—but retrieves him. Before her pious sister-in-law, Grusha is compelled to pass the child off as her own and play along with her pusillanimous brother's fabrication that she awaits her husband's return from the front. Through autumn and winter she rears Michael on the farm, teaching him to speak and to play the games that prepare him for a life of farmwork. For the sake of a marriage certificate Grusha's brother arranges for her to wed Yussup, a dying peasant. Although Grusha is already engaged to Simon, a soldier in Persia, she agrees reluctantly with the plan, convinced that Yussup hasn't long to live. Yussup, however, recovers when news breaks that the war has ended—and with it conscription. In a poignant scene Simon arrives to claim his bride, only to find her married. Even as Grusha tries to explain how she acquired a husband and child while remaining faithful, soldiers appear and seize Michael. Here the plot takes a twist. Prince Kazbeki has been beheaded, and the governor's wife, Natella Abashvili, seeks to establish maternity in court in a bid to claim the Abashvili estates as Michael's regent.

The focus in act five is on Azdak, poacher and intellectual turned judge. In staging notes Brecht describes Azdak as a "disappointed revolutionary posing as a human wreck." For having unwittingly sheltered the grand duke, deposed on the same day as his vassal Georgi Abashvili, Azdak denounces himself to the martial authorities. He becomes judge by chance, chosen as a joke by soldiers called upon by Prince Kazbeki to appoint a successor to a lynched judge. Azdak travels the district trying cases, taking bribes from the rich, and dispensing his singular justice. "It's men with nothing in their pockets who alone are able to corrupt Azdak." To save time he occasionally hears two cases at once. When the grand duke is returned to power, he confirms Azdak's authority, who by now is about to be lynched.

The stories of Grusha and Azdak converge in the final act. It is Azdak who hears Lady Abashvili's appeal and Grusha's contesting of it. Natella's counsels bribe Azdak accordingly, whereas Grusha brings friends who perjure themselves on her behalf. Azdak elects to hear an elderly couple's divorce case simultaneously. He curtails testimony over Michael and has the bailiff draw a circle on the floor and place the boy in it. Natella and Grusha are each then charged to seize a hand and attempt to pull Michael out of the circle on Azdak's signal. Twice Lady Abashvili jerks him to her side, twice Grusha lets go to prevent his injury.

Azdak awards Michael to Grusha, confiscates the estates for a public park, and pronounces an errant verdict in the divorce case—divorcing Grusha from Yussup that she may marry Simon. The singer intones the moral: "Things should belong to those who do well by them / Children to motherly women that they may thrive / . . . And the valley to those who water it, that it may bear fruit."

—Albert E. Gurganus

CHANDOGYA

See UPANISHADS

LA CHANSON DE ROLAND

See THE SONG OF ROLAND

LA CHANSON DU MAL-AIMÉ (Song of the Ill-Beloved)
Poem by Guillaume Apollinaire, 1913

Guillaume Apollinaire's "La Chanson du mal-aimé" is from his first collection, *Alcools*, in which poems from his early years embrace a variety of emotional upheavals and random events in the poet's psyche, presenting what Roger Little has called the "protean life of the imagination" (*Guillaume Apollinaire*, 1976). *Alcools* generally presents the loss of the labours of love, or an elegy to lost love, and this poem was written at the end of Apollinaire's romance with Annie Playden. Through a combination of a number of disparate sources and fragments, "La Chanson du mal-aimé" mixes this sense of sad loss with self-pity, frustration, excitement, and retrospective and proleptic views of the narrator's life, all of which add up to a veiled celebration of rhetorical and linguistic power.

"La Chanson du mal-aimé" is carefully structured around a main narrative divided into four sections by three interpolated episodes. Walks across two cities, London and Paris, provide the narrative framework for the poem and act as the prompting for an exploration of the narrator's mind and memory. Thus, the chronology of "real" time is played off against the pressures of emotional time. Written in a series of five-line octosyllabic stanzas (or quintils), the poem maintains a tight rhyme scheme (ababa) that provides a strict formality within which the poem runs the gamut of emotions—hope, despair, madness, jealousy, hatred—all caused by the demise of love. The poem works through a series of metamorphoses of the narrator, as he merges his personal emotions with analogous narratives and images.

The poem opens with the narrator wandering through the foggy London streets. His beloved appears in various forms (a ruffian, or a drunk staggering from a pub), which he chases as vainly as Pharaoh pursuing the Israelites. Clutching at these apparitions in the London streets, he realizes that he is not Ulysses with a patient Penelope, or King Dushyanta with a loyal Sakuntala. Evoking paradigms for testing the qualities, commitments, and fidelity of his past love, he is someone who, having lost love, now needs to seek a new identity and to rebuild his life. The predominant imagery of powerful kings in the poem, "rois heureux," "rois maudits," "rois persécuteurs," and "rois fous," and "les rois du monde"—only serves to stress the impotence and emptiness of the narrator's actions.

After the refrain about the former beauties of love, the mood switches to the fresh albeit clichéd joys of pastoral love in the "Aubade chantée à Laetare un an passé" ("Aubade sung at Laetare a year ago"). Here "L'aube au ciel fait de roses plis" ("The dawn makes pink folds in the sky") and gods dance in accompaniment to Pan's music. Yet this apparent state of happiness takes an ironic twist, since "Beaucoup de ces dieux ont péri" ("Many of these gods have died") and the narrator returns to his previous despair.

The narrative then breaks to a comparison of his former love with the fidelity of the Zaporogian Cossacks to their habitat of the Steppes and Christianity. The poem exemplifies fierce loyalty and fidelity, by narrating the Cossack's mocking refusal to obey the Sultan's demand for their allegiance to Islam. In the "Answer of the Zaporogian Cossacks to the Sultan of Constantinople," the poem presents a series of calculated insults delivered to the Sultan in defiance of his command.

The refrain of the poem concerning the issue of lost love in the image of the Milky Way returns, before the poem finally introduces the third interlude, a section on the symbolism of "Les Sept Épées" ("The Seven Swords"). This section oscillates between the eroticism of the phallic swords and the Christian religious symbolism of the seven swords piercing the heart of Our Lady of Sorrows, and is a good example of how Apollinaire attempts to turn legends into psychological truths. Linked to his earlier sorrow as "Sept épées de mélancolie / Sans morfil" ("Seven swords of melancholy / with no blunt edge"), each sword is carefully described with its attributes. The refrain returns, before a final meditation on destiny occurs, in which the narrator's madness finds an analogue in the story of the mad King Ludwig of Bavaria, and exemplifies the results of power being brought low by fate. The poet finds himself back in sparkling Paris, although with his sorrow unalleviated, musing over the demise of his love and of his power to articulate his emotions.

The principal focus of the poem is on a return to clear comprehension after illusion and hallucination. In making such a progression, the narrator seeks to define what constitutes true and false love. As the epigraph to the poem suggests in the image of love as a phoenix rising from the fire, the poem charts a movement from despair to a reconciliation with loss and a new optimism for the future born out of the trials of the past misfortune. Yet it also suggests the ways in which private sorrow is inextricably linked to public expression. In gesturing to various forms like the ballad, the epic, and the pastoral lyric, and demonstrating a debt to the aesthetic preoccupations and penchants of Symbolist and Parnassian art, the poem establishes the self as the site of narrative construction, and the individual psyche as an amalgamation of social myths.

—Tim Woods

CHARACTERS (Characteres)
Prose by Theophrastus, c. 319 BC

Characters, probably written in or around 319 BC, is comprised of 30 vignettes, each representing one man who displays a particularly unpleasant or ridiculous characteristic (''Mistrust,'' ''Petty Ambition''). The social attributes of each character are roughly the same: male, landowner, slaveholder, engaged in some form of commerce, prominent in public affairs, with enough means, if not always the will, to fund various forms of public and private generosity. With one exception (''Boorishness''), the characters are all city dwellers, but in every case their setting is Athens in the late 4th century BC. In this regard, *Characters* is an important document in the history of private life, offering a view of what was considered improper (and by inference, proper) behaviour for a gentleman of the day. The sketches contain clear and concentrated examples of what R.C. Jebb called ''the social language of Athens,'' the language of manners, dress, conversation, business practices, family and social life.

The tone throughout is satiric, though seldom harsh. No completely positive types are represented, but some are clearly more sympathetic than others. The characters do not mirror society's unfortunates. That is, the skinflint (''Penny-Pinching'') is not mocked because he is poor, but because he behaves as if he were poor. The offensive man (''Repulsiveness'') is lampooned not because of his disgusting skin condition, but because of the pride he takes in it. Some try too hard to impress (''Flattery,'' ''Petty Ambition''); others (''Obnoxiousness,'' ''Moral Apathy'') flaunt their outrageous behaviour and delight in the discomfort they create among their fellows. The most innocent and risible of the characters (''Late-Learning,'' and ''Overdoing'') simply seem unaware of what is done and not done. In short, these characters are transgressors of social norms. They do not behave in a way appropriate to the normative group, that of gentlemen.

The characters' offences can be divided into roughly three categories of behaviour that are not mutually exclusive: 1) offending others, either deliberately or haplessly; 2) attempting to elevate their status by pretending to be better informed, wealthier, braver, or more influential than they are; and 3) carrying a common fault or small peculiarity to excess, such as wanting to be young again, talking too much, being cheap, superstitious, or cowardly. Each character is described according to the same formula. The first sentence is a general definition of the characteristic (''Insensibility is a slowness of mind, both in words and actions''), followed by a descriptive series of characteristic actions (''The insensible man is the sort who, as the defendant in a lawsuit, forgets to appear at court and instead goes to the country'').

The man who represents the knack of saying and doing the right thing at the wrong time (''Bad Timing'') is one of Theophrastus' more deft vignettes. This sketch represents *Characters* well not only because of the subtlety of its delineation but because it affords a view of contemporary social norms. Theophrastus shows a fine comic flair in the instances he chooses to illustrate this type's behaviour. The character's action are not themselves criticized, only their timing. We can therefore deduce that it was perfectly acceptable for a gentleman to serenade his girlfriend (but not when she was sick), launch into a harangue against women (but not at a wedding), and be present at the beating of a friend's slave (but without commenting that he beat a slave like that once, who hanged himself after). He may dance at a party, but not with someone who is still sober, and, presumably, not when he is sober himself. He may ask outright for interest on his loan, but not when the other party is making an outlay for a sacrifice.

The character representing surliness (''Self-Sufficiency,'' or literally ''not needing anybody'') is another instance of bad manners, but this character's offences are entirely intentional. He responds curtly to simple requests for information; he remains angry about minor accidents, such as being splashed or having his foot stepped on; he does not lend money graciously; and he will not do his part to entertain his fellow banqueters by making a speech or singing.

Even in a work whose focus is largely on personal qualities, the man with oligarchic tendencies (''Authoritarianism,'' as Jeffrey Rusten translates) has his place. His unfashionable politics, rather than his way of eating or behaving at the theatre, make him egregious.

Theophrastus' penchant for telling detail not only creates lively characters but imparts the kind of cultural information difficult to obtain except through the comic playwrights. Through the sketch of the ostentatious man (''Petty Ambition'') one learns that Maltese dogs and trained canaries conferred status as household pets, and in ''Superstition'' we are told what the fearfully pious did when chance brought them near a madman.

The collection contains no representative types of ''the many,'' of slaves, women, children, or resident aliens. That this majority could be represented by comic types is clear from the New Comedy, but to do so was clearly not Theophrastus' aim, although his purpose, and hence the genre into which *Characters* should be placed, has long been disputed. If the genre of *Characters* remains in question, its literary influence is clearly traceable and, given the work's minor status in the author's *oeuvre*, nothing short of astounding. *Characters* served as the explicit model for what became a popular genre in English, French, and German literature. Many famous names are linked directly to the Theophrastan character sketch (Jonson, Addison, and La Bruyère, to name a few), and many more indirectly, in that the development of Elizabethan drama and of the novel may be said to have depended on the delineation of character.

—Elizabeth Bobrick

THE CHARTERHOUSE OF PARMA (La Chartreuse de Parme)
Novel by Stendhal, 1839

The Charterhouse of Parma was Stendhal's last completed novel and traditionally ranks with *Scarlet and Black* as one of his two masterpieces. Loosely based on a malicious early 17th-century manuscript biography of Alessandro Farnese (later Pope Paul III) that he had chanced upon in Rome, it was composed (by dictation) in Paris with extraordinary speed between 4 November and 26 December 1838 and published on 6 April 1839. Poorly received, it was nevertheless warmly praised 18 months later by Balzac, who admired its insights into the subtle arts of politics and diplomacy and who considered it a modern version of Machiavelli's *The Prince*. Balzac was also good enough to point out how Stendhal might have improved the novel. Like most of Stendhal's work, it was then largely neglected until the 1880s, only achieving its present status in the early 20th century, notably when André Gide dubbed it one of the two greatest French novels (with Laclos's *Les Liaisons dangereuses*).

Set amid the petty principalities of northern Italy in the early 19th century, but heavily imbued with the Renaissance atmosphere of its principal source, *The Charterhouse of Parma* is notable for its eventful plot in which elements of romance, epic, and fairytale blend in a tale of swashbuckling adventure: much comedy, a tragic love story, and astutely observed political intrigue combine to present a picture of Stendhal's beloved Italy that sets the values of passion, vitality, honour, and courage above the (implicitly French) characteristics of vanity, calculating self-interest, and prosaic caution.

The novel traces the life of Fabrice del Dongo from conception, as in Sterne's *Tristram Shandy*, to death at the age of 27 in the eponymous and hitherto unmentioned charterhouse. Ostensibly the son of a marquis, but probably fathered by a Lieutenant Robert in the Napoleonic army which enters Milan (in 1796) in the first sentence of the novel, Fabrice enjoys a gilded childhood by Lake Como before departing quixotically to join Napoleon at Waterloo. The battle is described brilliantly from the innocent observer's viewpoint (in a manner which was to influence Tolstoy's *War and Peace*), and the hero returns home requiring a newspaper to confirm that this was what people actually called a battle. He is now *persona non grata* with the Austrian authorities, and his return is concealed by his mother and her beautiful young sister-in-law Gina, who, after the early death of her heroic husband Count Pietranera, is about to become the Duchess Sanseverina in a marriage of convenience (the convenience being not only a sizeable fortune but also a cover for her relationship with Count Mosca, prime minister to Ranuce-Ernest IV, Prince of Parma). Following attendance at theological college in Naples and embarking upon an ecclesiastical career, Fabrice returns to Parma where his aunt now adorns the Prince's court. Smitten by a young actress, Marietta, he accidentally meets her in the company of her villainous lover Giletti: in the ensuing knife-fight and believing he has been disfigured, Fabrice kills Giletti, thereupon absconding to Bologna where he proceeds instead to pursue a famous opera-singer, la Fausta.

In Part II, with Gina threatening to abandon Parma for Naples, Ranuce-Ernest signs a document agreeing not to condemn Fabrice—at present, for unbeknown to Gina, the politic Mosca has omitted the exclusion of future proceedings orally agreed with the duchess. Fabrice is subsequently imprisoned in the infamous Farnese Tower in the custody of General Fabio Conti. Gina, now much infatuated with her "nephew," plans his escape: Fabrice, meanwhile, falls in love with the general's daughter Clélia. Happy where he is, Fabrice is obliged by his aunt's plotting to escape, an exploit which the vengeful Gina follows up by engineering the assassination of the uncooperative Prince of Parma with the assistance of Ferrante Palla, a doctor and ardent revolutionary. Increasingly jealous of Fabrice's love for Clélia, Gina seeks the latter's marriage to the eligible Marquis Crescenzi and intrigues at court to secure Fabrice's acquittal, a plan requiring him voluntarily to give himself up. Missing Clélia, Fabrice goes not to the town jail but to the Farnese Tower, thus placing himself again in the dangerous hands of a no less vengeful Fabio Conti. Fearing he may be poisoned, Clélia flies to his cell where their love is somewhat unceremoniously consummated; while Gina hastens to the new prince, who promises her Fabrice's acquittal and succession to the archbishopric in return for an hour of her favours. She accepts, vowing in angry despair to leave Parma for ever. Following his release and Clélia's marriage to Crescenzi, Fabrice begins to preach, hoping that Clélia will attend his sermons: his eloquence and lovesick asceticism earn him a considerable ecclesiastical reputation. With the

famous words, "Enter, friend of my heart," Clélia finally agrees to regular trysts—at night, for she has vowed never to see Fabrice again—and three years pass in happy deception. But they have a child, Sandrino, ostensibly Crescenzi's son. Fabrice, on a "tender whim" to have him as his own, plans to abduct Sandrino having pretended that he is ill, much against Clélia's better judgement pretence becomes reality, fate is tempted, and the child dies. The final page shocks with its succinctness: brokenhearted Clélia dies; Fabrice resigns as archbishop and retires to the charterhouse of Parma, to die within the year. Gina scarcely survives him, and only Mosca lives on, a lonely witness to the empty prosperity of the new prince's reign.

Dedicated at the end to the "Happy Few" and narrated (as we learn from the Foreword) by a former Napoleonic soldier revisiting Padua in 1830 and using both the annals of a Paduan canon and the first-hand information of a friend of the duchess, the novel owes its status to a "miraculous" air of improvisation, combined with a subtle challenge to conventional moral values and an unsettling ability to present violent emotion, unsavoury politics, and deep human suffering beneath a veil of delightful inconsequence. Seemingly quaint attention to astrology and auguries combines with suggestive narrative patterning to raise two age-old questions: is there a logic in human destiny? how should a storyteller tell his story? *The Charterhouse of Parma* is not only a profoundly political novel: it is also a cross between Diderot's *Jacques the Fatalist* and Mozart's *opera buffa*.

—Roger Pearson

CHATTERTON
Play by Alfred de Vigny, 1835

The phenomenal success of *Chatterton* at the Comédie-Française on 12 February 1835, like Hugo's *Hernani*, performed on the same stage some five years earlier, marked one of the summits of the Romantic movement in French theatre; like *Hernani*, it has also remained more a monument of literary history than a viable stage work. Alfred de Vigny had already dealt with the troubled life and suicide of a young English poet in 1832, in his novel, *Stello*. There Chatterton's story was told, together with those of French poets Nicolas Gilbert and André Chénier, by "Le Docteur Noir" ("The Black Doctor" or "Doctor Black") to illustrate the poet's suffering, neglect, and premature death at the hands of any form of government, whether an absolute monarchy (Gilbert), a revolutionary republic (Chénier), or a parliamentary regime (Chatterton). The good Doctor's prescription for the poet-"narratee" was an unflinching stoicism in the face of society's ill-treatment.

In a lengthy preface to *Chatterton* entitled "Final Night of Labour, June 29–30, 1834," Vigny summarized the drama's plot in one sentence: "It is the story of a man who has written a letter in the morning, and who awaits the reply until evening; it arrives, and kills him." Despite this claim to linear simplicity, his three-act play expands considerably and complicates the story presented in *Stello*. In fact, the play is a conflation of biographical information on Chatterton with imagined events, some of them contradicting historical fact, involving the story of the poet's rejection by society and a love-plot between the poet and his landlord's wife, Kitty Bell.

The heroine's role is greatly expanded, in part at least to meet the exigencies of the stage. Although Vigny, who was known as the most "philosophical" of French Romantic poets, referred to his work in the preface as a "drama of ideas," it seems now more akin to Romantic melodrama than to philosophy. That would help explain the public's frenetic response to the play. Certainly the fact that at the première Marie Dorval, playing Mistress Bell, did a previously unrehearsed fall down the stairs in the play's culminating scene contributed powerfully—most unphilosophically—to its effect.

Vigny gives extensive descriptions of physical qualities and garb for his principal characters at the outset of the play, both because it was a costume drama set in London in 1770 and because the author visualized them as symbolic figures in his "drama of ideas." Chatterton, representing the Poet (Vigny was fond of capitalizing, as a means to generalization), is a "young man of 18 years, pale, energetic of expression, weak in body, worn out from late nights and thinking." Kitty Bell is a "young woman, around 22, melancholy, graceful, elegant by nature rather than by upbringing"; in accordance with the prevailing English Protestant (and Romantic) sobriety, she is dressed in black and grey. Her husband, John Bell, meant to represent a typical English industrialist, is a "man between 45 and 50, vigorous, red-faced, swollen with ale, porter, and roast-beef." Around this triangle, Vigny places three major characters: an elderly Quaker friend of Bell's who acts as the poet's mouthpiece throughout the play and whose description is the lengthiest of all, in keeping with his importance to our understanding; Lord Beckford, a "rich, self-important old man" who, as Lord Mayor of London, represents officialdom; and Chatterton's college friend, the wealthy young Lord Talbot, "foppish and pleasant at the same time, thoughtless and lively in manner, opposed to all hard work and happy . . . to be freed from any sad spectacle and serious concern." Talbot's tactless chatter about Kitty Bell, as much as Beckford's condescending offer of employment, precipitates the tragic conclusion of the play—Chatterton's suicide and Kitty's death.

In the first act, young Chatterton, who for some reason is lodged in the home of Bell, a factory-owner, is anxious about the reception awaiting a collection of his poems that he has published as the work of a medieval monk, Rowley. His tender concern for his host's brow-beaten wife, Kitty and her two children is innocently returned by the young woman, who has set aside money from her accounts to help pay his rent. Much of this is learned from the Quaker's interrogation of one character or the other as well as his asides and comments (for local colour, Vigny has all his characters except the Quaker who typically says *thee* and *thou*, use the formal *vous*). The second act introduces Lord Talbot, with his young companions, Lord Kingston and Lord Lauderdale, and his well-meaning intrusion into Chatterton's literary and supposed amatory affairs. Kitty Bell is hurt by this revelation of her lodger's lofty connections, which contradict his apparent poverty. The Quaker, aware and fearful of the potential love between the two young people, tries to warn them away from each other. In the final act, later the same day, Chatterton contemplates suicide; only hope of suitable employment and the Quaker's hint that he might thus hurt Kitty Bell keep him from carrying out his design. When the Lord Mayor answers Chatterton's request by offering him a menial position as his personal secretary, the poet goes up to his room and drinks the poison he has prepared. Kitty Bell, discovering the poet's body despite the Quaker's efforts, falls dead at the foot of the stairs: it was here that Mme. Dorval was inspired to faint and fall on her way down.

Vigny's lament on the fate of poets in an indifferent society received considerable public acclaim, but he was also accused of glorifying suicide. His Chatterton can be seen as one of the earliest models for the "poète maudit" ("doomed poet") in French literature. Among the play's most celebrated scenes is one in which Chatterton develops for Beckford a lengthy metaphor on the poet's role as navigator and watchman aboard the ship of state.

—David Sices

CHÉRI
Novel by Colette, 1920

Possibly Colette's best-known novel, *Chéri* was published in final form in 1920. Having been first conceived in 1912, the year in which the action of the novel begins, *Chéri* began in the form of a play. As such, the work retains some of its original dramatic structure, being easily divided into three sections. Only the middle section, however, focuses entirely on the title character, a young man emerging from adolescence, referred to as Chéri by those who know him best—the two women who, in their own way, raised him: his mother and her confidante Léa, called La Baronne de Lonval. The first and third parts of the novel concern for the most part Léa, and Léa's amorous but ambiguous relationship to Chéri, some 25 years her junior.

This novel, appearing at a time when Colette's penchant for the unconventional, if not scandalous, both in her life and in her novels, was already well known, continues in the vein of unorthodoxy. Although acclaimed for its prose artistry, the book was criticized for its milieu and for the portrayal of Chéri. Firstly, the setting is the world of courtesans, the *demimonde* of Paris. Léa and Chéri's mother are two materially successful courtesans who have somehow escaped damaging scandals so as to "retire" from their profession peacefully and comfortably. Léa, at 49, considers her now seven-year-old liaison with Chéri to be her last (although she is concerned at such a notion), and Madame Peloux has not had an encounter since Chéri was at college. These are two businesswoman who have profited from the life they lead and who enjoy a certain "modern" independence. Secondly, Chéri's personality construction was controversial. Beautiful, childlike, spoiled, irresponsible, and somewhat effeminate, Chéri is vain and greedy. In the first pages of the novel he pleads with Léa to give him her glorious strand of pearls, which she refuses to do. Having known Chéri since his birth, she is fully aware of his capriciousness. In this relationship Léa is both lover and strong maternal figure for a boy who whines and plays. Here Colette reverses sex role stereotypes: Léa is world-wise, premeditative, practical: Chéri is carefree, young, naive. While Léa is able to define her needs and satisfy them, Chéri is incapable of even expressing himself in adult speech (at one point Léa hints at being frustrated by Chéri's inarticulateness, saying she never really knew him beyond a certain physical level).

As must happen, however, Chéri passes into adulthood by way of his betrothal to a young girl who is, actually, the foil of the mature Léa. Ironically, this young couple is a couple of children, uninitiated into the world of adults. The aftermath of Chéri's wedding heralds the second section of the novel. Léa, heartbroken without Chéri, goes off mysteriously to the south of France, leaving in her wake gossipy whispers concerning her supposed replacement companion (in fact, she is travelling alone). Her departure, and Chéri's frustration over being married to a needy child, results in his own flight. On a walk one evening (the first of many during which he will spy on Léa's vacant house), he decides to return home. Instead, he takes up residence with a bachelor friend and remains in his company for over six weeks, frequenting restaurants, bars, and opium dens, all characterizing his new-found freedom. Although Chéri never smokes the opium offered to him, there is an element of self-destruction inherent in his actions. Never having been very healthy (Léa had once taken it upon herself to fatten him up), he sleeps little, eats badly, and reminisces frequently about Léa. Not until he knows that Léa has returned to Paris (with or without a lover; this thought has not yet crossed his mind) does Chéri return home to his young wife, assured that he can now be a legitimate husband.

The last section of the novel, however, finds Chéri abruptly back in Léa's arms, and the themes Colette sketched in the first part of the novel come to fruition. Here we learn that love cannot conquer all, obstacles such as age play an essential role. Wanting to find again the Nounoune (as Chéri calls Léa) that he had left only months earlier, Chéri wakes in Léa's bed to discover an ageing woman with a sagging chin, roughened skin, and a lack of the freshness that he now, by contrast, witnesses in his bride. His words ''Tu as été pour moi'' (''You have been for me'') explain everything, parting the lovers for the last time.

Colette's prose is rhythmic, cadenced, eloquent, lyric, even musical. Her narrator (given a semi-omniscient point of view) allows her a wide perspective on character, and her dialogues artfully express the cattiness of competitive *demi-mondaines*. Added to this is the carefully treated question of sex. Colette inverts sex roles to create a strong woman/weak man dichotomy that moves one step beyond the simply caricatural male of her earlier fiction. Playing into the definition of sex role is Colette's genius for depicting sense perceptions, illustrated here by her use of the colours pink, white, and blue. Pink and white are symbolic of strength (Léa's room, the light, her skin), while blue (Chéri's silhouette against the window, for example) intervenes in an almost sinister way, contrasting with the maternal strength of the woman. Interestingly, woman's strength lies not in her physicality (the flesh which ages and betrays), but in her spirit, which comprehends the need for another to find life elsewhere than in a mother's arms, granting him an adulthood which excludes her.

It is perhaps noteworthy that *Chéri* precedes an era in Colette's life when she became a Léa-figure to her stepson. Colette, however, unlike Léa, did not find the inner strength to let her young lover leave. Although the two eventually parted ways, Colette found she was not the independent woman that she had created in the character of Léa, having hoped to present a new female image.

—Jennifer Brown

THE CHERRY ORCHARD (Vishnevyi sad)
Play by Anton Chekhov, 1904

The Cherry Orchard is Anton Chekhov's swan song. The Moscow Art Theatre first performed the play on 17 January 1904, and Chekhov died on 2 July of the same year. As a physician, Chekhov knew that he had only a short time to live, and this would be his last major work. Thus, he went beyond the themes of his earlier plays to include the decline of the nobility and the rise of an entrepreneurial class in Russia. In so doing, he was giving his own distinctive treatment to themes that had previously appeared in such important works of Russian literature as Tolstoi's novel *Anna Karenina* (1875–77)

and Aleksandr Ostrovskii's play *The Forest* (*Les*, 1871). The opposition between Liubov Ranevskaia, the elegant but hopelessly impractical aristocrat, and Ermolai Lopakhin, the hard-working entrepreneur whose father and grandfather had been serfs on her family's estate, also owes something to the somewhat similar opposition between Julie and Jean in Strindberg's *Miss Julie* (1888). Yet Chekhov made that opposition more subtle and complicated than Strindberg did. At first Lopakhin genuinely wants to help the aristocrats resolve their financial difficulties, but when they cannot understand the need to act, he buys the estate himself.

Only by understanding the delicate balance between all the sets of oppositions in *The Cherry Orchard* can we remain true to the vision that informed Chekhov's art. Thus, a balance exists between the charm of the aristocrats' way of life and the immorality of serfdom that made it possible; and between the aristocrats' ready empathy with others in personal relationships and their indifference to their own fates and those of others who depend on them.

The play itself remains balanced between the characters, who cannot quite say what they mean, or do what they want to do, and their symbolic environment. The cherry orchard itself, which symbolizes the old ways, is thus connected with the billiard cue that Epikhodov, the clown-like clerk, breaks during the ball scene in Act III. This incidental action, which occurs offstage, suggests that by playing billiards Epikhodov is encroaching on gentry prerogatives. It forms a subtle analogy for Lopakhin's far more disruptive encroachment on gentry prerogatives in buying the estate and chopping down the cherry orchard. Billiards links Epikhodov to Leonid Gaev, Ranevskaia's feckless brother, who hides his incompetence by pretending to play billiards. He can neither work nor play, so he plays at playing.

Arrivals and departures frame the drama, as they do for each of Chekhov's four major plays. The play begins in the manor house, as Lopakhin impatiently awaits the arrival of Madame Ranevskaia and her entourage from Paris, and ends—almost—as they leave. In a typically anti-climactic touch, Chekhov has old Firs, the senile butler, wander on stage after everyone else has left. They have forgotten about him, and locked him in. Serfdom has so deprived Firs of a sense of self that he cannot think of himself; he can only wonder whether Gaev has worn the right coat. He lies down to take a nap and presumably to die, and a way of life will die with him.

The principle of balance holds for the relationship between the past and the present, too. The continuity in Russian life appears in the similarities between Gaev and Petr Trofimov, a university student from the proletariat and a former tutor of Madama Ranevskaia's son who drowned several years previously. Despite their differences in class origin and attitudes, both of them engage in the very Russian tendency to make speeches for the sake of making speeches. Gaev makes a speech to the bookcase in Act I, and his sister later rebukes him for making a speech to the peasants. Similarly, Trofimov makes speeches welcoming the new life that will come after the passing of the gentry. Both resort to speechifying in an unconscious attempt to mask their inability to cope with life's challenges. In a way then, to understand the balance of the play is to understand that the French saying ''Plus ça change, plus c'est la même chose'' applies fully to *The Cherry Orchard*. The theme of the passing of the gentry way of life has served as the subject for a number of major 20th-century works, such as George Bernard Shaw's play *Heartbreak House*, Jean Renoir's film *The Rules of the Game*, and Bernard Bertolucci's film *1990*. All three of these works derive to a greater or lesser extent from *The Cherry Orchard*. The play also marks the end of an era in Russian culture. After Chekhov's death, Russian theatre became known more for its innovative stage sets and great directors than for its plays. No Russian play written since 1904 has enjoyed more than occasional performances in other countries.

—Jim Curtis

CHIN PING MEI

See GOLDEN LOTUS

THE CHRIST OF VELAZQUEZ (El Cristo de Velázquez)
Poem by Miguel de Unamuno, 1920

The subtitle given by Miguel de Unamuno to *The Christ of Velazquez* is "poema," and the polyglot philologist/philosopher often called his work poetry in the original etymological sense (*poesis* = creativity). Spanish literary histories frequently term the work a long poem, but it is more precisely a collection of poems with a single inspiration and unifying theme and a single metric form—2,538 unrhymed hendecasyllabic lines—without fixed strophes (each poem is one stanza, regardless of length). The 89 poems vary from seven lines to four pages; many have titles but some are only numbered. The four unequal parts contain 39, 14, 27, and nine poems, respectively. Although each is a complete entity, independently readable (and some have appeared separately in anthologies), Unamuno conceived the work as a unit.

Perhaps the best-known aspect of Unamuno's life and work is his struggle with doubt during a series of deepening religious crises from adolescence through maturity. Raised in a devout Catholic environment, Unamuno none the less realized the limitations of orthodox theological demonstrations of the existence of God. Fruitlessly searching ancient and modern philosophies and religions, he concluded that none could rationally or scientifically prove the existence of God—or the contrary. But agnosticism could not satisfy Unamuno. His hunger and thirst for immortality—the resurrection of the flesh promised by Catholic dogma—demanded orthodox belief. His anguished swings from faith to doubt were reversed repeatedly by religious experiences rekindling his faith, and during one such period of temporarily restored orthodox belief he conceived *The Christ of Velazquez*, half celebration of his recovered faith, half act of contrition or penance for his doubt. Although his faith faltered again while writing the work, he determined to complete it nevertheless.

The Christ of Velazquez is a prolonged meditation on the inspired, larger-than-life painting of Christ on the Cross by the 17th-century Spanish master, Diego Rodrigo de Silva Velázquez, which hangs in Madrid's Prado museum—a gigantic canvas depicting Jesus with a cloth carelessly draped around his loins and half of his face covered by a thick veil of falling hair. Unamuno had previously devoted poems to other representations of Christ—"El Cristo de Cabrera" ("The Christ of Cabrera") in his *Poesías*, and "El Cristo yacente de Santa Clara de Palencia" ("The Supine Christ of Santa Clara of Palencia," 1913)—neither of which pleased him, especially the latter. Remorse over this "ferocious" poem influenced Unamuno to undertake *The Christ of Velazquez*, using as his point of departure the biblical prose of Fray Luis de León's *On the Names of Christ* (*De los nombres de Cristo*), which amplifies the meanings of metaphoric

characterizations of Christ in the Scriptures. Many cantos of Unamuno's liturgical epic bear headings to indicate the biblical origin of interpretive commentary or metaphors, and marginal citations of chapter and verse are provided for most poems. Other intertextual allusions are utilized more rarely, as are metaliterary figures (e.g., viewing the Passion within the context of traditional Spanish miracle plays or discussing Christ's death and resurrection in relation to the paradox of life as a dream/death as awakening).

Paradox, metaphor, similes, word-play, repetition with variation, and the gentle cadence of the Spanish counterpart of blank verse are the major poetic devices. Unamuno was especially attracted by the English poets, Wordsworth and Coleridge, and his extensive familiarity with English poetry prompted experiments with versification and rhythms intended to introduce the subtle flexibility of English metrics to Castilian verse.

Although Unamuno scorned aesthetics *per se*, harshly criticizing modernism and "pure" art as empty and superficial, he was well-informed on technical aspects of lyricism, and his knowledge of 18 modern languages (in addition to his academic speciality in classical languages) allowed him to utilize many sources. Numerous echoes of Spanish Golden-Age and Baroque rhetoric (hyperbaton, oxymoron, and occasional Latinate syntax) remind readers that Unamuno was an accomplished exegete of Cervantes, Calderón, and Quevedo, while classical allusions (to Homer, Socrates, Apollo, etc.) recall the professional philologist. Incorporating these antecedents and drawing upon liturgy, Unamuno rarely creates novel images; the nature of the subject combined with his longing for orthodox faith precludes much innovation. Nevertheless, occasional audacious metaphors do occur: one presents Christ as a white eagle, another as a white sacrificial bull, still others as an eternal book written in letters of blood, lily of the valley of sorrows, a white dragon who overcame the original dragon (Satan) by absorbing all venom, etc. The cross is metaphorically a boat of the soul, a loom on which God's thoughts are woven, Jacob's ladder, the manger, and a lever whereby faith can move mountains, while the nails become keys opening the gates of death. Elsewhere, the cross is a tree whose leaves are souls.

Each of the four parts has some internal cohesiveness, more visible in shorter and better-unified subdivisions. Part I, the longest and most varied, includes meditations on common names of Christ (the Way, the Truth, and the Light; Lamb of God, Holy Dove; the Good Shepherd; Sacred Host; the gate of heaven). Unamuno develops one poem largely around whiteness, pallor, and lunar imagery, another on the opposites light and darkness, a third on peace in battle (conflicts of life), and yet another on thorns and flowers. Wheat and the harvest, sheaves of grain and Eucharist inspire another poem, followed by one on wine, while linen (Christ's garment) inspires images of textile production, cuts, weaves, and fabrics. Velázquez's depiction of flowing black hair is metamorphosed by Unamuno into black clouds, a shadow cast by the angel of darkness. Part II emphasizes the moments of crucifixion, the loneliness of Christ abandoned by his Father, Nature's cataclysmic reactions to the deicide, the words spoken by Christ on the Cross, his pain and sorrow, emotions of spectators who knew him, his solitude and suffering, and the anguish of the soul torn from the body. The common denominator is the humanity of the Son of God, his human emotions, helplessness, and doubt. Each poem in Part III describes some detail of the paintings: facial features and body parts, the inscription, the crown of thorns, the earth beneath. Christ's head, hair, forehead, face, eyes, nose, mouth, ears, cheeks, breast, shoulders, arms, hands, knees and feet, the wounds in his side, all inspire poems evoking acts from the Saviour's life that involved these anatomical particulars. Part IV, comprising final meditations and recapitulation, concludes with a noteworthy and original final prayer, Unamuno's most personal, existential plea for mankind's salvation.

—Janet Pérez

CHRIST STOPPED AT EBOLI (Cristo si è fermato a Eboli)
Prose by Carlo Levi, 1945

In *Christ Stopped at Eboli*, Carlo Levi recounts the year of political exile he spent in the god-forsaken region of Lucania in southern Italy, because of his anti-fascism. The title of Levi's book is a proverbial phrase often repeated by the local peasants and which "in their mouths may be no more than the expression of a hopeless feeling of inferiority. We are not Christians, we're not human beings." Levi explains its much deeper meaning: Eboli is "where the road and the railway leave the coast of Salerno and turn into the desolate reaches of Lucania. Christ never came this far, nor did time, nor the individual soul, nor hope, nor the relation of cause and effect, nor reason nor history."

The richness of the book's motifs lies in the diverse ways in which Levi penetrates the peasant's soul. The work's complexity makes it impossible to categorize: it could be called, variously, a novel, a prose poem, a collection of sketches, a diary, a sociological, ethnological, economic, political, psychological, or mythological essay. These different genres testify to the author's versatility, show him as a brilliant "scientific" observer, and make the work important and moving. What makes the book beautiful and unforgettable is the author's empathy with the world he is depicting; a feeling so powerful that the reader is at times under the impression that Levi created it from within, rather than simply observing it. One could say, metaphorically, that with this book the Lucanian peasant enters for the first time into an awareness of civilized man. The narrator succeeds in mediating the gap between the peasant's primitive condition and civilized man with his self-conscious compassion, and in a style without trace of facile sentimentality.

There is no organizing principle to *Christ Stopped at Eboli* save the passage of the seasons, which "pass today over the toil of the peasants, just as they did three thousand years before Christ." Between the author's entrance and the official conclusion we could interchange many pages. However, it is revealing that the first scene the reader witnesses between Levi and the peasants is the one where Levi, a physician, is called to assist a dying man. The scene is presented at the beginning of the book, in spite of the fact that, as we have been clearly told, the author has already lived in Lucania for months and has already met many peasants. In the economy of this book, this peremptory introduction of the narrator-persona and his protagonists in the presence of death lends an existential significance to their relation which will colour every aspect of the work.

At first Levi lives in Grassano, then suddenly, to his chagrin, is transferred to the smaller village of Gagliano. Soon here, too, a relationship develops between the exile and the peasants who feel respect, admiration, and affection for him because of his genuine understanding and participation in their suffering, although he belongs to a higher social class.

Levi's peasants are not picturesque or picaresque. They consider themselves "beasts of burden" who in darkness walk for two or three hours to their malaria-infested fields. Men, women, and children live, literally, with animals, in one-room huts with goats, pigs, and chickens, and are presented metaphorically by means of constant reminders of the animal world, a technique, of course, not meant to dehumanize the peasantry but to suggest its closeness to the natural world. The narrator presents his subjects in their pristine, prehistorical reality. The place, itself, is experienced at times in its virgin wilderness ("an animal-like enchantment lay over the deserted village"). It seems as if Levi enters these Lucanian villages—places without individual soul, without time, or relation of cause and effect—through intuitive empathy rather than reason. In fact, he not only distances his subjects in their relationships with the animal world, but, more importantly and more effectively, he transports his reader into a time and place where "there is no definite boundary line between the world of human beings and that of animals and monsters," a world crowded with witches, gnomes, spirits, goat-devils, cow-mothers, werewolves, love-philters and poisons, and wild myths and legends; a world where, in a Christian church: "were preserved the horns of a dragon which in ancient times had infested the region . . . Nor would it be strange if dragons were to appear today before the startled eyes of the country people." It is as if Levi had delved into his own subconscious and, concurrently, into the pre-conscious state of western civilization.

The peasants "had always to bow" to all the "invaders who passed through their land." They never protested. Centuries of resignation and a sense of fatality weigh on their shoulders, but when their "infinite endurance" is shaken, their "instinct for self-defence or justice, their revolt, knows no bounds and no measure": they become brigands. It is an "inhuman revolt whose point of departure and final end alike are death." Brigandage is their only defence against an enslaving hostile civilization. Brigands are the peasant's only heroes; they become his legends and myths, his "only poetry," his "epic." When Levi was forbidden from practising medicine, the villagers wanted to act "with grim determination" like their heroes. "With guns and axes on their shoulders," they were ready to "burn the town hall and kill the mayor."

The peasants share a common consciousness and subconsciousness, yet Levi individuates some of them. Among them, unforgettably, is Giulia, the author's housekeeper, the most powerful of Gagliano's 20 witches, mother of 16 illegitimate children, who "taught [Levi] all sorts of spells and incantations for the inspiration of love and the cure of disease," and finally on Christmas Day—although even then "its communication was not entirely sinless"—she revealed to him "the art of bringing about the illness and death of an enemy."

The peasantry is exploited continually in feudal fashion by the village's petty middle class, the families who command city hall but who also envy and hate each other. The reader also feels disgust at the "ridiculous spiderweb of their daily life, a dust-covered and uninteresting skein of self-interest, low-grade passion, boredom, greedy impotence, and poverty." Among them, only Lieutenant Decunto has a "unique beam of conscience that sets him apart," and makes him aware of the decay and spiritual poverty around him. Yet he hates his fellow-citizens, and self-hate makes him "spiteful and bitter . . . [and] capable . . . of any evil." Out of despair he will not become a brigand, as a peasant would, but chooses instead "an escape into a world of destruction." He is the only volunteer from Gagliano for the war in Africa.

The book deals cogently with such problems as malaria, poverty, deforestation, emigration, and ignorance, and concludes with some thoughtful suggestions for political, economic, and social reforms.

These add, usefully, to our knowledge of the author and of southern Italy during the Fascist period, if not to the magic of the book.

—Emanuele Licastro

THE CID (Le Cid)
Play by Pierre Corneille, 1637

Inspired by the Spanish "romanceros" and in particular by Guillén de Castro's *Youthful Deeds of the Cid* (*Mocedades del Cid*), *The Cid* is Pierre Corneille's first major play and probably the finest affirmation of the neo-classical dramaturgy which swept France in the 17th century. While *The Cid* presents a modern picture of man in charge of his own fate, it is also a strong commentary on the society in which Corneille was living. The strengthening of the king's power against the nobility, a Spanish invasion of France, and Richelieu's new social order and prohibition of duels provide the historical, moral, and social backdrop of the play. Key Cornelian words such as "glory," "honour," "merit," and "duty" reflect the concerns of the dominant class of the period. The groundwork for Corneille's subsequent production is laid in *The Cid*: the hero undergoes a test in which his force and lucidity are revealed, while the final act of generosity and royal pardon bring the climax to a happy ending.

The Cid was a public triumph but led to a famed literary dispute, the "Querelle du Cid," because Corneille did not follow strictly the rules of the dramatic genre of the times. A daughter marrying her father's murderer offended the "bienséances," or ethical conventions, while Corneille's liberties with the three unities also came under attack. In *The Cid,* the unity of time is used to its maximum of 24 hours; the unity of place extends to a whole city (private homes, King's palace, port); the action is multiple yet remains unified in its focus on the testing and assertion of the hero's valour, both individual and political.

The Cid holds a particular place in the Frenchman's heart: Corneille's style exemplifies "classical" purity, and every French schoolchild knows the most famous lines of the play.

The action takes place in Seville, in the days of the Reconquista against the Moors. While Chimène awaits her father's decision to allow her to marry Don Rodrigue, the Infanta, Doña Urraque, confides to her servant that she herself loves Rodrigue, "a simple cavalier," but gave him to Chimène since "none but kings are fit" for her royal blood. In the meantime, Don Diègue, Rodrigue's father, has been chosen by the King to be the preceptor of his son, the heir apparent. Don Gomès, count of Gormas, Chimène's father, feels that the ageing Don Diègue was unjustly granted a position that he himself was entitled to on account of his more recent military valour. In the ensuing argument, he slaps his older rival, whose only recourse is to call on Rodrigue to avenge the family's honour.

Torn between love and duty, Rodrigue expresses his dilemma in the famous "stances du Cid" a monologue of lyrical asymmetric stanzas during which he decides that he must confront Don Gomès since he will lose Chimène in either case: "J'attire en me vengeant sa haine et sa colère / J'attire ses mépris en ne me vengeant pas" ("If I avenge myself, I incur her hatred and anger / If I take no revenge, I incur her scorn"). The young and untried Rodrigue kills his father-in-law to be, the exemplary warrior of Castile. Chimène then seeks justice from the King, while Don Diègue appeals for forgiveness.

Rodrigue visits Chimène and offers her his life. While she insists on avenging her father's death, she cannot disguise her love for her enemy (offering a famous understatement: "I do not hate you") and vows "never to breathe a moment after [him]."

An invasion by a Moorish army that very night enables Rodrigue to further prove his valour. He defeats the invaders, capturing two of their kings, who call Rodrigue their lord, or "Cid" in their language. The King deceives Chimène by telling her that Rodrigue has died; she faints, but again asks for justice when she is told the truth. Don Sanche, one of her suitors, will fight for her in a duel against Rodrigue. The victor will marry the young woman. Although he wishes to die, Chimène encourages Rodrigue to live. After the duel, Chimène displays her grief, and then her love for Rodrigue when she learns that he won but spared his rival. The King then proclaims that Chimène will let one year pass to mourn her father while Rodrigue, who is pardoned for killing Don Gomès, goes to fight the Moors. Don Fernand, the King of Castile, imparts the final wisdom of the play: "To still that honour that cries out against you / Leave all to time, your valour, and your King."

These words situate Corneille's work within a conflict between the redefined French state and the old feudal system: the centralization of political power in the 17th century required individuals to work for their country, disregarding petty rivalry and pride. Don Gomès arrogantly believes in the self: "To disobey a little is no great crime / In order to preserve all my good fame"; yet some statements have a prophetic ring to our modern and democratic ears: "Great though they are, kings are but men like us." While Rodrigue asserts the power and courage of the young ("in a well-born soul / Valour awaits not an appointed age"), this new nobleman will nevertheless bow to the king's power for the greatest benefit of all. One should stress that Corneille's depiction of a valiant young Rodrigue reflects Richelieu's efforts to attract competence rather than noble blood to important positions in the administration of a renewed France. This is also supported by Corneille's creation of the Infanta, a character frequently attacked by critics as superfluous, and left out of shortened versions of the play; in fact, the Infanta represents a new social order whose values enlightened individuals like Rodrigue rather than undisciplined noblemen like Don Gomès.

Chimène also shares in this depiction of a new society. With all the reserve expected of a 17th-century woman, she is the exact female counterpart of Rodrigue. She could love only a man who would avenge his family's honour. Torn between love and duty, she will play the part of the worthy daughter; despite her body's weakness (fainting, crying), she embraces the same belief in heroism as Rodrigue.

The classification of *The Cid* as a "tragi-comedy" is explained by the happy ending as by the healthy, vital forces at work. The optimism expressed in the appeal to the present and the future, as opposed to the past glory of old men, certainly contributes to the prodigious success of *The Cid*.

—Pierre J. Lapaire

LE CIMETIÈRE MARIN (The Graveyard by the Sea)
Poem by Paul Valéry, 1920

"Le Cimetière marin" is about mortality and immortality, body and soul, life and death, the inexorable passage of time. It was published in 1920, when Paul Valéry was nearly 50, although he had started work on it some years before after revisiting the graveyard by the sea at Sète, a town on the Mediterranean coast, where he had been born and brought up and was later to be buried. It begins on a note of supreme tranquillity as Valéry gazes out between the pine trees and the tombs over the calm, roof-like expanse of the sea, stretching away into infinity, with what seem to be doves moving slowly and peacefully across it:

> Ce toit tranquille, où marchent des colombes,
> Entre les pins palpite, entre les tombes.
>
> (Quiet that roof, where the doves are walking,
> Quivers between the pines, between the tombs.)

He has the impression of looking down on an age-old golden temple and he experiences an overwhelming intimation of immortality, as if his soul has been absorbed into the glittering sea so that he too reflects back to the sky above the intense light of the noonday sun. But a reflecting surface supposes a darker underside—''endre la lumière Suppose d'ombre une morne moitié''—and this thought leads Valéry to turn his gaze away from the sea towards the marble tombstones of the graveyard which sharply remind him of the mortality of his body. Though the motionless sea may appear infinite and eternal, time, he is forced to recognize, does not stand still; he cannot remain in that state of suspended animation he had experienced at the beginning of the poem; he must accept the challenge of life, instead of waiting serenely for death in the belief that beyond the grave lies immortality. This change in him is matched by a change in the sea. The wind rises and breathes into him a fresh vitality as he rushes forward to plunge into the invigorating waves:

> Brisez, mon corps, cette forme pensive!
> Buvez, mon sein, la naissance du vent!
> Une fraîcheur, de la mer exhalée,
> Me rend mon âme . . . Ô puissance salée!
> Courons à l'onde en rejaillir vivant!
> Le vent se lève! . . . il faut tenter de vivre!
>
> (Break, body, break this pensive mould,
> Lungs, drink in the beginnings of the wind!
> A coolness, exhalation of the sea,
> Gives me my soul back! . . . Ah, salt potency,
> Into the wave with us, and out alive!
> The wind is rising! . . . We must try to live!)

The poem comes full circle when, in the final line, the doves of the opening line are seen to be white sailing boats, joyfully dipping their bows into the breaking waves that dispel the illusion of the sea being the peaceful roof of some timeless temple:

> Rompez, vagues! Rompez d'eaux réjouies
> Ce toit tranquille où picoraient des focs!
>
> (And break, waves, rejoicing, break that quiet
> Roof where foraging sails dipped their beaks!)

It is typical of Valéry's complex craftsmanship that not until the end of the poem is the mysterious image of the doves elucidated, and even then only indirectly with the word ''picorer,'' meaning ''to peck,'' recalling the earlier image and being unusually associated with the word ''foc,'' meaning ''jib-sail,'' used here as a metonym for ''boat.'' Many other examples could be quoted of a similarly original and expressive use of imagery, as when, in a striking oxymoron, the

dead are described as having dissolved into a ''dense absence'' and, in a vivid colour contrast and a startling use of the word ''boire,'' the red earth is described as having ''drunk'' their white bodies:

> Ils ont fondu dans une absence épaisse,
> L'argile rouge a bu la blanche espèce.
>
> (They have melted into a dense unbeing,
> The red clay has drained the paler kind.)

Just as the final line of the poem recalls the first line, so these two lines recall and contrast with Valéry's earlier and very different evocation of how he had savoured, like fruit dissolving deliciously into nothing in his mouth, the foretaste of the disembodied soul he believed he would become:

> Comme le fruit se fond en jouissance,
> Comme en délice il change son absence
> Dans une bouche où sa forme se meurt,
> Je hume ici ma future fumée.
>
> (As a fruit dissolves into a taste,
> Changing its absence to deliciousness
> Within a palate where its shape must die,
> Here can I savour my own future smoke.)

> (translations by David Paul)

The last of these four lines is a notable example of the audacious use of assonance and alliteration that is another remarkable feature of Valéry's poetry and of which again many other instances could be quoted, as when he describes the group of white marble tombstones as: ''Le blanc troupeau de mes tranquilles tombes'' and picks out the particular detail of a tiny insect scratching in the dry and dusty soil of the cemetery: ''L'insecte net gratte la sécheresse.'' Even the rhythm chosen by Valéry is seen as significant by some critics, who would contend that it is no accident that a poem concerned with the passage of time is made up of 24 stanzas and that there are 60 syllables in each stanza of six ten-syllable lines. There can be few if any poems in which form and content are so intricately and so persuasively interwoven.

—C. Chadwick

THE CITY OF GOD (De civitate Dei)
Prose by St. Augustine, c. AD 413–26

Although St. Augustine was, by training, a rhetorician, which allowed him to speak movingly about matters he himself did not necessarily feel strongly about (as he confessed), his greatest works were deeply felt and emerged from profound crises. The autobiographical *Confessions* derived from his own tormented conversion to Christianity. By contrast, *The City of God* responded to a spiritual crisis of national proportion.

On 24 August AD 410, Alaric and Goth and his army entered the city of Rome, initiating three days of looting and burning that sent shock waves through the Empire. Although the Empire, divided into East and West, had been officially Christian for almost a century, and the imperial residence and administrative centre of the Western Empire had moved to Ravenna, Rome remained the spiritual and symbolic centre for both pagans and Christians. To the pagans, the sack of Rome by the (Christian) Goths signified divine retribution for the abandonment of the old gods. For the Christians it raised doubts about the relationship between religion and the secular state. Augustine, Bishop of Hippo from AD 396, took up both issues, working sporadically from AD 413 to 426, drawing on his vast command of history, philosophy, and classical literature, as well as theology and the Bible, to produce the monumental work, *The City of God*. The work represents both an articulate and sophisticated defence of Christianity against its pagan critics and, more fundamentally, an attempt to elaborate a comprehensive philosophical explanation of Christian doctrine in order to create a Christian vision of history and universal society.

In a letter to the priest Firmus, Augustine suggested that the 22 books (*quateriones*) of *The City of God* should be subdivided into five sections. The first (Books I to V) was explicitly polemical, defending Christianity against the charges related specifically to the sack of Rome. The second (Books VI to X) shifted to an examination of Christian ethics in relation to the classical schools of philosophy. The third (Books XI to XIV) explained the creation of the two cities as it related to philosophy and religion. The fourth (Books XV to XVIII) traced the parallel historical development of the two cities. Finally, the fifth (Books XIX to XXII) envisioned the ends of the two cities, the goal of God's plan, and man's place in history.

The Donatist philosopher Ticonius had earlier distinguished between the cities of God and the Devil, using imagery from the Psalms. Augustine appropriated this distinction, transforming it according to his own philosophical and theological conception. Throughout his later writings he described the secular city, embodied in the City of Babylon and manifest historically in the Assyrian and Roman empires. This he contrasted with the City of God, embodied in Jerusalem and manifest in the Christian community, especially the Catholic Church. Looking specifically at the sack of Rome, Augustine sought to defend Christianity by pointing out that the sack was not the first disaster to assail the city. Indeed, what was unique to this disaster was the willingness of the Goths to spare those Christians and pagans who took refuge in churches. More to the point, however, the city of the Christian is not a physical place in space and time, but the otherworldly city of God. Thus, lamentably, while many may have suffered, if they were true to Christianity their true substance remained unviolated. Pointing to a parallel with the ancient story of the rape of Lucretia, he cited approvingly the statement that only Lucretia's assailant was guilty of adultery.

The fundamental philosophical problem for Augustine was how to account for the apparent dualism between matter and spirit, and to reconcile the presence of evil in the world with the notion that everything derived from a single omnibeneficent creator of the universe. Both problems looked back to his early obsession with Manichaean doctrine. Revealing a great debt to Plato and Platonism, Augustine argued that all reality emanated from God, positing a qualitative hierarchy that stretched from pure reality or absolute order (God) to nothingness or absolute disorder (chaos); from pure spirit to pure matter and inertia. In effect, the world is perfect, but incomplete. Humankind stands midway in this qualitative hierarchy, less real than God, more real than chaos, a mixture of spirit and matter. In this way Augustine accounted for the apparent dualism of spirit and body as a mixture of one substance in varying degrees of creation, thus preserving the notion of one reality created by God.

Accepting the classical philosophical model, Augustine equated the ethical good with the pursuit of happiness, linking this with the exercise of free will. When the ethical model is correlated to Augustine's conception of reality, human beings fall into one of two camps, according to the disposition of their wills. Either they are oriented toward absolute order and by extension God, or they are oriented toward disorder. The former is the basis of an ethical and moral good, the latter, the basis of evil. The community of those oriented toward the good form the City of God, the other the secular city. Here, Augustine argued, was the uniqueness of the Christian message. Classical philosophy and even Platonism had focused on a physical happiness, pointing ultimately toward chaos. Only Christianity (embodied in Christ) seeks true happiness, which is found only in an orientation toward God. Thus in its ultimate sense, the whole problem of the sack of Rome is irrelevant. Such a concern informs a will directed towards illusory happiness and, in reality, evil. The history of the two cities traces in time the unfolding and fulfilment of God's plan in a movement toward absolute order. This, Augustine suggested, is the eighth and final day of God's creative labour. ''On that day we shall rest and see, see and love, love and praise—for this is to be the end without the end of all our living, that Kingdom without end, the real goal of our present life.'' Only in this City of God will true happiness be possible.

The City of God stands as Augustine's attempt to defend Christianity. In so doing, he transcends polemics to articulate a comprehensive ethical and metaphysical vision of Christianity that makes it an integral contribution to the western philosophical tradition, inspiring philosophers and theologians from the Middle Ages to the present. If *The Confessions* are perhaps Augustine's literary masterpiece, *The City of God* is his philosophical *magnum opus*.

—Thomas L. Cooksey

CLOUD IN TROUSERS (Oblako v shtanakh)
Poem by Vladimir Maiakovskii, 1915

In all his poetry, Vladimir Maiakovskii set himself the task of living up to the 20th century. Believing that traditional and revered forms like the lyric could no longer serve to express the complexities of modern life, and rejecting the values of the Russian literary tradition he inherited, the poet sought to produce radically new forms, in which the urgencies of the moment could be conveyed. He was concerned that conventional poetry was unable to articulate the pressures of history on individuals, and that the extraordinary rapidity of change in the new century needed a new language. In his long poem *Cloud in Trousers*, written a few years before the Russian Revolution, these themes emerge clearly, in a characteristically strident and highly charged voice.

Interrogating the role of the poet in society, it is at once an intimate love poem about personal rejection and a fervent call to arms:

> How dare you bear the title of a poet
> and chirrup like a sparrow, drab and dull?
> Today like a blackjack, you should do it,
> bashing the world's rotten skull.

Maiakovskii's conception of the poet's role in this poem modulates from being that of the conventional rejected lover to the more vital and innovative one of being the social activist, in the vanguard of historical change. At the heart of the poem, the poet's role is unambiguously seen as being that of the political agitator:

> Pubcrawlers, pull your hands out of your pants.
> Grab bombs, cobblestones, knives, or instead,
> those of you who haven't got arms and hands
> batter at walls with your heads!

This inquiry into the responsibilities of the writer may be the poem's most distinctive feature, and the one it shares with much of Maiakovskii's early writing. Yet within this poem there is a simultaneous quieter voice, seeking dialogue with "Maria." She rejects him, despite his most agitated protests:

> Maria!
> Your body
> I'll love and tend
> the way a soldier,
> chopped short by war,
> cherishes his only leg; nay, more!
> No?
> You don't want to?

The dialectic between the poet's private and public selves remains unresolved, and provides *Cloud in Trousers* with its most provocative points of tension. At the end of the poem Maiakovskii places himself in the vast context of the universe, and seems to turn his back on the none the less attractive claims of carnal love:

> Hey you,
> heavens,
> I'm coming,
> d'you hear?
> Take off your hats,
> or. . .

The belief in the inevitability and the imminence of sweeping social change is always present in Maiakovskii's writing, and in this poem it takes over from the more self-absorbed soul-searching of the dialogue with the lover.

To make sense of Maiakovskii's work, it is necessary to see him as part of a concerted movement called Russian Futurism, with which he was involved at this time. Although his later work (especially his plays) moved beyond Futurist concerns, his pre-revolutionary poetry worked within the confines of a movement. Russian Futurism was an aesthetic tendency which drew together painters and writers (Maiakovskii was both) in an onslaught against the conventions of bourgeois society, most energetically in the years 1912–14. Its most prominent members, besides Maiakovskii, were David Burliuk, Elena Guro, Vassili Kamenskii, and Velimir Khlebnikov, and all were committed to a programme of progressivist activity, in which writing was only one part of a larger political project, designed to take creative activity out of the academies and museums and into more public places. In 1913–14, just after completing *Cloud in Trousers*, Maiakovskii and Kamenskii went on a tour of country towns, broadcasting their ideas and filming themselves in the process. The points of stress in this enterprise, between the artist's desire to outrage and his desire to entertain, lie at the heart of *Cloud in Trousers*.

This particular poem may thus be seen as beginning the transition in Maiakovskii's work from the confessional style of his early writing

to the more bombastic and innovative work of the great post-revolutionary period. At first, his powerful writing was suppressed. Speaking of *Cloud in Trousers*, he said, "When I brought the poem to the censors, they asked me, 'You want to go to a hard labour camp?' 'By no means,' I answered, 'that would not suit me at all.' After that, they crossed out six . . . .''

The first publication of the poem in 1915 was heavily mutilated by such interference, and the full text did not appear until 1918. It stands now as one of the most invigorating of the Russian Futurist poems, maintaining the persistent debate about the role of the poet and seeking to accommodate political and personal concerns. Perhaps this particular poem reveals these conflicting demands to be points of tension rather than areas of solidarity, but the energy of the writing gives the lines tremendous momentum. The poem remains one of Maiakovskii's most widely-debated, and its admirers include Louis Aragon, Pablo Neruda, Bertolt Brecht, and Hugh MacDiarrnid.

—Ian A. Bell

THE CLOUD MESSENGER (Meghadūta)
Poem by Kālidāsa, 5th century AD

The literary reputation of Kālidāsa is based chiefly on his dramas and epic poems. However, lyric poetry plays such an essential role in all his works that many critics consider him the first great Sanskrit lyric poet. Many of his plays, notably *Śakuntalā*, contain numerous fragments revealing his excellent mastery of poetic formalism. However, Kālidāsa's lyric genius is without a doubt at its height at the time of the poem *Meghadūta* or *The Cloud Messenger*.

The Cloud Messenger consists of 100 four-line stanzas, written in one of the most difficult metres of the Sanskrit language, the *mandākrāntā* (the "slow approaching"). The poet seems to have borrowed the subject-matter of this poem from the epic poem *Rāmāyana*, and allusions to Rāma's story are found on numerous occasions. However, Kālidāsa is interested not in the creation of an original plot so much as in the opportunity to display his descriptive skill and mastery of traditional poetic conventions.

The Cloud Messenger is the monologue of a *yakṣa*, a sort of demigod, who has been exiled from his home and his beloved wife for neglect of his duty. While in exile, he asks a cloud to convey a message to his wife. In a series of brilliant sketches the *yakṣa* describes to the cloud the path it must follow in order to reach his home in the Himalayas. These passages show how intimately the author knew the cities and the countryside of North India. In the second part of the poem the *yakṣa* first describes the city of Alakā, where his castle stands, and then the beauty of his wife, whom he imagines in a state of prostration due to his absence. In the message, he assures her of his faith and asks her to think of their ultimate reunion.

Kālidāsa is unquestionably a master of poetic style. Not only does he masterfully handle the elaborate metre throughout the poem, but he also makes use of superb descriptions of landscapes in which nature's moods blend with human feelings. The power to convey sentiment, and the fact that he prefers suggestion to elaboration—in contradistinction to later imitators—is for many critics a proof of his poetic genius. His striking mastery of language, characterized by its beauty and, at the same time, by its apparent simplicity, is evident, for instance, in the picture of the *yakṣa's* mourning wife:

Thou shalt know her, my second life, by the scantness of
   her speech,
Like a lonely chakravaki-bird, while I, her mate, am afar;
As these days pass heavy with intense longing, I imagine the
   hapless girl
Changed in form, as a lotus blighted by the cold season.
Surely the eyes of my beloved are swollen with passionate
   weeping,
And the hue of her lip now changed by the heat of her sighs;
Resting on her hand and half-hidden by her drooping locks,
Her face wears the sad look of the moon when thy approach
   eclipses its beauty.

(translated by F. and E. Edgerton)

The admiration that *The Cloud Messenger* has elicited has not deterred some critics from pointing out the apparent flaws of the poem. The most striking of these is the element of unreality of the story: the *yakṣa* is an immortal being, and his addressing the cloud seems unconvincing. However, these apparent flaws are for many critics a poetic advantage. Furthermore, the love of these two immortal beings has been interpreted by many scholars as a symbol of human love, which is skilfully described by Kālidāsa. Therefore, it can be said that the *The Cloud Messenger* expresses human sentiment in a highly poetic form.

Kālidāsa's erotic poem is too distant from the conventional genres to fit into any of the lyric categories determined by Indian tradition. The poem is ranked among the epic poems by Indian critics because the lyric verses have an epic frame; but it is the lyric element that predominates in the poem. *The Cloud Messenger* is in fact a blend of the existing lyric genres, too original to be properly understood by Kālidāsa's contemporaries. None of the numerous imitations of the poem in later Indian literature is capable of attaining the stylistic perfection or the beauty of imagery of the original poem, suggesting the difficulty of following Kālidāsa's pattern.

Nevertheless, *The Cloud Messenger* has been considered the first ''modern'' poem of Indian literature for its influence on later poets, not only Indian, but also Western. It won the admiration of Goethe, who praised it in his *Zahme Xenien*. Schiller drew on the idea of Kālidāsa's poem in his *Maria Stuart*, where the captive Queen of Scots addresses a pitiful speech to the clouds that fly towards her native land (Act III, scene i). The beauty of the language, the intensity of the poet's feeling for nature, and the powerful depiction of human sentiment which pervades the poem turn the work of the Indian author into a classical masterpiece of world literature. As G. Meyer wrote in *Essays und Studien*, II(99), *The Cloud Messenger* is ''the most beautiful lament of a sorrowing lover which one can read.''

—Ana M. Ranero

THE CLOUDS (Nephelai)
Play by Aristophanes, 423 BC

The Clouds, as it exists today, is not the play of 423 BC performed in the city Dionysia. That play, much to Aristophanes' chagrin, failed, only obtaining third prize. What we have is an unperformable revision whose date is not certain. How much of the original has been left intact is still a matter of controversy. The play takes its title from its chorus, whose members are introduced as the only divinities accepted by the new enlightenment, but in a volte-face at the end of the play reveal themselves as guardians of the old morality. In this, perhaps his most ambitious play, Aristophanes confronted one of the great issues of his day, the moral effect of the Greek 5th-century intellectual revolution. The so-called sophistic movement, which, among other things, sought to explain the workings of the universe in terms of scientific necessity rather than divine causation, undermined traditional worship and traditional morality. In *The Clouds* we are shown what happens when the man in the street becomes involved with representatives of the movement. An old farmer Strepsiades, beset by debts incurred by his son Pheidippides in his manic pursuit of equestrianism, decides to enlist the help of new thinkers. One of their specialities is training in public speaking, and Strepsiades has heard that in their college (*phrontisterion*, literally ''think-shop'') there are to be found two ''arguments,'' ''the better'' and ''the worse,'' and that the worse argument is capable of defeating the better. If Pheidippides can master this argument, Strepsiades will be able to dismiss his creditors without having to pay up. Pheidippides, however, refuses to have anything to do with this suggestion and Strepsiades himself attempts without success to acquire a sophistic education. After his failure he coerces his son into following him to the college, where the young man is confronted by the physical embodiments of the two arguments. In a formal contest (the *agon*) they debate the merits of traditional and modern education. The worse argument (in other words ''Wrong'') wins hands down and Pheidippides is taken into the school. He proves an apt pupil and with his advice Strepsiades deals confidently with his creditors.

The new training, however, has a less pleasant outcome for Strepsiades. Taught to reject traditional morality, Pheidippides now sees no reason why he should not beat his father if he so wishes. A second debate takes place in which Strepsiades takes on the defence of older morality and Pheidippides shows off his new sophistic powers. Naturally he wins the argument, ending by saying that he is also perfectly entitled to beat his mother. Realizing that he has a monster on his hands, Strepsiades turns on the chorus and blames it for leading him on. The chorus reveals that it has been dissembling and that in reality it is part of a divine plan to teach respect for the gods. With the help of his slave, Strepsiades attacks the college, demolishing and setting fire to it. The play ends as the inmates rush out in terror, fleeing for their lives.

One issue dominates critical reaction to *The Clouds*. The avaricious proprietor of the college and arch-sophist who is a professed expert on every subject under the sun—language, astronomy, biology, etc.—is none other than the famous Socrates. His portrayal in the play is a stark contrast to what we are told about him by his admirers Plato and Xenophon. Their Socrates does not teach for money, is vehemently opposed to the great practising sophists like Protagoras and Hippias, and disowns any claim to expertise in the field of learning, science, or the arts. The contradiction between the two portraits becomes explicable if one bears in mind that to the laymen the historical Socrates may not have appeared to be different in kind to his opponents, the sophists. Both parties were, after all, talking about the same things and Socrates' association with Athenian aristocrats might well have suggested that he accepted some kind of subsidy from the rich. Moreover, Aristophanes is dealing not so much with an individual as with a comic type, the bumptious intellectual. He has collected a multitude of traits associated with contemporary intellectuals (some of them contradictory) and foisted them on the character of Socrates.

How serious the intent behind this assault on the new learning may have been is debatable. It must be borne in mind that the normal stance of Old Comedy is backward-looking and philistine. As elsewhere in Aristophanes, however, the old does not escape penetrating satire any more than does the new. The better argument is represented as a spluttering incompetent who cannot conceal his own sexual obsession with boys' genitals.

The ending of the play with its stark portrayal of the conflict between generations and the violent assault on the college and its inmates leaves a slightly sour taste, paralleled only in Aristophanes perhaps by the ending of *The Wasps*. If this was how the play ended in its production at the Dionysia, we may have an explanation for its lack of success.

—David M. Bain

THE COLLOQUIES (Colloquia familiaria)
Prose by Desiderius Erasmus, 1518

The Colloquies are a masterpiece of literary satire and an invaluable source of information about a host of aspects of the Renaissance. Yet this substantial work was apparently produced almost by accident. There is some evidence that Desiderius Erasmus was far from pleased to discover, in November 1518, that his friend Johannes Froben, a printer in Basle, had, without asking his permission, published a small volume of Latin dialogues dating from some 20 years earlier. Erasmus had written them when, as an impoverished student in Paris, he had been employed as tutor to some boys. One of his duties was to train them in the use of Latin as a conversational medium, for speaking that language fluently still had its importance in intellectual spheres and, to some extent, in practical life too, and he came up with the idea of composing a number of model dialogues illustrating, for instance, the forms of address appropriate to people of varying status. In other words, *The Colloquies*, like his *De conscribendis epistolis* (*On the Writing of Letters*) and *Adagia* (*Adages*), a collection of classical proverbs and idioms, began life simply as a textbook designed to teach correct Latin in an attractive way.

A man of wit, responsive to all that took place around him, Erasmus was not, however, content to leave things at that. He never undervalued his pedagogic role, and possessed the encyclopedic scholarship needed to play a significant part in the Renaissance revival of a pure classical style that would not reflect the development (or, as he and his contemporaries saw it, the corruption) of Latin in the Middle Ages. In 1522, four years after the first, unauthorized, edition, Froben brought out an enlarged version of *The Colloquies*. Erasmus dedicated it to Froben's young son, illustrating not only that the author was now on good terms with his printer, but also that he had become more aware of the rich potential of the intrinsically humble form he was using. As well as teaching sound Latin, it would serve to inculcate good manners (or ''civility,'' as it was often termed in the Renaissance). More important still was Erasmus' use of some of his *Colloquies* to express his opinions about what was wrong in Europe generally and what, in particular, was amiss in the Church.

Euntes in ludrum litterarium (*Off to School*) is an example of *The Colloquies* in their simplest form. There are two short dialogues; the first features two boys chatting on their way to lessons, while the second, a conversation between two others about their pens and ink, is enlivened by a flash of schoolboy vulgarity. *De lusu* (*Sport*) gives some idea of how youngsters amused themselves in the Renaissance, for example, playing real tennis. As if to remind us that schooldays were not all fun and games, *Monita paedagogica* (*A Lesson in Manners*) presents a master who sharply reprimands a boy slouching around untidily dressed and unable to speak properly to his superiors. Erasmus was not, however, content for long with this sort of subject. *Hippoplanus* (*The Cheating Horse-Cooper*) reveals his knowledge of the ways of the world, his psycological insight, and his ear for dialogue in an entertaining account of the way a rascal is cheated out of his ill-gotten gains.

In *Ementita nobilitas* (*The Ignoble Knight*), Erasmus reveals his satiric side. Like many in the Renaissance, Harpalus seeks to rise to the nobility, though he does not come of good family and lacks any personal distinction. Nestor, with his tongue very firmly in his cheek, gives him an outspoken lesson in the art of social climbing without merit, which includes, typically for Erasmus, some particularly acerbic remarks about soldiering. In this colloquy, as in a number of others, there are indications that the spur to Erasmus' indignation was his animosity towards a particular acquaintance, but the point he raised was one of general interest in the period.

However, it is about religious matters that Erasmus is most outspoken. Either out of innate caution or, more likely, because of a theological conviction that the Roman Church alone offered the way to salvation, he was never prepared to follow Luther and countenance a schism. Nonetheless, he was conscious that there was much in Catholic religious life and practice in the early 16th century that was greatly in need of reform, and his attacks on abuses in *The Colloquies* and elsewhere made him and his works suspect in orthodox quarters.

Virgo Poenitens (*The Repentant Girl*) concerns a girl who objects to being pressured into taking religious vows, while fasting is under attack in *Ichtyophagia* (*A Fish Diet*). However, Erasmus' religious attitudes are perhaps best exemplified in *Peregrinatio Religionis ergo* (*The Pilgrimage for Religion's Sake*), a colloquy that reflects his visits to the Marian shrine at Walsingham in Norfolk, England. The bitter complaint that Erasmus makes time and again is that grasping and ignorant clergy wickedly lead gullible layfolk into mechanical devotional practices and encourage mindless superstition, when the clear message of the Gospels is that Christ sought to replace mere religious observance with deeply held conviction and a true change of heart.

—Christopher Smith

THE COMIC THEATRE (Il teatro comico)
Play by Carlo Goldoni, 1750

The Comic Theatre is one of a prodigious corpus of comedies written by Carlo Goldoni in 1750 for Girolamo Medebach, director of the Sant'Angelo theatre in Venice, with which the dramatist was associated until his move, in 1753, to the San Luca, another theatre in his native city. Although enjoying the favour of the theatre-going public, Goldoni was subjected to repeated attacks from literary rivals such as Piero Chiari and Carlo Gozzi, spokesmen for an academy of conservative purists, the Granelleschi, who opposed the innovations that were beginning to manifest themselves in Italian society, politics, and literature. The Granelleschi was dedicated to preserving the stylistic and linguistic purity of Italian authors and to re-establishing the *commedia dell'arte* (improvised comedy) as the prevailing comic theatre of the time. Goldoni, who dared to bring spoken, everyday language to the comic stage and, even more outrageously, replace improvised comedy with premeditated, "character" comedies, was thus a natural target for concerted public criticism. It was against such criticism that Goldoni produced, during 1750 and 1751, a number of new comedies: *The Comic Theatre, La bottega del caffè (The Coffee House), Il bugiardo (The Liar), L'adulatore* [The Flatterer], *La Pamela (Pamela), Il cavalier di buon gusto* [The Man of Taste], *Il giuocatore* [The Gambler], *Il vero amico* [The True Friend], *La finta ammalata* [The False Invalid], *La damma prudente* [The Cautious Woman], *L'incognita perseguitata dal bravo impertinente* [The Unknown Woman Persecuted by the Bumptious Braggart], *L'avventuriere onorato* [The Honourable Adventurer], *La donna volubile* [The Fickle Woman], *I pettegolezzi delle donne* [Women's Gossip], to establish himself as the leading comic writer of his time.

In a prefatory note, "The Author to the Reader," included in the first volume of the Paperini edition (Florence, 1753) of Goldoni's works, the author expresses his desire that *The Comic Theatre* serve as a foreword to all his comedies. Together with the preface to an earlier collection of his comedies (Bettinelli, 1750), this particular drama is a statement, in comic form, of the principles on which he based his comedies of character. As Goldoni himself explains in "The Author to the Reader," he chose this form for the statement of his poetics over a more conventional introduction as "the latter would probably have bored readers more easily" (*The Comic Theatre*, translated by John W. Miller, 1969). The play is simultaneously an explicit statement of the defects, prevalent in improvised comedy, which he sought to avoid in his own new style of comedy.

Compared to the rest of Goldoni's dramatic output, *The Comic Theatre* is innovative in both its form and content. Like Pirandello's *Sei personaggi in cerca d'autore (Six Characters in Search of an Author)*, it is a theatrical production in the making, a behind the scenes look at a rehearsal (of a Goldoni play) in progress, liberally interspersed with conversations between the existing cast members, and interrupted by two new arrivals, an impoverished poet and a virtuoso singer, both seeking work. Most of the 13 members of the cast with speaking roles play two parts: their "off-stage" character as well as the character they play in the rehearsal within the play. Hence Orazio, the head of the company of actors and mouthpiece for Goldoni himself, is called Ottavio in the rehearsal; Placida, the leading lady (a role written for Teodora Medebach), also plays the part of Rosaura; Eugenio, the second *amoroso*, is also Florindo, and so on. Three of the characters: Tonino/Pantalone; Anselmo/Brighella; Gianni/Harlequin, speak Venetian dialect when rehearsing the company's latest comedy, *A Father His Son's Rival*. Gianni and Petronio at times resort to Latin aphorisms in making their point (see, for example, Act I, scenes 8 and 9), while Anselmo and Gianni occasionally use rhyming couplets, typical of their stage' persona, before exiting (Act I, scenes 6 and 8). Unity of place is maintained throughout the comedy with the scene, the comic stage itself, remaining unchanged.

The Comic Theatre begins with Orazio and Eugenio discussing the requisites of successful comedy as they await the arrival of the other members of the company. Rehearsals are essential, and the most can be made of an actor by giving him a part that is good and not merely long. In the ensuing scenes they are joined firstly by their fellow actors, then by Lelio, a thin, impecunious author of plot outlines for the old style improvised comedies, followed by Eleonora, a singer of similarly old fashioned melodramas, which Orazio at first dismisses as new comedy, has no need of music to be successful. What then ensues is not so much a debate between the proponents of the old and the new comic theatre as an exposition (begun in the first act by Orazio and taken over in the second by Anselmo) of the salient

characteristics of comedies of character, addressed to two representatives of superseded theatrical schools only too willing to be converted if it means finding work in Orazio's company. Thus *The Comic Theatre* is not so much a statement of an intended reform as a declaration of a reform that has already been realized. Anselmo stresses the moral purpose of premeditated comedies: they have been purged of all immorality and are suitable entertainment for young ladies. In the old improvised, masked comedies, moral purpose, edification, had been sacrificed to the merely ridiculous. Identification, essential if edification is to be achieved, is now possible between the audience and the characters who will appeal to people of all social classes. Placida points out to Lelio (Act II, scene 2) that conceits (stock soliloquies, dialogues, tirades) have been replaced by plausible speeches and a familiar, naturalistic style. Gone are the metaphors, antitheses, and rhetoric of improvised comedies. Nor are Lelio's translations of French plays any more acceptable to Orazio. Unity of action and a simple title are required, yet masks (that is to say, such stock characters of the *commedia dell'arte* as Harlequin, Brighella, Pantalone, etc.) are not to be eliminated completely so that they may contrast with the serious characters. (Goldoni himself dispenses with this injunction in his later comedies in which these traditional characters no longer appear.)

Where the acting style of new comedy is concerned, Orazio stresses to Lelio the importance of credibility and realism; it is now inadmissible to address the audience directly, and all soliloquies must be plausible. Actors should learn by observing other actors in their free time, since practice and the observation of others are better teachers than theoretical rules. Goldoni implicitly acknowledges his indebtedness to the Latin theoretician Horace (Orazio is the Italian for Horace) when Orazio clears up (Act III, scene 9) Lelio's misinterpretation of a passage from the *Art of Poetry* regarding the number of actors appearing on stage at any one time. And when Lelio butchers lines from *Didone abbandonata (Dido Abandoned)*, Orazio, appalled, acknowledges the theatre's debt to its author, another reformer of Goldoni's century, Metastasio.

Besides being concerned with the quality of his actors as performers, Orazio also holds the off-stage atmosphere important; peace is essential: "Harmony among colleagues makes for the success of plays" (Act III, scene 1). The audience, too, should be educated as well as the actors: spectators should not spit, nor make a noise during the performance.

There is a certain complacency in *The Comic Theatre*, a self-congratulatory tone as when Lelio states (Act III, scene 2) that he hopes one day to compose comedies like those of the company's author. Comic reform has already been achieved by Goldoni and implemented with success. The comedy ends with the end of the rehearsal within the play, and with a statement to the effect that the day's proceedings have demonstrated how the Comic Theatre ought to be.

—Nicole Prunster

THE CONCEITED YOUNG LADIES (Les Précieuses ridicules)
Play by Molière, 1659

Although this play was given its first performance in 1659, at a time before Molière came into prominence as one of the three great dramatists of 17th-century France, and indeed before he had written anything else of real substance, it became a very successful farce, and has continued to be popular to this day. For the literary historian an additional interest lies in the fact that it contains in embryo many of his major preoccupations as a mature dramatist.

The French title—*Les Précieuses ridicules*—points directly at the target of Molière's acid wit: the affectation of two young provincial girls, Magdelon and Cathos, who reflect a tendency within certain elements of contemporary French society towards preciosity, coupled with aspirations and pretensions far beyond their proper place in society.

The play blends three elements in a successful and outrageous cocktail: the literary comic tradition, the tradition of the farce, and contemporary high society.

The play consists of 17 scenes, rather than the normal five acts, and the performance time is around an hour. Gorgibus has selected two gentlemen, La Grange and Du Croisy, as marriage partners for his daughter Magdelon and his niece Cathos. Gorgibus learns that the two young *précieuses* have rejected their advances.

He confronts the wayward young ladies, and it is clear that their precious escapist visions of life hardly match the rigours of everyday bourgeois reality. Their affectations are now unmasked by the arrival of a Marquis de Mascarille, so called, and the Vicomte de Jodelet: these supposed gentlemen are in fact the valets of the two rejected lovers, but Magdelon and Cathos swallow their blandishments hook, line, and sinker. By falling willing victim to their advances, the two ladies are now convinced that they have arrived in the "beau monde."

At this point, comedy has become farce as La Grange and Du Croisy break up the burlesque ball that takes place, rounding on their valets and literally stripping them of their fine feathers. The girls are disgraced and Gorgibus ends the piece by condemning the empty phrases and foolish extravagances of preciosity and wishing to send them packing "to the devil."

At the centre of the comedy and its principal target are the eponymous *précieuses*. There are three particular characteristics that mark out the *précieuses*: an obsessive preoccupation with external appearances, an artificially inflated approach to language, and excessive prudishness.

The linguistic affectations of the two young aspiring ladies are marked primarily by a process of accumulation: a wealth of superlatives, and the rejection of any common or ordinary turn of phrase in favour of an abstruse formulation and an obsession with euphemisms are just some of the elements of the linguistic contortions which serve, in their view, to indicate sophistication of manner and an elevated social position. Their verbal antics are not unlike those of the ethereal young ladies in Gilbert and Sullivan's *Patience*.

Natural objects assume fanciful appellations: a mirror is referred to by Cathos as "conseiller des grâces" (counsellor of the graces), which causes the servant Marotte to demand that her mistress speak plain comprehensible French. Cathos rejoins: "Fetch us the mirror, ignorant creature that you are, and beware of sullying the glass with the communication of your image." The terms she uses for mirror, together with that last phrase "communication of your image," serves to underline a central feature of preciosity: the strong tendency to take ordinary objects and to inflate their significance beyond all reason by seeking to turn them into abstractions. By a reverse process, human beings become all appearance and no substance, and human physicality tends to be devalued, if not actively shied away from. Cathos describes marriage in these horrified terms: "I find the idea of marriage utterly shocking. How can one possibly entertain the notion of sleeping next to a man who is entirely naked?"

Apart from being a farce of merit on its own terms, the play contains a number of pointers to the principal preoccupations of Molière in his more mature work. First, it marks him clearly as a social critic whose chief weapon is a barbed and highly accurate wit. Second, he holds up a mirror—or should we say "a counsellor of the graces"?—to absurdities and affectations within society which reduce human character to "the rigidity of an automaton" (Bergson) and devalue the life and vitality of true human nature. Thirdly, it demonstrates his awareness that there is no curative effect in comic drama: he can seek only to reinforce the vitality of genuine human beings—for those who have hardened into risible types there is no salvation.

These themes are later translated into the miserliness of a Harpagon, the false piety of a Tartuffe, or the misanthropy of an Alceste (in which society itself is implicated) and so it can rightly be said, in the words of Martin Turnell, that preciosity as depicted in *The Conceited Young Ladies* "leads straight to psychological perversion, to the obsessions that are studied with marvellous insight in Molière's greatest plays."

—Rex Last

THE CONFERENCE OF THE BIRDS (Manteq al-Tayr)
Poem by Farid al-Din Attār, c. 1177

The Conference of the Birds is the most important narrative poem of Farid al-Din Attār, the 12th/13th-century Persian poet. It is a long narrative poem of 4,600 rhyming couplets (*masnavi*), consisting of 45 discourses, each containing several embedded stories. The poem, which is a collection of Sufi tales, is an allegorical account of Sufism (Islamic mysticism). The art of storytelling enables Attār to communicate his subtle and complicated mystical ideas in a simple language which would otherwise be difficult for the reader to understand.

The book begins with the praise of God, the Prophet, and the Four Caliphs (Abu Bakr, Omar, Osmān, and Ali). The story then starts with the quest of the birds of the world for a king who can protect them from the perils of life. The hoopoe (*hud-hud*), known as Solomon's messenger to Belqays, the Queen of Sheba, is spiritually the best qualified bird to lead them to their king. Their king, who is called the Simurgh, abides behind the far-away Mount of *Qāf* (a legendary mountain imagined to surround the world).

The hoopoe explains that the journey to the Simurgh is long and difficult and that it requires dedication and effort to find one's way to his court. As soon as the birds find out about the difficulties of the journey, their eagerness disappears and they try to excuse themselves from undertaking the journey. Their apologies illustrate the typical characteristics of each species of bird. The first bird to withdraw from this journey is the nightingale, who cannot renounce his passionate love for the rose. The other birds, including the parrot, the peacock, the duck, the partridge, the *homa* (royal eagle, also a bird of happy omen), the falcon, the heron, the owl, and the goldfinch, follow the nightingale, each giving a reason why it is impossible to make the journey. The hoopoe resorts to storytelling in answering their excuses and other subsequent questions. The stories, which are thematically linked to each other, are meant to awaken the soul of the birds to the Divine Reality, and thus to encourage them to embark on the journey to the royal court.

Inspired by the hoopoe's stories, the birds set out to meet their king. The path to the Simurgh's court, however, is filled with obstacles, and the birds need further encouragement and clarification of their goal and path. The hoopoe explains the seven valleys (spiritual stages) that they have to cross before reaching their goal, the Absolute Being. First is the valley of quest (*talab*) in which the seeker has to go through thousands of tests in order to be purged from any impurities. At this stage the seeker of the path has to leave the material world behind and prepare himself to receive divine grace. Second is the valley of love (*ishq*) which will set the seeker's soul and body on fire. The ardent lover who is consumed in the fire of love is beyond good and evil. Third is the valley of esoteric knowledge (*ma'refat*). Esoteric knowledge transcends rational and logical knowledge; it is not to be learned from books but acquired by meditation and intuition. Fourth is the valley of independence (*isteghnā*) in which the seeker becomes completely independent of the outside world and detaches himself from the material world. He becomes so rich spiritually that the outside world is worth nothing to him. Fifth is the valley of unity (*towhid*) in which the seeker achieves a unitary vision. Duality disappears and everything becomes a part of the whole. There is no more talk of "I" and "Thou." There is no being except the Absolute Being. Sixth is the valley of bewilderment (*hayrat*). This is the valley of lamentation and confusion. The seeker does not know himself any longer; he does not know to which religion or nation he belongs. In fact, he has gone far beyond these artificial boundaries; he has achieved a cosmic consciousness by which he transcends the binary definitions of the material world. The last is the valley of poverty and annihilation (*faqr* and *fanā*). This is the last stage on the path of the Sufi where his individual self is annihilated and he becomes one with the Absolute Being. Finally the seeker who has constantly been looking for his Beloved becomes one with Him, like a drop of water joining the ocean. In other words, the lover is totally absorbed in the Beloved, and thus achieves the highest stage of spiritual growth.

Many of the birds die on their way to the royal court from the insurmountable hardships they encounter. From hundreds of thousands of birds who had initially started the trip, only 30 birds complete the journey. When these 30 birds finally reach His Majesty's court, they are exhausted, but they soon find out that the whole universe is nothing but dust in comparison with His Majesty. They wonder if a bunch of miserable creatures like themselves are worthy of meeting him. In fact, His Majesty's chamberlain receives them very coldly and sends them back. But the birds have no intention of going back now that they have had a glimpse of His Majesty. First they must be purified from all their previous sins. When they are finally admitted to his presence, they discover that His Majesty, the Simurgh, is only a mirror in which they see their own image. They are the Simurgh.

Actually the whole story is based on a pun. The word *simurgh* in Persian can be the name of a mythical bird, referred to also as *anqā* (the phoenix), and is usually associated with the Divine; it also means "30 birds" (*si* = "30," *murgh* = "bird").

The 30 birds in *The Conference of the Birds* represent 30 mystics on their path to perfection, to God, the Absolute Being. The dedicated pilgrims blessed by His grace depend on a spiritual master (*pīr* or *morād*) for direction and guidance. The real search is within and the ultimate goal is annihilation in God (*fanā fel-lāh*), and the discovery of everlasting life in God (*baqā bel-lāh*). The 30 birds eventually find eternal life through mystical union with the Simurgh.

In the conclusion Attār recounts the hardships he has gone through while composing *The Conference of the Birds* and hopes that his readers will find his book a source of guidance and inspiration on their path to the Divine Reality.

—Alireza Anushiravani

THE CONFESSIONS (Les Confessions)
Prose by Jean-Jacques Rousseau, 1782–89 (written 1764–70)

Jean-Jacques Rousseau completed *The Confessions* in 1770, but they remained unpublished until several years after his death. The book remains one of the most influential and provocative texts of the Enlightenment and one of the formative early documents of European Romanticism. As he opens the first part, Rousseau boldly sets his terms of reference:

> I have resolved on an enterprise which has no precedent and which, once complete, will have no imitator. My purpose is to display to my kind a portrait in every way true to nature, and the man I shall portray shall be myself. Simply myself. I know my own heart and understand my fellow man. But I am made unlike anyone I have ever met; I will even venture to say that I am like no one in the whole world. I may be no better, but at least I am different.

That his enterprise was unprecedented seems more than probable. Earlier attempts at the self-analysis and self-advertising of autobiography had taken other forms. The *Confessions* of St. Augustine, for example, were clearly exemplary in exploring the religious experiences of the writer—the author interpreted his own life and errors so that others might learn valuable lessons from them. Such was not Rousseau's aim. He was much more concerned with defining his personal identity, with the operation of memory, with trying to pin down exactly what sensations and feelings were most important to him, and, although the experience is mediated through the process of narration, he resolutely refuses throughout his long book to moralize or sensationalize events. In putting before the reader his shabby exploits as well as his more noble deeds, frankness (or at least the illusion of frankness) seems to be his guiding principle.

Rousseau's work is highly individualist, not just in the sense that it carries a personal stamp, but also in its belief in the intrinsic interest of his own personality. It is not because of his renown that he writes, but because he places value on introspection as a process of self-discovery. He sees himself not as integrated within society, living a predominantly public life which is communal and shares its most important features with others, but as a unique feeling individual, whose most valuable experiences are complex interior and private emotions. By chronicling his emotional responses, dwelling on his sensitivity and sensibility, Rousseau concentrates upon his personal development, upon the growth of his being, in a way that profoundly influenced many later Romantic writers, equally concerned with their own inner states—Wordsworth's *The Prelude*, subtitled "the growth of a poet's mind" is perhaps the best-known inheritor of Rousseau's mantle.

Also deeply influential was the way Rousseau emphasized the importance of childhood experience. In the first part of *The Confessions*, his own curious childhood is nostalgically presented as a special period of innocence, in need of protection and preservation against the enfeebling compromises and pressures of maturity. After the sudden death of his mother in childbirth, Rousseau was brought up by his father, and he turned inward, finding comfort in books, which he saw as giving insight into feelings at the expense of rational understanding: "I had grasped nothing. I had sensed everything." Yet although he talks of the "serenity" of his childhood, and although it is recollected with great tenderness, it still seems overshadowed by a sense of imminent loss, by a consciousness that this brief period of life is the most precious and the most vulnerable. In this, Rousseau not only influenced many subsequent writers on the formative period of childhood, but also acted as a precedent for the introspective narration of Proust and others. Indeed, the vast body of subsequent writing on subjectivity and the "self" owes a great debt to Rousseau.

The first part of *The Confessions* covers the period between 1712 and 1741, taking Rousseau through pastoral accounts of a relatively uneventful youth and young manhood, dealing with the growth of affecting feelings and many tender episodes between the sexes. The pleasures of a comfortable life in the country amid agreeable companions like the attractive Merceret and the urbane Marshal de Luxembourg figure prominently. The candour with which he recounts his sexual exploits also shows a remarkable freedom of spirit, even if his highly-charged responses to small stimuli now seem rather tame. The second volume, however, immediately employs a different tone, deepening the sense of loss:

> After favouring my wishes for 30 years, for the next 30 fate opposed them, and from this continual opposition between my situation and my desires will be seen to arise great mistakes, incredible misfortunes, and every virtue that can do credit to adversity except strength of character.

The sense of injustice and unfairness visible even in the earlier volumes in Rousseau's apparent hypochondria, emerges as a crippling anxiety about his standing in the face of others and a constant fear of persecution. Rousseau's feelings here, minutely presented, seem adrift from the provocations of the world, and the book becomes very revelatory of a particular state of mind, even when there seems to be inadequate justification for that state of mind. Yet the detailed accounts of his relationships with his companion, Thérèse Le Vasseur and his encounters with the literary intelligentsia of the day make compelling reading. Even if the later episodes lack the charm of the childhood adventures, they still add to the most compelling and revealing self-description written in pre-revolutionary Europe, and one of the most profoundly influential narratives in European culture.

—Ian A. Bell

CONFESSIONS, BOOK I
Prose by St. Augustine, late 4th century

No ancient book begins in a more disconcerting way for the modern reader than St. Augustine's *Confessions*. Knowing only that he desires to praise God, and so find rest in him, Augustine begins by raising a series of acute theological problems: should one know God before invoking him; how can God come to a human being; in what sense does God fill somebody or something; who or what, indeed, is God?

As well as a confession of sin and a confession of praise in the sense of the Psalms (as ever, a strong influence on Augustine's thinking), his work is the dialogue between a highly intelligent and relentlessly inquiring mind and its creator. No sooner has he begun his life story than he raises the vexed question, which he does not resolve even in the more exclusively philosophical later books of the *Confessions*, of whether the soul has an existence before entering the body. A discussion of the nature of time (developed in a later book) arises out of an apparent quibble about where his infancy went when it left him and was replaced by adulthood. It is not surprising that many of his ideas appear modern, for example his observation that an infant, far from being "innocent" (witness the jealousy of a twin), is resolutely manipulative and intent only on making others conform to its wishes, or his stress on the educational importance of giving free rein to the curiosity of children. These are, however, related to theological concerns such as original sin and the chastisement of God, whose law restrains curiosity, whether in the classroom or in the wider world. The classroom is a microcosm of the world; it is a "stony path" that adds to "the toil and sorrow of the sons of Adam." Augustine takes all his early recollections very seriously, even though he realizes that other adults, and even God himself, might smile indulgently at such foibles.

Augustine's account of the upbringing and education that he received—Book I takes him up to the age of 15—is another major source of the book's appeal, but it must always be borne in mind that the memories of the child are strongly overlaid by the comments of the bishop that Augustine, in the last years of the 4th century, had now become. It is clear that as a child he disliked Homer (too many Greek words to learn), but loved Virgil's *Aeneid*, written as it was in the language that he had learnt instinctively and by imitation from an early age, and was touched by the tragic story of Dido for much the same reasons as its modern readers, although they would express their reasons very differently. He seems, however, to have lived for his games and for playtime, and found the three Rs pure drudgery. His judgements on the fictions of Virgil, or rather his own stupidity in preferring them to subjects of greater utility, are clearly a later construct, as is his unrelenting criticism of the hypocrisy, inertia, and commercialism of the whole system and its inverted values. Teachers beat children for enjoying games, but they have their own adult games to play, and parents side with the tormentors in spite of the fact that they want their children to grow into adults who can win status and prestige by pandering to the universal desire for entertainment. (Augustine does give credit at least to his mother Monica, who was very concerned for his spiritual and physical health, especially on one occasion when he was dangerously ill.) The Latin language is learnt through texts which are not only fictive, but immoral and obscene, and the system produces people who take more pride in following the rules of grammar than in avoiding the spiritual dangers of envy or dishonesty.

Augustine writes as one not immune from such faults himself—indeed he calls himself the lowest of the low and an outstanding liar—but he is not so lost in his sins and the sins of the world that envelop him that he cannot see some good in his upsetting experiences. He says that as well as a dislike of pain and depression he has acquired an aversion to ignorance, a respect for the evidence of his senses, a high regard for friendship and truth, and a good memory and command of words. The style of the *Confessions*, as of his other works, illustrates that these intellectual qualities remained with him. A mind trained to observe and memorize every detail in a classical text was put to fruitful use in building up an astonishingly thorough knowledge of scripture from which he constantly drew new insights by his learned juxtaposition of diverse passages. Notwithstanding his strictures about the uselessness and perversity of the system that had developed them, his verbal skills—especially his expertise in rhetoric, of which he later became a professor—were consciously turned to the new task of articulating theological insight and divine praise. The power of its style contributes to the impact of this book no less than the intensity of its feeling and the profundity of its ideas.

—R.P.H. Green

CONFESSIONS OF FELIX KRULL, CONFIDENCE MAN
(Bekenntnisse des Hochstaplers Felix Krull)
Novel by Thomas Mann, 1954 (written 1910; first chapter published 1922, enlarged edition 1937, complete version, 1954)

Felix Krull, son of a Rhineland champagne producer who goes bankrupt and commits suicide, finds his early confidence and acting abilities enable him as a child to carry out increasingly daring pranks, which he continues in adult life by feigning an epileptic fit at his medical for military service to avoid conscription, and in Paris leads a double life, as both waiter and man-about-town. His charm, command of foreign languages, and bravado not only win over naive and experienced women and a Scottish lord, but also offer him the chance of travelling around the world as the Marquis de Venosta. In the meantime the real Marquis, unknown to his mother, continues his life of easy dalliance in Paris. Krull sets off with his false identity and papers on the Marquis's Grand Tour and is soon welcomed into the Lisbon home of the palaeontologist, Professor Kuckuck. He is also accepted into the circle of the Portuguese upper class and has a successful audience with the King who rewards Krull's vulgar witticisms with an Order. At the end of the first part of these memoirs (the second part of his journey to South America is never written), Krull/Venosta is involved simultaneously in an affair with both Professor Kuckuck's wife and his daughter.

In these so-called "confessions" (written in 1910, 1922, and 1937 and finally rewritten in the early 1950s) Thomas Mann deliberately set out to hoodwink the reader on several levels. In doing so, he allowed his central character to fascinate and reveal how easily criminal acts can be passed off as works of artistry, performed against the artificiality of social behaviour. From the first sentence it is not clear who is writing. Is it an 80-year-old writer having overcome a major operation and produced a major work, *Doctor Faustus*, on the collapse of German civilization into barbarism and now eager to correct his image of a "ponderous philosopher" (Thomas Mann's letter to Erika Mann, November 1948); or is it an experienced prisoner who has regained his liberty and is now living comfortably on his earlier gains whose charlatanism now consists of producing memoirs that will give him a certain immortality as an innocent victim of society? Felix Krull's anxiety that his style should show good breeding and natural talent is a sign both of his weakness from childhood days and of a gigantic trick to be played on his readers. That he now claims to counter his former picaresque dealings with the world by losing himself in an act of "dreamless" introspection invites, like every event in the book, a double interpretation: either Krull is worthy of sympathy or he overplays his self-pity. The

boyhood pranks are reinterpreted as reasons for the successful exploits of the young man in his various guises and of the fantasy of the now 40-year-old writer.

If the reader believes in this façade, he has been conned by the lasting sophistication of a parvenu who is more subtle and insidious than Heinrich Mann's Dietrich Hessling in *Man of Straw* (*Der Untertan*). One of his diversionary tactics as a writer is to draw the reader's attention away from his present situation as an ex-criminal to extol his virtuosity in the past, despite his claimed great mistake of hurrying forward too quickly. Such a manipulation of time levels, bringing together the past and a false future, is highly suited to Krull's own ambivalent temperament and fits in with his view of the world as a dual structure. The theme of life's double-sidedness is, in fact, an expression of the narrator's duplicity. Krull can even present himself as a person who has lost all self-definition, as an actor with no identity. He is cursed in a Faustian way with a double persona. He is afflicted with the boredom of his present and perpetually needs new forms of excitement to sharpen his awareness of the potentials of life. Change and renewal, and a total existential revolution in taking on new roles bring him fulfilment, but that fulfilment is revealed as illusory through Thomas Mann's use of epithets for him, for example, as a dreamer.

Krull has been interpreted as an absolute artist by an analysis of the loneliness motif. However, Krull has social as well as psychological reasons for being an outsider. Wysling has pointed out how Mann found Nietzsche's 361st aphorism in his copy of *Human, All Too Human* (*Menschliches, Allzumenschliches*) to exemplify his unease about the artist-figure so closely related to the actor whose deceptive skill is practised with a good conscience. Krull becomes the compound artist-rogue, whose double-faced combination explains his wish to lead a double life. Even the "confession" of the title may be interpreted as a piece of literary deception, as it is rarely Krull speaking as Krull, but Krull as Venosta who "confesses." The writer of the memoirs repeatedly casts himself as self-interpreter by taking on another role. Thus what is passed off as an uneasy conscience at work is a masterly confidence trick, for not only does Krull falsify the content and style of his life, but also as narrator falsifies the genre of the work he is writing. He offers the reader a Bildungsroman whose subject and style ought to make it a *Schelmenroman* (picaresque novel). Thomas Mann succeeds in parodying a Bildungsroman through the device of a *Schelmenroman* by deliberately encouraging the permanent ambivalence of Krull's position. The picaresque tradition in which this work stands has never been so elastic in its implications and, ironically, never so compressed. Whereas *Schetmenromane* were expandable to interminable length, here the form is made internally elastic, that is it can be read on several levels at once, and at no time can the reader assume any one of these is its golden mean.

—Brian Keith-Smith

CONFESSIONS OF ZENO (La coscienza di Zeno)
Novel by Italo Svevo, 1923

Confessions of Zeno is as unorthodox a novel, in structure and perspective, as Laurence Sterne's *Tristram Shandy* or Mikhail Lermontov's *Geroi nashego vremeni* (*A Hero of Our Times*) or its near-contemporary, James Joyce's *Ulysses*. It opens with a one-page "Preface" signed by a psychoanalyst, Dr. S., who announces that he is taking the extraordinary step of publishing the intimate confessions of his patient, Zeno Cosini, in revenge for the latter's jibes and withdrawal from treatment just when his condition is on the point of being cured. Dr. S. warns the reader of the jumble of truth and falsehood that is to follow.

Faced with an unreliable first-person narrator in Zeno and an even less trustworthy editor, the reader is thus constructed as the site of judgement in a discursive universe where intuitively subjective as well as would-be scientific objective modes of knowledge or models of truth have equally been problematized. High farce and high seriousness (often disguises for one another) are hard to separate as Zeno's dubious personality unfolds. Categories of value disintegrate. Zeno's mysterious psychosomatic symptoms cannot be related to any definable illness. An imaginary invalid, he discovers that those around him enjoy (or suffer) imaginary health. The issue of health shifts from the physical to the psychic to the moral to the social and ultimately to the metaphysical level. Zeno's wife is admirably sane, but when Zeno analyses her sanity, it takes on the appearance of an illness. Is analysis itself a malady, or the only mode of health?

Semi-schooled in psychoanalysis, Zeno attempts to turn the tables on his analyst and plays the game of hide-and-seek with his conscience or consciousness or conscious (highlighted in the polysemic *coscienza* of the Italian title) with a maximum of guile. He disingenuously mixes admitted lies with unadmitted ones, truths told in order to deceive, and startling moments of honesty in an anxiety-driven quest for enlightenment that often appears to come close to its goal but eventually ends in the most triumphant, entertaining, and blatant bad faith.

His confessions start with a brief "Preamble" in which he peers into his psyche only to recoil from the faces that jeer back at him. The next chapter recounts his lifelong compulsion to smoke and to stop smoking, whose outcome is an endless series of last cigarettes. The amusing buffoonery of this theme already hints strongly at the conflict from an early age with his father, whose competitive mercantilist values Zeno simultaneously rejects and absorbs. As a result, he suffers from strong feelings of both guilt and failure, and a deeply divided will. The farce turns serious in the chapter on the death of Zeno's father: the latter's dying slap reinforces Zeno's guilt feelings with the implication that Zeno has wanted his father dead.

Zeno then recounts how he proposes marriage on the same evening to three of the daughters of a surrogate father-figure and is accepted by the one he does not want. This involves him in a psychological duel with Guido, his rival for the hand of the beautiful Ada. Not only is Zeno visibly worsted, but he is tormented by his failure to act on impulse and tip Guido off a high wall to his death.

Non-linearity is the characteristic of this narrative that weaves nimbly between various moments in Zeno's past and the present moment of intermittent lucidity as he writes. Zeno turns his freedom with chronology to advantage in the two overlapping episodes relating his affair with Carla and his business association with Guido. The effect is to obscure his continuing interest in Ada and his part in Guido's commercial downfall and death.

In the final section, "Psychoanalysis," fictional time unexpectedly converges with historical time and Zeno's private obsessions merge with the catastrophe of World War I. Four dated diary entries take Zeno from May 1915—when his town of Trieste, then part of Austria, had been at war for over nine months, but Italy had not yet intervened to wrest the town from Austria—to March 1916, when the outcome of the war was most uncertain. On the very day when Italy declares war on Austria, Zeno is enjoying a country holiday right on the frontier.

He takes a stroll on the Austrian side, only to find himself cut off from his coat, his coffee and his wife on the Italian side. Back in Trieste, he discovers his vocation as a war profiteer, smoking to his heart's content, and cured of his compulsion to seek a cure for his condition, amid the terminal sickness of the old Europe. He ends the book with his celebrated prophecy of the ultimate weapon that will destroy our planet and rid it forever of parasites and diseases.

Italo Svevo affirmed that he began writing the autobiographically based *Confessions of Zeno* shortly after the end of World War I, and after abandoning a project to ensure perpetual peace. The fact that there is no overt trace in the novel of this suggestive connection shows how well Svevo has covered his tracks. Just as he turns psychoanalysis against itself, he also turns the novel against itself, opening it up to diverse and, indeed, opposed interpretations. Truth appears to be as inaccessible as are reliable ethical norms and values. Yet truth and values are visible in their negation. Falsehoods can be identified, implying a standard of discrimination. The possibility of innocence is predicated upon Zeno's sense of guilt.

The necessity of a social ethic is underscored by the final scenario, eloquently understated, of the world war. The novel's strength is that these all-embracing issues, with their still remarkably contemporary accent, are articulated in terms of the utter ordinariness, the banality, of everyday life and its potential to erupt into catastrophe.

—John Gatt-Rutter

CONSIDERANDO EN FRIO (Considering Coldly)
Poem by César Vallejo, 1939

Among César Vallejo's most famous and frequently anthologized poems, "Considerando en frio" ("Considering Coldly"), from his *Poemas humanos*, is also one of his more perplexing in both form and theme.

Vallejo, masterful at matching form to substance, was uniquely fond of "hiding" his poems, fundamentally traditional verse form, and this poem's formal characteristics reveal it to be much less "free verse" than a first glance suggests: perhaps two examples will suffice here. In their printed form lines 4–5 are highly uneven, yet when taken together form a perfectly symmetrical alexandrine (7 + 7 metric syllables); the long line 26 is really a fusion of the two dominant line-lengths of both this composition and Hispanic poetry in general: the heptasyllable and the hendecasyllable (7 and 11 metric counts; the Hispanic system of metrics is based primarily on syllable-count rather than "feet"). Similar metrical "tricks" abound. The question is why is there this contrast between surface and substance, appearance and reality? Precisely because these conflicts are the heart of the poem's themes.

The conflicts given voice in "Considerando" are characteristic of Vallejo: hope versus the harshness of lived reality; isolation versus community; aspiration toward a better life versus an unyielding and restrictive socio-economic system; logic versus emotion; and finally God and Man (union or conflict?). Hence the poem's discursive format, that of a legislative resolution or a judge's decision: the speaker repeatedly weighs the evidence and attempts to reach a rational conclusion on a "case" which is nothing less than the value, if any, of humanity itself.

Yet the cold distance of logic falters, over and over, as the "judge" (the speaker) is irresistibly drawn to the pathos around or below him:

humanity does nothing but "compose himself with days," "his desperation, upon finishing his atrocious day, erasing it." Reason, witnessing a life structured not on the basis of reason but the harsh laws of Latin American reality, can only recognize conflict, not resolve it. Hence, as the poem progresses, the attempt to impose order and sense on life yields to emotion, as the speaker yields to the unrelenting uselessness of objectivity, for all the external evidence proves to him is that humanity "was born very tiny." Finally, he surrenders, in the syntactically fragmented rush of pure feelings of the last line: "Moved . . . Moved . . . ." The judge finally judges himself, and transcends his inhuman isolation in an act of total compassion and identification with his Others.

Who is this "judge," who in attempting to come to a decision on human life finally changes within? A persona of Vallejo? Everyman, attempting to come to grips with his Others and hence with himself? Or is it the reader, finally, being judged and judging him or herself, worldly existence and life?

All these readings, of course, are equally valid, because of the universality of the poetic persona. It is Vallejo, humankind as a whole, the reader and even God (the final Great Judge of our individual and communal worth), for redemption is shown to lie only in our capacity to identify with the pain shared by all. Reason, logic, and order must give way to spirit, for Vallejo the world makes sense to the soul rather than the mind, and not in the epiphany of an abstract and possibly illusory salvation, but in that of inner human reality.

—Paul W. Borgeson, Jr.

THE CONSOLATION OF PHILOSOPHY (De consolatione philosophiae)
Prose and verse by Boethius, early 6th century

The Consolation of Philosophy is the spiritual and psychological autobiography of Boethius, written while its author was in prison awaiting execution for treason. Composed in the form of the so-called Menippean satire, with alternating sections of prose and poetry, the work also conforms to the generic dictates of the classical consolation and the dialogue style made famous by Plato. Generically a composite, *The Consolation* takes shape most substantially as a dialogue, however, for in the ongoing debate bruited between Boethius and Lady Philosophy much of *The Consolation*'s wisdom emerges. Appearing to him at the work's opening as the guide Boethius seeks in his time of sorrow, the task of Lady Philosophy is to lead Boethius to heart-wholeness, to freedom, and to the mental and spiritual consonances that proffer happiness.

To achieve this end, several preliminary tasks are required. First Lady Philosophy asks Boethius to consider the distinctive activities Fortune pursues. That consideration serves as the foil for much of *The Consolation*'s subsequent arguments about true, as against chance, happiness. Then, although Boethius has suffered a grievous blow to his social and physical well-being, Lady Philosophy shifts the burden of her argument for happiness entirely to the mental realm, ratifying the focus of her task under the rubrics of spirituality and psychology. Owing to the initial questions raised by Boethius, Lady Philosophy then finds it necessary to affirm the implicit order of all creation, an order, it seems, not easily discerned by humanity's imperfect vision, and an order condensed at the work's opening in the dilemma now facing Boethius whose very life hangs in the balance.

While the present dilemma of Boethius forms the backdrop against which *The Consolation* takes shape, the work develops along its own internal logic, and turns increasingly to consider the problems it raises from more abstract and formally philosophical angles. The necessity to articulate the nature and qualities of human happiness, for example, are presently considered from the wiser purview of Lady Philosophy herself, at a distance from Boethius' sorrowful plight. In the event, as Lady Philosophy makes clear, only a level-headed, logical approach of the kind she is about to offer can proffer to Boethius the sort of mental hygiene he seeks. Wallowing in his problems will only serve to make matters worse.

It is hard to be happy because happiness is not an obvious quality of human existence. Indeed, there are two kinds of happiness, chance happiness and true happiness, the former governed by those things that are subject to change, the latter by those things such as emotions and ideas that abide in and out of time. True happiness, in the event, is governed by a larger principle, divine love, articulated poetically in Book II as the acme of divine order. That order, written on the heart of humanity, is all that humans require, for happy would be "the race of men / if the love [*amor*] by which heaven is ruled / ruled your hearts."

Love is good and, in its third book, *The Consolation* articulates the central place that love holds in the attainment of true happiness. Humankind holds a variety of mistaken notions of happiness, Lady Philosophy repeats. Neither wealth, nor high office, nor power, nor fame, nor bodily pleasure, are paths by which true happiness is attained, ". . . because they can neither produce the good they promise nor come to perfection by the combination of all good." The essential ingredient in the attainment of happiness is the comprehension of one's own self-sufficiency, grounded in the cosmic notion of unity, articulated poetically near the mid-point of Book III. The superb and timeless coherence of God's creation symbolizes the potential for humans to participate with God. The unity obtained through participation with divinity forms the key ingredient in the therapy by which true happiness is achieved.

If love is good, then evil is not, and the problems presented by evil require attention. The good are always strong, Lady Philosophy tells Boethius, and the evil always lack power. Moreover, the good seek what is good in the proper way, for which reason they are happy, while the evil seek what is good in a perverse and, therefore, ineffective way, which explains their depravity. More than being unable to achieve the happiness they seek but do not know how to find, those who are evil do not exist, according to Lady Philosophy, because "a thing exists when it keeps its proper place and preserves its own nature. Anything which departs from this ceases to exist, because its existence depends on the preservation of its nature."

However, a fundamental difficulty remains in Lady Philosophy's presentation. Having staked so much of her argument on the consonance and implicit order of God's creation, Lady Philosophy must now explain how order can be defended in the face of the patent disorder of human affairs. She addresses herself to this problem by positing the nurturing oversight of God's thought, which she calls Providence, and the unfolding of those thoughts in time and space, which she calls Fate. Fate, which proceeds in the cosmic order from Providence, appears to those who experience it to be disjointed, disconnected, now chaotic, now inchoate. But it is, Lady Philosophy asserts, part of the divine and abiding order of God. "Whenever, therefore, you see something happen here different from your expectation, due order is preserved by events, but there is confusion and error in your thinking."

This affirmation of cosmic unity brings Lady Philosophy around full-circle at the conclusion of Book IV, for Fortune is recalled by her there as a means to enjoin Boethius to "the middle way," a way depicted by negation in Poem Seven, where the immoderate histories of Agamemnon, Odysseus, and Hercules are recounted as a means to embolden the truly strong to be on their way. This injunction is squarely a function of self-knowledge, the focus of *The Consolation* from its opening lines. It is fitting, therefore, for Book V to deal with the problems of divine knowledge and for it to conclude with an explanation of God's perfect ability to know. However, human self-knowledge is no less glorious, even if it is imperfect by comparison to God's providential consciousness. Because it is itself a reflection of God's intimate and all-expansive intellect, it is a profound and beautiful thing in its own right, offering a wisdom which eventually supercedes the bounds of its own language, the surest measure of its success:

Go now, ye strong, where the exalted way
Of great examples leads. Why hang you back?
Why turn away? Once earth has been surpassed
It gives the stars.

—Joseph Pucci

CONVERSATION IN SICILY (Conversazione in Sicilia)
Novel by Elio Vittorini, 1939

Conversation in Sicily is the masterpiece of the prominent Italian left-wing intellectual, Elio Vittorini. Published in 1938–39, during Mussolini's Fascist regime, the novel was banned by government censors in 1943, although today it is unanimously regarded as one of the major achievements of Italian literature in the 20th century. Indeed, Italo Calvino declared the novel to be the manifesto of modern Italian fiction on account of its stylistic innovations and the bold political agenda inherent in the work. The novel is one of the first examples of neorealist fiction.

Silvestro, a 30-year-old Sicilian labourer in Milan, receives a telegram from his father about his mother's delicate health, and returns to his village for the first time in 15 years. The novel focuses on the people Silvestro meets and talks with on the island of his birth. The work is divided into five parts. The first section describes the long journey by train and ferry to Sicily. Here Silvestro encounters other Sicilians for the first time on his voyage. In part two, he travels back in time to his childhood through conversations with his mother, Concetta, before accompanying her on nursing visits. In part three, Silvestro rediscovers his town through his neighbours, as his mother calls on invalids to give them injections. In the final two sections of the novel, Silvestro meets with the men in the local bar and later goes to the cemetery where he encounters the presence of his brother at the latter's tomb. Thus the entire novel is about returning and rediscovery. As Silvestro goes further back—to Sicily, to his mother, and to his town—he learns progressively more about himself on deeper and deeper levels until he reaches the most intimate communion with the spirit of his dead brother. Silvestro is the figure of Everyman on a voyage of rediscovery and purification.

The most distinctive feature of the novel is its style. Vittorini was a scholar of American literature as well as an accomplished translator of English language literary works. His writing in *Conversation in Sicily* demonstrates the influence of such writers as Ernest Hemingway and William Faulkner. Before Vittorini, the Italian novel had been weighed down by rhetoric in D'Annunzio's generation, and this new style, based on American models, was in stark contrast. Vittorini's prose is simple and linear with brief sentences, balanced clauses, and extensive use of dialogue and repetition. The range of vocabulary is limited to the most everyday phrases and expressions, making the style the opposite of the heavy, ornate, and empty political rhetoric of fascism.

The clear, linear, humble style of the novel is a very suitable complement to its content. Italian neorealism in the post-war period attempted to give an almost journalistic account of the stark, harsh realities of the proletariat class. The south was a favourite subject for neorealists because of the bleak situation in the rural areas of Italy.

The Sicilians he meets are poor, ignorant, and fatalistically resigned to a life that has no hope for improvement. Neorealism is different from realism, usually referred to in the context of Italian literature as *verismo*, because, although both present a documentary portrait of life, only neorealism implies a committed social and political agenda.

The style and content of *Conversation in Sicily* gave the work a mythical quality and indeed, in his introduction to the novel, the author refers to its allegorical quality. Silvestro is Everyman and Sicily is only Sicily by chance. The protagonists all have their own symbolic functions within Vittorini's ideology. The poor Sicilians with oranges are part of the "mondo offeso," the downtrodden of society, whereas the Great Lombard is a true man ("mas hombre"), like Silvestro's grandfather. The voyage to Sicily is also an interior voyage to a greater understanding of self. The book opens in a desolate setting as Silvestro leaves behind the concerns of his difficult existence ("gli astrati furori"), yet the protagonist's quest is also the universal striving for positive solutions for the lost human race ("il genere umano perduto").

In this work, allegory functions as a parable. The story of Silvestro's journey to understanding can be interpreted as the political itinerary of the anti-Fascist intellectual who feels that his own moral dignity has been lost in the events of the Spanish Civil War. Silvestro's conversations allow him to rediscover his infancy, just as the "engagement" of the opponents of Franco's regime in Spain and Mussolini's rule in Italy leads them to rediscover the true values of the human condition.

—Jordan Lancaster

LA CORTIGIANA (The Courtesan)
Play by Pietro Aretino, 1534 (written 1525)

La cortigiana [The Courtesan], written while Pietro Aretino was still living in Rome, but first published in modified form in 1534 after the author's transferral to Venice, is constructed on two distinct yet interconnected planes. The first of the two intertwined plots involves the Sienese Maco, who arrives in Rome determined to become firstly a courtier and then a cardinal with the help of Andrea (a character derived from a friend of the dramatist's, a Venetian painter celebrated in Rome rather more for his witticism and jesting than for his art). The second involves the Neapolitan Parabolano, a courtier duped by his servant Rosso who learns of his master's infatuation for a noblewoman, Livia, and ridicules him by arranging a tryst not with Livia, but with

Togna, the baker's wife. It is these two plots that provide the basis for the comic action, and from which the anti-court satire emerges.

There are no less than 24 characters appearing in the comedy, who use a variety of linguistic registers as they move through the streets of Rome, including the colloquial Italian, at times mixed with Spanish, of servants, the Latin of pedants and religious hypocrites, and exaggerated Petrarchisms. An essential innovation of *La cortigiana* is its break with the fixed setting characteristic of erudite comedy. Here, the streets of Rome are the physical, material link between tavern and palace, just as such characters as Rosso and Andrea are the social and psychological link. The street endows all characters with full theatrical citizenship, be they nobles, servants, priests, procuresses, doctors, fishermen, and so on, while simultaneously providing a reason for their interrelationships.

Developed upon the dual plot of *La cortigiana* is a discussion of the nature and function of comedy itself. The drama is the theatrical "fixing" on stage of one of the "one hundred comedies" being enacted daily on the natural stage of the Roman streets and within its palaces. It was inspired by a real, everyday spirit of buffoonery, transformed from life into theatre. Various characters had also been transplanted from "real" life onto the stage; all are aware of their comic role and strive to maintain it, together with the abstraction "Monna Commedia" herself. It is in the final scenes of the comedy that this discussion reaches its climax. From being participants in their own comedies, the characters emerge, regarding themselves objectively as instruments of a comic form. Thus the servant Valerio indicates to Parabolano (Act V, scene 18) the face-saving device of taking his own misadventures in good spirit so as to minimize his ridiculousness in the eyes of the others. Parabolano emerges from the comic plot when he urges the baker to refrain from violence because "it would be a shame if such a fine comedy were to finish in tragedy" (Act V, scene 21). Thus, his role in the play changes: from being simply a comic type he develops into a complex figure aware of his own theatrical function. His final role in the play is that of guardian of the comic form which, up to that point, had protected him from harm: "Step back! Don't do it! Don't do it! Don't kill our comedy!" (Act V, scene 24). *La cortigiana* thus illustrates the process of life becoming theatre, with Parabolano fully aware of the transition.

Society, as it is represented in *La cortigiana*, is divided into two principal levels: the courts, in which a man is powerful due to his inherited title or acquired wealth—as is the case with Parabolano—and the world of the lower classes, consisting of servants, tradesmen, and so on, in which the powerful are those who use their wits to exploit others less wily than themselves. It is a social hierarchy in which the balance of power is continually shifting: the servant dupes his master who, in turn, dupes his employees and punishes unjustly his few faithful servants. Moreover, true social position and character may be easily misrepresented: the Giudeo is mistaken for a friar: the fisherman is thought to be possessed by devils; Valerio is wrongly believed to be disloyal; Rosso is mistaken for a nobleman twice because of the clothes, stolen or borrowed, he wears. It seems, then, that little is required for one to become a member of the court beyond possessing adequate amounts of money and maintaining appearances. What Aretino laments, in this comedy, is the loss of the society of ancient Rome, with its well-defined aristocracy and impeccable values: the Livias, Camillas, and so on.

While Maco's criticism of Rome—the city in which he intends ascending to the ultimate heights of courtier—is unintentional, direct criticism is levelled frequently at it by representatives of the lower classes. As the deterioration of social and political conditions is directly attributable to the machinations of the court institution, and only indirectly to the presence of the Spaniards in Italy, the blame lies squarely with the hegemonic class. Taverns are described as everything the courts should be but are not, while the happy reflection on them gives rise naturally to references to the Rome of Julius Caesar's time. Thus, while the court lords are perennially occupied in ridiculous amorous escapades, their servants prefer the multiple pleasures of the taverns.

Two of the principal characters of *La cortigiana* are Rosso and Parabolano: the former creates the comic situations that others then enact; the latter has created his own comedy (as the *innamorato*) and lives it out from within the play. The other main source of comic interest is the Sienese Maco, a character that had traditionally enjoyed fame as a fool. Aretino's contribution to the development of this character-type is in Maco's language, childish and usually lacking in logic. His answers are random and irrelevant, and his every comment lacks consequence. He exists through his unpredictable language, oblivious to his own shortcomings, wholly temporal.

Despite the fact that much of the play's action depends upon women, only three female characters actually appear on stage: the procuress Alvigia, Togna, and, briefly, Biagina, a servant of the courtesan Camilla. This is due, in part, to Aretino's desire not to sully the virtue of such characters as Camilla and Livia who contribute to the idealized representation of ancient Rome. Those female characters who do appear on stage are portrayed favourably: Alvigia ranks equally with Rosso in guile, and Togna is to be admired for disregarding social edicts in seeking to satisfy her instincts. If the court is so markedly devoid of women it is because, according to Rosso, they are no longer needed there. Men, in their emasculated state, seek husbands. Yet Rosso's own position in court, like his relationship with Parabolano, is highly ambiguous. It seems that the servant, in his cynicism, obtains what he wants by whatever means are available to him.

Parabolano, at the end of *La cortigiana*, comments on the comedy, laughing at himself as one of its protagonists, suspended momentarily between life and pure theatre. His return to sanity has come too late to be of any benefit to the court. He has made the transition from life into art as a result of his own character, formed and nurtured by a society and an institution which, in ironic similarity to ancient Rome, is bringing about its own demise.

—Nicole Prunster

THE COUNTERFEITERS (Les Faux-monnayeurs)
Novel by André Gide, 1926

The Counterfeiters is the only work by André Gide to which he assigned the term "novel." Although he wrote other fictional works, he either gave them no label or called them "récits" (narratives) or "soties" (roughly, farces). The term "novel" was chosen to indicate a departure from his previous work—especially his stylistic and compositional classicism—and to suggest a more ambitious project, a three-dimensional slice of life, a "crossroads of problems." The dedication—to Roger Martin du Gard—points to the role Gide's friend played in helping him elaborate the novel; the work also reflects his spiritual crisis during World War I and his reading of Dostoevskii and Fielding.

The Counterfeiters is divided into three parts: the first and last, set in Paris, have 18 chapters each, the middle, set in Saas-Fée (Switzerland), has seven chapters. There are symmetrical pairs of families and characters and numerous parallels and contrasts. The episodic plot seems disjointed but is, in fact, carefully contrived and balanced. The title, with its reference to counterfeit coinage and—by extension—other falsehood, furnishes a major theme. Fraudulent and inauthentic characters, things, and actions populate the novel—bastards (false sons), infidelity (counterfeit love), derivative, inflated (false) literature, lies (false words), hypocrisy (false morality). Another major theme is adolescence, its challenges and possibilities. The discovery of his illegitimacy by the young Bernard Profitendieu, whose development makes *The Counterfeiters* a bildungsroman, precipitates his departure from home; this plot thread soon becomes entangled with others. His adventures include meeting by chance the writer Édouard, who is the uncle of his friend Olivier Molinier and—Bernard learns—loved by Laura Douviers, a married woman whom Vincent Molinier, Oliver's older brother, has made pregnant but callously abandoned. Later, Bernard comes to love Laura platonically, and meets other members of her family (the Vedel-Azaïs) at their boarding-house.

Another theme is fiction itself. The book, which displays the decentralization of plot, the multiple perspectives, and the relativization of character seen in some other modernist fiction, is a metafiction, concerned with the aesthetic, ontological, and epistemological status of fiction, Édouard, who resembles his creator, is trying to write a novel called "The Counterfeiters," in which *his* hero is a writer attempting to compose a novel. None of Édouard's book is finished, but he keeps a notebook in which he jots down ideas and dialogues. This notebook constitutes much of Gide's novel, making Édouard one of the main narrating voices. This structure of embedded self-reflexive images, called by Gide *composition en abyme*, allows the author to play with the topic of reality and speak directly of the novelist's craft. Moreover, as Gide composed *The Counterfeiters*, he kept two notebooks: his regular diary, which records some stages in the composition, and what he later called *Journal of the Counterfeiters*, which contains observations on fiction, embryonic episodes, and dialogues not included in the final product. The different perspectives and levels of reality within the novel are thus expanded by reflections outside of it, and the various texts together constitute a modernist treatise on fiction and prefigure works by Butor and Robbe-Grillet, with their embedded, self-reflexive plots and violations of narrative frame.

The plot here is dependent upon coincidence, and the novel is marked by the oppositions and reversals characteristic of melodrama; but Gide's concern is to show, under the apparent simplicity of motivations and actions, a complex moral field in which authenticity is precarious and moral choice is suspect. This field is marked by the presence of evil, compared to which freedom to choose the good seems feeble, perhaps because human life is governed by an oppressive fate, or because knowledge of good is inadequate when self-knowledge is insufficient. The self, its contours, and its criteria for choice are the constant preoccupation of Édouard and Bernard, who reject societal models. Opposed to them are those who follow standard social patterns without reflection, or who consciously choose either evil or a simplistic good—Laura's father, for instance, who leaves unexamined the religion by which he makes his living. A shadowy, ambulatory devil, who occasionally seems to intervene in the plot, can at first be taken lightly, but the ultimate consequences point to a powerful malevolent principle, which is realized in human action but seems also to dictate it.

This principle is visible in Strouvilhou, a circulating character who expresses Nietzschean concern for replacing traditional morality with one built on power; it appears also in Vincent, whose descent down the slope of irresponsibility—from an initial concern for Laura to a cultivated indifference and finally fascination with systematic egotism—concludes when, in Africa, after having murdered his companion, he takes himself for the devil. Edouard's old piano teacher, La Pérouse, expresses the omnipresence of evil when he concludes that the universe is a vast, sadistic joke: God and the Devil are one.

In a final disaster, La Pérouse's illegitimate grandson, Boris, is killed by a fellow student at Vedel's boarding house, in an episode of schoolboy sadism masking as an initiation rite. Other characters must bear some responsibility: the shots are fired from a pistol belonging to La Pérouse, and apparently innocent acts contribute to the murder. Beyond that, the role of Strouvilhou in the event suggests also a sombre fatality. After Boris's death, Bernard returns to his family, Georges Molinier (one of the schoolboys) to his, Laura to her husband; and Oliver, after a false start with the posturing writer Passavant, discovers love with Édouard (homosexual desire is a secondary theme).

Offsetting the sombre themes and unhappy events are insight and wit, ingenuity in plot handling, and, paradoxically, sometimes a sense of the characters' freedom; Gide wished to create a world that would obey its own laws, not respond to the wishes of the novelist. The wide range of tones suits Gide's ambition to create a multi-dimensional work, with numerous plots and characters, in which simple lines and explanations are replaced by a complexity more nearly mirroring human reality.

—Catharine Savage Brosman

UN COUP DE DÉS JAMAIS N'ABOLIRA LE HASARD
(Dice Thrown Never Will Annul Chance)
Poem by Stéphane Mallarmé, 1914 (written 1897)

It was in 1897, the year before his death, that Stéphane Mallarmé wrote what is undoubtedly one of the most original and complex works of 19th-century French literature. Its enigmatic main clause, printed in large capitals and in bold type, is broken into four sections: UN COUP DE DÉS JAMAIS N'ABOLIRA LE HASARD, distributed over 20 pages with a number of long and complicated subordinate clauses, some in small capitals, some in standard lettering, and some in italics, inserted between the sections. The resultant highly convoluted text is not set out in conventional fashion with equal spacing between words and lines; on the contrary, some lines are left blank or contain no more than one or two words irregularly placed; on one occasion even a whole page is left blank, except for the one word "n'abolira" at the foot of the page. Conventional punctuation is abandoned as unnecessary, since the use of different typefaces and the uneven spacing of lines and words indicate the way the various parts of the text relate to one another. Furthermore, it is the double page rather than the single page which forms the "frame" within which the text is set, so that sentences sometimes flow across from the left-hand page to the right-hand page. This introduces a pictorial element into the work to complement its meaning, in that the way the words trail across the double page, like a drawing of the wake of a ship, or are sparsely distributed across the wide expanse of paper, like black stars in a white sky, or black dots on white dice, reinforces the theme of a storm-tossed vessel which finally sinks beneath the waves while high above, like a distant reflection of the dice which the master of the ship holds in his hand and tries in vain to throw, shines a constellation, watching and wondering as it rolls across the sky:

> veillant
> > doutant
> > > roulant
> > > > brillant et méditant.

As for the significance of these events, there can be little doubt that the catastrophic shipwreck symbolizes the failure of Mallarmé's poetic ambitions. The same image of the storm-tossed ship occurs in two sonnets, "ien, cette écume, vierge vers" and "A la nue accablante tu," written just before *Dice Thrown*. In the first of these poems, dating from 1893, the vessel nevertheless presses steadily onwards through the hostile waves, although uncertain of reaching its goal; but in the second of the poems, dating from 1895, it has been wrecked in a "sépulcral naufrage," an expression echoed near the beginning of the prose work two years later:

UN COUP DE DÉS

JAMAIS

QUAND BIEN MÉME LANCE DANS DES
CIRCONSTANCES ÉTERNELLES

DU FOND D'UN NAUFRAGE

(A throw of the dice / never / even when made in / eternal circumstances / from the depths of a shipwreck)

The master of the ship, who fails in this last desperate attempt to throw the dice and thus play a part in deciding his own destiny, is clearly Mallarmé, who has failed to complete the *Grand Oeuvre* by which he had hoped to attain the immortality he had proudly predicted for himself some 30 years before in the sonnet "Quand l'ombre menaça de la fatale loi" and which he had celebrated in the case of fellow-poets in his elegies to Gautier, Poe, Baudelaire, and Verlaine. At the age of 55 and in failing health, Mallarmé knew that the grandiose project with which he had been struggling for so long, of giving poetic form to the ideal world, would never be completed. He finds consolation however, if only of a negative kind, in the thought that even if he had succeeded in publishing his *Grand Oeuvre*, it might still have sunk into oblivion; to seize the chance of publication, as every writer knows, still leaves open the chance that what one has published remains unread—"un coup de dés jamais n'abolira le hasard." But, in a long and involved epilogue after the completion of the main clause, the dice, despite the sinking of the ship and the death of its master, are nevertheless mysteriously thrown and form the constellation that calmly presides over the disaster. This suggests that Mallarmé finds further and more positive consolation in the thought that, even if he has failed to complete his *Grand Oeuvre*, his ideas still have a chance of being disseminated in other ways. "Toute pensée émet un coup de dés" ("every thought emits a dice-throw") is the modest concluding line, printed in appropriately modest lettering, of this extraordinary work. And it has in fact proved to be the case that, although his *Grand Oeuvre* never saw the light of day, Mallarmé's ideas have survived and flourished, largely because of the few dozen

poems that he himself dismissed as mere preliminary works—"études en rue de mieux" ("sketches with a view to doing better")—but that are now recognized as major contributions to 19th-century French poetry and have indeed made of Mallarmé one of its brightest stars.

—C. Chadwick

COUSIN BETTE (La Cousine Bette)
Novel by Honoré de Balzac, 1847

Cousin Bette is one half of a diptych that includes *Cousin Pons*, Honoré de Balzac's last major achievement. Its action takes place entirely in Paris between 1838 and 1946. Never elsewhere in *The Human Comedy*, and seldom elsewhere in literature as a whole, has the explosive force of love been so vividly presented. This love takes numerous forms, all of them responding to, or exploiting, physical attraction rather than the cash nexus of the marriage market.

Adeline Hulot loves her husband; with wifely modesty she practically worships him, forgiving him any number of marital indiscretions precisely because of the force of her sexual love. In the relationship between her daughter Hortense and Wenceslas Steinbock we see the "normal" love of a young couple. Adeline's cousin Lisbeth (or Bette) Fisher loves Steinbock with a semi-maternal affection that he does not reciprocate in the same possessive sense, and which perhaps does not include any element of physical fulfilment. Crevel loves the courtesan Josépha Mirah with physical passion; he finally marries Valérie Marneffe, with whom Montès de Montéjanos has also had a strong physical bond. Valérie (if we exclude her husband!) has two other admirers: Steinbock loves her with carnal and adulterous passion; so too does the latter's father-in-law, Hector Hulot, who takes his place in *The Human Comedy* as one of Balzac's eight great monomaniacs; for, besides the four incidental affairs mentioned in *Cousin Bette*, Hulot also loves Josépha Mirah, stealing her from Crevel. There have been many such women throughout Hulot's life and, it seems, things will continue in this way.

Another of Balzac's eight great monomaniacs is Bette, whose jealous love for Steinbock prompts insatiable yearnings for revenge when she loses him to Hortense. *Cousin Bette* is the only fiction in *The Human Comedy* in which two monomaniacs are presented side by side with virtually equal prominence. Balzac shows his eponymous heroine shaking and trembling from head to foot, glaring like a tigress and burning like a volcano: Bette is destroyed by her monomania, whereas Hulot's, like Vautrin's, does not destroy him physically.

But although *Cousin Bette* focuses on sexual love, that is by no means its only concern. Other important themes are chastity, artistic creativity, the decline of the notion of honour, and the imperfections of the modern world. By means of direct speech, the symbolic event, and also some authorial intervention, the narrator voices his own attitude towards this aftermath of the Napoleonic era. It is a time, says Hulot's son Victorin, when children ought to, but cannot, teach their parents how to behave; a time when all ethical integrity appears to be dead. After the discovery of Hector Hulot's embezzlement of public funds, his brother, Marshal Hulot hands him pistols with which to do the honourable thing: but to no avail! Even amid the mass warfare of the Napoleonic era, when normal moral codes were partially suspended, there was, it seemed, a sense of honour and moral responsibility that has ceased to exist under the July Monarchy.

The five-franc piece is the only god worshipped in Louis-Philippe's reign, a fact proclaimed by Crevel, the retired perfumer who (in the tradition of César Birotteau) is the ultimate embodiment of philistine bourgeois values in *The Human Comedy*. In Crevel's sexual rival Hulot Balzac goes even further than this. Detesting the July Monarchy for its double standards, he shows corruption in the higher administrative echelons of government. A key symbol of these double standards is Valérie Marneffe, who conveys the impression of being a respectably married woman. The very outrage unleashed by the publication of this novel was a further sign of the public two-facedness to which Balzac took strong exception.

Cousin Bette does not adopt a moralizing attitude with regard to private virtue, even though its narrator explicitly—and its author personally—deplored what appears (from *Les Deux Frères* [*The Black Sheep*] and elsewhere) to have been a general contemporary decline in moral standards. Adeline Hulot may well turn the other cheek, yet it is impossible to say whether the narrator of *Cousin Bette* considers her a ''virtuous'' woman. Like her husband, and like Bette, she is a force of nature, endlessly predetermined by her own nature: endlessly forgiving, just as Bette is endlessly vindictive, and just as Hulot's lechery seems as ardent as ever—though, by the time when *Cousin Bette* ends, he is already 74 years old. It is through melodrama that Balzac can provide some sort of moral commentary, as when Monthès infects both Valérie and Crevel, thereby causing the deaths of both. Not only melodrama but drama itself is the stuff of this novel: in his later years Balzac took an increasing interest in the writing of plays. Drama juxtaposes viewpoints without the need for authorial commentary; and this narrative ambiguity is essential to the presentation of issues of private morality in *Cousin Bette*.

There is, on the other hand, plentiful and unambiguous authorial commentary concerning the dramas of artistic creation. For, even at the very end of his own creative life, Balzac still upheld the Romantic view (previously expressed in *Illusions perdues* [*Lost Illusions*] and *The Black Sheep*) that art is a sacred calling and that, as also in religion, the sacerdotal function—that of Execution rather than Conception—is essentially male. Hence Steinbock's importance, and the varying nature of Bette's, Hortense's, and Valérie's influence upon him, while the statues of Samson and Delilah, a subject also memorably treated by Vigny, aptly symbolize the downfall of Steinbock's artistic talent. Hence too the early idea of beginning *Cousin Bette* with a description of the young sculptor. But, as the novel's actual first pages show, Balzac (building upon the examples of *Histoire de César Birotteau* [*Cesar Birotteau*] and *Ursule Mirouët* [*Ursula*]) had become to prefer the vivid opening *in medias res*—partly because of the influence of the theatre, and partly because of newspaper serialization.

—Donald Adamson

LE CRÈVE-COEUR
Poems by Louis Aragon, 1941

Le Crève-coeur consists of 22 poems and a brief theoretical essay, ''hyme in 1940'' (''La rime en 1940''). Thirteen of the poems were written between September 1939 (when Louis Aragon, aged 42, was enlisted into the army) and May 1940 (when his unit went into action). The last of these, ''The Interrupted Poem'' (''Le Poème interrompu''), was literally and dramatically interrupted when Aragon's regiment was ordered into Belgium in advance of the Allied armies. Aragon escaped via Dunkirk, returned immediately to France, and was involved in action right up to the ceasefire in June. He was demobbed in July, and began to compose the nine remaining poems of *Le Crève-coeur*, which appeared in book form in 1941.

The first 13 poems are Aragon's response to the *drôle de guerre* (phoney war) and the final nine his memories of combat and defeat. Several of the poems are also inspired by Aragon's separation from his beloved wife, Elsa Triolet.

Aragon had not in fact published any poetry since 1934, preoccupied instead with journalism, fiction, and politics. It was the traumatic nature of the events of 1939–40, together with the enforced inactivity of eight months of ''phoney war,'' which caused his return to the genre in which he had begun his literary career. In many of the poems the historical is intertwined with the personal. Indeed, it is part of Aragon's purpose to convince us that these two levels of experience are inseparable. In ''The Time of Crossword Puzzles'' (''Le temps des mots croisés''), looking back regretfully and self-critically on the pre-war years, Aragon writes:

> Too little have we prized those double hours
> Too little asked if our dreams were counterparts
> Too lightly probed the look in troubled eyes
> Too seldom talked of our concurrent hearts

The ''we'' is the poet and Elsa; but it is also ''we'' the French people and even ''we'' the human race. Sometimes Aragon's love for Elsa serves as a counterpoint to humanity's inability to love. This is the case in ''Printemps'' (''Spring''):

> But we were eyeless, loveless, brainless, phantoms,
> Ghosts parted from ourselves. . .

Throughout the poems written before the defeat Aragon's love for Elsa acts as a kind of foil to the collapse of human values, to the sense of impending disaster. Underlying a number of these poems is the anxiety that poetry may not be sufficient to the tasks Aragon has assigned to it, to convey love in a context that denies love:

> My love we have only words
> Our lipstick
> Only frozen words. . .
>
> (''Les Amants séparés'' [The Parted Lovers])

or to reach out with words to the ordinary people caught up on the apocalypse:

> But the sergeant
> I show these verses to
> Gets lost in my analogies. . .
>
> (''Romance du temps qu'il fait''
> [Romance of the Present Time])

The central, dominant image of the poems looking back on defeat comes in ''The Lilacs and the Roses'' (''Les Lilas et les roses''): ''June with a dagger in its heart.'' This poem uses its central flower imagery to explore the many different realities and emotions experienced by the poet as he witnesses defeat. The imagery is paradoxically delicate, in sharp contrast to ''Tapestry of the Great Fear''

("Tapisserie de la grande peur"), where it has a nightmarish and grotesque quality, reminiscent of Aragon's Surrealist youth:

> This landscape, masterpiece of modern terror
> Has sharks and sirens, flying fish and swordfish. . .
> A tame bear. A shawl. A dead man dropped like
> An old shoe. Hands climbing the torn belly. . .
> Evening soars down with silent wingbeats, joining
> A velvet Breughel to this Breughel of hell.

But at the same time as allowing his imagination full scope, Aragon is also concerned to point to historical continuities. The poems overflow with references to France's past: Richard II, Joan of Arc, the Crusades. He sees himself as a *national* poet, creating together with personal, idiosyncratic imagery references recognizable to the national community.

In *Le Crève-coeur* Aragon confronts implicitly some of the central dilemmas of modern poetry. He confronts these same problems explicitly in the appended essay "hyme in 1940." Aragon believes that poetry, because of its flexibility and inherent adventurousness, is the medium best equipped to respond creatively to the unprecedented nature of contemporary historical events. But poetry has become remote from ordinary people. According to Aragon, *rhyme* is at the centre of this problem, and also its potential solution. Rhyme, poetry's surviving link with popular song, is indispensable to a popular poetry. But rhyme has fallen into disrepute in modern poetry. Through renovating rhyme, Aragon believes, both the energy and popularity of poetry can be renewed. In *Le Crève-coeur* he experiments extensively with rhyme. For example, he employs what he calls "rime enjambée" (rhyme astride the line) in "Little Suite for Loudspeaker" ("Petite Suite san fil"):

> Ne parlez pas d'amour J'écoute mon coeur *battre*
> Ne parlez plus d'amour Que fait-elle là-bas
> *Trop* proche. . .
>
> (Don't speak of love I listen to my heart-beat
> Don't speak any more of love What is she doing there
> Too near . . .)

where "battre" rhymes with "bas" + "Tr"; or, in "The Unoccupied Zone" ("La Zone des étapes"), he uses a *rime complexe* (complex rhyme):

> Nous ne comprenons rien à ce que nos *fils aiment*
> Aux fleurs que la jeunesse ainsi qu'un *défi sème*
> Les roses de jadis vont à nos *emphysèmes*
>
> (We don't understand what our sons love
> The flowers youth throws down like a challenge
> The roses of long ago go to our emphysemas)

where "fils aiment" is rhymed first with "défi sème" and then with part of the single word "emphysèmes."

Le Crève-coeur is not simply a spontaneous response to events. It is highly ambitious, artistically and culturally. Interweaving intimate and collective experience, it appeals to a common patrimony and seeks a poetry both innovative and popular.

—J.H. King

CRIME AND PUNISHMENT (Prestuplenie i nakazanie)
Novel by Fedor Dostoevskii, 1867

In the complexity of its narrative and psychological structure, the many-facetedness and interlayering of its setting and characterization, *Crime and Punishment* is almost unique in world literature. Few works of fiction have attracted so many widely diverging interpretations. It has been seen as a detective novel, an attack on radical youth, a study in alienation and criminal psychopathology, a work of prophecy (the attempt on the life of Tsar Aleksandr II by the nihilist student Dmitri Karakozov took place while the book was at the printer's, and some even saw the Tsar's murder in 1881 as a fulfilment of Fedor Dostoevskii's warning), an indictment of urban social conditions in 19th-century Russia, a religious epic, and a proto-Nietzschean analysis of the "will to power." It is, of course, all these things—but it is more.

The story itself is fairly simple: Raskol'nikov, a young St. Petersburg ex-student, plans and executes the murder of an old woman pawnbroker, ostensibly for money, but in fact to prove to himself that he can "overstep" the limits laid down by society and the law. In the days that precede his arrest, we encounter his student friends, the policemen who are tracking him down, his prostitute girlfriend and her impoverished family, his sister, her arrogant lawyer suitor, and the character of Svidrigailov, a sinisterly omnipresent St. Petersburg dandy and ex-card sharper, who seems to know everything about Raskol'nikov. In the end, under the intolerable pressure of his conscience and the psychological manipulations of his pursuers, Raskol'nikov breaks down, confesses to the murder, and is sent into exile in Siberia. The novel's complexity derives from the minutely subtle way in which inner thought-processes are inextricably fused with the urban streetscape of St. Petersburg during a heatwave at the beginning of July 1865.

Perhaps the most cogent explanation of Dostoevskii's intentions in writing the novel was given by the philosopher Vladimir S. Solovev (1833–1900), who knew Dostoevskii and in the summer of 1878 travelled with him on a pilgrimage to the monastery of Optina Pustyn. In the first of his three commemorative speeches (1881–83), Solovev states the matter with utter simplicity. In a discussion of *Crime and Punishment* and *The Devils* he writes:

> The meaning of the first of these novels, for all its depth of detail, is very clear and simple, though many have not understood it. Its principal character is a representative of that view of things according to which every strong man is his own master, and all is permitted to him. In the name of his personal superiority, in the name of his belief that he is a *force*, he considers himself entitled to commit murder and does in fact do so. But then suddenly the deed he thought was merely a violation of a senseless outer law and a bold challenge to the prejudice of society turns out, for his own conscience, to be something much more than this—it turns out to be a sin, a violation of inner moral justice. His violation of the outer law meets its lawful retribution from without in exile and penal servitude, but his inward sin of pride that has separated the strong man from humanity and has led him to commit murder—that inward sin of self-idolatry can only be redeemed by an inner moral act of self-renunciation. His boundless self-confidence must disappear in the face of that which is greater than *himself*, and his self-fabricated justification must humble itself

before the higher justice of God that lives in those very same simple, weak folk whom the strong man viewed as paltry insects.

(translated by David McDuff)

Solovev's analysis is doubtless coloured by his theories concerning the Russian Church and people, but even so, in its simplicity and straightforwardness, based on a personal knowledge of the author, it is hard to refute. Far from moving towards a religious dogmatism or alignment with reactionary political views as some critics have considered he did, in the period that followed his incarceration in the labour camp Dostoevskii began to discover a "true socialism"—the "*sobornost*" ("communion") of the human spirit as it expressed itself in the shared identity of the Russian people and their self-effacing acceptance of God. *Crime and Punishment* shows us the steps along this way—Raskol'nikov's sin of pride is also Dostoevskii's, and his expiation of it through suffering is what the novel is really "about."

The intensity of suffered life that fills its pages lends a strange, electric brilliance to the action and plot. Above all, as Konstantin Mochulskii was one of the first to observe, the brilliance of the sun is everywhere. Its light and heat seem to increase as the novel progresses—and the light is surely the light of God, and the heat the warmth of His love. Raskol'nikov moves in the sunlight ever more pressingly conscious that there can be no concealment for him, that there is no corner where that brilliance will not reach and find him. Other gripping features of the novel are the vividness with which the sights and sounds of everyday St. Petersburg street life are recorded, and the satirical acuteness of Dostoevskii's caricaturing of the liberal, Fourierist intelligentsia of his time. Among the novel's most memorable passages, apart from the axe-murder itself, are the descriptions of Raskol'nikov's dreams, which merge with reality in a strange and disturbing manner. The characters of Marmeladov and his wife Katerina Ivanovna are drawn with a Dickensian panache, and in some ways stand out from the rest of the novel. This is probably because they derive from another novel, called *The Drunkards*, which Dostoevskii never completed, but which he cannibalized in order to help to build his greatest novel.

In the end, western readers must make a leap of the spirit and the imagination in order to penetrate the inner essence of this very Russian work. It was Nicholas Berdiiaev who viewed Dostoevskii not as a psychologist but as a "pneumatologist," a researcher of souls. In his book *Dostoevsky—An Interpretation* (1934), Berdiiaev characterizes the Russian soul as being fundamentally different in nature from the western soul. *Crime and Punishment* offers the clearest testimony to the nature of that difference, which hinges on the close association of individual identity with a divine conception of national belonging, in which "the people" are equivalent to God.

—David McDuff

CUPID AND PSYCHE
Story by Lucius Apuleius, c. AD 180

Cupid and Psyche appears as a long tale embedded in the *Metamorphoses*, also known as *The Golden Ass*, by Lucius Apuleius. *The Golden Ass* closely resembles the shorter *Lucius the Ass* of the satirist Lucian, leading some scholars to posit the possibility of some lost common source, although Lucian's satire does not include a version of the Cupid and Psyche story. Conventionally dated to around AD 180, *The Golden Ass* represents the only extant example of a complete novel in Roman literature. It presents the first-person account of the misadventures of Lucius, a naive young man who supposes himself sophisticated in the ways of the world. Driven by an unhealthy curiosity about black magic and witchcraft, as well as by lust for Fotis, the Venus-like slave girl of his host, young Lucius finds himself accidentally transformed into an ass. This begins a physical and spiritual pilgrimage that leads poor Lucius through a series of hardships that are only finally resolved through the intervention of the great mother goddess Isis. Here Apuleius is an advocate of the Alexandrian mystery cult of Isis and Serapis, which posited Isis as the universal Mother, the true godhead of all the goddesses of the world.

Like Boccaccio's *Decameron* or Chaucer's *Canterbury Tales*, both of which draw on Apuleius, *The Golden Ass* is a narrative containing many shorter narratives recounted during the course of the novel. *Cupid and Psyche* is presented in the form of a story told by an old woman to comfort a young gift named Charity, who has been kidnapped by bandits. This in turn is overheard by Lucius, the ass. The story parallels the fate of Charity and serves as an allegorical gloss of the larger narrative of Lucius, although it may stand on its own as a masterpiece of Silver Age Latin prose fiction.

The story, of *Cupid and Psyche*, like that of Lucius, revolves around the pattern of fall, trial, and salvation. Because of her great beauty, a young woman named Psyche has received the attention of many men, thereby earning the jealous enmity of the goddess Venus. Venus orders her son Cupid (Eros) to make Psyche fall in love with some outcast. Cupid, however, having himself fallen for the beauty of Psyche, disobeys his mother and arranges to marry Psyche secretly. Hiding his true identity, Cupid establishes his bride in a luxurious palace, attended by magical servants. Psyche may enjoy everything in this earthly paradise with the one stipulation that she never look at her husband, who remains invisible except at night. All goes well until Psyche, driven by a combination of curiosity and uncertainty about the identity of her mysterious husband, looks on his sleeping form one night. Seized by lust, she spills hot oil from her lamp on his leg. Enraged, Cupid flies off, and Psyche finds herself cast out, abandoned to the wrath of Venus.

In the hands of Venus, Psyche is compelled to perform a series of progressively more dangerous and difficult tasks in order to expiate her guilt. First she must sort seeds from a great heap, then she must get a piece of wool from ravenous golden sheep, then water from the middle of a waterfall on the River Styx guarded by dragons, and finally a box of beauty from Proserpina, goddess of the dead, a journey that involves resisting many dangers and temptations. Because of her beauty and goodness, in each case she is secretly helped by various creatures, and in the last test by her husband. Thus reconciled with both Cupid and Venus, Psyche is made immortal, and in due time bears her husband a daughter named Pleasure [Voluptas].

The old woman's tale comforts Charity with the prospect that she may be rescued from misfortune and indeed she is, through the courage of her fiancé. At the same time, Psyche's misadventures, caused as they are by her lust and curiosity as well as her trials at the hands of Venus, echo the trials and misfortunes of Lucius. On a deeper level, the allegorical relationships suggested by the characters' names point to the philosophical themes at the heart of both the tale of *Cupid and Psyche* and the larger narrative of *The Golden Ass*. Influenced by the philosophical school of Middle Platonism, and especially the Platonic doctrine of love found in Plato's *Symposium* and *Phaedrus*, Apuleius uses his narrative to dramatize and describe the transformation of the soul (Psyche), as she is driven by love (Eros/Cupid) towards salvation and enlightenment. Psyche's development follows that described by the stairway of love in the *Symposium*, which begins in the love of bodies and culminates in the love of the form of beauty. Thus Psyche begins with the physical love represented by Venus, and ends with a pure love represented by that of a mother for her child (Pleasure). Psyche's salvation, through the redirection of erotic passion towards pure beauty and enlightenment, anticipates that of Lucius through the actions of the mother goddess Isis. Both stories point to the importance and power of erotic passion and beauty as the driving forces in the life of the soul. The problem, as Plato noted, is the direction, whether the soul be guided by an empty desire for trivial matters and idle curiosity, or by the desire for true beauty and enlightenment. Both Psyche and Lucius must triumph over their physical passions if they are to enjoy spiritual metamorphosis.

Apuleius' allegory of the eros and the soul presents a masterful synthesis of Plato's philosophical doctrine with religion and the nature of religious experience. Self-contained, and yet commenting both on the immediate narrative of Charity and the larger story of Lucius, the tale of *Cupid and Psyche* is an exquisitely carved gem set into an intricately wrought work of art.

—Thomas L. Cooksey

CUTTLEFISH BONES (Ossi di seppia)
Poems by Eugenio Montale, 1925

A book of lyrics with which Eugenio Montale made his debut in the world of poetry in 1925, *Cuttlefish Bones* made much the same impact as did T.S. Eliot's *The Waste Land*, and brought him instant fame. It also signalled a break from the poetry of the "Crepuscular" poets as well as from that of Gabriele D'Annunzio—a break at least as decisive as the one effected by Giuseppe Ungaretti's *Allegria*, 1919. Moreover, it established a new canon as well as a new idiom that was to become the hallmark of modern Italian poetry. The peculiar kind of maturity, moral, poetic, and linguistic, that *Cuttlefish Bones* displays, Montale was not to repeat, still less to surpass in the course of his long poetic career, during which he published six further volumes of poetry. Little wonder, therefore, that critics have considered *Cuttlefish Bones* to be Montale's single most original book. Sergio Solmi, for instance, reviewed it soon after it came out, singling out such qualities as "a profoundly intimate, compact and necessary tone," an accomplished objectivity and immediacy, and a measured and subdued lyricism. Another critic, Alfredo Gargiulo, in his introduction to the second edition of *Cuttlefish Bones*, summed up the ethos of the volume through the celebrated phrase: "the critical corrosion of existence," entailing, among other things, "the intensity of so much negation" as well as the sense of a stagnant life, of one that is not lived.

What must have struck readers then and what strikes them now as one of the conspicuous features of this book is Montale's use of a new diction, a new imagery, and a new rhythm, cadence, and inflection, as if they were something quite natural and customary. Although he must have been aware of what was at stake, Montale goes about effecting a poetic revolution, to quote F.R. Leavis's noted phrase about Eliot's dislodging of John Milton, "with remarkably little

fuss." Images such as "a dead coil of memories"; "a crocus lost in the midst of a dusty meadow"; "a wall with pieces of glass stuck to it," and "a gunshot breaking the silence of the countryside," which occur in Montale's earliest poems, have something strikingly effortless, even casual about them. And yet they represent the very essence of what poetic modernity came to mean in terms of anti-D'Annunzianism and in terms of what was to follow. The same applies to the descriptive details and concrete objects in their luminous realism with which poems in *Cuttlefish Bones* bristle. As, for instance, "the lizard lying still on a bare rock"; "the shadow on an unplastered wall"; "the sunflower gone crazy with the light," and "the statue in the drowsiness of the moon." Such details and imagery give *Cuttlefish Bones* a throbbing vitality and concreteness, and its language a gripping power and perspicacity which Montale's subsequent books of poetry do not possess, or at least, not to the same degree. The essentiality of thought and feeling combines with the barest and most economic expression, so that, even in his first book of poetry, Montale seems to have achieved what he set out to, namely to be "rugged and essential," and to express his emotions through his own brand of what T.S. Eliot called "the objective correlative." This is demonstrated in such poems as "Often I have come across the evil of living," "My life, I don't ask for set features," and "Perhaps one morning going along in a glassy air."

The most impressive example of Montale employing the device of the objective correlative, however, is that group of nine poems called *Mediterraneo* (*Mediterranean*), where Montale treats the sea both as an *alter ego* and as a father figure, communion with whom takes him far beyond the descriptive or naturalistic level. There is something almost Wordsworthian about the way the poet bares his soul, pinpointing, as it were, the various stages of his moral and poetic development evaluated in terms of what the sea meant to him as a child and what it means to him now.

In other longer poems, like "Case sul Mare" ("Houses by the Sea"), Montale treats personal sentiment in a manner and through a technique that anticipate his future development as a love poet. "This little mist of memories"—which is how he sums up all the momentous events of his and his beloved's life as they appear to him now—is interpreted in such a way that the relentless passing of time and the imminent approach of "the hour ... when you will pass beyond time," are treated by means of luminously realistic and concrete details rather than through morally or philosophically loaded affirmations and concepts.

Another, longer poem that deals with Montale's childhood is "Fine dell'Infanzia" ("End of Childhood"). Though the recollections of childhood were not to play as decisive a role in Montale's poetry as they did in Wordsworth's, what Montale recalls of childhood in this poem has such a graphic and evocative quality that it makes it relive with a new poignancy and a new vigour. Even the sense of regret that those happy but short-lived years "vanished like days" indirectly attests to the poetry and vitality of the past rather than to the paucity and prosaic qualities of the present.

When we come to such poems as "Arsenio" [Arsenic], "Crisalide" [Chrysalis], "I morti" [The Dead], "Delta," and "Incontro" [Encounter], Montale's awareness of the present and his sense of modernity go beyond poetic diction and imagery. Tied up with his thought, perception, and intuition, they create a new kind of poetry, reflecting and analysing the mind, sensibility, and existential situation of a modern man. Such creatively paradoxical images and concepts as "going motionlessly"; the "too much known delirium of immobility," the "squalid limbo of maimed existences," and this "nameless torture'' of existence, constitute Montale's criticism of life—its crises, dilemmas, and perplexities—and convey it in a manner and an idiom that is both Dantesque and modern, realistic, and evocative.

Thanks to these qualities, *Cuttlefish Bones* bears that authentic and unmistakable stamp of freshness and originality which marks it off from any other book of 20th-century Italian poetry, including any others by Montale.

—G. Singh

CYRANO DE BERGERAC
Play by Edmond Rostand, 1897

When *Cyrano de Bergerac* was first performed in 1897 in Paris at the Théâtre de la Porte-Saint-Martin, famous for its spectacular shows, with Constant Coquelin, the greatest male actor of the age, playing the lead, it scored an immediate success, and this verse ''heroic comedy,'' as Edmond Rostand described it, has continued to enjoy great popularity ever since. Though film versions, notably those starring respectively José Ferrer and Gérard Depardieu, have been very well received, the play is best enjoyed when produced in the theatre, for every resource of 19th-century staging, including even the arrival of a coach drawn by trotting horses, is expertly deployed to create spectacle so magnificent as to leave the spectator gasping. In everything there is a sense of splendid extravagance, of fine excess and marvellous colour that leaves mere realism far behind.

What is striking about the setting is superabundantly true of the hero too. Rostand based him on the historical Savinien Cyrano de Bergerac (1619–55), but turned this relatively minor author, who wrote fantastic space-travel satires and a number of plays, including a comedy from which Molière purloined a scene for his *Les Fourberies de Scapin* (*The Rogueries of Scapin*), into a colourful figure of romance. Rostand's Cyrano comes from Gascony, and his origins are immediately apparent in his liking for brilliant swordplay that is combined with great readiness of tongue and wit. Like Dumas *père*'s D'Artagnan, who appears briefly to congratulate him on a particularly brilliant achievement, Cyrano is a strong-willed individualist who nonetheless also has a well-developed sense of comradeship; he also resembles him, in a play whose first four acts are set in the France of 1640, in his stout adherence to the values of the minor provincial nobility at a time when, under Richelieu, the country was moving towards centralized autocracy. Being poor does not upset Cyrano so long as he can still indulge a passion for quixotic gestures of generosity and independence.

But Cyrano has one grave defect that threatens to cancel out all his admirable qualities and deny him the woman's love that would make his world perfect. Like the historical Cyrano de Bergerac, he is cursed with an enormous nose, and it is out of the grotesque disproportion between the hero's appearance and his nature that Rostand fashions a play that may be seen as the culmination of the Romantic enterprise of reinvigorating the French dramatic tradition begun in 1830 with Hugo's *Hernani*.

Each of the five acts presents a brilliant contrasting spectacle, and each allows Cyrano to reveal himself in a different fashion. Act I is set in a theatre whose rowdiness partakes more of the Elizabethan playhouse than of the decorous routines of French classicism as it would develop in the 17th century, and we see Cyrano as a dashing duellist and a cheeky extempore versifier. Only at the end is it revealed that he is in love with Roxane and that his love is not returned. Next, in a bakery owned by a pastry-cook with a weakness for poets and poetry, Cyrano realizes that, to please the lady he loves, he must not only renounce her but protect the strikingly handsome but distressingly dim-witted Christian whom she prefers. At first it seems that this might involve no more than composing love letters suitably phrased to satisfy Roxane who, in the current fashion of ''preciosity,'' expects high stylistic elegance in amorous declarations. But in Act IV, a night-time balcony scene that owes something to *Romeo and Juliet*, Cyrano is obliged first to whisper sweet nothings for Christian to repeat and then, when he cannot manage to do even that convincingly, to emerge from hiding and actually speak out on his behalf. His heart-rending reward for eloquence is seeing Christian granted a kiss and, soon after that, Roxane's hand in marriage. At the siege of Arras the French troops are starving and dispirited until Roxane unexpectedly arrives with a coach full of provisions. Christian is only just learning that her inspiration for coming was the beautifully turned letters she had been receiving regularly from the front, only just beginning to realize that Cyrano, who had written them, was deeply in love with her, when he is killed in an attack, and Act IV ends in the confusion of battle. Act V, set 15 years later and in the convent to which his disconsolate widow has retired, is quiet and elegiac, with religious overtones, and Roxane divines the truth as Cyrano, who has been treacherously struck down by the servant of one of the gentlemen offended by his satires, dies in her arms.

Cyrano de Bergerac is a drama of action and spectacle, of excitement and rather sentimental emotion. But it is also a play of words. The range of vocabulary is enormous and inventive, the versification is witty and daring, clever to the point of virtuosity, and always the apt expression of the singular people who use it. The language in this play, no less than its characterization and its more overtly dramatic aspects, justifies Rostand's claim that he should be seen as the last and not the least of the French Romantic dramatists.

—Christopher Smith

D

DANTON'S DEATH (Dantons Tod)
Play by Georg Büchner, 1835 (complete version 1850)

Danton's Death was written in five weeks during January and February of 1835 while the 21-year-old revolutionary author was hiding from the police in his parents' house in Darmstadt. Georg Büchner claimed that he wrote the play simply to make money, much to the amusement of the militant liberal Karl Gutzkow, who published the play, first in a periodical in March and April 1835, then in book form later that year. The text was severely edited in order to manoeuvre it past the pervasive censorship. The play's public premiere did not occur until 1902, in Berlin, although there had been a private performance in Zurich about ten years earlier.

The action of the play takes place in the spring of 1794, near the climax of the Reign of Terror and of the French Revolution itself. Robespierre has disposed of the egalitarian Hébertists on his left and is heading for a showdown with the newly moderate Dantonists, who are pressing for a conclusion to the Revolution. Danton, a revolutionary leader with an energetic, even brutal past, is strangely passive at this crisis; he and his friends spend their time dallying with women and exchanging cynical or obscene *bons mots*. Danton claims to believe that the Jacobins will not dare to harm him, but in fact a sense of futility has overcome him. He defends himself too late to avoid the guillotine, a fate that Robespierre will later share. The external form of *Danton's Death,* unlike that of *Woyzeck,* appears relatively conventional: it is divided into acts and scenes, has an exposition, and a rising and falling action. In the background lies the model of Goethe's *Egmont,* especially in the interspersed folk scenes and the fatal indecisiveness of the protagonist, and there are echoes of Shakespeare too—Danton's wife, Julie (her name changed from the historical Louise), recalls Juliet; Camille Desmoulin's wife, Lucile, recalls Ophelia. In other respects, however, the play is astonishingly original.

It is, first of all, a pioneering example of what came to be called documentary theatre. Approximately one-sixth of the text is taken verbatim from historical sources. These are, primarily, the histories of the French Revolution by Adolphe Thiers and François Mignet, a memoir of Louis-Sébastien Mercier, and a German-language compendium of documents of contemporary history. There has been a great hunt for Büchner's exact sources; more have been adduced than he could possibly have had time to read in the circumstances. Judging from his own comments, he had an austerely realistic intention of putting history itself on the stage as objectively as possible. But a comparison with the sources does not strictly bear this out. For Danton and his friends evince a preoccupation with sexual libertinage and luxuriant sensuality for which there is practically no warrant in the sources. This, in turn, generates the most original dimension of the text: a slangy, vulgar, colourfully obscene language never before seen in a German literary work and not soon to appear again.

Danton's Death has been the object of endless critical disputes. The main problem has been to locate Büchner in his play. As a revolutionary activist in his time he ought to be a partisan of the French Revolution. But the Revolution is imaged with grim ambiguity. The Dantonists are certainly to some degree attractive. But in their cynicism and self-indulgence they seem to have become irrelevant to the Revolution and its social issues, while Danton is haunted by the memory of past atrocities committed in the name of political necessity. Robespierre, on the other hand, is pinched and puritanical; an imagined soliloquy shows him no less at odds with himself than Danton, and his vaunted virtue in its savage ruthlessness has the appearance of a neurotic symptom. St. Just, whose terrifying speech to the Convention Büchner invented, sounds like a fascist. As for the common people, they complain justly that the Revolution is giving them heads instead of bread, but they are crudely comic, easily duped, and fickle. Some critics have tried to identify Büchner with the engaging Camille and his sensualism. While working on the play, Büchner read Heinrich Heine's just-published essay ''On the History of Religion and Philosophy in Germany'' and attributed to Camille its doctrine of sensual emancipation as the true revolutionary issue. But others see Camille as a self-indulgent adolescent. Marion's laudation of totally amoral sensualism, the most lyrical moment in the play, is qualified by the Dantonists' mocking insolence toward the diseased prostitutes Rosalie and Adelaide.

Few critics have been able to avoid the impression of contradictoriness in the play and in the characters themselves, especially Danton. Not only is it difficult to reconcile his lethargic present self with his activist past; his whole tone becomes abruptly more resolute when he at last defends himself before the Convention. But here Büchner, returning to his sources, may be showing something about the autonomy of revolutionary rhetoric, as verbal machinery running by itself, detached from the realities of those who employ it. The play is relentlessly anti-heroic; the condemned can no longer even devise dignified last words that are not scoffed at as trite by the public and their own comrades. It is in any case important to remember that Büchner was a very young man with intense but by no means settled ideas: the scientist's materialistic determinism collides with a sympathetic awareness of the suffering of real human beings; his revolutionary ardour becomes entangled with scepticism born of the failures of 1789 and 1830; the youthful excitement of sexual liberation clashes with the insight that neither it nor anything else the revolutionary leaders say or do is relevant to the plight of the people, and the people know it. The play is best understood, not as an ideological manual, but as the fervent engagement of an uncommonly powerful creative spirit with the dilemmas of his age.

—Jeffrey L. Sammons

DAPHNIS AND CHLOE (Daphnis et Chloe)

Pastoral romance probably written by Longus (fl. 2nd or 3rd century AD) who may have been born on Lesbos, the setting of the romance. One of five remaining Greek novels of the Classical period.

PUBLICATIONS

Daphnis et Chloe, edited by Michael D. Reeve. 1982; as *Daphnis and Chloe*, edited and translated by William D. Lowe, 1908; translated by Angell Daye (from French), 1587; also translated by George

Thornley, 1657, revised by J.M. Edmonds [Loeb Edition], 1916; James Craggs, 2nd edition, 1720; C.V. Le Grice, 1803; Jack Lindsay, 1948; Paul Turner, 1956; Philip Sherrard, 1965; Christopher Gill, in *Collected Ancient Greek Novels*, 1989; Ronald McCail, 2002; as *The Pastoral Amours of Daphnis and Chloe*, translated by Roland Smith, 1882; as *The Pastoral Loves of Daphnis and Chloe*, translated by George Moore, 1924.

*

Critical Studies: *Longus* by William E. MacCulloh, 1970; *Daphnis and Chloe: The Markets and Metamorphoses of an Unknown Bestseller* by Giles Barber, 1988; *Myth, Rhetoric, and Fiction: A Reading of Longus' Daphnis and Chloe* by Bruce D. MacQueen, 1990; *A Study of Daphnis and Chloe* by Richard L. Hunter, 1993; *Sexual Symmetry: Love in the Ancient Novel and Related Genres* by David Konstan, 1994; *Greek Fiction: The Greek Novel in Context,* edited by J.R. Morgan and Richard Stoneman, 1994; *The Search for the Ancient Novel,* edited by James Tatum, 1994; *Love in a Green Shade: Idyllic Romances Ancient to Modern* by Richard F. Hardin, 2000.

* * *

Daphnis et Chloe (*Daphnis and Chloe*), by a writer named (in all probability) Longus who lived in the 2nd or 3rd century AD), perhaps on the island of Lesbos, is one of five long prose narratives to survive from Greek antiquity. All take as their subject the love between a young couple, male and female, who overcome various obstacles in order finally to be united in wedlock. These five works—Chariton's *Chaereas and Callirhoe*; *The Ephesian Tale* by Xenophon of Ephesus; *Clitophon and Leucippe* by Achilles Tatius; and Heliodorus' *Aethiopian Tale,* in addition to *Daphnis and Chloe*—are conventionally designated ''romances'' but may equally well be classified as novels.

Among the Greek novels, however, *Daphnis and Chloe* is unique for its pastoral setting, and the charming naivety of its protagonists, two young foundlings who have been raised, he as goatherd, she as shepherdess, by foster parents in the countryside near Mytilene, and fall innocently in love before they have heard of the word or can recognize its symptoms. The novel traces their initiation, over a single cycle of the seasons, into desire and sexuality, as well as their steadfastness in the face of rivals and marauders. In the end, the pair are revealed as the offspring, exposed in infancy, of rich parents from the city. By the kind of coincidence that is characteristic of the genre, Daphnis' family owns the estate on which the boy was reared.

The style of the narrative is elegant and suave, exploiting the rhetorical figures and balanced clauses that found favour with the writers of the so-called Second Sophistic, a cultural movement that rejoiced in classicizing diction and artful prose. Longus invites the reader to smile at the simplicity of his hero and heroine, which is underscored by the sophistication of the literary technique and by occasional cameos of urban manners. In this, Longus associates himself with the pastoral poetry inaugurated by Theocritus and perhaps by Philetas, a 3rd-century BC erotic poet whose name is borne by an old farmer in *Daphnis and Chloe*. Philetas offers the young pair their first lessons in love-making, instructing them that, in order to allay their desire, they must kiss, embrace, and lie naked next to each other. They follow Philetas' advice punctiliously, but discover that it falls short of satisfying their passion.

A married woman from the city, named Lycaenium, takes a fancy to Daphnis, and elects to alleviate his plight by initiating him into sex.

Daphnis is set to race straight for Chloe so that he may share with her his new discovery before he forgets. But when Lycaenium warns him that Chloe will weep with pain and bleed when she is penetrated, Daphnis recoils at the idea of inflicting harm on her, and returns to the procedures recommended by Philetas. Only at the very end, when the couple, now revealed as free citizens of Mytilene, are wedded, do they at last consummate their passion.

Various incidents and subordinate narratives punctuate the amatory plot. Raiding pirates and a war party from another city on Lesbos threaten to separate the couple. Just before Daphnis' identity is revealed, one Gnatho, a crony of the urbane youth Astylus who will turn out to be Daphnis' brother, conceives a passion for Daphnis, and succeeds in obtaining him as his servant. After the recognition of Daphnis, a rival cowherd named Lampis carries off Chloe, but she is rescued in the nick of time by Gnatho, who gathers some of Astylus' men for the purpose in hopes of appeasing his new young patron. Gnatho is a figure out of New Comedy, and bears the same name as a parasite in Terence's *Eunuch*. Here again, Longus reveals his flair for incorporating previous literary genres into his novel.

The presiding deities in the pastoral world of Lesbos are Pan and the Nymphs, and the entire tale is presented as an explication, provided by a professional interpreter, of a picture seen at a grove sacred to the Nymphs and dedicated to them, along with Love and Pan. Pan is a lustful character, and stories of his pursuit and attempted rape of Syrinx, who eludes him by turning into a reed (from which Pan constructs his pipes), and of Echo provide a counterpoint to the main narrative. The mutual adolescent desire of Daphnis and Chloe is in contrast to Pan's aggressive and selfish lust, and the protagonists, while grateful for his protection, distance themselves from his erotic violence and fickleness.

The pair's wedding night is described in the final words of the novel:

> Daphnis and Chloe lay down naked together, embraced and kissed, and had even less sleep that night than the owls. Daphnis did some of the things Lycaenium taught him; and then, for the first time, Chloe found out that what they had done in the woods had been nothing but shepherds' games.

Longus does not pause to explain why, on this night, Daphnis suddenly overcomes the fear of harming Chloe in the sexual act. Presumably, it is enough that she has moved from the status of unwed maiden or *parthenos* to that of wedded woman, ready now to assume a full sexual role. Yet, despite the knowing wink on the part of the author, the innocence of Chloe's previous life with Daphnis remains as an image of a simple, childlike way of sex in a pastoral world alive with rustic deities. To this world, in the end, the couple elect to return.

—David Konstan

DEAD SOULS (Mertvye dushi)
Novel by Nikolai Gogol', 1842

Dead Souls, according to its author, was based on a theme furnished by Aleksandr Pushkin. As a person with an exceptionally fertile imagination Nikolai Gogol' was always afraid of being accused of fanciful invention, so it may be that Gogol' fabricated this statement both to ward off such criticism and underline the parallels between his work and Pushkin's novel in verse, *Eugene Onegin*. Gogol's work was to be the reverse, an epic poem in prose, a genre conveniently removed from the realm of the novel with its female readership and preoccupation with the love story. Early draft chapters were evidently comic and mildly satirical, but as time went on Gogol's growing sense of the high calling of the artist—his moral mission to reveal the vices afflicting Russia and point the way to a better future—made him place much more serious demands upon his work. Now it was to be a trilogy strongly linked to Dante's *Divine Comedy*, with divisions into Hell, Purgatory, and Heaven. It took him seven years to complete the first part, which was published in 1842, while the remaining decade of his life saw him struggling and failing to complete the second. Fragments which escaped being burnt remain as a sad reminder of a great writer who destroyed himself trying to force his genius into an appropriate mould. Part Three, in which the hero would be transformed into a positive character, was never more than a dream. Fortunately Part One of *Dead Souls* is complete in itself and a brilliant testament to Gogol's genius.

The basic idea, whether Pushkin's or not, was retained in its simplicity: Pavel Chichikov appears in a small town, makes the acquaintance of local landowners, and while visiting them on their estates buys from them dead serfs (known in Russia as souls) on whom landowners have to pay taxes until the next census. His reasons for so doing and his background are revealed at the end of the book, by which time the secret is out and the townsfolk swing from adulation of Chichikov to savage rumour. Chichikov leaves town.

The structure of the first half of the book is based on a series of separate encounters with different landowners. The strength of the book lies in its characterization. Each landowner represents a set of negative characteristics: Manilov is sugariness, idleness, and pretension; Sobakevich crude vigour and solidity; Pliushkin miserliness. Each is introduced in the same way through amazingly colourful and detailed descriptions of his or her estate and house, family relationships, hospitality, physical appearance, manner of speaking, and reaction to Chichikov's proposition. These word portraits are so vivid and distinctive that in the company of the landowners Chichikov acts as a mirror, adapting his smooth exterior like a chameleon to reflect the character of his host. His role as the travelling link between the landowners is reminiscent of that of the hero of the picaresque novel who enjoys a series of encounters and adventures on his travels. So idiosyncratic are the landowners that they might well have appeared to be grotesques with no relevance to real life, but Gogol's epic poem employs a number of devices to give them and his book a broader relevance to Russia. One is an adaptation of the Homeric simile, where a simple comparison develops into a separate picture of a different aspect of Russian life, another his habit of generalizing from the particular (''Manilov was the type of man who. . .''). This latter method is developed extensively in the second half of *Dead Souls*, which is given over to group portraiture of the townsfolk, seen especially in their hysterical reactions (pro and anti) to Chichikov. Above all, Gogol' takes the device of digression so popular in 18th-century novels, and through it adds moral comment.

Despite the colourful and frequently comic detail, the book as a whole reveals a pessimistic view of mankind: there is no single positive character, but neither is there a real villain. Evil in Gogol' is petty, and dangerous because it is so banal. The apparently solid, respectable, charming Chichikov turns out to be the devil-knows-what, while other characters have little depth and are not much more than products of their surroundings. By describing people as vegetables (''a woman's face in a bonnet as long and narrow as a cucumber,

and a man's as round and broad as the Moldavian pumpkin.. .'') Gogol' implies that his characters have something more than just appearance in common with vegetables. While keeping a careful balance between comic and serious, Gogol' recognized that his book needed something to lift it from the mire of petty vice and make it worthy of the title of epic poem. To this end he added notes of lyricism, showing Pliushkin's garden splendid in its luxuriant neglect, lamenting his own lost youth, or comparing Russia to a hurtling troika, rushing one knows not where.

As was frequently the case with Gogol's works, his efforts not to be misunderstood by his readers were in vain. The book achieved instant notoriety because it was viewed as an attack on serfdom despite the evidence in the book to the contrary. Far from being an attack on an institution, the book is a damning portrait of a whole world. It can be said to fulfil Gogol's intention of depicting the whole of Russia, but not in a crude photographic sense. Gogol's characters are dazzling linguistic artefacts, their colours concentrated and their petty failings intensified. Take these away and it is clear that the dead souls of the title are not the deceased peasants Chichikov wishes to purchase but the living characters of the book.

—Faith Wigzell

DEATH AND THE COMPASS (La muerte y la brújula)
Story by Jorge Luis Borges, 1942

''Death and the Compass,'' now part of his *Ficciones*, definitive edition 1956, reveals Jorge Luis Borges at his best: densely labyrinthine, ironic, and multilayered.

The image of the labyrinth is one of Borges's favourites. In their repeated appearances in varied guises Borges's labyrinths all point to the same general idea: the near-impossibility of achieving full understanding and control of our own fate. Some of his characters cannot solve the puzzle of the labyrinth; those who do, through miraculous interventions, find destruction and even humiliation awaiting them. The labyrinth, then, symbolizes that which remains permanently out of reach of human abilities and aspirations, that which we could reach only through the loss of our humanity: it represents the frustration of the universal desire for transcendence.

The labyrinth also serves as an apt symbol of Borges's tales themselves, whose ''architecture'' is filled with tricks and false paths, and whose true way is complex and sometimes obscure. In ''Death and the Compass,'' Borges takes his reader along his own literary labyrinth, just as Red Scharlach leads Lönnrot on the path he has built for him.

Lönnrot's immediate problem, as a detective, is to solve a murder (and also to avoid being murdered by his arch-enemy Scharlach). Ironically, the solution is presented immediately by Commissioner Treviranus, but rejected by Lönnrot on the grounds that this explanation lacks ''interest''; for the death of a rabbi he prefers a ''rabbinical'' explanation, whether Treviranus is right or wrong. (While he never actually rejects his colleague's hypothesis, he simply is compelled, for reasons we understand only later, to find a more aesthetic solution.) ''Truth,'' for Lönnrot, matters less than the appropriateness of things and the elegance of reason.

Unfortunately for Lönnrot, Scharlach knows him very well indeed, and flawlessly anticipates his reactions. Planting a series of ''clues,'' he leads his evidently unwitting victim, just erudite enough to interpret them, through a labyrinth constructed just for him. Following Scharlach's path, Lönnrot reasons that there will be a fourth crime after the series of three he attributes to his rival, and in this he is correct; what he learns in the last paragraphs is that this last crime consists of his own murder.

We now enter the multiple ironies of this story. Firstly, Lönnrot is led to humiliation and destruction by the very values Borges (and his presumed reader) hold: intelligence, diligence, and learning. Hence the first real theme of the tale is the limitations of these same qualities, for they are never enough to solve all the mysteries we face. Lönnrot makes the fatal mistake of assuming causality in things that turn out to be unrelated: the first crime was unintended, the second (the murder of an accomplice of Scharlach) merely a matter of mob justice; the third is a simulated kidnapping. The second theme is that life continues to resist our desires and needs for things to make sense, and that in seeking meanings where there may well be none we may in a sense be "noble," but we are mistaking a pleasant illusion for reality.

Scharlach, then, traps Lönnrot in a multilayered labyrinth: geographical (following the layout of a city, possibly Paris), intellectual, aesthetic, and numerical (numerical symbols lead his enemy to his denouement at Triste-le-Roy). And of course, we readers are also trapped, led to follow the same clues to the same finality—our "death" as readers as we finish the tale.

This last irony (Borges is to the reader as Scharlach is to Lönnrot) is developed fully in the startling final pages. We have seen how the two main characters of this "fiction" exist as each other's counterpart, in terms of their rivalry only; we now also see how our identity as readers, and the artist's as writer, are another dependent duality wherein both exist only during the act of reading (a common subtheme of Borges). So, firstly, both dualities form a single identity. This is why Scharlach detests duplicated images and speaks so bitterly of the two-faced—but single-headed—god Janus: duality reminds him that he, although nearly omnipotent, is still bound to his Other. (They even share the same single name, since both mean "red.") Therefore, his murder of the detective is also a form of suicide.

There is yet another twist to these matters. The text tells us that Scharlach fires his gun at his rival; it does not actually tell us Lönnrot dies. In fact, we are led to assume he does not, for in the obligatory "explanation scene" (where the criminal tells how he pulled off his deed) we learn of an extraordinary aspect of the Janus-like pair of rivals: they fully expect to live again, to re-enact their pursuit and vengeance and for the outcome to be the same. They are, then, in a circular existence, entering into new *avatars* (the word is used by Lönnrot) at the close of each "chapter" of their ongoing series of fatalistic incarnations. It seems that Lönnrot's only hope of "escape" is to make the next pursuit a more "interesting" one, in a different sort of labyrinth, one made of a straight line instead of the geometric patterns of this sequence. Now at last we understand his obsession with the subjective adequacy of explanations, why he rejected Treviranus's interpretation: the individual who knows he or she is trapped can do little but try to make the paths leading to destruction aesthetically and intellectually interesting. The truth, in such a situation, is pitiful, melancholy, and, so to speak, must be transcended.

What, then, of Lönnrot's fate the next time? It is possible he hopes that Scharlach will be unable to overtake him in their new labyrinth. Sadly, however, the manner in which he asks for this more "interesting" labyrinth suggests little or no real hope: "when, in some other

incarnation, you hunt me." His feeling of inevitability is echoed when his enemy indeed promises to murder him again.

Clearly, this is a complex narrative. It is at once a detective story, a reflection on the limitations of the intellect, an exposition of the conflict between materiality and the ideal (or, to put it another way, between reality and what could be), and an allegory on the nature of reading and writing. Like those of many of Borges's "fictions" (a blend of the essay and the short story), the underlying themes of "Death and the Compass" are in the end melancholy, but there is a compensation to this basic fatalism. The labyrinth to which literature is assigned is, in fact, lineal (as Lönnrot wished his own to be), for literature cannot escape linearity because it can only be read according to the flow of time. Borges, our "Scharlach," in fact gives us the aesthetic satisfaction that his Lönnrot seeks. It may not solve the mysteries or the traps of life, but readers the world over enjoy Borges's (and their own) walks through the labyrinth of his art, and are, each in their own way, reborn with each new reading.

—Paul W. Borgeson, Jr.

DEATH FUGUE (Todesfuge)
Poem by Paul Celan, 1952 (written 1948)

Theodor Adorno's famous statement, made in 1949, that "to write poetry after Auschwitz is barbaric" reflects not only the cultural dislocation in Germany at the end of World War II but above all a sense that, since the enormity of Nazi crimes seems to place them beyond aesthetic treatment, the only fitting artistic response must be silence. Paul Celan's "Death Fugue," however, written in 1948 (although it was not widely published until 1952) by a Romanian German of Jewish extraction who lost both parents in the death camps, illustrates that the language of poetry, with its compressed metaphors, its suggestive allusions, and its emotional intensity, is capable of confronting even such horrors and indeed can articulate them with a force and immediacy that prose, let alone bare statistics, would struggle to match.

In just 36 lines "Death Fugue" seeks to convey the Jewish experience of Auschwitz. From the opening oxymoron of the "black milk" which the inmates must drink, to the closing juxtaposition of the golden-haired German girl and the ashen-haired Jewess, the poem is built upon contrast. Murder is carried out to the background of music performed by the prisoners themselves, the victims are promised death as if through the generosity of the perpetrators, while the officer in charge of the carnage, having killed Jews by day, writes love-letters home at night. And the whole deranged world is evoked by the poet within the structure and discipline of a fugue. It is this last contradiction which is probably the most shocking, as the beauty of a form normally associated with praise of the divine clashes with the vileness of the material it sustains.

Like its musical counterpart this verbal fugue establishes a theme, repeats, develops, and modifies it, at the same time introducing contrasting matter which is interwoven with, and played off against, the original. So the Jews drink their "Black milk of daybreak" at evening, at noon, at morning, at night, in varied and anachronic sequence. This sinister image, running throughout the poem, may well carry associations of the gas with which the Jews were killed, or the smoke from the crematoria that filled the air, but it is a mistake to pin it down to a single static meaning, for it signifies the depravity of a whole system, one which violated the order of nature and compelled the victims to become agents in their own destruction. The only other action in which the Jews here are seen engaging, apart from playing violins to accompany the slaughter (in Auschwitz there was indeed an "orchestra" of inmates), is the digging of their own graves.

In counterpoint to this helplessness there appears in line five the man who gives the orders. With the enigmatic statement, made on four occasions, that he "plays with the serpents" he is aligned with the archetypal emblems of evil, and he shows his malign power by whistling up "his Jews" as he would whistle out his dogs, commanding the musicians to play "more sweetly" while deriding his victims for their imminent fate. Menacingly he reaches for the gun in his belt, then closes one of his blue eyes to take careful aim and fire: "he strikes you with leaden bullet his aim is true." In the last third of the poem Celan introduces what has become one of the best-known phrases from the literature of this period, a sombre incantation which is repeated at intervals three more times, like a dark chord drowning out the other instruments: "death is a master from Germany."

His day's work done, the man retires to his house to indulge in romantic thoughts and write to Margarete in Germany. This symbol of Aryan womanhood is contrasted throughout the poem with the figure of Shulamith, her Jewish counterpart. In the Old Testament Song of Solomon the beautiful Shulammite woman had possessed hair "like purple" (7:5), but now it is ashen, consumed by fire. Resonances of the Old Testament recall the timelessness of Jewish persecution. In Babylonian exile too the Jews had been forced by their captors to make music against their will (Psalm 137), and the Book of Lamentations recalls a time when the servants of God had been "whiter than milk," as against their present condition with faces "blacker than a coal" (Lamentations 4:7–8). Such Old Testament experiences, however, are usually in the context of Israel departing from the Lord and receiving just retribution, and there always remains the hope of restoration. In Celan's poem there is no such underlying moral order: the Jews, so it seems, have been deserted by both God and man, left to suffer for no reason other than their race, in a world devoid of logic or compassion.

One critic, L.L. Duroche, has suggested that in the poem's final couplet, "your golden hair Margarete / your ashen hair Shulamith," there is a hint of reconciliation, even of redemption through the power of love, but this is a grotesque misreading. "Death Fugue" offers no explanation and holds out no comfort; its conclusion is not harmony or resolution but an obscene discord. Celan later repudiated the poem as too explicit, and it is certainly more accessible than his later work. Yet with its haunting imagery and its incongruous marriage of form and meaning, it expresses something of a reality whose full terror must, in truth, remain beyond words. It is a chilling and deeply memorable poem.

—Peter J. Graves

DEATH IN VENICE (Der Tod in Venedig)
Novella by Thomas Mann, 1912

Published in 1912, *Death in Venice* is perhaps the most widely admired of all Thomas Mann's shorter fiction, although it never attained the general popularity of "Tonio Kröger" (1903). It tells the story of the established writer Gustav von Aschenbach, who is tempted by the appearance of a mysterious stranger into a visit to the city of Venice. Here he succumbs to the fascination of a world very different from the ordered world of his previous life as a respected and successful writer. He becomes increasingly infatuated with a young Polish boy, Tadzio, who is a guest in the same hotel, and although he tries to persuade himself that the passion is merely aesthetic, at worst "platonic," his love reveals its unmistakably homosexual nature, even though the two hardly speak. His love for Tadzio causes Aschenbach to stay unwisely and too long in a city where cholera has already broken out, and Aschenbach falls victim to the disease. He dies on the Lido, where he has long sat staring at the object of his forbidden love.

Death in Venice is a perfect example of Mann's skill as a writer of parody. The story's original intention was to give a scurrilous and disrespectful account of the hardly respectable passion of an aging Goethe for the 17-year-old Ulrike von Levetzow (original title for the novella had been "Goethe in Marienbad") and its high-flown style, crossing over into pomposity, and the over-abundance of literary, reference never lose their parodistic intention. At the same time, the story problematizes not merely the perennially difficult relationship between the artist and the world of the senses (the artist is by definition the person whose road to the spirit leads "via the senses" and the artist must "inevitably fall into the abyss" of chaotic feeling), but also many aspects specific to Mann's own life and situation. It was a difficult time for Mann: he was uneasy about the respect society paid him as a writer, unsure if he could live up to it either in terms of his own productivity or simply on ethical grounds. Questions of his own sexuality were also on his mind, and Aschenbach's actual experiences in Venice are by no means remote from Mann's own biography.

The novella combines two very different narrative voices. There is a sharp psychological study of the process by which a repression revenges itself. Aschenbach has for too long attempted to suppress the tendency towards chaos in himself and can no longer sustain the violence he is doing to his authentic self. No less prominent in the story is the evocation of the city of Venice laden with myth and extraordinarily rich in allusion, both to classical antiquity and to the significant figures in German culture history associated with the city: from Goethe himself, to the mid-19th-century poet August von Platen and to Richard Wagner, whose death there in 1883 transformed Venice for Friedrich Nietzsche into a forbidden city. The two poles of the story—myth and psychology—were identified by Mann and subsequently by his interpreters as reference points for his entire work, and as the key to later novels, such as *Joseph and His Brothers* (*Joseph und seine Brüder*).

Death in Venice has been used by many artists as the basis of their own works, sometimes in respectful parodistic intention (as is the case with Wolfgang Koeppen's *Der Tod in Rom* [Death in Rome, 1954]), sometimes more directly, as in Benjamin Britten's opera *Death in Venice* (1973, libretto by Myfanwy Piper). The novella was brought to its widest public when filmed by Luchino Visconti in 1971. Visconti appropriately used Mahler's music (Mann had based the appearance of Aschenbach on that of Gustav Mahler) and suggested through quotations from Mann's *Doctor Faustus* and the recasting of Aschenbach as a composer the role of music—the Dionysian art—and of Nietzsche in the text. In its original version and in its adaptations, *Death in Venice* has established a reputation both as a historical text and as a focus of personal statement. Its tragic conclusion has often been associated with the collapse of civilization just before the outbreak of World War I; at the same time Mann's ability to communicate the intensity of Aschenbach's experience of beauty through his feelings for Tadzio, however questionable their origin and fatal their outcome, has been seen as one of his greatest artistic accomplishments.

—Hugh Ridley

THE DEATH OF IVAN ILYICH (Smert' Ivana Il'icha)
Novella by Lev Tolstoi, 1886

Lev Tolstoi's tale takes Ivan Il'ich from life to death and through pain and reflection. Ivan Il'ich goes to law school and graduates with an average grade. He is liked by everyone and does what is expected of him. He knows what he is to do in life and he follows the rules religiously. The point of life is to live properly and pleasantly, like all the other good people, and this is what Ivan Il'ich does. After law school he practises in the provinces, where he meets his wife Praskovia Fedorovna. He marries her not because he is madly in love with her, but because she is appropriate. She is not bad looking, has a little money, dances well, and fits into his set. The marriage starts off well, but when Praskovia Fedorovna becomes pregnant and suffers from some of its effects, Ivan Il'ich begins to ignore her. He had married to acquire pleasure not pain. His wife's suffering and complaints are not part of how he wants his life to be.

With the years Ivan rises in the ranks, has children, settles into a *modus vivendi* of calculated indifference to his wife, and makes his way into the right groups of people. His rise in his profession goes smoothly at first, but then unexpectedly he is passed over for promotion, an event that leads him to argue with his superiors. This in turn leads to further setbacks in his profession. He takes a leave of absence, reflects on his life, and determines that at all costs he must receive a position that pays 5,000 rubles. Only then would he be happy. Unexpectedly, he receives an even better position than he had hoped for. It is in the midst of this happiness that a small event takes place that is destined to have a momentous effect on his life. While he is decorating a new apartment and showing a draper how to hang a curtain, he falls off a ladder and hurts his side. He is injured slightly and takes little notice of the bruise. But with time he experiences a persistent pain. The pain interferes with his work, his bridge, and his relations with people. The doctors cannot help him, and he receives only perfunctory and largely indifferent from his friends and his family. The only person who shows him real compassion is a house serf, Gerasim, who takes care of the most unpleasant needs of the increasingly helpless Ivan. For the first time Ivan reflects upon the meaning of his life, and he can find no answer as to why he has been afflicted. He goes over his life and can find nothing wrong with it. He had always done what was expected of him. We too, as readers, must, in coming to terms with the story, explain why Ivan Il'ich has been bludgeoned by pain and then death. There is the added complication that in the last moments of his life Ivan Il'ich experiences what seems to be a religious illumination. Many critics have objected to what seems to be a "forced" didactic ending.

Ivan Il'ich arranged his life so as to live pleasantly and properly following the social conventions of the time. Pain and death have no place in this arrangement. Since both exist, real acknowledgement of the existence of pain and death is ignored by formalized pretence.

When Ivan Il'ich's wife suffers from her pregnancy, Ivan Il'ich wants no involvement in her pain and spends as little time at home as possible. When Ivan Il'ich becomes ill, Praskovia Fedorovna blames the illness on Ivan's refusal to follow the doctor's orders. A society without the acknowledgement of pain and death is a society without compassion, love, and shared feeling. Only Gerasim, a simple house serf, accepts without question pain and death as natural, and it is only Gerasim who alleviates the pain for Ivan Il'ich. When Ivan Il'ich slips through the black bag and into the light at the end of the tale, he accepts the pain and with the acceptance it is alleviated. Tolstoi seems to be saying that the "cement" that holds human beings together is the consciousness of death, and if we try to construct our lives without such a consciousness, we end up with the kind of society that Ivan Il'ich lives in: a society of isolated and "dead" people.

Tolstoi's narrative style is superb. The tale is cast in the form of chronicle and the tone is biblical and portentous. It begins with Ivan Il'ich's wake, so that Tolstoi forgoes any sense of surprise and suspense. What he achieves instead is a relentless sense of impending doom. Since we begin with Ivan Il'ich's death, the narration of his life—his successes, triumphs, and pleasures—is ironically undercut by our knowledge of what will happen. The tale, too, has a surprisingly contemporary air about it, despite the fact that it was published more than 100 years ago. The middle-class values of late-19th-century Russia and the moral and emotional conditions of life then are relevant to our lives today. Indeed, the tale has universal relevance—there is something of Ivan Il'ich in all of us.

—Edward Wasiolek

THE DEATH OF VIRGIL (Der Tod des Vergil)
Novel by Hermann Broch, 1945

Hermann Broch's meditative and essayistic novel about the death of the Roman poet Publius Vergilius Maro (70–19 BC) started inconspicuously as a short stop, "Die Heimkehr des Vergil" [The Return of Virgil]. It had been commissioned by RAVAG radio in Vienna (which broadcast the first half of it on 17 March 1937) as a fictional contribution to a topic that was much discussed at the time: the role of art at the end of a cultural era. Broch's major source of information was Theodor Haecker's book *Vergil—Vater des Abendlands* (1931), which interprets Virgil as a prophetic precursor of a Christian Europe. An expanded fragmentary version titled "Erzählung vom Tode" [Tale of Death], written during winter 1937–38, suddenly assumed an immediate personal relevance for its author when he was jailed in March 1938 in Altaussee, Styria, on suspicion of "cultural bolshevism." Broch feared for his own life and continued to expand his manuscript "as a private confrontation with the experience and reality of death" (letter to H. Zand of 12 February 1947). After his flight to London and then to St. Andrews in Scotland and directly upon his arrival to New York City on 9 October 1938, he resumed work on a story that by then had grown to the dimensions of a novel. He made good progress during his stay at the artists' colony Yaddo in Saratoga Springs, New York in summer 1939, where he met the poet Jean Starr Untermeyer who became his translator. But the precarious circumstances of his life in exile and his preoccupation with studies of mass psychology impeded the completion of the *Virgil* book. It underwent several revisions and was not published until June 1945 (by the exile publisher Kurt Wolff's Pantheon Books), its concurrent editions in German and English receiving considerable critical attention. The translation was often praised as more accessible because it has reduced the excesses of Broch's at times overly abstract and hymnically "mystic" style.

The Death of Virgil recounts the dying poet's last day in four sections of uneven length that, in tracing the course of his (and all) life back to its earliest beginnings, evoke the four elements of ancient philosophy. In the first section, "Water—the Arrival," after landing in Brundisium with the imperial fleet on his return from Greece, Virgil slowly advances through the destitute urban masses of the harbour as he is being carried to his apartment in the palace. His encounters with human misery, especially as personified by throngs of howling women, the "mass animal," make him despair of his poetic ideals so that he curses the dignified aloofness of his privileged life as an aesthete. His disenchantment turns into disorientation when a boy, Lysanias, appears as his psychopomp, the guide of his soul into the underworld. The second section is "Fire—the Descent," in which, in imitation of Orpheus and Aeneas, Virgil's mind, feverish at night, leads him into the abyss of self-castigation. He vows to destroy the unfinished *Aeneid* in sacrificial atonement for his irresponsible life of aesthetic self-sufficiency. Disturbed by nightmarish visions he listens to three drunkards outside his window whose quarrels almost end in murder. Terrified by his helplessness he condemns all creation of beauty as a frivolous game, cruel for its lack of ethical values. In the third section, "Earth—the Expectation," on the next day Virgil's literary friends Lucius Varius and Plotius Tucca and the court physician Charondas visit and express their utter disbelief over his decision to burn his poetic *chef d'oeuvre*. A long conversation with Augustus convinces him, however, that his act of contrition also demands humility and love and understanding of the needs of others, and it is as a sign of his appreciation for the emperor's practical purposes that he leaves the *Aeneid* to posterity. Hallucinations begin to haunt him as he relives episodes from his earlier life: his beloved Plotia whom he had left appears to him in an arcadian landscape; Lysanias turns into his *alter ego* and evokes further reminiscences of his life as a youthful poet; a slave persuades him to relinquish any pretence that salvation may be obtained through art, and admonishes him, in an allusion to the "Christ-prophecy" of the *Fourth Eclogue*, to place his trust in a child-saviour. As Virgil dictates his last will, his visions take him back to the harbour and out onto the infinite sea. In the last section, "Ether—the Homecoming," as his consciousness gradually returns to its origins, Virgil's mind traverses creation in reverse order. All material manifestations dissolve and are transformed ultimately into an Orphic "dark radiation." The metamorphosis of his self as he submerges into cosmic totality progresses until a new "reversal" takes place: he apprehends the (Christian) figure of a mother and child, the last in a sequence of archetypal images. It may signify both the promise of his salvation and his rebirth, as his soul, at last, experiences God's presence as a gust of wind in a primal realm that lies "beyond language."

The novel is a lyrical exploration of the limits of art and life. It balances precise and imaginative descriptions of a distant physical world with extensive dialogues and various forms of inner monologue. Its distinct feature is the use of a great variety of mythical images, archetypal symbols, and mathematical signs together with a hymnic, mystically paradoxical, and ecstatically abstract language that seeks to evoke a supernatural reality. In the final analysis, *The Death of Virgil* conveys a contradictory message, though. For Virgil's abjuration of aesthetic autarchy and his moral awareness that most people must contend with a very ugly life does not preclude the "beautiful" process of his euphoric dying. The vindication of the poet as a mediator of knowledge about a transcendent world and about the fundamental verities of life conflicts with the historical reality of mass extermination and the millions of anonymous dead. This is a dichotomy Broch was unable to solve artistically but which he sought to alleviate through complementary activities: his charitable work, his political programmes, and his studies of mass psychology.

—Michael Winkler

DEEP RIVERS (Los ríos profundos)
Novel by José María Arguedas, 1958

Generally regarded as José María Arguedas's best novel, *Deep Rivers* marks a break with his earlier work in that he abandons conventional realism in favour of a lyrical manner more appropriate to the Andean magical-religious worldview he seeks to communicate. Another significant evolution in his style relates to the problem of translating into the medium of Spanish the sensibility of a people who express themselves in Quechua. Whereas previously he had sought to modify Spanish so as to incorporate basic Quechua syntax, here he chose to write in correct Spanish adroitly managed so as to communicate Andean thought.

This book also differs from his other novels in that while the latter are social in essence, being concerned to present a totalizing overview of Andean society, here he draws on his own experience for his portrayal of the conflict between the indigenous and the Western at an individual level, and concentrates on the situation of a young boy pulled in both directions. The poor relation of a powerful landowning family, his protagonist, Ernesto, rejects the "white" world to which he belongs by birth and identifies emotionally with the native peoples among whom he spent the happiest period of his childhood. However, in the early chapters he is uprooted and sent to boarding school to receive the education that will enable him to assume his role in "white" society.

The Church-run school, whose value system is that of the landowning class it serves, stands as a microcosm of Andean society at large, and in its oppressive atmosphere Ernesto finds himself alienated. However, he is able to recharge himself emotionally by listening to native Andean music in the native quarter of the town and by making trips into the countryside to renew his bonds with nature. These excursions become a vehicle for insights into Andean culture, for not only does the novel abound in observations on Quechua music, language, and folklore, but it conveys the functioning of magical-religious thought by showing it at work at the level of Ernesto's subjective experiences.

For most of the novel Ernesto's perspective is an ambivalent one as he confusedly adapts to his new circumstances. He is partially absorbed into white society, for though he feels himself to be different, he has inherited many of the attitudes of his class, and his teachers and comrades embrace him as one of their own. Furthermore, his experiences conspire to undermine his faith in native values by calling into question their effectiveness in the world of the whites, for not only does he see the native people downtrodden and humiliated at every turn, but even the magical forces of nature seem to lose their power when they come into confrontation with Western culture.

In the latter part of the novel, however, a series of events occurs that further estrange Ernesto from the ''white'' world and consolidate his allegiance with the native Andeans. First the *chicheras* (female vendors of maize beer) challenge the established order by breaking into the government salt warehouses and distributing the contents among the poor. Then, following an outbreak of plague, the *colonos* (hacienda tenant labourers) shake off their servility and mobilize themselves. Believing the plague to be a supernatural being which can be destroyed only by religious means, they march on the town to demand that a special mass be said for them, and force the authorities to accede.

The novel thus ends with a victory of the native peoples over the social order, a triumph that is paralleled on the internal plane by Ernesto's unreserved adherence to the Quechua ethos. His identification with the *chicheras* and *colonos* against his own kind is more than solidarity with the downtrodden, for his faith in the Quechua values he has grown to live by depend on the outcome of the conflict between the two ways of life. In a very real sense his personal salvation hinges on the ability of the native peoples to assert the validity of their culture by asserting themselves socially. With the victory of the *colonos*, his faith is vindicated.

Nonetheless, the ending is somewhat problematic. On one level, if Ernesto appears to have resolved his inner conflict by embracing Quechua culture with complete faith in its effectiveness, he clearly faces a future fraught with tensions, since he must live by its values in the alien world of the whites. On another level, there is a pathetic disproportion between the strength the *colonos* acquire and the tragically limited purpose to which it is put. Here the native peoples' magical-religious outlook reveals itself to be both a strength and a weakness, for if it gives them the capacity to challenge the dominant order and win, it also substitutes a mythical enemy for the real enemy (the society that condemns them to live in subhuman conditions) and diverts them from practical political struggle. However, it would seem that Arguedas was concerned to demonstrate that the strength they display in pursuing religious objectives is capable of being harnessed to a social and political consciousness. Likewise, Ernesto's faith in Quechua culture would seem to reflect Arguedas's own newfound confidence in the ability of that culture not only to survive, but, with increasing migration to the cities of the coast, to spread beyond its traditional geographical boundaries to permeate and change the character of Peruvian society as a whole.

—James Higgins

THE DEVIL IN THE FLESH (Le Diable au corps)
Novel by Raymond Radiguet, 1923

The Devil in the Flesh was published when Raymond Radiguet was just 20 years old. A masterly analysis of emotions, this semi-autobiographical novel recounts in the first person an affair between an adolescent and a young married woman, Marthe, whose husband is serving in World War I.

The French title suggests the adolescent's longing to grow up and sow his wild oats, World War I providing the freedom that facilitates the fulfilment of this longing. The novel opens with the disclaimer: ''Is it my fault that I was 12 years and a few months on the declaration of war?'' Such casual shrugging-off of responsibility goes hand-in-hand with lucid insight into motives; adolescent irrationality is

combined with analytical maturity in a way that was quite new in literature. In addition, the narrator's capacity for irony and self-derision have the effect of making the reader suspend judgement on actions of deliberate callousness.

The narrator is still a schoolboy when introduced by his parents to Marthe, the daughter of family friends, who is already making arrangements for her marriage to Jacques. The young 15-year-old is struck by the respect with which Marthe listens to his conversation, and, making a conscious effort to fall in love with her, is subsequently surprised to find that his love is real. Anxious to prove his power, he indulges in senseless exercises, like persuading her to buy furniture he is certain her future husband will dislike. Such displays of power are, however, of limited scope when it comes to knowing how to seduce Marthe. In the end, it is the young woman who initiates the narrator, once her newly-wed husband has safely returned to war.

Despite his new-found sense of adulthood, the narrator is, of course, still a schoolboy who has to forge parental letters to excuse his frequent absences from school while staying with Marthe. His worldly façade collapses when he faints at the sight of the maid of a local councillor throwing herself from the roof of her house. Setting off for an assignation with Marthe, he is humiliated by his mother's insistence that he take a picnic basket with him. The conflicting demands of adolescence and adulthood become increasingly hard to reconcile as he passes through moments of cruelty, passion, jealousy, and tenderness. Above all, he is possessed by the compulsion to analyze every emotion, constantly questioning the nature of his love for Marthe and hers for him, and in the process risking its loss. The techniques of literary analysis that have served him well at school are inadequate in the real-life situation.

In the meantime, daily life continues around the couple, who have by now shocked the whole community. They quickly discover, though, that reactions can be unpredictable. The family who live beneath Marthe express their prurient horror by inviting friends to come and listen to the sounds of the couple cavorting upstairs; the couple respond by maintaining strict silence. The narrator's mother becomes jealous of Marthe, his father smugly proud of his son. Marthe's mother, a pious Catholic, is less afraid for Marthe's eternal soul than for her reputation. The couple remain aloof from convention, thereby revealing the hypocrisy of the society in which they live.

However, the war that has allowed them such freedom draws to a close. Marthe is by now pregnant, and her family insists that she go and live with them. In a desperate bid for freedom, the couple runs away to Paris, but the young narrator is too embarrassed to ask for a double room, dragging the ailing Marthe from hotel to hotel in the pouring rain and blaming her for his lack of decisiveness. Inevitably, Marthe catches pneumonia and dies giving birth to their son. When his two younger brothers announce the death to him, he is overwhelmed with grief, but still jealous of her: ''I wanted oblivion for Marthe rather than a new life in which I might one day rejoin her.'' His grief is assuaged when he learns that Marthe has named their son after him and that the husband remains in ignorance.

The Devil in the Flesh is an idiosyncratic masterpiece in the way that it uses a strictly classical style to analyse the raw emotions of adolescent love. Indeed, Radiguet's prose frequently reads like poetry, fully justifying Cocteau's accolade: ''Raymond Radiguet shares with Arthur Rimbaud the terrible privilege of being a phenomenon of French literature.''

—Jane McAdoo

THE DEVILS (Besy)
Novel by Fedor Dostoevskii, 1872

The Devils, also translated as *The Possessed*, is the third of Fedor Dostoevskii's great novels and was written during the years 1869 to 1871, after *The Idiot* and before *The Brothers Karamazov*. Whereas *The Idiot* examined the evils of money as it affected contemporary Russian society, in *The Devils* Dostoevskii reverted to themes raised in *Crime and Punishment*: radical socialism, revolution, and godlessness. But while in the epilogue to *Crime and Punishment* Dostoevskii hints at Raskol'nikov's personal regeneration through belief in God, in *The Devils* he intended to put forward the idea of the regeneration of the whole country through a return to Russian Orthodoxy. In the event his multi-faceted negative depiction of the revolutionary movement carries far more weight than the tragic figure of Shatov, who comes to believe in national regeneration through Orthodoxy.

Dostoevskii had already begun writing the novel when he learned of the case of the student revolutionary Nechaev, who had fled to Geneva in 1869 where he gained the confidence of the exiled radicals, in particular Bakunin. Returning to Russia, Nechaev began forming a revolutionary movement with a cellular structure, five members in each cell of whom each would also be a member of a different cell. With iron discipline and the minimum of contact between groups, infiltration by the police would be unlikely. When one of the members of his cell (it is doubtful there ever was more than one) rejected blind obedience, Nechaev arranged for the others to murder him. He himself then fled abroad. Dostoevskii saw in Nechaev the epitome of the amorality of the Western-influenced revolutionaries and, deciding on a pamphlet novel, turned Nechaev into the figure of Petr Verkhovenskii who arrives in a provincial town to organize a cell of the same type. One of the plot strands shows how one member of the cell, Shatov, is killed for his betrayal of revolutionary ideals.

Dostoevskii also blames contemporary revolutionary madness on the older generation of liberals: in a commentary on Turgenev's *Fathers and Sons* (*Ottsy i deti*), Dostoevskii depicts in Petr's father Stepan an ageing, weak liberal whose ideas have engendered the ruthless and tyrannical face of the modern radical because he was the first to reject God. For Dostoevskii, when man set himself up as a master of his own fate, there ceased to be any moral prohibitions. Furthermore, once man decided he knew what was best for mankind, there was nothing to prevent dictatorship. It is not surprising that the equation of socialism with tyranny made the book extremely unpopular with the Soviet authorities, while in the West, and in recent years in Russia, it has been regarded as in many respects prophetic.

Petr gathers around him a group of people who represent aspects of the radical movement, of whom Shigalev and Kirillov are the most interesting. Shigalev represents the theoretical aspects of Petr Verkhovenskii's destructive actions starting from the idea of unlimited freedom, and ending up with unlimited despotism. Kirillov, also interested in absolute godless freedom, argues that what holds man back from total freedom is his fear of death. Hence out of love for humanity he proposes to commit suicide to demonstrate to mankind that the fear of death is vain, in effect arrogantly taking on the role of Christ. The scene in which he commits suicide is one of the most horrifying in what is an extremely powerful book.

Both Shigalev and Kirillov as well as Shatov, who is murdered Nechaev-style at the instigation of Petr Verkhovenskii for rejecting revolution for Russian Orthodoxy, owe their ideas not to Verkhovenskii but to Nikolai Stavrogin, son of a local landowner. Here the novel transcends the political pamphlet to become a discussion of the nature of evil. Stavrogin possesses the ultimate freedom that the others seek in their various ways, a freedom to do just whatever he wants, and yet like Milton's Lucifer he is supremely bored and ultimately lonely. An enigma, part charismatic, part repellent, his behaviour ranges from cruel to capricious to apparently kind. Nonetheless almost all the characters (women find him almost irresistible) try to please him or placate him. In the absence of any clear beliefs, he has toyed with ideas and even with actions, for example secretly marrying the deranged, handicapped Maria Lebiadkina. The reasons for his marriage are unclear: he is kind to her, so perhaps he is experimenting with kindness, or else atoning for his appalling behaviour towards a young girl many years before, offending his aristocratic mother, throwing down a challenge to common sense, or perhaps revealing his own spiritual deformity by allying himself with someone physically challenged. With Dostoevskii actions are always to be explained by the ideas and motives behind them rather than the conventional meaning assigned to them, but in the case of Stavrogin these reasons, though no less important, are obscure, and aspects of his intellectual development are more clearly reflected in Shatov, Shigalev, and Kirillov. His ultimate suicide suggests the bankruptcy of an approach to life that embraces evil.

With this explosive mix of characters, the action of *The Devils* whirls to a frenzied conclusion. On one level the focus is on a grand occasion put on in the provincial town by the wife of the new governor, which is to culminate in a speech by the veteran liberal and grand old man of Russian letters, Karmazinov (a thinly disguised attack on Turgenev). Petr Verkhovenskii and the revolutionary rabble who follow him succeed in causing total disruption. This rather pathetic manifestation of revolutionary activity is contrasted with a series of murders, deaths, and suicides, in one way or another involving most of the many characters, in which the destructive and negative power of godlessness is made manifest. In *The Devils* Dostoevskii wove a range of interrelated and contrasting characters into a highly complex and dramatic, even terrifying indictment of the ideas he felt were destroying Russia. Whatever the reader may think of his pessimistic views, the force of the book and its ideas is undeniable.

—Faith Wigzell

THE DEVIL'S ELIXIRS (Die Elixiere des Teufels)
Novel by E.T.A. Hoffmann, 1815–16

Although known principally as a writer of tales, E.T.A. Hoffmann also published two novels, *The Devil's Elixirs* and *Lebens-Ansichten des Katers Murr*, the story of a philistine tomcat intertwined with that of the unhappy musician Johannes Kreisler. The first part of *The Devil's Elixirs* was written in the spring of 1814 at the end of the author's period in Bamberg where he had worked since 1808, principally as composer for the theatre but also as freelance music teacher. The figure of Aurelie in the novel is based on Julia Marc, a young girl to whom Hoffmann gave singing lessons and who proved to be as unattainable to Hoffmann as Aurelie is to the monk Medardus. Although completed in four weeks, the second part was not finished until the summer of the following year. This delay, untypical of Hoffmann, was due primarily to the change in his circumstances; his position at Bamberg was terminated in 1814, but through the help of a friend, he was able to return to Berlin and re-enter the Prussian civil service as a lawyer. He finally secured a publisher in Berlin and Part I appeared in the autumn of 1815, Part II the following spring. Although widely read it did not win critical acclaim and there was no second edition in the author's lifetime. The first English translation appeared in 1824 and was followed in the course of the century by occasional English versions of selective passages from the novel. A new translation by Ronald Taylor in 1963 coincided with the beginning of an intense critical interest in Hoffmann which has yet to wane and which has placed particular emphasis on psychological depths in his work overlooked by much earlier criticism.

The story of the Capuchin monk Medardus who drinks from the forbidden elixirs, leaves the monastery, and becomes involved in deceit, incest, and murder, seems on first reading so heavily indebted to contemporary stories of horror in monastic settings, and in particular to that recounted by Matthew Lewis in *The Monk* (translated into German a year after its appearance in 1796), that what is unique to Hoffmann is often submerged under established Gothic features. These include Medardus's excessive pride in his powers as a preacher, the anguish caused by sexual desire, the unattainability of the beloved, and a Faustian lack of concern for convention exhibited by Medardus's half-sister Euphemie with whom he enjoys a brief incestuous relationship before exchanging glasses and unwittingly causing her to drink from the poisoned wine which she had prepared for him. In accordance with Romantic notions of the fragmentary nature of human knowledge the interconnections between the characters are only gradually revealed—both to Medardus himself and to the reader. Thus fate and the power of heredity operating as a curse on the unsuspecting hero are central themes of the novel and are graphically represented by a family tree of a ferocious complexity typical of Hoffmann the lawyer. Both Medardus and the reader are left in doubt as to the reality of many of the events of the novel; often the doubt is removed by an ensuing rational explanation, but this is not always the case. The novel also offers a succession of terrifying and grotesque moments, including Medardus's vision of his double rising through the floor to speak to him and the murder, by the double, of Aurelie, the focus of Medardus's sexual anguish, at the moment of her consecration as a nun. But the temptation to classify *The Devil's Elixirs* as no more than an example of the Gothic novel does less than justice to the intricacies of its form and to Hoffmann's abiding concern, supported by a sound knowledge of contemporary medicine, with the workings of the human mind. In particular, Hoffmann's employment of the double, discussed by Freud in his essay on "The Uncanny" ("Das Unheimlicher") in 1919, underlines what is the most fascinating and enduring theme of the work: the struggle of the individual to maintain sanity and establish a distinct personality in the face of forces which he can only partially comprehend. With his lack of free will and his acquiescence in many of the incidents which befall him, Medardus can be seen as an archetypal anti-classical hero and forerunner of the figures of late 19th-century naturalism.

Many critics have rightly pointed out that *The Devil's Elixirs* is not about religious doubt. Medardus does not question the existence of God, nor does he seek to deny the reality of the sins to which he has succumbed. The strange figure of the painter who mysteriously appears at crucial moments in Medardus's earthly pilgrimage is both a reminder of the curse which lies upon his family and which it is Medardus's task to expiate and also the power of conscience which enables him to overcome his adversary, in his case the impulses inherited from his forebears. Religion provides only the background

to the novel, in the form of descriptions of monastic life, based upon Hoffmann's happy experiences as a guest among the Capuchin monks of Bamberg, and of the edifying effect of religious music.

—Roger Jones

DIARY OF A MADMAN (Zapiski Sumasshedshego)
Story by Nikolai Gogol', 1835

"Diary of a Madman" is one of a group of tales from the 1830s that have a Petersburg setting. It is the only work by Nikolai Gogol' to be given a first-person narrator and to be presented in the form of diary entries. Originally the tale was to be called "Diary of a Mad Musician," reflecting the Russian response to Hoffmann's tales, but this idea became intertwined with Gogol's own experience of life as a civil servant, of being a tiny cog in a huge dehumanizing wheel, where obsession with rank and mindless routine dominated the lives of an army of underpaid drudges. At the same time Gogol' was responding to popular obsession with grotesque accounts of madness as well as the terrifying information published in a newspaper that in one Petersburg asylum the majority of inmates were civil servants.

The hero of the "Diary of Madman," Poprishchin, is a minor civil servant whose lowly duties include sharpening quills for his superior. He has fallen hopelessly in love with the latter's daughter Sophie, but this is no clichéd situation of poor boy loves rich girl or of noble unrequited love. Poprishchin is 42 years old, stuck on the Table of Ranks at a point just below the desired rank that gained hereditary nobility for its holder, in name a noble himself but with nothing noble about his life or his values. This does not prevent him from being a snob, despising those who cannot write and fellow civil servants because they do not go to the theatre. Thus rejecting literary cliché and using the first-person narrative as a means of creating a close relationship between narrator and reader, Gogol' widens the gulf by making Poprishchin's snobbery ridiculous to his more educated and possibly even more snobbish readers: Poprishchin's own taste in poetry and theatre is of the most vulgar kind, and the newspaper he reads, *Severnaia pchela* [The Northern Bee], is the one that published mocking descriptions of lunatics. He emerges as a pathetic nonentity struggling to maintain his illusions.

Pathos is kept at bay until the very end of the tale by the comic and absurd nature of Poprishchin's madness. It is at the end of the very first diary entry for 3 October that Poprishchin, desperate to enter Sophie's world (his head has whirled as he glanced into her boudoir) suddenly hears her little dog Madgie talking to a canine friend Fidèle. In typically Gogolian manner, this preposterous event is viewed by Poprishchin as strange but not alarming. To one brought up on sensationalist stories in *The Northern Bee* and lacking personal insight, the event does not seem so startling. Spying on the two dogs, he discovers they are conducting a correspondence, a humiliating fact to a man for whom the ability to write is a sign of nobility. He seizes a pile of letters, composed in a style appropriate to frivolous upper-class young ladies like Sophie and her friends: to his fury Madgie proceeds to laugh at his appearance, but worse, the dog notes that Sophie finds him ludicrous. The most cutting blow is the information that Sophie is in love with a gentleman of high rank and means, a fact confirmed in the following entry for 3 December. From this point Poprishchin descends rapidly into insanity, bolstering his illusions about his rank and importance by imagining himself the King of Spain. Carted off to the asylum, he maintains this creative fiction about his life against increasing odds and with increasing incoherence: the inmates are courtiers, the warder the Grand Inquisitor who beats him unjustly. In the final entry, reality intrudes in the form of cold water poured on his head, and he seeks escape from the world in a troika (a frequent Gogolian escape symbol) and by calling on his mother for protection (''Mother, save your poor son! Shed a tear on his aching head! See how they've torturing him'').

Gogol' plays with his reader's reactions, taking him/her from laughter and even contempt for Poprishchin to the concluding moments of pathos, when the reader, like Poprishchin, cannot escape the tragedy of madness. And yet even at this point he cannot resist a final twist, with a last sentence in which his hero reverts to grotesque lunacy: ''And did you know that the Dhey of Algiers has a wart right under his nose?'' Such narrative tricks were highly innovatory for the time though they were not appreciated fully until much later. More obvious to contemporary audiences was Gogol's satire on the widespread obsession with snobbery and rank over genuine human values. Poprishchin's aims were consistent with his world, but he lacked the money, rank, or appearance to realize his dream of capturing Sophie's heart and thereby become an accepted member of that world of false values. In linguistic terms too the work broke new ground, as it combined colloquialisms and contemporary chancery jargon with, in the canine passages, a parody of the language of upper-class young ladies. ''Diary of a Madman'' may well make the reader uncomfortable as he or she reads, but this is what Gogol' intended.

—Faith Wigzell

THE DIFFICULT MAN (Der Schwierige)
Play by Hugo von Hofmannsthal, 1921

Hugo von Hofmannsthal's earliest recorded notes (dating from 1909) on his comic masterpiece, *The Difficult Man*, sketch out his original idea for a ''character comedy,'' light in atmosphere and comprising ''a chain of conversations'' which lead eventually to a resolution kept *in suspenso* over three acts. Later there is a shift in emphasis to the traditional Viennese ''Konversationsstück,'' or social comedy as the theatrical model from which he derives his form. The original plot consisted of no more than this: a young lady with several suitors has to decide between them, and the obliging but inept confidant, caught up in the match-making, finally ensnares himself. The finished play (1921) involves 16 characters of greatly contrasting personalities, manners, and modes of speech, who interact in the pursuit of their diverse aspirations, ambitions, and ''intentions'' (a key term), creating a network of subtle social relationships, full of ironic nuances and verbal subtleties. It is both a play about the passing historical moment which marked the end of the Hapsburg era with its culture and class structure, while it is also a finely gauged critique of language as the badge of that culture. The somewhat precious, artificial diction the playwright employs shows up language as the flawed but indispensable vehicle of communication. The terms ''misunderstanding'' and ''confusion'' are leitmotifs of the text. Though the action is set towards the end of World War I (the year is 1917), references to these momentous times are always kept peripheral and deliberately low-key. Hofmannsthal was not a Naturalist; he was heir

to the tradition of high comedy which followed the classical models of Molière, Goldoni, and Lessing. His dramatic technique was suggestive rather than representational, allusive rather than mimetic, and he was naturally given to symbolic statement as he indicates in one of his aphorisms: ''Whoever takes the social idea in any but a symbolic sense misses the mark.'' In choosing a contemporary subject, he insinuates a timeless element.

This ironic comedy deftly captures the salient features of that section of Viennese society which had outlived itself and merely perpetuated a shadowy charade of aristocratic ways. As the pompous Prussian Baron Neuhoff is moved to remark: ''All these people you meet here don't in fact exist any more. They're nothing more than shadows. No one who moves in these salons belongs to the real world in which the intellectual crises of the century are decided.'' Hofmannsthal's conviction that ''reality'' may not be embodied in the theatre, that it cannot be translated wholesale onto the stage in the manner advocated by the Naturalists, but remains an illusion, gives rise to his technique of a selective perspectivism. The vivid illusion of a complete unit of society, differentiated, full of interesting contrasts, levels of intelligence, tone, and points of view, is produced by the playwright through a kaleidoscopic method of ever-changing groupings and relationships. It is a dramatic technique comparable to Chekhov's, as is his choice of the essentially passive hero. The 48 scenes which make up the three acts of *The Difficult Man* display an ever-shifting pattern of relationships or significant links between characters. Each encounter and interaction is nicely calculated for its ironic effect, as contrasts are explored: convention is opposed to the unconventional, posing to sincerity, pretention to veracity, philandering to love. The new and the old order of social values are brought into confrontation from the very first scene when the retiring manservant, the image of his master in discretion and decorum, attempts the hopeless task of instructing his uncouth, inquisitive replacement in the niceties of serving a ''difficult'' master whose every mood should be judged by dumb gesture.

At the centre of the play with its shifting configurations there stands the passive figure of Hans Karl Bühl, a bachelor aged 39, a man who has difficulty in making his mind up about everything, not least in the use of words. He is also at the centre of speculation by all and sundry. As the embodiment of social complications, he is an unfailing source of misunderstanding and involuntary embarrassments. Whether he says something or remains silent, he creates confusion. He causes endless misunderstandings not by design, but because the society about him consistently misreads him. They attribute intentions to him where he has none. They seek for nuances of meaning where none are to be found. While most find him infuriatingly enigmatic, others believe they can read him like a book. All are mistaken, except the beautiful Helene Altenwyl whose intuition and intelligence afford her privileged insight into the heart and mind of the man she has loved since her teens. In two exquisite private exchanges between them (Act II, scene 14 and Act III, scene 8) the wavering complexities of the hero find more than their match in the profound sensibilities and certainties of the loving woman. The first of these dialogues opens with a statement by Hans Karl on the uses of that fickle medium, language: ''Everything in this world is brought about by speech. Of course, it's a little ridiculous for anyone to imagine that the carefully chosen word can produce some God-almighty impact within a life where everything, after all, quite simply depends on the ultimate, the inexpressible. Speech is based upon an indecent estimation of oneself.'' The problematical nature of language (a constant theme in

Hofmannsthal and most consummately expressed in *A Letter* of 1902) is identified with, and given voice through, the complicated character of Hans Karl. In this comedy theme and form converge to the point of total interdependence, creating the perfect ironic construct in which the medium and the message are one. Though Hans Karl may call himself "the most uncomplicated person in the world," the action is strewn with evidence of his propensity for causing misapprehension and confusion. He may believe that he is an unmotivated free agent as he moves about trying to avoid "chronic misunderstandings," but he himself becomes a victim of that "bizarre notion" of a "higher necessity" which he professes to his apish nephew Stani. When this difficult hero attempts to plead another suitor's cause to Helene, ultimate questions of a "higher power," predestined love, and the sanctity of marriage are playfully introduced and glimpsed, as it were, through a veil of mystical allusion. "Necessity lies within you" he openly confesses to his intended. Gradually, yet inescapably, he becomes engrossed in the business of proposing, and as his sense of purpose falters, he grows more eloquent. He tells her of his dream-like experience of being buried within the trenches at the Front, thereby divulging how he gained revelatory insight into the external meaning of marriage. This artless and moving confession assures Helene of what Hans Karl scarcely knows himself: that they are and always have been destined for each other. Moral seriousness is so finely interfused with a lightness of ironic texture in this comedy that no trace of gravity remains. The author's achievement wholly conforms with his own remark: "Depth must be hidden: where? On the surface."

—Alexander Stillmark

THE DIVINE COMEDY (Commedia)
Poem by Dante Alighieri, 1472 (written c. 1307–21)

The Divine Comedy is the first great poem in any European language which, to quote Thomas Carlyle, gave expression to "the voice of ten silent centuries." It can be compared only with the greatest works of world poetry—those of Homer and Shakespeare. In order to gauge the depth, intensity, variety, and universality of *The Divine Comedy*, one has to imagine Shakespeare's four greatest tragedies all rolled into one and yet still something will be missing: the entire matter and substance of *Il paradiso* (*Paradise*). For this reason T.S. Eliot described *The Divine Comedy*, which he ranked with the *Bhagavad-Gita*, on the one hand, and with Lucretius' *De rerum natura* (*On the Nature of Things*), on the other, as a philosophic poem, representing "a complete scale of the depths and heights of human emotion" and having the "width of emotional range" of no other poem.

The only comparison that has sometimes been made—as, for instance, by Hazlitt, Arthur Hallam, and Thomas Babington Macaulay in the 19th century—is between *The Divine Comedy* and *Paradise Lost* as religious poems. Neither Dante Alighieri nor Milton specialists will consider this comparison to be valid, not only because of the widely different form and style, technique, and expression of the two poems, but also because of the different modes of dealing with the mystery of the divine, the hereafter, and the ineffable. This was dictated not only by Dante's and Milton's individual poetics, but also by their personal ethics, religious beliefs, and convictions. Ezra Pound, a Dantist to the core, sums up the difference with characteristic forthrightness, though not without partisan bias:

Dante's god is ineffable divinity. Milton's god is a fussy old man with a hobby. Dante is metaphysical, where Milton is merely sectarian . . . Milton has no grasp of the superhuman. Milton's angels are men of enlarged power, plus wings. Dante's angels surpass human nature and differ from it. They move in their high courses inexplicable.

Another difference between *Paradise Lost* and *The Divine Comedy* is that while the former is universally regarded as the greatest authentic epic in any modern European language, the latter, for all its impressive compactness, symmetry of design, and the daunting regularity of its *terza rima* cannot, strictly speaking, be so regarded. For some like Leopardi and Croce, it is "a long lyric" or "a series of lyrical compositions of varying tone." For others it is a long narrative poem with dramatic and lyrical elements woven into its fabric.

Whatever the difference of form and style, *The Divine Comedy*, like Milton's epic, is a repository of its author's philosophical, theological, and religious beliefs, as well as his moral and political convictions. It exemplifies on a grand scale, and in the context of Dante's vision of the hereafter, what Samuel Taylor Coleridge calls "the living link between religion and philosophy." Written over a period of 15 to 20 years, and started perhaps before his exile from Florence in 1302, Dante's poem seems to be anchored more to autobiographical facts than to any mystical dream or vision, or to any particular religious or philosophical system.

Dante's political exile from Florence had a crucial bearing on the composition of *The Divine Comedy*, making him see not only Florentine and Italian history and politics, but also his own sufferings and hardships, in larger perspective. The uses of adversity in Dante's case could not, therefore, have been sweeter. For, in spite of the separation from his family, and his having known by experience "how salt is the taste of another man's bread, and how hard the way is up and down another man's stairs," his exile inculcated him with a sense of mission and of prophesy. The very theme he was dealing with as well as the particular circumstances of his life made him feel greater than himself.

Different epochs, both in Italy and outside, reacted to *The Divine Comedy* and to its author in different ways. For the English Romantic poets Dante became a sort of Romantic freedom-fighter, a symbol of political liberty, national freedom, and personal courage. Re-echoing this sentiment in their own poetry, Wordsworth, Byron, and Shelley—the last two also translated parts of *The Divine Comedy*—had as much Dante in mind as Milton. Hence, when Wordsworth talks of "love, and man's unconquerable mind," when Byron exalts the "Eternal spirit of the chainless mind! / Brightest in dungeons, Liberty!" or when Shelley observes how "Most wretched men / Are cradled into poetry by wrong: / They learn in suffering what they teach in song," Dante's example looms as large in their minds as does Milton's. And it also does in the mind of his compatriot Giacomo Leopardi who, even though he was very different from Dante in thought, philosophy, and outlook, bore eloquent testimony in his poetry to Dante's poetic and moral greatness as forming a cornerstone of Italy's glory.

The attitude of the modern poets to *The Divine Comedy* is varied. T.S. Eliot and Mario Luzi, for example, were drawn to it principally because, in the former's words, "it seems to me to illustrate a saner attitude towards the mysteries of life" than anything in Shakespeare. Ezra Pound and Eugenio Montale, were, for the most part, attracted by its qualities of style and expression, verbal economy and directness of presentation, as well as for its poetic realism based on the dynamic luminosity of metaphor, imagery, and detail.

Pound was also influenced and inspired by Dante's moral and political perception, shared his sense of values, including "the scale and proportion of evil, as delineated in Dante's Hell," and whole-heartedly endorsed Dante's condemnation of usury. Quite early in his life he had come to believe that there was nothing of any importance "in the lives of men and nations that you cannot measure with the rod of Dante's allegory."

The historical personages Dante dealt with so memorably in *The Divine Comedy*, such as Francesca da Rimini, Farinata degli Uberti, Pier della Vigna, Ulysses, Count Ugolino—*Inferno* (*Hell*); Matelda—*Il purgatorio* (*Purgatory*); San Tommaso, San Benedetto, and San Bernardo—*Il paradiso* (*Paradise*) are so many protagonists of that allegory. To each of them he dedicated an important *Canto*, as a result of which they, like Shakespeare's characters, have become embedded in literary and cultural history, and have attracted a large body of critical and exegetical commentary. In English alone, poets like Thomas Gray, Leigh Hunt, Tennyson, Browning, Rossetti, Pound, and Eliot wrote poems either dealing with some of these characters, or based on Dante's portrayals of them. Each character represents a particular sin or virtue, through which Dante covers the whole gamut of sense and sensibility, feeling and emotion: the tragic, the pathetic, the reverent, the indignant, and the compassionate.

The Divine Comedy was written and can be interpreted, as Dante himself explained in his dedication of *Heaven* to his host and patron Can Grande, in four senses: the literal, the allegorical, the anagogical, and the ethical. In the literal sense it is an account of Dante's vision of a journey through the three kingdoms of futurity, realms inhabited by the spirits of men after death—Hell, Purgatory, and Paradise. It can also be regarded, as Pound sees it, as a "journey of Dante's intelligence through the states of minds wherein dwell all sorts and conditions of men before death" whereas Dante's intelligence itself may be considered as "a symbol of mankind's struggle upward out of ignorance into the clear light of philosophy" and his journey as an allegorical representation of Dante's own mental and spiritual development. Thus Hell, Purgatory and Paradise are not places, but states of mind.

The poem is divided into three sections: *Hell, Purgatory*, and *Paradise*, and each section has 34, 33, and three sets of three cantos respectively, containing about 14,000 lines. In his journey through Hell and Purgatory, Virgil, symbolizing classical learning, poetry, and philosophy, is Dante's guide, and in Paradise, Beatrice, representing divine wisdom, takes over that role. The idea of the descent to Hell comes from the sixth book of *Aeneid* (230–900), where Virgil describes Aeneas' descent to Hell. The sins punished in both Hell and Purgatory are lust, gluttony, avarice, extravagance, wrath, sloth, heresy, violence, fraud, and betrayal. In describing both the sins and the sinners, as well as the kind of punishment meted out to each sinner and their reaction to it, Dante's poetic realism triumphs over the boundary between the real and the illusory, the terrestrial and the extraterrestrial, so that whatever he describes in minute topographical detail seems to belong as much to this world as to the hereafter. "In Dante's Hell," Eliot tells us, "souls are not deadened, as they mostly are in life; they are actually in the greatest torment of which each is capable." The sinners' inner character, psychology, and emotional state are so closely probed and so movingly portrayed by Dante that they become, to use Shelley's words, "forms more real than living men, / Nurslings of immortality."

There is in Dante the power of making us see what he sees, rendering, especially in *Paradise*, the spiritual not only visible, but

also intensely exciting. Dante is thus a master in expressing, vividly and concretely, experience that is remote from ordinary experience, the very matter and substance of *Paradise*.

Shakespeare, as Carlyle says, is worldwide, Dante world deep—or, in the words of Eliot, *The Divine Comedy* expresses everything "in the way of emotion between depravity's despair and the beatific vision, that man is capable of experiencing." Dante and Shakespeare divide the modern world between them, he says, for "there is no third."

—G. Singh

DOCTOR FAUSTUS (Doktor Faustus)
Novel by Thomas Mann, 1947

Doctor Faustus, begun in 1943 and published in 1947, was Thomas Mann's last major novel and the most ambitious and moving of his works. His idea for describing a 20th-century artist as a modern Faust dated back to 1905, but his lifelong interest in the pathology of genius and in the conflict of aestheticism and morality took on an overwhelmingly political dimension when he saw that the horrors of Nazism and the problems of modern art were symptoms of the same cultural development. In exile in America, where he functioned as the representative of a Germany opposed to Hitler and awaited the total destruction of his country, he asked himself if he too was a guilty German who had embraced an irrationalism which constituted an arrogant and disastrous negation of civilized values. He had himself voiced stridently nationalistic sentiments during World War I. It was this exhaustive reckoning of his personal past and the political madness of the times, which lead to the writing of *Doctor Faustus*.

The novel tells of the life and works of the fictional composer Adrian Leverktühn (1885–1940) who believes that music has been strangled by convention. Spontaneous creation is no longer possible, so he seeks abnormal stimulus and finds a paradoxical freedom in an arbitrarily chosen order and a radical departure from the conventions of tonality. He dreams of an art which will not strive for self-sufficiency but serve the deepest interests of a longed-for community. He deliberately infects himself with syphilis and makes his pact with the devil in order to overcome an artistic impasse. His self-identification with Faust reflects his Lutheran background and a twisted desire to relive myth and to wallow in anointed doom. He swings between periods of debilitating migraine and bouts of intense productivity. His revolutionary works remain virtually unknown, and he ends in paralysis and madness.

Mann drew on many sources, among them Arnold Schoenberg's serialism, the critic Theodor Adorno's theories on modern music, the lives of composers, and on his own experience, his memories of personalities and intellectual debates and his thoughts about music and the problems of a self-critical artist threatened by sterility and conscious of the need to break with tradition. He took his overall framework and many details from the Faust chapbook of the 16th century, and, though the reader is never told this, from the life of the philosopher Friedrich Nietzsche, including his strange courtship arrangements. The Nietzschean Apollonian-Dionysian dichotomy runs throughout the novel, where the Dionysian as an aesthetic and a psychological category is equated with the demonic.

Leverkühn (the name has Nietzschean overtones of living boldly) functions both as a representative modern artist and as an allegory for

Germany. The novel documents an era of cultural history lived under the influence of a debased and dogmatized Nietzsche: vitalism is here turned against life and inspiration is sought in evil. The hero who aims to escape from inhibiting self-consciousness and the epoch which thrust aside the restraints normally imposed on primitive instincts are juxtaposed by Mann's narrator figure, the Catholic schoolmaster Serenus Zeitblom. He writes during the years 1943–45 when the madness of the impulses he records has become only too manifest. As the bombs fall around him, this old-fashioned, marginalized spokesman for moderation and reason insists that the Germans have sold their soul to the devil Hitler, and descended into drunken, self-destructive barbarism. His friend Leverkühn, too, slid back into archaic patterns of thought and behaviour. In his disease of intellectual arrogance he reverted to the time of Luther and the original Faust. But his story is also open to psychological interpretation: his visit to the prostitute who gives him syphilis and musical inspiration follows a youth of sexual repression, and his life entails regression into infancy. Through Zeitblom, Mann condemns Germany's path to catastrophe, but Zeitblom's stance is tempered by love. His desperate prayer that the nation might be forgiven is linked to his belief that his friend was a genius who deserves sympathy and awe, not utter damnation.

In Leverkühn and Zeitblom, Mann exaggerates two aspects of himself. Zeitblom's style is almost a caricature of Mann's, but his verbosity serves to underline the abstractions which connect the various dramatic and realistically detailed strands of the narrative, and to relate the hero's music to general trends in society. In his all too staid worthiness and his mannered formality, the narrator unwittingly introduces a certain humour that makes a horrific story bearable. He highlights the difficulty of passing unambiguous judgements on complex matters. As an inexperienced writer he does what the fastidious Mann could not do in his own name: he can be an omniscient author, mount a direct assault on the reader's emotions, and betray the existence of authorial calculation in, for instance, the number symbolism that runs through the vast text. (Mann's montage technique remains his own poorly guarded secret.) Mann exploits clichéd traditions on novel writing, yet maintains the ironic distance typical of his devilishly hyper-intelligent hero who relativizes everything and rarely speaks or writes except by quoting others. The links between the author and his hero culminate in the similarities between Leverkühn's last composition, ''The Lamentation of Dr. Faustus,'' and the novel itself. Both works are tightly constructed according to a preconceived plan and yet intensely confessional. They stand in deliberate discordant contrast to Beethoven's Ninth Symphony and Goethe's *Faust*.

With its erudition in matters of music, disease, and cultural history, this novel makes enormous demands on its readers. An even greater difficulty is to be found in Mann's interweaving of literal and symbolic meanings, of realism, myth, allegory, allusion, and ironic ambiguity. He works with parallels that are seldom direct equations. Furthermore, Mann consciously undermines the oppositions at the core of his elaborate thematic structure. A fundamental paradox is that the hero is involved in trends from which he remains detached: he stands for the forces of fascism and yet is distinct from them. The task Mann set himself was to grasp the dialectics of compulsion and freedom, subjectivity and objectivity; the links between art and politics, individual psychological impulse and collective experience, in order to conjure up and explain an apocalypse. Total success in this immense undertaking was scarcely conceivable. Nevertheless *Doctor Faustus* is one of the greatest 20th-century novels. Its wide-ranging diagnosis of cultural phenomena is impressive indeed. It is skilfully orchestrated (the word is apt for a work about music which adopts musical structures) by means of a dense system of cross-references whose intricacies lurk beneath an appearance of straightforward narration. Here Mann displays an amazing mastery of language and of literary techniques both old and new, combines harrowing tragedy and cool critique, and shows that intellectual calculation and emotional depth, self-conscious artistry and moral responsibility need not be mutually exclusive.

—John Hibberd

DOCTOR ZHIVAGO (Doktor Zhivago)
Novel by Boris Pasternak, 1957 (written 1946–55)

Although Boris Pasternak was primarily a poet, he remains best known abroad for *Doctor Zhivago*, the novel that helped make him a Nobel laureate just a year after its publication in 1957. The book is very much that of a poet—not only does it contain an epilogue of 25 poems composed by Zhivago/Pasternak, but it is filled with patterns of imagery and written in a dense yet rhythmic style whose flow is extremely resistant to translation. Still, the observations on the relationship of the individual to society, on death and immortality, and on the historical significance of the Bolshevik Revolution are accessible to readers in any language and have helped make *Doctor Zhivago* a modern classic.

The novel's fame rests in part on its notoriety as well as on its merits. Pasternak worked on it from 1946 through 1955; however, the notion of writing a large prose work had come to him much earlier, and stories and prose fragments from previous decades contain motifs that eventually found their reflection in the finished work. The novel was submitted to the journal *Novyi mir*, which published many of the more notable literary products of the ''thaw'' that followed Stalin's death in 1953. Despite the more open atmosphere, the editors felt that certain sections dealing with the revolution made the book unpublishable in the Soviet Union. Meanwhile, an Italian publisher, who had received a copy of the novel from a compatriot working for Italian radio in Moscow, went ahead with plans to publish it. Soviet officials, viewing the book as anti-Bolshevik, began a public campaign against Pasternak, which grew sharply in intensity after the Nobel prize was announced. Pasternak was expelled from the Writers' Union and, under fear of not being allowed back to his homeland, refused the award. Although rumours of the book's impending publication surfaced at various times in the years following Pasternak's death, only in 1988, with the policy of *glasnost'* well-established, could it finally appear in his homeland.

Pasternak's hero has a more ambivalent attitude toward revolution than the attacks on the novel would indicate. Iurii witnesses the 1905 uprising, serves as a doctor at the front during World War I, and experiences both the Bolshevik Revolution and the Civil War. His instinct is to admire the boldness with which the new sweeps away the old, but he continues to adhere to the values that were instilled in him earlier. As a result, he is opposed not to the revolution itself, but to the belief in fulfilling abstract goals at whatever cost. A key moment occurs when Zhivago, who has been pressed into service by a Red partisan group during the Civil War, saves the life of a wounded

White soldier. The passage was seized upon by Pasternak's critics as evidence of his anti-revolutionary leanings, though it would be more accurate to see it as a reflection of the importance that Zhivago (whose own name comes from the word for ''living'') places on human life.

The narrative describes Zhivago's evolution into a poet. Following the death of his mother and the suicide of his father, who had abandoned the family, Iurii is raised by well-to-do distant relatives. He trains to become a doctor after rejecting poetry as a full-time profession and eventually marries Tonia, the daughter of the couple who had cared for him. Lara, a young woman who had come to Moscow from the Urals, crosses his path several times, and Zhivago eventually becomes involved with her when he is living in the Urals. Still later, after his escape from the partisans, he and Lara have a brief interlude together, and it is then that Zhivago writes some of the poems that appear in the appendix. Zhivago himself goes into a decline after he is forced to part from Lara; he makes his way to Moscow, takes on relatively menial work, and, following a final burst of creative energy, dies of heart failure.

A brief outline of the story cannot do justice to the novel's rich fabric. Pasternak attempted to go beyond 19th-century realism and to express his sense of the wonder of life by purposefully including numerous coincidences, so that characters' paths intersect with a frequency that strains credulity. What is more, many of the figures are less important for their role within the plot than for the way in which they function symbolically. Thus Lara can be seen as representing Zhivago's muse; her husband—originally called Antipov and after the revolution known as Strelnikov (''the shooter'')—comes to embody the revolution's unwavering drive toward its goals; Evgraf, Zhivago's mysterious half-brother, is the powerful force that aids him at moments of duress; Komarovskii, Lara's seducer and later the person who takes her from Zhivago, by contrast stands for the presence of evil. The novel's imagery is equally striking. Trains play a key role throughout: Iurii's father commits suicide by leaping from a train, Zhivago races back from the front to Moscow in a special express, his entire family go out to the Urals in a slowly moving train that seems to take them to another world, stopped trains symbolize the revolution's reversal of historical progress, and Zhivago's fatal heart attack occurs as he rides on a poorly functioning streetcar. Recurrent references to windows as well as clusters of meanings assigned to such objects as a rowan tree and a sign advertising ''seeders and threshers'' further augment the text's poetic intensity.

Pasternak's early training in philosophy influences the novel's themes as much as his poetry affects his manner of writing. Zhivago comments that the ultimate goal of art is to meditate on death in order to create life. In the early pages of the novel Nikolai Vedeniapin, Iurii's uncle, talks about history as the story of people's efforts to overcome death, and he connects the teaching of Christ with the beginning of this effort. If Zhivago's medical profession and his poetry in different ways link him to the attempt to further life, to establish a link with immortality, then the revolution is presented as a throwback to earlier, almost pagan, times, and its imagery is tied to death rather than to life. Pasternak's Soviet critics were correct, but only in part: *Doctor Zhivago* actually celebrates the change that revolution brings about and the turn to new forms as a potential step forward. If Iurii Zhivago finally turns away from Soviet society, then it is because that society and its leaders have imposed an order antithetical to the progress of mankind and to the ideals represented by the highest strivings of human thought.

—Barry P. Scherr

A DOLL'S HOUSE (Et dukkehjem)
Play by Henrik Ibsen, 1879

A Doll's House is a landmark in drama, but it is confined in its range of social setting to the middle class. For Henrik Ibsen, this class denoted a community limited not only in its means of livelihood but also in its outlook. It is preoccupied with work and money, leading to a reduction of values from a moral to a material plane.

Torvald Helmer upholds these values because it is in his interest to do so. He knows that his dominant quality, self-interest, will be protected by his adherence to conventional morality. He imposes it on his wife, Nora, because it satisfies his vanity and makes her subservient to him. To him the man is the superior being, holding the economic reins and thereby concentrating in his hands all power and responsibility in the household, making the woman his slave. This conventional view also applies to the attitude to sex; in the kind of relationship that exists between Nora and Torvald, she is his plaything. Ibsen even adds a touch of perversity to Torvald's character, who confesses that he likes to indulge in fantasies about his wife that will enhance her erotic appeal. His purchase of a fishergirl's costume in Capri for Nora and his insistence that she dance the tarantella in public manifest the same desire.

It is against conventional middle-class values that Nora rebels. Of course, she has been made to believe that she was happy, that she was an ideal wife, and that her husband loves her, and she was living with the belief that an ideal husband like hers would, if the necessity arose, sacrifice his life to save her reputation. It is these illusions that are shattered at the end. In her final revolt against her husband, we see the play as dealing with the subject of freedom for women. It has been said that the banging of the door as Nora leaves the house was the first action of women's liberation. (Ibsen was aware of the controversy surrounding his play, and was obliged to provide an alternative happy ending for its German production where Nora melts at the sight of her children. He described it as ''a barbaric outrage.'')

Ibsen himself tried to bring the controversy to an end. He said: ''I . . . must disclaim the honour of having consciously worked for women's rights. I am not even quite sure what women's rights really are. To me it has been a question of human rights.'' This, in fact, suggests the main theme of the play. It is true that the rebel, trying to claim what she considers her legitimate rights, is a woman, but Ibsen also conveys a more general theme of freedom from constricting circumstances of life, often observing that those circumstances are social in character. Whether they belong to his own century or to some other period, whatever the nature of the circumstances, there has always been a conflict between the sensitive, intelligent individual and social pressures and circumstances. Ibsen invests the topical and the contemporary with a universal significance, succeeding because of the creative force of his play, projected mainly onto the chief character, Nora. Her vitality is evident in the way she reacts to the life around her and the changes she undergoes in the course of the play. In fact, the most fascinating aspect of the play is Nora's consciousness, and an important theme is the development of a mature sensibility.

At the beginning, Nora makes her energetic temperament subservient to her love for her husband, but even at this stage her spirit of independence manifests itself as a kind of irresponsibility, making her forge her father's signature and surreptitiously eat macaroons, which Torvald has forbidden her to do. More remarkable is her deeply passionate and devoted heart. Her crime, after all, was motivated by an unreflecting love for her husband: without his knowledge and for his sake, she raises a loan by forgery. Nora also possesses a developing intelligence which enables her to acquire a mature conception of freedom. These qualities create a complex and many-sided personality and together constitute Nora's morality, fresh, vigorous, and unorthodox, which is pitched against the conventional morality of Torvald. What the play dramatizes is not a clash of characters but of values and of different ways of looking at the world. In Torvald Ibsen portrays a character who is lacking in the vital qualities of the heart and is a victim of social conventions. It is only gradually that Nora acquires a true awareness of her husband's character and what he represents.

The explosive impact of the play tends to deflect attention from Ibsen's dramatic skill. The construction has something in common with the "well-made play," but his technique is generally richer and far more meaningful. Ibsen also employs his characteristic retrospective method whereby he gradually lifts the veil over ominous events in the past, despite the resistance of the main character. Nora conceals her crime from Torvald, but events beyond her control result in his discovering it. She expects Torvald to take upon himself the responsibility for the past, but he does not and is thus stripped of all his pretensions, while Nora is jolted into a realization that she has been living in a doll's house.

Ibsen introduces a sub-plot centring upon two other characters, Mrs. Linde and Nils Krogstad. This is not handled as adroitly as the main plot, but is essential to the play. Ibsen's mode of presentation is realistic, but he incorporates symbolism and visual suggestion, too. For instance, when Nora dances the tarantella, the frenzied dance is an image of the torment in her mind. Indeed, Nora's very language, though prose, is vibrant with emotion and acquires a poetic intensity. The play confirms Ibsen's view: "I have been more of a poet and less of a social philosopher than people generally suppose."

—D.C.R.A. Goonetilleke

DOM CASMURRO
Novel by Joaquim Maria Machado de Assis, 1899

"Lord Stubborn" might be one translation of the title of this, the third of Joaquim Maria Machado de Assis's great novels, though its narrator insists that that dictionary version of his nickname is not the appropriate one: the more colloquial meaning of "retiring, quiet," suits him better. As Bento Santiago introduces himself to us, we become aware that he has his quirks: he has decided to build himself, in the 1890s, an exact replica of the house he lived in as a child, miles out in the suburbs of Rio (where the whole novel is set): the book itself, which he is writing, is a similar attempt to capture the past.

That past begins when Bento is 16, and he overhears a conversation between the older members of the household: Dona Glória, his mother; José Dias, a permanent retainer who has achieved considerable influence in the wake of his father's death; and two other relatives. José Dias is anxious for Dona Glória to fulfil her promise, made before Bento was born, to make him a priest, but he has seen a possible impediment: the girl next door, Capitu, Bento's 15-year-old playmate. The fact that their relationship might mean anything to anybody is a revelation to Bento: but he does know that the priesthood is not for him.

So we are introduced to a tussle that lasts most of the novel and concludes in the marriage of the two lovers. Its first stage is the

enlisting of José Dias on their side: as Bento is quite well aware, he is to be the head of the household, and so theoretically the one with the power to make others obey his will. But Capitu has the intelligence and insight to see that he is pliable and without the strength of character to make decisions: Bento, spoilt by his timorous and over-religious mother, has to practise the appropriate tone of voice. Capitu's father, a minor civil servant, is much less well-off than the Santiagos (Bento's father had owned a sugarplantation and been an important politician). So we are gradually introduced to an undercurrent of social tension in the "Romeo and Juliet" story of the young lovers. Capitu was "more of a woman than I was a man," and she has to conduct a campaign to get her way—she is, as generations of readers have witnessed, the epitome of the fascinating woman. Parallel to this, we become aware of the intense insecurity of Bento's nature, which manifests itself in irrational outbursts of jealousy. He has, as he says, an over-active imagination, which, like Tacitus' Iberian mares, can be made pregnant by the wind.

In the end, Capitu gets her way by a series of compromises: Bento does go to the seminary, but with the tacit understanding that if his vocation fails to appear he will not be forced into the priesthood. While there he meets Escobar, who also has no desire to take orders—"commerce is my real vocation"—and it is he who devises the final scheme by which Dona Glória is released from her vow: they simply pay for a young man to substitute for Bento. Bento and Capitu are happily married, though he does complain that she seems anxious to return to Rio from idyllic Tijuca rather too soon. The marriage is a happy one, however, marred only by the lack of children, made the more frustrating by the fact that Escobar, married to Sancha, has a girl. However, finally, even that wish is granted, and a son (Ezequiel, named after Escobar) is born.

We are now more than three-quarters of the way through the book, and, innocent of the ways of writing as he is, Bento is beginning to run out of paper. The novel thus becomes more and more episodic, though the reader also begins to get the sense of a sickening truth about to be revealed. All is clarified when tragedy strikes: Escobar is drowned in the bay of Guanabara, and Bento sees Capitu wiping away a few tears at the funeral. Soon, Bento begins to notice that his son looks more and more like the dead Escobar, and reaches the only possible conclusion: "it was the will of destiny that my first girlfriend and my best friend, so affectionate as well as so beloved, got together and tricked me." The marriage becomes impossible, and Capitu is eventually taken by her husband to Switzerland, where she dies: the son conveniently dies as a result of typhoid fever on an archaeological trip to the Holy Land, financed by his "father." Bento is left with his memories, several lady friends, and his collection of pictures.

Did the adultery take place? Is Ezequiel Bento's son? For all Bento's confident knowledge of the truth and his winning ways as a narrator, some critics (though only some 60 years after the novel's publication) have raised perfectly legitimate doubts, pointing out that everything is in the eye of the beholder/narrator, who is much less innocent than he appears to be: the narration, too, contains repeated hints of other possible readings, such as a remark that people totally unrelated may look strangely alike. There is no way of telling, though some hanker for the old certainties (including one of Brazil's best short-story writers, Dalton Trevisan, who recently published an intemperate article trying to prove—again—that of course she did). All the polemics have added to the fascination and popularity of what was already perhaps Brazil's best-known novel. But Machado de Assis wanted to create a work that forces the reader to make choices, ask questions, and think about the social and other forces that condition people's actions and their views of others. If this seems a touch sophisticated for a 19th-century Brazilian, perhaps we should remember that Henry James did a not dissimilar thing in *The Turn of the Screw* in 1898.

—John Gledson

DON CARLOS
Play by Friedrich von Schiller, 1787 (written 1783, published in parts 1785–86, complete version 1787)

Designated a dramatic poem, Friedrich von Schiller's *Don Carlos* is at the same time historical tragedy in the great Aristotelian manner. The main protagonists of the action are Philip II King of Spain, his wife Queen Elizabeth of Valois, and the infant Don Carlos. Other major characters drawn from history are Pater Domingo, formerly Inquisitor and now the King's Confessor, and Herzog von Alba, the Supreme Commander renowned for his ruthless suppression of the Netherlands at a time when it was one of the richest provinces in the Empire. Originally written in prose, the play became the first of Schiller's to be printed in verse, specifically in non-rhyming iambic pentameters. Schiller's sublimation of the dramatic action in this way allowed him considerable freedom: the deaths of Don Carlos and the Queen occur only after the defeat of the Armada in 1588, where history dates their demise 20 years earlier; one of the principal characters, Don Rodrigo Marquis von Posa, is wholly fictitious; and the political intrigue is forged out of the mere rumours of history which told of an incestuous relationship between Don Carlos and his stepmother.

The three main levels of the dramatic action are domestic, political, and historical. The family tragedy centres on a tyrant King who doubts his son's potential to govern, a Queen who, once in love with Don Carlos, is now faithful to his father whom, for the sake of the Catholic alliance, she married, and a son who, while feeling bereft of his father's affection, cannot cease loving the woman who has recently become his stepmother. The emotional tension arising from this situation permeates the whole play. Domingo and Alba's pernicious exploitation of the rumours of incest intensify the lonely King's suspicions to the point of frenzy, even to the extent of his doubting whether or not he is the father to the Infanta Clara Eugenia. For Schiller the domestic situation cannot be divorced from the political one. The inevitable loneliness of the office of an absolute monarch, who uses the Inquisition to control an empire reaching from the borders of Turkey to the new continent of South America, is mirrored in the human isolation of a father whose dutiful wife can offer him little more than a holy alliance with France, whose clandestine lover, Princess Eboli, can provide him with little more than sexual gratification, and whose son seems to offer him little more than rebellious presumption. Domingo and Alba's machinations aim to destroy what little remains of the relationship between Philip and Don Carlos, so that, as Philip himself understands, neither his entire Court nor his family can provide him with true counsel, nor he place his trust in them. Only the Marquis von Posa, who, as one of the few heroic survivors of the Siege of Malta, has overcome the inhibiting fear of torture and death, is free, as a result, to reject the King's magnanimous offer of an exalted position at Court, which would nevertheless have made him his servant, and to speak honestly to him about the gruesome crucifixion of heretics in the Netherlands, the unmitigated

cruelty of his Inquisition and government, and the undignified state of his subjects' thralldom. In private audience the Marquis pleads eloquently and persuasively for the dignity of mankind, for the individual's right to think and to worship freely. While these sentiments echoed those of Immanuel Kant and of the 18th-century Enlightenment, they were not unheard during Philip's reign. They are articulated in Schiller's sources for his play, his history of the Netherlands and his unfinished play about the Knights of St. John's heroic defence of Malta in 1565. After all, as Schiller wrote in his *Letters on Don Carlos* in defence of the Marquis von Posa's idealism: "It is in prison where most we dream of freedom." The King is so impressed by the Marquis's outspoken courage that he grants him full authority to determine privately whether there is any truth to the rumours of incest.

The economic handling of the material was almost as difficult for Schiller as it was to prove for Verdi in the even more stringent treatment which his transformation of the play into opera inevitably demanded. The dramatic intrigue is complex and Schiller could allow only a single meeting between Philip and the Marquis von Posa (III, 10). Nevertheless a masterly degree of unity is achieved, not via the traditional neoclassical inheritance, but by focusing the entire action on the eponymous Don Carlos. Born, like Hamlet, for kingship, Don Carlos demonstrates his persistent immaturity in the exclusively self-centred love which he still feels for Elizabeth even after her wedding. Just as Philip had hoped for his son to be fitted for inheriting his empire, so had the Marquis invested in him his albeit different political hopes for enlightened humanitarian government. Briefly, but in the end vainly, Don Carlos responds at last to the Marquis's highest expectations of him when exhorted by Elizabeth to transform his love of her into the love of mankind so that the Netherlands might be liberated from the Inquisition. He makes plans to leave for the Spanish Province. It is their humanity and their political vision of an enlightened republic which unite Elizabeth, Don Carlos, and the Marquis in friendship unto death, one for which even Philip shows momentarily sympathetic understanding. The vision is destroyed, however, in the final tragedy when the Marquis's hazardous undertaking to save Don Carlos for posterity, by diverting the King's suspicions of himself, founders, the King has the Marquis assassinated and his son handed over to the Inquisition. Although the idea is born, it remains, for the time being, an ideal.

—Edward Batley

DON JUAN (Dom Juan; ou, Le Festin de pierre)
Play by Molière, 1665

Don Juan, a prose comedy in five acts, is one of Molière's most enigmatic plays. First staged at the Palais-Royal on 15 February 1665, it proved an immediate box-office success but disappeared from Molière's repertory after only 15 performances. The play was revised in 1677 in an edulcorated verse adaptation by Thomas Corneille. This was the only version performed at the Comédie-Française until 1847. Thereafter, Molière's text was infrequently performed. Its complete rehabilitation was brought about largely through post-war productions by Louis Jouvet (1947) and Jean Vilar (1954). It is now generally accepted by both critics and producers as one of Molière's masterpieces.

The play provoked hostility from the outset. After its premiere cuts were made, including the suppression of the entire scene in which Don Juan challenges a religious hermit's belief in divine providence by offering him a *louis d'or* on condition that he swear an oath (Act III, scene 2). At the end of April 1665 an anonymous pamphlet (later identified as the work of a Jansenist writing under the nom-de-plume ''le sieur de Rochemont'') branded Molière a free thinker who had made a double attack on religion by putting the arguments against Christianity in the mouth of an atheistic master while entrusting the defence of the faith to a cowardly, credulous, superstitious valet incapable of distinguishing between the bogeyman and a messenger from heaven. Even though Rochemont's impassioned attack is mainly of historical interest nowadays, the play still tends to be seen as a polemical piece and, in particular, as the expression of Molière's frustration over the interdiction of *Tartuffe* after only one performance on 12 May 1664.

There were, however, commercial and theatrical reasons for the choice of subject. The Don Juan theme had been exploited successfully on the Spanish, Italian, and French stages. Two different French versions had been performed in 1658 and 1659. In addition, in the 1660s, machine plays had become very popular.

From a dramatic standpoint, Molière's *Don Juan* has been criticized for lacking unity. The apparent loose construction has been attributed to hasty composition and the fusion of disparate sources. The play's coherence has been justified in terms of interlocking themes. It is however possible to see an underlying dramatic unity if the play is viewed as a parody of certain conventions of so-called classical tragedy. Molière makes light of the unities, one of the central features of the period's serious drama. The unity of place: instead of the required single set, five different locations conjure up a world of fantasy—a palace in one of the maritime towns of Sicily (Act I); a coast frequented by peasants (Act II); near the coast a wood in which the disguised master can encounter a hermit, brigands, and, without his being recognized, his next-of-kin (Act III); a room in which Don Juan receives unwelcome and unexpected guests (Act IV); an unidentified place, inhabited by a spectre and a walking-talking statue (Act V). The unity of time: within one revolution of the sun, the Don's odyssey encompasses an attempted abduction, a shipwreck, proposals of marriage, a discussion on metaphysics, swordplay, invitations to dinner, a religious conversion, and his final descent into hell. The unity of action (unification of plot): in charting Don Juan's fatal attempt to rise not just above his peers but above the divine being, Molière departs from traditional comic plots constructed around the lovers' struggle to overcome parental opposition to their marriage or around conjugal strife. The plot exposes Don Juan as an anti-tragic hero, as a development of the *miles glorious* or of Matamore, an inveterate wordspinner whose protestations are undermined by events. Don Juan's portrayal of himself as sexual conqueror (he compares himself to the legendary womanizer Alexandre for whom all kinds of women would readily sacrifice themselves) is belied by a succession of failures: in Act I his mansuetudinous retreat at the approach of his wife, Elvire (his behaviour evokes the henpecked husband rather than the romantic hero); in Act II the abortive kidnapping issuing in his being soaked and forced to divest himself of his finery (a reported incident); the rather banal wooing of the pleasant Charlotte; the unseemly scuffle with her fiancé and his rescuer, Pierrot; his embarrassment when asked publicly to choose between the two peasants claiming his love (Charlotte and Mathurine). In Act III Don Juan's intellectual superiority, demonstrated in his demolition of his valet Sganarelle's defence of medicine and of Christianity and in his claim

to be a free thinker, is called into question by his lack of success with the hermit, by his bull-headed charge to rescue a nobleman (who turns out to be his arch-enemy, his brother-in-law, Don Carlos), by his refusal to perceive what the audience and even Sganarelle all too readily apprehend, the reality of the nodding statue. In Act IV his unwillingness to accept any obligations, be these social and financial (towards his bourgeois creditor, Monsieur Dimanche), filial (towards his long-suffering father, Don Louis), or conjugal and moral (towards his wife whom he had abducted from a convent), betrays his self-centred individualism. In Act V the vanity of his heroism is seen in his fake conversion, his quixotic attack on the spectre, and the self-deceptive offer of his hand to the stone executor of divine justice. The unity of tone: given the rigid separation of genres in 17th-century French drama, the juxtaposition of elements of farce, high comedy, tragi-comedy, and even tragedy in *Don Juan* has disorientated critics. A parodic intention may be discerned from the mock-heroic framework provided by Sganarelle's opening and closing lines: the ludicrous equation of virtue and tobacco and assertion of the fatal consequences of neglecting the weed (''who lives without tobacco is not fit to live''), and the trivialization of the Don's death in the valet's self-pitying complaint about being left unsalaried.

In recent years the play has given rise to a number of innovative productions on the French stage which have secured an international reputation for its directors. The eponymous hero has been interpreted as an ''outsider,'' a manifestation of Satan, a cross between a freemason and Jack the Ripper, a revolutionary anarchist, an intellectual lacking the means to change the world, a Brechtian spectator, a western outlaw pursued by a posse of victims, and an adolescent folk hero. The diversity of interpretations gives abundant proof of both the complexity of the role and the dynamism of the text and provides a lasting testimony to the richness of Molière's creation.

—Noel A. Peacock

DON QUIXOTE (El Ingenioso Hidalgo Don Quixote de la Mancha)
Novel by Miguel de Cervantes, 1605–15

Miguel de Cervantes was 58 when Part One of *Don Quixote* was first published in Madrid in 1605, and 68 by the time Part Two was brought out. By then he had had a varied life that might have provided him with all the inspiration needed for his masterpiece. It is, however, more fruitful to suggest that his experiences brought into particularly sharp focus a set of issues that plainly were major preoccupations of his contemporaries all over western Europe and especially in Spain. Cervantes's father was an impoverished gentleman who had been obliged to train as a surgeon, which was hardly the sort of career a person of his status would have sought, yet the fact that it was understood he had no real choice but to earn a living is revealed by the readiness of another impecunious member of his class to allow his daughter to marry him. Equally significant, however, was Miguel's refusal to follow in his father's footsteps. Instead, after acquiring what education he could, he proposed to put it to good use by turning to writing. It was a way of attracting attention. Another way of coming to the fore was accepting the risks of warfare: he fought heroically at the Battle of Lepanto in 1571 when the Turks were heavily defeated. Cervantes was, however, taken prisoner by the Turks some four years later and spent half a decade in captivity. On his return to Spain,

Cervantes again divided his time between literature, with scant success, and attempts to earn a living in the public service. It was the era of the Spanish Armada, and its defeat is a symbol of the decline of the once great state in whose decayed nobility Cervantes aspired to play a minor role. Literature could offer an escape into idealism, and in 1584 he brought out a pastoral romance called *La Galatea*. Finally he found a more satisfactory outlet for his frustrations in the irony and humour of *Don Quixote*. It struck a chord, as is shown by the fact that it was soon translated into all the European languages, with Thomas Shelton's English version appearing in 1612.

Cervantes's story of the adventures of a knight of shreds and patches who embarks on a long series of adventures with his steed Rosinante and his squire, Sancho Panza, has counterparts in a long series of works of fiction that reflect Europe's long fascination with the ideal of chivalry. This led first to romances, then to their reversal in spoofs that are often all the funnier for being addressed to a lower-class readership. At the origins of the tradition stand, if not Alexander and the Greek heroes, then King Arthur and Charlemagne, and the Middle Ages developed the genre, presenting in the mounted knight's quest a figure of all that was noblest in human aspiration. At the start of the 16th century *Amadis de Gaule* swept Europe, appearing to reinvigorate the tradition, but reaction soon set in, in response both to excessive idealization and to the evident decline of nobility as monarchs became absolute and the bourgeoisie claimed a status to match its increasing material prosperity. In France, Rabelais invented *Gargantua*, adding an attack on scolasticism to a satire on chivalric romance as handed down by the chapbooks, and in Italy Ariosto wrote *Orlando furioso*. Meanwhile in Spain the anonymous *Lazarillo de Tormes* gave a worm's eye view of the shams of Spanish society in the mid-16th century, and after that the rich picaresque tradition developed to provide an ironic reflection of the endeavour of knightly romance in an inconsequential rogue's progress. It was from these literary origins and with personal experience to reinforce the impression that Spain was a great civilization in decline that Cervantes derived his comic masterpiece, finding in laughter a release from disgust.

The narrative, a true one, as we are assured tongue-in-cheek, is long and digressive, but it is held together by the characters who have become almost proverbial. Chapter headings lead the reader on, often undercutting the events described by lauding them in extravagant terms that cannot be taken seriously. Sancho too sets up perspectives that ensure we are not tempted to take his master more seriously than he does. Above all we have the figure of Don Quixote, thinking yet not truly reasoning, going on his way from one setback to the next with a self-assurance that would be heroic if it were not crazy. Don Quixote is an unexpectedly upbeat epitaph to a grand tradition that had to die at the start of the early modern period.

—Christopher Smith

A DREAM OF RED MANSIONS

See THE DREAM OF THE RED CHAMBER

THE DREAM OF THE RED CHAMBER (Honglou meng)

Chinese novel, written largely by Cao Xueqin (c. 1715–63), about whom little is known. He probably completed the first 80 chapters of the novel; the later 40 chapters are generally considered to have been "edited" or revised by others.

PUBLICATIONS

Honglou meng. Edited by Gao E (120 chapters), 1792; modern editions: (80 chapters) 1912; (80 chapters, after 1770 manuscript) 1955; (120 chapters, after 1792 edition) 1957; (after 1912 edition, with last 40 chapters of 1792 edition) 1958; (80 chapters) 2 vols., 1961; (80 chapters after 1760 manuscript, last 40 chapters after 1792 edition) 3 vols., 1982; as *Hung lou meng; or, The Dream of the Red Chamber*, translated by H.B. Joly, 2 vols., 1892–93 (abridged); as *The Dream of the Red Chamber*, translated by Wang Chi-Chen, 1929; also translated by Florence and Isabel McHugh (from the German), 1958; as *The Story of the Stone*, translated by David Hawkes and John Minford, 5 vols., 1973–86; as *A Dream of Red Mansions*, translated by Yang Hsien-yi and Gladys Yang, 3 vols., 1978–86; as *Dream of Red Mansions: Saga of Noble Chinese Family*, translated by Huang Xinqu, 1994; as *The Dream of the Red Chamber*, translated by David Hawkes, 1995.

*

Bibliography: *Studies on Dream of the Red Chamber: A Selected and Classified Bibliography* by Tsung Shun Na, 1979, supplement, 1981.

Critical Studies: *On "The Red Chamber Dream"* (includes bibliography) by Wu Shih-ch'ang, 1961; *The Classic Chinese Novel* by C.T. Hsia, 1968; *The Dream of the Red Chamber: A Critical Study* by Jeanne Knoerle, 1972; *New Interpretations of the Dream of the Red Chamber* by Klaus-Peter Koepping and Lam Mai Sing, 1973; *Masks of Fiction in the Dream of the Red Chamber: Myth, Mimesis and Persona* by Lucien Miller, 1975; *Archetype and Allegory in the Dream of the Red Chamber* by Andrew Henry Plaks, 1976; *Ts'ao Hsueh-Ch'in's "Dream of the Red Chamber"* by Zhang Xiugui, 1991.

* * *

The Dream of the Red Chamber (*Honglou meng*) is perhaps the most beloved and widely read traditional Chinese novel. It appears to have been written some time before 1763 by a man named Cao Xueqin, the impoverished grandson of Cao Yin, a notable political and literary figure of the early Qing dynasty and the Kangxi Emperor's trusted servant. For several decades the book circulated in an 80-chapter manuscript version under the title *The Story of the Stone*. The first printed edition, in 120 chapters, appeared in 1792, with prefaces by Gao E and Cheng Weiyuan, who claimed to have pieced together various old manuscript fragments in order to complete the earlier version. The exact proportion of mere editing to actual creation *de novo* in their edition is still the subject of debate, as is the literary merit of the last 40 chapters. However, this version soon supplanted the earlier one, and it was not until the early 20th century that the old manuscripts came to light. Their accompanying commentary, mostly by a friend of the author known to us as Zhiyan zhai ("Red Inkstone"), has allowed us not only to trace the evolution of the text itself, but to glimpse some of the historical persons and events behind the novel. The book clearly incorporates certain features of the Cao family history as Cao Xueqin experienced it.

On this level, *The Dream of the Red Chamber* is the story of the fictional Jia family's fall from wealth and position. As the novel opens, their splendour is already said to be waning. Yet they are still dazzlingly wealthy and powerful: the junior and senior branches of the family, four generations of them and scores of servants and dependents, live in vast and elegant adjoining mansions in the imperial capital. Their fortunes, moreover, appear in some ways to be on the rise. When their daughter is made an imperial concubine, the family spares no expense to build a magnificent garden in which to entertain her—though only for a few brief hours—as befits her rank. Throughout the account of the garden's construction which leads up to the elaborate reception itself, there is a note of sadness for the fragility of worldly splendour—a note which recurs more and more insistently through the slow-moving idyll of garden life which takes up the novel's inner 80 chapters, until the imperial concubine's untimely death heralds the family's final precipitous fall from imperial favour, and the confiscation of their estate.

The Dream of the Red Chamber is also the story of the boy Baoyu's initiation into the mysteries of love and loss. Baoyu—whose name, ''Precious Jade,'' refers to the magic jade he bore in his mouth at birth, the ''stone'' of the novel's fantastic frame-tale—is tenderly solicitous of the girl cousins and maids who live with him in the family garden. Most of all Baoyu loves his cousin Daiyu, who is equally devoted to him, though they quarrel constantly. Daiyu's fragile health, her acerbic tongue, and her morose and solitary turn of mind lead the elder Jias to marry Baoyu, instead, to an equally beautiful and talented cousin who is in every other way Daiyu's opposite: Xue Baochai. Having been deceived into thinking that she is Daiyu, Baoyu marries the veiled Baochai at the very moment of Daiyu's death. Already in ill health from the loss of his magic jade, and deeply grieved by Daiyu's death and the trick that has been played on him, Baoyu eventually has a dream which parallels his dream-initiation into love near the novel's beginning. At last he begins to understand the connection between that first cryptic dream and the sorrowful events of his own recent life. In the end, his accumulated grief and disillusionment lead him to leave his family for the life of a Buddhist mendicant.

At one stroke, therefore, the Jias lose both their fortune and their heir-apparent. Their fall, though, is not a sudden blow of fate, but the delayed consequence of their own corrupt machinations. Very early in the novel their high position at court saves their relative Xue Pan from prosecution for murder. Later, their ambitious and scheming daughter-in-law, Wang Hsi-feng, embarks on a spiralling scheme of illegal loansharking; her abuse of the family's influence causes the deaths of several people and plays an important part in the Jias' disgrace and financial ruin. Some of the Jia family men are wastrels with a penchant for bribery and extortion; others are sexual profligates whose tastes run to incest. Though these dark details impinge only very gradually on the garden enclave where Baoyu and his cousins practise poetry, calligraphy, and other elegant and scholarly arts, multiplying signs of decay eventually suggest that even the garden-dwellers are not immune to the corrupt passions of the world outside.

Most critics agree that *The Dream of the Red Chamber* is unsurpassed in the tradition of the Chinese novel for its magisterial portrayal of literati culture and for its subtle depiction of interior states. Beyond these rather obvious points, however, there is little unanimity. Throughout its history the novel has been the object of a wide variety of interpretive schemes, some of them quite fanciful. It both invites and frustrates interpretation: the text is replete with erudite puns, riddles, and complex patterns of word and image which hinge on the ambiguous relation between the ''real'' and the ''illusory.'' Its multitude of sub-plots and the sheer vastness of its scale also ensure that any neatly consistent reading will fail to do it justice. Any reading, though, must take into account the centrality of the garden, which in the long course of the novel lapses from its original perfection to become a haunted, weed-infested wilderness. It is in this central image that Baoyu's story and the larger story of his family's fall are fused. Like Baoyu's perfect and unattainable love and his family's visions of splendour, the garden is an expression of the unquenchable human longing for riches, honour, beauty, and pleasure, and of the loss and dissolution which are the inevitable consequence of that longing.

—Mary Scott

E

THE EARTH (La Terre)
Novel by Émile Zola, 1887

In Aldous Huxley's 1928 novel *Point Counter Point*, Maurice Spandrell suggests that this world might be another planet's hell. Marianne Péchard, née Fouan, more commonly known as La Grande, who is one of the characters in Émile Zola's *The Earth*, published in 1887 as the 15th in the Rougon-Macquart series, rejects the priest Godard's threat that she will be punished in the next world for the cruelty she has shown to her grandchildren, Palmyre and Hilarion, with a similar argument. Hell, she says, already exists for poor people and it is on this earth. Perhaps because there is no God in Zola's world to chastise her or, more probably, to reward her for speaking the truth, such blasphemy goes relatively unpunished. At the end of a novel in which her brother, Louis Fouan, is smothered to death by his son, Buteau, and daughter-in-law, Lise, and then set alight in what proves to be a successful attempt to hide the crime, and in which La Grande's niece, Françoise, is held down by her sister Lise, so that Lise's husband Buteau can more conveniently rape her, La Grande is one of the few characters still on their feet. Françoise is dead, the fact that she was five months pregnant at the time of the rape having done nothing to stop Lise from throwing her on to a scythe, whose blade also penetrates the child she is carrying. Another character, the rich farmer Hourdequin, is also dead. He is murdered by his shepherd, Soulas, whom he has dismissed at the urging of his mistress, Jacqueline Cognet, of whose multiple infidelities Soulas is a frequent, if accidental, witness. At one point, La Grande almost gets her come-uppance. Her grandson, Hilarion, driven mad by being bullied by her and struck by her walking stick, turns against her in blind fury and rapes her. He is, of course, suffering from sexual frustration at the time. His sister, Palmyre, who had committed incest with him on a fairly regular basis in the hovel in which they lived, has dropped dead some months earlier from sunstroke while working at the harvest. Although 89, La Grande splits Hilarion's head open with an axe. She also ensures that the evil she has done in her lifetime lives after her by drawing up an extremely complicated will, specifically designed to keep her descendants at one another's throats for many years to come.

The only member of the Rougon-Macquart family to appear in *The Earth* is Jean Macquart, son of Antoine Macquart. He has given up his original trade as a carpenter, joined the army, fought at the battle of Solférino in 1859, and is proposing, at the end of the novel, to sign up again, ready to fight in the Franco-Prussian war of 1870. This he does in *La Débâcle* (*The Debacle*), the 19th in the series, which describes the defeat of the French and the horrors of the repression of the Paris *Commune* in May 1871. *The Earth* describes Jean trying his luck in the countryside but, since he is a character in Zola, he does not have any, except for an occasional roll in the hay with Jacqueline Cognet. It is his wife, Françoise, who is raped by her brother-in-law, Louis Fouan's youngest son, Buteau. At the end of the novel, Jean leaves the village of Rognes, near Chartres, where the action takes place, as poor as he was on the day he arrived.

This is partly the result of the laws of inheritance laid down in the Napoleonic Code of 1802, which play something of the same role in *The Earth* that the distillery machine does in *L'Assommoir* or the mine in *Germinal*. In order to avoid the reconstitution of the large landed estates that had been a feature of the pre-revolutionary France, the *Code Napoléon* abolished the principle of primogeniture. All children, illegitimate as well as legitimate, boys as well as girls, had to receive an equal share of the family property. For a country of small peasant farmers such as France, this meant that the birth of more than one child was a disaster. A farm that was already small had to be farther subdivided, making French agriculture even more inefficient and uncompetitive.

Although they live in La Beauce, one of the most fertile wheat-growing areas of Western Europe, the peasants in *The Earth* are all desperately poor and regard the birth of even one child as such a catastrophic addition to the number of mouths to be fed that *coitus interruptus* is the normal way of conducting any sexual encounter between a man and a woman. (There is no mention in *The Earth* of either homosexuality or bestiality; perhaps an indication that there were limits to what even Zola could write.) The Napoleonic Code also had the effect, according to Zola, of ensuring that, even when married, a woman kept the property she had inherited from her parents. Françoise does not love Jean enough to make a will in his favour, and the reluctance to give up the right to her minute piece of land is a major cause of her death. It is not only, or even mainly, through sexual jealousy that her sister Lise throws her on the scythe. She knows that her sister has not made a will leaving her property to Jean, so that if Françoise dies intestate, she and her husband will inherit the land and will also be able to evict Jean from the house that is still, legally, Françoise's property. This they duly do, not even allowing Jean back in to collect his clothes.

Except for some very good descriptions of the countryside, showing how effective an influence the Impressionists he so admired could have on Zola's work, *The Earth* is not one of the better novels in the Rougon-Macquart series. If Zola had a sense of humour, the book might have been seen as an exercise in self-parody, comparable to Stella Gibbon's satire of the English novel of rural misery in her 1930 masterpiece, *Cold Comfort Farm*. It is unfortunately obvious that Zola is in deadly earnest throughout, even in his presentation of the one financially successful branch of the Fouan family, M. et Mme. Charles. Laure Fouan, Louis's younger sister (considerably; she is 62 when the action begins in the early 1860s, when La Grande is coming up to 80 and Louis is 70) has married a not very successful café owner, Charles Badeuil. None of their enterprises flourishes until they get the idea of running a brothel in Chartres. Such institutions were perfectly legal in 19th-century France and were not outlawed until Marthe Richard introduced a bill abolishing what were officially known as *les maisons choses* in 1946. *Le 19* (No. 19) as it is referred to, prospered considerably, enabling M. et Mme. Charles to retire and lead a highly respectable life at Rognes, admired and respected by all. They have one daughter, Estelle, to whom they give the most austere of convent educations, before marrying her off to a handsome young customs officer, Hector Vaucogne. On reaching woman's estate, Estelle sees no reason why the business should leave the family; M. and Mme. Charles would have had no worries but for the fact that their son-in-law, Hector, proves a most incompetent manager, going against the basic principle of the trade to the point of enjoying the favours of some of the young ladies of No. 19 himself. Fortunately, all ends well.

Élodie, Estelle's daughter, has also been very strictly brought up, spending most of her time with her grandparents at Rogues, who keep a very close eye on her. However, on learning that one of her cousins, Nénesse Delhomme, who has been working in Chartres and had his eye on No. 19 for some time, would like to take over the business and replace the inefficient Hector, she leaps at the chance of marrying him and keeping the family tradition going.

The Earth has exactly the same number of pages as *Germinal* or *L'Assommoir*, reinforcing the impression that Zola is writing to a formula. After dealing with mining, alcoholism, department stores in *Au bonheur des dames* (*Ladies' Delight*), he decided to "do" the countryside. The novel ends, like *La Bête humaine* (*The Beast in Man*), with the impending disaster of the 1870 war. The technique of narration is also similar to the one used in *Germinal*, in that Jean Macquart, like Étienne Lantier, arrives from outside and leaves at the end of the novel. Unlike Étienne, however, he plays a relatively minor part in the plot, where disasters need no help from him to work themselves out. Since no other member of the Rougon-Macquart family either appears or is even mentioned, there is less insistence on the implacable weight of heredity than in *The Beast in Man* or *Nana*. In so far as there is an explanation for the doom-ridden atmosphere of Rognes, it is in the equally irresistible pressure of the environment. The land has fashioned these men and women in its own image, tempting them by its fertility, crushing them by its sudden caprices, inspiring them with a desire for possession which destroys them eventually. Even the unjust society of the Second Empire, the main conscious target of Zola's wrath, plays only a minor role, its inefficiency visible mainly in the fact that the introduction of free trade in the 1861 treaty emphasizes the vulnerability of French agriculture to competition from the New World.

—Philip Thody

THE EDDA OF SÆMUND

See THE POETIC EDDA

EFFI BRIEST
Novel by Theodor Fontane, 1895

Effi Briest, Theodor Fontane's greatest novel, has been compared with Flaubert's *Madame Bovary* and Tolstoi's *Anna Karenina* in its treatment of adultery. Yet Fontane, an enemy of the sensational, does not make Effi's sin the central issue of the novel. Instead he focuses on the destructive conventions of a society that condemns individuals to a life of boredom, frustration, and disillusionment.

While Fontane's contemporary social portrait sheds light on the whole of late 19th-century industrial, bourgeois European society, the primary object of his criticism is Prussia and the Germany it brought into being. This Prussia, its values and mores, is mirrored in the characters of *Effi Briest*. Effi's husband, Geert von Instetten, is committed to the discipline, authority, love of nation, and professionalism that typify the Prussian civil servant. He allows abstractions of moral convention to dictate his behaviour, killing Crampas in a duel and shunning his wife, in his own words: "for the sake of mere representations." While Instetten, after a short term of imprisonment for his involvement in the duel, continues his advance up the bureaucratic ladder, he nonetheless recognizes the ultimate meaninglessness of his success: "the more I am honoured, the more I feel that all of this is nothing. My life is ruined . . . ." Instetten recalls "the 'little happiness'" he had once enjoyed with his wife, and resigns himself to its loss.

The teenager Effi is seduced by a naive ambitiousness of her own. Enamoured of the idea of marrying a respected civil servant, she submits to engagement with her 38-year-old suitor on the day when he proposes it. But even on their honeymoon tour of Italy, boredom becomes the primary experience of Effi's married life. The birth of Annie does little to remedy the situation of a woman who must spend her days in loneliness while her husband disappears for long hours at work and her child is cared for by a governess. Effi succumbs irresistibly and against her better judgement to the seduction of Major von Crampas, who himself is chained to an unbearable wife and an outwardly successful existence that he despises. Effi witnesses her descent into sinfulness with a kind of horror and is profoundly relieved by her husband's news that his promotion to *Ministerialrat* means their relocation to Berlin, away from the disturbing monotony of their life in remote Kessin. When, more than six years later, Instetten learns of the adulterous relationship his wife has come to view as an unfortunate, yet forgettable episode of her past, she accepts her punishment: life as a social outcast and irreconcilable estrangement from her daughter, with resignation. The reader stands aghast at her tragic ability to accept the morals that have destroyed her when the dying Effi asks her mother to inform Instetten of her conviction that his entire handling of the situation was justified.

Fontane's realism is not intended to dictate an absolute reality to his readers. Reality is necessarily a matter of perception, and in *Effi Briest* the real work is unfolded from a multiplicity of individual perspectives and communicated primarily via dialogue. The reader learns nothing more about the society in which the characters exist than what they themselves reveal through their conversations, letters, and thoughts. The reader is left to decide whether to agree with Johanna, who, as a proper Prussian, regards Instetten's decision to banish Effi and turn her daughter against her as correct, or with the Catholic Roswitha, who believes Effi has suffered far more than she ever deserved and leaves Instetten to live with the melancholy divorcée. Each character sheds a different light on Prussian culture and society, and the final portrait mirrors reality in its multi-dimensional breadth.

Yet the reality recorded in *Effi Briest* is also *poetic*, making the novel a prime example of 19th-century German poetic realism. Fontane's "real world" is an artistic structure created with the aid of a meticulous selection procedure and an elaborate symbolic apparatus. Scholars have determined that *Effi Briest* underwent seven versions before the author was satisfied with it. The plot is based on real-life events: the discovery by Baron Leon von Ardenne that his wife, Elisabeth von Plotho, had once had an affair with painter Emil Hartwich; the duel in which Hartwich fell; and the couple's divorce. While several details from the experience of this real-life couple went into the composition of *Effi Briest*, the novel is anything but a biographical record of their lives. Frau von Plotho lived until the age of 99; Effi Briest dies of tuberculosis at age 29. Fontane merely got the *idea* for his novel from the Ardenne divorce. What he developed from it is a selective, fictional view of contemporary society created first as a work of art, and only secondly as an instrument of social criticism.

Fontane's use of symbols in *Effi Briest* likewise exemplifies the movement of poetic realism. Fontane is a master at taking real objects from everyday life and loading them with symbolic content. Thus the picture of the Chinese man to which Johanna is so attached assumes a whole spectrum of possible meanings based on the adventurous and tragic stories told about the man and the reactions of the various characters to his likeness. The natural boundaries present in the landscape around Instetten's home in Kessin, the sea, and especially the woods, take on profound importance as the symbols for Effi's fateful transgression into the realm of the forbidden.

In the final analysis, resignation is the overriding theme in *Effi Briest*, as it is in so many other novels by Fontane and by other representatives of German realism: Wilhelm Raabe, Gottfried Keller, and Friedrich Spielhagen. Those who accept society's limitations, like Geert von Instetten, survive, though happiness may forever elude them. Those who attempt to assert their individuality in the face of moral oppression, like Effi, will only be destroyed. This is the ultimate message of 19th-century realism.

—Virginia L. Lewis

EGILS SAGA

Icelandic prose narrative, written anonymously during 13th century, or possibly written by Snorri Sturluson (1179–1241), *q.v.*, and concerning events of the 10th century, in particular the life story of the poet Egil Skalla-Grímsson. One of the sagas called *Íslendingasögur* [Icelandic Family Sagas], quasi-historical accounts of leading citizens during and immediately after the period of settlement during the 9th–11th centuries, using a combination of prose and verse.

PUBLICATIONS

Egils saga skallagrímssonar, edited by Finnur Jónsson. 1886; revised edition, 1924; also edited by Sigurur Nordal, 1933; as *Egils Saga*, edited and translated by Christine Fell, 1975; as *The Story of Egil Skallagrimsson*, translated by W.C. Green, 1893; as *Egil's Saga*, translated by E.R. Eddison, 1930; also translated by Gwyn Jones, 1960; Hermann Palsson and Paul Edwards, 1976.

*

Bibliography: *Bibliography of the Icelandic Sagas and Minor Tales* by Halldór Hermannsson, 1908; *A Bibliography of Skaldic Studies* by Lee M. Hollander, 1958; *Bibliography of Old Norse-Icelandic Studies* by Hans Bekker-Nielsen and Thorkil Damsgaard Olsen, 1964–, and *Old Norse-Icelandic Studies: A Select Bibliography* by Bekker-Nielsen, 1967.

Critical Studies: *The Origin of the Icelandic Family Sagas* by Knut Liestøl, 1930; *The Sagas of the Icelanders* by Halldór Hermannsson, 1935; "Egil Skallagrímsson in England" by Gwyn Jones, in *Proceedings of the British Academy*, 38, 1952; *The Sagas of the Icelanders* by Jóhann S. Hannesson, 1957; *The Icelandic Saga* by Peter Hallberg, 1962; *The Icelandic Family Saga: An Analytic Reading* by Theodore M. Andersson, 1967: "The Giant as a Heroic Model: The Case of Egil and Starkar" by Kaaren Grimstad, in *Scandinavian Studies*, 48, 1976; "Fighting Words in *Egils saga*: Lexical Pattern as Standard Bearer" by Michael L. Bell, in *Arkiv*, 95, 1980.

*   *   *

Egils Saga ranks beside *Njáls Saga* and three or four others as one of the major Icelandic Family Sagas or Sagas of Icelanders, prose narratives written in Iceland mainly in the 13th century, but dealing with events of the century or so following the settlement of Iceland by Scandinavians c. AD 900. These sagas are anonymous, but there are reasons for thinking that *Egils Saga* is the work of Snorri Sturluson, author of the prose *Edda* and of the sequence of Kings' Sagas known as *Heimskringla* [The Orb of the World], which includes *Óláfs saga ins helga*. *Egils Saga* falls into three parts, ending respectively with the deaths of Egil's grandfather, Kveld-Úlf, his father, Skalla-Grím, and himself, his own career being dealt with from the beginning of the second part onwards.

The first part takes place mainly in Norway. Kveld-Úlf and his elder son Skalla-Grím refuse to join Harald the Shaggy-Haired in his struggle to become king of all Norway, but Kveld-Úlf's younger son, Thórólf, does join him. Thórólf is named as heir by Harald's retainer Bárd, who dies in the battle at which Harald gains control of Norway, and duly inherits Bárd's property, in which the two sons of Hildiríd, the second wife of Bárd's grandfather, claim a share. When Thórólf rejects their claim, Hildiríd's sons proceed to slander him to King Harald, with the eventual result that Harald kills Thórólf. Vengeance is taken on the sons of Hildiríd by Thórólf's kinsman Ketil Hæng, who kills them and then emigrates to Iceland, and on Harald by Kveld-Úlf and Skalla-Grím, who kill two of the king's retainers before themselves leaving for Iceland. Kveld-Úlf dies on the way; Skalla-Grím settles in western Iceland at Borg.

In the second part of the saga, Skalla-Grím's elder son, also named Thórólf, and Egil are born. Egil's precocity reveals itself in his ability to compose poetry at the age of three. In Norway, Björn, a chieftain, abducts Thóra, the sister of another chieftain, Thórir, against the latter's will, and brings her to Borg after first marrying her in Shetland. Reconciled with Thórir at Thórólf's instigation, the couple return to Norway, leaving their daughter, Ásgerd, in Skalla-Grím's care. In Norway Thórólf becomes friendly with Harald's son and successor, Eirík Bloodaxe, and his queen Gunnhild; he brings Ásgerd to Norway and marries her. Egil, who has meanwhile performed killings at the ages of seven and twelve, also comes to Norway, and makes friends with Thórir's son Arinbjörn. Meeting King Eirík and Gunnhild socially, he causes offence with his excessive drinking, and kills their steward after destroying the drinking-horn with which Gunnhild and the steward try to poison him. Thórólf and Egil, both now in trouble with the queen, leave Norway, and Thórólf is slain in a battle in England at which they help King Æthelstan against the Scots. Rewarded by Æthelstan with two chests of silver, Egil marries Ásgerd in Norway, and claims her patrimony when Berg-Önund, also a son-in-law of Ásgerd's father, himself claims it on the grounds that Thóra and Björn were not legally married when Ásgerd was born. With Arinbjörn's help, Egil takes the case to court, but Gunnhild disrupts the proceedings, with the result that Egil kills Berg-Önund and a son of the royal couple, plunders Berg-Önund's estate and, by setting up a pole topped with a horse's head and inscribed with runes, urges the spirits of the land to expel Eirík and Gunnhild from Norway. Skalla-Grím dies after Egil's return to Iceland.

In the third part, Eirík and Gunnhild are forced to leave Norway by the accession of Harald's son Hákon; Arinbjörn accompanies them. Intending to revisit Æthelstan, Egil is shipwrecked near York, Eirík's residence. He visits Arinbjörn there and, at his suggestion, saves himself from execution by composing his long "Head-ran-som" poem in King Eirík's praise. In Norway he finally wins Ásgerd's inheritance after killing a brother of Berg-Önund, and accepts money from Arinbjörn when King Hákon denies his claim to the brother's property. He restores to Hákon's favour Arinbjörn's nephew Thornsteinn, frowned on by Hákon because of Arinbjörn's support of Eirík's son Harald Greycloak, by undertaking on Thorsteinn's behalf a tribute-collecting expedition, in the course of which he cures a sick girl by runic magic and kills 21 assailants single-handedly. Back in Iceland he composes two long poems on the death of two of his sons and in praise of Arinbjörn respectively. After assisting his third son Thorsteinn in a lengthy dispute with one Steinar, Egil in old age hides the two chests of silver, which, contrary to King Æthelstan's wishes, he had never shared with his family, and dies.

Egil's family history reflects the ambivalent relationship of Iceland to Norway, the mother country from which, as the saga has it, settlers of Iceland broke away in defiance of the king's power. The sense of contradiction in this relationship must have been felt by many Icelanders at the time of *Egils Saga*'s composition, with the aspira-tions of Icelandic chieftains to become part of the Norwegian royal aristocracy, from which they were nevertheless mostly excluded. The saga may be seen as a mythical narrative in which these contradictions are mediated by a central episode in Egil's career, his visit to York, which takes place on "neutral" ground (neither in Iceland nor in Norway), and in which Egil balances a poem in praise of King Eirík against his earlier blatant defiance of him with the impaled horse's head. The immobilization characteristic of the hero and/or villain, often a feature of such mediating episodes in myth, is apparent in the fact that Egil is initially held up in his composition of the poem by a swallow twittering at his window, most probably Queen Gunnhild in disguise, and in the fact that, as he recites the poem, King Eirík sits upright, glaring at him, a position reminiscent of that in which Egil had placed the horse's head. Forming a bridge between the second and third parts of the saga, to which the first part forms an introduc-tion, this episode brings together many of the central themes and preoccupations of the saga as a whole.

—Rory McTurk

EIN FESTE BURG
Hymn by Martin Luther, 1531 (written 1528?)

"Ein feste Burg," Martin Luther's song of faith and assurance, long deemed the "battle hymn of the Reformation," has achieved an acclaim paralleled by few hymns in Christian tradition. Luther sang this hymn in the Coburg fortress in 1530 and his associates drew comfort from it during their banishment in 1547. Johann Sebastian Bach based his *Cantata for the Feast of the Reformation* (1735) upon the hymn and also set the tune twice in his *Chorales*; Felix Mendels-sohn used the melody in his Fifth Symphony, as did Giacomo Meyerbeer in his opera *Les Huguenots*.

The hymn has been translated into some 200 languages (over 60 times in English alone) and figures in hymnals all over the world. Thomas Carlyle's rendering "A Safe Stronghold Our God Is Still" (1831) is the dominant version in Britain, while the translation by the Unitarian Frederic Hedge, "A Mighty Fortress Is Our God" (1853), provides the basis for the composite version used in Lutheran worship in North America.

The earliest recorded appearance of the hymn is in an Erfurt hymnal of 1531, but it probably first appeared in the no longer extant Wittenberg hymnal of the publisher Joseph Klug in 1529. The date of composition has been the subject of much speculation, but since Luther wrote hymns for congregational use rather than for self-expression, the hymn is likely to have been published shortly after its composition, probably in 1528. This accords with Luther's increasing understanding, evident in his translation, of Psalm 46 upon which the hymn is based.

"Ein feste Burg" describes the faith and assurance of Christians who are confident in the knowledge that God stands by them and will prevail in the cosmic battle fought over mankind by God and the devil. In four strophes of nine lines each, the hymn articulates Luther's theology in trenchant manner. Monosyllables abound, re-sulting in a rugged rhythm, and the sparing but vigorous use of adjectives enhances the hymn's pugnacious mood. Alliteration un-derscores qualities of both God and the devil, and there are verbal repetitions within the thematic parallels and antitheses between strophes which lend cohesion. The first strophe establishes the power of a sheltering, rescuing God, the mighty fortress, and pits against him the age-old adversary whose devices include force and cunning and whom none on earth can match. In the second strophe, human powerlessness is resolved in the saving work of the proper champion, Christ, who will prevail in battle. However menacing the forces of evil, Christians have no cause for fear because the devil's threats are vain. The third strophe affirms that judgement has already been passed upon him, while the final strophe proclaims the certainty of victory, for the Word of God will prevail. Here the only action required of human beings is stated: to have faith in Christ and renounce worldly goods.

Luther's text is a free adaptation of Psalm 46: verbal parallels are not numerous. The disasters which befall Creation in the Psalm, mountains crashing into the sea, are transmuted into the assaults of the devil upon humankind. Interpreting the Psalms, through the perspec-tive of the New Testament, as valid for the Christian faithful, Luther treats Psalm 46 as the voice of the Church proclaiming its faith in an all-powerful God whose work of redemption is done, but ongoing; this yields an eschatological dimension to the hymn. The devil does not appear in the Psalm but derives from St. Paul's account of the warfare of the faithful Christian in Ephesians 6:10–17, which Luther brings to bear upon the Psalm. The application to Christ of the Old Testament title "Sabaoth" (Lord of the Heavenly Hosts) in strophe two emphasizes the hymn's Christological dimension, in which the three persons of the Trinity figure in succession. The Holy Spirit is conjoined with Christ, The Word, in strophe four, and the hymn depicts the whole history of salvation from the Fall (strophe one) to the threats of the Antichrist (strophes three and four). It has been argued that the final strophe is a later addition which alters the character of the hymn, but a Christological interpretation of the work confirms its unity.

Reformation hymns share with secular songs of the period formu-laic melodic frameworks, have expressive devices associated with specific modes, and copy typical melodic openings and conclusions. In this way a hymn could seem both familiar and yet original and creative. The melody of "Ein feste Burg" seems to have been composed by Luther himself. The hymn is in repeat-serial barform: the opening couplet is repeated, contrasting material makes up the bulk of the second half of the strophe, and elements of the opening recur at the conclusion. The hymn is in the Ionian mode, a recently developed melodic structure which governed the permissible span of notes employed in the range of the octave; to this mode belong also other, personal hymns of Luther: ''Ein neues Lied wir heben an'' (''A New Song We Raise''), ''Vom himel hoch'' (''From Heaven Above''), and ''Vater unser'' (''Lord Jesus Christ, True Man and God''), as well as French and Italian secular songs. For all that he deployed traditional elements (text and music) to produce contrafacta for most of his hymns, Luther was very much up-to-date in his composition. Melodically ''Ein feste Burg'' is characterized by its stepwise descent over the whole octave in the first two lines (and therefore repeated; see also ''Ein neues Lied wir heben an'') and a similar octave descent in the final line (so also ''Vom himel hoch''). This octave-space technique, deemed a personal feature of Luther's style, is known also as the ''Reformation-cadence.'' The hymn's other melodic feature is its confident, emphatic rhythmical opening, with repetition of notes at the top of the range. There have been repeated, inconclusive attempts to identify specific occasions for the work's composition, but this hymn is not directed against Catholics, Turks, Zwinglians, or any specific adversaries; at stake rather is the steadfast Christian community assailed by the temptations of the devil, yet certain of God's succour. Nonetheless the defiant tone issuing forth has caused ''Ein feste Burg'' to be regarded from the outset as a denominational battlesong. From as early as 1531 a peasant parody is recorded (''And if the world were full of priests, yet they shall not oppress us''), and in 1579 Johann Fischart refers in his *Bienenkorb* (Beehive) to the Lutherans as *''Festeburgsinger.''* Given the combative nature of Luther himself and the constant threats to his Reformation, the aspect of confrontation is not easily excluded from the meaning of the hymn. In 1834 Heinrich Heine called the hymn ''the Marseillaise of the Reformation,'' and it was deployed in a military nationalistic sense in the ''Luthercult'' of Wilhelmine Germany during World War I. After the term ''das Reich'' (the Kingdom of God) in the final line was misused during Hitler's regime, the function and meaning of the hymn have been reassessed in contemporary Germany. The kettle-drums and trumpets or oboes which accompany the voices in Bach's *Cantata* (BWV 80) embody the confidence and force of ''Ein feste Burg'' at its finest.

—Lewis Jillings

THE ELDER EDDA

See THE POETIC EDDA

ELECTIVE AFFINITIES (Die Wahlverwandtschaften)
Novel by Johann Wolfgang von Goethe, 1809

August Wilhelm von Schlegel's pronouncement ''Not to know Goethe, is to be a Goth'' is applicable particularly to those unacquainted with *Elective Affinities* which, Johann Wolfgang von Goethe insisted, was his best work. It has been called an infinite masterpiece; Thomas Mann regarded it as the most sublime novel of the Germans; Rilke wept an entire evening after he had read it. *Elective Affinities* has also been called immoral and dangerous, a book that makes a mockery of marriage. It is a work of mystery and ambiguity and no

other work of Goethe, perhaps not even Faust, has been as variously interpreted. It is a modern study of love and duty and guilt and renunciation. Goethe portrays the conflicts between marriage and passion, between Classicism and Romanticism. It is also a novel about the contemporary superficial Weimar society and its loose morals. It is a novel of marriage and spiritual adultery.

Like all of Goethe's writings, *Elective Affinities* can be considered an autobiographical fragment. Goethe maintained that he never could invent, that his power of imagination was never as vivid as reality. He writes that in his novel ''No one will fail to recognize a deep passionate wound that is hesitant to heal, a heart that is afraid to convalesce.'' Here we have a *Werther* novel of the married author: but instead of resorting to suicide, the hero renounces. Goethe was 60 when he wrote *Elective Affinities*. Three years earlier he had decided to marry Christiane Vulpius, his companion of 18 years, out of gratitude for her brave behaviour in protecting him from soldiers invading his house. Shortly after the marriage, however, he suddenly fell in love with 18-year-old Minna Herzlieb, and, as was the case with most of his passions, the sublimation was transformed into poetry. As a married man Goethe had to become an earnest and emphatic critic of the laxity of morals: the sanctity and indissolubility of marriage must be preserved, the values of society must be upheld, yet love as a force of nature triumphs; passion, although punished, is glorified.

The novel is divided into two parts, each consisting of 18 chapters; the novel's duration is 18 months: from spring, the season of youth and fermenting passion, to autumnal silence and the season of chrysanthemums, one and a half years later. The title of the novel is explained in the fourth chapter of Part I: *attractio electiva* is a technical expression taken from 19th century science to describe the affinity between certain elements in chemistry and applied by Goethe to human relationships to explain magical attractions, elemental and magnetic natural forces that cannot be resisted. In *Elective Affinities* the situation involves the emotional relationship between four people: Charlotte and Eduard (actually named Otto)—the A and B of our chemical formula—and Ottilie and the captain (also named Otto), the C and D elements. In chemistry these elective affinities—A will be attracted to B, just as B will be to C, leading to new combinations— are predestined and unavoidable. When these terms are transferred to personal relationships, passion and attraction may result with the same force. Whereas inanimate substances, however, obey the laws of nature, civilized human beings can choose behaviour, they can yield to eros or they can renounce on moral and ethical principle. Charlotte and Eduard, our A and B, belong to the country nobility; they are of an early middle age, just recently married (for the second time), without money worries, financially secure; they spend their days in leisurely activities of gardening, building, making music. Charlotte is a pragmatic, disciplined, prudent woman who, above all, wishes to preserve order and stability. From her domestic realm she wants to remove all dangers and disarray and lead a life of quiet responsibility. Eduard, on the other hand, is impetuous and self-indulgent, a narcissistic dilettante whose life of leisure has become tedious, and in the first chapter already we witness his restlessness. Invited, reluctantly on Charlotte's part, to their country estate, are C and D, Ottilie, the orphaned niece, adolescent, fragile, ethereal, and the captain, an old friend of Eduard's, sober, responsible and correct. These two have been asked to share the leisurely long hours, to celebrate birthdays, to plant and prune and build and to make music and indulge in a comfortable idleness, which inevitably lead to inextricable emotional turmoil. Eduard's fatal fascination with Ottilie, his soul-mate, is revealed in their mysteriously similar handwriting, their complementary migraine headaches, their harmonious music-making, the symbolic intertwining of their initials on a goblet. All are signs of their spiritual kinship. In the characters of Eduard and Ottilie, Goethe explored and revealed his interest in Romanticism, in the supernatural, in the realm of fantasy and the miraculous; but he criticized it severely and rejected it. Charlotte and the captain, equally drawn to one another, recognize the dangerous path the free-spirited Eduard and Ottilie have undertaken and are not willing to imitate their companions' excessive and impatient behaviour. They renounce in order to prevent the disintegration of society. Not until after the tragic accident of the drowning of Charlotte's and Eduard's child, a Euphorion figure, a child conceived in moral adultery, the victim of immoderation, does Ottilie withdraw into silence and renunciation. All that remains for Eduard is to follow the inimitable, to be drawn upward and on by the eternally feminine, in a scene reminiscent of the end of the final image in *Faust*.

The novel has been said to deal with the question of the waning of vitality, of the decaying of human relationships, of the tension between the classical conception of man who determines his own fate and the romantic conception of his failure to do so, of the struggle between order and chaos, between old age and youth, between marriage and eros. In *Elective Affinities* order is sought but not attained. Goethe maintained that his novel should be read three times. Each reading will offer new interpretations, insights, and pleasures.

—Renate Latimer

ELECTRA
Play by Euripides, c. 422–16 BC

Though the Athenian tragedians regularly made use of the same myths, the Electra story is unique in offering a direct comparison between the styles and techniques of Aeschylus, Sophocles, and Euripides. The middle play of Aeschylus' *Oresteia* trilogy, *The Libation Bearers* (*Choephoroi*) begins and ends at the same point in the story of the house of Atreus as do the *Electras* of Sophocles and Euripides. *The Oresteia* was first produced in 458 BC, but no firm date can be given for either *Electra*. If scholarly opinion is divided over whether the Sophocles or the Euripides came first, there is general agreement that both were performed about the years 416–413 BC.

Such details are of more than simple academic interest in the case of Euripides' *Electra* because it contains certain sequences which appear to parody the handling of similar ideas by Aeschylus. After the murder of Agamemnon by Clytemnestra and her lover Aegisthus, the baby Orestes was sent into exile to prevent him growing up to avenge his father. His sister Electra remained at home and grew up as an outcast, deprived of status but longing for her brother's return. Euripides' version is set before a humble farmhouse and opens with a prologue from a peasant farmer who reveals that Electra has been married off to him but that he has declined to consummate the marriage out of respect.

Electra is an embittered figure who undertakes unnecessary household chores and rejects any attempts to rebuild her life, yearning only for the return of Orestes to punish her oppressors. When he does arrive, accompanied by Pylades whose family has raised him, Orestes

proves to subscribe little to the picture of heroic avenger that Electra has envisaged. The key recognition scene between brother and sister, which Aeschylus places early in *The Libation Bearers* and which Sophocles delays in order to set up the plot against Clytemnestra without Electra's involvement, happens almost by accident when a diffident Orestes is recognized by the old man who rescued him as a baby.

That Euripides intended his audience to make a comparison with Aeschylus' treatment of the recognition is made abundantly clear when the old man suggests to Electra that Orestes must have visited Agamemnon's tomb in secret. He offers the exact recognition tokens, a lock of hair, footprints, and a piece of woven cloth, that once served to persuade Aeschylus' Electra that her brother had indeed returned. Euripides' Electra scornfully rejects all such tokens on practical grounds. She is only convinced when the old man confronts the two strangers and recognizes a scar on Orestes' brow. Then and only then does Orestes confess who he is and Electra is forced to admit that this reluctant avenger is the brother on whom she has pinned all her hopes.

This echo, pastiche even, of a previously familiar version of the story is typical of Euripides' approach throughout the play. Audience expectation is constantly confounded as all the characters turn out to be other than they seem. Orestes is a coward, driven to murder Aegisthus and then his mother by the combined pressures of his sister, his companion, and the old man. He chooses the least honourable method possible, accepting an invitation from Aegisthus to take part in a sacrifice as an honoured guest, then cutting him down from behind. Clytemnestra, one of the great villainesses of mythology, is treated with some sympathy. Invited by Electra to attend her after the supposed birth of a child, she shows regret for her past life but is unceremoniously hacked to death by her children, Orestes with his eyes covered by his cloak.

In such a vicious telling of the story, though one whose realism is thoroughly plausible, Electra is the real driving force. Obsessed and obsessive, her sanity hangs by a thread which snaps when her mother is finally dispatched. Where Aeschylus had created a subdued victim and Sophocles the wreck of a noble character, Euripides' Electra is a monster, the true daughter, perhaps, in dramatic terms, of Aeschylus' Clytemnestra. Even the chorus of local girls, initially well-disposed and friendly, appears by the end of the play to have turned from her. It is left to Castor and Pollux, the heavenly twin brothers of Clytemnestra and Helen, to arrive as *dei ex machina* and restore the myth to a more traditional ending.

This conscious iconoclasm is a regular part of Euripides' dramatic technique and is frequently used for comic effect. The peasant husband is roundly told off by the shrewish Electra for inviting ''superiors'' to dinner only to respond that ''a woman can surely find enough to fill their guts for one meal.'' Electra's warning to her mother to take care not to dirty her dress as she enters their cottage is particularly macabre when she knows that Orestes is waiting inside to murder Clytemnestra.

Euripides' *Electra* shows the story to be a bloody and unheroic episode in an unsavoury and savage saga. Human passion is the only driving force and religious sanction is sidelined. Extreme violence is fringed with domestic trivia and the blackness of the humour anticipates the Jacobean world of Webster or Middleton. As an antidote to the heroics of Aeschylus and Sophocles it has a supreme and precocious dramatic power.

—J. Michael Walton

ELECTRA
Play by Sophocles, c. 418–410 BC (?)

Sophocles' *Electra*, treating similar events to Aeschylus' *The Libation Bearers* (*Choephoroi*) and Euripides' *Electra*, occupies the middle ground with its innovations and emphasis on characterization. Aeschylus and Euripides were concerned with the legality and the criminal aspect of murder within the household; Sophocles shifted emphasis from Orestes' predicament to Electra's experience and anguish. Her role, extended and fundamentally lyrical, is one of the most demanding in Greek tragedy. The chorus and the choral odes lack distinction. The indecisive morality and marginal tragic nature of the action may indicate that the play was prosatyric, after the pattern of Euripides' *Alcestis*.

The play opens at Mycenae with Orestes, his companion Pylades, and an elderly Paedagogue, harbinger of the "clever slave" of New Comedy. Electra's thoughts and words run counter to the need for action; her mourning for Agamemnon's death, ten years ago, is shared by the chorus of local women and portrays her essential weakness: her dependence on her father (rather than on Clytemnestra) and her solitary role (*electra* = "unwedded"). Her hopes reside in Orestes. Aegisthus, the sole murderer of Agamemnon in Sophocles' version, is her arch enemy. Chrysothemis, her sister, favours compromise over righteous indignation and so quarrels with Electra. She carries libations to Agamemnon's tomb to allay Clytemnestra's distressing dream involving Agamemnon and Aegisthus. The chorus's appeal to Justice and prayer for an end of suffering derives from Aeschylus' trilogy. The confrontation of Clytemnestra and Electra explores the rationale for the murder of Agamemnon. Electra counters with charges of lust and injustice on her mother's part. The Paedagogue's news of Orestes' death at a chariot race provides a brilliant account of hair-raising anger at the centre of the play. Clytemnestra's maternal grief is a pretence to cover her sense of relief, but the lament for Orestes (technically a *kommos*, a dirge shared by an actor and the chorus) is deeply moving. Chrysothemis brings new libations to Agamemnon's tomb and discovers a lock of hair, still unidentified. Electra and Chrysothemis decide on retributive action, to kill Aegisthus. The return of Orestes and Pylades excites Electra's celebrated lament over the urn containing her brother's alleged ashes. Chrysothemis returns with the glad tidings that the report of Orestes' death is greatly exaggerated! Orestes recognizes Electra and is greatly distressed by her affliction; he clinches her recognition of her brother by the use of a signet ring. Joy and rapture reign supreme. Electra appeals to Artemis or to Ares for assistance in the impending murder.

Orestes and Pylades proceed to the murder of the mother, and Aegisthus, marred by a brutal, authoritarian nature, is doomed. Electra's presence outside the palace door waiting for the repetition of the death blow marks a distinct shift from her characterization in Aeschylus' *The Libation Bearers*. The play ends with all of the problems resolved, with Justice restored, without recourse to Furies or a trial by jury or assembly, the recourse of Aeschylus and Euripides respectively.

Melodramatic elements, deep-dyed villainy, and deception, support the identification of the play as pro-satyric. Electra's addiction to daydreaming and to words over action contrasts with Orestes' energetic behaviour, prompted and supported by Apollo. From the theatrical standpoint, the play is distinguished by the "messenger" speech, Electra's lament over the urn, and the recognition scene. The chorus

fails to measure up to the intensity of Electra's hatred for her mother: their roles as bystanders make them less interesting.

—Alexander G. McKay

EMILE (Émile; ou, De l'éducation)
Fiction by Jean-Jacques Rousseau, 1762

Emile, subtitled as a treatise on education, is the first great modern work of developmental psychology, synthesizing the view, arising in association with the growth of school systems in early modern Europe, that childhood, like the interest of the educator, should be considered as extending to the end of adolescence. The concomitant idea that childhood develops in distinct stages (the infant without speech, the child with speech, the mature child within an excess of energy over needs, and the adolescent) is the basis of the work's organization into its first four books. To this synthesis of early modern views, *Emile* adds the more radical proposition that the child has an entirely distinct nature from that of the adult, and has the right to develop and enjoy that nature to the full and consequently to be protected not only from the influences of modern society (which Jean-Jacques Rousseau regards as irredeemably corrupt and to be resisted) but also, as determined by the law of stages, from precocious development of its own powers. Provocatively, Rousseau describes the application of these notions of appropriateness and protectiveness as "negative education," which is sometimes interpreted as an injunction to "leave the child alone." However, it is clear that these principles imply a high degree of attention, and intervention, by the educator, so much so that other interpreters have taxed Rousseau with "manipulation"! A most difficult, and important, aspect of the work is the conception of the individual (here the child) as separate from, and indeed opposed to, the society in which it develops. This notion is perhaps Rousseau's single most significant contribution to Romanticism, and this in a work which, with *A Discourse on Inequality*, he himself describes as setting out the core of his philosophy. That core is the opposition of Nature to Society.

At one level this opposition constitutes an "anthropological dualism," whereby Rousseau envisages two distinct modes of human subjectivity: first ("natural man" or the uncorrupted child), a mode where the individual is totally self-contained, "solitary," or living only for itself (even if in proximity to others); and second (the adult of developed society), a mode in which the individual lives typically "in the opinion of others," deriving therefrom all essential goals and sense of self-worth. While *A Discourse on Inequality* presents only the first mode as legitimate, *Emile*, at another level, attempts to validate the second mode by evoking in Book IV (on adolescence and the entry of the child into social life) norms of society (or "living in the opinion of others") that contrast with actual social practice. This involves a reversal of educative method: whereas, in Books I and III, Rousseau is concerned with guaranteeing the child's autonomy and true perception of the world by insisting, under the influence of the philosophies of Locke and Condillac, on direct sensory experience of surrounding realities (the "education of things" as opposed to book-learning by rote), in Book IV, by contrast, the adolescent is to be protected against his own precocious sexual development by "arms-length" instruction from the educator (including instruction through books) about the realities of social and moral life that await him. The

principle of protection remains, but with new methodological consequences. The key factor in the child's move from one mode of being
to another is his imagination, understood in the old rationalist sense of
the power to "project" new (and usually illusory) objects of desire
and wants, over and above the basic appetites essential to survival.
Such wants are potentially limitless, and Book IV argues that they
must be checked by keeping the real condition of Emile's milieu
constantly before his intelligence. The early drafts of the work
(particularly what is known as the Favre manuscript) reveal some
perplexity concerning the treatment of Emile's sexuality: is it an
inexorable bodily function developing from within or is it one of the
many aspects of social life that depend on the activation of imagination? Rousseau finally adopts the second position, which gives the
educator and moralist maximum scope. He opines that if imagination
(in the sense of the projection of wants) did not function, then the
child would remain sexually inactive to the end of its days.

Emile thus pictures an alternative (normative or ideal) growth of
the individual in contrast to what generally happens in real society. In
that sense it is a pendant to *The Social Contract*—an account of
legitimate society and government in contrast to corrupt everyday
political society pictured at the end of *A Discourse of Inequality*. The
relation of *Emile* to *The Social Contract*, is however, a problem: must
a choice be made, as the opening lines of the work say, between
educating Emile for himself and making a citizen for a particular
state, or, as is suggested by his educative travels at the end of Book VI,
does Emile emerge capable of being the citizen of any state? At all
events, with both works, Rousseau ran into trouble (and eventual
exile) over the issue of religion. Book IV of *Emile* includes the
separately drafted *Confession of Faith of a Savoyard Curate*, the
presence of which proclaims his conviction that there can be no sound
morality in the absence of religious belief. This interpolated text
propounds a doctrine of natural religion and (unitarian) Christian
theism that was bound to upset Calvinist and Catholic orthodoxies
alike: Christ's miracles are doubtful, God's self-revelation in the
world is not historically unique but ongoing, and, so far from being
indoctrinated by catechisms when children, young people, in close
consultation with their real and intimate friends, should decide on
their religious stance at the approach of adulthood and maturity.

More controversial still for the modern reader is Book V: "Sophie,
or Woman." Its opening lines state that in everything not pertaining
to her sex, Sophie is a man, hence the principles of Books I–IV apply.
However, it emerges that woman's differences (and a leitmotif of
Rousseau's philosophic output is the respect for difference) destine
her for domesticity and ultimate obedience to a husband. This is a
typical 18th-century view, though, and so less essential a weakness
than the fact that Book V takes *Emile*, which is a utopian fiction
already, into the world of the sentimental novel. We follow Sophie's
preparation of life as a wife, her courtship and eventual marriage to
Emile and, in a sequel called *Emile and Sophie*, subsequent unfaithfulness and reconciliation (with capture by Barbary corsairs in
between). The utopian fictional aspect of *Emile* is on the other hand an
essential part of its force. Rousseau does not expect his ideas to be
applied literally according to the examples which, at all points, he
gives. Rather the fiction of a Tutor and his pupil Emile illustrates key
concepts in human nature and education. Its function is philosophical
and not practical: practice will depend on circumstances. The point is
made explicitly several times. It is true, nevertheless, that many of the
illustrative examples, including famous negative ones like the rejection (for children) of La Fontaine's *Fables*, have a verve and air of
practicality that might tempt the reader, wrongly, to treat the text as an
educational manual.

—Philip E.J. Robinson

THE EMPEROR'S NEW CLOTHES
Story by Hans Christian Andersen, 1837

Hans Christian Andersen wrote this story, about a vain emperor
who would rather spend his time in his dressing room than in the
Council Chamber, in 1837, borrowing the plot from a Spanish tale. It
is one of his most popular stories and has been translated into at least
25 languages. The story tells how one day two rascals come to the
emperor, claiming to be the best of weavers. Not only was their cloth
unusually beautiful, but clothes made from it were invisible to
everyone who was either incompetent or exceedingly stupid.

The emperor thought this was an excellent opportunity to learn who
was stupid and incompetent and who was not, so he employed the two
impostors. They immediately began work, asking for the finest silk
and gold, which they put in their bags, while they pretended to work
on the empty loom. After a while, the emperor wanted to know how
much they had done but, as he was a little hesitant about going
himself, he sent his old and trusted Prime Minister. The old man
looked at the loom and saw nothing. He was not, however, about to
admit to this, because he did not believe himself to be either
incompetent or stupid. Thus he praised the invisible cloth and
memorized the weaver's description of it. A little later the emperor
sent another trusted statesman who also pretended to see the fabric in
the empty loom. Everyone was talking about the marvellous cloth.
Finally, the emperor himself, together with a select group of trusted
advisers, went to see the weavers who demonstrated the "fantastic
fabric." Everyone, including the emperor, pretended to see the
beautiful cloth and it was decided that the emperor was to wear the
clothes made from it at the next great parade.

Soon the rascals set out to make the clothes and, when the day for
the parade arrived, the emperor stepped out on the street stark naked,
under the banner heading the parade. Everybody admired his new
clothes and commented on how magnificent they looked, until a little
child said: "But he has no clothes at all." Soon people began to
whisper to each other what the innocent child had said. The whispers
grew louder until all the people shouted the truth. The emperor
himself believed them to be right but nevertheless finished the parade
in style.

This ending was an afterthought, as Andersen initially ended the
story with everyone admiring the new clothes. Not until he had sent
the manuscript to the printer did he come upon the present ending. A
major change from the original Moorish version was the quality of the
cloth itself. In the original it was invisible to any man not a son of his
presumed father, which makes it a tale about men's fear and suspicions about women's fidelity and trustworthiness and their power
over men's honour. Andersen, however, made it a tale about human
weakness in a more general sense. To borrow some phrases from Bo
Grønbech, he made it a tale about how people are afraid of other
people's opinion, how people are afraid to see things as they are, and
how people do not dare to be honest to themselves. Interestingly, in
Andersen's tale it is the adults who believe in magic, and the child
who sees reality.

''The Emperor's New Clothes'' has posed a special challenge to illustrators, despite being a popular subject. How, after all, do you draw an emperor without clothes? A popular solution, particularly with the earlier illustrators such as Vilhelm Pedersen, was to picture him in his undershirt, decently covering his body down to his knees. Some early illustrators did show the emperor naked, but placed members of the crowd so that decency was maintained. Arthur Rackham drew him in silhouette, somewhat ridiculous with a fat stomach. The tale's potential for political satire was used by a Czech artist in 1956 who pictured the emperor as a fat pig. A 1923 woodcut from Germany displays mean and power-hungry faces on the emperor and his retinue.

As time has progressed and the rules about decency have become more relaxed, the emperor has become gradually more naked. In a number of children's books from the 1980s he is a fat, jovial ruler with bare buttocks. It should be remembered, however, that Anderson's emperor kept his dignity even as the whisperings around him grew stronger, and continued the parade carrying himself more proudly than ever. Thus, while he did not set out to be a good role model for emperors and others, he ended up as such.

—Torborg Lundell

ENDGAME (Fin de partie)
Play by Samuel Beckett, 1957

Over four years elapsed between the premiere of *Waiting for Godot* and that of Samuel Beckett's next play, *Endgame*, in April 1957. The plays share some similar features particularly in the ratio of three down-like characters to one ''serious'' character. In *Endgame* the paralyzed blind man, Hamm, is central, and dictates the overall tone of the play.

Of the four characters, Hamm's servant, Clov, is the only one who can walk. Confined to an armchair, which is on castors, Hamm orders him about, depending on him to push the armchair into different positions, while Hamm's ancient parents, Nagg and Nell, are confined to bobbing up and down in their dustbins. The interdependence of master and servant is reminiscent of that between Pozzo and Luck in *Godot*; Hamm and Clov are similarly interdependent—Hamm can't stand, while Clov can't sit. But the restrictions on movement limit possibilities for the kind of knockabout comedy that was so important in the earlier play. Clov, like Lucky, rushes frantically about, mostly in obedience to orders from his master, fetching whatever Hamm wants, appearing whenever he's whistled for, fetching, carrying, climbing up and down ladders. Beckett is inventive within the limits he sets for himself, but these are so narrow that the play seems to contain much less physical action than *Godot*.

Blind from the beginning of the play—Pozzo goes blind halfway through *Godot*—Hamm is in some ways like a god who has abdicated control of a world that is rapidly approaching its end. All he can do is wait, with the few other survivors, for non-entity to supervene. The powerful central image is derived from chess, and we have to watch the game from the viewpoint of the players, understanding why neither Hamm nor Clov can merely walk away from the chess-board, though both wish the stalemate could be checkmate. Allusions to *Oedipus* and *King Lear* suggest that art is part of the game which is ending, but the text is mined with self-deflating devices that discourage us from regarding it as art.

HAMM: We're not beginning to . . . to . . . mean something?
CLOV: Mean something! You and I, mean something! (*Brief laugh*) Ah that's a good one!

The action is less circular than that of *Godot*. Both plays move in the direction of an indeterminate viewpoint situated somewhere outside space and time, but the set of *Endgame* presents an outsized visual pun that admits the possibility of equating the action with life inside the brain. Two windows can be taken to represent eyes and Clov's opening the curtains and removing the dust-sheet that has been covering Hamm parallels the process of waking up in the morning. The two dustbins that house Hamm's parents are like receptacles for useless memories of the past.

There are many built-in contradictions, and the evidence that supports an equation between Hamm and God is counterweighted by indications that he represents the void:

HAMM: I was never there.
CLOV: Lucky for you. (*He looks out of the window*)
HAMM: Absent, always. It all happened without me. I don't know what's happened.

Underneath his dark glasses, his eyes have gone all white, and seeing nothing, he can see nothingness.

The play progresses by cancelling itself out; there are sequences that appear to have no function except to discredit the vision which has already been presented. Hamm talks about a madman who thought the end of the world had come:

I'd take him by the hand and drag him to the window. Look! There! All that rising corn! And there! Look! The sails of the herring fleet! All that loveliness! (*Pause*) He'd snatch away his hand and go back into his corner, Appalled! All he had seen was ashes.

When Clov looks out of the window, he reports ''nothing'' and ''zero,'' but if Hamm is mad to think the world is ending, Clov may be no more than a function of his madness.

At the end of the play, the appearance of a small boy contradicts all the indications we have been given that nothing has survived outside. Not that we have to choose between these mutually exclusive versions of the overall situation. Beckett maroons us between them. The play fights abrasively against our habit of assuming that information contained in dialogue and action should be self-consistent, that a situation should be coherent, that a character must seem to exist as a whole personality, that the total work of art represents ''reality.''

Occasionally it is the words that contradict each other, as when Hamm says: ''The bigger a man is the fuller he is . . . And the emptier.'' More often it is the indications about situation and action that cancel each other out. What's going on in the world outside the space we're watching? The contradictions have the effect of making the words more like objects in their own right and less like component elements in a theatrical reproduction of reality. In an article about painting, Beckett wrote ''each time that one wishes to make words do a true work of transference, each time one wishes to make them express something other than words, they align themselves in such a way as to cancel each other out.'' In *Endgame* he encouraged them in this tendency.

—Ronald Hayman

ENVY (Zavist')
Novel by Yury Olesha, 1927

Envy is Yury Olesha's most important work. Published in 1927, at the time of the relative literary freedom in the Soviet Union, it placed Olesha among the top young Russian writers after the revolution. As practically all writers, he could not escape the demands of the new life brought on by the change of the political system. Olesha related this confrontation with the new order in a highly artistic manner in *Envy* and other works, by creating two camps facing each other—the old and the new. The old world is represented by Ivan, an elderly vagabond, who lives in his world of fantasy, believing that fantasy is the beloved of reason. He refuses to accept the new world of the machines; in fact, he dreams of inventing a machine that would kill all other machines. Ivan also bemoans the loss of feelings and wants to organize a conspiracy of feelings and to lead "the last parade of the ancient, human passions." His wrath is directed against his own younger brother Andrey, "the new Soviet man," who manages the food industry trust and whose goal is to make nourishing, clean, and inexpensive food. Needless to say, he returns the hatred of his brother and desires to kill him. Both Babichevs have their young followers. Andrey is imitated by Volodya, an ambitious engineering student and accomplished soccer player, who calls himself a human machine and a heavy industry man, and wants to be the Thomas Edison of the 20th century. Ivan is looked upon by Kavalerov, a young drifter, who was picked drunk from a gutter by Andrey but, instead of gratitude, Kavalerov hates him and all he stands for. At the same time, however, Kavalerov realizes that he actually envies Andrey and Volodya, for he too wants success now but cannot achieve it because of his inner make-up. The ensuing split personality prevents him from achieving anything of importance and relegates him to the lower strata of society forever.

In *Envy* Olesha also created a visible and invisible world, the visible being pragmatic, utilitarian, and utterly materialistic, creating a new way of life and a new man personified in Volodya. The invisible world, based on fantasy and feelings, prefers Shakespeare over sausage, so to speak. Because the visible world has the upper hand, Ivan and Kavalerov are doomed to defeat. The fact that Kavalerov wants to be a part of both worlds but fails, makes his downfall that much more tragic. Thus, collectivism triumphs over individualism. Olesha has tackled this theme in other works as well, so that he is often dubbed by critics as a one-theme writer. Moreover, *Envy* has been rewritten into a play entitled *Conspiracy of Feelings*.

In reality, the confrontation of the two camps reflects Olesha's own confrontation with the new world. He was not averse to accepting the new world, but he was reluctant to abandon the old as the new rulers insisted upon. He himself was having great difficulties reconciling his own ideas and inclinations with the demands of the new way of thinking and writing. He voiced his dilemma at the first congress of the Soviet writers in 1934, pleading with the powers-that-be to let him follow his own artistic instincts since he could not abandon them for the sake of a blind acceptance of outside dictates. Olesha admitted that he is Kavalerov, whose envy of Andrey Babichev reflects Olesha's envy of those who easily accept the new, which he could not. Needless to say, his pleas fell on deaf ears and Olesha, one of the most talented and promising young writers in Russia in the 1920s, fell silent never to write anything else of substance for the rest of his life. Thanks to his artistic acumen, however, *Envy* remains one of the best literary testimonials of the struggle not only among the writers and intellectuals in Russia in the decade after the revolution and later, but in the entire world where the conflict between an individual and a restrictive society becomes a burning issue.

—Vasa D. Mihailovich

EPIC OF GILGAMESH

Ancient Sumerian poem cycle, later written down in Akkadian language of Babylonia (now Iraq). Oldest version exists on 12 stone tablets from the 7th century BC, discovered by A.H. Layard in Ninevah in the 1840s. The story of the eponymous hero is based on legends surrounding real-life ruler of Uruk of c. 2700 BC, and describes the adventures of Gilgamesh and his companion Enkidu.

PUBLICATIONS

Gilgamesh, translated by Derrek Hines, 2002.

*

Critical Studies: *The Babylonian Story of the Deluge and the Epic of Gilgamesh, with an Account of the Royal Libraries of Nineveh* by E.A.W. Budge, 1920; *The Gilgamesh Epic and Old Testament Parallels* by Alexander Heidel, 1949; *History Begins at Sumer*, 1956, and *The Sumerians: Their History, Culture, and Character*, 1964, both by Samuel Noah Kramer; *Gilgamesh et sa légende* edited by P. Garelli, 1960; *The Bible and the Ancient Near East: Essays in Honour of W.F. Albright*, 1961; *Sumerian Sources of the Epic of Gilgamesh* by Aaron Schaffer, 1963; "On the Sumerian Epic of Gilgamesh" by J.D. Bing, in *Journal of the Ancient Near Eastern Society of Columbia University*, 7, 1975; *The Treasures of Darkness* by Thorkild Jacobsen, 1976; *Das Gilgamesh-Epos* edited by K. Oberhuber, 1977; *L' Épopéé de Gilgamesh* by Abed Azrié, 1979; *The Evolution of the Gilgamesh Epic* by Jeffrey H. Tigay, 1982; *Enquête sur la Morte de Gilgamesh* by Yannick Blanc, 1991; *The Archetypal Significance of Gilgamesh: A Modern Ancient Hero* by Rivkah Scharf Kluger, 1991; *Gilgamesh and Akka* by Dina Katz, 1993; *Gilgamesh: A Reader*, edited by John Maier, 1997.

* * *

Gilgamesh is one of the oldest surviving literary epics. In its most complete form it is a compilation of the 7th century BC written in Akkadian (Old Semitic) on 12 tablets in the cuneiform script. This is a synthesis of older versions, the earliest written in the non-Semitic Sumerian language of Mesopotamia in the early 2nd millennium BC and probably based on oral traditions of the 3rd millennium. Other versions and fragments come from Hittite Anatolia, Syria, and Egypt. The 7th-century tablets were found at Nineveh in the library of Ashurbanipal, King of Assyria, by A.H. Layard in the 1840s; the first translation was attempted in 1872 by George Smith of the British Museum. Since then much fresh material has come to light and many translations have been made.

Gilgamesh was a historical king of Uruk, a city state in southern Iraq, who probably lived in the early 3rd millennium BC. From then until the fall of Nineveh in 612 he was remembered as a mighty hero throughout the Middle East. According to the epic tradition Gilgamesh was two parts god and one part man, inheriting from his mother, a minor goddess, beauty, strength, and ambition, and from his father mortality. According to the fullest Assyrian version, as a young king he oppressed the people till they complained to the gods who sent him a companion Enkidu, who is uncivilized "natural" man, and with whom he first fights, then forms a deep friendship. Together they go to the "Cedar Mountain" where they kill its monster guardian Humbaba, bringing back cedar-wood and a famous name. Gilgamesh is then wooed by the capricious goddess of love and war, Ishtar (Inanna in Sumerian). He rejects her and in revenge the goddess sends the "Bull of Heaven" to revenge the land. The two friends kill the bull but Enkidu fails sick and dies. Gilgamesh mourns his friend and in despair he sets out to find Utnapishtim the "Far Away," the Akkadian Noah, who alone survived the flood, to learn from him the secret of immortality. After much wandering in the wilderness he reaches the waters of death which he crosses with the help of the ferryman; but Utnapishtim gives him little comfort, though he recounts the story of the Flood (Tablet XI) which in the Sumerian is a separate account. Gilgamesh obtains a plant of "Eternal Youth," but it is stolen from him by a snake which promptly sheds its skin, so he returns to Uruk alone and empty-handed.

The diction of the Assyrian version is a loose rhythmic verse with four (in earlier versions two) beats to the line. The language is unadorned, with many repetitions but also with striking and memorable expressions. The overriding theme of the epic is the contrast between human aspirations and the reality of loss and death. Gilgamesh is a hero with whom it is possible to feel sympathy and human understanding in spite of the great age of the epic:

> Gilgamesh answered her, "And why should not my cheeks be starved and my face drawn? Despair is in my heart and my face is the face of one who has made a long journey, it was burned with heat and with cold. Why should I not wander over the pastures in search of the wind? My friend, my younger brother, he who hunted the wild ass of the wilderness and the panther of the plains, my friend, my younger brother who seized and killed the Bull of Heaven and overthrew Humbaba in the cedar forest, my friend who was very dear to me and who endured dangers beside me, Enkidu my brother, whom I loved, the end of mortality has overtaken him. I wept for him seven days and nights till the worm fastened on him. Because of my brother I am afraid of death, because of my brother I stray through the wilderness and cannot rest."

—N.K. Sandars

EPIGRAMS
Poems by Martial, late 1st century AD

The philosopher Seneca remarked, "magni artificis est clusisse totum in exiguo" (it is the mark of a great artist to have enclosed everything in a little space). Such an observation aptly applies to the maker of the epigram. Originally in Greek, the term *epigram* meant "to write on" something, but even in early times this term referred specifically to short, concise statements suitable to be carved and fitted upon a monument, pedestal, or tombstone. Of necessity, what was needed was an artful saying in a few brief lines that quickly got to the point. As a result, epigrams were admired as poetry for being able, despite their brevity, to build wittily to a climax at the close. Because terseness, wit, pungency, and point were called for, most epigrams tended to be satiric. We possess many a caustic epigram that a collector has preserved for us in the *Greek Anthology*.

Martial is by far the best known and most prolific of the Latin epigrammatists; he is the Roman satirist *par excellence*, dealing with urban scenes from a metropolitan culture. Society is eager for show, and corruption and deceit are part of the price civilization pays for its vanity and affectation. For instance:

> Thais habet nigros, niveos Laecania dentes.
> quae ratio est? emptos haec habet, illa suos.
>
> (Thais' teeth are black, Laecania's snowy white:
> What causes such extremes of day and night?
> One's true and tarnished, the other false—and bright.)

Here, the poet strikes a major satiric note about a world that is topsy-turvy in its values: honesty and truth are dark and dull and even beset by tooth decay. While the fake and the phoney gleam and glitter as if they were genuine. Satire often sharply reminds us that we live in an upside-down world where, in the words of W.B. Yeats, "The best lack all conviction while the worst / Are full of passionate intensity" ("The Second Coming"). Such a world is presented as being a carnival world, full of disguises, grotesquerie, and shallow pretence.

Thus the satirist's job, in his epigrams, is to lay bare this unnatural world with comic absurdity and acerbity. It is no accident that a number of Martial's poems address the unusual topic of an insect captured by chance in a drop of amber, so that it is enshrined inside a valuable piece of jewellery and curiously preserved for future ages to contemplate. This image is deftly analogous to the satirist's own practice in his epigrams. There, in a valuable poetic setting, are interred, "accidentally," all of society's typical, paltry, sordid, and ludicrous grubs—captured, when the poet is first-rate, forever. As Martial says, "solaque non morunt haec monumenta mori" (these monuments alone will never die).

Moreover, the satirist does not necessarily operate from deliberate malice. Indignation may fashion his verse, as Juvenal asserts, but his is often a spontaneous, even casual, gut reaction. One famous illustration of this response is Epigram 1.32:

> Non amo te, Sabidi, nec possum dicere quare:
> hoc tantum possum dicere, non amo te.
>
> (I dislike you, Sabidius; can't say why.
> But this I can say: I dislike you.)

The poem's very nonchalance is insulting; it implies that the poet hardly needs reasons for his aversion: Sabidius is the kind who exudes a general aura of unlikeableness. However, the poem also demonstrates satire's potency. In an instant, such verse can relegate an unknown into the arena of exposure and public ridicule.

Although Martial claims to spare the individual and only to denounce the vice (Epig. 10.33) and that his little barbs are innocent and harmless, his satire can be exceptionally personal and very poisonous indeed. And the fact that the satirist plays the naive innocent merely adds spice to his decoction.

Dotatae uxori cor harundine fixit acuta,
sed dum ludit, Aper. ludere novit Aper.

(Aper's arrow struck his wealthy wife in the heart;
But Aper is a good sport. Aper is merely making game.)

Here is society scandal at its most titillating. In an apparent archery ''accident,'' Aper has slain his opulent wife and become her heir. In reporting this juicy titbit, Martial never openly states that the sportsman committed a calculated slaughter; hence, Martial cannot be accused of libel. Rather, he merely drops hints wickedly, with outrageous puns, off-handed wit, and murderous irony. Needless to say, such rumour and *Fama* will spread like wildfire, and this satire's victim will be convicted of murder by innuendo. That is the power of satire.

Such are Martial's best achievements, and he has left us many: over 1,500 of his epigrams survive, arranged in 14 Books. They vary in length, from tightly honed poems of two lines to many of four, six or eight lines, a few running into 20 lines. Obviously, with such vast productivity, the quality of his poetry varies; as Martial himself justly concedes, some of his poems are good, some fair, and a host of them poor. But when his poetry is good, it is very good indeed. For Martial has given us lucid (and sometimes bawdy) satiric snapshots of almost all areas of society and life in a great capital city. Moreover, his work is almost never dull. That in itself is a considerable achievement.

—Anna Lydia Motto & John R. Clark

EREC AND ÉNIDE (Erec et Énide)
Poem by Chrétien de Troyes, c. 1160–70

Erec and Énide is the first of Chrétien de Troyes's romances, and one of the earliest Arthurian romances. Like most works of this type, it focuses not on King Arthur, but on one of the knights of the Round Table: in this case, Erec, son of Lac, a Breton king. Chrétien de Troyes claims to be writing this story in order to do away with mistakes made by previous storytellers, who ''usually mutilate and spoil'' tales. His version, he claims, ''will be remembered as long as Christianity endures.''

The poem, comprising 6,878 lines of rhymed couplets, can be divided into three sections: Arthur's and Erec's parallel hunts, which culminate in the marriage of Erec and Énide; the series of tests which Erec and Énide must endure to prove their love; and the Joy of the Court episode, which establishes their love firmly within their social setting. Integrated into these episodes are folkloric elements which were extremely popular in the oral tradition of the time.

The initial episode, that of the hunts, is, in itself, a unified tale. Arthur hunts the white stag in the hope of winning the traditional reward, a kiss from the fairest maiden in the court. Erec jousts for the beautiful sparrowhawk, for the reward of a lovely maiden of his own choosing. In doing so, he revenges himself on Yder, son of Nut, who has insulted him through his disrespect for the queen. Erec falls in love with and betroths himself to Énide, whom he takes back to Arthur's court, where she is admired by one and all.

Their wedding feast is sumptuous and is followed by a month's celebration. Marital bliss, however, causes Erec to forget his chivalric duties. Énide blames herself for this and begs her husband to prove himself once again by seeking further adventures. The two ride out

together and soon are obliged to affirm their love for one another: Erec, through battles with knights, a dwarf king, and others: and Énide, through various tests of wifely devotion.

The concluding episode, that of the Joy of the Court, features Erec's test in a fantastic garden, inhabited by a fair lady and a strong knight who is defending her, and decorated with a row of heads impaled on stakes and one horn. Erec and the knight, Mabonagrain, engage in battle. Finally yielding, Mabonagrain tells Erec the story of his imprisonment by the fair lady and asks him to blow the horn. Once Erec has done this, Mabonagrain is released from the garden, leaving only the lady, who is somewhat comforted when she learns that she is Énide's cousin. The poem ends with the crowning of Erec and Énide on Christmas Day.

While the three episodes can stand separately, they do flow easily from one to the other. The opening section characterizes Erec as a valorous knight by paralleling him structurally with Arthur. Énide, while appearing to be poor, displays noble attributes of beauty, modesty, and faithfulness. In the next section, the two display their worthiness and love through their tests. While they seem to be estranged for a while by their trials, their eventual reconciliation serves to strengthen the bond between them. The final episode allows them to prove their love even further, not just to each other, but to all the court as well. The earlier opposition of love and knightly duties fades as the two are joyfully accepted by their people as king and queen.

Chrétien de Troyes's first romance proved to be extremely popular. Shortly after its composition it was adapted into German by Hartmann von Aue, the traces of it can be seen in many other medieval works. It appears in Old Norse as the *Erex Saga,* and similarities to it can be seen in ''Gerain Son of Erbin,'' one of the tales in the Welsh *Mabinogion.* It was adapted by Alfred, Lord Tennyson in his *Idylls of the King* as ''Geraint and Enid.''

Not simply an adventure or a love story, *Erec and Énide* teaches that a balance must be reached between love and duty, and that both the man and the woman must share in seeking this equilibrium. Chrétien de Troyes weaves this lesson masterfully into a tale that is replete with both physical and psychological adventures, ably realizing his intention that ''it is right that all always aspire and endeavour to speak eloquently and to teach well.''

—Lisa M. Ruch

THE ETERNAL DICE (Los dados eternos)
Poem by César Vallejo, 1919

''The Eternal Dice'' exemplifies César Vallejo's mastery of poetic language and form, and the anguished yet irate voice of the poet who suffers for both himself and humankind at large. Published in 1919 in *Los heraldos negros*, it is included in the section subtitled ''Truenos'' [Thunderclaps].

Formally, ''The Eternal Dice'' shows Vallejo's characteristic tension between the regularity of classic verse-form and the irregularities (often more apparent than substantial) expressive of the thematic tensions mentioned above. In metrics, this poem is quite regular in that, with lines exclusively of seven and 11 syllables and its overall rhyme scheme (with the occasional unrhymed line), it fits the pattern of the *silva*, frequently used in the later Hispanic Golden Age (roughly the 16th–17th centuries). Yet this regularity is not total: the placement of the shorter lines is not regular (as the *silva* permits); the rhyme scheme varies with each stanza; nor is the stress-pattern uniform (for example, several initial syllables are stressed while the majority are not; the overall pattern of five stresses per line is violated, or at least pushed to the edge in line 17). The result is that the poem gives the impression of being freer in form than it actually is, an effect of which Vallejo was uniquely fond. This balance between order and disorder, reason and emotion in poetic form perfectly echoes the poem's principal themes.

This poem is highly representative of Vallejo in both form and theme. In his verse he struggled constantly to express the anguish of questions eternally unanswered, the search for a pattern amid the apparent chaos of life and a resolution of the multiple conflicts given to humankind as its ironic and even bitter birthright. In seeking such answers, Vallejo's speaker looks inward to the self, then outward to God, questioning and challenging both.

The rhetorical form of the poem is that of a prayer: the speaker addresses "My God" directly and repeatedly, in a tone at times supplicating but more often reproachful; hence the "prayer" becomes a blasphemy in which Vallejo finally inverts the traditional hierarchy to assert "And the man who suffers you: he is God!"

Yet the blasphemy born of the realization that God simply seems not to care alternates with the self-doubt and pain of both his personal suffering and his guilt. God continues as impassively detached from human lives, be they individual or universal, as the gambler from his opponent (the conflict, rather than co-operation, of gamblers is not coincidental to the poem). Hence the answers are not given, and the pain is unceasing.

"You have no Marys that abandon you" the poet reminds God, contrasting the faithful constancy of the Biblical Mary with the personal loss of a young woman beloved of Vallejo. He insists on his pain, in the hope God will listen, respond and (dare he hope?) heal. He contrasts his anguish with God's complacency—"Today, when there are candles in my witchlike eyes, / as in the eyes of a condemned man," and "I am weeping for the life that I live."

The pathos of this poem derives from the speaker's ongoing abandonment, doubt, and anguish, in the face of his intense desire to resolve them. So he feels anger when God remains distant, cold, and unmoved: "you feel nothing of your own creation." And as if in response to Einstein's assertion that God does not play dice with the universe, Vallejo says that He surely does: "and we will play with the old dice," "the Earth / is already a die nicked and rounded / from rolling by chance." Hence God is not only unmoved; he is a creator who coldly uses his own work for amusement and then, like Vallejo's María, leaves the scene having set in motion an eternity of pain and loss.

The poem's apparent simplicity belies a highly complex symbolism. Firstly, what does Vallejo mean when in line 1 he says he "weeps for the life" he lives? His individual anguish, to be sure; but also his identification with humankind, of whom his spirit is but a single manifestation. But this reality has still another corollary: the speaker is also a creation of God, in His image; a "thinking piece of clay" formed and inspired by the divinity of whom he is but a powerless parody, inferior and guilt-ridden.

Whence guilt? Line 2 gives numerous suggestions: "I am sorry to have stolen your bread." Herein the speaker alludes (as mentioned) to having human form and existence: limitations, inevitable death, flaws. He also admits that this form, as a caricature of the divine form, affirms his human inferiority. In addition, he expresses specific and personal guilt: he regrets having taken and eaten of God's bread

because had he not eaten it someone even more needy could have done so. Meeting one's needs, however legitimate they may be, implies someone else's inability to do so, and hence a crime of sorts against one's Other.

Line 2 is also a rejection of Holy Communion, for the speaker clearly feels unsaved; the Eucharist has not absolved him, but instead seems to have reaffirmed the falsehood, or at least the elusiveness, of Christianity's beautiful promises. Thus, the first stanza moves between guilt, pain, and anger; love of God and rejection; and from being identified with Him to cosmic abandonment. It presages the irresolution—Hell is, after all, stasis—of the composition, and life, as a whole.

What, then, is left to humanity? Pain even unto death, the only "resolution" Vallejo found until his political conversion in the 1930s. The earth, already described as a die, finally becomes rounded by use and age, wears away into nothingness and finally drops into an "enormous grave." God himself is portrayed as powerless, or unwilling, to set death aside, and chance itself is a lie, for it implies hope in a world without hope. Every cast of the die of the world can lead only to the universal grave (15–18, 23–24). The complex images of the third stanza verify this fate: "the circled eyes of Death will turn up, / like two final aces of clay." The "aces" cannot bring victory when the game is pre-ordained to be lost, and thus represent but another desperately false hope. They are made of mud to stress their incarnation of humanity's own fate ("from dust to dust," previously alluded to in the clay of line 3). Furthermore, the word "as" (ace) also alludes to a Roman coin, thus completing the circle of death, whose baggy eyes are already visible, by suggesting the ancient ritual of covering the eyes of the dead with coins. The final blasphemy of this poem, then, is that God is impotent, or unmoved, even in the glare of the cosmic tomb.

Finally, then, this poem protests against and even condemns a world that cannot be solved, that makes no sense: an apparent something that ends only in nothingness, and hence was never anything at all. God does not intervene in any meaningful way, nor does He care about his own creation's fate. Thus the poet finds himself even more abandoned than Christ, whose anguished "Why have you abandoned me?" reflected only temporary separation from the Godhead. But humanity's separation from the godliness to which we aspire is, *per* Vallejo, forever, and our permanent crucifixion on earth without meaning.

—Paul W. Borgeson, Jr.

EUGENE ONEGIN (Evgenii Onegin)
Novel by Aleksandr Pushkin, 1831 (written 1823–31)

The most famous work of Russia's national poet, *Eugene Onegin*, combining features of "an encyclopedia of Russian life" (Belinskii) and "a phenomenon of style" (Nabokov), is above all a chronicle of its author's life in literature, an elegant and sophisticated *ars poetica*.

The story, as with many Russian novels, is simple: Evgenii, a bored Petersburg fop, visiting the estate he has newly inherited, unwittingly wins the heart of his neighbour's charmingly shy daughter, Tat'iana, who, with far more experience of literature than life, confesses her love in a passionate letter, only to receive a dry lecture in return. Onegin, partly in reaction to his own behaviour, flirts outrageously with her far less sensitive sister Ol'ga, kills the latter's poet fiancé

Lenskii in an ensuing duel, and departs. When he returns to Petersburg after years of futile travel Onegin finds Tat'iana a sophisticated woman, married to a general, and a pillar of society. Though not indifferent to his impassioned declaration of love, she chooses fidelity and he is rejected for ever.

Eugene Onegin consists of eight chapters (or cantos), each with about 50 sonnet-like stanzas, so-called ''Onegin stanzas'' which comprise 14 iambic tetrameters ending in a couplet. The work's genre bears some resemblance to a mock epic combined with a Byronic poem such as *Beppo* (it was begun during Aleksandr Pushkin's Byronic period), but novelistic features are paramount. The mood changes noticeably in the course of the eight chapters (1823–31 was the richest period in the poet's creative life) from the effervescent, humorous, and highly referential description of Petersburg high life in the opening chapter to a more sombre, reflective narrative mood, albeit with many flashes of wit, in the later chapters. *Eugene Onegin* differs from a typical Byronic poem in various ways that are characteristic of the novel, such as, for instance, the wealth of major and minor characters, the use of letters, dreams, epigraphs to individual chapters, dialogue, and the mingling of conversations, authorial digressions, and detailed (if not encyclopedic) descriptions of many aspects of urban and rural life, from contemporary trading practices to card games and folk beliefs. Onegin and Tat'iana are characterized in psychological depth (for all Pushkin's constant lightness of touch, and despite the tolerant and humorous scepticism with which he describes fashionable society's attitude to the eligible young dandy), but Ol'ga and Lenskii are treated more superficially and satirically, the former so stereotyped as to require no description, the latter as a Germanized Romantic poet whose obscure and sluggish verses are the exact opposite of Pushkin's lightness and sparkle. The unusual, if not unique, genre of *Eugene Onegin* had virtually no direct imitators in Russian literature, but it may be observed that Pushkin's novel in verse had as much influence on the development of the 19th-century novel as did his prose works. Particularly notable is the contrast between a strong heroine and a weak or ''superfluous'' man that continued to figure in the novels of Lermontov, Turgenev, and Goncharov, among others. Also characteristic of later Russian novels is the relative open-endedness and lack of emphasis on the plot as such.

Like Mozart, to whom he has often been compared, Pushkin in *Eugene Onegin* combines subtle sophistication with apparent simplicity. The first chapter in particular is a *tour de force*, portraying a whole society with details of food, drink, fashions, manners, education, and much else, the specificity adding greatly to the reader's pleasure. Evgenii, as a much admired product of this society, clearly has something in common with Pushkin himself, though the author is always glad to distance himself from his hero. This does not prevent his introducing many personal digressions from the very start, some as short as one or two lines, on his own youthful experiences, sexual and alimentary tastes (the former with humour and discretion), his educational background, and, above all, his views on contemporary literature and aims in the novel. Throughout, the digressions, often embodied or culminating in a witty end-of-stanza couplet, far from being extraneous to the body of the novel are an integral part of it, and constitute a major part of its charm and fascination, enabling us to trace, among other things, Pushkin's literary development, his attitude to many of his contemporaries, and his changing views on such current obsessions as German philosophy and Romanticism.

Many attempts have been made to put *Eugene Onegin* into English verse, but none has achieved significant success, for the effortless rhymes and taut grace of Pushkin's iambic tetrameters too easily turn into doggerel in a non-inflexive language. The work is most easily approached through Tchaikovskii's opera which, however, replaces the novel's neo-classical elegance and scepticism with full-blown Romantic passion. As literature, *Eugene Onegin*, an unparalleled masterpiece, has to be taken on trust by readers without knowledge of the original. It may, on the other hand, serve as an ideal reason for learning Russian.

—Arnold McMillin

EUGENIE GRANDET
Novel by Honoré de Balzac, 1833

Eugenie Grandet is one of Honoré de Balzac's earlier works, and one of the very earliest of his writings for which it is possible to claim the status of a novel rather than a short story. In common with about half of his fiction, it is set in the provinces: in this case in Saumur, in the Touraine where Balzac was born and which he knew well. It is sometimes considered to be the first of his four inheritance novels. More importantly, it is the first of his major works to deal with the theme of monomania: in this instance, Félix Grandet's miserliness.

Grandet, a self-made multimillionaire, has an only child, the eponymous heroine. Her cousin Charles comes from Paris in 1819 to stay with his uncle and cousin after the bankruptcy and suicide of his father Guillaume. Charles is the epitome of the Parisian dandy, fashionable and ultimately calculating and self-seeking but because of the cultural divide separating Paris from the provinces he does not realize his uncle's immense wealth. Charles and Eugenie fall in love; the young man goes off to Java to seek his fortune; but before he leaves Saumur, he and Eugenie exchange tokens: they promise to marry on his return home.

A sub-plot is the rivalry of two unattractive suitors, pillars of the Saumur community, for Eugenie's hand in marriage. (The Saumur families have only a limited awareness of Grandet's wealth.) Charles meanwhile has engaged in the slave trade in the Dutch East Indies. Failing to appreciate that his cousin is one of the richest of French heiresses, he marries a young aristocratic woman on his return home, a comparatively rich man, in 1827. Heartbroken, Eugenie bestows her hand upon one of her Saumur suitors. The marriage is never consummated and Eugenic, soon widowed and ever mindful of the betrayal of her early and only romantic love, austerely devotes her life and fortune to the doing of good works: not least the repayment in full of Guillaume Grandet's still remaining debts.

Money, rather than the subject of an inheritance as such, is central to *Eugenie Grandet*, a novel which is the first of Balzac's full-length works to be acutely concerned with this theme. It provides a detailed and artistically convincing description of financial and economic activity in a provincial setting. *Eugenic Grandet* is also one of the first novels—indeed, one of the first works of literature—ever to ascribe such huge importance to financial matters. More than at any other time in human history, Balzac writes, money ''dominates the law, politics and social morality'' and, in so doing, it also undermines religious belief: this is the spirit of bourgeois capitalism, and he dreads the time when the working classes will adopt the same outlook. Thus Grandet is not only a monomaniac but a larger-than-life symbol: not, however, a symbol of the industrialism that was gaining ground in England at this same period. Although concerned with enhancing agricultural productivity, he still lives in, and does nothing to change, an agrarian economy. His non-agricultural wealth arises exclusively from speculation in Government stock. At his death he leaves a fortune of 17 million francs. When a friend expressed her reservations about the likelihood of his amassing such a huge sum, Balzac was little moved by such criticism—evidently viewing Grandet as a mythical representation of emergent capitalism: not, however, a fully convincing one at the level of historical accuracy.

Written, broadly speaking, before his invention of the system of recurring characters, *Eugenie Grandet* is one of the few of Balzac's works to have a strong flavour of self-containment which comes from being set apart from the rest. The description of the Grandet household has many of the characteristics of a Dutch genre-painting: stillness, reserve, and mystery. The character of Félix Grandet is one of the most memorable in French fiction; he is a counterpart to Molière's Harpagon. Mme Grandet and Nanon the maidservant are also sharply individualized. A still finer creation is Eugenie herself; her love-story—the blossoming and blighting of her love—is the finest thing of its kind ever achieved in *The Human Comedy*. Balzac's use of tricks of speech surpasses even Molière's. Whereas Harpagon has his "without a dowry," Félix Grandet has his "we'll see about that." But something never achieved by Molière is the transmission of the trick of speech from one generation to the next, as Eugenie herself uses the same trick of speech towards the end of the novel. Balzac skilfully describes the daughter's rebellion against her father while at the same time showing how she gradually grows to resemble him. Eugenie's rebellion is quite unlike that of Harpagon's children: it represents the coming to full strength and maturity of a person who is as strong-minded as her father but who was prepared, within limits, to submit to his paternal authority for as long as he was alive.

Such is one aspect of Balzac's "realism": recognizing both the transmission of genetic characteristics and also the determinism that implies. Another aspect is the vastly intriguing portrait of Saumur. No novel gives a more "realistic" picture of what it must have been like to live in French provincial society around the years 1819–33. Yet beneath this solid "realism" Balzac delights, as so often in *The Human Comedy*, in revealing all the strange and unexpected realities that lie close to the surface. These realities are as mystifying to us, his readers, as were the outer appearances of Grandet's house to Charles. Balzac, therefore, is as ludic towards his readers as (on the novelist's own admission) Grandet is towards his wife and daughter and indeed towards the whole of Saumur.

This "realism" is well contrasted with the "romantic" yearnings of unselfish love, a love shared by Eugenie and Charles (and symbolized by her store of gold coins, his mother's sewing-box, and Grandet's walnut tree) in the earlier part of the novel.

—Donald Adamson

THE EUNUCH (Eunuchus)
Play by Terence, 161 BC

The Eunuch was Terence's most successful play in his own lifetime. It is said to have been staged twice in one day and to have earned the highest fee ever paid for a comedy. The qualities that earned it this acclaim were not the purity of diction which Romans of later generations admired in Terence, nor the humanity which has been emphasized in his work down the ages. Rather, Terence had learned from the failure of *The Mother-in-Law* (*Hecyra*) that the

Roman audience wanted more than the sophisticated comedy of manners that appealed to Terence himself and to the tastes of his immediate literary circle. For *The Eunuch*, therefore, he chose as his primary model a play by Menander which already included an audacious eunuch substitution by which an ebullient young man gained access to his girl and raped her. To this he added the colourful stock characters of the soldier and his hanger-on Gnatho (the so-called "parasite") from a second Menandrean play called *The Flatterer* (*Kolax*). The result was a play which, in its general tone, bore a closer resemblance to those of Plautus and the rest of the Roman comic tradition than did any other of Terence's plays.

The plot is centred on the affairs of two young brothers. The elder brother Phaedria is in love with the courtesan Thais, who has asked him to withdraw for a couple of days while she secures from her soldier-lover Thraso the gift of a young slave girl. By coincidence, this is the same girl who had been brought up as Thais' sister in their home on Samos and had subsequently been sold into slavery. Thais believes the girl to be of Athenian citizen parentage and is hoping to gain protection for herself as a foreigner in Athens by restoring her to her family. However, the younger brother Chaerea sees the girl in the street and is captivated by her beauty; and, when the family slave Parmeno suggests that he should gain access to the girl in Thais' house by changing places with the eunuch whom Phaedria is about to present to Thais, Chaerea eagerly takes up the suggestion. Meanwhile, Thais herself attends a dinner party at Thraso's house, from which she returns with news of a quarrel and of the imminent arrival of Thraso intent on taking the gift back. After the attack has been beaten off, Thais learns of Chaerea's rape of the girl and agrees to allow him to marry her. Thais has now lost hope of gaining support from the gift's family but instead persuades the father of Chaerea and Phaedria to take her under his protection. All is now set for a resumption of the affair between Thais and Phaedria and for the banishment of Thraso but, by a surprise twist, Gnatho persuades Phaedria that Thais should also keep on Thraso as a harmless dupe who will continue to pay for her extravagant tastes.

The ending of the play has given rise to much critical discussion. To many it has seemed strange that Thais, who appeared throughout as a strong and independent woman well able to manage the menfolk with whom she has to deal, should have her affairs arranged for her behind her back. It also seems unlikely that Phaedria, who has been portrayed as a jealous lover, unhappy to think of Thais spending time with a rival, should so easily agree to her keeping Thraso. Nor is Gnatho the endearing kind of parasite (like Phormio in Terence's *Phormio*, with whose final victory the audience is likely to empathize). There are two approaches to this question. One is to look for some deeper meaning in the play which the ending is designed to underline. The simplest moral is that an affair with a courtesan, in contrast to an affair with a citizen-girl, can never be permanent or exclusive, but this is a point which scarcely requires a contrived or controversial ending. Rather more subtly, the triumph of the parasite has been seen as a pointer to the necessity of human dependence or, indeed, to the triumph of selfishness in human affairs, but neither of these attitudes to life seems to be characteristic of Terence. The other approach is simply to assume that Terence has sacrificed consistency for dramatic effect; on this view the ending is merely an amusing tailpiece designed to send the audience away in good humour. In any case, Terence had to modify the ending of Menander's *Eunuch* to include the two characters taken over from *The Flatterer*, and it may be that he substituted the ending from *The Flatterer* for the original

Eunuch ending. The courtesan in *The Flatterer* was not an independent woman like Thais but a slave-girl in the hands of a pimp, whose affairs could more reasonably have been settled without her being consulted.

The Eunuch is a play of colourful characters and vivid incident. Thais stands out as the most sympathetically drawn courtesan in Roman comedy, if not quite the "good courtesan" of the ancient commentator Donatus. She combines self-interest with genuine feeling both for Phaedria and for her supposed sister, and she handles Chaerea with the right mixture of humanity and reproof. Parmeno is also notable as an inversion of the "tricky slave" character favoured by Plautus; so far from bringing the affairs of his two younger masters to a successful conclusion, he tries vainly to withdraw his suggestion of the eunuch substitution, and is in the end fooled by Thais' vindictive maid Pythias into blurting out the truth to Chaerea's father. The most striking scene is the "siege" scene, in which Thraso and Gnatho, coming to recover the girl with a motley army of cooks and slaves, are repulsed by Thais. Also good are the early dialogue in which Gnatho shamelessly flatters Thraso; the narrative of the rape by the exuberant Chaerea to his friend Antipho; and the interrogation of the real eunuch by Phaedria which reveals the truth of the substitution.

—John Barsby

F

FABLES
Stories by Jean de La Fontaine, 1668–93

Jean de La Fontaine's first collection of fables, published in 1668, consists of 118 poems based on Aesopic models. Unusually, for a 17th-century work, they deal with the world of nature, albeit in a stylized form. The first fables are short poems evoking a magical world of cicadas and frogs, foxes and gods.

La Fontaine's achievement was the creation of poetry from a humble teaching aid. Before him, the Aesopic fable was used in schools, but had no literary pretensions. Hence his modest title, "Selected Fables Translated into Verse." As the subject matter was familiar, it had the aura of authenticity that suited the literary taste of 17th-century France. But the age was intolerant of pedantry and the fable's association with the schoolroom was a problem. La Fontaine's solution lies in a liveliness of style that he achieves by a variety of means.

Perhaps the most striking is his use of dialogue. Unlike his prosaic models, his fables are little dramas. His protagonists define their natures by the way they speak. In "The Wolf and the Lamb" ("Le Loup et l'Agneau"), the lamb's integrity is mirrored by the calmness and courtesy of its language; whereas the moral ambiguity of the wolf's position is reflected by the stridency of his reasoning: he loses the argument, but still eats the lamb.

Another quality is the attention to detail. These brief tableaux are painted with economy and wit. The creatures have fur and feathers and exist in their own right. If the animals in Aesopic fables are animals in name only, those in La Fontaine's world are brought alive by a charming rightness of scale. The dove saves the ant from drowning in "The Dove and the Ant" ("La Colombe et la Fourmi") by lowering a blade of grass into the water; the Cicada promises to repay with interest a borrowed grain of wheat in "The Cicada and the Ant" ("La Cigale et la Fourmi").

The fables abound in burlesque mythological references. There is humour in a cat being compared to Attila in "The Cat and the Old Rat" ("Le Chat et un vieux Rat"). But the effect is frequently pathos rather than parody. The shepherd's wretched fate is contrasted with Virgil's pastoral heroes in "The Shepherd and the Sea" ("Le Berger et la Mer"); while in "The Old Woman with Two Servants" ("La Vieille et les deux servantes"), the description of the girls' dreary labour is interleaved with references to the more romantic reaches of classical mythology. This is not gratuitous erudition: the brutality of the contrast heightens the impression of drudgery. And the modest little saga acquires a hint of the magic associated with the legends of antiquity.

Above all, in an age wedded to fixed forms and the alexandrine metre, La Fontaine's poetry has an air of freedom. His metre varies according to the movement of his subject: in "The Crow and the Fox" ("Le Corbeau et le Renard"), the scene is set with nimble lines of eight and ten syllables, while pompous alexandrines are used to express the fox's bogus compliments. And the rocking seven-syllable metre used in "The Earthen Pot and the Iron Pot" ("Le Pot de terre et le pot de fer") beautifully evokes the awkwardness of these unlikely travellers. The musicality is remarkable: sounds and rhythm are subordinated to sense, rather than the reverse. If the vocabulary is simple, La Fontaine finds ways of combining it that achieve Racinian reverberations: a line like "Sur les humides bords des royaumes du vent" ("On the dank shores of the wind's realm") from "The Oak and the Reed" ("Le Chêne et le Roseau") contains a wealth of suggestion almost impossible to translate.

At the same time, lightness of tone is maintained by the constant presence of the author. This can range from the throwaway "I read somewhere that a Miller. . ." in "The Miller, His Son and the Ass" ("Le Menier, son fils et l'âne"), to feigned uncertainty over whether a fox comes from Gascony or Normandy in "The Fox and the Grapes" ("Le Renard et les raisins"), to expressions of sympathy for the sufferings he describes. In addition to the stories, we have a kind of ironic commentary that brings the tales alive and puts the moral into perspective.

The latter is the aspect of La Fontaine's first fables that best illustrates his aesthetic awareness. In the Aesopic fable the moral is invariably introduced by the formula "This fables shows. . ." Such prosaic language is absent from La Fontaine. Fable and moral are usually united in a seamless unit. In "The Crow and the Fox," the moral, smugly delivered by the fox, completes our understanding of the character. In "The Cicada and the Ant," there is no explicit moral at all: the sense of the anecdote pervades the whole poem and La Fontaine pays the reader the compliment of leaving him to draw his or her own conclusion. But even this is not straightforward. The traditional moral is clear: the industrious ant is right and the hedonistic cicada wrong. Yet we also sense a feeling of regret that things are thus, that it is a pity the beautiful cicada has to die and that the ant is actually a self-righteous prig: the simplest of the fables is also a model of ironic ambiguity.

This quizzical attitude was one reason La Fontaine never found favour at court. The world of the fable is a world in conflict. But the conflict is between the strong and the weak, the foolish and the cunning, rather than between good and evil. Might is right and virtue is no protection against the arbitrary use of power. The political dimension would become more explicit in later fables. But even in this first collection, chiefly remarkable for its poetic qualities, we sense La Fontaine's reservations about the nature of the hierachical society in which he lived.

—David Shaw

THE FALL (La Chute)
Novel by Albert Camus, 1956

The Fall is a confession of a moral decline. In an unbroken monologue, Jean-Baptiste Clamence recounts to a stranger how, far from being the model citizen he once believed himself to be, he has come to realize that he is no more than an egocentric hypocrite who treats others with disdain. He cannot bear to be judged, however, and sets about finding a means of averting this seemingly inevitable consequence.

The confession begins in an Amsterdam bar, where Clamence introduces himself to a chance acquaintance as a *juge-pénitent* (judge-penitent). To begin his explanation of this "profession" he recounts how several years earlier he had been leading a successful life as a well-known, charitable Parisian lawyer always ready to defend worthy causes. His virtues extended to the social sphere, where he was also highly regarded. One evening, however, his self-satisfaction and good conscience were suddenly dispelled when he heard a mysterious and apparently judgemental laugh. This triggered a sequence of memories that jolted him into becoming conscious of the fact that what lay behind his virtue was, in fact, vanity and egotism. Gradually he recalls various proofs of this duplicity (vices within virtues). He realizes that when, during a confrontational traffic incident, he had been humiliated and embarrassed in public, his primary concern was revenge and that, therefore, although outwardly philanthropic, on a deeper level he was motivated by a desire to dominate. This, in reality, was his reason for championing the weak and for making women suffer in relationships. But his sense of shame centres on a more specific incident: he had ignored the cries of a woman drowning in the Seine. This made him guilty of not having helped someone who was dying. Later, he was to remember an even worse crime: while imprisoned in a war camp, he had stolen the water of a dying comrade and had thus precipitated his death. Clamence became aware that he was not as "admirable" as he had previously thought, that, in fact, he had enemies and was the subject of derision. He began to examine himself and soon discovered that his duplicity was central to his nature: each of his virtues had another side. Realizing that people are quick to judge to avoid being judged themselves, he sought to ward off ridicule in various ways. He became cynical and mocked all human and social values. Incapable of either falling in love or of maintaining chastity, he adopted a life of debauchery, which he found equally "liberating." But, when he subsequently mistook a piece of floating debris for a corpse, it was brought home to him that he was unable fully to escape his deep sense of guilt. The only way of averting this demise of his self-esteem and of recapturing his former sensations of superiority, Clamence explains, was by adopting the role of "judge-penitent." By being a penitent and accusing himself of the blackest deeds he would gain the right, he maintains, to judge others (and so dilute his own guilt feelings in the general guilt extended to all) without the risk of being accused in return. What is more, this venture is facilitated by the fact that his confession is, as he sees it, simultaneous with an accusation of others: the self-portrait which he creates "becomes a mirror," which reminds his interlocutors of *their* culpability. It is through self-accusation then that Clamence finds a long-sought comfort, being in a position to "judge the whole world" while escaping the repercussions, without *being* judged. This release can only occur, clearly, at the expense of others, as a result of their concomitant fall. To achieve his objective, so save himself from falling, Clamence is ready to condemn the rest of humanity.

Guilt is the central theme in *The Fall*. Clamence presents his personal guilt as being indicative of the true nature of all humans: he regards everyone as being guilty of shameful acts, as having fallen. He proclaims universal corruption. Even Christ is seen as guilty in that he is indirectly responsible for the murder of the innocents and, consequently, the ideals of purity and innocence based on his model themselves become hollow and dishonest. The fact that Clamence is bent on the downfall of Christianity has led critics to identify him with Lucifer, an anti-Christ. Indeed, his various allusions to religious imagery are consistently blasphemous. It is with derision that he adopts the name "Jean-Baptiste" for, while the biblical precursor

used water to baptize *out* of sin, in Clamence's case water (the Seine in which the woman drowned) is the instrument of his fall *into* culpability. Equally, in his role of "pope" in the war camp he increased suffering. Clamence says that people's most deeply-rooted belief is that they are innocent. In attacking this conviction and precipitating their "fall" into guilt, he becomes the enemy of humanity. His fundamental rationale is to secure innocence for himself by depriving everyone else of it. At the end of his monologue he invites his interlocutor (and presumably the reader) to examine his conscience and to confess *his* sins.

—Silvano Levy

THE FALSE CONFESSIONS (Les Fausses Confidences)
Play by Marivaux, 1737

By the time that *The False Confessions* was first staged by the Comédie-Italienne in Paris, Marivaux had been creating comedies for the company for 17 years. Its repertoire was always more dependent on fairytale plots and sheer spectacle than that of its more prestigious rival, the Comédie-Française. But over time Marivaux's writing reflects the Italian company's tendency to take on more and more of its rival's characteristics.

Like all classical French theatre, *The False Confessions* has a plot that is intrinsically extraordinary and theatrical, consciously set apart from the expectations of the everyday: theatre is viewed, in the Aristotelian tradition, as possessing its own inner coherence and rationality that does not directly depend on close resemblance to the real world, but rather on the working out, according to principles of dramatic necessity, of an initial imaginative supposition or hypothesis ("what if?"). A rich widow, Araminte, has employed, without her interfering mother's knowledge, an impoverished nobleman (Dorante) as new steward for her estate. Dubois, his former valet who is still in league with him, has been in Araminte's employ for some time and undertakes to reveal to her (the "false secret") that Dorante is madly in love with her and has only taken the job in order to approach her more closely. Araminte takes to Dorante at first sight and the infallible *machiniste* Dubois, through further "false revelations" of the truth, engineers their ultimate betrothal.

Through the classical theatrical formula Marivaux is posing (as the initial "what if?") a universal moral question relevant in all ages: "How is a wealthy woman to be approached by a poor man and how is she to know that he is not simply after her money?" The theatrical imagination allows Marivaux to posit the conditions of an answer. Obviously, since all is fair in love and war, such a man may ruthlessly apply what is known of female psychology and indulge in all sorts of tricks (he may even, in this case, hurt the feelings of Araminte's female companion Mutton) in order to come near his beloved and win her heart, but he must in the end be willing to risk the entire enterprise by kneeling before her and confessing (this time utterly genuinely) the whole elaborate conspiracy.

The play (in three acts and therefore designed as the principal item in a show) is one of the best of Marivaux's many comedies of sentiment and shows the vacuity of the oft-repeated claim that his plays all have one theme, the "surprise by love": not only is love one of the essential human experiences, it is as richly variable as the many different circumstances of life may make it. The moral dilemmas of the widow are not the same as those of the virginal young bride in *The Game of Love and Chance*.

In any case, Marivaux is not consciously using the theatre as a vehicle for moral lessons or illustrations, he is rather using what is known of human psychology in the crucial domain of love in order to create unique theatrical experiences. Like other great dramatists of the classical period (including creators of opera), he takes for granted the "specificity" or irreplaceability of the theatre (later elucidated by Adamov) and would not for a moment expect the stage to provide an exact copy of contemporary life. The figure of Dubois, perhaps the best developed "valet" role of Marivaux's entire theatre (and certainly an ancestor of Beaumarchais's Figaro), offers an excellent example of the point. Realist psychology would interpret him as somewhat "sinister" in his manipulations of Araminte and Marton, but this would be to overlook the fact that he is utterly infallible, hence entirely theatrical and not to be considered in realistic psychological terms at all. He is a kind of Cupid, allegorical in the best sense of representing some of the more inadmissible sides of the nature of human love. Because the Dubois role so frequently commands the stage, the Dorante figure of this play is sometimes judged as "weak" or "passive" but this again amounts to anachronistic expectation of "rounded" realistic psychology and ignores the fact that Marivaux's main focus is upon the moral dilemma of the woman, Araminte. She, by deciding to legitimize her love for Dorante against all the powerful social pressures which bear in upon her, demonstrates a freedom that was available to few women of the time. Indeed, his centrality of the female role is one of the constant general features of Marivaux's output and may even help to explain some of the traditional critical dismissals of his work. It is true that, as part of the Comédie-Italienne's tendency at this time to emulate the rival Comédie-Française, this play has not a fairytale or even a pastoral setting but a rigorously "domestic" one in the apartments of Araminte's mansion. It is also true that references to contemporary social conditions occur throughout the play (quite precise amounts of money are owed as debts or envisaged as dowries, Araminte is expected to resolve through marriage a lawsuit that she has with Dorante's rival the Count, and there is a strong sense that Dorante has an actual estate to manage as steward). But these features are part of the "surface" of the play, while its essential structure remains firmly embedded in the characteristic theatricality of classicism: characters are essentially distillations or concentrations of isolated aspects of human nature (in this case love). The theatre, like utopia, is a "land of nowhere" where the imagination reigns, but is nonetheless coherent for that. The attraction and excitement of this theatre is precisely the opposite of the modern "soap-opera": we are not taken into a replica of what we are assumed to know already, but into an alternative rational world where human potentialities are pushed to their limits and freed from the dead weight of the everyday.

The theatrical prose that Marivaux invented as vehicle for his multiple explorations (and validations) of love, namely *marivaudage*, is not, in this play, in the extreme Italianate form seen in *The Game of Love and Chance*, with its very rapid repartee, frequent use of *reprise* (picking up the word rather than the thought of the interlocutor) and parodic linguistic role for the valet (through his Arlequin of that play, Marivaux provides a gentle satire of his own dramatic style). But the use of a basic "double register" remains: characters' language is not only the unequivocal statement (as in Molière) of their own essential nature, it is also, through its hints at a nature that is unspoken (unconfessed feelings and intentions) and through its constant "running commentary" on the language of other characters, Marivaux's

means of sustaining an authoritative moral viewing-point, to which dramatic irony is essential. His spectator is always a god-like voyeur into the heart of the (usually female) principal character, always knowing more of her nature than she does herself and nearly always sympathizing and approving. The inescapable artificiality (or preciosity) of this language, derided from a late classical viewpoint by bitter rivals such as Voltaire, or more recently from the realist perspective, is the mark of its specific poetic theatricality: love explored and celebrated through the imagination.

—Philip E.J. Robinson

FAMILY STRIFE IN HAPSBURG (Ein Bruderzwist in Habsburg)
Play by Franz Grillparzer, 1872

Franz Grillparzer's drama *Family Strife in Hapsburg* grew out of the predicament many liberal-minded Austrians found themselves in during the first half of the 19th century, when demands for democratic liberties for the individual inevitably threatened to destroy the fabric of the multinational Hapsburg Monarchy. Stretching back to the 13th century, the Hapsburg Monarchy was essentially a dynastic creation. Its very success in amassing territories had been achieved at the expense of homogeneity of any sort. Hand in hand with the expansion outward went an inner consolidation of domestic power until it approached absolutism, legitimized by the doctrine of the divine right of kings and the concept of hereditary succession, both of which Grillparzer subjected to stern scrutiny in his play.

Anti-Hegelian in his outlook on history, he understood history as a series of events, largely unintelligible to the contemporary and in constant need of interpretative re-evaluation by later generations on whose development they had a bearing. In 1807 when Grillparzer first started historical research for a drama on Rudolf II, who was emperor of the Holy Roman Empire from 1576 to 1612, at a time of the intense religious and political tensions, the Hapsburg dynasty had just been dealt a severe blow by Napoleon, who in 1806 had decreed that the Holy Roman Empire should cease to exist. His edict completed a process that had started with the Reformation which spelt the end of medieval universalism in Germany as the Hapsburg emperors had pursued it and gave rise to particularism: Emperor Francis II of the Holy Roman Empire became emperor of Austria, a secular prince, like any other. Grillparzer did not finish the revision of his play till a year or two after the abortive revolution of 1848, which with its local and national demands threatened the foundations of the Hapsburgs' dynastic power in their own territories. As in all Grillparzer's stage dramas, the times represented in *Family Strife* mirror, figuratively, the time of representation and the author's understanding of his own time.

From the very first words of the first scene, strife and confusion reign in the drama. The many-layered meaning of *Bruderzwist*— "Conflict among Brothers"—is played out in all its nuances. Brothers and nephews of the emperor jostle for power, eager to replace the irresolute monarch, using his hesitancy as an excuse for usurpation. Intrigue is rife in the imperial household, lawlessness threatens in the streets, religious differences are on the point of turning into full-blown civil war. By skilfully delaying the emperor's entrance in the first act, Grillparzer not only gives ample scope to the theme of violence and scheming but arouses the reader's expectation that a strong personality is needed to put down the burgeoning rebellion. However, when at last Rudolf makes a ceremonious entry all conventional hopes for law and order are dashed by the spectacle of a weak old man in an advanced state of paranoia who thrusts aside important state documents and soon dismisses all those present by uttering a sevenfold "alone!" It is not until Archduke Ferdinand, a fanatic representative of the Counter-Reformation, elicits a kind of "Credo" from his uncle that Grillparzer affords us deeper insight into Rudolf's innermost thoughts. To Ferdinand's accusations that the emperor has allowed himself to be influenced by the dark prophecies of the astrologers he has drawn to his court, Rudolf replies with the revealing words: "I believe in God and not in the stars, but those stars, too, come from God. They are the first works of His hand, in which he laid down the blueprint of His creation." Rudolf's vision of the stars obeying God's every word from time immemorial to eternity "like a flock of silvery sheep obeying the shepherd's call" is by extension a blueprint for absolutism on earth, every subject willingly accepting the king's authority. Deeply upset by the gulf separating vision and reality and perturbed by the task confronting him of having to rule over a world torn asunder by dissension, he views man as an excrescence of the creation. Man has broken away from God, betrayed Him. Only up above among the luminous spaces of heaven is order; down among men there is nothing but falsehood, arbitrariness, and chaos. He wishes he had a huge ear to listen to a divine message or could stand guard on a tall tower eavesdropping on the stars as they surround God's throne. Grillparzer gives us the incongruous, almost bizarre spectacle of the head of the Holy Roman Empire, by tradition the defender of the Catholic faith, flying in the face of the fundamental tenets of Christian doctrine: that man and the world are in constant need of redemption. Rudolf has recourse to neoplatonic ideas but he knows that he does not have the intellect to penetrate to philosophical clarity. His speech breaks down. His confused and anguished mind conjures up Maleficus, the malignant stellar constellation, and he falls silent. Throughout the play, with great psychological perception, Grillparzer develops further the theme of the emperor's doubts. It becomes increasingly clear that he is longing for a sign from heaven indicating to him whether the dreadful schism that has occurred was ordained by God or was the work of the devil. Yet Rudolf's fears about the schism reveal not so much a concern with religious matters, such as the salvation of the soul, but the realization that doubts in the one apostolic faith lead to the loosening of all ties of reverence and respect and ultimately to the destruction of that hierarchial order that guarantees the survival of the empire and from which he derives his own raison d'être and power. He recognizes the democratic thrust in Protestantism. In his ravings he sees a Leviathan-like monster rising from the depths, for ever wanting more and never satisfied. Yet all that he has to set against this vision of a barbaric levelling down and the rule of the masses are outdated symbols of a past glory: "Our dynasty will last for ever for it does not march at the head of the new nor go along with it . . . and so, resting in the centre of its own gravity, it awaits the return of the souls that have gone astray!" Characteristically, Rudolf, when forced to abdicate, does not follow the example of his illustrious uncle Charles V, who entered a monastery, an act of Christian humility at least in gesture, but prefers to say in his castle in Prague, the fortified symbol of dynastic power.

The play ends on a deeply pessimistic, almost nihilistic note. Grillparzer re-creates the stage-setting of Act I, except that now we are in the imperial palace in Vienna, not in Prague. As in Act I members of the imperial family and other personages are waiting to

be received by the new emperor, Rudolf's brother Mathias, who has usurped power. Strife and intrigue are thriving as before in an atmosphere of hesitancy and impotence. Archduke Ferdinand and Wallenstein, his general, have just left vowing to wage a war of attrition on the Protestants even if it means eradicating a whole generation of heretics for the sake of their souls. The curtain goes down on a visually impressive, telling scene. The bejewelled insignia of the empire have been brought from Prague where Rudolf has died. They are arranged on a table in the background. Mathias is in the foreground on his knees, beating his chest and muttering "mea culpa, mea culpa, mea maxima culpa!" while shouts of "Long live Mathias!" are heard from the streets. A spectator of this scene might jump to the conclusion that the new emperor was feeling guilty towards his dead brother and asking God's forgiveness. But Grillparzer makes it clear in his stage-direction that the actor must keep his eyes on the table and not turn them to heaven, presumably because he wanted to suggest that Mathias's real guilt-feelings were concerned with his having endangered the continuity of the empire which is powerfully symbolized by the insignia on the table.

The play strikes home with the masterly psychological portrayal of Rudolf, which is underwritten both by a perceptive understanding of human frailty and by a sharp critical awareness of the limits of defensible behaviour. The other figures remain shadowy in comparison; their link with the protagonist appears often merely episodic. Seen as a dramatic whole the play is a vivid and incisive indictment of the Hapsburg "dunces by divine right" as Grillparzer called them, and their claim to everlasting power. But it goes much further than the Austrian context. It raises the urgent and topical question whether any unifying government drawn up along humanist, democratic, and peaceful lines will ever be able to hold down the will to power of conflicting national, ethnic, religious, economic, and social interests.

—Eve Mason

FANTASIA: AN ALGERIAN CAVALCADE (L'amour, la fantasia)
Novel by Assia Djebar, 1985

Fantasia: An Algerian Cavalcade is the first volume in a quartet by Algerian writer Assia Djebar which includes *Ombre Sultane* (1987); *Sister of Scheharazade* (1987), and *Vaste est la Prison* (*So Vast the Prison*, 1995). It proceeds along two main trajectories: a historical path that recounts the conquest of Algeria in 1830 and casts a look at women's involvement in the war of independence; and an autobiographical narration of the author's childhood memories, with very few incursions into her adult life and subtle references to her literary career. The historical nature of the novel is reinforced by the inclusion (in the English translation of the novel) of a chronology of important dates tracing Algeria's history, beginning with Turkish rule.

The two main sections intertwine as the author reveals the impact of the French colonial policy on her education. Djebar returns incessantly to the issue of the French language, explaining, justifying, and sometimes even apologizing for the use of French as a writing tool. She establishes an interesting parallel between the freedom of writing in French, allowing the discussion of taboo subjects without embarrassment, and Algerian women's reluctance to cover before a Frenchman, "his gaze, from the other side of the hedge, beyond the taboo, cannot touch them'' and ''so it was for me with the French language'' (126). She has a sentimental attachment to her mother tongues, Arabic and Berber, however, and deplores her failure to use them to tell her stories. Djebar personifies her relation to the two languages in a these words, ''when I sit curled up like this to study my native language it is as though my body reproduces the architecture of my native city: the medinas. . . . When I write and read the foreign language, my body travels far in subversive space'' (184).

Yet, what transpires from *Fantasia: An Algerian Cavalcade* is a special preoccupation with the word and its power, the spoken word and the written word. Stressing the importance of expressing her thoughts and feelings, Djebar is nevertheless more concerned with the release of the words than with the channeling language. She views the words as wings carrying their authors beyond the walls of their houses, the way they were experienced by her childhood friends, the daring sisters who corresponded with Arab pen pals to overcome their cloistered life.

Beyond the colonial history and the narrative of the author's memoirs, the novel is a hymn to the word and its ability to rekindle the memory of the past and give life to the dead. It is thanks to the written accounts of some members of the French military corps, in the form of personal memoirs or letters, that the story of the early years of the conquest and people's resistance became known, because ''between the lines these letters speak of Algeria as a woman whom it is impossible to tame'' (57). It is through the victimizer that Djebar learns about the victims and she in turn tells their story that moved her to the core, ''their words thrown up by such a cataclysm are for me like a comet's tail, flashing across the sky and leaving it forever riven'' (45). She is well aware of the double-edged nature of words, which can be manipulated to the interest of some at the detriment of others. Yet the words surpass the visual, as ''the word is a torch'' (62) and ''armed solely with the written word, our serious attention can never be distracted'' (62). The written word comes to the rescue of the oral word, the said word, as the novelist narrates Cherifa's story ''who in fact did not submit to anything'' (202) and that of many other *moujahidat*.

The novel sheds light on gender relations in Algerian society in the context of the traditional married couple, discussing simple yet significant matters like referring to a husband by a mere personal pronoun or his proper name, or a husband referring to his wife as al-Dar (the house), as a part of a collective entity, or sending her a postcard and provoking a scandal comparable to placing her naked in a public place. Through her parents' relationship Djebar reveals, in a subtle manner, the milieu in which she grew up, the freedom she enjoyed, taking pride in the matter, contrary to her friends and playmates who endured a life of confinement.

The story of the conquest of Algeria has the advantage of being told in *Fantasia: An Algerian Cavalcade* by a novelist historian who provides a personal, humane angle missing in history books. To write her novel, the author excavates events that received only superficial coverage, such as the fumigation of civilians during the early years of the conquest and the victimization of women during the war of independence. In many ways she is reproducing in written words the events and emotions recounted in folk poems. Like a present day oral historian, Djebar is decrypting the accounts of the conquerors to relive the victims' state of mind, to give voice to those who cannot testify to the atrocities they endured.

—Aida A. Bamia

FARSA DE INÊS PEREIRA
Play by Gil Vicente, 1523

This satire, first acted in Tomar in 1523, was commissioned as a test of Gil Vicente's poetic originality. The dramatist was invited to write a play to illustrate the popular refrain, ''Better an ass that carries me than a horse that throws me.'' This he achieved, with no little success. His characters are clearly delineated through their use of different linguistic registers; the plot is episodic in structure, but because of Inês's continued presence on stage, does not lack coherence. The narrative action is extremely compressed, which produces both comic and shock effects concerning the rapid transformation of the squire from courtly lover to blustering wife-beater and the brevity of Inês's mourning period. The play is also important because of its intertextual relationship with other literary works and traditions: virtually all of the characters and themes have their ancestry in medieval Galician-Portuguese satirical poetry, while some are found even earlier, in the comedies of Plautus and Terence, and there are distinct goliardic touches.

Inês longs for the freedom she believes she will achieve through marriage to an educated, sensitive, husband. Consequently she refuses the suit of rustic Pero Marques, choosing instead to marry the impoverished squire Brás da Mata. Her illusions are destroyed when the squire turns out to be a domestic tyrant who has married her for her dowry and then abandons her in order to go to war in Africa. Fortunately Inês is given a second chance for happiness. Her first husband, the ''noble steed'' of the proverb, is killed at war. She remarries immediately, this time accepting Pero Marques, the ''ass,'' whom she proceeds to cuckold with a less than saintly hermit. The play is undeniably entertaining because of its humour and word plays, but it also criticizes greed and hypocrisy.

Inês is the direct descendant of the young girl whose voice is heard in the *cantiga de amigo*, longing for love and marriage, but protected and kept chaste by her mother. She has much in common with the *malmaridada* of medieval folk poetry, and prefigures the unhappily-married Líva in António Ferreira's *O cioso* and *La bella Malmaridada* of Lope de Vega, both of which also date from the 16th century. Inês also recalls other frustrated heroines—Flaubert's Emma Bovary, or Luísa in Eça de Queirós's *O Primo Basílio* (*Cousin Bazilio*). Inês's reading of romantic literature has distorted her perception of reality so that her expectations are unreal and she makes faulty judgements. However, Inês has a stronger personality than her more wistful sisters in literature. When given a second chance for happiness she seizes it joyously and embarks on married life with every intention of savouring her freedom to the full. From being the victim, Inês turns into the dominant partner. Once married to Pero Marques, she sings a song that proclaims her infidelity and even asks him to transport her on his back carrying two jugs that give him the appearance of a beast with horns, the visible symbol of his cuckoldry.

Inês's mother, the confidante, performs a dual role: she acts as guardian and enforcer of domestic discipline, urging her daughter to work hard and present a respectable appearance in order to attract a good husband. But she also seems to act as vendor, allowing Inês to sing and dance in public, and leaving her unchaperoned when Pero Marques comes to press his suit. There are contradictions in the advice and instructions she offers and her moral stance is ambivalent. When Inês insists on making her own arrangements, calling the Jewish matchmakers Latão and Vidal, her mother lets Inês have her own way.

Lianor Vaz is another traditional figure, the procuress. She displays all the physical and verbal characteristics of her profession: her bustling entry on to the stage and her recourse to a particular register of language, which consists of justification of her professional activities by reference to religious practices and Christian values. On her first approach to Inês and the mother, she claims to come in the name of a blessed angel. When describing an encounter with a lustful priest, she mentions her olive-grove, alluding, perhaps, to the biblical Mount of Olives. Her speech is littered with endearments and pseudo-maternal pronouncements designed to inspire confidence and to reassure, as much part of her persuasive technique as her reliance on popular sayings, proverbs, and the kind of *exempla* found in vernacular sermons. Lianor's perception of sex and marriage as mere monetary transactions are in strong contrast to Inês idealized view.

The squire is instantly recognizable, present in numerous Galician-Portuguese satirical poems, other Vicentine plays, and elsewhere in other Peninsular literature, notably *Lazarillo de Tormes*. He owns no land, has no real status, and is characterized by his poverty and hunger. He is a ridiculous parody of the courtly lover or chivalresque knight, undermined by the comments that other characters make about him. He plays a musical instrument, sings, and hunts, badly. Far from being a courtier, he is a mere hanger-on. Instead of displaying courage he is killed by a lowly shepherd when running away from battle. Ironically, the squire's materialistic values are far more in tune with those of the bawd, not his virginal bride.

The matchmaking Jews are included for comic effect, a double act who use cross-talk, repartee, and pseudo-hebraic expressions. Responsible for finding Inês the husband she thinks she wants, they also cast doubt on the wisdom of her choice.

In direct contrast with the apparently sophisticated squire is Pero Marques, an exaggeration of the stereotypical bumpkin. His speech is uncouth and countrified; he does not know how to sit on a chair, has to rehearse his marriage proposal to Inês, and forgets the words of the marriage ceremony. However, he is honest in his intentions, and concerned for her reputation and her safety when she is left alone. Guilty of neither greed nor hypocrisy, he represents a certain naive innocence associated with life in the countryside.

Social comment and dramatic irony are key elements in the play, with the emphasis on the situation of women, human frailty, and anti-clericalism. Lianor Vaz recounts a one-sided version of her encounter with the local priest, and Inês's mother has a similar anecdote. In a mock-recognition scene towards the end of the play, Inês's meeting with the hermit permits the dramatist to parody the standard beggar's plea and play on the notion of giving alms to the needy. The essential irony of the play lies in the marked discrepancy between ideal and reality, characters' aspirations and lived experience. The work is a farce, but it does not cease to present moral and social problems. Because of its dramatic irony, social comment, and depiction of human psychologies, it is considered to be one of Vicente's finest works.

—P.A. Odber de Baubeta

FATHERS AND SONS (Ottsy i deti)
Novel by Ivan Turgenev, 1862 (written 1860–61)

Perhaps no work in the entire history of Russian literature has provoked such a critical storm as Ivan Turgenev's fourth and greatest novel. Written in 1860–61 and first published in 1862, *Fathers and Sons* reflects the seemingly insoluble tensions which beset Russian society early in the reign of Aleksandr II. The novel's topicality may be gauged by the fact that its main action takes place during the summer of 1859, while the emancipation of the serfs followed in 1861. Turgenev's evenhanded treatment of his characters and their dilemmas inevitably perplexed and infuriated partisans of all persuasions, much to the author's own discomfort. The work's abiding popularity indicates, however, that it transcends the vagaries of mere ideology, embracing subtler and more profound areas of the human soul.

The novel's plot unfolds in a leisurely and lucid manner, pausing where necessary to provide flashbacks and pre-histories. The protagonist is a young medical student, the "nihilist" Evgenii Bazarov. All four centres of the action serve to highlight aspects of Bazarov's personality and to demonstrate his essential homelessness.

Fathers and Sons divides easily into distinct segments. After the relaxed introduction of three leading characters, Nikolai Kirsanov, his son Arkadii, and Arkadii's friend Bazarov (chapters 1–3), the novel's main ideological clash develops at Nikolai's estate Mariino, between the plebeian radical Bazarov and Nikolai's brother, the aristocratic conservative Pavel (chapters 4–11). To relieve the tension, Bazarov and Arkadii move to the local town, where Bazarov's superiority over the pseudo-radicals of his own generation is illustrated (chapters 12–15). The central love-theme flares up and fades at Nikolskoe, when Bazarov's animal-like passion is rebuffed by the ice-cold Anna Odintsova (chapters 16–19). The two friends finally visit Bazarov's doting parents, but Bazarov departs after only three days (chapters 20–21). Thereafter the place of action changes more frequently, as the paths of Bazarov and Arkadii increasingly diverge. Bazarov and Pavel fight an inconclusive duel, Arkadii falls in love with Anna's younger sister Katia, and the characters' fortunes variously evolve towards marriage or isolation (chapters 22–26). Bazarov dies, after neglectfully contracting typhus (chapter 27). The final chapter is a kind of epilogue, reporting several marriages and Pavel's self-imposed exile abroad. A concluding tableau portrays Bazarov's grieving parents by his graveside, and speaks yearningly of reconciliation (chapter 28).

Fathers and Sons is undoubtedly dominated by the controversial figure of Bazarov. Rejecting blind adherence to any "principles," the utilitarian "nihilist" single-mindedly repudiates all existing institutions, including the aristocracy, the church, and, presumably, the monarchy. While inclining towards the natural sciences and empirical materialism, Bazarov views his task as fundamentally destructive. This aim of clearing the way for the future perhaps partly motivates his rampant philistinism: Bazarov evidently regards all the nicer subtleties of human sensitivity and creativity (such as individual uniqueness, love, appreciation of nature and the arts) as "romantic rubbish" or aristocratic privilege.

The uncouth barbarism of Bazarov's most extreme pronouncements is manifest. "A decent chemist is twenty times more useful than any poet" (chapter 6); "Nature is not a temple, but a workshop" (chapter 9); "aphael is not worth a brass farthing" (chapter 10); "People are like trees in a forest: no botanist would dream of studying each individual birchtree" (chapter 16). At various points he appears brash, immature, arrogant, insensitive, rude to his hosts, and unbending towards his parents. When, to his immense chagrin, he falls in love with Odintsova, Bazarov's previous denial of his common humanity is revealed as groundless. After his rejection in love he becomes an ordinary mortal, conscious of his insignificance in time and space. Yet while, on the one hand, this defeat leads to vulnerability and death, it also enables Bazarov to grow immeasurably as a person, investing his lonely strength with a tragic grandeur.

Striving to be an objective observer, the impartial chronicler of his times, Turgenev had unerringly detected the emergence in Russia of a younger generation of hard-headed, materialistic, utilitarian "revolutionary democrats." In this sense, the ruggedly determined, frog-dissecting Bazarov was a forerunner of what was to come, standing, as Turgenev noted in a letter of 1862, "on the threshold of the future." Turgenev's letters and reminiscences indicate that the author was unsure whether to love or hate his hero, although he basically appears well-disposed towards a character so dissimilar to himself. At various times, Turgenev described Bazarov as tragic, truthful, honest, and doomed, "a democrat to his very finger-tips" and a "revolutionary" (1862), "my favourite child" (1874), "the most sympathetic of all my creations" (1876).

Yet, despite Turgenev's claim in 1862 that his "entire story" was "directed against the nobility as the leading class," his attitude towards Bazarov and the Kirsanov family was patently ambivalent. As a liberal aristocrat, lover of the arts, and man of moderate views, Turgenev seems spiritually akin to Nikolai Kirsanov. Significantly, the novel ends with the exclusion of the extremists (Bazarov and Pavel) and the flourishing of the moderates (Nikolai, Arkadii, and their families). The "democrat" Bazarov despises, and is disdained by, the peasants, whereas the "noble" Nikolai wins and marries the peasant girl Fenechka.

When *Fathers and Sons* appeared, Turgenev found himself caught in a bewildering crossfire between the two wings of conservative reaction and radical rebellion. Yet his novel is so much more than the provocative portrait of an angry young man or "superfluous man." Richard Freeborn has remarked (in *Turgenev: The Novelist's Novelist*, 1960) that in all his greatest work Turgenev achieves "a subtle balance between the poles of human experience, between love and death, joy and sadness, youth and age, innocence and maturity."

Turgenev interweaves idea-content and love-plots (notably Bazarov-Odintsova, Nikolai-Fenechka, and Arkadii-Katia), presenting a rich gallery of individual, yet universally typical, characters. David Allan Lowe has noted (in *Turgenev's Fathers and Sons*, 1983) that the strong, egoistic, sterile characters (Bazarov, Pavel, Odintsova) are unfavourably contrasted with the meek, altruistic, fertile figures (Arkadii, Nikolai, Katia, Fenechka, Bazarov's parents).

N.N. Strakhov perceptively discerned (in *Vremia* [*Time*], [4], 1862) that Turgenev "stands for the eternal principles of human life," for "the enchantment of nature, the charm of art, feminine love, family love, parents' love, *even* religion." *Fathers and Sons* portrays not only the conflict between individuals, classes, and generations, but also eventual reconciliation and co-operation.

—Gordon McVay

FAUST
Play by Johann Wolfgang von Goethe, Part I, 1808; Part II, 1832

Johann Wolfgang von Goethe began *Faust* in the early 1770s with verse and prose scenes showing a high-minded scholar who seeks through magic to escape from academic sterility. Soon this Faust, in the unexplained company of the cynical devil Mephistopheles, loves and seduces, then deserts and destroys Margarete, a small-town girl who atones for killing their child by refusing to be rescued as she is about to be executed for infanticide. In the late 1780s Goethe composed further scenes with Mephistopheles and published them—without the still unversified denouement of Part I—in 1790 with revisions of what he had written as *Faust: A Fragment*. He worked out his definitive conception of a two-part tragedy (and at last motivated the introduction of Mephistopheles) in the last decade of the 18th century, when at the urging of his friend Friedrich Schiller he largely finished Part I and began Part II, most of which was then actually written from 1825 to 1831. Its genesis at the end of the Age of Reason largely explains the slowness with which *Faust* was completed: its supernatural motifs, deriving from beliefs no longer taken seriously, could only be reconciled with its secular theme of innate human potential when Goethe replaced the traditional bartering of immortal soul for wealth and power by Faust's Promethean discontent, his defiance of Mephistopheles ever to see him permanently satisfied with any pleasure or achievement.

In the scenes from the 1770s—basically those published in 1887 as *Goethe's Faust in Its Original Form* and known as the *Urfaust*—simple, often colloquial verse and prose is skilfully blended with contemporary lyricism and powerful rhetoric; a deliberately simple dramatic technique evokes the folk dramas and puppet plays ultimately deriving from adaptations of Marlowe's *Doctor Faustus* performed in Germany by travelling players through which the figure of Faust was then best known. Into what had become the drama of a representative of highest human aspiration who is seen in a wide range of important contexts, Goethe introduces a correspondingly wide variety of poetic forms and dramatic styles (e.g., classical Greek meters, old Germanic charms, hymn-like chants, Renaissance Italian verse, pastiches of ancient Greek tragedy and comedy, Elizabethan masque and history play, Calderonian lyric drama, and Baroque opera libretto), adding not only the relief of scintillating formal variety to a now abnormally long theatrical text, but also individuating stylistically the various times and places of Faust's real and imagined experiences.

The tragedy's main action is the thematic illustration of the rightness of the premise of its Prologue in Heaven, that anyone truly human intuitively knows what course of conduct is properly to be followed. Faust, who feels that all he has learned and taught has only alienated him from normal life, scornfully rejects the magical pleasures and powers soon proffered him by Mephistopheles, authorized by the Prologue's Lord to test his intrinsic worth, and instead challenges this "Spirit of Negation" ever to provide him, in exchange for his life, any moment of lasting satisfaction. With Mephistopheles at his service to obviate material—but not moral—obstacles to his desires, a rejuvenated Faust discovers the essence of common human experience in his love for Margarete (Gretchen), whom he nevertheless temporarily deserts for purely sensual pleasures represented dramatically by a phantasmagoric witches' sabbath (Walpurgis Night). Publicly shamed as an unwed mother, the distraught Gretchen kills their child and, when a profoundly shaken Faust seeks to rescue her with Mephistopheles' help from execution for infanticide, accepts death as necessary atonement. Part I ends with Faust, broken and helpless, borne off from her prison cell by Mephistopheles.

Part II opens as Faust, at last recovered from a long breakdown, regains the will to live, this time resolved to experience life in its noblest manifestations. Like his legendary model, he becomes an adviser of the German Emperor and—unfortunately, in so far as the wisdom he offers in the long poetic masque of Act I is disregarded by all whom it might benefit—also his Master of the Revels. Commanded to entertain the court with a dumbshow of Helen and Paris of Troy, with Mephistopheles' assistance Faust projects a Helen (possibly Margarete idealized as a neoclassical heroine) so beautiful that, ignoring her unreality, he embraces her figure only to fall into a paralytic trance as it explodes. He now experiences as syncopated dreams (grand-scale parallels to the Walpurgis Night of Part I and its less substantial Dream of the golden wedding of Oberon and Titania) the great cultural traditions that revitalized the Renaissance world to which he historically belongs: in a classical Walpurgis Night quest of Helen the great myths and best ethical insights of ancient Greece, and in his syncopated life with Helen of Act III—originally published separately in 1827 as a "Faust-Intermezzo" with the title *Helen: Classico-Romantic Phantas magoria*—its poetry both in substance and in forms imitating classical models and their later literary reincarnations. When Faust reawakens after Helen, their rashly heroic son Euphorion, and his classical dream world have vanished, he resolutely assumes socio-political responsibility and, for his (actually Mephistopheles') services to the Emperor is granted the right to create a new state on coastal lands reclaimed from the sea and still in Faust's old age imperilled by it. He is, however, not completely satisfied by all he has acquired and reminded by Mephistopheles' presence that what he has achieved is not entirely his own doing. An elderly couple own an area of land Faust covets and he asks Mephistopheles to remove them. Faust is shocked into a renewed sense of responsibility when Mephistopheles burns down the house, murdering the couple. He accordingly renounces magic, at last accepting full human finitude. Recognizing that no high achievement can be sustained without unceasing effort (here the cooperative labour of a whole people resisting the sea's encroachment), a now blind Faust dies content and is granted poetic redemption in a half Swedenborgian, half Renaissance-Catholic afterlife where, instructed by a beatified Gretchen, he once more begins a teaching career.

That *Faust* is a secular tragedy by a late-Enlightenment poet has for many often been obscured by its elements of traditional magic and folklore and by its ironic use of religious symbolism (particularly in the prologue in Heaven and the scenes with Faust's death and last ascension). It has accordingly sometimes been misread as a morality play whose hero is a figure warning against the evils of hubristic secularism, even though Goethe repeatedly emphasized that in the course of its dramatic action Faust experienced ever nobler and more worthwhile errors and has Mephistopheles concede in his final speech that he has been "robbed of a great, unequalled treasure—the noble soul that pledged itself to me." That *Faust* embodies the highest values of a fundamentally secular German-classical humanism is evident from its satire in Part I on scholasticism, sectarian religion, vulgar superstition, and utilitarian philosophy, and in Part II on irresponsible absolutism, transcendental philosophy, romantic Hellenism, medieval revivalism, and the regressive, post-Napoleonic politics of Europe in Goethe's last years. Despite the importance of allegorical devices in it, *Faust* is not a mystery play but—however freely and eclectically constructed—a tragedy by Aristotelian standards. It is, however, in every part "all theatre" (as Giorgio Strehler has said, well representing many contemporary stage directors), even if never intended to be performed all at once in its entirety. Radically cut versions (usually of Part I, but ever more frequently of Part I with substantial sections of Part II) have recently been staged with considerable success in Germany, England, France, Canada, and the United States, confirming that as imaginative and intelligent drama Goethe's

Faust deserves its acknowledged status as the preeminent symbolic vision of quintessential modern Western man.

—Stuart Atkins

FERDYDURKE
Novel by Witold Gombrowicz, 1937

Ferdydurke is Witold Gombrowicz's first and most influential novel. Even critics like Ewa M. Thompson who prefer Gombrowicz's post-war prose agree that this novel is "a key to [all] Gombrowicz's works." The title itself is meaningless—Gombrowicz, when questioned, claimed to have borrowed it from a character in one of H.G. Wells's stories, where it appeared as "Ferdy Durke." This novel illustrates one of Gombrowicz's basic antinomies, i.e. "maturity versus immaturity." It consists of five parts, two introductory and "philosophical" and three narrative. Joey (Józio), the 30-year-old hero, is a drifting and unsettled individual, whom Mr. Pimko, his former schoolmaster, visits in his home and by the sheer force of his schoolmaster's authority transforms into an adolescent. As in a bad dream, Joey is thrown back into the arena of fermenting immaturity, the grammar school. There he experiences both competition between immature schoolboys (the duel of grimaces between the "idealist" and the "materialist" in his class) and a struggle for influence over the minds of the schoolboys, all this signifying that all classroom education is a mishmash of lofty truisms and meaningless formulas. Our hero cannot get rid of his immaturity in school, so he tries to achieve this next in the household of the "progressive" Youthful family and then in a conservative country house where his uncle lives. Joey is disgusted with his own greenness, but cannot accept the barren and fake maturity of the grown-ups and the rules of behaviour laid down by "mature" society. This inability to come to terms either with oneself or with society is the attitudinal axis of *Ferdydurke*, while the protagonist's elaborate but futile attempts to self-liberation provide the absurd but very amusing plot.

Critics, by and large, offer two models for the interpretation of Gombrowicz's novel, a realistic and a philosophical one. The former regards the novel as a social satire, and specifically as a satire on pre-World War II Poland. Arthur Sandauer emphasized this view, pointing out that *Ferdydurke*, in fact, ridiculed most values cherished by the generation that had created independent Poland: education in a "national" spirit, the cult of scientific and technological progress, and the belief that the duty of educated Poles was to help the peasants to educate themselves. The second approach, which could be defined as "non-mimetic," stresses form and structure. In Gombrowicz's novel form (or the lack of it) takes precedence over ideology, ideals are undermined by biological urges, and language is shown to camouflage rather than reveal reality.

Ferdydurke was published in 1937, but it is a pioneering work in a sense, and it can be claimed that with it Gombrowicz created a general structural model of the human situation and inner human relations. Man is not authentic, because he is dependent on others: he is constantly influenced and shaped by the opinions, attitudes, and actions of others. This is not a uniquely Polish situation, but one that appears almost universally in the age of mass media and victorious mass culture. Artistic creation in itself is no remedy against the ''manipulation by forms'' which can be broken only by some act of self-liberating violence. All narrative parts of *Ferdydurke* end in a break-out attempt, in a ''wriggling heap'' of bodies.

As Bruno Schulz put it, *Ferdydurke* is ''bursting from ideas'': it is a grotesque, almost picaresque novel, packed with striking psychological observations and interesting philosophical propositions. Human biology is also important inasmuch as in each narrative part of the novel a different part of the body plays a central symbolic role; the school is the kingdom of the ''bum'' (people are ''fitted out with bums''), the house of the ''progressive'' Youthfuls emanates a cult of the emancipated schoolgirl's calves, while the country house reflects the insoluble conflict between the gentlemanly ''faces'' and the ''mugs'' of the peasants. ''There is no escape from the bum,'' declares Joey at the end of the novel: what he means is that there is no escape from one's social roles and obligations.

Some of Gombrowicz's linguistic jokes became everyday coinage in the Poland of the 1950s when as a result of Marxist indoctrination most individuals felt that they were indeed ''fitted out with a bum,'' having endured endless sessions of ''verbal rape'' by Party bosses. This strange topicality helped to make the book much sought after at the time it was reissued in 1957, and focused attention on Gombrowicz, who had lived abroad since 1939.

—George Gömöri

FILUMENA MARTURANO
Play by Eduardo De Filippo, 1946

The protagonists of *Filumena Marturano* met long ago at a brothel where Filumena worked to relieve her family's abject poverty. The hero, Domenico Soriano, was attracted to her, and decided to save her from a life of prostitution by taking her home with him, allowing her even to choose her own servant. She fell in love and, as if married, performed the duties of a faithful wife, loving Domenico, keeping house, and watching out for his business interests during his frequent travels. Symbolically, she is the whore with the heart of gold, and he is the knight in shining armour—an exemplary, fairytale for Hollywood or Broadway. But the story takes place in Naples, not Hollywood, and she conceals her love for him, while he continues to regard her as a kept woman.

Filumena Marturano is written in the Neapolitan dialect, in which a great deal of comic and sentimental literature has been produced, and, for most of the play, Eduardo De Filippo's serious use of it succeeds in estranging the characters from the maudlin and mawkish. His genius imbues this fairytale with a stark reality that cannot be concealed by laughter.

When the play opens, the two characters have been living together, unmarried, for 25 years. Filumena, however, wants to get married, and pretends to be mortally ill and on her deathbed so that Domenico will comply. We do not witness the ceremony but Rosalia, Filumena's servant and confidante, cannot stop laughing as she remembers how, after it, Filumena jumped happily out of bed, wishing her husband and herself the best of luck.

The main action of the play starts just after the ceremony, in the dining room, with Filumena still in her nightgown. Domenico is furious. He believes that the reason for her deception is to prevent him from marrying his new young girlfriend, 22-year-old Diana. Their bitter confrontation evokes their past lives: Filumena says she has always loved him, and he acknowledges that he has always considered her a kept woman and intends to have the marriage annulled. At the end of Act I, Filumena reveals that she had three children before going to live with Domenico and has been secretly supporting them, unbeknown even to the children. She did not deceive Domenico out of jealousy or greed, but in order to give a name to her now grown-up sons.

In Act II, the following day, Filumena brings her sons to the house and tells them that she is their mother. When Domenico's lawyer proves to her that the marriage is illegal, Filumena decides to go and live with one of her sons. Before leaving, however, she reveals to Domenico that one of the three sons is his, although she refuses to say which one.

In the first two acts we come to understand Filumena's plight: the mask of a kept woman conceals her existence as a lonely, loving mother and is her shield against circumstance. She has never cried. The illegitimacy of her own birth creates an obsessive yearning for her sons' legitimacy. De Filippo is aware of the quiet desperation underlying everyday life—a contrast expressed in his plays by their surface comedy and the searing sadness upon which they are founded.

In Act III, ten months later, we learn that after the annulment of their illegal marriage, Domenico is now willing to marry Filumena and has agreed to give his name to all three sons, since Filumena still refuses to reveal which one is his. The ceremony is about to be performed. It is a happy moment: Filumena seems rejuvenated and the young men finally feel they can call Domenico father. Humour is provided by Domenico's unsuccessful attempts to discover which son is really his. Just before the curtain falls, Filumena finally, for the first time, is able to cry. Her last words are: ''How wonderful it is to cry!''

The conclusion is predictable: the structure of the whole play must lead to such a finale. The mock death at the beginning is a clear indication of a happy ending, but there is no real happiness in De Filippo's world, and this happiness is false. Both protagonists have slowly become aware of the bitterness of their predicament. Domenico knows, and declares, that they are not getting married like two youngsters believing in love's illusion: ''We have had our lives,'' he says. They are only giving a name to the sons. His is not a sudden metamorphosis devised by De Filippo in order to end the play. In the second act we have already heard him reflect upon the passage of time:

I'm through. No will, no enthusiasm, no passions, and if I try anything, it's only to prove to myself that it isn't so . . . that I can get the better of death itself. And I do so well I believe it!

It is as if Filumena's feigned death has jolted him into contemplating his own decay. For her part, Filumena feels a deep grief for a life that could have been, and is painfully aware of having lost all the pleasures of motherhood. She tells Domenico: ''We have missed the beauty of having children.'' She regrets not having felt the joy of living with her sons when they were small. Ironically then, like the wedding at the start of the play, this ceremony, although legal, seems to be performed by the two main characters *in extremis*, at the end of their days. Life is mocking them.

—Emanuele Licastro

THE FIRE RAISERS (Biedermann und die Brandstifter)
Play by Max Frisch, 1958

Max Frisch's diary for 1948 contains in outline the story that forms the basis of this play: that of the anxious bourgeois who invites strangers into his house whom he soon suspects to be arsonists, yet cannot confront—and pays the price. In 1949 Frisch sketched a radio play on the same subject, but the work itself was not started until three years later. A radio success, the play was then reworked for stage performance in Zurich in 1958, and has gone on to world-wide success since.

That success has undoubtedly something to do with the play's sustained comic inventiveness and its openness to interpretation; as its subtitle proclaims, it is a morality play without a moral—no urgent message is forced upon the attention of the audience as it is with the much darker *Andorra*. Yet while it is clear that the Communist takeover in Prague in February 1948 and Beneš's supposed collusion gave Frisch the original idea for his diary sketch, and that other political scenarios can be adduced (e.g. Hitler's rise to power on the backs of the bourgeoisie), it adds little to our appreciation of the text to see it in this allegorical way, and indeed detracts from its aesthetic inventiveness and specific effect.

In some senses *The Fire Raisers* is a very undramatic work; there is a simple structure without genuine antagonists or subplots, and minimal suspense since we very quickly infer who the "visitors" are. The interest is provided precisely by fascinated anticipation of how this will all end, which derives from our familiarity with the vocabulary of dramatic irony. Yet this is a two-edged effect: we feel ourselves superior by our insight to the foolish protagonist, yet our capacity to anticipate his fate marks us as sharing the same cultural roots—and much else in this play has the same ambivalence. The presence of a chorus, for example, made up in this case of firemen: we recognize and laugh at the parody of Greek theatrical convention, the absurd mix of high rhetoric and modern jargon. However, it is our very cultural awareness and attentive response which also traps us into recognition of the occasional sharp relevance of what is said to our lives in general (e.g. their reading of belief in Fate as a mask for stupidity points to the suspicious nature of all such intellectual pretention). In fact our laughter throughout is similarly "dual"—we revel in our separateness and superior understanding, yet just that general cruelty and our specific enjoyment of individual comic scenes marks our unwilled but unmistakable identity with the protagonist's character and attitudes. This identity is then explicitly enacted when he addresses the audience and directly and asks "well, would you have behaved differently?"

What this play focuses on, then, are general middle-class attitudes, perhaps even broader modern attitudes in a post-Christian, media-driven world. The very "decency" enshrined in the protagonist's name, Biedermann, is the key. It is what most audiences would lay claim to, but it is also his downfall because it has become a class and cultural icon rather than an instinctive morality: that which apes aristocratic generosity with an implied recognition of desirably "higher" values, while also providing a comforting mask for cruder exploitative roles. It is self-congratulatory in its manners and rituals, but also a source of vulnerability because of its inherent element of bad faith. Frisch's dialogue and stage action capture this duality brilliantly, especially in the rituals of hospitality which are shown up for the manipulative pretence they are by being taken as sincere ("How did you sleep?" "Thank you, I was cold.. .."). Frisch also brilliantly captures bourgeois inability to replace these formulaic rituals with direct speaking, to name what threatens even in crisis, for fear of losing face—and the fact that plain-speaking of a very crude kind is not felt to be inconsistent with "decency" outside the home, in the factory or pub, only underpins the play's emphasis on received norms of behaviour. It is crucial to the meaning of the play that Biedermann effectively allows these men into his home, they do not force their way in; nor is he exceptionally gullible—on the contrary, he is at first very suspicious indeed. It is not true to say that he is simply cowardly or ingratiating either: rather the fire raisers deflect any element of resistance by calling Biedermann's bluff. For example, they describe "others" duplicity in first receiving them and then betraying them to the police, thus anticipating and defusing Biedermann's own self-preservatory instincts by foregrounding just that "decency" he also seeks to project. As they pinpoint bourgeois hypocrisies these become impossible to perform, and the self-sprung trap of bourgeois self-image is laid bare, to be finally enacted in a parody of heroic honour as Biedermann hands over the matches to the arsonists.

All this is deeply serious, yet uproariously funny too because we cannot fail to recognize that the pattern of events replicates the good old circus routine of the clown who trips over his own bucket of water and gets wet; Frisch's play, like many enduring comedy classics, has an underlying formula of traditional farce. Yet is also highly modern, twice for example explicitly breaking the separation of stage and audience in a way that both denies us the comfort of separate superiority and also actively foregrounds artifice as a theme. Such devices, and the many provocative incongruities, are reminiscent of Brecht, yet the spirit of this play is ultimately un-Brechtian. Frisch's world is not one of socially conditioned victims but of fallible, foolish human beings—and the Epilogue in Hell added for the first performance in Germany merely confirms this. Biedermann is unreflective and unregenerate, and it is a moot point whether audiences will themselves "learn" anything, or simply relish the cultural eclecticism and so re-enact Biedermann's complacency. The explosion with which the main play ends says it all: the only truth is in action, not words.

—Mary E. Stewart

FIRST LOVE (Pervaia liubov')
Novella by Ivan Turgenev, 1860

Published in same year as the novel *On the Eve*, *First Love*, according to the author, is the most autobiographical of all his fiction. Late in his life he wrote that *First Love* was the only one of his writings that still gave him pleasure to read again, "because it is life itself, it was not made up . . . it is part of my own experience." It was dedicated to Ivan Turgenev's friend, the critic P.V. Annenkov, somewhat bizarrely as Annenkov had just got married, and to Turgenev's belief that one's first love is the most important event in one's life—even though it is necessarily ultimately unhappy and everything afterwards is but an epilogue, it is a valuable and rewarding experience.

The basic construction of the story is one used frequently by Turgenev in his shorter works. A group of men meet to tell each other a story. Here the theme is first love. With the first man it was for his nanny; with the second for the woman he married. The third, however says that he would prefer to write it all down and read it to the others at their next meeting. As a 16-year-old boy the narrator, Vladimir, and his family moved for the summer from Moscow to their country estate. There, his parents pay him little attention; his father is a handsome man who married for money while his mother is a nervous, jealous woman. Their nearest neighbours are the Zasekins who have a 21-year-old daughter, Zinaida, a tall, slender, beautiful, and charming yet coquettish young woman. Vladimir immediately falls in love with her and is duly teased and flirted with. Depending on the mood or caprice of Zinaida he goes from ecstasy to despair and will obey her slightest command. He is delighted and flattered to be treated as her page-boy. He then discovers that Zinaida and his father are meeting secretly and an anonymous letter reveals the fact to his mother. The family returns to Moscow. Later Vladimir enters university and his father dies. He learns that Zinaida has married and is in St. Petersburg with her husband. He goes to see her but finds she has died in childbirth.

The story contrasts the almost innocent yet ardent love of the narrator with that of Zinaida—more mature, sexually passionate, and tragic. It is the clearest example in all of Turgenev's fiction of the impossibility of happy, successful, or lasting love between the sexes, here not only that between Vladimir and Zinaida, but also that between Zinaida and Vladimir's father. It might be added too that his parents' life is hardly idyllic or even affectionate and that Zinaida's presumably happy marriage is short-lived. "Beware the love of a woman," the narrator's outwardly cold yet fascinating father tells him, "that ecstasy . . . that poison."

The fascination of the story, which many consider Turgenev's best, rests on the portrayal of Zinaida; if Turgenev had failed with her, *First Love* would have failed too. But he didn't. Vladimir sees her from a viewpoint untainted by experience. It is fresh, clear, illuminating. He cannot appreciate the flirtatious side of her personality which is something his father uses to gain his control over her. The young boy idealizes her and worships her in a vision of his own creating. Her character is, as it were, ennobled in the process. Zinaida's relationship with Vladimir's father shows the other side to her nature. There is obvious sexual attraction and animal passion but little love. Turgenev rarely describes the physical aspects of the relations between the sexes. His methods are more subtle, more oblique, yet the scene where the uncomprehending Vladimir watches his father firmly stroking the face of Zinaida with his horse-whip which she seizes and kisses passionately is one of the few occasions where Turgenev permits himself to hint at the physical aspect, even the darker side, of love between a man and a woman.

Turgenev's most enduring opinion of a love relationship was that it is inevitable that one of the participants is always the slave of the other. Here it is expressed through Vladimir and Zinaida and, conversely, through Zinaida and Vladimir's father. Zinaida is therefore both temptress and victim. She has a dual personality. With all her young admirers she wishes to control, dominate, overwhelm, but to remain largely unaffected herself. With the narrator's father, however, she desires to submit, to be overpowered, to succumb. For Turgenev, love also demanded sacrifice and Zinaida, while not fully understanding it herself, combines both the need to experience the pleasures love can bring and equally the pain it involves. With all his undoubted skills at painting portraits, among all his accurately depicted heroines Turgenev never achieved anything more convincing than Zinaida. As illustration of a man's understanding of the

character, personality, moods, and patterns of behaviour of a young woman, she can be compared only to Tolstoi's Natasha Rostova in *War and Peace*.

First Love, if not pessimistic about the human condition, has an air of nostalgia and sadness. Vladimir's final memories of Zinaida recognize that youth and love are equally ephemeral; they "disappear like wax, like snow in the heat of the sun." The story cannot fail to create a feeling of regret in the reader, not only for the characters in the story, but also more personally. First love when it has died, as die it will, remains a "fugitive and momentary vision" and leaves us "with no more than a sigh, a nagging sense of loss."

—A.V. Knowles

THE FLAME (Il fuoco)
Novel by Gabriele D'Annunzio, 1900

The Flame exists in three English versions, two of which are well known. First published in Italy in 1900, there was an English version entitled *The Flame of Life* (1900) and in 1991 a new translation, *The Flame,* was published. The anomaly in the two English titles reflects the complexity of Gabriele D'Annunzio's use of symbolism, drawing as he does on two disparate traditions: the use of fire as a purifying force as exemplified in Dante's *Commedia* (the novel is prefaced with a line from Dante—"do as Nature does in fire") and the Wagnerian idea of the flaming forge in which the creative masculine spirit is shaped. Wagner appears as an actual character in *The Flame,* and it is with Wagner's funeral that D'Annunzio concludes this autobiographical novel which, in many ways, is a manifesto of his theories of art and of Italian culture.

When *The Flame* first appeared, D'Annunzio was already well established as a poet and novelist, and had begun to turn his hand to writing for the theatre, chiefly because of his relationship with Eleonora Duse, the greatest actress of her day. Duse and D'Annunzio began their *affaire* in 1894, and it lasted until 1904 when Duse left him, driven to despair by his infidelities. *The Flame* is in many respects a *roman à clef,* because it traces the relationship between a young writer, Stelio Effrena (D'Annunzio himself) and La Foscarina (Duse), a world famous actress. Although there was only a slight age difference between Duse and D'Annunzio, in the fictitious version Stelio is depicted as a virile young man, avid for life and full of springtime energy, while Foscarina is an ageing woman, terrified at the prospect of losing her beauty, the personification of Autumn.

Because of the immediately identifiable characters, the novel caused a scandal when it first appeared. D'Annunzio courted scandal throughout his life, and earlier novels had also caused a furor because of their sexual explicitness. *The Flame* crossed the boundary line between autobiography and fiction in ways that also transgressed contemporary conventions of good taste. Sarah Bernhardt was so appalled at what she saw as a betrayal of the intimate life of a fellow actress, albeit her greatest rival, that she returned her copy to the author unread. D'Annunzio had clearly kept notebooks detailing Duse's conversations in bed and in intensely private moments, and chose to make them public through the character of Foscarina. The heroine's account of her childhood and adolescence in the theatre, of her debut in the arena at Verona as Juliet, all derive directly from

Duse's own life. That Duse was an exceptionally private person only made D'Annunzio's exposure of her thoughts and feelings the more unpalatable to large numbers of readers.

D'Annunzio structured his novel in terms of binary opposites: youth and age, male and female, spring and autumn, life and death, fire and water. Set in Venice in the 1890s, it is full of lyrical descriptions of the city as the summer ends and autumn approaches, which remind us of D'Annunzio's poetic talents. He divided it into two parts, the first entitled ''The Epiphany of Fire,'' the second ''The Empire of Silence,'' Part One, which opens with the lyrical description of the protagonists sailing across the lagoon in a typically Venetian halcyon evening of absolute stillness, traces both the move towards physical consummation of the *affaire* and Stelio's rise to artistic success. Part Two follows the gradual disintegration of the relationship, as Stelio is driven by his inner desire for absolute freedom both in artistic and personal terms, and Foscarina is tormented by the realization that she is growing old and must inevitably lose him to a younger woman. By the end of the novel, Foscarina has decided to leave him and go back to her former life on tour with her company, and Stelio has been inspired to write his first play. The details show striking parallels with D'Annunzio's own play, *The Dead City,* written in 1895.

A substantial section of Part One is devoted to Stelio's speech to the elite of Venetian society. Based on one of D'Annunzio's own improvised speeches on the sublime power of beauty, it is intended here to show the power of Stelio's intellect and also to establish the aesthetic core of the novel. Because of its inordinate length, however, it does not work, and Part Two is a much stronger piece of writing. D'Annunzio could write magnificently when he chose, and his psychological insights into both his central characters are very well handled. However, when he decides to abandon narrative and use the novel as a political platform, his writing is much weaker. Stelio's great set-piece comes across as self-indulgence at best, megalomania at worst, and readers move with some relief back to the passages that trace the relationship between the writer and the actress. Particularly powerful are the sections (the novel is not divided into chapters, but into a series of unmarked quite distinct narrative segments) describing Stelio's feelings of entrapment after the couple have made love, Foscarina's anguish when she is lost in the maze during a visit to a decaying country house, and the lovers' quarrel after they have seen the glass-blowing furnaces on the Island of Murano.

The Flame is an uneven novel, and can be both moving and infuriating. The problem, however, is D'Annunzio's overidentification with Stelio: he wants his readers to approve of his character, but does not have the necessary critical distance to enable him to gauge their boredom threshold. The character of Foscarina, which contemporary critics felt was a cruel caricature of Duse, is ultimately the most memorable figure, and his account of the struggle for supremacy between the lovers shows narrative skills that recall other writers of the time, such as D.H. Lawrence.

D'Annunzio's work declined in popularity from the 1930s onwards, and for decades his plays and novels were regarded as period pieces, and examples of the excesses of Decadent symbolist writing. In the 1990s, however, there are signs of a reassessment, and *The Flame* is probably the novel most likely to appeal to a contemporary readership, focusing as it does on the battle between the sexes: between a powerful woman and a man desperate to enjoy the same

public recognition. Gender criticism has enabled us to look at D'Annunzio in a new way, and this novel is an ideal place to start.

—Susan Bassnett

A FLEA IN HER EAR (La Puce à l'oreille)
Play by Georges Feydeau, 1907

This spirited tale of suspected and would-be adultery is propelled by an intricate, coincidence-laden plot. It opens in a typically solid bourgeois interior, the drawing-room of the highly respectable director of the Boston Life Insurance company of Paris, Victor-Emmanuel Chandebise, whose wife, Raymonde, believes he is being unfaithful to her. After years of satisfactory performance in the marriage bed her husband seems to have lost interest in coition, and the arrival in the post of a pair of his braces, left behind at a louche suburban establishment by the name of the Hôtel du Minet-Galant, serves to confirm her worst suspicions. In point of fact the blameless Victor-Emmanuel, whose matrimonial problem is purely psychosomatic, has given the braces to his secretary (and cousin) Camille, an apparently innocuous individual with a cleft palate but something of a roué on the quiet, who is currently engaged in an illicit affair with the housemaid and valet's wife, Antoinette, and to whom the hotel has been recommended as a suitable love-nest by the family doctor, Finache, another of its habitués. Still, fired by jealous indignation, Raymonde confides in her old convent-friend, Lucienne, and together they concoct a scheme to trap the supposedly errant spouse. Lucienne pens a passionate declaration of love, ostensibly from an unknown admirer who has seen him at the Opéra and inviting him to an intimate assignation in the late afternoon at the same hotel, where Raymonde will be waiting to unmask his infidelity. Receiving the missive, Victor-Emmanuel is at first flattered, then modestly concludes that he must have been mistaken for his colleague and companion at the theatre, Romain Tournel, a noted womanizer who is secretly intent on seducing the half-willing Raymonde, and it is agreed that Tournel will keep the appointment in his stead. However, when Victor-Emmanuel jokingly shows the same letter to Don Carlos Homénidès dé Histangua, an insurance client who is married to Lucienne, the hot-blooded Spaniard recognizes his wife's handwriting, draws a revolver, and rushes out threatening to shoot Tournel *in flagrante delicto* and leaving panic in his wake. The narrative ground is thus richly prepared for an action-packed second act at the hotel itself. Here the stage is divided in two, one half occupied by the lobby with, opening off it, a corridor, a staircase leading down to the street and up to other floors, and the doors to four bedrooms; the other half is given over to one of these rooms, with a small bathroom off and a bed on a revolving platform designed, in an emergency, to whisk any adulterous couple into the safety of the next room and replace them with a bedridden old codger complaining of rheumatism. This multiple arrangement of spaces and points of access generates a rapid succession of inopportune arrivals and encounters, frantic concealments and discoveries, desperate flights and pursuits involving all the characters from Act I in turn and complicated still further by the libidinous antics of a drunken English hotel guest and the fact that Poche, the hotel porter, is the exact double of Victor-Emmanuel, the two being repeatedly mistaken for each other, particularly after Chandebise is forced by the proprietor into Poche's uniform and the latter dons

Chandebise's discarded jacket. Act III returns to the Chandebise household, where the abashed victims seek refuge from their evening's escapade only to be pursued by its consequences in the shape of the look-alike porter, still dressed as Victor-Emmanuel, then the still uniformed Victor-Emmanuel himself, and later the hotel proprietor. Further confusions and further changes of costumes ensue until true identities are established, explanations are exchanged, and three married couples are reconciled, with varying degrees of conviction.

The general contours of Georges Feydeau's dramatic technique are evident from this extended synopsis. In essence, it leans heavily on the Scribean formula of the "well-made play," especially as refined by such later vaudevillists as Labiche, who brought added depth to characterization, Henri Meilhac, whose strength lay in vivid, inventive dialogue, and Alfred Hennequin, who was a master of fast-moving, situational farce. Consciously borrowing from all three, Feydeau perfected a version of the genre which discarded the term "vaudeville" in favour of the less frivolous "comédie" or quite simply "pièce," as was the case with *A Flea in Her Ear*, one of his later plays, first performed at the Théâtre des Nouveautés on 2 March 1907. A customarily quite leisurely exposition allows him to flesh out his dramatis personae and give them a ballast of individual reality to keep them afloat in the torrent of improbable adventures that befall them. It is, in fact, an entirely credible personality trait, like a discontented wife's mistrust of her husband, that unleashes this torrent, engulfing the characters in painfully compromising situations or subjecting them to public indignity and humiliation. At the end, beached once more in domestic security, they remain basically unchanged, though somewhat chastened by their experiences.

Within this orderly but complex framework Feydeau's control of the dynamics of comedy is mesmerically compelling. He runs the gamut of visual slapstick, repartee, quid pro quo, repetition or inversion of situations, running gags, and the like; he is adept at bringing the wrong people together at the worst possible moment and at accelerating the pace towards a manic climax in each act, as with the successive brandishings of Homénidès's gun; he ruthlessly exploits the sound of foreign tongues or mangled French: and he does not scruple to use physical affliction—deafness, a speech impediment, halitosis—to devastating comic effect. The streak of cruelty already implicit in this becomes more marked in the grotesque, almost ritualized suffering he inflicts on some of his characters, which seems out of all proportion to their sins and reduces them to the level of helpless, semi-inanimate objects in the toils of a malign destiny. This distinctive quality has led some modern critics to see in Feydeau's comedy a parallel to the inexorability of fate that drives classical tragedy, and his plotting does indeed possess the unrelenting, geometrical logic and escalating momentum of some "infernal machine," reminding us of Brian Rix's dictum that farce is "tragedy with its trousers down." Other commentators have suggested that the unblinking, clinical eye Feydeau casts on the mores, particularly the sexual mores and marital relations, of the *belle époque* has given him the status of a true moralist, while still others have detected in what Norman Shapiro calls his "merciless and often gratuitous imbroglios" and the impotence of his characters within them an analogy with theatre of the absurd. Such assessments provide a measure of the critical rehabilitation of Feydeau's work and help to explain why, despite a partial eclipse in the two decades following his death, he has since become, after Molière, the most popular and widely performed of French comic playwrights.

—Donald Roy

FLEURS (Flowers)
Poem by Arthur Rimbaud, 1873

"Fleurs" is one of the 45 prose poems known as the *Illuminations*. The date of their composition is not known precisely but in all probability Arthur Rimbaud began to write them in the latter part of 1872. He had expressed his dissatisfaction with conventional poetic forms as early as May 1871 in his "Lettre du voyant," but it was not until a year later, in a group of poems dated May 1872, that he began to break away from traditional patterns of rhyme and rhythm and to experiment with blank verse and free verse. It was an inevitable next step that he should then go beyond even these loose verse forms and move towards the still greater freedom of the prose poem, of which "Fleurs" is no doubt an early example judging by the traces of standard poetic practices that it still retains. It is set out in three separate paragraphs like the stanzas of a poem. In the first of them there is an obvious use of attenuated rhymes in the form of alliteration and assonance as Rimbaud, gazing out over a mysterious and unreal landscape, describes how, from a golden step, amid silken cords, grey gauze, green velvet and crystal discs darkening like bronze in the sunshine, he sees a foxglove opening against a background of silver threads, eyes and strands of hair:

> D'un gradin d'or,—parmi les cordons de soie, les gazes grises, les velours verts et les disques de cristal qui noircissent comme du bronze au soleil,—je vois la digitale s'ouvrir sur un tapis de filigranes d'argent, d'yeux et de chevelures.

There is also a certain flexible rhythm to the paragraph which is even more marked in the second "stanza," where four parallel phrases describe golden objects laid out on an agate surface, pillars of mahogany supporting an emerald dome, bouquets of white satin and thin rods of rubies surrounding a water rose:

> Des pièces d'or jaune semées sur l'agate, des piliers d'acajou supportant un dôme d'émeraudes, des bouquets de satin blanc et de fines verges de rubis entourent la rose d'eau.

The final paragraph too, in which the sea and the sky, looking like a god with huge blue eyes and snow-white limbs, draw up towards the marble terraces the host of strong young roses, has a rhythmic quality to it, with what might be described as rhymes between "dieu" and "yeux bleus" and between "énormes" and "formes," as well as assonance and alliteration in "attirent aux terrasses de marbre":

> Tels qu'un dieu aux énormes yeux bleus et aux formes de neige, la mer et le ciel attirent aux terrasses de marbre la foule des jeunes et fortes roses.

But more than these vestiges of traditional versification it is the accumulation of brilliant colours and the scintillating images of gold and silver, crystal and bronze, silk and satin, emeralds and rubies, agate and marble that give the passage a particular poetic quality characteristic of the *Illuminations* as a whole.

As for the content of "Fleurs" rather than its form, in his earlier poems, such as "Le Bateau ivre," Rimbaud had displayed a remarkable capacity for transforming everyday reality into an exciting fantasy world, and many of the *Illuminations* continue and develop this process. Although it can sometimes be difficult to identify either the starting point or the end product of these metamorphoses, in ''Fleurs'' it seems to be a forest glade, carpeted with flowers, which is transformed into some kind of exotic temple. Thus the ''gradin d'or'' is no doubt in reality a bank covered with yellow flowers; the silken cords, grey gauze, green velvet and crystal discs could well be transformations of spider's webs, stretches of grass, and shimmering pools of water; the ''tapis de filigranes d'argent, d'yeux et de chevelures'' may originate in a background of interlaced branches, flowers, and blades of grass against which the foxglove is seen. The golden objects laid out on an agate surface are easily comprehensible, in the forest glade context, as yellow flowers on a mossy bank and it is surely the trunks of trees and a sunlit canopy of leaves overhead that are metamorphosed into mahogany pillars and a dome of emeralds. The two components of Rimbaud's equation are fused together in the bouquets, not of flowers, but of white satin, and it may be the purple foxglove that occurs again, under the guise of vergers' staffs, in the ''fines verges de rubis,'' while the ''rose d'eau'' can be interpreted as a pool of water reflecting the colours of the flowers around it so that, in the temple context, it looks like a rose window. Finally patches of blue sky and glimpses of blue sea are imagined as the eyes of a god-like figure formed by white clouds, and outcrops of rock as marble terraces towards which roses swaying in the wind seem to be moving.

In the section of *A Season in Hell* entitled ''Alchimie du verbe,'' describing the process of poetic creation he had followed, Rimbaud was to write, in 1873: ''Je m'habituai à l'hallucination simple; je voyais très franchement une mosquée à la place d'une usine.'' But the chapter where these words occur is significantly and dismissively entitled ''Délires,'' for he had by then become disenchanted with his verbal alchemy, and regarded as a kind of delirium the hallucination to which he had accustomed himself, and the readiness with which he had imagined mosques in place of factories, or exotic temples in place of forest glades.

—C. Chadwick

THE FLIES (Les Mouches)
Play by Jean-Paul Sartre, 1943

Jean-Paul Sartre began to work on *The Flies* during the summer of 1942, when he was on holiday from occupied Paris. This was a period in which French writers were packing subversive messages into innocent-seeming stories taken from Biblical or classical sources. ''The play I'd have liked to write was about a terrorist who, by ambushing Germans, becomes the pretext for the execution of 50 hostages.'' After an ambush, Resistance fighters could save the hostages' lives only by giving themselves up; the play argues that they should neither do this nor feel guilty about causing the deaths of innocent people. Sartre also wanted to demonstrate that even the gods are powerless to interfere with human liberty.

Like Giraudoux, who had already retold the Orestes story in his play *Electra*, Sartre deprives the gods of both dignity and power. The way Jupiter befriended Aegisthus, the usurper, parallels the way destiny was still befriending Hitler, while Thebes, infested with flies, represents Paris under German occupation. The oppressed citizens have little freedom, but a hero can show them how to preserve their integrity by accepting responsibility for their situation and rejecting the role of helpless victim.

In the *Oresteia* only superhuman powers can rescue Orestes from his guilt, but Sartre's hero follows Heidegger in believing conscience is the will to escape the guilt that is inescapable. While the occupying army makes it impossible to fight for the future without putting other people's lives at risk, Orestes is exemplary in ignoring the collaborationist arguments of Jupiter and Aegisthus, the proto-Fascist god and king, who try to scare him away from Thebes or bully him into accepting the *status quo*.

At first Orestes finds freedom a burden. He feels no urge to avenge his father Agamemnon's death. A king should share the memories of his people, and after growing up in exile, Orestes has different memories. The queen, Clytemnestra, represents the docile conformism of occupied France, but her daughter, Electra, is more rebellious, reviling the god who has allowed the people to condone the murder and accept the rule of Aegisthus, the usurper.

Aegisthus takes little pleasure in living: ''Almighty God, who am I, unless it is the fear other people have of me?'' Orestes is uniquely dangerous, because he knows he is free, and as Jupiter admits, ''Once freedom explodes in a human soul, the gods can do nothing against that man.'' Aegisthus is killed on-stage, Clytemnestra off-stage, but the killer Orestes has chosen to become is different from his sister in his reaction to the dog-like Eumenides. Though she has taken no part in the killing, she is so overwhelmed with remorse that she cannot stand up to them. Sartre generates rhetorical electricity out of Orestes' defiance:

> I *am* my liberty. You had scarcely created me when I stopped belonging to you . . . For I, Jupiter, am a man, and each man must find his own way. Nature hates men, and so, god of gods, do you . . . As for me, I don't hate you. What have I got to do with you or you with me? We'll pass each other, like boats in a stream, without touching.

Before leaving Argos he displays his pride in the crime which is his *raison d'être*. ''You can neither punish me nor reprimand me, and that's why I make you afraid. Yet I love you, my people, and it's for that I killed.'' This is a Resistance Orestes, a hero who sees it as his duty to destroy, not to stay on in Thebes as a monarch.

The importance of the play lies partly in the place it has in the evolution of Sartre's Existentialism. He was working simultaneously on his first major philosophical book, *Being and Nothingness*. Neither book nor play would be what they are if they had not been written in an occupied city, where the authority of the German army could be challenged only through underground activity and through actions that in normal circumstances would be criminal. The Occupation was giving a new cutting edge and a new resonance to the passion Sartre had already had before the war for liberty. In the play he highlights the freedom inalienably available to the man who refuses to view himself as a criminal, a sinner, or a victim of circumstances. The individual is still free to choose—and especially to choose his own identity—within a historical situation that appears to enslave him. You can be born as a worker, a Frenchman, a hereditary syphilitic, or you can have tuberculosis. You must obey Nature in order to command Nature.

Oddly enough, the Nazi authorities allowed the play to be staged. The director was Charles Dullin. A newcomer to professional theatre at the age of 37, Sartre learned a lot from watching him in rehearsal. Dullin believed in staging Dionysian violence with Apollonian restraint. As Sartre testifies:

Intangible richness arose out of poverty; violence and bloodshed were suggested with serenity, and, evolved with patience, the union of these opposites ... contributed an astonishing *tension*, which had been missing from my play.

(*Cahiers Charles Dullin*, March 1966)

Without asking for cuts or revisions, Dullin could make dialogue less rhetorical by telling the actors not to play the words but the situation. Nothing if not a good student, Sartre would later order himself to write the situation, not the words.

When the play opened on 3 June 1943, it was impossible for audiences to miss its political meaning, but most of the critics prudently ignored it.

—Ronald Hayman

FONTAMARA
Novel by Ignazio Silone, 1933 (written 1930)

Fontamara was published during Ignazio Silone's period of exile in Switzerland. Despite expulsion from the Italian Communist Party, he still had to flee Mussolini's Italy because of his socialist views. The novel was born in controversy and constantly aroused it. The first Italian editions were printed outside Italy and were distributed as anti-Fascist propaganda by the Allies during the war. For its first publication in Italy in 1949, Silone produced a revised edition. Despite having enjoyed considerable success in English translation, Italian critics attacked it on political and aesthetic grounds. Politically, in the eyes of left-wing critics, the book was tainted both because of its association with the Americans, and because of its author's rejection of communism in favour of a Christian socialism. Aesthetically, it was criticized because of an unrealistic plot, loose structure, and inelegant Italian.

Silone seems at least to have anticipated if not answered these criticisms since in the Preface he points out that the novel was narrated to him by three Fontamaresi, for whom Italian was like a foreign language. If this explains the stylistic deficiencies, the rest of the Preface deals with the other defects. The story was told, says Silone, like the old tales told at night beside the loom, even like the art of weaving itself, using simple and traditional motifs.

The novel consists of six lengthy chapters documenting the Fascists' abuse of the *cafoni* (the peasants)—the removal of their water, their land, their right to free speech, then the rape of their women—followed by four briefer chapters in which the hero Berardo admits to a crime he did not commit in order to allow his cell-mate, the socialist agitator, to go free and continue the revolt against fascism. In the final chapter the Fontamaresi print and distribute their own newspaper before the Fascists massacre the villagers.

The major theme of the work is the contrast between the old peasant attitude of fatalistic resignation and minding one's own business in the face of exploitation, and the new sense of solidarity and friendship epitomized by Berardo and the agitator. There is also a profound emphasis on the importance of language: bureaucratic jargon, which allows the corrupt middle classes to deprive the *cafoni* of their rights, is contrasted with the peasants' direct way of talking. The limited triumph of the *cafoni* occurs when Berardo uses language to deceive the authorities, and the printed word of the peasant newspaper spreads the gospel of socialism to other villages.

Silone's simple style suits the tale perfectly. He indulges in few stylistic devices, which reflect the peasant tradition of narration: lists of nouns or verbs, repetition of set phrases each time a character appears, like leitmotifs in opera, similes and metaphors drawn only from the rural world and religion, the two areas coalescing in the many pastoral images. The very first simile of the book compares the church tower and village houses to a shepherd with his sheep on the hillside. This image, like many others inserted into the second edition of the novel, prompts the question: who is the true shepherd of Fontamara?

The novel reveals that it is not the traditional claimants to this role, the corrupt priest and lawyer, but Berardo who will be the real defender of the *cafoni*. Again the imagery is consistent: Berardo is a Christ-figure who, like the Good Shepherd, rescues his girlfriend Elvira after she has fainted in the belltower, lifting her up "with the ease and gentleness of a shepherd carrying a lamb," and who in the end sacrifices himself for the others. Along with these appropriate stylistic measures, Silone also deploys effective humorous touches, thus preventing the novel from becoming too solemn and hagiographic. There is much linguistic humour: the bureaucrats speak in jargon, the maid, as befits her station, speaks in diminutives, and the pope, in a dream sequence, scatters fleas over the peasants, intoning: "Take, my beloved children, take and scratch, so that in your moments of idleness something will distract you from sinful thoughts!" There is also a hilarious episode in which the Fascists round up the peasants and "examine" them with the question "Long live who?" This examination is not just humorous in itself, but is carefully placed to relieve tension after the harrowing scene of the rape of the village women by the Fascists.

Fontamara is, then, an authentic and powerful picture of Southern Italy under fascism, but its appeal is not limited to one time or place, as is proved by its countless translations into many languages, particularly in the Third World. It may lack sophistication in *characterization* and structure, but its apposite style and humour ensure that its denunciation of injustice still rings out in countries and epochs far removed from 1930s Italy.

—Martin L. McLaughlin

FRAGMENT 1 (Address to Aphrodite)
Poem by Sappho, 7th century BC

The "Address to Aphrodite" is Sappho's only complete surviving poem. It is quoted in full by Dionysius of Halicarnassus, as an example of polished style, and in part by Hephaestion, to illustrate the so-called "Sapphic stanza." Scraps of the first 21 lines also exist in a papyrus fragment dated to the early 2nd century BC—that is, some 400 years after the time when Sappho is thought to have lived. Thus the poem has been retrieved from both sources through which the remains of Sappho's work have come down to us: quotations in ancient authors and papyrus fragments excavated in Egypt.

Sappho's poetry is classified as "melic" or "true lyric," and dates from a time when lyric poetry was in its infancy. Characteristically written in lines of varying lengths arranged in uniformly patterned stanzas, Sappho's poetry was probably sung with a single lyre accompaniment by one voice or (in the case of the wedding songs) by a chorus. The Alexandrians divided Sappho's work into books according to metre. The first of these books (which have been lost) is known to have contained poems in "Sapphic metre," that is, hendecasyllables—a form later to be revived in Latin poetry by Horace and Catullus. The "Address to Aphrodite" is in stanzas, the first three lines of which are hendecasyllables while the fourth is a pentasyllable, the so-called "Sapphic stanza." It is thought to have been the first poem of the first book.

The "Address to Aphrodite" has had a number of distinguished English translators, including Herbert and John Herman Merivale. Swinburne also included a paraphrase of the poem in his "Anactoria." More recently, the Nobel prize-winning Greek poet Odysseus Elytis has arranged all the existing fragments into "whole poems," filled the lacunae, and made a free translation into Modern Greek, thereby creating two parallel sets of poems, ancient and modern. The most recent translations into English (such as Josephine Balmer's *Poems and Fragments*) also exercise a fair degree of licence with the texts. The translation by the great classical scholar Denys Page has therefore been preferred here, as scrupulously faithful to the text. It should be pointed out that no surviving Sapphic poem includes a title and that Page refrains from supplying one, although the poem in question quite clearly constitutes an address to the goddess of love.

The "Address to Aphrodite" is an appeal to the goddess to release the speaker (who identifies herself as Sappho) from the anguish of unrequited love. In the opening lines of the poem, Sappho addresses the goddess as "Richly-enthroned immortal Aphrodite, daughter of Zeus, / weaver of wiles" and "Lady." Whilst "immortal" and "Lady" are conventional terms of respect, and "daughter of Zeus" is a Homeric commonplace, "richly-enthroned" and "weaver of wiles" are striking Sapphic coinage (modelled on Homeric epithets) and call attention to Aphrodite's intricate physical backdrop and complicated psychological machinations respectively.

A kind of dialogue ensues, in which Sappho attempts to enlist Aphrodite's support by reminding the goddess that she has not failed to come to her rescue in the past. She describes Aphrodite's descent to earth in an invisible chariot drawn by sparrows (birds sacred to the goddess of love) and how the goddess had asked her, smiling, what the matter was *this* time. Denys Page has pointed out the significance of the threefold repetition of the word "now" in the goddess's solicitous questions: there have clearly been many similar occasions in the past and the outcome has always been the same. Aphrodite is smiling with amusement at the transience of Sappho's desires once fulfilled. That Sappho depicts her patron thus is also indicative of a certain rueful self-awareness on the part of the poetess.

By recalling and repeating Aphrodite's words, Sappho appears to be reassuring herself, on the basis of her memories, that her present wish will be fulfilled. Aphrodite is quoted as saying to Sappho, of a previous love: "For, if she flees, she shall soon pursue; and if she receives not gifts, yet shall she give; and if she loves not, she shall soon love even against her will." Thus Aphrodite's part in the "dialogue" is not only anachronistic, since it takes the form of a quotation of her response to a similar appeal in the past, but also apparently dictated by past memories and present desires on the part of Sappho.

The poem concludes with a repeated plea to the goddess to come to Sappho's aid and the request that Aphrodite should become Sappho's "comrade-in-arms." This closing image functions as a metaphor, replacing the terms of love with the terms of war. Its emphatic

position in the final line suggests that this metaphor has been at work all along: Sappho has been planning an amorous campaign comparable to a military one.

Sappho's poetry is deeply personal and largely concerned with love; it is also highly polished and (even in the rare instances where complete or almost-complete poems, as opposed to fragments, have survived) elliptical. The "Address to Aphrodite" bears the typical Sapphic hallmarks of intensity, detachment, and self-knowledge.

—Sarah Ekdawi

FRAGMENT 31 (Declaration of Love for a Young Girl)
Poem by Sappho, 7th century BC

The "Declaration of Love for a Young Girl" is Sappho's second most complete surviving poem and among her most celebrated. Variously dubbed by tradition (for there are no surviving Sapphic titles, nor is it known whether Sappho employed them) "The Ode for Anactoria," "To a Beloved Woman," and "To a Maiden," the poem was used by Longinus (c. AD 250) as a perfect illustration of the Sublime in poetry, because it describes the signs of passionate love in faultless phrasing, and spoken of by Plutarch (c. AD 50) as "mixed with fire." The poem inspired a famous translation by Catullus ("Ille mi par esse deo videtur") and has been translated by W.E. Gladstone, among others, into English. Here, Denys Page's faithful rendering has been preferred to more modern and more free translations. (Page does not supply a title.)

The question of Sappho's sexuality has exercised generations of critics; her love-lyrics are addressed almost exclusively to women. Opinion remains divided, but it seems quite probable that Sappho's role in Lesbian society was that of a teacher who prepared young aristocratic girls for marriage. Educational organizations for girls of the kind which Sappho may have directed are known to have existed in ancient Sparta, as a female counterpart of the boy's military organizations. Boys were prepared for war and girls for marriage (and war is not an infrequent metaphor for love, in Sappho's work). Homosexual love played the same prominent role in the education of both sexes.

The "Declaration of Love for a Young Girl" is a poem of passionate love in the context of jealousy: the young girl in question is sitting laughing and talking with a man, whom the speaker regards as "fortunate as the gods" because of his proximity to her beloved. Some have argued that the poem is a bridal song, intended for performance at a wedding; its content, would, however, as Denys Page has pointed out, tend to call into question its suitability for use on such an occasion. It has also been suggested that the poem constitutes a farewell to a much-loved pupil on the occasion of her marriage. No textual evidence lends support to either view, however, and brides or bridegrooms are conspicuously lacking from the poem.

The poem consists of four "Sapphic stanzas"—verses of three hendecasyllables followed by one pentasyllable—and the first line of a fifth. It is not known how much more of the poem there once was. The poem belongs to the first of the lost books of Sappho's work, arranged by the Alexandrians according to metre, and is in the hendecasyllablic "Sapphic" metre admired and revived in Latin by Horace and Catullus. The latter used the "Sapphic stanza" for his translation of the present poem.

In the "Declaration of Love for a Young Girl," Sappho details the physical symptoms of the passion which overwhelm her whenever she looks upon her beloved. The lack of control which characterizes this experience is counterbalanced by the detachment and precision of the description of it, which displays the typical Sapphic self-knowledge and absence of self-pity. The vision of her beloved enjoying the company of a man has set Sappho's heart fluttering, she says:

> For when I look at you a
> moment, then I have no longer power to speak,
>
> But my tongue keeps silence, straightway a subtle flame has
> stolen beneath my flesh, with my eyes I see nothing, my
> ears are humming
>
> A cold sweat covers me, and a trembling seizes me all over,
> I am paler than grass, I seem to be not far short of death. . .

Beginning with her heart, representative of her innermost feelings, Sappho progresses through ever and ever more external bodily reactions: the tongue with which she would normally express those feelings is silenced; there is fire just below the surface of her body and her eyes are blind while her ears are ringing. Next, Sappho moves to the most external symptoms, which are observable to others: sweating and trembling. Finally, she describes her outward appearance as observable only to others, not herself: pallor and the appearance of being close to death (she "seems" rather than "feels" close to death). Thus we are presented with a description which moves from hidden interior to visible exterior.

The missing fifth stanza begins "But all must be endured, since. . ." It is impossible to establish whether the poem would have gone on to speak of the impossibility of requital for the love described, or of the patience requisite to contriving its requital, although it is tempting to speculate that the latter explanation is more tenable, in view of the broad hint conveyed in Sappho's "Address to Aphrodite" to the effect that she was used to victory (imaged as the support of the goddess of love) in affairs of the heart. In support of this view, the tone of the poem is far from despairing: it is matter-of-fact and faintly self-deprecating, but also a little coquettish, since Sappho invites her reader to imagine her powerless and aflutter in the throes of passion.

The "Declaration of Love for a Young Girl" is among the few surviving shreds of evidence for what the ancients viewed as Sappho's lyric genius. Its lasting popularity is testified by the generations of poets and scholars who have attempted to translate, adapt, and comment on it. In the English tradition alone, it has inspired Byron (via Catullus' version), Swinburne (in "Sapphics") and Tennyson ("Eleanore" and "Fatima"). The "Declaration of Love for a Young Girl," although incomplete, conveys even today the passion and precision of Sappho's lost art.

—Sarah Ekdawi

FRANCESCA DA RIMINI
Play by Gabriele D'Annunzio, 1901

The first run of *Francesca da Rimini* at the Costanzi theatre in Rome began on 9 December 1901 and was a lavish affair: it was then the most expensive production ever staged in Italy. The central part was written for the famous actress Eleonora Duse who was Gabriele D'Annunzio's lover at the time, but the play was considered too long and only met with any success after being cut. It was written in the middle of D'Annunzio's most intense period of theatrical output, but, like almost all of his plays, has not enjoyed the lasting success of some of his other work. D'Annunzio aimed to produce a "poetic theatre," but the result is a rather static play which relies heavily on set-piece lyrical passages. *Francesca da Rimini* is written in a flexible non-rhyming verse, based on lines of eleven, seven, and five syllables. The language, with its preciosity and many archaisms, aims to conjure up the rhythms of medieval speech.

The story of *Francesca da Rimini* is one of the most famous in Italian literature: Francesca is the central character in what is arguably the most powerful episode in Dante's *Inferno* (Canto V). Although Dante and his cultural milieu are mentioned by D'Annunzio (Act III, scene 5) and there are many stylistic echoes of the *Divine Comedy* in the play, D'Annunzio's approach is very different. Indeed, *Francesca da Rimini* is less a dialogue with Dante than a projection, in typical fashion, of D'Annunzio's own "decadent" themes onto Dante, whose story is removed from the judgemental context of the Inferno and suffused with a mood of mystery, fatality, and eroticism which is in tune with pre-Raphaelite medievalism.

Francesca da Rimini is a tragic love story set against the pitiless world of the medieval nobility. The handsome and cultivated Paolo Malatesta is sent to the Polenta household to arrange the marriage of Francesca to the elder of his two brothers, Gianciotto, an ugly, coarse and soldierly man. The marriage is part of a political and military alliance arranged by Francesca's brother Ostasio and his adviser, who fear that the strong-willed Francesca might object to being the instrument of their plans. Accordingly they have used Paolo, who is already married, as bait to catch her. In Act I, we see Francesca's ladies-in-waiting in an idyllic setting and a playful mood. In stark contrast are Ostasio's scheming, and his cruel treatment of both his feeble brother Bannino and a hapless minstrel. Francesca's sense of foreboding about her marriage emerges in a delicate scene with her sister, but when she sees Paolo, through the bars of a gate, she is captivated and silently hands him a rose.

Act II is set in Rimini, some time later, in a room of the Malatesta fortress which opens out onto the battlements. Even Gianciotto's soldiers are aware that Francesca's marriage to him is not a success. A battle is imminent, and the room is full of arms. Oblivious to the danger, Francesca appears and displays a self-destructive fascination with the lethal incendiary concoction which the tower-keeper is preparing to hurl down at the enemy. When Paolo enters to survey the field, it is clear, despite Francesca's hostile words, that her love for him has survived his implication in the cruel trick played on her. Tortured by remorse, and by his love for Francesca, Paolo agrees to give her his helmet, thus exposing himself to even greater danger. However, when Paolo survives the battle uninjured, Francesca gratefully takes it as a sign that he is cleansed of his deception. Gianciotto, pleased with Paolo's martial prowess, announces that he has been elected Captain of the People in Florence.

With the youngest of the Malatesta brothers, the warlike and sadistic Malatestino, D'Annunzio successfully adds an element of the macabre to his play. In Act III, Francesca tells her faithful slave of her fear of Malatestino who, having been blinded in one eye during the battle, succumbed to her beauty while she was nursing him. Paolo arrives back early from his duties in Florence, full of tales of the cultural life of the Tuscan city, but more eager to tell of the torment his thoughts of her have caused him. He asks Francesca to read with him. Their hoarse and nervous progress through "The History of Lancelot of the Lake," with Francesca reading the part of Guinevere, comes to an end when they act out the kiss recounted in the text.

In the opening scene of Act IV, the screams of a captive under torture can be heard from the dungeon as Malatestino tells Francesca of his violent lust for her. She fends him off, but is horrified when, on her request to him to stop the screaming, Malatestino sets off with an axe to kill the prisoner. Malatestino returns with the prisoner's head in a cloth and finds Gianciotto who jealously demands to know what he has done to upset his wife. Dropping ever clearer hints, Malatestino tells his brother of the affair between Paolo and Francesca, and proposes a plan to enable Gianciotto to catch them *in flagrante*. In the brief fifth act, Paolo and Francesca meet in the middle of the night, more in love than ever. But they are caught by Gianciotto. Francesca dies trying to protect Paolo from her husband's attack. Paolo is cut down, defenceless. Gianciotto stoops on one knee to break his sword.

Perhaps the most interesting aspect of *Francesca da Rimini* is its intertwining of the themes of violence and desire. D'Annunzio refuses to draw a platitudinous line between the pacific world of the lovers and the bloody times in which they live. Even the rose that Francesca gives to Paolo is "more living / than the lips of a fresh wound," and Paolo himself has a "scarcely repressed violence." Beauty is seen as fearsome and fragile, inviting jealousy and destruction. Passion pushes its victims into psychological turmoil and hurls them against the conventions of a society which is itself profoundly brutal. In D'Annunzio's hands, however, the recognition that desire *is* violent seems to topple over into an amoral and aestheticizing desire for violence.

—John Dickie

FREE UNION (L'Union libre)
Poem by André Breton, 1931

First published anonymously in 1931, "Free Union," a blazon of the female body, is widely regarded as one of André Breton's finest poems. It has been claimed that the inspiration was Suzanne Musard, but Breton is alleged to have told both his second and his third wives that "the poem could refer to the essence of woman, in a universalized sense," as Anna E. Balakian explains in *André Breton, Magus of Surrealism*.

The title could imply that the poet had in mind the alchemists' concept of the free union of two autonomous principles, in addition to the free union of man and woman.

Although its 60 lines of free verse are not divided into stanzas or obvious sections, the poem is structured in terms of little blocks of images, most of which are devoted to one part of the body, but there are gradual shifts, for instance from the shoulders to the wrists to the fingers.

At first glance the portrait of woman in this poem is composed of a quick-fire succession of images, the vast majority of which are Surrealist in their apparent gratuitousness, but a few come as less of a surprise. The "hour-glass waist" in line 3 is virtually a cliché, but the "champagne shoulders" (line 15) and the "armpits of marten and beech-nuts / Of Midsummer night / Of privet and wentletrap nests" (lines 20–22) are novel and bring the imagination of the reader fully into play.

In fact, the poem is not really a portrait of the beloved or of woman but rather an amorous or erotic litany in which the verbal is arguably more important than the visual, though the reader inevitably and immediately visualizes some of the images; the reader "sees" the matchstick wrists, the fingers of new-mown hay, the tongue of rubbed amber and glass, the tongue of a stabbed host, the tongue of a doll whose eyes open and close, the tongue of incredible stone.

At the same time, however, the reader's ears are stimulated by the bonds that the words themselves seem to seek out and generate. In places these links are semantic ones: the image of the woman's back "of a bird in vertical flight" (line 39) prefigures the reference to a swan's back in the evocation of the buttocks ten lines later; in the presentation of the hips the thought of the feathers of an arrow in line 45 leads instantly to that of the scapes of white peacock feathers.

Elsewhere the links are more phonic. Because they are easily lost in translation, it is better to cite some of them in the original, for instance the transition from "Ma femme au cou d'orge imperlé" ("My wife with her neck of pearl[ed] barley") to "Ma femme à la gorge de Val d'or" ("My wife with her throat [or bosom] a Golden Valley"), or the syllabic repetition in the line "Ma femme au *ventre* de dépliement d'*éven*tail des jours" ("My wife with her stomach like the spreading fan of days"). Words appear to attract or conjure up other words, there seems to be an accumulation of subtle shifts, modifications, metamorphoses.

At times the links are simultaneously semantic and phonic. Some of these are inherent in the French language: the juxtaposition in lines 11 and 12 of the evocation of the "cils" (eyelashes) and "sourcils" (eyebrows). Others, like the coupling of the first half of the word "hasard" and "as" in the presentation of the fingers, "Ma femme aux doigts de hasard et d'as de coeur" ("My wife with fingers of chance and ace of hearts") are illustrations of what the concept of verbal alchemy may mean in practice.

The poem moves to an apparent climax in the evocation of the sex in terms of, successively, a gladiolus, a placer (deposit where precious metals such as gold or platinum may be found), a duck-billed platypus, seaweed, old sweets, and a mirror. The surprise and the erotic excitement are engendered most of all by the diversity of the imagery discovered or devised to evoke this particular part of the female anatomy.

The real and ultimate climax is constituted by the last six lines devoted, quite characteristically for Breton, to the eyes. He proceeds from utterly simple statement (eyes full of tears), via the imagery of eyes of purple panoply and a magnetic needle, of savannah eyes, eyes of water to drink in prison, eyes of wood ever under the axe, to an amazing fusion of the elements in the final line (eyes of water-level, air, earth and fire-level). It is as if woman opens the eyes of her lover to the whole universe, as if she is indeed the microcosm and it the macrocosm.

Yet it has been claimed, not wholly implausibly, by Christine Martineau-Genieys "Autour des images et de l'érotique surréalistes: "L'Union libre," Étude et synthèse," in *Réflexions et recherches de nouvelle critique*, 8, 1969) that there are two persons present in the poem: in this scenario Breton is undoubtedly the lover as well as the spinner of words or the creator of images. As its title implies, this poem was meant to be a celebration of free union, and its cascading words are the expression of this celebration of an extramarital passion to be savoured to the full.

—Keith Aspley

THE FROGS (Batrachoi)
Play by Aristophanes, 405 BC

Along with *The Birds, The Frogs* may fairly claim to be Aristophanes' masterpiece. A brilliant mix of fantastic humour and serious matters, it brings together contemporary politics, literary criticism, gods, and religion into a comedy that won not only the first prize at the festival but also the unusual honour of a repeat production (though exactly when is debated).

Like all of Aristophanes' extant comedies, *The Frogs* is a flight of comic imagination based on the contemporary city of Athens. The "plot" depends on the recent deaths of Sophocles and Euripides, two of the three "Masters" of tragedy; Dionysus, the patron god of drama, struck by the loss of good poets, descends to Hades to bring back Euripides ("a creative genius who can utter a good phrase"). *The Frogs* reverses the normal comic structure, in that the episodes and adventures precede the resolution of the great idea. In the first half the cowardly Dionysus encounters a corpse, is forced by Charon to row across the lake of death, defeats an invisible chorus of frogs (for whom the play is named), and falls in with a group of initiates who form the real chorus. Four door-scenes follow, full of slapstick, changes of identity, and general discomfort for Dionysus and his faithful servant Xanthias.

After the parabasis, the play re-opens with Dionysus invited to judge a contest between Aeschylus, the grand old master of tragedy, and Euripides, the clever modern iconoclast; the winner is to hold the throne of tragedy and to return with Dionysus to Athens. The change in the plot from Dionysus' original intention to retrieve Euripides has bothered some scholars unnecessarily; consistency is not an Aristophanic hallmark. The second half features a formal *agon* (contest), in which Euripides claims for his drama realism, relevance, and common sense, and Aeschylus grandeur, nobility, and moral excellence. There follow investigations of Aeschylean and Euripidean prologues—the latter's ruined by a little oil-flask—parodies of Aeschylus' lyrics and Euripides' monodies, and a weighing scene where Aeschylus' ponderous grandeur overwhelms the scales. Finally Dionysus asks each "how to save the city," and despite clever and revealing answers, decides finally for "the one in whom my soul delights," Aeschylus. The play ends with a rousing send-off for Aeschylus and a general disparagement of current politicians.

The Frogs mixes three recurrent themes: religion (comedy was part of Dionysus' worship and the chorus a "sacred band"), politics (and not just in the parabasis where the comic poet advises the people to re-instate disenfranchised oligarchs and compares present political leaders to debased coinage), and poetry ("For what does one admire a poet?—For cleverness and for his teaching because we make people better citizens"). These strands are interwoven with consummate skill and come together forcefully in the parabasis ("it is right for the sacred chorus to advise and teach what is good for the city"), but especially in one telling moment near the end ("I came down for a poet.—Why?—So that the city might be saved"). Although the play is ostensibly about tragedy's role in the state, it is a short step to that of comedy, for which Aristophanes seems to claim a role like that of Aeschylus.

Critics have discussed endlessly the significance of the contest and Aeschylus' eventual victory. Elsewhere Aristophanes is a devotee of Euripides, and the words he uses of that tragedian (*sophos*—smart; *dexios*—clever) are words he uses of himself. Is Aeschylus' victory assured from the outset, or is it a close match with points scored on both sides? And what does it say about Aristophanes' own attitudes to these poets? The attentive reader will notice that Aeschylus has the second role in the *agon* (the traditional place of the victor), but also that neither the *agon* nor the parodies is actually resolved. Aristophanes is a traditionalist, and the victory of Aeschylus accords well with his other appeals to "the good old days" (e.g. in *The Knights* and *Lysistrata*). As much as he appreciates brilliant art, the poet as teacher is serious business for Aristophanes. The exchange at 1052–56 not only sums up most of subsequent Western literary criticism (freedom of artistic expression versus the moral responsibility of the artist), but seems also to reflect the comedian's own thoughts:

> Did I make up the story of Phaedra?—No, but a poet must hide what is bad, not put it on the stage. Little boys have a teacher to instruct them; grown-ups have the poets. What we say must be good and proper.

Some critics have found in *The Frogs* far more sophisticated and even metaphysical levels of meaning. For C.H. Whitman, Dionysus is Athens in search of its identity; for Charles Segal the theme of descent and rebirth "concern the regeneration of the *polis* through this general attempt to unify religion and art." Kenneth Reckford views the heavy presence of death as a sign of the death of "the old tragedy, the old Athens, and even the old comedy." For T.K. Hubbard, *The Frogs* was Aristophanes' final attempt to reconcile his "Euripidean side" (realism and modernism) with his "Aeschylean side" (imagination and moral purpose). One does wonder, however, if the essentially transitory and frivolous nature of comedy can really bear the weight of such sophisticated interpretations. Aristophanic humour is brief and to the point. There is much to commend in W.B. Stanford's assessment:

> In planning *Frogs*, he seems to have thought of something like this: "Let's send Dionysos off to Hades in search of a poet, give him plenty of adventures, have a contest between Euripides and Aeschylus, decide it quite whimsically, and end up with the usual victory-scene." The more variety and absurdity he can insert into this loose framework, the better.

Set in the shadows of the last year of the War, *The Frogs* is a marvellous comic fantasy revolving around the city and its cults, the city and its politics, the city and its poets. A legitimate classic, it bids an elegant farewell to Athens' greatness.

—Ian C. Storey

FUENTEOVEJUNA
Play by Lope de Vega Carpio, 1619

The action of *Fuenteovejuna* takes place in and around the year 1476 and centres on three interrelated, historical subjects which Lope de Vega Carpio combines into a single action in the play. The first is the uprising of the town of Fuenteovejuna against Fernán Gómez de Guzmán, the Comendador of the military Order of Calatrava in the year 1476; the second is the attempt by the Order of Calatrava, against the efforts of the Catholic monarchs Ferdinand and Isabela of Spain, to seize the strategic town of Ciudad Real in that same year; the third is the larger conflict between the Catholic monarchs of Spain and

Alfonso and Doña Juana of Portugal. Lope de Vega Carpio centres the principal action of the play upon the Comendador's depredations in the town of Fuenteovejuna and their consequences, while the secondary action revolves around the Comendador's treason against Ferdinand and Isabela. These two actions are portrayed against the backdrop of life in a village characterized as an innocent and harmonious pastoral paradise. In Act I, the Comendador attempts violently to assert himself over the townspeople and to interrupt the planned wedding of two of its members, Laurencia and Frondoso. In the second act the villagers confront the fact of the apparent inability of any one of their members to confront the Comendador and demand justice against him. In Act III the townspeople collectively rise up against the Comendador and behead him in an act of nearly ritualistic violence. The conclusion of the play turns on the attempt by the Catholic rulers to locate the perpetrators of the crime against the Comendador. In response to the inquest and attempts at torture by the agents of the Crown, the townspeople claim collective responsibility for what they have done and express their unity with the cry ''Todos a una Fuenteovejuna lo hizo!'' (''All together: Fuenteovejuna did it!''). When confronted with this response, the rulers decide that they can only pardon the townspeople; the village is placed directly under the jurisdiction of the Crown, and the alliance between the people and the monarchy is triumphantly restored.

Lope de Vega Carpio draws his historical information about the events of *Fuenteovejuna* from the chronicle by Rades y Andrada (the *Crónica de las tres órdenes militares*, 1572), as well as from traditional ballads, some of which also depend on Rades's text. This is a history play, but one in which Lope de Vega Carpio adapts the details of historical events to larger ''poetic'' purposes. In its overall structure, *Fuenteovejuna* resembles a literary romance. The action moves from a moment of harmony, through a period of trial, to the reconstruction of a more perfect world. As in romance, an idyllic land is placed in danger by a demonic figure and is then rescued from his threats. But unlike the typical romance, the tyrant-monster of this play is not defeated by any alien or mysterious knight. Rather, he is routed by the peasants themselves, who act *en masse* to slay him. *Fuenteovejuna* is in this sense a collective play, and its true hero is the entire town. The popular uprising, the revenge slaying of the Comendador, the cleansing of the villagers' honour, and their defiance of the authorities who come to extract a confession from them, are all collective actions, as are several ritual moments in the play— the celebratory entrance of the Comendador in Act I, the celebration prompted by the wedding of Laurencia and Frondoso, the ritual slaying of the Comendador, and the ceremonial recognition of the villagers by the rulers at the close of the play. Through the incorporation of such ritual moments *Fuenteovejuna* itself served to gather people together so that they could celebrate, in communion with each other, those ideals and values concerning honour that they held in common.

In addition, *Fuenteovejuna* may be seen as one of the many plays in which Lope de Vega Carpio recognizes that the concept of honour does not apply only to those noble enough to claim it by birth, but may extend to the peasants of society as well. In *Fuenteovejuna*, Lope de Vega Carpio's belief in the potential nobility of the peasants is buttressed by a platonic notion of ideal love. This love is represented in amorous terms in the relationship between Laurencia and Frondoso and is shown to be superior to ''natural'' love or desire. At a more general, interpersonal level the principle of love is revealed to be at work in the relationship among all the people of the town as a principle of mutual respect. Thus it is Mengo, one of the humblest

among the villagers, who, before the play's close, comes to demonstrate his solidarity with the group, to gain their respect, and to recognize the superiority of platonic over natural love.

During the historical course of its interpretation and reception, *Fuenteovejuna* has been taken as a revolutionary play, and has been seen as a symbol of popular freedom and independence. To be sure, *Fuenteovejuna* attempts to re-imagine social relationships along more just lines, but despite its depiction of mob violence it is a decidedly pre-revolutionary play, and recent studies have cast doubts on the plausibility of attempts to read it as a revolutionary drama. Lope de Vega Carpio attempts to imagine a purer or more perfect image of the relationship between peasants and monarchs, not to overturn that relationship in favour of the independence or equality of all members of society. Lope de Vega Carpio reaffirms the alliance of the monarchy and the people against their common enemy, the feudal nobility.

—Anthony J. Cascardi

THE FUGITIVE (Perburuan)
Novel by Pramoedya Ananta Toer, 1950

The Fugitive is one of the most representative and satisfying of all of the works of the major Indonesian prose-writer, Pramoedya Ananta Toer. This short novel was written while he was being held as a prisoner of war during the Indonesian struggle for Independence against the Dutch (1945–49), and smuggled out of prison by a sympathetic Dutch scholar.

The story is set on the last night of the Japanese Occupation of Indonesia at the end of World War II, 16 August 1945. It tells of the relentless pursuit of a rebel young military commander, Raden Hardo, by the Japanese and the unintentional betrayal of him to them by his own father. Hardo is captured and only just escapes execution when the Independence of Indonesia is first announced by a passing group of school children.

Although Pramoedya describes it as ''a story based on the imagination,'' the story has a firm basis in Indonesian history. Its background derives from the revolt of a Peta (Auxiliary Military Force) unit in Blitar, East Java, which took place early in the same year, on 14 and 15 February 1945. The troops took the munition depot and seized a number of key-spots in the city, including the Military Police headquarters and the telephone exchange. A significant number of Japanese soldiers and local Chinese merchants were massacred, before the revolt was quickly suppressed. The scholar, Benedict Anderson, has considered this revolt as ''the most serious single attack on the Japanese authority during the Occupation.''

Raden Hardo is one of three *shodancho* (platoon commanders) who were called upon by their comrades to support the revolt in Blora. His friend is Dipo, whose name significantly refers to one of the Javanese 19th century leaders of the early struggle against the Dutch, the aristiocrat Diponegoro, who was arrested at the end of the Java War in 1830 and exiled to Macassar. The third *shodancho* is Karmin, who betrayed Hardo and Dipo by unexpectedly refusing to support their units at the last moment, and he is charged at the end of the novel with their execution.

Underlying the contemporary nature of the story are many parallels with the traditional Javanese shadow theatre, or *wayang*. One of the major sources of the multiple plots of the wayang is the great Indian epic, the *Mahabharata*, which tells of a war led by five princes, the Pandawa, against their cousins, the Kaurawa.

Hardo has many similarities to Arjuna, the most sympathetic of the five Pandawa, in his guise as an ascetic. Like the self-denying Arjuna, Hardo's appearance is coarse and unkempt and he wears only a loin-cloth. His right hand bears an identifying mark, just as Arjuna's does. And despite his present suffering, Hardo is still refined and modest, yet extremely spiritually powerful, just as Arjuna was. Dipo is similar to Bima, the second of the Pandawas, in his bluntness and physical strength. And Karmin, the apparent traitor, is no traitor because he has maintained his allegiance to his masters, the Japanese, even though he now knows that they are in the wrong. This same nobility character-izes Karno, the half-brother of the Pandawa, who was raised by the Kaurawa and refuses to renounce his allegiance to them, even when he knows that they must certainly lose the war in the defense of their unjust claims.

The plot also follows the structure of a shadow play performance. It opens with a mock audience scene, in which the army (Hardo himself) is sent into the forest. The conventional hermitage scene, in which the hero's ascetic success is acknowledged by a priest or an old man, takes place in the second chapter, when Hardo meets his father in a hut in a rice-field. The chapter includes an early, inconclusive, battle scene, and the appearance of an ogre, here a Japanese officer.

The main battle scenes occur in chapters three and four. Here, too, the army of the enemy is defeated, and there is a "running amok battle scene" in which most of the major characters participate. As in the wayang, Dipo (Bima) has the major role in this part of the story, and it is he who performs the brief, exultant battle scene. There is one significant deviation from the traditional narrative at the end of the story. In the *Mahabharata*, Arjuna kills Karno with a special weapon he has earned for his asceticism. In *The Fugitive*, Hardo shields Karmin from the anger of Dipo and the mob. Perhaps Karmin's previous betrayal is forgiven, as an act of a particular sort of morality; the reconciliation is also a plea for a reconciliation of all Indonesians, those who supported the Japanese and those who didn't, to work together for the coming liberation of the Republic of Indonesia from the returning Dutch colonial forces.

Told in a plain, almost understated, style, *The Fugitive* first brought the importance of Pramoedya's writing, and the depth of his political commitment to the full independence of Indonesia, to the attention of the wider world. He has been nominated several times for the Nobel prize, and is sometimes considered "Indonesia's Solzhenitsyn." The story, even when one knows nothing of the Javanese archetypes which underpin it, is clear, the characterization strong, and the resolution of the story satisfying. It is a graphic tale of the problems of trust and betrayal, personal survival and death, in a time of great inhumanity.

—Harry Aveling

G

THE GAME OF LOVE AND CHANCE (Le Jeu de l'amour et du hasard)
Play by Marivaux, 1730

The Game of Love and Chance was first performed at the Comédie-Italienne in Paris in 1730. Using disguise and misunderstanding, and the conventional device of the arranged marriage, it deals with the theme of love, courtship, and deception, and offers delicately witty criticism of contemporary French society. Like Marivaux's well-known and influential novel, *The Life of Marianne* (*La Vie de Marianne*), which greatly influenced Samuel Richardson and later "sentimental" writers, the play is confined within the domestic world, and also like the novel, it gives unusual priority to female experience.

The plot is a conventional, self-consciously artificial one. Silvia Orgon, a beautiful and headstrong young woman is, by the arrangements of her wealthy bourgeois father, to marry Dorante, the eligible son of a nearby family. When she hears of the plan, about which she has not been consulted, her natural rebelliousness comes to the fore and she wishes to resist. Before she will consent to any arrangement, she disguises herself as her own maid, Lisette, and tries to discover more about the man she is required to marry. Dorante, meanwhile, has also been informed of the arrangement, and has disguised himself as his own servant, Arlequin, for the same reason. They meet, in disguise, ignorant of each other's true identity, and gradually discover a mutual attraction. Since Silvia thinks she is attracted to a mere servant, and Dorante thinks he is bewitched by a maid, each character is comically disturbed by a breach of strict social decorum. In a parallel plot, the real lower-class characters of Lisette and Arlequin mimic the high-flown language of the upper classes, and give an amusing parodic version of romantic love. Dorante bravely proposes marriage to Silvia/Lisette, still unaware of who she really is, and she accepts. The potentially radical conclusion that love recognizes no social distinctions is extenuated by the fact that, at the time of accepting, Silvia knows Dorante's true identity. The play ends with the betrothal of Silvia and Dorante, and that of Arlequin and Lisette, showing a conventional return to stability and order after a brief period of comic disturbance.

Typical of its theatrical tradition, this drama is made up of many small scenes of heavily stylized and ornate dialogue, with two or at most three characters on stage at any time, and the physical action is severely limited. The play's language has been characterized (not always sympathetically) as *marivaudage*, a witty, bantering style, sensitive to the nuances of status and class difference, concerned primarily with the complications of romantic love and with overcoming obstacles in courtship. The author produced at least one play a year between 1718 and 1757, all performed in Paris. Although some toy with the more cerebral and political ideas he entertained in his journalism, especially *The Double Inconstancy*, his own favourite play, the majority follow the regular pattern of *The Game of Love and Chance* and concentrate exclusively on lighter domestic subjects.

This particular play has always been one of his most popular and accessible and it may stand as representative of Marivaux's stagecraft, in the deftness of its treatment of disguise and its parallel plotting. However, it also stands apart from the others in its creation of a complex female figure in the leading character of Silvia. Whereas the other main characters (M. Orgon, Dorante, Arlequin, Lisette, Mario) are more or less familiar "types," Silvia stands out as a woman potentially capable of undergoing internal conflict. Her willingness to resist her father's pressure towards marriage, and her subsequent discovery that she is attracted to a man who appears to be of inappropriate social status, lead to an unusually intense psychological presentation, and raise questions about the particular pressures imposed on women by the system of arranged marriages. However, these remain little more than gestures, unfulfilled by the more complacent reordering of events at the end. For modern readers and audiences, it is disappointing that Marivaux seems unwilling to follow this dilemma through, or develop it more intensely, and Silvia's rebelliousness is diminished by the fact that when she accepts Dorante's proposal, she knows who he really is. So although there are undeveloped signs of greater depth in this play, it remains within the general style of Marivaux—elegant, amusing, stylish, but perhaps lacking in real substance. Marivaux's plays quickly fell out of fashion in the later 18th century and they are now only rarely performed.

—Ian A. Bell

GARGANTUA AND PANTAGRUEL
Novels by François Rabelais, 1532–34?

In 1532, for reasons not entirely clear, a man in holy orders, close to 50, with a degree in medicine from the University of Montpellier, and a thorough knowledge of the law and of the ancient world and its languages, published under an easily decipherable pseudonym (Alcofrybas Nasier) a book called *Pantagruel*, a story about a family of giants. What is more, the learned man in question, François Rabelais, had friends in high places, and, presumably, a lot to lose. The reason being that his book is couched in exuberant and often coarse language and is a veritable firework display of outrageous vulgarity. What, then, was Rabelais up to? Was he writing merely for fun, or to thumb his nose at conventional attitudes or, more likely, to make some money for himself? In the prologue to his work, he refers to the success of a book of stories about the giant Gargantua (the anonymous and frankly tedious *Chronique Gargantuine*) noting that "more copies of it have been sold by the printers in two months than Bibles will be bought in nine years." *Pantagruel* largely follows the pattern of the popular "chronicles" of the time and is obviously aimed (in part at least) at the same somewhat undemanding market. The book is not very carefully structured, and there is no real attempt at characterization or narrative coherence. Not that the author cared much about such things. His purpose—like the good doctor he was—was to raise his reader's spirits and to help them forget for a while the troubles of the world. *Pantagruel* is, then, largely escapist, and its special magic works almost as much today as it did four and a half centuries ago.

Rabelais's first venture into fiction is mostly a string of *bons roots*, anecdotes (some of which can still cause offence in some quarters) and pretty slapstick comedy. The main character in the book is Panurge, who is befriended by the giant early on and who quickly outshines him. A teller of tall stories (many about his sexual prowess) and traveller's tales, he is a fund of good jokes and high spirits. But the book does have some serious moments, too: notably when the giant receives a letter from his father Gargantua that sets out the educational programme he should try to follow and which is a hymn to the glories of the new enlightened humanist education. One cannot help wondering what Rabelais's more lowbrow readers made of this excursion into high seriousness.

These same readers must have been baffled by the tone and contents, too, of the sequel to the story, Gargantua (Rabelais now chose to write about the father of his first hero), which, though it keeps its popular touch, is much more concerned with matters "concerning not only our religion but also our social and private life" (Prologue). As M.A. Screech has shown, there is every reason to believe that the book was published in 1535 (and not 1534 as is usually thought), after the famous *Affaire des placards* in which placards attacking the Mass and the Church authorities in general went up all over Paris (October 1534), causing a backlash on the part of the King, a backlash that inevitably rebounded against the progressive ideas Rabelais and his friends believed in. This would explain the subdued and slightly melancholy tone on which the books ends. Otherwise, though, *Gargantua* represents the high noon of Evangelical and humanist optimism in France. The jokes are still there from *Pantagruel* but the humour has somehow become less important than a feeling of joyful good fellowship. The world is changing, and for the better. Rabelais's *Gargantua* is designed to give it a further nudge in the right direction.

The book can be conveniently divided into three main themes. These are education, warfare, and the Abbey of Thelema, which represents for its author a sort of ideal court where an intellectual and moral aristocracy learns to live at peace with itself (and eventually with the wider world) far from the persecutions of its enemies.

None of these themes is treated in an entirely serious fashion, however, although the section on Thelema is written in an unusually sober style. The educational reforms that Rabelais and like-minded people wished to see brought about are outlined in the section on the giant's upbringing. At the end of his schooling the giant Gargantua will look and sound like a Renaissance prince, albeit one with the correct political orientation. He will be prepared to fight the good fight on behalf of his subjects when danger threatens during the war with Picrochole, who unwisely invades the giant's lands, but the military action he reluctantly undertakes will be carried out with as little bloodshed as possible. In this he will be aided by what is probably Rabelais's finest creation, the irrepressible Benedictine monk Frère Jean (Brother John) who lays into his adversaries with gusto and who provides comic relief in what risks at times becoming too didactic a novel. In all this we see the strong influence of Erasmus, whose pacifism, humanism, and tolerant views Rabelais greatly admired. What separates the two, however, is the Frenchman's verbal creativity. Even when dealing with major issues of politics, religion, or morality, he enjoys spicing his text with puns, rude plays on words, and deliberate coarseness. He also delights in keeping his reader guessing about his real intentions. The prologue to *Gargantua*, with its teasing reference to Plato, Socrates, and the habit of dogs of breaking open and licking marrow-bones, invites the reader to look for the "substantial marrow" of his book, although quite what it is exactly is hard to see. Perhaps we should give up trying to find any

abstruse philosophical message and instead bear in mind the words with which the book ends: *grande chiere*—"good cheer."

—Michael Freeman

THE GAS TRILOGY: THE CORAL (DIE KORALLE), GAS I, GAS II
Plays by Georg Kaiser, 1917–20

Georg Kaiser's three plays *The Coral, Gas I*, and *Gas II* illustrate the expressionist ideal of the "New Man" against a background of class struggle in increasingly futuristic settings. *The Coral*, first performed in Frankfurt in 1917, although usually accepted as the first part, is a complete five-act account of a millionaire industrialist whose tragic parental origins he seeks to overcome by making money and by sparing his son similar hardships. His wish to fashion his son's life is thwarted when the son becomes a stoker on a cargo-boat while the father entertains guests on his private yacht. Shattered by his son's revolt (which is paralleled by an explosion in his main factory) the millionaire, instead of shooting himself with the gun left by his son after failed patricide, kills his secretary. The secretary, the millionaire's double who often represents him, carries a piece of coral for final identification. The millionaire takes the coral, is arrested for murdering his "employer," and can only accept the son's offer to identify him as the millionaire provided the son renounces his revolt. The millionaire is led off to execution seeing his ideals carried on by the "man in Grey" who has recognized, in the first act, how the millionaire has identified his own inner *doppelgänger* in his son.

The play is full of ironic twists which not only demonstrate that the New Man concept will remain a vision, but also relativize all genuine efforts to break down social differences and ease human suffering. Physical suffering caused by poverty or exploitation is counterbalanced by inner uncertainties. The millionaire, through an act of violence and deception, theoretically overcomes the arrogant demands of his will and reaches a higher state of awareness where, like a piece of coral, he can drift on the tides of life and death. He no longer needs a subservient *doppelgänger*, for the coral has given him the open-eyed wonder of the childhood he was never able to enjoy. In becoming inwardly certain he must die as both Millionaire and, as the judges insist, as Secretary.

Gas I, first performed in Düsseldorf in 1918, in five acts, introduces the millionaire's son who now controls his father's former huge gas factory. He has innovated worker participation in a form of socialist part-ownership, where success depends on ever-increasing achievements and productivity and the individual is of value only as a skilled mechanical operator. Gas has become the state's prime industrial power source and its failure would spell economic disaster. Even the safety mechanisms cannot prevent an explosion that destroys the works, since the workers are no longer able to master the latest technology used. Appalled by this, the owner refuses to rebuild and re-start production. Instead he tries to persuade the survivors to construct an ideal garden city and develop a community independent of advanced industrial processes. The workers, however, do not wish to become "human" but continue as wealth-earning and affluent automata. They elect the Chief Engineer to replace the owner and rebuild the factory to answer the demands of the state and other industries profiting from re-armament. The factory is nationalized and the state has to protect the owner from his workers' revenge. In parallel with the end of Bernard Shaw's *Man and Superman*, the owner's daughter looks forward to giving birth to a New Man, the first of a more hopeful and human generation.

In the three-act *Gas II* Kaiser explores his ideas further in a vision of the future with a new factory where gas is held in reserve for an expected war. The Chief Engineer is in charge and the workers are divided into coloured teams, operating control and information systems that are removed from the actual production of gas and demand endlessly repetitive responses. A struggle ensues between strikers who call for freedom from their machine-controlled existence and those who fear invasion. The "Blue" control figures are quickly overrun by enemy "Yellow" figures who force renewed production of gas with no shared profits. Act III repeats the opening situation, but when production falls the "Yellow" forces surround the factory and threaten to destroy it. In the ensuing confrontation between the Chief Engineer, the so-called Millionaire Worker, and the masses, a new invention, poison gas, is offered as a means of regaining power over the "Yellow" forces. The Millionaire Worker tries to persuade them to undertake a new spiritual way that would free them from dependence on material gain. The masses opt for the poison gas and, as the Chief Engineer throws his phial into the air, the enemy begins to open fire. Workers and enemy forces alike are hideously destroyed in the final holocaust.

Where *Gas I* depicts the end of the individual voice, *Gas II* extends this to predict, in dramatic form, the end of the world. The final result depends on the gullibility of the masses and their inability to support various utopian solutions proposed. Kaiser's repeated and balancing devices in the plays' structures, individual speech patterns, colour symbolism, and growing abstractionism and foreshortening of language, establish a growing feeling of inevitability. None of the characters act freely and the crowd scenes are marked by the power of rhetoric to produce propagandist visions of futures either under totalitarian regimes or as garden-city utopias. Central ideas are unfolded with deliberate control, thus making the two plays prime examples of Kaiser's so-called *Denkspiele* (thought plays). Huge swings of opinion responding to clear and compressed speeches, especially in Act IV of *Gas I*, represent the climax of expressionist dramatic art and mark growing interest in the problems and fate of man in the mass rather than the isolated individual. Gas, as the central focus of these two plays, is a symbol perhaps of the power of man to wring from nature a product to ease his own existence and provide the means to economic progress; but it also poses a threat. Not only technical skill but also correct emotional and ethical attitudes are needed by those who exploit and use such a commodity. Lack of proportion and the ruthless exploitation of the production formula and the control mechanisms to their utmost limits cause the explosion. Just as the machines become unpredictable when overworked, humans, when reduced to automata, can be equally self-destructive.

As with other examples of expressionist drama, the text is only one factor within a total theatrical experience. The *Gas* trilogy is a *Gesamtkunstwerk* (total work of art) where a variety of technical devices combine to produce an intense experience. Spatially, Kaiser used abstract, geometric forms in the stage-settings, in the constellations of characters, and in the representative use of a sliding roof to reveal the vault of the sky or a foreshortened mechanical reproduction of it. Structurally the scenes in both plays are paralleled and within each pair of scenes numbers and pairings of working figures emphasize the fatal repeat mechanism from *Gas I* to *Gas II*. The timing of the first performances of the plays supports the interpretation that they are meant as a warning to man not to repeat the catastrophe of World War

I and the industrial processes that led to its outbreak. Rhetorical use of language, using compressed, repetitive speech rhythms, especially in the crowd scenes, suggests an emotional response to the ideas expressed rather than a reasoned reaction to them. Above all clipped, emphatic phrases and stichomythia, dialogue in alternate lines of verse, produce an intensifying effect that heightens the sense of unavoidable, head-on clashes and eventual catastrophe.

—Brian Keith-Smith

THE GAUCHO MARTÍN FIERRO (El gaucho Martín Fierro)
Narrative poem by José Hernández, 1872–79

The Gaucho Martín Fierro (usually known as *Martín Fierro*) first appeared in Buenos Aires in 1872. Written in six-line stanzas of octosyllabic verse it imitated the gaucho custom of the *payador*, or guitar singer (at the end Fierro smashes his guitar in rage), and because of the political circumstances of the day became immensely popular, selling over 72,000 copies in the first seven years. This narrative poem, or novel in verse as Jorge Luis Borges called it, was continued by José Hernández with a second part in 1879, with chilling details taken from a pampas (rich grazing lands, a Quechua word) native peoples camp, but then breaks down into discursive elements. The second part lacks the anger and artistic unity of the first, which ends with the outlaw gauchos Fierro and Cruz abondoning the tamed pampas to live with the savage nomadic indigenous peoples. Over the years *Martín Fierro* has become Argentina's national poem, obligatory reading in schools, where passages are known by heart by most Argentinians.

The fact that Hernández wrote this narrative poem with a political purpose means that the historical moment of its writing and his intention are important. Argentina was already opening its doors to immigrants to populate the empty plains. The pampas peoples had lead a life completely bound to the cattle and horses that had multiplied since they first arrived with the Spaniards. The nomadic peoples lived on mare's meat and were expert horsemen. As the Europeanized Argentinians pushed the native peoples back from the port of Buenos Aires, the men who worked for them also had to depend on the cattle and horses, like the natives. These men were called gauchos (from an Araucanian word, *guacho*, for orphan). These gauchos prided themselves on their independence from the centralized State and the soft European way of life. They also despised foreigners. Indeed, in *Martín Fierro* a gringo (here meaning an Italian, one of the predominant immigrant groups) appears and is mocked because he cannot ride a horse. By the 1870s cattle were being exported not only as hide and jerked (or dried) beef, but frozen. In 1882 the first meat packing factory was installed, called frigorífico, and land became fenced in as railways were constructed to link the interior with the capital. With this development came a deliberate policy of chasing the native peoples off this land in what was called General Roca's Desert War. It was, in effect, a pogrom. The point of this historical context is that Hernández wrote his poem at a time when the gaucho's way of life was at a virtual end. Its appeal was partly nostalgic, and partly a reaction to the violent change in national identity that millions of immigrants brought to those who owned and lived off the land. The freedom-loving gaucho would end up as a hired farm hand, or *peón*. It is clear that this poem caught the national mood of shock and hostility to the abrupt changes, and came to be regarded as extolling freedom against state interference, conscription, and corruption.

The intellectual proponent of modernizing Argentina was Domingo Sarmiento (1811–88), who, in exile in Chile, penned his political pamphlet against the tyrant Juan Manuel Rosas, *Civilization and Barbary: Life of Juan Facundo Quiroga*, in 1845. For Sarmiento the gaucho epitomized Argentinian backwardness: ''El gaucho no trabaja; el alimento y el vestido lo encuentra preparado en su casa'' (''the gaucho does not work; food and clothes he finds ready-made in his house''). However, for Hernández's rebel gaucho, Fierro, work is a European plague: ''Allí no hay que trabajar / vive uno como señor'' (''Out there you don't have to work / and you can live like a king''), he says as he joins the wild native peoples.

The plot of this protest poem is simple. Fierro is conscripted and abandons his wife and hut. After killing a black singer, he is on the run from the law, joins up with the man sent out to capture him, called Cruz, and both leave for the native population. Hernández wrote this poem respecting gaucho Spanish, modifying the words to make the poem as oral and colloquial as possible. When Fierro decides to turn into an outlaw he swears: ''y juré en esa ocasión / ser más malo que una fiera'' (''and I swore then / to be more evil than a wild animal''), which gives us a clue to his symbolic surname Fierro—*fiera* means ''wild beast,'' while *hierro* means ''knife,'' the gaucho's main weapon, called in Spanish a *facón*, and used to slit animals' throats. His crime is not killing a black person, but simply being a gaucho: ''El ser gaucho es un delito'' (''Being a gaucho is a crime''). Through Fierro's conscription Hernández attacks corruption: ''Hablaban de hacerse ricos / con campos en las fronteras'' (''They spoke of getting rich / with frontier land''); and Fierro adds: ''He visto negocios feos'' (''I have seen dirty business deals''). Against this modernizing, capitalist state Fierro chooses freedom, ''juir (huir) de la autoridá'' (''to flee authority'') in order to live: ''mi gloria es vivir tan libre'' (''my glory is to live free'').

But *Martín Fierro* is far more than a political tract, and Hernández created vivid characters, knife fights, a close bonding of men, with abundant detail about the pampas way of life. A good example of Hernández's vividness is Fierro's knife fight with the person whom he kills, gaucho-fashion, to become a fugitive. In the second part there is another fight, over a *cautiva* (a white woman taken as prisoner by the native peoples), with vivid and unpleasant descriptions of the woman's dead baby: the *cautiva* tells Fierro ''Me amarró luego las manos / con las tripas de mi hijo'' (''He tied up my hands / with the guts of my child''), and she helps Fierro defeat the physically superior native in a duel.

One last element that stands out in this ''epic'' is what Borges called Hernández's poetry, the laconic descriptions of the flat pampas landscape and the wide horizon—''solo vía hacienda y cielo'' (''I could see only cattle and sky'')—or of the experience of horseback riding on the empty plains: ''Viene uno como dormido / cuando vuelve del disierto'' (''You arrive like a man asleep / when you return from the deserted lands'').

—Jason Wilson

THE GENTLEMAN FROM SAN FRANCISCO (Gospodin iz San-Frantsisko)
Novella by Ivan Bunin, 1915

The gentleman from San Francisco is a 58-year-old American who had made his fortune through hard work but also as a result of the hard work of others. To reward himself for his efforts he plans an extended trip abroad with his wife and daughter. He makes the journey across the Atlantic in the steamer *Atlantida*, which is outfitted with every amenity guests may desire. During the trip—on the island of Capri—he dies suddenly while waiting for dinner, and his body is unceremoniously hidden from the other guests. It is carried back to America ignominiously in a soda box, in the hold of the same ship that carried him to Europe. The structure of the story is an ironic commentary on the materialism of the New World and its insignificance in the face of nature and death.

The gentleman from San Francisco (he does not have a name) is crude, self-satisfied, commanding, and insensitive to others and especially to man's place in the cosmos. He has lived so long for pleasure and power that he has come to expect them as his just due. Ivan Bunin is at pains to show that such power is really powerless before the eternal truths of the world. Bunin was convinced that 20th-century man was progressively insulating himself from his place in nature, and confining himself to a world of his own making. This is revealed through Bunin's depiction of life aboard the *Atlantida*. It is described in exquisite detail as a vessel catering to human needs and pleasures—defiant of the storms that rage outside. In the thoroughly ''civilized'' and artificial world of the ship, the gentleman from San Francisco, and others like him, can command the satisfaction of every whim. Life is a continual round of eating, drinking, bathing, relaxing, and untaxing conversation. While the gentleman from San Francisco, ''his face cleaned and rubbed to a high lustre,'' sits in his white dinner-jacket in the comfort of the brightly lit salon, sipping cognac and other liqueurs and discussing the latest stock-market news with other gentlemen, sailors on watch freeze on deck in a raging storm and a ''great host of servants work below in the kitchens and wine cellars.'' In the very bowels of the ship, workers, half-naked and red from the furnaces, labour to carry him to the old continent, and when the *Atlantida* reaches Naples, crowds of Italian porters rush to help him. All these people, he believes, serve him willingly and in good faith. Bunin, it will be noticed, is at pains to show the injustice of the class system that has arisen in the New World of power and money. The gentleman from San Francisco and his like assume in their arrogance that they have the right to command, and they take for granted the ministrations of the obsequious help that caters to their desires.

But the social structure of the ''haves'' and the ''have-nots'' is not, in Bunin's view, natural and real. The gentleman from San Francisco lives in the thoroughly artificial and unreal world of modern civilization. He does not have the power he assumes he has; those who serve him do so in pretence and hypocrisy, and the pleasures he seeks and ''enjoys'' are unsatisfying and short-lived. What is real for Bunin is the world of nature, of both the physical world and the human heart. In the world of men the gentleman's will meets no obstacles, but in the world of nature his will is constantly thwarted. He had planned to enjoy the sun of Italy, but the sun that appears for a short time like some deceptive allurement at Gibraltar disappears as the *Atlantida* draws close to Naples. Once the gentleman from San Francisco and his family have landed, the weather behaves capriciously, deceiving him with its momentary rays of sunshine, fog, and unpromising skies. The family departs for Capri hoping to find it sunnier, warmer, and more comfortable there. The sun does not break out in its full splendour until the morning after his death.

Bunin is a superb craftsman and stylist and constructs the story on a series of delicately-wrought contrasts: power and powerlessness, nature and civilization, the natural and the artificial, light and dark, and upper and lower classes. Each of these contrasts is qualified paradoxically. The gentleman from San Francisco goes abroad in the splendidly-lit *Atlantida* and returns in the bottom of the ship and in the dark. He commands the lower classes, but after his death they mock him. He seeks light and warmth and ends in darkness and cold. Bunin's ''message'' is thoroughly objectified in his style and craft. There is little commentary from the author himself; he lets the events and the details speak for themselves. What they have to say is portentous and ominous for the new man and the new world of pleasure and power.

—Edward Wasiolek

GEORGICS
Poem by Virgil, c. 35–29 BC

The *Georgics* is a didactic poem on agriculture, presented in four books of slightly over 500 lines each. Begun around 35 BC and completed in 29 BC, the work coincides with Octavian's final consolidation of power as leader of the Roman state and also marks an important transitional stage in Virgil's poetic development, moving beyond the idealized rustic landscape of the *Eclogues* and paving the way for his epic of national duty in *The Aeneid*. Unlike the *Eclogues*, but like *The Aeneid*, the *Georgics* highlights as its theme Man's never-ending obligation to labour.

Virgil's most immediate source of inspiration for the *Georgics* may have been the prose treatise on agriculture by Mareus Terentius Varro, published in 37 BC. But its poetic sources extend back to the *Works and Days* (*Opera et dies*) of Hesiod, an 8th-century collection of peasants' wisdom combining mythology with practical instruction. Hesiod's poetry was revived and imitated by the Alexandrian poets of the 3rd century BC, particularly Aratus, whose astronomical treatise *Phaenomena* was also a major influence on the *Georgics*. Within the Latin tradition, Lucretius' philosophical epic *On the Nature of Things* (*De rerum natura*) provided models both of phraseology and of scientific exegesis. Virgil's unique achievement within this long tradition of didactic verse was to create a poem which was more than merely didactic and about more than its nominal subject. Indeed, the *Georgics* cannot be taken seriously as technical instruction, omitting necessary details and presenting as fact much that Virgil knew was superstition. Instead, Virgil uses agriculture to provide a metaphor for man's eternal struggle with nature and the human condition, and thus to reflect on the frailty and temporality of human achievements.

The *Georgics* has often been viewed as an alternation of straight didactic material with digressive ''purple patches'' on historical, mythological, or moral themes. The digressions seem designed to illuminate the broader significance of the agricultural lore and have been the focus of most critical discussion concerning the poem. Scholars have been sharply divided over the general tone of these passages and of the *Georgics* as a whole. Some have seen the poem as an optimistic glorification of the new political order under Octavian (Augustus), exhorting all Romans to a paradigm of self-sacrifice like their farmer-statesmen forebears; while others have seen the tone as deeply pessimistic, emphasizing the defeat, loss, and frustration which the farmer encounters. These opposing reactions may be part of Virgil's design, which seems consciously to promote ambiguity, indeterminacy, and self-revising reinterpretation of material. The poem's tone is best characterized as neither optimistic nor pessimistic, but as a mood of pervasive uncertainty about human progress, perhaps expressive of lingering doubts about Rome's political future after the tumultuous series of civil wars it had experienced over the last two decades. Human labour is seen as constructive and ennobling, but also as fragile and potentially even futile.

Book I of the *Georgics* concerns the cultivation of fields and begins with a prayer to Octavian among other gods interested in agriculture. Although the prayer is clearly based on Alexandrian encomiastic forms, it gives pause in light of the Roman disinclination to worship living rulers on the Eastern model and in view of Octavian's own refusal to encourage such a cult in Italy. The most famous passage of Book I is its theodicy of labour, in which Man's fall from the primitive Golden Age is justified as the unpleasant but necessary precondition of material progress: ''Labour has conquered all, / wicked labour and pressing need amid harsh affairs.'' Book I includes notable passages on the lucky and unlucky days of the month (modelled on Hesiod), the destructiveness of storms, and weather signs (modelled on Aratus), concluding with a list of the evil omens which occurred after the death of Julius Caesar. Fearful of the future, Virgil prays to the gods to allow Octavian's salvation of the Roman state; here, Octavian's success seems far less assured than in the prayer at the book's beginning, as Book I closes with the image of Rome as a chariot hurtling out of control.

Book II turns its attention to the cultivation of tree and vine, and is often perceived as more optimistic in tone. The book is punctuated by three laudatory digressions, the first on the glories of Italy, the second on Springtime, and the third on the country life. The praises have seemed to many critics too rosy and saccharine, coloured by manifest falsehoods (no snakes, two crops a year) and silly hyperbole (Caesar defending Rome against ''the unwarlike Indian''). The praise of the country life idealizes a pastoral primitivism which had been rejected as too easy a destiny for Mankind in the theodicy of Book I. The surface optimism of Book II may be as problematic as the botanically impossible grafts which Virgil presumes to describe at the beginning of the book.

Book III progresses to the cultivation of livestock: the book is neatly divided into two equal halves, each with its own prologue and epilogue, the first half treating cattle and horses, the second sheep and goats. The theme of horse raising and breeding is introduced with an elaborate proem, combining programmatic motifs from the epinician poetry of Pindar and Callimachus. Some critics have constructed the temple of song with its statue of Octavian in the middle as a forward-looking allusion to Virgil's epic design in *The Aeneid*. Equally memorable, however, are the two epilogues: the first on the destructive effects of love (modelled on the epilogue of Lucretius, Book IV) and the second on the cattle plague of Noricum (modelled on Lucretius' description of the Athenian plague at the end of Book VI). In both we witness forces of nature bringing to nought human cultivation and effort, and in both we see the animals' suffering as a paradigm for the seemingly incurable effects of passion and disease on Mankind itself.

Book IV focuses on beekeeping. The beehive is seen by some critics as a communitarian ideal for humanity, by others as a regimented totalitarian state without leisure, love, or art. The high point of Book IV is the description of the amazing *bougonia* ritual, in which bees are miraculously generated out of a steer's pummelled carcass. The ritual's origin is related through an Alexandrian-style epyllion, in which the farmer-hero Aristaeus is instructed how to regain his bees after losing them to nymphs angry over his role in the death of Orpheus' wife Eurydice. This passage is famous as the first literary rendition of the Orpheus myth in the form in which it came to be known by later centuries. In Virgil's contrast between the farmer Aristaeus and the singer Orpheus we see the opposition between economic man and artistic man; in the fantastic and ultimately illusory *bougonia* we see problematic success in man's quest for life out of death, even as we see that quest's devastating failure in the story of Orpheus and Eurydice. Like so much in the *Georgics*, the outcome is ambiguous and riddled with doubt.

—Thomas K. Hubbard

THE GERMAN LESSON (Deutschstunde)
Novel by Siegfried Lenz, 1968

An associate of the post-war writers league Gruppe 47, Siegfried Lenz was known chiefly for his deft short stories before the novel *The German Lesson* was published in 1968. Its popular and critical success took even the author by surprise. In the next year it became Germany's bestseller, translations were hurriedly commissioned, and Lenz was ranked with Böll and Grass as an eminent German novelist. By 1975 a million copies had been printed in German. An indictment of fascism and its lingering effects, Lenz's tale takes the form of a Heimatroman (novel of provincial life) gone awry. He constructs the setting of the central action, the northwestern coastal village of Glüserup and its environs, in such a way as to endow the region with a mystical essence, a communal temperament, and an earthy hero characteristic of the genre, only to scuttle these delusions and to illustrate in personal terms—the lives of two friends, the painter Max Nansen and the policeman Jens Jepsen—the disastrous consequences for Germany of a virulently particularist mentality. Their conflict is chronicled in retrospect by Jepsen's son Siggi, inmate at a Hamburg reformatory, with assistance from his psychologist. Siggi begins a three-year sentence for art theft in the autumn of 1952. The motive emerges as his reminiscences, grown of a composition on "The Pleasures of Duty" assigned in a German lesson, recount the years 1943–46. Siggi's prison life and his attempt to come to grips with the assigned theme serve to frame his narrative of the war years and their aftermath. The focus shifts repeatedly from frame to reminiscence and back again.

Siggi is nine years old in April 1943 when the recollections commence, youngest son of Jens and his wife Gudrun, who have another son Klaas (Lenz's autobiographical counterpart) and a daughter Hilke. All three siblings serve as models for Max Ludwig Nansen (an amalgam of Beckmann, Kirchner, and Nolde), internationally recognized Expressionist and the man whom Siggi addresses as Uncle Nansen. It is he who through his seascapes, marsh scenes, and windmills has conveyed the regional essence in watercolour and oil to an admiring world. In 1934 his paintings were removed from German museums, and after working in isolation on his farm since then, he has just been forbidden by the Nazis to paint at all. The character who emerges as antagonist is Siggi's father, as it falls to him to convey and enforce the ban. Jens understands the proscription less than the painter, but with Max's refusal to comply the professional conflict becomes personal provocation. Jens feels that Max has taken advantage of their friendship by continuing to paint in secret when he knows that Jens is bound by duty to uphold the law. Gudrun objects to Max's painting on more purely ideological grounds. She believes that the vaguely Jewish art dealer Teo Busbeck, whom she considers "a slightly superior sort of gypsy," has alienated Max from his own kind, an alienation reflected in "the sort of people he paints—those green faces, those mongol eyes, those lumpy bodies." Accordingly, she spurns Hilke's fiancé, an epileptic musician of Polish ancestry, and forbids Siggi from looking at mentally retarded children out of fear that the mere sight is enough to pervert a healthy outlook. Even as Jens's vigilance in monitoring the painter becomes an obsession, he himself becomes suspect to the Gestapo when Klaas deserts the army (as Lenz did the navy). It is Max who, at considerable personal risk, provides sanctuary. Far from being reconciled, Jens disowns his son and hounds Max more than ever. Hilke in turn secretly poses nude for Max, who portrays her as an exultant, dancing gypsy. She too is banished.

After the war the art world once again pays homage to Nansen. An English General who has come to induct Max into the Royal Academy reveals that he has on his walls in Nottingham several Nansens purchased in Switzerland. The very works the Nazis had labelled "degenerate" and ordered Jens to confiscate had been sold as treasures abroad by those who purported to have destroyed them. Jens, however, persists in harassing the artist by burning a cache of sketches he discovers. Under the pressures of delusion and obsession the Jepsen family disintegrates: Klaas and Hilke flee to Hamburg where Klaas settles with Nansen's goddaughter and Hilke with her musician. Siggi is jailed for stealing Nansen canvases from public displays in order to prevent his father from somehow destroying them. His fellow inmates, he claims, are all incarcerated in lieu of someone more highly placed. Nansen, the prophet vindicated, resumes painting the province and people he once thought he knew.

Like Grass, Lenz became an enthusiastic supporter of the Social Democratic Party's reformist programme. At a time when critics and friends alike surveyed the unrest in both German states and wondered if Germans were, in the words of one French observer, "fit for democracy," Lenz provided an unsettling answer. That Siggi's autobiography takes shape in the reformatory is telling. The lessons Lenz teaches are that the obverse of excessive pride in heritage and ancestry has its reverse in xenophobia and racism, that unquestioning acceptance of convention and authority is criminal, that fanaticism breeds fanaticism, and that the sins of the fathers are visited upon the children—to be revisited then upon the fathers. The latter proved oracular indeed; the year of the novel's publication former student Andreas Baader and his confederates, sons and daughters of the repatriated bourgeoisie, launched the campaign of terror aimed at annihilating their parents' preserve.

—Albert E. Gurganus

GERMINAL
Novel by Émile Zola, 1885

Germinal, published in 1885 and still highly popular in France, is the 13th of the 20 novels in the Rougon-Macquart series. It tells how Étienne Lantier, the son of Gervaise Macquart, the laundress from *L'Assommoir*, arrives in his quest for work at the mining village of Montsou in northern France. He finds a society marked by poverty, exploitation, and imminent disaster. Étienne, appalled by the conditions in which the miners have to work, takes advantage of the discontent created by the employers' attempt to introduce a new wages structure and organizes a strike. Since the miners are already so badly off that few of them have food supplies for more than two or three days, this inevitably collapses, especially after the army is called in to protect the right to work of the blacklegs brought in to help break it. As the miners go back, however, the Russian anarchist Souvarine decides to show that his version of social revolt is better than the early socialism and faith in trade union activity that inspire Étienne. He saws through the mineshaft, so that when the lift descends to carry the miners down to the coal face the mine collapses and is flooded. Étienne, in company with the young Catherine Maheu, with whom he has fallen in love, is trapped by the rising water on a narrow shelf. Earlier, Étienne has had a fight with Catherine's former lover, Chaval, and killed him. As Chaval's body is carried again and again by the waters against the shelf on which Étienne and Catherine have just made love for the first time, they push it away with their feet until it is eventually carried downstream. After staving off the pangs of hunger by chewing his leather belt, Étienne finally climbs up from the mine. Catherine, however, is already dead, and the ending of the novel, in which Étienne hears the seeds of social revolt germinating in the soil beneath his feet, leaves a bitter and ironic note rather than an optimistic one.

Germinal has been much criticized. The Rougon-Macquart series is an attack on the Second Empire, and the action of the novel takes place, according to internal chronology, in 1865. But the anarchist views that lead Souvarine to bring about the final catastrophe were developed 20 years later, when Émile Zola was writing the novel. The situation at the beginning of the novel is already so awful that not even Zola's imagination can overcome the objection that if the strike lasts as long as he says everybody would be dead of starvation. These reflections do not, however, occur while one is reading the book. The sweep of the narrative carries you along, as do the contrasts that provide the symbolic structure for the novel. The miners are always hungry, but they have plenty of sex. The rich owners of the mine, like the manager, Hennebeau, have plenty to eat, but their sex lives are either non-existent or disastrous. The red glare of the flames on the slag heap evokes both the hell in which the miners live and the flag of revolution, the black dust in which the miners are coated the despair that informs their lives, the green of the surrounding countryside the permanence of the nature as yet untouched by man. This, one feels, is how the working class lived in the 19th century. It is a sign of their instinctive feeling for what life was like for their ancestors, as well as their natural interest in sex and violence, that keeps the attention of the commuters of the late 20th century so riveted to the pages of *Germinal*.

Unlike Zola's 19th-century critics, they are not likely to be shocked by the realism with which he talks about sex, or particularly interested in the theories of scientific determinism that Zola was trying to prove by what he described as "the experimental novel." Zola was the first novelist to point out that, for the working class, the attraction of pre-pubertal girls lay in the fact that the men could make love to them without risking the creation of another mouth to feed. He wrote his novels in order to try to prove that human beings are entirely determined in their behaviour by the atavistic drives of humanity in general and, more particularly, by the vices and desires they inherit from their ancestors. The violence that leads so many of his characters to kill either their rival or, as in the case of Jacques Lantier, the hero of *The Beast in Man*, the women with whom they have just had sex, is presented by Zola as a throwback to the primitive behaviour of the caveman. He depicts the alcoholism that brings about the ruin of so many of his characters as the consequence of the hereditary defect they derive from the first of the Macquarts, the dissolute and drunken Antoine. These theories are not obtrusive in the novels and are soon forgotten in the excitement of the action. The principal interest of these themes lies in the intellectual framework they provided for Zola's own creative drive. They gave him the confidence that enabled him to put his own obsessions down on paper and organize his own emotional world. His first marriage was unhappy and there were no children. His second, to a woman 27 years younger than himself, Jeanne Rozerot, who had been his wife's seamstress, was happy and fertile. The quality of his novels declined dramatically.

—Philip Thody

THE GHOST SONATA (Spöksonaten)
Play by August Strindberg, 1907

The play *The Ghost Sonata* was intended for performance in August Strindberg's newly established Intimate Theatre in Stockholm, although its requirements, in term of staging and cast, would be more appropriately satisfied by a larger stage than that of what was essentially a studio theatre.

The Ghost Sonata was innovative in both its dramatic structure and its theatrical expression. As its title tantalizingly implies, the play bears some association with music. Strindberg himself revealed that the reference in the title is to Beethoven's Piano Sonata No. 17 in D minor, which the dramatist calls "The Gespenster Sonata," and the same composer's Piano Trio No. 4 in D major, known as the "Ghost Trio." Various critics have attempted to draw close analogies between the emotional or thematic structure of the play and the movements of the Sonata or Trio. Generally such analogies can, however, be applied only partially and are therefore ultimately unsatisfactory in illuminating Strindberg's innovative dramatic structure. A clearer indication of the nature of the play's debt to music appears in a remark made early in the play by the Old Man, Hummel: "My whole life's a book of fairy stories, sir," he tells the Student, Arkenholtz, "and although the stories are different, they are held together by one thread, and the main theme constantly recurs."

Strindberg's conception of *The Ghost Sonata* is intensely theatrical. Judging by its stage directions, in production the play should have the visual sharpness of detail which prefigures that of surrealist painting. Its symbolic characters, such as the shrivelled Mummy who talks at times like a parrot, or the grotesque Cook who consumes the goodness of the meat she prepares, leaving only fibre and water for the family, and the non-realistic treatment of time and causality are features which were to be adopted by later surrealist and expressionist dramatists.

Strindberg's acute awareness of the visual effect of the play is emphasized by the description of the set which is angled to create a strangely disturbing perspective of its interior rooms arranged one beyond the other. In addition, for some minutes before the commencement of the play's action with the entrance of the Student, Strindberg requires a tightly choreographed dumb show in which a number of the inhabitants of the house move, speak to each other or, in the case of the Lady in Black, remain motionless on different levels of the stage. Sound effects of church bells, a steamship bell, and an organ accompany the dumb show and establish the atmosphere of an unremarkable Sunday morning; an illusion soon dissipated with the arrival of the Student. Hummel's inability to see the milkmaid to whom the Student speaks on his entrance and his horrified reaction when told of the Girl's presence initiate a dislocation of reality which turns awry what initially appears to be a realistic situation. No longer can the audience interpret the play in an objective intellectual manner. Instead it must adopt a more subjective response to the stage imagery and verbal revelations, in a manner not unlike that demanded by music.

The student, like a fairytale hero in search of a beautiful princess, takes a journey through life (represented here by the house and its social cross-section of inhabitants) to learn that death, the "Liberator," is the only release from its pain. His quest takes him from the street outside the apartment house into the centre of the house itself, only to discover that behind the elegant façade, which seemed to him to promise a beautiful and gracious interior, reside only deception, guilt, revenge, moral corruption, and physical decay. Thus the set does not merely provide a naturalistic environment but instead makes a dynamic contribution to the communication of the play's themes.

The play has no plot in the traditional sense but is made up of three "movements" represented by its three scenes. Contained within these "movements" are the various stories of the past lives of Hummel and the inhabitants of the apartment block, all of whom are united by the "one thread," the theme which runs through the whole play, that of the conflict between seeming and being. The first scene is expository and reveals both to the Student and to the audience information about the inhabitants of the modern apartment block which dominates the set. The second scene, which takes place within the house, brings into conflict Hummel and two of its residents, the Colonel and his wife, the Mummy. Hummel is bent upon revenging himself for the Colonel's crime of stealing his fiancée, the Mummy. He exposes the Colonel as an impostor and reveals that it is he, not the colonel, who is the Girl's real father. In retaliation, the Mummy discloses that Hummel himself is also hiding a guilt-ridden past involving the physical and spiritual destruction of others. Offering him a rope with which to hang himself, she consigns Hummel to the cupboard in which formerly she hid from the world in order to conceal her decaying beauty. The final scene, which is interspersed with music and song, is lyrical and melancholy and ends with the death of the Girl, represented by her disappearance behind a screen similar to those used in hospitals. At this point the musical and the visual elements dominate the play and, as a white light fills the stage, the Student chants or sings his song accompanied by a harp. Gradually the room dissolves into a slide-projection of Böcklin's picture The Island of the Dead and the music becomes "soft, sweet and melancholy." Whereas the dumb show, which opened the play, prompted the audience to contemplate the actions of daily life, the picture and music with which it concludes inspire, in contrast, a quiet consideration of the sombre beauty of death.

—D. Keith Peacock

GHOSTS (Gengangere)
Play by Henrik Ibsen, 1881

Like its immediate predecessor A Doll's House, Ghosts announces itself as a domestic drama in three acts. Apart from its similar structure, Ghosts shares with A Doll's House a single interior location, concentration of the action on a few individuals, and an acute sense of personal catastrophe. Furthermore, in the way that Nora's increasing self-awareness is charted in A Doll's House, through lighting and mise en scène, the inner states of Henrik Ibsen's characters in Ghosts are indicated through extensive visual suggestion. All these means of intensifying the stage action produce what is probably Ibsen's starkest, and what was widely regarded as in its day as his most shocking, dramatic experience.

Ghosts concerns the fate of Oswald Alving, a Paris-based artist, who has returned to his native land of western Norway in order to be present at the dedication of a memorial to his father. Exiled at an early age by his mother so that he would be outside the influence of licentious Captain Alving, Oswald has remained ignorant of his father's past and is eager to discover life and joy in the bleak, rain-swept terrain of his birth. Oswald finds such qualities in his mother's servant, Regina Engstrand (a dramatic creation similar to Jean in Strindberg's Miss Julie [Fröken Julie, 1888] and Dooniasha in Chekhov's The Cherry Orchard [Vishnevyi sad, 1904] in her social displacement and personal pretensions). However, Oswald's attraction to Regina is doomed, as all the certainties of his family life are revealed as being founded on lies, with the revelation that his mother's servant is in fact his half-sister who was adopted, for payment, by the rascally carpenter Engstrand. Even more shocking is the realization that he has inherited syphilis, like Dr. Rank in A Doll's House, from his supposedly respectable father. Here, as in An Enemy of the People (En folkefiende), the presence of illness hints at murky and disguised truths. In a chilling final tableau, Ibsen shows us the long awaited reunion between mother and son, the beloved adult child reduced to babbling early babyhood as the hereditary illness attacks mind and body.

With its limited cast, close-packed action, time, and location, Ghosts is an attempt by Ibsen to emulate the tautness and severity of Classical and neo-classical drama. This 19th-century tragedy moves, like its French and Greek models, inexorably to a harrowing outcome, the consequences of past deeds bearing down, Eumenides-like, on the victim Oswald. Layers of illusion are shed and the truth about the past is revealed. Unlike its Classical predecessors, however, the moral questions raised are wholly secular, despite the omnipresence of the complacent Pastor Manders, to whom Mrs. Alving once fled on account of her husband's behaviour. The play shows the consequences of human deeds, and, as in many of Ibsen's dramas, the ways that people elect, or feel forced, to live are shown as life-denying and designed to inhibit vitality, creativity, and original thought. As with other naturalistic plays, Ghosts demonstrates how a particular milieu shapes behaviour and character. In this play, however, the environment exists more as a climate of ideas. Expressed in the "Ghosts" of the title, these ideas are handed on from generation to generation, and find expression in false notions of propriety and outdated beliefs in particular codes of conduct.

Although Ghosts depicts Oswald's tragedy, it is Mrs. Alving who is the central character in the play, and the main part of Ibsen's drama concerns her system of values and behaviour in relation to those of the other visitors to her household. Ibsen saw Mrs. Alving as a successor to Nora in *A Doll's House*. While Nora slammed the door on her constricting circumstances, Oswald's mother has chosen to stay in her home. In her isolation, Mrs. Alving has come to recognize more enlightened ideas of social and moral behaviour, and has grown scornful of the cowed and bigoted attitudes of her society. However, she is incapable of marrying action to belief, as is evident in her building an orphanage to her husband's memory in order to preserve an untarnished image of him. Her acts of bad faith, shown in her inability to reveal the truth, persist even to the end of the play when she glosses over the reality of Oswald's condition.

The representative of convention and respectability in the play is Pastor Manders who, like Helmer in *A Doll's House* and Aline in *The Master Builder*, has subordinated self-fulfilment to duty. Manders's measured and tightly patterned pronouncements are replete with platitudes, as he lays down the values of the patriarchal system that he has allowed himself to support without question. However, Manders is depicted as being in part a moral hypocrite with his lascivious interest in Regina's well-being and his anxiety to cover up his involvement in the careless burning-down of the orphanage that he has failed to insure.

Oswald, with his progressive ideas on living based upon his "beautiful, glorious and free" Parisian experience, becomes, as does young Hedwig in *The Wild Duck*, the innocent victim of a society based upon dogmatic beliefs and concealment of unpleasant truths. His idealism and lack of guile prevent his free existence, unlike Regina and her adoptive father Engstrand who have learned to survive by pandering to the outward respectability of their social superiors.

The idea of sacrifice to society, and also the way that truth cannot be quenched, is graphically shown at the end of the play by Oswald being burnt up by his disease, and is further accentuated by accumulating references to light and fire. The conflagration at the orphanage reduces to ash the very foundations upon which Mrs. Alving has maintained appearances of happy family life. Eventually the sunrise at the end of the play (the only time that rain has made way for sunshine) does not appear to represent a new beginning, but rather demonstrates how nature can cruelly overwhelm the nurturing process, as the ever-present natural landscape, ignored throughout the play, eventually pervades the elegant and outwardly ordered trappings of the Alving household.

—Anna-Marie Taylor

GILGAMESH, EPIC OF

See EPIC OF GILGAMESH

GĪTĀ

See BHAGAVADGĪTĀ

THE GLASS BEAD GAME (Das Glasperlenspiel)
Novel by Hermann Hesse, 1943

Hermann Hesse's longest and most ambitious novel took 11 years to complete. It depicts a quasi-monastic realm in which the competitiveness and sensationalism of the present have been superseded by the outwardly serene environment of the pedagogic province of Castalia, where the high-minded scholars of the future are nurtured in the benign but austere surroundings of elitist schools and institutions. The opening chapter acquaints the reader with the rudiments of the new culture, and the life story of Josef Knecht is told in 12 episodes by an anonymous narrator whose disposition is hard to describe as other than pedantic.

Knecht ("a servant") is a loyal member of the Castalian hierarchy, a committed scholar who eschews mundane pursuits, has no recorded love-life, and immerses himself in the affairs of the republic of aesthetes in a spirit of unquestioning obedience. His crowning achievement is to be nominated Master of the Glass Bead Game, which provides the central activity of the province.

This Game remains a mysterious, hallowed institution to which the narrator alludes with the utmost reverence. It is to be thought of as similar to a game of symbolic chess of infinite complexity, in which each piece and each move refer to an idea taken from the cultural history of the world. Castalia may sound like the revival of a medieval ideal, where the invariably male scholar is divorced from the need to earn a living and the arts enjoy the attention of teams of well-trained devotees, but nothing can disguise the fact that the new world envisaged by Hesse is profoundly, even wilfully sterile: overt manifestations of originality are proscribed. The paradox at the heart of Castalia is that her scholars are incapable of generating new ideas, her musicians are unable to compose, and her art experts have long abandoned any creative work. All that seems to count is mastery of the Glass Bead Game.

The minor characters come across as shadowy figures who are either heavily idealized (the Music Master, Pater Jakobus, Ferromonte), whimsical loners with neurotic tendencies (the "Chinese" Elder Brother, Tegularius, Petrus, Anton, Bertram), or faceless representatives of an impenetrable bureaucracy (Headmaster Zbinden, Master Alexander, Thomas von der Trave, Dublois). In the end, Knecht's individualism places him at odds with the administration; encouraged by his childhood friend Plinio Designori, he applies to leave the hierarchy and sample life in the world outside. From now on he is cold-shouldered by an increasingly hostile bureaucracy, and in the last chapter, "The Legend," an unverifiable story is reproduced, according to which he meets his death in a mountain lake. The biography ends with voluminous supplements containing Knecht's posthumous writings.

Early drafts indicate that Hesse intended to celebrate the Game as an invention worthy of our loftiest aspirations. The novel was to have culminated in a confrontation between Knecht and a "*Führer* of the Dictatorship" determined to stamp out such undesirable practices. The planned satirical vignettes had to be dropped from the final version, which Hesse vainly attempted to publish in Nazi Germany during World War II. With its rigid laws, constant surveillance, restrictions on travel, and overweening bureaucracy, Castalia mirrors a flawed world Hesse knew only too well; whether the Game itself is more than an empty ritual remains a matter for debate.

As soon as *The Glass Bead Game* appeared in Switzerland, two contradictory interpretations were put forward. According to one opinion, Castalia is a utopian state in a positive sense, while the other maintains that the province is shot through with evidence of human fallibility and decadence. Hesse repeatedly stressed the "utopian" dimension, but it seems unlikely that he would have endorsed the many authoritarian practices rife in Castalia. Ziolkowski suggested an answer to the critics' dilemma by distinguishing between the original community of intellectuals, the restrictive bureaucracy, and the improved Castalia represented by the narrator, which he supposes to have benefited from the lesson of Knecht's untimely demise. There are, however, few signs that conditions have improved since then, and the narrator's fawning attitude towards the "Board of Educators" is a disturbing feature not easily reconciled with Ziolkowski's optimistic account of him.

Hesse did not supply the continuation which some readers thought would resolve the issue, but by putting forward a wholesome, contemplative ideal contaminated by an all-too-human greed for power and abused until it seems no less pernicious than the evils it sought to combat, he created a masterpiece of tantalizing ambivalence, projecting his vision of man's enduring spiritual potential on to a disturbing background of crass authoritarianism and political intrigue. Castalia needs the Game to give itself credibility, but since culture must rely on social organization, the Game is wholly dependent on the new state. In its definitive form, the novel is utopian in its acceptance of this paradox, while warning against entrenchment, extremism, and the cultivation of collectivist ideals which can all too easily serve as convenient power bases for unscrupulous tyrannies.

—Osman Durrani

THE GODS ARE ATHIRST (Les Dieux ont soif)
Novel by Anatole France, 1912

The title *The Gods Are Athirst* was taken from the last number of the seventh and last issue of Camille Desmoulins's newspaper, *Le Vieux Cordelier*, whose motto, "Vivre libre ou mourir" [Live free or die] was an appeal for moderation launched at the height of the Terror, in December 1793. Desmoulins was arrested as he was correcting the proofs of the last issue and executed on 30 March 1794, on the order of his former classmate, Maximilien de Robespierre. The novel expresses Anatole France's own horror of the revolutionary violence which led some 2,600 people to be guillotined for supposed political crimes in Paris alone between 5 September 1793 and 27 July 1794. Its principal character, a rather mediocre painter called Évariste Gamelin, becomes an ardent supporter of Robespierre, having previously shown equal enthusiasm for other revolutionary leaders such as Mirabeau, Pétion, and Brissot before they had been revealed as traitors to the cause they were pretending to serve. In emphasizing the tendency of the French revolution to devour its children even more unmercifully than its enemies, *The Gods Are Athirst* anticipates the criticism of all revolutions, which was to become more acute after the Moscow purges of 1936–38 showed Stalin as an even more remorseless fanatic than Robespierre. Gamelin's enthusiasm for the revolution leads him to send to the guillotine not only an aristocrat, whom he wrongly suspects of having seduced his mistress, Élodie, but also his sister Julie's aristocratic lover, Fortuné de Chassagne. Like Robespierre, Gamelin is also a prig in sexual matters. It is only after he is, literally on one occasion, stained with the blood of his victims that he and Élodie begin to enjoy sex. When Robespierre is overthrown on 27 July 1794 (10 Thermidor, An II in the revolutionary calendar introduced on 21 September 1792), Évariste tries to commit suicide. He fails and is guillotined, after Robespierre himself, in the Thermidorian reaction.

The Gods Are Athirst is not a book by an erstwhile progressive who has made the great betrayal. Although France was one of the early socialists and a leading figure in the struggle to ensure a fair trial for

Captain Alfred Dreyfus, a French officer sentenced to life-imprisonment on Devil's Island for supposedly selling military secrets to the Germans, but innocent of any charge other than those brought against him by an organized campaign of anti-semitism, he had never been a supporter of any kind of political extremism. His attack on the cult of Robespierre stemmed from a characteristically 19th-century appreciation of reason, justice, and humanitarianism. It went hand in hand with an equally typical French anti-clericalism, which tended to present Robespierre's intolerance as the mirror image of the intolerance of the Catholic Church and all the more dangerous for that. In *The Gods Are Athirst*, the spokesman for France's own agonisticism is an elderly former nobleman, Maurice des Ilettes, now known as *le citoyen Brotteaux*, who carries in his pocket a well-thumbed copy of Lucretius' *De rerum natura*, (*On the Nature of Things*). Its doctrine of universal mortality, like its cult of physical pleasure and private friendship, provides for him and for the reader a preferable alternative to the puritanism and adulation of civic virtue that characterize the revolutionary attitude. France was, like his spokesman, a sceptical Epicurean. He pointed out, as other conservatively-minded thinkers were to do in the 20th century, how harmless the pursuit of sexual pleasure was compared to the havoc and bloodshed produced by puritanical revolutionary enthusiasm.

The Gods Are Athirst is not a novel in which one wonders what is going to happen next. From the opening page, it is inevitable that all the main characters are going to die. Its interest is political and its place in literary history a stepping stone between Dickens's attack on the French revolution in *A Tale of Two Cities* and 20th-century novels, such as Arthur Koestler's *Darkness at Noon* or George Orwell's *1984*. Just as these novels, like Orwell's *Animal Farm*, depict what went wrong in Russia after the Bolshevik revolution of 1917, so *The Gods Are Athirst* offers an analysis of why the ideals of 1789 lead to the Terror of 1793–94. The answer, suggests France, is not in the remorseless ferocity of the Gods evoked by the title. He was no more a believer in pagan divinities than in the God of Christianity. Revolutions go wrong, he suggests, because human beings invent ideas to which they attribute a truth so absolute that it justifies the destruction of everything and everybody that seem opposed to it. Together with *Penguin Island*, a satirical account of French history and especially of the Dreyfus case, *The Gods Are Athirst* is France's most popular novel and has never been out of print.

—Philip Thody

GOETZ OF BERLICHINGEN WITH THE IRON HAND
(Götz von Berlichingen mit der eisernen Hand)
Play by Johann Wolfgang von Goethe, 1773

Goetz of Berlichingen with the Iron Hand is Johann Wolfgang von Goethe's deliberate attempt to produce the kind of Shakespearean play which he and his *Sturm und Drang* contemporaries greatly admired for capturing so much of the dynamic, unresolved, self-contradictory vitality of Nature that the straitlaced, classicizing rationalizations of many Enlighteners had necessarily left out of account. In the towering figure of the eponymous hero—lustful, generous, brave, loyal, above all autonomous (he would rather die, he says, than be dependent on anyone but God, or serve anyone other than his emperor), and yet tender, sympathetic, and vulnerable—Goethe presents an unforgettable portrait of a human being tragically destroyed during a historic crisis in which the (old German) values he is committed to heart and soul cease to be operative in the new age, to which he finds it impossible to adapt. But equally impressive in its own way is the strangely sympathetic portrayal of Weislingen, Goetz's alter ego, who, in pushing personal freedom to the point of amoral licence and adapting to every twist and turn of political intrigue, betrays not only his beloved Goetz and his betrothed (Goetz's sister) but also his own professed values, and himself. And in the entrancing Adelheid (who so fascinated the author that she threatened to dominate the drama in the first version of 1771) Goethe gives us one of his many depictions of the ''man-made woman,'' the first precursor of the Helen of his *Faust*. Here the anima is clearly a projection of the woman in two men: what Goetz projects onto Weislingen is projected in intensified form on to her, a larger-than-life embodiment, beyond good and evil, of the apparent chaos of existence itself.

Shakespeare's influence is blatant, in the (notoriously coarse, though prose) language, and in its episodic structure (the plots and sub-plots are, on the surface at least, so provocatively open-ended—though, as some recent critics have demonstrated, in fact painstakingly composed out of a wealth of formal correspondences which produce a delicate underlying patterning—and at times so intricate, that would-be helpful résumés crop up with irritating frequency; events are distributed over several years and in as many as 36 different settings—in 56 scenes). But Goethe's teacher and foremost Shakespeare enthusiast J.G. Herder, echoing Garrick's famous phrase, savagely criticized the play in its first version, telling his pupil that ''Shakespeare has completely spoilt you!'' ''It's all mere *thinking*,'' he added, making brutally clear that, for all its outward theatricality, the play, in the detail of its language, lacked that intricate marriage of sense and bodily texture that alone constitutes poetry. In producing the far leaner version of 1773 Goethe left out whole chunks of text, sharpened the motivation of the characters (particularly of the demonic Adelheid), rounded out the enormous number of vivid characterizations, and cut out many of the linguistic crudities and archaisms. Above all, he brought into clearer relief the ''inner form'' of the drama, giving a fine and powerful aesthetic articulation to the notion that freedom entails limitation as surely as limitation entails freedom. This is evident, for example, in the metaphorical network drawn across the length of the play, from the subtitle of the final scene which establishes a close association between the ''hand'' and the ''eye,'' metonyms in the German 18th-century world of discourse for the interdependent polarities of physical and mental experience respectively. It surfaces at the very end (V, 13) in Goetz's dramatically ironic lament about what ''they'' have done to him: ''Little by little they have mutilated me, taking away my hand, my freedom, my property, and my good name.'' In fact, it is Goetz's necessarily mediated relationship to the world, with which he tragically craves immediate contact, that is symbolized by the, at times highly efficacious and yet ultimately (self-)destructive, insensitivity of his iron prosthesis. His pathetically confused and bewilderingly moving apostrophe to Freedom at the point of death is thus at once a defiant affirmation of the value of his heroic attitudes *and* a passionately tragic-ironic comment on his blindness to his own socio-historically conditioned, necessary limitations:

> All I said was freedom: all Weislingen said was some sort of order. To put the two together: all the world is broken up, and yet we must break it and break it and break it. . .

For the theme Goethe is articulating is the age-old polarity of individual and group, person and society, set at one of the great turning-points of European history, the dawn of the modern age in the Renaissance-Reformation, and given the peculiarly modern accent of the problematic interplay between endowment and environment, nature and nurture, subject and culture—between the values of the private sphere of the communal lifeworld and those of the public realm of the social system. (It is revealing of Goethe's historical awareness that the most explicit expression of this theme is put into the mouth of the rebellious monk Brother Martin, so obviously reminiscent of Martin Luther.)

The combination of Goetz's powerful and courageous energy with the brilliance of the language and the colourfulness of the presentation made the play a sensational success among Goethe's contemporaries, establishing his reputation and spawning a flood of *Ritterstücke* (''plays of knights-and-robbers''), characterized by a bustling stage-business analogous to that of the action movie (though, in theme, closer to the 20th-century Western). Instead of hi-tech gadgetry there is the (for the German stage of the time, novel) clash of swords, the clank and glint of armour, the clip-clop of horses' hooves; dark, mysterious dungeons and vaults, secret tribunals, the pomp of the Imperial Court of Maximilian I, the castle in the woods—in other words, all those aspects of ''medieval'' settings which helped inspire Sir Walter Scott (who translated the play in 1799) to write his Waverley novels. All of this of course contributes to the play's lasting presence (often in pageant performance) on the German stage and in film. But it is the poetic expression, especially clear in the second version (so different from the first that it maybe merits the status of a distinct work), of the paradigmatic human situation that Goethe saw as the central hub of Shakespeare's drama (and which, he insisted a mere month before writing the first version, lies beyond the grasp of any logical theorizing)—namely, that nexus of activity in which our much-vaunted free will comes up against ''the necessary order of the whole''—that makes the play, for all its technical faults, enduringly meaningful.

—R.H. Stephenson

GOLDEN LOTUS (Jin Ping Mei)

Anonymous Chinese novel of the middle or late 16th century. Based on part of the *Shuihu zhuan* (*Water Margin, q.v.*) which deals with Ximen Qing's seduction of Golden Lotus, the novel also borrows from other literary sources. Earliest manuscripts date from c. 1590. For much of the 18th century the novel was on the Chinese index of banned books, for its supposed licentiousness (ban rescinded, 1789).

PUBLICATIONS

Jin Ping Mei. c. 1617 (some sources give 1610); modern edition, 21 vols., 1933 (reprinted 1963); as *The Golden Lotus*, translated by Clement Egerton, 4 vols., 1939; as *Chin P'ing Mei: The Adventurous History of Hsi Men and His Six Wives*, translated by Bernard Miall (from the German), 1939.

*

Critical Studies: ''The Text of the *Chin P'ing Mei*'' by P.D. Hanan, in *Asia Major*, new series, 9, 1962; ''*Chin P'ing Mei*: A Critical

Study'' by Ono Shinobu, in *Acta Asiatica*, 5, 1963; *The Classic Chinese Novel* by C.T. Hsia, 1968; ''The *Chin P'ing Mei* as Wisdom Literature'' by P.V. Martinson, in *Ming Studies*, 5, 1977; ''Chang Chup'o's Commentary on the *Chin P'ing Mei*'' by D.T. Roy, in *Chinese Narrative: Critical and Theoretical Essays*, edited by Andrew H. Plaks, 1977, and *The Four Masterworks of the Ming Novel* by Plaks, 1987; ''Family, Society, and Tradition in *Jin P'ing Mei*,'' in *Modern China*, 10, 1984, and *The Rhetoric of Chin P'ing Mei*, 1986, both by Katharine Carlitz; *Renditions*, 24, 1985 (includes articles by D.T. Roy and S.P. Sun); ''Aspects of the Plot of *Jin Ping Mei*'' by P. Rushton, in *Ming Studies*, 22, 1986; *How to Read the Chinese Novel* by D.L. Rolston, 1990; *The Jin Ping Mei and the Non-Linear Dimensions of the Traditional Chinese Novel* by Peter H. Rushton, 1994.

* * *

The dating and authorship of the *Jin Ping Mei*, or *Golden Lotus*, are still a mystery. The novel's first known circulation was in manuscript form and goes back to the 1590s, its first printing to about 1617. The author was perhaps a well-known literary figure but kept his name secret because of the erotic contents of the work. He seems to have written his novel over an extended period of time, and, because of certain glaring inconsistencies, not even to have finished it. It may safely be said that he wrote in the second half of the 16th century (though some scholars say earlier), the beginning of an especially productive period in the history of Chinese fiction.

Golden Lotus, containing 100 chapters, is about a wealthy but uneducated merchant named Ximen Qing whose main activities consist of celebrating with friends and sleeping with concubines, courtesans, and other people's wives (his name may be translated as ''Celebrations at the Gate of Death''). The novel starts with an episode of adultery (lifted from another important 16th-century novel, *Water Margin* [*Shuihu zhuan*]) in which he and his paramour, Pan Jinlian (her name translates as Golden Lotus), poison her husband in order to bring her into Ximen's household. Subsequently he steals yet another man's wife, Li Ping'er, whom he then favours over the jealous and insatiable Pan Jinlian. Li Ping'er's status soon rises when she bears him his first son, but she and the son die within a year, mainly on account of the plotting of Pan Jinlian. The inconsolable Ximen Qing enters the last stretch of his life. Having already obtained a marvellous aphrodisiac from a Buddhist monk, he has been all along expanding the sphere of his sexual activities. But after Li Ping'er's death he gradually allows both sexual and financial powers to drain away, and finally dies when Pan Jinlian accidentally gives him a lethal overdose of the aphrodisiac. The last quarter of the novel tells of the decline of his estate, the dispersal or death of its members, and the survival of his main wife Yue niang and his only son by her, Xiaoge, who is Ximen's reincarnation, and who ends up becoming a monk.

Golden Lotus is unique among other novels of the period because its story matter is largely the creation of a single author. To be sure, the novel absorbs many sources (including current popular song, drama, and short story, not to mention the initial episode from *Water Margin*), which are at times quoted verbatim; but it is common for the Chinese novel to do so. For that matter, the reader of *Golden Lotus* should not expect a high degree of uniformity in style, plot sequence, or characterization. Scene changes are often extremely abrupt. The author uses diverse styles and language. Character types seem ill-fitting set against others, while individual characters seem inconsistent within themselves.

But upon close examination the novel betrays an astounding degree of unity and organization, particularly if one is attuned to certain generic features of Chinese fiction and discursive prose. Most important of these are the techniques of interlocking patterns of recurrence and alternation. In the 16th century such compositional techniques were central to prose theory and criticism and were reflected in both structure and image. In the *Golden Lotus*, for example, on a simple structural level, the novel consists of a first half in which the narrative world is steadily filled-in and a second in which it is emptied. In addition, polar images of heat and cold frequently accompany scenes of prosperity and decline, or sexual frenzy, frustration, or depletion. At times a cold figure is used as an ironic comment on an otherwise hot scene. Recurrence of image is also common, a notable example being that of the woman on top of the man. At the beginning of the novel, when Pan Jinlian has poisoned her husband, she smothers him with a blanket while straddling his body. Later she is astride the semi-conscious Ximen Qing when she gives him his fatal overdose of the aphrodisiac. Finally, at the end, after Pan is dead, her maid Chunmei (who continues in her footsteps) dies of sexual exhaustion while in the superior position.

Golden Lotus is most renowned as a pornographic novel and has been therefore censored throughout its history. But despite such a reputation there are in fact relatively few scenes which portray sex in a positive way. Sexuality is essentially the scene of a battle in which opponents attempt to score gains and recover losses. On a large scale, this battle is symbolic of all social struggle depicted in the book. It is remarkable that this novel took advantage of eroticism at such an early point in the history of Chinese vernacular fiction, especially since to this day (in contrast to the West) eroticism has been absent from all great Chinese art.

—Keith McMahon

THE GOOD PERSON OF SZECHWAN (Der gute Mensch von Sezuan)
Play by Bertolt Brecht, 1943

Like Bertolt Brecht's other three most celebrated plays (*Mother Courage, The Life of Galileo*, and *The Caucasian Chalk Circle*) *The Good Person of Szechwan* was written during the author's period of exile from Germany. It remains one of Brecht's most frequently staged plays. Its popularity may be ascribed to the almost folksy simplicity of the action, perhaps also to the fact that it may be interpreted—like so much of Brecht's work—both at a harmless, superficial level and in a more radical way: what some spectators will see as a slightly sentimental story of a tart with a heart of gold is in fact a striking condemnation of capitalism. The action consists of ten scenes, a prologue, short ''interludes'' that serve as commentary to the main action, and a verse epilogue.

The play begins with three gods, who are in search of a good person, looking for a night's shelter in Szechwan province. They are doing this in response to the complaint which has been heard for ''almost two thousand years,'' that the commandments of the gods are too strict, and economic reality too harsh, to enable men both to be good and to survive. The gods finally find shelter with Shen Te, a young woman who is spontaneously kind and who ''cannot say no,'' an ironic description given the fact that she has been forced into prostitution through poverty. Divine gratitude takes the form of a substantial sum of money, with which Shen Te buys a small tobacco shop which she hopes will enable her to do good deeds. Her unquestioning generosity soon leads her into both financial and emotional trouble. At the suggestion of one of the people she is trying to help, she "invents" a stern male cousin, Shui Ta, by asumming a male disguise. Shui Ta is as callous as Shen Te is generous, motivated totally by self-interest and cold calculation. Shen Te finds recourse to this bizarre "helper" increasingly necessary, particularly when she discovers she is pregnant by her lover, Yang Sun, who exploits her goodness like all the others. Shen Te spends so much time in the guise of Shui Ta that she is accused of Shen Te's murder. At the trial the gods arrange to take the place of the normal judges and try Shui Ta. When the court is cleared Shen Te reveals her secret and admits to the gods both her desperate plight and her equally desperate attempt to remedy it. The gods withdraw on a pink cloud, benignly smiling and waving, leaving Shen Te in despair.

The epilogue follows. By now it is clear that the gods are nothing but convenient dramatic fictions. From the outset they lack substance: although we are assured that they exhibit an excellent likeness to their images in the temple (which temple? which religion?), they are both ineffectual—they are forbidden to "interfere in the economic sphere"— and all-too-human. Whereas the first god tends to deny anything is ever amiss, ("Shall the world be changed? How? By whom? No, everything is in order!"), the second seeks rational explanations— flooding is caused by poorly maintained dykes, it is not a punishment for ungodly behaviour—while the third god always has a kind word at hand. The gods are mere ciphers, they motivate the action but are totally incapable of useful intervention. Their elevation to the role of judges at the end is merely authorial sleight of hand (a parallel to Azdak's service on the bench in *The Caucasian Chalk Circle*), and in no way confers authority. Their abandonment of Shen Te at the end of the play does indeed cry to heaven—but even the gods admit that the heavens are a void. If a solution is to be found, it must be found on earth. The gods are in fact the *reverse* of the *deus ex machina* of ancient tragedy. As they drift upwards, smiling and waving like superannuated royalty, we realize that their function is merely to pose the problem; they cannot even conceive of a solution.

On one level the transformation of Shen Te into Shui Ta is simply a comic device, effected by a mask, a change of clothing, a lowering of the voice, and a replacing of female body-language by its male equivalent—a stage fiction which is abundantly clear to the audience. More importantly, however, it is a powerful symbol for the way in which a world based on ruthless exploitation literally tears apart a person who seeks to behave with that decent, kindly, humane gener-osity that Brecht always sought, so infrequently found, and so convincingly invented. Although there is a sentimental streak in Shen Te, which emerges most clearly in the early days of her infatuation with Yang Sun, her "goodness" is never seriously called into question, merely its potentially destructive nature in the exploitative society in which she lives. It is most convincingly demonstrated in her stubborn resolve to provide for her as yet unborn child, linking her positively with Brecht's other great mother figure, Grusha in *The Caucasian Chalk Circle* (which might equally well have been entitled "The Good Person of the Caucasus"). The counter example is, of course, Mother Courage who, ostensibly dedicated to the preservation of her three children, loses them all because of her blind addiction to business.

Shen Te's creation of Shui Ta does not in any sense "save" the situation into which she is forced by her generosity. Shui Ta merely substitutes kindness for brutality. A proponent of "Victorian values"

of the least savoury kind, he sets up a tobacco factory with illegal working conditions in complicity with the corrupt authorities. Behind a façade of "entrepreneurial" efficiency, he creates an industrial jungle where dog eats dog for minimal wages, turning Yang Sun, ever the cynical opportunist, into a willing slave-driver who seriously contemplates supplanting his master. In an earlier prose version of the story, Brecht speaks of a "sweatshop of the worst kind," and the stage directions describe the workers as "horribly huddled together"; like animals. In fact their conditions are illegal, and Shui Ta has to allow them more space. The authorities agree to turn a blind eye, if he employs no more than *twice* the legal number of workers per unit space. Shui Ta's "solution" is merely a desperate, brutal—and illegal—response to a world based on exploitation. It compounds the evil. (In an alternative version of the play, Brecht turns the tobacco factory into an opium factory, to demonstrate the true nature of Shui Ta's beneficial activity.)

Like the gods, Shui Ta is part of the problem, not part of its solution. The dilemma is presented with dramatic mastery. But is there a solution? The epilogue, which Brecht added in the final version of the play, is both clear yet characteristically hesitant. The mock apology is not out of place: indeed "the curtain is dosed and all the questions open." But are the questions so open now? That the solution cannot be brought by "merely" another set of gods, or no gods at all, needs no further demonstration. Should it be a different set of people, or a different world? We do not get a clear call to a Marxist revolution at any price, as in Brecht's earlier play, *The Measures Taken*, which is also set in China. Yet it remains undeniable that the agonizing questions raised in this challenging theatrical parable could be answered by a society that puts people before profit.

—Bruce Watson

THE GOOD SOLDIER ŠVEJK AND HIS FORTUNES IN THE WORLD WAR (Osudy dobrého vojáka Švejka za světové války)
Novel by Jaroslav Hašek, 1921–23

In Jaroslav Hašek's novel, as in most of the best fiction relating to modern war, the diaphragm between history and invention is at its most transparent. The author's own experiences in fact provide the basis for much of the narrative. Hašek addresses the reader directly in a brief preface which presents the shabby Švejk as a real person whom one may encounter in the streets of Prague. But he goes further, overturning the grand perspectives of traditional historiography by asserting that Švejk is one of the "unknown heroes" whose glory eclipses that of an Alexander or a Napoleon, though he himself is quite unaware of it. The novel is a tellingly comic demonstration of this assertion.

The narrative opens with the middle-aged ex-soldier Švejk, now a forger of dog pedigrees, bathing his feet for rheumatism, when his landlady brings the news of the assassination at Sarajevo that will be the prelude to the outbreak of World War I. Since Švejk is never again troubled by rheumatism, the reader must presume that he has consid-erable foresight, and that his rheumatism is an insurance against military call-up. In fact, when war is declared, he propels himself through the streets of Prague on a wheelchair to volunteer for the front, crying "To Belgrade! To Belgrade!" to the huge amusement of the Czech population, who have no great enthusiasm for risking their lives fighting their Serbian (or Russian) fellow-Slavs on behalf of their Austrian Habsburg masters.

Švejk's inspired ruse, however, is no match for the efficient Austrian war-machine, which inexorably ingests him into its system. This provides one dimension of the novel's narrative system, propelling Švejk through the military hospital for would-be draft-dodgers shamming disabilities of one sort to another, and then through the whole gamut of situations, from the relatively secure and privileged status of regimental chaplain's orderly to eventual entrainment to the Galician front. Hašek thus creates for himself the opportunity for a systematic satire of Habsburg power as it impinges most directly on its unwilling Czech recruits, with a strongly physiological aspect, as the hegemonic control is imposed through the bowels. Much of the narrative is in fact an appalling comic saga of hunger, voracious eating, emetics, and excreting.

Here we have one feature of the book that from the first provoked a hostile reaction, both in Czech and in international literary circles, on moral and aesthetic grounds and also on patriotic grounds. Indeed, the very figure of Švejk was seen as a demeaning reflection upon the newborn Czechoslovak nation. All these grounds may be subsumed within class politics: Hašek's book shows all the characteristics of a subversive, perhaps anarchic, realism coming from below, and has many points of contact with the picaresque tradition (especially in its Spanish origins), with which it has frequently been compared. Apart from the overt challenge to the by then already defunct Austrian Habsburg authority, it presents a barely concealed challenge to a literary establishment and norms determined by class and, indeed, to authority of any kind. This is also evident at the level of language and style. The narrative is conducted in an idiom closer to the demotic speech of the Czech people than to the highflown literary tradition. The dialogue, especially the loquacious exchanges between Švejk and his peers, is freer and more broadly colloquial still, even phonologically. The German characters speak a frightful mishmash of German and broken Czech.

If the Austrian military machine and the historical script of World War I provide one part of the narrative propulsion of the book, Švejk's subterfuges or misadventures provide the other part, unfailingly involving him in scenarios that collectively add up to a coherent perspective on the situation of the Czech people at the outbreak of war. There has been much discussion as to whether Švejk is an idiot or a rogue, sowing confusion all around him through incompetence or by design. Hašek consistently avoids turning his hero into a subject of moral introspection or decoding his behaviour for the reader, just as Švejk carefully avoids allowing his military superiors to read his motives. It is only to his trusted Lieutenant Lukaš that he divulges one of his favourite techniques: overwhelming his antagonist with inane chatter (Part I, chapter 14). Nevertheless, Švejk's actions speak for themselves. All his blunders, ruses, or escapades have the effect of either delaying his approach to the bloodbath of the trenches or throwing the Austrian war effort into disarray, or both at once. He muddles the key to the Austrian military cipher and finally gets himself captured by his own side. Thus the definition of Svejk as "an idiot of genius," espoused by Ivan Olbracht and Julius Fučík, needs to be modified to "a genius at feigning idiocy."

Švejk's compulsive chatter, however, is not merely a defensive strategy. In the course of the novel, he tells hundreds of preposterous-sounding stories and anecdotes, typical pubtales very similar to those Hašek himself revelled in, which range in length from one-liners to a page or so. These have been characterized by Milan Jankovič as "absurdist" in their logic, and in that respect serve further to subvert

the purported rationality of the established order. But they go beyond that, building up collectively to a mosaic of the subject Czech people. Švejk also meets numerous tellers of other similar demotic tales that contribute to the overall picture of Czech ethnicity, the basis of the new nation that was to arise out of the cataclysm of the war. Though unfinished at the author's death, *The Good Soldier Švejk* established the oral history of the common Czech people as their comic national epic.

—John Gatt-Rutter

GÖSTA BERLING'S SAGA
Novel by Selma Lagerlöf, 1891

Selma Lagerlöf's first novel, *Gösta Berling's Saga*, won a prize for the best novel on the basis of five chapters submitted to *Idun*, a woman's magazine. Swedish critics in general received it coolly and it did not become a critical success until Brandes reviewed it positively, thus giving it the stamp of male approval. Lagerlöf struggled with its form, one that was new and difficult to categorize. One day she envisioned how it was to be written. The street in front of her heaved and she was overcome with a feeling similar to falling in love, an appropriate reaction to the conception of a novel that deals so much with love in all its passionate, destructive, and redeeming aspects.

The novel has 36 chapters, each constituting a story in itself. Elements from myth and fairy-tale are mixed with realism and social commentary. The style is Romantic, full of superlatives and exclamations. Lagerlöf is a storyteller whose roots are in the oral tradition. The setting is Värmland in the 1820s. Apart from the introductory chapters about Gösta Berling, the time span of the novel is one year, from Christmas Eve to Christmas Eve. The novel deals with "profound emotional experiences and important existential choices," to borrow a line from Vivi Edström. In his preface to a new edition of Lagerlöf's work in 1984, Sven Delblanc sees the novel as an expression of Lagerlöf's belief in "the liberating and redeeming power of woman's love." She also says that "the man is worthy of love in spite of all his faults and shortcomings," and, as Delblanc points out, "there is no lack of weak, fragile or violent and destructive men in Lagerlöf's work." This is especially true of *Gösta Berling's Saga*.

The plot concerns a group of adventurers, 12 so-called cavaliers, living on the Major's estate as guests of his wife, Margareta Samzelius, the most powerful woman in Värmland. The cavaliers, who are granted control of the estate for a year, represent a revolt against formality and rigidity but also "genuine, expansive love" (Edström). The hero of this fairytale, or "saga," Gösta Berling is a defrocked priest who must fight dragons and trolls before he marries his princess. The demons, however, are within himself; he must love women and be loved by them. Lagerlöf's description of him evokes an image of a fantasy figure and some earlier male critics tended to smile condescendingly at this male ideal drawn by a spinster:

> The priest was young, tall, slim and dashingly beautiful. If you had placed a helmet on top of his head and equipped him with a sword and armour, you could have sculpted him in marble and named the statue for the most handsome of Athenians.
>
> The priest had the deep eyes of a poet and the firm, round chin of a general. Everything about him was beautiful, fine, articulate, radiating genius and spiritual life.

He drinks, however, and ends up in a snowdrift hoping to die, when he is rescued by the Major's wife ("majorskan på Ekeby"). He joins the cavaliers and soon becomes a favourite among them in their hedonistic life.

The beautiful Anna Stjärnhök falls for the passion in his eyes, but when he tries to elope with her, the wolves pursue them across the ice. Not even his black stallion, Don Juan, can outrun them. Only by throwing a book at them, can the wolves be fended off long enough for him to bring her safely to her parents' estate on the other side of the lake. They must renounce their love to save their lives.

Another beautiful woman, Marianne Sinclair, flirts with Gösta Berling at a dance and her irate father drives home without her, leaving her to walk back in her thin dancing shoes only to find the door locked. The cavaliers find her half-dead in a snowdrift and carry her back to Ekeby to be nursed. She is not to be Gösta Berling's bride, nor is Ebba Doña, the fair sister of the stupid Count Henrik Dohna. She dies for her love.

The rich estate of Ekeby is wasted during the reign of the cavaliers while its mistress Margareta Samzelius walks the road like a beggar; she must be reconciled with her mother who cursed her when she struck her in anger. Instrumental in her being exiled from her own estate by her husband is Sintram, the villain who enjoys dressing up as the Devil. The "princess" of this fairytale is the young Countess Elizabeth Dohna, brought from Italy by Henrik Dohna as his wife. She is pure in her gaiety, taking pleasure in the dances held on the estates. She, too, falls in love with Gösta Berling but her conduct is blameless and their relationship innocent. Eventually, however, her jealous mother-in-law succeeds in making her son believe that Elizabeth is an adulterous wife. Dohna places her under his mother's control but with Gösta Berling's help she escapes the torment and pain imposed on her. The marriage, which was wrongly contracted, is not legitimized; the gentle countess is forced to earn her bread weaving for strangers. Weak and miserable, she gives birth to a sickly child, her husband's. She learns about the dissolution of her unfortunate marriage and turns in despair to Gösta Berling, begging him to marry her to give the child a father and a name. This he does.

Much happens to the proud estate of Ekeby before it is returned to its rightful owner. The spring flood comes crashing through the dam. The iron foundries, the pride of Ekeby, are mismanaged but, miraculously, the cavaliers manage to deliver the promised ore on time, thus saving the honour of Ekeby. Ekeby burns but is rebuilt. The Major's wife returns to Ekeby at the end of the year and work is gradually resumed.

The novel is rich in masterful characterization. Lagerlöf's blending of realism and superstition, drought, crop failure, and magical creatures and people, is breathtaking. The novel is at the same time a celebration of life's pleasures and an affirmation of the necessity of hard work. The book was made into one of the masterpieces of Swedish silent movies in 1924 by Mauritz Stiller, starring Gösta Ekman and Greta Garbo.

—Torborg Lundell

THE GOVERNMENT INSPECTOR (Revizor)
Play by Nikolai Gogol', 1836

Nikolai Gogol's great dramatic achievement *The Government Inspector* was also his first full-length play, written when its author was a mere 27 years of age. Gogol's background had prepared him as well for a career as a dramatist as was possible for a member of the minor gentry. In his childhood he had taken part in amateur dramatics organized by his father at the house of a wealthy relative, and his father was himself the author of a number of undistinguished Ukrainian comedies. Gogol' was also fascinated by the Ukrainian street puppet theatre. On arrival in St. Petersburg in 1829 to seek fame if not fortune, he had briefly considered a career as an actor, satisfying himself instead with frequent attendance at the capital's theatres. A discriminating theatregoer, he deplored the popular taste for overblown patriotic melodramas and above all for vaudevilles, hackneyed comedies interspersed with dance and song, at best mildly satirical, at worst merely silly. His own play had to reflect Gogol's own lofty views of true art which, while it might depict real life, even "low" subjects, should be informed by a serious purpose that would justify the subject matter. At the same time Gogol' had to work within the stage conventions of the period, bearing in mind constantly the dramatic experience of his audience.

This careful application of serious purpose and rethinking of current stage practice resulted in *The Government Inspector*, a play which, while employing traditional devices, recasts them in a highly innovative manner. The plot, which is far slighter than in a conventional comedy, depicts the comic misunderstandings that result when the officials and other inhabitants of a provincial Russian town mistake Khlestakov, a penniless minor clerk from St. Petersburg, for a government inspector sent to investigate their corrupt administrative practices. Gogol' takes the device of mistaken identity traditionally employed as part of a love intrigue, and turns it into the mainspring of the action, furthermore psychologically motivating it by showing town officials too terrified of discovery and too impressed by a visitor from the capital to see the obvious truth, while Khlestakov is firstly too fearful of imprisonment for non-payment of his hotel bill and secondly both too vain and too featherbrained to understand. To make the unwitting deception more credible, Gogol' gives the play terrific pace and concentrates the action into a few hours.

The traditional emphasis on love intrigue, normally the keystone of the action, is downgraded in *The Government Inspector* to the point of parody, Khlestakov alternately making advances to the mayor's wife and daughter, overcome by lascivious delight at finding women whose admiration of his supposed rank and city origins knows no bounds. However, the greatest innovation in the play is Gogol's deliberate refusal to introduce any positive characters; in conventional comedy the audience could conveniently ally itself with the innocent young lovers and wise adult figures who helped outwit the foolish and wicked. By rejecting positive characters entirely, Gogol' created a world of overwhelming mediocrity, where the characters are not black villains but people who bend their morals to get on in the world, who are vain, boastful, gluttonous, self-seeking, materialistic, and ambitious—in fact, have common human failings, even if to an exaggerated degree. Evil on a grand scale was instantly recognizable, whereas moral mediocrity merged imperceptibly into moral failing and was insidious and hence dangerous.

To make this point clear Gogol' adapted the stage aside to the audience, which in traditional comedy was designed to inform the audience or to gain their support. In *The Government Inspector* Gogol' uses the aside at the end of the play to turn the satirical spotlight on the audience. "What are you laughing at?" says the mayor, "you are laughing at yourselves." This was backed up by an original last scene. An intercepted letter from Khlestakov, who has now left the town richer by a large number of bribes ("loans" to him), reveals the truth to the officials, but before they can recover the real inspector general is announced and the characters freeze in a tableau of horror during which Gogol' hoped the audience would grasp the serious point of the comedy. Some modern critics prefer to see the real inspector as equally open to bribes and thus view this scene as merely a pause before the merry-go-round starts again, but this was not what Gogol' intended. In either case, the characters do not reform at the end, and good does not triumph—a much less comfortable ending than in conventional comedy.

Unfortunately the play's first audience, which included the Tsar and high officials, missed the point. Though the Tsar was amused, others were not, seeing the play as a dangerous calumny on the state. Indeed, in the repressive atmosphere of the 1830s anything that could be construed as critical was usually censored before it reached the stage, and it was only by imperial decree that the play was put on. Through his play and short stories about St. Petersburg Gogol' acquired an undeserved reputation as a radical. It has taken until well into the 20th century for the play to be seen for what it is, an exceptionally funny and well-written moral satire. Gogol' left town shortly after the first performance, horrified by the furor about his play. Fame he desired but not notoriety. The failure of Russians at the time to comprehend the dramatist's purpose has not prevented the comedy from enjoying uninterrupted success and achieving a world-wide reputation. Its portrayal of common human failings makes it universally applicable, and adaptations are numerous.

—Faith Wigzell

THE GREAT STAGE OF THE WORLD (El gran teatro del mundo)
Play by Pedro Calderón de la Barca, c. 1649 (written c. 1633–35)

The Great Stage of the World is one of Pedro Calderón de la Barca's many *autos sacramentales*. These are one-act dramatic compositions in verse, generally allegorical in nature, which always refer to some aspect of the Christian Eucharist and often incorporate a Eucharistic celebration. Many *autos*, including this one, were written specifically for the celebration of the feast of Corpus Christi. The *autos* have a liturgical and didactic function, and dramatize fundamental theological or doctrinal issues in a forthrightly allegorical manner.

The *Great Stage of the World* begins with the appearance of the Author, who creates the stage setting and the characters who will figure in the work and summons the World to appear on stage. World explains the history of man on earth according to a salvationist narrative. The first epoch of human history contains the story of existence from creation to the time of the great flood, and goes on to include man's salvation from the flood, and the covenant of peace, to the institution of natural law. The second epoch of human life corresponds to the period of the written law (i.e. to the Old Testament), and the third to the law of grace or of Christian salvation.

After the scene has been made ready, the characters themselves appear on stage. Author once again speaks, and creates the allegorical characters of Rich Man, Worker, Poor Man, King, Beauty, and Discretion. Before these characters are fashioned they lack free will

and so are unable to choose their roles in life; but afterwards it is up to them to choose to do good or evil according to their free will. They will be rewarded according to the way in which they exercise their capacity for choice. Calderón de la Barca affirms that the social and material differences among men may be radically contingent; the distinctions of social status are not arbitrary creations of men but correspond to the needs of social life. But it is essential to do good works regardless of one's station in life: "Obrar bien, que Dios es Dios" ("Do good, for God is God"). Each man who plays one of the assigned parts thus also has an individual purpose—to gain his own salvation.

As the play proceeds, Author watches the theatre-like actions or "representation" of the various characters he has created. He himself intervenes on only two occasions: at the beginning, in order to indicate his transcendent position with respect to his characters and to warn them that what they do will be seen from on high; and later in order to remind them that they can mend their ways but must always act in accordance with their freedom of will. In the representation itself the characters are associated in terms of contrasting groups: Discretion and Beauty, Poor Man/Worker, and Rich Man. When World declares the representation concluded, and when the celestial globe is closed, he asks each one what they have done. All are required to return the gifts with which they were endowed at the opening of the representation, except Child and Poor Man, who had nothing to begin with. The characters seek out the banquet of rewards promised by the Author to all those who played their roles well. This is the Eucharistic moment of the *auto*, when the celestial orb is once again revealed, along with the chalice and host, and the Author is seated on his throne. Discretion and Poor Man are called directly to share in the glory of the Eucharist, while King and Worker are sent to Purgatory. But since King assisted Religion in its time of need, he is pardoned and allowed to share directly in the Eucharistic reward.

The Great Stage of the World must first be understood as a theological and allegorical work, one that is fully informed by Calderón de la Barca's knowledge of theology through his Jesuit education. Its teachings are those of post-Tridentine Spain, and are influenced heavily by Calderón de la Barca's Christian neo-scolasticism. At the same time, the play cannot be isolated from its social and political content and represents an alliance of three important spheres of culture in Golden Age Spain: religion, theatre, and state power. The work is representative of Spanish culture in the declining years of the Golden Age, when the influence of the Council of Trent was still indirectly felt, yet when the theocratic State had gained ideological control of the means of representation.

The Great Stage of the World stands out among Calderón de la Barca's *autos* as the one that is simplest in its diction and most straightforward in its execution. And yet the play is not without its internal complexities. *The Great Stage of the World* is one of the most important examples of Calderonian metatheatre. Theatre and the allied, moral concept of role serve as the vehicles of a theological allegory, which teaches a Christianized version of the moral lesson to be drawn from the awareness that the world is a stage and that men are but actors on it. Yet Calderón de la Barca's representation of the play within a play also displays a high degree of artistic self-consciousness, and the *auto* must be appreciated for the sheer brilliance of its language and the elegance of its allegorical construction as well as for its doctrinal lessons.

—Anthony J. Cascardi

GRODEK
Poem by Georg Trakl, 1915

Bertolt Brecht and Georg Trakl, both served as medical orderlies during World War I. While Brecht responded to the inadequate patching up of wounded soldiers in characteristic *Good Soldier Schweik* fashion, by covering up emotional pain with sardonic humour and cynicism, Trakl's much less resilient personality was unable to withstand the horrors of the front. When faced by mass slaughter and sordid conditions, Trakl's already shaky (and often drugged) hold on sanity was severely tested, with the poet suffering a breakdown and dying in late 1914 at the age of 27 through an overdose of cocaine.

Ironically, Trakl's apprehension that his external and inner worlds were falling apart, and the articulation of these feelings of disintegration, gave rise to some of the most delicately composed and suggestive poems in 20th-century German literature. Trakl's best-known poem of his war experience is ''Grodek,'' a haunting poetic memorial to the bloody battle fought in Galicia, where as a trained apothecary, he was left single-handedly in charge of wounded men. ''Grodek,'' posthumously published in 1915, describes in its opening lines, rather as Arthur Rimbaud's ''Dormeur du Val'' (1870) does in its closing lines, human aggression and pain invading a natural landscape:

> Am Abend tönen die herbstlichen Wälder
> Von tödlichen Waffen, die goldenen Ebenen
> Und blauen Seen, darüber die Sonne
> Düstrer hinrollt; umfängt die Nacht
> Sterbende Krieger, die wilde Klage
> Ihrer zerbrochenen Münder.

> (In the evening the autumn woods ring
> With deadly weapons, the golden plains
> And blue lakes; above, the sun
> Darkly rolls by; night embraces
> Dying warriors, the wild lament
> Of their crushed mouths.)

However, despite the spare and almost banal way that the natural landscape is summoned up, it becomes clear as the poem progresses that this is far from a neutral setting. Rather as his contemporary Georg Heym presented a demonic vision of the natural world as alive with sinister and destructive forces in *Der Krieg* [War], Trakl's countryside is imbued with a primitive and vengeful spirit of sacrifice:

> Doch stille sammelt im Weidengrund
> Rotes Gewölk, darin ein zürnender Gott wohnt
> Das vergossne Blut, mondne Kuhle
> Alle Strassen münden in schwarze Verwesung.

> (But quietly in the willow grove gather
> Red clouds, in which an angry god resides
> Spilled blood, the cool of the moon;
> All roads end in black decay.)

Trakl's elliptical style, with its fondness for compression and inversion, and his tantalizing use of images from classical and Christian precedents and from his private imagination, perplex the reader here as in earlier poems. Having indicated the scene of the pain, Trakl now elaborates upon the quasiclassical references and develops his poem as a praise-chant for lost warriors. For out of this angered natural world:

> Es schwankt der Schwester Schatten durch den
>   schweigenden Hain,
> Zu grüssen die Geister der Helden, die blutenden Häupter;
> Und leise tönen im Rohr die dunklen Flöten des Herbstes.

> (The sister's shadow sways through the silent thicket,
> To greet the heroes' spirits, the bleeding heads;
> And softly sound in the reeds the dark flutes of Autumn.)

The archaic, seemingly pre-Christian, greeting of the heroes' spirits, with the appearance of the mysterious sister (who may be Trakl's own desired and ailing sibling, but who remains unidentified and enigmatic), is undercut by the final lines of the poem, that revive the sacrifice and destruction of the opening. ''Grodek'' ends on an elegiac note, with a melancholy lament not for the dead on the battlefield but for those deprived of birth:

> . . . ihr ehernen Altare,
> Die heisse Flamme des Geistes nahrt heute ein gewaltiger
>   Schmerz,
> Die ungebornen Enkel.

> (. . . you iron altars,
> The hot flame of the spirit feeds today a mighty sorrow,
> The unborn grandchildren.)

The overlapping of the human and natural worlds in ''Grodek'' is typical of Trakl's poetic vision, as is the dreamlike, hymnic way that the battle is evoked. Trakl's pessimistic view of the world in decline and decaying (expressed throughout his writings) is, paradoxically, suffused with great spirituality. The attraction to a world in decline, and the morbidity of Trakl's poetic vision, may recall the *fin de siècle* decadence of writers such as Stefan George and Joris Karl Huysmans. But Trakl's later poetry goes well beyond exotic aestheticism and flirtation with unhealthiness. His poetry searches for religious meaning, banishment of guilt, and spiritual feeling, in a world devoid of belief (and in which the fragile Trakl had to participate and not languish away des Esseintes-like in a beautiful boudoir).

This search for revitalized belief is of course common to a number of poets that have been collected together for literary convenience under the term of ''German expressionism.'' Trakl shares other features with writers of his time that include Gottfried Benn, the aforementioned Heym and his acquaintance Else Lasker-Schüler, as well as with painters resident in Germany during the period such as Max Beckmann, Wassily Kandinsky, and Oskar Kokoschka. These characteristics include extensive use of colour symbolism, image-laden and compressed expression, the fostering of a sensual response, and an apocalyptic vision of a culture coming to an end, evoked by morbid and violent subjects and emotions. Trakl's elusive work, with its shimmering evocation of the spiritual in an inchoate universe, is far less histrionic and strident than much German expressionist verse and art. His influences seem to come less from his contemporaries, and to reach back, to the religiosity of Höldedin and Novalis and the melancholy sensibility of Rilke in German poetry, as well as to the elaborate creation of a poetic reality of French symbolists such as Baudelaire, Mallarmé, and Rimbaud.

—Anna-Marie Taylor

THE GROUCH (Dyskolos)
Play by Menander, 316 BC

The Grouch was produced at Athens in 316 BC, when Menander was about 26 years old. The text continued to circulate for centuries in book form, but it—along with the rest of Greek New Comedy—eventually vanished from sight in late antiquity when readers lost interest in the genre. One copy, however, survived to modern times. The play had been included in an anthology of Menander's plays that probably dates from the late 3rd century AD, and this papyrus codex somehow found its way into a private book collection in Geneva. Since publication of the text in 1959, substantial portions of several other, often richer and more complex plays by Menander have also come to light on papyri, but *The Grouch* remains our one virtually complete example of its genre. It therefore continues to attract much critical interest, though on first sight it may not seem very appealing.

The plot is fairly simple: a rich young man named Sostratos, hunting in the countryside near Athens, falls suddenly in love with a beautiful farm girl, daughter of a misanthropic recluse named Knemon. Sostratos' honourable intentions soon win him the help of the girl's stepbrother, Gorgias, a poor but honest farmer. All approaches to Knemon are rebuffed, however, until the old man falls down a well and is rescued by Gorgias. Shaken by this misadventure and moved by Gorgias' selflessness in saving him, Knemon surrenders responsibility for his daughter to the young man, who promptly betrothes her to Sostratos. Sostratos then persuades his father—newly arrived in the country to perform a sacrifice—to permit Gorgias' marriage to his own sister. A double wedding is prepared, and Knemon, who had expected to withdraw again from the world, is dragged off by force to join the festivities.

The play as we have it confirms some important assumptions about New Comedy. The text is punctuated every 200 lines or so by a formulaic stage direction calling for a choral performance, and the stage action is clearly designed to rise and fall in tempo around these interludes. Nevertheless, the text includes no lyrics for the chorus's songs, nor do the choral performances seem to have had any organic connection with the action. They may not even have been the dramatist's responsibility to provide. Hints of such a separation between dramatic and choral functions are discernible in Aristophanes' last plays, which date from the early 4th century BC, and the growing trend was a source of complaint in Aristotle's *Poetics*. Critics of later antiquity, Horace among them, regularly speak of act breaks. *The Grouch* now provides clear evidence that by the last quarter of the 4th century BC a formal five-act structure had emerged and that Menander used the act, rather than the individual scene, as the basic unit of dramatic organization. That organization is itself quite tight. Menander paid careful attention to details of plot construction: Knemon's mishap is elaborately foreshadowed and its mechanism gradually developed. A series of broad comic scenes are both effective in their own right and provide the device for integrating Knemon into the finale. Actions and rewards are always consistent with the characters' personalities and values. Many of these characters are familiar stock figures. Some, such as a cook and faithful slave, are minor, while others, such as the misanthrope and young lover, are central, but all are carefully drawn. There is also striking use of tragic motifs, reminding us that by the later 4th century BC, comedy had become the intellectual heir of both the great 5th-century genres. The play is introduced by the god Pan, whose prologue is reminiscent of Euripidean tragedy, and Knemon is brought onstage after his accident with the familiar trappings of a tragic hero.

Yet there are also some important surprises. The love interest, while central to the plot, does not actually provide the play's focus. Knemon, whether absent or present, dominates the action. *The Grouch* is not the story of a young man in love. Menander's real interest is in the old man who abandons his social responsibilities: Sostratos' romance is simply the means for providing that demonstration. Nor is the plot in any significant sense the result of divine intervention. Pan's appearance is a structural, not thematic, device. He sets the scene, and the sacrifice that brings Sostratos' family to the country is in his honour. He promises at the outset to reward Knemon's daughter for her piety by arranging the marriage, but, given the conventions of the genre, Sostratos' love hardly requires such motivation. The motives that receive the dramatist's attention are made to develop from within the human characters themselves. While Euripidean divinities like Artemis (*Hippolytus*) and Dionysus (*Bacchae*) rightly claim responsibility for the dramatic action because piety and the price of impiety are part of Euripides' thematic design, Menander's interest is ethical rather than religious. His central characters therefore rise above their stock attributes to claim our interest as personalities in their own right. They play out standard roles, but each in a unique way. Their problems—and the solutions to their problems—are their own.

The Grouch is not in itself a great play, but it displays the mastery of New Comedy's basic elements that would in time make Menander himself a great dramatist.

—Sander M. Goldberg

GROUP PORTRAIT WITH LADY (Gruppenbild mit Dame)
Novel by Heinrich Böll, 1971

Group Portrait with Lady, published in 1971, was Heinrich Böll's most commercially successful novel, selling 150,000 copies within six months.

Böll develops the rather ironic, pseudo-objective narration of his previous novel, *The End of a Mission* (*Ende einer Dienstfahrt*), a device that was to be developed further—and most successfully—in *The Lost Honor of Katharina Blum*. In *Group Portrait with Lady*, the narrator is a researcher, whose attempt to construct an objective study of the central character demands almost as much attention as the completed study itself (even generating a plot of its own: the narrator falls in love with a nun whom he interviews about the case in hand, and she leaves her order to become his collaborator). This structure effects to allay doubts about the uses of fiction by reducing the novelist to a finder of facts (and the rather sloppy, non-literary style reinforces this impression and disguises the narrator's real depth of emotion, as in Max Frisch's *Homo Faber*); but in reality it allows him even greater freedom than the traditional narrator, since he can envisage two or more interpretations of the same "facts" without having to commit himself.

At first cogitations about the business of collecting evidence prevail, but gradually these are brought to a conclusion and the main plot gains in prominence, only to issue forth suddenly in a description of the present-day state of affairs. The central character, Leni Gruyten, is the daughter of a builder whose business enjoys a meteoric success during the Nazi period until he is caught defrauding the government his main customer). After the death of her fiancé and soulmate Erhard and a short marriage to the less congenial Alois Pfeiffer, killed in the war, Leni has to cope with her father's imprisonment, the death of her mother, and the death of her childhood mentor Rahel in distressing circumstances. (A nun in the convent where Lent is educated, a qualified doctor of Jewish birth, Rahel falls foul first of Catholic orthodoxy which demotes her to menial tasks because of her outspokenness, then of Nazi anti-semitism which makes her an "unperson" with no food allowance.) Leni, falling on hard times, works through the war and post-war years making wreaths for the florist Pelzer; the great passion of her life is for a Russian prisoner-of-war, Boris Lvović Koltowski, who is allocated to Pelzer's workshop as a labourer. Boris, victim of a confusion of identities in the chaos of the ending of the war, dies as a German prisoner-of-war working in a French mine. Their son, Lev, a difficult child, eventually becomes a refuse collector. Living in straitened circumstances (and quite impractical with money), Leni sells the house containing her flat cheaply to the Hoyser family, with whom she was thrown together during the war. In the flat, the last remnant of the one-time riches of the Gruytens, filled with her inherited furniture, well-read books, and an ambitious painting she is working on (of the surface of a retina with its millions of rods and cones), she collects sub-tenants from the lower reaches of society, notably Lev's Turkish colleagues. The Hoysers, objecting to this diminution of the value of their house, determine to evict Leni, whose rent is in arrears, but her admirers prevent this, by organizing "accidents" with dustcarts which block the streets against the bailiffs and by taking up a collection to pay her back rent.

The novel rambles, and has puzzling features. The period from 1945 to about 1970 is almost entirely neglected in the narration. The narrator spends much time (and fictitious money, carefully accounted for by a fictitious tax-office) collecting a confusingly long series of informants from all walks of life, and commenting on their various degrees of reliability; but the perspective Böll wishes to give on Leni's life is clear enough, so the invitation to the reader to make up his or her own mind on the basis of the evidence is an empty one. The content is sometimes fantastic (the roses which stubbornly grow in winter on the grave of Sister Rahel, much to the embarrassment of the determinedly modern-minded ecclesiastical powers-that-be), and sometimes needlessly embarrassing (Rahel's views on the training of girls to defecate without needing any toilet paper, and on the diagnostic value of inspecting the results). And could a Russian really have recommended Kafka to a German woman during the war—with the result that she has to be told not only that Kafka was a Jew, but also that Jews' writings and Jews themselves are frowned upon in Germany.

Böll returns to some of the themes of his earlier works: anti-militarism, anti-clericalism, and the defence of the social outsider. Another related attitude, manifesting Böll's rejection of the Cold War, is an emphatic sympathy for Russians. But he is perhaps overemphatic. Boris becomes a quite improbable paragon of tenderness and culture. The episode of Rahel's roses is created mainly in order to satirize the Catholic hierarchy, and diverts attention from the plot. Another mystical incident, the appearance of the Blessed Virgin Mary to the non-church-going Leni on the television screen after close-down, is self-parodying—especially when interpreted at the end of the novel as an optical illusion that produces an image of Leni herself! Böll's coquettish heresies about the sacramental value of erotic fulfilment are equally *de trop*. Rhineland separatism and anti-Prussianism is another sub-theme that lacks weight and relevance here.

Leni herself is a dunce at school who somehow gains enough intellectual awareness to read Trakl and Kafka; she plays a limited piano repertoire of Schubert to a good professional standard; once nominated as a member of the board of her father's company, she is, however, unable to look after even the small amount of domestic property left to her. On the dustjacket of the first edition, we see the negative of a photo of a group of people, the face of the woman in the centre being a blank: an all too true representation of the novel.

Group Portrait with Lady does have its high points. The narrator's interview with the distasteful Hoyser family (in their ultra-modern skyscraper where nobody dares open a window for fear of confusing the air-conditioning) shows that Böll's satire is not blunted; the way the press distorts its reporting of the dustcart blockage foreshadows *The Lost Honor of Katharina Blum*. The scene in which Leni offers some of her own coffee, the best available, to the despised prisoner-of-war in her workplace, cutting through the whole ideology of race and all the war-time propaganda with a few pointed gestures, is an object-lesson in how to make a moral point in literature without preaching.

—Alfred D. White

GUIGAMOR (Guigamar)
Narrative poem by Marie de France, late 12th century

Guigamor was composed in the second half of the 12th century and survives in the Anglo-Norman dialect of Old French comprising 886 lines of octosyllabic rhyming couplets. *Guigamor* stands first in the collection of 12 narrative poems, the *Lays*. Although the 12 poems are preceded by a Prologue of 56 lines, *Guigamor* itself contains a 26-line general Prologue in which the author asserts herself in the face of envious critics as an author worthy of esteem, and states that the stories she is presenting are based on Breton lays.

The Celtic connection is established in the figure of Guigamor, son of a baron in the service of a king of Brittany. Guigamor is an outstanding young knight marred in the eyes of his contemporaries only by the fact that he shows no interest in love. On a hunting expedition he encounters a white hind with stag's antlers, the androgynous nature of this creature symbolizing perhaps the fulfilling sexual relationship which he has yet to experience. The arrow with which he wounds it rebounds to wound him in the thigh. In Celtic tradition the white hind has supernatural connotations and against such a background it is no surprise that the hind speaks to him, predicting that he will be cured only by a woman who will suffer for love of him, as he will likewise suffer for her love.

Setting forth alone in pain and perplexity, Guigamor follows a path leading to a harbour where a magnificent boat stands. The boat carries him to an ancient city, and straight to a tower where a fair and noble young woman lives. She is the archetype of the traditional Old French figure of the *malmariée* (unhappily married wife), a young wife imprisoned by an old and jealous husband. Helped and encouraged by her capable young maid—another traditional figure in the literature of the day—the lady tends the knight's wound, while at the same time smiting him with the wound of love (the metaphor being Ovidian in origin). Attraction is mutual, and when Guigamor enjoins the lady to be his passion swiftly runs its course.

Guigamor and the lady live in blissful communion for a year and a half, untroubled by the outside world, until she voices a dreadful presentiment that they will be discovered. Each pledges to love the other come what may, and as tokens of fidelity the lady ties a knot in

Guigamor's shirt which no other woman will be able to undo, while Guigamor fastens round her body a belt that cannot be unbuckled. That very day the lady's husband breaks in upon them, and Guigamor is packed off again to Brittany in the ship that brought him. On his return, many ladies, desiring his love, try to untie the knot in his shirt, but in vain.

The focus now turns to the lady he has left behind. At the end of two years of grieving she decides to drown herself. Leaving her prison without hindrance, she finds the mysterious ship conveniently waiting to take her to Brittany. On arrival she immediately falls into the hands of a lord named Meriadus, who wishes to make her his, but who cannot undo the belt, the symbol of her faithfulness to Guigamor.

The narrative at first concentrates on the solitary figure of the young knight, up to the point of his first voyage, and encompasses the pair of lovers. After the lady's parallel voyage, it moves into its final phase, where the wider social context is uppermost. Meriadus has heard of Guigamor and the knotted shirt, and invites him to participate in a tournament which he is organizing as part of a war against a neighbouring baron. The invitation is a ruse, as he suspects Guigamor to be the lady's true love. Guigamor and the lady recognize each other, and the lady easily undoes the knot while Guigamor immediately knows where to place his hands to find the belt. Their love, which had been conceived and lived out in clandestinity, is now clear for all to see. But Meriadus refuses to give up the lady, and Guigamor must win her by force of arms, joining with Meriadus's enemy to besiege his rival, and, when victorious, to carry away the lady. The lovers' tribulations are over.

Although no trace remains of a specific Breton lay or lays on which Marie de France may, as she claims, have based her tale, the white hind with supernatural powers, as well as the Voyage of Healing to the Other World, are themes well attested to in Celtic mythology. In *Guigamor* Marie has woven together these strands of Celtic tradition with elements of the courtly literature of her day and classical allusion. She mingles traces of the supernatural with a concern for realism in both the psychological and material spheres.

In the *Lays* as a whole the dominant concern is love, explored from a variety of angles. The central theme in *Guigamor* is the awakening of love, its growth in two noble young people, and its ability to withstand separation and to inspire deeds of prowess. Through their experiences the knight and his lady are presented as progressing towards personal maturity and fulfilment. The adulterous nature of their relationship is outweighed by their mutual commitment and by the fact that her husband is a tyrant; and their love is ultimately brought fully into the social arena. Marie de France is not alone among authors of 12th-century French courtly literature in presenting the view of love that she does in *Guigamor*; her achievement within the relatively brief compass of the work is to have presented it with the delicate care and economy of a skilled miniaturist.

—Heather Lloyd

H

HANSEL AND GRETEL (Hänsel und Gretel)
Story by Jacob and Wilhelm Grimm, 1812

Near the borders of a large forest dwelt in olden times a poor woodcutter, who had two children—a boy named Hansel, and his sister Gretel.

These words usher the reader or hearer of "Hansel and Gretel" into the world of fairytale. The archaic language of its first line—"dwelt" and "olden"—signals our removal from the everyday to the timeless and ever-accessible imaginative realm of fairy land. The status of the lowly woodcutter, and the presence of a boy and girl, ensure that by the end of the sentence its audience has identified with the two children of the title. The indefinite geography—a large forest—conjures to the imagination whichever body of woodland the listener knows best. Having imaginatively located ourselves within the wood, and within the tale, we are prepared for a story which, like most fairytales, involves a perilous journey, a trial of wit or courage, and a happy homecoming. Features such as the wicked stepmother, the evil enchantress, and the animals which aid the hero, are part of the constant "language" of the fairy world, yet "Hansel and Gretel" creates its own unique and highly memorable atmosphere: one of darkness, cruelty, and capture. The anxieties which the tale evokes are, for a child, profound ones: the story opens with the children lying awake at night listening to their parents talking—their stepmother is arguing that they should be left to the mercy of the wild beasts. As the story continues, its emotional power is generated by primal fears: of abandonment, of being lost, of starvation and murder. These fears are first conjured and then exorcised in Aristotelian catharsis leaving Hansel and Gretel free and happy. The basic, instinctive nature of the story's concerns is best exemplified by its obsession with food and with hunger.

To attempt to understand such a tale rationally is misplaced. It has its own order, an unconscious order lying deeper than the intellect, one which combines the most instinctive of urges with subtle perceptions of the possibility of magic in the universe.

Like a dream, then, the story involves unconscious fears and intuitions, and like a dream the tale resolves its complexes not by logical progression but by means of developing patterns of images. Like a dream, it functions by means of recurrence, development, substitution, and transformation. The elements of recurrence and development are evident in the division of the tale, like a dream, into a number of "moves." Each move deals with the complex inherited from the previous move in a new way. It re-casts its symbols into a new situation which offers a new perspective on, and heightened awareness of, the initial problem. The element of recurrence in the narrative leads to the creation of a series of parallels and echoes between the images of the story. The first image represents an object from real life, the second image represents that same scene transformed by the "greater life" of the unconscious. Thus the wicked stepmother twice builds a fire, while the wicked ogress has a fiery oven. These parallels serve to enrich the real world with a layer of fantasy: the "magical reality" of the unconscious. Thus the woodcutter's humble cottage is replaced by a cottage of sweets, and pockets weighted down with white pebbles become pockets full of pearls.

Substitution is most obvious in the handling of the wicked stepmother. The stepmother, while terrifying, cannot be attacked directly, so the story shifts to a new location, where an even more hateful woman is dominant. There she can be defeated and killed. When the children return home at last, their stepmother has, naturally enough, died—for in another incarnation she has been tackled and disposed of.

A magical world is evident in the story, one which serves always to help and guide the protagonists. One could term this the "white world." The moon's light makes the white pebbles silver, and transforms them into gleaming markers. Hansel attempts, but fails, to achieve the same effect with white crumbs, disguising his actions with references to his white pigeon and white cat. The image of the white bird is one which haunts "Hansel and Gretel." The fictional white pigeon he invents seems to summon the real bird which leads them into danger through ultimate victory, in the candy cottage. At the moment of triumph Hansel escapes from captivity "like a bird from a cage." The phrase seems more than coincidental, for after this identification of Hansel with the bird the plot is, apparently unnecessarily, prolonged by a further final trial. The children's return is blocked by a stretch of water, but now at last the white bird is realized as a helpful figure. The white duck appears, to ferry both children home.

The story shifts, at its ending, to focus not on the children but on their father, leaving behind the terrors of the forest. For the children who form its audience, it offers at last an image of happiness and security, as both Hansel and Gretel are embraced within their father's arms. The crisis of the opening paragraph has been overcome. The final sentence forms an echo or redemption of the first lines: "From this moment all his care and sorrow was at an end, and the father lived in happiness with his children all his life."

The language of the story is typical of the traditional tales that were collected by the Grimm brothers. It is simple and straightforward in both vocabulary and grammatical structure. As with other traditional tales the "bare bones" of the story are designed to be easily memorized. The narrative proceeds in a series of tableaux—the children lying in bed, the moon shining on the pebbles, and so on. Direct speech is kept to a minimum, and is encoded in distinctive formulae. The use of repetition serves as a mnemonic device. The written text is subject to endless variation in the hands of its tellers, but the Grimms' version offers a story whose complexity belies the simplicity of its language.

—Edmund Cusick

HARD IS THE ROAD TO SHU
Poem by Li Bai, written c. 744

"Hard is the Road to Shu" (otherwise translated as "The Road to Shu is Hard") is one of Li Bai's most important poems in terms of the poetic imagination and descriptive power with which Li Bai handled the theme.

Shu, now a Sichuan province in west China, is surrounded by sheer mountains and is well-known in history for its inhospitable location and hazardous road conditions. Originally, ''Hard Is the Road to Shu'' was the title of a *yuefu* ballad describing difficulties and dangers involved in travelling to Shu. This poem was written in about 744 when Li Bai was staying in Chang'an, the then capital. He wrote it as a farewell poem for a friend who was going to make a journey to Shu. Though using the same title and subject as the *yuefu* ballad, this poem of Li Bai's excels all previous poems and folk songs in its description of the hardships and perils of travelling on the road to Shu. The way to Shu, a rich and, for many people, a fantastic land, is so hard that ''Since the two pioneers / Put the kingdom in order, / Have passed forty-eight thousand years / And few have tried to pass its border.'' As described in the poem, there has been, for a very long time, no walkable footpath to Shu from the neighbouring region of Qin. Only the flight-path of birds cuts through Emei [Mount Eyebrows]. A rocky path was hacked along the cliffs only after ''the crest crumbled'' through the effect of legendary force. The journey is not only hard for humans. ''Even the Golden Crane can't fly across; / How to climb over, / gibbons are at a loss.'' The poem presents a breathtaking picture of travel over inaccessible mountain peaks and precipitous cliffs: scaling the mountain, one can touch the stars; and one has to run away from man-eating tigers at daybreak and from long blood-sucking snakes at dusk.

The line ''The road to Shu is harder than to climb to the sky,'' a sigh breathed by the poet, is repeated three times—at the beginning, in the middle, and at the end of the poem, deepening the intensive impression of the hardships and despair suffered on the journey. However, the scenes unfolded before the reader are not unpleasant or depressing, but varied and enchanting. The poet invites the reader to share in the rare experience of the journey by following the traveller's footsteps in the poet's imagination. The rugged paths, cliffs upwards toward the sky, ancient trees, dashing torrents, birds flying in the forests are all knitted into extraordinary and picturesque visions.

What attracts the reader is not only the scenery, described in a vivid and dynamic way, but also the legend and mythology that are interlaced in masterly fashion and which give the poem strong romantic colouring. For example, the ''two pioneers,'' the two legendary kings who ruled Shu 40,000 years ago, evoke an atmosphere of mystery. ''Five serpent-killing heroes'' are five legendary brave men sent by the ruler of Shu to meet and protect five women whom the king of Qin promised in marriage to the ruler of Shu. On the way, they encountered a huge serpent. While the five men were pulling its tail, trying to drag it out of a hole, the mountain crumbled and all the men and women died and were transformed into five mountain peaks. This legend lends the poem a strong tinge of heroic tragedy and mystery. And the cuckoos, which, according to legend, wept after Du Yu, a king of Shu, had left the palace on his abdication are a symbol evoking memories of the sad past.

Opinions differ about the theme of this poem. An early annotator noted that, in a parabolic way, the poem tried to persuade the foolish and self-indulgent Emperor Xuanzong of the Tang dynasty, who had fled to Shu from the chaos of war, not to stay in Shu for too long. Some modern scholars disagree, pointing out that this is an anachronism, the poem having been written before the war in question actually started. Whatever the argument over the theme, it is frequently suggested that the last few lines may allude to the possible rebellions of warlords in Shu.

Li Bai used some traditional writing techniques often seen in *yuefu* ballads. For example, ''Alas! Why should you come here from afar?'' asks the poet. It is a rhetorical question. ''The Town of Silk,'' today's

Chengdu, and the capital of Sichuan province, may be a place for one to make merry, ''But I would rather homeward go,'' Li Bai states near the end of the poem. It is a kind of general warning to all hearing or reading the poem.

Li Bai, nevertheless, broke with tradition to develop a style of his own. Critics through the centuries have admired the superb description of the natural scenes and miraculous traveller's experiences, the subtle allusions, the flowing style without ''purple passages,'' the romanticism, and the author's unconstrained manner all fused in this poem. It is always considered the masterpiece of Li Bai's romantic style. On reading this poem, He Zhizhang, another well-known poet and a contemporary, marvelled at it, exclaiming that Li Bai was a ''celestial being banished from Heaven.''

—Binghong Lu

HECALE
Poem by Callimachus, 3rd century BC

The *Hecale* has come down to us in a highly fragmentary state, but this century has seen some remarkable papyrological discoveries and feats of reconstruction which have greatly enhanced our knowledge of the poem and are now conveniently assembled by A.S. Hollis in his 1990 edition, *Hecale*. We can now tell the poem, in heroic hexameters, must have been about 1,000 lines in length, though possibly somewhat more, and we are in a position to understand the peculiar genius which made it so influential in subsequent classical poetry (Ovid's debt in the Philemon and Baucis story in *Metamorphoses* being only a more familiar example).

The beginning of the epic refers to its titular heroine and her generous hospitality. From there we pass to the arrival of the young Theseus at Athens from Troezen, where his father, Aegeus, king of Athens, had sent him to be reared. Theseus' stepmother, Medea, tries to poison him, but he is saved in the nick of time by Aegeus, who places him under strict surveillance for his safety. We next find Theseus longing for adventure and pleading with Aegeus to let him slay the Marathonian bull, but he is forced to escape against his father's will. In the evening of his journey to Marathon a storm bursts upon him, and he takes refuge in Hecale's hut. Her reception of him was evidently described in some detail, from the moment he shakes the rain off his cloak to the moment she sits him down, washes his feet, and gives him a meal. Theseus explains his mission, and asks Hecale to tell him why she lives in such an isolated place in her old age. She reveals that her present poverty is not ancestral, and goes on to narrate how her husband was killed at sea, sent to fetch horses from Laconia by Peteos, who was in fact an enemy of Theseus' father. She describes how she lost her elder son and then her sole support, her younger son; he was killed when forced to wrestle with the murderer Cercyon, whom she curses, wishing she could stick thorns in his eyes and eat his flesh raw. Theseus tells her that he himself has killed the bandit, so that another link is forged between the two. They go to sleep, Hecale having improvised bedding for the young hero. Theseus rises early the next day, and we are possibly given a final picture of the old woman as she comes out to bid Theseus farewell.

The actual fight between the Marathonian bull and Theseus seems to have been narrated quite briefly, and we next take up the story as the hero drags the animal along, with one horn smashed off by Theseus' club, and is greeted on his way back to Athens by countryfolk who cannot even look at the huge man and the monstrous bull until Theseus asks someone to go ahead to Athens to tell Aegeus that he is alive and victorious, whereupon the bystanders sing a paean to Theseus and honour him with a ritual shower of leaves.

During a gap of some 22 lines in the text, the scene has changed to a conversation between a crow and another bird (an owl?), perched on a tree in the night. The crow tells the story of how she once brought the news to Athene that her child Ericthonius, whom the goddess wanted to be reared in secret, had been discovered, for which reason Athene forbade crows from entering the Acropolis. The crow also prophesies how Apollo will punish the raven for bringing him news that his human beloved, Coronis, had made love, while pregnant with Apollo's child, with the mortal Ischys; the raven will be changed from white to black. The connection between these digressions and the narrative frame seems to be the motif of relaying bad news; the crow is advising the other bird not to tell Theseus that Hecale has died in the interim. The two birds fall asleep, and we are given a graphic picture of the dawn that follows soon after as humans light their lamps, fetch water, are woken up by the creaking of wagon axles, and are tormented by the noise of the blacksmith.

Theseus returns from Athens to Hecale's cottage to thank her, but finds the neighbours preparing her funeral. Her neighbours celebrate her hospitality, Theseus laments her, and institutes in her memory a deme named Hecale, an annual banquet, and a sanctuary of Zeus Hecaleius.

Even in its fragmentary state, the *Hecale* amply demonstrates the broad tonal range, allusiveness, and innovative literary approach of Callimachus. On the level of diction, we find words taken from the different dialects of Greece, though of course Attic is highlighted in the interests of local colour, and lowly words for couches and the like contrast with words on a higher stylistic register, in Hecale's autobiography and in the mythological sections, for example. An analogous contrast exists between the recondite nature of Callimachus' deployment of myth and the lowly and the visually vivid images of human life and likewise with the allusions to earlier Greek literature: Hecale's impassioned curse of Cercyon for killing her son reminds us of Hecuba in the *Iliad* (44.212f) cursing Achilles for killing her own Hector, while the whole hospitality motif draws self-consciously on the reception of Odysseus by Eumaeus and Eurycleia in the *Odyssey*. Callimachus' foregrounding of a poor woman is innovative: she may indeed be of noble blood, like her literary forebears in the *Odyssey* or the farmer in Euripides' *Electra*, but she is the first figure of reduced circumstances and low social standing to play a leading part in epic, displacing Theseus' traditional heroism from centre stage, and her generosity is the theme of the beginning and the close of the whole epic. Callimachus seems to be deliberately subverting the grander traditional expectations of the epic hero.

—G. Zanker

HEDDA GABLER
Play by Henrik Ibsen, 1890

A tiny incident, but a significant one, is carefully planted by Henrik Ibsen at the start of this play which is a masterpiece of characterization, even if its meticulous craftsmanship, in an almost classical dramatic style, seems by now to be rather old-fashioned. Auntie Julle is all of a-flutter at the prospect of welcoming her nephew, Jörgen

Tesman, and his new bride, Hedda, after their extravagantly long honeymoon trip, in the rather grand home that has, we soon learn, been furnished with funds raised by way of a mortgage on the annuity providing her with the bare necessities of life. Anxious to make a good impression, she has also bought herself a new hat, which she takes off and places on a chair. Not long after, Hedda enters, sees it, and at once says that she really does not think that Berte, who has been engaged as a maid for the Tesman household, will be at all suitable. How could she be when she has shown her slovenly ways by thoughtlessly leaving her old hat lying about in the drawing room? At once there is electricity in the air, with the old busybody of an aunt offended and her nephew embarrassed, by what they take to be Hedda's dreadful *faux-pas*. Only Hedda does not seem embarrassed, and before long we discover that she dropped the brick intentionally. She was bored, she was resisting every attempt to be absorbed into the bosom of the family into which she had married, and she was frankly pleased to have the opportunity of stirring up trouble.

A lady of 29 and with a certain aristocratic elegance about her, Hedda feels that she has married beneath herself. We are not allowed to forget that her father was General Gabler, whereas her husband, her elder by some four years, is a cultural historian who is short of money and has only fairly tenuous prospects of becoming a professor. The fact that the title of the play is not *Hedda Tesman* but *Hedda Gabler*, like the way some of her admirers know how to flatter her by calling her by her maiden name, is a clear pointer to her unwillingness to accept her role as a wife to an unprepossessing husband whose undoubted infatuation with her is attenuated by his desire to continue collecting material for a work of what appears to be dry-as-dust scholarship. There are, as is perhaps to be expected after a honeymoon, some more or less discreet enquiries whether she might be pregnant, but she impatiently brushes them aside and, though she first appears in a fairly loose-fitting morning gown, she insists that her figure has not filled out. All in all, it seems that she has not yet found sexual fulfilment in marriage, and now, as autumn begins to set in, there is not much to please her in the prospect of life in the dreary Norwegian town to which she has returned.

Some idea of her frustration is given by the way she responds when Thea Elvsted arrives. She is a couple of years younger than Hedda, and though they were at school together, it is understandable that Hedda cannot immediately recall her Christian name accurately, but she insists that they both were and must continue to be great friends. Now the plot begins to thicken, as Hedda recalls how once she too had dallied with Eilert Lövborg. He is a scholar who had worked in much the same field as her husband, but his ways had been dissolute and his chances of making the most of his talents had been slim until Thea, who had left her husband, took him in hand and helped him write a book that none other than Tesman recognizes as an imaginative scholarly masterpiece. Jealousy now consumes Hedda. Though Eilert had wisely decided that teetotalism was the only safe policy for him, Hedda inveigles him into going off on a drinking bout with her husband and the sinister Judge Brack. In his drunken stupor he drops the only copy of the manuscript of his book, but Tesman finds it. When he brings it home, Hedda loses no time in consigning it to the stove. As she commits the pages to the flames, her language shows that she sees Eilert's great work as a love-child born to him and Thea. After that she has the ambition to inspire in Eilert a great, tragic passion, and she hands to him one of her father's pistols that she once had aimed at him in a tense moment. He must use it now, "beautifully," as she insists.

In fact the unfortunate Eilert does not kill himself with a romantic bullet in the heart, but by accident, in the abdomen, and while in a house of ill-repute. To make matters worse, Judge Brack realizes what has been afoot and sees how this may give him a hold over Hedda. Well may she say that everything she touches seems fated to turn into something like a mean farce. There is only one grand Romantic gesture left to her, and, typically enough, it is a futile one. She leaves the drawing room, pulling the curtains behind her before launching into a wild piece of music on the piano. Then a shot rings out: she has put General Gabler's other pistol to her temple and pulled the trigger. The dramatic style is classical in its avoidance of on-stage violence, the violence is melodramatic, and the predictable patterning of the drama with some well-formulated, quotable statements amidst the everyday talk belongs to the period of the well-made play. Within that framework, Ibsen has, however, portrayed a character in which many see not only the frustrations of women in 19th-century society but also the plight of mankind in general.

—Christopher Smith

HENRY IV (Enrico IV)
Play by Luigi Pirandello, 1921

Henry IV (also published in a close English adaptation as *Enrico Four*) translates the illusion and reality debate common to most Luigi Pirandello plays into a debate between sanity and madness. It is a poignant comment on 20th-century society's preoccupations with "normality" and individualism, with Freud and the human psyche, and on the nature of identity—impersonation in life and in the theatre—in short, on the masks we all wear, be they theatrical costume or facade adopted in life to shield, comfort, or project ourselves in different circumstances. Performed regularly since its premiere in Milan in 1922, the play has attracted some of the world's finest actors to the part of the protagonist, wavering (through different styles of performance) between insanity—feigned or real—and lucid sanity, costumed for a historical role, but using the facade to conceal deep-seated emotional turmoil.

Using the mask of the German Emperor Henry IV, donned as a disguise for a masquerade party where a jealous rival for the love of the Marchioness Matilda had caused him to fall from his horse, causing him to become (or seem to become) mad, a wealthy nobleman becomes fixed in his masquerade reality, surrounding himself with period fixtures and fittings including a group of retainers dressed in period costume, who live out the charade for their master. Henry's nephew, the Marquis di Nolli, carrying out the wishes of his late mother, Henry's sister, attempts to facilitate a cure for his uncle by bringing a doctor and the woman Henry had loved, Matilda, with her daughter Frida, and the Marchioness's lover Baron Belcredi to perpetrate a species of Freudian shock therapy to effect a cure. The strategy is to dress the daughter in the period costume of the Marchioness of Tuscany, the costume that her mother had been wearing when the accident occurred, which was preserved as a relic from the past by Henry as a painted portrait. They plan to show the portrait apparently coming to life 20 years after it was painted, and thereby to jolt Henry's memory into a cure. But the mad Henry IV (whether really mad or cured long before and now feigning insanity for convenience) does not fall for this trick—he rather sees it as a cheap device to disturb his comfortable illusion. Pretending to play

along with this charade, he eventually stabs his rival Belcredi and is obliged to return to the masquerade as a defence against the charge of murder.

The story is a metaphor for all masks or facades assumed for convenience or protection, the contest (the theatre) the logically ideal setting. The audience is hardly ever sure (depending on the skills and style of the actor) whether Henry is insane or playing a part—at least in the early stages. The wig and costume worn by the actor, the stylized make-up, the portraits in their fixed immutability, even the discussions between the hired courtiers, pile layer upon layer of meaning on the central questions of identity, impersonation, and role-play. The play moves through humour to tragedy (largely depending on the style chosen by the director and actors), reflecting the 20th century's deep concern about identity, schizophrenia, and conformity to society's norms.

There are echoes, too, of traditions as diverse as the *commedia dell'arte* (in the pedantry of the doctor and his panacea) and Freudian concepts of the conscious and unconscious mind. Powerful, too, is the part of the madman who may not be mad—about the most exquisitely theatrical of all creations—since he is constrained by no bonds of naturalism or psychological realism, but is free to project the playwright's imagination with no holds barred, as modern drama has discovered time and again. And the whole business of playacting is explored in depth by Pirandello (aware of the fragile boundaries of the mind as no other after the institutionalization of his wife) when Henry IV may dramatize the speech of the mentally disturbed by darting from subject to subject in a rapid sequence of penetrating lucidity and ranting incoherence.

Perhaps Pirandello's greatest play, with its range of resolutely modern preoccupations—taken up again in modern drama since Freud—*Henry IV* also projects the results of becoming victim of a closed system (perhaps fascism), adherence to an ideology (compare *Rhinoceros*), or the dictates of society's arbitrary norm-setting (*One Flew Over the Cuckoo's Nest*). In the end, our illusions become these closed systems, and the effects of their coercion may be the retreat from the everyday into a dream or other-worldly reality. Play-acting has become more real than reality: witness those actors who become schizophrenics, or the prisoner of war who escaped from a concentration camp by feigning madness and hoodwinking doctors—only to be institutionalized on repatriation.

—Christopher Cairns

A HERO OF OUR TIME (Geroi nashego vremeni)
Novel by Mikhail Lermontov, 1840

Mikhail Lermontov's novel *A Hero of Our Time*, which was completed in the year of his death, is his most famous work and the culmination, in a number of ways, of all his writing.

In *A Hero of Our Time* Lermontov presents the most complex treatment of his dominant and recurrent preoccupation, the figure of the Romantic hero, a subject which had received its apotheosis in verse in the long poems *The Circassian Boy* and *The Demon*. There are also echoes of many other motifs from his shorter lyric verse: for example, the extreme ironic world-weariness of "I skuchno i grustno" ("Oh, Boredom and Sadness"), or the bitter condemnation of the poet's generation in the civic poem "Duma" ("Meditation") with its opening line: "With sadness do I look upon our generation." On the other hand, in the novel Lermontov at last makes a successful move into prose, in tune with the direction in which the mainstream of Russian literature was moving at the time. A desire to diversify from poetry on Lermontov's part is already evident in the early 1830s, but his first prose work *Vadim* (written c. 1833–34) suffers from a Romantic identification of author and hero. In his next attempt, the society tale ''Kniaginya Ligovskaia'' [Princess Ligovskaia] (c. 1836–37), which features a hero called Pechorin, Lermontov is again confronted with the problem of narrative perspective. Yet again this is not resolved and the work is unfinished, but it provides a germ for ''Princess Mary,'' the society tale in diary form which is the longest part of *A Hero of Our Time*.

A Hero of Our Time has a highly distinctive composition. It is made up of five stories told by three different people, with two forewords. Collections of stories, usually brought together by a fictitious editor as in Pushkin's *The Tales of Belkin* (*Povesti pokoinogo I.P. Belkina*), play a prominent role in the development of Russian prose in the 1830s, but Lermontov develops this into something different by making the hero of all the stories the same. Until relatively recently the main focus in approaches to *A Hero of Our Time* has been the portrayal of Pechorin, the hero. The novel has been read as a character portrait of the so-called ''superfluous man,'' that type of alienated, initially Romantic, hero found in a series of Russian works from Pushkin's *Eugene Onegin* onwards; Lermontov's novel has been seen as highly significant in the development of the psychological novel and the transition to realism. But any reading of *A Hero of Our Time* has to take into account the manner of narration. In fact this is so central that our perception of character can only arise out of, or through, a consideration of narration and narrative structure, which can easily come to occupy the foreground in itself.

The introductory foreword, which was added by Lermontov to the second edition (1841), is the only place we hear the author's unmediated, though still ironic, voice. In the main body of the text three narrators take over. The first is an anonymous hack travel writer: he is the publisher of the whole book, and the author of the first two stories ''Bela'' and ''Maxim Maximych'' and of a foreword to Pechorin's ''Journal.'' The second is Maxim Maximych, a staff captain, whose oral narration concerning Pechorin and Bela is embedded in the travel writer's own text in ''Bela'' in a way that produces the opposite of a ''seamless'' composition: instead the difference and alternation of voices and viewpoints is emphasized. Narrative devices such as retardation are very much to the fore as the contrasting narrators exploit their position as storytellers. In addition, however, the voices may be contaminated, since the travel writer has clearly edited Maxim's story: Pechorin's confession, for example, presents a Romantic stereotype in a style that cannot be that of the uneducated military man.

Then, in the second story ''Maxim Maximych,'' a chance meeting allows the travel writer to give a description of Pechorin's appearance, the objective value of which he himself undermines by concluding that ''maybe his appearance would have created a completely different impression on someone else.'' The third narrator is Pechorin himself, whose writings comprise ''Taman,'' a parodied Romantic adventure story, ''Princess Mary,'' a diary account with the makings of a society tale, and finally ''The Fatalist,'' a sketch with leanings towards the philosophical tale. Whereas the travel writer commends Pechorin to us for his sincerity, the novel invites an ironic deconstruction of his narration. In ''Princess Mary'' Pechorin writes and acts as though he were an omniscient narrator, but this posture breaks down into limited comprehension and moral blindness. At the same time his presentation of himself and other characters can become a case study

for psychoanalysis in Jungian terms, rather than an objective portrait of the world (see Andrew Barratt and A.D.P. Briggs, *A Wicked Iron: The Rhetoric of ''A Hero of Our Times,''* 1989).

Thus the novel's composition brings us gradually closer to the central hero, but not in a straightforward way. The inadequacies of the narrators, the gaps and discontinuities, and the incompleteness of the picture (it is hard to speak of any development of character) work strongly against any authoritative interpretation of Pechorin. This is reinforced by the circularity of the structure—in chronological terms the final story precedes the first—and by the recurrent motif of relativity and uncertainty. ''The Fatalist'' concludes with an assertion of doubt as the way forward and the co-existence, yet again, of at least two points of view. The circularity is complete when the final sentence takes us back to the narrative situation at the beginning of ''Bela,'' as Pechorin, like the travel writer earlier, tries to get some discussion going with Maxim Maximych.

—Robin Aizlewood

HÉRODIADE
Poem by Stéphane Mallarmé, 1864–98 (unfinished)

Hérodiade is not, as it stands, a single, coherent poem but a series of seven pieces and fragments, the first dating from Stéphane Mallarmé's early twenties, the last from his final years. Three of them, ''Ouverture'' (''Overture''), ''Scène'' (''Scene''), and ''Le Cantique de saint Jean'' (''The Canticle of St. John''), have traditionally been published as a triptych of completed poems, but only ''Scene,'' begun in 1864, was ever published by Mallarmé himself. Letters and manuscripts of the 1890s show Mallarmé reworking the subject as *Les Noces d'Hérodiade, mystère* [The Marriage of Herodias, Mystery] but the new material he hoped to incorporate remained unfinished at his death in 1898. Possible arrangements of this material have been mooted but its fragmentary state and characteristic Mallarméan obscurity prevent any firm conclusion concerning the final work. This analysis concentrates therefore on the three poems that can be considered as having definitive or near-definitive status and that together provide the essential outlines of Mallarmé's project as far as it can be known.

The Biblical episode of Herodias, Salome, and St. John the Baptist was to become an extremely popular late 19th-century subject among artists, writers, and composers, but when Mallarmé first conceived his poem in 1864 his only immediate precedent was Banville's sonnet ''Hérodiade,'' itself drawing on Heine's *Atta Troll*. Mallarmé's version is in any case strikingly idiosyncratic. Though writing at a time when poetry and the history of antiquity were closely linked in the Parnassian emphasis on classical beauty of form and documentary objectivity of presentation, he vigorously rejected historical referentiality or visual picturesqueness. Rather it was, he claimed, the suggestive power of the ''divine name'' Hérodiade, ''red as a bursting pomegranate,'' that attracted him. Paradoxically though, despite the erotic connotations of the remark, he was not interested, either, in the traditional symbolic value of the Herodias/Salome couple as an emblem of lust. Significantly he explicitly avoided the celebrated episode of Salome's dance. His protagonist is not a symbol of the physical, but of the Absolute, a figuration of a Beauty utterly beyond the human grasp, forever virginal, uncontaminated by the physical world.

Hérodiade's unifying theme is the separation of the worlds of physical existence and metaphysical or aesthetic essence. "Scene," which Mallarmé conceived with a view to theatrical performance, expresses this dramatically in a dialogue structured on a triple refusal by Herodias of the human contact offered by her nurse, followed by a triple rejection, in response to the nurse's probings, of the idea of an earthly spouse. In "Overture" and "The Canticle of St. John" theatrical presentation is abandoned. Nevertheless the two pieces are "spoken" by nurse and saint respectively and develop further the contrasting principles established in "Scene." "Overture," substituting description for stage presentation, evokes the chamber from which Herodias is absent and the park and castle still inhabited by the nurse, priestess of a physical order, now rejected by her mistress. In contrast, in "The Canticle of St. John" the saint represents not earthly principles but spiritual ones. Decapitated, reduced to the "pure look" of his severed head, he figures the gaze of the spirit which, released from its physical bondage into the contemplation of the Absolute, provides the external validation that confirms the existence of Beauty.

Imagery across the three poems supports this dramatic structuring of physical absence and spiritual presence. "Overture" offers an intricate elaboration of motifs of death and abandonment. Dawn hovers like a bird of ill-omen over the tomb-like tower and mournful gardens where pools that once reflected swans and stars now mirror only the falling leaves of autumn. Herodias's inner chamber likewise is filled with objects evoking dead glories, ancient weapons, shadowy tapestries, fading flowers, an empty bed draped in a shroud of lace. In "Scene," her very existence is problematized by an emphasis on shadow and reflection. "Are you alive or do I see here only the shadow of a princess?" asks the nurse, while Herodias gazes, absorbed, at her own spectral image in the mirror. Her beauty, for all its insubstantiality, is portrayed as dazzling—golden hair, diamond-like eyes—but also as inhuman, hard as metal, cold as the stars, or as ice and snow, unmoving and unmoved, virgin and forever sterile. "A kiss," says Herodiade, "would kill me, if Beauty were not already Death." "The Canticle of St. John" extends the imagery of light and coldness to suggest the saint's ascension from the darkness of bodily contingency to the icy radiance of Herodias's non-contingent world. Death, the mark of her domain, is for him a second baptism. The knife, flashing in the sunlight, liberates him as spirit to bear witness to her glory.

Hérodiade marks a crucial stage in the development of Mallarmé's poetic theory and technique. Grandiosely conceived as moving towards a perfect union of Language and Essence, it gives birth to a new aesthetic of suggestion, which promotes apprehension of the Absolute through its reflection in the contingent and which depersonalizes content and deconstructs syntax to release the full expressive potential of language *per se*. These techniques are intensively present from the earliest stages of "Herodias." "Scene" retains vestigial traces of the language of classical theatre, the dramatic formulation of itself guaranteeing the principle of authorial effacement. "Overture" experiments with extended play on phonetic and semantic patterns based on the "musical" techniques of Edgar Allan Poe. "The Canticle of St. John," written much later, replaces florid elaboration with the hermetic compression characteristic of Mallarmé's maturity. The intensity of vision towards which "Herodias" aspires and the perfection of expression envisaged for it made the writing of the poem as much an experience of anguish as one of elation. Perfect beauty or the impossibility of its achievement? The Absolute or the Void? Mallarmé, like Herodias before her mirror, is assailed with doubt:

"Some evenings, in your pitiless clarity, I have known with horror the naked emptiness of my dream."

—Rachel Killick

HEUREUX QUI, COMME ULYSSE, A FAIT UN BEAU VOYAGE (Sonnet 31)
Poem by Joachim Du Bellay, 1558

Heureux qui, comme Ulysse, a fair un beau voyage,
Ou comme celui-là qui conquit la toison,
Est puis est retourné, plein d'usage et raison,
Vivre entre ses parents le reste de son âge!

Quand reverrai-je, hélas, de mon petit village
Fumer la cheminée, et en quelle saison
Reverrai-je le clos de ma pauvre maison,
Qui m'est une province, et beaucoup davantage?

Plus me plaît le séjour qu'ont bâti mes aïeux
Que des palais romains le front audacieux,
Plus que le marbre dur me plaît l'ardoise fine,

Plus mon Loire gaulois que le Tibre latin,
Plus mon petit Liré que le mont Palatin,
Et plus que l'air marin la douceur angevine.

In the Spring of 1553 Joachim Du Bellay left Paris for Rome, where he was to spend the next four years. At the age of 30 he had begun to make his mark as a poet in Parisian literary circles and had caused a stir with the publication of his controversial *The Defense and Illustration of the French Language*. But he had not yet managed to find a patron or a steady income, and when the chance came up to accompany his influential relative, Cardinal Jean Du Bellay, on a diplomatic mission to Rome he naturally took it—especially as Rome was the Mecca of the Renaissance, the city at the heart of the humanist dream of intellectual elegance and renewal.

As so often, reality did not live up to expectation. Du Bellay was probably not well suited to court or diplomatic life and he found his duties tiresome and humiliating. Nor did Italy—and more particularly the Italians—prove as attractive as he had imagined. He gave vent to his feelings of disappointment in the collection he wrote mostly during his stay in Rome, appropriately named *The Regrets*.

These 191 sonnets are a fine example of how a poet can turn his private feelings to account in a way that on the face of it appears public and (almost) impersonal, at least in the satirical sonnets. There are, in *The Regrets*, two distinct strains, although these have, as we have seen, a common source in the poet's bruised sensitivity and despair. Du Bellay is by turns sardonic and elegiac. In his satirical sonnets he criticizes Italians for their venality and lack of scruple, while in his elegiac sequence of sonnets he gives voice to his nostalgia for France, which he increasingly "regrets."

Satirical poetry inevitably fades with the object of the poet's scorn, and many of Du Bellay's sonnets about Roman life have lost their impact. The poet, himself, however, undoubtedly set great store by them and expected them to help establish his reputation as a latter-day Horace. For a modern reader it is rather the poems in which he expresses his longing for France and his disillusionment and bitterness at his situation that have the more immediate appeal. Among these melancholy poems of exile, the most famous is without doubt Sonnet 31, in which the homesick young Frenchman compares his lot to other sad travellers and looks forward to a happy homecoming.

Anyone who has ever felt lost and lonely in a foreign and unfriendly environment will be able to respond to Du Bellay's immortal sonnet, which articulates the emotional and irrational sense of loss and abandonment that provokes homesickness. By referring, from the opening line of his sonnet, to Ulysses, the archetypal wanderer, Du Bellay transcends everyday emotions and lifts his distress to a higher plane. It may well be that what caused him so much anguish was his inability to adapt, to take Rome and its inhabitants at their own evaluation; he cleverly suppresses any mention of the causes of his bitterness and looks forward instead to his eventual return, to the day when like Ulysses and Jason (alluded to in the second line) he will return home to live the remainder of his days among his friends and family, ''plein d'usage et raison'' (full of experience and reason). He comforts himself, therefore, with thoughts of home and peaceful security. Happy Ulysses to have returned home, unhappy Du Bellay who does not know when he will next see his beloved France! The second quatrain crucially shifts the emphasis from doleful complaint to wistful questioning. Lines 5 to 9 are in fact a question (which must by its very nature remain unanswered), punctuated with a poignant ''alas!'' as to when the poet will be able to return home. They also focus the reader's attention on the modesty of his aspirations. Not for him a return to a high position or to luxury. All he pines for is his ''petit village'' (''little village'') and his ''pauvre maison'' (''poor house''; in fact not as poor as all that, for he was of noble blood) with its little garden. This is a carefully constructed antithesis: the greatness of Rome would be willingly sacrificed for the chance to go home to these humble surroundings which to him are ''a province'' (note the careful choice of word) and ''much more.'' The two tercets (lines 10–14) develop this opposition between Rome and the simple pleasures of Du Bellay's native province of Anjou. The point is beautifully made in line 11, where the soft slates of the houses are contrasted with the ''hard marble'' of Rome's buildings, already characterized as being both ''palaces'' (and therefore opulent) and ''audacious.'' The last three lines of this sonnet accentuate the difference between proud Rome with its Tiber and its Palatine Hill and the humble but sweet province of Anjou; the reference to ''la douceur angevine'' with which the poem ends has become proverbial.

Du Bellay's poem was born of his despair, and for contemporary readers it no doubt had resonances lost on us today. Elsewhere in this collection Du Bellay plays what might be called the nationalist card, scoring points off the Italians and praising all things French, especially if they were homely and unpretentious. But this sonnet owes its fame to the undoubted chord it strikes in readers of all countries and all centuries, capturing more than any other the voice of the involuntary exile who longs for his own home, looking to a future in what is very often an idealized past.

—Michael Freeman

HIPPOLYTUS
Play by Euripides, 428 BC

Euripides was not popular in his lifetime, achieving only four victories in 22 or 23 competitions. But one of these rare victories came in 428 BC with a production that included his *Hippolytus*. One

ancient commentator calls it ''one of his best,'' and we can only agree. A tragedy in a major key, it is full of strong characters, ideas, and images, where men and gods meet and interact, where the world of reality and an ideal realm collide with tragic results.

Hippolytus is an instance of the ''Potiphar's wife'' theme (see *Genesis* 39), a love triangle involving an older man (here Theseus, king of Athens), his wife (Phaedra), and a younger male bound to him by a tie of authority (here Hippolytus, his son by ''the Amazon woman''). The woman falls in love with the young man, expresses her love, but is rejected by him, usually for virtuous reasons. To cover her shame, she falsely accuses the young man of rape to her husband. The older man punishes the younger, who in most instances survives by miraculous means. But in *Hippolytus* the youth is cursed by his father, and on his way to banishment his horses are frightened by a bull from the sea and he is dragged to his death. In remorse Phaedra kills herself.

It is crucial to realize that the play we possess is a revision of a lost earlier version (c. 435 BC?). From what we can tell of that earlier *Hippolytus* (see W.S. Barrett and Kenneth Cavander), it was an orthodox ''Potiphar's wife'' play, but this revision is in many ways a deliberate inversion of that genre. Note the setting, Troezen (Hippolytus' home, not the older man's). Phaedra is hardly the shameless seducer of tradition, but a noble woman in love against her will, who will not yield to her passion. In fact, Phaedra and Hippolytus never meet; a nurse acting on her own reveals Phaedra's love to Hippolytus. The young man refuses it, not just because he is noble and pure, but because he hates women: ''I shall have enough of hating women, and even if they said I am forever talking of this, remember that women are wicked forever.'' Phaedra kills herself halfway through the action, not from remorse or guilt, but for shame, with a note wrongly accusing Hippolytus.

But Euripides' greatest innovation was to set this play within a divine framework. Aphrodite (Love) speaks the prologue, revealing that she will punish Hippolytus for his excessive devotion to Artemis (the chaste goddess of the hunt). She has caused Phaedra's love, so that the revelation will destroy Hippolytus (and incidentally Phaedra) and thus satisfy her slighted honour. At the end Artemis appears to blame Theseus for the death of his son, to promise the dying Hippolytus honours after his death, and to revenge herself on Love (''I shall kill with these arrows whatever mortal is most dear to her,'' an illusion to the myth of Aphrodite and Adonis).

This is the first play we have demonstrating Euripides' celebrated excursions into theology. He sets up traditional anthropomorphic deities (Aphrodite, Artemis) with human passions (jealousy, pride, spite) and superhuman powers and little concern for men. Both Aphrodite and Artemis are cut from the same inferior cloth. Ironically, men must worship these unworthy beings and, like Phaedra and Hippolytus, strive for virtue. Yet Love is real, a cosmic force; so too is Purity, but Euripides juxtaposes his ideals (''Gods should not be like men in their passions'') with the grim reality. In his plays men have a superior view of gods and divinity. Note the ending where Theseus and Hippolytus forgive each other; gods cannot.

On a psychological level the playwright is exploring the human reality behind characters from myth. Must the woman always be a shameless seductress? This Phaedra is a woman of virtue, in some ways a continuation of the empathetic portrait developed in his *Medea*, and a real human figure. Likewise, must the young man be a paragon of virtue? Could he be so in reality? In Hippolytus we meet a man apart, devoted to Artemis and the wild. His virtue is real, his song to Artemis beautiful and sincere, and he does keep his oath of silence to the nurse. It is not incidental that he is Theseus' *bastard* son.

Hippolytus repays a variety of critical approaches. Anne Burnett has shown how it fits well into a Levi-Straussian dualism (a tension between the solitary hunter and the promiscuous city woman), resolved or ''mediated'' by the institution of marriage. This explains the rather unusual honours bestowed on Hippolytus (brides on their wedding eve will dedicate to him a lock of hair) and the joining of male and female choruses. B.M.W. Knox and Barbara Goff have explored the theme of speech and silence as dominant and motive symbols, while C.A.E. Luschnig stresses that the play revolves around knowledge and knowing. In fact, as in *The Trojan Women* and *Ion*, men come to a tragic knowledge about the universe—Desmond J. Conacher is especially good here.

Underlying and running through the drama is an untranslatable concept, *sophrosyne* (chastity, moderation, self-control, virtue). The dramatist seems to be asking who is truly *sophron*, the woman in love who will die to protect her honour or the young man whose ''virtue'' is undercut by his immoderate misogyny?

Full of vivid imagery from the wild and the hunt (animal imagery is particularly prevalent—the Bull from the Sea can be seen as Hippolytus' repressed sexuality which destroys him), of water and sea, or escape to distant lands, this play breathes the great outdoors, and displays brilliantly Euripides' favourite themes of psychology, realism, innovation, and theology. It deserves its place among the greatest of Greek tragedies.

—Ian C. Storey

THE HOLY TERRORS (Les Enfants terribles)
Novel by Jean Cocteau, 1929

Jean Cocteau's *The Holy Terrors* is a novel that recounts the lives of a group of adolescents in early 20th-century Paris. Published in 1929, the narrative portrays the realistic, functional world of the French bourgeoisie that envelops, and eventually overtakes, the private fantasies of childhood innocence. Somewhat autobiographical, Cocteau's account of these interacting and blurring realities incorporates scenes of Paris, as well as the brutality of bullies, intellectual oppression, and the emotional torments that characterize the French lycée. This actual world, though, collides with a mythical reality, and the naive games enjoyed by children are a subterfuge that reflect the cruel ploys conceived and executed by adults. The child's room, then, is a shadow that outlines the horrors of reality. Like Cocteau's dramatic representations of Orpheus or Oedipe in *The Infernal Machine,* these characters are destined to proceed from play to pain and from illusion to illumination.

The narrative opens with images evoking tension and disparities: the staid scene of Paris apartments, protected and darkened by drapes; the restless tumult of schoolboys engaged in reckless play. Dargelos, a pupil who exercises authority over weaker boys, throws a stone which, encased by snow, hits, and inflicts injury on his admirer, Paul. Gérard, sensitive to Paul's weakness, sees that his friend is taken home. Paul's sister Elisabeth nurses her brother, as well as her mother who, abandoned by her husband, is incapacitated. Secluded from the conflicts of daily life, Paul, Elisabeth, and Gérard create an imaginary world: Paul's cluttered room replaces the streets and courtyards of Paris, and children's amusements substitute for adults' machinations. External events, however, penetrate this artificial reality: for Dargelos,

expelled from school for throwing pepper at the headmaster, recognizes the ambivalence of adolescent fun and adult aggressions and is biding his time for a final blow, and Paul's mother dies unnoticed during an innocuous quarrel between Paul and his sister. Fantasy, though, continues to cloak actuality. Paul and Elisabeth treasure a photo of Dargelos dressed to play in a school performance the sinister role of Racine's biblical heroine Athalie; and they avoid entering their mother's room, thereby erasing her death from their consciousness.

Nevertheless, children's play reflects adult realities. Paul and Elisabeth participate in grotesque games which, like life's anxieties and inhumanities, instil terror and torment within others. The passage of time, moreover, impels changes in perspectives and interrelations, and adolescence as a *rite de passage* between childhood simplicity and adult sophistication ends in a discovery of the transparency of fictions and the reality of existence. In determining Paul's actions and attitudes, Elisabeth assumes Dargelos's place in a psychological hierarchy and thereby defines her identity. But through her marriage to Michaël, a rich American, she conforms to social expectations and simultaneously seeks to resolve her previous role of older sister with her present situation as wife. Although Michaël dies accidentally, external realities disturb the viability and complacency of a contrived, inner order. The themes of fate and futility influence characterization, and enable Cocteau to present a picture of desolation and death that define the human predicament. As a young man, Paul retains the calm innocence of childhood but, as an adolescent becoming a man, is attracted to Agathe, whom Elisabeth had invited to reside with them. Similarly, Gérard hopes to marry Elisabeth. This love that develops duly and naturally disrupts relationships, disturbs social roles and psychological identities, and displaces innocent fantasies with cruel contentions. Elisabeth, jealous and fearful of Paul's attention to Agathe, who resembles the photograph of Dargelos, attempts to preserve her position of control, secretly thwarts Paul's attempt to communicate his love to Agathe, and encourages a marriage between Agathe and Gérard. Paul suffers the distress of unrequited love and, dejected and reclusive, is enlivened momentarily by Dargelos's gift of poison which he consumes. Paul's death drives Elisabeth to suicide. Fatalism, masked by play and misconstrued, surfaces: the snow-enwrapped stone is transformed into a parcel enclosing poison and, subsequently, into a black bullet that kills Elisabeth. Man teeters between desolation and death. Dreams dissolve. In submitting to the exigencies of chronology and maturity, Cocteau's characters confront the shock of reality which emerges as the solitude and silence experienced by Agathe and Gérard in a loveless and lifeless marriage, and which marks for Paul and Elisabeth disintegration and oblivion.

Character portrayal and imagistic patterns reinforce the themes of destiny, desolation, and death. Defended by dream-like delusions, Cocteau's personages are puppets which, similar to ships tossed in a raging storm, writhe with anxiety and apprehensions. As sentient beings, they resist violence and elude agitation. But figured by the novel's pervasive imagery of shimmering shadows produced by moonbeams, or refracted light emitted by a chandelier, or the tenuous whiteness of falling snow, their world is ephemeral and undelineated. Fantasy contests, but coalesces, with truth. Objects appear inanimate and inconsequential, but they possess hidden powers: for a protective scarf and a plaster sphinx result respectively in Michaël's death and the pronouncement of tragic destiny. Rituals are games; but insults, sanctioned or teasing, remain tactics of pain. In retreating from reality, these characters are entrapped, destined to endure agitation and anguish. Abusive words, axe-like throbs in Elisabeth's heart, and a bloodied kerchief indicate violence and announce destruction. For Paul, the basilisk and mandrake seem magical and glorious; but, like Dargelos's present of poison and the bullet lodged in a revolver, they conceal agents of death. Paul and Elisabeth are tragic victims who, in seeking a shielded innocence, suffer, sadly and ironically, delusion and destruction. Elisabeth's final vision of the paradisiacal island inhabited by Bernardin de Saint-Pierre's romantic young heroes, Paul and Virginie, is ultimately a hallucination that appears as a vortex descending into a void. The whiteness of the snow that hides the stone surfaces as the blackness of the bullet that devastates and annihilates.

Cocteau's portrayal of destiny and his use of imagery denote parallels between this narrative and his plays, and may have facilitated this novel's adaptation into a film directed by J.-P. Melville in 1950. Like the dramatization of fate in *The Infernal Machine,* which Cocteau describes as a ''masterpiece of horror,'' the depiction of agony and anguish in *The Holy Terrors* defines the human situation in terms of destroyed delusions and inevitable death.

—Donald Gilman

THE HOMECOMING (20 Still ist die Nacht, es ruhen die Gassen)
Poem by Heinrich Heine, 1824

The night is calm; the streets quiet down;
Here lives a lass who was dear to me.
Long years ago she left the town,
But here is her house, as it used to be.
And here is a creature who stares into space
And wrings his hands in a storm of pain.
I shudder when I see his face:
It is my own self the moon shows plain.
You double! You comrade ghostly white!
Why have you come to ape the woe
That tortured me, night after night,
Under these windows—long ago?

(translated by Aaron Kramer)

Heinrich Heine's *Book of Songs* (*Buch der Lieder*), first published in 1827, is an edited collection of poems, almost all of which had been published previously over the space of a decade. In most cases we do not know the dates of origin very exactly. ''The Homecoming'' 20 perhaps best known, like many of Heines's poems, in a musical setting, in this case Franz Schubert's *Schwanengesang* (also 1827), may have been written in July 1823 or somewhat later that year. It was first published in a periodical in March 1824, as number 6 of ''Thirty-Three Poems by H. Heine'' (his tendency to publish poems in cycles of 11 is one sign of the formal control exerted on a poetry that has an appearance of emotional immediacy). In the first volume of *Pictures of Travel,* 1826, it took its final place as number 20 of the 88 poems of ''The Homecoming.'' Unlike other poems of Heine, it underwent little change from its earliest version to the definitive *Book of Songs* edition of 1844.

Heine's tendency to organize poems in clusters and cycles always makes it somewhat problematic to isolate them for interpretation. They echo and modify one another, creating a continuously varying

perspective on what appears to be his one subject, unrequited love. There are images elsewhere of the speaker of the poem standing outside the house in which his beloved once lived; in one of these, ''Lyrical Intermezzo,'' 38, he wanders through the streets accompanied by his shadow. In addition there are in the *Book of Songs* a great many echoes of other contemporary late-Romantic poets, down to specific images and rhymes. In the case of ''The Homecoming,'' 20 one can point to poems by Wilhelm Müller, Ludwig Uhland, Joseph von Eichendorff, and others, including a fabricated ''folk-song'' of Achim von Arnim. It is this synthetic quality of Heine's verse that has led some critics to regard his manner as derivative manipulation of ready-made materials. But he brings to these resources a new complexity and intensity, combining them into a sceptical metapoetry reflecting upon the poetic possibilities of his time.

An example is the image of the ''double,'' the *doppeltgänger* in Heine's spelling, which he may have taken over from the fantasy writing of E.T.A. Hoffman. But Heine does not employ fantastic or special images to Gothic effect, except in some of his very early, immature verse; they serve as metaphors of psychological and poetological anxieties. The double is the image of a split self brooding irritably on an emotional condition that should have been outgrown but continues to hobble and even shame the present self.

There are three temporally layered fictional personae in the poem. The most primitive is the self of the past who has loved and lost. Then there is the double, contorted in melodramatic emotion, ''aping'' the sufferings of the past to no rational purpose. The speaker of the poem recognizes the identity of the figures with himself and asks why this anachronistic grieving continues. Heine often distances himself from the impassioned content of his own poetry, deconstructing, so to speak, its emotionally laden and, to some extent, borrowed diction. He is notorious for a jarring break of mood within the poem itself, sometimes achieved by a lurch to a more colloquial or even vulgar stylistic level. The use of the word ''ape'' in this poem is a mild example of that. He will also hold up his own feelings to amused or satirical contemplation. In several places he addresses himself as ''dear friend,'' as one might speak to a foolishly behaving companion. The staring, hand-wringing double is hardly an image of tragic or even dignified stature. These devices, though not without precedent, constitute in their ingenuity and variety of nuance the genuine originality and unmistakable tone of Heine's early poetry.

This tone in its quite aggressive articulation has been misunderstood in two ways. In the past it was sometimes regarded merely as blatantly malicious cynicism, malevolent subversion of genuine, sincere feeling and true poesy. In more recent times there has been a tendency to give a similar reading a more positive evaluation. In this view Heine simply surpasses the poetry of Romantic delusion and emotional self-indulgence by parodying and exposing it in the interest of progress and reason. Both views gravely underestimate the level of stress in the *Book of Songs* and the difficulties of resolving it. ''The Homecoming,'' 20 is a key poem in its earnest depiction of the poet's dilemmas. It is an error to suppose that Heine was always a laughing poet or that his wit is univocally liberating. The past self is obsolete and ridiculous but cannot be fully exorcized. One might notice how quickly the ''lass'' is made to disappear from the poem; the poet is forever banishing her but she continually reappears, ever flaunting the impregnable indifference that calls his very ego ideal into question. His only resource for handling his situation is poetry. But poetry, in Heine's understanding of it, is implicated with the feelings that are causing all the disruption and are doubtful in their integrity. Thus the problem of the self is a problem of poetry, to which the only available solution is poetry. This incomparably astute perception of the dilemma of poetry at the decline of Romanticism is what gives the *Book of Songs* its historical importance, and the exploitation of it by poetic means its aesthetic endurance.

—Jeffrey L. Sammons

HONGLOU MENG

See THE DREAM OF THE RED CHAMBER

THE HOUSE BY THE MEDLAR TREE (I Malavoglia)
Novel by Giovanni Verga, 1881

In his Preface to the novel, Giovanni Verga calls *The House by the Medlar Tree* a "study of how the first anxious desire for material well-being probably originates and develops in the humblest social situation, and of the perturbations caused in a family, which until then lived in relative happiness, by vague yearnings for the unknown and by the realization that they are not very well off or that they could be better off."

The novel was supposed to be the first of a series of five, called *I vinti* (The Defeated), which would have depicted the struggle "for material well-being up to the loftiest ambition." And while "the fateful, incessant, often difficult and feverish course that humankind travels to achieve its goal is grandiose when seen as a whole, from a distance," the author, as an "observer," is interested only in the "weak who fall by the wayside . . . in the doomed who raise their arms in despair and bend their heads."

If *The House by the Medlar Tree* were only the presentation of a struggle for material well-being, it would have social interest and perhaps be sentimental, whereas the feature that helps make the novel a masterpiece is that this struggle appears as an *agon* of man against destiny, of will against circumstance, of possibilities against impossibilities.

Three generations of the Toscano family, nicknamed Malavoglia—Padron 'Ntoni, grandfather and patriarch; his son Bastianazzo and his wife Maruzza, called La Longa; and their five children—live in the family house by a medlar tree in Aci Trezza, a Sicilian seaside village. For centuries the family has earned a living by fishing from their boat, the *Provvidenza*. When the oldest child 'Ntoni is drafted into the army, Padron 'Ntoni, hoping to repair the loss caused by his grandson's departure, buys on credit a cargo of lupins to sell for profit in another seaside village. This change from fisherman to merchant is an act of hubris, a daring challenge to age-old ways. It will be the beginning of misfortune. In fact, Bastianazzo drowns in a storm that scatters the cargo and ruins the boat.

With his father dead, 'Ntoni chooses to return home instead of finishing the few remaining months of military service which would have exempted his younger brother, Luca, from conscription. Luca is soon to die in a naval battle.

The *Provvidenza* is repaired and the grandfather and 'Ntoni work to repay the debt of the lost cargo, but the deadline cannot be met. Grandfather 'Ntoni, old-fashioned and honest, pays with the house, refusing to accept the fact that he is not legally obliged to pay the debt or forfeit the house since it is part of his daughter-in-law's dowry.

From this point on, the requisition of the house becomes an obsession. Grandfather, the very young Alessi, and the less willing and grumbling 'Ntoni, work as much as possible, yet another violent storm almost drowns them all. When they are on the verge of recovery, cholera kills La Longa. 'Ntoni cannot be persuaded to stay by his grandfather's entreaties and leaves Aci Trezza in search of a better life.

Alone and old, with young Alessi and the two nieces Mena and Lia, no longer able to manage his boat, Padron 'Ntoni decides to sell it. No longer owners, the two men work as hired hands on other people's boats, always hoping to buy back the house whose image assumes increasing importance, as if the continuation of the family depended on it.

A final catastrophe is impending. 'Ntoni returns penniless and angry. With no desire to work, he spends his time drinking, knifes a customs guard in a smuggling incident, and ends up in jail. Lia, the younger sister, becomes a prostitute; the older, Mena, is thus dishonoured and will never be able to marry. The sick grandfather is taken to a hospital far from Aci Trezza where he dies alone, the day Alessi comes to fetch him after buying back the family house.

The requisition of the house, Alessi's success, and his bouncing children, the only carefree images in the novel, do nothing to cancel out the bitter defeat of the family's attempt to improve their lot. In fact, instead of ending the novel with images of hope represented by the children, Verga adds a kind of coda: after five years of jail 'Ntoni comes home but realizes that he no longer belongs to the world of his fathers: unchanging, stable, and naturally cyclical when experience from within, but monotonous, stifling, static, and unnatural when viewed as an outsider. As night turns into day and the villagers recommence their eternal life of work, joy, and suffering, 'Ntoni leaves Aci Trezza forever. They seem to have a glimmer of consciousness of a world beyond but no desire to explore or conquer it. Mena, for example, thinking of her beloved Alfio, a cart driver, becomes conscious of the existence of the many roads in the world which do not lead to Aci Trezza.

The idyll between Mena and Alfio is a rare, lyrical element, yet even this small joy is doomed. Their union is initially impossible because Mena has a large dowry, and her family arranges her engagement to a rich man. Later, poor, she cannot marry anyone because she has been dishonoured by her sister. The iron laws of tradition will crush small as well as big dreams and adventures. The requisition of the house does not imply or symbolize the redemption of the individual.

An atmosphere of epic grandeur surrounds the characters in their doomed efforts and silent resignations. The novel is an epic—D.H. Lawrence called it Homeric, because its protagonists are not only the Malavoglia but the entire village of Aci Trezza, indeed an entire civilization. The villagers are not only co-protagonists, they are the very tellers of the story. Verga, true to his belief in the impersonality of the author who is supposed to tell the tale "without passion," does not mediate between the events and his readers. Most of the action is presented not directly but through the villagers' reactions and comments, and characters are almost always introduced through the eyes of the community. This choral quality is the more powerful because it speaks in its own original language and style which Verga created by immersing Italian in Sicilian rhythms and patterns.

—Emanuele Licastro

THE HOUSE OF BERNARDA ALBA (La casa de Bernarda Alba)
Play by Federico García Lorca, 1945

The House of Bernarda Alba is, like *Blood Wedding*, set in the Spanish countryside and tells the story of the 60-year-old Bernarda's domination of her household, including her five, spinster daughters. The beginning of Act I announces a period of eight years of mourning following the recent death of Bernarda's husband and reveals at every step Bernarda's harshness towards her servants, her mother, and her daughters. Of these, the eldest, Angustias, is to marry Pepe el Romano, a circumstance that stirs up feelings of envy and resentment, particularly in the youngest and most attractive daughter, Adela, and the older and unattractive Martirio. In Act II, existing tensions intensify. Adela grows more rebellious, Martirio more resentful. Her theft of Angustias's portrait of Pepe draws from the servant, La Poncia, warnings to which Bernarda responds with a demonstration of even greater intransigence. Act III reveals that Adela has been meeting Pepe secretly at night. Her discovery by Martirio results in Bernarda attempting to shoot him as he escapes. Convinced by Martirio of Pepe's death, Adela hangs herself, and Bernarda announces a second period of mourning, for her daughter, who, others must believe, died a virgin.

Like *Blood Wedding, The House of Bernarda Alba* had its source in real life, for as a child Federico García Lorca had a next-door neighbour, ''an old widow who exercises an inexorable and tyrannical watch over her spinster daughters,'' one of whom was said to have a lover, Pepe de la Romilla. On the other hand, there are also literary sources. The insistence which Bernarda places on the good name of the family, deeply ingrained in the Spanish temperament, had its literary antecedent in the plays of the 17th century, notably in the ''honour'' plays of Calderón, with which Lorca was very familiar. The obsessive concern with the good opinion of others, which drives Bernarda to incarcerate her daughters and leads finally to Adela's death, is the motive which in Calderón's *The Surgeon of Honour* obliges a husband to murder an innocent wife. Another possible source was the novel *Doña Perfecta* by the 19th-century novelist Pérez Galdós, in which, in a narrow-minded, provincial town, the intolerant Doña Perfecta becomes increasingly opposed to the marriage of her daughter, Rosario, to the young liberal from Madrid, Pepe Rey. When the couple attempt to elope, she arranges Pepe's murder, after which Rosario loses her sanity. Finally, as in the case of *Blood Wedding*, the influence of Greek tragedy is very clear: the play's title suggests a household or a lineage; Bernarda brings about, through her actions, the end she seeks to avoid; there is a powerful sense of fatality; and the final scenes are strongly cathartic. But if the literary debt is evident, the themes of the play are pure Lorca: passion and frustration, exemplified above all in Adela; passing time, personified in the ageing of all the daughters; and death, physical in Adela's case, emotional in the other girls. Not only does the play constitute another powerful expression of Lorca's own situation, it also anticipates the divisions which would tear apart the family of Spain in the summer of 1936, only months after the play's completion.

Lorca's assertion that *The House of Bernarda Alba* is a ''*documental fotográfico*'' (a ''photographic record''), together with his deliberate stripping-away of obviously poetic elements, has encouraged the belief that, in contrast to *Blood Wedding* and *Yerma*, this is a naturalistic play. An examination of its style and techniques suggests that nothing could be further from the truth. While it is true that more

of the characters have real names than is the case in the other plays—Adela, Amelia, María Josefa, La Poncia—the names of others are decidedly symbolic: Angustias and Martirio suggesting suffering incarnate, and Bernarda Alba ironically suggestive of the illumination of dawn. Indeed, each of the characters embodies to some degree the clash of the opposites longing and denial which, concentrated in Bernarda's family, has its counterpart in other families wherever natural instinct comes into conflict with narrow-minded tradition.

Despite their apparent naturalism, the play's three settings are highly stylized, with the white walls evoking purity and virginity but also sterility and the endless monotony of imprisoned lives. Within the frame of the settings, movement and posture enhance the image: the daughters seated at the beginning of Act II, sewing passively; or later in the act the despairing Martirio, seated, head in hands. In contrast, bursts of activity suggest from time to time Adela's defiance, as does her green dress, suddenly bringing a splash of colour into the darkened house. Lighting too has a crucial role to play. In Act I the opening of a door momentarily floods the room with light, suggesting the world beyond the house. Act II sustains the idea when the girls observe the harvesters through a half-open shutter, but by Act III it is night, with Adela and Martirio engulfed by a darkness that is as much emotional, suggesting despair and mutual hate, as it is physical. The studied interplay of setting, movement, and lighting exposes the inner lives of the characters and affects the response of the audience in a way that naturalism could never do.

The language of the play, mainly in prose, is also carefully shaped, stripped of the inconsequential trivia of everyday speech. Almost every word exposes character: Bernarda's outbursts are the verbal equivalent of the stick with which she beats the ground; Adela's speech is alive with defiance, while Magdalena's is heavy with despair. When songs are introduced, on two crucial occasions, their rhythm pinpoints the importance of the moment, as in Act II when the vibrant harvester's song encapsulates a world for which Bernarda's daughters long but which they cannot reach.

The trajectory from the highly poetic *Blood Wedding* to the much more austere *The House of Bernarda Alba* is typical of Lorca's constant experimentation. But the differences between the two plays are less important than their similarity, which lies ultimately in the importance for Lorca of the poetic and the imaginative in the theatre.

—Gwynne Edwards

HOUSE OF LIARS (Menzogna e sortilegio)
Novel by Elsa Morante, 1948

House of Liars is Elsa Morante's first novel, and was published in 1948. In this work, two of the main characteristics of Morante's subsequent fiction are already present—the depiction of reality as a dream, and passions that lead to tragedy, deception, and despair.

The plot of the novel is extremely complex. The narrator of the story, Elisa, is a young woman who lives alone, having lost both her parents as a child and then also her adoptive mother Rosaria, a brash but generous prostitute. It is after Rosaria's death that Elisa locks herself away in her room to write the story of her family. Her wish to put pen to paper does not spring from a need for self-understanding, or a desire to explore the causes of the destruction of her family, but rather, as E. Siciliano (1967) has indicated, to reshape the reality of the past through lies of her own making. Thus, the mundane lives of the people she knew are transformed, in Elisa's narrative, into legends, almost myths.

Elisa starts her spellbinding storytelling with her grandmother, Cesira, a poor schoolteacher who spurns the young men who belong to her own class. Desperate to acquire a high position in society, she marries an old aristocrat, Teodoro Massia, who, unknown to her, is almost destitute and has been disowned by his rich family. When the little money he has runs out, Cesira finds herself living in poverty, trapped in a loveless marriage. She even dislikes her beautiful daughter Anna, who has inherited the aristocratic bearing of the Massia family, and Cesira is hated by her in return.

Anna, the narrator's mother, is in fact the main character of *House of Liars*. She is portrayed by Elisa as extremely proud of her father's family (which she has never met), and as leading an idle and futile life in abject poverty, living on Cesira's meagre earnings as a private teacher. Like a princess in a fairytale waiting for her prince, she dreams of being released from hardship by the man she loves, her rich cousin Edoardo Cerentano, whom she has seen only once when she was a child.

Edoardo is at the heart of *House of Liars*. Even Elisa, the narrator, who has never known him personally, is in love with her created image of him. He is, in her characterization, a godlike figure who can beguile and manipulate everybody with his blond good looks and capricious charm. Anna's second meeting with her cousin takes place in the city, which is covered in snow, in a landscape which becomes magical and enchanting in the southern light.

Edoardo, who had not even known of Anna's existence, is momentarily taken by the girl. The love she is ready to give him, even to the point of offering herself to him, amuses the young man for a while. He plays with the girl's feelings, conscious of the great power he has over her; he even goes as far as marking Anna as his property by burning a brand on her lip, then, annoyed by her submissiveness, he abandons her without any explanation, apart from a cold note he has a servant hand to her.

With no other resources except her beauty, Anna persuades Francesco De Salvi, a penniless student, to marry her. The pock-marked Francesco is a tragic character. The son of peasants, doted on by both his parents, he is deeply ashamed of his poor origins. On learning from his mother that she had been seduced by an outsider in the village when she lived with her husband and that he himself is the fruit of her adulterous encounter, he prefers to believe that his real father is a baron. After a chance introduction to Anna through Edoardo, he falls in love with the girl's beauty and aristocratic connections. The only offspring of the ill-fated union between Francesco and Anna is Elisa, the narrator, who describes herself as a "little lost animal" in childhood, ignored by her mother most of the time.

The novel reaches its climax with Edoardo's death. Anna, who hears of it by chance, refuses to accept it. Gradually she slips into an imaginary world where she thinks she can take her place beside Edoardo. Completely rapt in her dream, she even starts writing letters to herself, signing them with the name of her beloved, and then showing them to his mother, who is equally incapable of believing that her adored son is no more. Elisa, only ten years old at the time of these events, uses her narrative, when a grown woman, to transform these pitiful episodes of prosaic madness into a spellbinding tale that depicts the "ceremonies" these two women perform to their god Edoardo. Anna is portrayed throughout these events as a tragic heroine, a certain regal composure being one of her main attributes. Finally, consumed by her passion for the Edoardo she has created for herself, Anna confesses to her husband that she has a lover, but

refuses to tell him his name. Francesco, who has spent his entire life with Anna trying to win her love, and who has never known about Anna's feelings for Edoardo, is astounded by this revelation. He tries time and time again to get Anna to admit the name of her lover, but without success. Anna drives him into deeper isolation by telling him that Edoardo, the great friend he had lost touch with, is dead. Francesco, desperate and lonely, starts dreaming of Edoardo.

The presence of the dead man seems to permeate the whole atmosphere of Anna and Francesco's life at this point, but Edoardo's spirit is never malevolent. Both Anna and her husband see him as they had known him. For Anna he is the tyrannical and bewitching lover, for Francesco he remains the generous and understanding friend of his youth. The child Elisa lives in these hallucinatory surroundings carrying out her domestic chores like a slave to her idolized mother, who sleeps all day in her room, trying to reach her dearest Edoardo.

Tragedy strikes when Francesco, worn out by his unrequited passion and deep loneliness, dies in an accident. Anna follows him shortly, but not before having realized that she did truly love her husband and has wasted her life pursuing an illusion. The child, unknowing witness to this tragic denouement, is rescued from poverty and solitude by Rosaria, the prostitute whom her father Francesco had known as a young man and to whom he had turned in later years for comfort in his despair.

The plot of the novel unfolds in a Sicily that is never actually named: the city is referred to in the book as either "the capital" or simply "P." (Palermo). The action takes place in a society that is still feudal in its values, and is characterized by "dark passions, superstition and megalomania" (C. Sgorlon, 1972). The novel has been interpreted mainly in two ways: some critics (P. Pancrazi, E. Cecchi, G. Manacorda) consider it a representation of a magical world without any links with time or history, while others (G. Lukács, L. Stefani) see it as the portrayal of an archaic and decadent world symbolizing the lack of values in western civilization.

—Vanna Motta

THE HOUSE OF THE SPIRITS (La casa de los espíritus)
Novel by Isabel Allende, originally published in Spain in 1982. Translated by Magda Bogin, 1985

The House of the Spirits Isabel Allende's first novel was inspired by memories of her family and the political turmoil of her native Chile. It was originally written as a long letter to Allende's grandfather, in Chile, who was dying. Unable to publish her work in Venezuela, because she was an unknown writer and because of the lengthy manuscript, she sent the novel to a literary agent in Spain where it was first published by Plaza y Janés. The novel became an instant success and catapulted her to international recognition as it was translated into fifteen languages. Copies of the book needed to be smuggled into her native Chile and photocopied until the government authorized its publication. Several critics have compared Allende's novel with Gabriel García Márquez's *One Hundred Years of Solitude* (translation, 1970) for its scope as a saga of a family as well as its magic realist vision of Latin American society as it blends the real and the fantastic. Other critics acknowledge her usage of magic realism but focus on her narrative voice, which emerges in her clear journalistic dealings with the events. The novel thematically explores feminism, politics, and writing as a fundamental act.

The House of the Spirits made Allende one of the most important and widely read Latin American women authors. It is an epic saga about the members of the Trueba del Valle family at the turn of the 20th century and follows them for some fifty years in an unnamed country in South America. It contains striking images that dramatize political experiences and their consequences, while at the same time showing solidarity with the poor downtrodden who confront the established social order.

The novel while containing autobiographical elements recreates Chilean history during the same period. It is a era of great political and social turmoil with the women's movement gathering force. Clara del Valle who will become the matriarch of the clan is a young girl with telepathic abilities, can read fortunes and predict the future. After the death of her sister, Rosa the beautiful, she remains mute for nine years, only breaking her silence to make known her plan to marry her dead sister's fiancé, Esteban Trueba. He is thirty-five years old and returned to the city from his country estate to visit his dying mother and find a wife. Esteban is an aggressive and proud man who becomes obsessed with his wife Clara who he cannot totally possess. He builds a magnificent house for her where her spiritualist friends and the artists she takes in can gather and where Esteban's politico pals mingle along side of them. Their daughter Blanca develops an intimate and permanent relationship with the foreman's son. This liaison produces a daughter, Alba, a headstrong women, who falls in love with a radical student, finally winding up being tortured despite her family's power and influence. Alba's story parallels that of so many other women tortured in Chile after the military coup. As a journalist Allende is able to compel her readers into making the connection between fiction and real events, thus urging us to focus on the fact that no matter what happens we must move forward and embrace the future. The female characters may also symbolize or mark different stages in women's struggle to attain self-determination, freedom and justice as each female character corresponds to a different epoch.

The House of the Spirits is not about the patriarchy, although Esteban Trueba is a force to be reckoned with throughout the novel. He builds a plantation out of nothing and makes a name for himself among the powerful, finally becoming a senator. Allende has been criticized by some critics for her portrayal of the traditional male dominated society as being too patriarchal and *machista*. Trueba deceives, dupes, tyrannizes, and even rapes. He oppresses the peasants for his own benefit representing an on-going power struggle since the time of the conquest. He has an illegitimate son who gains power over others through his position and status as a police officer, representing the corruption and repressive nature of the controlling forces or military.

Women are seen as coping with and conquering the male's domain and they all subvert the system one way or another. Alba's great-grandmother Nivea worked to gain women the right to vote. Clara, her grandmother is a humanitarian serving the poor. Blanca, Alba's mother does not base her love on social class as she is educated to do and chooses her own career and identity. The narrator, Alba, attends the university and becomes involved in underground politics, is captured and tortured. Alba's testimony about her capture as Linda Gould Levine affirms in "A Passage to Andorgyny: Isabel Allende's *La casa de los espíritus*," is "a mirror reflection of Allende's novel— . . . that underlies the major principles of her life her author believes in: the need to remember and continue onward." Thus, Alba chronicles not only her history but her family's and country's as well.

Throughout the novel, there are references to verifiable historical references such as "the Great Poet," Pablo Neruda, winner of the 1971 Nobel prize in Literature. In addition, Pedro Tercero, who fathered Blanca's daughter Alba, is a recreation of Chilean folk singer and musician Victor Jarra, whose hands were crushed as punishment after the takeover by General Pinochet. The novel was adapted for the screen by Danish director Bille August in 1994 with an unlikely but star-studded cast including Antonio Banderas, Meryl Streep, Glenn Close, Jeremy Irons, Winona Rider and María Conchita Alonso. While the movie is mildly entertaining and is reasonably faithful to the text, it appears that *The House of the Spirits* is devoid of spirit on screen, at least. The novel, however, based on real events and inhabited by real people pulses with life and spirit.

—Beth Pollack

HSI-YU-CHI

See JOURNEY TO THE WEST

THE HUNCHBACK OF NOTRE-DAME (Notre-Dame de Paris)
Novel by Victor Hugo, 1831

Contrary to received opinion, enshrined in early translations and popular films, the preface and the structure of *The Hunchback of Notre-Dame* show that the main character is not the "hunchback," Quasimodo, but the archdeacon Claude Frollo. The preface recounts a visit to Notre-Dame when the author found the Greek word "ΑΝΑΓΚΗ" graven in the stone in an obscure corner. This is presented as the origin of the text: "He . . . sought to divine who might be the troubled soul who had not wished to leave this world without leaving this mark of crime or misfortune on the surface of the old church." The word, which means "fatality," is Frollo's. Not only is it inscribed in his cell (VII, 4), but in a scene which is emblematic of the novel as a whole (VII, 6), he prevents a visitor from saving a fly caught in a spider's web, crying "Let fatality have its way." In relation to La Esmeralda Frollo is the spider, but in relation to fatality he is the fly. Moreover he is placed in a relation of power towards all significant characters: his younger brother Jehan, for whose death he is ultimately responsible; Pierre Gringoire, whom he teaches; Quasimodo who is his adoptive child, and not least Esmeralda, whom he desires and over whom he has the power of life and death. Frollo is central: he is an agent of fatality, but also its victim.

Fatality has several dimensions. A key image in the novel first occurs when Quasimodo is being described. The Cathedral has become metaphorically the hunchback's "shell" and he has become its soul; were the narrator able, however, to scrutinize the soul of Quasimodo, within its "cave," he would probably find it hunched up ("rabougrie") "like those Venetian prisoners who grow old, bent double in a stone box which is too low and too short" (IV, 3). This image stresses oppression and incommunicability, themes which are present in the central section (VI), when the deaf Quasimodo is brought before a deaf judge and sentenced, and also in the scene where Louis XI is discussing with his treasurer the cost and the measurements of a cage, while ignoring the prisoner inside it (X, 5). Medieval justice is deaf; the voice of the oppressed is unheard. In that scene, while the ''truands'' are about to storm Notre-Dame to release Esmeralda, the King is at the Bastille. The theme of imprisonment is political as well as psychological.

Escape is illusory. The door which love might have opened leads only to frustration or death. Quasimodo loves his master Frollo, and Esmeralda, but both die. Esmeralda loves Phoebus, who does not return her love, and when she is in prison escape without death is only possible if she yields to Frollo, which she refuses. Frollo nourishes two kinds of illusion: to be loved by Esmeralda and to succeed through the alchemical quest in his search for knowledge. These two desires are incompatible, but the text of the novel unites them through variants of the image of inaccessible light: the gold of the sun, which is an emblem of the alchemist's aim, but also used of Frollo's vision of Esmeralda dancing (VIII, 4).

Fatality works therefore against love in human relationships, against individuals and peoples of a social or political level, and against the quest for knowledge. Breaches in this fundamental pessimism are rare: Jacques Coppenole, who insists on having himself announced as a cobbler (I, 4); the gourd of water that Esmeralda offers to Quasimodo in the stocks (VI, 4).

When *The Hunchback of Notre-Dame* was written, the most influential novelist in France was Walter Scott. In 1823 Victor Hugo had praised *Quentin Durward* for its ''magical'' evocations of the past and its mingling of the ugly and the beautiful. *Notre-Dame* is an historical novel (the year 1482 marks a transition from the Middle Ages to the Renaissance, from sculpture to printing as a means of instruction), but there are two important differences from Scott. The first is that in the Hugo novel historical characters, such as Louis XI, have minor rather than major roles, and the second is the narrator's ironic stance: he makes clear that he is pulling the strings, and also makes frequent parallels with the time of writing: ''If Gringoire were living nowadays, how well he would hold the middle ground between classic and romantic!'' (II, 4). His attitude towards his characters varies from ironic detachment (Gringoire), to sympathy (Quasimodo); he sees them mostly from outside, or through the eyes of other characters, but on rare occasions, such as Frollo's hallucinated anguish when he believes Esmeralda hanged (IX, 1), he writes from within.

Notre-Dame is not, as has been said, a ''character'' in the novel, but its architecture is doubly important: firstly in the immediate context (1830), when some were defending Gothic monuments against depredations on aesthetic but also political grounds (Gothic architecture was ''of the people''); secondly as a structuring principle of the whole book. The Cathedral is a hybrid construction, part romanesque, part gothic (Quasimodo is also *hybrid*) and Paris is described (III, 2) as a hybrid (city, university, town). Hybrid means that what is ugly in detail may not be so in the whole. The facade of Notre-Dame, this ''symphony in stone'' (III, 1), is an exemplar of that harmony in multiplicity which the total construction of the book embodies at one level, and complex sentences (or sustained metaphors), powerfully welded into unity by their clear syntactic structure, at another. The proliferation of living detail—popular speech, minutiae of early documents, architectural features—and the author's capacity to work such detail into new and ever-widening forms of unity are in creative tension with his pessimism. This creative tension, palpable at best in the prose style, makes of *The Hunchback of Notre-Dame* not a melodrama but a novel in which the pessimism induced by the operations of fatality is fought with the tools of art. At the end

Quasimodo and Esmeralda have become dust, the word ΑΝΑΓΚΗ has been effaced, but the cathedral, and the book, remain.

—Tony James

HUNGER (Sult)
Novel by Knut Hamsun, 1890

The story, of how *Hunger* came to be published could almost have served as an incident for the novel itself. Edvard Brandes, one of the great campaigners for naturalism in Scandinavia and editor of the radical newspaper *Politiken*, was visited in his office by a young Norwegian writer (''He had a manuscript with him, of course''). About to reject it on the ground of unsuitable length, Brandes was suddenly gripped (''though I am not sentimental'') by the desperation of the author's face. Reading over the manuscript later, Brandes was still more impressed. He arranged for the publication, anonymously, of the first fragment (in fact, what is now Part II) of the novel, which was to be published in full as *Hunger*.

Germane to the fragment of narrative Brandes read in 1888 was the desperate poverty out of which it was conceived and in which it was written. Equally characteristic of the novel, as of its *Entstehung*, was the sudden shift of fortune which transfigured defeat into survival. On one level *Hunger* is an account (based in the naturalistic manner on authorial research, but research of a kind that makes Zola and the Goncourts seem like the merest dabblers) of the effects of hunger and extreme poverty on the inner life of an individual. The first-person narrative of the novel is, in a literal sense, constructed by the hunger of its narrator. As James W. McFarlane notes in his classic study of the early novels (*PMLA*, 71, 1956), the fragmented narrative is only quickened into life by hunger; each section describes a bout of suffering. The interstices of relative well-being are a narrative silence. Such plot as the novel possesses is built upon the desperate levels to which poverty, hunger, uncertainty, and total lack of income, reduce the narrator. Significantly, the novel's ''I'' has no proper name, though he takes on various fictive identities to satisfy the police or welfare authorities, or just to conceal, out of self-defence or for his own amusement, who he ''really'' is. His single great dream is to attain the freedom to write, and through writing to escape the poverty which gives *this* fiction life. To this end, he tries to live independently of the demands of a society that, in the person of landladies and policemen, creditors and indifferent editors, alternately harries and rejects him. He lies, cheats, temporizes, all the while fascinated by his own inner reactions to an external world which seems sometimes alluringly contingent (as he watches, enraptured, the behaviour of an insect roaming across the page), sometimes threateningly invasive or distantly absurd.

However, though it hangs on the cusp of naturalism, *Hunger* is anything but a naturalistic novel. Where naturalism seeks always to place individual experience within the patterns of a wider world, *Hunger* focuses on the world inside the individual. The novel may be set in Christiania (now Oslo)—that raw, newly urbanized society which contemporaries called *Tigerstaden*, the City of Tigers. It is indeed the greatest literary evocation of those lower depths into which Hedda Gabler loves to peep and through which Brack and Løvborg go slumming. (Appropriately, Ibsen's play was published in the same year as *Hunger*.) But what fascinates Knut Hamsun are exactly the areas of experience that refuse the social, the ethical, the logical and reasonable. "People don't *do* that sort of thing!" exclaims Ibsen's Brack. They do; and that is exactly the psychological territory Hamsun sets out to explore.

Yet the narrator of *Hunger* is anything but an everyman; and his narrative refutes any attempt to see it as representative. He sees himself as (in Hilde Wangel's phrase) "one of the chosen." He tries to live by a code of individual chivalry towards (some of) those even poorer and weaker than himself, a code which satisfies his craving for self-respect even though too often it proves self-defeating or even self-destructive. Even more important, doubly so in this most self-reflexive of fictions, he is a *writer*. While what he writes seems dreadful—and sometimes unnervingly prophetic of what is weakest in Hamsun's own later work—it is clear that the central fiction of his life, what makes it worth experiencing and writing, is the experience of surviving against all the odds an unsympathetic world can stack against him.

It is the representation in prose narrative of "the unconscious life of the soul," "the whispers of the blood," which so fascinated the slightly younger generation of writers who (after Hamsun himself had regressed to more outwardly traditional narrative forms) created that Modernist fiction of which *Hunger* is so important an innovation. What Hamsun had achieved, as he suffered and wrote feverishly in Christiania and Copenhagen in the 1880s, was to create, in its subjective intensities, its narrative discontinuities, what might very well be seen as the first European Modernist novel.

—Robin Young

THE HUSSAR ON THE ROOF (Le Hussard sur le toit)
Novel by Jean Giono, 1951

The Hussar on the Roof was published in 1951. Although belonging to a four-book cycle—*Mort d'un personnage* [Death of a Character] (1949), *Le Hussard* (1951), *Le Bonheur fou* (*The Straw Man*) (1957), and *Angélo* (1958)—*The Hussar* can be read as a work of fiction complete in itself. A complex and demanding novel, it has been interpreted variously as quasi-medieval epic, chronicle, allegory, or romance. However, Jean Giono's novel and its hero owe as much to Stendhal and to the tradition of the plague novel established by Defoe and Manzoni.

Angélo Pardi, the hero, is a young Piedmontese officer under sentence of death in his own country for having killed a fellow officer in a duel. We first meet him wandering in a dream-like landscape where strange manifestations of the natural world are encountered at every turn. The heat is palpable, but the sky is an unnatural, chalky white. The silence is so total that "the presence of the great, speechless trees seemed almost unreal." Shade becomes as dazzling as the light, and rocks are barely distinguishable from vegetation. Life in the villages seems to be disrupted as people move around in "air as viscous as syrup."

Into this menacing atmosphere, a plague of cholera suddenly erupts. Henceforth Angélo's simple quest to rejoin his foster-brother and return with him to Piedmont is transformed into an epic journey across the Provençal Alps, a journey that will become a voyage of self-discovery. At first, disgusted by the manifestations of the illness, he tries to detach himself from the scenes of desolation he encounters. Gradually, however, the solider in him realizes that this is a battlefield

in which death in the shape of the plague is the real enemy, and that only by tackling his enemy head-on will he liberate himself from fear.

A meeting with an heroic young doctor provides Angélo with the opportunity to learn how to tend cholera victims and offers him a model of selflessness which he vows to follow as the doctor dies. As he wanders cross-country to avoid the certain death of quarantine camps, Angélo's devotion proves unequal to the task as he sees victim after victim die. Giono constantly counterpoints scenes of devastating horror where the reader's sensibilities are disturbed profoundly by the well-researched descriptions of the plague, with scenes that demonstrate the hero's courage and nobility of spirit. Desire of self-preservation has turned the population into animals. High on the roofs of Manosque village, seeking refuge from a lynch mob, Angélo watches as the crowd kick a cholera victim to death. Such bestiality can only be wiped from the memory by acts of devotion, and Angélo spends some weeks helping an old nun seek out bodies to prepare for burial. The grimness of their situation is alleviated by the nun's equally grim sense of humour.

Angélo later encounters a very different situation when he meets with a young aristocrat, Pauline de Théus, who is travelling to rejoin her elderly husband. Now, much of the mystery inherent in the narrative begins to resolve itself as the two refugees divulge their personal histories. Giono recreates a world of courtly love in which Angélo's admirable qualities, courage, tenderness, devotion, and generosity are fused into a spiritual affection for a married lady whose respect he has deserved. She in turn, like the heroine of *Orlando Furioso*, journeys as a liberated woman with optimism and bravery in the face of all obstacles. The loving but innocent friendship between the two faces an ultimate trial when Pauline succumbs to the plague. Angélo battles all night to save her, and, because he has treated her with love and honour, is for the first time rewarded with success. Their friendship, in which restraint, humour, and affection have all played their part, has proved to be stronger than the plague. Angélo is finally able to return Pauline to her home before continuing on his personal journey to Italy.

The Hussar on the Roof represents a clear break with Giono's previous works. Although the lyrical descriptions of nature and powerful characterization of his earlier work remain, this novel is primarily an adventure story which revives medieval genres in a modern context while celebrating love in a pure and joyful way. Its achievement is perhaps best summed up by Marcel Arland: "It is a novel in which the former poet and the new narrator join hands."

—Jane McAdoo

HYMN TO AUTUMN (Hymne de l'Automne)
Poem by Pierre de Ronsard, 1563

Most anthologies of Pierre de Ronsard's poetry give pride of place (and understandably so) to his love poems, which are still accessible and remarkably fresh despite the passage of time. But this most prolific of poets also distinguished himself in many other genres, and he himself might not have expected to be remembered today mainly for his lyric output. Modern readers do, however, have some difficulty appreciating his political and philosophical poetry, and could at first sight find it hard to understand the opinion of Etienne Pasquier, Ronsard's eminent contemporary, who felt that in the four "hymnes"

Ronsard wrote on the four seasons of the year he had arrived at the very acme of his art.

The "Quatre saisons de l'an" ("Four Seasons of the Year") were published in 1563 in the *Recueil de trois livres des nouvelles poésies* and dedicated to powerful statesmen. The "Hymn to Autumn," for example, praises its dedicatee Claude de l'Aubespine, a secretary of state and according to Ronsard, in the last verse of his long (470 lines) poem, a patron of the arts.

The four hymns share a similar structure and a similar poetic outlook. Here, after an introductory description of Ronsard's views on poetry and its practice, there comes the hymn proper, a mythological explanation of the seasons of the year that combines allegory with anthropomorphism and which inevitably makes demands on 20th-century attitudes and knowledge. A modern reader can never be entirely comfortable with poems that describe nature in terms of gods, goddesses, nymphs, and sprites and that sees Autumn as a young girl flirtatiously looking at herself in her mirror and decking herself out in the finest colours. We are clearly dealing with a shift in sensibility here which tends to make such poetry of academic interest today. But for Ronsard and his original audience this was a daring and poetic way of making sense of the mysteries of life, and it remains true that however alien the general drift of the poem is to us nowadays, this "Hymn to Autumn" does contain some memorable and moving lines. It also bears witness to the poet's own intense relationship with Nature. As I.D. McFarlane has noted, "what must strike any reader of Ronsard is the instant delight he takes in certain fundamental aspects of nature, not merely for the further associations they may possess, but in themselves." These hymns are humorous and deliberately far-fetched at times but they also throw up beautiful descriptions of natural phenomena, portraits of pastoral scenes and landscapes, and some delightful vignettes. As always in Ronsard there is, too, an element of sensuality. Images such as l'Aurore à la vermeille bouche ("red-mouthed" Dawn), for instance, or the ten-line description of Autumn prinking and preening herself like a young girl thinking of winning the heart of a potential suitor.

But what makes the "Hymn to Autumn" especially significant is the long introduction (86 lines) in which Ronsard sets out his poetic credo, his views on inspiration and his discussion of the role of the poet in society. He tells us with evident pride that he feels he was born for poetry. It was ever his destiny to be a poet. As such he knew that he would never amass great wealth—"richesses vaines," he calls them—in this world, but he was blessed with another kind of treasure, namely inspiration ("fureur d'esprit") and the ability to write. He was also blessed with a fertile imagination and, above all, the "don de Poësie," the gift of poetry, a rare gift indeed but one that brings with it great powers, but also obligations. When a man is touched with the gift of poetry, he becomes a prophet, able to communicate with nature and the secrets of the world (in Ronsard's words the "segrets des cieux"—secrets of heaven—even), raised to the level of a god himself. However, a poet must accept certain sacrifices, too. Virtuous and solitary, he must avoid the contaminating influence of the Court above all, portrayed by Ronsard as a place of envy and ambition.

This leads him on to an autobiographical description of himself as a young man fleeing court society as soon as he could to wander among the hills and the woods with which he entered into communion. Such an attitude, he tells us, one which is essential to the real poet's vocation, inevitably causes unpopularity and incomprehension among the "vulgaire" ("the crowd"), who look upon poets as uncouth, wild, dreamy. What a poet can hope for, instead, is the promise of immortality and, in this life, the boundless wealth of nature. Thus a poet will never have material possessions, but the man who lives "for the muse and for himself" will inherit the forests, the meadows, the mountains, and the sea. What is more, he will be free. There is a decidedly epicurean tone to this manifesto (for that is what it is) but also a statement of the dignity of the poet's calling. The poet alone has the power to pierce the mysteries of nature and also to cloak them in a "fabulous mantle," in other words in the enchantment that great art can bring.

—Michael Freeman

HYMNS TO THE NIGHT
Hymns by Novalis, 1800 (written 1799)

The word "Hymn" is not used here in the religious but in the Greek sense of poetry addressed to a great being or, as here, to a personified cosmic force. The six *Hymns to the Night* exist in two versions, the earlier in short-line free verse, unrhymed except for interspersed stanzas in the last two. With this same exception, the final version in *Athenäum*, the Schlegel brothers' journal, 1800, is in rhythmic prose, the solemn movement of the language heightened by assonance and alliteration. Both versions should be considered together, as printed on facing pages in the definitive edition. Seen together, the two versions are a record of the psychological and poetic process by which Novalis gradually came to terms with the death of his bride, Sophie, and with his own deathwish. He believed that "the magic power of assertion," of poetic formulation, was in itself the actual achievement of what a poet desired. In his case this was the longing to live an emotionally and professionally committed life in the world of day, while keeping faith with the mystic realm of night and death, with Sophie in the world to come. He saw her as the messenger and wise enabler of this faith and its power of which the *Hymns* are the record.

In *Hymn One* Novalis praises light which makes manifest the beauty of the created world, then mourns light's disappearance in the dark grave. Turning to this darkness (*Hymn Two*), he discovers that night is a loving mother who opens her eyes to the hidden beauty of her own realm of love, sleep, and ecstasy. Night, not ruled by the giant clock of time, is eternal, the sphere of legend, romance, and past ages. *Hymn Three*, the central poem and focus of the whole cycle, tells of a mystical vision at Sophie's grave, where she draws him across to her own timeless realm of night by a glittering chain forged, as it were, out of his tears of mourning for her. He sees eternity in her eyes as Dante sees Paradise in and through the eyes of his beloved. Now Novalis understands the true meaning of death and night as a paradise of fulfilment even on earth. His graveside vision helps him to re-establish himself in the world of day (*Hymn Four*), to build a dwelling-place of peace on the frontier mountains from where he can survey both this world and the next, day and night, thus living in a new state of consciousness with Sophie in eternity and faithful to night.

Integrating his personal experience in a wider historical context, Novalis now tells of mankind's changing attitude to death in past ages, before Christ and his triumph over death. He now writes, in *Hymn Five*, in conscious opposition to Schiller's "Die Götter Griechenlands" (1788 version), where classical Greece is seen as the poet's true creative realm, now shattered by Christian gloom. But in Novalis's thinking the figure of Christ now gradually merges with that of his beloved, her grave is as the Holy Sepulchre, Golgotha, the place of initiation, Christ alone having unriddled death's mystery and thus given life meaning. His life story is told in general terms, as a legend or myth, the magic of poetic diction purporting to effect a creative change of belief in Novalis. Where Schiller implied that the poet's task had vanished with classical civilization, the Romantic poet finds creative work to do in the Christian setting. *Hymn Five*, the longest of the cycle, ends in a poem of seven short-line verses celebrating the joy of those who, even on earth, have been called to the marriage feast of death where God is the eternal sun in the night, Mary and the saints are awaiting those who have understood the paradox of light in darkness so that no one now need weep by a grave. This poem is reminiscent of Novalis's "Geistliche Lieder" (1799) written shortly before the poet's own early death.

The regular iambic verses of *Hymn Six*, entitled "Longing for Death," summarize what the poet has learnt by exploring and poetically stating the ideas and emotions in this cycle. Mindful of past ages when man was prepared to suffer and die for his faith, not only to live for and by it, he realizes that his mourning has now been transformed into the joy of a new way of life. Both in content and form this Romantic hymn-cycle is original, even revolutionary, carried along on a sustained, powerful rhythmic impulse of mounting tension which gives the language incantatory appeal and a firm sense of conviction. What matters to the poet is the magical power of poetry to break *new* ground: his own correct accentuation of his pseudonym, an old family name of the Hardenbergs, was "Novalis," meaning "what is new." He saw his name as a symbol of his belief in the power of poetry to discover and reveal what had hitherto been hidden in "night," the mystical element addressed and hymned in these poems.

—Elisabeth Stopp

THE HYPOCHONDRIAC (Le Malade imaginaire)
Play by Molière, 1673

This "comédie-ballet" in three acts is interspersed with sung and danced *intermèdes*. After a musical prologue, the opening scene finds Argan, the hypochondriac, alone in his room, laboriously scrutinizing and making deductions from his apothecary's exorbitant monthly account. He summons the maidservant, Toinette, to clear things away and is then joined by his daughter Angélique, for whom he says he has received an offer of marriage. Assuming it to be from Cléante, the young man she has met recently and loved at first sight, she is initially overjoyed, only to discover that her intended husband is Thomas Diafoirus, not only the son of a doctor but newly qualified himself and therefore ideally placed to supply Argan's every medical need. Toinette endeavours to argue Argan out of his selfish plan in an extended piece of comic repartee before they are interrupted by his second wife, Béline, whose wish to place both her stepdaughters in a convent masks a desire to become his sole beneficiary. After cossetting her husband with pillows and extravagant endearments she calls in a notary conveniently waiting in the next room and her financial designs are made abundantly clear, to the audience if not to the gullible Argan.

The first *intermède* is followed by the arrival first of Cléante, disguised as a replacement music master for Angélique, and then of the Diafoiruses, father and son. Thomas, as official fiancé recites his stiff, prepared compliments with ludicrous ineptitude, while Cléante and Angélique openly declare their love for each other, under Argan's

very nose, by singing a so-called "impromptu" operatic duet. Seeking to postpone the projected wedding, Angélique has a pointed verbal skirmish with Béline, concerning women's motives for marriage. Argan solicits an instant (and free) consultation from the two doctors, whereupon Béline alarms him with news of seeing a man in Angélique's room and he peremptorily quizzes his younger daughter Louison about the incident.

After the second *intermède*, Béralde, by questioning Argan's choice of son-in-law, initiates a lengthy, heated argument with his brother about his over-reliance on doctors and the efficacy of medical practice in general, ultimately persuading Argan to defer a prescribed enema and provoking a breach with his regular practitioner, M. Purgon, who threatens him with a litany of the direst pathological consequences. Enter Toinette, masquerading as an itinerant physician specializing in hopeless cases, who contrives to dismay even so seasoned and determined an invalid as Argan by recommending amputation of an arm and removal of an eye. Reverting to her true identity, she convinces her master that he should pretend to be dead in order to prove to Béralde how loving a wife he has. This charade serves to expose both Béline's hypocrisy and Angélique's dutiful affection, thus undermining his objection to Angélique's marriage to Cléante. Finally, Béralde proposes a more elaborate charade designed to resolve his brother's problem by enabling him to qualify as his own doctor through the simple expedient of donning an appropriate cap and gown and taking part in a graduation ceremony. This ceremony constitutes the closing *intermède* of the play.

Notwithstanding its musical and choreographic elements, *The Hypochondriac* functions in the same way as Molière's other "comedies de caractère," as an exploration, through action, of an obsessive state of mind and its various ramifications. Argan's energetic howling, his haranguing and chasing of Toinette, to say nothing of his shrewd fiscal economies, make it obvious that he is no invalid, but he is certainly "sick in the head," to an extent that endangers his own well-being and the welfare of others. The very structure of Act I describes a graph of this dynamic process. An unusually long opening monologue, with Argan confined to his chair, poring over prescriptions and surrounded by medicaments, not only signals everything the audience needs to know about the nature of his complaint but also underlines its ominously solipsistic bent. A two-handed scene with his servant, followed by a three-hander with his daughter and a four-hander with his wife, show his sick-room to be the epicentre of a delusion whose shock-waves spread out progressively to engulf the entire household. Even the use made of the few stage properties can be seen as iconic: Argan's stick, in particular, without which he affects to be unable to walk and which serves as a prop to his illness and as an aggressive weapon against Toinette, becomes an objective correlative of his incipient tyranny over the immediate family. Broadening the focus to incorporate further characters in Act II and again in Act III, Molière demonstrates the impact of outside forces on this domestic unit, in the form both of exploitation by a venal medical profession and of the potential for salvation represented by Cléante's love for Angélique and Béralde's robust anti-medical reasoning. Doctors (or mock-doctors), deriving ultimately from the *dottore* of Italian comedy, had of course long been familiar to French audience, their awesome pedantry, their constant mouthing of obscure Latin phrases, and their arrogant assumption of infallibility providing ready butts for satire or slapstick, not least in Molière's earlier farces, and the Diafoiruses duly share these traditional characteristics. But, more importantly, they are also portrayed as recognizable contemporaries, and M. Purgon's hieratic expulsion of Argan from his flock of patients for the crime of "lèse-faculté" explicitly calls into question the entire medical establishment of the day. Against their dogmatic, system-bound scholasticism Molière pits the post-Renaissance empirical thinking of Béralde in a dialectical opposition of profound import. In purely dramatic terms, however, Béralde's polemic has no effect on the action and significantly enough, the plot is fully resolved only when he takes a leaf out of Toinette's book and organizes a final masquerade in which Argan's obdurate mania is suitably indulged, indeed apotheosized. The protagonist himself remains fundamentally unchanged: the notion that reason is in the last analysis powerless to unseat the eternal follies of mankind lies at the heart of Molière's comic fatalism.

The "comédie-ballet," a form devised by Molière essentially as a festive court entertainment for Louis XIV, here relinquishes none of the playwright's seriousness of purpose. Of the musical items, which were scored by Marc-Antoine Charpentier, the prologue and first two intermèdes all bear on the play's theme in their appeal to life and the life-giving force of love, and the final intermède is central to it. Moreover, Molière's sudden death immediately after the fourth performance on 17 February 1673, when against his colleagues' advice the genuinely ailing, possibly consumptive author played the self-deluding hypochondriac, has invested his last work with a powerful dimension of irony. Even without yielding to the romantic temptation of seeing it as a valediction to the make-believe art of theatre, one still cannot resist the poignancy of Toinette's words as the mock-doctor when she ascribes all of Argan's imagined troubles to "the lungs."

—Donald Roy

I

THE IDIOT (Idiot)
Novel by Fedor Dostoevskii, 1869

Of all Fedor Dostoevskii's great novels, *The Idiot* was written with the greatest difficulty, and yet it contains some of the author's boldest and most cherished ideas as well as an intriguing plot and a plethora of fascinating characters.

During the years 1867–71 Dostoevskii lived abroad, mainly in Dresden, to escape his Russian creditors. *The Idiot*, in which he invested much emotional and creative capital, represented for him possibly the only path to financial salvation. Although it took 18 months to write, elements of haste may be observed, particularly in the middle (second and third) parts of the book where elements of didacticism, inconsequential characters, and incomplete plotlines slow the novel's initial momentum which is, however, regained in the final part.

The book opens with the childlike "idiot," Prince Lev Myshkin, returning to St. Petersburg by train after treatment in a Swiss sanatorium. In the carriage he meets Parfen Rogozhin, a violent and passionate merchant who both repels and attracts him, and who subsequently becomes in some sense his rival for the hand of the wronged and vulnerable but arrogant beauty Nastas'ia Filippovna. The gentle Prince, epileptic and sexually impotent but possessing unbounded charity and understanding, manages in the course of the book to ruin not only Nastas'ia but also her rival Aglaia, one of the three daughters of the Epanchin family upon which he settles on arrival. At first, however, the "idiot" is welcomed into their midst as a slightly comic, immensely humble figure who seems able to read his interlocutors' thoughts and comprehend their motives. But the novelty of the Prince's clairvoyance and Christian forgiveness wears off for the worldly and venial people he meets, and before long we understand the validity of one of the characters' remarks about him: "humility is a terrible force." This apparent paradox is also reflected in the Prince's names that signify both strength and meekness, meaning "lion" and "mouse." He represents Dostoevskii's first major attempt to realize a longstanding ambition and create a "positively good man" to contrast with and redeem the materialistic and egotistical Russian society that had so shocked him on his return from Siberia. From the notebooks we know that Dostoevskii believed goodness could only be portrayed convincingly in a character who was unaware of his own worth and also, perhaps, comical or even ridiculous like Don Quixote or Mr. Pickwick. Greatly fearing failure, he took the bold step of making his positively good man an epileptic "idiot," somewhat akin to the *iurodivyi* or holy fool of Russian tradition.

Dostoevskii's success in realizing his dream was only partial. Though often consulted by other characters, Myshkin is very passive, and the reader learns relatively little of his ideas (Dostoevskii's own views, insofar as they are represented in the novel, are mostly vouchsafed to another character, Radomskii). One concept, however, namely that "beauty will save the world," recurs as a leitmotif throughout. Dostoevskii appears to be offering this aesthetic concept in opposition to the utilitarian and legalistic ethics prevalent in contemporary Russian society. Beauty here may perhaps refer to the Prince's moral beauty. Moreover, if humility constitutes a large part of the Prince's beauty, then it would seem that the novel's two most memorable aphorisms, "beauty will save the world" and "humility is a terrible force," support each other. In purely aesthetic terms, however, the great beauty of, for example, the two rival women is in both cases flawed by insecurity, unhappiness, weakness, and malice; each (like many others of Dostoevskii's "broad" characters) contains elements of both the "Madonna" and "Sodom." Myshkin's most vivid visions of almost mystical harmony and beauty are in any case associated, indirectly, with disintegration and death, for they come in the seconds of heightened awareness immediately preceding an epileptic fit, and it is just such a fit that saves him from Rogozhin's knife on a dark stairway (having earlier exchanged crosses with him in a similar place). At the end of the novel Nastas'ia Filippovna meets her death by this same knife, and her murder is followed by a night-long vigil conducted by her murderer and her would-be saviour before the latter relapses into idiocy.

The Idiot operates on the levels of realism and allegory, reason and the irrational, virtue and vice, comedy and tragedy. The dying student Ippolit provides an intellectual discourse to match those of the underground man, Raskol'nikov, or Ivan Karamazov. Condemned by nature to an early death, he counters the Prince's ideas on happiness, beauty, and humility. He is one of the most articulate and strongly depicted condemned men in all Dostoevskii's fiction, like Rogozhin playing the role of half-brother to the condemned Myshkin. Rogozhin himself is an unforgettably dark character epitomizing fanaticism and death. The scene in which Nastas'ia Filippovna throws Rogozhin's packet of 100,000 rubles onto the fire to test her weak and mercenary supposed fiancé's courage is one of the most dramatic in all literature.

Dostoevskii's vision of a messianic saviour, a Russian Christ to revive the Russian Christian ideal, proved impossible to realize in the face of dark fanaticism, nihilism, and capitalism; his idea of creating a "positively good man" had to be held over for a later novel. But *The Idiot*, a flawed masterpiece, is rich in psychology, moral and social ideas, high drama, and possesses some of the most memorable characters in all of Dostoevksii's *oeuvre*.

—Arnold McMillin

IDYLL I
Poem by Theocritus, c. 270s BC

Theocritus' Idyll I stands as the seminal text within the subgenre of the pastoral lament. Even within the Alexandrian period, it spawned imitations in Bion's *Lament for Adonis* and the anonymous *Lament for Bion*. It was subsequently the polemical model for Virgil's Eclogue V, together with which it inspired a whole tradition in later European pastoral, including such notable works as Sponsor's *November*, Milton's *Lycidas* and *Epitaphium Damonis*, and Pope's *Winter*. Idyll I is also important for its prominent position within the Theocritean corpus, standing at the beginning of the collection in virtually all extant manuscripts and thus achieving an implied programmatic status.

The poem is framed as a dialogue between the shepherd Thyrsis and an unnamed goatherd. They exchange compliments on each other's musical abilities. The goatherd declines Thyrsis' invitation to play a song on his pipe, for fear of waking Pan during his noontime slumber. Instead, the goatherd offers Thyrsis gifts to perform a song such as he once sang in competition with the Libyan Chromis (whom some scholars see as a mask for Callimachus of Cyrene).

The goatherd regards his most valuable gift as the opportunity to milk one of his she-goats three times, but the gift which attracts our attention is a carved wooden cup. Its description has long been recognized as an ecphrastic emblem of Theocritus' poetry in its epic context. The cup's name, *kissybion*, is a rare word out of Homer's *Odyssey*, where it refers to a crude cup used by the primitive Cyclops Polyphemus and again to one owned by the poor swineherd Eumaeus; the word's connotations are thus epic, but at the same time also humble and rustic. The three scenes enchased on the cup also bear allusive resonance. First, we see a woman flanked by two contending lovers; they recall the elders judging the two litigants on the Homeric shield of Achilles (*Iliad*, Book XVIII). We then see a sinewy old fisherman straining as he casts his net; he recalls a similar figure on the pseudo-Hesiodic shield of Heracles. The first two elements of Theocritus' ecphrasis thus neatly enfold allusions to the major ecphrastic descriptions of the two principal epic traditions which vied for authority in Greek consciousness, particularly of the Alexandrian period, when Hesiodic epic came to be taken seriously as a generic model challenging the Homeric. Finally we are shown a picturesque scene of a boy sitting on a wall, absentmindedly weaving a cricket cage while foxes raid the vineyard he is supposed to be guarding. This tableau evokes a complex network of programmatic references: weaving as poetic composition, the cricket as a paradigm of sweet song, the child as a symbol of Alexandrian playfulness and rejection of grandeur, his neglect of the vineyard as a suggestion of indifference to practical utility. The progression of scenes on the cup thus moves allusively from the Homeric (most archaic) to the Hesiodic (also archaic, but favoured by Alexandrian aesthetics) to the purely Alexandrian vignette of the sort that Theocritus' *eidyllia* ("little pictures") aimed to capture. Bought from the Calydnean ferryman for a goat and a round of cheese, the goatherd's cup is an import from abroad, ferried into bucolic Cos and Theocritus' Alexandrian aesthetic from the world of epic. Handed over to Thyrsis as a reward for his splendid song of the dying Daphnis, the cup becomes a precious heirloom, representing the sum of poetic traditions and styles which pass from the hands of one poet into those of another.

Thyrsis' song, punctuated by a repeated and progressively modulated refrain, tells of the dying Daphnis, legendary shepherd-hero and poet. He is mourned by all the animals, both wild and tame; in response to his death Nature will turn itself upside down. The scene is structured around a series of three divine visitors to Daphnis—first a puzzled Hermes (god of flocks and shepherds), then Priapus (the god of ithyphallic sexuality), who tries to reason with Daphnis in vain, and finally the love goddess Aphrodite, who mocks Daphnis and is angrily insulted by him in turn. Theocritus never makes the reason for Daphnis' death altogether clear; although the story seems to have been as old as the lyric poet Stesichorus (c. 600 BC), none of our extant sources for it agrees completely with the details assumed in Theocritus' version. Some scholars believe that Theocritus' Daphnis dies out of a self-imposed commitment to chastity, but the reference to his love for Xenea in Idyll VII, combined with allusions to the story in other authors, makes it more likely that Daphnis was constrained by a vow of fidelity to a nymph.

Whichever version Theocritus presupposes here, the point of his story is the incompatibility of erotic passion with the ideal freedom of the pastoral existence. Light-hearted promiscuity, as offered by Priapus, is the bucolic norm: Daphnis' stubborn resolve estranges him from that Epicurean freedom and leads to his destruction.

—Thomas K. Hubbard

IDYLL IV
Poem by Theocritus, c. 270s BC

Theocritus' Idyll IV has sometimes been regarded as the exemplary paradigm of pastoral realism, but like much of Theocritus' work, it reveals a structure of nuanced literary allusiveness and complexity beneath its surface of rustic simplicity. The poem consists of a dialogue between two shepherds—the cynical and abrasive Battus and the apparently younger, more straightforward Corydon. Corydon has been entrusted with the care of Aegon's cattle, while Aegon is off to Olympia to compete in the boxing contest. The cattle waste away in longing for their absent master; through a series of sharp questions, Battus implies that Corydon's neglect is responsible for their condition. After revealing that Aegon has left his pipe in Corydon's care as well, Corydon sings an ode of praise for Aegon's athletic achievements. Battus waxes nostalgic at the mention of his late beloved Amaryllis, but the cattle wander away and draw the shepherds' attention back to their pastoral duties. As Battus gazes at a heifer, he is wounded by a thorn in the foot, which is then extracted by the patient hand of the once abused Corydon. The poem closes with some lascivious gossip about an unnamed old man and young girl.

Critics have often viewed the poem as a study in opposed character types—a waggish and sophisticated Battus versus a naive Corydon, or a sentimental Battus versus a crude and earthy Corydon, or a townsman Battus versus a rustic Corydon. But the interaction of the characters is more dynamic; we see in the poem a progressive diminution of Battus' status and a corresponding elevation of Corydon. Battus' initial pose of superior condescension and mockery is replaced by a moment of genuine human sentiment when he is reminded of the dead Amaryllis. However, the straying cattle guide his attention back to the present bucolic reality; instead of wistfully recalling Amaryllis, he gapes at a heifer and steps on a thorn. The reduction of Battus to the grossly physical dimension is completed with his expression of interest in the old man's lechery. The intellectual and sentimental sides of love are replaced by a descent into physical pain and perversion; Man becomes like the beasts over whom he nominally has domination.

In Corydon, however, we see an opposite development: from his defensive responsiveness to Battus' hostile questions, he progresses toward a more self-confident posture with his outburst of song in praise of Aegon at the poem's midpoint. By the poem's last third, Corydon moves into a position of magisterial dominance, extracting the thorn from Battus' foot and lecturing him on the dangers of going barefoot in the countryside. Corydon's development can in many ways be seen as that of a young poet discovering his voice. Corydon is clearly presented as a successor to Aegon, who has left the bucolic world for greater pursuits and handed over both his cattle and pipe to his younger friend. Announcing that he now possesses Aegon's pipe, Corydon gives a demonstration:

... I am something of a player myself, and can strike up Glauca's tunes, or Pyrrhus's, well enough. I sing the praise of Croton—"A bonny town Zacynthus is"—and of the Lacinian shrine that fronts the dawn—where boxer Aegon devoured 80 loaves all by himself. There it was, too, he seized the bull by the hoof and brought it down from the hill and gave it to Amaryllis. The women shrieked loudly, and the herdsman laughed.

(translated by A.S.F. Gow)

Corydon opens in a self-deprecating vein, merely "something of a player," a poetic neophyte able to imitate the female musician Glauca or Pyrrhus, the writer of obscene doggerel. But the song he goes on to compose is something quite different from the trivial work of Glauca and Pyrrhus—a high-flown Pindaric epinician praising the athletic feats of his mentor Aegon. In the manner of Pindar, Corydon's praise of the victor Aegon begins with praise of his native city Croton, here styled in the form of a priamel comparing it to other cities such as Zacynthus; also like Pindar is the reference to local cults of the city, such as the Lacinian shrine.

The 19th-century scholar Richard Reitzenstein made Idyll IV the exemplary paradigm for his theory of the "bucolic masquerade." In his view, Battus was a mask for Theocritus' fellow Alexandrian Callimachus: Battus was the name of Callimachus' father as well as the royal founder of his native Cyrene, and Callimachus calls himself *Battiadēs*. Battus' last two lines, deriding "satyrs and scrag-shanked Pans," are seen as an allusion to Callimachus, directed against the tragic poet Alexander of Aetolia (whose father was Satyrus). On this basis and in view of Alexander's authorship of some doggerel verses like those of Pyrrhus, Reitzenstein regards Corydon as a mask for Alexander. While this is less convincing than the identification of Battus with Callimachus, Reitzenstein was right to see Corydon as a likely mask for some contemporary poet. Idyll IV, like most of Theocritus' bucolics, is programmatically concerned with the practice of learned, allusive poetry under the cover of rusticated primitivism.

—Thomas K. Hubbard

IDYLL VII
Poem by Theocritus, c. 270s BC

Idyll VII is set on the island of Cos. It is narrated in the first person by a character whose name is identified at line 21 as Simichidas. Simichidas and two friends, we are told, once walked from Cos, the islands' capital, to a harvest festival on the property of two landowners of illustrious Coan parentage, who farmed in an area called the Haleis, some nine kilometres south-west of the city. Less than halfway through the walk, and at midday, the three friends, who are firmly characterized as town-dwellers, happen to meet a goatherd named Lycidas, whose rustic attire (and smell) are described in realistic terms. Lycidas adopts a sarcastic tone at the sight of the city people bustling along in the midday heat of July or August, and Simichidas, feigning respect and deference, throws out a challenge to Lycidas' acknowledged superiority as a piper, explains the goal of his journey in the countryside, and invites Lycidas to join his party and sing country songs, while deprecating the opinion of all and sundry that he is the best singer, and claiming with mock modesty that he cannot as yet stand comparison with Sicelidas of Samos (known more

commonly as Asclepiades) or Philetas of Cos. Lycidas agrees to this, offering to give Simichidas his goatherd's staff, on the ground that he hates pretentious poets who contend with the great Homer as much as he hates builders who try to build houses as big as Mount Oromedon, the highest mountain on the island, which would have been visible to the party on the left at just this point on the journey.

Lycidas offers his song without further ado. A melancholy piece, it pictures Lycidas wishing his lover a fair voyage away to Mitylene if the man will only assuage Lycidas' love for him. The song imagines Lycidas alone, celebrating his friend's safe arrival (and, presumably, his own successful suit) with a feast all to himself, with two shepherds piping to him, and Tityrus singing of the legendary neatherd Daphnis' love for Xenea, and of the goatherd-poet Comatas, who, it seems, had been imprisoned in a chest by his master but had been sustained by honeycomb sent by his protectresses, the Muses, for his poetry. Lycidas breaks off his song with the nostalgic wish that he had been alive in Comatas' time to hear his pastoral singing.

Simichidas prefaces his offering by claiming it as one of the things that the Nymphs have taught him as he tended his herd on the hills and as one whose fame may have even reached the throne of Zeus, probably in fact a reference to Ptolemy Philadelphos. For a song claimed to be a country piece, Simichidas' has an oddly urban setting, and this may be an intentionally ironical reflection on his status as a town-dweller. Simichidas sings how his friend Aratus is suffering from unrequited love for a boy called Philinus. He prays to the rustic deity Pan that Philinus will comply with Aratus' passion, unbidden, but he threatens the god with various painful consequences for any failure to help. Then he turns to the Loves, whom he asks to wound Philinus with their bows. After all, he points out, women are already saying that the young man is losing his youthful charm. Finally, he begs Aratus that they give up their vigils outside Philinus' door until the cold of morning, suggesting that peace of mind (*hasychia*) is the more sensible option.

The singing match concluded, Lycidas hands over his staff as a "gift of friendship in the Muses," and heads off to the left to Pyxa, while Simichidas' party makes for the harvest festival, after a gorgeously sensual description of which Simichidas asks the Castalian Nymphs whether the wine was comparable with the wine served up to various figures from the mythic past, Heracles and Polyphemus. With the poem's second major reference to the world of Hellenic myth, Simichidas closes his narrative with a prayer that Demeter repeat the prosperity he has enjoyed.

This beautiful pastoral has inspired several matters of interpretation. To what extent is Simichidas meant to be identified with Theocritus? They are both poets; Simichidas engages with literary debates of Theocritus' own day, especially over Asclepiades, who was critical of Callimachus, and Philetas, for whom Callimachus expressed reserved admiration; if we are indeed meant to see a reference to Ptolemy Philadelphus in Simichidas' mention of Zeus, this would square with Theocritus' known activity as a court poet at Alexandria; and Lycidas' favourable comparison of Simichidas with the Homer-imitators of Theocritus' day would put him in the literary camp of Callimachus, whose programme for short poems of high polish Theocritus' poetic output shows he shared, if not followed. Thus there seems to be no real difficulty in identifying Theocritus and Simichidas, not that Theocritus need at all be describing an actual occurrence in his life on Cos. Lycidas, for his part, has various divine motifs in his characterization, the staff in particular reminding us of the sceptre given to the poet Hesiod by the Muses. However, despite various attempts to see him as disguising a deity, it seems more attractive to take him as representing an earthy goatherd, whose emphatic rusticity is meant to contrast with the hallowed deities of poetic investiture; this would tally with the noticeable tension in the Idyll between the realism of the description of the route of the walk and the fauna and flora of the poem on the one hand, and the nostalgic reminiscences of the mythical past on the other (see W.G. Arnott, "ycidas and Double Perspectives: A Discussion of Theocritus' Seventh Idyll," *Estudios Clásicos*, 87, 1984).

—G. Zanker

IF ON A WINTER'S NIGHT A TRAVELLER (Se una notte d'inverno un viaggiatore)
Novel by Italo Calvino, 1979

Metafiction—a fiction about the reading and writing of fiction—is the business of this book, which can barely be defined as a novel. It opens with the words: "You are about to begin reading Italo Calvino's new novel, *If on a Winter's Night a Traveller*," and ends correspondingly. Calvino cunningly contrives a story out of the semiotic, structuralist, and post-structuralist insights of the 1960s and 1970s, and out of the material processes of writing, producing, distributing, and consuming the literary artefact. "You," the Reader, a male subject, are the central character, and the Reader finds, on coming to the second chapter of *If on a Winter's Night* that, thanks to a binding error, it, and all the succeeding chapters are repetitions of the first. Thus begins the potentially endless quest for the text, which takes the Reader back to his bookseller, then to the publisher, then into academe, the library, and so on. On each occasion the Reader lights upon the beginning of another novel, whose reading in turn is similarly interrupted.

The series of false starts (and false ends) produces ten foreshortened narratives that are actually virtuoso short stories, alternating with the chapters that relate the story of the Reader's quest for the complete authentic story. This brings the Reader into contact with the female Other Reader, who is on the same trail. Two trails now intertwine. The pursuit of the text leads to ever more exotic adventures involving revolutionary aircraft hijackers (for whom the authentic text is powerfully subversive), samizdat circles, the elusive Ermes Marana, a counterfeiter of texts, and the burnt-out bestselling novelist Silas Flannery. Extreme ways of producing or consuming texts are encountered: computers may replace either readers or writers; a sculptor sculpts books instead of reading them. The book itself, as commodity or contraband, is the protagonist of this trail.

The other trail is the love story, which leads the two Readers to an erotic reading of each other's bodies and to marriage as the end of reading. The female Reader acquires a name—Ludmilla—and a distinctive character—femaleness. She is a Reader with a difference.

While these intertwined trails pursue never-ending narrative as a metaphor of (male-centred) desire, conjugality, and continuity, it is the eternal ending of death that dominates the ten inset narratives, ten short versions of different subgenres. Their consecutive titles spell out a long question that ends "Around an empty grave what story down there awaits its end?" Each deadly tale is itself a metanarrative, brilliantly telling itself by displaying the technique of its own composition. The very first one, for instance, opens: "The novel begins in a railway station, a locomotive huffs, steam from a piston covers the opening of the chapter, a cloud of smoke hides part of the

first paragraph." The ten tales progress from the pole of detached impersonal narration to the opposite pole of solipsistic notation, taking in along the way a dazzling variety of formal techniques. The book as a whole is Calvino's celebration of storytelling as mankind's profound game-playing analogue to its game of love and death, and the 11th chapter contains a fitting tribute to the narrative archetype of *The Thousand and One Nights*.

If on a Winter's Night a Traveller may be viewed as a fruitfully delayed product of the debate over the relationship between literature and industry, which took place in Italy in the late 1950s and early 1960s, and in which Calvino himself, and his friend Vittorini, figured prominently, particularly in their journal significantly entitled *Il Menabò* [The Printer's Dummy]. The argument focused on the impact of the second industrial revolution and on the need for writing itself to match the new techniques of mass reproduction, with their seemingly inexhaustible capacity to transform anything into something else. The post-modern writer's interest thus appears to be displaced from substance (themes, referential content) to process.

Yet this novel, far from negating the specifics of place, time, ethnicity, and individuality, realizes a multiplicity of these specifics with remarkable intensity—the epic of a small Baltic nation, the fate of a Paris hoodlum, a Mexican vendetta, and seven other equally diverse situations. They are more than pastiches, but they produce a paradoxical effect. On the one hand, the disdainful virtuosity of the storytelling makes all storytelling appear obsolete. On the other hand, the intense impression produced of authenticity and seriousness in the manner in which the diverse experiences are rendered is a triumphant vindication of the power of storytelling to negotiate "reality." Likewise, in the frame-story of the Readers, many problematic aspects of the role of textuality in the tendentially homogenized order characteristic of the westernized world are captured with diagnostic precision in their up-to-the-minute historicity. Calvino is no apostle of the inability of language to refer to anything but itself: his is a transitive semiotic, in which communication concerns something of moment to both sender and receiver, though there can never be any last word. We produce meanings, not truths.

—John Gatt-Rutter

THE IGOR TALE
See THE TALE OF THE CAMPAIGN OF IGOR

IL PLEURE DANS MON COEUR. . .
Poems by Paul Verlaine, 1874

"Il pleure dans mon coeur. . ." ("The tears fall in my heart. . .") appeared in *Romances Without Words*, and is the third of a group of poems numbered I–IX and bearing the general title of "Ariettes oubliées" ("Forgotten Ariettas")—a double paradox, since the "songs" consist only of words, and the "forgotten" airs are there on the printed page. The "Ariettes" are the most typical, in this volume, of Paul Verlaine's famous "musicality." But nothing in Verlaine's art is simple. His "songs without words" create both music and elusive pictures recaptured from memory. Though it is not described in detail (only the words "town," "ground," "roofs" refer to a physical locality), the sense of a visible world is so strong in the first two of this poem's four stanzas that critics have argued about its exact location (the favourite is London, where Verlaine and Rimbaud stayed in 1872). But that is to miss the point. This poet's tears are not determined by place or indeed by time: he carries them with him.

The formal structure of Verlaine's short lyrics, which appears as a regular pattern on the page, is overlaid, and often almost obliterated, by a pattern of musical sound. This poem is one of the most complex in that respect. Music is not made of equally weighted sounds but of their succession and repetition, and of variations in stress, pitch, volume; it is sound structured in both time and space. Verlaine exploits all of these elements, so that his "music" is made not only of the sound of individual words but more importantly of the relations between them and their place in the poem as a whole. Verlaine remarked that the one essential feature of poetry was not rhyme but rhythm; but rhyme and assonance play a vital part in this text. The poem has a hypnotic effect on the reader, the sense of the words becoming obscured so that one is chiefly aware of a misty melancholy that is by no means unpleasant. That effect is produced by both sound and rhythm: the poem contains an unusually large number of mono-syllables, which slow the pace of the verse, so that the vowels create a lingering effect of lassitude:

> Il pleure dans mon coeur
> Comme il pleut sur la ville;
> Quelle est cette langueur
> Qui pénètre mon coeur?
>
> (The tears fall in my heart
> As rain falls on the town;
> What is this languor
> Invading my heart?)

Of course the effect is not produced by sound and rhythm alone; the word "langueur" ("languor" or "lassitude") placed strategically in the poem's third line, to rhyme with the repeated "coeur" ("heart"), implants the idea of lassitude in the reader's mind from the start. Dragging monosyllables are combined with that idea, and with images of tears and rain (not only named but also suggested by the onomatopoeic effect of the letter *p*), to set the scene. In the second stanza the alliterative *p* is preceded and modified by its softened form, *b*, which also introduces an assonance with "pluie" ("rain"): "oh bruit doux de la pluie. . ." ("oh soft sound of the rain"); but again the word "doux" expresses the idea of softness and sweetness (the word has both meanings) as well as having itself a soft sound. Only one word in this stanza is not a monosyllable: "s'ennuie"), rhyming with the repeated "pluie." The word is nicely ambiguous: "un coeur qui s'ennuie" may be bored (the commonest meaning); and, given the tears in this heart, also melancholy or distressed. Here the reflexive verb ("s'ennuie"—"bores/distresses *itself*") turns the attention inward: the languor "penetrates" his heart, and may be partly the effect of the rain, but the heart creates its own distress, to which the rain is an appropriate accompaniment. The unusual impersonal form of "Il pleure" ("it's weeping," on the model of "il pleut," the normal way of saying "it's raining") expresses the fusion of inner and outer worlds, and the landscape of wet roofs and pavements becomes the "objective correlative" (to borrow Eliot's phrase) of the poet's mood.

The third stanza finds no reason for the tears in "ce coeur qui s'écoeure." The internal rhyme is audacious, and draws attention to the verb, whose reflexive form is again unusual, and strongly suggests

that the poet's suffering is self-inflicted. "Écoeuré" means both "sick at heart" and "disgusted"; here the poet's heart is certainly sick, but also, it seems, sickened by its own complaint, for which there is no cause. Thus it is sick of its own nature, and perhaps of its very existence. The rhetoric of "Quoi! nulle trahison?" ("What! no betrayal?"), which might come straight from neo-classical tragedy, is so incongruous in this poem of elusive half-tones that its effect is ironic. What appears to be a key word, occupying the strategic position at the end of the stanza's third line, is emphatically in the negative: "no betrayal at all"; there has been no tragedy, no cause for grief, and thus (the mocking tone implies) no excuse for striking a dramatic pose.

But the last stanza has the last word. It insists on the reality of the poet's causeless grief, and intensifies it by stressing the *p* sound, associated with both raindrops and teardrops: "C'est bien la *pire peine*? De ne savoir *pourquoi*. . ." ("It's the worst pain of all? Not to know the reason why. . ."). The poet feels neither love nor hatred, but would clearly prefer either to the lassitude that he feels. In "Laetiet errabundi" ("Joyfully wandering"), which appears in *Parallèlement* [In Parallel], he echoes the terms of "Il pleure. . .": "Ah, quel coeur faible que mon coeur! / Mais mieux vaut souffrir que mourir? / Et surtout mourir de langueur" ("Oh what a weak-willed heart, my heart! / But rather pain than death for me, / Especially death from apathy").

The poem's complex music intensifies the mood and encloses the reader in a narrow mental space that looks out on a desolate, rain-soaked landscape. If Verlaine is generally considered the most untranslatable of poets, that is because his finest poems depend not only on what is said (and can be paraphrased), but chiefly on how it is said. The rhythm of Verlaine's poems, which often reminds one of English verse, can be caught in translation, but the sound-patterns are difficult (frequently impossible) to reproduce. The reader without French is advised to struggle with the original alongside a translation, so as to catch a glimpse of the spell that this poet can create: Verlaine without his music can be very prosaic.

—Norma Rinsler

THE ILIAD
Poem by Homer, c. 750 BC

Composed around 750 BC, probably the earliest surviving work of Western literature, *The Iliad* is astonishingly complex. The main plot, the wrath of Achilles, criss-crosses a number of sub-plots, such as the tragedy of Troy, and the quarrels and peace of the gods. The theme of heroism versus love is thereby extended beyond the context of Achilles' career, permitting the varieties of love to be set forth and exemplified, the quest for value to be located politically, and human aspirations glimpsed in the light of what heaven encourages, permits, and disallows. Value-conflicts occur within the psyche as well as between individuals and nations, and some characters are very subtly drawn.

Apollo sends a plague upon the Greeks to force Agamemnon, the Greek commander, to return the woman Chryseis, Agamemnon's prize, to her father. Agamemnon wants another prize in recompense; Achilles demurs; Agamemnon, enraged, demands Achilles' prize, the woman Briseis; and Achilles, equally enraged, withdraws his troops from the battle. Facing disaster, the Greeks offer Achilles a vast array of gifts, including Briseis, for his return. Achilles, initially scornful, first threatens to return home but, moved by Ajax's appeal to love for his comrades-in-arms, he agrees to stay, though not yet to fight. Next day the Trojans, led by Hector, set fire to the Greek ships. Achilles' beloved companion, Patroclus, persuades Achilles to allow him to lead his troops into battle, but after many victories is slain. Achilles, devastated, returns to battle and kills Hector (whom he considers Patroclus' killer) after slaughtering countless Trojans. Finally Hector's father, Priam, persuades Achilles to return Hector's body.

As this plot develops, Achilles too develops. His initial passionate self-concern and quickness to anger reflect the heroic personality. Then, his idealism shattered, he rejects heroism, realizing that it can be undermined by the antics of an unstable commander. Thanks to Ajax's appeal, love for his friends then becomes central, and he remains in Troy, though rage still keeps him off the battlefield. Love for the dead Patroclus turns that rage towards Hector, and Achilles now fights for vengeance (though the old heroic urge is not entirely dead). Later his wrath abuses Hector's corpse, seeking to nullify Patroclus' death; and even as he responds lovingly to Priam, Achilles simmers over a breach in manners.

We can debate whether to call such transcendent anger neurotic, but neurotic is the correct modern term for Agamemnon. In Book I his megalomania leads to *hubris* (presumptuous pride, dishonouring others and/or the gods); in Book II his guilt over alienating his best warrior impels him to an irrational test of his men's devotion; in Book IX, with defeat impending, he first urges flight, then, acknowledging his previous madness, offers staggering amends. Books XIV and XIX reveal the same pattern: urge flight, accept rebuke, later confess and offer compensation. Priam, in contrast, is the idealized gentle father who accepts his sons' need to fulfil themselves although the city may perish thereby; he is just the person to guide Achilles to the final act of love. And Patroclus is a simple, decent man who naturally wants to help the hard-pressed Greeks and merits Achilles' affection.

Sub-plot characters include Ajax, dedicated warrior and loving companion, deeply insightful into Achilles; Paris, romantic lover, indifferent to heroism, who wounds Diomedes and will kill Achilles; Helen, whose guilt induces incessant self-condemnation without dulling her awareness of the fame awaiting her and her lover; Andromache, Hector's wife, who (like Priam later) urges a defensive strategy upon Hector but accepts his need to be heroic. Hector's tragic subplot rivals the wrath of Achilles in prominence. At times the egocentric would-be hero, abusive to his brother Paris, insensitively detailing to his wife the horrors he will suffer after his death, at other times Hector is deeply kind and compassionate to both. He often fights bravely, yet always falls short of the great heroic deed. In Book XVIII the lure of heroism overpowers sound strategy, and he persuades the army, disastrously, to face Achilles returned to battle. With Achilles descending upon him he rejects his parents' appeals and makes the heroic, tragic, decision to fight; suddenly a yearning for love emerges from behind his heroism, as he fantasizes speaking to Achilles "as a young man and maiden speak erotically to each other"; then as Achilles draws near he runs. Athena (goddess of self-realization) appears, ostensibly to help Achilles but in effect to cause Hector to stand and die heroically, with a spear in his throat and not his back.

The poem's main themes are values: heroism and love, success and power. Heroism exalts the value of the individual male, as demonstrated through valour with the heroic weapons, sword and spear, and

as recognized socially by the prize symbolizing honour and glory. Heroism can conflict with love (which ultimately affirms life over death), with success (which may exalt winning no matter how, and subdue the hero with the non-heroic bow and arrow), or with power (which permits an irrational commander to trample on anything). The varieties of love include the companionate (Achilles and Patroclus), the romantic (Paris and Helen), the connubial (Andromache and Hector), and the parental (Priam and Hecuba).

The quest for value occurs in the context of politics and religion. The Greek heroes are mostly absolute monarchs heading states loosely allied under Agamemnon; their economy is essentially military, based on plunder, so they naturally value heroism alongside success and power. The Trojans belong to an alliance headed by Troycity, Ilios (Ilium), Troy itself being nominally a monarchy but in fact an oligarchy run by a council of elders. The Trojans achieve tragic beauty by honouring a plurality of values, including freedom (which keeps them from imposing their will upon Paris and Hector) and material gain (which enables Paris to bribe the council into fighting). Though most of the poem's great decisions are made without divine intervention, the Olympian gods form a constant background, imposing certain eternal conditions upon the search for value: self-limitation (Apollo), the need for self-fulfilment (Athena), and the fact that so much is beyond our control (Zeus).

—William Merritt Sale

I'M NOT STILLER (Stiller)
Novel by Max Frisch, 1954

With *I'm Not Stiller* of 1954 Max Frisch placed himself in the forefront of modern narrative art. It is a work which is typical of Frisch in its thematic focus but also highly innovative in technique.

The Stiller of the title is a Swiss sculptor, who feels that he has failed in his dual roles as artist and husband. He has fled to America and undergone a profound existential crisis of self-assessment and "rebirth," assuming a new identity as Jim White. Yet he is drawn to return to Switzerland; he is arrested at the border, and in prison records memories, reflections, and encounters with figures from the past, including his wife. The novel opens with the words "I'm not Stiller": thus we are faced with anything but an objective narrative. The sub-text from the very start is one of need: a need to assert new identity by rejection of the old, and these two threads are then intertwined with extraordinary complexity in the main body of the novel.

At the simplest level this novel functions as a kind of whodunnit; the reader remains unsure for some time who the central figure "truly" is. But even at this level the simplicity is deceptive, the reader both trapped and liberated. On the one hand the diary-like form makes us try to recuperate the text as the product of an identifiable person, and there is pleasure in uncovering "clues." Yet we are forced to recognize that the very notion of circumscribable identity presupposed by this exercise is profoundly questionable, for all the information is filtered through others' subjectivity and their will, or ability, to communicate verbally—there is no direct access to some seat of consciousness. We are made very aware both that traditional realist characterization is a kind of reductive image-making, and that language itself is problematic. Yet precisely these issues liberate our thinking on the problems inherent in cognition and the creation of "identity."

Stiller is both a perpetrator and victim of images. There is something deeply disturbing about how authority and family immediately perform the act of simple resolution denied the reader and assume White is Stiller. Differences is blotted out by a desire for order, which Stiller interestingly sees even in Swiss architecture and general resistance to change. But the problem is broader too. Travel may open up new horizons, Stiller/White argues, but the vicarious experience offered by modern media forecloses the expression of what is truly individual. Yet ultimately we see that this is also a problem of language itself; when Stiller/White claims that he has no words to express his reality he is touching on the inevitable gap between language and "truth," and man's need for recognition and mutuality only re-enacts and exacerbates the slippages and distortions of language.

Despite such scepticism, however, this novel also allows the reader to comprehend something of the processes that further restrict the search for "truth," imposing images more limiting than those inherent in language itself. Though we can never make final statements about Stiller's relationship with his wife, we can surmise a complex pattern of cross-determination—perhaps Frisch's finest study. Stiller's need to prove himself forces Julika into the role of "needing redemption," yet her complicity with that role casts him as aggressor and reinforces the insecurity he seeks to escape. However, the image-making is not only inter-personal. Other textual patterns suggest that Stiller/White's view of himself—even at his moments of profoundest crisis—is fraught with problems and evasions. The very discursiveness of his notebooks, intended as an assertion of freedom, is a self-laid trap, for they reveal obsessions and weaknesses all the more clearly. For example, in the early days after his arrest "White" tells many stories as a way of expressing obliquely his claim to unique experience: stories like that of Rip van Winkle, Isidor the bourgeois who breaks out, the discovery of the Carlsbad Caverns as a kind of modern "descent into Hell and rebirth" myth, or stories of his own highly coloured adventures in the United States. Yet these stories fade out of the text, or are unintentionally relativized by later incidental comment, and that change indicates not only that others' "stories" come to dominate (i.e. that society is stronger), but that Stiller/White's stories are unsustainable in themselves. They are not metaphorically encoded "truth" after all, but inflated elaborations which reveal precisely weakness not strength as their source as they break down. Ironically such patterns thus suggest the very craving for recognition in White that he has detected in Stiller; in trying to prove that he is not Stiller he in fact moves ever closer to that identity.

This process does not obliterate or resolve Stiller's powerfully captured anguish, however. The State Prosecutor's Epilogue, telling of Stiller's life after he is legally deprived of the identity "White," seems to offer a message of necessary compromise, of self-acceptance, yet the view is seemingly as subjective as Stiller's, the product of personal need. What is left, then, between the poles of self-refusal and passive acceptance? The answer is perhaps best represented by the performance of the text itself; it engages us as readers while refusing to do our thinking for us. That is, it puts us in the role of ideal communicative partner, able to see both the unchanging constants and also the fluidity in personality. We can both accept biographical data and allow existential openness, we "finish" the book yet we also go on thinking about its issues. Frisch forces us, unlike Stiller/White's very gullible warder Knobel, to distinguish between art and life by foregrounding story-telling as an act, but in doing so we also perform

("realize" in both senses) what his characters so rarely achieve—an ongoing harmonization of structuring artifice ("fiction") and openness that must be the model, if there is any possible, for the best of human "knowing."

—Mary E. Stewart

IMMENSEE
Novella by Theodor Storm, 1851 (written 1849)

During his lifetime, none of Theodor Storm's stories (apart from his final novella, *The White Horseman*, 1888) approached the popularity of his first major work, *Immensee*, which was published in book form in 1851—indeed, Storm was still alive when the first of its many translations into English (by Helene Clark in 1863) appeared. The mood of Biedermeier melancholy resignation which prevails throughout this tale of unrequited love could not be further removed from the turbulence of the political age in which it was written—this is, though, probably one of the reasons why it appealed to a German middle-class public only too happy to forget the failures of the 1848 revolutions.

A classic example of an *Erinnerungsnovelle* (novella of reminiscence) the story has an outer framework in which an old man, Reinhard, recalls incidents from his childhood and youth in a series of separate scenes. The events of the inner story chart Reinhard's increasing consciousness of his love for his constant childhood companion, Elisabeth. Yet simultaneously, the couple appear to be progressively drawn apart, not only by social pressures, but also by their own reticence, their inability to communicate with each another. While Reinhard is away at university, Elisabeth, under pressure from her mother, marries Erich, a wealthy childhood friend, at the third time of asking. The final scenes of the story, recounting Reinhard's visit to Erich's estate at Immen's Lake two years later, demonstrate that Reinhard and Elisabeth, though still fervently in love, only now fully realize that their love can never be fulfilled. Their final meeting, as Reinhard resolves to go away and never return, underlines the tragedy of their situation—two people, who could have made each other happy, are driven apart. The last section returns the reader to the outer framework, with Reinhard, now an old man, sitting alone in his room.

Any attempt at a short summary of the plot does an injustice to a feature of the novella which is typical of much of Storm's early writing—its elusive quality which consists in its poetic evocation of *Stimmung* (atmosphere), its indirect (often under-)statement of its central themes (isolation and transience), and its suppression of clear causality. This is largely a consequence of the narrative stance which Storm adopts, constructing this and the majority of his other stories without recourse to a conventional omniscient narrator. Although *Immensee* is related in the third-person, the narrator puts himself and the reader in the position of onlookers—in the first sentence of the story, Reinhard is described as a stranger would see him: "One afternoon in late autumn, an old well-dressed man walked slowly down the street." The narrator then chooses not to give the whole story but only the individual scenes which form the content of Reinhard's memories. The overall effect is typical of Storm's brand of poetic realism—the revelation of poetry in everyday events is achieved by the reduction of the story to a series of finely distilled episodes. Moreover, the gaps in the narrative leave a great deal to the reader's imagination—by avoiding direct authorial analysis of the characters' motives, for instance, Storm leaves open convincing psychological explanations of his characters' behaviour. Recent criticism has interpreted such concealment of character motivation not as a fault, but as evidence of Storm's solipsistic vision—his modernity is reflected in the extreme subjective standpoint which he adopts in stories such as *Immensee*, where the narrative stance admits of no certainties and underlines how little human beings can know of realities outside themselves. The narrative technique of *Immensee* is thus seen to underscore its central theme—the isolation of both Reinhard and Elisabeth.

Earlier Storm criticism regarded *Immensee* as derivative, citing Goethe's *The Sufferings of Young Werther*, Mörike's *Maler Nolten* [Nolten the Painter], and novels by Eichendorff as literary models. More recent critics, though, have recognized its literary borrowings as a virtue, praising the way in which Storm exploits well-worn literary motifs and, above all, the *Volkslied* style, to express his own unique vision of human dilemmas. Folk-songs (some of Storm's own invention), fairy stories such as the three spinning women, and folk tales such as the Biblical story of Daniel in the lion's den are used as structural devices, being interpolated in order to create *Stimmung*— they are part of Storm's technique of hints and poetic evocations rather than confident statement of facts. However, more importantly, they are employed above all to emphasize the universality of the issues and problems at the heart of the novella. They also function as commentaries on the story and vice versa—they anticipate motifs and events in the main story or are themselves alluded to.

Sentimentality was early recognized as an element in Storm's literary make-up, and *Immensee* has been criticized for frequently bordering on the overly sentimental. Yet such criticism has been counterbalanced by the recognition of the work's symbolic density, which gives expression to its tragic undercurrents. Gestures, usually associated with hands and eyes, have striking symbolic force in *Immensee*. When, for instance, Reinhard takes his final leave from Elisabeth, their emotions are expressed solely by means of gestures: "She stood motionless and looked at him with lifeless eyes. He took a step forward and stretched his arms out towards her. Then he forced himself to turn away and went out through the door." The most famous symbol in the story is that of the waterlily—one sultry evening during his visit to Immen's Lake, Reinhard sees a white waterlily on a lake a stone's throw from the land. After taking off his clothes, he swims out towards it. Suddenly he is whirled beneath the water; he then struggles back to the surface and almost reaches the lily only to become entangled in weed. Unnerved, he gives up and swims back to the bank. The lily lies "distant and solitary as before above the dark depths." As Ritchie comments: "the tension . . . is produced by this electric atmosphere with its hints at wild passions raging just beneath the surface threatening to tear the idyllic peace of the family scene asunder and hurl the lovers and all concerned into tragedy."

Immensee is also the first of Storm's works to testify to his ironic view of nature—nature harboured no romantic or sentimental illusions for him at all. Far from functioning as a quaint backcloth or as conventional pathetic fallacy, nature is portrayed as a force which is supremely indifferent to the fate of men, underscoring the bitter and tragic nature of existence through ironic contrast: on the morning that Reinhard leaves Elisabeth for the last time, "the first lark ascended jubilantly in the sky."

—David Rock

THE IMMORALIST (L'Immoraliste)
Novella by André Gide, 1902

The Immoralist is the first of André Gide's *récits*, a French genre halfway between a short story and a novel. Perhaps the best starting point to enter the world of *The Immoralist* is a phrase by the author himself: Is the end of Man God, or is it Man? In this *récit*, Gide postulates and pushes to the extreme the hypothesis that Man's final aim or end is Man. The main character, Michel, lives in a universe from which God has been ousted, rejects traditional notions of morality and convention, and sets himself up as the measure of all things. His tragedy lies in the fact that having liberated himself from morality and Christian mores, he is unable to find fulfilment or pleasure in immorality.

It is necessary to consider *The Immoralist* in relation to *Strait Is the Gate* (*La Porte étroite*), a later *récit*, published in 1909. Together they form a diptych, an unstable balance devoted to exposing opposing human tendencies. Alissa, the heroine of *Strait Is the Gate*, espouses a point of view contrary to that of Michel. She finds Man's end in God, to the detriment of her human, physical self. Gide sees the two extremes as being equally undesirable, potentially tragic and based on denial, either of the soul or of the body. It has been said that Michel and Alissa are both dangerous fanatics and hopeless romantics. This is true. Gide presents two victims of excess. The two quests of a total blind adherence to Man or to God fail, leaving behind a string of other victims and a hope for the just medium.

In the preface to *The Immoralist*, Gide outlines not a problem but a drama. In Part One of the *récit*, Michel, a learned puritan of Protestant background, is stricken with tuberculosis while, accompanied by his wife, Marceline, he is in North Africa. He has lived a life of austerity at great intellectual expense, but his sickness causes an inner change: he discovers what was up till now denied any expression or importance, his body. Gide describes the discovery of Man's corporal dimension; Michel discovers his senses and exults in a newly-gained consciousness of the flesh. The author in fact gives us a caricature of the cult of the body. Michel relishes sensuousness, what Baudelaire would have called *volupté*. In his revolt against convention, religion, God, and the spiritual, lies the protagonist's drama. Knowing how to free oneself from these constraints is nothing, the narrator writes on the first page, the hard thing to do is to know how to be free. This is Michel's failure. What he does after his spiritual and physical crisis only brings misery and loneliness.

Part Two of *The Immoralist* takes place in Paris and at La Morinière, Michel's property in Normandy. Michel deserts his pregnant wife to involve himself in the low life of the peasant workers under his control. In his attempt at discovering his true personality, the authentic self, ironically called the Old Adam by Gide, Michel abandons the New Adam, typified by the example and the teaching of Christ. Instead he selfishly pursues a hedonistic ideal in the name of individualism and personal liberty, at the expense of his wife, whom he betrays in Part Three by sleeping with an Arab woman. He exacerbates his wife's ill-health and leaves her dying alone while he enjoys promiscuous pleasures. The quest of the hero finally leads to destruction, vice, debauchery, and a moral abyss.

It is possible to see some typically Nietzschean themes in *The Immoralist*; however, one must not run the risk of attributing too close a dependence on Nietzschean philosophy, which was extremely popular in the literary world of Paris in the 1890s. Rather, Gide found a curious correlation of his ideas with those of the German thinker whom he eventually came to read after the seeds of *The Immoralist* were already growing in his mind.

The tripartite structure of *The Immoralist* presents an ascending and descending pattern. Two arcs are dialectically opposed: the physical decline of Michel in Part One leads to a primacy and ascendancy of the body in Parts Two and Three, paradoxically at the cost of a spiritual decline. Marceline's spiritual and physical health, established in the first part of the *récit*, gradually decline towards extinction. The two settings (North Africa and France) are neatly juxtaposed to form a circular pattern. A recurrent technique of Gide makes a geographical and metaphysical quest coincide. Repetition of symbols and incidents in Parts Two and Three make for a balanced and often ironic juxtaposition in the moral and physical decline of the two main characters.

Michael supposedly dictates his *récit* to three friends after Marceline's death. He thus becomes a sort of lamenting Job. Gide does not want to either excuse or accuse. The first-person narrative helps to give the *récit* a strong colouring of irony, essential to Gide's vision of Man's plight. There is a constant gap between Michel's perception of his noble ideal and the reader's increasing appreciation of a solipsistic, hard, and deluded sensualist. We realize the harshly ironic import of the initial quotation taken from the Book of Psalms: ''I will praise thee: for I am . . . wonderfully made.''

Gide's classical, literary style is a major success. There is a voluptuousness and harmony in the writing, a lyric passionate intensity, and effusion of poetic images characteristic of Gide's sometimes overwrought and precious language. The easy inversion of subject and verb, the placing of adjectives before nouns for a literary effect, and the more than frequent use of the now rare imperfect subjunctive give to *The Immoralist* a highly artistic and masterly style. Gide, like Chateaubriand or Flaubert, has a fondness for a ternary rhythm which gives to the sentences either a clipped terseness or a lyrical, rhetorical flow and ease.

Finally in its treatment of the problem of being and nothingness, *The Immoralist* prepares us for the French Existentialists, Sartre and Camus.

—David Coad

IN DEFENCE OF MARCUS CAELIUS RUFUS (Pro M. Caelio)
Prose by Cicero, 56 BC

Cicero's *In Defence of Marcus Caelius Rufus* was a lighthearted but clever labour of respect and affection for Caelius' father, who had assigned his son to Cicero's charge from 66–63 BC, and for the young man of 26 whose sometimes reckless nature, energy, and qualities of mind had already won the regard of the celebrated statesman. Caelius had earned his own reputation for courtroom oratory' in 59 BC by prosecuting Gaius Antonius Hybrida, Cicero's colleague in the consulship of 63 BC. Cicero defended Antonius but lost the case to his protégé Caelius.

Caelius' own trial was the result of an accusation of *vis* (violence) against the father of Lucius Sempronius Atratinus. Atratinus brought the case in collusion with Clodia Metelli, widow of an ex-consul, with whom Caelius had conducted a two-year affair, ending in a quarrel. Cicero and Crassus appeared as defence counsel at this trial, held on 3–4 April 56 BC. Caelius probably spoke first in his own defence, with

a fusillade of insults, objectionable remarks, and witticisms, often directed against Clodia; Crassus spoke second, and Cicero third. Clodia's hand in the indictment was transparent; damage to her social status by Caelius' desertion had provoked her animosity. In the end Caelius was acquitted and pursued a political career. Clodia lost her leading role in high society and vanished from public view.

Cicero's oration in defence of Caelius is carefully designed following generally accepted patterns: *exordium* (1–2); *praemunitio* (3–50); *argumentatio* (51–69); and *peroratio* (70–80). The *exordium* enables Cicero to indicate that the trial is exceptional in being held during a public festival. It also establishes Cicero's position: that the formal charges are negligible and that the real accuser is Clodia. The *praemunitio*, literally a ''build-up'' which replaces the *narratio* (statement of facts) which normally followed the *exordium*, dispels the insinuations against Caelius' father, against Caelius' popularity with his townspeople, and against Caelius' morals and his attachment to Catiline (whose attempted revolution Cicero quelled as consul in 63 BC). Caelius' complicity with the Catilinarian conspiracy and charges of bribery and corruption against him are all summarily dismissed. Caelius' fortunes changed after he left his father's house and, like a latter-day Jason, he met his Medea of the Palatine. Charges of assault and battery and sexual assaults are swept aside along with the charge that Caelius was somehow connected with the murder of the philosopher Dido, leader of an Alexandrian embassy to Rome. Prosecutor Herennius Balbus' earlier extended lecture on the wages of sin and the moral decadence of modern youth should not, in Cicero's view, influence the jurors' attitude to Caelius. The only substantial charges (Crassus had dealt with three others) refer to gold (ornaments) and poison, and both relate to Clodia. Cicero proceeds to ridicule Caelius' former mistress by uproarious jest and stagecraft: first by calling up a ghostly ancestor, Appius Claudius Caecus, censor in 312 BC and builder of the Appian Way, to speak in character and rebuke his descendant; secondly by introducing Clodia's notorious brother, in another impersonation, to advise his sister to abandon Caelius for better game. Cicero enhances this parade of impersonations by presenting two characters (a stern father and an indulgent father) from comedies of Caecilius and Terence. Both discourage the jurors from treating Clodia's charges of misconduct as serious. The tone changes with more serious, personal remarks on Caelius' character: earnest and industrious, but susceptible to the lifestyle of the age.

The *argumentatio* disposes of the charge of Caelius' acceptance of gold and of his evil intent to poison Clodia. A skilful digression, with the suggestion that Clodia may have poisoned her consular husband, intervenes before Cicero responds to the charge of intent to poison as being farcical. While the jurors are shaking with laughter, Cicero moves briskly to his concluding statement on the serious nature of the case, and the need to save the exemplary Caelius for his father and for the state. The elevated tone of the finale, accenting the promise attached to Caelius, is a fitting postlude to the largely comic nature of the speech.

Cicero's defence of the wayward youth was clearly designed to persuade as much by jest as by serious argument. Because the jurors had been forced to renounce a holiday (the *Ludi Megalenses*, sacred and theatrical events in honour of the Magna Mater, Cybele) in order to hear the prosecution, Cicero cannily supplied them with an alternative holiday experience in the confines of the lawcourt. By appealing repeatedly to theatrical topics and conventions; by introducing the gibes of contemporary lampoons and scatological verse; by a series of impersonations; by exciting their parental instincts and so their proper concern for his client; by dramatic shifts from merriment and naughty assaults to serious austerity; and by appeals to their avuncular natures, Cicero pulled out every stop of his rhetorical genius. Light-hearted repartee and episode, with a rich measure of hilarity, farcical situations echoing the antics of popular mimes, with their grotesque caricature and surprises, are all part and parcel of Cicero's courtroom masterpiece.

—Alexander G. McKay

IN THE LABYRINTH (Dans le labyrinthe)
Novel by Alain Robbe-Grillet, 1959

Alain Robbe-Grillet's fifth novel, *In the Labyrinth*, is a round refutation, in the form of a contest between New and Old novels, of the belief that there can be any virtue, much less necessity, attached, in the mid-20th century, to the tradition of realism come down from the 19th century.

While it may seem to record the very process—effortful and uncertain—by which setting, character, and plot are brought into being (and so confirm the place of these standard elements within the work of fiction), *In the Labyrinth*'s divergence from realistic conventions is situated at a quite different level of depth from a mere exposure of the authentic travail of creativity: one where the link between word (and therefore work) and world is essentially severed, it being the world found in a word, where man-made rules replace versions of what nature imposes, that the novel consists in.

In the Labyrinth is the supreme example of the puzzle-text, challenging the reader to find the concealed centre on which its component parts converge, the clues provided being scandalously unorthodox features such as the initial reification of character and elevation of the object to the stature of protagonist; the substitution for plot of a principle of descriptive antithesis-cum-alternation; and an insistent emphasis, at the beginning, on the work's absent content. No moment of insight, clearly, can be promised as part of the experience of reading; but whether through reflection or in some more sudden act of comprehension these features and others may be perceived to coalesce at a point where a word with its linguistic outgrowth supposes both physical forms and symbols of nothingness quite subverting their reality: *In the Labyrinth* consists in an expansion on "morpion"—French for noughts and crosses.

This lexical label itself is mined semantically to furnish the main human elements realized, a soldier who dies after days tramping snow-covered streets as he attempts to hand over a package ("mort pion" meaning dead footsoldier) and the boy guiding him who causes his death ("morpion" in the sense of bothersome child). It also suggests the plot assembled in *In the Labyrinth*, which, reduced to a skeletal scheme, consists in "(la) mort (du) pion"—the soldier's decline into death. And while the grid required for the game of noughts and crosses gives rise to the preternaturally formalized street-plan of the novel's town, the symbols employed in playing it explain the proliferation of Os and Xs among its features and furniture (the halos of innumerable streetlamps, for example, and myriad snow-flakes; the long vistas of crossroads and multiple intersections of check table cloths). At the same time, O and X (whose obligatory alternation in the game accounts for the whole system of oppositions mounted in *In the Labyrinth*, chiefly the exchange of indoors for outdoors) provides too the fundamental structure of the text, which

describes a circle within which is drawn a cross formed by the changing relationship the reader witnesses between New and Old novels.

This relationship involves a transfer of ascendancy in the progress of a game of chess—for noughts and crosses is itself crossed here with the more complex adversarial game with which its conventions are compatible. Once physically constituted in the book's opening section, Robbe-Grillet's New Novelistic (cham)pion ("pion" also means pawn, the footsoldier in the stylized warfare of a chess-match) is juxtaposed with a 19th-century engraving, whose human contents are the animated antithesis of the lay figure represented by the soldier himself at this stage, and where what is suggested of its subject ("The defeat at Reichenfels") constitutes a concise visual equivalent of the strong, actuality-related plots favoured by a novelist like Zola. The literary battle-lines are drawn: what *In the Labyrinth* conveys thereafter is the pawn/soldier's advance, then defeated retreat—an initial phase where characters derived from the engraving (the boy, a woman who turns out to be his mother, and a medical man) are the means of his making progress, and a second phase where these representatives of novelistic reaction gain fatal control over him: wounded through the fault of the boy, he is carried back to his mother's home where he is vainly tended by the doctor.

The New Novel predominates at the start of *In the Labyrinth*, but novelistic convention, born out of 19th-century realism, asserts itself at its expense as the work continues, with character forming, plot emerging, and past tenses (although not quite historic) replacing the present which had at first effaced chronological relief. But this does not mean that Robbe-Grillet acknowledges defeat for his New Novelistic endeavour—for what should seal the triumph of tradition, closing text and argument at the same time (the investigation, after his death, of the soldier's box) is turned into the means of asserting the inanity of contemporary naturalism (the box contains letters too clichéd to publish) and renewing the literary challenge: the dead soldier proceeds to live again, and *In the Labyrinth* to revert to the "new" manner of its beginnings.

The rhetoric of the text is loadedly ambiguous, something sustained by the way Robbe-Grillet effects the integration of two myths (crossed like the games of "morpion" and chess) into his exercise in radical modernity: Theseus and the Minotaur, of course, but also Oedipus. Ariadne confects a black sail of her clew as she knits beside a dying Theseus who slays the minotaur only if the reader prefers the New Novel in *In the Labyrinth* to its conventional content: Oedipus is blinded (by driving snow) from the start and never meets the father (a dead comrade's) for whom the box he carries is intended—unless, that is, the engraving be synonymous with that father, when, once again, he may murder him (but may not). These ancient narratives may appear topsy-turvy in Robbe-Grillet's fictional anti-reality; but being, by their very nature as myth, resistant to revision, they in fact affirm what Robbe-Grillet cannot allow himself to claim: success in ending the jejune practice of a now etiolated realism.

—Dorothy Bryson

INCANTATION BY LAUGHTER (Zakliatie smekhom)
Poem by Velimir Khlebnikov, 1910

In Velimir Khlebnikov's enormously varied and rich *oeuvre*, "Incantation by Laughter," one of his earliest poems, is far from the most important or semantically dense work. But it is a small masterpiece of linguistic imagination, which acquired fame very early on and has been his most widely known poem ever since, in spite, or perhaps because, of a persistent perception of him as the kind of poet who is only for the initiated:

O laugh it out, you laughsters!
O laugh it up, you laughsters!
So they laugh with laughters, so they laugherize delaughly,
O laugh it up belaughably!
O the laughing stock of the laughed-upon—the laugh of the
    belaughed laughters!
O laugh it out roundlaughingly, the laugh of laughed-at
    laughians!
Laugherino, laugherino,
Laughify, laughicate, laugholets, laugholets,
Laughikins, laughikins.
O laugh it out, you laughsters!
O laugh it up, you laughsters!

              (translated by Gary Kern)

''Incantation by Laughter'' was published first in 1910, and a couple of years later, as Russian Futurism was attempting to establish—and announce—itself, it could not only be seen to exemplify a number of the movement's tenets concerning art and the ''self-sufficient'' word, but also stood out as an accomplished piece. Despite the ridicule it initially received from a number of reviewers, it has the great polemical advantage that it cannot be dismissed in this way, for to laugh is precisely to engage with the poem; and its very effect as an incantation is confirmed by the spell it has cast on so many readers and, especially, listeners who would otherwise be shy of Khlebnikov.

The most obvious aspect of Futurist poetics in general, and Khlebnikov's poetics in particular, that is manifested in the poem is word creation. This is upheld as the first ''right'' of poets in the infamous manifesto *Poshchechina obshchestvennomu vkusu* (*A Slap in the Face of Public Taste*), 1912: ''To enlarge the *scope* of the poet's vocabulary with arbitrary and derivative words (word-novelty).'' In ''Incantation by Laughter'' such novelty is achieved by the extensive use of suffixes and prefixes on the root for ''laugh,'' creating nouns, verbs, adjectives, and adverbs—''conjugating'' a root, as Khlebnikov called it. In doing so he exploits the distinctive function of suffixes and prefixes in Russian, so that the original effect is extraordinary but in the spirit of the language, while in translation the effect is interesting but un-English. Other aspects of Futurist poetics that are manifested in the poem include the orientation towards sound, relegation of syntax, and loose rhythm, and yet also the ''difficulty'' of reading the poem if one stops to struggle with the possible meaning of each word.

In fact, ''Incantation by Laughter'' is emblematic of far more in Khlebnikov's poetry than just some of the tenets of Russian futurism. Above all, it shows his concern for the roots of words, which were ''of God,'' and for meaning, since each creation on the root for ''laugh'' is intended to draw out latent semantic possibilities in the language. Furthermore, the poem shows Khlebnikov's orientation towards popular, folk forms, such as proverbs, sayings, riddles, and chants, and in general towards the language of the common Russian people, since for him it was the ''will of the people'' which could grant the ''right to create words.'' But the poem also shows the almost scientific nature of Khlebnikov's attitude to the word, because if the poem is read with attention to word formation and semantics, then it seems to approach a linguistic exercise.

Thus ''Incantation by Laughter'' anticipates the unique paradox and synthesis of Khlebnikov's art: it is semantically dense and cerebral, and yet also immediate, popular and —in the famous term ''*zaum*''—transrational. It is an art that is both philological and magical, for the poem is, after all, an incantation; it is an art of extraordinary imagination.

Later, in 1919, Khlebnikov wrote that ''minor works [such as ''Incantation by Laughter''] are significant when they start the future, in the same way as a falling star leaves behind itself a fiery trail; they must have sufficient speed to break through the present. . . ''; he concluded that ''the home of creation is the future. It is from there that blows the wind of the gods of the word.'' The particular significance of ''Incantation by Laughter'' for Khlebnikov is further evident in the way that it is echoed in a poem written shortly before his death, ''Once again, once again. . .'' (1922), a poem which critics have called his ''testament.'' At the end of his life the poet felt ignored, mocked, and misunderstood. Now, returning one last time to the root ''laugh,'' he warned his audience, who had ignored his guiding light as a star, that the underwater rocks would ''laugh at [over] you,'' just as ''you have laughed at [over] me.''

              —Robin Aizlewood

INDIAN SUMMER (Der Nachsommer)
Novel by Adalbert Stifter, 1857

Indian Summer appeared in 1857, the same year as Flaubert's *Madame Bovary* and Trollope's *Barchester Towers*, and has been described as the most fascinating achievement, as well as the peak of the German 19th-century prose tradition. Nietzsche was among the first to place the didactic three-volume Bildungsroman among the most significant German writings, and he felt that it deserved to be read again and again. Although the novel is an eminent example of the Austrian Biedermeier epoch, it has attained a classical stature similar to Goethe's *Wilhelm Meister* and Keller's *Der Grüne Heinrich*: it is a work that stresses the power of art to educate, that portrays lives clinging to great unchanging values, that states the gentle law of nature and humane actions based on self-control, simplicity, and the restoration of the beautiful.

The idyllic, utopian world of the *Indian Summer* is inhabited by people whose lives are dedicated to restoring humanistic ideals, rescuing the past from oblivion, resuscitating lost beauty, and renovating art objects, paintings, sculptures, altars from the horror of decay and formlessness. With reverence and fastidiousness, with composure and constancy, Freiherr von Risach and the narrator Heinrich Drendorf's father, both men of means and moderation, shape and form things and lives until they have all attained ripeness and maturity. The word *Gestalt* is perhaps the most important word in the novel: trees, cacti, roses, art works, jewels, the human figure are all shapes patiently created and cultivated to form a stable harmonious whole, until man, art, and beauty fuse to become one.

What must be banished from this ideal *Indian Summer* world are passion, violence, impatience, and eroticism. The vehemence of emotions and the rage of jealousy lead to downfall and destruction. Above all, *Sitte* (ethical behaviour) must be maintained. It is the stormy, youthful Mathilde whose impatient passion turns to anger and rejection. Such passion drives Risach to resignation and renunciation and forces them to experience merely an after-glow, an *Indian Summer* of their love. The narrative of this passion serves as a warning to young Heinrich and Natalie to observe moderation and propriety in all emotions.

Adalbert Stifter has created his utopian world in contrast to his contemporary, degenerating, chaotic society. The novel is set in the 1820s, in the days preceding the revolutions of 1848 and the decades of pessimism and disillusionment which Stifter attributed to a general absence of moral education. Stifter claims to have written *Indian Summer* because of the rottenness prevailing in politics, life, and education. He wished to confront the degenerate conditions with an affirming, positive moral force. He has created fences and glass walls between his idyllic world of the Rose House and that of his contemporaries. His linguistic fences are evident in his use of archaisms and the avoidance of foreign words, jargon, dialect, and regionalism. There is a persistent demand for purity in language. Whereas his contemporaries often strove to capture the rare, the sensational, and the transient, Stifter longed to escape the superficial present, to portray a profound and rich life, to preserve the old and speak about the eternal nature of man. Just as Freiherr von Risach is committed to the restoration of old treasures, Stifter restores a language that has begun to decline into noisy outcries. The isolated, secluded realm of the Rose House serves as a place of refuge for Stifter's pristine vocabulary.

In the first chapter of *Indian Summer*, Heinrich Drendorf is told by his father that man's first responsibility is to himself, to improve himself, and by cultivating a higher life, he is also useful to society. But first he must live for himself, live apart and become independent. He studies science, he travels, collects, and gradually becomes acquainted with art and beauty and gains an appreciation for the sublime. He is instructed by private tutors and is financially independent. Middle-class occupations are virtually scorned. Heinrich is alienated from most people of his age; he shares neither their interests nor seeks their company. His happiest hours are spent in the intimacy of the family or alone on solitary walks, away from the festivities of the city. Heinrich seeks refuge in the country, in the Rose House, and flees the social spheres of the city. Thus to create a distance between the world of the city and of the country, between his contemporary society and his utopian, aristocratic creation, Stifter seeks a linguistic seclusion, avails himself of archaisms, and bans the colloquialism of the *Young Germany* movement.

Since the two fundamental activities in *Indian Summer* are the collecting and cherishing of all that has been of enduring value in the past, Stifter the purist attempts to evoke a sense of the traditional values in antiquated, purified vocabulary in the rarified atmosphere of the Rose House, where the height of isolation and seclusion from society manifests itself in a paradise on dearth, where there are no wilted leaves, where wild birds have been tamed, where Natalie and her family are compared to works of art, resembling figures on cut stones. The daily activities in the Rose House are regarded as sacred: its inhabitants perform sacrosanct rituals, the conversations sound liturgical, and words are purged of all temporariness. It is here that Heinrich Drendorf blossoms into maturity and comes to understand art and nature, beauty and love. Stifter lets his hero escape the harsh realities of the urban proletariat and the industrial age. The chaotic and ugly have been banished from the serene, apolitical, and timeless Stifter landscape.

It is a sacred and safe world, without toil and turmoil. Fences and locks protect the characters from reality. Propriety and piety guide them with a predictable rhythm and convey the impression of a fragile stability.

—Renate Latimer

THE INFERNAL MACHINE (La Machine infernale)
Play by Jean Cocteau, 1934

This play, first performed in 1934, was to be Jean Cocteau's definitive reworking of the Oedipus story, but he had already drafted both a libretto for Stravinsky's oratorio *Oedipus Rex* for translation into Latin and a free adaptation of the Sophocles tragedy, similar in its contracted form to the earlier *Antigone*.

The precise significance of the title-image (an apparatus for producing destructive explosions) is revealed in the final paragraph of the prologue: "Spectator, contemplate how the spring of one of the most perfect machines constructed by the infernal gods for the mathematical annihilation of a mortal, wound up as tight as possible, slowly unwinds throughout one human life."

Previously in this prologue, recited by Cocteau himself in Louis Jouvet's original production, the author emphasizes the inevitability of the denouement as he ruthlessly takes the audience step by step through the plot. As he does so, he brings in the ancient tragic theme of *hubris*, which paves the way for the reminder from Anubis at the end of Act II that the Sphinx is also the incarnation of Nemesis.

In his attempt to reinforce the tragic quality of the play, Cocteau manifestly modelled his first act on aspects of *Hamlet*, even if it is essentially a parody of Shakespeare. The ghost of Laius appears on stage but is neither noticed nor heard by Jocasta and Teiresias.

It is not immediately clear to what extent Cocteau was aware that Freud refers to Hamlet in his presentation of the Oedipus complex first raised in *The Interpretation of Dreams*, where it is claimed that "the enigma of . . . Shakespeare's procrastinator . . . can be solved by a reference to the Oedipus complex, since he came to grief over the task of punishing someone else for what coincided with the substance of his own Oedipus wishes."

However, in the opening act Cocteau launches into a series of hardly veiled allusions to Freud and the famous complex. One speech by Jocasta begins: "All little boys say: 'I want to become a man in order to marry mummy.'" The repeated word-play on "crever les yeux," with the interaction between the literal meaning of "putting out someone's eyes" and the figurative sense of "something staring one in the face," in this particular context is a reminder that Freud referred to the Oedipus legend when discussing the castration complex. Cocteau manages to blend extremely well the old and the new: for instance, the long scarf with which Jocasta will eventually hang herself is made to remind the audience of the scarf that was instrumental in Isadora Duncan's death.

In the second act Cocteau points out links between the Greek and Egyptian pantheons, not only through the presence of the Sphinx but also through the question that one character puts, semi-rhetorically, to Anubis: "Why in Greece a god from Egypt?"

The second act differs markedly from the Sophoclean original in its enacting of the encounter between Oedipus and the Sphinx. Cocteau's brainwave of casting the Sphinx as a young woman in a white dress makes her a possible alternative bride for the hero and she even spells out to Oedipus the one sure way of cheating the oracle: if he were to wed someone younger than himself, he could not possibly marry his own mother.

If there is an obvious weakness in the play, it is found in the stultification of Oedipus, whose intelligence is undermined by the fact that the solution to the riddle has to be given to him by the Sphinx in a rehearsal of the real interrogation. Even the Sphinx, though she is apparently in love with Oedipus, refers to him as an imbecile.

Cocteau has frequent recourse to dramatic irony. More than once the comical mother in this act ridicules her little son when he in fact hits on the truth concerning the identity of the Sphinx. Then in response to Oedipus's claim, "Queen Jocasta is a widow, I shall marry her," the Sphinx remarks: "A woman who could be your mother." Yet it is later in Act II that Anubis points out to the Sphinx that Oedipus is indeed Jocasta's son.

The symbolism of the décor of the bedroom, the setting for Act III, "The Wedding Night," "red like a little butcher's shop," is perhaps too obvious for words, as is the way in which the Oedipal tension between father and son is transferred to the relationship between the hero and the substitute-father, Teiresias, Jocasta's erstwhile companion.

The denouement proper commences near the end of Act III when Jocasta notices the scars on Oedipus's feet, but the whole truth finally emerges for the protagonists firstly when a messenger from Corinth tells how his king, Polybos, on his deathbed, had ordered him to inform Oedipus that he was only an adopted son and then when a shepherd announces that Oedipus is the son of Jocasta. In the final twist Cocteau created a *regina ex machina* situation when the ghost of Jocasta appears to the newly-blind Oedipus to assist Antigone in guiding him off the stage.

Despite the almost inevitable anachronisms, despite the jokey nature of some of the references to Freudian theory, *The Infernal Machine* was a genuine, serious, and inventive attempt to rework the Oedipus story for a 20th-century audience. The play is a potent illustration of the powerlessness of man in face of the inexorable will of the gods. It is likewise a demonstration of Cocteau's belief in the importance of the force of destiny.

—Keith Aspley

THE INFINITE (L'infinito)
Poem by Giacomo Leopardi, 1831 (written 1819)

"The Infinite" is part of the collection of poems, *I canti*, lyric poetry characterized by a type of language that aims at communicating vague and indefinite sensations through a precise choice of archaic words (*parole peregrine*), and words eliciting feelings of vastness, multitude, space, time, infinity. Giacomo Leopardi's *Canti* are divided into two chronologically distinct groups: the *Piccoli Idilli* (1819–21) and the *Grandi Idilli* (1828–30); these *idilli* ("idyll" is a Greek word meaning "small picture," "little vision") were defined by Leopardi as "situazioni, affezioni, avventure storiche dell'animo" [situations, emotional states, intimate experiences of the soul] of which "The Infinite," with its immediacy and compactness, is the most outstanding example. The *idillio*, in its poetic form, conveys also philosophical insights and meditative moments in the poet's life; "The Infinite" bears testimony to the poet's yearning for the infinite

and liberation, his passionate attempt to move from the geographical limitations of a small country town (Recanati)—boxed in between the Apennines and the Adriatic sea—to endless vistas of time, space, and eternity. What is limited and real, he felt, was furthest from the infinite; there are no present joys, only joys remembered, desired, or dreamt. Man's imagination, indeed, is the prime source of human happiness creating for itself the infinity not available in the "real" world. We cannot experience the infinite but we know that its opposite is the definite, the delimited, the *hic et nunc*. This explains Leopardi's fondness for memories of childhood, a time in which our impressions and ideas are vague, hazy, undefined. In his voluminous work, *Lo Zibaldone*, Leopardi makes the following remarks regarding the craving for the infinite and its relation to memories of one's childhood:

If, as a child, a view, a landscape, picture, sound, tale, description, fable, poetic image, or dream please or delight us, that pleasure and delight is always vague and indefinite; the idea that it awakens in us is always undefined and unbounded; every comfort, pleasure, expectation, plan, illusion (and almost every idea) at that age is always directed towards infinity. . .

(translated by Iris Origo and John Heath-Stubbs)

This lonely knoll was ever dear to me
and this hedgerow that hides from view
so large a part of the remote horizon.
But as I sit and gaze my thought conceives
interminable spaces lying beyond
and supernatural silences
and profoundest calm, until my heart
almost becomes dismayed. And as I hear
the wind come rustling through these leaves,
I find myself comparing to this voice
that infinite silence: and I recall eternity
and all the ages that are dead
and the living present and its sounds. And so
in this immensity my thought is drowned:
and in this sea is foundering sweet to me.

(translated by J.-P. Barricelli)

The poet's vision is impeded by the hedge, thus he cannot appreciate the hidden panorama; but this does not frustrate the poet since he has a chance to turn his vision inwards and transcend reality: the poet can now contemplate with his mind a limitless expanse, an endless succession of spaces that he conceives in the plural—*interminati spazi* (interminable spaces). The work of the imagination, triggered by finite means (the blocked view), is explained by Leopardi himself in *Lo Zibaldone*:

For then it is our imagination that is at work instead of our sight, and the fantastic takes the place of the real. The soul imagines what it cannot see, what is hidden by that tree, that bush, that tower, and goes off wandering in an imaginary space . . . Thence the pleasure that I felt as a boy, and sometimes do even now, in seeing the sky through a window or a door or between two houses.

(translated by Origo and Heath-Stubbs)

The concept of infinity is present at the beginning of the poem (''always'') and is represented at the end by the image of the sea: this is one of the many examples in which language and imagery combine to communicate the underlying thematic core of the poem. The experience of spatial disorientation (ll.7–8) when the poet's heart hovers on the brink of fear—reminiscent of Pascal's *Pensée* 206—gives way to a perception of time marked by the passing of the seasons; the rustling of the leaves and the sound of the wind act as a catalytic device which jolts the poet back to reality. It is especially in this passage of the poem that the use of the polysyndeton is most effective since it conveys, by stringing together a series of events, the juxtaposition of time and space, of the finite with the infinite. The judicious usage of a series of enjambments (*interminati/spazi; sovrumani/silenzi*, supernatural silences), of the diaeresis (*quiete*, profoundest calm,), of adjectives (*caro*, dear and *dolce*, sweet) coupled with the different tenses of the auxiliary ''to be'' when describing the poet's attitude to nature, highlights his mastery and control of language.

The conclusion—the sensation of sweetness when foundering in the sea—may appear to be pessimistic and nihilistic but only if we attribute too much philosophical weight to the poet's words which, instead, should be interpreted for what they are: an instrument through which he can release his inner self. Leopardi was trying to break away physically from his home town and family. In the summer of 1819 he attempted to obtain a passport and planned to escape, and so it is all more poignant if we contextualize the ending of ''The Infinite'' in the poet's own life. Independent of such biographical considerations as these, this idyll, as a poetic meditation, forms the basis for future philosophical speculations to appear subsequently in his prose works.

—Bruno Ferraro

THE INSECT PLAY (Ze života hmyzu)
Play by Karel Čapek, 1921

The Insect Play (subtitled *And So Ad Infinitum*) was written in 1921 by the Czechoslovakian playwright Karel Čapek in collaboration with his brother Josef, a cubist painter and writer. The play, which exhibits the influence of German expressionism, is divided into a prologue, three acts, and an epilogue, and is a combination of dream allegory, in which a narrator is transported in sleep to another world, and animal allegory, in which animals are used to represent human qualities. The ''dreamer'' is, in this case, the lowest common denominator of mankind, a tramp. It is he who in the prologue transports the audience into the world of the insects, is at hand to underline the moral embodied in each act, and conveys humanity's mortality by dying during the epilogue having learned from his observation of the insects to live and let live. Throughout the play runs the theme of the continuity of the life force of which humans and insects are merely a part.

Humanity is divided in the play into four broad types—hedonists, materialists, parasites, and workers. In Act I the hedonists are butterflies whose romantic dalliance and quest for superficial enjoyment evokes the world of the carefree ''gay young things'' of the 1920s. Towards the end of the act the Tramp makes clear in verse the moral to be drawn from their selfish devotion to the pursuit of pleasure:

Ho! 'Igh Society, what? Powder yer nose,
Strip to yet waist—and let the *rest* show through!
Put it blunt-like—Lord All and Lady Rose
Be'ave exactly like them insec's do.

While the first act satirizes those who simply live for pleasure, the second represents more harshly the selfishness generated by humanity's desire for material possessions. Those who hoard their wealth are represented by two beetles whose ''capital,'' in the form of a huge dung-ball, is stolen by another beetle while they are away looking for a place to hide it. The aggression generated by the competitiveness of human society is represented by an Ichneumon Fly who kills other insects in order to feed his spoiled child. The amorality generated by this struggle is seen in the behaviour of the Parasite who, masquerading as a ''working man,'' steals what he can from those around him. In the second act we are introduced to the figure of the Chrysalis who, here and in the third act, is poised to be reborn. Its speeches are poetic and idealistic and serve to counterpoint the much less idealistic behaviour of the other insects. Again, at the close of the scene, the Tramp draws explicit parallels in verse between the insect and human worlds.

In the third act the Tramp is introduced to a society whose members work to a ''general scheme'' and are prepared to fight and perish for the State. This socialist state is represented by an Ant Heap in which the individual ants work as an efficient industrial unit for the general good. The capacity for industrial efficiency is however turned to the production of a weapon of mass destruction, while the sense of common purpose that inspires the Ant society is employed by a Dictator to create a disciplined army. Although initially the Tramp finds this form of society attractive, he soon learns that state control may easily be employed in a struggle for world domination which, in totalitarian double-speak, is justified as a means of ensuring world peace. The ensuing lengthy battle with the Yellow Ants offers opportunities for vivid stage action which culminates in the victory of the Yellows whose triumphant leader is destroyed by the Tramp in disgust at the madness of war.

As in other dream-allegories, the play's Epilogue returns the focus to the dreamer. The Tramp wakes to a reprise of voices from the earlier scenes and to a ballet of moths who, joined by the moth that has now liberated itself from its chrysalis, celebrate the continuity of the life-force and expire. Their death is followed by that of Tramp himself. Thus is represented once more the eternal round of life and death already conveyed throughout the play. The audience is brought back to present reality by the arrival of a woodcutter and a woman carrying a new-born baby who discover the Tramp's corpse. ''One's born and another dies,'' remarks the Woodcutter, ''No great matter, missus,'' and the play ends with the arrival of children, the next generation, singing and dancing with the carefree spirit of youth.

The play was extremely popular during the inter-war years and was performed in translation in both Britain and America. The satire of the modern industrialized state and of the stupidity of war must have appeared particularly pertinent to contemporary audiences recently faced with the foundation of the Soviet State and the mechanized killing of World War I. Although it must be admitted that the play's philosophy is hardly profound, its revue-like combination of satire, verse, song, dance, and comedy and the opportunities it offers for imaginative, non-realistic staging, extravagant costume, bold lighting, and evocative sound effects, make it a play still worthy of production.

—D. Keith Peacock

THE INTRUDER (L'Intruse)
Play by Maurice Maeterlinek, 1890

Maurice Maeterlinck had been hailed as a new Shakespeare when his first drama, *The Princess Maleine*, was published in 1889. *The Princess Maleine* was a highly individualistic neo-Romantic drama, evoking a make-believe world at the mercy of invisible forces. With his second play, *The Intruder*, Maeterlinck revealed his genius in another mode. Here all is economy and understatement. The play is set in the present. The scene is a sombre and spacious room in a country house; the time, the last three hours before midnight condensed into one sustained act. A group of people—a grandfather, an uncle, the husband, father, and three young girls—wait during the lull that has, it seems, succeeded a crisis. In a bedroom leading off and invisible to the actors and audience, the husband's young wife is recuperating from childbirth and ensuing illness. In another room, also off-stage, her baby too is asleep. The danger over: they can all relax, or can they?

At the centre of the drama is the grandfather. He is blind, but his sightlessness makes him aware of sounds and sensations that the others do not notice. Physical blindness gives him a degree of insight they lack. To them his apprehension that all is not well appears unjustified. They are simply waiting for the arrival of the mother's sister-in-law. He, hearing the sound of someone walking through the garden and approaching the house, is actually witnessing the approach of an invisible intruder: Death. A breeze rustles the trees. The nightingales suddenly fall silent, the swans swim anxiously on the pond, the dogs do not bark, a scythe can be heard being sharpened, there is a sound of footsteps, a servant reports that a door to the house has been found open. The sequence of occurrences that signal Death's approach are in no way supernatural; they can all be explained by natural causes. But paradoxically their anchorage in reality only serves to reinforce the atmosphere of mounting apprehension that spreads from one member of the family to the next, and from the stage to the audience.

Maeterlinck developed the dramatic potential of blindness in his next play, *The Blind* (*Los Aveugles*), while in *Interior*, death is watched from the outside as it approaches a group of people cosily sitting in their home, unaware of what is about to strike them. In *The Intruder* we experience its remorseless approach from within, not fully realizing what is happening. At one point the uncle asks ''What are we going to do while we wait?'' ''Wait for what?'' (''En attendant quoi?''), the grandfather replies. The exchange seems to point directly towards *Waiting for Godot* by Samuel Beckett, whose art owes much to Maeterlinck's pioneering example.

The Intruder demonstrates Maeterlinck's skill at generating an atmosphere of growing malaise and claustrophobia. Shortly before the end, the oil lamp flickers and goes out, leaving the stage in darkness. Anxiety mounts. A window is opened to provide relief, but

this produces the most atmospheric touch of all—total silence. This silence is so unbearable that it almost comes as a relief when a faint sound of movement becomes audible in the mother's room. The baby starts crying, then silence falls again. The waiting group watch, immobile, until the door opens and a sister of charity appears: with a sign of the cross she indicates that her patient has passed away. As they file into the bedroom off-stage, the blind grandfather is left to grope his way around the table in the dark. His last words (''They have left me all on my own'') provide the bleak and memorable curtain line.

In *The Intruder* Maeterlinck's uncanny ability to create tension and suspense through the unlikely medium of desultory conversation is already fully evident. Phrases casually uttered take on unintended layers of meaning, words have resonances, and the listener or spectator gradually becomes aware that the hypnotic verbal fabric and its visual accompaniment of movement and lighting are as finely tuned and subtly orchestrated as chamber music. Although the play was written for the stage its technique often anticipates radio drama. Dramatic action and theatrical effect have acquired a new relationship. *The Intruder* is virtually static—the only thing that ''happens'' does so off-stage—and its dialogue seems unrelated to what actually takes place. Yet much of what is said relates unconsciously to the metaphysical and existential implications of its action and the inscrutable mystery of life and death that neither the characters nor the audience can escape. Dark and questioning though it was, it proved an unexpected success when it was first performed on 21 May 1891 at the Théâtre d'Art in Paris as part of a benefit programme for the painter Paul Gauguin and the poet Paul Verlaine.

—Peter Skrine

THE INVESTIGATION (Die Ermittlung)
Play by Peter Weiss, 1965

On 19 August 1965, after a trial lasting some 20 months, sentence was passed by a West German court in Frankfurt upon 18 of the men who had operated the Auschwitz death camp during World War II. Exactly two months later, Peter Weiss's play *The Investigation* received its premiere in 15 theatres simultaneously throughout Germany. A prime example of documentary drama, it presents scenes from the Frankfurt trial, with a text based almost entirely upon a published transcript of the court proceedings. Yet despite the apparent objectivity of its material, the resulting play is no impartial reportage. This form of theatre, in Weiss's own definition as set out in his ''Notes on Documentary Theatre,'' far from being a dispassionate mode, is in reality ''partisan,'' for although it works with authentic material and ''refrains from any invention,'' it consciously selects and shapes its subject matter in order to reveal a particular tendency, mostly social or ideological in character. In this conception, therefore, documentary theatre belongs firmly in the Brechtian tradition of viewing the stage as a forum for political statements.

The immediate impact of *The Investigation*, however, is emotional rather than political. Weiss has cast his play as an ''Oratorio in 11 Cantos'' and has set it in free verse, but the superficially poetic structure is in marked contrast to the bitter content. Where a traditional oratorio is devoted to a sacred theme, the audience here must listen to a sickening litany of human viciousness. Similarly, although the division of each canto into three sections recalls the comparable structuring of Dante's *Divine Comedy* (*Divina Commedia*), the notion of any higher meaning to events is ruthlessly absent. Starting at the loading ramp where the trains bearing the victims arrive, the play moves into the camp itself, then on past scenes of torture and medical experiment to the gas-chambers, and finally into the fire-ovens, the ultimate Inferno where the bodies are consumed and individual existence extinguished. In its modern version the Divine Comedy has become a parody, in which merited punishment and God's justice are replaced by meaningless slaughter and brute force.

In contrast to Rolf Hochhuth's play, *The Representative*, which sets its final act in Auschwitz and succeeds only in trivializing the suffering, no attempt is made in *The Investigation* to reproduce any of these scenes on stage. Indeed, Weiss declared that even the courtroom should not be reconstructed. Instead the horror of the death camp is reduced to the level of bare language, as participants in the trial engage in ritualized exchanges and recite lines shorn of rhetorical trappings. To hear the vilest atrocities described in cool detail is shocking in itself, but the effect is intensified by the attitude of the defendants, who respond to the evidence with dismissive laughter and protestations of self-righteousness. Unlike the witnesses, who remain as anonymous as they were in the camps, the defendants are given their original names, but the purpose, as Weiss explains in a foreword, is not to try them again: rather, they serve as "symbols of a system that imposed guilt on many others who never appeared before this court." The "investigation," in other words, concerns not so much what happened in individual cases as the structures that made such crimes possible in the first place. It is here, in its attempt to lay bare the origins of the Holocaust, that the play's political sub-text comes to the surface. In keeping with the Marxist convictions at which Weiss had arrived shortly before writing *The Investigation*, he lays the blame firmly at the door of capitalism. As one of the witnesses asserts:

> We all knew the society
> which had produced the regime
> that could bring about such a camp. . .
> and so we could still find our way
> even in its final consequences
> which allowed the exploiter
> to develop his power
> to a hitherto unknown degree
> and the exploited
> had to deliver up his own guts

German firms, such as Krupp and IG Farben, which had been involved in the construction and operation of Auschwitz and were flourishing again in post-war West Germany, are publicly indicted for their part in the killings, and attention is also drawn to the way in which the defendants had been able to settle comfortably into West German society after the war. The ideological message is clear: capitalism contains the seeds of fascism, and the bacillus continues to lurk, untreated, within the Federal Republic. The point is reinforced by the play's conclusion: it ends, not with conviction and sentencing, but in mid-trial, as one of those in the dock, to the cheers of his co-defendants, loudly declares that "we did nothing but our duty" and calls for the Federal Republic to concern itself with "other things than with recriminations."

The Investigation is a powerful play because the events with which it deals cannot fail to move the spectator. Such extreme horrors certainly resist any naturalistic reproduction on stage (as Hochhuth's attempt shows), and Weiss's use of a narrative mode and stylized

dialogue is undoubtedly effective. It is also true that post-war West Germany did not always confront the Nazi past as wholeheartedly as it might have done, and it is entirely legitimate to highlight the complicity in the Holocaust both of named firms and of countless unnamed individuals. But in other respects Weiss's political analysis is trite and simplistic, and despite its force as a piece of drama there remains at the heart of the play an unresolved conflict between its documentary form and its tendentious purpose.

—Peter J. Graves

INVITATION TO WINE
Poem by Li Bai, written 752

"Invitation to Wine" (or "The Song of Wine") is one of the best-known of Li Bai's poems. Its title is the same as that of a *yuefu* ballad which is mainly about wine-drinking and singing. This poem was written in 752, when Li Bai was staying with a friend during his second period of wanderings after he had left the Emperor's palace. With his ambition to help the administration and the country unfulfilled, and his talents stifled, he felt depressed and, as he implied in the lines "kill a cow, cook a sheep and let us merry be, / And drink three hundred cupfuls of wine in high glee," he found a way to vent his frustrations by indulging himself in wine. Wine is like a thread running through the whole poem.

The poem (translation by Xu Yuanzhong) begins with two most impressive lines, "Do you not see the Yellow River come from the sky, / Rushing into the sea and ne'er come back?" which imply that time passes fast and life is short. The shortness of life is further emphasized and expressed directly in the lines that follow immediately: "Do you not see the mirrors bright in chambers high / Grieve o'er your snow-white hair though once it was silk-black (at daybreak)?" To enjoy a brief life to the full before it comes to an end, the poet proposes that you "drink your fill in high delight, / And never leave your wine-cup empty in moonlight." These lines, infused with a gloomy ambience, reflect Li Bai's attitude towards life, especially after his unhappy days at court. He was summoned to the palace but, contrary to his expectations, given only a low post as a literary attendant writing poems to please the Emperor. Later, slandered by influential officials and in disfavour with the Emperor, he had to leave the court. To "wash away" the bitterness in the depths of his heart, he took to drink. He set little store by fame, an attitude reflected in the line "But great drinkers are more famous than sober sages." Examples are cited from history to drive the point home: the Prince of Poets (Cao Zhi, 192–232 AD) "feast'd in his palace at will, / and drank wine at ten thousand a cask and laughed his fill," and a Confucian Scholar could "drink three hundred cupfuls of wine" at a time "in high glee." Li Bai's negative attitude towards life permeates the whole poem. However, his state of mind was complicated. He was not totally dejected. In the line "Heaven has made us talents, we're not made in vain" he emits out of his downcast mood sparks of hope and self-confidence.

This poem creates a self-indulgent image which, to a great extent, is a self-portrait of the poet. It is not only a genuine reflection of his melancholy mood but a portrayal of his character. Though Li Bai tried all his life to find a way to use his talents in politics, he did not intend to make a fortune through politics. He thought one should not care about wealth. The poet asks here, "What difference will rare and costly dishes make?'' and states, ''A host should not complain of money he is short [of],'' and ''To drink with you I will sell things of any sort.'' For the poet, wine is more important then wealth and has almost become his lifeblood. Even ''my fur coat worth a thousand coins of gold / And my flower-dappled horse may be sold / To buy good wine that we may drown the woes age-old.'' This last line reveals Li Bai's melancholy and brings out his deep grievance over the failure to fulfil his political ambition. It is the focal point of the poem, presenting a picture of an anguished poet. Artistically it brings out a sharp contrast between the pleasures of wine described up to this point and the pent-up sadness for which the poet wishes to find an outlet. Thus the theme is fully expressed and the artistic effect superbly achieved.

This poem has proved itself over centuries to be one of Li Bai's masterpieces. Lines like ''Do you not see the Yellow River come from the sky, / Rushing into the sea and ne'er come back?'' and ''Heaven has made us talents, we're not made in vain'' have become catchphrases known in almost every household in China. Li Bai's frustrations can be sensed between the lines, and his bohemian style of life is very evident. Nevertheless, his self-confidence and philosophical spirit in the face of setbacks in his career lend great appeal to the poem. His brilliant artistry is displayed through the skilful use of language and in figures of speech such as hyperbole (''the Yellow River comes from the sky'' and ''My fur coat is worth a thousand coins of gold'' and so on) and metaphor (for example, the change of the colour of hair described to indicate ageing, and the contrast mentioned above). No wonder the poem has always had a wide readership and is learned by heart by many Chinese.

—Binghong Lu

ION
Play by Euripides, c. 421–13 BC

Of the 19 Euripides plays to survive, all but the satyr play *Cyclops*, and, possibly, *Alcestis*, performed fourth and in the satyr position, can be classified as tragedies. Among these 17 there is considerable difference of emphasis and treatment, with several of the lighter plays appearing to explore the territory *Alcestis* opened up. Savage war plays, such as *The Trojan Women* and *Hecuba*, and plays of individual passions, such as *Medea* and *Hippolytus*, may have earned Euripides the soubriquet from Aristotle of *tragikotatos*, ''most tragic,'' but the gentler works, *Ion* among them, equally demonstrate the touch of a master playwright.

Ion, indeed, suggests in its plot and characters more the world of 4th-century BC New Comedy than that of formal 5th-century BC tragedy. Here is the story of a foundling, of recognition tokens, of intrigue and deception, all ending happily, or relatively so, for all the major characters. The play does have its serious side with a jaundiced look at Apollo and his fellow Olympians, and a possible parochial significance in the establishment of Ion's lineage which is lost on any modern audience, but nothing more harrowing happens than the poisoning of a dove. The date of the first performance in Athens is not known, though it is thought to have been produced during the Peloponnesian War and probably between 421 and 413 BC.

The play opens with a prologue from the god Hermes in which he tells of the rape by Apollo many years ago of Creusa, daughter of the Athenian king Erechtheus. At Apollo's wish, Creusa left the child of the union, complete with a necklace and a shawl, in a cave from which Hermes rescued him and deposited him on the steps of the temple at Delphi. The child comes to be known as Ion. He is brought up by the priestess of the temple and at the beginning of the play is serving as its steward. Back in Athens, Creusa married Xuthus but they have no children. They have now come to Delphi to ask advice from Apollo's oracle.

So much is simple setting of the scene, but Hermes continues by anticipating the oracle's reply. Apollo will give his son, Ion, to Xuthus, telling Xuthus that he, Xuthus, is Ion's real father. Creusa will come to recognize her son and everyone will be satisfied with an edited version of the truth. It is not unusual for the progress of the plot to be given away in Greek New Comedy and even in tragedy. It is of major importance that it happens in *Ion* because so much of the rest of the play is taken up with the various characters trying to work out what is really going on.

Xuthus is delighted to be informed that the first person he meets when he emerges from the oracle will be his real son and embraces Ion enthusiastically. Ion is less enthusiastic and Creusa is furious to find that the result of the consultation is for Xuthus to be awarded a fully-grown son and that she is expected to welcome his bastard when her own son died in the cave, as she imagines, so many years ago. The chorus suspects fraud. Creusa's old retainer assumes that the whole thing has been concocted to foist the illegitimate child of Xuthus onto Creusa. Creusa reacts by trying to poison Ion, barely restraining the old retainer who would quite cheerfully murder Xuthus and burn down the oracle to boot.

The complex task for a modern director or reader is to work out how much of this is to be taken seriously. The twists and turns of the plot are so rapid and convoluted that the Hermes guide to what really happened is indispensable. Creusa's attempt to murder Ion fails when the cup is spilled and a dove drinks the poison. Creusa has to seek sanctuary from both the angry locals and Ion, who now wants to kill her. At this moment of crisis, the priestess of Apollo arrives with the cradle in which Ion was found, together with the shawl and the necklace.

Even now the outcome is not resolved because the tokens of recognition look suspiciously new. Ion is thoroughly sceptical of Creusa's version of what happened to her and seems to be happier with the idea that he is the illegitimate son of Xuthus than that he is the illegitimate son of Apollo. However, convinced at last that Creusa really is his mother, he still has doubts about Apollo being his father. Determined to storm into the oracle and demand the truth from Apollo himself, he is forestalled by the goddess Athena who confirms Hermes' version from the prologue but suggests that Xuthus is better off believing Apollo's version from the oracle: and so to everyone living happily ever after.

Whatever direction the play is seen to take, towards tragedy, romance, or social comedy, *Ion* is a play of great sweep and flow. Plot developments may dominate our attention but the main characters are memorable and the handling of individual scenes does far more than simply anticipate a new direction for Greek drama. The chorus, comprised of servants of Creusa, has a remarkable *parados*, or opening song, in which it marvels at the decoration on Apollo's temple, either in tribute to the set designer, or in a curiously backhanded theatrical in-joke about the plainness of the scene-building. Ion, still confused about details of his past, as well he might be, takes his mother to one side so that he can talk to her ''in private''—in front of an audience of 17,000. All this is part and parcel of the theatre game, with the audience co-conspirators, as it were, with the author. *Ion* is a play of potential rather than actual tragedy in which humans are less the victims of the vicissitudes of fate than of arbitrary and barely respectable gods and goddesses. For Euripides this is as comic as it is serious.

—J. Michael Walton

J

JACQUES THE FATALIST (Jacques le fataliste et son maître)
Novel by Denis Diderot, 1796 (written c. 1780–84)

Having completed his massive endeavours on the *Encyclopedia*, Denis Diderot worked on his most experimental novel *Jacques the Fatalist* from the late 1760s until sometime around 1778, attracting some enthusiasm from eminent writers like Goethe, but causing greater puzzlement with the general public. The first full publication of the book came in 1796, 12 years after its author's death.

That the initial reaction to the novel was largely one of bafflement is not surprising for *Jacques the Fatalist* is a curious and complex book, both a narrative of its own and a self-conscious examination of the procedures of fiction. As well as telling its own story, it offers a critique of rival fictional forms, being particularly hostile to the facile conventions of contemporary fiction. Like Sterne's *Tristram Shandy* (1760–67), to which Diderot respectfully refers, it is both fiction and meta-fiction. The book's opening paragraph shows the dialogue between this text and other texts, and the constant challenging of the reader:

> How did they meet? By chance like everyone else. What were their names? What's that got to do with you? Where were they coming from? From the nearest place. Where were they going to? Does anyone ever really know where they are going to? What were they saying? The captain wasn't saying anything and Jacques was saying that his Captain used to say that everything which happens to us on this earth, both good and bad, is written up above.

The unidentified narrator presents the exchanges between Jacques and his master, interrupts them, digresses, and attests to the authority of what we read—"everything which I have just told you, Reader, I was told by Jacques." This game-playing and its distrust of the orthodox distinctions between illusion and reality permeate the whole novel, and give it a uniquely teasing philosophical quality more attractive to 20th-century readers than to their 18th-century predecessors.

At first, the narrative strives to persuade readers of its truth by great precision in the handling of names and dates, by the incorporation of "real" historical events into the tale—like the battle of Fontenoy in 1745, where Jacques received his knee wound—and by paying due attention to the method by which the narrator describes things. However, at the same time, our attention is constantly drawn to the processes of fabrication and invention by which the story is made possible. The interpolations and digressions keep reminding us that the gap between narration and experience is unbridgeable. Indeed, the effect of these copious devices of authentication gradually becomes paradoxical, and the more we are reassured of the book's veracity, the more of a construction it seems.

Although this self-absorbed dramatization of the processes of storytelling is the most prominent feature of *Jacques*, it is not its sole concern. Again echoing Sterne, and anticipating Beckett, the narrative is beset by anxieties about the passing of time, and the inconstancy of human beings. This emerges through the concerns with compulsive behaviour, be it jealousy or the code of honour, and with the human capacity for deceiving and being deceived. The persistently deferred and interrupted accounts of Jacques's amatory adventures reinforce both the motif of duplicity and the interaction of appearance and reality that sustains the whole fabric of narration. A further reversal and disruption within the book is that the eponymous servant, Jacques, takes precedence over his anonymous master, easily outwitting him and yet staying with him, mirroring the equally fraught relationship between Sancho Panza and Don Quixote. In this area of the book's concerns, the world is turned upside down in every sense, and the revolutionary potential of Jacques's disagreements with his lordly master give the book its political energies. Yet Jacques is no radical. Instead, he voiced Diderot's philosophical determinism, where everything that happens is preordained, "written up above." In philosophical terms, the book investigates the limited powers of human beings, and makes traditional comic play of people struggling against destiny. Yet the role of the narrator complicates the apparent fatalism of the characters. Jacques may be enslaved by what has been written for him, but we can easily see the hand of the writer at work, Diderot himself. Yet it seems inappropriate to read such a persistently playful book as this as articulating a philosophical dilemma. Without turning it merely into a series of trivial games, we must see it as deliberately paradoxical and frustrating, what an equally experimental and serious contemporary Czech writer calls "a feast of intelligence, humour, and fantasy." Like Tristram Shandy, or like Joyce's Leopold Bloom for that matter, the fatalistic servant Jacques is at once an intellectual conceit and a vividly-realized human being. Diderot's book deserves its great reputation first and foremost for the way it humanizes its intellectual playfulness, and the way it rejoices in the mutability of us all.

—Ian A. Bell

JERUSALEM DELIVERED (Gerusalemme liberata)
Poem by Torquato Tasso, 1580 (complete version, 1581)

The first authorized edition of Torquato Tasso's *Jerusalem Delivered* appeared in 1581 and represented a peak in Italian Renaissance poetry that was never to be regained. Perhaps more than any other work, it achieved that synthesis between classical models and vernacular traditions that had been the chief aspiration of Italian writers since Petrarch. It also realized in practice the theories about the epic poem which Tasso advanced in his two treatises, *Discourses on the Art of Poetry*, and *Discourses on the Heroic Poem*.

Despite the enormous success of Ariosto's *Orlando Furioso*, Tasso was dissatisfied with a number of aspects of the chivalric romance, and wanted to achieve a closer imitation of classical epic. His theories, which embraced subject matter, structure, and style, were influenced by two main cultural factors, the rediscovery of Aristotle's *Poetics* with its stress on unity, and the militant Catholicism of the

Counter-Reformation. The appropriate subject for the epic, Tasso decided, should come not from Carolingian legend but from a historical episode of the not too remote past, and any magical episodes should strictly accord with the beliefs of Catholic orthodoxy. All actions should be noble and illustrious, unlike some of the episodes in Ariosto. The length and structure of the poem was to be guided by the average reader's memory, and there should not be a proliferation of sub-plots. The tone should oscillate between the stark gravity of tragedy and the florid eroticism of the lyric, while the language should be sublime, with Latinate words and periods. Tasso remained remarkably faithful to his own precepts.

The poem, divided into 20 cantos of about 100 stanzas each, recounts the capture of Jerusalem by the Christians in the First Crusade under Godfrey of Boulogne. Although Godfrey is the leader, he is rather an uninteresting figure, a flawless Christian version of "pius Aeneas." It is Rinaldo who is the main hero: he undergoes a fall from grace when he succumbs to the beautiful Armida and is banished from the Christian camp, but is recalled to his sense of duty in Canto 16, returns to help the Christians enter Jerusalem, and kills the Saracen hero Solimano. Similarly flawed is a secondary hero, Tancredi, who is also in love with a Saracen female warrior, Clorinda. In a tragic episode he unwittingly kills her in combat, but is roused to great deeds at the end and slays the giant Saracen Argante. The poem ends in Christian triumph, not only with the capture of Jerusalem, but also with the conversion to Christianity of the Saracen heroines, Clorinda as she dies, and Armida at the end of the poem. In fact, throughout the poem, Tasso introduces religious ritual, such as prayers and processions, on several occasions, as well as portraying God and his angels fighting on the Christian side against the forces of evil.

Tasso was aware that the love episodes were necessary to balance the military/religious material. Indeed, it has often been argued that the finest poetry in the poem was inspired by the former not by the latter topic. However, this is too naive a dichotomy and it ignores Tasso's own specialist interest in military tactics and duels, as well as some fine exploration of the psychology of the warrior. It is in his portrayal of amorous psychology and erotic clashes that Tasso excels. The love scene in Armida's luxuriant garden (16) is one of the great set pieces that Tasso relished. Armida is stereotyped as both the great seductress, and, by the end of her affair with Rinaldo, as the rejected woman. There are finer shadings in the portrayal of Clorinda's complex make-up. She can be both aggressive and humane, the former in her nocturnal sortie and duel with Tancredi (12), the latter in her rescuing of the unjustly condemned Christians, Sofronia and Olindo (2). Erminia, another Saracen, but not a warrior, who is in turn in love with Tancredi, is evidence of Tasso's ability to vary his female characters. The unwitting slaying of Clorinda by Tancredi is one of the moments of the poem, notably in its delicate admixture of military and erotic motifs (12.64). Tasso's poetry also proves sublime when dealing with descriptions of nature or nightfall: his sense of the supernatural powers inherent in natural phenomena is conveyed powerfully in lines that incorporate both his own personal vision as well as classical topoi (2.96).

The structure of the poem also reflects Tasso's fidelity to his own theories. The harmony and symmetry of the construction combine to create that sense of diversity contained within unity that he believed indispensable to the epic. If Rinaldo leaves to follow Armida exactly a quarter of the way into the poem (5), he returns as the poem enters its last quarter (16); Jerusalem is sighted first in canto 3, and is entered in 17; the pastoral interlude of Erminia among the shepherds (7) is contrasted with the journey to Armida's garden (14–15); Argante

appears in the second canto and is slain in the second to last; and when the poem enters its second half, the pagan debate (10) gives way to Christian ritual (11). This symmetrical structure is not merely dictated by a sense of Renaissance balance, but it also reflects Tasso's counter-Reformation belief in the harmony of God's world.

The symmetrical laws governing the poem's overall construction permeate even microtextual units, with each octave, and even many individual lines, deriving force from a complex mechanism of balances and contrasts. Tasso is also a master of varying the rhythm of the octave, often engineering strong pauses within the single line. When Tancredi drives his sword into Clorinda's breast, the disrupted rhythm of the penultimate line enhances the erotic pathos of Clorinda's realization of imminent death: "e la veste, che d'or vago trapunta / le mammelle stringea tenera e leve, / l'empie d'un caldo fiume. Ella già sente / morirsi, e 'l pié manca egro e languente" [and her tunic, which embroidered with fine gold, / held her breasts lightly and tenderly, / was filled with a warm flow. She already feels / herself dying, and her foot gives way in her pain and languor] (12.64). Tasso's nuanced exploitation of balance and rhythm, as well as his pursuit of a sublime poetic lexis, which is difficult to achieve outside Italian, certainly also contribute to his epic, being translated more rarely than the less stylized narrative poetry of Ariosto. Yet despite his own dissatisfactions with it, which led to his rewriting the poem as *Gerusalemme conquistata*, the verdict of posterity has always preferred the poetry of the *Liberata* for its sublimity and symmetry as well as for the light it sheds on the darker aspects of late Renaissance psychology.

—Martin L. McLaughlin

LA JEUNE PARQUE
Poem by Paul Valéry, 1917 (written 1912–17)

"La Jeune Parque," five years in the writing, is generally considered Paul Valéry's poetic masterpiece, its 512 lines celebrated both for their thematic complexity and intensity and for their exceptional musicality. Valéry had published no poetry since 1892 when in 1912 André Gide and Gaston Gallimard urged him to make a collection of his earlier pieces. Confronted by what now seemed to him the imperfect relics of his youthful poetic self, Valéry was stimulated to write a new poem bridging the 20 years' gap, which would incorporate and further develop his mature preoccupation with the functioning of the individual as a composite of body and mind and his exploration and analysis of the nature of consciousness. World War I provided an extra impetus. Inhibiting Valéry's ability to pursue his abstract speculations, it encouraged him to re-engage with the less oppressive if equally intractable difficulties of artistic expression with the additional hope that the poem might constitute a monument to the beauty of French language and culture in a new barbarian age.

Valéry's subject is at once totally specific and endlessly imprecise: the living self in its ceaseless modulations between being and knowing, always distanced by its distinguishing consciousness from pure physicality but constantly seeking an impossible union between these two aspects of its existence. The title, setting youthfulness alongside an allusion to three ancient Fates of Antiquity, who together represented the inexorable progression from birth to death, strikingly summarizes the problematic situation of the self, individualized and limited in time and space, yet in its inmost sense of its own being all-embracing and ever young. Significantly Valéry rejected both titles too closely tied to specific protagonists ("Hélène," "Pandore," "Psyché") and depersonalized titles with a thematic or formal orientation ("Îles" [Islands], "Larme" [Tear]; "Ébauche" [Draft], "Pièce de vers" [Piece of Verse]). His poem is centred not on a particular individual or motif but on the Self, any self, as universal and as anonymous as possible.

The poem, "a monologue for two voices" (Octave Nadal), is divided between a nocturnal and a diurnal setting. In the opening lines the young Fate weeps alone in darkness by the sea, her gaze fixed on the remote stars. Unable to see even her hand before her face, she experiences herself as fragmentation and loss, her very weeping seemingly the voice of a stranger. The source of her grief seems to lie in the conjunction of the dark cosmic vastness that surrounds her and the dream from which she has just awoken. In her sleep she seemed to follow and identify with a serpent whose bite engenders self-aware-ness and the control of the conscious mind over pure sensation. But this sense of mastery is inescapably linked with regret for an uncon-scious self existing in harmonious symbiosis with the physical universe. Awareness of difference and separation leads paradoxically to the urge towards reabsorption within the cosmos, either in an involuntary physically impelled participation in the rebirth of spring-time or in the conscious suppression of individuality that is suicide. Earth, the apparently stable foundation of physical existence, is thus transmuted into the slippery seaweed-covered rocks, down which the young Fate seems ready to slip into oblivion. The second section of the poem counters however with a strong assertion of individual survival. As dawn breaks, the young Fate regains conscious posses-sion of her person from the darkness, while simultaneously being caught up in the joyous celebration of the new day over land and sea. The struggle between these two contradictory urges remains however unresolved, and throughout the latter section the themes of suicide, seduction of the physical, and temporary surrender of the conscious self in sleep continue to oscillate, with an affirmation of the crucial significance of self-awareness and a recognition of the extremes of ecstasy and distress that are the inevitable result. Beyond linguistic expression, the young Fate's tears are the visible sign of the tragedy—and the richness—of the living self.

Though the poem can be presented in terms of a narrative sequence—Valéry calls it "a depiction of a series of psychological substitutions in the course of a night"—it is important to underline the essentially interchangeable and cyclical nature of the phenomena described. The serpent, traditionally a notoriously ambivalent symbol, simultane-ously figures body and mind. Light is associated both with intellectual illumination and physical elation. The "secret sister" revealed by the serpent's bite, is both the corporeal and the conscious self. Moreover the night of confused self-questioning experienced by the young Fate is not a unique event but rather, as the persistent interplay of past and present tenses and the chiastic reversing in the second section of initial motifs of consciousness, sleep, and self-annihilation suggest, a constant cycle of dynamic, self-regulating being.

The dedication to André Gide describes the poem as an "exer-cise," a tangible intervention of the conscious mind in the inchoate substance of physiological being. The aim is to render the "modula-tions of the self" by a poetry of musical modulation, analogous to the recitative of Gluck's *Alceste*, and reminiscent also of the lyrical voice of Racine's "Songe d'Athalie" ("Athalie's Dream"). Structurally this is achieved by the sinuous intertwining of repeated thematic motifs, tears, stars and diamonds, shade and sunlight, earth, sea and islands, wind and trees. Rhythmically and phonetically, Valéry bril-liantly exploits all the resources of balance, repetition, and symmetry

of the traditional 12-syllable alexandrine rhyming couplet to achieve a union of analytical inquiry and musical profusion unparalleled in French poetry. The poem is thus in itself an illustration and a celebration of the sublime compensations offered by the physical and mental worlds to our awareness of the limitations of our living being: a restitution, as Valéry puts it in lines 346–7, of "the eager tomb / To the gracious state of universal joy."

—Rachel Killick

THE JEW'S BEECH TREE (Die Judenbuche)
Novella by Annette von Droste-Hülshoff, 1851 (published in serial form, 1842)

The Jew's Beech Tree, one of the most famous novellas in the German language, was first published in serial form in the *Morgenblatt für gebildete Leser* in 1842, and appeared in book form in 1851.

Friedrich Mergel, the central character, is born in a village, Dorf B, to poor parents. His father, a drunkard, dies in mysterious circum-stances when Friedrich is nine. When the boy is 12 years old, he comes under the influence of his uncle, Simon Semmeler, who is involved in petty crime and may be linked to the *Blaukittel*, the wood thieves who work at night stealing wood from the forest. Friedrich's *Doppelgänger*, his cousin Johannes Niemand, a pale imitation of Friedrich himself, is introduced at this stage. When Friedrich is 18 he is instrumental in sending the forester, Brandis, to his death at the hands of the wood thieves. A public enquiry into the incident fails to solve the crime, but Friedrich's guilt is shown when Simon persuades him not to go to confession.

At the age of 22 Friedrich is depicted at a village wedding where he is publicly humiliated when his protégé, Niemand, is caught stealing butter. Later the same night Friedrich is humiliated again when a Jew, Aaron, publicly accuses him of not paying for a watch he has bought. Three days later Aaron is found murdered and Friedrich, the obvious suspect, disappears. The local Jewish community purchases the beech tree where Aaron was murdered and carves a Hebrew inscription on it. Friedrich's name is later cleared of the murder when someone else makes a confession.

28 years pass. A wanderer returns to the village on Christmas Eve and is taken in for the night. He is declared to be Johannes Niemand, who left with Friedrich, and he does not deny his identity. He recalls his years of slavery in far distant Turkey, and is now apparently content to settle down to a new life back in the village. However, he disappears one day as suddenly as he had returned, and all attempts to find him are in vain. The son of Brandis, the forester who many years earlier lost his life because of Friedrich's involvement with the wood thieves, is wandering in the wood when he discovers the badly decomposed body of "Niemand" hanging from the beech tree. A scar on the body reveals that the man was in fact Friedrich Mergel and he is subsequently buried in the knacker's yard. Only now is the Hebrew inscription translated: "If you approach this place then what you did to me will be done unto you."

The strength of the story lies in its dense structure and complex interweaving of various, sometimes conflicting, themes and motifs. While it is unified by its episodic structure, which focuses on key events in Mergel's life, the story's emphasis shifts from an attempt to understand the process of criminalization to the uncovering of Mergel's crimes. The early part of the story concentrates on the social milieu in which he grows up and seeks to explain why he develops as he does; for example in a striking piece of dialogue his antisemitism is shown to be learned directly from his mother. It is a society with a strong group identity to which Mergel is anxious to conform, a society which expels those who do not fit. Annette von Droste-Hülshoff herself referred to the work as a "story of a criminal, Friedrich Mergel," and her source was an article by her uncle, Freiherr A. von Haxthausen, about the murder of a Jew by a farmhand, called *The Story of an Algerian Slave*. In the latter half of the story, however, the emphasis shifts to the attempt to solve Mergel's crimes and places the reader in the position of investigator by supplying clues. But it is more than a detective story, for there are many unanswered questions in terms of the plot (what does happen to Johannes Niemand? What are we to make of the—presumably false—confession?), and the use of detective work alone will not tell the reader how to interpret the other, larger questions the story raises about reason and superstition, Old Testament justice and New Testament salvation, social conditioning and free will.

The narrative perspective, crucially, does not seek to guide, for it shifts frequently, sometimes appearing omniscient but at other times being close to the action and withholding vital information. The text does, however, accord the reader a unique insight into both the social and psychological processes at work and the insufficiency of human agencies: none of the crimes reported in the story are ever "solved." Much of the depth of meaning of the story is achieved through the use of symbolism, for example the beech tree itself and the use of Johannes Niemand as Friedrich's alter ego.

The painstaking attempt to depict realistically the life of a local community (the subtitle is *A Portrayal of the Life and Customs in Mountainous Westphalia*), while also looking below the surface for deeper meanings, and the conscious artistry of the composition make this an outstanding example of 19th-century German poetic realism,

—Brigid Haines

JOURNEY TO THE END OF THE NIGHT (Voyage au bout de la nuit)
Novel by Louis-Ferdinand Céline, 1932

The appearance of *Journey to the End of the Night* provoked scandal and controversy in French literacy circles. It was included in the 1933 list of candidates for the coveted Goncourt prize with Léon Daudet vigorously campaigning in its favour, but it narrowly missed, receiving shortly thereafter the Renaudot prize. Whereas that year's Goncourt nomination has passed into oblivion, Louis-Ferdinand Céline's novel ranks among the great novels of the 20th century. As Leon Trotskii remarked in "Céline et Poincaré" (1933), "Céline walked into great literature the way others walk into their own homes."

Belonging to that category of novels with famous opening sentences, the *Journey*'s first sentence defied accepted literary and grammatical conventions with its colloquial use of the contraction ça (that, it) instead of the correct form of *cela:* "Ça a débuté comme ça" ("Here's how it started"). Such double emphasis announced, as Céline called it, his modest invention of a prose style patterned on popular, spoken French. Céline thus broke away from the naturalist tradition that generally confined popular speech to phonetic transcription and passages of dialogue. The *Journey*'s originality lay in its

implicit rejection of the popular *roman à thèse;* it was not a safely contained slice of life so much as a way of life that aesthetically revolutionized the French novel with the rhythmic flow of its slang and its linguistic post-positions and prepositions (unfortunately, these do not translate well in to English), which are so common to French speech patterns but innovative to prose. Céline's conception of language as a living entity in opposition to writing's arrested state would have much to do with the *Journey*'s major themes. In one famous passage, speech is considered a physical calamity:

> When you stop to examine the way in which words are formed and uttered, our sentences are hard put to it to survive the disaster of their slobbery origin. The mechanical effort of conversation is nastier and more complicated than defecation. That corolla of bloated flesh, the mouth, which screws itself up to whistle, which sucks its breath, contorts itself, discharges all manner of viscous sounds across a fetid barrier of decaying teeth—how revolting! Yet that it what we are abjured to sublimate into an ideal. It's not easy. Since we are nothing but packages of tepid, half-rotted viscera, we shall always have trouble with sentiment. Being in love is nothing, it's sticking together that's difficult. Faeces on the other hand make no attempt to endure or to grow. On this score we are far more unfortunate than shit: our frenzy to persist in our present state—that's the unconscionable torture.

The connection between speech's "viscous sounds" and bodies as "packages of tepid, half-rotted viscera" forecloses aesthetic idealization (i.e., writing) and triggers other considerations on the human condition as decay and the frenzy of exacerbated psyches on the verge of mass destruction and biological breakdown.

Lauded nevertheless by many critics and writers at the time as a left-wing novel, the *Journey* explores through the eyes of its hapless first-person protagonist, Bardamu (pushed on through life by his burden; *barda* = knapsack, *mu* = driven, propelled), the profound cruelty of the powerful and the deep despair of the ragged, rationalized "minions of King Misery." But Céline's aim is not to idealize their social condition. From a psychological and biological perspective, he examines man's egoism and vanity in collusion with his self-destructive biological cells. The famous Freudian hypothesis of the death drive lies just below the surface of Bardamu's explorations and reflections on the human condition.

If Céline's language was ground-breaking, the *Journey*'s narrative development, as is evident from its title, is organized around the cliché often found in the novel, "life is a voyage." Céline begins his second epigraph by stating: "Travel is useful, it exercises the imagination, all the rest is disappointment and fatigue. Our journey is entirely imaginary. That is its strength." The epigraph concludes with the affirmation that the *Journey* is a work of the imagination, but this first sentence interestingly establishes the link between travel and work ("exercises" translates *travailler)* through the etymological root that *travel and travail* have in common. This equation both popularizes the novel and aestheticizes the popular.

Although its episodic sections (not chapters) loosely imitate picaresque, narrative structure, the *Journey* can be broken down into two basic parts. The first half contains Bardamu's experiences as a brigadier in World War II, his wound, mental trauma, and breakdown, and his passages to Africa and America. The second half contains his return to Paris to finish his medical degree, his routine life as a doctor for the poor, and his continued encounters with Robinson, Bardamu's double, who, first encountered by Bardamu in the dark during the war, in the first half is the object of the protagonist's wanderings in Africa and America and later, in the second half, becomes the protagonist's dependent. Bardamu's role shifts from follower to followed, a reversal predicated on the decline of Robinson's self-esteem and health and on Bardamu's change in social position from poor itinerant worker to established doctor for the poor.

Céline's account of the war counts among some of the most critical and irreverent pages on the experience of modern war: ''Horses are lucky, they're stuck with the war same as us, but nobody expects them to be in favour of it, to pretend to believe in it. Unfortunate, yes, but free! Enthusiasm, the stinker, was reserved for us!'' Bardamu suffers a mental breakdown, which he attributes to his great fear of death. Refusing the unimaginative vocation of death, he opts for cowardice, a survival tactic, bringing him down in the eyes of his zealous American girlfriend, Lola, a nurse of the American Expeditionary Force stationed in Paris; but, for Bardamu, survival means placing imagination (i.e., fear) above suicidal patriotism (i.e., courage). Discharged from the army, Bardamu embarks for the French Congo.

As in Gide's scandalous exposure of colonialism in his *Voyage au Congo* (1927), Bardamu encounters depraved colonials intent on making their fortunes by robbing the native population of their dignity and the fruits of their hard labour. These colonials are, however, victims too, being ill-equipped for the heat, moisture, and malaria, which only accelerate their physical and moral decay. In a malarial delirium, Bardamu sets fire to his isolated encampment and escapes the jungle only to find himself a purchased galley slave aboard a boat headed for America. He lands at Ellis Island where he finds employment as a flea statistician. He manages to escape to Manhattan, a concrete jungle of money temples and distant people: ''The bigger and taller the city, the less they care.'' Penniless, he eventually tracks down his old girlfriend, Lola, who bribes him to leave town. From here he travels to Detroit, where he will find employment at the Ford factory. Rationalization and Fordism convert the poor and the handicapped into machines, while the factory's deafening noise is reminiscent of war: ''It's not shame that makes them bow their heads. You give into noise as you give in to war.'' Life at the factory is only made bearable by Bardamu's love affair with the magnanimous prostitute, Molly, whom he leaves behind with regret in order to pursue a new identity in Paris.

Among his responsibilities as doctor, Bardamu finds himself mixed up with Robinson, who has accepted payment from the Henrouilles to murder Grandma Henrouille, one of Bardamu's patients. Robinson, however, temporarily loses his sight in a botched attempt to rig a rabbit hutch with explosives destined for Grandma Henrouille. With the help of Bardamu and the Abbé Protiste (whose mouth it was that led to the description above of grotesque speech), the Henrouilles manage to rid themselves of Robinson and Grandma Henrouille by sending them to Toulouse to work in a catacomb run by a convent. Robinson becomes engaged to a young dressmaker, Madelon, who also works part-time at the vault. Realizing that his solitary nature goes against married life, Robinson tries to extricate himself from his commitment to Madelon, who becomes increasingly possessive and paranoid. Matters between them go from bad to worse and Bardamu is unsuccessful in his attempts to help his friend. During a violent dispute in a taxi cab, Madelon shoots Robinson in front of Bardamu and his companion, Sophie. The novel ends with Robinson's death.

A mixture of slang and lyricism, black humour and aphorisms, verging at times on the sentimental, *Journey to the End of the Night* was not only a turning point in Céline's career but also a turning point in the French novel.

—Andrea Loselle

JOURNEY TO THE WEST (Xiyouji)

Also known as *Hsi-yu-chi* or *Monkey*. Chinese novel of 100 chapters by Wu Cheng'en (c. 1505–80), based on the 7th-century story of a Chinese monk's pilgrimage to India to find Buddhist scriptures. Other versions of the tale existed, and there is an ''Urtext'' fragment in the *Yongle dadian* encyclopedia dating from c. 1403–08.

PUBLICATIONS

Monkey, Folk Novel of China, translated by Arthur Waley, 1943; as *The Monkey King*, edited by Zdena Novotna, translated by George Theiner (from the Czech), 1964; as *Monkey: A Journey to the West: A Retelling of the Chinese Folk Novel by Wu Ch'eng-en* by David Kherdian, 1992.

*

Critical Studies: ''*Journey to the West*'' in *The Classic Chinese Novel* by C.T. Hsia, 1968; *The Hsi-yu chi: A Study of Antecedents to the 16th-Century Chinese Novel* by Glen Dudbridge, 1970; ''On Translating the *Hsi-yu chi*'' by Anthony C. Yu, in *The Art and Profession of Translation*, edited by T.C. Lai, 1976; *The Mythic and the Comic Aspects of the Quest: Hsi-yu Chi as Seen Through Don Quixote and Huckleberry Finn* by James S. Fu, 1977.

*   *   *

Xiyouji (*Journey to the West* or *Monkey*) is a novel based on the historical pilgrimage of Tang Sanzang (also known as Tripitaka or Xuanzang), the Chinese monk who went to India in search of Buddhist scriptures in the 7th century. The earliest story of Sanzang appeared in the Southern Song period and was entitled *Da Tang Sanzang qujing shihua* [The Shihua Version of Sanzang's Quest for Scriptures]. The main story is about Sanzang's spiritual quest, but Monkey (Sun Wukong) emerges as a prominent character in the story as Sanzang's disciple. They encounter various fantastic adventures, often involving gods, demons, and animal spirits. The legend of Sanzang also provided materials for plays of the Yuan Dynasty (1272/79–1368), the most famous being Wu Changling's *Tang Sanzang xitian qujing* [Tang Sanzang in Quest of the Scriptures from the Western Paradise]. In the *Yongle dadian*, a partially preserved encyclopedic compilation dating from the Yongle period of the Ming Dynasty (1403–24), there is an entry of some 1,200 Chinese characters which relates the slaughtering of a dragon king by the Tang minister Wei Zheng. This episode has its fuller counterpart in the 100-chapter novel *Xiyouji* (*Journey to the West*), by Wu Cheng'en, who lived approximately between 1505 and 1580 at Huaian in Jiangsu Province. The standard modern edition of *Journey to the West* was published by the Zuojia Publishing Society of Beijing in 1954.

The story of *Journey to the West*, as we have it in the modern edition, can be divided into the following four sections:

1. The first seven chapters tell of the birth of the Monkey, who is hatched from a stone egg under the influence of the sun and moon. He lives on the Mountain of Flowers and Fruit and has acquired such tremendous powers under the tutoring of Subhodi that only Buddha can subdue him under the Mountain of Five Phases. He is released 500 years later by Tang Sanzang after he promises to protect Sanzang on his journey to the West and to be Sanzang's disciple.

2. Chapters 8 to 12 describe the background and birth of Sanzang and the origin of his mission to India. Major episodes include Buddha's intention to impart the Buddhist canon to the Chinese, preparation for the journey by Guanyin (the Goddess of Mercy), Sanzang's revenge on his father's murderers, Wei Zheng's execution of the Eastern Dragon King, the journey of Tang Taizong to the underworld, his convening of the Mass for the Dead, and the appointment of Sanzang as the pilgrim to seek the scriptures after the epiphany of the Goddess of Mercy.

3. Chapters 13 to 97 tell of the pilgrimage to India of Sanzang, his disciples—Monkey, Pig, and Friar Sand—as well as Sanzang's white dragon horse. The 14-year journey is developed primarily through a series of captures and releases of the pilgrims by animal spirits, gods in disguise, demons, and monsters, which together constitute the 81 ordeals preordained for Sanzang. Each episode is a self-contained story running from one to five chapters in length. In each, the pilgrims are presented with a problem which they must overcome before continuing their travels. Once the problem is solved and a new episode begins, the place and characters in earlier episodes are left behind and seldom mentioned again.

4. The last three chapters tell of the successful completion of the journey: the meeting with the Buddha, the return with the scriptures to China, and the final reward of the five pilgrims (including Sanzang's white dragon horse).

Wu Cheng'en gives shape and coherence to the tradition of the Sanzang legend by writing it in the style of the storywriters of the Tang and Song dynasties. The 100-chapter narrative consisting of self-contained episodes, is abundant in dialogue as well as in accounts of events and passages of descriptive verse. The reader is occasionally addressed directly and urged to listen to the next chapter. Since the story is already well-known, the main interest of the reader is hardly in experiencing suspense or wondering whether Sanzang will survive his adventures, but in the manner in which Monkey will overcome the monsters confronting them all in each case.

Interpretations of the theme of the *Journey to the West* vary among critics. The novel is widely regarded as an allegory in which Tang Sanzang represents the ordinary man, easily upset by the difficulties of life, while the Monkey stands for human intelligence, and Pig the physical aspects of human beings. A Buddhist interpretation considers the basic plot of the story to be the religious quest for Buddhist scriptures. Titles of the *sutras* and of Buddhas and *bodhisattvas* recur in the novel. For example, a complete transcription of the "Heart Sutra" appears in chapter 19 and reappears as a subject of repeated discussion between Sanzang and Monkey. Also, the wisdom and mercy of Buddha—the novel begins with the benevolent intention of the Buddha to send Tripitaka (Sanzang) to the people of the East—are

often emphasized. There are also elements of Daoism in the novel: Daoist symbolism, such as the Five Elements, is often referred to. The novel is also interpreted as a treatise on internal alchemy through an elaboration of the use of alchemical, yin-yang, and Yi jing lore. Interpreted with the focus on the quest as a way to the classic Confucian doctrines of virtue and rectification of the mind, the novel can be seen to carry a Confucian message. Scholars, however, also look to the advice Monkey gives the King of the Cart-Slow Kingdom in chapter 47, and find the preservation of equal reverence for Buddhism, Daoism, and Confucianism to be a major theme in the novel.

The comedy and humour in the novel lie in the vivid characterization. The triangle of Sanzang, Monkey, and Pig is the central structure of every episode. Sanzang is presented both as a Buddhist monk and as an ordinary mortal. As a pilgrim monk, Sanzang has the unyielding determination to reach his goal and obtain the scriptures. He is also saintly in that his flesh can give the monsters and demons everlasting life. As a common mortal, he is fretful, credulous, and self-pitying. Though master of his animal disciples, he shows little spiritual improvement during his journey. In fact, it is always Monkey that reminds him of the wisdom of the *sutras*. From this perspective, Sanzang in the modern edition scarcely suggests the heroism of his historic namesake. Rather, his every manifestation of human weakness helps define his role as a comic figure in the novel. Monkey is Sanzang's first and most celebrated disciple. In spite of all of Sanzang's credulity and peevishness, Monkey remains loyal and selfless. Discontented with the pastoral life as a leader of monkeys on the Mountain of Flowers and Fruit, Monkey seeks immortality through the patriarch Subodhi, symbolizing to some extent Monkey's quest for spiritual understanding. His promotion from animal rebel to Buddha's submissive servant and eventually to a Buddha himself depends not only on his magical powers but also on his wits— knowing or being able to discover the background of the monsters he and the others confront. The only pilgrim able to detach himself from all human desires, Monkey, whose name, Wu kong, means "aware of vacuity," stands as the spokesperson for the doctrine of emptiness.

Pig serves in every respect as a foil to Monkey. If Monkey represents the mind, Pig then represents the body and its appetites— vanity, greed, lust, and jealousy. While Monkey is intelligent enough to survive on his wits and valiant enough to be a champion fighter, Pig is not too stupid to avoid responsibilities and dangers whenever possible. With the serious Monkey and the joking Pig, the *Journey to the West* becomes a great literary source of pleasure. In comparison, Friar Sand turns out to be the most colourless of the four main characters, retained from earlier versions and existing as a shadowy figure throughout.

—Ying-Ying Chein

JUSTICE WITHOUT REVENGE (El castigo sin venganza)
Play by Lope de Vega Carpio, 1632

"*Cuando Lope quiere, quiere*" ("When Lope wishes, he will"): this subtitle, added to a 1647 edition of *Justice without Revenge*, emphasizes the carefully executed quality of this work, widely acknowledged to be one of its author's most outstanding achievements. Reputedly an instinctive artist rather than a conscientious craftsman, Lope de Vega Carpio was also capable, particularly in the later years of his extended career, of revising what he had, at first, rapidly composed. The autograph manuscript of *Justice without Revenge* contains many corrections which confirm that even late in his career Lope was influenced by the thoughtful attitudes and meticulous techniques of his own follower, Calderón de la Barca.

The subject-matter of this admirably executed play, the product of scrupulous attention to unity of theme and structure, is derived from a *novella* by Bandello based on a real event in 15th-century Italian history. The play dramatizes the fatal love-relationship between Federico, bastard son of the Duke of Ferrara, and Federico's step-mother, Casandra. When the Duke discovers their adultery he deter-mines to punish his wife and son without making public their offence and his dishonour. He persuades Federico to execute an unidentified traitor, bound and hooded, whom Federico recognizes as his step-mother and mistress only after he has committed the horrifying deed. Falsely accused by his father of having deliberately murdered Casandra in order to prevent her bearing a legitimate heir to Ferrara, Federico is then himself summarily executed by the Duke's command.

Golden Age audiences delighted in dramas of illicit love and affronted honour, and in plays with a political dimension, especially those in which rulers conflicted violently with their sons. *Justice without Revenge* contained both such preferred elements but it was originally staged for only one day and then withdrawn for reasons that the playwright mysteriously declined to reveal, and subsequently arousing many hypotheses among critics as to possible reasons why. Francisco de Rojas Zorrilla dramatizes, likewise in the 1630s, a daring case of feminine dishonour in a work entitled *Cada cual lo que le toca* (*Each to His own Concern*). This play, in which a nobleman discovers that he has unknowingly married a woman who has already been violated by another man, was hissed at its first performance in Madrid by an audience offended by its lack of moral decorum. Casandra's blatantly immoral conduct might have provoked the first audience that attended *Justice without Revenge* to a similarly extreme reaction of disapproval.

Described in its final lines as "tragedy," an exalted category to which Lope allocated few of his numerous plays, this complex and sombre drama has been the subject of much critical controversy. United in admiration for its artistry, scholars disagree vehemently as to its interpretation. Opinions differ particularly concerning who is the tragic hero; whether, in the final act, the Duke's professed change from libertine to faithful husband is genuine; and what meanings the drama's ambiguous title is truly intended to convey. All three principal characters are tragically blameworthy for the catastrophic denouement, though in significantly different degrees. Federico is guilty of consummating his illicit passion for Casandra. But his father's dissolutely bad example and his stepmother's seductive persuasion are decisive influences upon his behaviour, at once lessening the measure of his offence and diminishing the tragic importance of his role. Casandra is a more interestingly complex and strong-minded individual than is Federico. Married for reasons of state to a middle-aged libertine, this deeply humiliated young woman deliberately commits adultery less from motives of love than of revenge. But the Duke is, surely, the central and most profoundly tragic figure in Lope's drama. The Duke's womanizing activities and indifference to his wife—whose bed he shares only once—impel Casandra and Federico into adultery, which, in turn (when the Duke finds out), leads inevitably to their violent deaths. The Duke discovers their crime upon his return, apparently a reformed man, from a military campaign in defence of the Pope. Some critics have judged as sincere the Duke's declared intention to change his wanton ways, though too late to prevent his wife's adultery. But had Lope intended us to believe in the Duke's reformation, he would surely have provided us with a more credible witness than his disreputable manservant, Ricardo. His declaration that his master "is now a saint" is much less convincing than the comment of a less biased figure, the wise fool Batín, that the Duke is a "false saint."

Unlike Casandra and Federico, the Duke does not die at the end. But his survival, far from reducing, instead intensifies his tragic stature as hero. A childless widower, he lives on in a torment of spiritual isolation and inwardly-acknowledged responsibility for the death not only of Casandra, but of the one person he has truly loved—his son. It is known that Lope hesitated over the title of his play. As the autograph manuscript reveals, he considered "evenge Without Justice" before deciding upon "Justice Without Revenge." His finally chosen title confirms that the true crime for which Federico and Casandra died (their adultery) was not publicly revealed. They were punished "sin venganza" because the Duke's dishonour was never openly acknowledged nor officially avenged. More importantly, however, the title is used to signify the punishment suffered by the Duke himself, which, though bloodless and invisible (apparently "unavenging"), cruelly denies him quick release through sudden death, condemning him, instead, to imprisonment for life in the solitary confinement of guilt. A Roman-Catholic playwright, com-posing for religiously-minded audiences, Lope doubtless also in-tended his public to understand that, when he dies at last, the Duke will be punished in the hereafter for his wickedness, through the eternally just vengeance of the Lord.

—Ann L. Mackenzie

JUSTINE (Justine; ou, Les Malheurs de la vertu)
Novel by Marquis de Sade, 1791

Justine, unlike its heroine, evades easy capture. While it begins in adherence to the literary conventions of its day, it plunges into a dark private world which, for detailed savagery, has no point of compari-son in published literature. Its stylistic triumphs, the dazzling moral debates in the form of Socratic dialogues between Justine and her persecutors, are matched by the graphic and prolonged descriptions of torture. Both are directed against its eponymous heroine. All this, we are told in a prefatory letter, is for a moral and religious purpose. Justine, the purest champion of virtue, is released into a world rapacious beyond belief, a fictional world which forms a specially created alembic for the Marquis de Sade's experiment. The experi-ment is to bring unparalleled pressure against her in order to subvert, or corrupt, her faith. The philosophic model for the novel is thus the Book of Job, with the author playing the part of both God and Satan—a fair comparison in the light of the Marquis's religious obsessions. Behind this experiment, claims Sade, is the deeper moral purpose of seeking to prove the triumph of virtue: thus the novel, which lingers over passages of virulent misogyny and violence, is presented as an essay in moral philosophy—a conceit which the author exploits to the full.

Justine is never simply an object in the voyeuristic sense, perceived from without as a source of sexual gratification. She is always the subject, describing her sufferings from within. The reader and her sympathies (the novel is dedicated to a woman) are always with the heroine. The division between author as persecutor and both character and reader as victim adds moral complexity and psychological interest to a story which, if it were related in the third person, would be simply pornographic. This division is most shrinkingly evident when Sade places in Justine's lips a prayer pleading to God for deliverance. The prayer cannot be answered—Sade has removed God from his world.

The atrocities recounted in this book are themselves shocking. This shock is likely to be compounded by the disorientation of the reader who is introduced to a world in which the conventional norms of the novel—the sanctity and power of chastity, the guiding protection of Providence over the heroine—are at first respected and then systematically violated. While exposed to a variety of horrors, Justine's virginity is at first shielded. Having witnessed her escape from her first captors, the reader might breathe a sigh of relief—only to see Justine casually raped, robbed, and beaten senseless by the man whose life she has saved.

From that point on, Justine is endless victim in a hellish counterworld where every man is a fiend, awaiting his chance to abuse her. The universe created by the book ventures into territory unknown to the novel of its day—detailed descriptions of homosexual intercourse, for example. In this sense, *Justine* could be seen to form the dark shadow cast by the 18th-century novel, exploring its absences and repressions, saying the unsayable.

In structural terms, the plot forms a repetitive sequence of moves on the Gothic pattern of threat, enclosure, and escape. Yet from each escape the heroine falls victim to yet more horrifying captivity. The narrative trajectory Sade has established must inflict greater and greater pain on her, pushing back yet further the distorted horizons of expectations he has established. Thus Justine's journey takes her from rape, to mass torture of children, to dismemberment, to slavery, and the murder of siblings. The narrative is forced to wilder and wilder

extremes. At its most effective it approximates to the landscape of a medieval vision of hell: where, as in Roland's castle, women are kept underground as beasts of burden and tortured until their death. At its weakest, however, it topples into farce, as in the description of the gigantic proportions of her attackers' penises and the huge quantities of their semen.

The violent hatred of women expressed by Sade's diabolical villains is combined with another, equal hatred: that directed against Christianity. Blasphemy is one of the most persistent discourse of *Justine*: its villains insult and rape against God, while their orgasms are marked by sacrilegious oaths. A series of elaborate rituals are staged in order to enact this hatred: a child is dressed as, and venerated as, the Virgin Mary, then raped in the same costume; Justine (an appropriate Christ figure in the light of her purity and her suffering) is tied to the thorny cross and tortured: the consecrated host—"the body of Christ"—is pushed up her rectum; she is placed on the chapel altar and buggered.

Justine should be understood in terms of its literary context which it both acknowledges and perverts. In some respects, it is an extreme extension of, rather than an aberration from, its contemporaries. While the 18th-century novel of sensibility exposed its heroine to a maximum of emotional torment, the Gothic novel took the process a stage further by threatening its heroine with violence and terror. Sade calls the Gothic's bluff by bringing out of the shadows horrors which the Gothic novel only dared to suggest. Roland's underground cavern (stocked with skulls, an open coffin, an effigy of death, and a wax image of a tortured woman) and Count Gernande, who gains sexual gratification from sucking women's blood, both seem to be homages to the genre. Yet these are only the external trappings of the Gothic, for, crucially, Sade's work denies even the suggestion of the supernatural. Justine's only enemy is man.

—Edmund Cusick

K

KALEVALA
Epic poem compiled by Elias Lönnrot, between 1828 and 1846

Finnish national epic poem; compiled by Elias Lönnrot (1802–84), doctor of medicine and later professor of Finnish at Alexander's University in Helsinki, from traditional oral poetry of northeastern Finland and the Finnish-Russian border, together with about 600 lines written by Lönnrot himself. Title means "Land of Kaleva."

PUBLICATIONS

Kalevala, edited by Elias Lönnrot. 1835; revised, enlarged edition, 1849; *Selections from the Kalevala,* translated by John A. Porter, 1868; translated by Selma Borg, 1882; also translated by John Martin Crawford, 2 vols., 1888; William Forsell Kirby, 2 vols., 1907; Aili Kolehmainen Johnson (in prose), 1951; Francis Peabody Magoun, Jr. (in prose), 1963; Eino Friberg, edited by George C. Schoolfield, 1988; Keith Bosley, 1989.

*

Bibliography: *Elias Lönnrot and His Kalevala: A Selective Annotated Bibliography* by Elemer Bako, 1985.

Critical Studies: *Hiawatha and Kalevala: A Study of the Relationship Between Longfellow's "Indian Edda" and the Finnish Epic* by Ernest J. Moyne, 1963; *The Kalevala and Its Background* by Erik Alfred Torbjörn Collinder, 1964; *Kalevala Kommentar* by Hans Fromm, 1967; *Epic of the North: The Story of Finland's Kalevala* by John I. Kolehmainen, 1973; *Finnish Folk Poetry: Epic* by Matti Kuusi and others, 1977; *Kalevala* issue of *Books from Finland,* 19(1), 1985; *Studies in Finnish Folklore: Homage to the Kalevala* by Felix J. Oinas, 1985; *Religion, Myth and Folklore in the World's Epics, the Kalevala and Its Predecessors,* edited by Lauri Honko, 1990; *Mind and Form in Folklore: Selected Articles* by Matti Kuusi, translated by Hildi Hawkins, 1994; *Finnish Folk Poetry and the Kalevala* by Thomas A. DuBois, 1995; *Finnish Magic: A Nation of Wizards, a World of Spirits* by Robert Nelson, 1999.

* * *

The preliminary 1835 edition of the *Kalevala* contains 16 poems, and 5,052 lines. The 1849 definitive edition known as "the Finnish national epic" is considerably longer, containing 50 poems, and 22,795 lines. However, the latter represents only a fraction of the oral poetry in the Kalevala metre handed down from generation to generation and saved by collectors. By comparison, the 33-volume *Suomen Kansan Vanhat Runot* [Ancient Poems of the Finnish People] published by the Finnish Literature Society (Helsinki) between 1908 and 1948, contains approximately half of some 1,270,000 lines of collected material in the society's archives, the rest of which remains unpublished. The wealth of oral poetry which Elias Lönnrot recorded during his field trips, principally to north-eastern Finland and Karelia,

made possible not only the compilation of *Kalevala* but also the publication of companion volumes, the best known of which is *Kanteletar* [Lady of the Kantele], the collection of lyric poetry to which female singers, specifically, made their contribution. Traditionally men tended to sing heroic poetry while women favoured lyric, legends, and ballads.

The epic poetry of the *Kalevala* can be divided into four strains. Myth poetry describes the creation of an ancient world at the dawn of time, a world in which animistic powers governed the human environment. It belongs to the oldest strain of Kalevala poetry, the arbitrary starting point of which comparative evidence sets at some two-and-a-half millennia ago. Its predominant characters are the "eternal sage" Väinämöinen and the smith Ilmarinen. The origins of the second type, magic and shaman poetry, can be dated from about the birth of Christ to AD 500–600. Besides female characters, the shamans Lemminkäinen and Joukahainen also now make their appearance. Adventure poetry dates from AD 600–1000, and reflects contacts of the Baltic-Finns with the East Vikings. The poems give notable prominence to male-female relationships, courtship, marriage ceremonies, and conflicts between female desire for a peaceful, stable, family-centred life and male desire for adventurous combat. Finally, there are poems of the Christian period (AD 900–1450), in which the arrival and establishment of Christianity have a profound effect. The lines chronicle the onset of the modern era when the ancient heroes will make way for a new one, a boy-child miraculously conceived by the virgin, Marjatta.

The particular structural and metrical form of Kalevala poetry is a distinctive feature of great antiquity. The unrhymed, non-strophic, trochaic tetrameter carries the name "Kalevala-metre." The prominent stylistic devices of the *Kalevala* are alliteration, parallelism, and repetitiveness, such as in the following example in translation:

> Then the Mother of the Waters,
> Water-Mother, maid aerial,
> From the waves her knee uplifted,
> Raised her shoulder from the billows,
> That the teal her nest might 'stablish,
> And might find a peaceful dwelling.
> Then the teal, the bird so beauteous,
> Hovered slow, and gazed around her,
> And she saw the knee uplifted
> From the blue waves of the ocean,
> And she thought she saw a hillock,
> Freshly green with springing verdure.
> There she flew, and hovered slowly,
> Gently on the knee alighting;
> And her nest she there established,
> And she laid her eggs all golden,
> Six gold eggs she laid within it,
> And a seventh she laid of iron.

Soon after its publication in 1849, the *Kalevala* was recognized as an epic of major significance, along with the *Iliad,* the *Poetic Edda,* and *Nibelungenlied.* In assembling the *Kalevala,* Lönnrot created a national mythology; hence the work compels the reader to view it against the background of the emerging Finnish nation-state. The *Kalevala* not only gives structure to the roots of Finnish national culture, but the work can be seen as evidence of the extent to which historically pre-literate art shapes a nation's self-perception and the high cultural expression of its later ages. In a wider context, and aside from its anthropological and historical connections, the *Kalevala* represents the epic as a genre of imaginative world literature which provides a rich source of aesthetic appreciation and varying approaches to literary criticism. Whether we read about the tragic lives of the girl Aino or the boy Kullervo; the adventures of Väinämöinen, Ilmarinen, and the gallant Lemminkäinen; the struggle between the land of Kaleva and Pohjola; or the interplay of pagan and Christian ideas and ideals, the *Kalevala*'s creative variants supply a wide range of interpretative possibilities, from the allegorical to the symbolic and historic. Appropriately its open ending, in the words of the eternal bard Väinämöinen, embodies what is central to *Kalevala*, its relevance to all ages:

> Here the course lies newly opened,
> Open for the greater singers,
> For the bards and ballad singers,
> For the young, who now are growing,
> For the rising generation.

(translations by William Forsell Kirby)

—Seija Paddon

KATUHA

See UPANISHADS

KAUSÚĪTAKĪ

See UPANISHADS

KENA

See UPANISHADS

THE KINGDOM OF THIS WORLD (El reino de este mundo)
Novel by Alejo Carpentier, 1949

In the now famous prologue to this novel, Alejo Carpentier introduced his term, ''lo real maravilloso'' (''marvellous reality'') as a concept that gives access to a deeper, more authentic understanding of Latin American reality. He criticizes the utterly trivialized images of European surrealism and turns to Latin America in search of a genuinely marvellous essence in its racial, geographical, and historical realities. Carpentier affirms that what is truly magical and mystical can be observed in the primitive vestiges of the New World: the opposition between civilization and barbarism is inverted by him to

elevate the authentic power and innocence of nature in opposition to alienated and degraded (European) culture. For Carpentier, surrealism exists in Latin America as a commonplace, everyday aspect of reality; the magical beliefs of primitive religions keep the real marvellous aspect of reality alive. In *The Kingdom of This World*, the author embodies this opposition between magical nature and decadent culture in the virility and vitality of the black slaves who, through their collective faith, always retain their essential links to nature, in contrast to the effeminate and impotent French landowners for whom ritual is an empty gesture.

The novel is set in Haiti during the period of the French Revolution. While it is based faithfully on a series of real historical incidents and figures, the plot is developed in a seemingly chaotic manner and appears to lack unity. In effect, the free flow of the fictionalized events corresponds to the image of history Carpentier wishes to project in this novel, a history whose order comes from a non-linear source. History can be understood as a series of cyclical repetitions: the fall of the French ruling élite in Haiti, the rise and fall of the black dictator Henri Christophe, and the rise at the end of the novel of a new mulatto ruling class (all these narrated from the perspective of a slave named Ti Noel) make it impossible for the reader to conclude that this tale ingenuously pits evil whites against virtuous blacks.

A runaway slave named Mackandal escapes to the mountains, where he builds up his magic powers and begins to send poisonous mushrooms back to the other slaves, who kill livestock and Frenchmen in order to prepare the way for a slave uprising. Mackandal acquires the power to metamorphose into an insect, an animal, or a bird, and his faithful followers believe him to be invulnerable. When he does return finally in human form, he is captured by the French and burned at the stake; the slaves are not at all agitated by the execution, as it is their belief that the African gods have saved him. A second rebellion 20 years later is crushed and followed by fierce repression. Eventually a former cook named Henri Christophe seizes power at the moment of the French Revolution. Christophe's tyrannical and grotesquely Europeanized dynasty, however, comes to resemble the one recently overthrown in France, and the new black dictator ruthlessly exploits his subjects even more harshly than the white settlers ever did, forcing them into an abominable and violent continuation of slavery.

The collapse of Christophe's dynasty occurs and Ti Noel, now an old man, observes the rise of the new mulatto ruling class, as anxious to dominate and exploit forced black labour as all of the leaders, both black and white, who preceded them. Ti Noel transforms himself into a series of creatures in an attempt to understand history and mankind: an ant, toiling endlessly and anonymously; a powerful stallion subject to enslavement at the hands of mankind; a goose, who attempts to enter the aristocratic order of the clan only to be shut out. The principle of society, Ti Noel discovers, appears to revolve around the eternal recurrence of oppression and exclusion; history repeats itself endlessly, mankind exploits mankind (even those from its own clan), but the old man continues to affirm that human greatness can be discovered in the agonistic and conflictive kingdom of this world. Ti Noel proclaims once more his declaration of war against the new ruling class, in the never-ending cycle of revolution and renovation. He dies at the end of the narrative *or* he is transformed into an old vulture: the final ambiguity reinforces Ti Noel's magical and mystical links to nature as well as his acceptance of the eternal cycle of birth, death, and transmutation.

—Susan Isabel Stein

KISS OF THE SPIDER WOMAN (El beso de la mujer araña)
Novel by Manuel Puig, 1976

Manuel Puig's fourth novel, published in Spain in 1976 and in English translation in 1979, deals with the polemical nature of the relationship between sexuality and revolutionary politics. The conflict between power and sex, and their functions in society, is embodied in the two protagonists, Valentín Arregui Paz and Luis Alberto Molina. The isolated setting of the novel, a prison cell, emphasizes the problem of language and communication between two individuals who experience different realities. Molina, a male homosexual who feels that he is a woman, colours his world with images of the silver screen of the 1930s and 1940s. Valentín, a heterosexual leftist, expresses himself in the rhetoric of Marxist ideology.

In order to fill the empty space between and around them, Molina narrates films to Valentín. The films become a form of metaphorical displacement for the two men—as they identify with or reject characters and actions in the films, they expose themselves to each other and to the reader. In addition to this major concern of interpersonal communication, there is a sub-plot of intrigue and possible betrayal which gives the flavour of a mystery story to the novel and also ties the two men to the larger social world outside the womb-like existence of the prison cell. The prison officials have offered Molina a lighter sentence in exchange for information about Valentín's political activities. Valentín, then, may be victimized by Molina. When Valentín asks Molina to risk his life to deliver a message to the revolutionaries, Molina is put in the position of potential victim. Thus, personal allegiances are pitted against larger social forces.

Puig's innovative narrative techniques are inextricably connected to the novel's theme of language and its social uses. Various types of discourse—dialogue, interior monologue, film and song texts, bureaucratic documents, footnotes, and letters—are presented without the traditional guiding voice and manipulative power of a third-person narrator. The reader must fill in the gaps, a process which reveals the reader's own preconceptions and ideological framework. How one feels about homosexuality and left-wing politics will determine in part how one judges the actions of the characters.

The novel begins with unattributed dialogue. No names are given, and there is no ''he/she said.'' One speaker is describing a woman, and the details of the description (clothing, colours, emotions) may lead the reader to believe a woman is speaking. The other speaker is oddly antagonistic, interrupting to question the details and objecting frequently. Only much later in the novel are the gender and the enforced cohabitation of the characters explained. This technique exposes the connections between interpreting language and interpreting gender.

Because the characters have trouble communicating with each other—the text is filled with the ellipses of unfinished sentences—Molina narrates films he has seen. These are standard Hollywood potboilers, with the addition of a Nazi propaganda film. Film narration, however, is different from film viewing. The plots may be familiar, but what the reader sees is Molina's and Valentín's identification with character. Molina becomes the heroine and Valentín the male love interest. With the Nazi film, however, Valentín's knowledge of history makes him refuse to participate, while Molina sees it as just another romantic love story. In all of the films there are outside social forces that defeat the lovers' relationship. The identification

process is also taking place at the level of the reader. Which character in this dialectic confrontation elicits the reader's sympathy? Readers also identify by gender and by ideology.

The footnotes present an unfamiliar interpretive problem in fiction. In them, Puig presents various historical and contemporary explanations of homosexuality in chronological order. Both famous and obscure experts are named, but the references are paraphrased and not in any standard format. Moreover, their authority is undermined by the inclusion of part of the Nazi film in footnote form. When the film switches from Molina's voice to footnote form, its hyperbolic fascist content becomes clearly evident. The discourses of the state and academe are both manipulative, and thus suspect.

The prison documents presented in the text are another manifestation of the language of power. The State's obsession with proper names, hierarchical titles, dates, times, and gender contrasts with the absence of all these features in the dialogue between the two men and with Molina's emotionally-charged recounting of the films. Language in these forms is divorced from an individual voice and assumes a mask of objectivity and authority. The documents also fulfil the plot function of portraying the effects of a malevolent exterior reality on the lives of the protagonists. The real confrontation is not between two men of different world-views, but between the individual and the state.

The themes and techniques in this novel make it almost a display text for current trends in literary theory. Puig's questioning of the assumptions of gender identity is also a concern of feminist theory. He shows that language is not a unified monolithic system, but rather a set of conventions particular to use or function. The novel is self-deconstructive in its various discourses. Reader-response theorists can experience a step-by-step manifestation of the process of reading in the beginning of the novel. And finally, Puig exposes the weak links in both psychoanalytic and Marxist theory: Marxism's lack of a theory of the individual and Freud's inadequate explanation of both the female and the homosexual.

—Barbara P. Fulks

THE KREUTZER SONATA (Kreitserova sonata)
Novella by Lev Tolstoi, 1891

One of the embittered fruits of Lev Tolstoi's old age, *The Kreutzer Sonata* is a powerful but unbalanced work that created a sensation when it first appeared on account of its outspoken statements on sexuality and jealousy. Sometimes seen nowadays as marking Tolstoi's approach towards feminist positions, the story is more often interpreted as a violent and twisted, very personal outpouring of guilt and anguish.

Rewritten five times over a period of many years, *The Kreutzer Sonata* had circulated extensively in typed and handwritten copies before it was first published, as a result of which Tolstoi was able to print an Afterword with it, in which he attempted to explain further some of his ideas. As early as the late 1860s he had begun but not completed a story to be called ''The Uxoricide,'' but it was much later, in June 1887, that his interest was aroused by a story told him by an artist friend of a travelling companion who had murdered his wife. A first draft of the story was made in that year, although as yet the theme of music was absent, for the lover was a painter rather than a musician. A particularly strong stimulus, however, came in March

1888 when Tolstoi attended a performance of Beethoven's Kreutzer sonata, played by his son Sergei with the violinist Liasota. The experience made a profound impression on the 60-year-old writer who, though not very musical himself (he describes the music inaccurately in the story), perceived clearly the great intimacy implied in a musical partnership. Later, in *What Is Art?* (1898), he was to take a strictly functional view of music and other arts, acknowledging, for instance, only utilitarian music—a march to make soldiers more resolute or a lullaby to help a baby to sleep; all other music he regarded as simply stimulation of feelings and emotions to no good purpose, and, indeed, possibly to sexual arousal which, for Tolstoi at this time, racked with guilt as he was over his ruined marriage and frequent extra-marital escapades, could only be harmful, signifying degradation, exploitation, and corruption.

The story is set in a railway carriage and falls into two badly linked halves, with an Afterword that bears little relation to the story. In the first half, a carriage full of people discuss various sexual topics, including the desirability of total chastity and the merits of free love, all presented by Tolstoi as aspects of degeneracy and hypocrisy. The atmosphere is forced, much of it little more than a one-sided didactic tirade, and it is notable that Tolstoi is particularly harsh in his portrayal of the "modern" woman who participates in the discussion. Eventually the majority of the passengers leave the carriage, and the narrator is addressed by a passenger who has hitherto remained silent. After a somewhat forced transition this Pozdnyshev becomes the narrator of the second half, and the story he tells of jealousy and murder occupies the remainder of the story. Increasingly affronted by the supposed intimacy of his wife and a musician who partners her in Beethoven's sonata, he detects in this (stylish, classical, hardly erotic) music evidence of a sexual liaison, and, in a fit of uncontrollable jealousy, plunges a knife through his wife's corset in one of the most graphic descriptions of murder ever written. Tolstoi's message (and none of his later stories lacks a strong moral lesson) is that physical, sexual love destroys the true human bonds of friendship and understanding (even though Pozdnyshev never knows for certain the nature of his wife's relations with the musician). It is only when she lies battered and dying that the tormented husband recognizes in his wife a human being and not just an object of jealousy.

Although total sexual abstinence is advocated in *The Kreutzer Sonata* it is plain that the main theme is jealousy, a central and very personal concern of Tolstoi's old age; hardly less so are the themes of hypocrisy and death, and the railway context acts as a harmful heightener of emotions, familiar from *Anna Karenina*. In the unmistakable Freudian symbolism of murder as sex, when Pozdnyshev's knife penetrates his wife's corset, Tolstoi is proclaiming the stark message that sex is not merely a degrading, violent act, but even a form of murder. His own lack of abstinence and even fidelity are well known, and these together with the fierce jealousy he felt concerning his wife Sof'ia, help to explain the passion that informs this somewhat clumsy narrative and makes it so gripping. It is notable that Countess Tolstoi, after reading the story, commented, "What a clear link connects Lev's old diaries with his 'Kreutzer Sonata'."

An inflammatory and daringly outspoken work in its time, Tolstoi's story, always embarrassingly extreme even to his contemporary disciples, is now not only clumsy and unbalanced, but also dated. It shows nothing of the breadth of vision or brilliant characterization of his major novels. As a historical curiosity, however, it retains much of

its passion and tells us a great deal about the miserable last years of one of the world's great writers.

—Arnold McMillin

KRISTIN LAVRANSDATTER
Novels by Sigrid Undset, 1920–22

In the autumn of 1919, Sigrid Undset was 37 years old. Her marriage had disintegrated. She had just moved to a house in Lillehammer. In her care were her three young children, the oldest of whom was six, the middle one mentally handicapped, and the youngest a baby a couple of months old. Caring for them was taking up most of her time. During quieter hours, her new novel was "trickling gently through her mind, the images glowing and shining," but when she sat down to write, her head seemed filled with "sand and stagnant water." But write she did. Every night, when the house was quiet, she sat down with black coffee and cigarettes, and wrote until the early hours of the morning. These were her circumstances during the period she was working on her great medieval masterpiece, the trilogy *Kristin Lavransdatter*.

When *Kransen* (*The Garland*), the first book of the trilogy, was published in the autumn of 1920 it became a resounding success throughout Scandinavia. The second volume, *Husfrue* (*The Mistress of Husaby*), was published in the autumn of 1921, and the autumn of 1922 saw the publication of the last volume, *Korset* (*The Cross*). The trilogy is set in the first part of the 14th century and includes a realistic description of the Black Death, which, according to Icelandic annals, wiped out two-thirds of the Norwegian population.

Why was *Kristin Lavransdatter* such a success? Probably because with its many facets it offers most people some point of identification. The novel has a host of interesting characters, as well as universal themes. There is the strong protagonist (the eponymous Kristin) set against the strict conventions of her time. There is Kristin's conflict between her love and loyalty towards her wise and caring parents and her love for the handsome but unsuitable Erlend Nikulausson. There is Kristin's relationship with the Catholic Church and the old and kindly monk Brother Edvin. Her parents are deeply religious, and Kristin is drawn to the Church, but her all-consuming love for Erlend is an obstacle; hence, there is a conflict between heavenly and earthly powers: Kristin wants to marry the disreputable Erlend *with* the blessing of her parents and God.

After constant pressure from Kristin her father agrees unwillingly to her marriage. But by marrying Erlend Kristin wins the disapproval of her father and the Church as well as society. Her father seems broken. She learns that happiness built on other people's unhappiness is incomplete.

During the trilogy the protagonist experiences murder, suicide, death of a sister, death of a child, the imprisonment and torture of her husband, jealousy, character assassination, and of course the Black Death.

Although it depicts a woman who rebels against convention and whose life is far from bleak, *Kristin Lavransdatter* is not a feminist work in the modern sense of the word. Kristin brings much of her misfortune onto herself by refusing to conform and insisting on marriage. The setting may be that of the 14th century, but the pressure to conform was nearly as strong in the 1920s.

From her father, the famous archaeologist Ingvald Undset, Sigrid had inherited a scientific approach and knew that it was important to know one's background material. Her father had also given her a love for and familiarity with the Middle Ages. As she explained about her view of the past:

I think the reason I understand my own time so well is because from my earliest childhood I've always had a sort of living memory of an earlier age with which to compare it. The style is not a hardened copy of a mental life that is dead and gone. If one strips away the layer of concepts and things that are characteristic of one's own time, one enters directly into the Middle Ages and sees it from that viewpoint. It coincides with one's own.

—Margrethe Alexandroni

L

THE LADY WITH A DOG (Dam s sobachkoi)
Story by Anton Chekhov, 1899

Vladimir Nabokov considered "The Lady with a Dog," which Anton Chekhov wrote in 1899, "one of the greatest stories ever written." Throughout the 20th century, critics have hailed it as a masterpiece, and it has influenced several generations of writers, particularly in England and America. Moreover, Joyce Carol Oates has even reworked the story and given it an American setting in her version, "The Lady with a Toy Dog."

Chekhov began work on "The Lady with a Dog" in August or September of 1899, and published it in the December 1899 issue of a major journal of the day, *Russkaia mysl'* [Russian Thought]. He later made some revisions to the story for the edition of his collected works that appeared in 1903.

Like most of Chekhov's works, the story has a simple plot. Dmitrii Dmitrich Gurov, who is vacationing in the resort town of Yalta on the Black Sea, meets a woman, Anna Sergeevna von Dideritz. They have a love affair, after which he returns to his wife and children in Moscow, believing that they have had only a brief encounter. However, he finds that he cannot forget Anna, and seeks her out in the provincial town of S. (usually considered to be Saratov), where she lives. He astonishes her by appearing without warning in a theatre, and she promises to come to Moscow to see him. When they renew their affair in Moscow, they realize that they truly love each other. "And it was clear to both that it was a long way to the end, and that the most complicated and difficult part was only beginning."

"The Lady with a Dog" provides a good example of the way Chekhov often acknowledged the masterpieces of the past, while simultaneously reacting against them. In "The Lady with a Dog" he is reacting against the treatments of the theme of adultery in Flaubert's *Madame Bovary* and Tolstoi's *Anna Karenina*. In both novels, the heroine is a married woman who has an affair, and commits suicide as a result. In Chekhov's story, however, the married woman who has an affair finds true love. Chekhov was also reacting against the portrayals of love in popular fiction which, in his day as in ours, tended to equate love with happiness. Thus, Anna neither commits suicide nor finds lasting happiness.

The story has a similar relationship to Impressionist painting. The story begins in the summer, at a resort, which was a setting that the Impressionists often depicted. In fact, the artist Konstantin Korovin, a good friend of Chekhov's, painted an Impressionist work, *Cafe in Yalta* (1905), which the story probably inspired. Just as the Impressionists often used arbitrary, asymmetrical framing in their pictures, Chekhov used open endings in his stories and plays, which rarely come to a clear resolution. However, Chekhov reacted against Impressionist painting by emphasizing psychological development, as Monet and Renoir rarely did.

The principal psychological interest in "The Lady with a Dog" lies in Gurov's development. At the beginning of the story, he has a cynical attitude towards women, to whom he refers as a "lower race." After he and Anna go to bed together for the first time, she wants reassurance that he still respects her. He cannot respond to her need, however, and merely eats a slice of watermelon. But when he returns to Moscow, and finds that he cannot forget her, he attempts to tell a dinner companion about her. "If you knew what an enchanting woman I met in Yalta," he says. But his friend can only reply, "You were right: the turbot was a bit off." When his friend cannot respond to him, as he could not respond to Anna, he begins to understand what she experienced. As his capacity for empathy increases, his capacity for love and self-awareness increase as well. Chekhov signals this change when he and Anna are in a hotel room in Moscow at the end of the story, and he looks in the mirror. He notices that his hair has turned grey; "And only now, when his head had turned grey, did he fall in love, as one ought to, really—for the first time in his life." It is one of the great moments in modern literature.

"The Lady with a Dog" shows Chekhov at the height of his powers. The story's subtlety, its masterful understatement, and interplay of character and environment place it among the masterpieces of modern short fiction.

—Jim Curtis

LANCELOT
Poem by Chrétien de Troyes, c. 1170–80

Lancelot, also known as *The Knight of the Cart*, is Chrétien de Troyes' third Arthurian romance. Its inspiration can be found in the Celtic abduction tale, in which a maid or maiden is captured, a knight sets out to rescue her and must undergo many trials, and they are brought together through his prowess. In this case, the maid is Guinevere, wife of King Arthur, and the brave knight is Lancelot, champion of the Round Table.

The poem—7,112 lines of rhymed couplets—follows the structure of its Celtic model, but elaborates on it with its multiple adventures and tales of knightly prowess and chivalric acts. Through this elaboration, we see Lancelot compared to Gawain, another favourite of Arthur's court. Lancelot consistently appears as the better of the two, and thus proves his worthiness as Guinevere's lover.

Chrétien de Troyes dedicates the poem to his patroness, Marie de Champagne, declaring that she provided him with the *matière* and the *sen:* the subject matter and the meaning. Chrétien de Troyes states simply that "he undertakes to shape the work, adding little except his effort and his careful attention." Curiously enough, he did not finish the tale himself, but left it to his clerk, Godefroi de Lagny, to conclude. Godefroi states unequivocally that he followed Chrétien de Troyes's directions in doing so, and added nothing of his own.

As the poem opens, an unknown knight rides into Arthur's court and informs those gathered there that he is holding many of its subjects captive in his own land. He then challenges Arthur to release Guinevere to him as the prize for a tournament. Kay insists on being her escort, but is swiftly defeated by the stranger once they are outside Camelot. Gawain, who is in pursuit, meets with Lancelot, who, travelling incognito, is also after Guinevere and her captor. Both knights continue on, Lancelot always surpassing Gawain in his deeds. He commits his one error when he hesitates before boarding a cart, which is a test of his humility and love. He successfully copes with other tests, such as a flaming lance and a perilous bed. As the knights travel along, they meet a number of maidens, one of whom informs them that Guinevere's kidnapper is Meleagant, son of Bademagu, the king of Goirre. In another adventure, Lancelot visits a cemetery in which the gravestones are reserved for the future dead. He lifts the heavy stone on a tomb reserved for himself, which proves his role as the messiah-figure who will free the imprisoned subjects in Meleagant's land. This land is bounded by water, which can be crossed by means of a Sword Bridge or an Underwater Bridge. Gawain opts for the Underwater Bridge, the easier of the two, leaving the Sword Bridge for Lancelot. Lancelot's love for Guinevere helps him to forget the pain as he crosses the bridge with bare feet and hands. Later he is obliged to rescue Gawain, who is having difficulties with his crossing. Lancelot fights with Meleagant and betters him, although Meleagant will not admit defeat and imprisons Lancelot after catching him in bed with Guinevere. Lancelot is eventually released from his prison by Meleagant's sister, and battles with Meleagant once again, this time killing him. Thus, the freedom of the captives is ensured.

One of the most striking additions to this abduction tale is Chrétien de Troyes's concern with the psychology of his characters. Lancelot's love for Guinevere is displayed by his complete absorption in thoughts of her. By concentrating on her, he can overcome the pain of his injuries, and the mere sight of her renews his energy in his first tournament with Meleagant. However, she tests his psyche even more completely when she spurns him at her rescue because of his hesitation at the cart. The following scene, in which both of them react to rumours of the other's death, allows us to glimpse into both of their minds. By portraying both the external and the internal trials of his protagonist, Chrétien de Troyes creates a fully-rounded character who is both active and contemplative.

This poem, the earliest surviving tale of Lancelot, portrays the love affair that supplanted that of Mordred and Guinevere as the factor that brings about the fall of the Round Table in Arthurian legend. It was incorporated into the French Vulgate cycle of the 13th century, and developed further in the *Queste del Saint Graal* (*Quest for the Holy Grail*). Malory drew from this tradition when he wrote the *Morte d'Arthur*, and the love of Lancelot and Guinevere is still the focus of many writers of Arthurian works in the 20th century.

—Lisa M. Ruch

THE LAST POEMS (Les Derniers Vers)
Poems by Jules Laforgue, published separately, 1886 and 1890

The Last Poems, published three years after Jules Laforgue's early death from tuberculosis, comprises 12 poems, which originally appeared in 1886 (except for XII, posthumously published in 1888), mainly in the experimental periodical *La Vogue*. The question of coherence in the collection has been much debated. Some critics argue a perceptible linear progression, others stress the absence of authorial imprimatur and treat the individual poems as discrete units, while nevertheless recognizing their mutually reinforcing similarities of theme, imagery, and technique and the unifying perspective of a first person narrative voice, poised precariously between lyricism and irony.

The poems, focused on the twin themes of love and personal identity, revolve around the "blocus sentimental" ("sentimental blockade") evoked in typically punning fashion (cf. the "blocus

continental," the continental blockade or Continental System, planned by Napoleon against England) in the opening words of the collection. The poet/protagonist, torn between the opposing 19th-century philosophies of idealism and positivism, continues to yearn for an absolute spiritual love even while despairingly convinced of love's all too earthy nature as physical sensation. His unhappiness is projected onto a fiancée, who figures in the poems not in her own right but as the poet's frustrations made manifest. Ardently desired, she is also doubly reviled, paradoxically condemned both as an unthinking creature of natural instinct, an affront to the poet's idealizing dreams, and as a body and mind hidebound by bourgeois codes of morality and naively and ignorantly resistant to his erotic desires.

These themes of inadequacy and disenchantment are of course far from original. The view of woman proposed in *The Last Poems* has obvious affinities with Baudelaire's *Les Fleurs du mal* (*The Flowers of Evil*). Meanwhile Laforgue's poetic persona, "pauvre, pâle piètre individu" ("poor, pale, paltry individual"), is the direct descendant of the central figure in Sainte-Beuve's *Vie, poésies et pensées de Joseph Delorme* (1829), the first expression in French poetry of the inverse of Romantic lionization of the individual. Where Laforgue breaks new ground is in the mixture of irony and seriousness that suspends those themes in an unresolved tension between tragic despair and comic detachment. Pain is both agonizingly immediate and skilfully distanced through a series of masks, notably that of Hamlet, too undecided a figure even to make his way explicitly into the body of the text, but pervasively and subliminally present through epigraphic quotation at the beginning of the collection and again before the final poem. His luckless partner is Ophelia, Antigone, or Philomela, or, in a characteristic switch of register, Little Red Riding Hood, venturing forth, alone and unprotected. But, executioner as much as victim, she is also the prim young "miss" in her Sunday best, demurely engrossed in her prayer book or her mechanical piano scales, an Emma Rouault lying in wait for a gullible Bovary whom she will betray with the first silver-tongued fly-by-night who chances along.

The problematizing of Romantic stereotypes is also evident in the modernization of the symbolic landscapes of Romantic melancholy. The inevitable falling leaves of autumn mix with the swirling rubbish of old theatre bills in city streets; grey drizzle or lashing rain shroud factory chimneys; the bitter wind wails through rusted telegraph wires that stretch endlessly along desolate highways. Similarly the conventional imagery of sunset is transformed by a starkly realistic vocabulary of illness and death. The sun, like "a gland torn from a neck" agonizes, "white as a drunkard's spittle," on a gorse-covered hillside. The failure of its fruitful light is tied both to a failure of sexuality and ultimately to a more general failure of physical vitality manifest in the anaemic aspect of the poet and his fiancée and the tubercular cough that punctuates their forlorn attempts at communication. Meanwhile the winding of the hunting horn echoes through the collection, its traditional suggestion of loss and aspiration serving simultaneously as a mocking reminder of the emptiness of sentimental dreams.

Versification reinforces the contradictory and complementary impulses of lyricism and irony. *The Last Poems* is the first collection of French poetry entirely in modern free verse. Laforgue's translations of Walt Whitman's *Leaves of Grass*, general contemporary interest in Wagner and Impressionist art, and the prosodic debate in which Laforgue participated along with Gustave Kahn and the rest of the *Vogue* circle, all combine to facilitate a brilliant fusion of form and theme where the swings of psychological mood achieve tangible expression in the flexibility of prosodic structure. Strophic arrangements are endlessly variable, moulding themselves to the syntactic patterns of interior monologue; metre, following oral inflexion, moves from a fixed syllabic count to a more elastic system based on tonic accents. Rhyme disregards traditional rules of gender and number, sometimes disappearing altogether. Nevertheless Laforgue remains close enough to conventional procedures to allow ironic appreciation of deviation from them. Popular language conceals literary quotation, for example the reduction of Lamartine's high-flown ''L'homme n'a point de port, le temps n'a point de rives'' (''Man hath no port, time hath no shores'') to the laconically colloquial ''Y a pas de port'' (VII, 31). Metre plays with diaeresis and synaeresis to perturb anticipated rhythmic patterns but retains the basic syllabic groupings underlying traditional verse. Rhyme displays sufficient orthodoxy to highlight subversive aberration. Laforgue thus achieves a versification that aptly mimics the uncertainties of a self defined by its deficiencies and caught in an endless circle of stop-gap compromises.

The Last Poems, except in a literal sense, is a misnomer, since the poems it contains were seen by Laforgue himself, particularly in the technical area, as a new initiative. Psychologically too they suggest perhaps an advance. Love may be possible as ''humains échanges,'' a communion between two similarly finite beings that transcends sexual misunderstanding; the protagonist may find the maturity to confront his psychological inadequacies; above all, as in VII, ''Moonlight Solo,'' his poetry may liberate him finally to dance, light and carefree, above the grey disappointments of life, Hamlet no longer but Ariel.

—Rachel Killick

THE LAST TEMPTATION (O Telefteos Pirasmos)
Novel by Nikos Kazantzakis, 1955

Nikos Kazantzakis's *The Last Temptation* attempts what no other work of fiction has attempted—to rewrite the New Testament in the form of a novel from the point of view of Christ. To the accounts given in the Scriptures Kazantzakis adds the post-modern device of the double ending—the ''last temptation'' of an alternative destiny for the Messiah as a comfortable family man.

The problems inherent in such a work are considerable: the impossibility of expressing the psychological inner life of a divinity as the novel form demands, and the necessity of creating dialogue worthy of God. The problems for the author, however, are matched by the difficulties for the reader. Kazantzakis's narrative is continually compromised by the ''authorized version'' of the material it would make its own: a weighty problem of intertextuality. In scenes such as the wedding in Magdala (chapter 15) where Kazantzakis inventively contextualizes the parable of the foolish virgins, the author seems to add to his overshadowing source. Elsewhere, however, he seeks to question the notion of holy writ. His novel provocatively explores the contradictions involved in enclosing divine truth within the written word, thereby opening a space for speculation and creativity in which his own work may have validity. Thus we see Jesus angrily rejecting as lies the stories Matthew, the evangelist, has written about him.

When, however, Matthew replies that he has been compelled by an angel to write what is untrue, Jesus ponders the existence of different layers of truth: ''If this was the highest level of truth, inhabited only by God. . . ? If what we called truth, God called lies. . . ?'' Later, Paul openly proclaims his willingness to propagate falsehood, if it is necessary to save mankind: ''Whatever gives wings to man . . . that is true.''

The level of truth inhabited by Kazantzakis is, as he tells the reader in the prologue, one of confession. The novel is a dramatization, through a fictional Christ, of his own religious struggles. Hence the ''Holy Land'' of the novel is in fact the world of Kazantzakis's own psyche. The hallmark of this inner world is its obsessive fascination with the body. The early chapters in particular are dominated by descriptions of blood, heat, and pain. This emphasis on the physical is only further stressed by the author's use of demotic Greek, which renders the abstract in terms of the concrete, the metaphorical as the literal.

Kazantzakis seeks to establish the reality of his action by anchoring it to the senses. Jesus plunges himself into this world of the senses with the mortification of his flesh. The same language of sweat and wounds is used to describe his beloved, the prostitute Mary Magdalene.

Equally characteristic of the author's vision is the profusion in ancient Palestine of giants, dwarves, and deformed cripples. It is typical of Kazantzakis that when two monks espy Jesus emerging from the desert, one is an elephant-like man with a mouth like a shark, the other a hunchback who drags an enormous backside.

As these grotesqueries indicate, Kazantzakis's confessional novel has little interest in historical realism: inaccuracy and anachronism abound. Rather the tale draws on other sources—those of traditions of folktale and rural religious art. Signs of this are everywhere. The narrow cast of characters and the lack of any coherent geography shrinks the Holy Land to the dimensions of a village. Comic tales of wily trickery hark back to rustic fables, such as that of Simon the Cyrenian obtaining a larger share of the lamb's head supper by reminding the disciples of John the Baptist's beheading. Through all these devices Kazantzakis's Messiah is memorable but profoundly human: not so much divine as embarked on a Nietzschean struggle to attain divinity, that struggle referred to in the prologue as the battle between the flesh and the spirit. As this struggle is an evolutionary one, the book presents not one Christ but a developing sequence of different Christs: the madman possessed by God, the holy fool, the loving simpleton, the fiery prophet, and, finally, the sensible, and sensual, worldly man.

It is, however, this last version of Christ that remains in the imagination. The novelist must always be more convincing when speaking of human desire than when attempting to create the divine. The Jesus of the book's final section, who achieves his long-desired consummation with Mary Magdalene, is inevitably more appealing than the Christ who voluntarily chooses the agonies of crucifixion. This section is, further, as the title suggests, the creative *tour-de-force* of the novel. It alone has the originative value of myth, rather than the frisson of novel reinterpretation. The mythos it offers—of Christ saved from his destiny—has some value. Jesus, after all, only does the reasonable thing. Here, arguably, is the true reason why the book has been blacklisted by the Vatican. The last temptation, declined by Jesus but likely to be accepted by the reader, is too hard to resist.

—Edmund Cusick

LAZARILLO DE TORMES

Anonymous 16th-century Spanish novel; the first of the picaresque genre. Earliest extant editions date from 1554, although there may have been a 1553 edition which is no longer in existence. Popular throughout Spain, but disliked by the authorities because of its satirical content; banned by the Inquisition, 1559; Philip II ordered that offensive material be removed. Authorship is uncertain: in 1605, it was attributed to Fray Juan de Ortega; by 1607, it was thought that Diego Hurtado de Mendoza (1503–75), the Spanish poet and historian, and son of a governor of Granada, may have been responsible. More recently, other authors have been suggested, including: Sebastián de Horozco, c. 1510–80 (one of his works features a character called Lazarillo); the Valdés brothers, Alfonso (c. 1490–1532) and Juan (c. 1491–1541), writers of prose and dialogues; Cristóbal de Villalón, c. 1505–58 (or possibly a pseudonym for several writers of the mid-16th century). There have been several attempts at sequels or copies; these are usually by inferior writers and fail to capture the flavour of the original, including: *La segunda parte de Lazarillo de Tormes* (1555); *El Lazarillo de Manzanares*, by Juan Cortés de Tolosa (1620); *Segunda parte*, by Juan de Luna (1620); and *The Life and Death of Young Lazarillo* (1685).

PUBLICATIONS

La vida de Lazarillo de Tormes y de sus fortunas y adversidades. 1553/54; edited by R.O. Jones, 1963; also edited by A. Blecua, 1974, and Antonio Rey Hazas, 1984; as *The Pleasant History of Lazarillo de Tormes*, translated by David Rowland, 1586, many subsequent reprints; also translated by William Hazlitt, 1851; Michael Alpert, in *Two Spanish Picaresque Novels*, 1969; as *The Life and Adventures of Lazarillo de Tormes*, translated by Thomas Roscoe, with a translation of Alemán's *Guzmán de Alfarache*, 1880; as *The Life of Lazarillo de Tormes*, translated by Clements Markham, 1908; as *The Life of Lazarillo de Tormes, His Fortunes and Adversities*, translated by Louis How, 1917; also translated by J. Gerald Markley, 1954; Harriet de Onís, 1959; as *Lazarillo de Tormes: His Life, Fortunes, Misadventures*, translated by Mariano J. Lorente, 1924; as *Blind Man's Boy*, translated by J.M. Cohen, 1962; *Lazarillo de Tormes*, translated by Fernando Fernán Gómez, 1994; *Lazarillo de Tormes*, adapted by Marcel C. Andrade, 2000; as *Lazarillo de Tormes*, edited by Roberto L. Fiore, 2000; as *Lazarillo de Tormes*, edited and translated by Stanley Appelbaum, 2001.

*

Critical Studies: ''Literary and Artistic Unity in 'Lazarillo de Tormes''' by F.C. Tarr, in *Publications of the Modern Languages Association of America*, 42, 1927; ''Sebastián de Horozco y el 'Lazarillo de Tormes''' by F. Márquez Villanueva, in *Revista de Filología Española*, 41, 1957; ''The Death of Lazarillo de Tormes'' by S. Gilman, in *Publications of the Modern Languages Association of America*, 81, 1966; *Introducción al ''Lazarillo de Tormes''* by José F. Gatti, 1968; *La novela picaresca y el punto de vista* by Francisco Rico, 1970; ''On Re-reading the 'Lazarillo de Tormes''' by D.W. Lomax, in *Studio ibérica*, 1973; *Lazarillo de Tormes: A Critical Guide* by Alan David Deyermond, 1975; *Ediciones y traducciones inglesas del Lazarillo de Tormes, 1568–1977* by Julio-César Santoyo, 1978; *Language and Society in ''La vida de Lazarillo de Tormes''* by

Harry Sieber, 1978; *The Spanish Picaresque Novel* by P.N. Dunn, 1979; *Lazarillo de Tormes* by Robert L. Fiore, 1984; *Problemas del Lazarillo* by Francisco Rico, 1988; *El borrador del Lazarillo: Texto íntegro* by Joaquín Aguirre Bellver, 1994; *Play and the Picaresque: Lazarillo de Tormes, Libro de Manuel, and Match Ball* by Gordana Yovanovich, 1999; *Las dos caras del Lazarillo: Texto y mensaje* by Aldo Ruffinatto, 2000.

*   *   *

The earliest known editions of the anonymous Spanish novel *Lazarillo de Tormes* date from 1554, although some scholars believe that an earlier text may have been lost. A short work of no more than 20,000 words, its authorship remains unclear, but a number of critics believe the most convincing candidate to be the prolific writer and humanist Diego Hurtado de Mendoza. As well as enjoying great success in Spain, the book was translated widely throughout Europe in the second half of the 16th century (the first English translation was in 1586) and it quickly proved highly influential. With the benefits of hindsight, it takes on great historical importance by being the first of the genre of tales known as picaresque novels, a group including Mateo Alemán's *Guzmán de Alfarache*, 1599, and Francisco de Quevedo's *El Buscón* [The Rogue], 1626, and many subsequent adaptations.

In explicit opposition to the contemporary chivalric or idealized romance, as represented by *Amadís de Gaul* and as satirized in Cervantes's *Don Quixote*, the picaresque novel deals exclusively with first-person testimonies from low-life characters placed in the most difficult circumstances. The central figure, the *pícaro*, or rascal, travels through a hostile environment, learning quickly that he (or occasionally she) has to survive by his own efforts, principally by his ingenuity in outwitting others. Without undue self-examination or recrimination, the *pícaro* recounts his adventures with unapologetic frankness and a racy taste for bawdy episodes. Where the chivalric tale is sacred, the picaresque is profane; where the romance idealizes, the picaresque strives after harsh realism in its depictions of money, sex, and food. The eventual aim of these narratives is to combine elements of contemporary social satire with a more general stripping away of illusions about human dignity.

Initiating what were to become the literary conventions of the picaresque novel, *Lazarillo de Tormes* involves a catalogue of pranks and tricks played by the *pícaro*, carried out initially in retaliation for his own mistreatment, but later taking on a momentum of their own. The cumulative effect is to present a highly unflattering cynical picture of a volatile society in which the cravings for money and the operations of desire are only barely concealed, and in which competition and rivalry are of much greater importance than collaboration or friendship. Chronicling its hero's mishaps and triumphs, *Lazarillo* acts as an ironic revelation of the material, unsentimental features of contemporary society, as they appear to the knowing eye of the trickster, who harbours no illusions. The unpredictability of life is typically made prominent at the opening of this narrative, when the young Lázaro, born on the river Tormes near Salamanca, loses his father immediately. In less than a page, his mother fails foul of the law and becomes destitute, unable to provide for her son. She entrusts the young Lázaro to the care of a blind beggar, whose gratuitous cruelty and unsparing treatment instruct him very quickly in the harsh realities of life. After suffering severe physical abuse, Lázaro turns the tables on his teacher, and runs off to start his solitary and peripatetic existence in earnest.

As he is successively taken up by a priest, a seller of Papal indulgences, a tambourine-painter, a down-at-heel gentleman, a constable, and other representatives of contemporary Spanish society, the unprotected Lázaro comes to realize that there can be no room in his life for indulgence or mercy, and that only guile will save him. If he seems naive, he will be exploited, but if he seems quick-witted, no one will employ him. So Lázaro has to pretend to be more simple-minded than he is, confiding his real motives and ambitions only to the reader. If there is a common point of reference to which this diffuse text returns, it is in its insistent anti-clericalism—the book was banned by the Inquisition in 1559—but the satire on hypocrisy and self-deception is generalized, and none of the figures from any walk of life emerges with dignity.

As he breaks off his account of his inglorious career so far, Lázaro has become a town-crier. Ironically, part of his job involves shouting out the crimes of malefactors as they are taken to be punished. In private, he tells us of his own misdeeds, whereas in public he publicizes those of others less fortunate. He has also married, unhappily, but neither the steady job nor the more settled domestic life has provided security, and as Lázaro makes his farewell, he knows that the wheel of fortune may turn for him again at any time. So, like other picaresque novels to come, *Lazarillo de Tormes* offers glimpses of an unstable and violent world, where everyone has to look after themselves, and where there can be no confidence in any of the protective institutions of society. Life seems without obvious meaning or pattern, and there is little sense that these injustices will be rectified in the hereafter. The picture of contemporary Spain Lázaro paints is a disquietingly unheroic one, but the darkness of the vision is balanced by the raciness and energy of the descriptions, and in its willingness to describe life ''from below.'' *Lazarillo* is one of the most important precursors of realist literature in Europe, influencing writers like Lesage in France, Grimmelshausen in Germany, and Smollett in Britain.

—Ian A. Bell

LÉLIA
Novel by George Sand, 1833

This lyrical, symbolic, and enigmatic novel provoked strong reactions when it was published in 1833, largely because it features the subjective outpourings of woman who is incapable of finding fulfilment in her relationships with men. Analogies were (and still are) made with George Sand's own varied and rather public love life, a response exacerbated by her remark to her friend, the critic Sainte-Beuve, that ''I am utterly and completely Lélia.''

Lélia is not merely a novel about frigidity however, but a gloss on the immensity of human desire, emotional, sexual, and spiritual, and the impoverishment of the reality with which the individual is confronted. The anguished conflict about sexual fulfilment is just part of what Dostoevskii called Sand's ''immense ethical quest.'' Sand herself referred to it as a ''work of anger,'' which brought her to ''the depths of scepticism,'' and she produced a revised version in 1839 that omitted some of the more flagrantly outspoken passages, changed the ending, and forgrounded a more optimistic picture of religious faith.

Essentially a novel of emotions, *Lélia* consists of loosely linked episodes of often violent, melodramatic action interspersed with passages which, though superficially giving the impression of an exchange of letters, are deeply subjective and declamatory monologues, more akin to operatic arias, in which the characters explain themselves to one another. There is no clear exposition of setting in time or place: the overall effect, however, is of a highly dramatized and remote world of extremes of luxuriance and depravity in, perhaps, the late Middle Ages or the Renaissance. The novel, in fact, manifests many of the elements of full-blown Romanticism: the cultivation of the emotions, the preoccupation with the individual and the exaltation of personal suffering, a responsiveness to nature, revolt against social and religious conventions, and a longing for the absolute, as well as an authorial penchant for vivid, melodramatic description.

With Lélia, the beautiful, brilliant, desired, and tortured protagonist, Sand constructs the typical Romantic hero as a woman. Her unassuaged longing, cold pride, sense of estrangement and alienation, almost obsessive introspection, and alternating rebelliousness, despair, and scepticism are characteristic of the Romantic *mal du siècle* (''sickness of the age''). Her profuse doubts, her anguished questionings about the nature of God and of human relationships are intensified by her preoccupation with the nature of woman and her place in a society that imposes artificially defined roles on her. The duality of spiritual and sensual love is epitomized in the alternative images of the religious recluse and the courtesan.

For the most part, Lélia is seen through the eyes of the men who aspire to be her lovers—Sténio, the young, possessive, and emotionally fragile poet, and Magnus, the priest whose religious vows are besieged by confusion and lust—and hence as an object of male desire. Physical description of her is minimal: the emphasis on her long, flowing hair (a cliché of femininity but in its massy darkness suggestive of dangerous power and fatality), her cold, pale brow and hands and her dark, brooding eyes, suggesting intellectual and spiritual strength, evokes in the reader the same sense of mystery and fascination she exerts over others in the text. Repeatedly, she is seen as a ''statue,'' ''dream,'' or ''shadow,'' or as possessed by demons, by the men who deem her an ''incomplete woman'' because of her apparent lack of sexual responsiveness as they understand it. Her very unobtainability, evoked in images of marble, ice, and water, inspires Sténio and Magnus to excesses in thought, word, and deed, the former eventually drowning himself for love of her, and the latter, in the final pages, choking the life out of her in a frenzy of despair. A more shadowy male companion and confidant is Trenmor, a world-weary stoic who has paid for a life of gambling by five years in prison and now, repentant, without plans or personal desires, views the suffering of his fellows with compassion and humility, offering advice and support where he can.

Lélia is contrasted with her courtesan sister, Pulchérie, who is warm, sensual, and totally devoted to a life of hedonism, in a literary ''doubling'' common in Sand's works. In a scene of intimate confession that is central to the text and which Sand excised from 1839 version, Lélia discusses with Pulchérie her inability to find fulfilment in love and her hitherto fruitless search for a God to curse for her misfortune. The coldness of her senses and the exaltation of her thoughts distance her, she feels, from both men and other women. She recounts her strange history, revealing that her experience of all-embracing passion alerted her to the self-hatred which self-abnegation in love can create so that she revolted against the ''misery and enslavement of women'' and underwent an awakening from the deceptive ''illusion'' of love. Fleeing from this slavery of the senses, she sought spiritual and emotional regeneration in solitary retreat in a ruined monastery, but found neither consolation in faith nor respite from the turmoil in her emotions. Rescued during a violent storm by a passing priest (Magnus) who became obsessed with her, she was returned to a sterile life of suffering in the world, a prey to a libertine imagination masked by an austere outward existence.

In a scene worthy of grand opera, Lélia resolves to allow the ever-persistent Sténio to believe he is enjoying a night of love with her at a masked ball at a gorgeous palace in order to appease his cravings. When he discovers that he has slept with the disguised Pulchérie in her place and Lélia appears singing on a craft on the lake beneath his window, he is so distressed that he embarks on a life of embittered debauchery from which he is rescued after a year by Trenmor, and taken to a monastery to be healed. Here he meets up again with the tormented Magnus, who is further destabilized by Sténio's anguished questions and accusations. After Sténio's suicide, the now insane Magnus attempts to exorcize his obsession by strangling Lélia as she kneels weeping by Sténio's body. Trenmor buries them in identical tombs on opposite shores of the lake and watches two glimmers of light embracing over the water at night like the loving souls of his friends, before going on his way to pursue his life of expiation.

In her *Journal intime* (*Intimate Journal*), Sand listed the qualities the characters of *Lélia* represented: doubt (Lélia), youthful credulity (Sténio), superstition and repressed desire (Magnus), the senses (Pulchérie), and the stoicism of age and experience (Trenmor), and states that they are all aspects of herself. Though the characters only intermittently transcend mere philosophical abstractions, their suffering, revealed in poetic and highly charged rhapsodic monologues, haunt the imagination, and the novel, despite its roots in 19th-century Romanticism, reveals conflicts that continue to preoccupy the modern world.

—Penny Brown

LES LIAISONS DANGEREUSES
Novel by Choderlos de Laclos, 1782

The only significant imaginative work of Choderlos de Laclos, *Les Liaisons dangereuses*, is a masterpiece that apparently grew fully-armed (but not without multiple revisions during its writing) from his mind. Probably the most perfect epistolary novel of any ever written, it tells of the beautiful, dissolute, but brilliantly hypocritical young widow, the Marquise de Merteuil and the handsome libertine Vicomte de Valmont who, bored with their perfect love affair, decide to break it off in order to write to each other with the utmost candour of their further sexual exploits. They hold society in contempt and treat it as a field for manipulation of others through sexual conquest.

Valmont is in pursuit of the respectable 22 year-old Présidente de Tourvel, who from his description we realize is already in love with him; meanwhile Merteuil dallies with the Comte de Belleroche. Having previously been jilted by yet another lover, Gercourt, she wishes Valmont to procure the deflowering of Gercourt's 15-year-old prospective bride, the wealthy heiress Cécile de Volanges, newly emerged into society from her convent education. The best instrument for this purpose appears to be the young Chevalier de Danceny, madly in love already with Cécile but, it proves, too decent and romantic to be enterprising enough for Merteuil's liking.

Valmont shows little interest in Merteuil's "commission" until Cécile and her mother (Mme. de Volanges, who infuriates him by attempts to damage him in Tourvel's eyes) find themselves under the same roof as the Présidente, at his aunt's (Mme. de Rosemonde's) country house. This is the arena of his rape-cum-seduction of Cécile, achieved by pretending to further the designs of Danceny, and of Valmont's relentless pressure on Tourvel to yield to him. This second seduction he later achieves at last, by arranging a supposedly final renunciatory interview with Tourvel through a priest.

Throughout his narratives of these events to Merteuil, Valmont has boasted that he will return to her bed as a reward for his conquest of Tourvel. Merteuil, however, despite having in a long exposé of her "principles" vaunted her own intelligence and self-control, superior to that of any man, and despite demonstrating her powers in the course of the novel by ruining the social reputation of another famous rake, Prévan, has from the beginning clearly been jealous of the Présidente. She sends Valmont the draft of a contemptuous letter of abandonment, challenging him to use it on his new lover. This he does and Tourvel eventually dies broken-hearted and insane. Valmont, however, is only mocked by Merteuil after he discovers that she has seduced Danceny. Full of rage and growing remorse, Valmont persuades Danceny to abandon a rendezvous with Merteuil and she in revenge reveals Valmont's seduction of Cécile. Challenged to a duel by Danceny, he approaches the fight half-heartedly and receives a mortal wound. The dying Valmont is reconciled with his adversary and gives him his correspondence with Merteuil. The Chevalier, entrusting the correspondence to Valmont's aunt, reveals the contents of selected letters in society. Merteuil's reputation is in ruins; she has to leave Paris, loses an important lawsuit, and subsequently receives the further "punishment" of disfigurement by smallpox. Cécile, having earlier miscarried Valmont's child, now retires permanently to a convent.

Laclos's use of the letter form takes pseudo-history (the convention of claiming a fictional narrative to be true) almost to its limits, so that the claim is only with difficulty shown to be false. He explains in an almost watertight way how the "correspondence" came to be before the reader; each of his fictional letters has a characteristic personal style; the use of reported speech is sparing, so that a narrator's verbatim memory is hard to challenge; and above all few of the letters are mere "reports": most themselves constitute acts in the drama by the very fact that they are sent. If this seems implausible in real-life terms, we are told that repetitive letters have been edited out! The reader is frequently placed in a position of dramatic irony with regard to the correspondents, knowing more of their situation than they do as they address or receive a communication. This resemblance to drama is an important key when interpreting the work and certainly helps to explain the success of a recent stage play and two films based on the novel.

At a structural level, the work owes more to classicism than to realism. Like one of Racine's or Marivaux's comedies, the plot begins from a basic (and extraordinary) supposition (the libertine lovers' "pact"), which the action then works out according to psychological verisimilitude. As in classical French theatre, the initial supposition ("what if?") is less interesting by its (doubtful) resemblance to the possibilities of ordinary life, than by the moral issue which it distils for our concentrated dramatic attention: even if the wicked are self-deceiving and their own worst enemies, what help is that to the lives they destroy? One may be tempted by the novel's technical perfection and inclusion of specific social detail to treat it as a realistic portrayal of late 18th-century French aristocracy (as if Merteuil and Valmont were in some way typical!) or to interpret Merteuil as a feminist campaigner against an essentially phallocratic *ancien régime* (as if she did not take delight in destroying other women!). Such misinterpretations are a huge compliment to Laclos's powers of persuasion and are implicit, from the time of the book's initial popularity, in the ongoing quest for historical real-life "keys" to its fictional characters. However, while Laclos had many sources to inspire him in both fiction and real memoirs and while his ethical and social concerns (for example over the education of women and the harmfulness of cloistering girls with nuns in their early years) are undoubtedly reflected in his novel, his leading characters are hyperbolic statements and exist nowhere but in his art. For them God is dead, conventional morality an object of disdain, and all behaviour permissible (provided it can be masked). The fascination that they exercise compared with their more virtuous victims is central to the work's moral ambiguity and helps to explain its continuing popularity in our own time.

—Philip E.J. Robinson

LIFE A USER'S MANUAL (La Vie mode d'emploi)
Novel by Georges Perec, 1978

Generally thought of as Georges Perec's masterwork, *Life A User's Manual* is by any standard one of the most complex and intriguing novels of the 20th century. It is a massive novel by current norms, running to 700 pages. Perec tells many different stories in it (107 of them, by his own reckoning), stories that interweave and complement each other in a variety of ways. Together, they center upon an apartment building in Paris and the lives of its inhabitants, each story focusing upon a different resident, but presenting in their totality as rich a panorama of society as contemporary French literature has to offer. One story among all of them occupies a place of centrality in the novel. It is the tale of Percival Barnabooth, a very wealthy man who conceives a vast project intended to occupy fifty years of his life. He takes lessons in watercolor painting for ten years, then spends twenty years traveling to port cities around the world and painting a picture of each, until he has accumulated 500 paintings. As each painting is finished, he arranges for a workman named Gaspard Winckler to mount it and cut it into a jigsaw puzzle. Upon Barnabooth's return to Paris after his wanderings, he devotes twenty years to solving those 500 puzzles. As a final gesture, when each puzzle is completed, he sends it back to the port in which it was painted, and has it dipped in the sea until nothing remains but the empty paper with which he began.

Hailed shortly after its publication as an exceptionally well-told novel, *Life A User's Manual* was awarded the prestigious Médicis prize. It gradually became apparent, though, that Perec had followed certain very complicated principles of construction in writing it. Two of those bear mention here. First, Perec conceived the apartment building as a square of ten spaces by ten (ten apartments on each of ten floors). He used a modified version of a classic chess problem called the Knight's Tour in order to structure the sequence of chapters in his novel. Each of those chapters deals with one of the spaces in the apartment building, and no space is dealt with twice. Second, Perec used an arcane mathematical algorithm known as the "orthogonal Latin bi-square order 10" to distribute sets of 42 elements (situations, objects, allusions, and so forth) in each of his chapters according to predetermined rules of permutation. The formal principles that guided Perec's composition are by no means obvious, however; and what results is an avant-garde novel that can be read, as Perec himself suggested, "stretched out on one's bed."

Many suggestive parables of art and artistic interpretation circulate in *Life A User's Manual*, and many ironies, too. Perec compares Barnabooth's project to his own task in ways that are both wry and canny. Throughout the novel, he asks questions about the role of the artist and about the way the artist conceives his or her task. Perec also asks his readers to think about the conventions of reading and interpretation. Putting the dynamic of the puzzle-maker and the puzzle-solver so centrally on stage in his novel, Perec reflects upon the relationship of artistic production and reception, encouraging us to join him in that reflection and to consider literature itself in astonishing new ways.

—Warren Motte

THE LIFE AND ADVENTURES OF LAZARILLO DE TORMES
See LAZARILLO DE TORMES

LIFE IS A DREAM (La vida es sueño)
Play by Pedro Calderón de la Barca, 1636

Life Is a Dream is the story of Segismundo, a Polish prince, imprisoned from birth by his father, King Basilio, as a result of omens and prophecies predicting disaster for the kingdom. Act I reveals that, despite Segismundo's violent behaviour, Basilio has decided, 20 years later, to give his son an opportunity to rule, and in order to do so he has him transported secretly to the palace under the influence of a powerful drug. Act II sees Segismundo awakening in the palace and, informed of his new power, proceeding to take revenge on those who have wronged him in the past or displease him in the present: his jailer, Clotaldo; his father, Basilio; a prince, Astolfo; a young woman, Rosaura; and an upstart servant. Convinced that the omens were true, Basilio imprisons his son again and instructs Clotaldo to inform him that the palace experience was merely a dream. When in Act III Segismundo is released by soldiers supporting his claims to the throne, he is unable to decide if he is dreaming or not, but feels he should behave more prudently. Confronting those people he saw previously in his "dream," he resists the impulse of the moment and, having defeated his father in battle, forgives him. The prophecy that he would see his father at his feet is fulfilled, but in a way that rejects vengeance in favour of forgiveness.

The sources of Pedro Calderón de la Barca's play are many. The story of the awakened sleeper occurs in the *Thousand and One Nights*, as well as in the work of Spanish writers from the 14th century. The theme of the individual seeking to avoid, but merely confirming, what is foretold was also common, as in the collection of stories, *Barlaam and Josaphat*. And the idea of life as fleeting and dream-like was central to both oriental and Christian religions. But the direct source of *Life Is a Dream* was Calderón's earlier play written in collaboration with Antonio Coello, *Yerros de naturaleza y aciertos de la fortuna*, in which, despite differences of detail, the basic ideas are the same: a prince who recovers his throne; a young man who, apparently unfit to rule, learns to do so, suggesting in the process that men can shape their destiny.

Life Is a Dream is, however, a much more complex play. The idea that men can shape their destiny is linked now both to the process of self-discovery and to the realization that the objects of human ambition—power, wealth and pleasure—are insubstantial in comparison with true spiritual values. Moreover, these are themes that are embodied in all the characters and incidents of the play. The affairs of Segismundo and Basilio are paralleled by the efforts of Rosaura, abandoned by Prince Astolfo, to recover her honour, which she achieves through Segismundo's recovery of his throne and his appreciation of the worth and rights of others. Basilio's initial irresponsibility towards his son has its counterpart in the self-interested behaviour of many other characters, all of whom grow wiser through disillusionment, achieving knowledge of themselves and of the world. In terms of the complex interlocking of incident and character in a meaningful and illuminating way. *Life Is a Dream* is one of Calderón's most accomplished plays.

Like Don Juan, Segismundo is one of the truly memorable characters of 17th-century Spanish theatre: a man-beast initially at the mercy of his volatile emotions, subsequently bewildered by his inexplicable changes of fortune, and finally groping his way towards a greater understanding of himself and his fellow-men. But the play has other interesting characters too: Basilio, tortured by his son's predicament; Rosaura, passionate in her pursuit of honour, confused by her loss of it; Clotaldo, her father, confounded by the arrival of a child he has never seen: Astolfo, as powerful as he is insincere; and Clarion, Rosaura's servant, the self-interested seeker responsible for his own death. The gallery of brilliantly drawn characters answers the charge that Calderón was much more interested in plot than characterization.

The characters have their counterpart in highly evocative settings, suggested, of course, by the dialogue itself. The opening scenes take place as darkness descends and they conjure up a gloomy tower, a flickering light, and a chained man dressed in skins. In total contrast the subsequent palace-scenes shimmer with silks, brocades, jewels, music, and beautiful women. The effect is truly of *chiarowscuro*, splendidly dramatic, but while the changing landscapes of the play are effective backdrops, they are also reflections of the characters' emotional and mental conflicts, evoking the movements from darkness to light that in one way or another affect all the characters of the play.

Calderón's language, here as elsewhere, is highly stylized, even "operatic." Segismundo's opening soliloquy, for example, is not unlike an aria, as are other long speeches in the play. They reveal Calderón's liking for repetition, symmetry, and pattern in the structure of his verse, as well as an overall sense of musicality. The effect of such stylization is not, however, to mute or straightjacket the emotional charge of the lines but, by channelling it into a disciplined form—lines of eight syllables in a variety of stanza forms—to intensify it further. In emotional terms the language has enormous range, from the violence of Segismundo's outbursts to his lyrical praise of female beauty.

Life Is a Dream, written in a strongly Catholic climate, is not a religious play, though it does, in a more general way, expound the theme of the triumph of free will, at the heart of Calderón's particular brand of catholicism. Rather it is a play about man at any time and in any place, at the mercy of deficiencies within and without himself, and struggling to overcome them. It is this more general relevance that accounts for its lasting appeal and allows for varying interpretations that may embrace existentialism on the one hand or the efforts of post-war Poland to resist Soviet authoritarianism on the other.

—Gwynne Edwards

THE LIFE OF GALILEO (Galileo)
Play by Bertolt Brecht, 1943

The Life of Galileo follows Galileo from his "invention" of the telescope through his confrontation with the reactionary power of the Church to his writing of the Discorsi in old age under virtual house arrest. It is unique among Bertolt Brecht's plays in taking as its central character a major figure from history. Many of the other characters with whom he interacts are also powerful historical figures, and many of the events portrayed in the play are based in reality, although Brecht does attribute to Galileo an entirely unhistorical sense of being at the dawn of a "new age" of science for the people. Brecht holds Galileo responsible both for the frustration of the hopes of the people for social change and the subsequent development of "pure" science. When Galileo confirms the validity of the Copernican system by observation with his telescope, he places science at the barricades for progress towards the possibility of a new social order and the rejection of blindly accepted authority, represented by the Church's adherence to the Ptolemaic system. With his recantation, Brecht's Galileo allows that authority to reassert itself, to stifle legitimate research, and to appropriate for its own benefit the results of scientific enquiry.

With its concentration on the fate of its central character and its indoor locations, *The Life of Galileo* lacks the epic breadth of his other major plays. It does, however, contain some of Brecht's most theatrically effective scenes demonstrating on stage the concrete nature of the truth Brecht was seeking to represent. In the robing scene Brecht develops a stunningly telling image. The mathematician Pope Barbarini starts the scene with rational acceptance of the truth of Galileo's discoveries. As the scene progresses and he puts on the vestments, he physically becomes the image of the head of the Church, and his rationality is progressively overwhelmed until he accepts the authority vested in him. As the scene ends he is ready to deny Galileo's discoveries, rejecting what he knows to be the truth to preserve the power of the Church. Equally effective is the play's first scene in which, after visibly enjoying his bath, Galileo demonstrates the movement of the earth around the sun to Andrea by physically picking him up on his stool and moving him.

With this concrete demonstration of a complex scientific concept Brecht's Galileo shows his intensely physical nature. The excitement he shows in his explanation of the movement of the earth is as sensual as the pleasure he takes from a bath. His scientific research derives from the same motivation as his eating and drinking. He is a glutton. His appetite is as keen for a goose dinner as it is for discoveries in astronomy. As with many self-indulgent people, however, he is a physical coward, and recants on sight of the instruments of torture. While not a consciously cruel man, his self-absorption in his work, which amounts to monomania, loses his daughter her husband, and might have cost his landlady her life in the plague.

The first version of *The Life of Galileo* was written in Denmark in three weeks during 1938 as the first major play of Brecht's exile from Germany, and performed in Zurich in 1943. In it the cunning Galileo is presented in a positive light, recanting in public only to continue his ground-breaking work in private. This stratagem is adopted by a number of Brecht's characters in the face of overwhelming opposition. It was indeed not unfamiliar to Brecht himself, and he might be seen as propounding it as a way for dissenting thinkers to survive under the Nazis. However, in 1945, after revelations of the Nazi abuse of science and the dropping of the first atom bomb on Japan, Brecht in his second version of the play gives the aged Galileo a moving speech in which he accuses himself of releasing scientific research from legitimate responsibility. Brecht no longer believed in the primacy of free scientific enquiry which he saw during World War II as being subjected to immoral exploitation by the scientists' political masters. His Galileo rejects this stratagem of deceit, calling instead for a version of the Hippocratic oath for scientists, to force them to face the consequences of their research and for them to assume a proper responsibility for it.

For the stage premiere of the "American" version of the play at the Coronet Theatre, Beverly Hills in 1947, Brecht himself produced an English translation with the actor Charles Laughton. As Brecht spoke poor English and Laughton no German the translation was the result of a search for English equivalents by Laughton for Brecht's "gestic" performances of the German. This version was later translated into German for staging in Cologne in 1955, and, altered further by Brecht, was performed at the Berliner Ensemble in 1957 in a production started by Brecht and continued after his death by Erich Engel.

The character of Galileo, with its dynamism, confidence, and energy so quickly collapsing at his recantation into self-loathing and recrimination, is one of Brecht's most impressive inventions and a marvellous opportunity for character actors of the calibre of Ernst Busch in 1957 and Ekkehard Schall in 1978 at the Berliner Ensemble, and Michael Gambon at the National Theatre, London, in 1980. But the split in the characterization between the essentially sympathetic and positive portrayal of the first part of the play and the judgemental picture of the traitor to science presented in the penultimate scene has for some actors proved unbridgeable, despite Brecht's insertion of more negative elements in the third version.

Galileo's moral and physical weakness may lead him to recant, but his character embodies for Brecht the essence of scientific enquiry— an insatiable thirst for experimentation arising out of a conviction that one should doubt everything, only accepting an idea when, despite one's best endeavours, it cannot be disproved. It is this questioning attitude when applied to society and human interaction that is at the heart of Brecht's concept of a "Theatre for a Scientific Age."

—A.J. Meech

THE LIFE OF LAZARILLO DE TORMES

See LAZARILLO DE TORMES

THE LIME WORKS (Das Kalkwerk)
Novel by Thomas Bernhard, 1970

The Lime Works, which, together with *Gargoyles* (*Verstörung*), marks the culmination of Thomas Bernhard's early fiction, is characterized by a narrative structure which is at once both complex and lucid. The main narrator, an insurance agent, collects, sifts, and compiles an objective sounding account of the events which ended in the murder of a handicapped woman, Mrs. Konrad, by her husband in the isolated lime works where they had lived for the previous five years. The narrator himself remains in the background. He reports information given by the few men of the village, such as Fro and Wieser, with whom Konrad had social contact and to whom he had

spoken about his daily life. Much of the narrative takes the form of reported speech, as the narrator records details of what his informants in turn have been told by Konrad. The narrator thereby attempts to formulate a precise and objective account of what occurred.

Think of it, my dear Fro, everything I am telling you, intimating to you, Konrad is supposed to have told Fro, basically goes on here every day, over and over again! Everything that goes on here goes on day after day, it's the height of absurdity, and by dint of being the height of absurdity it is the height of terribleness, day after day. It's true, Fro's testimony agrees in every respect with Wieser's testimony, the works inspector confirms everything Fro and Wieser have said, and conversely, both Wieser and Fro confirm what the works inspector says, basically one confirms the other, they all confirm each other's testimony.

The sense of detachment and objectivity, created by the apparent presence of multiple narrators, is simultaneously undermined by the fact that the narrative is largely a monologue based on Konrad's words, the man at the centre of the story. The relentlessness of the style reflects his own obsessive pursuit of the scientific study of "hearing." He believes that his investigation, which he is attempting to put in writing, will be enhanced by living in the remote lime works, where he anticipates few external distractions. However, the harder he tries, the less he succeeds in writing up his ideas: often he blames the difficulty he experiences on intrusions from outside. Yet the distractions are largely internal: the more obsessional Konrad's ideas become, the less he is able to communicate them in written form.

Konrad's tendency to extremes is graphically conveyed through superlatives and spatial extremities of height and depth. Through practice, he has succeeded in hearing sounds not normally accessible to human hearing, such as those which occur at the bottom of the lake on which the lime works is situated. His "hearing things" becomes a metaphor for his incipient madness. His inclination to pursue everything to its ultimate point also characterizes his relationship with his wife, whom he subjects to the rigours of the "Urbanchich method." This series of hearing exercises, named after the scientist Victor Urbanchich, was intended to provide a means of re-integrating deaf people into society. By contrast, Konrad's obsessive practice of the method is self-indulgent and self-delusory, and it merely intensifies his wife's, and his own, isolation from the villagers.

The novel depicts the sterile inner world of Konrad, the scientist and intellectual. His wife, who is also his half-sister, offers a mirror image of his obsessiveness. While Konrad is engaged in his "study," she pursues an equally futile activity, knitting mittens which he would never wear: she constantly unpicks her work and starts again with wool of a different colour as if never satisfied with her work. The complementary nature of the relationship between Konrad and his wife is also apparent in their intellectual preferences: while his favourite reading matter is the anarchist scientist Kropotkin, his wife is occasionally rewarded by his reading Novalis to her, a Romantic poet who combined scientific leanings with a mystical approach to life. Both these writers had utopian visions which caused them to reject modern society. The incongruity of their idealism in the Konrads' life shows up the author's attack on Konrad's misuse of scientific endeavour. It is also science, in the form of incorrect medication, which is to blame for Mrs. Konrad's physical incapacitation and general decline. Konrad's debility, on the other hand, is largely psychological: his concentration on the sense of hearing, to the exclusion of all else, suggests the alienation of the scientist, and perhaps of modern man in general, from the wholeness of the healthy human being, an approach ironically at variance with that of his own humanistic heroes, Kropotkin and Urbanchich.

The abandoned lime works, which had long since ceased production, itself offers an external representation of Konrad's mindset. First obsessed with acquiring it from his nephew Hörhager (the name suggests "poor hearing"), his desire to withdraw to it from the world, and his paranoia, are represented by the heavy bolts which he has had fitted to all entrances. The layout of the building, too, epitomizes the conflicting, but complementary, patterns displayed by the Konrads: while Mrs. Konrad occupies the smallest room, near the top of the house, he is more concerned with plumbing the depths of the lake and cellar. As a result of a series of expensive lawsuits, Konrad has been forced to sell most of the furniture, so that, although inhabited, it has a desolate atmosphere. External space reflects the emptiness and sterility of Konrad and his enterprise, and the lime works offers a powerful metaphor for human decline, alienation, and madness.

—Juliet Wigmore

THE LITTLE CLAY CART (Mṛichchhakaṭikā)

Ancient Indian Sanskrit play, the preface of which asserts that it was written by "King Śūdraka," of whose existence there is no other evidence. Date of composition extremely uncertain: suggestions include 1st century BC, 1st century AD, mid-2nd century AD, and even 5th century AD.

PUBLICATIONS

The Mṛichchhakaṭikā. 1904 (2nd edition, with commentary of Prithvadara); edited by Rangacharya B. Raddi, 1909; also edited by M.R. Kale (bilingual edition), 1924, R.D. Karmarkar (bilingual edition), 1937, and V.G. Paranjpe, 1937; as *Mrichchhakati; or, The Toy-Cart*, translated by H.H. Wilson, 1901; as *The Toy Cart*, translated by Arthur Symons, 1919; also translated P. Lal, in *Great Sanskrit Plays*, 1957; as *The Little Clay Cart*, translated by Arthur W. Ryder, 1905, reprinted 1965; also translated by Satyendra Kumar Basa, 1939; Revilo Pendleton Oliver, 1938, and in *Six Sanskrit Plays*, edited by Henry W. Wells, 1964; J.A.B. van Buitenen, in *Two Plays of Ancient India*, 1968; Barbara Stoler Miller, 1984; A.L. Basham, 1994.

*

Critical Studies: *Introduction to the Study of Mṛcchakaṭika* by G.V. Devasthali, 1951; *Preface to Mṛcchakaṭikā* by G.K. Bhat, 1953; *Śūdraka* by C.B. Pandey, 1958; *Theater in India* by Balwant Gargi, 1962; *The Sanskrit Drama in Its Origin, Development, Theory and Practice* by Arthur Berriedale Keith, 1964; "Producing *The Little Clay Cart*" by J. Michel, in *Asian Drama*, edited by H. Wells, 1965, and "Artifice and Naturalism in the East" by Wells in *Quest*, 1(1), 1965–66.

* * *

The Little Clay Cart ranks with Kalidasa's *Śakuntalā* as one of the great masterpieces of the Indian theatre, but nothing is known of its

author except what the preface of the play itself reveals. According to Stage Manager, the play is the work of a "King Śūdraka," an expert in the *Rig-Veda*, the *Sāamma-Veda*, mathematics, the arts of courtesans, and the training of elephants, who lived 100 years and ten days, and after establishing his son as successor cast himself into the flames. No such king is recorded in history, and most scholars assume that he is purely legendary, a dramatic mask for the unknown real author who sought perhaps in this way to give his work a patina of nobility and antiquity.

Early in the 20th century a group of dramas by the pioneer Sanskrit dramatist Bhāsa were discovered, among them one called *Chārudatta in Poverty* which, it was soon observed, tells essentially the same story, occasionally in almost the same words, as the first four acts of *The Little Clay Cart*. Clearly the author of that work appropriated this material as the basis for his much longer ten-act work. While the longer version is compatible with the original material, the major characters are considerably deepened and enriched, many new and striking minor characters are added, and the perspective is broadened so that the private affairs of the hero are intertwined with the fate of the city and the kingdom.

Although pious Brahmins and wealthy courtesans are common figures in the Sanskrit theatre, *The Little Clay Cart* is the only play to show a love affair between two such figures. Chārudatta's poverty is the result of his generosity, and although it has cost him friends and physical comfort, he is happily married with a son when he sees the courtesan Vasantasenā in the temple and they are strongly attracted to each other. Fate works to bring them together. Vasantasenā rejects, yet is pursued by, Prince Saṁsthānaka, the half-mad brother of the ruling King Pālaka, and by his attendant and a servant. In an elaborately choreographed sequence, they stalk her about the empty stage, representing the city streets at night, reciting in turn balanced poetic stanzas, each in a different dialect. The attendant, betraying his evil lord, aids Vasantasenā to seek refuge in Chārudatta's humble home.

Vasantasenā leaves a casket of jewels in trust with Chārudatta, initiating an elaborate subplot. These jewels are subsequently stolen by a thief who is seeking wealth to buy and marry one of Vasantasenā's serving women. Vasantasenā accepts the jewels in payment for her servant, but before she can inform Chārudatta of their recovery his wife volunteers her own rare pearl necklace as recompense, providing the courtesan with further proof of Chārudatta's love and honour.

At this point, during the fourth act, a political action (not found in the original version) begins. Sarvilaka, the thief, hears that his friend Prince Āryaka has been arrested by the King on the advice of a soothsayer. He leaves his new bride to aid the prince, who is reported to have escaped. The private and public actions now develop in tandem. Vasantasenā uses the pearl necklace as an excuse to return to Chārudatta's house. Another famous scene, paralleling in certain respects the night scene of the first act, shows Vasantasenā hurrying through a spring storm with her confidante, a slave-girl, and a slave with an umbrella, in an elaborate dance and poetic sequence, the alternating stanzas of which develop parallels between the upheaval in nature and that in the lovers' hearts.

The storm forces the courtesan to spend the night in Chārudatta's house and the next morning she meets his son, who complains that his only plaything is a little clay cart. She gives him jewels to buy one of gold. Chārudatta arranges to meet her again in a nearby park, but when he sends his carriage to fetch her, it is appropriated by the escaping Prince Āryaka. As a result Vasantasenā mistakenly takes the carriage of her evil pursuer Prince Saṁsthānaka.

When Prince Āryaka arrives in Chārudatta's carriage, Chārudatta shields him and goes in search of Vasantasenā. But she has encountered Saṁsthānaka who, enraged that she has not come to him willingly, orders his servants to kill her, and when they refuse, beats her himself until she falls unconscious. He buries her under some leaves and goes to the court to denounce Chārudatta as her murderer. Meanwhile, a monk whom Vasantasenā helped in the past finds and revives her. Chārudatta, accused of murder and also implicated in the escape of Prince Āryaka, is condemned to death.

The final act is the richest and most complex of the drama. It begins with the reading of Chārudatta's condemnation in the four sections of the city, and is primarily made up of the progress of the funeral procession through the city, interrupted several times by vain attempts by various minor characters to gain pardon for Chārudatta. The executioner's first blow is miraculously deflected, and before a second can be struck, Vasantasenā and the monk appear to save him. As the lovers rejoice, word comes that Prince Āryaka has slain King Pālaka and taken over the throne. Naturally he restores his helper Chārudatta to wealth and honour and frees Vasantasenā from her profession so that she may marry him. Even Saṁsthānaka is pardoned, at the request of the merciful Chārudatta.

This brief summary indicates only the principal features of this huge and complex work, written in verse and prose, and in several dialects along with the aristocratic Sanskrit. The cast of almost 30 characters represents every stratum of society, and even the minor ones are drawn with care and detail. Dance, pantomime, and music add to the verbal richness, providing a texture as varied as any work of world drama. The language which, as in all the greatest Sanskrit poetry, brilliantly mingles the sensual and the pious, natural phenomena and human feelings, defies the skill of the translator, but the complex fabric of human society and human emotions, suggesting the elaborate dramatic worlds of the Western Renaissance playwrights, has nevertheless made this drama highly appealing to Western readers.

—Marvin Carlson

LIVES OF LYSANDER AND SULLA
Prose by Plutarch, 1st/2nd century AD

Plutarch's *Lives* have suffered somewhat from the modern tendency to treat them as a quarry for historical information rather than the polished work of literature that they are. Some popular contemporary translations split up the pairings and remove the comparisons, and it must be admitted that some of Plutarch's pairings appear a little strained; but in Lysander and Sulla he found two great historical figures whose lives and characters displayed very real similarities. Both were born to old but impoverished families and had to make their way in the world by ambition and talent; both were notable war-winners; both were grossly indulgent to their friends; by an interesting verbal echo, both combined the lion and the fox in their nature—Lysander in his own words, Sulla in the words of his enemy Carbo. More superficially, perhaps, both captured Athens. Possibly for this very reason, the closing comparison stresses the no less real differences between the two men.

Plutarch was astonishingly well-read and had a retentive memory, but for facts he could only be as good as his sources. It is clear that he knows nothing of Lysander's early life, apart from his poverty; nor of Lysander the private man—it is only his career that we see. The

effective narrative covers just 14 years, from his first appointment as Admiral of Sparta in 408 BC to his death in 395 BC. For much of this material Plutarch is indebted to the sober, unadorned narrative of Xenophon, who lived through the events described; some of the choicest anecdotes and sayings, however, come from elsewhere, such as "dice to cheat boys, oaths to cheat men," a saying also attributed to others, but to no one more memorably or aptly than to Lysander. Plutarch seems to be conscious of a possible thinness of material, since he pads out the *Life* with a lengthy digression on meteorites (introduced on a very slight pretext) and an extended commonplace on the corrupting influence of money. Despite this, however, he succeeds in presenting to us a picture of a character that is both coherent and credible.

Plutarch's introduction to the main narrative is magnificent. The Peloponnesian War has been going on for 23 years; five years have passed since Athens' shattering defeat in Sicily, yet Sparta still seems unable to deliver the *coup de grâce*. Enter Lysander: he immediately brings new energy and ideas to the war effort, conjuring fresh subsidies out of Persia to pay his sailors, fostering cells of political sympathizers in the cities of Athens' empire, and winning an opportunistic naval victory. After a year, however, Spartan law obliges him to hand over the command to another. By devious means Lysander undermines his successor's position, then, after the latter's defeat and death in battle, is reinstated. By a brilliantly executed stratagem he catches the entire Athenian fleet beached and defenceless. Apart from the formalities of the capture of Athens, the war is over.

Plutarch is always interested in the effect that success has upon a man's moral character. With his partisans now in power all round the Aegean, Lysander was the dominant figure in Greece, and he now appears in his true colours: his arrogance, cruelty, and favouritism made him widely hated. Expecting to cement his power he secured the succession to the Spartan throne for his protégé Agesilaüs, against the claims of a rival candidate; but Agesilaüs soon showed his independence and actually went out of his way to humiliate his former patron. As his influence waned, Lysander dabbled in schemes to change the Spartan constitution, but nothing came of them; and it seems somehow symbolic that this most wily of commanders should have thrown his life away in a futile skirmish in Boeotia, during a campaign of no military importance. Always a kindly and generous writer, Plutarch leaves Lysander, not with a recapitulation of his faults, but with a paragraph of praise for his undoubted incorruptibility: of all the vast sums that passed through his hands, he kept nothing for himself, but ended his life as poor as he began it.

For the *Life* of Sulla, by contrast, Plutarch has almost too much to go on, and there is no phase of Sulla's sensational life and career that he does not cover (though he still finds room for a substantial digression on the merits of divination). For us, much of the interest lies in his use of Sulla's *Memoirs*, which have not survived. It might be imagined that this would result in a strong bias in favour of Sulla, but it is balanced by plenty of material stemming from a hostile standpoint.

The *Life* opens with a telling sketch of Sulla's youth: a patrician he may have been, but he lived in poor rented accommodation, was of unprepossessing appearance, and drew his friends from the ranks of professional actors and musicians—a raffish taste he retained to the end of his life. The first manifestations of his good luck (he gloried in being fortune's favourite) came in the form of legacies that enabled him to make a start in public life.

Plutarch shows flair in selecting the salient points of Sulla's career for full treatment. His first military appointment was under Marius in

Africa in the war against the rebel prince Jugurtha: it was Sulla's coolness and courage that secured the surrender of Jugurtha by his father-in-law and ended the war (105 BC), but the boastful way he celebrated this achievement aroused Marius' jealousy and sowed the seeds of hatred between them. After further military successes he ran for political office, but Plutarch shows that it was not all plain sailing for one of such a background: he met with more than one setback and only became consul (seven years above the normal minimum age) because of his distinguished service as general in the Social War (against Rome's rebel Italian allies, 90–88 BC).

This office saw the first great crisis of Sulla's career, and Plutarch narrates it superbly. By seditious means the aged Marius has got the command of the projected Eastern war (against King Mithridates) transferred from Sulla to himself. Sulla's reaction is to appeal to his army for support. They march on Rome, capture it by force, expel Marius and his partisans, and reverse the measures taken by them. Here we see, in combination, Sulla's ruthlessness, cunning, and willingness to take a desperate gamble. This was the first full-scale coup in Rome's history—a taste of things to come. More than once Plutarch points to Sulla's unorthodox attitude to military discipline: he indulged his soldiers with lavish donatives and often overlooked serious offences on their part. He is also struck by Sulla's cavalier approach to religious scruples: in his Greek campaign he lays hands on the temple treasures of Delphi with complete insouciance.

The highlight of Plutarch's account of the Mithridatic War is the siege and capture of Athens (86 BC). The privations of the besieged are contrasted with the luxurious living of their tyrant Aristion, who had delivered the city to Mithridates; some observant soldiers spot a possible way through the defences, Sulla brings his men in at midnight, and gives them free rein to loot and slaughter, something Lysander had refrained from doing in 404 BC. Then there are the *bons mots*: when an Athenian delegation came to parley with Sulla during the siege and went on about the glories of the Persian Wars, he replied "Rome did not send me here to learn history but to subdue rebels!" and when he finally calls a halt to the sack, he "spares the few for the sake of many, the living for the sake of the dead."

The rest of the military narrative, including two battles on Greek soil against Mithridates' generals, confirms Sulla as a master tactician, but is of less biographical interest and is not the sort of material that shows Plutarch to the best advantage. He is back to form in the account of the negotiations to end the war: Mithridates himself cannot stand up to the steel and charm that Sulla alternately deploys.

On his return to Italy Sulla is faced with a domestic war against his political opponents who were supported by the last of the rebel allies. Plutarch does not, this time, dwell on the details until the climax, the Battle of the Colline Gate: a bold attempt by the Italian leader Telesinus to capture Rome undefended is narrowly forestalled by Sulla in a terrible battle that he all but lost.

He is now master of Italy, and once again Plutarch draws attention to the way a man's character is either changed, or revealed for the first time, by power. The first of his cruelties is the massacre, in the Circus, of 6,000 survivors from the rebel Italians. As their shrieks are clearly audible in the senate-house, Sulla unconcernedly tells the senators to pay no attention: "I have ordered some criminals to be admonished." Then follows the murder of his political opponents, at first haphazardly, then systematically according to lists of names posted in public; the property of these victims is confiscated and auctioned. He is proclaimed dictator, with the special provision that all his actions, past and future, should have the force of law.

Rather surprisingly Plutarch does not stress, indeed barely mentions, the Jekyll-and-Hyde aspect of Sulla's dictatorship: beside the appalling cruelties, he was a prolific legislator who made a systematic attempt to reform the bases of the Roman constitution. Perhaps Plutarch ignores this side because the reforms were a failure: most of them did not outlive their author by more than about ten years. Instead, we get Sulla's triumph, then his retirement into private life (79 BC). Now a widower, he married a much younger woman— something that Plutarch comments upon censoriously—but soon died from a painful intestinal illness. In death, however, as Plutarch says, his good luck held: the rain did not come until his funeral pyre was burnt out. So ends one of the most unforgettable of the *Lives*.

—John Hart

LORENZACCIO
Play by Alfred de Musset, 1834

Although—in part because of his brother Paul's undependable biography—for a long time it was thought that *Lorenzaccio* was the fruit of the 23-year-old poet's trip to Italy with his lover, George Sand, more recent scholarship has shown that the play was largely completed by December 1833, prior to the couple's departure. However, Sand's "historical scene," "A Conspiracy in 1537," along with Benedetto Varchi's *Storia fiorentina*, was both an impulsion and an example for Alfred de Musset's creation of the drama, which followed the general plot line of the former and enriched it with historical and biographical details from the latter.

Whatever its "sources" may be, *Lorenzaccio* has remained the most important and the most theatrically viable of French Romantic historical dramas. It differs from its two immediate literary models— the so-called "scènes historiques" ("historical scenes") of the 1820s and the historical tragedy of the 1830s—by seeking greater thematic unity than the first, and by not using alexandrine rhymed verse as in the works of Victor Hugo. More importantly—in this its primary influence would seem to be Shakespeare's *Hamlet*—it is an immensely complex dramatic construct, centring around a puzzling character, Lorenzo de'Medici (Lorenzaccio, the suffix of whose name indicates the opprobrium of those around him), but enriching the story of his assassination of his cousin, Alexander, Duke of Florence, with political and sentimental sub-plots, a large number of characters (some 12), and a "shakespearian" dramatic structure that interweaves 38 scenes, whose settings shift and whose temporal interrelationship is not always linear, into the standard five acts of French neoclassical and romantic tragedy. This dramatic and intellectual complexity has not prevented the drama from achieving success on the modern stage, notably in Jean Vilar's 1952 production at the Théâtre National Populaire, starring Gérard Philipe as Lorenzo. It did, however, lead to postponement of its première until 1896, many years after the author's death, when Sarah Bernhardt staged it as a vehicle for her cross-dressing talents. She had already played Hamlet, and created a precedent for female impersonators of Lorenzo that lasted until after World War II, in a highly modified version that simplified and condensed Musset's unwieldy creation, both intellectually and formally. Since Musset had written the play for reading rather than performance, publishing it with *Un spectacle dans un fauteuil* ("Armchair Theatre") in 1834, that is not entirely surprising.

The drama's central plot, interwoven among scenes devoted to the sub-plots, involves Lorenzo's intention to execute Alexander, whom he and others around him see as a tyrant imposed on Florence by Pope Clement VII. In order to achieve acceptance by the Duke, Lorenzo has become his drinking companion and purveyor to his orgies. This has led to his being an object of suspicion to those who would normally be his allies, the republicans, who want to restore democracy—in reality an oligarchy of the great families—to the city. The plot reaches its climax at the end of the fourth act, when Lorenzo, who has promised to bring his adored and idealized aunt, Catherine Ginori, to Alexander's bed, murders the Duke. By this time Lorenzo has realized the meaninglessness of his long-meditated gesture, both because his "mask" as debauchee has ended by becoming his real identity and because the republicans lack the courage and the unity to follow it up. The final act illustrates the truth of this realization, as it demonstrates the inaction of the republicans, the willingness of his fellow-Florentines to accept a new Duke (Cosimo) imposed by the Pope, and the ultimate futility of Lorenzo's act. It culminates in the latter's ignominious assassination in Venice (Musset telescoped historical events: Lorenzo died 11 years later) and Cosimo's insipid speech of acceptance of the throne of Florentine, proclaiming his submission to the Pope and the Emperor.

The two principal sub-plots, interwoven with this, involve Lorenzo's older friend Philip Strozzi's idealistic attempts to restore republican rule to Florence (he takes too long to move, and abandons everything when his beloved daughter, Louise, is assassinated); and Marquise Ricciarda Cibo's bid to convert Alexander to the republican cause by allowing herself to be seduced. Both these actions, along with Lorenzo's deed and the several scenes in which we see Florence's citizens standing by and futilely commenting the actions that they witness, illustrate Musset's predominant theme: the failure of men to act meaningfully in accordance with their principles, as well as the prevailing meaninglessness of political action when it does occur.

The play can thus be seen as both a very personal expression of Musset's besetting psychological themes—also present in his novel, *The Confession of a Child of the Century*, and some of his best poetry, particularly the "Nights" ("Nuits")—and an allegory for contemporary events in France, namely the Revolution of 1830, which had ended by putting a constitutional monarch, Louis-Philippe, on the throne of France rather than re-establishing the republic. Some recent productions of the play have tried to temper this disheartening message by emphasizing the moral independence of the young artist, Tebaldeo, who is represented painting Lorenzo's portrait in several scenes: this was notably true of a 1969 revival by the Za Branou Theatre of Prague, following the Soviet occupation of that city, when *Lorenzaccio*'s evocation of foreign domination made it particularly relevant to modern political history. That, however, seems contrary to the author's intentions, as revealed in the text of the play as well as in its variants.

—David Sices

THE LOST HONOR OF KATHARINA BLUM (Die verlorene Ehre der Katharina Blum)
Novel by Heinrich Böll, 1974

Heinrich Böll exemplifies the post-war German tradition of socially engaged literature, but while all his works betray concern for the political and moral health of the Federal Republic, the social antecedent is most specific in *The Lost Honor of Katharina Blum*. On 22 December 1971 a bank in Kaiserslautern was robbed and a policeman murdered. Assuming that this had to be the work of West Germany's then most notorious terrorists, the sensationalist newspaper owned by the press magnate Axel Springer, *Bild*, ran a front-page headline the next morning: "Baader-Meinhof gang kills again." Two weeks later Böll wrote an essay in the news magazine, *Der Spiegel*, in which he launched a virulent attack upon *Bild*, accusing the paper of stirring up lynch justice, of condemning without evidence, and of creating an atmosphere in which Ulrike Meinhof could never give herself up for fear of "landing in a cauldron of demagogy like some medieval witch." He finished by pleading that the terrorists be offered the prospect of fair trial rather than death in a hail of bullets. *Bild* responded with a campaign of character-assassination against Böll, calling him a terrorist sympathizer and likening him to Goebbels. Asked the following month by a Swiss newspaper whether he might one day turn the whole experience into a novel, Böll replied: "No, though it may be that one or two elements will be adapted and used for revenge. Even a writer sometimes wants to avenge himself." That vengeance came, two and a half years later, with the publication of *Katharina Blum*.

From the outset Böll makes no bones about his primary target. Having declared, in the traditional author's disclaimer, that characters and plot are fictitious, he continues (in an addition curiously omitted from the English translation): "Should the depiction of certain journalistic practices suggest similarities with the practices of *Bild*, such similarities are neither intentional nor coincidental but unavoidable." Katharina Blum, the victim in this case, is an unexceptional woman, 27 years of age, housekeeper to a professional couple, working hard to pay off her mortgage and rebuild her life after a broken marriage. At a masquerade party during Carnival in February 1974 she encounters a young man called Götten and spends the night with him, unaware that he is under observation as a suspected terrorist. Next morning he slips through the police net, and she is interrogated as an accomplice. Despite the rough handling she receives from the police, her real ordeal begins when the press becomes involved, specifically a newspaper called simply "*News*" (the capitalized German original, *ZEITUNG*, conveys better than the English the paper's meretricious tone). With no more than circumstantial evidence their screaming headlines and histrionic reporting present Katharina as a criminal and a slut. Her private life is publicly dissected, her friends are harassed, and facts are shamelessly twisted to fit the preconceived picture. Finally one of the journalists, in search of a quote, invades the hospital where Katharina's mother is seriously ill, and the old lady subsequently dies. Katharina arranges a meeting with the reporter concerned and, as he is making a crude sexual advance to her, she shoots him dead.

Böll's works are generally constructed on a dualistic pattern, one in which individual values such as integrity, love, and faith, are set against, and frequently overcome by, a social environment with different priorities, whether these are the war aims of the Third Reich or the materialistic preoccupations of the Federal Republic. *Katharina Blum* shows a similar configuration: a fundamentally decent citizen (whose name, to put the point beyond any doubt, means "pure flower") is crushed by agencies allegedly existing for her benefit. Throughout the text there is a sense of powerful forces behind the scenes, not just the press but also the police, politicians, and the business community, working together to protect their own interests above everything else. The story's subtitle, "How violence develops and where it can lead,'' makes plain that the source of the violence should be seen, not with the woman who shot the journalist, but with those who perpetrated the character assassination that brought her to that point. The revelation at the end that Götten was, after all, not a terrorist but simply an army deserter who had absconded with some cash serves further to put the authorities in the wrong and emphasize Katharina's role as victim, albeit one who, unusually for a Böll heroine, strikes back.

The story is presented by an unnamed narrator who affects the viewpoint of a detached observer trying to piece events together, but his protestations of impartiality are constantly undercut by irony. He cannot disguise his sympathy for Katharina nor his dislike of her persecutors, who show themselves in a persistently negative light and are also made the butt of several satirical digressions (rather heavy-footed ones, it must be said). Böll himself called *Katharina Blum* a ''pamphlet disguised as a narrative,'' and the anger beneath the surface composure is very apparent. But it is also here, in the priority of polemical intent over aesthetic quality, that the text's main failings lie. The narrative structure, for instance, is at times self-consciously arch, and touches of sentimentality, never far from Böll's writing, creep into his portrait of Katharina. There is, in addition, for all the passion of the message, a distinctly contrived aspect to the plot, with the boundaries between vice and virtue too tightly drawn. The story created a considerable impact when it was first published, and Volker Schlöndorff turned it into a highly successful film, but it seems likely to survive more as an interesting social document than as a work of great literature.

—Peter J. Graves

LOST ILLUSIONS (Illusions perdues)
Novel by Honoré de Balzac, 1837–43

Lost Illusions resembles another of Honoré de Balzac's novels, *The Black Sheep*, in that it is set partly in Paris and partly in the provinces. It is unique, however, among the novels and short stories of *The Human Comedy* in the even-handedness with which it treats both Paris and the provinces.

Lucien Chardon de Rubempré is the pivotal figure of the entire work. Even as Part I, *Les Deux Poètes* (*The Two Poets*) begins, he has already written a historical novel and a sonnet-sequence; his friend David Séchard is a scientist. But both, according to Balzac, are ''poets'' in that they creatively seek truth. Theirs is a fraternity of poetic aspiration, whether as writer or as scientist: thus, even before David marries Lucien's sister, the two young men are spiritual brothers. At the very end of *The Two Poets* Lucien is carried off to Paris by the provincial bluestocking Mme. de Bargeton.

In Part II, *Un grand homme de province à Paris* (*A Great Man of the Provinces in Paris*), Lucien is contrasted both with the journalist Lousteau and with the high-minded writer Daniel d'Arthez. Jilted by Mme. de Bargeton for the adventurer Sixte du Châtelet, Lucien moves in a social circle of high-class actress-prostitutes and their journalist lovers; soon he is the lover of Coralie. He becomes a reviewer, thus prostituting his literary talent. But he still nurtures the ambition of belonging to high society and longs to assume by royal warrant the surname and coat of arms of his mother's family (now sadly fallen in the world). In the furtherance of this social ambition, and urged on by Coralie's well-meaning advice, he switches his allegiance from the

liberal opposition press to the one or two royalist newspapers that support the government. This act of betrayal earns him the implacable hatred of his erstwhile journalist colleagues, who destroy Coralie's theatrical reputation. In the depths of his despair he forges his brother-in-law's name on three promissory notes: this is his ultimate betrayal of his identity. After Coralie's death he returns in disgrace to Angoulême, stowed away behind the Châtelets' carriage: Mme. de Bargeton has just married du Châtelet, who has been appointed prefect of that region.

Part III of the novel begins as a long flashback. At Angoulême David Séchard is betrayed on all sides but is supported by his loving wife Ève. He invents a new and cheaper method of paper production (the commercialization of paper-manufacturing processes is closely interwoven, at a thematic level, with the commercialization of literature). Lucien's forgery of his signature almost bankrupts him, and he has to sell out the secret of his invention to business rivals. The whole of Lucien's world has collapsed around him too. He is contemplating suicide when he is approached by a sham Jesuit priest, the Abbé Carlos Herrera, alias the escaped convict Vautrin whom Balzac had already presented in *Le Père Goriot*. Herrera takes Lucien under his protection; and off they drive to the capital, there to begin the assault on Paris anew.

Balzac revels in strong contrasts: Lucien and David, art and science, Lousteau and d'Arthez, journalism and literature, Lucien and Ève, Coralie and Ève, Paris and the provinces. Metaphorical hyperbole intensifies these contrasts: thus, Daniel d'Arthez and his followers in the upper room are like Jesus and his disciples (and Lucien/Judas betrays him), while Lucien's crucially testing week in Paris is compared to Napoleon's retreat from Moscow. Lucien's return to Angoulême behind the Châtelets' carriage stands in stark contrast to his departure from Angoulême in a carriage with Mme. de Bargeton: no other symbol—and a symbol of such simplicity—could so powerfully have conveyed the extent of his downfall.

Such contrasts, at a less superficial level, are features of technique rather than of substance. Characters and viewpoints are polarized, usually for structural and therefore narrative reasons. This polarization reaches the point of melodrama as Balzac appears to draw moral distinctions between ''vice'' and ''virtue.'' Coralie is the Fallen Woman, Ève an Angel of strength and purity; yet Balzac also describes Coralie's love for Lucien as an ''absolution'' and a ''benediction.'' Thus he underlines what he considers to be the fundamental resemblance of opposites: a philosophy of hypostatic monism. (The same point is made by Blondet, in discussion with Lucien, Lousteau, and Vernou. This theme is present almost everywhere in *The Human Comedy*, except notably in *The Black Sheep*.)

Like all the major works of *The Human Comedy*, *Lost Illusions* preeminently focuses upon the social nexus. Within the nexus of love, in her relationship with Lucien, Coralie is life-giving; her love has a sacramental quality. In an environment of worldly manoeuvring her influence upon him is fatal. She is, in other words, both a Fallen and a Risen Woman; all depends upon the nexus within which she is viewed. In the unfavourable environment of Angoulême Mme. de Bargeton is an absurd bluestocking; transplanted to Paris, she undergoes an immediate ''metamorphosis,'' becoming a true denizen of high society—and rightfully, in Part III, the occupant of the *préfecture* at Angoulême.

Even the change of tempo from Part II to Part III is but a superficial point of contrast between life as it is lived in the capital and life in the provinces. Everywhere the same laws of human behaviour apply. A man's downfall may come from the rapier thrust of the journalist or from the slowly-strangling machinations of the law. But duplicity is omnipresent in the world: that two-facedness of human life in all its aspects, from the universal to the specific, both in Paris and Angoulême.

In so many ways Lucien has two ''faces''; he even has two surnames! But is he endowed with real talent? Is he, despite the title of Part I, a true poet? Is his downfall brought about by a philistine commercial world, or does it result from a multiplicity of accidental factors? Does it arise from some deep-rooted shortcoming within himself? Balzac, criticized by Zola (among others) for his authorial commentaries and interventions, offers no real clue to this enigma.

—Donald Adamson

THE LOST STEPS (Los pasos perdidos)
Novel by Alejo Carpentier, 1953

Regarded by many critics as Alejo Carpentier's most important novel and the one that cemented his fame at the international level, *The Lost Steps* contains autobiographical elements (it parallels the author's experiences in Venezuela in 1947) and depicts as well in its nameless protagonists the general malaise of the post-war intellectual whose struggle against an alienated and inauthentic existence leads him to search for his own lost identity in the jungles of Latin America. It is a tale of the return through time to the lost origins of nature; by the same token, the narrative insists upon the impossibility of such a return to original innocence: the civilized man—the artist-intellectual—can never reclaim such innocence.

The narrator is a composer living in a large, cosmopolitan North American city with his wife Ruth, an actress whom he hardly ever sees. He feels himself to be lost in a dissolute and meaningless existence in which his artistic talents are commercially exploited and all of his friends are pseudo-intellectuals. He bitterly counts himself among them, and seeks escape through alcohol, sex, and self-recrimination. He portrays himself as a man without a country, a culture, or a profession; he resents the alienating, lonely life of the city and longs to be a different man with a different destiny. Nevertheless, his idealized yearning for an authentic existence and homeland is continually undermined by the facility with which he indulges in the behaviour he portrays as dissolute: he has no respect whatsoever for his French mistress, Mouche, but he cannot leave her bed. He sees himself as Sisyphus, condemned to a futility against which he cannot rebel.

The narrator accepts a commission from an old friend, the Curator, to go on an expedition into the jungles of Orinoco in search of primitive musical instruments, a trip that will offer him the opportunity to escape from his meaningless life and thereby rid himself of the guilt he suffers for having prostituted his talents. He is accompanied by Mouche, a vulgar woman who cannot withstand the harsh environment of the tropics and falls ill; the narrator has meanwhile fallen in love with a native woman named Rosario and abandons Mouche in order to join with his new lover and a band of travellers seeking to found their own city in the virgin interior. He is transformed once he leaves Mouche, the last vestige of his previous life, behind, and commits himself to Rosario; a striking contrast is established between his appetites and desires in the city as apposed to his basic needs in the jungle, where he grows lean, contented, and healthy on hard work, simple food, and Rosario's love.

When the travellers reach Santa Mónica de los Venados, the new city, the narrator perceives it as situated in the world of Genesis: he has travelled back to the origins of time. He decides never to return to the city, but he also discovers the urge to compose a threnody in the jungle, which makes the irony of his situation complete: he must return to civilization in order to obtain paper on which to compose his masterpiece, inspired by his escape from his previous existence! When a two-man search party arrives at Santa Mónica de los Venados, the narrator accompanies them back to the city, assuring Rosario he will return; she, however, turns away from him coldly, knowing he will not return. In the city, he becomes embroiled in a nasty divorce from his wife, and when, many months later, he does attempt to return to Rosario, he cannot find the secret opening in the jungle leading back to Santa Mónica de los Venados. The artist-intellectual is left, at the end of the narrative, to face a destiny and responsibility he cannot escape. He admits to himself that the creative act achieves nothing in a vacuum, and that he must affirm his legitimate place within the artistic community.

The narrative elements retrace the steps to a paradise lost and a reality regained. The contrasts between culture and nature, alienation and authentic existence, lust and love, the narrator's digressions on Romantic art, the horror and alienation of the 20th century, and his perception of the voyage he makes as a journey back through time to lost origins, are all woven together to form a reflection of the cosmopolitan artist's dilemma. His attempts to synthesize the reality of the culture he must be a part of with his longing for a lost innocence or lack of consciousness reinforce the fact that the artistic endeavour itself is as close as he will ever come to this lost utopian existence.

—Susan Isabel Stein

LOVE IN THE TIME OF CHOLERA (El amor en los tiempos del cólera)
Novel by Gabriel García Márquez, 1985

Gabriel García Márquez's 1985 novel is a masterpiece of sensuous prose, rivalling other contemporary texts such as Patrick Süskind's olfactory extravaganza of 18th-century France *Perfume* (1985) and Toni Morrison's vibrant account of Harlem life *Jazz* (1990) in its ability to summon up the textures, sensual pleasures, tastes, and smells associated with living in a particular place at a certain time. Overblown yet controlled, Márquez's story of life, love, and lust in a convention-bound provincial city on the Caribbean coast of Colombia displays great imaginative and narrative freedom coupled with almost novella-like discipline in its structuring of recurrent ideas.

Love in the Time of Cholera charts the love affair between a haughty, beautiful woman and her unfailingly devoted suitor, who for over 50 years (from late 19th- to early 20th-century) has pursued the object of his desire, both in silent observance and in torrents of exquisite love missives. His presence is not recognized until her husband, an eminent doctor and exemplary citizen, dies. As an elderly widow, she realizes that not all passion is spent; finally allowing herself the pleasures of spontaneity and physical freedom after a controlled upper-middle-class existence. This, though, is a meagre synopsis of Márquez's novel, for entwined within the central love story are the lives of other lovers, parents, children, and sundry relatives, as well as the ghost of a woman who drowned herself for unrequited love, a multilingual parrot and countless other personages—a remarkable feat of storytelling that takes off in all manner of exhilarating and surprising directions.

Despite its sprawling narrative style, Márquez's novel returns again and again to its central idea, that of the primacy of passion and feeling over order, honour, and authority. Love and sexual desire control, invigorate, and at times lay havoc to lives. Sometimes the participants are burnt up as if by cholera; after which they may completely recover, may be extinguished, or, as with the central suitor, may linger on in a state of perpetual convalescence. In Márquez's exquisitely meandering work, life, and love are shown as unpredictable and turbulent; forever surging and overflowing their bounds like the ever-present Caribbean sea and great Magdalena river.

Love in the Time of Cholera, however, is not just a plea for passion in a rule-bound world. The novel is also a meditation on old age and human memory. The main characters' biographies are laid out from childhood to near death, showing us lives actually lived, lives that could have been lived, and the way that memory can transfigure, keep alive, and obliterate the pain and ardour of earlier years. Such taking stock of lives spent is not wistful, however, for Márquez's characters have all got on with their lives successfully, despite the shimmering and beckoning half-presence of unrealized possibilities and unconsummated relationships.

Besides reflecting of love, old age, and memory, *Love in the Time of Cholera* gives the reader a richly detailed panorama of a provincial coastal city in times of cholera and civil war; its steamy and sleepy streets, rat-infested sewers, old slave quarter, decaying colonial architecture, and multifarious inhabitants evoked in loving and vital fashion. The novel, though, is not only social history, for Márquez, masterly practitioner of magic realism, heightens the historical material by weaving no end of fabulous tales within his account of Colombian life. In this way, he not only creates a marvellous piece of story-telling, but, perhaps even more pleasurably, Márquez shows us how our own lives are in many ways fabulous tales; each of us able to accommodate and transform the real through our own extraordinary, and even fabricated, versions of life stories.

—Anna-Marie Taylor

LOVES (Amores)
Poem by Ovid, c. 26–19 BC

Most people know when they have fallen in love; but not, apparently, the Ovid of this poem, which opens with his ruminating on whether an unexpected attack of love could conceivably be responsible for the sleepless night he is having. After concluding that, all things considered, this must indeed be the case, he next deliberates whether to put up a fight or give in. The most prudent course of action, he eventually decides, is to give in. This incongruously academic debate quickly introduces the reader to the emotional detachment which pervades the *Loves*. Not for Ovid the romantic pose of helpless subjection to a uniquely attractive woman (despite some superficial appearances to the contrary, e.g. II.17), and here no mention even of a woman at all; rather Ovid presents his condition as a matter entirely between himself and the love-god Cupid, the winged child with bow, arrows, and torch, so familiar in Western art and literature. He takes much the same line in *Amores* I.1, II.9A and 9B, and II.12.

The Greek poets of the Hellenistic period (3rd to 1st centuries BC), liked to depict Cupid physically attacking the lover with his traditional weaponry, while their Roman successors additionally portrayed the lover himself as a fighting man and love as a kind of warfare or military service. This had special significance in the principate of Augustus (31 BC–AD 14) because of his commitment to the glorification of martial prowess, particularly his own. By casting themselves as soldiers of love, the amatory elegists signalled their rejection of the military ideal in favour of an alternative life of love and art. Ovid, however, is bolder than the others, Tibullus and Propertius, in that he uses the concept to make contemporary militarism the butt of his deflating humour.

A fine case in point is the body of the present poem, where he transfers the warring Cupid—usually a puckish aggressor—to that most honorific of Roman military rituals, the Triumph. This was the formal distinction awarded to a victorious general for an outstanding success; it involved him being driven in a four-horse chariot through the streets of Rome to the temple of Jupiter Capitolinus, accompanied by his loyal lieutenants, and with his captives and spoils of war paraded in his procession (cf. Virgil, *Aeneid*, VIII, 370–453). With much the same ingenuity and wit as he adapts the conventional funeral dirge to suit a dead parrot in *Loves* II.6, Ovid here adapts the details of this spectacle to suit the god of love. Instead of the laurel wreath conventionally worn by the triumphing general, Cupid will wear one of myrtle, sacred to his love-goddess mother, Venus, and instead of the war-horses, he will have doves, also sacred to Venus and, then as now, symbolic of non-aggression. The triumphal chariot itself will be provided by Cupid's *vitricus*, ''stepfather,'' i.e. either Vulcan, the blacksmith-god, who could manufacture one, or possibly Mars, the war-god, who could lend one. (Both of them, the former usually and the latter sometimes, were credited with being Venus' husband, but Cupid's father was notoriously unknown.) Ovid then envisages Cupid's triumphal progress through the streets to traditional acclamation from the awed crowd. In his procession, however, young men and girls who have fallen victim to him, the newly-smitten Ovid included, will replace the conventional prisoners of war. Also among the captives ''with hands tied behind their backs'' will be the personified virtues ''Conscience'' (*Pudor*) and ''Common Sense'' (*Mens Bona*), while ''Flattery'' (*Blanditiae*), ''Passion'' (*Furor*), and ''Delusion'' (*Error*) will have pride of place among Cupid's supporters. For readers of Virgil's *Aeneid* this is a striking reversal of fortune for *Furor*, whose subjugation, ''hands tied behind its back,'' symbolizes in *Aeneid* I the peace and stability of the Augustan era (Augustus had set up in his forum Apelles' painting of *Furor* in chains at the victory procession of Alexander the Great). Venus herself will look on and enjoy the fun, we are told, but the mortal spectators will just present sitting targets for Cupid's further relentless assault.

Ovid then goes on to liken Cupid to Bacchus, god of wine and general tamer and civilizer of the world. So too, by implication, had the many artists who depicted groups of cupids in a chariot hauled, like Bacchus', by wild animals. In Ovid's time, however, the role of emulator of Bacchus had already been allotted to none other than Caesar Augustus himself, notably by Virgil in *Aeneid* VI, 804–5 (a passage which obliquely also compares Augustus with Alexander).

Finally, after setting up Cupid in competition with Augustus, Ovid suggests that he should take a leaf out of his book: like his ''cousin'' (the Latin word means ''relative'' in the loosest sense), the love-god should extend his mercy and protection to those he has conquered. Cupid could indeed be said to be related to Augustus in that Augustus liked to derive his descent from Aeneas, who, as the son of Venus by the Trojan Anchises, was technically Cupid's half-brother; and "clemency to the conquered" was a much-vaunted tenet of Augustan policy (cf. Virgil, *Aeneid*, VI, 853). However, Ovid's remark is no compliment. At various points in the poem he has, for fun, subverted the Augustan image presented especially in Virgil's *Aeneid* (though with no disrespect to Virgil himself) and systematically trivialized the public distinction by which Augustus set so much store (he was particularly proud of the triple triumph awarded him in 29 BC for the victories of Dalmatia, Illyria, and Actium) and which after 19 BC became restricted to members of the imperial family. Ovid's emphasis here on Cupid's kinship with Augustus (this disreputable candidate's one impeccable qualification for the honour now out of reach of sober citizens) must be recognized as nothing more or less than a final outrageous joke. It would be hardly surprising, however, if a ruler who stood on his dignity and was all but obsessed with his own image failed to appreciate it.

Guy Lee's unfettered translation conveys well the verve and elegance, the neatness, and the deceptively easy fluency of Ovid's elegiac couplets. Especially characteristic are the piling up of examples to reinforce a single point and the general liking for balance, antithesis, and wordplay, which a more literal translation of the Latin at lines 41–2 may serve to highlight:

tu pinnas gemma, gemma variante capillos,
ibis in auratis aureus ipse rotis.

(Your wings with jewels, with jewels your hair adorned,
you will ride, golden yourself, on gilded wheels.)

In style no less than attitude this is the quintessential Ovid.

—Joan Booth

THE LOWER DEPTHS (Na dne)
Play by Maksim Gor'kii, 1902

Of the more than one dozen plays that Maksim Gor'kii wrote, it is his second, *The Lower Depths*, that remains not just the most widely performed of his dramatic pieces, but also the single work that is most responsible for his literary reputation outside Russia. Like Gor'kii's first play, *Meshchane* (*The Petty Bourgeois*), it had its premiere at Stanislavskii's Moscow Art Theatre, which was also the first theatre to do justice to Chekhov's talent. The cast for the first performance included some of the finest actors in Russia: Ivan Moskvin played Luka, Vasilii Kachalov the Baron, and Olga Knipper (Chekhov's wife) had the role of Nastia. Stanislavskii himself took the part of Satin and later was to comment on the difficulty he had with the role as well as on the play's tumultuous reception.

Lacking a single dominant figure (or, more precisely, shifting from one key figure to the next), containing several structural flaws, and with a plot that is of only minor interest, *The Lower Depths* at first glance seems a surprising candidate for literary immortality. However, the very contrast with *The Petty Bourgeois* does much to explain the work's popularity with audiences. Gor'kii's first play is largely Chekhovian in its setting, in its types of characters, and in the atmosphere that envelops the action; indeed, several of the figures and incidents have direct parallels in *Tri sestry* (*The Three Sisters*). In *The Lower Depths*, however, Gor'kii—interestingly, for the only time in all of his plays—turns to the milieu that originally brought him fame as a writer of short stories. This is the world of the *bosiak* or vagabond, he who by choice or circumstance finds himself outside society. Gor'kii's vagabonds embrace a wide range of figures: some come from the lower classes, some are well-educated and know a better life; many are submissive before blows that life has dealt them, but others have made a firm decision to break with their past life and the social order. The more heroic of these characters may seem romanticized, but Gor'kii was the first to explore in detail a world of which most Russians had only been vaguely aware.

One of Gor'kii's strengths in all his writings is his ability to sketch characters quickly and memorably. Here the setting is a lower-class lodging, with both long-term residents who have sunk as low as they can (the literal meaning of the Russian title is "on the bottom") and others who pass through. For the most part the action is confined to a dank basement, lit by only a single window—thus an early title for the work was "Without Sunlight." Within this dreary world virtually every figure, both major and minor, is in some way memorable. There is the Baron, a person proud of his noble background and of his family's possessions, who professes a love for the truth and who attacks the dreams of others. He, however, in turn falls apart when his own vision of the better life that he presumably once lived is attacked as a lie. Vasilisa, along with her husband, the building's owner, beats her own sister, Natasha, who has plotted to run off to what she imagines would be a better life with the thief Pepel (who also happens to have been Vasilisa's lover). Nastia, a prostitute, escapes into the world of the romantic novels that she reads and tries to comfort others with her vision of a better life. Also prone to dreams is the Actor, who, like the Baron, has lost his real name and who appears to have dropped down the social rank. In contrast to some of the other characters in the play, he has never come to terms with his failure, and, at the end of the play, when he realizes the hopelessness of his yearnings, he hangs himself.

Also contributing to the play's success are the ideas expressed by two figures who are at its thematic centre even if Gor'kii never quite manages to work them fully into the plot. Luka, a wanderer who has only stopped by at the lodging, is prominent during the first three acts, while the fourth act contains a long monologue by Satin, a card sharp who has killed a man and has served time in prison. Luka tries to comfort others, encouraging Pepel in his desire to run off to Siberia, comforting a dying woman, and telling the Actor that there is a place where his drunkenness can be cured. Satin, like Luka, wants to help people, but he prefers a world without illusions: he wants people to confront the truth and feels that people can triumph over everything. It is he who utters one of Gor'kii's most quoted lines: "M-a-n! The word is magnificent; there's a proud ring to it! A man has to be respected! Not pitied . . . ."

In commenting on his play, Gor'kii himself later expressed a strong preference for Satin; Luka, he felt, offered only the consoling lie. That many have identified instead with Luka could be seen as a failing, as could the action of the last act, where, as Chekhov himself was the first to note, nearly all the important characters of the first three acts are absent. The latter is indeed a dramatic weakness—only the startling suicide of the Actor after Satin's long monologue imparts an emotional impact to the finale. And the play as a whole has sometimes been criticized as one of the works which make those living in the West believe that even uneducated Russians sit around in the evenings philosophizing about the meaning of life.

However, in posing the conflicts that lie at the heart of his play—between the soothing if possibly harmful lie and the harsh if possibly liberating truth, between the dreams that enable people to cope with the severity of their lives and the danger that those very dreams will leave them passive—Gor'kii has expressed irresolvable dilemmas with which audiences around the world have been able to identify. Dramatists, meanwhile, would appear to have learned from the play's seemingly chaotic structure. Such subsequent works as Eugene O'Neill's *The Iceman Cometh* and William Saroyan's *The Time of Your Life* employ the device of throwing together varied characters, some only tangentially related to the plot, and place an emphasis on self-revelation rather than on dramatic resolution. A few of Gor'kii's later plays are technically more perfect, but none matches *The Lower Depths* for originality of form or emotional impact.

—Barry P. Scherr

THE LULU PLAYS (Lulu)
Plays by Frank Wedekind, *Earth Spirit*, 1895, and *Pandora's Box*, 1904

Frank Wedekind's *Lulu Plays*—*Earth-Spirit* (*Der Erdgeist*) and *Pandora's Box* (*Die Büsche der Pandora*)—belong to the last years of the 19th century yet still retain their sensational and provocative impact. It is not diminished by recognizing them as important early documents of modernism, major precursors of Expressionism and Brecht, Surrealism and the theatre of the absurd. They were a deliberate affront to the conventions of contemporary naturalism, but also of "legitimate" theatre. They are entitled tragedies, yet they scorn sentiment and idealism and bring farce, melodrama, horror, and black humour. They manifest a flair for the grotesque, an irreverent spirit of parody and satire, and an enthusiasm for the stuff of penny-dreadfuls, vaudeville, circus, and *commedia dell'arte*. The characters, who display boastful arrogance, naive self-deceit, or a sense of humiliating doom, lack both dignity and psychological depth. They move puppet-like in an episodic action which flaunts its improbabilities (even through an element of self-reference). The dialogue aims at striking formulations and contains flashes of wit, but is often cryptic. Comic allusions to matters topical at the turn of the century go hand-in-hand with hints of timeless mythical significance, caricature with a promise of symbolism. The expressions of monomaniacal passion breathe an intense vigour which vouches for the dramatist's commitment to more than stunning theatricality. Yet the all-pervasive irony makes it difficult to determine what purpose, other than ridicule of the complacent acceptance of traditional values, underlies the defiance of aesthetic orthodoxy, and what audiences are meant to think after being exposed to Wedekind's assault on their emotions and expectations.

These plays would not present such a challenge to directors, players, audiences, and critics if it were not felt that they have something unusual and urgent to say. They concern the awesome mystery of the irresistibly attractive Lulu, whose relevance has few limits. A sex symbol, she stands, it seems, for woman and beauty, but also for instinct and sinful pleasure, for the power of undomesticated nature or a life force at odds with society's morals and institutions. A parallel is suggested between her situation and that of art subject to market forces. She defies rational understanding. Her would-be male tamers dream of enjoying sole possession of the ultimate happiness she appears to promise. Yet that goal is elusive or illusory, and she is a threat to their intelligence and self-esteem—and to their lives. In *Earth Spirit* her first two husbands die on her account before she

shoots the third, a ruthless operator who, enraged by her unfaithfulness, tries to make her kill herself. Her willingness to please men is stressed, but also the limits to her adaptability. Men proud of their success in other spheres prove incapable of coming to terms with their dependence on her. Their failure signals a basic flaw in a civilization that claims to master nature and instinct but is ludicrously and tragically blind to reality.

The colonization of woman and beauty (through marriage or prostitution) by the spirit of commercialism is prominent in *Pandora's Box*. The urge to possess and control her is again linked with a need to destroy her. It is, in Nietzschean terms, the product of a life-denying mentality. The convicted murderer Lulu, aided by her admirers, makes a miraculous escape from her German prison and joins the *demi-monde* of Paris, only to face blackmail and the threat of enlistment by a white-slave trader. Still accompanied by her most faithful and despondent admirers, but without her former good looks and the fortune and status obtained from her marriages, she becomes a miserable prostitute in London and falls victim to a sex murderer who believes he is cleansing the world of evil. Suggestions in the Paris scenes that some women might prefer the brothel to the marriage bed and, even more, Lulu's horrific death at the hands of Jack the Ripper, inevitably caused a notorious confrontation with the German censors before 1918. There are also other affronts to moral sensibilities. The action questions the meaningfulness of love, virginity, gratitude, and unselfishness. It implies that respectable society is, in essence, a collection of criminals; that the consciously selfish brute deserves admiration as a prototype superman; and that social norms and perversions both mirror the same deeply rooted pernicious attitudes. Lulu may just conceivably offer the basis of an alternative morality. Yet supporters of permissiveness may note that Wedekind does not argue that licence is synonymous with happiness. Nor are most feminists drawn to a heroine who seems to demand emancipation and yet to reflect male prejudices.

As Lulu points out, her admirers are willing to sacrifice everything for her, whether they do in arrogant hope or with sighs of despair. Everyone is in love with her: a doctor, a painter, a powerful newspaper owner and his son who is a poet, a circus strong man, a schoolboy, and a lesbian countess. So, too, is a strange old man on the verge of death who may be her father. He alone among her slavish adherents escapes the slaughter of the last act. His survival only underlines the impression that life without Lulu—without true vitality, detached from the hope or illusion that happiness is possible—is a sad thing indeed. No permanently satisfactory mode of involvement with her has been shown, only the superlative value she has for men, which has nothing to do with security, but much with excitement, and cannot be measured in money.

In his opera *Lulu*, Alban Berg captured the discordancy of Wedekind's plays and highlighted some of their important patterns of repetition by reducing the sprawling double-drama to a much neater work. Wedekind had indeed first written them as one five-act play. That "monster tragedy" then underwent a remarkably complicated history of continuous revision. The recent publication of his original manuscript version has increased critical curiosity about the changes he made to secure appearance of his work in print and on stage, to improve its dramatic effectiveness, and above all to placate or bamboozle the censors, who remained adamant that *Pandora's Box* was unsuited for public consumption. It has also raised hopes of unravelling the many paradoxes in the more readily available texts, and of confirming their contested claim to be modern classics by confidently establishing Wedekind's intended meaning. That meaning he evidently (but mistakenly) believed was clear enough to any intelligent person willing to question commonplace preconceptions of human dignity and the meaning of life and to react to the dramatic action as much as to the words spoken. It is likely, however, that the drama of Lulu, in any version, will continue to shock and puzzle, and to prove its strengths more often in enthusiastic experimental performances than in established repertoire.

—John Hibberd

LUO GUANZHONG

See WATER MARGIN

THE LUSIADS (Os Lusíadas)
Poem by Luís de Camões, 1572

Luís de Camões is the greatest poet in the Portuguese language, and *The Lusiads* is his finest achievement. Although a master of the Petrarchist lyric and the author of exquisite sonnets in this vein, he has always been best known for this epic poem, which is perhaps the best example of the genre in postclassical European literature. The 16th century believed firmly in the hierarchy of literary forms and placed the epic at the very summit of poetic creation. Camões responded by marrying the noblest style to the greatest heroic exploits of his time. *The Lusiads* is thus a poem fit for heroes.

The word takes its name from the mythical father of the Portuguese nation, Lusus, and is clearly meant to rival the great epics of antiquity. The author says as much in his opening stanzas, declaring—in an obvious reference to the first line of Virgil's *Aeneid*: ''Arma virumque cano'' (''I sing of arms and the man'')—that he will praise the deeds of those famous Portuguese heroes who left their Lusitanian shore to sail previously uncharted seas and discover new worlds, carrying to the very heart of the Infidel's territory the message of the Christian faith and the Portuguese empire. He calls upon the *tágides*, or nymphs of the river Tagus, to inspire him to write a work worthy of these intrepid adventurers whose exploits far outshine these of Ulysses or Aeneas, Alexander or Trajan. This is, then, a truly national epic and one which has truly great events to celebrate. In a poem of close on 9,000 lines, divided into ten cantos and just over 1,100 stanzas, Camões provides his public with a pageant of Portuguese history. Published for the first time in 1572, in the somewhat febrile atmosphere of the reign of King Sebastião (to whom it is dedicated), who dreamed of feats of arms and a Portuguese empire that would rival that of ancient Rome in glory, it exalts and exemplifies what many felt to be the country's special mission. The result is, in the words of Frank Pierce in his 1973 edition of the work, ''a remarkable poetic record of the rise of Portugal and its emergence as a power of European importance and the creator of the first modern overseas empire.''

Little is known about Camões's life, and this has allowed critics to embroider and fantasize. What is clear, however, is that he was a man of deep learning and justifiably patriotic sentiments. Taking his reader through Portugal's history, he selects the high points of its past to suggest that it has a unique place in the scheme of things. Very much a Renaissance man (he was probably born in 1525 and may have attended the University of Coimbra before embarking on a life of adventurous wanderings in Portugal's overseas possessions), he does not hesitate to call on the gods and goddesses of pagan mythology to help illustrate his heroic tale. Thus, in Canto I, the gods assemble on Olympus to debate whether or not to support the Portuguese as they watch Vasco da Gama's ships set sail on their voyage of discovery. Venus and Mars (representing the idealized Portuguese attributes of sensuality and valour) wish them well, but Bacchus comes out against them. By Canto II we see the ships, despite Bacchus' continued attempts to hinder them, rounding the coast of Africa and reaching Malindi (in what is now Kenya) and a warm welcome. In Canto III, for the benefit of his foreign hosts (and, of course, for Camões's public and potential patrons) Vasco da Gama surveys his nation's history. The most famous section deals with the tragic love-affair of Inês de Castro, which leads on to reflections on the power of love and, especially, the trouble it can cause. A typical litany of sinful lovers from King David and Bathsheba to Mark Antony and Cleopatra brings the canto to an end on a moralistic and melancholy note, although the real purpose of this apparent digression may well be elsewhere. As we know from his other poetry, Camões is sensitive to love's hurts. But there may also be a political consideration here: it is surely not without significance that the poet alludes to examples from Portugal's recent past (to Inês, and to the adulterous love-affair between the weak King Ferdinand and Leonor Teles) and concludes that ''um baxo amor os fortes enfraquece'' (''base love weakens the strong''). A message here perhaps for King Sebastião?

Cantos IV and V take us through the great age of Portuguese history, with the revolution of 1383 and the rise to power of King João I, naturally stressing the battle of Aljubarrota which sealed Portugal's independence, and the first overseas voyages. Here too, though, there are some discordant notes as Camões introduces the Old Man of Restelo, who watches the departing ships from the banks of the Tagus, warning against ambition and the vanity of restless endeavour. These Cassandra-like sentiments no doubt reflect Camões's humanist awareness of the limits of fame and of the active life in the search for human happiness. Similarly, in Canto V, which includes the famous episode of the giant Adamastor, there is a gentle reminder of the status of the writer (a typically humanist theme) and a plea for greater recognition. The following cantos continue the narrative of Vasco da Gama's adventures, interspersed with moralistic and philosophical comments (on life's injustices, the dangers of ambition, etc.) before finishing with an extraordinary episode—and one which has shocked some readers—in which the Portuguese are guided to the Isle of Love by amorous nymphs who delight in being ravished by the lustful mariners. The final and very lengthy canto (156 stanzas) is by turns descriptive and philosophical: it serves, above all, to extol heroic values and ends with an appeal for fortitude and high enterprise.

Camões's great epic is firmly rooted in the moral and political atmosphere of its time. Beneath the surface optimism and pride in Portuguese achievements there is an unmistakable note of doubt and criticism. But *The Lusiads* is beautifully written, eminently quotable and, to the Portuguese, the equivalent of the Bible and Shakespeare. It is, and deservedly so, the touchstone of Portuguese culture. Camões's is the voice of that ''Portuguese sea'' of which Fernando Pessoa speaks, perpetuating the memory of those discoverers whose birthplace was a small country but who chose the wide world as their grave.

—Michael Freeman

LYSISTRATA (Lysistrate)
Play by Aristophanes, 411 BC

Lysistrata is doubtless Aristophanes' boldest and bawdiest drama. Composed at the height of the devastating Peloponnesian War (431–404 BC), when Athens and Sparta were locked in a protracted battle for dominance in Greece—a war that rendered all of the Greek mainland a battleground, and a war that Athens would eventually lose—*Lysistrata* dramatizes the tale of rebellious women imposing an end to the hostilities. Tired of all the bellicosity and loss of life, an heroic Athenian housewife, Lysistrata, convenes a secret congress of Greek women. They agree to withhold all sexual favours from the men until peace is restored. The males soon grow half-crazed with frustration, deprivation, and desire. (Old Comedy is usually raucous and bawdy; choruses frequently wore large leather phalluses on stage—props especially appropriate for this drama.) Although the women, sexually agitated themselves, would just as well surrender their advantage, Lysistrata repeatedly and tirelessly shames them into upholding the sex embargo. Indeed, the Athenian girls seize the Acropolis, the sacred ground reserved for temples and shrines, and lock up the treasury—thereby establishing a first-rate blockade, which isolates the men from their gods, their money, and their women. The chorus of Athenian elders is ignominiously defeated, and all the so-called warriors of Greece are overcome and sexually disarmed.

Soon, male sentinels and ambassadors from every part of Greece converge on Athens, eager to surrender, rabid to restore sexual relations, and, as it were, win the peace. The women drive a hard bargain and carry the day. All the men are utterly defeated by the women's stratagems, are brought to the bargaining table, and are forced to yield to the women's terms and to a cessation of hostilities. The women, as the saying goes, come out on top; they conclude the play with a grand victory and a celebration party.

Clearly there is here a plenitude of controversial material: patriots would be upset by the women's consorting with the enemy; members of the war party would be shocked by the suggestion that there ought to be "peace at any price," especially a "peace without honour"; pious Athenians would be offended at the sacrilegious seizure of the holy shrines; and politicos would be nonplussed by the trivialization of government and of law and order. Furthermore, the play constitutes a direct blow to Athens' intellectual pride—for Athenians presented their society as a city-state founded upon principles of "wisdom," and perceived themselves as being engaged in a century of philosophical and cultural growth and sophistication. Instead, Aristophanes dramatizes irrationality and decline. Epic heroism is humbled in the dust, for the psychological implications of this dramatic fiction are that male aggressiveness, realized in its penchant for swordsmanship, is nothing more than the sexual urge run wild. Men are accordingly depicted as mechanical warrior-studs, helplessly gripped by carnal and disruptive instincts and drives. However, women hardly fare any better; throughout, they are portrayed as wavering and fickle, with tendencies toward nymphomania and alcoholism. No one is spared.

But hardest hit by the play's satiric ploys is self-satisfied male chauvinism. Athenian society was complacently and intransigently male-dominated, its women not even granted citizens' rights. A woman's place was in the home. It is in this area that Aristophanic satire is brought most heavily to bear, turning custom and convention upside-down. What would have outraged much of the audience is precisely this "women's issue": quite simply put, in Aristophanes' satiric plot, women take over. It was clearly a humorous—but galling—thesis, annoying enough to the audience, doubtless, to earn his play low grades in the annual dramatic competition.

In fact, however, Aristophanes liked this ploy well enough to utilize the theme of women coming into power in two more of his extant plays—*Thesmophoriazousai* (*The Poet and the Women*) and *Ekklesiaszousai* (*Women in Power*). Such a dramatic theme also allowed Aristophanes to mock Platonic ideas of an ideal utopian republic. Victorious feminism was a topic that disturbed his audience and captured their attention while doubtless making them uneasy.

—Anna Lydia Motto & John R. Clark

M

THE MABINOGION

Collection of Welsh oral tales, first written down by an unknown 14th-century author. Name derives from the word ''Mabinogi'' [Tale of Youth] from the 11th-century *Pedair Cainc y Mabinogi* [The Four Branches of the Mabinogi]. These four tales—''Manawydanab Llyr'' [Manawydan, Son of Llyr], ''Pwyll Penderic Dynet'' [Pwyll, Prince of Dyved], ''Math vab Mathonwy'' [Math, Son of Mathonwy], and ''Branwen Uerch Lyr'' [Branwen, Daughter of Llyr]—were augmented with folklore, the additional stories ''Breuddwyt Maxen Wledig'' [The Dream of Maxen Wledig], ''Cyfranc Llud a Llevelis'' [Lludd and Llevelis], ''Mal y Kavas Culwch Olwen'' [Culwch and Olwen], ''Breuddwyt Rhonabwy'' [The Dream of Rhonabwy], and three Arthurian romances—''Chwedyl Jarlles y Ffynnon'' [The Lady of the Lake], ''Historia Peredur vab Evrawc'' [Peredur, Son of Efrawc], and ''Chwedyl Gereint vab Erbin'' [Gereint, Son of Erbin]—to form the modern *Mabinogion*.

PUBLICATIONS

Owein (individual tale, modern edition), edited by R.L. Thomson. 1968.

*

Critical Studies: *The Mabinogion* by J.B. John, 1901; *Lady Charlotte Guest and the Mabinogion* by David R. Phillips, 1921; *Celtic Myth and Arthurian Romance*, 1926, *Arthurian Tradition and Chrétien de Troyes*, 1949, *Wales and Arthurian Legend*, 1956, and *Arthurian Literature in the Middle Ages*, 1959, all by R.S. Loomis; *Rhiannon: An Inquiry into the Origins of the First and Third Branches of the Mabinogi*, 1953, and *Folklore and Myth in the Mabinogion*, 1958, both by William J. Gruffydd; *La Civilisation française dans les Mabinogion* by Morgan Watkin, 1962; *Medieval Celtic Literature* by R. Bromwich, 1974; ''Early Prose: *The Mabinogi*'' by G.E. Jones, in *A Guide to Welsh Literature 1*, edited by A.O.H. Jarman and G.R. Hughes, 1976; *The Mabinogi* by P. MacCana, 1977; *The Four Branches of the Mabinogi* by Sioned Davies, 1993; *Medieval Welsh Literature* by Andrew Breeze, 1997; *A Century of Welsh Myth in Children's Literature* by Donna R. White, 1998.

* * *

The Mabinogion is the collective name for a group of Welsh tales, first written down in the 14th century and contained primarily in the *White Book of Rhydderch* and the *Red Book of Hergest*; at least some of these tales were undoubtedly in existence orally at a considerable time before they were written. The collective name ''Mabinogion,'' which has disputed meanings and does not adequately describe the contents of what we now know as *The Mabinogion*, was first used by Lady Charlotte Guest, who translated the text into English in the early 19th century, making it a popular Welsh and Arthurian source book.

The arrangement of the tales that most editors still follow (from Lady Guest's lead and from the *White* and *Red* Books) lends weight to the argument that, although the text of *The Mabinogion* is diverse in terms of the historical origin of its tales, there is a discernible thematic coherence in the written form in which they appear. *The Mabinogion* begins with ''The Four Branches of the Mabinogi'' (referred to as such in the text) which may once have formed a coherent and continuous narrative cycle, but which, in the form in which we have them, bear no strong narrative relationship to each other.

Like the other tales in *The Mabinogion*, the ''Four Branches'' deal with figures of, or associated with, the ruling aristocracy—Pwyll, Prince of Dyved; Manawydan, Son of Llyr; Math, Son of Mathonwy; and Branwen, Daughter of Llyr. The tale of the last of these has in it the most impressive villain in *The Mabinogion*, Evnissyen, whose patriotic pride leads him to maim the King of Ireland's horses and later to stab with his fingers the heads of one hundred Irish warriors who are hiding in flour bags hung on pillars. Indeed, the themes of aristocratic conflict and power games are heavily to the fore throughout *The Mabinogion*, and particularly in the Four Branches, in which we are given a picture of Wales and Britain divided into small kingdoms existing uneasily side by side, or ruled over equally uneasily by, for example, ''Bran,'' whose kingship might appear (from the fact that his head is buried in London looking toward France), to have been in existence due to the expediency of facing a common enemy.

As the tales in *The Mabinogion* progress it becomes clear that there is some sort of thematic change, as the concepts of ''courtliness'' and ''chivalry'' appear more frequently and affect the behaviour of the characters. This is best signified by the fact that in ''Culwch and Olwen'' (alternatively ''Kilhwch and Olwen'') King Arthur makes what is probably his first appearance in literature. In this tale he is already seen as an authoritative ruler, preparing the way for what is recognizably the Arthur of mainstream Arthurian literature, living by chivalric ideals and controlling his kingdom from the centre, either through his knights or by his own actions (the list of feats performed by Arthur and his men in ''Culwch and Olwen'' is Herculean).

The Mabinogion ends (modern versions tending to drop Lady Guest's ''Taliesin'') with ''Peredur, Son of Efrawc'' and ''Gereint, Son of Erbin,'' which bear remarkable resemblance to Chrétien de Troyes's *Perceval* and *Erec et Énide* (*Eric and Enide*) respectively. Whether the Welsh tales, in a form of which we are currently unaware, influenced Chrétien or whether the influence was in the opposite direction is less important than the fact that the correspondences of the texts reveals that the Celtic nature of the Welsh tales was being tempered by an awareness of other cultural ideals, and in particular that the Celtic religious content of the oral tales had been partly Christianized by the time they were written (though not necessarily by the scribes who preserved them). As modern scholarship has looked further into the sometimes unharmonious confluence of paganism and Christianity in Celtic literature, it has become apparent that texts such as *The Mabinogion* contain remnants of the pagan past in various forms. It is likely, for example, that the proliferation of kings, queens, princes, and princesses in the tales (especially in the ''Four Branches'') is the product of a Christian euhemerization of what were once ancient gods and goddesses of the Welsh Celts from whom the stories originate. Equally, the powerfully symbolic cauldron, which in ''Branwen, Daughter of Llyr'' is a site of the regeneration of dead warriors and is sought for in another land (Ireland), can be seen to be a prefiguration of the courtly/chivalric/ Christian grail story.

The Mabinogion is not, then, a text set marmoreally in a certain time-period. Firstly, the oral composition of its tales was deeply affected by changes in the cultural make-up of the society from which it originates, reflecting the difficulties inherent in the Christianizing of a pagan people. Secondly, its transference to written form may be seen in part to have affected perspectives of its ''coherence'' as a text, and it is therefore a significant artefact in the history of the move in cultures from the oral to the written. Finally, we need to be aware that what we understand today by ''The Mabinogion'' (in translation at least) is in many ways a product of the early Victorian culture which, through Lady Charlotte Guest's work, brought *The Mabinogion* to a greater audience. It still remains for the overlapping cultural ideologies at play in *The Mabinogion* to be disentangled and fully understood.

—Colin Graham

MAD LOVE (L'Amour fou)
Prose by André Breton, 1937

Published in 1937, *Mad Love* follows on from *Nadja* and *Communicating Vessels* to form the third element of a prose quartet completed by *Arcane 17* in which André Breton presents and examines various aspects of his affective life and his artistic preoccupations. All four works constitute a particular kind of autobiographical writing in which reflection and analysis complement and at times replace chronological narrative in the elaboration of the discourse. As in the two earlier works, Breton makes use of photographs, not just to eliminate the need for verbal descriptions but to accompany and illustrate certain phrases or references in the text.

Mad Love continues the account of the quest for a new love commenced in *Communicating Vessels*, but the fourth of the seven chapters contains an evocation of Breton's encounter with the woman, Jacqueline Lamba, who was to become his second wife.

In Chapter I Breton is more ostensibly concerned with the definition and illustration of the Surrealist concept of ''convulsive beauty'': indeed its final paragraph consists of the dramatic proclamation, ''Convulsive beauty will be.'' Among the examples of the concept that he cites are Prince Rupert's drops, crystals, alcyonarians, madrepores, corals—and poetic images, of the kind produced by automatic writing.

The value of the opening chapter as a prefiguration of what is to come later in the book is provided more obviously, however, by the pretty waitress in a little restaurant and the word-play on ''l'Ondine'' and ''on dîne'' (''the Udine'' and ''One dines''): she could be seen as a modern water-sprite, since she was a performer in an aquatic show.

Chapter II begins with the repetition of a pair of questions with which Breton and Éluard had launched an inquiry in the review *Minotaure*: ''Can you say what has been the most important encounter in your life? To what extent has this encounter given you the impression of being fortuitous? Or necessary?'' Breton goes on to consider various definitions of chance, including the one by Souriau ''the meeting of an external causality and an internal finality,'' and concluding with that of the modern materialists, according to which ''chance would be the form of manifestation of external necessity working its way into the human subconscious''; and the chapter

closes with a recognition of the manoeuvrings of desire in search of its object.

In Chapter III this abstract theme is made concrete in the account of a visit made by Breton and Giacometti to the Flea Market in Paris in the spring of 1934. The sculptor at that time was endeavouring to solve a problem posed by the face of a female statue: the discovery there of a mask-cum-helmet was to prove the decisive key. For his part Breton picked up a wooden spoon with a shoe at the end of the handle which satisfied his previous wish, inspired by a curious phrase ''le cendrier Cendrillon''; (''the Cinderella ashtray''), that Giacometti should make for him a glass slipper, Cinderella's lost slipper, to be used as an ashtray. In the postscript to the chapter the sexual connotations of the spoon and the slipper reminded Breton of Freud's theories (''Concerning Eros and the struggle against Eros'') and of Freud's proposition that ''the two instincts, both the sexual instinct and the death-instinct, behave like self-preservative instincts.''

Chapter IV gravitates around the account of Breton's encounter with the beautiful young woman who was soon to become his new bride, and subsequently by his commentary on his 1923 poem, ''Tournesol,'' a commentary which seeks to demonstrate its prophetic nature in relation to this meeting with Jacqueline.

The fifth chapter is essentially a lyrical presentation of the couple's reactions to the Canary Islands. Here the themes of love and desire are accompanied by suggestions of paradise regained. Breton refers to the title of the Buñuel and Dali film *L'Âge d'or* [The Golden Age] in contrast with the ''age of mud'' that contemporary Europe called to mind, before closing this part of the book with a passionate invocation to Mount Teide, the volcano that dominates Tenerife.

The study is pursued from a different angle in Chapter VI, where the author discovers that the mirror of love between two people can be clouded by circumstances totally foreign to their love, but the final chapter, in the form of a letter to their daughter Aube, intended to be read by her when she was 16, dispels the impression that life and love are full of vicissitudes. Breton expresses the hopes that Aube will embody the eternal power of Woman and that the idea of ''mad love'' will be her guiding principle, before closing with the words ''I wish you to be madly loved.''

The publication of *Mad Love* was an indication of the importance of the title-theme for members of the Surrealist movement. The precise significance of the word ''amour'' for Breton is revealed in a couple of sentences slipped into Chapter V:

Love, the only love there is, carnal love, I adore, I have never ceased to adore your pernicious shadow, your mortal shadow. A day will come when man will know how to recognize you for his sole master and honour you even in the mysterious perversions with which you surround him.

—Keith Aspley

MADAME BOVARY
Novel by Gustave Flaubert, 1857

Gustave Flaubert published his novel, *Madame Bovary*, in serial form in 1856 (first book publication 1857), using it to develop ideas, themes, and techniques already embryonically present in his earlier unpublished writing. He first conceived of it as tracing the destiny of a young Flemish woman leading an uneventful life in the provinces, escaping only through religious mysticism. This original anecdote, whose possibilities Flaubert explored further in his tale, ''A Simple Heart,'' was enriched in the novel by newspaper accounts of the life and death of a Normandy woman married to a health officer, by the diary of Louise Pradier, whose sexual adventures and financial predicaments seem to have suggested certain aspects of Emma Bovary's life, and by the personality of Flaubert's current mistress, the writer Louise Colet.

In its final form, the plot recounts the life of a young woman, Emma Rouault, who marries an unremarkable provincial health officer, Charles Bovary, in the expectation, based on her reading of sentimental novels, that love will transform the boredom of her existence and bring her happiness. Emma's reading, uncritical, incomplete, and incapable of distinguishing between fact and fantasy, feeds her yearning for passion and excitement. Part of the power of Flaubert's depiction lies in the combination of his own sharp awareness of the seductive nature of such romantic promises and his pessimistically clear-sighted vision of reality. When Charles, although he loves her, fails to satisfy her either emotionally or sexually, Emma tries to transform him, first into a romantic lover, then into successful doctor. This ambitious attempt leads disastrously to a botched operation on the club-footed stable boy of a local inn. Emma also seeks escape through motherhood, sexual affairs, religious mysticism, reading, and material possessions, but finds each venture doomed to failure—an endless repetition of the same. Emma's first lover, Rodolphe, a cynical and experienced philanderer, seduces her despite his initial concerns about the difficulties of getting rid of her, and brings the affair to an abrupt end on the evening before the two of them were to have run away together. The letter in which he announces this decision is a masterpiece of hypocrisy, egotism, and debased Romantic cliché.

Later, she meets a former admirer, Léon, at a performance of Donizetti's opera, *Lucia di Lammermoor*, which Emma characteristically leaves before the mad scene. The two soon become lovers. Despite superficial differences—Léon is weak, inexperienced, and vacillating, and Emma herself, submissive with Rodolphe, now assumes the dominant role—this second affair reinforces the novel's central theme, that of the eternal monotony of illusory passion.

The dreariness and insignificance of provincial existence is beautifully illustrated by a range of minor characters, and in particular by the pharmacist Homais, a walking encyclopedia of clichés and received opinions. In such circumstances, Emma's longing to find intensity of experience leads her to desire material possessions she cannot afford, and thence into a plummeting spiral of debt. On the point of bankruptcy she is rejected again by her first lover, refuses the possibility of selling her sexual favours to a rich neighbour, and chooses instead to commit suicide. Ironically, Charles, devastated by her death, arranges a funeral as romantic as she herself could have wished. He himself dies shortly afterward, leaving their young daughter Berthe obliged to earn her living in a cotton mill.

Flaubert's achievement lies in the deliberate choice of a banal subject and unremarkable characters, in his refusal either to elevate or condemn Emma's conduct, and in his subtle, sophisticated use of narrative focus. Insisting that the author should be present everywhere in his novel but visible nowhere, he rejected the authorial interventions commonly practised at that time and attempted instead to show events and individuals through the thoughts of his central characters. To do so, he used a technique known as free indirect discourse, where the thoughts of the inarticulate protagonists are conveyed through the discourse of the narrator, but in ways that uses the images, memories, and vocabulary typical of them. Thus we both share the perceptions of the characters and are forced to maintain a critical distance from them.

The critical distance is increased by the fact that recurrent images and structural patterning draw our attention to the repetitive nature of experiences that Emma initially perceives as unique, and by Flaubert's insistence that the characters, however richly complex they consider themselves, are seen by others not as individuals but as stereotypical members of a series.

Determined to create a sonorous and rhythmical style, Flaubert frequently complained in his letters that writing was a torment for him, yet for the reader much of the novel's pleasure springs from the sense of constant tension between struggle and spontaneity, mental disgust and physical delight. That delight, however ironic, is evident in many of the set-piece descriptions—the rural wedding with its elaborate cake, the agricultural fair in which Rodolphe's words of seduction are punctuated by the bureaucrat's speech, and the evocation of Rouen cathedral, where the guide's description of religious statuary and architecture counterpoints Léon's erotic longing for Emma. Distinctive, too, it is the precise detail of Flaubert's descriptions, most notably in the remorselessly realistic account of Emma's suicide.

The desire to draw on and analyse apparently banal elements of everyday existence within the context of a specifically modern French society, and to do so in ways that refuse to ennoble or embellish them, not only marked a change with much contemporary literature but also led to problems with government censorship. Both Flaubert and the review in which *Madame Bovary* had appeared were accused of offences to public morality, with the prosecuting lawyer arguing forcefully that not a single character in the novel is in a position to condemn Emma's behaviour from a position of unimpeachable virtue. Nevertheless, the government lost its case, and the novel was published in volume form in April 1857. Though much of the immediate critical response was stridently hostile, *Madame Bovary* has come to be seen as exemplary by readers, critics, and novelists alike.

Above all, perhaps, the depiction of the physical and intellectual limitations placed on women in mid-19th-century France, the exploration of the inadequacies of language, and the fact that Flaubert, far from setting himself apart from Emma, inscribes the same failure into his own desire to capture reality, all make this a novel of particularly haunting resonance.

—Rosemary Lloyd

THE MADWOMAN OF CHAILLOT (La Folle de Chaillot)
Play by Jean Giraudoux, 1945

The Madwoman of Chaillot is one of the most successful plays written by Jean Giraudoux. When it was first produced in Paris on 19 December 1945, its subject matter coincided perfectly with the feelings of the French people. France had just come out of the devastating effects of World War II and the humiliating experience of the German occupation. As a result, the French people were seeking to break loose from the shackles of the past few years and to look to a better future. At the same time, emotions were running high over the collaboration of some French citizens with the Nazis and over the resultant corruption. There was a tendency on the part of the French to see things as right or wrong. Giraudoux's latest work incorporated these elements and appealed immediately to the public of that time. *The Madwoman of Chaillot* had a direct, uncomplicated approach to good and evil. The play is a fantasy in which the ''good'' people succeed in ridding their world of the ''bad'' people, and it seeks a happy ending.

The protagonist of the play, the Madwoman of Chaillot, was based upon an eccentric figure whom the playwright had seen on the streets of Paris only once. This Madwoman, the Countess Aurelia, seems to be a ridiculous figure, clothed in an outlandish manner, as Giraudoux describes in his stage directions: ''the grand fashion of 1885, a taffeta skirt with an immense train . . . ancient button shoes, and a hat in the style of Marie Antoinette.'' When she first appears on stage at the Café Chez Francis, she asks the waitress: ''Are my bones ready, Irma?,'' setting the comic tone of the piece. The people who surround Aurelia include the flower girl, the ragpicker, the street singer—all the ordinary, humble people who represent the real essence of life and possess the true wisdom, in Giraudoux's view. Aurelia discovers that the ''evil'' people of the world—the financiers, the barons, the presidents—are planning to destroy the way of life of the common folk. These people are all representatives of the capitalist world, a surprisingly direct political reference on the part of the playwright, who was usually discreet in these matters. The capitalists have uncovered the fact that there is oil underneath the Café Chez Francis where the Countess and her friends congregate. They are determined to seek out this oil, even though in doing so they must destroy the beauty and charm of the area.

When Aurelia becomes aware of their intentions, she puts her own plans into motion. She calls three of her friends—the Madwoman of Passy, the Madwoman of Saint Sulpice and the Madwoman of La Concorde—to a meeting to discuss the situation. Their ''discussion'' is often senseless and non-sequential, as they have trouble sticking to the subject at hand, one of the Madwomen insisting on speaking to her long-since deceased dog Dickie and another demanding to consult her ''voices'' that she hears in her hot water bottle. While their comments are often far-fetched and fanciful, they end up with the correct conclusion that these ''evil'' people must be eliminated. A mock trial is held in which the humble people, like the sewer man and the ragpicker, assume the roles of the capitalists who are all found guilty. A trap door in Aurelia's apartment leads to the sewers of the city and, once having descended into them, no one is allowed to return. Aurelia invites all of the profiteers to her apartment and they greedily head down into the sewers looking for the oil. Once they have all gone down, Aurelia shuts the trap door and the world has been made safe.

The Madwoman of Chaillot is most characteristic of Giraudoux in its fanciful and whimsical tone, demonstrating the playwright's inventiveness and charm. In a sense, the fairytale atmosphere of this play is the perfect expression of the unique and creative mind of Giraudoux, allowing him to escape from the mundane world of reality into a delightful fantasy world. The playwright makes the chaotic and seemingly unreal world of the Madwomen seem more vivid and more truthful than the real world.

Although the play is a typical example of the imaginative Giraudoux mind, the work had a deeper meaning to the playwright. Underneath the amusing and witty façade of the comedy, the dramatist was expressing his concerns over the future of France and its urban life. At the time of the writing of this play, Giraudoux was increasingly preoccupied with the problems of everyday living. Basically, he was telling the public to beware, that people were out there ready to take away the quality of their lives. Aurelia recounts this concern to the other Madwomen:

> There are people in the world who want to destroy everything. They have the fever of destruction. Even when they pretend that they'e building, it is only in order to destroy. When they put up a new building, they quietly knock down two old ones. They build cities so that they can destroy the countryside. They destroy space with telephones and time with airplanes.

This attack on the greed and corruption of the capitalist profiteers was a political stance not common in Giraudoux's writings, and some observers have viewed this as a change of direction interrupted by his death. At the same time, however, it can be argued that this is, in its own way, an escape from reality. The playwright composed the work during the occupation of France by the Germans and *The Madwoman of Chaillot* sidesteps any direct reference to that situation. It is as if the dramatist had made up his mind to look to a different, better time, when problems could be solved simply and directly.

—John H. Reilly

THE MAGIC MOUNTAIN (Der Zauberberg)
Novel by Thomas Mann, 1924

The Magic Mountain is the story of a young man, Hans Castorp, of solid and respectable background who, rather worse for wear after his final examinations, takes his doctor's advice to postpone his engineering apprenticeship at a Hamburg shipbuilding firm and leaves for a recuperative three-week stay at Berghof, the pulmonary sanatorium in Davos, Switzerland. Castorp has an unshakeable respect for work but an understandable reluctance to engage in it himself. As luck would have it, the liquidation of his father's estate has left him 400,000 marks which, invested, makes his immediate return to work unnecessary while enabling him, for the next seven years, to pursue enlightenment and practise contemplative experimentation. As Thomas Mann is fully aware, Castorp's dependence on invested capital casts his later fascination for the usury-reviling, collectivist social theories of Leo Naphta in an equivocal light. Having lost both parents and a guardian grandfather while still young, Castorp is on familiar terms with death, the physical and disreputable nature of which is not entirely concealed by the powerful odour of the tuberoses at his grandfather's wake.

Some of the most lyrical writing in the novel is devoted to Castorp's systematic and loving research into the organic functioning of the human body. For a young man of such practical heritage and technical training, there is also a suspicious sensuality and indolence in his fondness for good food and cigars. This, together with his early talent for maritime watercolours, suggests not only artistic sensitivity, but a semi-conscious desire for freedom, an impulse intensified by his presence at the Berghof sanatorium. This institution is later compared by Lodovico Settembrini, the voice of self-denial and responsibility, to an ocean liner, an ark deluxe where the ease of life, the frivolity of its Belshazzar's feasting goes on, oblivious to its precarious separation from oceanic chaos and briny death. Thus is the allegorical nature of the Berghof prepared for in terms that recall not only the sinking of the *Titanic* in 1912, mentioned explicitly by Leo Naphta as a salutary writing on the wall for civilization's moribund softness, but also the *Lusitania* in 1915, the "gigantic pleasure ship" and "impudent symbol . . . of a still comfortable civilization," denounced personally by Mann, for a change indulging his unironic, naphthalene side, in *Betrachtungen eines Unpolitischen* (*Reflections of a Nonpolitical Man*), 1918. Unlike that other imperilled seaman, Odysseus, Castorp does not particularly want to return home, nor does he show the Greek's mastery of the Berghof Circe, Clavdia Chauchat. Like all heroes worthy of the name, however, he is allowed the opportunity to descend into the underworld to commune with the dead during Dr. Krokowski's seance, the *Nekyia* of the modern age. During this uncanny episode, Castorp sees the spirit of his cousin, Joachim Ziemssen, kitted out in the equipment of the war yet to come, that appalling "thunderclap" that will mean the end of magic mountain society. Castorp had mentioned that, with Joachim gone, he might never find his way back down. Here Joachim points the way, not necessarily to the catastrophic waste and the mass suicide of Europe in World War I so much as to responsibility, action, and racial solidarity, salutary alternatives to the shallow distractions, lechery, and ennui that life in the Berghof had become. As Mann points out in *Reflections of a Nonpolitical Man*, ". . . everyone wanted war and demanded it, could not do without it any more. Otherwise it would not have come." It is at least as true to say, therefore, that the "terrifying masculinity" of the war is the inevitable next stage in Castorp's education, the expansion, ennoblement, and refinement of his soul in the crucible of death, as it is to say that the war is the insane and loathsome sacrifice of all the possibilities of sensitivity, wisdom, and beauty latent in this "delicate child of life," The war, says Mann, is both liberation and atonement: liberation from an increasingly pointless enchantment, and atonement for a stage of sin and lawless indulgence. Despite this late appearance of the vocabulary of "sin," the transformation of the *Zauberberg* (magic mountain) into a *Sündenberg* (mountain of sin), Nietzsche's influence remains strong, especially on the bracing effect of combat. Indeed, the novel's title probably comes from Nietzsche's designation in *The Birth of Tragedy* of Mount Olympus, dwelling place of the Greek gods, those beautiful and radiant projections of the Greek artistic imagination striving to conceal the truth of life's abysmal horror in order to seduce Greek culture by means of illusion to life and joy. The hectic revelry and concupiscence typical of consumptives parody the daily preoccupations of Hellenic divinities to the point that the *Zauberberg* becomes also a *Venusberg*, and Castorp a modern-day Tannhäuser sojourning among the nymphs and sirens. Even Dionysus makes a late appearance in the form of a wealthy Java coffee magnate, Mynheer Peeperkorn, who is alcoholic and inarticulate but somehow powerfully appealing with his theology of feeling and his celebration of the elemental Holy Trinity of bread, wine, and sex. He is Castorp's rival for the love of Clavdia and lives in mortal terror of the one unpardonable sin, the unspeakable fiasco of not being able to rise to the challenge of woman, who requires of man merely that he intoxicate her endlessly with desire. Far from being threatened by Peeperkorn, Castorp becomes his friend and disciple, though a somewhat impertinent one, participating in his Passion, watching with him until Peeperkorn, abandoned by Priapus, injects himself with cobra venom.

The spiritual centre of the novel comes in the "snow" chapter, where Castorp, indulging his forbidden hobby of skiing, gets caught in a severe snowstorm and loses his way on the mountain. Exhausted and half-delirious, he leans against a hay-hut and takes an ill-advised sip of port. Soon he is at the point of falling asleep and freezing to death. He forces himself upright but slips into a waking dream in which he sees, in a Mediterranean setting, a beautiful bay, cypress groves, and groups of gentle people: shepherds playing their pipes, girls dancing, mothers suckling their children while goats leap happily among the rocks. These "people of the sun" are enviably civilized, friendly, and wise. Castorp is ecstatic to be there with them, until a young boy, his face suddenly grim, points to a temple of mossy columns and Cyclopian stones. Within, an anguished Castorp sees naked hags dismembering a child, cracking its bones in their teeth, their lips dripping blood. They curse Castorp in the dialect of his native Hamburg. At this point he understands that the children of the sun are courteous and gentle to each other because they live in perpetual awareness of the witches' feast. He will give his allegiance to these gentle people, not to his mentors at the Berghof, neither to Naphta, proponent of ego-obliteration in Bolshevist collectivism, nor to Settembrini, humanist proponent of progress and reason, loveable and well-meaning though the Italian is. Naphta lacks love, and Settembrini lacks a sense of the primal horror present in Castorp's dream-poem, the neolithic savagery still lurking like a virus in the human brainstem. It is love, then, that robs death of its mastery, that generates "form and civilization, friendly, enlightened, beautiful human intercourse—always in silent recognition of the blood sacrifice,"

From one point of view, the snow vision is a lesson contradicted or forgotten by Castorp when he gives himself so eagerly at the end of the novel to the "feast of death" that is World War I. A less rationalist, more Nietzschean perspective would see human life as a tragic alternation between Dionysian abandonment and Apollonian serenity, extremes rarely, if ever, in fruitful equilibrium, and then perhaps only in the sphere of art.

—Dan Latimer

MAHĀBHĀRATA

Indian epic of great magnitude, written in Sanskrit, usually dated to some time between c. 400 BC and c. 400 AD. Traditionally supposed to have been passed down through Ganeṣa, god of wisdom, and ancient sages, but later attributed to Vyāsa (compiler of the *Vedas, q.v.*). It includes 19 books of 106,000 double verses (*śloka*). The main story concerns a family feud over sovereignty. Also included are many other tales and myths, the poem *Bhagavadgītā, q.v.*, and a shortened form of the *Rāmāyaṇa, q.v.*

PUBLICATIONS

Mahābhārata. 5 vols., 1834–39; edited (as *Sriman Mahabharatam*) by T.R. Krishnacharya and T.R. Vyasacharya, 6 vols., 1906–10; also edited by R. Kinjawadekar (with Nilakantha's commentary), 7 vols., 1929–36, P.P.S. Sastri (southern recension), 18 vols., 1931–36, Vishnu S. Suthankar (critical edition), 21 vols., 1933–71, S.D. Satwalekar, 18 vols., 1968–77, and K.M. Munshi and R.R. Diwakar, 22nd revised edition, 1979; as *Mahabharata*, translated by P.K.M. Ganguli, 16 vols., 1884–94 (subsequent reprints wrongly credited to Protap Chandra Roy), revised by S.L. Bhaduri, 1919–25, in 11 vols., 1924–31, and selection, 1956; also translated by Manmatha Nath Dutt (in prose), 18 vols., 1895–1905, reprinted 1960; abridged translations as *The Mahābhārata* (either with or without accents) by R.C. Dutt, 1899; S.C. Nott, 1956; C.V. Narasimhan, 1964; J.A.B. van Buitenen (bilingual edition), 1973–; R.K. Narayan, 1978; other selections; Kamala Subramaniam, 1965; P. Lal, 1968–, in a single volume, 1980; William Buck, 1973; as *Nalopākhārata: Story of Nala*, translated by M. Monier-Williams, 2nd edition, 1879; as *Indian Idylls*, translated by Adwin Arnold, 1883; as *Five Sons of King Pandu*, adapted by Elizabeth Seeger from K.M. Ganguli's translation, 1967; as *Young Krishna*, translated by Francis G. Hutchins, 1980; as *Epics Ramayana and Mahabharata*, edited by S.D. Kulkarni, 1992.

*

Critical Studies: *The Heroic Age of India* by N.K. Siddhantha, 1929; *The Mahabharata: An Ethnological Study* by G.J. Held, 1935; *On the Meaning of the Mahabharata* by V.S. Sukthankar, 1957; *Conscience and Consciousness: Ethical Problems of the Mahabharata* by Norbert Klaes, 1975; *Political Ideas and Institutions in the Mahābhārata: Based on the Poona Critical Edition* by Brajdeo Prasad Roy, 1975; *Mahā Myth and Reality: Differing Views* edited by S.P. Gupta and K.S. Ramchandran, 1976; *The Ritual of Battle: Krishna in the Mahabharata* by Alf Hiltebeitel, 1976; *The Mahābhārata: A Study of the Critical Edition, with Special Reference to the Suparṇākhyāna of the Ādiparvan* by Mahesh M. Mehta, 1976; *Political Ideas and Ideals in the Mahabharata: A Study of the First Two Parvans* by N.K.P. Sinha, 1976; *Gods, Priests, and Warriors: The Bhṛgus of the Mahabharata* by Robert P. Goldman, 1977; *Geographical Horizons of the Mahā Bhārata* by Syām Nārāyan Pande, 1980; *The Concepts of Religion in the Mahābhārata* by Usmita Rani Trikha, 1980; *Valmiki's Ramayanam and Vyasa's Mahabharatham (the Immortal Epics of India): A Joint and Comparative Study* by A.K. Ganesan, 1981; *Mahabharata and Archaeological Evidence* by Gouri Lad, 1983; *Folklore in the Mahabharata* by N.B. Patil, 1983; *The Mahabharata; The Story and Its Significance* by S.L.N. Simha, 1983; *The Mahabharata: A Criticism* by C.V. Vaidya, 1983; *Kṛṣṇa Kathā and Allied Matters: A Critical Study of the Life-Story of Kṛṣṇa as Narrated in the Mahābhārata and the Appended Harivaṁśa* by Asha Goswami, 1984; *The Mahabharata: A Literary Study* by Krishna Chaitanya, 1985; *The Book of Yudhisthir: A Study of the Mahabharat of Vyasa* by Buddhaheva Bose, translated by S. Mukherjee, 1986; *The Mahabharata* by Shanta R. Rao, 1986; *Astrological Key in Mahābhārata: The New Era* by Paule Lerner, translated by D. White, 1988; *The Mahabharata and Modern Indian Literature* by Sitakant Mahapatra, 1988; *Who is Who in the Mahabharata* by Subash Mazumdar, 1988; *Mahabharata: Its Influence on Indian Life and Culture* by the Ramakrishna Mission Ashrama, 1988; *Elements of Poetry in the Mahabharata* by Ram Karan Sharma, 1988; *Social Philosophy of the Mahābhārata and the Manu smrti* by Pratima Verma, 1988; *Themes and Structure in the Mahabharata: A Study of the Ādi Parva* by Pardip Bhattacharya, 1989; *Moral Dilemmas in the Mahābhārata* edited by Bimal Krishna Matilal, 1989; *Gītās in the Mahābhārata and the Purāṇas* by R. Nilkantan, 1989; *An Episodic Interpretation of the Mahabharata* by Rabindra Nath Sarkar, 1989; *Mahabharata: A Military Analysis* by G.D. Bakshi, 1990; *The Concept of State in the Mahābhārata* by Diwakar Tiwary, 1990; *Essays on the Mahābhārata* edited by Arvind Sharma, 1991; *Political and Moral Concepts in the Santiparvan of the Mahabharata* by Y.S. Walimbe, 1991; *Forest Setting in Hindu Epics: Princes, Sages, Demons* by Thomas Parkhill, 1995; *Milton and the Indian Epic Tradition: A Study of Paradise Lost, The Ramayana, and the Mahabharata* by M.V. Rama Sarma, 1995; *Vyasa's Mahabharata: Creative Insights*, edited by P. Lal, 1995; *The Sanskrit Epics* by John Brockington, 1998; *Mystical Stories from the Mahabharata: Twenty Timeless Lessons in Wisdom and Virtue* by Amal Bhakta, 2000.

*   *   *

With over 100,000 verses, the *Mahābhārata*, the world's longest epic, is about eight times the length of *The Iliad* and *The Odyssey* put together. It had originally 18 books, with a 19th added later. Interwoven with the central story are a number of subsidiary ones, long enough to be epics in themselves. Though the Mahābhārata is replete with philosophical passages, it is essentially a literary work. It is believed to have been written about the 4th century or perhaps earlier, and its celebrated author was the sage Vyāsa. Tradition, however, atributes its origin to divinity.

The central story revolves round the enmity between the Kauravas and their half-brothers, the Pāṇḍavas, consequent to Yudhiṣṭhira of the Pāṇḍavas being nominated as the heir apparent of Hastināpura. Escaping a plot hatched by the Kauravas, the Pāṇḍava brothers flee to the forest in disguise. Sometime after, Arjuna, the Pāṇḍava leader, wins the hand of Draupadī, daughter of the king of the Pāchālas, and the brothers come out of exile. A settlement is finally made, the Kauravas getting Hastināpura, and the Pāṇḍavas, Indraprastha. But the Kauravas continue plotting against Yudhiṣṭhira, now Indraprastha's ruler, tempting him to a gambling match in which he wagers and loses everything, even his brothers, himself, and his wife. Draupadī is openly insulted, and this widens the gulf between the two clans. Yudhiṣṭhira's possessions are restored, but he again speedily gambles them away, forcing the Pāṇḍavas into exile again for 12 years. Nevertheless they resolve to regain their lost kingdom. Arjuna and Duryodhana, the Kaurava leader, both seek the assistance of Kṛṣṇa, King of Dwarka. Duryodhana is given Kṛṣṇa's entire army, while Arjuna wisely choses the divine Kṛṣṇa himself. So Kṛṣṇa becomes Arjuna's charioteer. In the great battle which follows, the Kauravas are destroyed. But Yudhiṣṭhira and the other Pāṇḍavas are filled with remorse for causing the bloodshed of their kinsmen. Yudhiṣṭhira abdicates the throne and, along with his brothers, retreats to the Himalayas to dwell in Indra's Heaven on Mount Meru.

The literature to which the *Mahābhārata* belongs is called Ākhyāna and Itihāsa. The work abounds in picturesque descriptions, like that of the sudden downpour while the Pāṇḍavas are in the forest in exile: "The rain poured and poured till hills, dales and rivers could not be distinguished, and all one could see was an endless sheet of water." Vyāsa often uses colours as symbols, as, for example, when he likens the orange flames of fire to the glory of a hermit even though he just wears rags, the warrior whose ire mounts, and the fiery rage of a chaste woman approached by a licentious man. Folk tradition is used to give keenness to language. Bhīṣma is like the flamingo who kept prattling about morality so that other birds trusted him with their eggs, which he promptly ate up. The inveterate gambler, Yudhiṣṭhira, who still preaches righteousness, is likened to a cat who practises austerities to entice mice. Aśvatthāma runs away from the battlefield and plans revenge. In the night he sees an owl who kills birds when they are asleep. Taking the cue he falls on his enemies while they are sleeping and slays them all. There are picturesque descriptions of lovely women, like those of Draupadī with eyes like the lotus leaves and waist slender as a wasp, and Urvaśī, the celestial nymph, "of finely tapering breasts, looking like the slender moon amid fleecy clouds."

The *Mahābhārata* represents Hindu culture at its best. Its fascinating episodes have inspired many writers to create masterpieces, for example Kālidāsa's renowned play *Śakuntalā*. Not without justification it has been said "What is not in the *Mahābhārata*, is nowhere."

—K.P. Bahadur

MAHĀNĀRĀYANŮA

See UPANISHADS

THE MAIDS (Les Bonnes)
Play by Jean Genet, 1947

In a letter to the publisher Jean-Jacques Pauvert to preface the 1954 edition of his one-act play *The Maids*, Jean Genet described his hopes for the play:

To achieve the abolition of characters—which usually stand up only by psychological convention—in favour of signs as remote as possible from what they should at first signify, but in touch with it none the less, in order to link the author to the audience by this one means . . . The highest modern drama has been expressed every day for 2,000 years in the sacrifice of the mass . . . Theatrically I know of nothing more effective than the elevation of the Host.

What equivalent can there be to the mass in a theatre where the only counterpart to the shared faith of the congregation is the audience's willingness to suspend disbelief? The task Genet sets himself in his plays is to engender belief in solitude, emptiness, transparency, and equivalence. He refuses to individualize his characters, stressing the lowest common multiples of humanity, and in each of his five extraordinary plays he creates an anti-society which he holds up provocatively as a mirror-image for a public naturally inclined to deny any resemblance. Why should the bourgeois audience identify with murderous maids plotting to kill their mistress?

When the curtain goes up, we see Solange impersonating Claire, while Claire impersonates Madame with grotesque exaggeration of her condescension, her patronizing mixture of benevolence and contempt. It is a game, a ritual, that makes the three overlap with the other two, and, reluctantly overcoming our resistance, we find ourselves overlapping with all three.

This wouldn't happen if the hatred on display were unambivalent, but underneath the envy that makes the maids want to kill their mistress is something that makes them want to *be* her, or, failing that, to play at being her. This is a kind of love. Their identity derives from their relationship with her: rebelling against their independence, they are fighting against themselves, and suicide is the culmination of the attempt at murder. It is apt that the ritual should end in self-sacrifice:

the instinct of self-betrayal was strongly at work while Genet was writing it. Its primary purpose, he said, was:

To disgust me with myself by indicating and refusing to indicate who I was. Its secondary purpose was to produce a kind of discomfort in the auditorium . . . I go to the theatre to see myself on the stage (reconstituted in a single character or through a multiple character and in the form of a story) in a form that I wouldn't be able or wouldn't dare to see or dream as an image of myself, in spite of knowing that is what I am.

("Comment jouer *Les Bonnes,*" *Ouvres complètes*, vol. 4.)

The play is based on a murder committed in 1933, when two maids, Christine and Lea Papin, aged 28 and 21, killed their mistress with an axe. Writing soon afterwards about the crime, Jacques Lacan said that in paranoia the aggressive impulse sometimes implies a wish for self-punishment and expiation. The intellectual content of the murderous delirium, he suggested, was a superstructure which at once justified and negated the criminal impulse. He felt sure there was no active lesbianism between the sisters, as reported. "The homosexual tendency would express itself only through a desperate negation of itself, which would lay the foundation for a conviction of being persecuted and an identification of the persecutor as the loved one." The hatred is partly an extroversion of self-loathing, the aggression an outlet for guilt.

In his first novel, *Our Lady of the Flowers* published three years before *The Maids*, Genet had written that if a play of his with women in it were ever produced, he had asked for their roles to be acted by boys. This would expose female elements in the male constitution, and male in the female. Penetrating as intimately as he does in *The Maids* into the fantasy lives of three women, he reveals something of his own femininity, and when the roles are played by boys, the self-betrayal becomes more complex. Exposing the femininity of the male actors, he is complicating their relationship with the play and with him.

Interdependent with self-betrayal is displacement of reality. While Claire will be imperfect in her impersonation of Madame, as Solange will be in hers of Claire, the boys' imperfection in impersonating females would lay extra emphasis on the point that Madame always puts on an act for the benefit of her maids, while they always play roles, both when trying to impress her with their subservient devotion and when they are alone together, not trying to be anything other than themselves but always aware of themselves as maids. As sisters they know each other too well to think they can impress each other, but they know themselves by knowing each other, and Claire is defining both herself and Madame when, speaking as Madame, she launches into a ritual of insults against maids, deriding the look of fear and shame on their faces, their scrawny elbows, their dowdy clothes, their bodies, apparently designed for wearing cast off clothes.

Exploring the emptiness, the transparency, the solitude, and the equivalence of the three characters, the play inverts moral values. As in *Deathwatch*, a play Genet had written before *The Maids*, though it was not produced or published until 1949, the violence is quiet, muted, decorous. However ugly the clumsy crime usually is in reality, Genet was making it look glamorous and elegant on the stage.

—Ronald Hayman

THE MAN WITHOUT QUALITIES (Der Mann ohne Eigenschaften)
Novel by Robert Musil, 1930–43

When the first volumes of *The Man Without Qualities* appeared in 1930–33 it was hailed as the representative work of its time. It has since been recognized as one of the great novels of the century and has been placed besides works like Proust's *Remembrance of Things Past (Á la recherche du temps perdu)* and Joyce's *Ulysses*. Like a platonic dialogue this novel is as much concerned with understanding the world as it is with telling a story. It strives everywhere towards the typical and general and, for this purpose, takes into the process of storytelling a wealth of ideas and problems from philosophy, psychology, ethics, and science.

The title of the book is derived from the definition of its protagonist, Ulrich. A typical product of the modern crisis of identity, he finds that his character is merely an intersection of impersonal qualities (derived from his membership of a particular nation, profession, sex, etc.) accidentally acquired during the course of his life. Thus he calls himself a "man without qualities." The formula, however, contains not only a threat but also a promise. Together with the principles of experiment, essayism, and irony, they form the basis of an essential openness and fluidity in his approach to the world. The story is of a quest for an authentic self and a true morality. Ulrich, taking stock in his 30th year, decides to take a year's holiday from life. His individual quest is submerged into a general one when he becomes the honorary secretary of a patriotic committee with the aim of finding a guiding idea for the 70th jubilee of the rule of the emperor of Kakania—from "k. und k.," referring to "kaiserlich und königlich," imperial and royal—the quasi-historical equivalent of the Austro-Hungarian empire, but just as much an analogy of any modern state, since Robert Musil's intention was always to write a topical novel (a *Zeitroman*) developing out of a historical novel.

The fact that the year just happens to be 1913, the last year before World War I, and the celebration of the "emperor of peace" is planned for 1918, puts the whole personal and general enterprise into an ironic frame, apart from giving it a certain sense of urgency. The world presents itself as a chaos of undigested ideas and unresolved contradictions which inevitably seem to lead into the war. The hero's general stocktaking allows Musil to introduce a spectrum of figures representative of the social and intellectual trends of the times: from the aristocrat who believes that everything can in the end be accommodated in the old order, to the revolutionary socialist, from the elegant Jewish industrialist and writer to the crude National Socialist agitator, and from the follower of the Nietzsche cult to the moral do-gooder.

Far from being a dry, intellectual exercise, the novel shows Musil as a sparkling satirist, lacking neither warmth nor venom, and possessed of a skill of character drawing which includes such gems as the general "with special cultural responsibilities," drawing up a strategic plan of the confusing array of modern ideas. Many of the figures are, in part, based on characters from public life or Musil's circle of acquaintances, for example, his fellow writer Franz Werfel appears thinly disguised as the expressionist poet Feuermaul, the darling of the salon, and co-formulator of the final contradictory resolution of the patriotic committee.

The breadth of Musil's achievement can be gauged from the fact that he can give a pertinent satiric description of a high level conference as well as finding the delicate touch for the portrayal of a mystical love relationship. While the first book is given over more to satire, the second book (entitled: "Into the Millenium," subtitled, "The Criminals") enters into the description of the relationship between the protagonist and his sister. All his other love relationships are found wanting in one sense or another. Love in *The Man Without Qualities* is explored from many angles. From the portrayal of the excesses of the nymphomaniac to a send-up of the pretentious quasi-mystical union of two self-important people, from the Socratic investigation of feelings to the utopian union between hero and the figure constructed, as it were, as a negative of the self in the other sex: the sister, the twin, the Siamese twin.

The novel is structured in individual chapters which allow the author to emphasize the principle of analogy and variation. All the characters and all relationships—in the system of ironic reflections—bear a resemblance to the protagonist's. They are all looking for a guiding idea or a state of "enthusiasm" in which their existence would become truly "moral" but all is revealed as illusory—until Ulrich embarks, with the consciousness of the post-Nietzschean vivisecteur—on the dangerous path of the mystics to experience the "ultimate love-story" between the "last Romantics of love."

Where exactly this "adventure" was to lead the hero is unfortunately uncertain, since Musil did not complete his novel. In his lifetime only Book One and a part of Book Two (38 chapters) were published. A further 20 chapters were given to the printers but then withdrawn again (1937–38) and Musil died in exile from the Nazis in Switzerland while still working on a revision. The last chapter he was working on entitled "Atemzüge. . ." seemed particularly to absorb him. It is taken by some critics as a kind of testament, even a kind of conclusion, of the novel in its portrayal of sublimated spiritual love, as brother and sister feel mystically united while sitting in their garden meditating on the spectacle of blossoms floating down. Other critics have disputed this and refer us to the earlier drafts and plans which Musil did not have time to complete but which would have taken him on to a "Journey into Paradise" where their union was to be physically consummated and finally, as with the hero in Thomas Mann's *Magic Mountain*, would have dismissed him into World War I, where he was to become a spy.

The English translation of the book is based on an edition published in 1952 in which the editor had attempted to reconstruct and round off Musil's fragments, using drafts from different periods and going back to the early 1920s. The newer critical edition in *Gesammelte Werke*, 1978, gives a much truer, more scholarly-though less easily digestible—picture of the state of the posthumous section of this tantalizing torso. It is hoped that a new translation based on this edition will soon be available.

—Lothar Huber

THE MANDARINS (Les Mandarins)
Novel by Simone de Beauvoir, 1954

Although Simone de Beauvoir was awarded the 1954 Goncourt prize for *The Mandarins* and the novel enjoyed great critical success at the time of publication, de Beauvoir's challenging account of post-Occupation manners and morality has suffered a degree of critical neglect in recent years.

There are several reasons for this oversight. Its reputation as a *roman à clef* may not endear the work to a readership no longer eager (or able) to identify the members of de Beauvoir's ''family'' described in fictional terms. Furthermore, just as the characters may seem locked into a particular period, the book's concern with political action and morality on the Left, and its discussion of the independent Left's relationship to the Communist Party, may seem less relevant in today's changed political climate. Similarly, the central Existentialist debate in *The Mandarins* about individual freedom and its curtailment by personal involvement and political practice may also seem to belong to a particular epoch and social group.

The Mandarins, though, is by no means a dull and worthy period-piece, and its depiction of life among a group of Paris-based intellectuals (the mandarin caste of the title) from Christmas 1944 to 1948 is still of consequence, thought-provoking and interesting 50 years on. De Beauvoir's longest novel provides us with a closely observed portrait of the hopes and endeavours of the French Left immediately after the Liberation, a picture that is multi-dimensional and finely drawn. To stress the complex nature of historical change, and the difficult ethical questions raised by involvement in political action, de Beauvoir constructs her novel around several different stories and viewpoints. The way her narrative is textured emphasizes the consequences of individual actions, with de Beauvoir threading in the various personal histories, each of which poses different questions about the nature of personal freedom and public action. As the novel consists mainly of satellite stories, it is hard to identify and summarize any central plot in the work, and perhaps easier to analyse the manner in which the structure of *The Mandarins* is organized. Each individual tale concerns one of a group of writers, journalists, friends, and political activists associated with the journal *L'Espoir* [''Hope'']. Foremost in these stories is the relationship between Henri Perron, the editor of the journal began during the Resistance, and the much older Robert Dubreuilh, a formidable political activist and writer. Dubreuilh is much more of a pragmatist and more accustomed to *Realpolitik* than Perron, and attempts to persuade the younger man to align *L'Espoir* to the independent socialist group that he is founding. The complex relations of these two men are set against a troubled background of political events and decisions that include the bombing of Hiroshima, revenge killings of collaborators by Leftist acquaintances, and the disclosure of the realities of Stalin's regime. Their friendship (and shared political ideals) eventually founder over Henri's decision to publish accounts of Soviet labour camps.

Although we are given a sure sense of what motivates Dubreuilh, *The Mandarins* is more concerned with the progress of Perron. Parallel to his post-war fate is the story of Anne Dubreuilh, Robert's wife. She is the same age as Henri (late thirties) and is a psychiatrist. Unlike Henri, who embraces experience and partakes actively in whatever befalls him, Anne is characterized as controlled and watchful, a witness to events rather than a participant. Her public and private lives are tested throughout the novel. Questions are raised about the basis of her work and about the validity of fostering individual happiness in a world of mass poverty and misery. In the personal sphere, she longs for some kind of reawakening before she moves towards old age and death, and finds her identity as wife and mother tested through her affair with an American writer, Lewis Brogan. Although Henri emerges as the more vital character, it is Anne who is accorded the first-person voice in a novel that is for the main part related in the third person. This directness of address, coupled with the descriptions of de Beauvoir's own visits to the United States (with Brogan resembling her former lover, Nelson Algren), and the echoing of her fears of ageing, may lead us to think

that Anne's voice is that of the author. However, it does not seem likely that this is the case, rather that de Beauvoir's own arguments, emotions, and experiences are dispersed throughout the various private histories so convincingly related in the novel.

The Mandarins was de Beauvoir's first novel after her analysis of women's place in society, *The Second Sex*, and it is interesting to look at the personal and political choices available for women here. De Beauvoir could be criticized for the novel's lack of adequate role models, as the female characters do not appear to share the confidence and vigour of her male creations. However, de Beauvoir's commitment to revealing true relations and circumstances, rather than idealized notions of action and behaviour, is seen in her positioning the women in the novel as caught between personal and public life. Their inability to seize authentic freedom, tied as they are to relationships with men, disempowers them from full and active involvement in the political and public sphere. The most extreme example is the passive and beautiful Paule, who has given up a career as a singer to devote herself to Henri, feeling that her love is sufficient. When Henri no longer loves her, Paule loses her reason for living and has a breakdown, rather like the betrayed wife in *The Woman Destroyed*. Paule's rival, the rich Josette, who wishes to make a career as an actress, is portrayed as equally vulnerable to male attention, her beauty even sold off during the occupation to German soldiers by her ruthless and *arriviste* mother.

Anne herself is seen as unable to change herself, haunted as she is by the certainty of death, and, although she rejects suicide at the end of the work, she resigns herself to life and to staying with Robert. Her relationship with her daughter, Nadine, is far from easy, with Anne often offering control and responsibility in the absence of love. The gawky Nadine herself is the most active woman in the work, but it is a restless activity born out of unpredictability and irresponsibility rather than conscious intervention and willed choice. And again and again, it is the question of choice, and how it is possible to act ethically when asked to choose particular courses of behaviour, that occurs in *The Mandarins*. What is fascinating in this work, and what marks it out as a novel that has contemporary resonance, is de Beauvoir's insistence that it is the political that is personal; that political action and public behaviour have their basis in personal relations and commitments.

—Anna-Marie Taylor

THE MANDRAKE (La mandragola)
Play by Niccolò Machiavelli, c. 1518–20

The Mandrake, written around 1518 when Florence had reverted to Medici rule, is set in 1504 during the republican interval so that the dramatist could criticize contemporary Florentine society without fear of further repercussions from patrons already ill-disposed towards him. The play's usual classification as an ''erudite'' comedy is due rather more to its formal elements than to any substantial derivation of its plot and characters from the classical Latin theatre of Plautus and Terence. *The Mandrake* begins with a chorus which, together with the four songs serving as intermezzos between the five acts, was added to the comedy for a performance planned for the carnival season of 1526. Sung by nymphs and shepherds, this opening chorus propounds the hedonistic theme of *carpe diem* (seize the day), fundamental both to much of Renaissance literature and to *The Mandrake*: since life is both short and fraught with woes, pleasure must be taken at every opportunity. The detached prologue, divided into two equal parts of four strophes each, serves as both an introduction to the play and a key to its interpretation.

After drawing attention to the originality of *The Mandrake* ("... let our troupe commence / To play for you ... / A recent case that's something new") and identifying the setting as contemporary Florence, the prologue alludes to the principal characters in seemingly contradictory terms: the lawyer Nicia is "doltish"; the priest is "venal"; Callimaco Guadagni, outwardly noble and worthy of respect, is also a "wretched swain"; Lucrezia, although a "circumspect young wife," is also "hotly and at length pursued ... falsely wooed ... At last ... brought to bed ...." Appearance, the prologue thus implies, may be deceptive, as the comedy itself then demonstrates. The focus of the second part of the prologue shifts from the comedy's constituent elements (characters, plot, themes) to the circumstances surrounding its composition. The prologue discloses that *The Mandrake* was written to distract the author, whose bitterness at having been excluded from the diplomatic and political life of Florence was further exacerbated by the Medici's indifference towards his political works *The Prince* and *The Discourses*. It is this particular frame of mind, as defined by the prologue, that determines the bitter cynicism which is the comedy's principal frame of reference.

In the first scene of the comedy, Niccolò Machiavelli employs a conventional artifice in having Callimaco convey to the audience the drama's pre-textual situation as he recalls to Siro events with which his servant is already familiar. After a 20-year sojourn in Paris, 30-year-old Callimaco Guadagni has returned to his native Florence, attracted by the fabled beauty of Lucrezia Calfucci. All his expectations having been exceeded, Callimaco despairs of becoming her lover as she is also renowned for her chastity. His only hope for success lies in the fact that Lucrezia's wealthy husband of six years, Nicia, famed in his turn for his foolishness, is no less anxious than Lucrezia for an heir. Callimaco has secured the help of the parasite Ligurio, an acquaintance of Nicia's.

The rest of the plot (Acts II–V) centres on deceptions devised by Ligurio so that Callimaco may spend the night with Lucrezia. By ensuring the complicity of the three people closest to her, that is, those whose every effort should have been directed at protecting her virtue rather than betraying it (her confessor, Friar Timoteo, her husband, Nicia, and her mother, Sostrata), Machiavelli thus implicitly criticizes the three institutions, fundamental to society, which these three characters represent: the Church, marriage, the family.

On Ligurio's bidding, Callimaco pretends to be a celebrated Parisian doctor who specializes in curing infertility by means of a potion made from the root of the mandrake. Nicia agrees to administer it to Lucrezia, but is temporarily disconcerted when Callimaco points out that whoever first makes love to Lucrezia after her treatment is likely to die. The solution which Callimaco proposes serves his own interests if Nicia agrees to it: the first man to happen by will be placed forcibly in bed with her, instructed in what he is to do, and then released the following morning. Nicia's reluctance to be cuckolded in this way is overcome easily when Callimaco states that the king and nobles of France had no such scruples. Lucrezia's participation in this immoral scheme can only be secured by making Friar Timoteo their accomplice. Ligurio first tests the priest's probity by promising him money in return for his assistance in a fictitious enterprise: a young niece of Nicia's, entrusted to a local convent, is supposedly pregnant.

Friar Timoteo is asked to take a potion to the abbess who, in turn, will administer it to the young woman to make her miscarry, thereby avoiding all scandal. By agreeing to help, Friar Timoteo discloses both the depth and breadth of the corruption in the religious community. (There are further references in the comedy to the general impiety of priests.)

With Friar Timoteo's complicity ensured, Sostrata agrees to accompany her reluctant daughter to the meeting with the priest. To his sophistical, captious reasoning (based on the Machiavellian philosophy that the end—here, the birth of a child—justifies the means—adultery and possibly homicide) Sostrata adds pragmatically that Lucrezia must have a child to guarantee her financial status should Nicia die.

The deception works flawlessly. Callimaco is overjoyed when Lucrezia, outraged at the betrayal perpetrated against her, cynically attributes it to divine will and resolves to remain Callimaco's lover, motivated as much by the desire to avenge herself against Nicia as to serve her own personal interests. Lucrezia, initially the sole morally incorrupt character in the comedy, ultimately adapts to a reality which she is powerless to oppose and far less to change. *The Mandrake* shows society and human nature as they are, without suggesting how they ought to be. It illustrates Machiavelli's belief that those endowed with the necessary *virtù* are able to overcome adverse circumstances. The bitter irony of *The Mandrake* is that virtue, in the English acceptation of the term, is lost in the process.

—Nicole Prunster

MANDUKY

See UPANISHADS

MANON LESCAUT (Histoire du chevalier Des Grieux et de Manon Lescaut)
Novel by Abbé Prévost, 1733

Abbé Prévost's *Manon Lescaut* introduces the first great *femme fatale* of European Romantic literature. Manon, unlike her antecedents in history and legend (Helen of Troy, Delilah, Cleopatra) adds a dubious social origin to the motifs of irresistible beauty and relaxed virtue. She is also presented in such a way as to suggest that, in her alienation from society, she is probably misunderstood. Through her, the *femme fatale* enters the modern novel and passionate love appears as an absolute requiring total sacrifice in any lover, be he only the younger son of a not specially distinguished French nobleman. For her, Des Grieux several times goes through a cycle of behaviour that involves the abandonment of his own social milieu, indulgence in a life of idleness and pleasure, and finally, in order to sustain income, crime and consequent punishment. The cycle only ends when Manon is exiled to the penal colony of Louisiana and when, with Manon on the point of at last marrying her chevalier and becoming a changed and decent woman, the pair have to flee the wrath of the colony's governor (whose son Des Grieux thinks he has killed) and take to the bush, where Manon dies. The picture of Manon as an enigmatic, and probably misunderstood, heroine is one which is sustained by the two famous operas that the novel has inspired: Massenet's *Manon* and Puccini's *Manon Lescaut*. It is now undoubtedly one of the canonical texts exemplifying Romantic love.

There is strong evidence, however, that Prévost's concerns, as creator of the work, are more with Des Grieux and the nature of the moral situation that he is in, a case that is couched in the terminology of rationalism and in language characteristic of classical rhetoric. First, the reader depends for the description of Manon (with no precise physical features), almost entirely on the besotted (and still unrepentant) oral account given by Des Grieux himself. The description is prepared, it is true, by a short introduction of Des Grieux and Manon by a "Man of Quality" (himself a fiction of Prévost's) who offers their story as the seventh (and final) volume of his own memoirs. The reader, then, is made to share the delusion of the chief narrator and hero and, if the Romantic view of love is taken on board, is in the same doubtful moral case as he is. This is certainly the stance adopted in the "Advice to the Reader," a preface to *Manon Lescaut*, which may be attributed either to Prévost or to his fictional Man of Quality, and in which Des Grieux (both as narrator and as hero) is described as a "blind young man" who "refuses to be happy and casts himself willingly into the utmost misfortune." This "advice" cannot be dismissed as merely Prévost's deference to a convention of claiming that one's fiction offers moral instruction (here as a cautionary tale). For one thing, it proclaims the chevalier's freedom of will, whereas Des Grieux himself speaks constantly of his love as an overmastering "destiny." An erstwhile student of theology, he is interpreted by his friend and constant provider of financial assistance, Tiberge, in Jansenist terms, as one claiming to be predestined to follow Manon (and hence to be damned) and to have no moral freedom in the matter. For Prévost, a man of wild passions who tried several times to come to terms with life as a religion, such theological issues were of immediate personal concern as well as objects of hot contemporary public debate. Des Grieux, of course, infringes the moral code of his class as well as the Christian one: his adventures with a floozie bring shame on his family, and his father, by vainly offering to procure other women for his son (as a distraction from his fatal passion), reveals which code matters most to him.

Technically, the work has high artistic merit. Presented in two well-balanced sections (marked by a break for dinner in the chevalier's oral account!), its language reflects the preciosity (the preference of noble to common terms), the concern for syntactical harmony, and the high level of abstraction that are typical of French classicism. In genre terms, it is a happy convergence of three important strands of the nascent modern novel: fictional memoirs (which by pseudo-historical conventions are presented as true), the picaresque (where the hero lives out a series of episodes on the margins of the law), and the comic (where contact with low life leads to undignified and sometimes funny incidents). In its presentation of background, it is also a strong reflection of some of the social realities of France at the end of the reign of Louis XIV and during the Regency. The beginning of the novel and the beginning of the denouement evoke the same scene of the piteous Manon in a group of captive prostitutes about to be transported to the New World, a process which began historically towards the end of the reign of the Sun King. The three hate figures of the work, who buy Manon's favours for money, are two tax-farmers and one tax-farmer's son: Prévost mirrors the resentment of the traditional aristocracy towards these *nouveaux riches* by attributing such ignoble practices principally to them. While he shows little concern to describe the precise physical appearance of his characters,

he offers several *tableaux* that graphically evoke contemporary life: the meeting of Des Grieux and Manon at the inn in Amiens, the convoy of prostitutes, a prison scene, and a scene outside a theatre, among others. These are not detailed descriptions in the manner of 19th-century Realism, but rather dramatized vignettes of what may typically arise in the society of the age.

Indeed, the work as a whole is probably best appreciated as a kind of drama. There is the obvious drama of the story proper, that is, the recurring cycle of events told by Des Grieux. But there is also, and perhaps most interestingly from a literary-historical point of view, the "drama" of Des Grieux's narration itself, a long monologue in which the reader (who is treated as a "listener") is present at (and may be seduced by) the continuing delusion of a sad young man. The form of the narrative is manifestly important to this last kind of interpretation, underpinned by the "Advice to the Reader," and might suggest some comparisons and contrasts with Constant's use of first-person narrative in *Adolphe*. But these narratological aspects scarcely alter the power of the story proper (the cyclic narrative of the lovers' adventures and misdemeanours) to establish the myth of the Manon figure, the bourgeoisie's *femme fatale* who, having found her way into opera, continues today to reappear in different forms in pulp fiction and film. In the 18th century the *Bibliothèque universelle des romans* (Universal Novel Library, a sort of upmarket *Reader's Digest*) proved the point by transcribing Prévost's text into a shortened third-person version, which, while it shows little respect for the moral and aesthetic subtleties of the original masterpiece, is thoroughly effective in evoking the power of love and in presenting the mythical figure of the heroine.

—Philip E.J. Robinson

MAN'S FATE (La Condition humaine)
Novel by André Malraux, 1933

Man's Fate, considered André Malraux's fictional masterpiece, stands out by the scope of its concerns and by its dramatic power, although detractors have criticized the handling of plot and theme. In seven parts, it is set during the 1927 Chinese uprisings. An omniscient narrator provides background information and insights into the character's psychology, sometimes by free indirect style; but, following Malraux's conviction that the novel of psychological analysis was outmoded, reflecting determinism rather than freedom and action, the characters often seem enigmatic, and their motivations must frequently be gleaned from their actions. Feelings are conveyed by images: light and dark, blood, sirens, animals, and water. The style, ranging from telegraphic to poetic, is frequently abrupt, incisive, with fast-paced dialogues and scene-switching.

In Shanghai, Communists and Nationalists are preparing together an insurrection against the government and foreigners who, by treaty, occupy concessions in the city. The insurrection is successful, after violent fighting. Shortly thereafter, the Nationalists, whose support comes from the petty bourgeoisie and who must protect private property, break with their Communist allies, whose aim is proletarian revolution and liberation of peasants from indebtedness. A campaign is launched to suppress the Communists and seize their arms. The ensuing struggle constitutes the remainder of the political plot line.

Most of the characters are associated with the Communist movement. The novel begins as a young revolutionary, Ch'en, must kill a man who possesses papers that will allow the insurgents to seize much-needed revolvers. Other important figures are Katow, a veteran of the Russian Revolution, and Kyo, half European and half Japanese. Kyo's father Gisors, a former professor, does not participate in the struggle but comments on the meaning of action. Kyo's wife May, one of two named women characters, participates, although the couple is temporarily alienated by an infidelity of hers that causes Kyo to question the meaning of their common undertaking. Other important figures are Hemmelrich, a miserable Belgian worker (misidentified in the translation as German) who joins the Communists to give meaning to his suffering; Ferral, a French capitalist with vast investments in Asia, who supports the Nationalists; König, the sadistic head of Chiang Kai Shek's police; and Clappique, a mythomaniac European.

Underlying the action of nearly all the characters is an effort to combat destiny, either through political action or by striving for absolutes, which the world cannot offer and to which death brings ultimate denial. What appears at first to be chiefly a political novel is thus equally concerned with the entire human condition, viewed as fatality. For Ch'en, political action is an outlet, not a solution. Initially anguished by his first murder, but then fascinated, he cannot explain his experience to his comrades. Combat does not satisfy him either: heroism is empty and the fraternity of blood excludes him because his chief concern is the enigma of the individual. Gisors believes in the revolution only through his son: saying that men suffer because they think, he dulls the pain of existence by opium. Ferral wants to achieve power and to impose his will, not just in Asia but on his political enemies in France. This undertaking, however, like eroticism, his other pursuit, requires the co-operation of others, on whom he then becomes dependent; he too suffers from fatality. To avoid facing destiny, Clappique has recourse to whatever masks it: lies, jokes, role-playing, alcohol, eroticism, and gambling. König tortures as a response to his own humiliation. Even Kyo needs May as a rampart against his inner demons and the weight of destiny. However, his response to fatality—the struggle to acquire dignity for the downtrodden—does not isolate him but rather creates solidarity with other sufferers. Katow is even more single-minded: without a family, and having learned to surmount his obsessions, he devotes himself wholly to the revolution.

In the struggle between Communists and Nationalists, the former are abandoned by the International, for reasons of political strategy; but Kyo, Katow, and their followers refuse to surrender their arms. Thanks to support from Ferral and Chinese bankers, and to the International's inaction, the Nationalists overpower their former allies. Ch'en, whose death wish becomes apparent, is unsuccessful in a first attempt to assassinate Chiang Kai Shek (whose death would disrupt the Nationalist movement); he then throws himself and his bomb at Chiang's car (empty, however), dying in a paroxysm of pain instead of euphoria. After Hemmelrich's wife and child are killed by grenades, he escapes and goes ultimately to Russia as a worker. Kyo, who is captured, is thrown into a foul cell where the guards' brutality and the bestial conditions serve as a kind of purgatory; when König offers safety in exchange for the hidden armaments, the prison experience helps Kyo refuse the humiliating bargain and counter König's will to power by claiming dignity for all. Kyo takes cyanide; Katow, who gives his poison to two young Chinese prisoners, is carried to a locomotive, in which he will be burned alive. (Earlier indications suggest he is a Christ-figure.) When May and Gisors retrieve Kyo's body, Gisors contemplates it lengthily, before throwing his opium—the temptation of serenity—through the window.

As for the non-political Clappique, who became involved none the less, he smuggles himself onto a ship bound for Europe, having lost his money at gaming. Ferral too leaves for France: although the Nationalists are successful, his floundering enterprises will not be supported by the government and he must concede defeat. Later May leaves to work as a doctor in Russia; Gisors, who has taken refuge in Japan, refuses to accompany her; he has resumed his opium habit.

The complexity of the novel (especially its political plot), its ideology, its sombre atmosphere, its portrayals of violence and death, make *Man's Fate* difficult or unpalatable to some. Yet in its investigation of suffering and metaphysical anguish, through powerful scenes and searching discussions of destiny, it has few rivals.

—Catharine Savage Brosman

MĀNŪDŪŪKYA

See UPANISHADS

MARAT/SADE (Die Verfolgung und Ermordung Jean Paul Marats, dargestellt durch die Schauspielgruppe des Hospizes zu Charenton unter Anleitung des Herrn de Sade)
Play by Peter Weiss, 1964

Ever since its first night in West Berlin on 29 April 1964, *The Persecution and Assassination of Jean-Paul Marat as Performed by the Inmates of the Asylum of Charenton under the Direction of the Marquis de Sade*—better known as *Marat/Sade*—has been regarded as one of the masterpieces of the German and European theatre since World War II.

Apparently observing the classical unities, Peter Weiss operates with a multitude of locations and incidents at three different levels of time. The play-within-the-play by the fictitious Sade, featuring the murder of the revolutionary leader Marat by the Girondist Charlotte Corday, is set in Paris on 13 July 1793; the frame-play, showing Sade's work in performance, is set in Charenton on 13 July 1808; and the whole text abounds in allusions to the 20th century. The action of 1793, with further flashbacks and repetitions, is linked with that of 1808 by the arguments of Sade and Marat, the interventions of the asylum's director Coulmier, and the actors' relapses into their madness which eventually bring both Sade's imaginary production and Weiss's real play to a close.

While the historical Sade never met Marat, he did produce plays during his internment at Charenton. Although Weiss thought Sade as a dramatist timidly conventional, *Marat/Sade* owes much to his other writings, notably the treatise *The Bedroom Philosophers* (*La philosophie dans le boudoir*). Oscillating between intellectual debate and physical violence, Weiss unfolds a grotesque tragicomedy of overwhelming proportions, omitting none of the techniques available to a 20th-century playwright. Combining the methods of mime, masque, cabaret, street ballad, musical, and horror film with those of epic theatre, documentary theatre, the theatre of cruelty, and the theatre of the absurd, he creates what, in Antonin Artaud's term, has often been praised as an extraordinary piece of ''total theatre.'' His compilation of mutually alienating devices may obscure the meaning, and his overindulgence in visual and acoustic sensations disguise a lack of unifying dramatic tension. Nevertheless, he provides both a stunning spectacle and a memorable dramatization of important issues.

The most obvious theme is political. Although the play is ostensibly about the French Revolution and its aftermath, the deliberate anachronisms highlight Weiss's notion of the problems of revolution facing capitalism and imperialism today. Between 1962 and 1965 Weiss prepared five different versions. While the basic message of these remained the same throughout, his theoretical comments varied substantially. In 1964 he labelled Marat as a radical socialist and Sade as an uncommitted individualist whose indecision he himself shared. After the first East German production, which opened in Rostock on 25 March 1965, he declared that he had shown how a reactionary society will crush progressive ideas, commending Marat as ''the revolutionary who wants to change the bourgeois order'' and condemning Sade as ''the representative of the bourgeois order,'' whose ''scepticism, cynicism, pessimism serve nothing but his own downfall.'' In the play itself Marat indeed speaks like a proto-Marxist agitator, but his emotional and physical traumas and his doubts ring truer than his ideological proclamations; while Sade's nightmarish view of revolution as all greed, aggression, frustration, and perversion let loose seems justified by the events.

According to Weiss, the central conflict takes place between Sade and Marat, but the two characters are not equal in dramatic status. While Sade is the protagonist in the frame-play, Marat is only an invention of Sade for the play-within-the-play, even though he sometimes assumes an autonomous existence. On the other hand Coulmier, as the antagonist in the frame-play, opposes Sade as his equal in the dramatic structure. Thus it is the conflict of Sade and Coulmier that lies at the symbolic centre of the play.

Sade is bedevilled by a twofold struggle. His arguments with Marat externalize his struggle with himself, while his clashes with Coulmier epitomize his struggle with his environment. Through Marat he voices his yearning for a just society, but he is too conscious of the power of despotic rulers, the totalitarian potential of collectivism, the contradictions inherent in revolutionary activism, and the frailties of human nature to believe in any social improvement. Both product and agent of a failed revolution, he desires commitment but is prevented by his nihilism from adopting it. The more he despairs of life the more he withdraws into scornful detachment, and the more he withdraws the more he despairs. At the same time he needs to express himself. Rejecting politics, he espouses art, not to offer solutions but to dramatize his bewilderment at the historical upheaval around and the psychological turmoil within. The tragic farce he enacts with the lunatics manifests his disillusionment with a society dominated by the perversion of all instincts: its chaotic atmosphere is that which, according to Weiss, characterizes the arts under repression. The repression is exercised by Coulmier, who interrupts Sade's production whenever he suspects subversion. Although Coulmier abhors both social and sexual liberation, it is not so much the liberation itself that he attacks as its reflection in Sade's art, and he does so as a pillar of the newly established bourgeois order under the Emperor Napoleon. Thus the conflict proves to be one between artistic and bourgeois values, and the play ultimately reveals the plight of the artist in a hostile bourgeois society, which is the recurrent autobiographical theme of Weiss's entire work.

In denouncing bourgeois repression, Weiss does not romantically glorify the artist. As the riot finally disrupts the performance Sade, having failed as a politician, also fails as an artist. But while the fictitious dramatist Sade is defeated by the pressures in and around him, the real-life dramatist Weiss succeeds in transforming the very destruction of art into a remarkable artistic achievement.

—Ladislaus Löb

MARIA MAGDALENA
Play by Friedrich Hebbel, 1844

Maria Magdalena, a domestic or middle-class tragedy in three acts, focuses on the family of Meister Anton, a master joiner who swears to his daughter Klara that he will commit suicide rather than endure the ignominy of ever having a pregnant, unmarried daughter as well as an apparently criminal son. The shame attached to his son Karl's arrest on suspicion of theft has already killed Meister Anton's wife. Klara is pregnant by her fiancé Leonhard, and half-suspecting Klara's plight, Meister Anton extorts from her an oath that, whatever else, she will never bring shame upon him. It is clear what is meant. Failed by her brother Karl, by Leonhard, and by Friedrich, her childhood sweetheart who she believes abandoned her, she jumps down a well to her death. The dread prospect of eternal damnation is less daunting than that of having her father himself commit a mortal sin.

In his preface Friedrich Hebbel argued that, far from having been superseded by philosophy, art—in particular, a specific type of drama—had a vital role to play in modern society. This supreme type of drama was only possible when a decisive change occurred in the relationship between the state of human consciousness, social structures, and institutions on the one hand, and the ''idea'' or ''moral centre'' on the other. Germany, in Hebbels view, was in such a phase: philosophers and poets had recognized that the idea too was governed by the dialectic principle. Put simply, current norms and ideals did not have any absolute, timeless validity; in fact, they needed reforming because they hampered the quest for true human fulfilment. *Maria Magdalena* thus echoes many of the concerns of Heinrich Heine, the young Marx, and the philosopher Ludwig Feuerbach.

Hebbel, however, claimed that modern human beings did not want revolutions or new, ''unheard-of'' institutions: they wanted existing ones to be built on more solid foundations. Marriage, for instance, which in the play is presented as frustrating and dehumanizing, would not be abolished; instead, relations in marriage between the sexes would be transformed.

Given that German society was in the ferment and fever of a transitional phase, one could not, in Hebbel's view, depict ideal individuals living in an unalienated society. By creating concrete characters and inventing an action rooted in everyday life, one could, however, exploit the specific resources of art to bring home to audiences the limitations, indeed inhumanity, of middle-class life in a north-German provincial town.

In a world where middle-aged artisans are still illiterate, the sermon and the Lutheran Bible continue to be the main shapers of consciousness. Humanitarian ideas make few inroads. The characters are racked by feelings of sinfulness and guilt, by mortal fear of judgement and damnation. The values of mercy and understanding, enshrined in Christ's treatment of the Biblical Mary Magdalena are strikingly absent; in contrast, pharisaical self-righteousness and ''pointing of the finger'' abound as traditional rituals are equated with godliness. Fear of God has been replaced by an all-pervasive pathological obsession with reputation and respectability.

The cult of work and thrift goes hand in hand with condemnation of all amusement and play. Indeed the general stress on the vanity of mortal, earthly life precludes and perverts any natural delight in physical beauty, love, and sex. Furthermore this ethos perpetuates the old hierarchial society of God-given estates, and by preaching contentment with existing life-styles hinders the growth of a more dynamic economy which could afford new possibilities of human self-realization. Certain professions are still deemed dishonourable and their members treated as pariahs. Criminals and bankrupts, too, are for ever beyond the pale of respectability.

The preoccupation with respectability has other dire consequences. Obeying the expectation that middle-class males secure a respectable position before seeking a suitable spouse, Friedrich leaves to study law at university oblivious to Klara's needs and her situation. His emotional immaturity and self-centred insensitivity are strikingly conveyed. He cannot simply love Klara and forgive her. Only if Leonhard can be murdered in a duel is silence guaranteed. Although mortally wounded in the duel, Friedrich does at the end at least achieve some insight, whereas Meister Anton is totally confused by a world which defies all his norms and expectations. Leonhard, for his part, progressed by various machiavellian ploys. Yet, despite this, he has been welcomed by Meister Anton as his future son-in-law once becoming town treasurer. While craving returned affection and shared sexual pleasure, he views marriage as a matter of dowries, social advantage, and status. Women too are subject to traditional notions of what constitutes a suitable match. In all this, mutual love and passion count for little. In fact, marriage is shown to violate a woman's natural feelings; sex is perverted.

Instead of being the framework which nurtures and supports its individual members, the family emerges as a hell. Relations between husband and wife, between parents and children, and between the children themselves are totally frustrating or destructive. In this authoritarian, puritanical family individuals vainly crave affection and understanding. Jealousy, resentment, and hatred are rampant. There is no frank communication, only veiled accusations, innuendoes, and circumlocutions. Characters talk past each other and are driven into silence or anguished soliloquies. In his preface Hebbel speaks of characters lacking any sense of dialectic, i.e. unable to relativize or change their traditional standards. Only when consciousness and conditions change can natural, spontaneous human aspiration be fulfilled.

Because all the characters are products of this society, there can be no division into heroes or heroines and villains. In all of them valid human needs and aspirations vainly struggle to assert themselves in the face of social pressures and ingrained values invested with divine authority. One cannot speak here of individual guilt, of incorruptible reason or conscience, of moral autonomy or spiritual freedom. Suffering does not ennoble or point the way to a truer understanding of man and the world. There is no supernatural redeemer or Christian providence. If human beings are to be rescued from this hell, they must redeem each other by creating a humane society.

—David Jackson

MARY STUART (Maria Stuart)
Play by Friedrich von Schiller, 1800

''Tragedy has the power, indeed the obligation, to subordinate historical truth to the laws of poetry and to adapt its given subject matter to its own needs,'' Friedrich von Schiller states in his essay ''Über die tragische Kunst.'' In *Mary Stuart* he strives to ''give the imagination freedom over history'' (letter to Goethe, 12 July 1799) by boldly modifying the sourse material which he took chiefly from William Camden's *Annales*, Johann Wilhelm von Archenholtz's and Friedrich Gentz's respective studies of Queen Elizabeth I and Mary Queen of Scots, and histories of England and Scotland by George Buchanan, Paul de Rapin Thoyras, William Robertson, and David Hume. In particular he overrides historical uncertainties by declaring Mary clearly innocent of any complicity in the Babington plot (which the fictitious Elizabeth uses as the final pretext for her execution) and clearly guilty of conniving in the earlier murder of her first husband Darnley by her second husband Bothwell (which is not included in the charges against her). He makes the Earl of Leicester love and betray Mary, and he invents Mortimer, who also falls in love with her. Blatantly contradicting history, he presents Mary as 25 years younger than she really was when she died, and he contrives an unhistorical meeting between the two queens, when Mary accuses Elizabeth of illegitimacy.

Although he sets the play against the authentic background of 16th-century religious and dynastic struggles, Schiller is more interested in the ''passionate and human'' aspects (letter to Goethe, 19 March 1799), which he dramatizes in terms of the Stoic philosophy he adopted largely from Immanuel Kant. In his treatise ''Über das Pathetische'' he argues that the purpose of tragedy is to exalt the individual's ''moral independence of natural laws'': it is the willing acceptance of suffering for the sake of duty that demonstrates this ''moral freedom'' or ''sublimity'' most persuasively. In his treatise ''On the Sublime'' he explains that the only way to overcome the degrading rule of necessity in the world of empirical reality is to ''destroy the very concept of a force'' by ''submitting to it voluntarily.''

It is then the achievement of sublime spiritual freedom that Schiller illustrates in the development of Mary. In her youth, ''destined only to experience and inflame fierce passions'' (letter to Goethe, 18 June 1799), she was subject to ''sensuality,'' which flares up for the last time when she challenges Elizabeth and seals her own fate. When she realizes that she cannot be physically saved she abandons all earthly desires. Taking Holy Communion, in a scene that was often censured and censored for its alleged blasphemy, she serenely accepts her undeserved death sentence in atonement for her earlier sins. She thus rises above the constraints of external necessity and natural instinct into the pure realm of the ''ideal.'' Elizabeth, on the other hand, becomes increasingly enslaved by sexual jealousy and by the manipulations she feels obliged to carry out in order to retain her throne. Her tyranny and hypocrisy are the inevitable outcome of her commitment to the ''real.'' Most of the other characters, although sharply drawn in their own right, represent further aspects of these moral conflicts: Shrewsbury pleading for mercy and fairness, Burleigh insisting on political expediency, Leicester conducting opportunistic intrigues, and Mortimer giving in to immature emotion to the point of attempting to rape Mary—another incident criticized in Schiller's day on grounds of decorum.

Planned from 1783, written and first performed at the Weimar court theatre in 1800, and first published in 1801, *Mary Stuart* has been praised as Schiller's supreme technical achievement. Schiller himself, with the Aristotelian concepts of fear and pity in mind, attributed its tragic effect chiefly to the fact "that the catastrophe can already be seen in the first scenes and is brought closer and closer as the action seems to be moving away from it," (letter to Goethe, 18 June 1799). Concentrating on the last three days of Mary's life in 1587, he begins with her death sentence, recapitulating the irrevocable antecedents in the Euripidean analytical manner and constructing a profoundly ironic plot in which the very attempts to save her precipitate her destruction. The structure, combining elements of French classicism and German baroque, is based on symmetry and antithesis. The scene alternates between Mary's prison at Fotheringhay and Elizabeth's palace at Westminster, the climax and turning point of the play being provided half-way through the action by the confrontation of the two queens in a park. Mary's moral rise, accompanied by the decline of her worldly fortunes, runs parallel to Elizabeth's consolidation of her power and her concurrent moral degeneration. Elizabeth is placed between Shrewsbury and Burleigh, who respectively urge her to spare and to destroy Mary. Leicester is torn between his love for Mary and his mercenary need for Elizabeth. The dialogue is written in the stylized blank verse of "Weimer classicism," with some interludes in more "romantic" lyrical forms. Violent events, notably the decapitation of Mary, are reported rather than shown on stage.

Despite its massive dramatic impact, which caused Madame de Staël to call it "the most touching and best thought-out of all German tragedies," the play has been criticized for its artificiality: Otto Ludwig, for example, accused it of showing "nowhere a trace of spontaneous nature." A standard German classic, and also successful in France and Italy, it has never been popular in England, possibly because of its unsympathetic portrayal of Elizabeth, although an English translation by Joseph Charles Mellish appeared as early as 1801. Brecht, who detested Schiller's idealism, wrote a travesty of the encounter of the two queens transformed into squabbling fishwives. For all its impressive stagecraft and magnificent rhetoric, *Mary Stuart* is too much a statement of Schiller's abstract philosophy and too chilly in its formal perfection to be a completely satisfying recreation of history and human life.

—Ladislaus Löb

THE MASTER AND MARGARITA (Master i Margarita)
Novel by Mikhail Bulgakov, 1965–66 (written 1934–40)

The Master and Margarita was essentially completed in 1940 but its origin goes back to 1928, when Mikhail Bulgakov wrote a satirical tale about the devil visiting Moscow. Like his literary hero, Gogol' (as well as the Master in his own novel), Bulgakov destroyed this manuscript in 1930 but returned to the idea in 1934, adding his heroine, Margarita, based on the figure of his third wife, Elena Sergeevna Shilovskaia. The novel went through a number of different versions until, aware that he had only a short time to live, he put other works aside in order to complete it, dictating the final changes on his deathbed after he had become blind. It remained unpublished until 1965–66, when it appeared in a censored version in the literary journal *Moskva*, immediately creating a sensation. It has since been published in its entirety, although the restored passages, while numerous, add comparatively little to the overall impact of the novel. It has

been translated into many other languages. (In English, the Glenny translation is the more complete, while the Ginsburg translation is taken from the original *Moskva* version.)

The novel's form is unusual, with the hero, the Master, appearing only towards the end of the first part, and Margarita not until Part Two. It combines three different if carefully related stories: the arrival of the devil (Woland) and his companions in contemporary Moscow, where they create havoc; Margarita's attempt, with Wotand's assistance, to be reunited with her love after his imprisonment and confinement in a psychiatric hospital; and an imaginative account of the passion of Christ (given the Hebrew name of Yeshua-Ha-Nozri) from his interrogation by Pontius Pilate to his crucifixion. Differing considerably from the gospels, the latter consists of four chapters which may be regarded as a novel within a novel: written by the Master, related by Woland, and dreamed of by a young poet (Ivan Bezdomnyi, or "Homeless") on the basis of "true" events. Correspondingly, the action takes place on three different levels, each with a distinct narrative voice: that of Ancient Jerusalem, of Moscow of the 1930s (during the same four days in Holy Week), and of the "fantastic" realm beyond time. The book is usually considered to be closest in genre to Menippean satire.

Despite its complexity, the novel is highly entertaining, very funny in places, and with the mystery appeal of a detective story. In the former Soviet Union, as well as in the countries of Eastern Europe, it was appreciated first of all for its satire on the absurdities of everyday life: involving Communist ideology, the bureaucracy, the police, consumer goods, the housing crisis, various forms of illegal activities and, above all, the literary and artistic community. At the same time it is obviously a very serious work, by the end of which one feels a need for more detailed interpretation: what, in short, is it all about? The problem is compounded by the fact that it is full of pure fantasy and traditional symbols (features associated with devil-lore, for example), so that the reader is uncertain what is important to elucidate the meaning. Leitmotifs (such as sun and moon, light and darkness, and many others) connect the three levels, implying the ultimate unity of all existence.

Soviet critics tended to dwell initially on the relatively innocuous theme of justice: enforced by Woland during his sojourn in Moscow, while Margarita tempers this with mercy in her plea to release a sinner from torment. Human greed, cowardice, and the redemptive power of love are other readily distinguishable themes. More fundamental ones are summed up in three key statements: "Jesus existed" (the importance of a spiritual understanding of life, as opposed to practical considerations in a materialistic world that denied Christ's very existence); "Manuscripts don't burn" (a belief in the enduring nature of art); and "Everything will turn out right. That's what the world is built on": an extraordinary metaphysical optimism for a writer whose life was characterized by recurring disappointment. There is indeed a strong element of wish-fulfilment in the book, where characters are punished or rewarded according to what they are seen to have deserved.

Thus the novel's heroes, the Master and Margarita, are ultimately rescued, through the agency of Woland, in the world beyond time. They are, however, granted "peace" rather than "light," from which they are specifically excluded: a puzzle to many critics. Here, on a deeper philosophical level, there is an undoubted influence of gnosticism with its contrasting polarities of good and evil—which, as I have argued elsewhere, are reconciled in eternity, where "peace" represents a higher state than the corresponding polarities of light and darkness. Another influence is the Faust story, with Margarita (a far more dynamic figure than either the Master or Goethe's Gretchen) partly taking over Faust's traditional role, in that she is the one to make the pact with Woland, rejoicing in her role as witch. A major scene is "Satan's Great Ball," a fictional representation of the *Walpurgisnacht* or Black Mass.

Bulgakov, however, reinterprets his sources—*Faust*, traditional demonology, the Bible, and many others—in his own way, creating an original and entertaining story which is not exhausted by interpretation. His devil is helpful to those who deserve it and is shown as necessary to God's purposes, to which he is not opposed. Bulgakov's Christ figure, a lonely "philosopher," has only one disciple (Matthu Levi)—although eventually Pontius Pilate, "released" by Margarita from his torments after 2,000 years, is allowed to follow him as well. Woland too has his disciples: Azazello, Koroviev, and a huge, comical tomcat called Behemoth. So has the Master, with Ivan Bezdomnyi. Like Faust, the Master is the creative artist, "rivalling" God with the devil's help; like Yeshua he is profoundly aware of the spiritual plane, but is afraid, cowed by life's circumstances.

Endlessly fascinating, the novel indeed deserves to be considered one of the major works of 20th-century world literature.

—A. Colin Wright

THE MASTER BUILDER (Bygmester Solness)
Play by Henrik Ibsen, 1892

One of the great strengths of Henrik Ibsen's dramas was to deflate bourgeois self-confidence, and to reveal that the cosiest and best furnished of drawing rooms could harbour grim secrets, dissatisfaction, and despair. The desire to expose the self-deception, constriction, and hypocrisy upon which middle-class life was founded can be seen most obviously in his socially realistic plays such as *The Pillars of Society* and *Ghosts*. However, such criticism of bourgeois living is also apparent in the plays that belong to Ibsen's final stage of writing. In the plays written in the 1890s he proved, however, to be more interested in probing the nature of artistic creativity, and was less concerned with showing how social environment could determine individual consciousness as he had done, for example, in *A Doll's House* and *An Enemy of the People*.

The Master Builder comes from Ibsen's last years as a playwright and is, like his final play, *When We Dead Awaken*, an examination of personal and artistic expression, with strong symbolist tendencies in its style. There are pronounced autobiographical elements in both plays, suggesting (rather neatly for literary biographers) that these late pieces could be the Norwegian playwright's final reckoning with his own art, life, and ambitions. Although the two late plays share much in common, *The Master Builder*'s setting, a carefully described and prosperous architect's residence, recalls the social dramas of the 1870s and 1880s much more directly than the dreamlike, semi-mythical mountain world of *When We Dead Awaken*.

Halvard Solness is a self-taught architect and builder from a poor country background, whose business has prospered despite personal tragedy. He believes that he has willed the burning down of his wife's childhood home, a fire that destroyed all of her most precious memories and possessions. As a result of the fire, Aline Solness was unable to feed their twin baby boys, who also perished. With Faustian overtones, Solness believes that this domestic misfortune has bought him success and artistic acclaim. He has been ruthless in exercising his will to power and has deliberately impeded the development of others. In order to be acclaimed, he has held back his assistant Ragnar Brovik out of fear that the younger generation will overtake him. He exerts great dominance over Ragnar's fiancée Kaja, who is his secretary and is infatuated with him. Despite the fact that his occupation is the building of homes, Solness's own home life is barren and miserable, unable as he is to help Aline who, always dressed in black, is in mourning for her lost life as a mother.

An unexpected emissary from outside Solness's world, the young, vital, and impulsive Hilde Wangel, brings enthusiasm and joy into Solness's solitary existence. The idealistic Hilde offers herself as his princess to be carried away by Solness the Troll, a fantasy that she claims was enacted ten years previously when he visited her village to place a wreath on top of the church tower he had designed. To Hilde, Solness reveals an almost fanatical sense of vocation, a belief that he has been chosen and is special. Yet Solness's belief in his mission as an artist is in crisis; his confidence is shaken by Ragnar's request to be allowed his own building commission. Spurred on by Hilde's adulation Solness, who is afraid of heights, is persuaded to repeat his climbing feat of ten years back, and scales the high tower of his new home. Unfortunately Solness plunges from the tower to his death. Just as the outsider Gregers Werle imposes an impossible notion of the ideal on the Ekdal household in *The Wild Duck* and destroys the family, Hilde also forces Solness to attempt to live up to an unattainable reality.

Although the setting is much more realistic than the expressionistic plays of writers such as August Strindberg and Georg Kaiser, this intriguing play has features that anticipate them. It is, like Kaiser's *From Morning to Midnight* (*Von Morgens bis mitternachts*, 1916), a monodrama, with the action centred almost entirely on the inner states of the central character. Also, as in Strindberg's *A Dream Play* (*Ett drömspel*, 1902) and *Ghost Sonata* (*Spöksonaten*, 1907), there is the sense that the events, particularly the attraction of Hilde and Kaja, stem from workaday reality suffused by fantasies, dreams, and desires. Like Solness's towers and palaces, which have no foundations in the ground, the dialogue here has a visionary quality which reveals Solness's forceful urges and guilt-torn fears that he has failed as an artist and as a human being. Behind the successful architect's domineering façade lurk anxieties about waning creativity and potency, expressed in his yearning to build higher towers, and his inability in recent years to do so. Creative talent is presented here as a painful process, born out of domination, egotism, and an inability to give love. Eventually this artistic ability, built as it is on dubious practice, is destroyed by the unexpected (and possibly willed) retribution of Hilde's irresponsible over-confidence in his powers. The younger generation destroys Solness, as he fears, but through worship rather than envy. However, the master builder's sudden death as a result of his *folie à deux* with Hilde is not tragic. Accompanied by Hilde's ecstatic adoration (and the earth-bound Aline's warnings), Solness's plunge to his death anticipates the transfiguration of the individual, found also in Rubek's triumphant recapturing of life in *When We Dead Awaken* and at the end of several German expressionist plays, where the hero transcends the everyday through heightened experience.

The idiosyncratic tone of *The Master Builder* has caused critics to reach outside the text to look for shared ideas and influences. It is possible to find affinities with Freud's contemporary ideas on the unconscious in the evocation of Solness's sublimated desires, subconscious fantasies, and dreams, to make sense of the patterns of imagery in the play. Solness too may resemble some kind of Nietzschean Superman, trying through his art to rise above the cowed masses.

However, the provincial architect appears to be a poor prototype, showing himself in his egotistic treatment of those who surround him as being all too human. It seems more fruitful to look at *The Master Builder* within Ibsen's dramatic *oeuvre*. The play's ideas revive preoccupations and patterns of interaction from earlier works in Ibsen's theatrical career, which are here reshaped. The relationship between self-fulfilment and duty, the desire for truth and authenticity of experience, and the tensions between life, art, and passion are all examined with different shifts of meaning from earlier plays. To such recurrent concerns, Ibsen, in his portrait of the artist as an ageing man, incorporates a wish for self-analysis, hinting at the exorcism of trolls in his own creative life.

—Anna-Marie Taylor

MASTER DON GESUALDO (Mastro-don Gesualdo)
Novel by Giovanni Verga, 1889

Critics have often attempted to determine which of Giovanni Verga's two most acclaimed novels is the greater: *Master Don Gesualdo* or *The House by the Medlar Tree*? The debate remains unresolved, but does indicate the superb quality of both masterpieces. *Master Don Gesualdo* follows *The House by the Medlar Tree* as the second work in the author's intended series, *I vinti*.

Verga is famous as the foremost exponent of the literary movement *verismo*. The aim of the *verismo* writers was the objective and faithful reproduction of the customs, unique features, and mentality of the various regions of Italy, with the goal of describing the diverse aspects and concrete problems of different areas. In his proposed series of novels, Verga presents the reader with three levels of Sicilian society: the oppressed, ignorant Malavoglia family, Gesualdo Motta, the worker who acquires wealth and social position, and finally the decadent aristocracy in the incomplete *Duchess of Leyra*. In the Preface to *The House by the Medlar Tree*, Verga states explicitly the literary itinerary of the second volume of his series. His intention in *Master Don Gesualdo* is to represent the greed for wealth of a typical bourgeois in a small, provincial town.

The novel is divided into four parts. In part one, the narrative opens with a fire in the decrepit home of the impoverished but noble Trao family. Their neighbour, a workman called Gesualdo Motta, helps to put out the blaze and, in the ensuing confusion, the young baron, Don Nini Rubiera, is discovered in the bedroom of his cousin, Bianca Trao. In order to remedy the scandal, a marriage is arranged quickly between Bianca and Gesualdo. Gesualdo is willing to forgo a dowry in order to marry into one of the area's noble families, whereas Nini Rubiera's mother opposes the match with the penniless Bianca. Upon his marriage to Bianca, however, Gesualdo must give up his faithful servant and companion, Diodata, who had shared his life for several years and had borne his children. In the second section of the novel, a daughter is born to Bianca, but she never confesses to her husband that Isabellina is not Gesualdo's biological daughter. Despite his marriage to Bianca, Gesualdo has found no business allies among his newly acquired relatives. He is isolated from the noble families who disdain his background and his marriage fares no better. Although Bianca is a docile wife, she is incapable of offering her husband the warmth and affection he found in Diodata. Isabellina is very much a Trao, and upon her entry into an exclusive convent school for

Sicilian noblewomen, she quickly distances herself from her father's humble origins.

The 1837 outbreak of cholera in Palermo results in the removal of the entire family to a country estate. Bianca is very ill with typhus and does not have the strength or the will to supervise her daughter. Isabellina falls in love with Corrado la Gurma, an orphan taken in by her father, and makes the same mistake as Bianca a generation before. To save the good name of the family, a marriage is arranged with the wealthy Duke of Leyra who is interested only in the sizeable dowry. The dowry for Isabellina's marriage is provided by her biological father, Nini Rubiera, in a strange twist of fate. Many years earlier, the young baron's dissolute lifestyle had made it necessary for him to borrow money from the wealthiest man in the town, Gesualdo Motta. He is unable to repay the loan and therefore must marry a wealthy woman he does not love. The dowry of Nini Rubiera's wife is thus passed on at the time of Isabellina's wedding and makes up the girl's dowry. After the death of Bianca, Gesualdo moves to Palermo where he lives in a remote wing of the Duke of Leyra's luxurious palace. At the end of his life, he is profoundly alone. His daughter and son-in-law have little interest in the old man and are intent on depleting the fortune he built up in a lifetime of hard work in order to enjoy a sumptuous life-style. Gesualdo dies alone and his last thoughts are of his calloused hands.

The ambiguous title *Mastro-don* is symbolic of the dichotomy inherent in the protagonist. He is both a worker (*mastro*) and a member of the upper class (*don*). Verga's portrayal of a man who attempts to make his way out of the class he is born into is a realistic description of family values, social conventions, and class differences in 19th-century Sicily. Like the proletariat class described in *The House by the Medlar Tree*, Gesualdo is obsessed with ''la roba,'' the accumulation of tangible assets. The nobility are uninterested in the accumulation of wealth because their wealth is inherited. The Trao family was too proud to recover their depleted resources by working, and Isabellina and her husband are interested only in the spending of their inherited wealth. It is for this reason that Gesualdo is never able to fit in with the nobility. The only aspect that Gesualdo and his noble relatives have in common is that they routinely subordinate sentiments to more practical concerns, such as social conventions and the accumulation of wealth. Thus most personal relationships are unhappy and based on calculation, as is clear in the marriages of Bianca, Nini, and Isabellina.

The reader is sympathetic to the protagonist through Verga's use of the technique of indirect discourse in order to explain Gesualdo's point of view in various situations and the internal logic of his thoughts, emotions, and motivations. Gesualdo Motta is a truly modern anti-hero. *Master Don Gesualdo* is often considered the first modern Italian novel because of the alienation of the protagonist, both from the social milieu into which he was born and that to which he aspires, as well as from the other characters.

—Jordan Lancaster

A MATTER OF DISPUTE (La Dispute)
Play by Marivaux, 1744

A Matter of Dispute, a prose comedy in one act (and therefore envisaged as a smaller supporting piece alongside a longer play), was withdrawn (and consigned to almost two centuries of oblivion) after its first performance by the Comédie-Française on 19 October 1744. A later play, written after the period of Marivaux's fruitful collaboration with the Comédie-Italienne, 1720–40, it was too avant-garde and experimental for its company's persistent declamatory style and highly conservative audience. Prefigured in certain respects by Autreau's *The Ignorant Lovers* (*Los Amants ignorants*), 1720, it is theatrically challenging in its staging of an anthropological experiment to find out which, man or woman, first invented unfaithfulness in love. Beneath the comic irony lurks a more general question about whether or not durable love is at all possible. The plot (traceable back to Herodotus' story of an Egyptian king's attempt to find the origin of language) is a reflection of the typical 18th-century philosophical method of "hypothetical history," whereby a return to the state of nature is postulated in order from that point to deduce the development (and hence explain the structure) of some human phenomenon. The Prince (who is not named) and Hermiane, the object of his love, agree that men were unfaithful first, and are witnesses to the results of an experiment initiated by the Prince's late father. Two babies of each sex (Azor and Mesrin, Eglé and Adine) have been raised in individual isolation from all human society, except for one black servant of the same gender assigned to each pair in order to sustain life and teach language (blackness in this hypothesis and at this period seems to imply that neither the male servant, Mesrou, nor the female, Carise, "really counts" as human society). The action of the play is the emergence in turn of the now grown-up young people, Eglé, Azor, Adine, and Mesrin in that order initially into self-perception (as reflections in stream or mirror), thereafter into appreciation of the opposite sex, and from thence to rivalry or (for the men at least initially) friendship with their own sex. Both pairs follow a pattern of progress, from narcissism to discovery of the opposite sex and love, to exchange of lovers in a "double infidelity," echoing the three-act play of that name. There is even the prospect that each will return to the original partner (or try to keep both)! *A Matter of Dispute* also, in the characters' emergence from animal "stupidity" into social and moral behaviour, incorporates the principal motif of *Harlequin's Lesson in Love*, Marivaux's first successful (one-act) piece for the Comédie-Italienne and the first to stage the typical marivaudian "surprise by love." While the case of the two unfaithful pairs is presented with the fine sense of dramatic necessity sought after by classicism, it is not on the other hand a universal moral necessity: in the last scene a previously unmentioned third pair (Meslis and Dina) emerge from their isolation, are shown to be impervious to the temptations of infidelity, and receive their proportionate reward from the Prince.

The play is remarkable, by comparison with Marivaux's earlier plays, first of all for developing the theme, hitherto only exploited fully in his journalistic essays, of narcissism and the mirror as both the *sine qua non* and the fatal flaw of love. Equally remarkably, in technical terms, it explicitly stages two worlds simultaneously: that of the Prince and Hermiane, conducting their own game of love and, from the fourth scene to the penultimate one, observing the experiment from hiding (but perhaps visible to the real audience), and that of their guinea pigs, the young people emerging from their isolation. The black servants, who are present throughout the play, provide the link between the two worlds and contribute indispensably to the typical marivaudian "double register" of language, whereby characters not only speak and feel as they are but also comment constantly on the utterances of others. For the real audience, therefore, the play offers two layers of action: firstly the "dispute" of the Prince and Hermiane who watch the experiment (the Prince denies that he disagrees about

infidelity) and secondly the behaviour of the guinea pigs themselves. It is as if Marivaux has explicitly staged an aspect of his dramaturgy that remains only implicit in his earlier output: his real audience is indeed quite normally the voyeur looking in on an imaginative "dramatic experiment" into the workings of the human heart. This is the "journey to the true world" (an exact mirror of our own world except that intentions are always clearly perceived) that is evoked famously in Marivaux's *Le Cabinet du philosophe* [The Philosopher's Study] (sixth to eleventh *feuilles*). There is thus here arguably even a "third layer" of meaning where we are invited to meditate upon what the theatrical art actually is as well as upon the play's ostensible subject. While the psychology of love is sketched with Marivaux's usual sensitivity and sureness of touch, there is obviously no question of realism or of commentary on the specific mores of an age. The world of the stage is a utopia, a "land of nowhere" (or "true world") where human acts are freed from everything that is contingent, relative, and trivial and where, paradoxically, human nature can be contemplated free of its masks. In *A Matter of Dispute*, where the many psychological steps are presented with the utmost brevity, this "otherness" of the classical drama is refined almost to the point of pure ritual: the (non)dispute which leads into the anthropological experiment is as typically human as the predictable rhythm and rapid progress of infidelity in love. At the end Hermiane's revulsion at the experiment's results likewise ritualizes a characteristic human reluctance to accept the truth. These things are presented as so well known (yet important) that it is pointless to seek any individual psychology: human truth parades before us with compelling coherence and in an almost perfect balance between the comic and dramatic atmospheres: Marivaux's humour invites emotional engagement with his creatures while maintaining comic distance from them. We are witnessing the summation of his art.

Renewed interest in the play arose among theatre people in the mid-20th century as part of the general reaction (led by Adamov and others) against the deadliness of naturalism. With its strong dramatic rhythms bordering on the ritual, it still appeals, despite period ideological features that challenge the producer of the piece for a modern audience: the dramatic convention, for example, that servants' black skin rules them out as genuine human contact; or the fact, hardly palatable to a feminist sensibility, that Marivaux's sequence of infidelity (like that of the book of Genesis) begins with the woman. On the second point, however, patience rewards the spectator, who finds that, as usual, the female interests Marivaux more than the male and that she is a superior being who is at the origin of civilization: the equal of the male in infidelity, she as least pays virtue the homage of being hypocritical about it! Marivaux's marking of the difference between dramatic and moral necessity is also a problem in the last scene, where the third pair of lovers remain faithful to each other. Morally this is easily interpreted as the "exception which proves the rule," but dramatically there is an element of (pleasant) surprise that it is not easy to relate to what has gone before.

—Philip E.J. Robinson

MAXIMS (Réflexions; ou, Sentences et maximes morales)
Prose by François La Rochefoucauld, 1665–78

François La Rochefoucauld's *Maxims* is a collection of dispassionate personal reflections on human nature, honed and polished by the tastes of 17th-century literate society. As such, they are a fine example of French classical literature. Five editions appeared between 1665 and 1678.

Military and political disappointments had destroyed La Rochefoucauld's illusions about human nature. The resulting tone of disenchantment, which is evident in the *Maxims*, challenged the official optimism of the age. The finished work was a product of salon society. La Rochefoucauld was a member of Mme. de Sablé's circle, which included philosophers, theologians, and scientists. Their conversations covered a variety of themes—human behaviour, the limits of free will, the relationship between morality and society, and the nature of love—which anticipated those of the *Maxims*.

It was in the context of these gatherings that La Rochefoucauld and Mme. de Sablé launched the fashion of expressing their insights in lapidary form; their maxims achieved widespread fame, and publication followed. It may seem strange today that such a work should be successful. But in La Rochefoucauld's day it expressed an important aspect of the intellectual climate. The 17th century had inherited from humanism a taste for moral precepts: the feeling was that virtue and happiness lay in the definition and application of a code of moral laws.

The central thesis of the *Maxims* is resolutely pessimistic. Humanity is flawed. At the heart of our corruption lies self-interest (*amour-propre*), which effectively controls our lives: "It is present in all estates and conditions; it lives everywhere, it lives on everything and it lives on nothing." Inseparable from egoism, pride, and vanity, self-interest is the motivating force behind all our actions, even those apparently inspired by altruism: "Self-interest speaks all sorts of languages and plays all sorts of roles, even that of unselfishness." Reason is powerless against it and sentiments conventionally thought noble are really self-interest in disguise. Love, stripped of its romantic façade, is concerned with possession and resembles hatred. Friendship masks a desire to exploit and we take pleasure in friends' happiness, says La Rochefoucauld, because we hope to take some profit from their good fortune. Even virtues such as humility and military valour are stripped of their prestige and systematically reduced to the hypocrisy of personal interest.

As striking as the doctrine itself is the vigorous form in which it is communicated. Expressed in less trenchant style, the maxims would be less provoking. La Rochefoucauld is a supreme exponent of the metaphors and antitheses enjoyed by the polite society of his time. "Virtues merge into self-interest, as rivers merge into the sea." Everywhere there is paradox and economy: a single thought reduced to a minimum of words and artfully expressed: "Constancy in love is perpetual inconstancy." The author's awareness of the importance of form is demonstrated by the care with which he revised his maxims in successive editions.

He was not alone in writing about the power of egoism. Influential works such as Descartes's *Traité des passions* (1649) and Cureau de la Chamber's *Caractère des passions* (1662) had already suggested that human judgement is influenced by "humours" over which reason has no direct control. In addition, Mme de Sablé's circle was deeply influenced by the growing force of Jansenism and by the feeling of disillusionment that permeated polite society after the disappointment of the Frondes: the *Maxims* are simply the most memorable expression of this strain of pessimism.

And yet they are not entirely negative. It would be wrong to imply, as some critics have, that they are solely concerned with egoism, or that La Rochefoucauld does not believe in the possibility of virtue. What saves this austere doctrine from hopelessness is the idea that a small élite is capable of rising above self-interest. La Rochefoucauld

states, for example, that if friendship is often a façade, the true article can exist. If we are to know ourselves properly, the first requirement is humility, "the altar on which God wants us to offer sacrifices." Linked to humility is the kind of lucidity that enables man to identify his true motives, admit his faults, and, ideally, act disinterestedly: "The true gentleman recognizes his faults and confesses them." If we cannot identify our defects, we cannot hope to correct them: if there is to be moral progress, lucidity is essential.

Far from being a negative work, the *Maxims* should be considered a high-minded manual of social etiquette in the tradition of Montaigne and Charron: true virtue, suggests La Rochefoucauld, lies not in conformism but in a deeper sense of personal greatness, the need to be true to oneself. Although he discussed his work at length with his friend, the Jansenist theologian Jacques Ésprit, the moral ideal that emerges from the *Maxims* is not religious but human, not submission to Divine Providence but independent nobility of spirit.

—David Shaw

MEDEA
Play by Euripides, 431 BC

Euripides' famous play *Medea* is set in Corinth where Medea is in exile. It depicts the revenge she takes against her errant Argonaut husband Jason who, despite owing his life to her and having sworn an oath of fidelity, has deserted her in order to marry the daughter of Creon, the king of Corinth. After disposing of her rival and Creon by means of poisoned gifts, a robe and chaplet, she completes her revenge by killing her own children, thus leaving Jason without issue. She makes her escape in a miraculous manner, using a winged chariot provided by her grandfather Helius, the sun, having already secured the promise from King Aegeus of asylum in Athens. Legends regarding Medea's stay in Corinth and the death of her children already existed in Euripides' time, but there is general agreement that the form of the story presented in the play is very much his own.

Two aspects of the play have been subjected, from Aristotle onwards, to adverse criticism—the "Aegeus scene" and the supernatural conclusion. The appearance of Aegeus at Corinth on his way from Delphi to Troezen has appeared to many to have been dragged in for the convenience of the plot. It should be pointed out, however, that by 431 BC the figures of Aegeus and Medea were closely linked in Athenian legend and that the scene contains a thematic link with the rest of the play, namely children: the purpose of Aegeus' journey is to discover if he can make his marriage fertile. The finale is a remarkable *coup de théâtre*. Medea appears, in a scene akin to the divine epiphanies so common in Euripides' work, as *dea ex machina*, announcing her own intentions and revealing to Jason what will happen to him in his future life. To see this as contrived is to miss the point. We have been reminded already of Medea's relationship to the sun and there is undoubtedly something inherently demonic about her character.

The dramatic structure of the play is hard to parallel. No other character in Greek tragedy dominates the stage to the extent that Medea does. The central action of the play is made up of scenes in which she converses at length with the chorus and scenes in which she confronts single characters acting as foils: Creon, Jason, Aegeus, Jason, the messenger, and finally, Jason once more. Her formidable character which this prominence highlights has been explained by many critics as the product of her non-Greek origins (''no Greek woman could behave like this!'') and her powers as a sorceress. But neither of these features, so prominent in later treatments of her story, is to the fore in Euripides' play. Her barbarian birth is certainly relevant to her isolation and need for protection in the Greek world: it is not used as an explanation for her conduct. She is, admittedly, an expert with potions (*pharmaca*), which she is able to use both for deadly purposes (the murder of her rival) and benign ones (ensuring that Aegeus has issue), but such skill is paralleled in tragedy in the case of other, female, Greek characters. It is not so much her magical powers as her acute intelligence and insight that are stressed. Most of all, it is her heroic nature—she has affinities with the great, unrecalcitrant Sophoclean hero figures—that stands out. Because of her acute sense of injustice she is driven to extreme action. After much soul-searching she conquers her strong maternal instincts and takes the ultimate step of killing her children because she knows that this is the way to inflict the greatest hurt on Jason.

Medea is also a spokeswoman for her own sex. (For most of the play she has the total support of the chorus of female Corinthians.) Her opening speech is a powerful description of the plight of women in the Greek world and includes the memorable response to the assertion that women do not have to undergo the same physical risks and discomfort as the Greek warrior male: ''I would rather stand three times in the line of battle than give birth once.'' Such a sentiment must have made uncomfortable hearing for the male audience in the theatre of Dionysus in 431 BC.

—David M. Bain

MEDITATIONS
Prose by Marcus Aurelius, c. AD 170

Although remembered as a virtuous and honourable ruler, Marcus Aurelius is most famous for his *Meditations*, a work his subjects never saw, the intimate notebook in which he recorded his own reflections on human life and the ways of the gods. Internal evidence suggests that he was past his prime when he wrote, and that parts, at least, were composed during his lengthy campaigns against the German tribes. The work seems to have survived almost by accident; it was unknown to the writers of his time and for long afterwards, but seems to have surfaced in the 4th century AD. It was written in Greek, the language of philosophy, and its content is largely philosophic in nature, especially reflections on morality and social virtue.

Although divided by modern editors into 12 ''books,'' the work seems not to have a clear structure (except for ''Book I''): rather, it represents the emperor's notes and self-admonitions as recorded in his leisure moments, perhaps before retiring at night. Brief epigrammatic remarks are juxtaposed with quotations (usually of moral tags) and with more developed arguments on, for example, divine providence, the brevity of human life, the necessity for moral effort, and tolerance of his fellow human beings. Frustratingly for the historian, these *pensées* are almost invariably generalized: we do not learn

Marcus Aurelius' secret thoughts about his family, his position, members of the court, or military policy. We do, however, get some idea of his personality and preoccupations, and also of the influence which philosophic doctrine (in his case, the teachings of Stoicism, particularly absorbed through study of the Stoic teacher Epictetus) might have upon an educated and thoughtful Roman statesman.

The first book of the *Meditations* is a different matter, and may have been composed independently. It forms a more coherent whole than the others. Here Marcus Aurelius goes through a list of his closer relatives and several teachers, recording what he owes to each: in some cases a specific lesson, but more often a general moral example. This list culminates in two long passages on what he owes to his predecessor Antoninus Pius, and to the gods. These passages, though often allusive and obscure, give us unique access to the mind of an ancient ruler.

Turning back to the main body of the work, certain recurrent themes stand out: the need to avoid distractions and concentrate on making the correct moral choice; the obligation of individuals to work for the common good (for example, ''What does not benefit the hive does not benefit the bee''); and insistence on the providence of the gods, often combined with vigorous rejection of the alternative view, espoused by the Epicureans, that all is random movement of atoms. Duty and social responsibility are strongly emphasized; and the emperor is also keenly aware of the temptations of power (''it is also possible to live well in a palace''; ''do not be Caesarified''). Thoughts of providence lead him to contemplate the vastness of time and space, and the guiding pattern that according to the Stoics gives order to the universe (''Whatever befalls you was prepared for you beforehand from eternity and the thread of causes was spinning from everlasting both your existence and this which befalls you''). There is also a more melancholy note, of resignation and pessimism, which sometimes seems in conflict with the positive strain of Stoicism. Though determined to persevere in his moral efforts, the author is often resigned to their futility (''Even if you break your heart, none the less they will do just the same''; ''who will change men's convictions?''). Hymns to the grandeur and order of the universe can give way to revulsion and disgust (''As your bath appears to your senses—soap, sweat, dirt, greasy water, all disgusting—so is every piece of life and every object''). Above all, Marcus Aurelius is fascinated by life's transience and the way in which all great men, even philosophers and emperors, pass on and are forgotten. Although it is presumably accidental that this passage ends the *Meditations* as we have them, xii. 36 provides a splendid coda, capturing the near-poetic quality of the emperor's sombre self-reproach:

Mortal man, you have been a citizen in this great city; what does it matter to you whether for five or fifty years? For what is according to its laws is equal for every man. Why is it hard, then, if Nature who brought you in, and no despot nor unjust judge, sends you out of the city—as though the master of the show, who engaged an actor, were to dismiss him from the stage? ''But I have not spoken my five acts, only three.'' ''What you say is true, but in life three acts are the whole play.'' For he determines the perfect whole, the cause yesterday of your composition, today of your dissolution; you are the cause of neither. Leave the stage then, and be content, for he who releases you is content.

—R.B. Rutherford

MEMOIRS (Les Mémoires d'outre-tombe)
Prose by Vicomte de Chateaubriand, 1849 (written 1809–41)

Vicomte de Chateaubriand's original intention, as his title indicates, was that the *Memoirs* would not be published until after his death. He was writing them, as he said, as a man would write sitting on his coffin. This would avoid the scandal which had accompanied the publication between 1765 and 1770 of Rousseau's *The Confessions*, the first great autobiography of French romantic literature and would also, be hoped, give a kind of objectivity to the account of a life which had involved exile, war, literary fame, prison, politics, and, finally, poverty. For it was the need for money that made Chateaubriand sell the rights of certain sections of the *Memoirs* to a financial company composed mainly of supporters of the exiled French king, Charles X. The first extract thus appeared in 1836, 12 years before Chateaubriand died. When the first complete edition did appear, in 1850, it had less success than Chateaubriand had hoped, George Sand commented that a ghost in ten volumes was rather long, and the book had none of the provocative honesty about his own failings which makes Rousseau's *The Confessions* still worth reading. The discovery, in 1930, of a complete manuscript revised in 1847 by Chateaubriand himself provided the basis for a completely new edition in 1948, exactly 100 years after the author's death on 4 July 1848, two months short of his 80th birthday.

Chateaubriand was a Breton aristocrat, the tenth child of Count René-Auguste de Chateaubriand, and his account of his eccentric and terrifying father dominates the opening volumes. The terror inspired by René-Auguste made François-René draw particularly close to his sister, Lucille, four years his elder but presented in the *Memoirs* as having been born in 1766, two years before his own birth on 4 September 1768. This attachment provided the emotional force behind Chateaubriand's first bestseller, the short story *René*, published in 1802. René is the archetypal romantic hero, of the same type as Goethe's Werther, Byron's Manfred, or the doomed heroes of Victor Hugo's later dramas, but one whose misery offers the additional interest of incest. It is his fatal love for his sister, Amélie, which is the root cause of his troubles, in addition to the world-weariness, loneliness, and pre-existential *angst* which made him so popular with the European reading public of the 1800s that Chateaubriand wished he had never created him.

René, like the companion story *Atala*, was taken from the work which Chateaubriand published in its entirety in 1802, *The Genius of Christianity* (*Le Génie du christianisme*). This put forward the argument that Christianity is better than other religions because of its moral superiority over paganism (Christ teaches a higher ethic than Socrates) and because works of art inspired by Christianity are better than those coming down to us from classical antiquity (Gothic cathedrals are better than the Parthenon, Dante a better poet than Homer, Shakespeare a better playwright than Sophocles). As the *Memoirs* insist, there was nothing deliberate about the fact that this attempt to restore to Christianity the artistic and intellectual validity taken from it during the 18th-century enlightenment was published within a year of Napoleon's signature of the *Concordat* with the Catholic church on 16 July 1801. In May 1798, while in exile in England, Chateaubriand had learnt of the death of his mother, had wept, and had believed. The total self-centredness which characterizes the *Memoirs*, Chateaubriand's insistence on having always been right (Louis XVIII agrees with him that the monarchy is finished; there is nothing to be said in favour of the greatest politician of his age, Talleyrand, other than the fact that when he appears in company with the regicide, Fouché, it is "vice leaning on the arm of crime"), his obsessive preoccupation with the double nature of his own personality are, nevertheless, redeemed by the way in which he writes. With him, French prose breathes a more rhythmic, colourful, and exotic air. He was one of the first Europeans to write poetically about North America, when it was still a land of virgin forests. His account of the changes which, in his lifetime, included the fall of the monarchy, the triumph and defeat of Napoleon I, two attempts at monarchical restoration, and the beginnings of the industrial revolution in France, is still worth reading. At one point, in the closing pages, he even anticipated the disappearance of frontiers between the European states. Chateaubriand's influence on the writers of his generation was considerable and he marks the beginning of a new mood in French literature as well as a new set of moral and intellectual attitudes. For the writers of the classical period, form mattered as much as, if not more than, content, and technique more than sincerity. It would never have occurred to Boileau to ask whether Racine or Corneille "really meant" what they wrote. For Chateaubriand, sincerity was everything, and there is no reason to disbelieve the portrait which he gives of himself in the *Memoirs*. He was highly emotional, he did lead a varied life, he did meet the people he claimed to know, he was very fond of his sister, he did believe in Christianity, he was convinced of his own genius. It is, nevertheless, unlikely that as he claimed in *The Natchez*, the epic from which the short stories *René* (1802) and *Atala* (1801) were extracted, he saw crocodiles in the Mississippi.

—Philip Thody

MEMOIRS OF A GOOD-FOR-NOTHING (Aus dem Leben eines Taugenichts)
Novella by Joseph von Eichendorff, 1826 (written 1816–25)

One of the best loved of all German tales, *Memoirs of a Good-for-Nothing* has influenced the popular image of German Romanticism more than any other single work. First published in 1826, it has gone through numerous editions and has been translated into many languages. There are three film versions and a vast number of often contradictory interpretations.

The protracted genesis of the work (1816–1825) and the extant manuscripts indicate that the impression of freshness, immediacy, effortless ease, and artless simplicity conveyed by the finished story is deceptive, achieved only after much painstaking revision and alteration. The most important change between earlier versions and the full published text was the author's decision to transform the hero's beloved, Aurelia, into a penniless unmarried orphan rather than a married countess, thus removing the obstacles to her eventual union with the non-aristocratic hero and permitting a happy ending. Traces of the earlier conception, however, still remain, giving a bittersweet tinge to this seemingly lighthearted tale of the miller's son who sets out into the world with his violin to make his fortune and finds a better prize than he had sought.

The plot is complicated and confusing, reflecting the confusion of life as Eichendorff saw it. In summary, it relates the hero's departure from home at the behest of his father, who calls him a "good-for-nothing," the only name given him in the story; his life as gardener's boy and subsequently toll-keeper at a castle near Vienna, where he is employed after his singing has attracted the attention of a countess; his adoration of Aurelia, whom he takes to be a noblewoman and idealizes in the manner of courtly love; his departure from the castle under the mistaken impression that she is married; his journey to Italy as servant to Count Leonard and Flora, the countess's daughter, who are eloping together; his adventures at Leonard's Italian castle and in Rome after his involuntary parting from his patrons; his return to the Viennese castle, reunion with Aurelia, and the prospect of marriage and life with her on a little estate presented to the couple in recognition of his services to Leonard and Flora, who are now to be married; and, finally, the clarification of all the mysteries and misunderstandings that had beset him. The story ends with his proposal to return to Italy and with the declaration that ''all was right with the world.''

The tale is narrated entirely in the first person, so that the reader is obliged to view all the events and characters through the eyes of the naive hero. From this perspective the natural world appears beautiful and unspoiled, whereas human society seems largely comic or grotesque. The superior point of view of the author, implicitly present throughout, gives rise to humour, irony, satire, and parody, which are used to defuse potentially dangerous situations, including those of erotic temptation, to counteract any tendency towards sentimentality, and to convey, from a Catholic Christian and Romantic viewpoint, criticism of the contemporary age for its philistinism, utilitarianism, acquisitiveness, self-satisfaction, and adherence to the bourgeois work ethic. Though quite different in tone and structure from Bunyan's allegorical novel, Eichendorff's story has justly been called a ''German *Pilgrim's Progress*'' (G.T. Hughes): the hero may be seen as an exemplary human being on life's journey, guided towards his goal by a beneficent Providence in which he places absolute trust. The name ''good-for-nothing'' is, then, ironic: conferred on the hero by a society which lives by false values, it reveals that society's own lack of true worth.

The literary models and the popular and artistic traditions on which Eichendorff drew for his tale are many: the novella, the picaresque novel, the German novel of personal development (Bildungsroman), chapbook, folktale and fairytale, autobiography, and travel literature, as well as baroque drama, the Viennese popular theatre, opera, folk song, and medieval court poetry. These disparate sources and styles of writing are fused in a seamless whole which conveys the impression of oral rather than written narrative and eludes categorization in terms of genre, just as its hero, in spite of his humble origins, eludes social categorization. He moves between social groups, occupations, and even gender categories, and disguise and mistaken identity play a large part in the story as a whole. These are, of course, traditional theatrical devices, but they have a deeper significance, too, since they raise the question of the identity of the self, a problem which Eichendorff also treats in other works.

Time and place in the story are as difficult to pin down as its genre and central character. There are a number of chronological inconsistencies and geographical inaccuracies: for instance, when the hero leaves home it is early spring and the snow is melting, but by noon the same day the sultry air hangs motionless over waving cornfields; similarly, the hero's approach to Rome at the beginning of chapter seven is described in non-realistic terms, while his journey from Italy back to Austria at the end of chapter eight is accomplished in a single leap. Times, places, objects, landscapes, flowers, birds and animals, episodes, and even human figures have a primarily symbolic rather than realistic function, pointing beyond themselves to a higher, spiritual meaning. This is crystallized in the numerous lyrics interpolated in the narrative. Although not always specially written for the

story, they are perfectly placed within it and give a strongly lyrical flavour to the whole. Like the narrative itself, they express the tension between the desire for home and the urge to travel, the longing for security and the fear of stagnation, a fundamental opposition which pervades all Eichendorff's work and can only be resolved through love and through faith in a transcendent sphere in which all the dualities of life are reconciled. *Memoirs of a Good-for-Nothing* offers a poetic image of how such a reconciliation might be achieved. This surely is the reason for its lasting appeal.

—Judith Purver

MEMOIRS OF HADRIAN (Mémoires d'Hadrien)
Novel by Marguerite Yourcenar, 1951

In 1924, a visit to the Villa Adriana was, for Marguerite Yourcenar, the beginning of a spiritual adventure, which 27 years later became *Memoirs of Hadrian*. She wrote some fragments of the work between 1924 and 1929. In December 1948, she received a trunk of personal papers from Lausanne. Among some letters dating from ten years before, there were a few old and yellowing typed pages addressed to ''My dear Marc. . . .'' From that moment on, until May 1951, she devoted herself entirely to the book. One year after publication, the critics applauded her achievement. In 1952, the book obtained the Académie française award, followed in 1955 by the Newspaper Guild of New York's Page One award.

Hours spent at the Yale and Harvard libraries provided Yourcenar with an impressive amount of historical documentation. Henriette Levillain in *Mémoires d'Hadrien of Marguerite Yourcenar* identifies the sources that provided direct and indirect inspiration for the book. One of the first is *The History of Rome* written by Dion Cassius at the end of the 5th century. This work is composed of 80 Greek books partially preserved thanks to a Byzantine monk's manuscript of the 10th century. A second source is *The Augustan History*, by an anonymous author of the fourth century, who assembled 39 emperors' biographies, including *Memoirs* published by Hadrian himself under his secretary's name, Phlegon. The indirect sources for the historical style are, among others, Tacitus' *Annals*, Suetonius' *Lives of the Twelve Caesars*, and Flaubert's *Salammbô*. Besides historical documentation, Yourcenar has provided ''eflections on the Composition. . . ,'' notebooks showing stages in the creative process. There are sections, seldom dated, relating to past or present stages in the novel's composition, which can be divided into three categories: historical data, comments on these data, and poetic thoughts; all this representing the book's contents before its finalization and publication.

Determining the book's genre is a problem. On the one hand, the title ''Memoirs'' indicates absence of fiction. This argument is reinforced by the presence of an historical character, Hadrian, narrating his experiences. The work goes beyond autobiography in that the character's vision includes social and political aspects of the epoch. On the other hand, this work is classified, in the Pléiade edition of the author's works, among *Oeuvres romanesques* (i.e. novels) and thus considered there as fiction. It is true that the narrator does not correspond exactly to the historical character, whereas in memoirs these two notions are generally identical. We can also observe that historicity is not, as it is in memoirs, a target in itself, but a means of self-knowledge before death. To simplify this problem, critics often speak of an ''historical novel.'' Recalling the author's definition of this genre—'a kind of costume ball in Technicolor'—Paul Horn questions this classification of the *Memoirs* because of the scarcity in it of historical customs and local detail. Let us bear in mind, though, that this text relates past events, while keeping the aspect of a fiction.

From a structural point of view, the book is composed of six chapters written in a style close to oratorical rhetoric. The exordium—*Animula, vagula blandula* [small, wandering, caressing soul]—brings the narrator and the discourse's subject upon the scene: Hadrian relates his life in the first person. The epilogue (*Patientia*) prepares the narrator for death and the reader for the outcome. The four central chapters narrate Hadrian's life in a more or less chronological order and received their respective titles from the currencies of the epoch: *Varius multiplex multiformis* [Varied, Multiple, Changing], *Tellus stabilita* [The Earth Recovers its Balance], *Saeculum aureum* [Golden Century], *Disciplina Augusta* [Augustan Discipline].

The story's starting point is a sentence from Flaubert's correspondence: "Just when the Gods had ceased to be, and Christ had not yet come, there was a unique moment in history between Cicero and Marcus Aurelius, when man stood alone." This announces a mainly humanistic, objective, and transparent message. In the first chapter, Hadrian, approaching death, decides to relate public and personal events of the past 60 years: he is meditating upon the world, art, and politics and preparing himself to die; his spirit is ready to leave his body and his soul begins to notice the aspect of his death. Yourcenar adds in her notebooks:

> Comme un peintre établi devant un horizon, et qui sans cesse déplace son chevalet à droite, puis à gauche, j'avais enfin trouvé le point de vue du livre.

> (Like a painter sitting in front of the horizon, continually moving his easel to the right, then to the left, I had finally found the book's point of view.)

The second chapter starts with Hadrian's childhood in Spain and his departure to Rome, where he discovers a way of thought and perfection by learning the Greek language. Following varied, multiple, and changing roads, he makes his career in a legal and military environment. Embracing each opportunity as an excuse for learning, he wins Trajan's esteem and becomes his successor. It is suggested that the transfer of power is owed mainly to Trajan's wife Plotina.

The empire recovers its balance in the third chapter through numerous commercial treaties and non-aggression pacts: Hadrian keeps order by compromising. Once the political situation has become stable—chapter four—he gets involved for several years in an idyllic relationship with Antonius, a young Greek-Asian boy, who considers Hadrian as a master and a god. Moved by a strange feeling of sacrifice, Antonius wishes to add the rest of his life to the emperor's by committing suicide. After Antonius' death, Hadrian dedicates a solemn cult to him by raising towns, temples, and many statues. Having turned his back on easy pleasure, he makes time from now on to think and to read. He immortalizes himself by the construction of the Mausoleum and a villa at Tibur, as well as by the choice of his successor: Lucius Ceionius, an old lover, who happens to die before Hadrian, who then in the last resort chooses Antonius, an excellent administrator and senator. Antonius is ordered to adopt Marcus Aurelius. The epilogue shows Hadrian renouncing suicide, considering it as an evidence of ingratitude and insipidity towards his friends: "Let us try . . . to enter death with open eyes. . . ."

—Sabine Madeleine Hillen

METAMORPHOSES
Poem by Ovid, early 1st century AD

Ovid's purpose in *Metamorphoses* is, he tells us in its first line, "to tell of bodies which have been transformed into shapes of different kinds." Ovid has another purpose too: to tell a history in stories. Thus the poem's descriptions of humans who are turned into different forms (birds, beasts, trees, stars, and gods) has a loose but continuous chronological structure. This begins with the creation of the world and proceeds through Greek myths and the Trojan War to the founding of Rome, the eventual divinization of Julius Caesar, and to a eulogy of Augustus, Ovid's emperor.

In narrative terms the work has another structure, one sufficiently flexible to handle the enormous size (the poem is literally of epic proportions) and multifarious nature of its material. To maintain his readers' interest, Ovid succeeds in guiding them through this narrative labyrinth by spinning a single, almost unbroken, yarn to follow: a line of stories that passes continuously from speaker to speaker. As this thread continues, our interest is constantly refreshed by the introduction of new tellers who invest their stories with their own distinctive styles. The thread is passed on by devices ranging from storytelling competitions to characters within stories telling further stories, often in an attempt to convince their hearers of some moral precept.

Despite their common thematic link, the stories differ greatly in tone. Some, like that of the blackening of the raven's plumage, read like moral fables, while others, such as that of Mercury stealing Apollo's cattle, resemble folk tales of trickery and deception. Some (for example, the tale of the plague of Aeacus' kingdom) are exploited for their spectacular or horrifying effects, while others, such as that of Ceyx and Alcyone, are developed into poignant love stories. Technically, the poem is distinguished by its vivid pictorial quality and gripping images, as in the description of Pyramus' wound:

> his blood spouted forth, just as when a waterpipe bursts, if there is some flaw in the lead, and through the narrow hissing crack a long stream of water shoots out and beats the air.

> (translated by Mary Innes)

Battle scenes in *Metamorphoses* are rare but treated with a similar visceral directness. In the great set-piece battle between the Centaurs and the Lapiths, no detail of dismemberment or disembowelling is spared. Elsewhere Ovid's poetic skills tempt him into virtuoso displays which verge on poetic conceit, such as the extraordinary catalogue of the pedigree and character of the hounds in Actaeon's pack, while they are hunting him to his death.

Through the ever-changing kaleidoscope of tales and voices, distinct themes emerge. The motif of the future foretold and then fulfilled recurs again and again, most dramatically in the case of Ocyrhoe, overtaken in the very act of prophesying by her metamorphosis into a horse. The idea of fate as an immutable force runs throughout. This fate is not an external law, achieving its ends by a conspiracy of circumstances, but an internal law, derived from the character's own inner compulsions. As with Pentheus' hubris, which leads him to ignore warnings and earn Bacchus' punishment, fate works through our own natures. For good or for ill, our own desires compel us to our destinies. Only once is an oracle attended to and a fate circumvented. This is the politically intriguing tale of Cipus, who is saved from himself by accepting exclusion from Rome, thus forestalling his potential as a tyrant. Elsewhere passion, the driving force of fate, brings ruinous consequences. Many of the metamorphoses of mortal women are the consequence of arousing a god's passion, while men and women who are gripped by unlawful passion are transformed in punishment or compensation as, for example, in the story of Procne, Tereus, and Philomela.

Ovid's pursuit of this theme takes him into darker and darker regions of the psyche. Two of his stories deal with women caught in incestuous love. Myrrha, who sleeps with her father, is portrayed in the language of horror and disgust. Byblis, who falls in love with her brother, receives more complex treatment. Her soliloquies communicate her anguish by the use of the language of lovers which in other contexts we are accustomed to respect. Applied to a forbidden object, her speeches force us to acknowledge the depth of her turmoil, and again present passion as a force beyond human control, to be suffered by those it smites.

Metamorphoses deals constantly with the gods: almost every transformation is at the will of a god. Its stories are, however, inspired by a spirit of entertainment rather than one of devotion. Only once does Ovid evoke a sense of awe or reverence for a divinity, in the prolonged description of Medea's rites before Hecate, Goddess of Witchcraft, where the atmosphere is heightened by fear and fascination with the occult. It is significant that this is the only occasion where a mortal, rather than a god, works a transformation.

Religious writing of a different order appears in the final book. Here narrative is at last suspended for a moment as Pythagoras speaks, teaching a mystic philosophy illustrated by a string of actual or fabulous instances of metamorphosis in nature. His miraculous biology includes such examples as the bear licking her formless cub into a bear's shape, and frogs generated out of mud. Metamorphosis, he teaches, is at the heart of the activity of the universe, a Heraclitan stream running through all the varied forms of life. Out of this all-embracing understanding comes serenity, for ''to die'' simply means to change into a new form. Pythagoras' philosophy, coming at the end of *Metamorphoses*, serves as a possible bridge between the phantasmagoria of the tales and the real world to which the reader must return.

Ovid closes the *Metamorphoses* with the proud claim that the work itself will be immortal. Ovid's reputation and the *Metamorphoses* have survived not only because our appetite for the fantastic is unabated, but because of the power of the myths he relates to transform our own world. The swan is indeed changed if we see it, if only for a moment, as Cygnus, cleaving to water and flying low in the sky, forever wary of the sun.

—Edmund Cusick

THE METAMORPHOSIS (Die Verwandlung)
Novella by Franz Kafka, 1915

The Metamorphosis, which tells of how a young man, Gregor Samsa, wakes to find himself transformed into a horrid beetle-like creature, is quintessential Franz Kafka and deservedly the most famous of his works. Written during Kafka's first period of intense creative activity in late 1912, it was one of the few pieces published during his lifetime.

The basis of the short story can be found in the author's tense relations with his father, his sense of isolation, failure and guilt, but also of unjust rejection. The role of Gregor's sister Grete, too, can be related to Kafka's feeling of betrayal by his sister Ottla, the one member of his family in whom he believed he had an ally. Despairing of his ability to write, he noted that he was good only to be swept up with the household rubbish, and that is the fate of his hero. Kafka senior had called his son's friend, a Yiddish actor, a flea-ridden dog and a vermin. It was a condemnation which the writer believed extended to himself. In the story the disgusting verminous creature of the metaphor becomes flesh. Kafka explores the narrative possibilities that emerge from taking a metaphor literally, and discovers a series of haunting images for his potentially suicidal inner condition. The hero's physical state, the details of his environment and his movements all assume symbolic significance. Because the grotesque fantasy set against a realistic background is like a bad dream, it seems to call for psychoanalytic interpretation and there have been no lack of Freudian commentaries on it, in which an Oedipus complex inevitably provides the focus.

The story concentrates on dramatic confrontations and says as much about family tensions as it does about the psychology of the hero or the author. Understanding between Gregor and his parents and sister, impossible after his physical transformation, was far from perfect before. However, neither that nor any other circumstance is advanced to explain his metamorphosis. Kafka describes its consequences. The family's first reaction of shock and horror becomes one of resigned frustration and finally of relief when Gregor dies. Unable any longer to rely on Gregor as sole breadwinner, his parents find a new sense of strength and purpose within themselves. That development, like Gregor's increasing hopelessness, appears absolutely logical and even inevitable. So, too, does the sister's growth in confidence and responsibility—another metamorphosis, one might say. The brief last scene of spring sunshine, family unity, and hope for the future after Gregor's death contrasts tellingly with the blackness of the preceding episodes. Grete, it is revealed, has ripened as Gregor has wasted away. Life, it seems, triumphs over a useless freak, but *The Metamorphosis* brings no Nietzschean glorification of vital strength. For here the life force is linked with social conformity and insensitivity. Gregor's demise is scarcely a victory for human values. The contrast between the outwardly animal hero and those around him brings some cruel ironies. The existence from which he is excluded hardly seems a desirable one. The three lodgers who, for a time, dominate the Samsa household reveal that conformity can mean loss of individuality. They insist too much on bourgeois values and show no appreciation of Grete's violin playing, which Gregor imagines might furnish the nourishment he cannot otherwise find. Despite strong hints that his attachment to his sister is potentially incestuous, his reaction to the music may be read as a longing for spiritual satisfaction, even redemption, which is absent in the materialist society of which the Samsas are part. His duty to his family has apparently been defined almost exclusively in economic terms. It is possible to account for his alienation as a product of capitalist labour relations which, as Marx argued, dehumanize the worker. Gregor certainly felt that his work as a travelling salesman was a denial of his freedom and dignity.

Yet the story establishes no cause for the hero's condition, nor does it allow a conclusive allocation of blame. It shows that love can scarcely be divorced from possessiveness, or responsibility from tyranny, but that a life without them is a form of living death. The demands of family, society, even of time (Gregor becomes oblivious to the clock and the calendar that once dominated his every moment) seem intolerable and yet to require recognition if the self-esteem of the individual is to be maintained.

The Metamorphosis is told largely from the hero's point of view. It offers no explanations. The dividing line between the third-person narrative and *style indirect libre* is very fluid and the narrator never reveals his identity or standpoint. The result is a remarkably open text which has elicited an immense number of different interpretations. It has been seen as a sadly sick, but more often as an acute, vision of reality. Yet critics have not even agreed whether the story's elusive meaning is essentially psychological, sociological, existential, or religious, and some have argued that it deals with the gulf between art and life or the relation of language to reality. For the text seems to imply much more than it states, to challenge its readers to explore the possible significance of its every detail, to escape from the hero's perspective in order to appreciate its black humour, and to discover its universal relevance.

It would be wrong, however, to place sole stress on the intellectual challenge of a story whose impact is dramatic and overwhelmingly emotional. Its three carefully paced sections each culminate as Gregor tries to make contact with his family and is met with determined rejection. The repetition lends weight to the impression of tragic inevitability. Its exceptional power to haunt the imagination, together with its undermining of certainties, has earned *The Metamorphosis* its place of prominence in the history of 20th-century world literature.

—John Hibberd

MÍA
Poem by Rubén Darío, 1896

Prosas profanas, Rubén Darío's collection of poems published in Buenos Aires in 1896, sought even in its title to be outrageous. The hint at blasphemy—"prosas" refers to a sequence in the Catholic mass—is developed in several poems, especially the erotic "Ite Missa Est." In fact, one element Darío had made his own stemmed from his Nicaraguan tropical exuberance, appearing in erotic poems that enshrined lust as the optimum state of the mind. This collection opens with what could be called Darío's manifesto, where he outlines his view of art, which for him was synonymous with freedom. One of his cultural heroes was the composer Wagner, and quoting from him Darío justifies his idiosyncrasies. Darío is not writing for a public but to awaken in a reader, in himself, his "reino interior" (inner world).

The poem that summarizes many of Darío's achievements, and his thinking about eroticism and passing time, is a sonnet "de arte menor," written in imitation of a Wagnerian *Lied*, and called "Mía" (both a woman's name, and the possessive pronoun "mine," differentiated in the poem by the use of capitals, as first pointed out by the poet critic Pedro Salinas). This name "Mía" and the allusion to Wagner underline Darío's fascination with the enchantment of music. The French symbolist poet Paul Verlaine's battle cry, "De la musique avant toute chose," is exaggerated by Darío so that from the opening poem of the collection "Era un aire suave" [It Was a Soft Musical Air] you have music both as sound predominating over sense, through alliteration and rhyme, and music as the ideal art form, hinting at a sensuous and mysterious world beyond verbal description, beyond referentiality, that could only be suggested through symbols.

"Mía" opens with a stanza whose rich sounds play with double meanings to suggest the plenitude of the senses of a male lover: "Mía: Así te llamas. / ¿Qué más armoní / Mía: luz de día; / mía: rosas, llamas" [O my Mía: so that's your name / what greater harmony / my Mía: Daylight / my Mía: roses, flame]. In what is almost poetic annotation, a rhythm of desire is built up by the short phrases broken by colons and semi-colons. Mía promises the poet the harmony (*mia* emerges from the word har*monía*) that he has always sought outside the harsh world of survival that Darío actually inhabited as a poet, bohemian, and freelance journalist. He defined art as the freedom to escape empirical reality and mundanity into fantasy, Darío transformed fantasy (normally seen as an inability to be) into the ultimate reality. For a moment his inner mental world becomes more real, with its roses (perhaps lips) and flames (passion of love).

The second stanza suggests how sensuality seeps into his soul, something quite pagan and alien to the Church's condemnation of pleasure. According to the critic Guillermo Sucre, Darío exalted pleasure. Octavio Paz has inserted Darío's view of love into a Western heretical tradition of love as access to a higher truth. Darío's poems parade centaurs, satyrs, Greek gods and goddesses promising a guiltless sexuality. Mía's "aroma" spills into the poet's soul. The second stanza ends with an orgasmic cry of ecstasy: "¡Oh Mía! ¡Oh Mía!"

Had the poem ended here, it would have been a condensed little song to possessive love. But the third stanza changes the tone. It is one sentence, and it brings the poet back down to earth: "Tu sexo fundiste / con mi sexo fuerte, / fundiendo dos bronces" [You melted your sex / with my strong sex / like melting two bronzes].

No doubt the reduction of the male and female lovers to their "sexo" scandalized the idealizing public of the 1890s, but Darío had hoped for more than sensual pleasure from ephemeral physical union. He wanted to remain in that moment of ecstasy for ever, as if that moment could be converted into a bronze statue, a work of art. Within the very poem Darío senses the negation of *eros* which is *thanatos*, death in the form of passing time, of running out of energy. Only a work of art can fix ecstasy, like Rodin's sculpture *The Kiss*. So Darío ends the poem with a note of melancholia, repeating Ovid's famous phrase about post-coital sadness: "Yo triste, tú triste . . . / ¿No has de ser entonces / mía hasta la muerte?" [I am sad, you're sad / Can't you stay mine / until the end of time?]. And the obvious answer to the poem's final question is no, she will not be his unto death. This parody of the marriage vows ("until death do us part") becomes the condemnation of the lovers. Darío's latent melancholia surfaces here in this poem, to become an emotive vein in his next collection *Cantos de vida y esperanza*, 1905, where Darío is forced to face a world that does not allow the poet to escape, for a world without fantasies for Darío is spiritual death. Darío associates woman and death: "La hembra humana es hermana del Dolor y de la Muerte" (The human female is sister to Pain and Death) he has Hipea say in his long discursive poem "El coloquio de los centauros" [Colloquy of the Centaurs]. What one can add concerning this sonnet "Mía" is that Darío's confusion of sexual possession, pleasure, and death makes the poem more than a pleasurable ditty, for it opens out into a 20th-century dilemma where lust and eroticism cannot replace God, and a poem cannot save you from extinction. It is a very human position, and one that Darío sought to avoid in many poems of *Prosas profanas*.

—Jason Wilson

MICHAEL KOHLHAAS
Story by Heinrich von Kleist, 1810

Michael Kohlhaas, Heinrich von Kleist's longest prose work, is loosely based on the historical Hans Kohlhase, who took up arms against authority, principally Saxony, in order to obtain justice. He was captured and executed in Berlin in 1540.

A fragment of Kleist's story appeared in Dresden in the periodical *Phöbus* in 1808 but broke off where Kohlhaas sets out to attack the nobleman Wenzel's castle. The complete story was published in Berlin in 1810. The inclusion of historical personages and geographical locations in the 1810 version makes the work more politically overt. The focus shifts gradually away from the perversion of justice, committed by a fictional nobility, to the Elector of Saxony. He has been party to the initial denial of justice and agrees to tricking Kohlhaas into writing an incriminating letter. The last section of the work is devoted to Kohlhaas's revenge on the Elector.

Wenzel's illegal retention of Kohlhaas's horses, the brutal treatment of Kohlhaas's servant, and the exploitation of family connections to prevent Kohlhaas from obtaining legal redress could be interpreted as social and political commentary, as could Kohlhaas's meeting with Martin Luther. Although he intercedes on Kohlhaas's behalf, Wenzel's utterances betray that he is also concerned that respect for authority, epitomized in the hereditary ruler, should not be undermined. Kohlhaas's untrained followers' humiliation of the various military forces dispatched to deal with him is perhaps an allusion to the unexpected defeats suffered by the German rulers in Kleist's own lifetime at the hands of the French Revolutionary army.

Such interpretations do not detract from the universality of the work. The narrator refers to Kohlhaas's anguish "at seeing the world in such monstrous disorder" after his case has been so disgracefully dismissed. The disorder Kleist portrays is existential as well as political, and chance is given a crucial role in all that happens. Kohlhaas's manner at the start of the story, when he haggles over the value of his horses, unintentionally plays a part in provoking Wenzel's illegal retention of the horses, done in a fit of anger rather than as a calculated abuse of power. Admittedly, Wenzel exploits his position in order to avoid paying compensation for the injustice suffered, but there is no evidence that he ordered the mistreatment of the horses and Kohlhaas's servant. The death of Kohlhaas's wife clearly precipitates the attack on Wenzel's castle, although the death, part of a chain of events set in motion by Wenzel, is an unfortunate accident not involving the nobleman. The reader is made to share Kohlhaas's sense of outrage and anguish at injustice, but against this must be set the role played by chance. The speed and complexity of events are also part of Kleist's strategy to show how ambiguous and confusing the situation is.

Kohlhaas's pursuit of legal redress takes a frightening course. The innocent as well as the guilty are murdered in his attack on Wenzel's castle. He threatens to burn Wittenberg to the ground unless Wenzel is delivered up and declares himself to be "St. Michael's deputy, sent to punish the evil into which the whole world had sunk." Commenting on all this, the narrator refers to Kohlhaas as "a monstrous villain." In so doing he is understandably being overwhelmed by the events of the moment, to the exclusion of all else. As with the other characters, circumstances, chance events, and the sheer complexity of Kohlhaas's situation cloud and confuse his judgement.

This theme of an unpredictable, chance-driven existence is continued when Kohlhaas is given safe conduct to come to Dresden to have his case reviewed. The reader is subtly made aware of a power struggle in the Saxon capital. Opponents of Wenzel's relatives treat the case as an opportunity to humiliate them and circumstances now seem to favour Kohlhaas. However, the arrival of the horses in Dresden (and the reader is left in some doubt as to whether they are the ones that Wenzel retained) sparks off a civil riot. This takes place in Kohlhaas's absence but the episode turns public opinion against him. Kohlhaas is so reduced to despair by this that he tries to resume contact with a former henchman, thereby condemning himself. All this reinforces Kleist's disturbing vision of a world in which circumstances, questionable motives, and chance events combine, with disastrous consequences for the individual.

Kleist's lengthening of the story to cover Kohlhaas's transportation to Berlin after he has been condemned to death, during which the Elector of Saxony makes desperate attempts to obtain from Kohlhaas the gypsy woman's prophecy concerning the fate of his dynasty, has been criticized as artificial, an unwarranted introduction of the supernatural, and detracting seriously from the unity of the work. It has to be conceded that this section was probably an afterthought on Kleist's part and the events involving the gypsy woman do strain the reader's credulity.

However, the sequence of events parallels other sections of the story and the work retains its thematic coherence. A power struggle, in which Saxony has to placate Brandenburg and which is irrelevant to Kohlhaas's case, results in the Elector having to back down and agree to deliver Kohlhaas to Berlin. Although all parties involved claim they are acting in the interests of justice, the reader is once more made aware of the destructive interplay of ambiguity of motive, the complexity of events, and sheer chance. The Elector is also the victim of this interplay, for it enables Kohlhaas to take the prophecy to his grave and so exact revenge.

The story ends with Wenzel's punishment, the restoration of the horses to their previous condition, and Kohlhaas's execution for the death and destruction he has caused. This could be interpreted as a resolution of the conflict in keeping with the ideals of classical literature. However, the concatenation of events that has led to this situation suggests the possibility that Kleist intended this ending to be ironic.

—D.J. Andrews

MILITARY SERVITUDE AND GRANDEUR (Servitude et grandeur militaires)
Stories by Alfred de Vigny, 1835 (written 1822)

Servitude et grandeur militaires (sometimes rather freely translated as *The Military Condition*) is not a novel in the conventional sense of being a single sustained fictional narrative. The three stories which it comprises were published separately in the *Revue de Paris* in the early 1830s, and it was only subsequently, in 1835, that Alfred de Vigny combined them in a unified collection linked by serious discussions of the issues involved. In its final form, the book stands as a notable endeavour by a young man of noble origins to come to terms with the problems confronting him in a very troubled period of French history and, more generally, to make sense of the role of the army within a civilized society in the modern world.

Born into an aristocratic family with strong military traditions in 1797, some eight years after the storming of the Bastille had marked the beginning of the French Revolution, Vigny witnessed the meteoric rise and disastrous fall of Napoleon, then hurried to take up a lieutenant's commission in the prestigious *Gendarmes du Roi* as soon as Louis XVIII was restored to his throne by the victorious allies in 1814. Less than a year later when Napoleon returned from Elba the French king retreated ignominiously to Ghent. Waterloo ended the Hundred Days decisively, but the omens for the French legitimate monarchy were not promising. Vigny, a sensitive, thoughtful young man who found a soldier's life tedious and was not fortunate in his marriage to an English girl either, found it hard to reconcile the forces that pulled him this way and that in a troubled period. In the 1820s Vigny wrote historical drama and fiction, as well as some poetry, but it was, significantly, after yet another violent flight of Charles X, Louis XVIII's very conservative brother and successor, and his replacement by his cousin, the so-called ''bourgeois'' monarch, Louis-Philippe, that he set to work on the stories that were later to constitute *Military Servitude and Grandeur.*

All three tales read as authentic first-person reports, but research has established that though they are based, in varying degrees, on historical fact, the material was substantially remodelled for artistic purposes. The first tale, ''Laurette; or, The Red Seal,'' starts with a young officer, whom we readily identify with the author, meeting an old soldier during Louis XVIII's retreat into Flanders, and then flashes back to the period of the Directory to relate how a sea captain is ordered to sail his brig out to Cayenne with a political prisoner on board. When the time comes to open his sealed instructions he realizes that despite the affection he feels for the young man and his pretty wife, who insisted on coming too, he has no choice but to obey. He promptly orders the execution of his prisoner in mid-ocean, but when Laurette's mind gives way he takes responsibility for her for the rest of her life. ''A Night at Vincennes'' has a more confused story line than ''Laurette'' and lacks its effectively simple use of symbolism. Set in the great fortress of Vincennes just outside Paris in 1819, and with some account of military life under the *ancien régime* whose relevance has been questioned by many critics, it dwells on the sterling qualities of an NCO. The focus changes, to centre rather on the experiences of a junior officer from the time of Napoleon's invasion of Egypt right through to the July Revolution, in ''The Life and Death of Captain Renaud; or, The Malacca Cane,'' the secondary title coming from the fact that after the killing of a young Russian boy in an attack which the hero commanded he resolved never to carry a weapon again.

The question of obedience to orders, something that became especially problematic when there were changes of regime such as those that France encountered between 1789 and 1830, is one of the major themes of *Military Servitude and Grandeur*, but this is subsumed in an even larger meditation on the nature of military service in modern times. A fine tableau in ''Captain Renaud'' depicting the Knights of Malta's surrender of their stronghold to the fleet carrying Napoleon's invading army to Egypt is emblematic of the eclipse of religious values, and Vigny considers the possibility of a code of honour serving as a substitute for them. At the same time, appreciating that since the time of Frederick the Great armies had become professionalized and lost their intimate connections with society in general, Vigny sees soldiers as modern pariahs, disconsolate outcasts from society for whom he, as a Romantic, feels the greatest sympathy. While making these points, he also feels the need to enter a solemn warning against the propensity the French have of losing all common sense when they idealize military heroes. This unfortunate tendency Vigny calls ''séïdisme,'' basing the word on the name of the Prophet's

fanatical disciple in Voltaire's play *Mahomet* (*Mohamet*). He shows how insidious it can be in scenes contrasting brilliantly the steady virtue of the British Admiral Collingwood with the duplicitousness and temperamental instability of Napoleon. Yet even at the end, Vigny cannot withhold some admiration for the enigmatic, charismatic Emperor, and that final touch reveals much about the conflict of loyalties that is fundamental to this unusual and thought-provoking work.

—Christopher Smith

MINNA VON BARNHELM
Poem by Gotthold Ephraim Lessing, 1767

Minna van Barnhelm was conceived in 1763 in the aftermath of the Seven Years War in which Saxony and Prussia were enemies and was completed in 1767, the year in which Gotthold Ephraim Lessing assumed his post as resident playwright and critic to the new National Theatre in Hamburg. In the play Lessing, a Saxon working as secretary to a Prussian general, makes an impassioned plea for tolerance and reconciliation, both themes central to his writing as a whole. In his theoretical writings on the theatre Lessing calls for a national repertoire for the German theatre.

In *Minna von Barnhelm* Lessing offers a model of a truly German comedy, as much of the humour and interest in the play arises from the interaction between the vivacious and witty Saxon Minna and her fiancé the unbending, high-principled Prussian Tellheim. Minna, a Saxon, has come to Berlin in search of Tellheim, a Major, newly discharged from the Prussian army. The act of generosity performed by Tellheim, in advancing money from his own funds to cover taxes he was supposed to collect in Saxony, which won Minna's love for him, has been misinterpreted by the Prussian authorities as dishonourable and dishonest. Tellheim is now without funds and awaiting the outcome of an investigation into the matter. Feeling himself both crippled physically (he has been wounded in the arm) and emotionally by this slight to his honour, Tellheim rejects Minna. He now feels unworthy of her and that he cannot depend on her for his happiness. Minna contrives to convince Tellheim that she herself is penniless and has been threatened by her uncle, and by this ruse tricks him into declaring his love for her again. However, this is not enough for her. She feels that she must punish Tellheim further. This punishment, inflicted after Tellheim receives notification from the King that his fortune and honour are both restored, goes almost too far. The situation is redeemed by the arrival of Minna's uncle, who approves the union, bringing the play to a happy conclusion.

In form the play is conventional. It is written in five acts, the scenes changing with characters' entrances. The main characters come from the minor nobility and their courting is mirrored in the developing relationship between Minna's pert maid Franziska and Tellheim's stolid Sergeant-Major Paul Werner. The play also follows convention in its observance of the classical unities of time, place, and action. Later Lessing would attack the French theatre of the day for its slavish adherence to the letter rather than to the spirit of the unities, suggesting that the German theatre would be better advised to imitate the freer construction of Shakespeare's plays than those of the French.

The true originality of the play lies in the freshness and contemporaneity of the characters and their concerns. The structure of the play might be reminiscent of classical comedy, but there is a striking quality of realism in the characterization and settings, as well as Lessing's rejection of verse and his choice of a supple prose for the dialogue, accurately matched to the standing of characters. Tellheim finds himself in the limbo of the discharged officer, a situation which must have been familiar to many in the original audience, as were frequent references to both good and bad features of the recent conflict. In the character of Riccaut de la Marlinière Lessing ridicules the fashion, prevalent in Germany at the time and at the court of Frederick the Great, of regarding the German language as incapable of expressing the subtleties necessary for cultured conversation and, by implication, literature. By refusing to speak in French with Riccaut, Minna (and Lessing) decisively takes sides in the argument current at the time. This, and the direct reference to the King himself in the play, led the Prussian authorities to discourage the production of *Minna von Barnhelm*, which was premiered in Hamburg, a free city beyond Prussian jurisdiction, in 1767.

The play's abiding appeal for audiences derives chiefly from the charm of the central character, Minna, herself. She might with justification be seen as the first emancipated woman in German comedy. Not deterred from setting out in search of her fiancé, nor afraid to go on ahead of her uncle when his carriage breaks down, she is well able to defend herself against the prying questions of the landlord and to win the hearts of the audience in her exchanges on love and romance with Franziska. Above all, she is a heroine of the German bourgeoisie, embodying the virtues and standards espoused by the new theatre audience who recognized in her self-confidence their own growing self-esteem. Despite this, however, the play owes a considerable debt to the *sächsische Typenkomödie* (the Saxon comedy of types). In this genre of comedy attempts are made to show a flawed character the unreasonableness of his behaviour, and, when reason fails, the other characters resort to intrigue. Thus it is that Minna, unable to persuade Tellheim to owe his happiness to her (his fault being his inability, as a generous man, to receive generosity), has recourse to trickery.

Here Lessing adds a new dimension to comic form and an increased depth to the play, for Tellheim is a more complex and sympathetic character than the traditional butt of this type of comedy. We are shown his positive qualities in his interaction with the widow of his captain-of-horse, and with Werner. We admire his honesty and sympathize with him when, after notification from the King of the restoration of his fortune and honour, Minna persists in deceiving him in order to teach him a lesson. Minna sees that she has taken the game too far. Tellheim is thrown into serious confusion by Minna's dishonesty towards him and only the arrival of Minna's uncle saves the play from an unhappy ending, Minna having lost control of the situation.

In the event *Minna von Barnhelm* was not taken as a model by the new movement of the *Storm und Drang*, the German romanticism of the late 18th century, whose inspiration lacked the balance necessary for the writing of comedy. However, the play has retained its place in the repertoire of the German theatre and is regularly performed throughout the German-speaking world.

—A.J. Meech

THE MINOR (Nedorosl')
Play by Denis Fonvizin, 1782

The Russian 18th-century neo-classical comedy of manners is largely a very paltry affair. Re-workings, copies, and adaptations of not even the best models abound and most of them have little even historical interest today. A few worthy exceptions do exist, for example Iakov Kniazhnin's *The Braggart*, Vasily Kapnist's *Iabeda (Chicanery)*, and most notably Denis Fonvizin's *The Minor*, which is still performed occasionally in Russia. Started in the late 1770s, *The Minor* was completed in 1781. Fonvizin gave a few readings of the play before it was first performed in Knipper's private theatre in St. Petersburg on 24 September 1782. It was published the following year. In its day it was seen as a highly topical play concerned with the dire results of ignorance, abuse of power, and man's (and woman's) inhumanity to their fellows. Catherine the Great's favourite, Prince Gregory Potemkin, is reported to have said to Fonvizin "Denis, you might as well die for you'll never write anything better." This was once somewhat more threateningly mistranslated as "If you write anything like that again, you'd better die."

Despite many attempts, especially by Russian critics, to suggest that *The Minor* is an early precursor of realism on the stage (despite the fact that it was written several years before the term was coined), this is at best wishful thinking or not very sensible special pleading. There can be no argument that it remains a thoroughly traditional neo-classical comedy, albeit influenced less by the example of Molière than by Holberg, whose plays, along with those by Goldoni, were extremely popular in Russia in the later 18th century. The three unities are adhered to strictly in its five acts, the action lasts scarcely more than 24 hours and occurs in one room, violence takes place off-stage, the characters have symbolic names and represent specific human vices and virtues, there is a pair of traditional young lovers, and good conquers evil in the happy ending. Within this restricting framework Fonvizin has written a well-constructed and, in parts, amusing play. The conflict between the old-fashioned, uneducated, and rough-hewn provincial gentry and the civilized, cultured, and wealthy representatives of the Enlightenment is reasonably well-balanced. Although it is clear that the positive characters have justice on their side and ultimately triumph, their speeches tend to the moralizing, didactic, and tedious, while the negative characters are far more interesting linguistically and dramatically and all the real comedy in the play stems from their words and actions.

The action takes place on the country estate of the meek and henpecked Prostakov (Mr. Simpleton). Everyone there is tyrannized by his ignorant, cruel, and domineering wife. Their 16-year-old son Mitrofan, the minor of the title, is a lazy, remarkably unintelligent, and spoiled adolescent who is adored by his mother. His only ambition is expressed in the now proverbial words: "I don't want to study, I want to get married." Staying on the estate is a nobleman, Pravdin (Mr. Truthful), who unbeknown to the Prostakovs has been sent by the government to verify reports that Mrs. Prostakov has been maltreating her serfs, which indeed she has. She hopes to marry off her ward, the young orphan Sof'ia, whose estate she has taken over illegally, to her brother Skotinin (Mr. Brute), who prefers the company of pigs to human beings. Sof'ia hears that her rich uncle Starodum (Mr. Oldwise) is returning after making his fortune, and Mrs. Prostakov thinks, for utterly selfish reasons, that Sof'ia should now marry her son. Sof'ia, though, is in love with Milon (Lt. Dear) a young army officer who soon arrives on the scene, closely followed by Starodum, who rejects as suitors both Skotinin and Mitrofan. Mrs. Prostakov attempts to kidnap Sof'ia but is prevented from so doing by Milon. Pravdin announces an official order removing the Prostakovs from control over their serfs and everyone turns on the wretched woman, even Mitrofan. Milon and Sof'ia are now free to marry.

Fonvizin's satire is directed not just at the grasping, narrow-minded provincial landowners. He suggests that their faults come from a lack of education and along with his contemporaries believed that all his country's ills would be cured once ignorance had been removed. The three tutors Mrs. Prostakov employs for her son are comically incompetent and are only engaged because of the legal requirement that sons of the gentry have to receive an education. The legal bureaucracy and sycophancy at the imperial court are denigrated as are many of the abuses of serfdom. However, Fonvizin did not wish that serfdom be abolished completely or for anything other than autocracy to be the form of government, but he does plead here that the abuses they clearly engender should be eradicated. One further important theme in *The Minor* is that of duty, the mutual duty of subjects and their monarch, that of the landowners to look after their serfs, of children to respect their elders, and of all citizens to serve their country. While none of the butts of Fonvizin's satire is original (and Catherine herself had used similar targets in her own plays), it was Fonvizin's dramatic sense, his fine and apposite use of language, his ability to portray recognizable Russian life and people, and the humour of many of his characters' speeches that made *The Minor* the most popular play of its day. It still remains pleasantly watchable and is more than the historical curio most other Russian plays of the 18th century have become.

—A.V. Knowles

THE MISANTHROPE (Le Misanthrope)
Play by Molière, 1666

The play begins with a lively dialectical exchange setting out the parameters of the comic dilemma that will inform it: what price sincerity in an irredeemably insincere and self-serving world? Alceste, the eponymous misanthrope, upbraiding his friend Philinte for having shown excessive cordiality to a person he scarcely knows, proclaims the moral imperative of honesty and total candour towards one's fellow creatures. He is outraged by the hypocritical manners of the age. Philinte's defence of the virtues of courtesy, restraint, and civilized tolerance of the failings of others is dismissed with an angry expression of contempt for the essential depravity of mankind in general, as typified by the conduct of Alceste's adversary in a lawsuit, which he is in danger of losing because he refuses to stoop to the accepted practices of cabal and judicial bribery. Contrariwise, he is prepared to concede the illogicality of his attraction to Célimène, a young widow renowned as much for her coquettishness as for her beauty.

The first test of his forthrightness comes with the arrival of Oronte, who solicits first Alceste's friendship and then his frank opinion of a sonnet he has written. When, after much evasiveness, Alceste speaks his mind, he offends Oronte deeply, an incident which leads later in the play to a summons to appear before the marshalsea in order to settle their differences. In the meantime we meet various other members of Alceste's circle of acquaintance. He reproaches Célimène for showing complaisance towards all her male friends and entreats

her to respond more openly to his love, but their tête-à-tête is interrupted by the announcement of further visitors, including two rivals for her hand, the marquises Acaste and Clitandre, who engage Célimène in an exchange of backbiting about absent friends and whom Alceste censures for encouraging her malicious wit. The depths such society gossip can plumb are revealed in a scene between Célimène and her ostensibly prudish friend, Arsinoé, which ends with the two women trading scurrilous insults in the most elegant language and prompts the written proof of Célimène's infidelity. Confronted by Alceste with the tell-tale letter she has supposedly addressed to Oronte, Célimène deflates his towering rage initially by suggesting that it was written to a woman, then by nonchalantly inviting him to believe his own interpretation and finally by observing that she cannot love a man who does not trust her. News that Alceste has lost his lawsuit provokes from him another choleric outburst against human iniquity and a threat to abjure the society of men altogether. The full extent of Célimène's duplicity is finally unmasked in a showdown with the marquises, who, by comparing the letters each has received from her, have discovered that she takes delight in maligning all her suitors equally, including Alceste, behind their backs. He none the less declares his devotion intact and offers to forgive her everything provided she will join him in abandoning the world. When she consents to marriage but not to self-imposed exile, he rejects her and departs in search of some remote and solitary refuge, leaving the loyal Philinte to pursue and remonstrate with him.

The play's originality as a comedy resides in the choice of so paradoxical a figure as Alceste as its focal point. Admittedly, Molière also paints a satirical portrait of an entire class or social enclave, the minor aristocracy and leisured bourgeoisie clustered about the French court, whose vanity, superficiality, and petty jealousies are incisively pilloried. But all these shortcomings are seen in relation to Alceste, and his extreme intransigence serves to throw them into still greater relief. On the face of it, his embattled idealism, beset on all sides by evidence of human frailty and malevolence, is scarcely a promising subject for comedy, but, as is so often the case with Molière's mature plays, a reflective laughter, a ''rire dans l'âme,'' is provoked by our perception of the gulf between appearance and reality, between what a character pretends or imagines himself to be and what is revealed about him by the progress of the action. Already in the opening scene Alceste's so-called integrity seems that less of a man of principle than of an intemperate egomaniac: he wishes to be singled out, to be acknowledged as the embodiment of scrupulousness in an otherwise corrupt society. Within minutes, however, scruple is abandoned is favour of the tact and diplomacy advocated by Philinte, as Alceste strives to avoid giving an objective assessment of Oronte's poem, only to lapse into ludicrous critical overkill when he can no longer sustain the requisite social posture. Célimène's allusion to his sporting of ''green ribbons'' suggests that he even has some pretensions, whether prudent or not, to emulate the fashionable dress of the society he supposedly abominates, and it is she who interprets his professed attitudes of mind as simply an exercise in contrariness. The sheer inconsistency of his position is, in fact, most clearly exhibited through his relationship with Célimène, who appears to be an incarnation of the very shallowness and deceit he affects to despise, yet for whom he avows an uniquely passionate love beyond his rational control, which he expects her publicly to reciprocate. However, no sooner does the unaddressed letter give him grounds to suspect ''betrayal'' at her hands than he abruptly offers his heart to her cousin Éliante by way of exacting revenge, before forfeiting any claim on sincerity by begging Célimène at least to feign innocence and a show of affection for him.

By Act V the predominance of calculation and self-regard in Alceste's behaviour is unmistakable: first he refuses to appeal against an unjust verdict because it affords him a martyr's privilege of railing against the entire age and reinforces his self-indulgent misanthropy; and then he makes his final offer of forgiveness to Célimène conditional on her willingness to share his own social alienation.

There can be no doubt that Molière saw Alceste as a comic figure: the oxymoron of the play's sub-title, "l'atrabilaire amoureux (the crosspatch in love)," and the fact that he created the title role himself in June 1666 are sufficiently conclusive. The extravagances and incongruities of the character would make him an absurd misfit in any society.

On the other hand, one does not have to accept Rousseau's dissenting view of him as virtuous and truly estimable, nor Sainte-Beuve's who, notwithstanding Molière's intentions, found him courageous, "almost heroic," in order to experience some intellectual sympathy for his plight; and, by contrast, it is not difficult to conceive of circumstances in which Philinte's phlegmatic acquiescence in the ways of the world would appear positively contemptible. Indeed, Alceste's final exit, his rejection of that world, can be regarded as the act of both a terminally defeated idealist and a petulant, self-dramatizing fool who will soon be back—such is the force of the play's irony.

—Donald Roy

THE MISER (L'Avare)
Play by Molière, 1668

Molière's *The Miser* is a prose comedy, produced in 1668 when he was 46 and had already written his best plays. As was the custom for French writers of the 17th century, he took his plot from a classical model, the *Aulularia* of Plautus. Unlike *Tartuffe* or *Don Juan*, *The Miser* was uncontroversial and is still frequently performed. It is useful as an introduction of Molière to young people and has provided the basis for some lively productions.

Harpagon is a rich miser and a widower. He has no affection for his two children, his daughter Élise and his son Cléante. He wishes to marry off the former to a rich old man, Anselme, whose principal merit in Harpagon's eyes is that he is prepared to take her "without a dowry." The scene in which the phrase "sans dot" is endlessly and obsessively repeated indicates the extent of Harpagon's monomania. Harpagon himself wishes to marry a young woman, Marianne, already in love with Cléante, and Rousseau strongly disapproved of the immortal effect that Cléante's defiance of his father over this and other matters was likely to have on the audience. Marianne's attraction in Harpagon's eyes lies in her rich dowry, and he is encouraged in his endeavours by the intriguing Frosine. Cléante steals the only real object of Harpagon's affection, his "chère cassette" ("beloved money box"), thus provoking one of the many scenes in which Harpagon's obsession with the physical possession of money borders, for modern audiences, on the tragic and goes well into the pathological. After an entertaining misunderstanding, in which the young man who loves Élise, Valère, is thought by Harpagon to be confessing to the theft of the "cassette" because he speaks of a purloined treasure with such affection when, in fact, he is talking about his beloved, everything is solved by the device of a *deus ex machina*. Anselme, it is revealed, is Valère's long lost father. He happily surrenders his claims on Élise to his son, on condition that Harpagon allows Cléante to marry Marianne. Harpagon, now back in possession of his "chère cassette," agrees and the play ends with everybody united to what they most desire.

It is improbable that the 17th-century audience took the happy ending seriously and equally unlikely that they saw anything verging on the tragic in Harpagon's behaviour. The distinction between the genres, which was carried to the point where it was considered more normal for tragedies to be performed in winter and comedies in summer, precluded the bathos to which audiences became accustomed after the outbreak of romanticism. Harpagon was seen as funny, for the same reason that Monsieur Jourdain in *The Bourgeois Gentleman*, or even Alceste in *The Misanthrope* were seen as funny: because he was what was known in the 17th century as "un imaginaire," a man held captive by one single idea. His obsession with money matches Alceste's insistence that everybody should be as scrupulously honest as he is, just as it runs parallel to Monsieur Jourdain's overwhelming desire to become a member of the nobility, and the conviction of Orgon, in *Tartuffe*, that Tartuffe, whom everybody else in the play rightly sees as an impostor, and whom Molière takes great pains to present as such, is a model of Christian virtue. Such departures from what the *raisonneurs* in Molière's comedy present as the golden mean were to be expected from members of a society that the 17th century saw as corrupted by the inevitable effects of original sin. The sympathy that Molière is alleged to have had for enlightened, non-Christian ideas did not extend to a belief in the natural goodness of man. The defeat of the "blocking character," Harpagon, which enables the young lovers to be united, is in the best traditions of the modern theories of comedy with which Molière, essentially a practical playwright with a company to be run and who wrote plays for money, was not acquainted.

The Miser is interesting more for historical than for theatrical reasons. Comedy traditionally dates more quickly and more finally than tragedy and the young lovers whose frustrations and final union are regarded as so integral and obligatory a part of the genre generally seem insipid and pretentious. This is often the case with Molière, and one longs for the funny man to come back on again. Harpagon is quite funny, especially when he interrogates one of his servants, Maître Jacques, whom he suspects of having stolen his money box. When Maître Jacques holds his two hands out before him, Harpagon asks where the other ones are. When, however, in an obsessive attack of suspicion, he grasps his own arm under the illusion that he has robbed himself, the modern audience feels that it is being asked to laugh at a madman and does not find him quite so funny. The play's interest lies more in the portrait it gives of a middle-class household in 17th-century France, and the choice of a miser as the principal comic character. The interdiction on usury, which led the Christians of the Middle Ages to have such an ambivalent attitude to Jews, presenting them as scapegoats but compelled to borrow money from them at the same time, was still producing some curious effects in the 17th century. Early capitalism needed money to circulate if the economy was to develop. The miser, who stored his gold in a secret place and prevented this from happening, was as legitimate a figure of fun as the old man who married a young girl and was cuckolded by the young man whom nature had intended her to marry. He was somebody at whom the audience could be invited to laugh for good economic reasons. At the same time, many of the qualities he embodied were essential to the development of a modern economy. Frugality, a sense of the right price for a particular service or object, was a necessary part of the Protestant work ethic that helped to bring about the rise of capitalism. The fact that Harpagon is not as funny nowadays as

Molière's other great monomaniacs is, perhaps, a reflection of the different attitude our society has towards money.

—Philip Thody

LES MISÉRABLES
Novel by Victor Hugo, 1862

Victor Hugo started to write in France a novel which was first called *Les Misères*, but he finished it in 1862 while he was in exile in the Channel Islands, during Napoléon III's régime.

As the double meaning of the title (Base Wretches/The Poorest of the Poor) indicates, the main character of the novel is the precarious social group, below the working class, which is led to commit crime (prostitution for women and theft for men) because of poverty.

Those people do not express themselves in literary French. In some dialogues, realism forces Hugo to use slang which he translates, through Gavroche, for instance, who explains certain expressions to his brothers, or in footnotes when the text contains too much of it.

Outsiders of society live in the margins of space, out of the city (in "les faubourgs") and of time: they only appear when night falls and the bourgeois go to sleep.

Among them, Hugo favours youngsters: children like Gavroche, his brothers and sisters, and Cosette in the first part of the novel, and teenagers (Montparnasse, Éponine, Azelma, and Cosette) in the second part. He compares them to small, cute animals—to cats, for instance: originally Gavroche's name was Chavroche—while adult thieves are compared to nasty, dangerous ones. The Thénardier and the Patron-Minette band are repulsive, according to Lavater's theory that the soul is reflected in the physical appearance. Children and teenagers should be beautiful because of their youth, but are in fact ugly as a result of their conditions of life, and women loose their femininity in poverty. But the younger ones succeed in being happy (they sing all the time) by keeping their sense of humour and of poetry because they are free.

The "misérables" move towards greater social and religious awareness by sacrificing themselves to others. Their evolution usually ends in death: Fantine dies for her daughter, Gavroche for the barricade, Éponine for Marius, and Jean Valjean for Cosette. Martyrdom is achieved and the characters cannot progress any further. The poor are seen as the people of God.

If the author shows the way out of poverty and crime to his characters, it is because he is portraying the readers of his novel: in his letters to his publisher, Hugo kept insisting that the volumes were financially accessible to all. He chose to show reality not out of complacency but in order to denounce it and, therefore, to change it. As his introduction points out, he addressed this book to all human beings who endure exploitation, suffering, and ignorance.

Was his wish fulfilled? Was *Les Misérables* read by the people Hugo intended it for? It was certainly very successful when it first appeared simultaneously in many European countries. The publication was even delayed because the workers were crying over the proofs . . . And the characters of the novel became "types" straight away.

Popular acclaim and doubts from critics have ever since characterized the life of the novel and of its many adaptations (drama, cinema, and the long-running musical). French education and teaching institutions everywhere seem reluctant to include it in their curricula,

although it is the most read novel in the world. As Jean-Paul Sartre said, Romantic writers—with the exception maybe of Musset—purported to write for the people, but only Hugo's *Les Misérables* actually reached its intended audience.

—Myrto Konstantarakos

MISS JULIE (Fröken Julie)
Play by August Strindberg, 1888

August Strindberg's great naturalistic tragedy *Miss Julie* or *Lady Julie* belongs to the avant-garde in theatre history and is his most frequently performed drama. The novelty of this play lies both in its psychology and its staging and dialogue. Strindberg's "Preface" to the play, written afterwards, is a no less important document in theatre history than the play itself. Strindberg believed that environment, heredity, time, and chance are the basic factors in the development of any human being, and that the dialogue should reflect actual conversation in its irregularity and fragmentation. He preferred a one-act play that would not allow for interruption of the audience's attention and advocated a realistic staging, eliminating artificial lighting effects.

Miss Julie was too advanced for the Swedes at the time, and Strindberg had difficulty getting it accepted for the stage in his homeland. It was first performed abroad in Copenhagen in 1889, with Strindberg's first wife, Siri von Essen, playing Miss Julie. The play became a sensation and was performed widely in Berlin, Paris, and New York before it was finally staged in 1906 at Lund, in Sweden. In 1950 Alf Sjöberg directed a successful screen version of the play with Anita Björk and Ulf Palme as the main characters, and the same year Birgit Cullberg choreographed a classical ballet based on the play, with Elsa Mariann von Rosen dancing Miss Julie. A drama about sex and class, it has been performed in the American South with a black actor in the male role, thus substituting race for class and making the tension perhaps more comprehensible to an American audience.

The play takes place during a Midsummer Night celebration at the estate of Miss Julie's father, the Count, who is absent but nevertheless strongly present in spirit. The Swedish midsummer, with its strongly erotic overtones, lack of inhibitions, and abandonment of normal social conventions, underlies the dynamic temperament of the play. There are few characters: Miss Julie; Jean, her father's valet; and the cook, Kristin. A group of estate workers appears in a dancing and singing interlude, illustrating the earthy and bawdy aspect of the Midsummer Night.

The plot is simple: Miss Julie entices Jean to seduce her, after which they are both struck with guilt feelings: Miss Julie because she feels she has degraded herself by becoming involved with a man from a lower class; Jean because he is afraid of what the Count will say, but also for the wrath of his "fiancée," the cook Kristin, representing religious consciousness. He has also lost respect for Miss Julie herself. To assuage their shame and guilt, they make plans to run away and open a hotel in Switzerland with money Julie has stolen from her father. Miss Julie even tries to make Kristin go with them, using words almost identical to those Jean used in persuading her to escape with him. However, Kristin preaches about sin and atonement and voices to Jean her lack of respect for Julie who has defiled herself by sleeping with him. Her values are firm and unyielding. Miss Julie and Jean are delaying their escape by their lack of strength. Julie asks: "What would you do if you were in my place?" and he answers: "In yours? Wait a minute—as a noblewoman, as a woman, as . . . a fallen woman. I don't know—yes, now I know'': *Julie (takes a razor and makes a gesture)*: ''Like this!?'' (translated by Walter Johnson). Shortly after the Count returns home and Jean, terrified at the sight of the Count's boots, is unable to make any decisions. Finally he tells Julie: ''It's terrible! But there isn't any other answer. . . . Go!'' This is the last word of the play.

The events are foreshadowed in the beginning of the play when Kristin is preparing a foul-smelling concoction for Julie's dog Diana, who has mated with the gatekeeper's mutt and needs an abortifacient. Julie's fate is more drastic: she must kill herself to erase her shame. Julie is the daughter of an emancipated woman who tried to bring her up as a boy until her father took over and allowed for her femininity to develop, but treated her like a fragile doll. Human instinct, nature, and a number of other components also explain her fate. As Strindberg says in his ''Preface'':

> I have motivated Lady Julie's tragic fate by means of a great many circumstances: her mother's basic instincts; her father's improper rearing of the girl; her own nature and the influence of her fiancé's suggestions on her weak degenerate brain; furthermore and even closer at hand: the festive mood during Midsummer Night; the absence of her father; her monthly period; her preoccupation with animals; the exciting influence of the dance; the night-long twilight; the strong aphrodisiac influence of the flowers; and finally chance, which brings the two together illicitly in a room, plus the excited man's aggressiveness.

Jean, however, survives and Strindberg explains his character in the following words:

> Aside from the fact that Jean is on his way up, he is also superior to Lady Julie because he is a man. Sexually he is the aristocrat because of his masculine strength, his more sensitively developed senses (but no more so than that he can easily kill Julie's finch when she wanted to bring it with her when they escaped), and his ability to take the initiative. His inferiority consists mainly of the social environment in which he is temporarily living which he most likely can put off along with his valet's jacket.

> (translations by Walter Johnson)

From these characterizations we glean that Strindberg was also very much a man of his time in his basic perception of man's and woman's nature and characteristics. This in no way diminishes the importance of his play, but may have contributed to the success of the tragedy and its Preface.

—Torborg Lundell

MIST (Niebla)
Novel by Miguel de Unamumo, 1914

Mist is the only one of Miguel de Unamuno's works of fiction specifically termed a *nivola*, a tongue-in-cheek variant of the novel invented as a burlesque response to critics who had considered his prior excursions into the genre as ''not really novels.'' Largely a negation of formulas of realism and naturalism, the *nivola* is an antecedent of the anti-novel, characterized by having no plot or plan, as the authorial *alter ego*, Victor Goti, explains to the protagonist Augusto in Chapter 27. One need not go beyond the author's affirmation in the prologue that *Mist* is a ''pornographic novel'' to find reason to discount other affirmations in the text as to characterization, style, structure, and technique of the *nivola*. In his correspondence, Unamuno refers to *Mist* as a novel of humour, and that humour is most convincingly borne out by the abyss between alleged theory and actual practice. The numerous and emphatic attacks on aestheticism found throughout Unamuno's essays undercut any notion of applying his counter-aesthetics to serious exegesis of his fiction.

Unlike realist and naturalist novels, the *nivola* contains no wealth of descriptive detail, no family chronicle or background of characters, no historical or geographical scene-setting. Not only does the action begin *in medias res*, without clues as to time or place or the character of the unheroic protagonist, but little information is ever given on these aspects; Unamuno's overpowering interest was in the souls of his ''agonists,'' and the few physical details that appear are almost without exception symbolic (e.g., Eugenia's cold, white hands denote her frigid, calculating nature). Unamuno calls his fictional city ''Renada'' (Double Nothingness) and its inhabitants ''renatenses'' (doubly non-entities), but in the absence of indications to the contrary, readers may be tempted to equate the setting with the provincial university town of Salamanca, where the author spent most of his adult life. Locale is in no way decisive, nor is the epoch, although readers will deduce that it is contemporary by the final chapters, when Augusto decides to make a trip to consult with Unamuno, whose articles he has read. Appearance of the author within the text on the same level as his fictional creations is not original to Unamuno, but a device found in *Don Quixote* (Unamuno was an exceptional Cervantine critic). More innovative is the confrontation between character and author, Augusto and Unamuno, although critics have suggested antecedents in Pirandello. The major coincidence, however, is with the latter's *Six Characters in Search of an Author (Sei personnaggi in cerca d'autore)*, which—like *Mist*—features a ''revolt'' of the characters, the existential search for being, and metaliterary devices (novel-within-the-novel, theatre-within-the-theatre), but Pirandello's play was not written until 1921, making Unamuno the precursor.

Augusto is initially a character almost without character, inactive, indecisive, unproductive, a creature of boring routine. The Spanish title *Niebla* means not mist but fog or cloud (it is related to ''nebula'') and Augusto, who is himself nebulous, lives in something of a fog. He personifies weakness of the will, which Unamuno and other members of the ''Generation of 1898'' such as Baroja considered the national illness of Spain. Augusto is at first existentially non-existent, not having experienced anguish, not exercising his liberty, not living authentically. *Mist* is a proto-existential novel, presenting the absurd sequence of events whereby Augusto becomes aware of his own existence through humiliation and suffering, fails in attempts to assume his liberty and take control of his life, and ultimately suffers existential anguish. Although he stops short of contemplating his life as being-toward-death, he faces absurdity and the abyss of nothingness when his creator—Unamuno—informs him of his fictitious condition. Augusto's awakening is sparked by his chance encounter with Eugenia, a young piano teacher who passes by his door and whom he follows to her home without forethought or planning. A conformist who feels constrained to behave in a socially correct fashion, he begins to court her because this is what is expected when a man follows a girl home. Her rejection, and Augusto's decision—based on literary models—to accept the challenge of winning her, lead him further into a labyrinth from which he cannot escape.

Although Unamuno stated that the *nivola* has no plot, *Mist* has one, camouflaged by the wandering, anecdotal structure, with prologues and epilogues, monologues or soliloquies, the numerous interpolated tales, and Augusto's abundant, prolonged dialogues with his friend Victor. The plot is trite and romantic: boy meets girl, falls in love, loses her to a rival, and decides upon suicide. The existential theme and presence of elements of both the anti-novel and meta-novel are sufficiently visible and interesting for readers not to have noticed the shopworn plot. And despite Unamuno's affirmations to the contrary, the stylistic coherence and metaphoric integration of the text convincingly demonstrate that *Mist* was not written without plans and without revision. Some of the attributes of the *nivola* listed by Victor do apply: like the personages in the novel Victor is writing, the characters of *Mist* are not presented as fully defined, but define themselves through what they do and say, and in this sense their "existence precedes essence" in classic existential fashion. And although *Mist* is not a *nivola*—a novel without a plan that develops as it goes along—this was the effect Unamuno intended to create, and he does so through concentration on Augusto, whose life is without plan other than one he develops as he goes along.

Perhaps the most interesting aspect of *Mist* is the ending, or lack thereof, for it is a novel without closure, deliberately crafted to intrigue the reader. Frustrated in his search for proofs of the existence of God, his metaphysical quest for guarantees of immortality, Unamuno postulated two lesser forms of survival: biological prolongation via numerous progeny, and enduring literary glory. One of his essays affirms that, "so long as a reader is shaken by what I have written, Miguel de Unamuno will not be completely dead." The final confrontation between Augusto and Unamuno—creature and creator—creates an enigma: who is more truly alive, the mortal author, or the fictional entity who cannot really die because he is not truly mortal? And who possesses the truth about Augusto's death? Unamuno informs Augusto that he cannot decide to commit suicide because Unamuno as author-creator has already planned to eliminate him. Returning home, Augusto eats in extravagant, gargantuan fashion (an affirmation of life and biological appetite) and is subsequently found dead, whereupon Victor and Unamuno (the author within the fiction, on the same level as his fictional entities) dispute whether Augusto was able to exercise existential freedom or whether his demise is strictly the result of authorial will. Conflicting signals are planted in the prologues and epilogues, and in the contradictory opinions expressed by various witnesses (the doctor, Augusto's servants) because the puzzle is not intended to be solvable. Metaphorically and allegorically, *Mist* raises questions about the existence of man without God or with a creator who wills death in a seemingly arbitrary fashion, and these are questions that Unamuno was unable to answer.

—Janet Pérez

MR. MANI (Mar Mani)
Novel by A.B. Yehoshua, 1989

Mr. Mani is one of A.B. Yehoshua's finest and most critically-acclaimed novels, an enormously popular best seller in Israel. The book is also one of the rare instances in which Yehoshua addresses Sephardism in his fiction. The novel, like Harold Pinter's play *Betrayal*, tells a complicated story in reverse order. Yehoshua creates the family history of the Manis, a fascinating and unique Jewish family that has lived in places such as Salonika, Jerusalem, Beirut, and Crete. In the novel, Yehoshua tells the story of ten generations of Manis during the course of five conversations between two people; in each case, the readers only have access to one side of the discourse and must fill in for themselves the other side of the dialogue.

The name "Mani" itself is unique. Throughout the novel, characters inquire about the family name, its origin and its meaning. Some characters liken the family name to the word "manic"; Hagar Shiloh calls Gavriel Mani "Mr. Mani-Depressive"; and Dr. Efrayim Shapiro, when describing Dr. Moshe Mani, says that the man is "Mani-fold." These puns, which are appropriate, suggest the complexity of Dr. Mani, Gavriel Mani, as well as the other generations of Manis. Dr. Shapiro's comment about the complexity of Dr. Moshe Mani holds true as he tells his father the horrifying account of his encounter with Mani, a 19th-century Jewish obstetrician who operates his own birthing clinic in Jerusalem. Moshe Mani meets Efrayim Shapiro at the Third Zionist Conference and succeeds in convincing him and his twenty-year-old sister, Linka Shapiro, to visit his clinic in Jerusalem. After visiting the clinic and spending time in Jerusalem, the Shapiros wish to return to their home in Jelleny Szad, in Galicia, Poland (near Cracow). Mani, however, does not want them to leave and even follows them as far as Beirut. Unable to convince them to return home with him and work in his clinic, Mani lies on the railroad tracks and allows a train to tear him apart. Shapiro is not entirely positive whether Mani has lured him to his Jerusalem clinic to provide him with donations, to be a partner in the clinic, to seduce Linka Shapiro, or to help him commit suicide.

The story involving Efrayim Shapiro and Moshe Mani illuminates the intricate structure of the novel. Moshe Mani's meeting of the Third Zionist Congress, his subsequent return to Jerusalem with Efrayim and Linka Shapiro, and his pursuit of them in the fourth conversation (in Jelleny-Szad in 1899) are alluded to by Mani's son, the spy Yosef Mani, in the third conversation (in Jerusalem, Palestine, in 1918). This connection between the third and fourth conversations manifests the intricate tapestry with which Yehoshua structures the novel. Yosef Mani, under interrogation for being a spy, mentions that his father has committed suicide because of his inability to win the heart of Linka Shapiro. Examining the same episode nineteen years earlier, Efrayim Shapiro tells his father, Sholom Shapiro, that Mani committed suicide because of a death wish, that the affection for Linka is merely a ruse that masks his desire for death. Sholom Shapiro later attempts to find the Mani family and compensate them financially for their loss, which suggests to the readers that he, like Moshe's son Yosef, believes that it was love of Linka that drove Mani to suicide. The complexity of the situation illuminates the varied and sometimes conflicting perspectives of the characters, which makes this novel so complex and unique. The readers view situations and events involving the Manis from various characters but rarely—primarily in the last conversation—from the perspective of the Manis themselves.

The theme of suicide pervades Yehoshua's novel. For instance, in the first conversation, Hagar Shiloh dates Efrayim Mani, the great-great-grandson of Dr. Moshe Mani. It is interesting that Yosef Mani, the spy who, as an adolescent, is jealous of the attention that his father gives to Efrayim and Linka Shapiro and blames them for his father's suicide, names his son Efrayim. This Efrayim Mani has a grandson named Efrayim, who is the man that Shiloh dates. This genealogy is crucial to the understanding of the novel yet also manifests the complicated and intricate nature of this book. Shiloh believes that she is pregnant by Efrayim Mani, who is away serving in the Israeli army. Efrayim Mani, worried about his father, Gavriel Mani, who has not answered the phone, requests that Hagar telephone him. Unable to get Gavriel, a judge, to answer the phone, she leaves school and finds him; she learns that he seems determined to kill himself. She follows him everywhere, equally determined to prevent him from committing suicide, partly because she believes that she is carrying the next generation of Manis and wants her baby to know his paternal grandfather. She succeeds in preventing his suicide attempts but discovers that she is not pregnant. She does, however, get pregnant by Efrayim Mani shortly thereafter and names the baby Roni Mani.

In the second conversation, in Heraklion, Crete, Nazi soldier Egon Bruner tells his grandmother, Andrea Sauchon, that his unit's assignment was a suicide mission: "Who but a dedicated suicide pilot could have thought that such a fantastic operation was possible." He then mentions that after being separated from his unit and losing his eyeglasses, he wishes that he would have been killed quickly by the enemy. Fortunate to have survived his ordeal, he encounters and takes prisoner a Jewish tour guide named Yosef Mani, who tells him about local archaeological digs and even gives him a tour guide brochure. Mani then dies calmly, as if he wants to do so and has the power to die at will: Bruner informs his grandmother that Mani was "taking his final leave of me and giving death the green light . . . ."

Readers discern that suicide appears to be a pattern in the family. Other traits include the love of languages and conversation. The Manis are charming and intelligent but have terrible luck. There are differences within the family, however; a strong bond exists between the Manis in the second conversation, for Yosef Mani's son, Efrayim, is clearly devoted to him. Moshe Mani, in the fourth conversation, appears to have little love or respect for his family, attempting to seduce Linka Shapiro before their very eyes, even inviting her to live with him in their house. In the novel, A.B. Yehoshua creates a complex and sophisticated family and traces their roots through different countries and three centuries. Although *Mr. Mani* includes members of the family who are suicidal, the novel nonetheless manifests the endurance and the strong will of the family to survive; this will to maintain the family is especially apparent in the last conversation in which a father, upon the death of his childless son, impregnates his own daughter-in-law to maintain the continuance of the Mani family.

—Eric Sterling

THE MISTRESS OF THE INN (La locandiera)
Play by Carlo Goldoni, 1753

As the most important dramatist in Italy since the Renaissance, best known for his gradual introduction of realistic characters and the psychological drama of the middle class and its values, supplanting the masks and fixed stereotyping of the *commedia dell'arte*, Carlo Goldoni wrote *The Mistress of the Inn* at a mid-point in this process of theatrical reform. From his early days when masked stereotypes were the norm in his native Venice—through comedies where a central protagonist sustained the comedy—to comedies of milieu, where the atmosphere and values of middle-class society were the subject,

Goldoni proceeded, in a substantial dramatic production, to introduce into 18th-century theatre an upholding of bourgeois values, together with a critique of Venice's decaying aristocracy and its mores (particularly the phenomenon of *Cicisbeismo*—the adopting of a close male friend by a married woman—and the duel).

The Mistress of the Inn introduces the position of woman into this scenario. Written for the well-known actress Maddalena Marliani, who had enjoyed previous successes in Goldoni's plays, it highlights the career of Mirandolina, left in charge of the inn after her father's death and courted, using a variety of "modern" devices, by two members of the aristocracy, the presumptuous marquis and the vain count, whose advances she disdains. The *cavaliere*, also staying at the inn, affects a total disregard for her, which spurs her to greater efforts to win his love, in which she is finally triumphant. With this moral victory secure, Mirandolina finally rejects his suit and marries her servant in deference to her late father's wishes, upholding the solid bourgeois values of hard work and just rewards.

Developed with psychological penetration, the character of Mirandolina is a fully realized portrait—she shows none of the sentimental affectations of many stage women—and strikes a blow for the independence of women in society. She uses a full range of feminine ploys—from flattery and kindness to cooking and fainting—to achieve her desired ends, and the triumph of commercial interests is celebrated in the play's conclusion. By contrast with the fixed values of the *commedia dell'arte*, Goldoni's portraits of his aristocrats have recognizable virtues and defects, his setting is a room in an ordinary inn, and the characters' relationships are motivated by the social values prevalent in 18th-century Venice. Realistic and naturalistic humour replaces the slapstick of the *commedia*, and the hegemony of the playwright in performance is ensured by scripted comedy which replaces the improvisation of the earlier comic tradition.

Forward-looking for its time, *The Mistress of the Inn* makes an implicit statement about the position of women. Always calculating, and always in control, Mirandolina uses her sex in a series of complex strategies to win over the male characters, implying every woman's right to decide and determine her own future in a male-dominated society. The ironing scene is a *tour de force* of feminine determinism and determination, and its setting strikes a blow for realism, far removed as it is from the set-piece gilded drawing-room of most contemporary theatre. Striking, too, is the use of "everyday" theatrical props—gifts, money, perfume, hot chocolate, linen—to link characters inextricably to setting, to show them as natural, in a situation audiences could recognize. Finally, the dialogue is believable, unlike the rhetoric of the straight or comic stereotypes of the *commedia dell'arte*.

Goldoni's critique of contemporary society—aristocrats apart—depicts a world short on morals and virtues, where most human activity is played out as a game, and where the protagonists are self-orientated to the point of obsession, driven by ambition or lust. The aristocrats are vacuous vehicles for a package of traditional characteristics that depend on forms, appearances, and outdated concepts of honour, dignity, and prestige. Even so, they are not empty stereotypes but are recognizable in Goldoni's Venice as the noblemen whose only claim to significance rests on the exploits and values of past generations. By contrast, the subtle and sceptical Mirandolina is a finely-drawn psychological portrait. In the end, her marriage to Fabrizio, her servant, in the play's conclusion, celebrates middle-class values. For the marquis, count and, ultimately, the *cavaliere* marriage is an old-fashioned romance in which the man offers protection to the woman (and demands obedience in return): Mirandolina, however, marries

Fabrizio as a commercial arrangement, offering partnership in the business and financial stability between (more or less) equal partners.

—Christopher Cairns

MOLLOY, MALONE DIES, THE UNNAMABLE (Molloy, Malone meurt, L'Innommable)
Novels by Samuel Beckett, 1951–53

The three novels *Molloy, Malone Dies*, and *The Unnamable* come together to form what is otherwise known as "The Beckett Trilogy" (all originally written in French). While each can be read as a separate piece there is some attempt at progression and coherence across these three "novels."

Indeed to say there is an attempt at progression through the works is to point to one of the major obsessions of the interior monologues of which these three works consist; each character is in search of something, on the way to somewhere, or wondering where it may be he is going. In *Molloy*, Molloy, incapacitated, sometimes on crutches, on his bicycle, or crawling, is going to meet his mother. Moran is in search of Molloy, though is reluctant to find him, having forgotten what it is he is meant to do with Molloy once he has found him. Malone, bedridden, is moving towards death. And the voice that speaks *The Unnamable* moves towards its objective, silence. Samuel Beckett, though, continually shies away from absolutes. The shift throughout the trilogy from physical movement (however sad, farcical, and restricted, as with Molloy) to Malone controlling his surroundings from his bed using a stick, to "the unnamable," seemingly egg-shaped and in a jar, is not pushed to its "logical" conclusion. There is not the final paralysis and silence which at times *The Unnamable* tends towards but instead *The Unnamable* ends, not in the ultimate static nothingness, but at "the threshold of my story" saying "you can't go on, I can't go on, I'll go on." And this, given the sense of decay, hopelessness, and loss of fixed identity which precedes it, is in many ways a final affirmation of hope.

These three novels together form a sharp questioning of accepted concepts of the "self," of the relation of character to action, and of the usefulness of language in conveying any sense of reality. Beckett's characters carry the full weight of these questions around with them, and at times their monologues are frantic with the panic which comes from worrying over these considerations. Molloy and his mother exemplify the inability of humans to communicate with each other. Molloy is able to make his mother understand him only by tapping her skull with his knuckles; since he decides that three raps means "money" and his mother seems to have the ability only to count to two, he then makes one thump on the skull equal "money." To counter the utter bleakness, Molloy at one point resorts to an intense experiment in order and the random. To pass the time more than anything, he sucks pebbles. His obsession is to ensure that he never sucks the same one of his pebbles twice in a row and this leads to a need to suck the pebbles randomly while ensuring that order is introduced to maintain the random nature of the sucking. Molloy speculates intensely on the different ways in which he could group the pebbles and the number of pockets he could use or would need. The effect of this is, above all, comic (an aspect of Beckett's writing that is often ignored). But while there is a futility in all of Molloy's calculations, there is in this futility the seed of the drive that persuades the voice of *The Unnamable* to end the trilogy by saying "I'll go on." Earlier the voice of *The Unnamable* has said "They taught me to count, and even to reason. Some of this rubbish has come in handy on occasions . . . I still use it to scratch my arse with." But even "the unnamable" gets "little attacks of hope" from an attempt to understand, in a way similar to Molloy's calculations with the pebbles, how to keep a constant water level in a series of jars. While they are undermined in Beckett's fiction until they almost no longer exist, the vestiges of a more solid sense of human character and knowledge are the shaky props to a fading but still existent hope in these characters.

Beckett's method of interiorizing the thoughts of his characters is obviously influenced by the modernist writers of the earlier 20th century and in particular Joyce (with whom Beckett was acquainted, and part of whose early work-in-progress on *Finnegans Wake* Beckett helped translate into French). In these three texts it is the questioning of the very ideas of self and character that makes the sustaining of the interior monologues so remarkable and important for 20th-century literature. The awareness that the "self" is a slippery entity intrudes further into the texts as they progress, until in *The Unnamable* it is apparent that the voice itself is primarily engaged in either proving to itself the concreteness of its existence or, having failed to prove it, lapsing into the relief of silence. It is difficult, especially *The Unnamable*, not to see Beckett rehearsing the questions which he, as a novelist, felt faced him in the creation of characters and texts. He does this partly through a self-referentiality in the three texts, which confuses the boundaries between author (as creator) and text: both Malone and "the unnamable" are the creators of fictive characters and scenarios (which are often indistinguishable from "reality"), and all three of the main protagonists in the trilogy show an awareness of characters from Beckett's other prose works, such as Murphy, Watt, and Mercier. It sounds like the voice of the writer when Malone says "with practice I might produce a groan, before I die" (a groan is better than silence?). Or, even less hopefully, when "the unnamable" says "When I think of the time I've wasted with these bran-dips, beginning with Murphy." The pronounless voice of *The Unnamable* is the ultimate acknowledgement of the unsustainability of the notion of the writer's only material ("blank words, but I use them," "the unnamable" says).

Yet given all these questions and uncertainties, the hopelessness of knowing anything, the desire to "go silent," there is among the despair still that which enables "the unnamable" to say "I'll go on." If it is as much Beckett as "the unnamable" speaking when he says "Ah, if only I could find a voice of my own, in all this babble," then one can only reply by saying that *Molloy, Malone Dies*, and *The Unnamable* contain a very distinctive "babble," out of which, against all expectation, emerges the will to continue, to "go on."

—Colin Graham

MONKEY

See JOURNEY TO THE WEST

THE MONKEY KING

See JOURNEY TO THE WEST

A MONTH IN THE COUNTRY (Mesiats v derevne)
Play by Ivan Turgenev, 1869 (written 1848–50)

A Month in the Country was the last-completed and is indisputably the best of Ivan Turgenev's plays. Written in Paris during 1848–50, it was first entitled *The Student* and then *Two Men*. It was sent to *Sovremennik* [The Contemporary], the leading literary journal of the time, and submitted to the censors. They demanded some substantial cuts, especially in some of the student Beliaev's radical speeches, and other major changes, notably that Natalia Petrovna be a widow (which removed her husband Islayev altogether). Turgenev objected mildly but agreed to the changes. The play, with its new title *A Month in the Country*, was passed in 1855 with the demands of the censors satisfied. It next appeared in an edition of Turgenev's works in 1869 with some minor changes and the part of Islaev restored.

The play was first performed in Moscow in 1872 with cuts with which Turgenev concurred. Some 20 years before, he had written that it was not really a play anyway but a novel in dramatic form, quite unsuitable for the stage. When it proved no great success with either the public or the critics, he was confirmed in his mistaken opinion. Seven years later the young actress Maria Savina chose it for her benefit performance. She asked Turgenev to cut it a little on the grounds of length (it would have taken almost five hours to perform) and played the role of Vera. It was a resounding success and Savina's acting ensured that it entered the Russian repertory. Much has been made of Turgenev's debt to Balzac's *La Marâtre* (*The Stepmother*) which was performed in Paris in 1848 where Turgenev probably saw it. There are clearly some similarities in plot. Both comedies (although it is strange that Turgenev should have described his play thus) concern the love of a young married woman (Gertrude/Natalia Petrovna) and her much younger stepdaughter/ward (Pauline/Vera) for a young man in the former's employment (Ferdinand/Beliaev). The older woman attempts to remove her rival by marrying her off to an old bachelor (Godard/Bolshintsov). There are also similarities in the roles of a cynical yet observant and dispassionate doctor (Vernon/Shpigelskii) and a young son (Napoléon/Kolia). However, the atmosphere and the entire dramatic conflict are different, if only because Turgenev gives a central role to Rakitin, the man unhappily in love, with all the bitterness and regret that involves, and because he sets the play in the milieu he knew best, the Russian country house inhabited by representatives of the minor landowning class. Gone too are Balzac's Romantic techniques and melodramatic tendencies. Moreover *La Marâtre* rests in deserved obscurity while *A Month in the Country* is still regularly and successfully performed not only in Russia but abroad as well.

The production at the Moscow Art Theatre in 1909, with Stanislavskii directing and playing Rakitin and with Chekhov's widow Olga Knipper as Natalia Petrovna, established the now standard interpretation of the play, at least outside Russia. Although Stanislavskii's collaborator Nemirovich-Danchenko thought the play a faithful reflection of a former but unchanging Russia with the social criticism that implied, Stanislavskii saw it more as a psychological study and played down its social or political aspects. Indeed the action of the play is almost entirely psychological. Although this aspect of the play has led many commentators to see it merely as the precursor of Chekhov's work, Turgenev combined his skill at portraiture with his ability to sketch the changing and often conflicting emotions that afflict men and women in love. With a delicate sensitivity to language and through skillfully constructed dialogue—often it is what is not said that is more important—Turgenev depicts the barely noticeable changes that occur in relationships, the elation and the doubts, the jealousies, justified or not, the hopes and fears, the rises and falls in emotional intensity, and the varying levels of love and hate among the characters. Crucial to this psychological interpretation is the role of Natalia Petrovna and her relations with and effect upon the people who have the misfortune to come under her sway. Her moods are constantly changing and she confuses and infuriates those around her. Extremely emotional and self-centred, she usually behaves without the slightest regard for the feelings of others. She discounts her husband and bullies and terrorizes Vera out of her love for the dithering Beliaev and into marriage with Bolshintsov. She herself falls in love with Beliaev who cannot cope with either the intensity or the fluctuations in her feelings and behaviour. Yet she refuses to go away with him, remains faithful to her unloved husband, and in the process loses her long-suffering and understanding friend Rakitin through whom Turgenev expressed much of his own view of himself. Overall the play is not optimistic about the human condition. Happiness is a possibility but it is apparently unattainable. Beliaev is almost alone in believing that love is a positive and welcome phenomenon but Rakitin, in the most bitter passage in the play, disillusions him. Love, whether in itself happy or unhappy, is transitory and can lead only to misery in the end.

While the psychological interpretation is the most satisfactory, there is also social and political comment. While this should not be emphasized, neither must it be overlooked. Couched in lyrical terms and set amidst the nostalgic charms of a Russian gentry class in decline, the play contrasts two social groupings: on the one hand the old, out-of-date, aimless gentry class of Natalia Petrovna, Rakitin, and Bolshintsov, doomed to ultimate frustration, and on the other the younger, idealistic, hopeful, and hard-working section of the community, that of Beliaev, Vera, and the servants whose day is yet to dawn. Such matters were not lost on contemporaries but to stress them at the expense of a fascinating if gently pessimistic examination of the lives of the characters is to lose the play's essential charm and interest.

—A.V. Knowles

THE MOON AND THE BONFIRES (La luna e i falò)
Novel by Cesare Pavese, 1950

The Moon and the Bonfires was the last novel that Cesare Pavese wrote before his suicide in August 1950. It was recognized instantly as not only his most representative work, since it contained a summary of all the themes and questions with which he had wrestled in his literary career, but also his finest novel, as his blend of lyrical evocation of landscape with American realism of dialogue achieved here its fullest synthesis.

Set in Pavese's home area, the hills of Le Langhe in Piedmont, the novel deals with the return of the narrator, Anguilla, from America to his home village, and with his meditation on the sameness and yet the differences that he discovers there. Anguilla concludes that he finds the changes so difficult to take because, having been born illegitimate, he never had any real family or roots there, which might have compensated for his sense of loss. In the end, realizing he does not belong, he moves on, a solitary rootless traveller.

The book, however, is not about Anguilla's present or future, but about the reconstruction of his past. There are three main sections:

chapters 1 to 13, in which he recalls his early life on the farm at Gaminella, and meets the surly Valino, its new tenant-farmer; chapters 14 to 25, which reconstruct his adolescence on the more prosperous farm at La Mora, where he falls in love with the owner's two elder daughters; chapters 26 to 32, the violent climax that shatters the lyrical evocation of Anguilla's rural past. The structure is more complex than this suggests, for each chapter begins in the present, with a meeting of a local character, or a *festa*, which then sparks off a chain of related memories. On three occasions there are powerful flashbacks to Anguilla's life in the United States, notably the authentic depiction of his night spent in the Arizona desert, a realistic scene paradoxically culled not from Pavese's own travels (he never left Italy), but from his reading of James M. Caine, John Steinbeck, and Ernest Hemingway.

The significance of the title is explained in chapter nine, when Anguilla recalls the old rural myths about grafting trees only in certain phases of the moon, and about the bonfires lit beside the fields in midsummer to encourage a good harvest. Anguilla's chief interlocutor is his boyhood friend, and *alter ego*, Nuto, who represents the rational, scientific, communist mind as opposed to Anguilla's intuitive tendencies. Anguilla is keenest to know the fate of the three beautiful daughters of Sor Matteo, owner of La Mora. By the end of the second section, Nuto has revealed to him that the eldest, the sophisticated Irene, had become ill with typhus; that the second daughter, Silvia, had sown her wild oats with a series of lovers; and that the youngest, Santina, was even more beautiful than the other two. It is at this point that the slow reconstruction of the past is shattered by the violence of the present: Valino, ground down by poverty, goes berserk, killing his wife and mother-in-law before burning down the farmhouse and hanging himself. Luckily, Cinto, Valino's handicapped son, whom Anguilla sees as a younger version of himself, has escaped to tell the tale. When Nuto finally resumes his story, Anguilla learns that Irene now lives in squalor, married to a violent man who beats her constantly; that Silvia had died after an abortion; and that Santina had during the war become both a whore and a double-agent for the Nazis and Fascists. The book closes with Nuto recounting how Santina finally was shot by the partisans, and how her beautiful body was burnt: "the other year you could still see the traces, like the bed of a bonfire," are the last words of the novel.

The Moon and the Bonfires constitutes the most mature elaboration of the motifs of Pavese's previous works, both in prose and verse. It provides the fullest exploration of his obsessive polarities between the city and the country, between myth and rationality, between the cyclical time of the seasons and religious *festa* and the linear time of history and the war. Like other novels of the period, it denounces the Fascist legacy in post-war anti-communism, as well as the continuing rural poverty and the *mezzadria* (sharecropping). But the novel's richness derives from its unique synthesis of realism and lyricism, and its treatment of themes of perennial concern. In bald summary the events narrated can sound melodramatic, but Pavese's sensitive prose is never strident or melodramatic. When Silvia dies, it is the austerity of a prose devoid of adjectival ornament which contributes to the impact: "She came back [from the abortion] with rings round her eyes, looking like death—she went to bed and filled it with blood. She died without saying a word either to the priest or to anyone else, only calling "Papà" in a low voice." Pavese's judicious oscillation in this novel between austere and, on other occasions, poetic prose, as well as his complex structuring of narrative, prove that he had indeed

reached the stylistic maturity to which he long aspired, before his death.

—Martin L. McLaughlin

THE MOSELLA
Poem by Ausonius, c. AD 371

River poems are not unusual in modern European literature, but Ausonius' poem in praise of the Moselle is a unique example of the genre from antiquity. It is also unsurpassed in any genre for its elaborate attention to visual detail. There is a series of intensely realized descriptions—of waving grasses on the river bed, of the dark spots on a trout's back, of the lengthening reflections of green foliage in the river at dusk—punctuated with a remarkably fresh set of similes in which, for example, he likens the reactions of sailors as they gaze into the clear water to a young girl's first experience of a mirror, or the struggles of an expiring fish to a pair of bellows hard at work. Similes are a traditional part of epic, but with his gift being for description rather than narrative, Ausonius seems to draw more from the didactic tradition than the epic. The main classical influences on this original poem are Virgil's *Georgics* and Statius' *Silvae*, with which the poem conducts a complex dialogue.

The presentation of the theme is systematic rather than impressionistic, but the snapshots, as they have been called, are not organized spatially, as a guided tour of the river, or chronologically, as the ordered experiences of a single day. If anything, the principle of organization is rhetorical, as the description moves upwards from the river bed to the overhanging crags and houses. In structuring his introduction as a journey from the Rhine frontier to Neumagen (on the Moselle, a little below Trier) Ausonius prepares a series of contrasts which are fully realized as he and his readers burst out of the wooded wastes east of the river into the dazzling air of the Moseltal. The river is as clear as the air is pure, and within it, upon it, and on its banks are life, peace, and beauty. The area is benign to its inhabitants, and the river convenient to its various users.

The first description is of the river's limpid depths; the second a portrayal of no fewer than 15 species of fish with an accuracy that suggests a close experience beyond the gastronomic. This *tour de force*, although obviously based on a common theme of mosaic pavements, excited the incredulous admiration of at least one contemporary. From a new vantage point, the river's gorge is compared to a theatre, though the only noise to disturb the almost pastoral stillness is the crude catcalling of a wayfarer. In a rare piece of mythological fantasy the poet pretends that in the heat of midday, an intrusive touch of the traditional Italian environment of Latin poetry, such pleasances are exploited by satyrs and naiads. Later, by contrast, the appearance of the river at twilight is rendered in exquisite chiaroscuro. At other times there is great bustle, much of it concerned with fishing. One of the poem's most elaborate vignettes presents a young angler who jumps in after an escaping fish and gets the soaking that he deserves. The final scene offers a composite view of the river snaking between banks crowned with villas of various shapes and sizes, likened with characteristic hyperbole to some of the seven wonders of the world.

By conscious choice little is said of the inhabitants. Although Ausonius claims in part of his long conclusion that he will one day write a poem to give them their due, this is just polite convention. Such individuals as do enter his verses are conspicuously placed in rather demeaning contrast to the world they invade. Particularly noteworthy, given the political conditions of the late Roman Empire and the importance of panegyric, is the scarcity of allusion to the emperor or the royal house, especially as they were his employers and had been responsible for bringing Ausonius to the region. Strangely but symptomatically, the Roman capital city of Trier, the centre of the area and the support of its prosperity, is never named and barely referred to. Apart from a reference to an important recent victory over a German tribe in AD 368 (the poem was written in about AD 371), there is little recognition of the imperial peace and those who preserved it by force of arms. All this serves a clear purpose, one of privileging the world of nature—a nature organized into neat fields and vineyards—and belittling the activities of man. When Ausonius breaks off his enthusiastic description of individual scenes, he appeals to the tributaries of the Moselle to add their own tribute of praise; and when, at the end, he considers what the reception of his poem will be, he thinks of the fellow rivers of Gaul rather than human readers. This world, "where every prospect pleases, and only man is vile," does not issue from a political stance. Ausonius was not a "green" *avant la lettre*, let alone a misanthrope or anti-imperialist, and goes beyond the limits of traditional rhetoric. The poem is in all probability an essentially personal construct and, like most of his work, directly founded upon personal experience.

—R.P.H. Green

MOSES (Moïse)
Poem by Alfred de Vigny, 1826 (written 1822)

While Alfred de Vigny's "Moses" should not be considered as belonging to the French Symbolist movement of the 19th century, the poem does foreshadow certain aspects of the movement, namely the use of a single prevailing image (a symbol) to represent the true subject of the poem. "Moses" first appeared in the 1826 collection *Poèmes antiques et modernes* [Ancient and Modern Poems], in the section *Livre mystique* [Mystic Book], the preliminary section of the collection. Curiously, it did not fall under the rubric "Antiquité biblique" ("Biblical Antiquity," of the *Livre antique* book), which could easily have been the category of a poem whose central character is borrowed from the Old Testament. "Moses," however, composed in 1822, rises above its apparently transparent title to evoke another, similar, but perhaps greater prophet-leader, the poet. Vigny's repositioning of the poem in the collection's second printing (1829) as the initial poem in the work proves its importance as an introduction both to the collection as a whole and to Vigny's views on the artist and his world.

This poem of 116 lines with the rhyme scheme aabb, written in the classically traditional French alexandrine verse of 12 syllables per line, is a concise account of Moses' final glory—his pilgrimage towards the Land of Canaan and his subsequent death on Mount Pisgah (identified as Nebo in the poem), as given in the books of Numbers and Deuteronomy. Vigny borrows rather heavily from these books, as well as from Exodus, condensing particular episodes and speeches to form his narrative poem. Vigny's poetic artistry, however, is readily evident in the imagery and language that Vigny uses to successfully intertwine episodes of Moses' life, synthesized into a climactic event and a single burning question.

Although the major part of the poem consists of a speech Moses makes to God in his final moments, "Moses" begins with a typical Romantic description of the sun setting on the tents of the Hebrews encamped at the foot of the mount, a descriptive detail which should be attributed fully to Vigny's poetic imagination. The description (representative of the orientalism of the Romantic period) is dotted with terms evoking heat and light, red and gold, establishing the geographical setting of the middle-eastern desert. Within this 1289 description is a language of sleep (the bed of sand, the sun setting or "sleeping" [*se coucher*], the sunlight "stretching" out [*prolonger*] on the tents) that serves as a backdrop for Moses' upcoming refrain "Laissez-moi m'endormir du sommeil de la terre" ("Let me sleep the earth's sleep"). The sun and Moses' people are preparing for their rest; Moses desires to do the same but cannot. God has already declared that Moses will not find his final resting place, death, in the promised land. For Moses, this means that he alone will not take part in the realization of the collective dream. Ironically, he will die before attaining his ideal.

Moses' plight is bittersweet. As the chosen one, Moses serves as the face, hands, and mouth of God, as frequent references to these parts of Moses' body attest (his shining and flaming forehead, his eyes, and his earth-moving voice are of particular importance). To the people, he is thus the prophet of God, their leader throughout generations. His chagrin, however, lies in the fact that he is not one of the people; he has been chosen out of them to be separated from them, to be different from them, superior in the eyes of God. His divine election causes his estrangement; Vigny's Moses says to God: "Sitôt que votre souffle a rempli le berger / Les hommes se sont dit: 'Il nous est étranger'" ("As soon as your breath filled the shepherd / Men said to themselves: 'He is a stranger to us'").

The people no longer know him as one of their own. Moses' alienation is artistically illustrated through a contrast between the vertical and the horizontal. As Moses climbs Mount Nebo, the Hebrews stretch out prostrate on the horizon under him. Another contrast is that between the thunderous, cloud-filled storm taking place at the crest of the mount, where Moses speaks face to face to God, and the arid heat of the desert below. Moses' torment (i.e., that he can see from above the promised land but knows that he will not be allowed to enter there) is made clear through yet another set of contrasts. Vigny includes in the poem the list of lands under Moses' gaze (included in Deuteronomy), and attributes to them either fertile or sterile soil. Finally, Canaan is fertile, but it is ironically sterile to Moses, because he will not be buried in that soil with the rest of his people.

Moses' dilemma, and, as Vigny has established it, the poet's as well, is that as a leader and prophet of the people, he is so estranged from them that he can be of no help to them—the people cannot possibly comprehend enough to follow, and are thus fearful. The poet is reduced to a state of lonely solitude, being understood by only himself and other poets, themselves in a state of isolation. Moses laments, "Je vivrai donc toujours puissant et solitaire?" ("So I shall always live powerful and solitary?"). So, even though the poet can command the elements and know the skies and stars, as does Vigny's Moses, he is alone and lonely in his successes; superiority brings alienation. The question lies not so much in why the poet is the chosen one, as in why he is feared and misunderstood, and alone as a result.

—Jennifer Brown

MOTHER COURAGE AND HER CHILDREN (Mutter Courage und ihre Kinder)
Play by Bertolt Brecht, 1941

Bertolt Brecht wrote the first version of *Mother Courage and Her Children*, probably his best-known play, in the autumn of 1939, although it is likely that he had been developing the idea for some years. At that time he was in exile in Scandinavia where he was deeply disturbed by the readiness of Scandinavian countries, especially Denmark, to trade with Germany despite what he regarded as the very obvious signs that Germany was planning an expansionist war of which the Scandinavians were likely to be early victims. The play sought to teach some timely lessons, namely that war is nothing but business conducted with other means and in other commodities (''instead of cheese it's now with lead''), that only those with a large ''pair of scissors'' can make their cut out of the business of war, and that, for the little man at least, there are no winners since ''war makes all human virtues deadly, even for those who possess them.'' His method of teaching these lessons was one he used in most of his ''classic'' later plays. It involved the techniques of ''estrangement'' or defamiliarization (presenting something all too familiar in a new light, so as to challenge common assumptions), and ''historicization,'' stepping back from the immediate present in order to gain a distanced, larger, and fundamental grasp of the issues. Hence he set *Mother Courage* in the period of the Thirty Years War (1618–48) which swept across most of the Continent, causing great loss of life not only among fighting men but also among civilians because of the famines and pestilence that followed in its wake.

Brecht's dramatic chronicle centres on the family of Anna Fierling, known as ''Mother Courage'' because of her willingness to risk her life for the sake of her business, an opportunistic camp-follower who sets out to make a living for herself and her children by selling wares to whichever army is willing to buy them. The play opens in the spring of 1624. Mother Courage's wagon, pulled by her two sons, is stopped by two recruiting officers on the look-out for new men. While Mother Courage is distracted by the chance of selling a belt-buckle, her ''bold'' son Eilif is lured away to join the soldiers. The scene ends with an explicit lesson which will be repeated and varied throughout the play: ''If from the war you would live, to the war you must give.'' Mother Courage is shown constantly in a double perspective, as an object both of criticism and of sympathy. She is criticized for her entrepreneurial approach to war as an opportunity for gain; as such she shares the guilt of all war-profiteers and thus only gets what she deserves when she loses her children one by one to the war. In each case where a child is taken away (Eilif), killed (Swiss Cheese), or mutilated (Kattrin), Mother Courage's business dealings are directly implicated. On the other hand she pursues her business not out of mere greed, but in order to provide for herself and her family. She is a ''great living contradiction,'' a mother who loses her children by trying to provide for them, the embodiment of a human virtue rendered deadly by war. She could also have lost them if, like other ''little people'' (e.g. peasants) in the play, she had simply worked the land peacefully, for war destroys by-standers as well as those who go out to meet it. Brecht constructed such situations of coerced culpability and in-escapable self-injury because, as a Marxist, he wanted the audience to recognize that there is no simple and, above all, no piecemeal-reformist solution to the dilemma. The contradictions which tear the family and Mother Courage apart are endemic to class society, the result of a competitive, self-centred form of social and economic organization. The play displays half-guilt and suffering in order to challenge the audience to reflect on the changes that would be necessary to make human virtues productive rather than destructive.

The play is an example of Brecht's epic theatre, a form of play in which events are mediated to the audience via a narrative voice in various guises, in the form of banners strung across the stage summarizing the content of the scene that follows, in the form of rhyming couplets or songs addressed directly to the audience (thus stressing the theatricality rather than the illusory reality of the performance), and in the manner of acting, whereby the actor is required to ''show'' the behaviour of his or her character critically rather than simply impersonate that character. However, Brecht's theatre did not eschew emotion entirely. No one can watch Mother Courage as she hears her son being executed off-stage, unable to scream lest she betray herself, without identifying with her pain. But for Brecht empathy was not an end in itself; it was only useful if it promoted critical reflection and the will to remove the causes of suffering. As a piece of epic theatre *Mother Courage* has no truck with the unities of action, time, and place typical of classical drama. The play is unified not by plot but by argument, each episode contributing to the ''dialectical'' demonstration of the lessons the playwright wishes the audience to learn. In many instances the lesson is left implicit, so that the spectator has to draw conclusions from the juxtaposition of contradictions, as when one scene ends with Mother Courage cursing the war while the very next shows her singing its praises again, seemingly mindless now of her bandaged daughter. When orthodox communist critics complained that the play seemed to lack a positive message and in particular that Mother Courage fails to learn from experience, Brecht's reply was characteristic: what mattered was not whether Mother Courage learned anything but that the audience should learn to see things differently.

—Ronald Speirs

MRUICHCHHAKATUIKĀ
See THE LITTLE CLAY CART

MYTHISTORIMA (Mythistorema)
Poem by George Seferis, 1935

Mythistorima is the third published work of the poet George Seferis, who became a Nobel laureate in 1963. It was published in 1935, and was one of the factors that served to make that year a landmark in the history of Greek literature. In the same year surrealism made its first significant appearance in Greece. These two events delineate the paths along which modern Greek poetry was to move for many years: an exploration of the possibilities of free verse together with the exploration of new associations between words and meanings that break away from any obvious logical connections.

Mythistorima, as Zissimos Lorentzatos, an important critic of the time, pointed out, marks the real "turning point"—Seferis's first published work, in 1931, was called *Strophe* [Turning Point]—in Greek poetry, since through its introduction of free verse and a new poetic language it provides a response to the poetic crisis dominating Greek poetry in the 1920s, when the need for a break with tradition was becoming apparent.

Mythistorima consists of 24 sections which have often been regarded as separate poems, so that *Mythistorima* has frequently been treated as a collection. Taking into account, however, the fact that the individual sections are numbered but not titled, and the title *Mythistorima* ("novel"), the reading of *Mythistorima* as one single poem seems the most convincing. Viewed from this perspective, the various episodes alluded to in the 24 sections can be considered as interconnected parts of a single adventure.

Seferis himself, when referring to the title of this poetic composition, has pointed out his twofold preoccupation with myth and history. The presence of ancient Greek mythology dominates *Mythistorima*, either through direct references to mythological figures and stories, or through borrowings from ancient literary sources. The mythological characters appearing in the poem can be divided into three main categories: characters from ancient tragedy, especially *The Oresteia* (Orestes, Clytemnestra); characters from the Homeric cycle (Odysseus, Astyanax, Elpenor) and, by implication, the Argonauts; and finally, characters drawn from different myths, but still connected with the notion of redemption, either through liberation from mortal danger (Andromeda) or through resurrection (Adonis). From another point of view, all these figures may be seen as connected with murder, quests, and redemption, a link between the first two categories, tragedy and epic, being Astyanax (the son of Hector, who, according to one tradition, was killed on Odysseus' orders), and a link between the second and third categories, epic and myth, Odysseus' visit to Hades and guidance by the dead.

The presence of history in the poems is less obvious; one critic, Timos Malanos, attributed the sense of tragedy and loss prevailing in *Mythistorima* to the Asia Minor disaster of 1922. Seferis himself, however, rejected this interpretation, defining the Asia Minor disaster as one cruel episode in a general Odyssey. One extract that has often been cited as a reference to that particular episode is:

Sometimes unfortunate women wept
lamenting their lost children
and others raging sought Alexander the Great
and glories buried in the depths of Asia.

Apart from its preoccupation with myth and history, *Mythistorima* focuses also on landscape. With the exception of a few references to northern, probably English scenery (Seferis began work on the poem in London), most references reveal a Greek landscape, with the emphasis on its barrenness: "Three rocks, a few burnt pines, a solitary chapel / and further above / the same landscape repeated starts again." Or on the sea: "The sea once so bitter to your soul [. . .] / now full of colours in the sun."

These two points of focus mark the character of the sections, which, as Roderick Beaton has pointed out, can be divided into poems of land and poems of sea, while a parallel categorization suggested in the same study divides the sections into poems of waiting and seeking.

The first section combines all four categories and refers to the object of the quest or waiting:

Three years
we waited intently for the herald
closely watching
the pines the shore and the stars.
One with the plough's blade or the keel of the ship,
we were searching to rediscover the first seed
so that the ancient drama could begin again.

It has been suggested by various critics that the three years of waiting refer to the time between the composition of *Strophe*, which states: "we wait for the herald as in the ancient drama," and that of *Mythistorima*. In this case the herald or angel ("*anghelos*") may also be that of poetry.

The object of the quest appears to be multiple; the chief objective, perhaps, a Greek identity, rediscovered or redefined by Greeks, as Beaton suggests. This is combined with a quest for some "other life" characterized by authenticity, and a validation of life and death. The journeys in *Mythistorima* often fail, as do the waiting or prayers (the 15th section ends with the plea, "Give us, outside sleep, serenity," while the 16th describes a scene that evokes the reverse of serenity). The quest finally ends ("Here end the works of the sea, the works of love") with death, and serenity is achieved: "Those who will some day live where we end [. . .]/We who had nothing will teach them peace." The speaker and his compatriots have finally acquired their identity, perhaps by finding in the myths a common language with the ancient Greek past—a language very different from the "carved reliefs of a humble art" brought back from their initial journey "towards the north" in section 1.

Nevertheless, if this part of the quest has ended successfully, other parts, such as those seeking authentic life and the realization of a life justifying both itself and its end, remain open and continue to haunt Seferis in his subsequent poetic work. Thus, *Mythistorima* constitutes not only a turning point in Greek poetry but also a landmark in the poetry of Seferis himself, introducing both a form (free verse based on iambs) and a subject matter that will persist throughout his work.

—Elli Philokyprou

N

THE NAME OF THE ROSE (Il nome della rosa)
Novel by Umberto Eco, 1980

The first work of fiction by the Italian Umberto Eco, professor of semiotics at University of Bolonga, became an unexpected success with more than 26 million copies sold in more than 20 languages. This long and multifaceted novel plunges readers directly into the world of a 14th century Benedictine Monastery where Medieval politics and religious intrigues intersect. The events take place over the course of seven days and serve as a microcosm of the conflicts rocking the late medieval world. The plot is presented as the memories of Adso of Melk, a monk who recalls an episode of his adolescence in the year 1327, when he assisted William of Baskerville, an English Franciscan monk dedicated to solving a number of crimes committed in the Abbey.

William of Baskerville, a student of Roger Bacon, uses his reason to interpret reality and inquire about the tragic homicides. In a way, he is a medieval Sherlock Holmes dressed in religious clothes. As a Franciscan, he incarnates one of the tendencies in Catholic Church that questioned the Pope for its wealth, material greed, and political power. The Papacy was undergoing a profound crisis at the moment as well as other institutions of Medieval culture affected by the growth of commerce and capitalism. The world around the monastery is far from stable. Increasing wealth in the cities is changing the social structure. Two main conflicts occur during this period. First, the Pope and the Holy Roman Emperor are fighting for preeminence; and second, the Pope and the Franciscans are battling over the question of poverty. Should the Church possess earthly riches and play a role in temporal politics; or should it work among the poor and outcast, emulating (as the Franciscans argue) the poverty of Christ?

The Franciscan monk has two main antagonists in the novel. The Abbot who runs the Monastery is a Benedictine himself and for that reason opposes the Franciscans. Also lurks Jorge de Burgos, the blind librarian, a character who's name and physical appearance allude to the Argentine writer Jorge Luis Borges, admired by Eco. The abbot and his henchmen carefully control access to the collection; only the librarian and his assistant are allowed into the labyrinthine stacks. The ostensible reason is that there are thousands of books by pagan, Jewish, and Arab authors, as well as the records of many heresies. While true Christians must understand error in order to combat it, only the strongest and most mature minds should be exposed to it. Naturally, scribes and scholars, who come from all across Europe, long to view the library's hidden treasures. Strange intrigues develop among the monks, and suddenly turn to murder. A gifted young illuminator is killed; the next morning a second monk is found dead, plunged head-first into a barrel of pigs' blood. The conspiracy around the library express the enormous amount of power amassed by Monasteries during the Middle Ages as archives and holders of unique pieces of knowledge in Christendom. The plot runs around the lost Second Part of the Poetic of Aristotle, which is kept in the Monastery Library but secured by its malicious librarian.

Adso of Melk is presented in the position of a young learner. He observes his mentor and rationalizes his behavior in order to understand what's going on. The book uses modern semiotic theory to inform much of the dialogue, and invests its cast of characters with

multi-layered allusions to philosophical and literary figures. However, the persistent reader can learn plenty from this exciting and shocking story, which blends erudition with entertainment. It can be read both as a murder mystery and as a work full of theoretical implications over the human ability to interpret the world, and about the ways of life in Europe during the 14th century.

Soon after the publication of the novel, the French film director Jean-Jacques Arnaud began making an internationally distributed film of *The Name of the Rose*, bringing Eco even more to the center of international attention—although he respectfully distanced himself from the movie, released in 1986. The film stars Sean Connery in the role of William of Baskerville.

—Alvaro Fernández Bravo

NATHAN THE WISE (Nathan der Weise)
Poem by Gotthold Ephraim Lessing, 1779

Nathan the Wise, with its expression of optimistic belief in humanity and its argument for religious tolerance, is a central document of the German Enlightenment. Its moral has special relevance whenever anti-semitism and sectarian fanaticism or bigotry threaten humane values and social harmony. Its effectiveness as theatre depends on its apparent lightheartedness.

Unlike Gotthold Ephraim Lessing's other dramas, *Nathan* was not influenced by his desire to write a model comedy or tragedy in a realistic mode. It was conceived as a vehicle for the propagation of ideas at a time when great hopes were placed on the theatre as a means of educating the public. After publishing fragments of another scholar's rationalist critique of Christianity, where doubt was thrown on the divinity of Christ, Lessing had become engaged in a bitter controversy which attracted such attention that in the summer of 1778 the Duke of Brunswick, to whom he was librarian, forbade him all further engagement in theological debate. Lessing, however, put his fundamental ideas on religion and morals into dramatic form. That same summer he began *Nathan*, whose action involves a rich Jew, Christians, and Muslims in Jerusalem during the Crusades. The setting calls for some local and historical colour, which the dramatist duly provides, but more importantly it serves to distance the action and to underline the symbolic function of a romantic comedy with an elaborate plot of mistaken identity. The symbolism is crystallized in the central scene in the parable of the three rings (a variation of Boccaccio's *Decameron*). By telling this story the Jew implies that none of the three religions can establish its historical truth. Their adherents must endeavour to justify their religion by behaviour which is pleasing both to God and to their fellow men. By this standard Nathan, who insists that he is a human being first and a Jew second, proves to be closer to the true faith than those around him, particularly the Christians.

The happy ending follows the reappearance of a fortune and the disclosure that Nathan's adopted child Recha, brought up as a Jewess, is the crusading Templar's sister and the Sultan's niece. The expected wedding of Recha to the Templar is thwarted but we are to understand that we are all members of the great human family and that mutually platonic love brings more than sufficient satisfaction, even to the confusedly ardent Templar. Thanks to Nathan's reading of coincidence, the young lovers and benevolent but irresponsible Sultan and his sister Sittah embrace the truth. The Christian patriarch, a fanatical bigot and enemy of reason, would have had Nathan burnt at the stake but he is presented as a grotesquely comic figure. The other characters, for all their foibles, evoke sympathetic smiles. A garrulous servant woman and a naively honest messenger who betrays his master's plot are recognizable comic types. The dialogue brings much wit, not least from the mouth of Nathan in whom Lessing lends dignity to stereotyped Jewish traits: he is associated with money, sentimentality, and a quizzical intelligence. The main figures are psychologically convincing and rewarding roles but Nathan, partly modelled on Moses Mendelssohn, a leading Jewish philosopher and friend of the author, dominates the stage.

The hero's exemplary wisdom is the wisdom of tolerance and of trust in the will of God which he has maintained after a Job-like experience when his wife and children were senselessly slaughtered by Christians (Lessing's wife and their newborn son had died in the winter of 1777–78). He is a deist with a faith in the potential goodness of his fellow men. The plot shows that proper human relationships are undermined by supposed differences of religion and race. Tolerance is the corollary of the right and duty of every individual to use his reason unrestricted by institutionalized authority. Virtue is not to be found in an impatient rejection of human imperfections and a flight from society.

One person's goodness, whatever its motivation, encourages goodness in others and is rewarded in this life. Wealth, used properly, is not to be despised. Fatherhood is to be judged by love for the child, not by paternity. Belief in miracles undermines the need for human deeds to solve human problems. Lessing's didacticism is packaged in a pleasing mixture of wit and humour, and a touch of pathos. His unpretentious blank verse with its colloquialisms, rough and ready rhythms, and avoidance of heroic grandiloquence, brings what might have been austere sermonizing down to earth.

—John Hibberd

NAUSEA (La Nausée)
Novel by Jean-Paul Sartre, 1938

Nausea, Jean-Paul Sartre's first novel, is undoubtedly his best. Originally called "Melancholia," it was retitled at an editor's suggestion. A critical work, it tears away illusions uncovering what truths, if any, remain. It parallels, and was nourished by, Sartre's phenomenological investigations of the 1930s into emotions, imagination, and the ego. It also reveals many elements of what would become his phenomenological ontology in *Being and Nothingness*, but it should not be taken only as an illustration of the treatise it antedates.

After a career that took him abroad, Antoine Roquentin, still youngish, has resigned his post and has come to Bouville (Mudville, based on Le Havre) to do research on an 18th-century diplomat,

Rollebon. He lives on his modest income and follows a routine of visits to the library, meals at restaurants, walks in the streets and park, and an occasional hour spent with a café proprietress to relieve his sexual needs. Solitary and marginalized, he is more suited than others to see through fraudulent social structures and myths. The novel, in the form of a diary, begins when he realizes that something strange has occurred in the relationship between himself and the world. He writes in order to understand; the work has elements of the quest-novel pattern. He has glimpses of the thing-ness of objects, their independence from him (once separated from their utilitarian function), their solidity and self-identity. Facing them, he feels empty, contingent. This realization gives him a feeling he eventually calls nausea. It leads him to sense his own inner nothingness, compared to the solidity of the world; he realizes that he has no being, but is only an organization of protoplasm and a consciousness that spins itself out in endless thought. He re-examines his work on Rollebon, whom he has tried to resuscitate through historical re-creation. He realizes that Rollebon, like all the past, is beyond his grasp, and that he must abandon his meaningless project: no dead man can justify a living one.

Other undertakings are equally meaningless; they merely mask human emptiness. Someone Roquentin calls the Self-Taught Man is trying to read all the library books in alphabetical order, to consume knowledge as an absolute, an essence, that will make him other than he is; moreover, he believes in abstractions such as humanity and socialism, which, according to Roquentin, do not exist. Love is no more satisfying as a project. Roquentin receives a letter from Anny, an actress he once loved passionately; he hopes she will give him some reason for existing, and later travels to Paris to meet her, but finds that although she too has lost her illusions, including her belief in "perfect moments" (a theatrical view of experience), she refuses to acknowledge any resemblance between them or renew their relationship, preferring to "survive herself" with a handsome Egyptian. As for the consolations offered by society, Roquentin rejects them entirely: patriotism, religion, family, duty, altruism, bourgeois conventions are all demolished under his pen, shown to be frauds that enable some to wield power over others and thus veil to themselves their nothingness.

Unenthusiastically, Roquentin accepts an invitation to lunch with the Self-Taught Man. The occasion allows the host to bare his soul and spew out humanistic nonsense; he is looking for complicity. Roquentin responds by a violent attack of nausea: the food becomes disgusting, and since there are no absolute values, Roquentin feels that he could as easily stab his host as eat his cheese. He flees, walks along the sea wall, and enters the public park, where he has a revelation of the utter gratuity, or groundlessness, of all existence. Nature has no purpose; it is just there. Objects lose the solidity he had seen in them; names and labels ("root," "black") veil a mass of undifferentiated being, which overwhelms him by its abundance. All existence, including his own, is without reason.

After this experience, rendered in powerful impressionistic prose, and the subsequent disappointment with Anny Roquentin has no reason to remain in Bouville. He decides to live in Paris, doing nothing. Before his departure, he revisits the library, and witnesses a scene where the Self-Taught Man is driven out in ignominy because he has surreptitiously caressed a schoolboy. Roquentin tries to help him, but the humiliated bookworm flees in shame; henceforth he will be recognized as an outcast. Roquentin sees himself also as an outcast, alone and purposeless. However, another revelation awaits him:

listening to a jazz record in a café before leaving, he discovers that, unlike existing things, the song is independent of contingency (one can break the record but not destroy the song itself); it is an absolute, and justifies the composer and singer. He resolves to create something similar, a book (not a history, of course) that will, as he says, make people ashamed of their existence but justify his.

Despite its gloom, occasional sordidness, and methodical dismantling of many cultural constructs, which make it unacceptable to many, *Nausea* is both poetic and comic. Roquentin's paranoia is amusing; his images for conveying concrete experience are arresting; the style is controlled, always suited to its topic; and the moments of discovery, conveyed partly as interior monologue, are psychologically persuasive as well as metaphorically powerful. Sartre demonstrates well that the phenomenological investigation of reality can be dramatized in terms of everyday experience. The aesthetic solution to Roquentin's dilemma, which is rejected in later Sartrean works, connects this novel to previous aesthetic enterprises such as Flaubert's quest for the supreme literary artefact, Proust's apotheosis of art, and the Surrealists' belief that art could remake the world; but the deconstructing of abstractions and of novelistic convention—since there are mainly mental events in *Nausea*, and the hero is most unheroic—points ahead to Sartre's later call for a radically different fiction suitable for the present time, and, ultimately, to his critique of all aesthetic values.

—Catharine Savage Brosman

THE NECKLACE (La Parure)
Story by Guy de Maupassant, 1884

''The Necklace'' is one of the most famous of Guy de Maupassant's short stories but also one of the most enigmatic. Its crux is the loss of a diamond necklace borrowed by the wife of a low-ranking official in the Education Ministry, who wears it at a ball given by her husband's employers. Mme. Loisel is a poor but an honest woman. She is determined to return an identical—or practically identical—piece of jewellery to Mme. Forestier, the wealthy schoolfriend from whom she had borrowed it. The price of a similar necklace is 36,000 francs. M. Loisel already has half that sum; he borrows the remainder. Husband and wife spend the next ten years in grinding poverty until they have finally paid off their debt. One day, not long after the last loan repayment has been made, Mme. Loisel happens to meet Mme. Forestier again. In the course of conversation she relates the tribulations she has been through since borrowing the necklace. Mme. Forestier explains that those glittering gems were mere costume jewellery.

The first feature of ''The Necklace'' that is also characteristic of so many of Maupassant's other short stories is that it deals with the genteel poor. He excels in the description of low-ranking civil servants, having been one himself for eight years. No writer has known better than he did how such men struggle to keep up appearances while living on the breadline. It is a prospect that seems to have no end until death. In his emphasis upon shabby gentility and dreary routine, no writer has known better how to describe such lives.

Into this static situation, a terrible crisis suddenly erupts: the necklace vanishes. The rest of ''The Necklace'' is concerned with the inexorable working-out of the crisis. This is the second characteristic feature of Maupassant's approach to the short-story form. Crises, in Maupassant's short stories, axe either single or twofold. ''The Necklace'' relates a twofold crisis: the loss of the necklace is but the prelude to the discovery, much later on, that the necklace was a sham.

A third feature of ''The Necklace,'' characteristic not only of Maupassant but also perhaps of his ''naturalism,'' is that the narrator does not overtly look into the minds of his characters. The characters in ''The Necklace,'' and there are only three, are viewed externally, being as it were characters in a drama rather than a prose fiction.

A fourth and final characteristic of ''The Necklace'' is its extreme brevity: it is nine pages long. But this is not because all so-called extraneous details have been ruthlessly pared away. For the story is not as straightforward as it seems. The storyteller in ''The Necklace'' is a ludic narrator, sometimes mischievously misleading his reader, and sometimes building suspense by indulgence in personal digression. The first two pages of the story—introspective, generalizing, even somewhat diffuse—are a meditation yet also a character portrait, in the manner of Flaubert's *Madame Bovary*, but two pages out of nine are devoted to such effects, and there is no mention in them of any necklace.

This tantalizingly ludic effect is heightened by the fact that ''The Necklace'' is narrated in the third person. Following Balzac, Flaubert, and other users of *style indirect libre*, Maupassant engages in free indirect discourse—though only very sparingly: at the most critical point in the narrative. Writing of ''her treasure,'' ''a superb diamond necklace,'' he misleads the reader into believing that the necklace really is valuable.

In fact, does not Maupassant employ too many artifices of narrative? It is likely that Mme. Forestier would not have said that the necklace was costume jewellery when it was borrowed? Is it likely that M. Loisel could so easily have borrowed 18,000 francs? Or that a similar and almost identical necklace could so quickly have been found, especially if Mme. Loisel's brief memories of it were somewhat imprecise? Or that Mme. Forestier (apparently) never looked at that necklace again during the next ten years?

As with aspects of so many other masterpieces of literature (the time-scheme of *Phèdre* for instance), the detail of ''The Necklace,'' when clinically analysed, teems with improbabilities. Yet, as we read it, we are content to undergo a ''willing suspension of disbelief'' and to accept it as a ''realistic''—perhaps indeed ''naturalist''—picture of the world.

—Donald Adamson

THE NEW LIFE (La vita nuova)
Poems by Dante Alighieri, 1295

The New Life, written when Dante Alighieri was 29 or 30 years old, is primarily an anthology of poems, composed over a number of years and compiled by the author into a single collection, connected by a narrative, together with explanations of individual poems. A literary tribute to Beatrice, it both celebrates and analyses the poet's elevated feelings for his beloved. As such, it clearly belongs to the courtly love tradition of the troubadours, brought from Provence into Sicily by

Giacomo da Lentini, and thence to Tuscany, where the Tuscan School, notably Guinizzelli, and Dante's great friend, Cavalcanti, refined the rough vernacular poetry of the Sicilians, and used it as a vehicle for expressing philosophic and literary ideas.

The collection opens with Dante's description of his first meeting with Beatrice when he was nine years old. At their next meeting, nine years later, he falls deeply in love: "I was filled with such joy that I departed from people's company like one who was drunk." A series of allegorical visions reveals Beatrice to him as both a bestower of blessings and a reflection of divine goodness. So profoundly moved is he by her presence that he composes poems to a "screen" lady to disguise his embarrassment, though this device is eventually abandoned when the offended Beatrice refuses to return his salutation. Dante resolves to remove the fictional screen and devote himself to singing the praises of his lady. He now moves into a new realm of poetic creativity, writing with supreme skill and self-assurance: "I felt I had to take up a new and nobler theme than before." One by one, he recounts the death of Beatrice's father, his anguish at the sudden realization that "one day, of necessity, the most noble Beatrice must die," and the moment of her actual death. Finally, he resolves to "say no more of this blessed woman until such time as I can write . . . what has never been written before in rhyme of any woman." This is clearly the first intimation of the role to be played by Beatrice in *The Divine Comedy* as guide and spiritual redeemer to the poet.

The New Life is closely structured around a numerical symmetry based upon the number nine with which Beatrice is associated (the poet is nine at their first meeting, and nine plus nine at their second encounter; Beatrice dies at the ninth hour of the ninth day of the ninth month) and upon the root of nine, three, the symbol of the Trinity. Three *canzoni* provide the framework, the first and third being preceded by one ballad and nine sonnets. The central *canzone* in turn forms part of a grouping of nine poems, being itself preceded and followed by four sonnets. Most of the poems are introduced by a prose passage describing the circumstances of their composition, usually some encounter or vision, together with an explanation of the poem itself. Dante deliberately counterpoises the poetic style of the prose narrative with the prosaic analysis of the poem's content. Sometimes, for special effect, he chooses to analyse the poem before presenting it, "so that it (the poem) might seem more widowed at its conclusion."

Critics have interpreted *The New Life* in various ways. For some, it is a youthful collection of poems in the courtly love tradition, drawn together by the medieval practice of textual glossary. For others, it is the essential groundwork for *The Divine Comedy* since it sets the living poet in a spiritual relationship with the beatified Beatrice in Heaven. Others again read it as a psychic drama, recounting the Neoplatonic ascent of the soul through love towards spiritual illumination. Recently, it has been viewed more as a treatise on poetry, a manual written by a poet for poets. All these interpretations are possible, and not necessarily conflicting.

For all that, it is a work of startling originality: the first literary autobiography, the first cohesive linking of poems, and the first attempt to write consistently poetic prose. It represents a major shift of focus, one in which the powerful expression of personal experience rather than poetic craftsmanship is at the heart of the poetry. Dante himself described it in this latter light in Canto XXIV of *Purgatory*: "I am one who, when love inspires me, takes note, and as he instructs me, writes it down." In other words, he saw *The New Life* not just as a poetic anthology but as something akin to what we would now call autobiography, and written in a *dolce stil nuovo*, "sweet new style." His judgement is sound.

—Jane McAdoo

NIBELUNGENLIED

German poem of c. 1200, probably composed in Austria; the author is possibly to be linked with the court of Wolfger von Erla, Bishop of Passau, 1191–1204.

PUBLICATIONS

Translations: by A.T. Hatto, 1965; D.G. Mowatt, 1962; Frank G. Ryder, 1962; Robert Lichtenstein, 1992.

*

Bibliography: *The Study of the Nibelungenlied* by Mary Thorp, 1940; *Bibliographie zum Nibelungenlied und zur Klage* by Willy Krogmann and Ulrich Pretzel, 1966; *Nibelungenlied-Studien* by Werner Schroeder, 1968.

Critical Studies: *Das Nibelungenlied: Entstehung und Gestalt* by Friedrich Panzer, 1955; *The Nibelungenlied Today: Its Substance, Essence, and Significance* by Werner A. Mueller, 1962; *Das Nibelungenlied: Stoff, Form, Ethos* by Bert Nagel, 1965; *The Nibelungenlied: An Interpretative Commentary* by D.G. Mowatt and Hugh Sacker, 1967; *Das Nibelungenlied in seiner Zeit* by Friedrich Neumann, 1967; *Nibelungenlied-Studien* by Werner Schröder, 1968; *Das Nibelungenlied: Problem und Gehalt* by Karl Heinz Ihlenburg, 1969; *The Nibelungenlied: A Literary Analysis* by Hugo Bekker, 1971; *The Nibelungenlied: History and Interpretation* by Edward R. Haymes, 1986; *A Preface to the Nibelungenlied* by Theodore M. Andersson, 1987; *Reading the Nibelungenlied* by Neil Thomas, 1995; *A Companion to the Nibelungenlied*, edited by Winder McConnell, 1998.

* * *

The events narrated in the *Nibelungenlied* fall into two distinct halves. In the first half, the hero Siegfried grows up in the Netherlands and moves to the Burgundian court at Worms. Here he eventually wins Kriemhilde, the King's sister, in marriage, but he is then murdered by his hosts. In the second half of the story his widow Kriemhilde marries Attila, moving to what is now Hungary. She induces the Burgundians to visit her from Worms and takes revenge for the death of Siegfried when the Burgundians are eventually massacred to the last man by their Hunnish hosts.

There are various sub-plots. The most important one is the complex theme of Kriemhilde's brother Gunther. He is married to the Icelandic queen Brunhilde, who however continually displays a relentless sexual affinity (presumably of extremely ancient origin in the development of the legend) with Kriemhilde's husband Siegfried.

It is established historical fact that the Burgundians were massacred by the Huns in 437, but Attila was not there and moreover his death in the bed of a woman of Germanic extraction did not take place until 453. In the *Nibelungenlied* she is promoted to his wife and the two events are chronologically reversed: she prompts the massacre of the Burgundians after the marriage. These and numerous similar observations show how the poem distorts history unrecognizably in the 750-year course of its development. It seems that adaptations were frequently made quite consciously in order to suit changing fashions of literary and cultural taste. The factual basis of many features of the poem must of course have been lost beyond redemption.

The version which we possess is itself unrestrained in its radical modernization of the tradition. All the characters exhibit the most exquisite courtly taste, breeding, and self-restraint. The poem tells of many festivals and contests and of much lavish and sensitive hospitality. The warriors are capable of displaying immense courtesy to each other even as they fight to the death. In Book 37 for example Ruediger gives his shield to his enemy Hagen.

Such noble behaviour is not confined in literature to the courtly warriors of the High Middle Ages. In this instance there is no real conflict between the traditional material and the tastes of the era in which our version was composed. But of very great interest are the numerous instances where the tradition proves incompatible with the intentions of the poet. The result is a large number of most interesting inconsistencies and evasions. The poet is reticent, for example, about the provenance of Siegfried's magical powers and about the background to Albrecht the Dwarf and his cloak of invisibility which could play no part in courtly behaviour. In a parallel version a quarrel between two queens is based on one of them dirtying the river water in which the other is washing her hair. The courtly version changes this to an essentially unconvincing argument about who should enter Church first. Furthermore why the quarrel should break out at this time rather than years earlier is never made clear.

There are countless similar weaknesses of construction of recent or less recent origin. One assumes that each one was consciously introduced because of some overriding cultural consideration valid at a given time. The work is of great length and there are parallel versions especially in Norse and German sources which must have diverged from the tradition represented in our version at different times. The events can be identified with historical events sometimes with certainty, sometimes vaguely, and sometimes not at all. These circumstances combine to make the pre-history of the *Nibelungenlied* and its gradual evolution a study of the utmost complexity and fascination.

The work also has a genuine appeal as a work of literature. The poet introduces emotional sensitivity to characters who in the hands of less gifted authors of parallel versions remain the fairly lifeless bearers of famous historical names. For all the myriad inconsistencies of detail, a powerful tragedy is told with a clear linear development in verses of sustained lucidity and power. There is not poetically weak line in the whole poem. There are many striking effects, such as the dead and wounded bodies of the Huns being thrown out of the hall in Book 34. If the poetry lacks the truly striking originality and lyrical beauty of some other contemporary work, the *Nibelungenlied* remains a monumental achievement. It is one of the most impressive and powerful of all medieval epics and preserved for Germany its most important national legends in a form which gives them a prominent place on the stage of world literature.

—G.P. Cubbin

NIGHT FLIGHT (Vol de nuit)
Novel by Antoine de Saint-Exupéry, 1931

Based in large measure on Antoine de Saint-Exupéry's personal experience of the pioneer years of civil aviation, this short novel was first published in 1931 and was awarded the Prix femina. It was dedicated to Didier Daurat, a former World War I air-ace who became director of operations for the Latécoère company in Toulouse. However, the action of the novel centres on Buenos Aires, where Saint-Exupéry served the company both as pilot and as director of operations in his turn. At the start of the novel, regular flights have already been established to and from Patagonia, Chile, and Paraguay and a crucial decision needs to be taken on whether or not to open up a new line to Europe. For the whole enterprise to compete successfully with the established surface freight-services, flights must continue throughout the night. The hazards are formidable: wild weather, savage terrain, primitive machines, and human frailty. The director of operations drives each mission on remorselessly. One of his pilots gets through against the odds, another is lost. In the end, he orders the European testing flight to proceed.

Characterization is not the novel's strong point. The director, Rivière, modelled mainly on Daurat, provides an interesting study of the loneliness and responsibilities of leadership. He is a despotic disciplinarian who insists that everything and everybody must be sacrificed to the success of the cause. Though the cause in this case is noble, one can appreciate why hostile critics have discerned in this aspect of the novel an apologia for fascism. To Rivière are ascribed most of the maxims with which the text is regularly punctuated: "Regulations are like religious rites: they may seem absurd but they make a man of you" or "You should love the men under your command but never tell them so." His pilots and mechanics respond with total loyalty; personal considerations are sacrificed to duty with never a pause or question. The consequence is that compared to Rivière, whom Saint-Exupéry tries, with some success, to humanize, all the other characters are one-dimensional. These include the company's chief inspector, Robineau, who is just as solitary as Rivière, without the rewards of responsibility and power, and whose main consolation, kept well concealed, is geology—"the only thing in life he had found gentle had been stones." The two principal pilots, Pellerin, who survives, and Fabien, who runs out of fuel and crashes over the mountains, are allowed to do little more than strike heroic attitudes. Their wives, whose one role in life is to watch, wait, and dry their tears, are merely sketched in.

The novel is memorable for the evocation of the perils and rewards of the early days of air transport: the insidious beauty of the cloudscapes, sea, and mountain ranges and the reassuring sight of houses and fields far beneath. All these are conveyed with poetic similes of light and dark and a profusion of images associated with the sea. Especially striking among a rich array of impressions of battling against hostile elements is Pellerin's encounter with a cyclone, or the final sight of the doomed Fabien and his radio operator, above the cloud-layer and beneath the stars shortly before they crash to earth: they are likened to tomb robbers, trapped in a vault of glittering treasures, unable to find their way out.

It used to be asserted regularly that Saint-Exupéry was the outstanding novelist of the air just as Conrad is the supreme novelist of the sea. *Night Flight*, which is certainly his most popular and accomplished venture into the world of fiction, does not really substantiate such a claim. The gifts of narrative and of poetic evocation are undoubtedly there but Conrad's awareness of the complexities and ambiguities of human behaviour are conspicuously absent. Because of Saint-Exupéry's preoccupation with the heroic virtues of duty, self-sacrifice, idealized love, and physical courage, a more apposite comparison would be with Froissart's chronicles of chivalry.

—Robert Gibson

THE NINTH TALE OF THE FIFTH DAY OF THE DECAMERON
Story by Giovanni Boccaccio, 1470 (written 1349–1351)

The Ninth Tale of the Fifth Day of *The Decameron* combines two of the leading strands of Giovanni Boccaccio's masterpiece: love and fortune. Fortune, however, is not conceived as the medieval ancilla of God's providence but as the erratically pagan force, and love is not presented in a familiar, fleshy, and saucy manner but rather on the courtly or *stilnovistic* conception on which the story is based: a conception, of course, which belongs not to the time of the writing but to the preceding age, where nine-tenths of the events and characters of all the tales come from.

Boccaccio succeeds in distancing the events of this tale even further from the present by placing them in an atmosphere of legend: in fact, Federigo, the protagonist, is a descendant of the Alberighi, one of the most ancient Florentine families, a family which Dante Alighieri's great-great-grandfather Cacciaguida mentions as noble in *Paradise* (XVI, 89). The name itself evoked for Boccaccio's contemporaries, more than for us, perhaps, a life where courtly love was possible. This chronological and imaginative distance is paralleled by a formal, aesthetic detachment: Filomena, the narrator, declares she will recount one "among the beautiful things" told by Coppo di Borghese Domenichi, who not only was an "excellent person . . . revered more for his manners and virtues than for his nobility of blood" but could also speak "better and in a more orderly way . . . and with more ornate speech than anyone else."

The stage is set for a romance, beautifully told. Federigo, the most accomplished young man in all of Tuscany, falls in love with Monna Giovanna, one of the most beautiful and graceful ladies in Florence. Boccaccio describes both of them as *gentile* (noble) which cannot fail to remind the reader of Guinizelli's and Dante's theories of love, and especially of Guinizelli's famous line, "Al cor gentil repara sempre Amore," the first verse of the *canzone*-manifesto of the *Stilnovo*. We are told that Federigo falls in love, "as often *avviene* (happens)" to a noble heart: there is a sense of fairytale inevitability, of enchantment or curse; only in choosing Monna Giovanna instead of someone else does his choice appear an act of will. In fact, the verb *avvenire* (to happen) will be a refrain in the story. All the main events are introduced by it or by a circumlocution. Fortune dominates the will of man, though a happy love story requires that "voluntary element" by which medieval courtly ladies distinguish marriage from love. Monna Giovanna, "not less chaste than beautiful," cannot be conquered by Federigo's jousts, tourneys, and feasts.

The defining characteristic of the medieval lord with a noble heart is his liberality: largesse implied a disregard for the material and a preference for the lofty. Federigo squanders all his riches for Monna Giovanna save his falcon, "among the best in the world." No longer able to afford city life, he goes to live on his small farm near Florence, where he spends his days hawking, "patiently endur[ing] his poverty." The falcon, a well-known symbol of victory over passion, is a metaphor of Federigo's contemplative life.

From this point in the story, however, Fortune rules. Immediately after learning of Federigo's poverty, we are told "[n]ow it happened" (*[o]ra avvenne*) that Monna Giovanna's husband, near death, left his patrimony to his wife "if it happened" (*se avvenisse*) that their only child died without heir. After his death, Giovanna passes the summer in the Florentine countryside in one of her farms "very close" to Federigo's. So "it happened" (*avvenne*) that her son grew friendly with Federigo and much admired his falcon. When later "it happened" (*avvenne*) that the boy got very sick, he asked his mother for the falcon. After some hesitation, Monna Giovanna decides to go to Federigo, but instead of behaving as a mother whose only child is near death, she presents herself with "womanly charm" (*donnesca piacevolezza*). She says she has come to dine with him to "make amends for the damage he suffered" because of her. Still devoted to her beauty, Federigo's noble answer is in content and style that of a *stitnovistic* poet: she has done him "no damage but so much good that if he was ever worth anything it was owing to her worth and the love he bore it." His speech is so lofty that it includes three hendecasyllables. His lordly largesse induces him to sacrifice his falcon, the only "food worthy such a lady." When their reciprocal misunderstanding is discovered, Federigo sighs that he "shall never know peace of mind again," whereas Mona Giovanna scolds him "for having killed such a falcon to make a meal for a woman," however inwardly she commends his magnanimity.

After her son's death, her brothers push her, since she is "very rich and still young," to remarry. "Remembering Federigo's worthiness and generosity," Monna Giovanna agrees to marry only the very poor Federigo. *Amor vincit omnia*, including Fortune; determinism seems to have been broken by will. In the beginning Federigo chooses Monna Giovanna for her beauty; in the end Monna Giovanna chooses Federigo for his magnanimity. Exceptionally, marriage and love are united in a tale appropriate to the Fifth Day on which "tales are told of those lovers who won happiness after grief and misfortune."

The tale's rich texture is not limited to the enveloping literary tradition of courtly love. As in all of *The Decameron*, one can perceive what critics call Boccaccio's "narrative contemporanization": he imbues his pages with the cultural myths and social structures of his time. In the tale of Federigo and his falcon, contemporaneity is suggested by the name of a Florentine family and more specifically by such routine details as the expense of living in Florence, the particulars of a last will, and the summer customs of Florentine ladies. Nevertheless, one must invoke "realism" cautiously in a tale where the combined lines required to kill off a father and his child are far fewer than those used to kill off a falcon.

At tale's end Federigo has become a *miglior massaio* (a more prudent administrator). Such routine information would be unimaginable in a love story of old. Only in a society of merchants, bankers, and incipient capitalism can it make any sense, although the detail can be read as a parody of courtly love: magnanimous, open-handed, and carefree Federigo becomes just another burgher. This detail also mocks the new ideals of Boccaccio's society. It is an ironic thrust aimed at those of his contemporaries much too interested in materiality, as if to say that the chivalrous ideal and the poetic ideal are no longer possible, just as liberality is no longer possible, and that all that remains is the prudent administration of property.

—Emanuele Licastro

NJÁLS SAGA

Icelandic prose narrative, written anonymously towards the end of the 13th century. One of the *Íslendingasögur* [Icelandic Family Sagas], quasi-historical accounts of leading citizens during and immediately after the period of settlement during the 9th–11th centuries, mixing prose narrative and versified speech.

PUBLICATIONS

Njála, udgivet efter gamle Håndskrifter af Det Kongelige Nordiske Oldskrift-selskab, edited by Konrá Gíslason. 1875; supplementary volume of commentary, with others, 1889; *Brennu-Njáls saga*, edited by Finnur Jónsson, 1908; also edited by Einar Olafur Sveinsson, 1954; as *The Story of Burnt Njal; or, Life in Iceland at the End of the Tenth Century*, translated by George Webbe Dasent, 1861; as *Njál's Saga*, translated by Carl F. Bayerschmidt and Lee M. Hollander, 1955; also translated by Magnus Magnusson and Herman Palsson, 1960.

*

Bibliography: *Bibliography of the Icelandic Sagas and Minor Tales* by Halldór Hermannsson, 1908; *A Bibliography of Skaldic Studies* by Lee M. Hollander, 1958; *Bibliography of Old Norse-Icelandic Studies* by Hans Bekker-Nielsen and Thorkil Damsgaard Olsen, 1964–, and *Old Norse-Icelandic Studies: A Select Bibliography* by Bekker-Nielsen, 1967.

Critical Studies: *The Origin of the Icelandic Family Sagas* by Knut Liestøl, 1930; *The Sagas of the Icelanders* by Halldór Hermannsson, 1935; *Studies in the Manuscript Tradition of Njálssaga*, 1953, and *Njáls saga: A Literary Masterpiece*, 1971, both by Einar Ólafur Sveinsson; *The Sagas of the Icelanders* by Jöhann S. Hannesson, 1957; *The Icelandic Saga* by Peter Hallberg, 1962; *The Icelandic Family Saga: An Analytic Reading* by Theodore M. Andersson, 1967; *Fire and Iron: Critical Approaches to Njáls Saga* by Richard M. Allen, 1971; *"Njáls saga," a Critical Introduction* by Lars Lönnroth, 1976; *Evil and the Earth: The Symbolic Background of Mörðr Valgarðsson in Njáls saga: A Study in Medieval Allegory* by Einar Pálsson, 1994.

* * *

Njáls Saga ranks beside *Egils Saga* and three or four others as one of the major Icelandic Family Sagas or Sagas of Icelanders, anonymous prose narratives written in Iceland mainly in the 13th century, but dealing with events of the century or so following the settlement of Iceland by Scandinavians c. AD 900. *Njáls Saga*, written near the end of the 13th century, is considered by many to be the greatest of the Family Sagas. An attempt may be made to outline its highly complex plot as follows.

After recovering his cousin Unn's dowry from her former husband Hrút, Gunnar becomes the third husband of Hallgerd, Hrút's niece.

Hallgerd's quarrel with Bergthóra, the wife of Gunnar's friend Njál, results in the killing of Thórd, the former fosterparent of Njál's sons. Gunnar's killing of Otkel in a feud initiated by Hallgerd prompts Njál's advice to Gunnar never to kill twice in the same family, advice he is forced to disregard when, after a feud between himself and the brothers-in-law Starkad and Egil, in which the latter is killed, Gunnar kills Otkel's son when he and Starkad's son join forces against him. Banished from Iceland for three years, Gunnar refuses to leave, and is slain by a group including Starkad and his son, and Mörd, Unn's son by her second marriage, whose envy of Gunnar has led him to plot against him from the time of Gunnar's feud with Otkel onwards. Njál's sons now kill Thráin, who had conspired to help a fugitive and brought them under suspicion. Njál, anxious to keep the peace, adopts Thráin's son Höskuld as a foster-son. After the saga has paused to describe Iceland's conversion to Christianity, Njál's sons, egged on by Mörd's slanders, kill the innocent Höskuld. This leads Flosi, the uncle of Höskuld's wife Hildigunn, to take vengeance on Njál's family by burning them to death with the help of a hundred followers. The one survivor of the burning, Njál's son-in-law Kári, starts legal proceedings against the burners, but when fighting breaks out at the Icelandic General Assembly as the result of a technical blunder in Mörd's prosecution of the case against Flosi, Kári shoulders the responsibility of vengeance independently. After he has slain some of the burners and others have fallen in the defeat of the Norsemen by the Irish at Clontarf, Kári and Flosi both make pilgrimages to Rome and are finally reconciled with the marriage of Kári to Hildigunn.

Njáls Saga falls into two parts, each culminating in the death of one of the two main characters, Gunnar and Njál. Manuscript evidence suggests that the second part was supposed to begin with the chapters describing Iceland's conversion. The two parts are linked thematically both by the fact that Gunnar and Njál are close friends, representing respectively, it has been argued, the qualities of *fortitudo* and *sapientia*; and in terms of plot by the father-son relationship between Thráin and Höskuld, since it is essentially their grudge against Thráin in the first part that leads Njál's sons to believe ill of Höskuld in the second.

Until very recently, there has been fairly general agreement among scholars that the conversion of Iceland marks a moral turning-point in the story, whereby the heroic ethic of the blood-feud is replaced by a Christian ethic of mercy and forgiveness. One version of this view is that the structure of *Njáls Saga* is comparable to that of the Bible, with its two parts corresponding to the Old and New Testaments, Höskuld's death to that of Christ, the battle of Clontarf to Armageddon, and the reconciliation of Flosi and Kári to the building of the New Jerusalem. Another view is that Höskuld's death, the burning, Njál's death, and Flosi's pilgrimage reflect a pattern of sin, punishment, expiation, and atonement respectively. In addition to the final reconciliation, the chieftain Sídu-Hall's rejection of compensation for the slaying of his son in the battle, following the legal wrangle at the Assembly, has been singled out as an example of the new Christian spirit.

Recent critics have, however, demonstrated that *Njáls Saga* is both simpler and more complex than this view suggests. Simpler, because it is easier to see Höskuld's death as part of a pattern of feuding and revenge than in terms of one of sin and expiation; and easier to see the reconciliation between Flosi and Kári as owing to a feeling by both that enough killing has been done to satisfy the demands of vengeance rather than as the result of any especially Christian impulse. The saga is more complex because, with the conversion of Iceland, the author seems to introduce an ironic tension between the requirements of Christianity and the persistence of most Icelanders in the bad old ways. This becomes only gradually apparent. At first, it looks as though Christianity is on the side of blood-vengeance, as when Njál's grandson, Ámundi the Blind, receives the miraculous gift of sight for just long enough to kill the slayer of his father. As soon as he has done this, however, he becomes blind again for the rest of his life. What would have happened if he had resisted the temptation to kill? Síðu-Hall's rejection of compensation for his slain son is indeed a handsome gesture, and wins such approval that he ends up receiving four times what is legally due to him—an ironic situation in itself. Its primary function, however seems to be to throw into relief the contrasting attitude of Kári, who is set on vengeance for his own son, slain in the burning. The text of the saga portrays the battle of Clontarf as a victory for the Christian Irish over the mainly pagan Norsemen, whereas a poem quoted at length in the saga just after its description of the battle (and in fact the original of Thomas Gray's *The Fatal Sisters*) presents it as a victory for the Norsemen. This discrepancy effectively underlines the tension in the second part of the saga between Christian and pre-Christian values, leaving the reader with the troubling question of whether Christianity does finally triumph in *Njáls Saga*'s world of ideas.

—Rory McTurk

NO EXIT (Huis clos)
Play by Jean-Paul Sartre, 1944

Jean-Paul Sartre's widely acclaimed one-act play, *No Exit*, was first performed in Paris in 1944 during the German Occupation. The play tells the story of three people who have died and gone to hell, where they are condemned to spend eternity with each other. The work is based on and masterfully illustrates Sartre's philosophy of Existentialism, and is valuable for that reason alone. The play's literary appeal transcends its philosophical implications, however, and its probing into the truths of human existence endows it with a measure of universal appeal.

No Exit is at once modern and traditional. It is especially modern in tone. The language is colloquial, and the characters are ordinary people who exhibit the concerns of their times. They are preoccupied with their roles in society and how society might judge them. One is a coward, another a lesbian, and the third a nymphomaniac, and their personal failures and appetites have led them to commit terrible crimes for which they must now accept responsibility.

Conversely, *No Exit* is linked by both its forms and its themes to traditional French theatre and to the classics. In almost every respect, the play observes the formal rules of 17th-century neo-classical French theatre. Sartre carefully observes the unities of time, place, and action, and to an extent even the *bienséances*, the rules governing the etiquette of the stage. None of the heinous deeds of the condemned characters is shown on stage, and although the language of the play is colloquial, it is in character and without gratuitous vulgarity.

Despite its modern ring, *No Exit* is solidly tied to important literary traditions. By situating the play in an existence beyond death, Sartre's work implicitly brings to mind Virgil's *Aeneid* and Dante's *Inferno*. In these writings, divine intervention in human affairs reminds us of the frailty of human endeavour and of mankind's dependence on the gods. Virgil and Dante construct their respective episodes in the underworld as visions designed to reveal the future. Virgil displays the coming greatness of Rome, and Dante warns us of the threat of damnation and of the future glory of Christian salvation.

Within this tradition, however, Sartre rejects the idea of a guide like Dante's character Virgil, who leads us through the inferno toward a heavenly realm. In Sartre's philosophical hell, we find no explanations of the fate awaiting those who act in bad faith, no guide to lead us on to the next realm (there is no higher realm), and no one to explain the meaning of what we find. There is no hope of redemption, no transcendency, only a tortuous voyage of self-discovery. Each of the three figures who people the staid atmosphere of the play will serve as the executioner and potential "saviour" for the others. Thus, Garcin tortures Inez, a lesbian, by constantly distracting Estelle, a nymphomaniac, with offers of love. So, because of Garcin's presence, she will always remain beyond the reach of Inez's advances. Conversely, Inez needs a woman, Estelle, who because of her preference for Garcin, becomes her torturer instead of her lover. Escape through love is thus rendered impossible for this unhappy trio. There simply is no possible relationship between any two characters that the third person does not destroy.

On the psychological level, the idea of each character as judge and torturer of the others is even more intense. Since Inez has figured out that Garcin is in reality a coward, and not the hero he claims to be, his only "salvation" would be to convince Inez of his heroism. However, since they are now dead, there is nothing he can possibly do to change what he has become—a coward. Hence Garcin's cry of anguish, "If you have faith in me I'm saved."

Garcin, on the other hand, decides ultimately to abandon Estelle to Inez and her caresses; but more importantly, he tortures her by discovering her earthly crimes and subsequently refusing to let her forget them.

Inez is the strongest character in the play. It is she who refuses to accept things as they appear and insists on a full disclosure of the truth. She is more of a realist and therefore the cruellest of the three. Her diabolical laughter at the end of the play characterizes perfectly their fate when she scoffs at Estelle's attempt to murder her by pointing out that they are already dead and destined to remain together for ever.

The dilemma of the dead in *No Exit* has clear existential implications for the living. Sartre's plea is for authenticity, which he sees as an acceptance of our inherent liberty and our decision to become engaged in life so as to affirm that liberty. In order to find the peace which Inez, Estelle, and Garcin so painfully lack, we must act in good faith, or we too could find ourselves locked in an evil world with no exit. That Garcin is a coward is especially important given the fact that the play was first produced during the war-time occupation of France, a hell, as one critic has observed, created by others, hence the oft quoted phrase, "Hell is other people."

Although the underlying philosophical framework of *No Exit* is complex, the play remains pertinent today and is one of the most accessible of Sartre's works.

—Gary M. Godfrey

NOTES FROM THE UNDERGROUND (Zapiski iz podpol'ia)
Prose by Fedor Dostoevskii, 1864

Notes from the Underground, one of Fedor Dostoevskii's most enigmatic and complex works, served as a prelude to his great novels, particularly *Crime and Punishment* and *The Devils*. It has also been claimed as an overture to existentialism, recognized by Nietzsche as the work of a kindred spirit, and acclaimed by, among others, Albert Camus for its prophetic qualities. However, the brunt of the underground man's (and through him Dostoevskii's) polemic is directed against specific phenomena in Russian social and political life: the Romantic dreamers of the 1840s and the social idealists of the 1860s, the latter epitomized by Nikolai Chernyshevskii whose novel *What Is to Be Done?* (*Chto delat'?*) had appeared in the previous year.

The book is in two parts. The first, showing the underground man as an embittered, malicious, and (as he himself declares in his opening sentence) sick paradoxalist, is the part that contains the essence of his thought and presents most clearly the underground mentality as a modern phenomenon. The second part, entitled "Apropos of Sleet," takes us back two decades to the 1840s and shows how the underground man in his youth sought status in a self-destructive way, his head filled with garbled Romantic ideas drawn from books (Schillerism or "all that is beautiful and lofty" in Dostoevskii's shorthand), and seemingly capable only of scandalous self-humiliation and petty debauchery. There is much satire here as well as vividly depicted social embarrassment: the "sleet" in the title was a cliché for literary descriptions of St. Petersburg by the "natural school" writers of the 1840s, and, indeed, it figures in Dostoevskii's own early novel *The Double*; the epigraph, which interrupts the poet Nikolai Nekrasov's self-lacerating lines about poverty and prostitution with "etc. etc.," is especially biting, for it was Nekrasov who had first introduced Dostoevskii to the literary world in 1846; the pathos of the underground man's speech to the noble prostitute Liza, which—like the reader—she easily recognizes as being derived from books rather than the heart, parodies not only Nekrasov but also Chernyshevskii; even the hero's aspiration for new clothes to give himself status seems to recall Gogol's *The Overcoat* (*Shinel'*), although in this case there is no pathos but only malicious self-assertiveness, as he simply wants a smart outfit in which to challenge an officer he imagines (or chooses to imagine) has insulted him.

Part Two is a brilliant portrait of psychological and social inadequacy, a warning against substituting literature for life, and a sour rejection of the ideals of Dostoevskii's youth. It is, however, the first part of *Notes from the Underground* that has made such an impact on modern thought. Beginning memorably, "I am a sick man . . . I am a nasty man. A truly unattractive man. I think there's something wrong with my liver," it comprises an extended dialogue, passionate, sarcastic, paradoxical, with an equally arrogant imaginary interlocutor against whom the underground man rails. *What Is to Be Done?*, the main catalyst for Dostoevskii's work, had created a sensation when it first appeared, being claimed as a "textbook for life." In it Chernyshevskii had advocated self-interest as the mainspring for all human behaviour, preaching "rational egoism" or enlightened self-interest. The underground man's attack centres on this attempt to align egoism with reason, against which he proposes a greater self-interest, "the most advantageous of advantages," which is the freedom to do exactly what one wants even if it means acting against one's own self-interest. The paradox is obvious, but the underground man is convinced that free will is more important than reason. Indeed, the seemingly irrational lies at the basis of all his thought. Living by reason, man is condemned to what Herzen called the ant-heap and what for Dostoevskii was epitomized by the crystal palaces dreamed of by Chernyshevskii's heroine (and reinforced by the one Dostoevskii himself saw without pleasure on his visit to London). For the underground man a crystal palace meant not only a lack of privacy but a perfection that is inhuman and therefore beyond all criticism, even that of a protruded tongue. Symbolizing the kind of rationality that codifies and orders everything, it by implication leaves man no freer than a piano key or organ stop. Perfection admits of no progression, and we are left with dead formulas like $2 \times 2 = 4$ and all the other laws of nature which the underground man boldly seeks to change (proposing the possibility of $2 \times 2 = 5$, for instance). Perfection, after all, is imperfect in that it takes no account of man's fear of perfection. Dostoevskii had intended that the underground man's challenge to nature and, by implication, God would eventually prove his (i.e. modern man's) need for God, but this part of his work (like several other religious passages in Dostoevskii's *oeuvre*) fell foul of the censor and was never restored.

It is obvious that in his extremes of arrogance and insecurity the underground man is afflicted by hyperconsciousness. He is also, as he tells us, ill (with a strong sado-masochistic streak) and can find pleasure and, indeed, significance in, for instance, his own toothache. "I am convinced that man will never renounce real suffering, that is renounce destruction and chaos; for suffering is the sole cause of consciousness." In *Notes from the Underground* morbid consciousness is revealed as the human tragedy. As a social phenomenon and as a literary type the underground man has achieved almost archetypal status.

—Arnold McMillin

OBLOMOV
Novel by Ivan Goncharov, 1859

Ivan Goncharov's *Oblomov* was first published in the literary journal *Notes of the Fatherland* and as a book in 1859. Although Goncharov saw it as the middle part of a trilogy—the others being *A Common Story* and *The Precipice*—which would describe three historical periods in Russian 19th-century life, it is now considered his masterpiece and a classic of the Russian realist school.

Writing about the earlier novel in 1866 Goncharov asked, "Was it not I, as early as the 1840s, who pointed out the need for everyone to work and showed my sympathy for the old uncle who rightly abused his nephew for his utterly despicable ways—his laziness?" Just exactly what work young men should do, though, Goncharov was chary of mentioning. None the less the critic Belinskii hailed *A Common Story*, along with Dostoevskii's *Bednye liudi* (*Poor Folk*), as examples of the way Russian literature should go, and the theme is continued in *Oblomov*.

The young Oblomov was brought up on an estate on the Volga, a thousand miles from Moscow, governed by tradition and lethargy. He is pampered and spoilt, surrounded by serfs who look after his every need. His family have to do nothing. In the chapter "Oblomov's Dream" Goncharov reveals Oblomov's memories of that peaceful, slumbering, overprotected, carefree life with its ample food, steaming samovars, feather beds, aimless conversations, and complete and enjoyable indolence. Later Oblomov goes to university but education has no effect on his temperament or his behaviour patterns. He enters the civil service but retires before he is 30. He can now lounge about all day (it actually takes him a whole chapter to get out of bed), lost in reverie and looked after by his equally lazy manservant Zakhar. He deserts his friends and neglects any social responsibilities. Life is a burden and he hides away from it. Yet he is intelligent, kindhearted, and generally amiable. The aim of life is tranquillity. His acquaintances term his "illness" Oblomovism. That tranquillity is disturbed when he falls in love with Olga, a charming girl who is no fool and has a desire for action. With her strong will and integrity she very briefly stirs Oblomov into almost doing something, but love requires responsibilities and Oblomov has neither the will nor the stamina to continue. Olga goes abroad and meets Stolz, the boyhood friend of Oblomov, whom she eventually marries. Stolz, characteristically half-German, is the complete antithesis of Oblomov. He studies life, travels widely, and gets things done. He is a successful businessman and an incipient capitalist. He is practical, innovative, materialistic, and rational. He is a representative of the new way of life that would rescue Russia from the Oblomovism of the decaying serf-owning society. He is also a new psychological phenomenon. Oblomov lives by his dreams and his imagination, Stolz by experience and facts. Oblomov is an idle gentleman, Stolz an enthusiastic organizer. Oblomov is superstitious, Stolz is rational. Oblomov wants to achieve nothing, Stolz achieves whatever he wants, with one notable exception. He cannot change Oblomov. After a brief illness Oblomov settles down to live with Agafya, a gentle, uneducated, but loving widow who sets about providing for her "gentleman" in the manner of the serfs of his childhood. They eventually marry and have a son, and Oblomov lives out the rest of his life in complete contentment.

Through his depiction of Oblomov Goncharov deprecates the whole way of life of the conservative and patriarchal minor gentry class and suggests that their attitude might well be a national Russian characteristic. The radical critic Dobroliubov set the tone of many future interpretations of the novel in his article "What is Oblomovism?" He argued that the "superfluous men" of the 1830s and 1840s—Pushkin's Onegin, Lermontov's Pechorin, Herzen's Beltov, Turgenev's Rudin, and Gogol's Tentetnikov—were all more or less suffering from Oblomovism. They all shared a penchant for day-dreaming and rationalizing and were all basically passive. Their yearnings bore little relation to everyday life. Although their personalities were not at all identical they were still impractical and socially useless. Oblomov differed from them all, however, in that he did not share their liberal aspirations. He was actually a supporter of serfdom, yet his Oblomovism was a direct result of that system and it affected not only landowners but also the civil service and the rising middle class. Consequently it was a clearly Russian defect. Later critics also suggested that Oblomovism contained a large element of fatalism. The individual can have no influence on current events so a perfect state of complete inactivity leads not only to happiness but also to wisdom. It was to Goncharov's lasting credit that he had so convincingly described the phenomenon.

Although Goncharov remained untouched by the various intellectual and historical currents of his time, he none the less became the chronicler of the real concerns of everyday life. In various matters, he wrote, he shared contemporary opinions about, for example, the emancipation of the peasants, the need for better methods of education, and the harmfulness of all forms of oppression and restrictions on progress. But he never passed through a stage of enthusiasm for utopias created by the socialist ideal of equality, fraternity, and the like. He might well have felt that Russia needed some radical change but he still regretted the passing of the old. While clearly admiring Stolz's qualities the fact that he makes him rather staid and wooden might point to a basic lack of sympathy for him and all he tried to make him represent, whereas the reader, despite—like Stolz and Olga—getting infuriated with Oblomov, takes to him, likes him, follows his uneventful life with interest and even compassion, and is sorry to see him go.

—A.V. Knowles

ODE TO CHARLES FOURIER (Ode à Charles Fourier)
Poem by André Breton, 1947

While in exile in the United States during World War II, André Breton came across the complete works of Charles Fourier, the French social theorist, in a New York bookshop. They were his reading during a journey to Arizona, Nevada, and New Mexico in the summer of 1945. This *Ode* is his response to this particular conjunction of circumstances.

The poem is divided into three movements after the basic manner of the Greek ode, but here two lyrical sections in free verse surround a seemingly more prosaic central part.

The first movement, the first address to Fourier, seeks to relate the state of mankind at the end of World War II to Fourier's early 19th-century philosophy. In the central section, consisting of 12 paragraphs, the balance sheet is drawn up between the Utopian dream and contemporary reality. The final part, the renewed invocation to Fourier, is inspired by Breton's contact with native American civilization and the beauty of the American countryside: the new Eden seems a little less distant.

References to the prospectors in the desert and images from classical mythology (especially Jason's voyage in search of the Golden Fleece) introduce the theme of the quest for gold: this helps to reinforce the dream of a Golden Age, which stems implicitly from the poem's overt invocation and tribute to Fourier.

Breton was fascinated by Fourier's law of ''passionate attraction.'' He could not fail to sympathize with Fourier's condemnation of the ills produced by the system of free economic competition, his disgust for war and armies, his conviction that the human condition in general could not improve before the condition of women was changed for the better. Breton shared Fourier's dislike of the domination of the family unit in modern civilization; he would have been impressed by Fourier's reasoning that the workings of society should be based on a scheme of natural association in which the gratification of individual desires and passions should serve the general good. Breton no doubt admired the absolute quality of Fourier's attack on ''civilization.''

Allusions to Fourier's thought constitute an important element of Breton's poem: Breton employs certain phrases or ideas of Fourier as springboards for his own imagination, or else some aspect of contemporary reality calls to mind observations made by Fourier. Concepts such as the ''gastrosophic régime'' and ''phanerogamous morals'' are incorporated into Breton's scornful survey of a world at war.

The central section, written in prose, rigidly follows Fourier's tableau of the 12 radical passions, divided into three branches of the tree of ''Unityism.'' In the first of these subsections Breton composes five analyses of the passion corresponding to the five senses. In the second subsection Breton evokes friendship, love, ambition and the family (for Fourier the dominant drives of the four ages of man: childhood, youth, maturity, and old age). The third subsection of the central movement is devoted to the three distributive or mechanizing passions: the Cabalist or intriguing passion, the Butterfly or alternative passion (the penchant for variety and contrast), and the Composite, the most beautiful of the passions for Fourier.

In the poem's third and final movement the style of the allusions to Fourier's thought reverts to that of section I, save for a long extract near the end from the third volume of Fourier's *Theory of Universal Unity*, evoking life in a Fourierist *phalanstère* (or community).

The contrast between the harsh contemporary reality and the Utopian dream runs through most of the poem. On the one hand there are references to shortages and the black market, the unscrupulousness and the scandal of the commercial world, the violence and the butchery of war. On the other hand there is the affirmation, near the end of the poem, of Breton's basic optimism:

> Filtering the thirst for greater well-being and maintaining it against all that could make it less pure even if and it is so I considered it proven that the betterment of human fate can be effected only very slowly and fitfully by means of down-to-earth demands and cold calculations the real lever remains

nonetheless the unreasoned belief in the movement towards an edenic future and after all that is also the only leaver of the generations your youth.

(translated by Kenneth White)

This contrast is symbolized to a degree by the change of setting from the Old World of the first movement to the New World of the third. Paris is the focal point of the imagery of the first part. The poem opens with the recollection of the sight one morning in 1937 of Fourier's statue on the Boulevard de Clichy. On its plinth Breton noticed a bunch of violets, placed there, he assumes, by a woman, to commemorate the centenary of the visionary's death. By the final movement there is a step forward in both time and place, as Breton is inspired by the environment in which the *Ode* was written. He employs the gallicized name of The Petrified Forest, a national park in Arizona, as a symbol of the state or culture at that time, and writes other stanzas from the Grand Canyon and Nevada. He realizes that the place where he was writing had once been the Eden of the native peoples: it is from a Hopi *kiva* (or underground chamber) that he draws the inspiration for the final stanzas of the poem, alluding at one stage to the celebrated Snake-Dance.

The poem acquires an epic grandeur partly because Breton resists the temptation to dwell on his personal reasons for the trip to Reno, a quick divorce and remarriage. Thanks to such features as the anaphoric leitmotif ''Parce que'' in the final movement, he is able to compose a persuasive and lyrical demonstration of his conviction that the end of the war could signal the dawn of a new era for mankind and the final word is, significantly, ''liberté'' (freedom).

—Keith Aspley

ODE TO JOY (An die Freude)
Poem by Friedrich von Schiller, published in *Die Thalia*, 1786, (written 1785)

Friedrich von Schiller's *Ode to Joy* celebrates, as the root of a civilized community, precisely that quality which Georg Wilhelm Friedrich Hegel, in his *Lectures on the Philosophy of History*, had deemed a trivial matter: namely, *happiness*. (The German word *Freude* is close to the French term *jouissance*, and has earthier connotations than does its English equivalent ''joy,'' indicating ''pleasure'' and ''delight'' as well as ''near bliss,'' as is evident in Faust's rejoinder to the devil's offer of earthly pleasures in Goethe's *Faust*: ''Von Freud ist nicht die Rede'' [''Pleasure doesn't come into it'']). Contrary to the received image of Schiller, there is no discrepancy here between duty and the joy of living; rather, what we have is a return to the Ancient view of a concurrence of the two. Like Leibniz, Schiller sees joy as embracing the whole of existence; and, like Alexander Pope, he seeks to give poetic form to this inspiring, life-enhancing feeling.

Both Hegel's and Faust's rejection of the kind of joyful happiness Schiller eulogizes in this poem is an accurate indication of the low status which this once great value had sunk to the end of the 18th century. Indeed, throughout the modern era pessimism has grown into the very badge of our modernistic sensibility, the mark of the truly intellectual, alienated, spirit. It is wholly typical of Schiller's philosophical poetry, still radically unfashionable, to take such material and to revalue it by means of what the rhetoricians call an "epideictic" presentation, that is, by a celebration, in the language of public discourse, of shared, communal values which would otherwise go without saying. What Schiller is doing in his *Ode to Joy* can be illustrated by recourse to a sardonic observation on the irresistible decline of common cultural property by his contemporary, G.C. Lichtenberg, who offers a summary of a debate stretching back to the impact made by the printing press:

> One thinker gives birth to the idea, the second lifts it out of the font, the third produces children with it, the fourth visits it on its deathbed, and the fifth buries it.

The thoughts deployed by Schiller in his philosophical poems are not simply commonplaces but—to borrow Lichtenberg's metaphor— "on their deathbed." Schiller shared his age's deep anxiety about the possibilities of cultural continuity: how was the apparent "triviality" of such in reality vital truths to be overcome, so that they would once more seem important and significant? Sharing, too, Dr. Johnson's opinion that "the task of an author is, either to teach what is new, or to recommend known truths," Schiller sets out in his *Ode to Joy* to recommend, to his mind, a disastrously underrated value. Unlike Johnson, Schiller is not content to appeal to the mind alone: if such apparent banalities are to come home to the reader, they must engage feeling; and to do this, they must be made sensuous. For it is the peculiar office of the poet—as Schiller insisted in one of his epigrams ("To the Poet")—to exploit the bodiliness of language, "as lovers use their physical bodies," to give expression to what discursive language cannot possibly capture.

Read, as it unfortunately so often has been, merely as a discursive statement, *Ode to Joy* traces an ever-widening perspective on the cosmic ubiquity of joy. From the apostrophe to its personification as the "daughter of Elysium" in the first strophe, where its revolutionary potential to transcend the conventional dimensions of society is celebrated; to the second, where the quite ordinary experiences of love and friendship are cited as paradigmatic cases of joy, requiring an ability to relate one to another; to the strophe in which the participation of "all creatures," in a realm beyond good and evil, is evoked:

> All drink joy from Mother Nature,
> All she suckled at her breast,
> Good or evil, every creature,
> Follows where her foot has pressed.

In the fourth, a definition of joy is offered as the driving force of life: "the spring of all contriving, / In eternal Nature's plan"; before, in the fifth strophe, we move back, in a way reminiscent of the baroque hymnal poetry to which Schiller owned so much, from the macrocosm to the microcosm, the joyful human experiences of the pursuit of truth, right conduct, and faith. The undisguised Christian morality of the sixth strophe—"the only *aesthetic* religion," as Schiller described it to Goethe in 1797—is integrated as an effect of joyful living, while in the seventh we return to the sheer exuberance of "the joy of sparkling potions / In the goblet's liquid gold." The eighth strophe—now the final one, since Schiller deleted the ninth—recapitulates the whole panoramic survey in an appropriately climactic condensation of language.

This whole, magnificent edifice is given cohesion and coherence not by logical links, nor by a self-consistent pattern of imagery, but by

a masterly rhetorical structure. The poem can perhaps best be seen as built up on a figure of thought, the technical term for which is *expolitio* (the presentation of a central thought by variation of the formulation, especially of subsidiary thoughts). This sense of development-with-return is underlined by the use of a dramatic chorus added to each strophe, one which is repeated over and over again, with more or less minor variations which signal important modulations. Similarly, a well-judged choice of synonyms, antonyms, homonyms and, perhaps most simply effective of all, plain repetitions (sometimes with tiny variations) make for a sense of coherence. The reader, addressed directly by the stirring imperatives and rhetorical questions, is drawn along (and then sent back) through a network of interrelated figures. For example, in the third strophe, the word "Küsse" ("kisses") sends us back to the chorus of the first strophe where the singular "Kuss" stands; and the changes rung in the epithets for "God"—"a loving father" (strophe 1), "the Unknown" (strophe 2), "the creator" (strophe 3), "The good spirit" (strophe 7)—provide an object lesson in the effective use of rhetorical synonymization, here with the purpose of pointing to, and yet avoiding dogmatic limitations of, the mystery of being. With these, and a variety of other techniques, Schiller enacts a semblance in language of that "holy circle" which the final strophe proclaims as the work of joy.

Schiller's talent for the grand manner of high rhetorical style, however, must not blind us to the fact that its function here is to transfigure and (to use a favourite term of his) "ennoble" what is an everyday experience. We are told, in the third strophe, it is true: "E'en the worm was granted pleasure, / Angels see the face of God." But the clear implication of this is that the human condition lies between these extremes, sharing something of both. For Schiller, "ennoblement" retains its alchemical meaning of "enhancement," of raising—without loss—to a higher degree of complexity. The reiteration in the poem of the motif of wine ("that maketh glad the heart of man") is enough to indicate that this no prim exhortation to some other-worldly purity of feeling. Rather, in its revaluation of radiant worldly happiness, it is as radically challenging to many of our modern cultural snobberies as is Nietzsche's summons to "love the earth." This earthiness of the poem is most powerful in the non-discursive, sensuous configurations which Schiller weaves into his rhetorical structures. In strophe 8, for instance, the original German evinces profoundly meaningful patterns that are simply untranslatable:

> Trinken Sanftmut Kannibalen,
> Die Verzweiflung Heldenmut
>
> (Savages drink gentler notions
> While the meek learn to be bold)

The syntactical ambiguity of the second line quoted expresses an exquisitely subtle thought (*something* like "heroism owes as much to despair as despair to heroism"), one amplified by the homeoteleuton play on "*Sanftmut*" and "*Heldenmut*": both seem like species of "courage" ("*Mut*"), a felt-thought utterly lost on the discursive level of translation. Similarly, the figure (again, a syntactical ambiguity—a favourite resource for Schiller) in the opening line of the strophe's chorus: "Den der Sterne Wirbel loben" ("Him whom the stellar eddies praise") can be taken to mean what the literal translation indicates, *and* "den" can also be taken as the definite article of (the singular) "Wirbel," and "loben" as an infinitive-imperative: we then have a wondrous articulation of the pantheistic identification of God and Nature. Or consider how, in the penultimate line of this chorus, the simple device of alliteration—again a much used Schillerian poetic technique—tethers the sublimity of ''God,'' or rather the ''good spirit,'' with the everyday yet powerful symbol of good cheer, the glass: ''Dieses Glas dem guten Geist'' (''This glass to the good spirit'').

As Frank M. Fowler has rightly insisted (in the best edited collection of Schiller's poetry to appear, in English and German, since the war) ''it is the emotional value of . . . ideas that is predominant in his poetry.'' It is surely this quality, of deeply felt thought, that inspired Beethoven's enthusiastic admiration for the poem (which Schiller himself judged harshly, and quite wrongly, in later years), using the first three strophes and the first, third, and fourth choruses in his Ninth Symphony. Doubtless, too, Schiller's poetic exploitation of the idiom of public discourse has also contributed to the success of Beethoven's melody as the ''national anthem'' of a united Europe.

—R.H. Stephenson

ODE TO MICHEL DE L'HOSPITAL (Ode à Michel de l'Hospital)
Poem by Pierre de Ronsard, 1552

Pierre de Ronsard's ''Ode to Michel de l'Hospital'' is an encomium dedicated to the chancellor of the humanist-reformer Marguerite de Navarre, sister of Henri II. In the ''Ode'' Ronsard extols l'Hospital's support of poetry and, indirectly, his reconciliation of Ronsard's attempts to adopt classical genres and styles to French verse with Mellin de Saint-Gelais's polemic defence of conventional medieval forms. But like many of Ronsard's occasional poems, this lyric goes beyond the conferring of praise and, in this case, describes the dynamics of inspired poetic creativity.

Structurally and stylistically, the poem is an imitation of the odes of Pindar (518–438 BC). Divided in to 24 triads of strophe, antistrophe, and epode, the ''Ode'' incorporates elaborate epithets, periphrases, metaphors, and mythological narratives that complicate expression and heighten tone. Unlike Ronsard's less elevated Horatian odes, which are more personal than public, and unlike his Anacreontic odes, which commemorate amorous and convivial experiences, this poem is serious in subject and, through subtle shifts of imagery, intricate in narrative and thematic development. As a member of the Pléiade, Ronsard aspired to actualize the dual aims proposed in Joachim Du Bellay's The Defence and Illustration of the French Language (La Défence et illustration de la langue française, 1549): 1) a renewal and enrichment of the French language through an accommodation of Greek and Latin words and a use of archaisms, neologisms, and sophisticated turns of expression; 2) the replacement of medieval genres (e.g. ballad, rondeau, virelay) with classical and Italian forms (e.g. epigram, epic, sonnet), more refined metrical patterns (e.g. rhyme, hiatus, enjambment), and more cultivated rhetorical tropes and techniques (e.g. sententia, copia, contaminatio). In publishing his Odes, Ronsard attains one of these programmatic aims (II, iv); and, in describing the poetic process, he expands Du Bellay's seminal statements on the source of poetic creativity (II, iii and xi).

The narrative of the ''Ode'' reworks an episode in Hesiod's Theogony (vv. 52–115). As the daughters of Jupiter and Memory, the nine Muses visit their father at a festive gathering. In the presence of the gods, they recount the Gigantomachy (the battle with the giants). Jupiter, victorious in the conflict, is enchanted by the tale, and he

authorizes the Muses to instil divine furor into the first poets. The quality of poetry, however, deteriorates from the lyrics of inspired singers to the verse of human poets who depend upon the resources of natural talent and learned techniques. Finally, poetry becomes the product of versifiers who, totally reliant upon acquired skills, slavishly imitate the lyrics of others. Public ignorance, moreover, stifles creativity. Defeated and discouraged, the Muses reascend to heaven. Fortunately, the Fates imbue Michel de l'Hospital with justice and compassion; and, through his courage and initiative, he promotes a renewal of inspired poetic creativity, and assures the Muses of a respected role and position in 16th-century France.

Through the combining of classical narrative and contemporary events, Ronsard stresses the significance of Michel de l'Hospital's support of the agenda set forth in Du Bellay's manifesto. But, in 1549, Pléiade poets continued to define the poetic process in ways consistent with established views of imitation. Poetry is a craft; and, even in the preface to these Odes (1550), Ronsard sees the poet as a copier of accepted literary examples. Although his selection of ancient genres and styles as appropriate models of imitation departed from contemporary practice, the integration of classical themes and structures into his verse conformed to a mimetic procedure advanced by the later 15th-century Rhétoriqueurs and their followers. Creativity, though, is neither an eclectic mingling nor a liberal translation of other works. Rather, the statement ''the Poet is born, the Orator is made,'' that Thomas Sebillet cites in his Art poétique français (1548) calls for the theorization of a process of inspired poetic creativity; and Ronsard prepares a response in the ''Ode to Michel de l'Hospital.''

A description of the nature and function of the ''Ode'' leads to a definition of the artistic process in neo-platonic terms and to an elevation of the social place and role of the practising poet. As Homer suggests in his characterization of the blind bard Demodocus (Odyssey, VIII, 479–81), the inspired poet is a passive agent of the gods who transmits divine insight to man in intelligible form. Plato develops the idea which, reworked in Marsilio Ficino's 15th-century translations of, and commentaries on, Plato's dialogues, enables Ronsard to present the operations of enthusiasm. Like the rhetor in Plato's Ion, Ronsard's inspired poet mediates unconsciously between divine vision and earthly reality, participating in a magnetic chain extending from the gods to man (II. 409–20). Ronsard's poet-seer, moreover, resembles Plato's winged charioteer who, in the Phaedrus (243e-245c), is infused and impelled by the prophetic, mystic, poetic, and amatory frenzies (425–32). As intermediaries between heaven and earth, the Muses are both mythological representations of this phenomenon and demonic sprits who, in forming links in a chain, inhabit the poet's mind, convey divine insight, and assure an accurate and artistic expression of truth. Like Orpheus, Ronsard's inspired poet is a prophet whose verse serves society and humanity.

Throughout his theoretical writings, Ronsard affirms the significance and viability of divine furor, Pontus de Tyard, in his Solitaire Premier (First Solitaire), 1552, published a few months before the ''Ode,'' also applies neoplatonic concepts to artistic creativity, and other humanists (e.g. Jacques Peletier du Mans and Louis Le Caron) endorse Ronsard's ideas on poetic inspiration. Later, in his Abrégé de l'art poétique français, Ronsard defines poetry as ''théologie allégorique'' (''allegorical theology''), a term that recalls the role of the Muses in the inspired poetic process. But the poet-seer depicted in the ''Ode'' is ultimately an ideal that poses two problems to be resolved later: firstly, the reconciliation of poetic inspiration of poetic inspiration and natural talent; secondly, the use of dialectical reasoning in the writing process. Despite these subsequent refinements, the

"Ode" demonstrates an achievement of one of the objectives of the Pléiade and presents a picture of the poet as a seer, and conveyer to men, of wisdom and morality.

—Donald Gilman

ODES BOOK I, POEM 5
Poem by Horace, 23 BC

The fifth Ode in Horace's first book is written in four four-line stanzas, each with two asclepiads, followed by a pherecratean and a glyconic. It deals with two erotic themes: the pursuit by an inexperienced boy of a girl who already knows how to play the game, and the retirement of a battered older man from the sport of love. The poem opens with a question:

What delicate boy, covered with liquid scents,
importunes you, Pyrrha, in this pleasant grotto,
amid the many roses?

This sets the scene, by establishing the inexperienced ardour of the youth and the worldly-wise attitude of Pyrrha, whose Greek name, meaning "yellow-haired," marks her as a recognizable Horatian type: one of those rather callous females who toy with men's affections, like Lydia in I.8 or Barine in II.8. Another question follows: "For whom do you bind back your hair, / prepared with tasteful simplicity?"

There is a contrast between the boy, who has drenched himself in perfume, sparing no expense in his efforts, and Pyrrha's careful, yet simple, preparations. The expectation naturally arises that the girl's unadorned and innocent appearance will be matched by her behaviour, but, as the poet muses on the scene, his thoughts take a different turn. The remainder of the poem is one long sentence, in which the poet's thoughts ramble over the relationship between the young couple and his own erotic experiences. It begins with *heu*, which expresses pity for the boy who is soon to be disappointed and disillusioned:

Alas, how often he will lament that she has broken faith,
and that the gods have turned against him,
and will look at the waters harsh with black winds,
in wondering innocence.

This introduces the notion of the pursuit of love as similar to sailing on the sea: as far as the average Roman was concerned, an action fraught with danger and unpredictability. The implication is that the youth will have to endure Pyrrha's frequent temper tantrums, and will soon find himself facing a storm which he, as a novice sailor, will be unable to handle. The notorious propensity of the sea to change from shimmering calm to raging tempest parallels Pyrrha's emotional mutability. In the third stanza, the boy is given the epithet *credulus*, meaning "naive" or "credulous," as he "enjoys" the "golden" Pyrrha, hoping that she will always be available and loving. He does not, however, know about "the deceitful breeze" which picks up the metaphor of the stormy sea in the previous stanza. When Pyrrha is "golden" she is like a sunny day at sea, but conditions can quickly change.

The poem concludes with a change of perspective as the poet focuses on his own situation and experiences:

The temple wall with its votive tablet
indicates that I have hung up my
soaked clothes, as a dedication
to the powerful god of the sea.

This alludes to the practice of placing a tablet on the wall of a temple to commemorate an escape from great danger, and also to the fact that shipwrecked sailors who survived sometimes made an offering of their clothes to the gods. Venus was connected with the sea, since in one version of the myth she was born from the foam of the waves, and so the idea of hanging up clothes has a double meaning here. The ode thus moves from boyish innocence to adult wisdom. The poet is the old, experienced sailor who knows the ways of the sea, that is, of women and, perhaps, of Pyrrha in particular. Having been shipwrecked in his time, as indicated by the soaked clothes, the poet has now apparently retired from seafaring. Yet he still has an interest in observing Pyrrha with her young lover and perhaps, like an old sea-dog, yearns for the excitement of past adventures. The poem also shifts scenes from Pyrrha's "grotto" of roses to a temple, expanding the theme of love from the particular to the general. The goddess of love is an important deity, who must be treated with respect. One cannot help thinking in this context of the cave where Venus brought Aeneas and Dido together during a storm in Virgil's *Aeneid* IV. There, too, the unwary Aeneas found a woman impossible to control.

Horace's poem draws upon several elements of the Greek and Alexandrian literary tradition: for instance, the comparison of women to the sea derives from the patriarchal bias of ancient myths which associate the female principle with the irrational and untamed aspects of the natural world. Semonides of Amorgos, who wrote vituperatively of women's supposed animalistic features, also utilized the sea comparison. Others made the connection with the goddess of love. The figure of Pyrrha is a stereotype, as is the innocent youth who pursues her. The assumption throughout the poem is that such a woman is difficult to control but that her beauty entitles men to attempt to control her. The retirement from erotic pursuits was also a commonplace in Greek and Roman poetry.

As is often the case with Horace, several words are ambiguous and repay detailed study; for instance, the boy is described as *gracilis*, which suggests a slim and fragile build, but can also have a pejorative sense of "thin" or "puny." There is, perhaps, the hint of a suggestion that Pyrrha ought not to waste her time on a mere boy who does not know what he is doing. It can also mean "graceful," which would be nicely ironic in this context, since the youth is obviously not a practised lover and has covered himself with perfume. Likewise, the youth hopes that Pyrrha will always be *vacua*, which means "available" or "empty"; again this serves to emphasize the ideology of possession, control, and even violence which permeates a superficially innocuous poem.

—David H.J. Larmour

ODES BOOK IV, POEM 7
Poem by Horace, 13 BC

The seventh ode of Horace's fourth book has seven stanzas of four lines each and is written in a variant of the Archilochean metre, with a dactylic hexameter followed by a dactylic trimeter catalectic. Each stanza is semantically complete although connected with the one that precedes it. The poem opens with an evocation of the countryside after the spring thaw:

> The snows have fled, now the grass returns to the fields
> and the leaves to the trees;
> the earth goes through its changes, and subsiding rivers
> flow past the banks.

The mention of the earth going through its changes introduces the idea of the cycle of life and death, which is later elaborated. In the second stanza, the poet turns to the mythological universe, with a picture of the naked Graces and Nymphs ''daring'' to come out and perform their dances, now that the weather has turned warm. This is a typical scene of the joyfulness of Spring, described elsewhere by Horace (Odes I.4 and IV.12), But then comes a reminder of the passage of time and the inevitable cycle:

> Lest you hope this goes on for ever, the year offers a warning,
> and also the hour which carries off the nurturing day.

This admonitory tone is continued in the third stanza, in which we see the winter cold being warmed by the spring zephyrs, then the summer ''trampling on'' the spring, to be followed by ''the fruit-bearing autumn'' with its crops, and soon ''sluggish winter rushes back.'' The seasons are personified in anticipation of the emphasis on human death in the latter half of the poem. Horace also shows considerable virtuosity in introducing the seasons in different ways.

The first three stanzas take the traditional type of poem about the joys of Spring and turn it into a more reflective and philosophical piece on the meaning of the cycle of the seasons. There is a sense of inevitability about the movement from birth to death. The first stanza opens with snow, and the third stanza closes with Winter. In the fourth stanza, the focus shifts to the legendary kings of Rome:

> When we sink down
> to where dutiful Aeneas, where wealthy Tullus and Ancus are,
> we are dust and shadow.

The reference to Aeneas is possibly an allusion to Virgil's *Aeneid*; Horace uses the epithet *pius* (dutiful), which is one of the most frequently used Virgilian adjectives for Aeneas. The theme of death now comes to the fore. The fifth stanza opens with a direct question to the reader: ''Who knows if the gods above will add tomorrow's time / to today's total?'' This echoes the well-known Horatian and Epicurean theme of living for the day, expressed most memorably by the phrase *carpe diem* (seize the day) in Ode I.11.

In the sixth stanza, the poet returns to the issue of death raised in the fourth stanza:

> When once you have gone down and Minos has made his
> shining judgement of you,
> then, Torquatus, neither lineage nor eloquence, nor
> dutifulness, will bring you back.

Death, therefore, is inevitable and terribly final. Torquatus was probably one of Horace's friends, perhaps an orator from a noble family. The mention of dutifulness (*pietas*) again alludes to Aeneas who, in the sixth book of Virgil's epic, went down to Hades to meet his father and came back to the world of the living. He could only achieve this, however, with the aid of the gods. For the rest of humankind, there is no way back. The last stanza restates this using more mythological examples: Diana would free ''chaste Hippolytus'' from the ''infernal darkness'' if she could, but she does not have the power. Likewise, Theseus cannot break the ''Lethaean chains'' of his dear friend Pirithous. Hippolytus was devoted to Diana as goddess of chastity and was driven to death by Theseus, who thought he had made sexual advances to his wife. Theseus went down to Hades with Pirithous in an attempt to carry off Proserpina, wife of Pluto; they were imprisoned, but Theseus was rescued by Hercules and taken back to the world above. Now, however, he has finally died, and cannot do anything to help his companion. Pirithous has, in fact, forgotten him (Lethe was the river of Forgetfulness). Thus, the *pietas* of Theseus is wasted. Hippolytus' devotion to virginity contrasts starkly with the reputation of Theseus and Pirithous for sexual aggression but, in death, Horace seems to suggest, vices and virtues do not really matter.

In the first part of the poem, the cycle of the seasons suggests movement, while the latter part emphasizes the finality and bondage of death. The penultimate word of the ode is ''chains'' (*vincula*), emphasizing that there is no escape from death. There is some ambiguity about the poem, however, as is often the case with Horace: the cycle of the seasons and of nature in general recalls the Stoic doctrine of the cycle of the universe, which is continually consumed by fire and then recreated. The mention of Aeneas similarly recalls the transmigration of souls explained in Virgil's sixth book. There is, then, some suggestion of an eventual ''escape'' from death's chains; this is particularly likely because of the mention of Lethe at the end of the poem: Aeneas learns from his father that the souls of the dead are purified for a thousand years, after which they drink from the river Lethe before returning to the upper world. Death is perhaps to be seen, therefore, as a period of immobility, paralleling the ''sluggish'' Winter mentioned at the end of the third stanza. The general pessimism of the poem is thus tempered to a certain extent in a reading which is cognizant of the Virgilian allusions.

—David H.J. Larmour

THE ODYSSEY
Poem by Homer, c. 720 BC

Composed around 720 BC, not long after *The Iliad* and perhaps by the same poet, *The Odyssey* neatly complements its predecessor. It focuses upon peace, the household, ingenuity, and domestic love, rather than war, society, heroism, romantic and companionate love. Its fairyland symbols of universal peril and enchantment contrast with *The Iliad*'s status symbols, the prizes of honour of this world. It is mythic and comic where *The Iliad* is tragic.

The narrative begins in the 20th year after Odysseus departed for Troy; he is far from his home in Ithaca, perhaps dead, so far as his family knows. His wife Penelope and his son Telemachus are besieged by 108 suitors for her hand who spend each day in Odysseus' palace devouring its livestock and wine. Athena (goddess of self-realization), perceiving Telemachus' helplessness, descends to inspire him to move towards manhood, summon the assembly, urge the suitors to disperse, then travel to Nestor in Pylos and Menelaus in

Sparta for news of Odysseus. Just before Telemachus' return, the narrative shifts to Odysseus, imprisoned amidst sensual delights on the nymph Calypso's island. He has turned down her offer of immortality, and longs to go home. Zeus, through Hermes the messenger, persuades Calypso to release him, and he crosses the sea to the Phaeacians, where Princess Nausicaa finds him and leads him to her father's palace. Received warmly, Odysseus tells the story of his earlier adventures, including the Cyclops, Circe, Hades, the Sirens, and Scylla and Charybdis.

The Phaeacians return Odysseus to Ithaca where, disguised, he encounters his faithful swineherd Eumaeus, and reveals himself to Telemachus. He goes up to the city and his palace, and begs from the suitors amidst their abuse. When they have left for the night, Odysseus, still disguised, talks with Penelope, who announces that next morning she will set up an archery contest (using the great bow that Odysseus left behind) to decide who is to win her hand. Telemachus tries to string the bow, shows that he can do it, but obeys his father's signal not to. After the suitors make their futile attempts, Odysseus succeeds, and turns the bow upon them. Helped by Athena, Telemachus, Eumaeus, and another loyal servant, he kills them all. Penelope then tests him by tricking him into revealing his knowledge that their bed was built upon a treetrunk, and husband and wife are rejoined.

All three main characters are depicted in depth. Telemachus is a likeable but immature youth, who grows up with the aid of Athena, Nestor, Menelaus, Eumaeus, and eventually Odysseus. His attempt to string the bow (and thus win Penelope for himself) is aborted by his father, to whose designs Telemachus must subordinate himself on the path to manhood. Penelope is subtle; she loves Odysseus, yet must keep the suitors interested in case he is dead, postponing remarriage until she knows the truth, while enjoying their attentions and accumulating gifts to compensate for their ravages upon livestock and cellar. Earlier she promised to make a choice when she finished weaving a shroud for Odysseus's elderly father, Laertes. Caught out undoing by night what she had woven by day, she finished the task, but instead of choosing she arranges the archery contest. Her strategy is double: if, as she half-suspects, the beggar in the palace is really Odysseus, he will string the bow and have a weapon against the suitors; if he is not, then probably neither he nor the suitors will succeed, and she can continue to postpone the choice. Penelope's games with the suitors are the erotic and intellectual counterpart to Odysseus' adventures in fairyland; and the ingenuity she displays in the bed-trick, outwitting the outwitter, makes her his perfect match and mate.

Odysseus too is subtle. Intensely curious, highly courageous, he thoroughly enjoys many of the adventures that postpone his return. But he has perceived a deeper truth by the time he refuses Calypso's offer of immortal life with her and elects to go home: human destiny, male as well as female, is ultimately domestic. (His choice is more poignant because as he has visited Hades, where the ghost of Achilles told him that any form of existence is preferable to death, non-being). Athena as goddess of self-realization stands by Odysseus' side when he is fighting at Troy to restore Menelaus' violated household, and when he fights on Ithaca to restore his own; but during his adventures, as he self-indulgently explores his self's limits, she is absent.

The varieties of meanings of Odysseus' name enrich his complexity: he is the giver and receiver of pain, the hater and the hated, the one who leads forth. For instance, he blinds the Cyclops, giving the giant pain and arousing his hatred, but allowing Odysseus to lead his companions forth from the Cyclops' cave to safety. Before this, Odysseus tells the Cyclops that his name is ''No-one.'' (The Greek word for ''No-one'' has the slightly hidden meaning, ''ingenuity'', one of Odysseus' chief characteristics.) As a result, when the Cyclops turns to his neighbours for help, he cries, ''No-one is killing me.'' Naturally they respond, ''Since no one is assaulting you, you must be mad.'' But then Odysseus reveals his ''proper'' name, ''Odysseus,'' and the Cyclops is able to call down Poseidon's wrath upon him. As No-one (the elusive, indefinite one) Odysseus is secure, but by putting his signature to the deed, he evokes the magical and divine forces that he must struggle against for the next ten years.

The poem's main theme, that human destiny is domestic, is greatly enlarged by the symbolism of the mythic world of Odysseus' adventures. Odysseus becomes an everyman, facing universal perils—Circe (erotic enchantment and bestial enslavement), the Sirens (deadly lure or artistic beauty), Scylla and Charybdis (lose part or lose all). Penelope in turn becomes everywoman confronted by the perils and pleasures of masculine desire, and all of us are seen caught between the competing needs for adventure (meeting risks and satisfying curiosity) and for home and family.

—William Merritt Sale

OEDIPUS
Play by Seneca, c. 48 BC

The best-known Greek tragedy is doubtless Sophocles' *Oedipus the King*. The story of Oedipus' attempt to escape his destiny is well-known. Told by an oracle that he will murder his father and marry his mother, Oedipus flees Corinth, the land of his supposed father, King Polybus. He does not know that he is, in fact, the son of Laius, King of Thebes. In his flight he meets and murders an old man upon a narrow road, after quarrelling about who has the right of way. He arrives at Thebes, victorious over a monster (the Sphinx) and becomes king, wedding Jocasta, his own mother. Years later, the truth begins inevitably to emerge. A plague infects the land, and oracles blame and denounce the slayer of the earlier King Laius. Sophocles shapes this relentlessly ironic story with masterful dramatic aplomb. Oedipus the hero volunteers to be the ''detective'' to search out and punish the offender. He is a well-meaning but firm ruler, touchy, temperamental, overly sure of himself. In scene after scene he meets with others, flares up at any contradiction or restraint, and slowly but surely proceeds to hunt himself down. When he ''cracks'' the case, becoming the successful public investigator, he simultaneously becomes, as he discovers to his horror, the abject criminal.

After the terrible shock of recognition, Oedipus, in another fit of anger, blinds himself (he does not wish to ''see'' or to face the facts of his case) and subjects himself to self-imposed exile. Like many a scapegoat, he is ousted but, unlike most, he is courageous: he insists upon heaping the blame upon himself and then enduring expulsion. Jocasta, his wife and mother, cannot endure the horror and the shame, and hangs herself. Oedipus claims that now he ''sees,'' although he is blind. He has indeed learned much about his origins and even about his conduct and nature, but there remain large stretches of his personality that he cannot fathom; indeed, his quick temper, his rashness, his remorseless drive are both the cause of his crime and the means to its detection. He is emblematic of flawed greatness. Sophocles shaped the plot of this drama relentlessly, and the play was an exemplary study of regal diligence and corrosive zeal. Aristotle, in the

Poetics, speaks of the *Oedipus Rex* more often than any other play. In short, it was rightly held, over the centuries, to be a model and a classic.

The Sophoclean *Oedipus* proves a difficult act to follow; critics use it as a yardstick for measuring ancient drama. Hence, Seneca the philosopher shows daring by even attempting another version. Almost inevitably, critics measure and compare the two; and many a study has pronounced that Seneca's version is unlike its forebear, and therefore not a traditional classic.

Although *Oedipus* is an early Senecan play (there are signs of immaturity in its composition), it is none the less accomplished. For Seneca's Oedipus is a creature of modern metropolitan ages. He is a far cry from a heroic, self-willed, self-reliant, or well-assured leader; rather, he continually reveals his ineptitude, and insecurity. He repeatedly engages in hand-wringing, is crippled by self-doubt and paralysed by feelings of guilt, foreboding, and dread. He suffers from despair and wishes that he were dead. In some ways he resembles that avatar of the modern condition, Prince Hamlet, for he is unprepared and incapable of confronting reality and of coming to terms with events. The chorus, too, is feeble, dour, and despairing.

Seneca adds to this pathetic situation a murky atmosphere in which Thebes is surrounded by grey clouds of smoke from the cremation of victims of the plague. In addition, the play details minutely the rites of divination and necromancy; these spirits, signs, and omens dramatize the play's "something-is-rotten-in-the-state-of-Thebes" theme. The drama is virtually a tone-poem of lamentation, stressing a world gone awry, a place where *Angst*, an evil fate, and the unnatural prevail. Like a hunted creature, Oedipus is tremblingly forced to discover his identity and is overwhelmed with horror at the discovery. He asks, like Dr. Faustus, for the Earth to gape and split open, and for lowest Tartarus to hide him from upper earth, from his shame, and from the sight of men. Then, in a fit of raging madness, King Oedipus tears out his eyes and peers uncomprehendingly at the world through empty, bleeding sockets. Nevertheless, he insists that he has "insight." Intransigently, he claims that he alone is guilty, that justice demands he pay the price for his sins. He serves simultaneously as prosecutor, judge, jury, criminal, and executioner. Thus, Oedipus claims to have righted the "balance," to have instituted "justice," and to have paid his "debt."

Yet, as the Messenger observes in reporting these dire events, Oedipus' fury is excessive, his wild ire exercised in vain. No "balance" of any sort can be restored when law and order and self-control are thrown to the winds. By a dreadful irony, Oedipus has missed the mark throughout this play. His fear and trembling reveal that he is no confident hero; neither do the last scenes of fury and rampage rectify that imbalance.

Seneca's drama is a fable of modern times, where classic order is absent from the scene. His unheroic characters rage or tremble, temporize or suddenly explode, but they have lost all sense of community, of calm, of self-assurance or self-restraint.

—Anna Lydia Motto & John R. Clark

OEDIPUS AT COLONUS (Oedipus Coloneus)
Play by Sophocles, 401 BC

Oedipus at Colonus is a singular play, eluding categories. Out of a remarkably wide variety of contrasting moods and incidents, it generates a sense of complex balance and harmony. This balance is revelatory and perhaps apocalyptic, almost a vision of all of life's patterns. A useful comparison would be with a late play of Shakespeare, such as *The Tempest*.

Oedipus at Colonus seems to be Sophocles' final work, written shortly before his death in 406 BC and produced five years later. It too has been read biographically, as a poetic last will and testament. Sophocles brings Oedipus, also old and on the edge of death, to Colonus, his own birthplace, from which Oedipus looks back on his life before departing it. Yet this elegiac note, often picked up by the chorus, is only one aspect of the play.

Sophocles had already used the Theban myth for the subject matter of his *Antigone* and *Oedipus the King*. As the dates suggest, the three are not a trilogy, though *Oedipus at Colonus* follows on fairly well from *Oedipus the King*, and draws on both previous tragedies for aspects of character and plot. This use of myth does not limit thematic concerns. For myth is neither detached from reality nor the product of the unconscious mind as early 20th-century scholars argued, but rather an interpretation and evaluation of the society that produces it. Nor would the myth have provided a constraining master text; myths tended to exist in variant forms, which tragedians commonly altered for their dramatic ends. Judging by the few other references associating Oedipus with Colonus, Sophocles may have had only a very slight tradition either to follow or to diverge from.

The plot is made up of two antagonistic strands. One is centred on Oedipus' journey, and progresses linearly, focusing on the future. Oedipus, now a blind and squalid old man, led by his daughter Antigone, arrives at Colonus. There he gains Athenian protection from its king, Theseus, and then leaves the stage to go to his "most marvellous" death. For he dies a *heros*: a man more than mortal yet not divine, whose influence over men's affairs will extend after his death, helping the land which possesses his grave and hurting its enemies.

His death is more than his own triumph, however. It is also the culmination of the play's exploration of the relationship between man and the gods, and, as part of that relationship, of divine justice. Moreover, it completes Athens' glorification, begun with the use of Theseus as a symbol of the contemporary city's (idealized) political practices. For it is Athens that Oedipus' grave will protect. The city needed such protection; it was facing defeat and destruction in the Peloponnesian war. By the time *Oedipus at Colonus* was produced, that defeat had already come; Athens' power and glory was past, only the stories of it, like Oedipus' influence, living on.

The second strand of the plot interrupts the linear progress of the first, as the past repeatedly attempts to keep Oedipus in the present. The chorus, to begin with, has a role, but more significant are the subsequent arrivals of Creon and then Polynices, both of whom need Oedipus' help for their present interests. Creon is a marvellous depiction of politicking hypocrisy (which is seen particularly as non-Athenian state-craft), the instant dislike he generates being another proof of Sophocles' power of characterization. Frequently in the play, appearance—whether physical or verbal—is far from reality. Polynices is less vicious, simply self-justifying. Begging for his father Oedipus' blessing, he is execrated, in poetry of a terrible violence. Such poetry is the reverse of the chorus's earlier tenderly lyrical description of the sacred grove at Colonus, famous as the greatest nature poem in ancient Greek. The range and power of Sophocles' poetry is plain, but it can be complex and subtle too; for though the language is simple and elegantly clear, its meanings are often multiple, ambivalences playing constantly across the words.

The Polynices scene has often been taken as the prime example of the play's episodic and incoherent dramatic structure. Though there is no single unifying dramatic action, the two strands of the plot are instead given structural unity by the use of parallelism. Oedipus opens the play by arriving at Colonus, and closes it by departing from there. Ismene, Oedipus' other daughter, arrives after the opening, and Polynices arrives before the close. And at the centre of the play Oedipus meets first Theseus and then Creon, the rulers of Athens and Thebes.

The stagecraft this structure allows is impressive. Entrances and exits produce considerable dramatic impact. When Oedipus enters the stage, he is led by Antigone. But in leaving he walks for the first time unaided, leading others, and his inner transformation is made concrete.

Finally, it is the linear strand of the plot that dominates. For the past's irruptions are all overcome. Oedipus' reversal, in fact, is the opposite to that expected of tragedy; he begins fallen and ends raised. Yet he still *suffers* this reversal. Throughout the play he is racked, finding rest then being denied it. After Theseus leaves, Oedipus seems to have found peace, but then Creon arrives and abducts his daughters; the blind old man can only hear Antigone's cries receding, and begs her to touch him. At moments, *Colonus* has that hallmark of tragedy, the audience's wish for an end to the pain.

But even when Oedipus dies, the play does not close. His release is his daughter's sorrow, as they look to a future of suffering. With typically Sophoclean irony, Oedipus' curse on Polynices will lead to his beloved Antigone being entombed alive. Yet at the end we are still left with a sense of mystery, grandeur, and awe at Oedipus' death. The blind old man, after all his sufferings and because of his endurance, eventually becomes something rich and strange. So there is hope, that most human and painful of faiths.

—John Lee

OEDIPUS THE KING (Oedipus Tyrannus)
Play by Sophocles, 430 BC

Oedipus the King is perhaps the best known of any Greek play. Lauded by Aristotle as the example of all that is best in tragedy, it appealed no less to Freud for its way of demonstrating through myth the most basic of all relationships, those between a child and its parents. The story was one that was tackled by all three of the Greek tragedians: Aeschylus, Sophocles, and Euripides. Only the Sophocles play survives, though episodes from later stages of the saga can be found in Aeschylus' *Seven Against Thebes,* Euripides' *The Phoenician Women (Phoenissae),* and Sophocles' own *Antigone,* performed several years before *Oedipus the King,* and *Oedipus at Colonus,* which was produced posthumously in Athens in 401 BC.

The unusual structure of *Oedipus the King* gives one reason for its abiding popularity. All the significant action has already taken place before the play begins. What the audience witnesses is the process of Oedipus uncovering the truth about his background, in order to justify the trust placed in him by the people of Thebes. Though of equal status with Jocasta and Creon, it is Oedipus who makes the decisions. He is the *turannos,* an unconstitutional ruler, a position which, as the revelation of his parentage will demonstrate ironically, he holds by right as the son of the former king. The truth is first hinted at by the blind prophet Teiresias and gradually becomes apparent to all the other characters, including his wife and mother Jocasta, until Oedipus can deny it no longer. Jocasta hangs herself and Oedipus puts out his eyes with the pin of her brooch. Only when he has become physically as blind as Teiresias does Oedipus appreciate the enormity of the situation.

Much of the comment the play has excited revolves around the extent to which Oedipus can be held responsible for what happens to him. His past is gradually unveiled during the course of the play in a series of revelations. Before he was born, his father Laius consulted the oracle at Delphi about his wife Jocasta's childlessness. He was informed that, were he and Jocasta to have a child, that child would kill its father. In Sophocles' version of the story, this was the only omen that Laius received. When Jocasta did become pregnant and had a child, Laius had it abandoned.

As inevitably happens to abandoned children in drama, the baby was rescued. A shepherd gave it to the king and queen of Corinth who brought up Oedipus, "swollen-foot," as their own child. Taunted by a drunk at a party about his parentage, Oedipus himself went to consult the oracle. Apollo's message was graver this time. Oedipus would marry his mother and kill his father. Determined to escape such a horrendous fate, Oedipus headed away from Corinth, never to return. On the way he met and killed an old man who tried to ride him down. A little later he encountered the sphinx that had been terrorizing Thebes and destroyed it by answering its riddle. He arrived in Thebes to be rewarded with the hand of Jocasta, the recently widowed queen, and an equal share in the government of the city with her and her brother Creon. Only several years later and after fathering four children on Jocasta, his own mother, did an outbreak of plague result in Oedipus sending Creon on a third visit to the oracle. Apollo's answer to Creon, that the killer of Laius must be found, begins the process which leads to the unmasking of Oedipus as the murderer of his father and the husband of his own mother. Sophocles' play deals simply with that process of unmasking, revealing all the other details of the story in retrospective dialogue.

One of the features of Sophocles' handling of the play is that he refrains from suggesting that Oedipus is simply an unfortunate who has been cursed by Apollo, or by Fate, for no good reason. The courage with which he searches to find the truth of what he has done is part of Oedipus' heroic stature, but he is much more than a worm wriggling on the end of the god's fishing-line. Apollo, far from condemning Oedipus to an arbitrary fate, has been seen by some to be offering to Oedipus, as he does to Laius and to Jocasta, a warning which they wilfully choose to ignore. As the god of prophecy, Apollo already knows the outline of the feature, not because he dictates it, but because he is not confined to seeing human life as a linear progression. It is no fault of Apollo that Oedipus tries to avoid what Apollo tells him is going to happen, at every stage making things worse by cursing the murderer of Laius and eventually blinding himself.

Part of the play's tragic power resides in human failing, *hamartia,* constantly underpinning any sense of the inevitable. Laius flaunts Apollo by fathering a child. The man who is meant to expose the child takes pity on it. The king and queen of Corinth decline to tell Oedipus of his origins. Oedipus is so stricken at the thought of marrying his mother that he never thinks twice before killing an older man who stands in his way, even though the second part of the oracle told him he would kill his father. The one survivor from that encounter on the road announces, back in Thebes, that the king's party was overcome, not by a single young man, but by "robbers." Jocasta, never warned that she would marry her son, is an innocent victim of incest, but did contribute to her child's survival. Oedipus, who always looks to the future, not the past, cannot see the truth until after it has become plain to everyone else.

This twin comment on the arbitrariness of fate and the manner in which individual character contributes to that fate is what makes *Oedipus the King* one of the true reference points in the drama and in all literature. The composite picture of a man who appears to have everything, and by doing nothing beyond seeking truth, loses everything, touches a universal anxiety. We pity Oedipus, as Freud tells us, because, at some level, his fate could be our own.

—J. Michael Walton

OLYMPIAN ONE
Ode by Pindar, c. 476 BC (?)

Olympian One is justly regarded as Pindar's most famous ode. Written in celebration of the 476 BC victory in the Olympic horse race of Hieron, tyrant of Syracuse, the poem was placed first in the collection of Pindar's *epinicia* assembled by Alexandrian editors. This position reflects not only the historical prominence of Hieron, but also the grandeur and scope of the ode itself. Its splendid opening was parodied by Pindar's contemporary and sometime rival Bacchylides; "Pelops' ivory shoulder," the starting point of its mythological narrative, became synonymous with Pindaric epinician for Roman poets such as Virgil.

The opening lines have long been admired as some of Pindar's most memorable:

> Best blessing of all is water,
> And gold like a fiery flame gleaming at night,
> Supreme amidst the pride of lordly wealth.
> But if you seek, beloved heart,
> To sing of the great Games,
> Then neither in the lonely firmament
> By day, look for another star more bright
> And gladdening than the sun, nor can we praise
> a greater contest than Olympia.

(translated by Geoff S. Conway)

The series of linked superlatives builds up to the praise of Olympia as the most glorious of athletic contests, even as water is pre-eminent among elements, gold among wealth, the sun among stars. The strophe proceeds to name Zeus and Hieron, who are by implication comparably pre-eminent among gods and men. The emphasis on being the best in a given domain embodies the competitive spirit of Greek athletics and society, as well as the ethos of aristocratic superiority with which Pindar's poetry is ideologically invested. The poem returns to this theme at the very end, declaring Hieron's kingship as the greatest destiny for any mortal and Pindar's celebration of such kings as his own claim to pre-eminence among poets.

There is, however, as always in Pindar, a cautionary side to his encomiastic rhetoric. "Further seek not to glimpse." Man's prosperity is always contingent on the continued favour of the gods. As in many of Pindar's odes, the bulk of Olympian One consists of an extended mythological narrative with morally paradigmatic overtones. The myth centres on the destiny of the hero Pelops, in whose

honour the Olympic games were instituted. Pelops did benefit from continued divine favour, but his paradigm is countered by the negative exemplum of his father Tantalus, who abused the gods' hospitality and was punished. Hieron is thus offered a choice of ethical paradigms —to be a tyrant like Tantalus, with presumptuous aspirations to immortality, or to be a hero like Pelops, duly acknowledging his reliance on divine patronage.

One of the most interesting aspects of Olympian One is its self-conscious mythological revisionism. Pindar explicitly rejects the traditional version of the Pelops story, which was the basis for preliminary sacrifices opening the ceremonies at Olympia. Although he begins to relate a story about the boy chopped into a stew for the gods, his shoulder consumed by Demeter, and his reconstitution in a cauldron with a gleaming new ivory shoulder, Pindar abruptly cuts himself short and declares the whole tale a malicious lie. He provides us with a corrected version in which Poseidon did not fall in love with the boy after the latter emerged reconstituted from the cauldron, but merely when seeing him at a feast; Tantalus' crime was not cooking his son in a stew, but stealing the gods' nectar and ambrosia and distributing it to his mortal friends. The rest of Pindar's story, however, appears to concur with other versions: Poseidon keeps Pelops with him on Olympus as a cupbearer and boy-favourite, Pelops returns to Earth and competes in a deadly chariot race against Oenomaus for the hand of his daughter Hippodameia, and defeats him with the aid of winged horses granted by Poseidon.

Pindar's expressed reason for rejecting the old story of the cannibal feast is to avoid imputing such a disgrace to the gods. This purification of the myth can be understood as a response to moral criticism of the Homeric gods, which seems to have become common with Xenophanes and other thinkers of the 6th century. However, it may also owe something to the radical Orphic critique of traditional Greek sacrifice: the Orphics rejected all animal slaughter and consumption of meat on the ground that it was a form of cannibalism, reenacting the Titans' primeval dismemberment and eating of the child Dionysus Zagreus. Pindar's substitution of the story about Tantalus' theft of nectar and ambrosia is modelled on Hesiod's story about Prometheus' theft of fire, which was also part of a complex of myths concerning the origins of sacrifice and the proper relations between men and gods.

As Pindar presents it, the Pelops myth has an improved narrative unity and even features a pattern familiar to many myths and rituals of adolescent initiation: first, Pelops' violent *separation* from his childhood home through rape by Poseidon; second, a period of *isolation* from humanity while he serves as a cupbearer to the gods; and third, *re-integration* with humanity through his competition in the chariot race, proving his full manhood by defeating the older father-figure Oenomaus. Pindar even enfolds within his narrative the rejected version of the myth, explaining it as a vicious rumour circulated by envious neighbours when Pelops first disappeared. But by rejecting this story as falsehood and poetic embroidery, Pindar challenges an important etiological myth at the core of the Olympic festival and in so doing elevates the power of poetry, including his own, to mould men's understanding:

> For Beauty, goddess who fashions
> All things that lovely are for mortal men,
> Her shower of glory many a time enriched
> That which deserves no firm belief
> To be a trusted tale.

—Thomas K. Hubbard

ON OLD AGE (De senectute)
Prose by Cicero, 44 BC

Cicero's *On Old Age* has been read for centuries. Among the many philosophical works by Cicero, the book has enjoyed a popularity equal to that of his *On Duties* (*De officiis*) and his *On Friendship* (*De amicitia*). The work itself was finished in the early days of 44 BC and belongs to the last years of Cicero's life, a period from 46 to 43 BC, known as his "marvellous years" (*anni mirabiles*) in which he wrote most of his philosophical works. It, like *On Friendship*, is focused upon a single theme, in this case the coming of age. The work was cast in a dialogue format patterned on that developed by Plato. It consists of a conversation invented by Cicero between Cato the Elder, then 84 years old, and a pair of younger visitors, Laelius and Scipio Aemilianus, each an actual figure in the Roman republic. The scene is a villa owned by Cato in some unspecified locale and the year is 150 BC, one year before Cato in fact died. After a brief introduction in which Cicero informs his best friend Atticus that not only has he written something on old age for Atticus but has also dedicated it to him, the remaining 81 paragraphs made up a series of gracefully posed questions designed to elicit long speeches full of advice from Cato. For the two younger men, about 35 or 36 years of age, have come to find out from Cato by what means they can most "easily sustain the weight of increasing years." Cato then examines and refutes in order four reasons why old age appears to be unhappy: that it takes us away from active pursuits, that it weakens our bodies, that it deprives us of almost all physical pleasures, and that it is not far from death. Although the work owes much to the various literary formats that popular philosophy assumed during the Hellenistic period such as the diatribe, how much or by what specific source Cicero was influenced is not known. Out of the Greek canon, scholars have perceived the influence of Plato, Xenophon, Aristotle, Aristo of Chios, Heraclides Ponticus, and Theophrastus. Among the Latin writers, one influence seems to have been Varro.

In *On Old Age*, as in Cicero's other philosophical writings, a clear effort has been made to emphasize the "Romanness" of things. Certain Roman values are therefore readily apparent such as the traditional respect the conservative Romans had for their elders. On a personal level, the energy used by Cicero to express a complex Greek idea in terms of the Roman experience was for him an act of intellectual "imperialism" by which he and his fellow citizens could benefit. Whether Cicero at age 62 actually believed the sentiments he committed to paper can never be determined with certainty. That Cicero, who was experiencing terrible trouble in both his private and public life during those years, might have steadied himself with thoughts of Cato, would not be surprising. Cato the Elder had long been something of a hero to Cicero. Cato represented a man born into the middle class, like Cicero, who had risen through his own industry and his own genius to the apex of political success in Rome, the consulship. Although Cicero in no way attempted to present a verbatim imitation of Cato's speech or vocabulary, he "set the stage" accurately. Cicero was thoroughly acquainted with works by and about Cato and his knowledge is revealed not only through this work, but through his many references to Cato in his other works.

The evergreen appeal of *On Old Age* is based upon its charming style and humanistic outlook. Its noble effort to dignify and find value in the hardships of old age and in the inevitability of death has comforted many readers experiencing their own senectude. Notable figures like Dante, Petrarch, Erasmus, Chaucer, and Milton read, quoted, and/or recommended the book.

On Old Age was also among the first works of Greco-Roman literature to be printed after Fust and Schoeffer's famous edition of Cicero's *On Duties* and the *Paradoxes of the Stoics* (*De officiis et Paradoxa stoicorum*) at Mainz in 1465. *On Old Age* was soon printed separately about 1467 by Ulrich Zel in Cologne and again two years later in 1469 as a part of a group that included *On Duties*, the *Paradoxes of the Stoics*, *On Friendship*, and *The Dream of Scipio* (*Somnium Scipionis*) at Rome by Ulrich Han. This is all the more significant when one realizes that Virgil's *Aeneid* was not published until late 1469 or early 1479 in Rome. Translations of the book appeared earlier than the printed editions. In 1405 Laurent de Premierfait (d. 1418), a priest from Troyes, translated it into French for an uncle of Charles the Wise. Drawn from this French version was the first translation into English which was printed in 1481 by William Caxton at Westminster. This edition, one that included a translation of *On Friendship* and a declamation on the nature of true nobility, foreshadowed the advent of Renaissance interest in the work. In 1517, a translation into Greek by Theodore Gaza (c. 1400–95), a professor of Greek at Ferrara and Rome, was published posthumously in Italy. *On Old Age* also made bibliographical history in America as the first translation of any work by Cicero into "American" English. This was done by the bibliophile James Logan (1674–1751) of Philadelphia and was printed on the presses of Benjamin Franklin in 1744.

With the eclipse in general of the classical curriculum this century, the readership of *On Old Age* has greatly diminished. However, as modern technology extends the human lifespan and the population of the elderly increases, this work, over 2,000 years old, seems more timely than ever. Perhaps it will find a new audience.

—Michele Valerie Ronnick

ON THE COMMONWEALTH (De republica)
Prose by Cicero, c. 51 BC

On the Commonwealth is a work in six books, one of Cicero's three political treatises, the others being *On the Laws* and *On Duties*. These works are closely connected in that they all deal with the complexities of contemporary Roman politics and the search for the ideal state and statesman. The titles *On the Commonwealth* and *On the Laws* are indicative of the influence of Plato, but Cicero's observations are based on his own considerable practical experience and are less concerned with abstract political theorizing than with perfecting the already advanced Roman constitution. *On the Commonwealth* accepts the prevailing order of the Roman Republican system, and assumes that the political crisis in Cicero's day is the fault of bad politicians rather than failing political structures.

The treatise takes the form of a debate on the nature of the "ideal state" between the eminent statesman Scipio Aemilianus and his companions, set in the year 129 BC, the year of Scipio's death. The subject matter and the dialogue format both recall Plato's *Republic*. In Book I, the guests arrive amid a discussion of the sighting of a mysterious second sun. This leads into a conversation about the political situation in Rome after the murder of the reformer Tiberius Gracchus by Senatorial forces in 133 BC. Scipio opens the discussion of the ideal constitution by defining the state as a group of people brought together by community of interest and a shared notion of

Law. The stress on legal institutions rather than ethical relationships marks a Roman rather than a Greek approach to the political question. Scipio goes on to list the three basic forms of government—monarchy, aristocracy, and democracy—and their degenerated forms—tyranny, plutocracy, and mob rule—and follows Polybius in presenting the "mixed constitution" as the ideal state. This is exemplified by the Roman system, in which the Consuls constitute the monarchic element, the Senate the aristocratic element, and the Assemblies the democratic element. This is a typically conservative formulation, combined with a notion of absolute "justice" in opposition to the will of the popular majority. Book II, indeed, after a historical survey of Rome and some discussion of the characteristics of the ideal statesman (the text is fragmentary), concludes with the statement that "a state is made harmonious . . . by a fair and reasonable blending of the upper, middle and lower classes . . . and such concord can never be brought about without the assistance of justice." From his other writings and speeches, it is clear that Cicero's "concord" means cooperation between the landowning Senatorial class and the Equestrian order, who made their money from business activities, with both these groups in turn being supported by the "good" citizens (those who own property). This alliance must then defend the state against extremist demagogues, who foment revolution among the discontented.

In Book III, one of the interlocutors puts forward the utilitarian view that government must be based on the interests of the ruler (i.e. injustice), but another counters with the traditional Platonic argument that justice is an absolute virtue, necessary in any government which is to be "good." Stoic influence is apparent in the idea of justice being innate in humankind and derived from the gods. Book IV is concerned with the class structure, the maintenance of moral standards and public order, and the education of the young. The ideal class structure again appears to be the Roman version, with Plato's Guardians finding their equivalent in the Senators and Equites. Both Spartan and Platonic communism are rejected: it is the state's duty to protect the rights of property owners, and a community of wives and children subverts the moral order.

Book V (again very fragmentary), after some generic remarks on the ancient Roman virtues, develops the idea of the "Director" of the state. This is Cicero's ideal statesman, who is just and wise, who protects the constitution, and who aims at both the happiness of the citizens and the strength and prosperity of the state. Exactly what Cicero had in mind here has been the subject of much debate. Possibly it is a plea for someone like Augustus to intervene and establish a Principate; alternatively, it may be a variation of the Stoic "wise man" who is supremely qualified to guide the state by personal leadership. He may well have had specific individuals like Scipio, Pompey, or even himself in mind. In Book VI, the treatise reaches an emotional climax, concluding with the famous "Dream of Scipio" in which Scipio tells the others of a dream he had 20 years earlier. This is a vision, modelled somewhat on the Platonic myth of Er, of the eternal life after death. It is startlingly different in tone from what has preceded, with its strange, otherworldly explanation of the nine circles of the universe, the music of the spheres, and the divine rewards of the good statesman. The dream ends with a typically Roman expression of patriotic duty: the best activities are those which promote the well-being of the native land.

On the Commonwealth exemplifies the best aspects of the Ciceronian Latin prose style. The dialogue flows easily in the first five books, and the more ornate language of the "Dream of Scipio" heightens the effect of the revelation of eternal life, which has been compared in emotional power to the visions of St. John and Dante. Cicero also

manages to adapt the Latin language to essentially Greek philosophical subjects: no easy task in itself, as Lucretius discovered. *On the Commonwealth* comes out of the Greek philosophical and political tradition and attempts to graft significant elements of it onto the Roman experience. This is sometimes highly successful; for example, the implications of the idea of universal law expressed in *On the Commonwealth* are far-reaching: if all citizens are subject to one law, they are all, in some sense, equal. Moreover, authority arises from the collective power of the populace, since the state and the laws ultimately belong to it. There are nevertheless certain gaps and tensions in the treatise: for instance, little attention is paid to the administration of Roman provinces, and the often tense relationship between the central government and the proconsuls with their large armies. Similarly, the material conditions of the poor and their exploitation by the rich are not considered as causes of social disorder. The stress on the afterlife at the end of the work trivializes the political difficulties of the here and now.

Ultimately, *On the Commonwealth* looks backward, rather than forward: it is a reaction to the inevitable political changes in the last decades of the Roman Republic, not a realistic prescription for dealing with them. Hence, perhaps, the use of the long-dead Scipio as the main speaker, and the concluding flight into the comforting vision of another, less turbulent, world.

—David H.J. Larmour

ON THE CROWN (De corona)
Prose by Demosthenes, 330 BC

The speech *On the Crown* is the last surviving speech by the Athenian orator and statesman Demosthenes; it is also one of his longest, and since ancient times has been regarded as his masterpiece. The title refers to the proposal of a supporter of Demosthenes, Ctesiphon, that the orator should be awarded a crown (i.e. an honorific wreath) in recognition of all that he had done for Athens. This proposal was attacked by Demosthenes' enemy Aeschines, who indicted Ctesiphon for unconstitutional action on a number of formal grounds but more fundamentally because, Aeschines maintained, Demosthenes' entire career had been disastrous for Athens. (Aeschines' prosecution speech survives in full, so that the pair of speeches offers a rare opportunity to measure two major orators against each other.) Consequently, in defending Ctesiphon, Demosthenes was also presenting a defence of himself and his past policy; and on the basis that the best form of defence is attack, he devotes extensive parts of his speech to a vitriolic indictment of Aeschines, whose policy of support for Philip of Macedon Demosthenes brands as treachery.

By 330 BC, when the case was brought to trial, Demosthenes' past policy of unswerving opposition to Philip of Macedon might well have seemed disastrous. Philip had crushed Athens and the other resisting Greek forces at the battle of Chaeronea (338 BC), and in 336 BC, when the Greeks sought to shake off Macedonian rule after Philip's death, the military brilliance of his heir Alexander the Great had made short work of this revolt. Although the Macedonian yoke was not as severe as those which later conquerors of Greece were to impose, the loss of independence was a bitter blow, and especially to democratic Athens, once mistress of an empire of her own. Demosthenes makes much of the Greek ideals of freedom in his speech, and one reason that it has been so highly valued is this stress on the best aspects of Athenian history and Greek ideals. In the perspective of history, *On the Crown* reads as an epitaph of Greek freedom. The eloquence of the orator has often dazzled even the sceptical historian, who can recognize that Demosthenes' pan-Hellenism is pursued in Athens' interests and may even suspect that there was more to be said on Philip's side than our sources allow us to see.

The structure and strategy of the speech are complex, but a few key points can be summarized. Demosthenes deals lightly and swiftly with the formal charges of irregularity, where Aeschines' case was strong. Instead he concentrates on his own record as a statesman, repeatedly contrasting it with Aeschines'. He surveys his career in phases, culminating in the role he, Demosthenes, had played in marshalling Greek resistance prior to Chaeronea (in particular by securing an alliance between Athens and Thebes). Throughout, Demosthenes presents himself as representing the highest and noblest ideals of Athens, whereas Aeschines stands for everything that is self-serving, inconsistent, and base. One of the least attractive aspects of the speech to modern eyes (though commonplace in Greek courts) is the persistent invective concerning Aeschines' upbringing and background: according to Demosthenes, he was of low birth and sordid profession (he was originally an actor), unable to live up to the high standards demanded of Athenian statesmen. It is enlightening, though depressing, to see how much weight such arguments were expected to carry even in a democratic society.

More admirable and more memorable is the heroic image which Demosthenes paints of Athens' past, and the lesson he draws from that past to vindicate the policy which, under his leadership, she has pursued against the invader from Macedon. In one crucial passage (192–210) he even insists that, despite defeat, they made no mistake; even if they had marched to Chaeronea knowing they were to be defeated, they would have been right to do so. Only thus could they sustain their record as the champions of liberty in the 5th-century wars against Persia:

> It cannot be, it cannot be that you erred, men of Athens, when you took upon yourselves to fight the battle for the liberty and security of all. Witness those of your ancestors who bore the brunt of the danger at Marathon, those who held the line at Plataea, those who fought on shipboard in the waters of Salamis or off Artemisium, and many other gallant men who lie now in the public tombs—all of whom the city deemed worthy of that same honour, Aeschines, and not just the successful and the victorious.

Much admired by ancient critics, and memorably discussed in Longinus' *On the Sublime* (chapter 16), this passage shows Demosthenes at his best: these are the tones which were imitated by Cicero in his *Philippics* and by Churchill in his war speeches.

Demosthenes won his case so resoundingly that Aeschines was unable to secure even a fifth of the votes, and was therefore obliged by Athenian law to pay a fine or go into exile. He chose the latter, and was said to have ended up teaching oratory on Rhodes. A number of anecdotes tell of his using his own speech and that of his enemy in teaching: when his students marvelled that he had lost the case, he wryly told them "You would not be so surprised if you could have heard the beast making his response."

—R.B. Rutherford

ON THE POWER OF THE IMAGINATION (De la Force de l'imagination)
Prose by Michel de Montaigne, 1572

In his chapter "To philosophize is to learn to die" ("Que philosopher c'est apprendre à mourir") (Book I, 20), Michel de Montaigne tells us that although he is not melancholy by nature, he is prone to morbid reverie ("*songe-creux*" in the original). In fact, intimations of mortality had troubled him from an early age. Like most of his contemporaries, he was deeply suspicious of the imaginative faculty and of its power to disrupt men's thoughts and lives. Robert Burton, in *The Anatomy of Melancholy* (1621), would warn against being solitary and idle, a condition that inevitably allows the mind to wander. As he prepared to embark on a life of contemplation, Montaigne must have worried about the dangers of letting his (by his own admission very fertile) imagination off the leash. For, as Richard Sayce pointed out, Montaigne took the view that imagination, like narrow-mindedness, is an obstacle to knowledge and self-awareness, causing us to "distort and falsify our vision of things." But Montaigne was fascinated by the unusual and by all manifestations of irrationality, and it was inevitable that he should be drawn to the subject of the unsoundness of the mind.

"On the Power of the Imagination" is relatively short (less than 6,000 words) and typically anecdotal. The chapter opens with a Latin quotation to the effect that a strong imagination produces the event, and it allows the author to launch into a description of his own hypochondria. The sight of a sick person quickly brings on in him the same symptoms, he confides, so much so that he would willingly "live only among healthy and cheerful people." He amusingly claims that it is enough to hear someone with a chronic cough to feel that he has himself an irritated throat and lungs, but the serious point he wishes to convey is made from the start: he is the victim of a powerful (and by definition wayward) imagination. He admits to being one of those who is *renversez* ("knocked over") by it. This chapter is, then, less a list of case-histories drawn up by an objective amateur psychologist than a sufferer's attempt to describe and to analyse his own condition. He delves into his reading and personal experience to give us examples of mind over matter. You can almost imagine him sitting round with friends after a good supper and asking them whether they had heard the one about the woman who wrongly thought she had swallowed a pin with her bread and who was cured by some clever chap who made her vomit and then discreetly slipped a bent pin onto what she had thrown up, with the result that she immediately felt better. And then there was the one about the gentleman who played a practical joke on his guests by telling them some time after the event that the pie they had eaten in his house had contained a cat. The prank backfired badly, for one of the ladies who had so enjoyed his hospitality fell into a faint, from which she never recovered. Even animals, Montaigne notes, "are subject to the power of the imagination," witness the dogs who pine away after the death of their owners. He also comments on the habit (which we must all have observed at some time or another) that dogs have of yapping and wriggling in their sleep. Who knows what dogs dream of?

But this chapter is more than a catalogue of psychosomatic disturbances and quaint occurrences. Montaigne widens the subject to include "miracles, visions, enchantments" and such like, and suggests that they are essentially the result of strong imaginations acting upon gullible souls. Many ordinary people, he writes, have been brainwashed to the point where they "think they see what they do not.'' One can imagine what he would have made of corn-circles or UFOs. Or, more to the point, of the religious movements that trap the unwary. At the end of the chapter he is clearly warning his reader against dogmatism and blind trust in so-called expert opinion. This is true Montaigne territory; he is for flexibility, openness, and clarity but only too aware of the limitations of the human intellect and powers of understanding. He goes so far as to imply that men of ''exquisite and exact conscience and prudence'' such as theologians and philosophers, can never really be trusted with giving us the facts.

This chapter is, then, something of an apology and a declaration of good faith: ''I do not consciously falsify one jot; for my knowledge I cannot answer.'' It is also one of the author's first attempts at complete frankness. In his introductory remarks to the reader at the beginning of the *Essays*, he says that he will paint his self-portrait in his *''forme naifve''* (''natural form'') in so far as public decency allows. At another time and in another place he would gladly have ''painted [himself] completely and quite naked.'' In this chapter on the power of the imagination he describes how the workings of the mind can interrupt the natural functioning of the body, commenting in some detail on cures for impotence and on the general unruliness of the male member, which pits its ''authority so powerfully against our will.'' Other parts of the body, too, cannot be controlled by reason or will-power. Is the imagination not just another of our unreliable senses? Can we be sure of anything, even ourselves? To try (*essayer*) to make sense of things is all we can hope to do, using our imaginations and our critical faculties but also being aware of their idiosyncrasies and shortcomings.

—Michael Freeman

ON THE SUBLIME (Peri hypsous)

Greek literary treatise, written by an unknown author known as ''Longinus.'' In the 19th century attributed to the Greek rhetorician and philosopher Cassius Longinus (AD 213–73), but internal evidence points to composition date during 1st century AD. Part of it is lost; about two-thirds survives. An examination of literary greatness, it was written as a reply to, and an improvement on, an earlier literary treatise of the 1st century BC by rhetorician Caecilius of Calacte.

PUBLICATIONS

On the Sublime, edited by A.O. Prickard. 1906; revised edition, 1946; also edited by D.A. Russell, 1964; translated by J. Hall, 1652; also translated by W. Smith, 1739; W. Rhys Roberts, 1899, reprinted 1987; A.O. Prickard, 1906; W.H. Fyfe [Loeb Edition], in *Demetrius on Style*, 1927; G.M.A. Gruber, 1957; D.A. Russell, 1966; as *A Treatise on the Sublime*, translated by Frank Granger, 1935; as *On Sublimity*, translated by D.A. Russell, 1965.

*

Critical Studies: *Longinus and English Criticism* by Thomas R. Henn, 1934; *The Sublime* by S.H. Monk, 1935; *Boileau and Longinus* by J. Brody, 1958; *Aristotle's Theory of Poetry and Drama, With Chapters on Plato and Longinus* by P.S. Shastri, 1963.

* * *

Longinus is the name given to the unknown author of *On the Sublime*, a Greek critical treatise of the 1st century AD. Tradition has established this title while time has rendered it misleading. For the sublime, in its literary sense, has come to denote since the 18th century ''a style expressing lofty ideas in a grand and elevated manner.'' But the subject of Longinus' treatise is far wider, though it sometimes coincides with this sense. Longinus seeks to identify not a style, but an effect: he attempts to analyse sublime moments of tragedy, comedy, lyric poetry, epic, history, oratory, and philosophy.

Longinus defines sublimity variously. This is not a result of vagueness or incoherence, but rather a function of his argument that sublimity is not codifiable; it is not an effect produced by certain elements which can be distinguished and then reproduced. Rather it is to an extent non-rational, like a force of nature, tearing everything up ''like a whirlwind.'' Longinus' initial definition, a kind of working premise for the exploration of one aspect of the sublime, holds sublimity to be ''the source of distinction of the very greatest poets and prose writers.'' It distinguishes at the same time as it irresistibly produces wonder and astonishment, and can be found in a single line. Yet it is not ephemeral; for sublimity is unforgettably striking and leads us into thought—it is a productive, questioning ecstasy. The more such moments are read, the more they are appreciated.

Longinus is here discussing sublimity mainly in terms of its impact on its audience's mind. Elsewhere he explores this interrelation beyond mere effect, in a critical approach we might think of as reader-response or psychological. Sublimity is so satisfying because it fulfils the audience's creative aspirations, recreating within them the sense of the artist's achievement and glory.

Moreover, sublimity is morally improving since it is ''the echo of a noble mind.'' Here, Longinus defines sublimity in terms of an expressive relationship with its author's mind. Sublime moments express the personality and genius of the poet. But the presence of the adjective ''noble'' is essential, for the only morally upright mind can ring out. Thus the echoes heard by the reader are those calling to nobility and truth.

In the context of English literature, such an expressive theory of literary creation is associated with the Romantic movement, and this movement was indebted to Longinus. For though he had little contemporary impact, *On the Sublime* had considerable European literary influence for about 150 years after Boileau's 1674 French translation. Ironically, it was the Romantic movement which also ended Longinus' influence, focusing on another strand of his treatise.

For alongside the private aspect of *On the Sublime*—Longinus' discussion of the intimate, and basically readerly, triangular relationship between author, work, and audience—lies a public aspect. This becomes manifest in Longinus' concern that his treatise should be ''useful to public men'' who are competent in speaking. Under this aspect, the treatise may be considered as a rhetorical handbook. Rhetoric must here be understood in its Hellenistic (and Elizabethan) sense, that is, not simply as the ornamentation of language but as a system for the appreciation and creation of literature, whose ultimate aim is to teach the art of persuasion.

This public aspect, with its pedagogic aim and concomitant objective, non-moral treatment of literary composition as a transmittable skill, is naturally antagonistic to the private and moralizing aspect of the treatise. Indeed, these two aspects derive from mutually exclusive traditions of criticism (Aristotelian and Platonic respectively).

On the Sublime's complicated relationship with both critical traditions has led it to be considered the culmination of ancient literary criticism. Certainly, the interplay between the traditions enriches both. Most importantly, Longinus sees sublimity not simply as the result of either innate genius or learned art, but as a complex question of the combination of the two. Hence he proceeds from asking ''What is sublimity?'' to ask, ''How can it be achieved?'' Being non-codifiable, it cannot be simply taught. Instead Longinus' argument proceeds by citing and analysing particular passages, under the rationale that through appreciation may be gained the literary judgement to recognize true sublimity. He is the first critic to root his criticism firmly in specific textual examples.

Recognition of sublimity facilitates its production, teaching us both the faults that destroy sublimity and the qualities that produce it. In listing the five qualities, Longinus puts forward his sense of the balance between genius and art. Two qualities—that of conceiving great thoughts and that of uniting thoughts with powerful emotion—can at most be nurtured. Emotion, however, may not be necessary; this is one of the few areas of uncertainty in Longinus' argument, probably the result of one of seven lacunae in the text. Later, Longinus argues that these qualities may also be acquired from great writers, whose genius acts as an ''oracular cavern'' whose ''effluences flow . . . into the minds of their imitators.''

The other three qualities are the more codifiable, rhetorical sources of sublimity: figures of thought and speech, noble diction, and correct composition. On their own they can produce only faultless works; and Longinus prefers flawed genius to correct mediocrity. Yet the treatise's rhetorical aspects have also been extended by the interplay of traditions. For figures are not simply defined and their effect noted. Instead Longinus goes on to consider why hyperbaton, for instance, produces its effect, providing a more subtle literary definition and anticipating the practical criticism movement.

The quality of his own prose is equally impressive; Pope declared it to be sublime itself. In his comparison of Cicero and Demosthenes, Longinus builds a cumulative magnificence out of dazzling single phrases. The vigour of his enjoyment of literature and his certainty of its value to all of us is irresistible; the inspiration of sublimity, Longinus believes, is the author's recognition that nature made man ''no humble or lowly creature, but brought him into life and into the universe as into a great festival.''

—John Lee

ON VANITY (De la vanité)
Prose by Michel de Montaigne, 1588

The two major themes of this essay are vanity and travel. They are treated in an erratic and unpredictable fashion. This has led one critic (Grace Norton) to suggest that Michel de Montaigne originally composed two essays, one on vanity, one on travel, and arbitrarily mixed sections from each together. This hypothesis is unnecessary since it was characteristic of Montaigne to build up his essays by a series of additions and insertions without making explicit the links between them, and he often discusses topics that seem remote from the title of the work. ''On Vanity'' is a good illustration of this. Most of the first part of the essay is devoted to travel and associated ideas; then he links travel with vanity and ends with an episode from his own life in which travel and vanity are linked. Since he is talking about his own travels and his views on vanity, this leads him to introduce refections on his project of self-description which constitutes the *Essays*. The way in which he composes his *Essays* becomes a subsidiary topic interwoven with the other two themes.

The travel alluded to is Montaigne's journey to Italy via Switzerland and Germany in 1580–81. His travel journal of this trip survives and recounts his visit to Rome, which provides the material for his observations on vanity at the end of the essay.

After a brief introduction in which he admits he shares with his contemporaries the vain urge to write, Montaigne gives his reasons for liking travel. He is fond of change, he dislikes managing his own household, and he wants to escape the turbulence of the civil wars that were raging on his own doorstep. He also offers a positive reason: travel broadens the mind. Next he replies to objections against his travelling. Some of this is cast in direct speech, giving the impression he is justifying himself to an interlocutor—perhaps his wife, or a member of his family, or a friend. The substance of the debate can be summed up as follows: ''You shouldn't travel because you are married.'' Montaigne replies: ''Husband and wife don't have to be together all the time.'' ''You are too old for travel.'' ''Why can't an old man enjoy himself?'' ''You may die away from home.'' ''So what? I travel for enjoyment and I would rather die away from home anyway.'' ''Why be so restless? You will not escape yourself. Travel is a vain pastime.'' With this Montaigne agrees and his conciliatory answer provides the link between travel, which has formed the substance of the essay so far, and vanity, which will be the main theme of the remainder. The actual words expressing this link are: ''There is vanity in this amusement [i.e. travel]—but where is there not? These fine precepts are vanity, and all wisdom is vanity.'' Then he develops his discussion of vanity in relation to three topics already raised earlier in this essay, namely the civil wars, his own book of *Essays*, and travel.

First he comments that private morality is vain in public life, especially during civil war. Secondly, he explains that the longer pieces in Book III of the *Essays* are disorderly in structure because he likes to let his vain thoughts shape his writing. Finally, his enthusiasm for Rome, which he visited on his travels in the winter of 1580–81, is vain, and vain also is the gift of Roman citizenship that was bestowed upon him on that occasion. He ends with reflections on the vanity of everything in the world, and the vanity of man himself. He cites the Delphic precept ''Know thyself'' and concludes with the god Apollo's words to mankind: ''There is no single thing so empty and destitute as you, who try to encompass the universe. You are the investigator without knowledge, the magistrate without jurisdiction, and, when all is said and done, the fool of the farce.''

Critics have responded in various ways to this work. Some have thrown up their hands in despair. Albert Thibaudet characterizes it as an example of the vanity of discourse itself in its disorderly and fragmentary treatment of vanity. Richard Sayce on the other hand argues that the various themes are connected and ''weave in and out of the fabric, threads of different colours composing a unified design.''

Others have gone beyond questions of structure and endeavoured to extract a message. For Joseph Zeitlin ''the principal thought of the essay concerns itself with the dominant strain of the whole book, which is the regulation of our life according to Nature, rather than according to the artificial and extravagant precepts of an over-subtle and over-exacting philosophy.'' In support of this Zeitlin quotes a passage near the close of the essay: ''I am angry at this kill-joy Reason . . . I make it my business to bring vanity itself into repute, and folly too, if it gives me any pleasure, and let myself follow my natural inclinations without exercising too close a check upon them.'' Certainly this quotation goes some way to summarizing the piece, since in the course of it Montaigne does assert his freedom to travel and to write in whatever way he wishes. But as always with Montaigne, any attempt to summarize the thought of an essay pales into insignificance beside the writing itself. ''I'm always going for change, incautiously and chaotically; my style and my mind go along like that too . . . Given that I can't hold my reader's attention by weightiness, it's not so bad if I can engross him with my complexity.'' These words occur shortly before the statement about ''kill-joy Reason,'' and are just as valid as a key to this essay, which is a fine example of Montaigne's ever-changing and always engrossing manner of writing, and of his infinitely complex view of himself and the world.

—David Maskell

ONE DAY IN THE LIFE OF IVAN DENISOVICH (Odin den' Ivana Denisovicha)
Novel by Aleksandr Solzhenitsyn, (written 1958)

One Day in the Life of Ivan Denisovich, the story by which Aleksandr Solzhenitsyn first became a household name in both his own country and the West, is in the fullest sense of the word a landmark in Soviet Russian literature, The first honest and realistic description of life in Stalin's camps, its sensational first publication seemed to herald a new age of openness, although this event was, in fact, related to Khrushchev's personal leadership struggles rather than to liberalization as such. Published four years after it was written, it has now come to be seen not only as a bold political statement but also as a remarkable achievement in purely literary terms—indeed, as one of the finest short stories in all 20th-century Russian literature.

Published exactly one hundred years after Dostoevskii's *Memoirs from the House of the Dead* (*Zapiski iz mertvogo domo*), it also sought to expose life in a prison camp to a wide public, but beyond that the similarities are few, although most readers making the comparison find the Tsarist prison regime relatively lenient. In any case Dostoevskii concentrates on the pathology of the criminal while Solzhenitsyn describes in graphic detail his hero's struggle for physical and (although he would not think of it in that way) spiritual survival, from stratagems to avoid not only starvation, exhaustion, and frostbite but also—and equally debilitating, indeed fatal—loss of self-respect.

For Ivan Denisovich Shukhov, his hero, Solzhenitsyn uses third-person direct speech; in other words, the narration, though not by Shukhov, is close to his point of view and thought processes, albeit with an element of commentary to aid comprehension. Much of the story is also told in Shukhov's language, untutored peasant speech heavily interlaid with prison-camp slang. This rich and inventive aphoristic discourse is, indeed, one of the major glories of the story, a bold innovation in a work written at a time when linguistic distortion and corruption by politicians and journalists had reduced the Russian literary language to a sorry state.

By limiting his story to one day and by including no thoughts deeper than might have occurred to a simple peasant, eschewing all generalizations, Solzhenitsyn creates a more powerful effect than if he had presented a broader view, since the microcosm leaves the reader in no doubt about the macrocosm of Stalin's Gulag. A wide cross-section of prisoners is presented, none of whom is politically motivated (a telling political point in itself—they are all innocent) and the story of how each of them came to be caught up in the nightmarish net offers a panorama of life under Stalin, from Shukhov's position as automatically a traitor, having been surrounded by the Germans after the Soviet army's retreat, to the pious Baptists, or Captain Buinovskii whose misfortune had been simply to receive a present sent after World War II by an unsuspecting English comrade-in-arms.

It is not difficult to interpret *One Day in the Life of Ivan Denisovich* symbolically: the wide social spread and the manifest innocence of the prisoners imply clearly that the camp represents a society of meaningless work and arbitrary authority, which was for many Stalin's Soviet Union. Nothing, moreover, could be plainer than the image presented by the prisoners' first task at the ''Socialist Way of Life Settlement'' they are building: to erect a perimeter fence to keep themselves in—Solzhenitsyn's story appeared exactly a year after the building of the Berlin Wall.

One Day in the Life of Ivan Denisovich gains immensely by presenting, almost without comment, a single day in the life of a Soviet everyman. The very ordinariness of Shukhov underlines the cruelty and injustice of the system to which he has fallen victim. Not only an indictment of Stalin's reign of terror, this story also offers an exceptionally vivid description of the battle for survival in an inhuman environment. As a work of literature it broke the stultifying mould of official Socialist Realism in a variety of important ways: by its decidedly un-Olympian narrator, its unheroic hero, the complete lack of overt ideology, its very original non-standard speech, and, not least, by its bold subject matter. After *One Day in the Life of Ivan Denisovich* Soviet literature was never to be the same again.

—Arnold McMillin

ONE HUNDRED YEARS OF SOLITUDE (Cien años de soledad)
Novel by Gabriel García Márquez, 1967

One Hundred Years of Solitude was first published in Argentina in 1967. Not long after its initial English translation in 1970, the novel had already established itself as one of the great works of 20th-century world literature inaugurating and popularizing the new wave of South American fiction (Carlos Fuentes, Jorge Luis Borges, Julio Cortázar, Mario Vargas Llosa, Isabel Allende), and bringing its hitherto little-known author into the forefront of the literary world. Gabriel García Márquez has consolidated his reputation with subsequent novels and short stories, most notably *Love in the Time of Cholera*, and in 1982 he was awarded the Nobel prize for literature.

One Hundred Years of Solitude is an extraordinarily ambitious and compelling tale, dealing with the entire history of the village of Macondo from its foundation, and recounting the saga of six generations of the Buendia family. But this is no orthodox anthropological or realist chronicle: it is instead a book of deep and powerful magic, describing and creating a fantastical world of dreams and visions, mysteries and prophecies. Right from the opening sentence the book's capacity to localize and articulate the marvellous becomes immediately apparent: ''Many years later, as he faced the firing squad, Colonel Aureliano Buendia was to remember that distant afternoon when his father took him to discover ice.'' The elemental struggle between fire and ice hinted at in this passage recurs through-out the book, but the way it is integrated into the history of Macondo and the Buendias is astonishingly skilful. Although every page is full of such symbolic resonance, the meanings remain suggestive and allusive, resisting any simple decoding.

Throughout the novel, García Márquez deliberately and exuber-antly disrupts conventional procedures of storytelling and characteri-zation, and his narrative is conducted through recollections, anticipa-tions, digressions, and confusions over the limits of reality. Without the overt intrusion of a controlling authorial narrator, the tale is carried on by virtual stream-of-consciousness techniques, dispersed around the characters, so that no single account ever achieves full narrative authority. Time is made to stand still when appropriate, conventional expectations about ageing are suspended, and each life story flows over and around those preceding and those following. The human imagination intrudes upon and transforms the world of Macondo time and again, transgressing the normally-understood limits of the possible and creating a sense of wonder and enchantment.

The novel is thus extremely difficult to categorize, being at once an attempt at symbolic epic, a historical romance, a family saga, a national allegory even, and, to use the appropriate jargon, an influen-tial experiment in magical realism. But the attempt to categorize the text remains less important than the need to experience the texture of the writing. Although García Márquez shares some of Borges's love of paradox and conundrum, and although he acknowledged his own interest in laying bare the mechanics of narrative, the author of *One Hundred Years of Solitude* is clearly an altogether more sensual and less starkly cerebral novelist than any of his Latin American contem-poraries. Indeed, for all its playfulness, this entire book may be read as a tribute to the human power to love and endure, despite everything, to survive wars and tempests and hardships and yet retain the capacity to dream and to love.

What García Márquez achieves in this novel is a remarkable and arguably unique balance between the literary experimentation of magical realism and the more conventional human-centred saga. Whereas for some post-modern writers the notion that there can be no transcendental reality and that all we have are stories can become debilitating and dehumanizing, García Márquez rejoices in his narra-tive freedom to produce a compendious account of enlarged human possibilities. The village community of Macondo is fantastical, and the Buendias and their acquaintances are extraordinary figures, but the book none the less becomes moving and involving. Early on in the tale, Jose Arcadio Buendia becomes heavily involved in alchemy, but he soon sees that the attempt to recover gold from base metals is a paltry project compared with the very joy of being alive: "Fascinated by an immediate reality that came to be more fantastic than the vast universe of his imagination, he lost all interest in the alchemist's laboratory." For García Márquez too, this "immediate reality" can be transformed and can yield more humane riches than any laboratory experiment.

For its sheer energy, for its combination of experimentation and humanity, and for the way it enhances the possibilities of seeing the world, there can be little doubt that *One Hundred Years of Solitude* will remain one of the key texts of 20th-century world literature for the foreseeable future.

—Ian A. Bell

THE ORDEAL (Sotnikaw)
Novel by Vasil Bykaw, 1970

The Ordeal is the second of Vasil Bykaw's works on the theme of partisans in World War II, and one of the finest examples of all his prose fiction, displaying many of the features that have made him perhaps the leading Belarussian prose writer today.

The story concerns a particularly difficult mission by two partisans in occupied Belarus, and the different reactions of the two, both highly committed and competent fighters, to the disaster of failure and capture. Bykaw is a realistic writer with a strong gift for portraying physical experiences, and the reader shares the partisans' discomfort, despair, and acute pain as they struggle against the harsh and punishing forces of the bleak Belarussian terrain in winter, despite the fact that one of the two, Sotnikaw (whose name forms the title of the original version of this work), is sick even before they set out and only volunteers through pride. For this reason, apart from its inherent hazards, the successful outcome of the mission is in doubt from the start. As things get worse Sotnikaw only fights to stay alive out of loyalty to his comrade, Rybak; for his part, Rybak begins to blame their fearsome predicament on his sick partner. Briefly shel-tered by some peasants, one of whom turns out to be the village headman, they are put to the supreme test by the ruthless Belarussian puppet police (*Polizei*) into whose hands they soon fall; Sotnikaw passes the test—and dies; his comrade, Rybak, under similar interro-gation and torture, makes first one (clearly rational) compromise and then another, ending as a collaborator and witness, indeed, helper, at the public hanging not only of his comrade, but also of two peasants and a 13-year-old Jewish girl. The test of courage in the face of adversity which Bykaw gives his characters in many stories has led some critics to compare him to Jack London (a well-known writer to all Soviet readers), but there is nothing gratuitous in Bykaw's unflinching portrayal of suffering, for example, as a result of torture inflicted by the *Polizei*: the Belarussian is more interested in motive than in results, and his works have a great deal more psychological substance than London's.

The story is told from two different points of view, those of Sotnikaw and Rybak, which lends the work not only objectivity but also exceptional psychological depth, bringing the reader to the heart of the partisans' appalling situation. Bykaw makes far from a blanket condemnation of Rybak's weakness; rather, by following his thought processes, he shows how thin a line there can be between bravery and cowardice; how a game of cat-and-mouse with ruthless captors, albeit inspired by the entirely reasonable motive of trying to win time, could lead in this instance to moral degradation. Bykaw's message is not so much one of no compromise, but of the ease with which things can go wrong in a maximally tense wartime situation: each case, each individual fate, the author is stressing (in the face, of course, of inflexible dogmatism and maximalism in Soviet attitudes to World War II) should be considered separately, not in terms of doctrine but of understanding. The reader is made not only to experience the physical fear and hardship of the partisans, but also to think what he or she would do in comparable circumstances. Throughout his writing Bykaw has consistently resisted dogmas that ignore real circum-stances: like Alexander Solzhenitsyn, at much the same time, he has defended those who, merely for the misfortune of having been surrounded by the enemy, have been classified as traitors, the victims of collectivization, the fates of simple German as well as Russian and Belarussian soldiers, even those who (sometimes for excellent and selfless reasons) accepted official posts, such as that of village headman, under German occupation. It is, incidentally, noticeable in *The Ordeal* that Rybak, the future quisling, adopts a far more intransigent attitude to the village headman than his morally sturdier companion Sotnikaw. It is Bykaw's very strength as a realistic and psychologically acute writer that makes his constant moral witness against "paper truth," the rigidity and cruelty associated with Stalin, and the simplification and trivialization of war, so moving for readers and so important in the whole context of Soviet morality.

The Ordeal is a powerful example of Soviet war literature, reflecting many of the strengths of Bykaw as a writer. Broadly referential (for example, to the notorious Finnish campaign) and unflinchingly realistic, this novel, written at a time of Soviet stagnation in literature, has become a classic example of psychological war-writing at its best.

—Arnold McMillin

THE ORESTEIA
Plays by Aeschylus, 458 BC

Aeschylus' Orestes trilogy is unique, providing three successive dramas on a single theme, the tragedy of the house of Atreus. Both Homer and Stesichorus, the 6th-century BC Sicilian lyric poet, were acquainted with the story of Agamemnon and Aegisthus. Homer tells the story of Odysseus against the background of the known story of Agamemnon and Orestes; but he does not consider the possibility that Agamemnon deserved his fate, that Clytemnestra may have had good cause to kill Agamemnon, and that Orestes committed a mortal sin in killing his mother. Stesichorus, however, was concerned with an interpretation of the old epic story that would be in keeping with the moral principles held at the time in the Greek world. Agamemnon's guilt in the sacrifice of his daughter Iphigenia, the rape of the priestess Cassandra, and the bringing of the latter home as his concubine, provided Clytemnestra with ample cause for killing her husband. Aegisthus, her paramour and consort, remembered the mistreatment of his brother Thyestes and the slaughter of Thyestes' two sons as a dinner-offering. The throne of Agamemnon rightly belonged to Thyestes, and after him to his son Aegisthus.

Aeschylus' first play of the trilogy, *Agamemnon*, enacts the return of Agamemnon, the confrontation of husband and wife, of the victim and his murderess. Cassandra, never believed, knows what will happen, but the chorus of Argive elders is ignorant and their fear and foreboding become binding elements in the action. Agamemnon's false vanity and modesty and the deceit of Clytemnestra are memorable, and Agamemnon's entry into his palace on a scarlet carpet reserved for divinities is prelude to his slaughter. Cassandra's vision reveals past, present, and future misdeeds of the house of Atreus, and so underscores the link between crime and punishment; she is herself a living symbol of Agamemnon's wickedness. He has defiled a priestess of Apollo and revealed his unfaithfulness to Clytemnestra. The sacrifice of Iphigenia, recalled by the chorus and Clytemnestra, also seals his fate; the Trojan War also resulted in the deaths of many Greeks and in the slaughter of many Trojans. So Aeschylus emphasizes the guilt of Agamemnon without justifying the deed of Clytemnestra. The connection between action and suffering is the theme of the first act of the trilogy. There is evidently a constant imbalance in human nature, either to suffer more than one deserves, or to inflict more evil than one has suffered. The poet also says that what

man suffers must be attributed to what man has done in the past. Deeds have consequences, and suffering has a cause.

The action of the second play, *Choephoroi* (*The Libation Bearers*), is based on the action of the first play and parallels it, just as the antistrophe of a lyric poem corresponds to the strophe. The tomb of Agamemnon occupies the position of Agamemnon's chariot in the first play; Orestes and Pylades enter and witness another sacrifice comparable to that in the first play. Both sacrifices are caused by messages from Agamemnon: in the first play, it was the fall of Troy and the return of Agamemnon communicated by beacons from the Dardanelles to Argos; in the second play, it is a dream announcing the coming of an avenger, Orestes. After the spectacular mutual recognition of Orestes and Electra, the plan is developed to kill the murderers. The murder of Agamemnon, the suffering of Electra, the tyranny of Aegisthus, and Apollo's command to Orestes all justify the deed of retribution. Orestes and Clytemnestra face one another, both deceitful, the one by nature, the other by design. Clytemnestra plays the part that Agamemnon played in the first play. Her vanity and her modesty are both false. She is as blind as Agamemnon was; she alone cannot see what it all means and what is about to happen. The play within the play is a marvellous innovation, the story of Orestes' death invented by Orestes to deceive his mother. Orestes, who reports his own death, witnesses the feigned grief of his mother whom he is set to kill. With the curtain of deceit drawn aside, the play within the play is over; Aegisthus lies dead, and Orestes once more faces his mother, who warns him of the Furies that will pursue the matricide; but Orestes cannot disobey Apollo's command, and expects that her death, inflicted by him and his sister Electra, will end the travails of the house. The noble avenger of the father becomes the killer of his mother; the Furies attack him, and he flees to Delphi.

The third play, *Eumenides* (*The Furies*), presents both the ritual and legal absolution of Orestes. The scene has shifted from Argos to the sanctuary of Apollo at Delphi where Orestes is still pursued by the Furies (*Erinyes*) although he has been purified. Apollo sends him to the sanctuary of Athena in Athens, where the main action takes place. Athena is confronted by the suppliant Orestes and by the Furies, like bloodhounds in pursuit of their prey. She decides to establish a court to resolve the issue of Orestes' guilt or innocence, the court of the Areopagus, the first criminal court in the Western world, and an important institution in the evolution of democratic Athens, particularly during the lifetime of Aeschylus. Before a jury of 12 leading Athenian citizens, presided over by the goddess Athena, Orestes is prosecuted by the Furies and defended by Apollo. The conflict involves the rights and privileges of an older pre-Hellenic dispensation—childish and barbarous, female, chthonic, the prosecutors of Orestes—and those of Apollo who represents a newer Olympian dispensation, youthful and enlightened, civilized, male, and celestial. The votes of the mortal judges are evenly divided, whereupon Athena casts a deciding vote for acquittal. Then, by the exercise of her Zeus-given power, and by the power of persuasion, the Erinyes are pacified and consent to dwell in Athens as "gracious, kindly goddesses," guarantors of justice in cases of homicide and of Athenian security.

So, with apparent religious (and political) change, the test case of Orestes, embodying the doctrine of "blood for blood," provides a solution in the principle of legal trial of a killer by a jury of his fellow-men. Such was the will and purpose of Zeus, working in his mysterious way through Apollo his prophet and Athena his daughter. *The Oresteia* is a parable of progress, from butchery and the blood feud to the rule of law.

The trilogy displays prominent themes and motifs: the light that comes out of the darkness; dread compulsion and involvement (evidenced in the images of robe, net, snare, yoke, bit, and goad); animals; medical allusions to recurring sickness; and the ship of state.

By 458 BC, theological drama proper had developed to the point where it was equal in importance to the choral part; the spectacle—in the visions of Cassandra, the pageantry of robes (the Erinyes change from black to crimson cloaks in the final torchlight procession), and horrifying creatures—is prominent and characteristically Aeschylean. Characterization has also developed greatly: although Agamemnon appears to be little more than *hubris* (arrogance) personified, Clytemnestra ranks with the greatest characters in Greek tragedy.

—Alexander G. McKay

ORESTES
Play by Euripides, 408 BC

Euripides' *Orestes*, his final production for the theatre of Dionysus at Athens prior to his retreat to Macedon, was designed to be a thriller, a murder plot to kill Helen, with a happy ending. The trilogy comprised *Oenomaus, Chrysippus*, and *The Phoenician Women* (*Phoenissae*) (extant), with *Orestes* as the satyr play. The play details what happened to the matricides. Its psychological examination of their abnormal natures, the transfer of a variant of the Mycenaean story of 5th-century Athenian conditions and contexts, its comic passages, and Euripides' original approach to traditional mythology, provide diversified entertainment. The aristocracy is basically degenerate: some antique virtues still survive, loyalty between Orestes and Electra, and (somewhat extravagantly presented) between Orestes and Pylades, but the loyalty is self-centred, disdainful of the law and of the common welfare, and capable of ruthless inhumanity to others.

Orestes appears in rags, a veritable stretcher-case, haunted by his mother's Furies, with no prospect of release or asylum. A trial by the Argive assembly lies ahead, Euripides' parody of the trial by jury in Aeschylus' *The Furies* (*Eumenides*). The forecast sentence is execution by stoning. Menelaus surfaces as the saviour figure, brought to Argos to recover his daughter Hermione who had been left in Clytemnestra's charge during the war overseas. Helen, wide-eyed and innocent, self-satisfied and elegant as usual, appeals to a depressed Electra to carry offerings to Clytemnestra's tomb. Electra's love for her brother is dominant. His mad scene, on stage, with visions of the Gorgon, can be diagnosed not as hysteria but as madness by design. Menelaus is assigned parenthetic scenes around the presence of Tyndareus, the maternal grandfather of Orestes, who comes to mourn the murder of his daughter Clytemnestra; his somewhat sophistic position, in the presence of Menelaus, is that the expected sentence to death by stoning seems excessive, until he sees and hears Orestes. Thereafter his earlier preference for banishment instead of death by stoning is rejected; he proposes to advocate the stoning of both Orestes and Electra, and leaves in consternation.

Orestes seeks Menelaus' assistance. A messenger reports the proceedings of the Assembly and the spokesmen for and against the execution of Orestes and Electra: Talthybius favoured condemnation; Diomedes spoke in favour of banishment; an anonymous, ill-trained speaker, encouraged by Tyndareus, favoured death by stoning; a peasant farmer spoke in defence of Orestes' matricide. Orestes, according to the messenger, left his sickbed to defend his action as

executioner within the family as having been a public benefaction. Condemnation followed. Electra responds with a song and dance calling on Persephone, goddess of the dead, and asks pity for those who once fought for Hellas. The house of Pelops (and of Atreus) has been destroyed by a democratic process and by the envy of the gods. Orestes and Pylades return to take their farewells from their grieving friends. Electra begs Orestes to kill her and faithful Pylades is prepared to join the suicide pact with Orestes. Orestes' criminal mind then proposes the execution of all the slaves and of Helen. Electra reveals her father-fixation and her addiction to violence and deceit by suggesting that Hermione also should be kidnapped and murdered.

Pylades and Orestes enter the palace to kill Helen, leaving Electra outside with the chorus. At the sound of Helen's screams from within, Hermione arrives and is rushed indoors where Orestes is waiting. The choral song drowns out the sounds behind the palace doors, at which point a slave emerges on the palace balcony, drops to the ground, and gives a breathless account, an almost unintelligibly garbled eyewitness report, of Helen's escape.

Orestes leaves the palace with drawn sword, threatens then releases the slave, and re-enters the palace. The chorus finally senses what is happening and catches sight of the torches which will set fire to the palace. Menelaus appears, alarmed by the news of Helen's disappearance, and orders his men to break down the palace doors. Orestes drags Hermione onto the balcony for execution; Pylades and Electra are beside him with torches at the ready. At this point, the insoluble (and intolerable) situation calls for a *deus ex machina* in the person of Apollo, with the divine Helen alongside. Apollo contrives a solution for every problem: Helen will become a star to guide sailors; Orestes, acquitted by the court of the Areopagus, will marry Hermione; Electra will marry Pylades; Orestes will administer Argos, Menelaus will rule over Sparta; and Apollo will deal with the Argive assembly. Helen disappears with Apollo, bound for Zeus.

Euripides' play comes close to chaos. Degeneracy, sickness, and manic blood-lust have brought the one-time celebrated House of Atreus to the edge, where only miracles can fend off impending disaster and strain credulity. The political context of 408 BC—a season of vulgarity in the assembly and ineptitude in the strategic command, a time when the citizens longed for the return of the disgraced traitor Alcibiades, onetime scion of Periclean democracy, although he was engaged even then in trying to negotiate an entente with Persia—must lie at the heart of Euripides' discontent and indictment of the democratic process. In light of these conditions, the ludicrous final scene seems more intelligible and prognostic. ''The final tableau is the direct prophecy of disaster,'' as William Arrowsmith deduced, ''complete, awful, and inevitable, while Apollo intervenes only as an impossible wish, a futile hope, or a simple change of scene from a vision that cannot be brooked, or seen for long, because it is the direct vision of despair, the hopeless future.'' The defeat of Athens in the Peloponnesian War came four years later.

—Alexander G. McKay

ORLANDO FURIOSO
Poem by Ludovico Ariosto, 1515–32

Orlando Furioso is the culmination of the Italian tradition of chivalric literature. The Renaissance saw a decline in the chivalric tradition, with Pulci's *Morgante*, a parody in the Florentine comic-realistic vein, and, in France, the satirical tales of Gargantua and of Pantagruel by Rabelais. Ludovico Ariosto was to remedy this situation. A courtier to the Este family, rulers of Ferrara, the poet wrote for a public of noblemen, knights, and ladies who were knowledgeable enthusiasts of the chivalric genre. It was the explicit intention of Ariosto to continue the unfinished poem written by a poet of the preceding generation at the court of Ferrara, Matteo Maria Boiardo. In *Orlando innamorato*, Boiardo tells of Orlando's unrequited love for the beautiful oriental princess, Angelica, and Ariosto goes on to complete the saga, by narrating how Orlando becomes mad ("furioso" in Italian) for love.

Ariosto continued the narrative with the same characters used by his predecessor, with a few orthographic changes to names: Ranaldo becomes Rinaldo, Ferraguto becomes Ferrau. Like Boiardo before him, the poet also follows the model of the united traditions of the Breton and Carolingian cycles. The genre of chivalric poetry had originated in France in the Middle Ages and came to Italy by way of the Franco-Venetian poets of the 13th century. The Carolingian cycle told of the feats of Charlemagne's courtiers whereas the Breton cycle relates the romantic tales of the knights of King Arthur's Round Table. Another element used by Boiardo and continued by Ariosto is the stylistic choice of the narrative octave, verses of eight endecasyllables, the first six with an alternating rhyme, followed by a concluding couplet (ABABABCC). Although the octave had been used often in chivalric and other forms of literature, it is Ariosto who is credited with ennobling the verse to the point that his are often referred to as "golden octaves." It is the ideal form for his conversational and yet elegant narrative style.

The chivalric tradition was also an oral tradition, and the stories of Roland (Orlando) and his knights were often related at court by wandering troubadours. Thus Ariosto's narrative follows tradition in that the narrator is omnipresent in the poem, providing the reader with occasional ironic commentary on the events related. In the first lines of the poem, the narrator declares: "Le donne, i cavallier, l'arme, gli amori, / le cortesie, l'audaci imprese io canto" ("Of women. knights, weapons, loves, courtly life and audacious feats I sing"). Thus the reader is given a ready catalogue of the multiple subjects of the work, a panorama of courtly life and wars rather than a straightforward narrative of the life of Orlando.

In the first verse of the poem quoted above, the poet promises to narrate not only tales of war, but also tales of love. Against the background of the Holy War between Charlemagne's knights and the Saracen army of Agramante, Ariosto tells two love stories. Orlando's love for Angelica is unrequited and, when he discovers that she loves the simple soldier Medoro, the knight in love becomes crazy with despair ("furioso"). He turns into a brute, and Astolfo must undertake a voyage to the moon in order to recover Orlando's brain. After recovering his reasoning faculties, Orlando is again a fearless knight and brings victory to Charlemagne's army. Boiardo had invented the character of Ruggiero in tribute to his patrons, the Este family. The second major love story of the poem is that of Ruggiero and the female warrior, Bradamante, destined one day to marry. Their descendants would then become the mythical ancestors of the Este family. Of course, because the marriage of Bradamante and Ruggiero must constitute the conclusion of the poem, both Boiardo and Ariosto place many obstacles in the path of their happy union in order to continue the other narratives of Orlando and Angelica, and the war.

The narrative skips between these tales, often leaving a dramatically crucial moment of the plot to pick up another interrupted adventure in midstream. In this way, dramatic tension is increased for the reader, using a technique common in serialized novels and today's television soap operas.

The definitive work is divided into 46 cantos and, despite the interweaving of story lines, does have a definite beginning, middle, and end, Boiardo's poem was left unfinished in the middle of a great battle between Christians and infidels. Before this battle, Charlemagne had asked old Namo to look after Princess Angelica, the object of the desires of the two feuding cousins, Orlando and Rinaldo. Namo was to give Angelica as the victor's prize at the end of the battle, but she escapes and Ariosto's poem begins with Orlando and others on the heels of the fleeing princess. The central canto of the work is dedicated to a description of Orlando's love sickness and ensuing madness. Finally, the work concludes, just as Boiardo had planned, with the wedding between Bradamante and Ruggiero.

The harmony of the poem makes it a symbol of its age. The theories of Castiglione's ideal courtier and Bembo's ideal Italian vernacular are exemplified in Ariosto's art. The *Orlando Furioso* is one of the great masterpieces of the Italian Renaissance.

—Jordan Lancaster

OUTLAWS OF THE MARSH

See WATER MARGIN

THE OUTSIDER (L'étranger)
Novel by Albert Camus, 1942

The principal character in *The Outsider*, Meursault, is a French Algerian clerk who kills an Arab, is imprisoned, tried, and sentenced to death. The novel begins with Meursault's unemotional announcement that his mother has just died. He goes to the funeral and when he returns he carries on with his daily routine as if nothing had happened: he goes swimming, meets a woman called Marie, takes her to the cinema, and begins an affair. For some weeks he works as usual and sees Marie on Saturdays. During that time he refuses an offer of promotion from his employer and also agrees to marry Marie even though he does not love her. One day Meursault's friend, Raymond, brawls with his Arab girlfriend whom he suspects of infidelity and, as a result of his efforts to help, Meursault becomes involved in the antagonism between Raymond and his mistress's brother and friends. These Arabs, on a subsequent occasion, wound Raymond in a fight on the beach. Later that day, Meursault, who has Raymond's revolver with him, encounters one of the Arabs, who is armed with a knife. Being suddenly confused by the blinding sun, Meursault mistakes flashes of light for a blade and shoots and kills the Arab. After the man falls, Meursault fires four more shots into the body.

The primary concern throughout the ensuing investigation and trial is not so much the killing of the Arab, which would not have been punishable by death, as Meursault's nonconformity with social norms. A large part of the case against him focuses on his relationship with his mother, his reactions at her wake and funeral and his involvement with Marie. By pointing out that he had not wanted to see his mother's body and that shortly after her burial he had gone to see a comic film with Marie and had then spent the night with her, the prosecution argues that Meursault is a moral misfit devoid of filial grief and that, consequently, he deserves punishment. To that extent Albert Camus engages in a critique of a self-righteous society that assumes the right to judge and condemn a man for not sharing its moral and religious values.

Meursault's whole way of life represents a defiance of those values. Far from considering himself to exist within a rational, justifiable, and comprehensible social order, he rejects even the idea that there can be a meaningful pattern of life. To him the notion of striving for social and economic progression is devoid of meaning and for this reason he rejects the offer of promotion from his employer. To have done otherwise would have meant believing in a coherent world based on logical principles and within which ambitions and hopes for a better future can exist. Meursault simply refuses to become involved in the mechanisms of a world, which, to him, does not make sense. He cannot see the point of having aims or of wanting to change his existence in a world impervious to human aspirations to determinism. To the extent that he consciously considers life as a sequence of inconsistent events that have neither reason nor purpose, his view of the world can be termed Absurdist.

This concept is based on the premise that the world is devoid of divine intention and that human existence arises from chance and arbitrary contingencies. Man can neither understand nor control the world, which unfolds in a haphazard manner regardless of human volition. According to Camus, the Absurd is a confrontation between man's determination to make sense of reality and a world which is essentially unmotivated and meaningless.

Meursault's attitudes acknowledge this ''divorce,'' to use Camus's term. Free from a belief in a system of values, Meursault lives in a way that is spontaneous and amoral. All that matters to him is the present, which he dissociates from the past and the future. He regards his relationship with Marie, for example, as momentary pleasure and he never places it within the more far-reaching permanence of love. His agreement to marry her is, to say the least, unenthusiastic. Equally, he does not see the purpose of connecting his mother's death with a subsequent feeling of grief or, indeed, with his desire to enjoy Marie's company. In fact, when he is asked by the *juge d'instruction* (examining magistrate) whether he loved his mother, a sentiment which would have implied a lifelong attachment, his reply is noncommittal. Above all, he refuses to attribute a cause or justification to his crime. When questioned, he simply repeats the nonexplanation ''because of the sun.'' Meursault admits that, in general, he has got out of the habit of asking himself for explanations. For him there are no meanings which either account for existence or formulate it into a continuum.

Once any notion of long-term or overall coherence in life has been discounted, what remains is a belief in the here and now. Throughout the first half of *The Outsider* Meursault is seen to base his existence on the present instant and on the impulsive, spontaneous sensations that it offers. His response to the world is dominated by a heightened sensitivity to physical phenomena; colour, smells, fatigue, pain, the heat of the sun. What is more, these are evoked within the transitory context of an immediate present, the word ''today'' appearing in the first sentence of the first three chapters. When the freedom to live in this ''instinctive'' way is taken away from Meursault by his incarceration and pressure is put on him to identify with the alternative values of religion and social responsibility, he accepts death rather than compromise his nihilistic stand. To the last Meursault remains at odds with the society which condemns him. He remains an outsider.

—Silvano Levy

P-Q

PALAU
Poem by Gottfried Benn, 1922

This poem first appeared in *Der Neuë Merkur*, 5(1), April 1922. Its original title "Rot" was changed to "Palau" in a subsequent publishing of the poem in the collection *Spaltung* and has since retained that title. The island in question is situated in the south west Pacific, north of New Guinea. Ever since Gauguin's trip to Tahiti, interest in the South Seas had been stimulated among German expressionists, not least the painters Max Pechstein and Emil Nolde. In literature too, that lure—as a means of flight into the exotic—was manifested. Here Gottfried Benn distances himself from the perceived tired and outworn civilization of northern Europe (it was the time of Oswald Spengler's major philosophical work *Der Untergang des Abendlandes* (*The Decline of the West*) to an island, redolent of the exotic, that serves as the goal of his escape.

The impression of exotic tropicality is deftly suggested with the briefest of images: heat, reefs, the smell of eucalyptus, palm trees (II. 9–10); Sepia, coral (II. 41–42). It is eventide ("The evening is red on the island of Palau") and the approach of darkness ("and the shadows sink" I. 2), ("soon it will be night and lemurs" II. 7–8) induces the poet to reflect on the vegetative and also the biological processes in the natural order. The richness of sexual experience ("it is good to drink from the cup of woman" II. 3–4) is then linked in the second stanza with the very primal biological processes of nature ("in the depths of the womb of the darkening seas" II. 15–16).

But the concomitant factor with life is death. This idea has been introduced at the outset of the poem with the mention in the opening stanza, as the red of the evening sky changes to black with the approach of night, of "Totenvögel" and "Totenuhren." In the third stanza—where the "refrain" of the poem's opening couplet is now incorporated into the text itself—death is further mentioned directly ("all the deaths in the world / are ferries and fords" II. 21–22). Indeed the poet allows himself then in the fourth and fifth stanzas the opportunity to call to mind some examples of the comparative nature of death rites, as he considers the functional similarities of such rites in Nordic and classical mythology, (the hammer of Thor, the ferryman Charon on the river Styx) in relation to the practices of the Micronesians.

The conjuring-up of the natural scene and the pursuant homing-in on the processes of life and death permit the poet to distance himself not only spatially, but also temporally, as he moves from consciousness of the transience of time to that of "static" timelessness. By means of a series of pairings of words and images, Benn seeks a poetic balancing of these polarities: "what still remains standing / also craves disembodiment down to a limbless state, / down to the void" (II. 11–14)—which in turn leads here of course to the very positive value of "the depths of the womb of the darkening seas" (II. 15–16); and in a repeated form, "what still holds and rises, / will also crumble" (II. 43–44); "never and always" (I. 20, I. 48).

In short, this poem does not belong to the early aggressive poems of Benn, where he often seeks to *èpater les bourgeois* in his first verse collection, *Morgue* (1912) (e.g. the poem "Man and Woman Go Through the Cancer Ward"). Here in this poem of regression, a calmer, more contemplative note is observable. Little more than half a year earlier, Benn had been writing in a mood of creative crisis: "I am now 35 years of age . . . I can't write anything anymore. I can't read anything any longer. I can't think any thought through to its conclusion." In "Palau," the contextual balance is further matched by its structural form—from the very composition of the poem with its six eight-line stanzas, coupled with the regularity of an alternating masculine and feminine rhyme scheme, down to the deliberate and careful repetition, or slight variation, of phrase and line interwoven into the different stanzas, to create musical and colourful patterns of imagery that help to persuade the reader, as Benn moves beyond the level of man and nature to embrace religious/mythical and cultural dimensions. Dissolution of consciousness, regression is what Benn seeks and effectively finds in "Palau."

—Ian Hilton

PAN TADEUSZ
Poem by Adam Mickiewicz, 1834

Pan Tadeusz; or, The Last Foray in Lithuania: A Story of Life among Polish Gentlefolk in the Years 1811 and 1812 has been gradually recognized in Poland as the most important national masterpiece. Written in Paris between late 1832 and February 1834, it was published there in June 1834. It contains 12 books and almost 10,000 13-syllable lines. As proved by specialists, the initial concept of the poem developed progressively from an idyll, similar to Goethe's *Herman and Dorothea* (*Hermann und Dorothea*), into a much broader attempt at re-creating the national revival at the beginning of the 19th century, when democratic ideas, upheld by Polish troops allied with Napoleon, undermined the old spirit of a "noblemen's republic," left by the Sarmatic past.

Pan Tadeusz, set in the country estate Soplicowo in the Lithuanian and Belarusian corner of former Polish lands, includes several storylines and many episodes. The action covers a few days in the late summer of 1811 (Books I-X) and just over a day in the spring of 1812 (Books XI-XII). The return of young Tadeusz from school in Vilnius to his native home and his subsequent romantic involvement with two women constitute the frame of all the stories, but not the most important development in the poem. The long-lasting dispute between the Soplicas and the Horeszkos about property rights to the castle makes a background for events, relating them to the past, shown in flashbacks, and to the future, that is, to the poem's optimistic forecast, embodied in its happy ending. This conflict is linked directly to the "last foray in Lithuania" referred to in the title, to the story of Jacek Soplica, later Father Robak, and to Jacek's son, Tadeusz, himself. The vicissitudes of Jacek's audacious and repentant life belong mostly to the past, brought back to life in a tale of vengeance, recounted by Gerwazy, and in Father Robak's confession. His ups and downs, however, merit much more than mere exposition, serving as a vehicle for the author's message about the national revival, and thus relating private matters to the grand image of liberation brought about by the Napoleonic army in 1812. The glory of this historic event coincides with the reconciliation of the two families at war, sealed by Tadeusz Soplica's marriage to Zofia Horeszko.

The singular form of this modern epic reflects Adam Mickiewicz's effort to strike a balance between high and low styles, poetry and reality, his personal yearning for the lost country of childhood and narrative detachment. The poet believed that nature, prominent in old songs, offered wonders capable of replacing Homeric gods and supernatural presence. Moreover, portraying common events, the poet had to employ novelistic techniques. The popular convention of family feud, frequent in Walter Scott's fiction, the dominance of ordinary heroes, including Tadeusz himself, and the detailed descriptions of domestic matters, considered too trivial for poetry, contribute to the poem's realism. The ''comedy of errors,'' when Tadeusz confuses mature Telimena with teenage Zofia, the ridiculous vanity of two noblemen contending about the alacrity of their greyhounds, and the medley of characters obsessed with something or someone, convey humour and satire. The description of fighting between Polish noblemen and Russian soldiers in Book IX introduces mock-heroic tones. Only the story of Father Robak, the secret emissary of independent Poland, has a definitely Romantic character, with its mystery and suspense, dramatically resolved by a Byronic confession (Mickiewicz translated *The Giaour* into Polish) in Book X.

Its variety of substance and literary genres is reflected in the work's narrative art. The poem starts from a lyrical invocation to the author's homeland, where the direct personal tone of loss and painful cravings for a return, at least in the imagination, to its rural beauty eventually converts smoothly into the objective novelistic account of Tadeusz's arrival in Soplicowo. In the same way a patriotic exaltation in the first stanzas of Book XI, which openly refers to the poet's childhood memories of Polish and French troops advancing into Lithuania in the spring of 1812, is followed by the impersonal narration of historical and fictive events. Consequently, lyricism is balanced by epic detachment, the high style of a rhapsody by the low style of a raconteur who often treats his characters with jocular familiarity or light-hearted mockery. The omniscient, digressive narrator turns sometimes into a pure observer or, conversely, into a personally involved speaker, identifiable with the real author.

Pan Tadeusz has been long admired for its descriptions of nature and everyday details. This was not often the case at the time of its publication. Cyprian Norwid, Mickiewicz's contemporary and an outstanding poet himself, resented the alleged triviality of numerous meals portrayed in the poem. Many modern writers, however, such as Czesław Miłosz, have found in *Pan Tadeusz* an amazing art of transforming the ordinary into pure poetry. Mickiewicz's epic vein embraces almost everything, from Lithuanian forest to Lithuanian coffee, from sunrises and sunsets to orchards, vegetable plots, and wild-growing mushrooms. His poetic imagery may depend on an impressionistic sensitivity to colours and movement, take on the air of fairy-tale wonders, or simply stay as accurate and prosaic as kitchen recipes, as in the description of *bigos* (cabbage with meat) in Book IV.

The way common events are transformed into poetry demonstrates the author's consciousness of a gap between illusion and reality (as in Goethe's *From My Life* [*Dichtung und Wahrheit*]), which often leads to unexpected counterpoints or aesthetic bathos. Mickiewicz plays poetic fantasy off against ordinary existence, pointing out that not only the Count, the most eccentric of his characters, has been possessed by the old malady of Don Quixote and thus confused teenage Zofia with a nymph (Book III). Mickiewicz himself enjoyed similar bathetic shifts from high to low styles and in accord with a

broader trend within Polish Romanticism (Juliusz Słowacki, Zygmunt Krasiński) portrayed reality from two points of view, poetic and factual. There are two Soplicowos: the appealing incarnation of the homeland, its charms and patriotic values, and the place where the long-lasting litigation, family feuding, and personal animosities subside only at the end of the poem. Even this optimistic denouement, caused by political liberation, seemed illusory at the time of publication, when everybody knew about the eventual defeat of Napoleon in 1812. Was not the final victory that of poetry over reality, in the poem that had reconciled Romantic fantasy with everyday events?

—Stanislaw Eile

PARIS PEASANT (Le Paysan de Paris)
Poem by Louis Aragon, 1926

Paris Peasant is commonly considered the most exhilarating and enduring of Louis Aragon's surrealist prose works. It appeared in instalments in *La Revue européenne* before being published as a single text in 1926. It comprises four sections: ''Preface to a Modern Mythology'' (''Préface à une mythologie moderne''), ''The Passage de l'Opéra'' (''Le Passage de l'opéra''), ''A Feeling for Nature at the Buttes-Chaumont'' (''Le Sentiment de la nature aux Buttes-Chaumont''), and ''The Peasant's Dream'' (''Le Songe du paysan'')— the last was added for the 1926 publication.

The first section is a quasi-philosophical diatribe against rational mental habits and the pursuit of truth. In keeping with ideas being circulated by the Surrealist group of which Aragon was a key member, the narrator sets out his intention to apprehend the sense of the marvellous suffusing everyday existence. ''The Passage de l'Opéra'' and ''A Feeling for Nature'' constitute the core of the text and are literary reconstructions or meditative strolls in two places in Paris, the first a 19th-century arcade in the Opéra *quartier*, and the second a park in the northeast of the city. The fourth section is a further pseudo-epistemological debate and a series of pronouncements echoing one of the Surrealists' elected predecessor's texts: Lautréamont's *Poésies*.

Breton chided Aragon for betraying surrealism in *Paris Peasant*. An essential aim of the movement was to undermine rational thought in order to reveal the hidden part of the mind. They derided narrative since it relies on logic and on coherent, commonsense temporality. Aragon creates a kind of narrative out of those fragments which were generally considered by the Surrealists to be outside narrative structure. Thus a collage of shop signs, newspaper cuttings and municipal inscriptions are incorporated verbatim into the text in what is teasingly a disruption of the narrative and at the same time a revitalizing of it. These signs are made to glow strangely by appearing in a literary text, just as in the real world they are imbued, for all their ordinariness, with the spirit of the marvellous. Aragon has described *Paris Peasant* as a work of ''surrealist realism,'' and this (collage) procedure is a textual imitation of how the marvellous erupts in reality. The implied dialectic here is that just as societal language can become poetic, so poetic language ought to be useful to society. Surrealist procedures imitate and parody both the serious philosophical debate about objective reality in which the Surrealists were then engaged, and the lyrical excesses inherent in automatism. *Paris Peasant* is full of extraordinary and ingenious arbitrary imagery, and there is a genuine parody of automatic writing in part V of ''A Feeling for Nature.''

The "Passage de l'Opera" section is in part a vociferous defence of the arcade's small traders against its proposed demolition by the Boulevard Hausmann Building Society in collusion with the City of Paris administrators. This defence includes collage material, and also involutes into the text the tradesmen who have read the early part of "Passage de l'Opéra," a literary trick possibly borrowed from Gide. The ironical pamphleteering embedded in the text hints perhaps at the revolutionary political position that Aragon was to adopt from 1930.

The walk in the arcade provides a pretext for abstruse musings and poetic observations on the following locales, trades and services: lodging-house (for liaisons), bookshop, the Certa café, restaurant, stamp-dealer, hairdresser, wine-merchant, tailor, shoeblack, lavatory, gunsmith, orthopaedist, massage-room, and (erotic) theatre. As the narrator on his stroll pauses (in his narrative) before each window, a series of panegyrics is delivered. In *Aragon romancier* Lévi-Valensi has drawn attention to the textuality of the arcade that can be seen as a metaphor for future novels. The arcade is also a microcosm of the city and of modern mental life. With its display of desired objects it is also a paradigm for the unconscious.

The Buttes-Chaumont park is as ambiguous an environment in which to take a stroll as the Opéra arcade. Where the arcade, as Benjamin has shown, is at the same time public street and private interior, so the park is a condensation of the countryside, both town and country, a public space for private thoughts "the town's collective unconscious." Reflection on how mythologies are created in cultures leads the narrator to the discovery that his own mind follows the same procedure when it contemplates objects. The charm of "A Feeling for Nature" relies chiefly on the collision of different discourses to humorous effect. In part VI Aragon meets Noll and Breton, who propose a stroll in the Buttes-Chaumont. They arrive by taxi, "drunk with openmindedness," and part VII then consists entirely of a physical geography of the park, complete with details of its roads and contours, followed in part VIII by a delirious monologue addressed to Night. Another collision follows with the inscriptions of municipal worthies, when Noll perceives a white spectre on the Suicides' Bridge. After a passage of Hegel-inspired thought ("the concrete notion emerging from the pure reedless waters"), Woman, the eternal female, is suddenly invoked as the cohesive force behind the world's appearances. In contrast, in the last pages the narrator tears his head from his body and it undergoes exaggerated metamorphoses into, for example, a blackberry, picked and discarded by a schoolboy, until the man finally becomes "a sign among the constellations."

"The Peasant's Dream" relaunches the inquiry into the purpose of metaphysics, concluding that it is "notion or knowledge of the concrete." The philosophical utterances are best read in the same way as the vertiginous imagery. The narrator proceeds to describe how the "general law" is accessible through a specific woman and falling in love. Among many bizarre and some unfathomable statements, the narrator-poet makes an impassioned plea for a poetry of the concrete.

Paris Peasant is a grand surrealist work, in its imagery, its obsession with identity and chance, its dream-evocations of "real" Paris, its discrediting of reality. It celebrates the ordinary, glories in anti-elitism, eulogizing waiters and hairdressers and spelling out a utopia in which everyone is an artist. It is a memorable experiment in constructing narrative from the raw material of the external world and in baring the process of its attempt.

—Rolf Venner

A PART OF SPEECH (Chast' rechi)
Poems by Iosif Brodskii, 1977

A Part of Speech is the title of Iosif Brodskii's second English collection and of his fourth Russian collection. The contents of these two collections are, however, different: while the Russian collection includes poems written after his exile from Russia (1972–76), the poems in the English book stretch from 1965 to 1978. Brodskii has been fortunate with his translators (who include Richard Wilbur, Anthony Hecht, and Derek Walcott): "every poem in the book reads as if English had been its first home" (Henry Gifford). It is no wonder that this book has established Brodskii as one of the major figures in the Western literary landscape. Apart from diversity of style and theme, this collection has immense breadth and cultural resonance: Greek mythology ("Odysseus to Telemachus"); the Old and New Testament ("Nunc Dimittis"); and the classical world of the Latin poets ("Letters to a Roman Friend"). One can also hear the voices of Samuel Beckett, T.S. Eliot, W.H. Auden, and Robert Lowell. Beckett had a very specific impact on Brodskii's poetics and *Weltanschauung*. The ninth part of "Nature Morte" opens with the simplest and most terrifying description of death in Russian poetry, a description which is reminiscent of Beckett: "A thing. Its brown colour. Its / blurry outline. Twilight. / Now there is nothing left. / Only a *nature morte*." In one of the most perfect poems in the collection, "The Butterfly," Brodskii exhibits an amplitude that no other Russian poet among his contemporaries can claim. His range is such that he combines the incompatible: a Pushkinian lightness and elegance of style and thought with Beckett's way of looking at the world, which demands a dotting of all the "i's" and then leaves only the dots: the butterfly is seen as merely a "frail and shifting buffer," dividing nothingness and man.

Three or four themes dominate this book: exile, empire, language, and time. Finding himself "in a strange place," he wrote the poem "1972," his "first cry of speechlessness," in which, amidst irony, wit, sarcasm, and philosophical digressions, we find the first serious reproach against Russia. But thanks to his poetic skill, the acute feeling of orphanhood and fear of silence are conveyed only indirectly, through his triple dactylic rhymes: "*otchaian'ia / odichaysn'ia / molchaniia*" ("despair / isolation / silence"). Other structural and semantic resources fulfil the almost Calvinistic function of the dismissal of pain and loss, so that "each poem becomes an exercise in stamina" (Czesław Miłosz). The poet has succeeded in placing the very tragedy of exile under the control of his art. The exile poet has become a unique tool of his native language: "A man gets reduced to pen's rustle on paper, to / wedges, ringlets of letters, and, due / to the slippery surface, to commas and full stops," Talking of linguistic isolation, he said: "It helps you to win a notion of yourself unimpeded. It's not pleasant, but it is a more clinical notion of yourself. The relationship with your own language becomes more private and intricate." He put language at the centre of his poetic world and created a solid ground for himself in exile. The supremacy of language is underlined by the very title of the book. For Brodskii, poetry is "an instrument of self-betterment," "a form of sentimental education," as well as "the highest form of linguistic activity." A poet is merely an embodiment of language: "I'm a mumbling heap / of words."

Empire is one of Brodskii's conceptual metaphors. It runs through several poems in the collection and stands for forced harmonization, for the state in general. Brodskii's witty elaboration on the imperial theme attains its full glory in "Lullaby of Cape Cod" (named after the jazz classic "Lullaby of Birdland"), where he achieves a baroque sense of wonder and displays his formal and linguistic virtuosity. But perhaps the most technically accomplished poems are those from the cycle "A Part of Speech," where the mastery of rhyme, enjambment, and trope is especially striking. This cycle can be seen as poetry of the psyche. His lyrical persona is influenced by the principal oppositions within the major themes: individual versus empire; man versus time; time versus faith, love, memory, and creativity. Among some excellent translations by Brodskii himself, the splendid "Elegy: For Robert Lowell" was composed in English. In both languages Brodskii is seeking to preserve "words against the time of cold." By his own admission, Brodskii writes "exclusively about one thing: about time and what time does to man, how it transforms him." It is identified now with cold, now with dust; things, too, can be regarded as masks for time. In the face of time, the generally accepted hierarchy of things appears to be defective and is replaced by the principle of relativity, and this is stated in many of Brodskii's poems: "What remains of a man is a part / of speech"; "From great things, the words of language remain." The tragic pathos of Brodskii's poetry can be felt in his attempt to overcome time and alienation by faith and creativity, and in his awareness of the illusory nature of this attempt. For Brodskii, an almost stoic resistance to all life's calamities forms the structure of the human soul.

—Valentina Polukhina

PARZIVAL
Poem by Wolfram von Eschenbach, c. 1200–10

Of the three narrative poems written by Wolfram von Eschenbach, *Parzival* is the longest and most complex. Writing during the course of the first decade of the 13th century, Wolfram von Eschenbach does not reveal the identity of his patrons, though references to places and individuals, including the Landgrave Hermann of Thuringia, from whom he later acquired the source of *Willehalm*, suggest that he was writing for an aristocratic public in Franconia but was also connected with the literary activity centred on Hermann's Thuringian court.

The identification of the sources of Wolfram von Eschenbach's work is hindered partly by his own contradictory comments on the matter. Despite his comments, most scholars are agreed that his main source was Chrétien de Troyes's unfinished *Conte du Graal* (*Perceval*). It depends on one's view of Wolfram von Eschenbach and the potential extent of his originality whether for the rest of the work one accepts his explanation that his source was an otherwise unknown French work by the equally unknown Kyot of Provence or instead sees him, as do most scholars, drawing on the logical implications of his own work and on a wide knowledge of medieval literature, in which case Kyot merely serves as a fictional source to legitimate his inventiveness.

Parzival is traditionally interpreted as an examination of the relative value of a superficial secular knighthood, the ethos of which is epitomized by the court of King Arthur, and a form of knighthood. The pursuit of this, identified with the search for the Grail (in Wolfram von Eschenbach's view, uniquely, a miraculous stone), leads to a higher plane of religious awareness.

In order to place Parzival's development in context, Wolfram von Eschenbach commences his work not with Parzival himself but with his father Gahmuret in whose activities Wolfram presents a concept of knighthood obsessed with the gaining of personal glory and sexual conquests through warfare. Gahmuret's two sons, Feirefiz and Parzival, are born of heathen and Christian mothers respectively, both of whom are abandoned in the search for further opportunities of knightly combat.

Using the bipartite structure of contemporary Arthurian romances, Wolfram von Eschenbach shows how Parzival, following, despite initial ignorance, the same concept of knighthood, seeks admittance as a knight to Arthur's court. On the way he commits acts that have baleful consequences: above all the unwitting killing in combat of a relative and the theft of his red armour—as the "Red Knight" he henceforth bears the stigma of this murder—and, running through the work as a constant motif, his failure to ask a question. This failure touches the centre of Parzival's fitness for membership of the Grail community, where through his mother he is ultimately destined to succeed his suffering grandfather Anfortas as King, provided he can ask the cause of the old man's suffering. It is this failure that precipitates Parzival's public disgrace, at the very moment that he appears to have achieved his goal of integration into Arthurian society.

One might here expect Wolfram von Eschenbach, following the traditional scheme, to present a new series of events leading to Parzival's rehabilitation, but instead he chooses to introduce a second narrative thread, that of the chivalric exploits of the knight Gawan. This sequence is interrupted by the ethical centre of the work, Parzival's encounter with his hermit-uncle Trevrizent, and elsewhere too Wolfram von Eschenbach does not allow the reader to lose sight of Parzival completely. He appears as a slightly mysterious background figure within the sequence of Gawan's exploits and their separate paths ultimately coalesce when, not recognizing each other, they fight a duel in which Parzival is spared the disaster of spilling a relative's blood for a second time. Gawan's exploits show him to be the perfect knight servitor of a lady and permit his reintegration into the Arthurian world. They are however, determined by a chivalric code in which the imperative of taking revenge and never refusing combat is paramount, and as such they culminate in a situation of some complexity in which adherence to the letter of the code would lead inevitably to results desired by none. It is Arthur's court that, relativizing the code, provides the diplomatic solution to these problems. The process of rehabilitation is thus doubled. A secular rehabilitation for Gawan at the court of King Arthur is balanced by a spiritual rehabilitation for Parzival, who, through his encounter with Trevrizent, eventually learns to understand the nature of his own sinfulness, the true nature of Christianity, of the Grail and of his own role as a member of the Grail community.

Parzival's installation as Grail King allows Wolfram von Eschenbach to incorporate the narrative thread of Parzival's half-brother and the Muslim world left dangling since the beginning of the work. This is achieved yet again through the image of a combat between relatives, in which God himself shatters Parzival's sword, thus saving him again from the sin of parricide. Some critics have argued that Wolfram von Eschenbach presents in the Grail community a utopian vision of the ultimate unity of mankind under one God. The genealogical detail provided by Wolfram von Eschenbach certainly shows that all figures of importance in *Parzival* are members of one family, extending, as Feirefiz shows, into the Muslim world. While the extent of Wolfram von Eschenbach's knowledge of this world is a matter of debate, it is also noticeable that throughout his work their "heathendom" never prevents the presentation of Muslim knights as the equals of their Christian counterparts: they too are welcome guests at Arthur's court. Only to the Grail community is access limited to Christians, and the work ends with the conversion of Feirefiz.

Most critics favour a gradualist interpretation of the relationship between the Arthurian and the Grail communities. Wolfram von Eschenbach is at pains to show the many links that exist between the two, not least Parzival's reintegration into the Arthurian world on his way to the Grail castle. While one is "higher" than the other, they are equally valuable and each individual must learn to serve the community to which he or she is called: Parzival, after all, is born to the Grail, Gawan is not.

—Alan Deighton

PASCUAL DUARTE'S FAMILY (La familia de Pascual Duarte)
Novel by Camilo José Cela, 1942

Essentially, the text of *Pascual Duarte's Family* is the autobiography of a man, Pascual Duarte, who, seemingly driven by circumstances to a series of senseless killings of people and animals, is garrotted in prison for the murder of a local wealthy landowner.

Pascual writes his own memoirs during the few months between the trial and his execution. Preceding the autobiographical tale there are three brief texts: a preliminary note by the transcriber, Pascual's letter to the recipient of his manuscript, and an extract from the last will and testament of Don Joaquín relating to this manuscript. The main text is followed also by a note by the transcriber, an affidavit by the jail's chaplain, and another affidavit by the prison guard who witnessed Pascual's execution: but these provoke suspicion and doubt about the story instead of convincing the reader of its veracity. From reading the texts one draws the conclusion that little can be trusted. There is nothing like an objective account here; there are only apparent truths, authorized ones, manipulated and mutilated ones, which preclude a naive and passive reading. These implications highlight the role of the narrator in the elaboration of the text, destroying the myth of a transparent correspondence of the text to an exterior reality. One infers the need for a critical reading, capable of deciphering that which is implicit, and which censorship does not permit to be exposed more openly. For all these reasons, the novel imposes its own method of reading. It tells us that in immediately post-war Spain, a critical reading was considered subversive, since against the passivity and the position of inferiority demanded by dictatorial discourse it requires the active participation of the reader in the creative process.

The autobiographical mode of *Pascual Duarte's Family* implies that the name of Pascual has two different functions—that of protagonist and that of narrator of his own story. A comparative analysis of both would allow us to determine the nature of the relationship between these functions.

Pascual has two inner characteristics—tenderness and a strong sense of justice—but he is uncultured. Such lack of education means not only a lack of knowledge about the world, but also ignorance about himself and an inability to reflect on his own behaviour. The narrator points out that the character fails to recognize the motivations of his acts. From this lack of knowledge come the inability to control himself and a tendency to be carried away by impulses. Another consequence of such a lack of culture is the reduced capacity for symbolic activity, which limits the possibilities of self-expression,

and prevents social communication. The only way of communicating is through violent actions. In the semantic organization of the novel, silence and violence are opposed to words and communication.

Pascual's first social experience is of violence in the family, which teaches him resignation in the face of the unavoidable. The key to the code of social values here is manhood, the defence of one's honour through physical aggression. This social law means reduction of the individual to the level of his physical power, and the regarding of others as aggressors and potential enemies, implying the institutionalization of violence as moral duty. According to the code of manhood, the innate qualities of Pascual—his affection and sense of justice—become feminine weaknesses; the assertion of manly strength is more important than expression of feelings: "You know that a real man does not cry like a woman." The code of violence transforms society into a battlefield.

Pascual draws another lesson from his social experience: the impossibility of choosing one's own destiny, amply illustrated by the metaphor of the pre-ordained path. But even though the stereotyped language of the uncultivated peasant attributes to God the responsibility for his destiny, the organization of the text makes it clear that the determinant of destiny is not divine but social. The habit of violence is a social inevitability. Its generalization in the community, and the lack of a reflective capacity which, in turn, generates routine and immobility, are symbolized by the dried fountain and the stopped clock in the square.

The inability to innovate implies denial of freedom. No choice is possible for him who plays an active role only in appearance. For the judicial system Pascual is the one who commits the crimes, but a thorough analysis reveals that he is rather the victim, dominated by circumstances instead of controlling them. What he does is merely the fulfilment of another's will. He merely responds to a previous aggression. The active and passive roles are superimposed on him. The distribution of roles assigned by the narrator and by the judicial system are radically different. The active-passive, aggressor-victim duality is reversed and, instead of opposing Pascual to society, it identifies him with the collective subject, thus rendering illegitimate the trial and the death penalty. The logic of the action is a war logic, in which the only alternatives are either to kill or to be killed, physically or symbolically (by loss of honour, of social consideration, and so on). These alternatives enclose the protagonist, and with him the collective subject, in an infernal spiral of violence from which it is impossible to escape. The memoirs are thus highly subversive, since they reverse the relationship between judge and criminal. They ascribe to the convicted man a natural goodness. The narrator accuses society of having institutionalized hate and violence, of not leaving the individual any alternative but to kill or be killed. In the light of this analysis, the final rebellion of Pascual acquires a new meaning, totally different from the one given by the guard and the priest. It is not a matter of cowardice but of legitimate rebellion, on the part of one who realizes that he is going to be executed for having applied in his life the laws that the collectivity taught him. We can understand now why in his letter to Don Joaquín he refuses to ask society for forgiveness.

The transformation of the character into narrator constitutes an authentic conversion. The passing on of his memoirs to Don Joaquín and their later publication shows the desire to communicate this process of individual conversion, making it a proposal for collective therapy. This transformation is made possible by Pascual's insertion into a new space, the jail. A place of confinement becomes a space of freedom. Rather than a denial of freedom, prison really represents the impossibility of acting. Pascual sees himself deprived of his usual mode of expression and immediate physical reaction. Jail interposes between him and his acts a distance that substitutes mental activity for physical action. He ceases reproducing, mechanically, a behaviour dictated by society and begins a personal and original consideration of such behaviour. The writing of his memoirs implies an effort of reflection, a process of learning about himself, which compensates for his deficiencies. The methodical exploration of the past allows him to acquire the abilities given to others by education. Whereas the protagonist let himself be controlled by circumstances and abdicated responsibility for his actions, the narrator is transformed into a subject in control of the story of his life. The roles, therefore, are reversed. His experience as a writer gives him the chance to learn symbolic behaviour and oral communication and thus to escape from the inevitability of violence. The memoirs, being a written artefact, require a reader.

So, the progression of this peasant transformed into a writer shows a progression from the denial of education to an affirmation of its necessity. *Pascual Duarte's Family* is thus a critique of the climate of the Spanish Civil War, still persisting in 1942, whose practices were in direct contradiction to the ideological principles upon which it based its legitimacy, those of Christianity.

Sending his memoirs to Don Joaquín, the narrator is advocating a social reconciliation, in the name of Christianity, among all Spaniards. If the reality of censorship at the time hindered an explicit presentation of the message, the real winner is literature itself: this masterpiece transcends its historical circumstances and continues to offer us the renewed pleasure of deciphering the enigma proposed in its own dedication: back in the 1940s, Camilo José Cela had already brought the Spanish novel into "the age of the reader."

—Francisco Carenas

PEASANT TALES (Bondefortelling)
Stories by Bjørnstjerne Bjørnson, 1856

The first of Bjørnstjerne Bjørnson's peasant tales appeared in 1856 in the periodical *Illustreret Folkeblad* which he was editing to assist an impoverished printer. The tales are contemporary portraits of Norwegian peasant life and although the place names and descriptions of nature are characteristically Norwegian they were sufficiently ambiguous to appeal to peasants of the entire nation.

According to Bjørnson himself, in an essay entitled "Hvorledes jeg blev digter" [How I Became a Poet] (1872), his poetic mission became clear to him on a trip to a student gathering in Uppsala (Sweden) in 1856 when he was gripped by "historical envy" at the Swedish security of national identity. Norwegians had been denied this by 400 years of Danish rule.

With a firm belief in the great heroic past of the Vikings and the view that the peasant was the key figure of national self-awareness—the custodian of the traditional Viking values of spiritual and moral existence—Bjørnson strove through his tales to stimulate national self-assertion against the superior foreign culture of Denmark. For Bjørnson, the peasant was the living embodiment of an exemplary way of life linking the people of contemporary Norway with the "Golden Age" before the throne had passed to the Danes. The peasant, like the Viking, was powerful but undemonstrative in

feeling, with a strength of will and purpose, self-disciplined, and supremely loyal to kinsman and friend. Bjørnson believed that upon these virtues a glorious national future could be built, and this is a predominant theme to which he returns throughout his peasant tales.

Unlike the overt national Romanticism of writers like J.S. Welhaven, Bjørnson's tales are not idyllically Romantic portraits of Norwegian life. The tales also address the social and political issues of the day, as in *Arne* where Nils Skredder represents the irresponsible, heavy-drinking peasant who terrorizes his family. However, the majority of the tales reflect Bjørnson's intention to present an alternative to the negative view of peasants being promoted by the sociologist Eilert Sundt around this time. Sundt's research revealed the high rate of unmarried mothers, illegitimate children, and alcoholism in the farming communities of Norway.

From the outset, Bjørnson's tales introduced the public to a stylistically fresher and more direct narrative technique, simultaneously inaugurating what was to become virtually a national campaign: a literary programme in national pride. The most important peasant tales are *Synnøve Solbakken, Arne, The Fisher Maiden, En glad gut (A Happy Boy), Brudeslåtten (The Bridal March)*, and "Fadren" ("The Father"). In a letter to Paul Botten Hansen, Bjørnson characterizes his own narrative style, declaring "Jeg respekterer intet Grammatik-Norsk: jeg bruger Bryst-Norsk!" [I have no respect for Norwegian grammar: I use Norwegian from the heart!]. The tales have a spoken quality about them, characteristic of the oral storytelling, and invoke comparison with the earlier sagas and folk literature of his day, such as the works of Asbjørnson and Hans Christian Andersen.

There are primarily two themes that dominate the peasant tales, the first being the stifling of talent, brought about by poverty or the misunderstanding of others. In the very first tale "Aanun," a gifted child whose family does not understand him is corrupted by an evil schoolteacher and an ignorant priest. The second theme concerns marriage between the social classes—for example, the lowly farm hand who either works hard or displays great feats of physical prowess and is rewarded with the hand of the farmer's daughter, like Thore in "Et farligt Frieri" [A Dangerous Courtship].

Like Thorbjørn in *Synnøve Solbakken*, who must overcome the savagery in his own nature, and Øyvind in *A Happy Boy*, who is hampered by his personal ambition and narcissism, all of Bjørnson's heroes must pass through a period of suffering before reaching a greater insight into their own nature.

Bjørnson's female heroes almost exclusively represent the male hero's "prize" and the majority of the tales end happily with the marriage ceremony, reminiscent of folktales and reflecting Bjørnson's belief in the church during this period of his authorship. Religion was expected to teach people to turn from self-love to neighbourly love and was part of his overall view that the nation required a national identity of which it could be proud.

The central stylistic achievement in these tales, although varying in quality and reminiscent of other literary genres, is found in Bjørnson's ability to give psychological insight to his characters by "showing" rather than "telling" the reader about their feelings. This is best seen in "The Father," where a conceited, demanding farmer, who has always pressured the local pastor to get the very best for his son, loses the son in a freak boating accident. When he visits the pastor to make amends for his arrogant life and to donate half the money he has received for the sale of his farm to the church, he appears as a broken man. The emotion of deep shame and newly acquired humility is implied by action and dialogue rather than the omniscient voice of the author.

Of all the tales the short story ''The Father'' and the novel *Synnøve Solbakken* illustrate the best qualities of Bjørnson's writing. They are well-constructed narratives, devoid of all unnecessary embellishment, and allow characters to come into direct contact with the reader through action and direct speech. This evokes psychological insight and pre-empts the work of the later Scandinavian writers of the 1880s and 1890s—the period of the ''Modern Breakthrough.'' Between them these works convey the dominant themes found repeatedly throughout the first 15 years of Bjørnson's prose writing, collectively known as the ''peasant tales.''

—J.M. Buscall

PEDAIR CAINC Y MABINOGI

See THE MABINOGION

PEER GYNT
Play by Henrik Ibsen, 1867

Henrik Ibsen wrote *Peer Gynt* in Rome, Ischia, and Sorrento in the early years of what was to be a 27-year absence from his native Norway. It is a five-act poetic drama, written for publication rather than for the stage, whose leading character and themes may be seen as complementary to those of Ibsen's previous play, *Brand*, written in 1865. Whereas Brand is ruthlessly singleminded in his beliefs, Peer is a compromiser who avoids facing up to reality and prefers to go ''round about.''

Peer Gynt takes the form of an epic narrative based upon the archetypal theme of the quest. Its eponymous hero travels from Norway to Africa and finally back again to Norway, passing from youth to old age and possibly death, in search of his authentic self. Although not intended for realization on the stage, these three locations visually complement the various psychological states experienced by the hero. The first three acts are set in the rural landscape of Norway with its mountains, valleys, and forests dotted with isolated farms and cottages and in the dark troll-world of rural folklore. During these scenes Peer is portrayed as an energetic young rogue who spins fantastic yarns and falls in love with a chaste and beautiful young girl, Solveig. His romantic image is, however, sullied by his surrender to an orgy of sexual indulgence which begins with the kidnap, seduction, and abandonment of a bride, continues in a sexual romp with a group of herd-girls, and is completed by his copulation with a green-clad woman who turns out to be a troll princess. This moral descent is reflected by the replacement of the objective material reality, represented by the rural landscape, by the nightmarish subjective reality of the troll kingdom, a world in which normal morality is reversed. Faced with the true implications of his behaviour, Peer refuses however to confirm his moral decline by submitting to the troll King's demand that his eye should be scratched so that his moral perception will remain irreversibly awry. In the following scene, still located in subjective reality, Peer's evasiveness and his inability to commit himself to a course of action are further conveyed by his struggle with the invisible Boyg. The dark world of Peer's sin-laden mind intrudes into day-to-day reality with the reappearance of the

green-clad woman who introduces him to his monstrously deformed son. Overwhelmed by guilt, Peer accepts the Boyg's advice to ''go round.'' In spite of Solveig's offer to share his burden, on the death of his mother who has hitherto offered him a refuge from life's realities, he flees from Norway.

In contrast to the green and fertile rural settings of the first three acts, the world of the middle-aged Peer of the fourth act is that of a flat and arid desert. Peer now attempts to discover his true self through worldly power and material success. In succession he adopts the roles of successful but amoral businessman, religious prophet, and academic historian, while considering in passing the foundation of a new state to be called Gyntiana. These attempts at aggrandizement end in a madhouse where he is crowned with a straw crown as the ''Emperor of Self.''

The bright and arid landscape of Act Four is replaced in the final act by a stormy North Sea night-crossing during which Peer, returning to Norway, meets a Strange Passenger emerging from nowhere, is ''cleansed'' in the sea when his ship is wrecked, and ultimately arrives home to a dark, purgatorial wasteland of dried river beds, burnt forests, and misty moorland. Here he is confronted, as in a morality play, by the metaphysically conceived figures of the Thin Person and the Button Moulder. The barrenness of these settings reflects Peer's gradual realization of the barrenness of his own character, a process dramatized in a series of visual images which include the auction of his past possessions and the peeling of an onion. The auction reveals that his life has been without significance, while the peeling of the onion, each layer related to a stage in his life, makes him realize that, like the onion, he has no centre and no heart. Once again the play slides between objective and subjective reality as Peer meets the Button Moulder who informs him that, because he has never committed himself with strength or purpose to any course of action, be it good or evil, he is worthy of neither heaven nor hell, and that his destiny is to be melted down, along with other anonymous scraps of wasted humanity, to be recast as someone else. With the Button Moulder poised to take him, Solveig's singing intervenes, and it is at this point that Peer makes the first positive choice of his life and completes the progress home to Solveig which he had earlier interrupted.

It is in Solveig that he discovers his true self for, during his absence, she has sustained him in her faith, hope, and love. Day is breaking and Peer is bathed in light as he buries his face in Solveig's lap. At this point the play, underscored by the singing of the now blind Solveig, seems poised to topple into melodramatic sentimentality. Ibsen attempts, however, to avoid this resolution by making clear that the matter of Peer's salvation is yet to be resolved, for he has yet to meet the Button Moulder at the last crossroads. In these final moments of the play Solveig is, however, portrayed not as a wife and equal but as Peer's surrogate mother. ''My mother! My wife! O, thou pure woman!'' he cries, ''O hide me in your love! Hide me! Hide me!'' He has returned to what he was at the beginning: a child in need of the support and validation of his mother. The play opens with Peer's mother's accusation that he escapes from reality into lies. It closes, ironically with Solveig's advice that Peer should ''Sleep, sleep and dream,'' and thereby escape from reality into unconsciousness.

In its delving into the murkier side of human psychology and in its recognition of the importance and power of the unconscious, *Peer Gynt* not only prefigures Ibsen's later symbolic plays such as *The Master Builder, Rosmersholm*, and *The Lady from the Sea* but also the concerns of 20th-century expressionism and surrealism.

—D. Keith Peacock

THE PEONY PAVILION (Mudan Ting)
Operatic libretto by Tang Xianzu, 1598

Written in 1598, *The Peony Pavilion* is considered the finest example of musical drama created in China during the later Ming Dynasty (1368–1644). A canonical work in the Kunqu tradition, a highly refined form of Chinese opera, it is one of four plays, known as *Lin-chuan's Four Dreams*, written by Tang Xianzu (1550–1617), whose life nearly parallels that of William Shakespeare. Tang Xianzu wrote the libretto to *The Peony Pavilion* in the form of prose dialogue, intoned verses, and arias that were initially performed using a variety of existing musical scores. It was not until 1792, however, that original music became available, in the form of the *Na Shu Ying* score edited by Ye Tang. Like other Kunqu operas, *The Peony Pavilion* makes use of the qupaiti musical tradition, which is based on a close harmony between word and melody and which employs the dizi, or bamboo flute, as a lead instrument. The Kunqu style was popular until the 19th century, when it was overshadowed by the more popular Beijing Opera style, though a Kunqu revival began in the 1950s. Important editions of the libretto were published by Xu Shuofang in 1958 and by Yang Xiaomei in 1963.

Tang Xianzu helped to revitalize the tradition of the Southern Song (Sung) dynasty in Chinese drama by creating elaborate productions in which characters engaged in animated musical dialogues; prior to this, vocalists tended to sing independent solos with less interaction. Unlike classical Western drama, epic plays like *The Peony Pavilion* were not limited to a single time, space, and action. Instead, these dramatic romances, according to Stephen Owen in *An Anthology of Chinese Literature: Beginnings to 1911* were "often vast, sprawling works" that were "often intricate, with numerous subplots, usually weaving together one or more love stories with political intrigue and/or warfare."

This is an apt description of *The Peony Pavilion*, a play with fifty-five scenes in all that takes nearly twenty hours to stage. For this reason, it had rarely been performed in its entirety in a single production until its controversial revival in the West in the late 1990s. Set in the later Song Dynasty (960–1279), the work narrates the fortunes of two lovers who have an affair in a garden called the Peony Pavilion: Liu Mengmei (Willow Dreaming Plum), a student, and Du Liniang (Bridal Du), the daughter of a government official. After encountering her beloved in a dream, the young woman is smitten with love and eventually dies of a broken heart. After her death, her remains are interred beside a plum tree, near to where her portrait had earlier been buried under a stone. The Du family then moves to the north, where her father takes up a government post. Soon afterwards, Liu Mengmei, recuperating from an illness in the Du residence, is greeted by an apparition of his beloved, who is disinterred and found to be alive. Reunited at last, the two enjoy a blissful marriage until Du Liniang sends Liu Mengmei to search for her father, who had been involved in a military campaign. Believing his daughter still to be dead and her grave to have been vandalized, Governor Du does not accept this man to be his son-in-law and has him arrested and whipped. The abused lover is freed only after an audience with the emperor, who validates his claim. The family is reconciled and all is well.

As in some the works of Shakespeare, Tang Xianzu's contemporary in the West, *The Peony Pavilion* draws on a variety of elements to create an overall effect of epic dimensions: ghost stories, romantic tales of young lovers, psychological and class conflict, scenes of ribaldry and comic relief, intrigue, war, historical allusions, and interaction with royal or imperial figures. It has also been compared with Western operas of the Baroque era for their sweeping portrayals of many layers of society.

Controversy surrounded *The Peony Pavilion* in 1998 when Shanghai's Kunqu Opera Company was to have presented it at New York's Lincoln Center, directed by Chen Shi-Zheng, a Chinese-born American citizen. Shanghai's Bureau of Culture ruled that its new staging of the opera was "feudal, superstitious, and pornographic" and refused to allow it to travel to the United States. Although the Kunqu production was cancelled, Chen eventually directed an American production of the opera at Lincoln Center in 1999. A condensed production of *The Peony Pavilion*, directed by Peter Sellars and with music by Tan Dun, was produced in Berkeley, California, that same year. Xiaoping Yen adapted the story for a novel published in English in 2000.

—Edward Moran

LE PÈRE GORIOT
Novel by Honoré de Balzac, 1835

In Honoré de Balzac's enormous literary production *Le Père Goriot* occupies a pivotal position. For the first time, Balzac wrote with the idea of using recurring characters to paint all of the French society of his period. Consequently, *Le Père Goriot* is as much about the education of the young and naive Rastignac as it is the story of old Goriot, a "Christ of fatherhood," a martyr of unworthy daughters. Rastignac and Paris—a Paris corrupted by money—are as important as the title character, and will survive him with a life of their own in other works of *The Human Comedy*.

In 1819, at Madame Vauquer's sordid and mysterious boarding-house, which is described in great detail, rumours abound about Monsieur Goriot, a retired vermicelli manufacturer. Every year he moves to a cheaper room on a higher floor; two rich young women visit him, although less and less frequently. Some say they are his mistresses; he protests they are his daughters. Among the other boarders are Eugelaane de Rastignac, a poor, provincial law student, and Vautrin, a rather menacing figure with an unusual knowledge of the ways of the world.

Little by little, Rastignac discovers Goriot's story: his two daughters, Anastasie and Delphine, now known respectively as Countess de Restaud and Baroness de Nucingen, thanks to successful marriages and solid dowries, are ruining him with their frivolous ways. Meanwhile, Rastignac's cousin, Viscountess de Beauséant, educates the ambitious student about Paris and opens the doors of society to him.

Rastignac discovers that Paris is "a heap of filth," "an ocean of mud," He himself is not cynical enough to accept Vautrin's invitation to court Victorine Taillefer, a boarder in the Vauquer house and prospective heiress to a large fortune. But he does follow Madame de Beauséant's advice to seduce Delphine de Nucingen in order to advance in the world; in so doing, he befriends Goriot, who relishes talking about his daughter. The old man expresses his fear of not keeping his daughters happy, since his financial resources are getting so meagre. As he becomes involved with rich people, Rastignac too is pressed for money; he requests and gets funds from his family, and finally agrees to court Victorine.

Two of the Vauquer boarders, Poiret and Mademoiselle Michonneau, motivated by greed, report Vautrin to the police who arrest him. Vautrin's true identity is discovered: he is the famous criminal Jacques Collin, also known as ''cheat-death,''

Goriot, Delphine, and Rastignac share some happy moments together. The young couple are to move into an apartment of their own, with Goriot occupying a room above. But Delphine is too financially dependent upon Nucingen to gain her freedom, and the prospect of happiness for all of them is soon shattered. At the same time, Anastasie is involved in a costly love affair, and both daughters beg their father with tears and cries for more money. Rastignac saves Anastasie by forging a draft made out to Vautrin.

His daughters' demands and misadventures prove too much for Goriot, who becomes ill and is cared for by Bianchon, a medical student and boarder in the Vauquer house. Despite Rastignac's pleas to the daughters to visit their dying father, the two women can think only of Madame de Beauséant's final ball. Goriot's condition worsens. During his agony (which is probably the most emotional scene in the novel), he realizes that his daughters will not come to see him on his deathbed and curses them.

Goriot is buried in a pauper's grave at Rastignac's and Bianchon's expense. The daughters, too preoccupied with their own lives, send their empty carriages to follow the hearse. From the highest point of the Père-Lachaise cemetery, Rastignac defies Paris and, ''as a first act in his challenge of Society,'' he goes to dine with the Baroness de Nucingen.

Balzac's characters are dominated by their passions. Goriot's single-minded devotion to his daughters is tainted by his absolute and selfish disregard for anything else: he will stop at nothing on their behalf, declaring himself ready to ''kill a man'' or ''go to the penitentiary'' for them. Vautrin and Rastignac prove equally extreme and corrupt in the pursuit of their goals.

Vautrin sees corruption as the law of all men: ''Man is the same at the top, in the middle, at the bottom of the social ladder.'' Indeed, all of the characters in *Le Père Goriot* are partners in crime: Goriot made his fortune during the Revolution by selling flour for ten times what it had cost him; Gobseck, the money lender, a recurring character in *The Human Comedy*, attends to the needs of rich and poor alike; Madame Vauquer, Mademoiselle Michonneau, Nucingen, Madame de Beauséant's lover, and Goriot's daughters all fall victim to greed.

Vautrin's vision of society (''*Succeed!* Succeed at any cost!'') is no different from Madame de Beauséant's, who foresees Rastignac's revelations: ''the world is ignoble and nasty. You will discover how deeply corrupt women are, and you'll measure the enormous and wretched vanity of men. Treat this world as it deserves. The more coldly you calculate, the farther you'll climb,'' By the end of the novel, Rastignac himself has become one of the people he first despised, one of those described by Vautrin for whom ''there are no such things as principles, there are only events: there are no such things as laws, there are only circumstances,''

Le Père Goriot is the unveiling of the modern world by a lucid conscience: ''Law and morality [are] impotent among the rich. In wealth [Rastignac] saw the *ultima ratio mundi*,'' Morality is foreign to both poles of society, as much to the Vauquer boarding-house as to the Beauséant mansion. In this respect, *Le Père Goriot* is a testimony to the beginnings of the modern age in France.

Balzac's stated aim in the novel is not to reason about right and wrong, but to show what simply is:

This drama is no work of fiction, no mere novel! It is all true, so true that everyone may recognize its elements within himself, perhaps in his very heart.

Indeed, it is for Balzac's remarkable attention to realistic detail, the breadth of his creative imagination, and the sense of inescapable fatality which pervades it that *Le Père Goriot* has been acclaimed as one of the major novels of modern literature.

—Pierre J. Lapaire

PERI HYPSOUS

See ON THE SUBLIME

PERIBÁÑEZ AND THE COMENDADOR OF OCAÑA
(Peribáñez y el comendador de Ocaña)
Play by Lope de Vega Carpio, 1614 (written 1605–08)

In the *Arte nuevo de hacer comedias en este tiempo* of 1609, Lope de Vega Carpio declared his special interest in a notably dramatic theme: ''Los casos de la honra son mejores, / porque mueven con fuerza a toda gente'' (''cases of honour are best, because everybody is extremely moved by them''). Among Lope's most memorably dramatized ''cases of honour,'' *Fuenteovejuna*, *The King, the Greatest Alcalde*, and *Peribáñez and the Comendador of Ocaña* form almost a trilogy, since all three are plays of peasant honour, in which base overlords are destroyed by nobly-minded peasants whose conduct is ultimately approved or forgiven by right-thinking Spanish monarchs. These are all plays in which Lope extols the unsophisticated pleasures of country life, contrasts naturally authentic love with destructively sexual passion, condemns the abuse of political power and social privilege, and distinguishes between surface honour (the immediate prerogative of high birth and rank) and the superior quality of inner honour, to which every man, regardless of his class, is entitled to aspire. Though its exact date of composition is unknown, internal evidence (preferred verse-forms, etc.) indicate that *Peribáñez* was written earlier than the other two dramas, and probably in the period 1605–08. Audiences in Madrid must have received the play with enthusiastic approbation, for its fame evidently soon inspired an unknown author to compose a burlesque version, entitled *El comendador de Ocaña*, which entertainingly parodies the Comendador's lascivious interest in his vassal's wife and Peribáñez's jealously offended reactions. Some decades later Lope's drama was reworked—and retitled *La mujer de Peribáñez* [Peribáñez's Wife]—by three anonymous imitators of Calderón. Theatre documents record that *Peribáñez*—perhaps this inferior adaptation, however, rather than the original masterpiece—was staged in Valladolid in 1681, and was still being performed in Madrid, at the royal palace in 1684, and at the *corrales* (public theatres) in 1689 and 1695.

The drama is set in the reign of Enrique III of Castile (1390–1406), a turbulent period of campaigns against the Moors and conflicts with powerful noblemen opposed to the king's authority. The play opens with a *boda de villanos*, as the village of Ocaña celebrates the wedding of a prosperous and respected young peasant to Casilda, his extremely virtuous and extraordinarily beautiful bride. Their overlord, the comendador Don Fadrique, injured during a bullfight that forms part of the festivities, is tended by Casilda with whom he falls passionately in love. At first he attempts to seduce Casilda and render her husband complaisant through flattery and gifts; but when persuasion fails he resorts to extreme measures of deceit and violence. Apparently he honours and ennobles Peribáñez by appointing him captain over 100 peasant-soldiers, but the honour which is intended, as the Comendador reveals to his servant, Leonardo, is ''honra aforrada en infamia'' (''honour wrapped in ignominy''). Don Fadrique's evil purpose is to separate the jealously protective husband from his devoted wife. Peribáñez is sent, at the head of his soldiers, to join the king in his campaign against the Moors. The Comendador enters the peasant's house prepared to rape Casilda if she resists him. But Peribáñez, aware of his lord's ignoble passion and suspecting his intention, returns home as Casilda struggles to oppose her aggressor. Peribáñez protects his wife's virtue and defends his own honour by killing the Comendador. Peribáñez almost pays with his life for the death of his overlord. Having heard the true facts, however, King Enrique is finally persuaded to pardon, even reward him. His noble rank of captain is confirmed and, a peasant no longer, Peribáñez embarks upon a career in the king's army, to serve in the war against the Moorish kingdom of Granada.

Despite the convincing authenticity of its medieval setting, and the presence among its characters of an impressively historical, Spanish monarch, *Peribáñez* differs notably from *Fuenteovejuna* and *The King, the Greatest Alcalde*, in that the main elements of its plot were not derived from chronicle-sources. The play was essentially developed from its author's imagination, uniquely stimulated to creativity by the sentiments of a traditional song:

> más quiero yo a Peribáñez
> con su capa la pardilla
> que al comendador de Ocaña
> con la suya guarnecida.
>
> (I love Peribáñez
> with his plain brown cloak
> more than the Comendador of Ocaña
> with his cloak so richly adorned.)

This song is worked into the dramatic centre of the action, where, in Act II, it forms part of the key speech that Casilda delivers, as she addresses Don Fadrique from the safety of a window in her locked room—the speech through which she rejects the aristocratic Comendador's dishonourably sexual advances and demonstrates her virtuous devotion to her honourable peasant-husband. The song also dramatically inspired Lope's symbolic use of contrasted costumes and different visual effects. Peribáñez usually appears dressed as a peasant in plain brown cloak, though he acquires a less humble costume, a sword, and even a plumed hat after the Comendador has appointed him to the rank of captain. Significantly, however, Peribáñez reverts to his peasant's plain cloak when he appears before the king to explain honestly and justify the death of the Comendador. As for Don Fadrique, in contrast to Peribáñez, he is always splendidly attired, which indicates not only his status but his vanity and arrogance. His dress is also used suggestively to prepare us for his violent death. Throughout the play he wears a tunic decorated with a blood-red cross, the insignia of the military order to which he proudly belongs. That same tunic, together with the red cloak which, ominously, he chooses to wear during his final visit to Peribáñez's house, will be fatally stained in the crimson reality of his own blood, ironically shed by a vassal whom he has personally armed.

Lope thoughtfully manages symbolism and imagery to motivate the central conflict and prepare us for its outcome. In the first scene the bull, through its horned presence at the wedding festivities, symbolizes sexual aggression, signifying that danger already threatens Peribáñez's honour and marital happiness. Still more significantly, the almost fatal injury which Don Fadrique sustains in his encounter with the bull leads us to expect that the violent passion that he immediately conceives for Casilda will ultimately destroy the Comendador himself. Another remarkable aspect of Lope's achievement is his lyricism—as illustrated by the poems in which Peribáñez and Casilda respectively recite their ''ABC''s of love, listing the qualities that each considers essential in a wife or husband. Equally noteworthy is Lope's sympathetic, yet realistically detailed, representation of country life: Peribáñez harvests his crops, tends his animals, embraces his wife in the stables; and their evening meal, bubbling in the pot, is seasoned with onions and garlic.

Lope also offers convincingly vital portrayals of the main characters. Casilda is less profoundly individualized than her husband or the Comendador. Nevertheless, besides extraordinary beauty and exceptional virtue, she is acceptably endowed with more ordinary qualities, such as good sense and quick wits, and she displays some naturally feminine weaknesses, occasionally indulging her fondness for pretty clothes and frivolous pleasures. Her husband is distinguished by a more interestingly ambiguous personality. To an extent he is happily active within the peasant community. Yet there are other still unsatisfied ambitions and undeveloped abilities in this man, which cause him to give up his humble occupation with alacrity when he is offered a notably different profession with distinctly elevated social status. The Comendador is an even more memorably complex individual. Far from being simply an evil-minded overlord, he is also a nobleman possessed of courage, intelligence, and self-perception. Moreover, the love he has for Casilda is passionately genuine. He longs to be her husband and the father of her children. These longings, however, are impossible to realize because of her already married state and her impossibly inferior social rank. Consequently his love, from its more exalted aspects, degenerates violently to levels of ultimately self-destructive lust.

In the final moments of life the Comendador recognizes, courageously and with dignity, that the fatal punishment administered by Peribáñez is justified, so that we are moved to appreciate his human qualities and to regret his death. At this point were are almost inclined to accord him the lofty status of tragic hero. However, since the action is not yet concluded, the impression made upon us by Don Fadrique's death soon diminishes when his accomplices—Inés and Luján—are also killed by Peribáñez. The latter's success in protecting his wife's virtue attracts our principal attention and holds our admiration, while his elevation in rank gains our lasting approval as an appropriate reward for his noble attitudes and honourable conduct. In its last lines Lope alludes to the play as a ''*tragicomedia*,'' which is an entirely accurate description. With its combination of sad and happy events and its finally optimistic conclusion, *Peribáñez* fulfils the main purpose of drama—as Lope understood it—by reflecting the variety in the reality of human experience.

—Ann L. Mackenzie

THE PERIODIC TABLE (Il sistema periodico)
Prose by Primo Levi, 1975

Scientific research and literature are often seen as opposite methods of interpreting reality: scientific research is defined as primarily analysis, literature as mainly synthesis. This collection is an attempt to convey to readers of literature some of the lessons learned by Primo Levi in the course of his diverse experiences, and at the same time something about the conflicts and ultimate joy of scientific learning.

The title refers to Dimitri Mendeleev's table of elements. The book consists of 21 stories, each named after an element, which are arranged in an order roughly corresponding to the course of Levi's own life—from the history of his Piedmontese Jewish ancestors to his youth under the Fascist regime, from his deportation from Italy to his return home, and finally to the moment when he turned from the trade of the chemist to that of the writer. Three basic themes are present, with varying emphasis—Levi's personal history and that of his generation; the pursuit of knowledge through trial and error; and the characteristics and changes of matter, presented first as enemies to be conquered, then as allies in physical and moral survival, and finally as the essence of life itself.

Levi denies this text the status of autobiography, "save in the partial and symbolic limits in which every piece of writing is autobiographical, indeed every human work." He calls it, instead, "a micro-history, the history of a trade and its defeats, victories, and miseries." Chemistry is thus represented not as an abstract science, but rather as a constant struggle, inseparably connected to daily life, history, politics, and personal development, as a metaphor for all kinds of learning: it is "a particular instance, a more strenuous version of the business of living." Although some of the processes and lessons learned in acquiring the chemist's trade, and even the structure of some molecules, are described in terms accessible to non-scientists, the text focuses on what individual human beings acquire personally from contacts with chemical transformations of matter. The elements of Mendeleev's table are thus occasionally personified, by being attributed anthropomorphic traits, and occasionally used as metaphors for aspects of the human condition.

In the first story, "Argon," Levi compares inert or noble gases, which do not combine with any other element, with his own ancestors, a dynasty of likeable eccentrics, gradually integrated but never fully assimilated into Italian society, each identified by an anecdote and by one or more sayings in Piedmontese dialect containing linguistically assimilated Hebrew expressions. "Iron," in the eponymous story, set in 1939, is metaphorically connected both to the imminent world catastrophe and to the courage of one of Levi's friends, who was to die heroically in the Resistance.

Interaction with the elements is represented as a source of practical moral instruction. Levi, as a student, sets fire to a laboratory by using potassium instead of sodium, and learns the hard way that "one must distrust the almost-the-same, the practically identical, the approximate, the or-even, all surrogates and all patchwork." There is a comic side: lipstick ingredients can be synthesized from chicken droppings, and acids can be stored in soup tureens, Art Nouveau chandeliers, and chamber pots. There is also a tragic side: the autobiographical story "Cerio" is set in Auschwitz, where the theft of some cerium bars buys Levi and a friend two months of life. Some stories are fictional interludes: a few brief vignettes and two fables set in the past share with the autobiographical tales a passionate interest in the changes of elements and in the relationships of these changes to the lives of human beings.

All the themes of the book are brought together in the last story, "Carbon": the journeys of an atom of carbon are followed through the centuries and through a variety of forms, until it enters Levi's own brain, gives Levi's hand an impulse, and leads it to impress the final full stop of the book on paper. The conclusion is thus a synthesis between a view of life as a series of chemical changes, the autobiographical strand, and the text's reflection on itself.

This inspiring, if at times slightly uneven, book is more than a mere attempt to bridge the gap between the "two cultures." Its power lies in the constant tension between science—seen initially, naively, as the key to truth, then exposed as dogmatic and unavoidably linked to politics, and finally accepted as a concrete way of testing oneself—and literature, "the trade of clothing facts in words," at first rejected as abstract and empty, then, in the final story, defined as "bound by its very nature to fail" but reclaimed as the only means of consciously shaping and communicating the writer's knowledge of the extra-textual world.

—Mirna Cicioni

THE PERSIANS (Persae)
Play by Aeschylus, 472 BC

Aeschylus' *The Persians* is the earliest extant tragedy, unique in the repertoire for its historical subject, the battle of Salamis (480 BC) and the defeat of the Persian fleet under Xerxes. Aeschylus himself was a participant in the action. The political character of the prize-winning trilogy *Phineus, The Persians,* and *Glaucus of Potniae* is signalled by the presence of Pericles, the celebrated democratic statesman, as patron (*choregus*) at an early age. The satyr play *Prometheus the Firebearer,* which would have followed the trilogy, no doubt featured a torch race for victory, and perhaps parodied the final play of the trilogy. The plays are linked thematically through subject matter relating to the conflict of east and west, a factor which Herodotus explored in his history of the Persian wars. The religious factor is repeatedly evident in *The Persians,* recalling the religious content of the beginnings of tragic drama. Aeschylus' play unquestionably extols the Athenian victory, not through nationalistic self-eulogy but through Persian eyes. The majesty, nobility, and dignity of the Persians, especially Darius, are noteworthy. Themistocles, the hero of Salamis, and his colleagues are unnamed; the roll-call of Persians is colourful and authentic.

The play is virtually plotless, although the other plays of the trilogy no doubt resonated with livlier librettos if not more exotic costumes, music, and dancing. *The Persians* is limited to two actors and a council of 12 Persian elders who comprise the chorus; the mood shifts, through choral response, from foreboding, through confirmation, to explication and extravagant emotional response at the close. The play opens in a council chamber of the palace at Susa, and later shifts to the tomb of Darius at Persepolis. The chorus plays a major role in the drama; its members' confidence and trust in their own nature, in Atossa, Xerxes' royal mother, and in the deceased Darius, are of major importance to the meaning of the play.

Foreboding and concern dominate the play; specific themes and symbols resonate though the drama, with repeated reference to a moral formula: excess wealth (*koros*), arrogance (*hubris*), persuasion (*peitho*), and ruin (*atê*). Age and antiquity are also pervasive, as embodied in the council of elders, and in the antiquity of the Persian realm. Compulsion, enslavement, and the cruel sea are omnipresent in the symbolic use of language.

Atossa, the queen mother, before whom the chorus lies prostrate, is a vehicle for the omnipresent gold (*koros*) theme, and also of disturbing dreams. In one her son Xerxes yoked two women, Persia and Greece; Persia is docile, but Greece upsets the chariot of Xerxes. The other dream centres on a falcon (embodiment of the sun god) clawing an (imperial) eagle, interpreted as the weaker resisting the stronger bird, which sought refuge at Apollo's hearth at Delphi, a probable allusion to Delphic complicity in the Persian advance into Greece. Atossa's emphasis on Xerxes' autocratic rule over an enslaved people excites the chorus to respond that Athenian soldiers are committed citizens, not slaves. A messenger reports that the Persian forces at Salamis have been totally defeated; Atossa finally learns that Xerxes is a survivor.

The chorus addresses an invocation to Zeus, and contrasts Xerxes with Darius as battle commander. Atossa assembles offerings for Darius' tomb, and the chorus appeals to his ghost to manifest itself. The ghost scene, charged with melodrama and lugubrious music, heightens the expectation of Xerxes' arrival. The ghost also excites reminders of the yoke, fetters, and manacles (and net) used earlier. Concern for Xerxes' clothes leads to Atossa's removal from stage. With the arrival of Xerxes, the play reverts to the original content of tragedy, lamentations exchanged by the actor and the chorus members; the passing parade of Persian names lends an exotic and colourful element to the grand finale. The final lesson is not that Zeus has been the saviour of Athens but that Athenians have been their own champions; Zeus' resistance to arrogance (*hubris*) is perennial and ultimately victorious.

The Persians falls short of being a great play, but attains some distinction for its exotic language, impressive imagery, elaborate spectacle, and dramatic effects.

—Alexander G. McKay

PETER SCHLEMIHL (Peter Schlemihls wundersame Geschichte)
Novella by Adelbert von Chamisso, 1814

Peter Schlemihl is the work by which the poet and scientist Adelbert von Chamisso is now best known. It was first published in 1814, at the end of the High Romantic period in German literature, and over 20 years after its French-born author and his parents had settled in Prussia after fleeing France during the Revolution. Chamisso served as a page at the Prussian court and in 1798 became an ensign in the Prussian army, but his parents had returned to France in 1801. The year after its publication he set off on a voyage around the world as the scientist attached to a Russian expedition commanded by Captain Otto von Kotzebue, the son of the internationally popular dramatist August von Kotzebue. His record of this expedition, published in 1836, is a classic of German travel literature.

Chamisso's story reflects his innate restlessness and his search for an identity. As it opens, Peter Schlemihl, its first-person narrator, returns from a perilous sea voyage. His return to familiar, safe surroundings is deceptive, however. He looks up a certain Herr Thomas John, to whom he has a letter of introduction. This innocuous action proves to be his introduction to a bewildering sequence of adventures in a world which does not operate according to the laws of normal, conventional reality. At Herr John's opulent home he encounters a mysterious, withdrawn, gaunt, and elderly man, dressed in grey, whose extraordinary actions the other members of the company take in their stride. Before long, the gentleman makes Schlemihl an offer he cannot resist: in return for the shadow he is casting that fine sunny day, he is offered the magic purse of Fortunatus which, as the old chapbook story has it, never runs out of money. Before Schlemihl realizes what is happening, he has parted with his shadow.

Until that moment, Schlemihl, like all human beings, had taken his shadow for granted. But Chamisso's tale brings home the terrifying enormity of its loss. A shadow is the visual proof of the physical existence of a solid body: from now on Schlemihl finds himself living his life without this vital proof of his existence. Wherever his adventures take him, someone sooner or later notices that he has no shadow; repeatedly and inevitably this leads to his rejection by his fellow men and to his social ostracism, for without a shadow he is "different." In fact his name is taken from the Old Testament Book of Numbers and means, "The unlucky one" or, literally, "The Beloved of God." a paradox which Chamisso was keen to explore, though not in religious or racial terms.

The central metaphor so tangibly presented by the story is open to a number of interpretations, which makes it fascinating without in any way diminishing its readability as a good yarn: not surprisingly, it has always enjoyed great popularity as a children's classic. In a discerning essay written in 1911, Thomas Mann argues that it is no fanciful allegory, but the penetrating portrayal of the romantic sensibility and the price that has to be paid for it. Schlemihl's shadow, Mann suggests, is a symbol of middle-class solidity and of "belonging": its loss is therefore a metaphor for the loss of social status. The ensuing story of Schlemihl's wanderings can be seen as an expression of Chamisso's search for stability which should be viewed in direct though ironic connection with his own apparently successful attempts to settle down to the demands of professional and domestic life both as an admired writer and as the keeper of the botanical garden and herbarium in Berlin.

Chamisso's story is a remarkably original and largely successful amalgam of disparate motifs given cohesion and credibility by its subjective truth and its close reflection of the economic facts of early 19th-century middle-class life. The result is a tale which, for all its superficial naiveté, subtly reveals the relationship between self and world. This is also apparent in its presentation, which is in the form of letters addressed by the fictitious narrator to Chamisso himself. Written towards the end of the German Romantic period, it succeeds in combining the mysterious and fantastic elements of the Romantic fairy tale, such as the wager between a human being and an emissary from the supernatural world, with the new preoccupations of 19th-century realism, such as the relationship of money to social identity and social acceptance. Schlemihl's ultimate rejection of the grey man and the bottomless purse brings about a change in his fortunes. As the story draws to its conclusion, he ceases to be the haunted outsider at the mercy of the world and of his own baser instincts. Released from the twin burdens of conformity and rejection, he finds a freer and more forward-looking fulfilment as his wanderings turn into travels in pursuit of the objectives of the scientific observer. Thus the story bridges the gap between necromancy and empirical science in a way which met with the approval of a wide spectrum of readers.

—Peter Skrine

PETERSBURG (Peterburg)
Novel by Andrei Belyi, 1916

Although compared by some critics to Joyce's *Ulysses* with its broad scope and challenging formal innovations, *Petersburg* has none the less remained a relatively obscure and little-known work. It appeared in 1916 to immediate acclaim and after Andrei Belyi's 1922 revisions, although suffering from the Soviet censors intent on establishing Socialist Realism, it nevertheless went through several reprints. Originally conceived as part of a projected trilogy about western versus eastern cultures and their conflicting representations of life, Belyi radically changed his conception of this novel during the process of its composition.

The novel is set in the autumn of 1905, a turbulent period of political instability with a series of mutinies, strikes, and assassinations, which create an air of being on the brink of cataclysmic change. This atmosphere of conspiracy, political anxiety, and fear propels the narrative. Nikolai Apollonovich Ableukhov, a student of neo-Kantian philosophy, who was once incautiously involved with a revolutionary group and their plot to assassinate a prominent government official, is now asked to plant the bomb. In a cruel twist, the eminent politician turns out to be his father, senator Apollon Apollonovich. Although the assassination plot ultimately fails, this main narrative thread weaves together a wide variety of subplots that involve linguistic and philosophical concerns, with a number of characters and ideological perspectives of Russian society. From the powerful and influential Ableukhovs and their circle, to the antagonistic and poverty-stricken Dudkin and the peasant Stepka, the multiplicity of characters in the text presents one with a cross-section of a society locked in struggle.

The novel's careful detail establishes a ''realism'' which is nevertheless constantly subverted by the question of ''unreality.'' A dichotomous tension between appearance and illusion is always evident, especially in the subplot of the elusive Red Domino, and the other frequent allusions to masks, disguises, and hidden activities. Even ''shadowy consciousness'' itself is regarded as a site of fantastic and duplicitous activity: ''Cerebral play is only a mask. Under way beneath this mask is the invasion of the brain by forces unknown to us.''

Thus, the novel makes the interrogation and exploration of the nature of reality a central concern. Various philosophies of consciousness are considered, including those of Kant, Comte, Nietzsche, Bruno, and Bergson. A tension emerges as subjects oscillate between desiring consciousness to be a stable centre for the self and finding that consciousness is constantly upset, distorted, and de-centred, as it verges on a chasm of darkness and emptiness: ''Consciousness struggled in vain to give illumination. . . . And there was no centre of consciousness.'' The certainty of subjectivity falls away into a morass of indescribable blankness: ''And the 'I' proved to be merely a black receptacle, if not a small cramped storeroom.'' Indeed, far from proving to be the manageable instrument of an autonomy that threatens to subvert the ''I'''s power, ''. . . there were swarms of thoughts thinking themselves; and it was not he thinking, but thoughts thinking themselves—something was being thought, was being sketched, was arising.''

Belyi utilizes various mythologies concerning St. Petersburg in the layered construction of this novel, alluding to the works of Pushkin, Dostoevskii, Chekhov, Tolstoi, and others. Belyi's principal text is Pushkin's poem *Mednyi vsadnik* (*The Bronze Horseman*), which focuses on the statue that is one of the principal landmarks of the city. In Belyi's personification of the city—the whirlwind, the caryatid, the buildings—this statue haunts the characters, as it hovers ominously and apocalyptically over both the city and the novel. As with many modernist texts, temporality and spatiality are important foci of the novel's interrogation. St. Petersburg's geography is always minutely detailed throughout the novel, as the narrative constantly relates the characters' imaginative relationship with the physical urban space of the city. The city is often the locus of delusion, almost indeed the limit of perception: ''There is an infinity of rushing prospects with an infinity of rushing, intersecting shadows. All of Petersburg is an infinity of the prospect raised to the nth degree.'' This boundlessness equally extends to the temporal dimension, since although the novel's final chapters are structured around the elapse of the 24 hours of the bomb, time nevertheless expands in the characters' consciousnesses. They frequently find themselves adrift in a timelessness which is profoundly disturbing. In order to preserve some sense of subjective integrity in the face of this temporal disorientation, characters construct various systems around them, like Apollon Apollonovich's fascination with ''proportionality and symmetry.''

The novel's philosophical explorations into the nature of reality are intricately linked to its formal experimentation, much of which derives from Belyi's interest in Symbolist aesthetics. A central feature of Belyi's aesthetic innovation lies in his conception and treatment of language. In a society where human subjectivity is splintered and uncertain, communication appears to be similarly fragmented: ''all the words jumbled and again wove in to a sentence; and the sentence seemed meaningless.'' Dialogues are often abruptly wrenched through unexpected interruptions and gaps; the text itself is fractured and dispersed into smaller units by a series of dashes and dots. Belyi recognizes that language can reinforce and create social abstractions and illusions if its partiality is ignored or forgotten. Therefore, he highlights the materiality of language, and emphasizes the production of words as sounds and contingent human ideas. To aid this aesthetic principle, the text utilizes clusters of certain sounds, as for example in Belyi's description of his use of the sounds ''ll,'' ''pp,'' ''kk,'' and ''rr'' (see Penguin translator's introduction, p. xvii). The text also makes extensive use of neologisms, puns, and letter games, such as Dudkin's confusion over Shishnarfne and Enfranshish. The recurrence of specific symbolic motifs, like the swirls of dust with their apocalyptic associations, reinforces the patterned structure of the novel.

Petersburg demonstrates an ingenuity, diversity, and intensity equal to that of the most significant 20th-century texts, while its formal and aesthetic experimentations broaden the boundaries and understanding of European modernism.

—Tim Woods

PHAEDRA (Phèdre)
Play by Jean Racine, 1677

Phaedra is Jean Racine's last public achievement as tragic poet. It was first titled *Phèdre et Hippolyte* but Racine later opted for the definitive title in the collected edition of 1687. After an initially mixed reception (due to the cabal of Racine's opponents), *Phaedra* has since enjoyed undisputed acclaim.

Inspired by the *Hippolytus* of Euripides, Racine was also influenced by several French predecessors to his play and, more significantly, by Seneca's *Phaedra* (from which he borrowed Phaedra's confession and the use of Hippolytus' sword as evidence against him).

At the outset of the play, Hippolytus is about to leave Troezen in search of his father Theseus, the king, but also to flee from Aricia, the young captive princess of Athens whom he is afraid to love, all the more so as her whole family was killed by Theseus. Phaedra, Theseus' wife and Hippolytus' stepmother, confesses to Oenone, her former nurse and confidante, that she loves Hippolytus, whom she has consistently treated harshly but in whom she finds all the virtue and bravery of a youthful Theseus. Soon after, Theseus' death is announced. To Aricia, who has secretly responded to his love, Hippolytus considers giving all of Attica, sending into exile Phaedra and her son, and keeping only Troezen for himself. Despite her resolve and past harshness to the young prince, Phaedra confesses her love to Hippolytus, who is stunned and runs away leaving his sword in her hands, It is discovered that Theseus is not dead. He arrives in Troezen, and is utterly puzzled by the behaviour of both Phaedra and Hippolytus. Oenone accuses Hippolytus of having offended Phaedra's honour. Questioned by his father, Hippolytus only confesses his love for Aricia. Theseus then banishes his son and calls upon Neptune to take revenge against him. Aricia and Hippolytus decide to flee together; however, by alluding to their mutual love, the young princess causes Theseus to question the justice of his punishment. Oenone, called for further questioning, commits suicide. Meanwhile, Neptune has a monster destroy Hippolytus. When Hippolytus' servant Theramenes, in a famous description, brings the news of the young prince's death, Phaedra confesses her guilt and drinks poison. Theseus then adopts Aricia as his own daughter.

Phaedra is one of Racine's and indeed one of France's grandest tragedies, not only because of the impetuous and fatal passion that consumes Phaedra, but also because of the overbearing presence of ancient Greece. The drama of the Athenean queen in love with her stepson is not merely a story of guilty and forbidden love: it becomes the conflict of the metaphoric forces of light and darkness. Love is the weapon of divine vengeance (''Venus hath wholly fastened on her prey''). Phaedra is a prisoner of her heredity, ''the daughter of Minos and Pasiphaë,'' associated with her father's role as moral judge and her mother's unnatural passion for the famed Cretan bull.

Racine's *Phaedra* stands out from earlier treatments of the theme thanks to the renewed violence of the queen and the element of tenderness introduced by the character of Aricia (whom Racine adapted from the *Aeneid*, book VII). The strength of Phaedra's personality transcends the traditional role of victim of god's revenge: Racine's Phaedra is the embodiment of an irresistible and dark love, a passion she knows to be criminal in itself, not just in the eyes of society. Phaedra is first described in the play as ''A dying woman, and one who longs to die / For Phaedra, languishing with some disease / Which she will not reveal, aweary is / Both of herself and of the light of day.'' At first, she unsuccessfully tries to stifle her love for Hippolytus: ''Thou wilt shake with horror, if my silence I should break,'' she announces to Oenone. One of the play's most famous scenes, and most representative of Racine's style, is Phaedra's

confession to Hippolytus of her love for him, a confession she calls ''shameful'' and ''involuntary'':

> PHAEDRA Do not think that while I love,
> Spotless in mine own eyes do I approve
> Of what I am; nor that of the perverse
> Passion that shakes my reason, I did nurse
> The poison by an abject yielding.—Nay,
> Of heaven's wrath the miserable prey,
> More than thou loathest me do I abhor
> Myself. I call the gods to witness, more!—
> Those gods that in my breast have lit the flame
> Fatal to all my race!

The originality of Racine's play resides in the awakening of a Christian conscience subjected to temptation and sin; sinful thoughts are considered as horrible as the sin itself. Therein lies the Jansenist heritage of Racine, despite his earlier break with the famous abbey of Port-Royal.

The sombre atmosphere that pervades the play is most noticeable in the depiction of human suffering. Phaedra's cries, the stating of her passion, incantations to ever-present gods, outpourings of jealousy and anger, all are supreme examples of Racine's lyrical poetry. Aricia, Phaedra, and Hippolytus all express their own brand of love (tender, tormented, or virile) in a palpitating or pulsating rhythm. This particular feature of Racinian diction pervades the phonetic structure of such verses as: ''Tout m'afflige et me nuit, et conspire à me nuire'' (''Everything afflicts and hurts me, and conspires to hurt me''); ''Mais fidèle, mais fier, et même un peu farouche'' (''But faithful, but haughty, and even a little fearful''); ''Le jour n'est pas plus pur que le fond de mon coeur'' (''The day is no more pure than is this heart''). This pattern of alliterations and assonances is a testimony to Racine's poetic skill and accounts for the lasting recognition awarded *Phaedra* through the centuries.

—Pierre J. Lapaire

PHAEDRUS
Prose by Plato, 5th/4th century BC

The *Phaedrus* is a less ambitious work than Plato's most famous dialogue, *The Republic*, but hardly less challenging to the interpreter. It features only two interlocutors, Socrates himself and Phaedrus, an enthusiastic and poetically inclined youth who is entranced by the eloquence of the orator Lysias. Lysias has just given a set speech on the theme of love, paradoxically advising a boy to yield his favours to a non-lover rather than a lover (''Love'' is to be understood as homosexual love throughout). Socrates settles down with Phaedrus in an idyllic spot by the river Ilissus (also a sacred place, it seems, watched over by Pan and the nymphs). There Phaedrus reads Lysias' speech, Socrates tries his hand at the same theme, and then recants, offering his friend a far richer and more poetic speech in praise of love: in that speech love is treated as a divine gift, and as the pathway to recollection of the other-worldly magnificence of the immortal Forms, which transcend all physical objects in beauty and goodness. The vision of the Forms (which, according to Socrates, the human soul has glimpsed in the period before birth) is described in an elaborate mythical passage, which also includes a mythical allegory of the divided impulses of the soul, seen as two horses of opposed natures driven by a charioteer. Afterwards the two friends discuss, in deceptively informal style, the faults of contemporary rhetoric (including Lysias' speech, now recognized by Phaedrus as deficient) and the dangers of trusting in writing and books. Hypothetically, Socrates paints a picture of a real orator, one versed in psychology and philosophy: such a man would do his work by conversation, and write little or nothing. The parallel with Socrates himself is patent.

As always in Plato, it is hard (and may be misguided) to separate serious thinking from teasing banter, or to distinguish incidental remarks relevant to Phaedrus from "lessons" which are intended as general principles valid beyond the dialogue itself. Some points may be taken as clear, at the risk of oversimplification. The dialogue in part presents a "conversion" story: Phaedrus is described as at the crossroads, divided in loyalty between rhetoric and philosophy. Socrates leads him into the more fruitful realm of the latter. (There is some evidence that Phaedrus may have deserted Socratic principle later in life, but the relevance of this to the dialogue is disputed.) Similarly, Lysias and Socrates stand on opposite sides in the debate on love, for Socrates elevates the power of love as a purifying and enriching experience which can lead to wisdom. Lysianic pragmatism and worldliness are set against Socratic idealism and mysticism (the experience of love as a process of ascent to revelation and insight is also explored in Plato's *Symposium*). Socrates' criticism of the oratory of contemporary Athens as intellectually and morally corrupt also finds analogies in other works of Plato, notably the *Gorgias*. What is unusual in the *Phaedrus* is the variety of tone and the seemingly whimsical way in which Socrates treats these themes. Towards the end of the work, indeed, he refers to their conversation several times as "play," and implies that little has actually been achieved. More clearly than in any other dialogue, Plato seems to be directing his irony, and that of Socrates, at his own work.

These qualifications and ironies have led some interpreters to question whether Plato intended any of the dialogue's "conclusions" to be taken seriously or literally; and in view of the concluding section on the inadequacy of the written word, this "deconstructive" reading has been extended to Plato's works in general. As already implied, this negative interpretation can be taken too far: even when referring to the "play" of their discussion, Socrates grants that the mythical speech may have allowed them to grasp some truth. But is certainly true that the *Phaedrus* is not a work from which the reader can take away a clear set of propositions: it is more like a complex prose-poem, in which analogies and connective ideas (for instance, the implication that Socrates himself is both the ideal lover and the model philosophic orator) are suggested or implied rather than spelled out.

The work (like the closely related *Symposium*) has often been regarded as a *vade-mecum* to homosexuality and indeed pederasty. This reading neglects the important point that Socrates sees the relationship between lover and beloved as best left unconsummated: the spiritual development, not the physical satisfaction, is the important side. It is through intimacy and dialectical discussion that the souls of both can rise above the physical world and renew their knowledge of the Forms. (This non-physical relationship is misrepresented and deprived of its real significance in the vaguer modern conception of "Platonic love.") Gregory Vlastos in an influential essay has argued that Plato's concept of love is seriously inadequate, in that the lover cares nothing for the individual personality and uniqueness of the partner, but uses the relationship as a vehicle for selfish self-improvement. The argument is important, but many critics feel that Vlastos has not done full justice to Plato (see A.W. Price's 1989 study, with earlier bibliography).

The *Phaedrus* will probably appeal more to the reader of Plato as literature than as philosophy, but it is one of the most attractive and intriguing of all the dialogues.

—R.B. Rutherford

PHILOCTETES
Play by Sophocles, 409 BC

The myth of Philoctetes is as old as Homer. Son of Poias, king of Malis (in central Greece), he received from the dying Heracles the latter's invincible bow and arrows. On the way to Troy he trespassed upon a sacred shrine and was bitten by the guardian serpent, a wound that failed to heal. The foul stench and his cries of pain drove Odysseus and the Atreidae to abandon him upon the island of Lemnos. Ten years later the Greeks learn from the prophet Helenus that Troy cannot fall without Neoptolemus (the young son of Achilles) and Philoctetes, with the weapons of Heracles. Odysseus is sent to fetch Neoptolemus, and Diomedes to bring Philoctetes from Lemnos. Philoctetes comes willingly to Troy where his wound is healed and he becomes part of the company in the Trojan Horse.

The dramatists chose the embassy to Lemnos and the persuasion of Philoctetes as the subject for tragedy. Aeschylus (who first used Odysseus as the appropriate person to retrieve Philoctetes), Euripides, and Sophocles all wrote Philoctetes plays. Dio Chrysostom provides some information about the first two lost works. The following details seem to be new with Sophocles: the presence of Neoptolemus with Odysseus; Lemnos is a *deserted* island; Philoctetes has had no human company for ten years; Neoptolemus is to deceive (rather than force or persuade) Philoctetes into coming to Troy; a scene with a trader (one of Odysseus' men in disguise), full of lies and intended to accelerate the plot; the audience does not know what Helenus' oracle actually specified; Neoptolemus' repentance and rejection of Odysseus, his return of the bow to Philoctetes, and his promise to take Philoctetes back to Greece; Heracles' epiphany *ex machina* to restore the traditional plot-line, that Philoctetes will go to Troy.

For all that Aristotle (*Poetics* VI) insists that plot (*mythos*) is essential to tragedy, and character (*ethos*) is secondary, *Philoctetes* above all Greek tragedies depends on the interaction among the three main players—"that intricate ballet of relationships" (R.G.A. Buxton). By the 5th century the character of Odysseus had become but a fragment of Homer's complete man, a symbol of deceit and verbal trickery. What Sophocles does is to add to this drama the role of Neoptolemus, an adolescent growing up—called "child" throughout, he becomes "this man" in the mouth of Heracles (1422)—who decides where he stands morally in the heroic universe. Although the pivot of the drama, he is not its main character, for that role belongs to Philoctetes, Sophocles' creation of misery, loyalty, affection, hatred, and nobility, reinforced by ten long years of loneliness. Sophocles' heroes are often solitary figures, and none more so than Philoctetes. But read his speech to the boy at 254–316, and one finds a hero who has survived, who has not given in to his misery, for whom the Greeks are still his people. It is this nobility and devotion to which Neoptolemus responds, and which ironically raise the possibility that the traditional ending may not occur.

1451

Sophocles explores also the world of heroes, distinguishing true heroes "of the hand," men of action who "prefer to act with honour and fail than to win dishonourably," from false heroes "of the tongue," for whom "it is sweet to gain the prize of victory and be honourable tomorrow." The old and noble heroes are gone, only the modern and wicked are left; Neoptolemus discovers where he stands, reinforces his status as Achilles' son, and sides with Philoctetes rather than with Odysseus. Thus he returns the bow "captured by foul and unjust means" and acquiesces in Philoctetes' refusal to go to Troy. Here is the great irony (and potential tragedy) that the espousal of noble values will lead away from Troy with its healing and glory. Note Philoctetes' reasons for refusing (1358–61):

> It is not the grief of woes gone by that stings me, but I forsee what I might suffer at their hands again; for those whose mind has given birth to evil, will have learned more evil deeds hereafter. Yet Philoctetes does go to Troy.

The double ending and the intervention of Heracles have made critics speculate widely on the "meaning" of this play. C.M. Bowra sees it as paradigm of human futility ("God proposes, man confuses"); others (Joe P. Poe, Harry Avery) view the ending as profoundly pessimistic. A.J.A. Waldock eschews any serious meaning; his chapter "Sophocles improvises" emphasizes an Aristotelian primacy of plot. Some (H.D.F. Kitto, H. Musurillo) see in Heracles the exemplar of the suffering hero redeemed—all will be well *in the long run*. B.M.W. Knox stresses Sophocles' fondness for themes dependent upon knowledge; this tragedy turns on the lack of true knowing. R.P. Winnington-Ingram considers the ending as deeply tinged with irony (characteristic of a flawed universe), for the same Neoptolemus will murder Priam on the steps of Zeus' temple (see 1440). Matters are not cut and dried in this play, and in performance a director has scope to bring out aspects in the characters of the three main figures, especially in the varied attributes of the title character. How much, for instance, of Neoptolemus' speech (343–90) is actually fiction? The only overt falsehood is his claim to be sailing home (383); the rest can be played as truth or invention.

Philoctetes shows the old playwright at the very top of his form. At the same time this is an unusual Greek tragedy. Because the audience must be kept in ignorance, Sophocles' famous dramatic irony is muted. The attentive spectator, however, will notice that the true details of the oracle are given by the trader (603ff.) in a scene otherwise replete with lies and deceit. The island setting with its double-entranced cave is most unusual—how was it staged? And Lemnos with its rocks, birds, and caves is as real and as vivid as the island in Shakespeare's *The Tempest*. Props and physical items are rare in Greek tragedy, but when they occur they possess a devastating impact. In *Philoctetes* the hero's wound and the bow of contention stand out as the central features of this powerful and engaging drama.

—Ian C. Storey

PHILOSOPHICAL DICTIONARY (Dictionnaire philosophique portratif)
Prose by Voltaire, 1764

Voltaire's *Philosophical Dictionary* is neither a dictionary nor philosophical in any modern sense of the terms. The alphabetical listings of articles provided a convenient vehicle for writings in a mixture of genres on a wide range of concerns rather than an objective and systematic analysis of arguments. Like Pierre Bayle's *Dictionnaire historique et critique* (1697–1702), from which Voltaire drew both arguments and inspiration, the *Dictionary* aimed to criticize religious orthodoxy and superstition. Like the grand *Encyclopédie* (1751–72) of Diderot and d'Alembert, to which Voltaire contributed some 40 brief articles, it assumed the conviction that knowledge and reason were the keys to liberty and enlightenment. But unlike either, Voltaire conceived his book as literature and predicated its success on a witty, playful style in an accessible format. As he noted in 1765, "Twenty folio volumes will never make a revolution: it's the small, portable books at 30 *sous* that are dangerous. If the Gospel had cost 1,200 sesterces, the Christian religion would never have been established."

While the *Dictionary* has a precedent in his early *Letters on England* (1734), Voltaire began the project in 1752, during his stay at the court of the Prussian King, Frederick the Great. The early articles, "Abbé" [Priest], "Abraham," "Âme" [Soul], "Athée" [Atheist], and "Batheme" [Baptism], were composed to display Voltaire's literary skills and to appeal to Frederick's anti-clerical sentiments. His eventual quarrel with the king as well as his subsequent travels delayed rapid progress on the *Dictionary*. The first edition appeared in June 1764, containing some 73 articles, including the long dialogue *L'ABC*.

The lack of a rigid format gave Voltaire the freedom to play with a wide variety of methods, perspectives, genres and styles. Articles such as "Abraham," "Miracles," and "Atheist," draw on the resources of the conventional essay. "Christianity" is a long, scholarly discourse on the doubtful historical sources about Christianity, while "Jephthah or Human Blood Sacrifices," is in the form of textual exegesis. "Pride" is about Pico della Mirandola and Pope Alexander VI. The article "Necessary" features a dialogue between the Persian gentlemen Osmin and Selim, while "Fraud" features one between the fakir Bambabef and the Confucian Ouang. "Paul" presents a series of questions and answers on the saint, while "Job" is an apostrophe addressed to Job. Many of the articles are filled with stories, fables, and other assorted narratives, some from history, some from world literature, and some of Voltaire's own invention.

While Voltaire's articles present a wide variety of forms, they are unified in their irony, playfulness, coyness, wit, and occasionally their malice. Underlying this is the objective: to ridicule and undermine superstition, hypocrisy, corruption, despotism, and the pretensions of authority, in society and especially in religion. Always polemical, Voltaire's method, suggests Eric Auerbach, is to pose a problem in a way that contains the solution. For instance, "Luxury" begins with the statement that "luxury has been railed at for 2,000 years, in verse and in prose, and it has always been loved." The irony, Voltaire suggests, is that it was the leisure and taste derived from luxury that allowed such verse and prose. "What did Sparta do for Greece? Did it ever have Demosthenes, Sophocles, Apelles, and Phidias? The luxury of Athens produced great men in every sphere; Sparta had a few captains." The article "Beauty" opens with the telling statement, "Ask a toad what beauty is, the supreme beauty, the *to kalon*. He will tell you it is his lady toad with her two big round eyes coming out of her little head." From this and other examples, it is evident that beauty is not a universal category, but relative to the nature and interests of the individual.

Underlying Voltaire's ridicule, perhaps paradoxically, was a spirit of toleration derived from an awareness of the limits of human understanding and an ethics that looks back to Montaigne. For

Voltaire, reason marked the limits of human understanding. What we may know, we know through reason. What falls beyond reason is inaccessible to us, and should be acknowledged honestly with ''I don't know.'' Ethically, this entailed attacking what is inconsistent, contradictory, or intolerant, or, lacking certainty, exercising moral restraint. This is well illustrated in the ''Catechism of the Japanese,'' a conversation on cooking between a man from India and a man from Japan, really an allegorical treatment of the relationship between the Church of England and the Church of Rome: ''If there are a dozen restaurateurs, each of whom has a different recipe,'' asks the Japanese, ''need we cut each others' throats over that, instead of dining? Quite the contrary; everybody lives well in his own fashion with the cook whom he finds most agreeable.'' The difference between religions are for Voltaire more a matter of taste than of substance. It is absurd, he suggests, to be intolerant of different forms of spiritual nourishment (whether transubstantiation or consubstantiation), since what was important was the nourishment and not the specific formula.

While Voltaire is now chiefly read and remembered for his novella *Candide* with its attack on follies of false optimism, the *Philosophical Dictionary* is in many ways Voltaire's masterpiece, not only for its breadth and variety, but for its literary virtuosity and for its use of satire and irony in the service of revolution.

—Thomas L. Cooksey

PHORMIO
Play by Terence, 161 BC

Phormio, based on a Greek original by Apollodorus, is essentially a lighthearted play of intrigue, in which an engaging trickster outwits two fathers in order to further the love affairs of their two sons. It depends for its effect on the neatness of its construction, the delineation of the major antagonists, the comic justice of the ending and, for connoisseurs of the genre, the skilful way in which the conventions are exploited and varied.

During the absence of Demipho and Chremes on separate trips overseas, their sons Antipho and Phaedria have both fallen in love. Phaedria has fallen for a music-girl owned by a pimp, Antipho for a poor orphan girl named Phanium. Antipho has, moreover, actually married his girl, thanks to the machinations of the ''parasite'' Phormio who, posing as a friend of the girl's family and alleging that Antipho was her nearest male relative, had obtained a court judgement compelling him to do so. Demipho, who is the first of the fathers to return, is predictably furious at Antipho's marriage; he summons Phormio, and a spirited confrontation ends with Demipho threatening to expel the girl and Phormio threatening to take Demipho to court if he does. Phaedria then appears, arguing with the pimp who is about to sell his girl to a soldier if Phaedria cannot himself produce the purchase price. Next Chremes returns from his overseas trip. It transpires that he has been to Lemnos to trace his illegitimate daughter, and that the two fathers have agreed to marry this daughter to Antipho to cover up the situation; it is imperative therefore that they undo Antipho's marriage to Phanium. Phormio now offers, through Demipho's slave Geta, to marry Phanium himself if they will provide him with a large dowry. Demipho refuses, but Chremes eagerly accepts the offer, and the money is duly handed over. At this stage Phanium's nurse recognizes Chremes as Phanium's father, which

means that the marriage planned by the two fathers has actually taken place, and they hasten to cancel their agreement with Phormio. Phormio, however, refuses to give back the dowry money, which he has used to buy Phaedria's girl from the pimp, and moreover reveals Chremes' guilty secret to his wife Nausistrata. The play ends with Nausistrata brushing aside Chremes' objections to Phaedria's affair, and refusing to forgive her husband until she has consulted her son.

This summary will serve to make clear the neatness of the plot and its morally satisfying denouement. As with most of Terence's plays, the plot is double, involving two fathers and two sons. The two halves are united by the close associations of all of the characters (Demipho and Chremes are in fact brothers as well as neighbours) and by the figure of Phormio, who confronts both of the fathers and solves the problems of both of the sons. The characterization of Phormio is unusual and impressive. He is not the standard ''parasite'' of Roman comedy, who is typically either a flatterer accompanying a soldier (like Gnatho in Terence's *Eunuch*) or a wit earning free meals from a patron by his conversational skills (like Peniculus in Plautus' *The Brothers Menaechmus*); he is a master schemer and plotter, and as such bears a greater resemblance to the ''tricky slave'' character as developed by Plautus. Moreover, he manages to dominate the play while being on stage for only a third of it: such is the force of his presence and the skill with which Terence contrives to keep him in the audience's mind. He has two major confrontations in person with the old men, one on Demipho's return and one at the end of the play. There is also a third confrontation, in which Phormio offers to marry Phanium in return for a dowry, but this is carried out for Phormio by proxy through the slave Geta. Geta, who might otherwise have played the tricky slave role in the play, is reduced to being Phormio's right-hand man but is by no means a colourless character. It was a bold move to split the trickery in this way, and it is interesting that Molière in his imitation *The Rogueries of Scapin* recombined the two into a single role. The two fathers are well contrasted and individualized. Demipho is by no means the typical gullible angry father, but proves a good match for Phormio, showing both determination and a good knowledge of the legal situation. Chremes, though terrified that his wife may find out his secret, is also concerned to do the best for his daughter and, though humiliated in the end, is treated rather more gently than the typical old lecher of Plautus. Nausistrata, too, is an interesting character, not the usual unpleasant dowried wife but a much more sympathetically drawn figure.

One interesting aspect of the play is the element of surprise. The audience does not find out the reason for Chremes' trip to Lemnos until the play is almost half over; and the true identity of Phanium is not confirmed until three-quarters of the way through. This means that much of the irony of the first half is lost, or at least enjoyable only in retrospect. The audience will begin by assuming (wrongly) that Demipho's opposition to the marriage is based on the usual rich father's aversion to a poor daughter-in-law; they will not appreciate at the time that Phormio's fiction is actually very close to the truth (Antipho and Phanium are in fact cousins) or that Demipho is opposing a marriage which he has already agreed to promote. It is often claimed that it was Terence who created the surprise element by omitting an expository divine prologue from the Greek original, but this must remain a matter of conjecture. The suggestion that Terence expanded the part of Antipho in the middle of the play is rather more plausible; if so, he was filling out the double plot by giving more prominence to the sons, and at the same time (since Antipho among other things takes Phaedria's side against the pimp) emphasizing the ideal of mutual helpfulness which is part of the general humanity of his plays.

—John Barsby

THE PHYSICISTS (Die Physiker)
Play by Friedrich Dürrenmatt, 1962

Friedrich Dürrenmatt's two-act comedy is played out in a villa which is part of a "private sanatorium" —a euphemism for a lunatic asylum which houses three mad physicists. The single set for the play is the drawing-room of the villa with the doors to the rooms of the three inmates opening off it. The play opens with the dead body of a nurse lying on stage and the police investigating the circumstances of her death. She has been strangled by one of the physicists, who thinks he is Einstein. Some three months earlier another of the inmates, who believes himself to be Sir Isaac Newton, had murdered a nurse. At the end of the first act the third patient, Johann Wilhelm Möbius, who apparently suffers from the delusion that King Solomon appears to him in visions, strangles his nurse when she tells him that she loves him and that she has obtained permission from the psychiatrist in charge, Fräulein Doktor Mathilde von Zahndt, for them to leave the sanatorium and get married.

There are several hints that, perhaps, all is not quite what it seems. Newton confides to the police inspector that he is not mad; he is only pretending to be Newton in order not confuse poor Einstein because he, Newton, is really Einstein. When the inspector reports this to the psychiatrist she assures him that Newton does, after all, believe he is Newton and that, in any case, it is *she* who determines who her patients think they are.

Möbius takes leave of his wife and three sons. She has divorced him and married a widowed missionary with six sons and has come to say goodbye before going off with her new husband to a post in the Marianas Islands. At first Möbius appears hesitant and confused, but he then has a brainstorm; he turns over a table, climbs onto it, imagines it is a spaceship, and declaims a new Song of Solomon which paints a picture of a desolate, lifeless, radioactive universe. When his nurse tells him he has been putting on an act he agrees; he has done so in order to make it easier for his family to abandon him without feeling guilty.

The purpose of these odd goings-on is quite unclear. What is certain is that there is a high degree of artifice in the action. This artifice is underlined in the beginning of the second act—which repeats almost exactly the beginning of the first: the police are investigating another strangling. There is one difference: the inspector, who had earlier been frustrated, is now resigned, even relieved. There is nothing he can do. In an asylum all normal rules are suspended. He departs with an assurance from the psychiatrist that male attendants will be installed to supervise the homicidal patients.

The physicists are left alone. Newton informs Möbius that he is not, after all, Newton—or even Einstein—but the secret agent of a superpower which believes Möbius to be a scientific genius; his mission is to recruit Möbius into the service of his country. Einstein joins them and indicates that he is the agent of a rival superpower with exactly the same mission. Möbius confesses that there has been method in his madness too. He has chosen to be locked away in the asylum because he fears the practical applications of his theoretical discoveries; he has played the fool in order to protect the world from

their potentially destructive consequences. The three then engage in a debate about their responsibilities as scientists. Möbius appeals to the principles of logic and reason and succeeds in persuading the other two that his investigations should be kept secret: "We have to take back our knowledge and I have taken it back." In a spirit of noble self-sacrifice they resume the masks of madness and prepare to live out the rest of their lives in the asylum.

So, it seems, the play moves to a solemn and serious climax. But there is a final twist. The psychiatrist returns and reveals that she has had Möbius drugged every night and his notes copied. She is now about to exploit his discoveries and, with her newly established police force headed by the male attendants, take over the world. The physicists will remain locked away as her prisoners.

The Physicists is a carefully constructed box of tricks, a Chinese puzzle of a play. It repeatedly leads the audience up the garden path and arouses expectations which are not fulfilled. It invokes the conventions of the detective thriller, the drawing-room comedy, and the morality play. But ultimately it fits into no neat category.

It is a play which depends crucially on the immediacy of theatrical performance. Its twists and turns are supported by a variety of stage effects and dramatic images which help to sustain a pervasive note of grotesque humour. It would be impossible to enumerate all the effects, but these are typical examples: while a nurse is strangled we hear Einstein playing classical music on his violin; the psychiatrist has a hump, a physical deformity which manifests her mental and moral deformity; the two secret agents draw guns on each other, a visual image of the balance of power; the scientists conduct their earnest debate over a sumptuous meal; when Dr. von Zahndt reveals that she knows their true identities the three inmates are caught in the beam of searchlights, their pretences glaringly exposed.

The lunatic asylum clearly stands as a metaphor of the world in which we live. In Dürrenmatt's work it is a world governed by Sod's Law, a world where the most carefully laid plans achieve the very opposite of their intention, where reason is forever defeated by unreason. The only certainty is that the unexpected and unpredictable will happen.

The final image of the play is that of Möbius withdrawing into the role of King Solomon. As Einstein once more plays his violin, Möbius's last words are:

> Now the cities over which I ruled are dead, the kingdom that was given into my keeping is deserted: only a blue shimmering wilderness. And somewhere, round a small yellow, nameless star there circles, pointlessly, everlastingly, the radioactive earth. I am Solomon. I am Solomon. I am Solomon. I am poor King Solomon.

The Physicists is a comedy of despair, the exuberant theatrical expression of a deeply ironic, apocalyptic vision.

—B. Ashbrook

PIERRE AND JEAN (Pierre et Jean)
Novella by Guy de Maupassant, 1888

Pierre and Jean is longer than a short story and shorter and less complex than the traditional novel of the 19th century. Guy de

Maupassant wrote a number of works of this length and this seeming hesitation between two literary forms led some critics to attack him on formal grounds alone. Maupassant responded by pointing out that no one had been able to arbitrate definitively on which prose writings through the centuries would qualify as novels and which would not. He caustically remarked that anyone capable of doing so seemed to him gifted with a type of perspicacity closely resembling incompetence. Maupassant's remarks were first published in the newspaper *Le Figaro*, and later in their complete form as an accompaniment to *Pierre and Jean*.

The *Preface to Pierre and Jean*, as it has come to be known, retains an important place in the canon of 19th-century critical texts on the novel form and a paramount position in the theoretical writings of Maupassant.

The story of *Pierre and Jean* takes us to the heart of 19th-century French social structure and values. A jeweller has retired from his business in Paris and come to live in Le Havre, in Normandy, to fish and enjoy the countryside. Two sons live with the couple, Pierre, who is 30 years old, and Jean, who is 25. When a family friend from the past suddenly dies and leaves his considerable fortune to Jean, the question this event raises have easy answers at first. He had no posterity of his own, but he was present when Jean was born and therefore feels some special kinship for the boy. Not content with these facile explanations, Pierre searches for more satisfying ones. Acting first out of a sense of jealousy, he later discovers something deeply mysterious about the whole situation. When he asks his mother about a portrait of the now deceased friend that once occupied a place on her dresser, he discovers the clues to this unexpected gift and the key to his own life.

As he gazes into the portrait, he discovers the resemblance between the friend Léon Maréchal, and his brother Jean. When his mother admits that Jean is Maréchal's illegitimate son, Pierre realizes he and his brother are very different. Pierre has black hair, his brother blond; he is smaller, weaker, his younger brother bigger, with muscles that ripple under his skin; he is nervous, his brother is calm. Suddenly many seemingly little things now make sense that never did before.

Ultimately this family is wrenched from its middle-class moorings by a biological fact. But beneath the calm surface of hypocrisy and respectability, an emotional storm boils between a mother and her sons. Their simple father delights in the superficial successes of each and never apprehends the deeper truth that so troubles the other members of his family.

According to the conventions of 19th-century France, the introduction of a foreign element into any cell of a society will pose a threat and risk destroying that cell unless it is expunged. The story details the working out of that axiom.

Maupassant was a master story-teller who paid particular attention to style. In his carefully constructed narratives every word is weighed, every sentence has its place, and every paragraph has its purpose. There are no forays into politics, no gratuitous commentaries on the arts or the professions, no extraneous discourses. The narrator is discreetly unobtrusive as he lets characters speak for themselves. He selects those events and details that will best delineate character and then sets them into motion so as to show us, without commentary, the traits and qualities each person possesses. So when Pierre and Jean are rowing across the bay and Pierre tires in a spasm of fatigue, Jean must take over and row alone for a while. This detail illustrates a biological difference lying at the heart of the story. Thus, every aspect of the narration fills a specific purpose, which is to communicate Maupassant's vision of life.

Maupassant's attachment to his surroundings penetrates his writings. When he describes places and people, they are people he has known, places where he has lived, and they are part of him. The Norman landscape and its peasants and farmers, bankers and boaters, young and old, come to life on the pages of Maupassant's tales. They speak their own dialect and reflect their own circumstances. But they are not free: their lives are determined by forces in the world they cannot control. Something pessimistic, even nihilistic lies at the base of this determinism. In some cases it is nature, or human nature; in others it is heredity or a combination of heredity and social imperatives, as in *Pierre and Jean*. But whatever the causes, life has a way of persistently crushing certain of its participants.

Pierre and Jean is the carefully drawn psychological portrait of a family and their immediate acquaintance. They are superficially happy, carefree, enjoying their easy life. But beneath it all boils an unrest, a malaise, that will soon change the tranquillity of their life for ever. The brothers must confront the fact of their mother's infidelity and her hate for their father and her circumstances. It seems so incongruous to Pierre when he discovers his brother's illegitimacy. But the secret could not remain for ever, the forces were there that would eventually betray the age-old hypocrisy to which Pierre's father himself remains so blind. And so Pierre and Jean, each in his own way, are both subject and object, actors upon life's great stage, but ultimately acted upon by the force of things.

—Gary M. Godfrey

THE PILLAR OF SALT (La Statue de sel)
Novel by Albert Memmi, 1953

Albert Memmi's first novel and best-known fictional work, *The Pillar of Salt*, is a *bildungsroman*, the story of Alexandre Mordekhai Benillouche's childhood and coming of age in colonial Tunisia. When the English translation was released in 1955, it was billed for English-speaking audiences as a glimpse of the exoticism of North Africa and of the old-fashioned traditions of the Sephardic Jews. Critics first interpreted the gradual disintegration of the Benillouche family as a consequence of modernization, whereas modern critics place more emphasis on Memmi's condemnation of colonization, shown through a child's naive point of view.

The novel's title is taken from the Biblical story of Lot's wife, in which, having been exiled from her home in Sodom, she ignores the prohibition to look back and is turned into salt. This epigraph introduces the motifs of prohibition and exile woven throughout the book. Beginning with the hero's earliest childhood, the novel chronicles his growing consciousness and psychological discomfort until, as a young man, he leaves for Argentina after World War II.

The novel's protagonist, like Memmi himself, is a Jew, raised in a Muslim neighborhood outside the Jewish ghetto in Tunis. The hero's tripartite name reveals a triple identity: Benillouche, a Berber-Arabic surname meaning "son of the lamb," reflects the North African homeland; Mordekhai, an unmistakably Jewish name, shows his religious Jewish upbringing; and Alexandre, from the French, is in the spirit of the colonizers and their European culture. A child of three distinct worlds, Alexandre ultimately feels at home in none of them; as a teenager he attributes his loss of a relatively uncontested Jewish-Berber identity to the alienation experienced when he began at age

seven to attend school, where all subjects were taught in French, a
foreign language. At school Alexandre is separated from his Jewish
classmates by his Arabic accent, yet since he is a Jew, the Arab
students think he is making fun of them. His situation is further
complicated when he successfully competes for entry to the French
lycée. For the first time Alexandre is exposed to students from the
bourgeoisie whose native language is French. The experience at once
humiliates the boy and galvanizes his desire to escape Tunis' Jewish
ghetto by success in his studies.

Alexandre dreams of winning the respect of both the native
Tunisian and the colonial French communities by becoming a physician, a goal heartily endorsed by his sponsor, his father, and his
bourgeoisie girlfriend. Although constantly threatened by the specter
of poverty, Alexandre is revolted by the casual anti-Semitism and
unchallenged egotism of the middle classes; he consequently decides
to abandon his plans for medicine and study philosophy instead. The
luxury of Alexandre's academic pursuits is juxtaposed to his parents'
intellectual and material poverty. All the other children in the family
leave school early to find jobs to supplement the household's meager
income. As the eldest son, Alexandre feels keenly the tension between
his family and his responsibilities to school and his scholarship
sponsor. His crisis of conscience is not resolved, and eventually
drives him to volunteer to work in a German labor camp and to try to
enlist with the Allies. Unfortunately, these attempts to connect with a
cause only succeed in emphasizing Alexandre's marginal status.

The Pillar of Salt is a fictional treatment of colonization's effect on
the colonized's psyche, a question examined in greater depth and
theoretical detail in Memmi's later fiction and non-fiction works.
Upon its French publication, *La Statue de sel* was awarded the Prix
Fénéon and named book of the month by the Société des Lecteurs de
France. Memmi met the influential existentialist thinker Albert Camus in
1955; the Algerian-born French intellectual, Memmi's senior by only
seven years, wrote an introduction to subsequent editions of the novel.
With its North African setting and theme of alienation, elements
found also in Camus' writing, the novel interested the older writer. In
1979 Memmi's novel became the basis for a 60-minute Israeli film,
entitled *A Pillar of Salt*, directed by Chaim Shiran; the film won the
UNESCO prize at the Munich International Film Festival. The charm
of Memmi's young hero combined with his sharp criticism of the
colonial dynamic has made *The Pillar of Salt* favorite reading in many
academic disciplines ranging from French and African literature to
post-colonial studies.

—Natalie Smith

THE PLAGUE (La Peste)
Novel by Albert Camus, 1947

The Plague is Albert Camus's longest and most elaborate work of
fiction. To this day, the novel has enjoyed unfaltering success and has
been read by several million readers worldwide. *The Plague* is an
allegory on the subject of evil, a reflection on the lessons that World
War II taught, or should have taught, mankind. One of the main
characters, Tarrou, claims that "each of us has the plague within him;
no one, no one on earth is free from it." *The Plague* is a search for the
meaning of life and an eloquent recognition of collective existence
and solidarity.

An unidentified narrator sets out to relate the "unusual events"
which take place in Oran, Algeria, in 194-. In April, rats come out to
die by the thousands in the streets, houses, and buildings. Soon the
people themselves start dying in increasing numbers, and Dr. Rieux
must fight an epidemic of plague that compels the authorities to seal
off the city. All must now learn to live in isolation, "exiled" from the
rest of the world, and from this point the narrator uses "we" rather
than "I" in his narration. Rieux rejects all metaphysical interpretations of that evil, unlike Father Paneloux, a learned and militant
Jesuit, who sees in the plague a divine punishment for human sins.
Little by little, all the characters are introduced: Rambert, the Parisian
journalist, whose only concern is to escape back to the woman he
loves; Cottard, a shady character, who rejoices at the relaxed enforce-
ment of laws during the epidemic; Tarrou, whose notebooks will be
another source of information to the reader; judge Othon, who
represents the established social order, in the same way as Paneloux
embodies religion; Grand, a clerk at the Municipal Office; old Dr.
Castel, who first encountered the plague in China; an old asthmatic
Spaniard, and others.

During the summer, the epidemic is at its worst. Burials are
expedited as mere administrative formalities; disposing of the corpses
is a major problem; isolation camps are created for relatives of the
dead; riots at the city gates are commonplace. All must now come to
terms with the plague. Tarrou best represents the new attitude:
although a non-believer, he sets up sanitation teams of volunteers,
thereby illustrating his moral "comprehension." There is now "only
a collective destiny, made of plague and the emotions shared by all,"
a life confined to the present with no values attached to anything.

In the autumn, while all still work feverishly and wearily without
any improvement in the situation, Rambert, who had the opportunity
to leave the city, decides to stay because "it may be shameful to be
happy by oneself"; the plague is now "everybody's business." Judge
Othon's young son dies in horrible agony while doctors try unsuccessfully to save him by means of an anti-plague serum created by
Castel. This death shakes Father Paneloux's beliefs, since the child
was obviously an innocent creature: after a confused sermon, Paneloux
dies, probably from the plague, but is listed as a "doubtful case."
During an evening together (followed by a temporary and illegal
escape to the beach), Tarrou explains to Rieux that even before the
plague struck he knew he would always take the victim's side as the
only way to be "a saint without God"; Rieux replies that he just wants
to be "a man."

By December, the new serum begins to work. Grand recovers from
the fever; however, Othon and Tarrou die. At the same time, Rieux
receives notification that his wife, who was away for unrelated
medical reasons, has also died. Finally, the plague recedes. The gates
of the city are reopened a few weeks later, allowing all those who had
been separated for so long to be reunited. Alone, Rieux then reveals
that he is the narrator and that he decided to write his "chronicle"
because "it was up to him to speak for all," so that other men would
know "what had to be done and what assuredly would have to be
done again in the never ending fight against terror and its
relentless onslaughts."

The epidemic of plague brings into shocking relief the mortality of
men; it makes daily life more perceptible. The style of Camus's
writing serves the same purpose: by writing a "chronicle," Rieux
displays objectivity and emphasizes factual narration. There are
moments of passion, such as the exchange between Rieux and
Paneloux at the time of young Othon's death, and the evening

conversation between Rieux and Tarrou, but Camus always restrains his lyricism in favour of the logical and the impersonal.

The Plague came under attack from some for avoiding the human side of evil. Rachel Bespaloff, echoing later critics (most notably Barthes and Sartre), noted in 1950 that *The Plague* "has no symbolic equivalent for the humiliation of the suffering inflicted upon man by man." She concluded that a moral based upon solidarity means that all "stubborn heroes of *The Plague* remain subjected to the precariousness which binds them to the *we*." In this respect, the allegory falls short of offering an absolute answer to the absurd divorce of man from his environment. More recently, the absence of both female and Arab characters has also attracted critical attention. Nevertheless, Camus's lesson in modesty and pragmatism has not been lost, as the warm reception of the novel attests to this day.

Camus called *The Plague* his "most anti-Christian" writing: in a world devoid of hope, it seeks to reaffirm human dignity amid the destruction wrought by World War II and its tangible illustrations of the Absurd. Coming after the revelation of the absurd and the need for man to rebel against his estrangement from his world, *The Plague* stands out among Camus's works as a balanced, yet optimistic, answer. Rieux states this moderately positive view in these terms: "there are more things to admire in men than to despise." The real hero of *The Plague* is Grand, the clerk who just does "what has to be done" while refusing to allow the "unusual events" to change his life. Despite the plague, Grand never gives up the quest for the perfect opening sentence to the novel he wants to write. He continues to compile statistics for the sanitary groups. But "this insignificant and obscure hero who ha[s] to his credit only a little goodness of heart and a seemingly absurd ideal" offers man's obstinate yet moderate answer to the absurd.

—Pierre J. Lapaire

PLAGUED BY THE WEST (Gharbzadegî)
Essay by Jalâl Âl-e Ahmad, 1962

Jalâl Âl-e Ahmad's "Plagued by the West" is a literary event in modern Persian literature. The first draft of the book was presented at two of the many sessions of the Congress on the Aim of Iranian Education, held in Tehran on 29 November 1961 and 17 January 1962, in the form of a report, but—due to its deeply critical and polemic nature—it did not appeared published in the proceedings of the Congress. Another attempt was made from the pages of the periodical *Ketâb-e mâh*, immediately suspended after the publication of the first one-third part of *Gharbzadegî*. The author succeeded in publishing it as a single work privately 1962. Since its publication the book has been debated, criticized, and analysed heatedly both in Iran and abroad. It is recognized by both admirers and detractors as a work of unique significance because of its content and of original methodological approach.

Gharbzadegî—a Persian compound word that can be translated as "weststruckness," "westoxication," "occidentosis"—is Jalâl Âl-e Ahmad's tryst with the infinite world of ideas, for which the stage is set in a quickly changing 20th-century Iran and the background is provided by the vast panorama of the East facing the challenge of the Western outgoing and contagious civilization. Addressing Iran's mounting social problems directly for the first time in Iranian literature, the book takes this omnipresent cultural intrusion to task. Teaching the various ways to serve a hot dog to students, Âl-e Ahmad states, who do not even know what a hot dog is, is a waste of time for both the teacher and his wards.

"Plagued by the West" is an essay written by a fiction writer and it is important to remember that it is not a historical work nor a sociological one in the strict meaning of the word. Its author was a high school teacher who, after two decades of thought and experimentation, had discovered an important and basic truth concerning his society and was in a hurry to communicate his discovery to others. This basic truth was the disastrous and increasing subordination of Iran to the West, and the fundamental role played by Iranian intellectuals in promoting this surreptitious colonisation.

The nature of the disease is depicted in terms that today are of indisputable relevance; in fact, Âl-e Ahmad says, ideological compartmentalization becomes superfluous and redundant: there exist only two blocks and they are not, as one may expect, communist East and capitalist West, but rather producers-of-the-machines and buyers-of-the machines and the boundaries of the blocks are floating and shifting. According to Âl-e Ahmad, when the Ottoman empire was disintegrated as an aftermath of the World War I, its provinces fell an easy prey to the ever-increasing lust of the west, and virtually became Western satellites. This was the end of national identity of all Islamic nations.

As a result the world is compartmentalized according to the interests of its masters who pull oppressed people's strings from behind the scene. In Jalâl Âl-e Ahmad view, the most dangerous of all the contradictions arising from weststruckness is an increasing ignorance of the reality of the situation in that part of world in which significant events are taking place.

Jalâl Âl-e Ahmad provides in his books a vivid description of Iranian "occidentotics," who seem to be a paradigma relevant to all countries affected by Westernization. they have been uprooted from their native soil, alienated from their own culture, society, heritage, and religion; they live in a vacuum, filled just by exported luxuries, "modern" ideas and fashionable trends: "The occidentotic is a man totally without belief or conviction, to such an extent that he not only believes in nothing, but also does not actively disbelieve in anything. [. . .] He is indifferent. He even goes to mosque at times, just as he goes to the club or the movies. But everywhere he is only a spectator. [. . .] The occidentotic is the most faithful consumer of the West's industrial goods [. . .] and he knows more about the staff of the *Time* or the *News Chronicle* than about some nephew way off in Khorasan. And he suppose more veracious than a prophet because all these have more influence on the affairs of his country than any domestic politician, commentator, or representative." (transl. by R. Campbell, 1984, pp. 94–98). The educated class is a typical breed of plagued by the West and the author must have been a direct observer of the Westernization of the Iranian educational system: "At their most advanced levels of training [universities] merely produce good repairmen for Western manufactures" (transl. by M. Hillmann in *Introduction* to Âl-e Ahmad's *The school principal*, 1974, p. 14). A further problem is that of the mass of European educated or the returnees from America "each and every of them having returned a candidate for a viziership at the very least," but ending up governmental dead weight: ''And contrary to the commonly accepted belief, however much of the horde of returnees from abroad increases, their power to act diminishes. [. . .] It is because these particulars that I feel that the time has arrived for us to refrain from sending students to Europe and America.'' (*idem*, pp. 16–18).

Though—as many modern progressive writers of the first post-colonial decades did—Âl-e Ahmad, in his diagnosis of the effects of Western influence, could not notice the danger of the West inspired nationalism and methodological approaches, his *Gharbzadegî* has been reined and made a flag by modern Iranian thinkers and remains a turning point and a key-notion for the actual rethinking of Iranian post-revolutionary cultural identity.

—Alessandro Cancian

PLATERO AND I (Platero y yo)
Prose poem by Juan Ramón Jiménez, 1914 (written 1906–16)

As one of the most famous prose poems in 20th-century Spanish literature, *Platero and I* stands as an early masterpiece in the long and distinguished career of the Nobel prize laureate, Juan Ramón Jiménez. Translations into more than 20 different languages and millions of copies testify to its vitality and to its status as a classic in world literature. Drawing upon a venerable tradition of Christian humanism from the Gospel to *Don Quixote*, it portrays the travels on the road of life of master and donkey, of poetic personality and Platero. One of the enduring charms of this lyrical story is the attribution of human sensibility to an animal, conceived as an innocent child, and the instruction of this humble creature in the ways of Christian love and morality. Indeed, the guidance of Platero on the road to spiritual perfection is the central focus of the work.

As the author himself has indicated, *Platero and I* was written nearly in its entirety between 1906 and 1912. It was first published in an abbreviated edition in December 1914. The first complete edition appeared in January 1917. It is important to note the enormous difference between the two. The edition of 1914 contains only a selection (made by the editors) of 64 chapters of the original 136 and was organized according to the wishes of the editors. The 1917 edition is the first that reflects in its structure the artistic intention of the author, and consists of the 136 original chapters plus the last two chapters, CXXXVII, ''Platero de carton,'' and CXXXVIII, ''A Platero en su tierra,'' dated respectively Madrid, 1915, and Moguer, 1916.

There are at least three fundamental influences that inform the content, vision, and style of *Platero and I*. The work is first of all inspired by the author's native village of Moguer, in the province of Huelva in south-west Spain. The beauty and charm of this coastal town and its countryside, the decline of its economy based on fishing and the export of wine, the social problems of poverty, violence, and persecution, and a redemptive ideal and morality leading to a better world all constitute essential ingredients of this lyrical narration. Secondly, the decisive influence of Spanish kraussism, of Francisco Giner de los Rios, and the Institución Libre de Ensenanzsa must be noted. Giner, the greatest educator of modern Spain, and the movement for educational and social reform that he and his followers

inspired, were to have a lasting influence on the ideals and values of Jiménez. In particular, the krausist interpretation of history, with its ideas of human progress and perfectibility, and its absolute confidence in the advent of a better world clearly informs the regenerationist vision of *Platero and I*. Thirdly, with respect to style and to the development of artistic prose in *fin-de-siècle* Spain, one must take note of a rich confluence of three related but distinct literary currents: the decisive influence of French symbolism (particularly the prose of Baudelaire, Rimbaud, and Mallarmé), the artistic prose of late Spanish romanticism (especially that of Gustavo Adolfo Bécquer), and the immensely important renovation of language and aesthetic sensibility of Latin American modernism, and, in particular, of the Nicaraguan, Rubén Darío, and the Cuban, José Martí.

In *Platero and I*, Jimenez brings to fruition the stylistic innovations and achievements of all three of the above currents as well as anticipates brilliantly all the expressive forms that characterize the great prose of his second period. His absolute mastery of prose writing exhibits the following essential characteristics: the construction of long melodic sentences; the artful modulation of the rhythm of the sentence; a great freedom and flexibility in the manipulation of syntax for expressive effect; an impressionistic mode of narration in which logical and causal connectives give way to sheer enumeration and juxtaposition; and, above all, a cultivation of the poetic image as the primary vehicle for a symbolic mode of presentation. Indeed, Jiménez's contribution to the renovation of artistic prose in Spain is as important as his fundamental contribution to the development of Spanish lyric poetry.

For full comprehension and aesthetic appreciation, *Platero and I* must be seen as a unified whole of interrelated parts. A first reading reveals that this work does not tell a conventional story. There is no strict narrative ordering of events, no causal relationship linking one lyric chapter to the next. There are sudden shifts of scene and changes of time; there is no apparent inner thread that links the chapters together. But careful study reveals that there are several key principles that account for the expressive organization of this poetic work. Several such principles govern both the beginning and the ending of the book. The first is that Platero dies in the month of February. The second is that the book begins in March, passes through the cycle of a year, and ends in April (*Platero and I* begins in later winter/early spring and ends in spring). The third principle, which reveals the significance of the first two, is that the book begins with the introduction of butterfly imagery and ends with a cluster of butterfly imagery, distributed throughout several of the final chapters. This pattern is elaborated in such a way as to reveal that Platero, at the moment of death, undergoes, like the butterfly, a process of metamorphosis and a resurrection. The underlying theme, then, of *Platero and I*, put in its most abstract formulation, is the theme of life, death and rebirth as a natural process of metamorphosis.

Finally, the organization of *Platero and I* into an expressive form involves the following sets of interrelated principles: the symbolic treatment of the sense and feeling of life embodied in the seasons of nature, and in accordance with the Christian vision of human destiny; the expressive manipulation and elaboration of the seasonal pattern to fit the special needs of Platero's death; the juxtaposition and distribution of expressive material in terms of life and death, light and darkness, violence and harmony, with the gradual reduction of death and violence and the triumph of life and harmony, in accordance with the krausist ideal of a better and more purified world for a more perfected humanity.

—Michael Predmore

THE PLEASANT HISTORY OF LAZARILLO DE TORMES

See LAZARILLO DE TORMES

POEM 85
Poem by Catullus, mid 1st century BC

Odi et amo. quare id faciam fortasse requiris?
nescio, sed fieri sentio et excrucior.
(I hate and I love. Why I do that you perhaps are asking?
I don't know, but I feel it happening and I'm tortured.)

This is the most famous distich in Latin, to whose unique combination of intense emotion and verbal simplicity no translation does justice. The one given here has deliberately been kept strictly literal and follows the Latin word order almost exactly. An interesting collection of freer and more creative versions, however, with perceptive criticism, is available in *Lines of Enquiry* by Niall Rudd (1976).

The elegiac epigram, a very brief poem, rarely amounting to more than ten lines and often to less, in elegiac couplets (a longer and a shorter line alternating, each basically conforming to a set rhythmic pattern), had a long history before Catullus. Love, and frequently what purports to be the author's own love, was a favourite subject of it in the Hellenistic Greek period (3rd to 1st centuries BC). Ambivalent and conflicting feelings, too, were expressed at times, as in the following poem by Philodemus of Gadara (c. 110–c. 40/35 BC):

My soul warns me to stop yearning for Heliodora,
acquainted as it is with tears and jealousies past.
It tells me, but I haven't the strength to stop; for she, the
    shameless creature,
warns me herself, and even as she warns is giving me a kiss.

For all his profession of mental conflict, Philodemus, in the typical way of the Hellenistic epigrammatists, is amused and amusing, wittily playing with words for intellectual and aesthetic pleasure, as in the artistic repetition of "warn" and "stop," and the tension between "warn" and "kiss"—neater still in the original Greek, with its greater conciseness and more manipulatable word order. Catullus, on the other hand, turns to traditional epigrammatic brevity and antithesis to convey emotional pain of searing intensity.

The ultimate cause of this pain must be assumed to be his obsession with the woman he calls Lesbia (probably she was the aristocratic Clodia Metelli, whose freewheeling behaviour Cicero famously attacked in *Pro M. Caelio [In Defence of Marcus Caelius Rufus]).* Catullus makes this the explicit subject of many other poems; the

affair went sour for him, he claims, because she failed to recognize or return the selfless spiritual affection he felt for her as well as physical desire. He pinpoints the difference between the two in Poem 72, where he attempts an objective analysis of his situation, and sees the persistence of desire without affection as the root of his anguished conflict:

You said one day you only knew Catullus, Lesbia,
And you'd refuse to embrace even Jove instead of me.
I loved you then, not only as common men their girlfriend
But as a father loves his sons and sons-in-law.
I know you now. So though my passion's more intense,
Yet for me you're much cheaper and lighter-weight.
"How can that be?" you ask. It's because such hurt compels
A lover to love more but to like less.

(translated by Guy Lee)

No such analysis is attempted in 85; indeed Catullus sets up his addressee as an imaginary interrogator precisely to reject the very possibility of a rational explanation for his suffering. The phraseology of the question suggests that his mental conflict is of his own making ("Why *I do* that. . ."), while that of his answer makes clear his utter helplessness ("I feel it *happening..* ."). Arguably his anguish seems all the more real and immediate because of the prose-like plainness of his vocabulary and syntax: seven verbs, six of them in the first-person singular, with present significance, and no nouns or adjectives at all. The nearest thing to a metaphor is tellingly kept for the very last word, *excrucior* ("I'm tortured"). The root meaning of this verb is "suffer on the cross," and crucifixion's agonizing pinioning of both upper and lower extremities vividly conveys Catullus' mental torture by two conflicting emotions, from neither of which he can escape. The concept of the love-hate relationship is one which most modern readers will instinctively understand; in Poem 72 Catullus himself attempts to understand it as hatred of Lesbia for her treatment of him and love of her for her sex appeal, though he does not use the terms "hate" and "love" antithetically in that poem. Here, however, by simply saying "I hate" and "I love," without specifying what or whom, and professing not to understand at all how such conflicting emotions can simultaneously co-exist, he contrives to invest a potentially banal observation with a peculiar menace. Nowhere else in surviving Latin love poetry is anything quite like it to be encountered.

—Joan Booth

POEM ON THE DISASTER OF LISBON (Poème sur le désastre de Lisbonne)
Poem by Voltaire, 1756

This poem has long suffered from its association with *Candide*, which was to appear three years later in 1759. Most critics have considered it only as a prologue, instead of in its own right. Yet it remains one of Voltaire's most important philosophical poems, an original personal response quite independent of *Candide*.

The Lisbon earthquake occurred on 1 November 1755, destroying the city. Never had such a catastrophe struck such a large population before. Of the quarter-million people then inhabiting Lisbon, it is now thought that around 10,000 perished. The awful novelty of such a disaster excited commentaries throughout Europe in the subsequent decades. But none was as immediate as Voltaire's. His first response dates from 24 November, probably the date he got the news. In a letter of that date he describes his bewilderment that a natural cataclysm of these dimensions could occur in ''the best of all possible worlds.'' Ten days later the poem on the Lisbon disaster was already in the hands of his publisher. The composition of a work 180 lines long in the space of about a week testifies to the way in which the earthquake took hold of his imagination and harnessed all his creative energies.

The sub-title of the poem indicates that Voltaire's intentions are polemical: ''Examination of this Axiom: All is well.'' From the start the author delivers an onslaught on the philosophical Optimists who hold such a view. Voltaire had long harboured growing doubts about such a doctrine, and the Lisbon earthquake represented for him the clinching proof of its falsity. Faced with the spectacle of the dead and the dying beneath the ruins of their homes, what explanation have these philosophers to offer? That it is the ''effect of eternal laws that constrain the choices of a free benevolent God''? That God is taking his revenge on the crimes of Lisbon—in which case, is Lisbon any more sinful than pleasure-loving London or Paris? Whatever the excuse, the Optimists are odious because they complacently accept the suffering of others. Was it all necessary? Surely not; God ''is free, He is just, He is not implacable.'' But we must cry out our grief and horror, as sensitive human beings.

The argument broadens out. Pain and death are seen to be the universal law for all sentient creatures. A terrible cycle of slaughter prevails: the predatory vulture is the victim of the eagle, who is shot by man, himself cut down by fellow-men on the battlefield, where his body becomes food for the vultures. This vision leads Voltaire to his central statement: ''Elements, Animals, Mankind, all is at war. / We must accept that *evil* exists on earth.'' How then can this be, since God is master? The enigma is insoluble. Voltaire considers four possible explanations: original sin and divine punishment for it; total indifference by God to human fate; the inherent defects of matter; God is testing us for the afterlife. None of them convinces or consoles. Leibniz fails to show us by what invisible links pleasures and pains are mixed together in ''the best organized of all possible worlds.'' Nor are Plato or Epicurus any more help. The only philosopher worth following is Bayle, whose scepticism teaches us that doubt is the one true stance to take.

So to the peroration, reiterating the total ignorance of human beings regarding their own nature, origins, destiny: ''What am I? Where am I? Whither am I going? Whence have I come?'' It remains for us only to accept suffering without complaint, in the hope that perhaps one day all will be well. The poem concludes on this note of hope, but it is fragile in nature and beset by all the apprehensions that have been present throughout.

This synopsis reveals that the structure of the work is not totally coherent. Some ideas are repeated or risk contradiction with others. This is scarcely a matter for surprise when one recalls the white-hot method of composition. The original version was subjected to numerous revisions, but in the form of interpolations and additions rather than by a recasting of the overall pattern. That said, a strong unity of tone informs the poem, born of Voltaire's eloquent protest of anger at the earthquake and more particularly at the insulting justification of such occurrences by the Optimists. It is this rhetorical urgency, expressed eloquently, that makes it memorable. Voltaire uses simple antithesis (''Lisbon is destroyed, and they dance in Paris'') or cumulative repetition (''But I live, but I feel, but my oppressed heart. . . '') or the austere purity of the lines about evil and about

human ignorance quoted above, all to trenchant effect. The poem quickly attracted attention, both in France (where Rousseau refuted Voltaire with a memorable Letter on Providence) and abroad. It is a landmark in the 18th-century debate on Optimism.

The comparisons with *Candide* are significant; in the *conte* Voltaire will repeat the same attack on Optimism. But the tone is quite different. Whereas *Poem on the Disaster of Lisbon* is built up on urgent questioning, the direct expression of genuine bewilderment, *Candide* achieves its effects by ironic distancing. The tragic note of the poem has given way to the tragicomic duality so characteristic of Voltaire's best *contes*. *Candide* is more subtle, constructed on a broader scale; but that should not be allowed to obscure the poignancy of Voltaire's troubled and doomed search for enlightenment about evil when confronting the recent disaster in Lisbon.

—Haydn Mason

POEM WITHOUT A HERO (Poema bez geroia)
Poem by Anna Akhmatova, 1963 (written 1940–62)

''*Poem Without a Hero* was for Anna Akhmatova as *Onegin* was for Pushkin—a compendium of all the themes, plots, principles, and criteria of her poetry . . . It is a survey of what she had to struggle against in life, and consequently of what she wrote'' (Anatoli Naiman, in Judith Hemschemeyer's translation of *The Complete Poems*, 1990).

This complex and cryptic poem proceeds via an abundance of enigmatic epigraphs, dedications, and prefaces (all containing clues to its deciphering) to its beginning on New Year's Eve 1940, when the poet sets up a magic ritual to summon her beloved (the eponymous but absent hero). However, she rouses instead the shades of her contemporaries from the Petersburg bohemia of 1913, all now dead except herself. The brilliant culture of the period is evoked, but in retrospect seems shameless and frivolous: the year 1913 is perceived as the last flowering of a free but irresponsible culture. The poet's conscience returns to the sins of her youth and at the centre of the ''hellish harlequinade'' of 1913 she perceives her own double, an alluring and amoral actress and dancer who pushes a young naive admirer to suicide by her evident preference for his rival. Part Two is set in 1941, when Russia is again on the verge of war. In this intermezzo the poet comments on the poem (hinting in riddles at the way in which it should be read) and reflects on what the 20th century has brought Russia: ''the decades file by, / Tortures, exiles and deaths.'' She begins to ask what it was in her own past and that of her contemporaries that called down this dreadful retribution. By the time of the epilogue Leningrad is under siege and in ruins, punished for its venal past, and the poet is parted from it, but she records her allegiance to her native city and her fellow feeling with all exiles. She has survived to tell of her experience of purgatory.

The poem reflects on the interrelation of Russia's past, present, and future (''My future is in my past''), on the responsibility of individuals for the shaping of history, and on the function of the poet in 20th-century Russia (''to demand the one and only highest Truth''—Akhmatova's description of Pushkin's purpose, and also a self-characterization). On the personal level the poem's theme is the necessity of acknowledging guilt and making atonement for it and the poem is a quasi-religious act of confession and expiation. Akhmatova also shows that the 20th century is "not unendurable chaotic suffering, but a strange and beautiful and yet cruel and horrible drama in which not to be able to play a role is to be seen as a tragedy" (Amanda Haight, *Anna Akhmatova: A Poetic Pilgrimage*, 1976).

Like most of Akhmatova's writing, the poem is concerned with historical authenticity and has a basis in Akhmatova's own biography. Her actress double is her friend Glebova-Sudeikina whose roles in the cabaret-theatres of the day are accurately recalled; the cigar-smoking Guest from the Future is Isaiah Berlin (with whom Akhmatova had a meeting of mind and spirit in 1946); the young suicide is the minor poet Kniazev, who was in love with Glebova-Sudeikina, and whose fate reminded Akhmatova of a catastrophe in her own life which she would not discuss. But "the box has a triple bottom." All the figures are generalized and symbolic, and unravelling the poem's allusions is a matter of collating multiple references so that the young poet is not only based on Kniazev but also associated with Mandel'shtam, whose words he quotes, and must further be seen as an analogy of Lenskii, the shallow romantic whose unnecessary death is enacted in Pushkin's *Eugene Onegin*.

The poem, which the poet calls a "cryptogram" written in "mirror writing," is a *tour de force* of periphrasis and quotation which locates the poem firmly as a late flowering of modernism and protected it from the onslaughts of censorship. It claims to be written on the first draft of Kniazev's poems, but quotation is not limited to Kniazev—or Mandel'shtam—and many others of the poetic voices of 1913 are to be heard (Blok, Lozinskii, Kuzmin, Kliuev, Akhmatova herself), alongside T.S. Eliot, Pushkin, and Byron.

Akhmatova listened with interest to interpretations of the poem but refused to explain it. However, commentators, the doughtiest of whom is Roman Timenchik, have elucidated many of the references, generated a vast corpus of exegesis, and offered a variety of hypotheses as to who or what is the missing hero of the poem (Time; Petersburg-Leningrad; Akhmatova's first husband and one of the first poet-martyrs of Bolshevism, Gumilev; etc).

The poem has its roots in the "Petersburg myth" in Russian literature (tracing its own descent from Pushkin, Dostoevskii, and Blok—as well as from Byron's *Don Juan*). Akhmatova was aware of the perils of imitating Pushkin's *Eugene Onegin* when writing a long poem in Russian, a problem that she solves through a typical paradox by following Pushkin in inventing a stanza form unique to this work.

The poem was begun in 1940, after several arid years. Almost possessed of a life of its own, it continued to haunt Akhmatova through the siege of Leningrad, her evacuation to Tashkent, and the 1946 political campaign against her, into the happier late 1950s, until after several false alarms it was finally declared finished in 1962. Lydia Chukovskaya's diaries of these years lovingly record the minutiae of the poem's difficult creation. In the course of writing, some separate poems were absorbed into it, and some passages evolved into poems which were then separated from it. Attached to the poem are various verse fragments, observations about it in prose, and an uncompleted libretto for its translation into a ballet. There are over 30 variants of parts or the whole: the definitive discussion of editions of the text is E. von Erdmann-Pandžić's "*Poema bez geroja von Anna A. Achmatova*" (1987), which also contains a bibliography of critical material.

—Wendy Rosslyn

THE POETIC ART (Ars poetica)
Poem by Horace, c. 12–8 BC

The Latin poet Horace discussed a number of artistic and critical problems in his extensive series of verse *Epistles*, but the long verse-letter known as *The Poetic Art* is the most sustained account of literary criticism written by a practising poet in the ancient world. Thought to have been composed towards the end of Horace's life (scholars now agree that it should be dated between 12 and 8 BC), it carries the informal and convivial tone of the poet's most characteristic work, and has the structure of an illustrated description of current thinking rather than a closely argued treatise. The poem is best seen as a witty and elegant synthesis of relatively familiar views, rather than as an exploratory or innovative manifesto, drawing as it does on the precedent work of earlier Greek and Roman models, including Aristotle and Cicero. It is addressed to an unidentified father and son, hailed only as "Piso," but the advice offered to the fledgling writer opens out into wider considerations about the role of the artist and the best techniques to be followed.

Although the poem is rather haphazard in its organization, its central concerns can be easily summarized. The recurrent themes are the need for unity and propriety in poetry, the interaction between the contemporary writer and the past, and the moral and educative function of creative writing. When dealing with consistency and unity, Horace's advice concentrates on the poet's technique, and his fundamental principle is that all works of art have an internal decorum, with each part fitting into the overall conception:

> Imagine a painter who wanted to combine a horse's neck
> with a human head, and then clothe a miscellaneous collection
> of limbs with various kinds of feathers, so that what started out
> at the top as a beautiful woman ended in a hideously ugly fish.
> If you were invited, as friends, to the private view, could you
> help laughing?

As always, this brief passage, the opening of the poem, shows Horace's recurrent concern with the audience, and his notion of "fittingness" is based on the predictable expectations of the intelligent reader or viewer. The idea of decorum had already been put forward by Aristotle and Cicero, but Horace made it more fundamental to the art of the writer for both pragmatic and more doctrinaire reasons. He believed that every component in any work of art should be appropriate for the kind of work it was part of, that the genre a particular work belonged to set out clear rules for the kind of characterization, language, metre, and tone it should include. If these rules were followed, the relationship between writer and reader could be one of mutual respect, and the dignity of writing be maintained.

In order to become aware of the rules of propriety, the aspiring writer must embark on a course of education: "Study Greek models night and day." By immersing himself in these "models," the new writer learns enough about technique to discover his own articulateness, seeing what to do and what not to do. Histories of kings and generals, dreadful wars: it was Homer who showed in what metre these could be narrated. Revered writers from the past are thus the models for imitation, but the poet should not neglect the world around him. "My advice to the skilled imitator will be to keep his eye on the model of life and manners, and draw his speech living from there." Horace does not develop his idea of imitation fully, but it is clearly central to his thinking, and along with the notion of the appropriateness of parts to the whole (''decorum''), it was exhaustively debated throughout the Renaissance and into the 18th century, forming the basis of neo-classical criticism.

Horace's third central idea was equally influential. For him, the poet must aim to combine delight and instruction in his audience and must seek simultaneously to entertain and edify them. ''Poets aim either to do good or to give pleasure, or, thirdly, to say things which are both pleasing and serviceable for life.'' The status of creative writing depends, for Horace, on its unique ability to combine pleasure and instruction, and this both empowered writers and laid responsibilities upon them. For the writer who managed to achieve the proper blend, the rewards were enormous. ''The man who combines pleasure with usefulness wins every suffrage, delighting the reader and also giving him advice; this is the book that earns money for the Sosii [booksellers], goes overseas and gives your celebrated writer a long lease of fame.''

So Horace's presentation of the writer's role is an unusually professional one. He has little time for the idea that the writer is an eccentric or inspired figure, and prefers to see him as an erudite, skilled commentator on the affairs of the day. Only by combining nature and art properly can a writer reach the status to which the artist is entitled:

Do good poems come by nature or by art? This is a common question. For my part, I don't see what study can do without a rich vein of talent, nor what good can come of untrained genius. They need each other's help and work together in friendship.

By adopting this position, Horace can be seen as an interim figure between the more formalist thinking of Aristotle, and the more inspirational concerns of Longinus. And although the *Poetics* and *On the Sublime* have stimulated enormous discussion, Horace's *The Poetic Art* has probably been more extensively influential on the practice of writers.

—Ian A. Bell

THE POETIC EDDA

Anonymous Old Norse poems, possibly composed between AD 800 and 1100; written down during 13th century. Main manuscript (Codex Regius) discovered in 1643 by Icelandic bishop Brynjólfur Sveinsson, who named it *Sæmundar edda* because of attribution to Sæmundr Sigfússon the Learned, 11th-century founder of Icelandic historiography, and the superficial resemblance to the prose *Edda* of Snorri Sturluson. Also called the *Elder Edda* (i.e., older than the prose *Edda*).

PUBLICATIONS

Poetic Edda: Essays on Old Norse Mythology, edited by Paul Acker and Carolyne Larrington, 2002.

*

Bibliography: *Bibliography of the Eddas* by Halldór Hermannsson, 1920, supplement by Jóhann S. Hannesson, 1955.

Critical Studies: *The Book of Edda Called Völuspá: A Study in Its Scriptural and Spiritual Correspondences* (with translation) by James John Garth Wilkinson, 1897; *The Edda: The Divine (Heroic) Mythology of the North* by Lucy W. Faraday, 1902; *The Elder Edda and Ancient Scandinavian Drama* by Bertha Surtees Phillpotts, 1920; *The Alliterations of the Edda* by Winfred Philipp Lehmann and Joey L. Dillard, 1954; *Old Icelandic Poetry* by Peter Hallberg, 1975; ''Eddic Poetry'' by Joseph Harris, in *Old Norse-Icelandic Literature: A Critical Guide* edited by Carol J. Clover and John Lindow, 1985.

*   *   *

As well as meaning ''to compose,'' the Latin verb *edere*, from which the word *edda* may derive, can also mean ''to compile.'' The term ''The Poetic Edda'' refers primarily to a 13th-century Icelandic compilation or collection of poems on mythological and heroic subjects preserved mainly in two manuscripts, Codex Regius 2365 4to and AM 748 4to, which together contain 30 poems, 19 of them on heroic subjects. Over 20 related poems, mostly on heroic subjects and preserved as quotations in prose sagas, are known as the ''Eddica minora,'' and a few of these, plus a few others preserved elsewhere and mostly on mythological subjects, are included in modern editions of the main collection, forming an ''eddic appendix'' varying somewhat in scope from one edition to another.

The eddic or eddaic poems, as all these poems are called, date variously from the 9th to the 13th century, and differ from skaldic poems, the other major Old Norse poetic genre of the period, with their preference for subjects remote in place and time from their audiences, their comparative straightforwardness of word order, metre, and diction, and their relative lack of attributability to known authors. The eddic poems are variously narrative, dramatic (in the sense that they often consist of dialogue), and gnomic; they use alliteration rather than rhyme, in the manner of traditional Germanic poetry, and are stanzaic, employing three main metres, known in English as ''epic,'' ''speech,'' and ''chant'' metre, the latter being found most often in dramatic and gnomic passages.

The mythological poems in the Codex Regius are as follows: *Völuspá*, a visionary history of the universe narrated by a prophetess; *Hávamál*, a compilation of originally separate poems presented as if spoken by the god Óðin, in which he gives advice on social conduct, relates his adventures with women, and parades his knowledge of runes and magic; *Vafþrúðnismál* and *Grímnismál*, in which Óðin reveals his identity by his specialized knowledge, in a dialogue and a monologue respectively (these two poems, together with *Völuspá*, are major sources for Snorri Sturluson's prose *Edda*); *Skírnismál*, about the wooing of a giant maiden on behalf of the god Frey; *Hárbarzljóð*, a competitive dialogue between the gods Thór and Óðin, the latter in disguise; *Hýmiskviða*, an account of some of Thór's exploits, including his fishing for the world-encircling serpent; *Lokasenna*, a dialogue poem in which Loki mischievously accuses his fellow-deities of various imperfections; *þrymskvia*, the story of Thór's recovery of his hammer from the giants; and *Alvíssmál*, a dialogue in which Thór prolongs his questioning of a dwarf until the latter turns to stone at sunrise. In AM 748 4to, but not in the Codex Regius, is found *Baldrs draumar*, in which the god Baldr's ominous dreams are interpreted by a dead prophetess, magically invoked by Óðin, as portending his death.

The mythological ''eddic appendix'' is represented by *Rígsþula*, preserved in manuscripts of Snorri's *Edda*, about the origins of the three orders of society: thrall, yeoman, and earl; *Hyndluljóð*, a dialogue between the goddess Freyja and the giantess Hyndla, preserved in the late 14th-century saga-compilation *Flateyjarbók*; and *Grógaldr* and *Fjösvinnsmál*, two dialogue poems sometimes treated by editors as one (called *Svipdagsmál*), about the wooing of Menglöd by Svipdag, and preserved in late paper manuscripts. Closest to the mythological poems among the *Eddica minora* are perhaps the riddles of Gestumblindi (preserved in *Heidreks saga*), a sequence in which Ódin in disguise finally asks, as in *Vafþrúðnismál*, a question only he can answer, thus catching out his interlocutor.

The heroic poems in the Codex Regius are *Völundarkvia* (the one heroic poem also preserved in AM 748 4to), about the grim revenge taken by the smith Völund on his captor King Nídud; the three Helgi poems, one dealing with the ill-starred love of Helgi Hjörvardsson and Sváva, and the other two with that of Helgi Sigmundsson and Sigrún; *Grípisspá*, a prophetic overview of the career of Sigurd; and *Reginsmál, Fáfnismál*, and *Sigrdrífumál*, dealing respectively with the early history of the gold guarded by the dragon Fáfnir, Sigurd's slaying of the dragon, and his coaching in runic and other wisdom by an armour-clad woman aroused by him from sleep. The Codex has a lacuna of eight leaves beginning towards the end of *Sigrdrífumál*; their contents have to be deduced from the 13th-century prose *Völsunga saga*, for which the sequence of heroic poems in the original Edda compilation formed the main source. Codex Regius resumes with part of a *Sigurðarkviðu*, about Sigurd's slaying by Gjúki's sons, and continues with *Gudrúnarkviða* I, on the grief of Gudrún, Gjúki's daughter and Sigurd's wife, at her husband's death; *Sigurðarkviða in skamma*, which views Sigurd's killing mainly from the point of view of its instigator Brynhild, married to Gudrún's brother Gunnar but in love with Sigurd; *Helreið Brynhildar*, in which Brynhild further defends her position in a conversation with a giantess; *Gudrúnarkvia* II and III, about Gudrún's reluctant marriage, after Sigurd's death, to Brynhild's brother Atli; and *Oddrúnargrátr*, about Gunnar's clandestine love affair, after Brynhild's death, with Brynhild's and Atli's sister, Oddrún. Two Atli-lays then deal in different ways with Gudrún's revenge on her husband Atli for his slaying of her brothers Gunnar and Högni; and in *Guðrúnarhvöt* and *Hamðismál*, finally, Gudrún persuades her sons by her third husband, Jónakr, to avenge her daughter by Sigurd, Svanhild, on King Jörmunrek, who had had her trampled to death by horses.

Representative of the heroic "eddic appendix" are *Gróttasöng*, preserved in manuscripts of Snorri's *Edda*, about two giantesses grinding the flour of peace, gold, and war for King Fródi; and such *Eddica minora* as *Hlödskvia*, preserved in *Heidreks saga*, about a tragic battle of the Goths and Huns in which the two warring leaders are half-brothers, and the death-song of Hildibrand, preserved in *Ásmundar saga kappabana*. Sometimes also included in the eddic corpus is the Christian religious poem *Sólarljód*, preserved in 17th-century manuscripts but thought to date from the 12th or 13th century.

—Rory McTurk

THE POSTHUMOUS MEMOIRS OF BRAZ CUBAS
(Memórias póstumas de Bráz Cubas)
Novel by Joaquim Maria Machado de Assis, 1881

First published in serial form in the *Revista Brasileira*, then as a book in 1881, this is Joaquim Maria Machado de Assis' first great novel, and the first great example of the genre to have come out of Latin America. In form it is strikingly original: the memoirs are posthumous in the sense that their narrator is dead at the time of narration, and they are dedicated to the "first worm that gnawed my cold flesh." In the opening address to the reader, Sterne's example is appealed to, and some of the mocking, digressive, insouciant familiarity of the tone comes from 18th-century sources, though, as Machado de Assis says in the prologue to the third edition, "the cup may be worked in that manner, but it contains a different wine." What that different wine is, is not quite plain. Machado de Assis seems to see it as something sharply pessimistic—more recent criticism sees the flippant manner as an appropriate expression of a class viewpoint.

The novel begins with the death of the narrator, Braz Cubas, in 1869, at the age of 64, in a Rio suburb: he is a typical (though unmarried) member of a wealthy family of the Brazilian ruling élite, and there are, already in the early parts of the novel, hints at an adulterous affair. But we are treated first to a long description of his delirium, which turns out to be a view of life and creation inspired by Darwin and above all Schopenhauer: it culminates in an encounter with Pandora, "mother and enemy," who reveals the pointlessness of existence, and the repetitiousness of history, which the 19th century, so full of itself, had done nothing to contradict.

The introductory section (about 15 pages and eight chapters) is distinctly disorientating in terms of normal expectations, and led one contemporary critic to ask if this was a novel at all. But we then return to a recognizable if original version of a Bildungsroman, to the narrator's birth, and his family: his social-climbing, snobbish father who wants his son to be a successful politician, his mother, "fearful of thunderstorms and her husband," uncles, aunts, and slaves, one of whom he uses as his whipping-boy. "From this manure grew this flower," as he says. His "career" is very largely an account of his affairs, since he lives happily off inherited wealth: first, the Spanish "courtesan" Marcela, who fleeces him of a huge sum of money before his father bundles him off to Portugal for a university education. On his return, he first comes across the unfortunate Eugenia, the illegitimate child whose conception, in an encounter in the bushes, Braz had been accidentally present at, some 16 years before. By means of a semi-allegorical fantasy involving black and blue butterflies, we are shown what the possibilities for a relationship between the two of them are, given mutual attraction: either she must reject him to preserve her only asset, her honour; or, she could become his mistress, briefly pampered and permanently insecure.

This short episode sets the tone for the novel's account of social relations, which, when people of different classes are involved, are sharply delineated as exploitative, even sadistic. Thus we are introduced to Braz's brother-in-law, Cotrim, a hardened slave-dealer, to Prudencio, Braz's ex-whipping boy, shown in a later chapter having bought his own slave and giving back all the punishment he himself received with interest, to Damasceno, the plantation-owner from the sticks who wants to marry his 19-year-old daughter off to the 45-year-old Braz.

At the novel's centre lies the relationship with Virgília, a woman of his own age and class, with whom Braz has a long-lasting adulterous affair. He could have married her, and only laziness and indecision make him lose out to the honest if dull Lobe Neves; but that is all to the good, because both are out for the excitement of an illicit "love." Eventually, they acquire a small house in a slightly shady part of town, complete with "housekeeper," the impoverished and dependent Dona Plácida. In some ways, *Posthumous Memoirs* is a parody of the realist adultery novel, with its conventional tragic ending: the whole city seems to get a kick out of conniving at the affair and gossiping about it, and it eventually ends out of sheer boredom (and probably because Braz is "unfaithful").

This affair is as close as the reader gets to having a "plot" in the usual sense, and after it is over the novel winds down in a series of anticlimaxes which end in its famous concluding chapter "of negatives": "I did not have children, and transmitted to no one the legacy of our misery." But Braz is not all pessimism. Towards the end of his life he encounters an old school friend, Quincas Borba, who has invented the perfect philosophy to counter all such notions: Humanitism, a combination of Darwinism and Comtean positivism, then in the process of becoming highly influential in Brazil. The survival of the fittest is turned into a justification of the *status quo*, and implicitly of the privileges of the caste to which Braz belongs: he is an instant convert. Humanitism crowns the novel, giving the final sophisticated (and more than slightly mad) touch to its exploration of ingrained selfishness in a slave society.

—John Gledson

THE POT OF GOLD (Aulularia)
Play by Plautus, early 2nd century BC

The Pot of Gold is centred on one of Plautus' most memorable characters, the poor miser Euclio. Euclio has a daughter who, unknown to him, is pregnant by Lyconides, a young man from a neighbouring family. The girl is a devout worshipper of the household god Lar who, in order that she can be married with a suitable dowry, has revealed to Euclio the existence of a pot of gold his miserly grandfather had buried beside the hearth. The plot revolves around Euclio's neurotic anxiety that the pot may be discovered, whether by his long-suffering old slave Staphyla or by his neighbour Megadorus, who excites Euclio's suspicions by asking to marry the daughter, or by the cooks who are hired to prepare the wedding feast. In the end, Euclio digs up the pot himself in order to hide it in a safer place; but his plans are overheard by Lyconides' slave, who steals it with a view to buying his own freedom from his master. The ending of the play is missing from all our manuscripts; but it is clear from the plot summaries and quotations that do survive from antiquity that Euclio has his pot restored, that he was persuaded to consent to his daughter's marriage to Lyconides and that, in the end, in order to preserve his peace of mind, he was only too happy to give the gold away as a dowry.

The character of Euclio is cleverly handled. At first he appears as an exaggerated caricature, expelling the hapless Staphyla from the house, going to collect state benefit to avoid any suspicion of his new wealth, and misinterpreting every approach of the well-meaning Megadorus as a design on the gold. This impression is reinforced by the tall stories swapped by the cooks on how he saves up his toe-clippings and even sleeps with a balloon on his mouth to avoid losing his breath. There gradually emerges, however, a picture of an honest poor man with ingrained habits of thrift who just cannot cope with his sudden wealth. He goes to the market to buy food for the wedding but cannot bring himself to spend extravagantly. Similarly, he has the poor man's realistic view of the gulf between the social classes and the difficulty of bridging it and he has quite sensible arguments to support his initial unwillingness to ally himself by marriage to the wealthy Megadorus. Euclio is duly distraught at the theft of his gold but he is not by nature a miser, and his giving away of the gold as a

dowry makes an entirely appropriate ending. Not only does this neatly solve the two problems of the plot (the future of the gold and the fate of the daughter), but it also achieves the classic comic reconciliation in which the blocking character is reintegrated into society.

The Pot of Gold offers the obvious moral that wealth does not bring happiness. It also raises the issue of rich—poor relationships and indeed of the function of the dowry in marriage. Megadorus' tirade against extravagant dowried wives may be seen as reflecting the social conditions of contemporary Rome, when laws were passed limiting women's luxuries. It is also a supremely funny play. Apart from the tall tales of the cooks mentioned above, much of the humour is based on dramatic irony: Euclio's behaviour is explicable only to the audience who know of the existence of the gold. The funniest scene of this kind is that in which Lyconides comes to confess the seduction of Euclio's daughter but in such hesitant and ambiguous terms that Euclio thinks that he is confessing to the theft of the gold. Other good scenes are Euclio's unavailing frisking of Lyconides' still empty-handed slave in the Shrine of Faith, where the gold is temporarily hidden, and his distraught cries to the audience to reveal the thief when the gold is finally stolen.

Euclio belongs within the tradition of comic misers and misanthropes and *The Pot of Gold* played a significant part in transmitting this figure from ancient Greece to the later European stage. The underlying situation of *The Pot of Gold* bears some resemblance to that of Menander's *The Grouch* (*Dyskolos*), where a prologue god similarly undertakes to forward the marriage of the dutiful daughter of a curmudgeonly old man. However, Knemon in Menander's play is a misanthrope rather than a miser, and the plot in fact develops along quite different lines. But, if we cannot now identify the precise Greek model of Plautus' play, there is no doubt of the direct link between *The Pot of Gold* and Molière's *The Miser* (*L'Avare*). Molière has expanded and to some extent transformed the plot, notably by making Harpagon into a thoroughly unpleasant miser who hangs on to his gold at the end. On the other hand he has taken over most of Plautus' most effective comic scenes, including the tall tales of miserly behaviour related by the cook, the distraught plea to the audience to reveal the thief, and the cross-purpose confession of the young man.

—John Barsby

THE PRAISE OF FOLLY (Encomium moriae)
Prose by Erasmus, 1511

The Praise of Folly began as a joke, an expression of what Erasmus termed his *jeu d'esprit*. In a letter to his friend, Sir Thomas More, Erasmus claimed that the inspiration came to him on horseback while returning to England from Italy in 1509, later expanding the idea while waiting for his books and luggage to catch up with him. The subtle play of irony, and the dense allusions both to Biblical and Classical literature, as well as the careful modifications carried on through a series of editions between 1511 and 1515, however, belie the off-handedness with which Erasmus seems to dismiss *The Praise of Folly*. Despite the surface playfulness, it represents, as M.A. Screech suggests, the mature effort of a sophisticated thinker at the height of his intellectual powers. The multilingual pun of the title, playing on the Latin form of More's name and the Greek word for folly, meaning thus both "in praise of folly" and "in praise of [Sir Thomas] More" is indicative both of the game and of its profundity.

On one level, Erasmus holds Folly up to ridicule, but at the same time advocates a serious vision of Christian folly.

Drawing on the methods of the Greek satirist Lucian, the work is in the form of a long Latin panegyric delivered by Folly (Stultia) in praise of herself. Erasmus uses, however, the Greek rhetorical model of the *Aphthonius* rather than the more conventional Latin model outlined by Quintilian, signalling his knowledge of Greek language and learning and his affiliation with Renaissance Humanism. This is important to Erasmus's concern as a Humanist theologian, pointing to the authority of the Greek *Septuagint* and *New Testament* over that of the Latin *Vulgate*, and to that of the ancient philosophers and early patristic writers over the schoolmen. The *Aphthonius* divides its topic into six parts: a *prooimion*, in which Folly introduces herself; a *genos* which outlines Folly's birth and origins; an *anatrophe* which describes the powers and pleasures of Folly; a *synkrisis* which enumerates Folly's followers; and finally an *epilogos*, which outlines the doctrine of the Christian fool.

The *genos* and the *synkrisis* look back to medieval allegory. Folly describes herself as the daughter of Plutus, the ancient god of riches, and Youthfulness. After being nursed by Drunkenness and Ignorance, she is attended by Philantia (Self-love), Kolakia (Flattery), Lethe (Forgetfulness), Misoponia (Laziness), and Hedone (Pleasure), among others. Her followers, like those portrayed in the medieval *danse macabre* or Sebastian Brant's *Ship of Fools* (1494), represent an anatomy of human types, cutting across all strata of society from professionals such as schoolmasters, poets, lawyers, and theologians, through kings and courtiers, to church prelates of various sorts, German bishops being the greatest fools of all.

The *Praxis* shows a more sophisticated irony and playfulness. The power of Folly resides in facilitating ecstasy. Here Erasmus plays on the semantic field of the Greek *Ekstasis* which ranges over drunkenness, madness, and rapture. Would it not be mad, Folly suggests:

if some wise man, dropped from heaven, should suddenly confront me at this point and exclaim that the person whom everyone has looked up to as a god and a ruler is not even a man, because he is led sheeplike by his passions. . . ?

The implicit answer is yes, but isn't this also the description of Christ? If this is madness or foolishness, then it is a holy madness, a Christian foolishness. Similarly Folly questions the virtue of the rational stoic who has stripped away all passion and emotion. Such a being, she suggests, "makes a marble imitation of a man, stupid, and altogether alien to every human feeling." Such a being becomes arrogant and isolated in his self-sufficiency. "He does not hesitate to bid the gods to go and hang themselves. All that life holds dear he condemns and scorns as folly." Who, Folly asks, would choose to be ruled by such a person? "What host such a guest? What servant such a master?" These questions point to the seriousness of Erasmus's intent. If Christianity is a rational religion, then it is effectively indistinguishable from ancient Stoicism, offering a vision that leads to pride and isolation from God. For Erasmus, however, the heart of true Christianity is not in its appeal to reason, but to an irrational passion that lifts individuals out of themselves.

The ultimate folly is that of God, for how, Folly asks, can the humiliation and sacrifice of Christ, the act of Divine grace, be understood except as an act of sublime and benevolent folly.

Christ himself, although He possessed the wisdom of the Father, became something like a fool in order to cure the folly of mankind, when He assumed the nature and being of a mortal? And that He was made "to be sin" in order to redeem sinners? He did not wish to redeem them by any way except by the foolishness of the Cross, and by weak and simple apostles.

Could humankind reasonably expect salvation from a rational God?

As with the knight Parzifal, or Dostoevskii's Prince Myshkin, Erasmus sees the saving grace of Christ in the innocence and foolishness of the Christian fool. Only through an irrational passion that allows us to love our neighbour or spurn our self-interests can we hope for salvation. Only by folly is folly redeemed. Thus in its intricate play of satire, *The Praise of Folly* advocates a humanism that conceives man not as a rational animal, but as a passionate one, and like itself, capable of serious folly, of moral *jeu d'esprit*.

—Thomas L. Cooksey

PRAŚNA

See UPANISHADS

THE PRESIDENT (El Señor Presidente)
Novel by Miguel Ángel Asturias, 1946 (written 1922–1932)

The President, Miguel Ángel Asturias's first novel, although not published until 1946, following the fall of the Guatemalan dictator Jorge Ubico, was written in Guatemala and Paris during the 1920s and early 1930s. Asturias wrote it as an attack against the dictatorship of Manuel Estrada Cabrera, but the novel comes to represent the horror of all Latin American dictatorships. The grotesque, violent, and nightmarish vision of despotism depicted in this novel is presented within a complex narrative structure punctuated by stream-of-consciousness subjectivity, multiple perspectives, punning onomatopoeia, and free association. The beauty of Asturias's literary language serves as a powerfully ironic means of highlighting the horror and violence of dictatorship. While the President himself rarely appears in the novel, he acts as the malevolent, invisible motivator of most of the action, his power and knowledge are a continual threat to everyone, and his command over their mental states is complete. Asturias created a gripping portrait of a nation controlled by fear.

One of the central motifs of the novel involves the forces of light against those of darkness, of angels pitted against Lucifer. In this infernal world, plots are continually hatched and assassinations planned against those who were previously allies, and individuals are thrown into the dungeon for no apparent reason, or tortured to death for telling the truth. At any moment, the President can turn against his allies for the most trivial infraction, real or imagined. It is useless to try to determine whether one should tell the truth or not: the system for torture and punishment is so arbitrary that some characters never know why they are in the dungeon—or why a lucky few are released.

The story begins with the murder of Colonel Parrales Sonriente by an idiot he has taunted, and the President decides to blame the colonel's death on two men he wants to get rid of: one of them, a lawyer, is arrested and shot; the other, General Canales, escapes to the mountains after being warned by Don Miguel Cara de Ángel, the

President's favourite. The narrator characterizes Cara de Ángel, whose name means "angel-face," as a fallen angel, one who is as beautiful and evil as Satan. A handsome and debonair young man, Cara de Ángel has never questioned his duties and obligations as the President's favourite, nor does he realize that his commission to warn Canales is actually part of the President's plan to assassinate the general. Canales, however, is successful in his escape thanks to Cara de Ángel's aid, and the young man is left to escort the general's daughter, Camila, to the home of one of her uncles. However, none of her relatives is willing to take her in as they are afraid of being compromised politically, and she falls gravely ill with pneumonia. It is while Cara de Ángel is taking care of the sick girl that he falls in love with and marries her. In so doing, he is transformed from a selfish and self-centred puppet of the President into a man who puts another person's welfare before his own for the first time in his life. This act of falling in love, of making Camila's life dearer to him than his own, constitutes Cara de Ángel's betrayal of the President, whose law is to control and destroy with hatred, violence, and fear. Although Cara de Ángel never has any intention of harming the President, he ultimately becomes the victim of the tyrant's most vicious and sadistic punishment. One character maintains that only love can oppose death; the President, who realizes that Cara de Ángel has committed no overt act of disloyalty, can none the less only respond to the discovery of this love as if it were an act of treason punishable by death.

Cara de Ángel plans to escape with Camila to Washington, but he is captured and tortured by the President's henchmen, and thrown into the deepest and darkest cell in the dungeon to die. And he does die, after many years in the dungeon, when a fellow prisoner, planted by the President, falsely insinuates to him that Camila has become the President's favoured mistress.

Asturias's novel, deeply poetic as it is, may be characterized as a metaphysical as much as a political treatment of dictatorship; Cara de Ángel's personal spiritual transformation and triumph over his previous existence would otherwise be seen as an empty victory, especially in light of the horrible and painfully slow death he meets, disillusioned and broken-hearted in the dungeon, defeated were it not for the conscious desire to do good that has freed him from the clutches of the President's dark forces and redeemed him. The President must eliminate him precisely because, as the embodiment of the force of evil, he senses, on an instinctual level, the threat of such goodness to his powers. Camila is left with a baby son at the end of the novel, a symbol of the couple's triumph over the forces of annihilation, which separated them, but which could not destroy the fruit of their love.

—Susan Isabel Stein

THE PRINCE (Il Principe)
Prose by Niccolò Machiavelli, 1532 (written 1513)

The Prince is a concise and powerful tract on monarchies written by a convinced republican. Read out of context, it gave Elizabethan England the figure of the "Machiavel" as the evil schemer for power and equated Niccolò with Old Nick. Rulers and seekers after power, up to Frederick the Great of Prussia, condemned the work while following what they took to be its precepts. But Niccolò Machiavelli's interest in *The Prince* centres on the new ruler who comes to power, in the words of the Latin title to chapter six "armis propriis et virtute"— by his own armed might and valour. "Virtù" is one of Machiavelli's key words that confound translation. It conveys "worth," with a strong masculine marking, and restores the currency of the ancient Roman military and political "virtus" under the ethical cover of medieval Christian and Renaissance humanist "virtue."

This dynamic leader is sharply distinguished from the opportunist who bases his bid for power on the support of other rulers, as was the case with the notorious Cesare Borgia (chapter seven); and also from the merely criminal power-grabber, like Agathocles in ancient Syracuse (chapter eight). Both are dismissed as inadequate models, yet they are also praised for their ruthless and clear sighted efficiency, and also for having mobilized "the people" against "the grandees." The same considerations are also paramount in chapter six and in the entire second half of the work from chapter 12 onwards, all dealing with the "new prince." In chapter six it is made quite clear that the prince's "own armed might" means, in fact, the people in arms, and the three central "military" chapters (12–14) stress that the new prince cannot succeed unless he is the military leader of his own army and does not rely (as was the current Italian practice) on hired mercenaries or foreign auxiliaries. It is evident from Machiavelli's other writings that he was inspired above all by the military success of the citizen armies of ancient Republican Rome. What interpreters of *The Prince* have often overlooked is Machiavelli's analysis in chapter six of the historical condition—"occasione"—essential to the durable foundation of the new realm. In this (with the final chapter 26, one of the two most intense chapters of the work), Machiavelli selects the loftiest examples of political creators: Moses for the Jews, Cyrus for the Persians, Theseus for the Athenians, and Romulus for the Romans. Fortune blessed each of them only in one respect: in offering an historical "occasione." However he defines this opportunity in terms of total political negativity. It is the helplessness and hopelessness of a people, their total lack of reliable institutions, that provides the raw "material" upon which princely "virtù" may stamp its creative "forma." Machiavelli is theorizing the birth of the state, political creation from zero. The greater the misery of the people the readier they will be to join in the act of political creation.

This is the theoretical context that explains the supposedly immoral precepts that many have found so shocking but that make of *The Prince* the starting-point for modern political science. Armed force as the ultimate sanction of political power, the ruthless suppression of dangerous enemies and the establishment of authority through fear rather than love, the use of deceit, careful economy rather than lavish expenditure—all these Machiavelli cites as necessary to the founder of a new state, in systematic opposition to the wishful thinking of the prolific conventional "mirror of princes" literature based on the political ethics of Christians and humanists. History is no longer a gallery of examples of elevated political virtue in the ethical sense, but a political laboratory in which the experiments of both past and present can be studied, compared and evaluated, with an eye to cause and effect and to the modalities of success and failure.

The Prince combines this general theoretical valence with an immediate application. The final chapter reveals the present state of Italy, lying helplessly weak and divided under the impact of foreign invasions, as just such an historic "occasione" awaiting a leader to create the Italian nation-state with a new model army of Italians. It ends with a stirring exhortation to Lorenzo de' Medici (grandson of "il Magnifico"), to whom the work is dedicated, to lead the Italians to freedom and dignity.

Machiavelli wrote *The Prince* while still confined to his country home after imprisonment by the Medici, who had in 1512 overthrown the Florentine Republic which he had served. During 1513 he had been working on his *Discourses*, a study of the conditions of success and expansion of ancient Republican Rome. As was first argued by Chabod in 1924 (now in *Machiavelli and the Renaissance*, 1958), the conception of *The Prince* seems to have been triggered by the question that Machiavelli posed in chapters 16–18 of Book I of the *Discourses*, namely, what political recourse is there for polities in total breakdown (''nelle città corrotte''): the case of Florence and, more broadly, of Italy. His answer in the *Discourses* was: none, unless a leader of extraordinary ''virtù'' restores the institutions of the state or creates them anew. *The Prince* transforms this despairing hypothesis into a rousing political programme.

The excitement of political discovery produces in *The Prince* an equally revolutionary style, in which humanist decorum is consciously abandoned for a direct and dynamic eloquence. The sentences are spare and functional as the Realpolitik, unremittingly pursuing a linear logic and resorting at key moments to pungent colloquialism and resonant similes. As a literary masterpiece the book remains a landmark in the discourse both of Italy and of the wider western civilization.

—John Gatt-Rutter

THE PRINCE OF HOMBURG (Prinz Friedrich von Homburg)
Play by Heinrich von Kleist, 1821

Described by Heine as ''written by the genius of poetry itself'' and by Hebbel as ''a German oak whose top is closer to heaven than to earth,'' *The Prince of Homburg* is one of the few dramatic masterpieces associated with German Romanticism. Begun in 1809 and finished in 1811, it was prevented from being performed in the year of its completion by Princess Wilhelm of Prussia, a descendant of the title hero, who objected to a scene which showed her ancestor as being afraid of death. The first production in Vienna in 1821 (also the year of first publication) was banned by Archduke Charles after a handful of performances, as was that in Berlin in 1828 by King Frederick William III, because of alleged slurs on the valour of the military aristocracy. From the Marxist camp, Franz Mehring accused Heinrich von Kleist of ''raising old Prussianism, with its mixture of brutality and stupidity, into the realms of art'' by his ''hymn on subordination,'' while Brecht called the hero a ''personification of warrior's pride and servant's intellect.'' After serving the nationalist cause from the mid-19th century to World War II, the play is now chiefly admired for Kleist's existential probings, his psychological insights, and his mastery of stagecraft and dialogue.

Based on Frederick the Great's *Mémoires pour servir à l'histoire de la maison de Brandebourg* and Karl Heinrich Krause's *Mein Vaterland unter den hohenzollerischen Regenten*, the action revolves around the battle of Fehrbellin in 1675. After a fit of somnambulism, the Prince—young, dashing, highly strung, and altogether different from the middle-aged, twice-married, mutilated veteran officer of history—ignores the delay ordered by the Elector Frederick William and leads a Prussian attack against the Swedes, winning a partial victory but jeopardizing the success of the campaign as a whole. The Elector sentences the Prince to death but reprieves him when he recognizes his guilt and accepts his impending execution.

At one level, by exalting 17th-century Prussia, Kleist purveys anti-Napoleonic propaganda, voicing the chauvinism he shared with the political theorist Adam Müller and other German contemporaries. At another level, by leading his hero from anarchistic self-indulgence to communal responsibility, he recalls the ideals of German classicism, as propounded in the drama of Schiller. Above all, however, he reveals his intensely personal preoccupations.

Kleist's central experience was his failure to find happiness through rational virtue. His famous misunderstanding of Immanuel Kant confirmed his feeling that the truth was inaccessible to human perception. As his essay *Über das Marionettentheater* (*On Puppetshows*) illustrates, he believed—partly under the influence of Rousseau—that ''reflection'' was liable to destroy the ''natural grace of man,'' which could only be regained, if at all, on a higher plane through the attainment of an ''infinite consciousness.'' To some extent the Prince's development follows the lines of this triad. While he expects his subjective desires to justify his disobedience, he feels at one with himself and the world. When, at the sight of his grave, he becomes aware for the first time of an objective reality outside himself, he breaks down in fear and confusion. When he assents to his punishment and takes leave of life, he may be said to have recovered his original poise through a higher kind of knowledge. This progress may seem to be of a rational kind, but although the Prince is pardoned as a result of a deliberate moral effort, it is his initial dream of love and glory that is fulfilled in a similarly dreamlike manner at the close of the play. Thus, beneath the deceptive appearance of a classical synthesis of reason and intuition, the romantic undercurrent or irrational visions and mysteries prevails.

Irrationality is also the hallmark of the Elector. He encourages the Prince to pursue his ambitious fantasy out of sheer curiosity. He is puzzled when the Prince objects to the death sentence. Granting the pardon, he disregards the Prince's own hard-won determination to atone, and he flouts the law that he has claimed to be upholding in all circumstances. Although the text itself explains that the state should be ruled by human feelings rather than by abstract principles, he remains an ambiguous figure. Owing to his position in society—and in the structure of the play—he seems to represent a rational order, but his conduct is inconsistent and arbitrary. In symbolic terms he thus conveys Kleist's own experience of a universe which, far from being rational, seems to be governed by capricious and unpredictable forces. These forces may appear indifferent, cruel, or beneficial to human beings, but they are always baffling and incomprehensible. In this instance, the conflict ends happily, but the happy ending is explicitly declared to be a dream.

At the technical level, Kleist's last play before his suicide shows him at the height of his powers. His artistic maturity manifests itself in the portrayal of complex characters; in the consummate timing of retardation and precipitation; in the suspense arising not from physical violence but from the clash of emotions between and within the protagonists; in the fusion of harsh near-tragedy in the central plot with the lyrical idylls of the frame; and above all in the blank verse which has a wider range and more relaxed atmosphere than in any of his previous plays. *The Prince of Homburg* is one of the most impressive demonstrations of Kleist's ability to re-create, through the very movement and rhythm of his language, the ebb and flow of feeling, the meeting of dream and reality, and the interaction of the conscious and unconscious layers of the mind.

—Ladislaus Löb

PROFESSOR BERNHARDI
Play by Arthur Schnitzler, 1912

Professor Bernhardi articulates social and political concerns which remained relevant for many decades to come. In it the proverbial levity and eroticism associated with many of Arthur Schnitzler's plays is absent. The dialogues are brief and to the point, the language terse without the usual hint of Viennese dialect. The character constellation reflects the sociology of the medical profession at the turn of the century with which Schnitzler was eminently familiar. Oskar Bernhardi reflects back on his own experience as an assistant at his father's clinic until 1893. *Professor Bernhardi* became the paradigm for later works dealing with anti-semitism among doctors, for example Friedrich Wolf's *Professor Mamlock* (1933) and the episodes involving the surgeon Edgar in Lion Feuchtwanger's novel *Die Geschwister Oppenheim* (1933). Neither the plot, the near destruction of the protagonist, nor the representation of characters justify the designation, ''Comedy in Five Acts''; however, the absurdity of the intrigues does. Although Bernhardi is rehabilitated in the end, the drama is a tragi-comedy at best. *Professor Bernhardi* is set in Vienna in the year 1900, ten years after the ''Central Association of German Citizens of Jewish Faith'' was founded to counteract anti-semitism, and four years since the publication of Theodor Herzl's *Judenstaat* and the formalizing of his Zionist programme in reaction to the Dreyfus affair. *Professor Bernhardi* is modelled after this famous anti-semitic scandal; Dreyfus was rehabilitated in 1906.

The play reflects the strained social situation in Austria in the wake of the economic and political upheavals. The emancipation movements of the Jews, women, and the working class seemed doomed as the Austrian government suppressed progressive parties and individuals. The attitude of Bernhardi's vice-director, Dr. Ebenwald, reflects a manifesto by Karl Lueger who was the mayor of Vienna in 1900, which called for the elimination of all Jews from the professions. Bernhardi's characters reflect the religious and racial anti-semitism of his time, a phenomenon which he, a Viennese Jew, had personally experienced. He uncovers the economic motivations which propel his gentile characters' supposedly philosophical or religious principles. *Professor Bernhardi* did not pass Austrian censorship. It was first performed in Berlin, 28 November 1912. After the collapse of the *Kaiserlich und Königlich* monarchy *Professor Bernhardi* was first staged in Vienna as late as 1921, after receiving an award from the Vienna Volkstheater.

Like some of Schnitzler's earlier works, for example the novels *None But the Brave* (*Leutnant Gustl*) and *The Road to the Open* (*Der Weg ins Freie*), *Professor Bernhardi* exposes the bigotry of the upwardly mobile middle and lower-middle classes as the breeding ground of ethnocentrism and misogyny. His autobiography *My Youth in Vienna* (*Jungend in Wien*), written between 1915 and 1920, further elucidates the background against which he created his anti-semitic students and professionals. According to Egon Schwarz, Bernhardi is a paradigm of the identity crisis faced by Schnitzler and other turn-of-the-century Jewish intellectuals, including Sigmund Freud, Ludwig Wittgenstein, and Otto Weininger. Other contemporary problems examined in *Professor Bernhardi* are chauvinism, cut-throat careerism in a capitalist society, and the oppression of women by keeping abortion illegal.

Dr. Bernhardi is the director of a clinic and a renowned physician of Jewish background who becomes the focus of a scandal because of his ethics. To a large extent he represents Schnitzler's position: religious or racial considerations have no bearing on the decisions of this enlightened scientist who is detached from the religious community and the Zionists. He is motivated by professional considerations when he refuses to disturb a dying patient by having a priest administer the last rites, not realizing that this refusal leaves him open to attack. His gentile colleagues who are jealous of him accuse him of anti-Christian intentions. Fanaticized by the biased press, the public is ready to condemn Bernhardi while, to the audience, the sincerity of Bernhardi's professional and personal commitment is obvious all along.

Among the fanatics and opportunists who place ideologies or personal interests above the welfare of others, Bernhardi stands out as truly humane: he wants to spare a victim of an illegal abortion unnecessary panic in the last minutes of her life. His sensitivity is shown in a variety of ways: his spontaneous affection for his son and assistant Oskar proves him a loving father; his interaction with his former student Feuermann, a young doctor accused of performing an abortion, reveals him to a concerned teacher and colleague. Toward his staff Bernhardi is fair beyond the call of duty; the Jewish professor practises charity, whereas the Christians do not. As an enlightened intellectual, Bernhardi judges his colleagues by their merits, even if they, like his assistant Pflugfelder, are by their own admission anti-semites. The conflict between Bernhardi and members of his staff, the clergy, the courts, and government agencies, allows Schnitzler to unveil a spectrum of attitudes. Bernhardi represents the individualism of apolitical, middle-class professionals and assimilated Jews. The pitfalls of their indifference to politics become evident; alone, Bernhardi is defenceless against his adversaries. To show this dilemma as universal, Feuermann is introduced as a parallel case. Wherever there is suspected wrongdoing, Jewish doctors are blamed, although they play by the rules in contrast to their gentile rivals. Schnitzler repeatedly exposes the hypocrisy of the would-be Christians. Even the most reactionary of them, the Tyrolian intern Hochroitzpointner, belongs to the secular society of his time. He only flaunts his Catholicism when it is convenient and he is entirely worldly when flirting with the nurse. Schnitzler depicts the medical profession, a microcosm of Austrian society, as a hotbed of ambition and ethnic strife. As soon as Bernhardi becomes vulnerable, the men whom he nurtured attack him. The conflict reaches its climax when Bernhardi is convicted after a highly irregular show trial. Schnitzler effects a solution in a manner reminiscent of Heinrich von Kleist's *The Prince of Homburg*, by a *deus ex machina*. After a short prison term, Bernhardi is released. Publications of the liberal press at home and abroad, but even more so, Prince Konstantin's wish to consult Bernhardi, help the latter to be reinstated. Rather than a happy ending, this is an indictment of the presumably educated bourgeoisie. Bernhardi owes his triumph over the system to a gracious benefactor and dissenting forces. Neither one is likely to have come to the aid of a less prominent man. Schnitzler's drama leaves the audience wondering whether these positive forces will prevail in the future.

—Dagmar C.G. Lorenz

PROFESSOR TARANNE (Le Professeur Taranne)
Play by Arthur Adamov, 1953

This short but disturbing play has the bizarre, remorseless logic of a nightmare. It begins abruptly with the eponymous professor in mid-peroration, attempting to rebut a charge of indecent exposure reported to the police by a group of children. In a blustering self-defence he pleads the palpable absurdity of divesting oneself of clothes in such cold weather, the notorious unreliability of juvenile witnesses, and his own international reputation as a scholar; he even alleges persecution at the hands of the children, who, he says, have pointed and jeered at him; but the chief inspector remains sceptically impassive. Taranne is then subjected to humiliation by a succession of unlikely visitors to the police station: a female journalist who denies ever having met him, two men far too engrossed in talking business to recognize him, and an elegant socialite who compliments him on a recent public lecture only to introduce him to the others as Professor Ménard. The scene ends inconclusively with the gradual dispersal of police officers and visitors alike, and the action shifts to the vestibule of a small hotel where Taranne is waiting impatiently for his mail. Two more police-men arrive, accusing him of having deposited litter in some bathing cabins. The policemen are also investigating the ownership of the notebook which Taranne immediately claims as his, although he cannot decipher the handwriting or explain its many blank pages. Again the stage empties as Taranne protests the simple absent-mindedness of a scholar. The hotel manageress brings in a large roll of paper addressed to him, which proves to be the dining-room plan of a luxury ocean-liner with a place mysteriously reserved for him at the captain's table. His sister Jeanne, the only other named character, enters with a letter from the rector of a Belgian university where Taranne has recently lectured: it complains of his general incompe-tence and, in particular, of his plagiarism of Professor Ménard's work. Indignant initially, Taranne ends by acquiescing to the charges, and on a bare stage, cleared of furniture by the manageress, he hangs up the plan against the rear wall, stares at it long and intently, then slowly begins to remove his clothes.

The oneiric quality of the action is no mere stylistic device: by Arthur Adamov's admission, the play is a direct transcription of a dream of his, completed in two days with only minor changes of detail. Given his long history of neurosis—childhood phobias and superstitions, an intense dislike of his commercially prosperous father, subsequently transformed into self-reproach by the latter's suicide, an abiding fear of persecution—which he recounts in his graphically confessional book, *Endless Humiliations*, it is tempting to see the play preeminently in personal terms. In particular, Adamov's sexual impotence and persistent alcoholism could have offered fertile ground for the dream's brooding sense of guilt, while the reiterated cry of the dream professor, "I am the author of *La Parodie*" (the title of an earlier play by Adamov), would seem to make the identification between playwright and protagonist complete. During his somewhat bohemian adolescence in Paris, when he mixed in Surrealist circles and assimilated their aesthetic, not least their interest in dreams and automatic writing, he had been deeply impressed by a production at Artaud's short-lived Théâtre Alfred Jarry of Strindberg's *A Dream Play* (*Ett Drömspel*), in which there is a similar identification between the personality of the author-dreamer and his dramatic creations. Such was Adamov's preoccupation with dreams and the unconscious that his first published work was a translation from Jung, *Le Mot et l'inconscient* (1938), and *Professor Taranne* itself contains more than a hint of Jungian thinking, enabling it to transcend crude autobiogra-phy and situating it on a broader symbolic plane. In his original dream, Adamov, the true author of *La Parodie*, found the legitimacy of his claim to it ignored and subverted by a nightmarish conspiracy of circumstances; in the ensuing dramatic text, however, he cast himself as a more ambiguous character with no external referent, who may be either upright citizen and eminent scholar or pathetic deviant and

academic fraud, or indeed someone combining elements of both. It is as if Adamov has reached down into the collective unconscious and produced a powerful image for the essential precariousness of our sense of identity, for the nexus of illusion, veracity, and pretence which holds it together and the link between self-knowledge and self-destruction.

In effect he has given the play some of the properties of an archetypal myth, of the kind advocated by his friend Artaud, whose notion of a theatre of cruelty deeply impressed him and whose contempt for orthodox psychological drama he shared. Atmospheri-cally, too, the play has much in common with the work of other dramatists writing in the two decades following World War II, whose anguished contemplation of the contingency and ultimate meaninglessness of human existence led to its being categorized as "theatre of the absurd." In fact, Ionesco's suggestion that burrowing into his own "darkness" was what allowed him to discover "the problems and fears of literally everyone" might almost be taken as a recipe for the genesis of *Professor Taranne*. On the other hand, Adamov never loses sight of the objective world altogether: the forces that threaten or oppress his characters come from outside as well as inside the individual—in this case from a somewhat Kafkaesque police force and the academic establishment, in which respects it could be said look forward to his later, so-called "Brechtian" plays and their overt concern for political and social realities. This may well have been what particularly recommended *Professor Taranne* to the young director Roger Planchon, who staged its first performance at his Théâtre de la Comédie in Lyon on 18 March 1953, since when it has remained the play by Adamov that commands most attention both in France and abroad.

—Donald Roy

PROMETHEUS BOUND (Prometheus Vinctus)
Play by Aeschylus, c. 466–59 BC

Prometheus Bound depicts the power struggle between the Olym-pian god Zeus and the Titan Prometheus. The former is presented as a violent and tyrannical divinity who wishes to destroy the human race. Prometheus, by contrast, is the champion of men, who brought them fire and taught them various arts and skills. He also possesses foresight. Zeus is the leader of the new generation of gods and has only recently gained his position of dominance in the universe, after battling with his father and the Titans (all except Themis and Prometheus) with the help of his Olympian brothers and sisters. He is not yet secure, however, and Prometheus alone has knowledge of a secret that will bring about his downfall: Zeus must stay away from the sea-nymph Thetis, who is fated to bear a son greater than his father.

As the play opens, Prometheus is being nailed to a cliff in remotest Scythia by Kratos (Strength) and Bia (Violence), the servants of Zeus. They are accompanied by the god Hephaestus, an Olympian who pities Prometheus. In spite of his torments, Prometheus is defiant, complaining bitterly of his unjust humiliation at the hands of Zeus, who formerly counted him among his allies. He also lists the many gifts he has brought to mankind—architecture, numbers, writing, farming, sailing, medicine, prophecy, mining—for which he is now being punished. In the course of the tragedy, Prometheus is visited by the chorus of Oceanus and his daughters, and also by Io, who herself is a victim of Zeus: she was raped by him and then his wife Hera vengefully turned her into a cow and had her chased all over the world by a gadfly. Prometheus uses his foresight to give Io a detailed account of her future wanderings, and also of her eventual deliverance from suffering by Zeus. In Egypt she will bear him a son, Epaphus. As the play ends, Hermes, the messenger of Zeus, threatens Prometheus with even worse torments: he will be plunged under the earth, and an eagle will gnaw at his liver every day. Prometheus' final words express his continuing defiance: "O majesty of my mother, O sky revolving the light common to all things: you see me, how I suffer unjust torments."

Any interpretation of *Prometheus Bound* is complicated by the fact that it was part of a trilogy, the other plays of which survive only in a few fragments. Their titles were *Prometheus Unbound* and *Prometheus the Firebearer*, and a judicious reconstruction of their content has been made by M.L. West ("The Prometheus Trilogy," *Journal of Hellenic Studies*, 1979, 130–48). Additional light is thrown on the matter by the detailed accounts of the Prometheus myth in Hesiod's *Theogony* (*Theogonia*, 507–616) and *Works and Days* (*Opera et dies*, 47–105). The central theme is the need for reconciliation and compromise between Zeus and Prometheus. Zeus must change his ways if he is to survive as the supreme deity of the universe. He must learn compassion and justice. Likewise, Prometheus needs to develop a respect for authority. In all probability, the trilogy ended with a reconciliation of the two gods, and a celebration of moderation on the divine and the human plane. In *Prometheus Bound*, Prometheus appears to foresee an eventual change in Zeus' attitude, and the prophesied end to Io's sufferings parallels the end of his own punishment. It is, in fact, one of the descendants of Epaphus, namely Heracles, who finally releases Prometheus from his bonds. Zeus learns the secret about Thetis, who later bears Peleus a son called Achilles.

The play has a political message relevant to life in the Athens of the mid-5th century: authority must be benevolent in order to be respected, and change and progress must be gradual and orderly. Whether or not the play was actually written by Aeschylus (see Mark Griffith, *The Authenticity of Prometheus Bound*), it contains conflicts which are quint-essentially Aeschylean, conflicts which reflect the societal disruption accompanying the birth of Athenian democracy: between old-fashioned authoritarianism and revolutionary reform, between violence and reason, between excess and moderation. The Prometheus trilogy, like the Orestes trilogy of Aeschylus, appears to have been founded on the basic idea that the old ways of violent confrontation will no longer work, and that a new system based on reason and justice is required. This is associated with the patriarchal Olympian religious system which supplanted the earlier matriarchal one, and remnants of this conflict between male- and female-centred orders can be seen in the unhappy union of Io with Zeus, and in the shadowy presence of the Earth goddess (Gaea), who gave birth to the Titans.

The action of *Prometheus Bound* takes place in a mysterious and marginal realm, in the space between the human and divine worlds. Zeus himself does not appear on stage: we see only his representatives. The lengthy geographical descriptions in Prometheus' speeches to Io, however, remind us of the extent of his power. Humankind is also very much in the background, evident mainly in Prometheus' words. The play is unusual in the static nature of the action, which consists almost entirely of various visitors coming to witness Prometheus' sufferings and lament the startling and ignominious spectacle he presents. The most frequent images in the play are those of disease and the yoking of animals, underscoring the web of suffering and domination in which the characters are trapped. The language of the play is also much concerned with sight and seeing: by the end, we realize that "sight" and "blindness" are not absolute terms, since all the characters, including Zeus and Prometheus, are in some way blind to certain necessities. Only by recognizing this fact can Prometheus and Zeus come to terms. None the less, Prometheus has proved to be, and remains for many, an inspiring and heroic figure just as he is: to some, he is the creator who stoutly defends his creation, even if it provokes his own terrible suffering; to others, he is the noble rebel who stands alone against oppression, secure in the knowledge that his values will prevail in the end.

—David H.J. Larmour

THE PROSE EDDA
Prose by Snorri Sturluson, 13th century

The prose *Edda* is a four-part introduction to the language, subject matter, and metrical forms of eddic and scaldic poetry, the two main types of poetry in Scandinavia from the ninth to the 13th century. It was written by the Icelander Snorri Sturluson, apparently with the aim of sustaining an interest in this poetry at a time when its popularity was in decline. Since scaldic poetry, in particular, made frequent use of the circumlocutory expressions known as kennings, often involving a knowledge of mythology (such as "Ægir's daughters" for "waves," Ægir being a sea-giant), Snorri's *Edda* appears in parts to deal more with mythology than directly with poetry and it is, indeed, the fullest and most accessible, if not always the most reliable, extant medieval source for Old Norse mythology. The word *edda*, according to a recent suggestion, derives from the Latin verb *edere*, meaning "to compose (poetry)."

The prologue tells how the Æsir, the inhabitants of Asia Minor or Turkey, migrated to Scandinavia under the leadership of Ódin, and were so distinguished that they seemed more like gods than men. Snorri thus hints at euhemerism in its medieval Christian form: the idea that pagan deities were human beings who, by devilish deception and magic, came to be regarded as gods.

The second part, *Gylfaginning*, "the tricking of Gylfi," has deception as one of its main themes. The Swedish king Gylfi visits the Æsir in their Scandinavian stronghold Ásgard, built on the model of their former home, Old Ásgard or Troy, to find out whether their success is due to their own nature or to the gods they worship. They are aware in advance of his coming, and subject him to various optical illusions. He meets three figures, High, Just-as-High, and Third, the first of whom tells him that in order to depart unharmed he must prove himself wiser than they. He then proceeds to ask them questions about their gods, as much with a view to exhausting their store of knowledge as to satisfying his curiosity. Their replies include some of the best-known stories of Norse mythology, not least the one in which the god Thór, visiting a giant's castle, fails to drain a drinking-horn or to wrestle successfully with an old woman, only to be told, once safely out of the castle, that the giant had been concealing from him by optical illusions the fact that what he had been drinking was the sea, and that the old woman was Old Age. When Thór, furious at being so deceived, raises his hammer to smash the giant and his castle, both vanish. When Gylfi finally brings High and his companions to the point where they can answer no more questions, they too, like the giant in the story they have been telling, vanish. In a sense, however, Gylfi has the last laugh, since he goes off and tells people what he has heard, including presumably the fact that the gods in the stories, the divine Æsir, are not identical with the human Æsir telling them; whereas the human Æsir, as emerges after Gylfi has left, wish it to be thought that they are identical. Their position is that of Alice's elder sister, who at the end of *Alice in Wonderland* equates the dream world with reality, whereas Gylfi's position is that of Alice, who is convinced of the dream world's otherness. The title *Gylfaginning* may be ambiguous; is the trick played *on* Gylfi, or *by* him?

The third part, *Skáldskaparmál* ("the language of poetry"), as its title suggests, deals more directly than *Gylfaginning* with poetry, but also makes use, if not so consistently as *Gylfaginning*, of a narrative framework in which mythical stories are told. Ægir, here described as a man from the Danish island of Læsø, visits what appears to be yet another Ásgard, the mythical home of the gods worshipped by the human Æsir. Here he finds himself sitting next to Bragi, the god of poetry, from whom he learns about, among other things, the poetic mead made from the blood of Kvasir, a man fashioned from the spittle of the gods. The framing story of Ægir tends to recede as kennings for deities, poetry, natural phenomena, men and women are illustrated, but is reactivated when kennings for gold are described. The point, it has recently been suggested, is to draw attention to a distinction between kennings for *animate* beings (including not only poetry, with its supposed origin in body-fluids, but also natural phenomena, endowed with life as in the "waves" example above) and kennings with *inanimate* referents, such as gold, battle, weapons, armour, and ships, which are dealt with, along with further kennings for humans and for Christ, as the framing story again recedes. Given Snorri's evident general preference for non-metaphorical kennings (he would have preferred "traverser of the desert" to "ship of the desert" for "camel"), his ready acceptance of kennings explicable in terms of pagan mythology betrays a respectful sympathy with that mythology. The remainder of *Skáldskaparmál* is taken up with an account of the non-periphrastic poetic expressions known as *heiti*, of which "targe" (for "shield") might be an English example.

The fourth part, *Háttatal*, is a poem of 102 stanzas, each containing a different metrical form, in praise of Norway's co-rulers King Hákon Hákonarson (d. 1263) and Earl Skúli (d.1240). It is set within the framework of a prose commentary, initially in the form of a dialogue between unnamed speakers. The prose *Edda*'s four parts may have been written in the reverse of the order in which they are treated here; if so, this might help to explain Snorri's greater control of framing devices in *Gylfaginning* than in *Skáldskaparmál* or *Háttatal*.

Like Chaucer's *Canterbury Tales*, Snorri's *Edda* exploits different narrative levels, illustrates many different literary forms, and leaves an almost deliberately unfinished impression. An investigation of "the idea of the prose *Edda*," somewhat on the lines of Donald F. Howard's *The Idea of the Canterbury Tales* (1978), would make a most rewarding and welcome study.

—Rory McTurk

PYTHIAN ODES FOUR AND FIVE
Odes by Pindar, c. 462 BC

The fourth and fifth Pythian Odes of Pindar are epinician songs, celebrating the victory of Arkesilas IV at the Pythian games near Delphi in 462 BC. Arkesilas, king of Cyrene, and his brother-in-law and driver, Karrhotus (Alexibiades), won a gruelling and dangerous 12-lap chariot race when some 40 other chariots crashed. Arkesilas was descended from the founder of Cyrene, Battus (the "stammerer"), who had led a Greek colony to North Africa from the Aegean island of Thera, and who claimed descent from Euphamus the Argonaut.

The fifth Pythian Ode, probably commissioned by Arkesilas himself, describes the blessings of honour wedded with wealth. As with all of the odes, Pindar was concerned with celebrating both the glory and limits of the individual. He approaches this by exploring the reciprocal relationship of the individual with his family, ancestors, and ultimately with mankind. Thus Arkesilas' achievement sheds glory on his family and community, but at the same time he is blessed by his roots. The poem is composed of four triads (12 strophes), linked thematically by two enveloping rings. In the outermost ring, Pindar celebrates Arkesilas' victory and what he owes to Apollo. This elides into a long description of the skill of Karrhotus the charioteer. In turn, this leads by association with Libya, a country of great charioteers, to the centre of the poem, a description of Battus and why he was favoured by Apollo, thereby linking Arkesilas with his ancestor. Speaking of the glories of Battus, and the prosperity of Cyrene, Pindar declares in the middle of the fourth triad:

> In this delight their son
> Arkesilas shares in his right.
> His name in the young men's song
> Let Phoebus of the Gold Sword cry aloud.

> (translated by C.M. Bowra)

Pindar returns to praising the charioteer, closing the inner ring around the legendary story of Battus, and finally concludes by hoping that Arkesilas will succeed at the Olympian games, closing the outer ring, and enveloping the whole.

The fourth Pythian is by most accounts Pindar's masterpiece. It is the longest extant work, some 13 triads (39 strophes), and differs from the other odes in that while its occasion is the celebration of victory, its intent is to win the sympathy of Arkesilas for Damophilus, a political exile. The centre of the ode is in a long account of the exploits of Jason and the Argonauts. As such, it represents the earliest known account of Jason. After a conventional invocation of the muse, Pindar recounts the prophecy of the Delphic priestess of Apollo that Battus should leave Thera and found Cyrene. In turn, the priestess recounts a long prophecy made by Medea to Euphamus about the founding of the city. Together the prophecies of Medea and the Delphic priestess form concentric rings around the narrative of the foundation of Cyrene. Then the figures of Euphamus and Battus, as the ancestors of Arkesilas, draw a line across these rings, joining the legendary and historic past with Arkesilas and the well-being of Cyrene in the present.

The link of Euphamus, Medea, and the Argonauts with Arkesilas, his family and community, leads to a long narrative (over seven triads) about Jason and the search for the Golden Fleece, a narrative in which Pindar approaches the scope and conventions of the epic. Warned to beware a man wearing one sandal, Peleus, the king of Iolchos, is alarmed by the sudden arrival of such a man, Jason, the son of a political rival. Jason had supposedly died as an infant, but had in reality been spirited away to be reared by Hieron. Confronting Peleus with words that anticipate Pindar's deeper intent, Jason declares:

The hearts of men are perhaps too quick
At choosing a smart advantage rather than right
(Though the next day the taste is wry in the mouth).
But I and you must rule our wrath
And weave our future fortune.

To defer his fate, Peleus agrees, but sends Jason on a quest for the Golden Fleece.

Pindar then describes a gathering of suitably glorious heroes who will accompany Jason on his quest, perhaps suggesting the divine and semi-divine company of Arkesilas' ancestors. The object of the quest was also felicitous, since Cyrene was an important centre in the wool trade. In turn Pindar outlines the high points of the Argonauts' voyage to the Colchias, Jason's encounter with Medea, the tasks he must perform (with the aid of Medea's magic) to win the Golden Fleece, and the return voyage. Here Pindar compressed his story (''The journey is long on the high road; / Time presses me, and I know a short path''), turning to his central theme with the aid of the Oedipean riddle of the lopped oak:

Though its fruit has perished, yet it gives
Witness of itself, when it comes at last
In winter to the fire,
Or rests on the upright pillars of a master,
Doing sad labour in a stranger's house
While its own land is desolate.

Everything is useful, even a damaged oak. Better, therefore, that its scattered limbs benefit its master than a stranger. Thus Arkesilas, the healer of his community, should forgive Damophilus, should ''stretch out a gentle hand, to dent / A sore wound.'' For all, like Jason, will eventually return home.

Together, the fourth and fifth Pythian Odes indicate the power and range of Pindar's poetic mastery, and his vision of humanity. Drawing on the resources of both the epic and the lyric, he weaves an elaborate pattern of mythical, historical, and contemporary material to praise the achievements of a hero, but at the same time to celebrate the community. As an individual, Arkesilas not only achieved victory in the Pythian games for himself, but focused the blessings of the gods on his family, his city, and ultimately the human community.

—Thomas L. Cooksey

QUAND VOUS SEREZ BIEN VIEILLE. . . (When You Are Old. . .)
Poem by Pierre de Ronsard, 1578 (written 1572)

Pierre de Ronsard's ''Quand vous serez bien vieille, au soir à la chandelle'' (''When you are old . . . '') is one of the most studied and celebrated poems in French literature. Published in his collection of amatory verse, Sonnets for Hélène in Oeuvres (1578), the sonnet is addressed to Hélène de Surgères who, admired for her beauty and virtue, had lost her fiancé in a conflict during the Wars of Religion. Responding to Catherine de Medici's request, Ronsard seeks to console and extol Hélène through these verses. Like his previously published ''Loves of Cassandre'' (''Amours de Cassandre''), 1552, and ''On Marie's Death'' (''Sur la Mort de Marie''), 1578, this sonnet cycle explores the dimensions and dynamics of unrequited love, and

demonstrates conventional and creative uses of 16th-century styles and structures. The Sonnets for Hélène, moreover, reflects the work of a mature poet who integrates the obscurities and complexities of expression in his poems addressed to Cassandre Salviati with the simplicity and directness of imagery in the cycle honouring Marie Dupin. Further, the theme of love extends beyond a catalogue of Petrarchan conceits, and enables the poet to portray a universal situation that incites attempts to reconcile the confusions of the earthly and human with the order of the heavenly and spiritual.

A petrarchan sonnet written in dodecasyllabic, or Alexandrine, verse, the poem comprises two quatrains and two tercets, with rhyme schemes ABBA/ABBA and CCD/EED respectively. In the quatrains the persona develops two themes: the passage of time and the benefits of poetry. A sense of fragmentation suggested by temporal perspective and different personages presents conflict and crisis. The poet, speaking in the present, imagines a future situation where Hélène, aged and alone, must confront the loss of beauty, infirmity, and impending death. Memories remain, and the poet-lover perpetuates present experience in verse. Hélène's vibrance and vitality will triumph over time, for the poet's lyric will incite a toiling servant to recognize an enduring beauty and to respond, ''blessing [Hélène's] name with immortal praise.''

Any vision of harmony, however, is more apparent than real. In the first tercet the persona describes the future directly and realistically: he will have died, resting among ''myrtled spirits''; Hélène will have become decrepit and deformed. Hélène's current indifference, the poet predicts, will evolve into regret for denying his love and for being arrogant towards him. This sorrow identifies the irretrievability of cherished experiences, and in the two concluding lines the poet-lover implores Hélène to seize present opportunities. Through use of imperatives, the poet dissolves temporal particularities; and the hidden but operative force of love unites him with his lady, and prompts the creation of verse which, transcending time, assures the commemoration of beauty and love.

Subtle uses of literary and mythological allusions enrich the development of the themes of unrequited love, the brevity of human existence, and the glory of poetry. Like Horace (Odes, 11), Ronsard employs the carpe diem (''seize the day'') motif to convey the urgency of the present situation and to suggest the distress of separation. But the poet joins this plea with a metaphorical request: ''Pick today the roses of life.'' Similarly, in the widely anthologized ode, ''Mignonne, allons voir. . .'' (''Darling, let's go to see. . . ''), Ronsard uses the convention of the roses to depict the ephemerality of youthful beauty and, like the 5th-century poet Ausonius (Idyll 6), combines this image with Horace's prayer in his lyric, ''Quand on voit sur la branche au mois de May la rose'' (''When one sees the rose on the branch in the month of May'') (Sur la mort de Marie, II. 3).

Further, through the rhetorical technique of contaminatio, whereby poets rework frequently cited literary passages, Ronsard incorporates into this Hélène sonnet Virgil's thoughts on the lasting nature of poetry (Georgics II, 174–76) and Tibullus' picture of an ageing Delia who is entertained with stories by a servant seated at a lamp (Elegies I, iii, 83–94 and I, viii, 41–46).

Ronsard, though, is not an indiscriminate or slavish imitator, and the name Hélène reflects an innovative use of mythological reference essential to the sonnet's thematic development. Hélène's name recalls Menelaus' wife who, abducted by Paris, instigates the Trojan War. Her beauty stirs passion, incites unrequited love, and ends in destruction and death. But Helen practises virtue and, upon her return to Sparta, remains faithful to her husband. Likewise, Ronsard's Hélène creates within the poet-lover an inner turmoil; but, through a redirection of intention, she can participate in a love that assures emotional healing and spiritual tranquility. The ambivalence of this mythological allusion, then, enables Ronsard to depict Hélène's dual nature: as an earthly Venus, she instils within the poet a desire for her sensual beauty, but through her indifference, inflicts anguish and frustration; as a heavenly Venus, she represents an ideal of grace and virtue that offers the persona hope in transforming present suffering and solitude into future rest and reconciliation. Differences in age deter the consummation of this love; but the poet's pleas, like Menelaus' heroic deeds, demonstrate the urgency of the call to respond to a shared will that will culminate in a love eternally binding and continually renewing.

Ultimately, death will defeat the particular players in this drama, but the poet's love inspired by Hélène's beauty and immortalized in verse defies time and circumstances. Like the hidden image of the spinning wheel, visually stationary but unrelentingly turning, time passes imperceptibly but inexorably. The light of the candle will expire; embers in the hearth will darken and die; and, like Hélène who yearns, the Fates beget, thread, and sever the strands of life. Individual roses will perish, but their beauty, engendered and remembered, will endure. Hélène's name suggests an inspiration (''haleine''—breath) that incites artistic creativity, and Surgères (''surgir''—to rise) offers an optimism in spiritual renewal. In a Renaissance sonnet that combines the resources of logic and lyric, Ronsard presents elegantly and eloquently the means to overcome temporal restraints and earthly disturbances, and describes personally but universally the attainable beauty of life and love.

—Donald Gilman

R

THE RADETZKY MARCH (Radetzkymarsch)
Novel by Joseph Roth, 1932

Joseph Roth's nostalgic, occasionally morbid, narrative on the Austrian-Hungarian monarchy, *The Radetzky March* treats the careers of four generations of Slavic Austrians, the von Trottas. A baronetcy is conferred on Joseph Trotta, infantry lieutenant, as a consequence of the Battle of Solferino (24 June 1859), during which he forces the young emperor Franz Joseph to the ground and is wounded by the bullet fired at the exposed sovereign by the enemy sniper. The glory resulting from this episode incites the jealousy and contempt of Joseph's father, a sergeant-major who had served under Radetzky and who is unable to resist belittling his son's unexpected advancement. Worse still, the Solferino events are rewritten by the propaganda ministry and read by all Austrian school children to inspire them with the spirit of patriotic self-sacrifice. When the erroneous account comes to the attention of the story's actual hero, he takes the extraordinary step of requesting an audience with Franz Joseph to have the story removed from the school curriculum. The glory of the episode in any event is tacitly undermined by the fact that the Battle of Solferino was a defeat for Austria and the occasion of the loss of Lombardy to France. From the beginning, then, the status of the Trottas is tied both to romantic distortion and to a cause of dubious success. There is irony as well in the novel's title, which refers to Johann Strauss's popular and bouncy march celebrating Field Marshal Radetzky's victories in Italy during the 1848 uprisings. The territory retained for the Empire by Radetzky was lost ten years later at Solferino. The tune, written in the euphoria of victory, is used by Roth to suggest loss. Moreover, the actual rescue of the emperor by Joseph Trotta is motivated only in part by concern for the sovereign's apostolic welfare; Trotta is driven more by the annoyance (*der ewige Groll*) that a foot-soldier always has for staff officers.

This rather desultory beginning, paired with Roth's sympathies for the brush factory strikers of chapter 12, make Roth seem miscast as a Habsburg Legitimist, which at his death he was proclaimed to be. A more natural allegiance would have been to the social democratic left, had Roth not associated these groups with revulsion for *chutzpa*, the aggression and arrogance that western Jews regarded as typical of their Eastern cousins, the *Ostjuden*, a group to which Roth himself unwillingly belonged. With the fascists on the right, the only path possible seemed to be the doomed monarchy, which at least professed supra-nationalism against the divisive self-determination of peoples, the ethnic chauvinisms shattering the Empire and leading to World War I.

The next two generations of Trottas are each overwhelmed by the memory of the "hero of Solferino," whose portrait hangs in the study of Joseph's son Franz, the Chief District Commissioner, whose dedication as an Austrian civil servant extends to affecting the side-whiskers of his now aging emperor. Franz's son, Carl Joseph, bound for the military career forbidden his father, is wont to stand on a chair on quiet afternoons and study the portrait, which with the passing years grows ever more remote and inscrutable. Carl Joseph longs to achieve something extraordinary, but his era, hollowed out by desuetude and decadence, provides him with no opportunity to do so.

Instead he repeatedly finds himself to be an agent of misfortune. He is seduced at the age of 15 by Kathi Slama, wife of a local gendarme. The woman dies in childbirth. Roth, in Carl Joseph's graveside revery, dwells on the worms crawling over Kathi's once comely, now rotting face. The baroque intensity as well as the frequency of such images of decay suggest perhaps metaphorical implications beyond their merely local application. Kathi's husband, the sergeant-major, loyal to the class hierarchy holding Austria together, returns Carl Joseph's numerous letters, permitting himself only a trace of bitterness, to which Carl Joseph responds with a corresponding trace of superciliousness. Authentic human decency seems impossible in this context of formality and subordination.

When Carl Joseph is commissioned by the Uhlans and stationed in Moravia, he meets Max Demant, the regimental surgeon, whose childhood memories are also dominated by a titanic grandfather, an orthodox Jew with a silver beard, an innkeeper at the far eastern frontier. This old man expresses revulsion for his own male issue, who, instead of remaining self-employed in the family business, become civil servants and intellectuals (*lauter Konzeptsbeamte*). Demant and Carl Joseph show their rectitude and patriotism by rescuing a portrait of the Kaiser from the flyblown wall of a brothel. Each man considers the other his only friend, but the brotherhood is spoiled by an incident involving Demant's aggressive wife, Eva, who allows Carl Joseph to accompany her home after the theatre. The incident provokes gossip. Demant is forced into a duel and killed. Carl Joseph exiles himself to an infantry outpost on the Russian border.

The pointlessness and monotony of frontier military life lead inexorably to alcoholism. A further dangerous element appears in the form of the casino and its dancing girls singing songs about their "pink panties full of folds." Carl Joseph's superior officers pressure him to co-sign their loans from the local Shylock, Kapturak. When one of the officers is arrested for espionage, Kapturak threatens to impugn Carl Joseph's honour unless he produces the 7,250 kronen owed by the arrested officer. After immense effort, Carl Joseph's father, Franz, manages an audience with the Kaiser, who rescues from dishonour the grandson of the man who saved his life at Solferino.

Carl Joseph is also befriended in his exile by the local Polish landowner Count Chojnicki, who, wealthy and cosmopolitan, not only shares his man-hungry mistress, Valery ("Wally"), with his young friend but articulates the reasons for the coming end of the monarchy: no one now believes in God, and with the end of religion is the end of the apostolic mission of the Kaiser. The religion of the people now is nationalism. Hence the monarchy is moribund, and progress will come in a blaze of electricity and nitroglycerine.

It is at the centenary celebration of Carl Joseph's regiment at Chojnicki's that a telegram arrives announcing the assassination of Franz Ferdinand in Sarajevo. Hungarian representatives are particularly disrespectful at the news but are squelched by the loyal Carl Joseph. Nevertheless his role in the army now seems pointless, and he makes plans to return to civilian life. After a brief Tolstoian interlude during which he adopts a rural existence, serving as estate steward for Chojnicki, learning the regional dialect, bargaining with the local Jews, Carl Joseph is mobilized in the declaration of war against Serbia. He is killed by Cossack snipers while carrying water to his thirsty men. Chojnicki ends his days in the insane asylum of Steinhof where the forlorn Wally, temporarily spared from the worms, serves as a nurse. Franz, Carl Joseph's father, keeps vigil in the rain outside Schönbrunn as the old Kaiser is dying. Unwilling and unable to survive Austria, Franz dies the day the emperor is laid to rest in the vault of the Capuchins.

—Dan Latimer

RAIN IN THE PINE FOREST (La pioggia nel pineto)
Poem by Gabriele D'Annunzio, 1903

"Rain in the Pine Forest" is one of Gabriele D'Annunzio's most famous lyric poems, and has become one of the best known Italian poems of the 20th century, despite the decline in popularity of its author from the 1930s onwards. Probably written in July 1902, it was published in the *Alcyone* collection in 1903, one of the four volumes in D'Annunzio's *Laudi del cielo, del mare, della terra, e degli eroi* [Praises of the Skies, the Sea, the Earth, and the Heroes], the other two being *Maia, Elettra* and *Merope*. The collection *Alcyone* also contains some of his equally famous lyrics, such as "a sera fiesolana" [Evening at Fiesote], "e stirpi canore" [Lineages of Melody], and "Il novilunio" [The New Moon].

"Rain in the Pine Forest" consists of 128 short lines, some comprising a single word. It is addressed to the poet's companion, named in the poem as Ermione (Hermione), a name with classical connotations (Hermione was a daughter of Helen and Menelaus, and Hermione, the place in Argolis, was the site of a shrine to Aphrodite in her role as goddess of the seas as well as goddess of love. The same Hermione was also said to be the place through which Pluto plunged back into the earth towards Hades, after abducting Persephone). From the dating of the poem, it is likely that the inspiration for Ermione was Eleonora Duse, who also inspired D'Annunzio's novel *The Flame*.

The poem is structured along heavily rhythmical patterns, with repeated sound clusters. The sibilant "s" sounds reflect the sounds of falling water:

Ascolta. Piove
dalle nuvole sparse.
Piove su le tamerici
salmastre ed arse,
piove su i pini
scagliosi ed irti,
piove su i mirti.

(Listen. It rains
down from scattered clouds.
Rains on tamerisk trees
salt-stained and brown,
rains on pine trees
spiky and scaly,
rains on the myrtles.)

Each new rhyming couplet moves the poem forward, so that as the lovers wander through the pine forest, their walk is reflected in the

rhythm of the verse. There is no rigid pattern to the rhymes, which happen in couplets or across three or even four lines. The principal characteristic of the poem is the careful use of repetition and the way in which D'Annunzio keeps the reader's attention by creating a series of dramatic sections, each with a clearly marked starting point that ends in a climax. The starting point is always an imperative: "Taci" ("Hush") says the poet in the opening line; "Ascolta" ("Listen") in line 8; "Odi?" ("Can you hear?") in line 33; "Ascolta" again, in line 40; "Ascolta, ascolta" in line 65; "Ascolta" again for the last time in line 88. From line 96, the poem changes direction, and the imperatives end as the focus changes. The final section of the poem is more reflective, less immediate, and the language marks a shift from the urgency of the speaker's endeavours to communicate with Ermione to a more introspective consideration of the destiny of the lovers who have undergone a kind of transformation and become at one with the natural environment in which they find themselves.

There are signs early on in the poem of this symbolic transformation. Even as he urges his beloved to listen to the sound of the rain on the leaves and on the pine needles, the poet uses a significant set of adjectives: their faces are "silvani" (sylvan), line 21, their hands are "ignude" (bare), line 23, their clothes are "leggeri" (light), line 25, and their thoughts are "freschi" (fresh), line 26. By line 51 he is describing how they are both steeped in the spirit of the wood, how her ecstatic face is "molle di pioggia / come una foglia" (damp with raindrops like a leaf), and her hair is the colour of broom.

In line 65 the urgency of the poet's voice increases with the greater force of the falling rain. The repetition of "Ascolta" marks the description that follows of the increasingly heavy rain drowning out the sound of the sea and the singing of the crickets. The wildness of this rain-music marks the transformation of the lovers into creatures of the woods:

Piove su le tue ciglia nere
sì che par tu pianga
ma di piacere: non bianca
ma quasi fatta virente,
par di scorza tu esca.
E tutta la vita è in noi fresca
aulente,
il cuor nel petto è come pesca
intatta

(The rain on your dark lashes
looks like tears
of joy; not white
but almost leaf-green
you seem to rise out of bark.
And all of life is fresh within us
sweet-scented,
the hearts in our breasts like peaches
on the branch)

Line 115 to the end is a repetition of lines 20–32, only now the transformation that was only suggested the first time has already begun to take place. What is particularly significant is the slight alteration of lines 29–32 into the final lines of the poem:

su la favola bella
che ieri
t'illuse, che oggi m'illude,
o Ermione

(on the fairytale wonder
that yesterday
deceived you, today deceives me
oh Ermione)

becomes:

che ieri
m'illuse, che oggi t'illude

(that yesterday
deceived me, today deceives you)

so that the poem ends on a slightly different note, one in which Ermione is no longer all powerful. Indeed, it is possible to read into the inversion of ''you'' and ''me'' a deliberate distancing device, so that the woman who has been the object of the man's adoration is seen ultimately to be the one suffering from the delusion of believing in the fairy-tale wonder of their love. Given the autobiographical nature of D'Annunzio's writing and the fact that his relationship with Duse was in trouble in 1902 (they finally parted in 1904) it is not too far-fetched to see the signs of the end in this poem. Some editors have chosen to see the inversion as purely technical, as yet another example of D'Annunzio's manipulation of language for musical effect, but this is unlikely. The process of transformation undergone by the lovers in the woods, and the shift of the speaker from directly addressing Hermione to the introspective reflection on what has been taking place between them and nature also contains signs of a change of emphasis, as the poet looks back at his own delusion and notes with sadness that those feelings are part of his yesterday.

The sadness of the final lines gives a note of melancholy to what is for the most part a lyrically beautiful poem about human passion in an evocative natural landscape.

—Susan Bassnett

RĀMĀYAṆA

Indian epic poem in Sanskrit, consisting of 24,000 double verses describing adventures of King Rāma, attributed to Vālmīki. Originally five books; two books added at a later date. A shortened version of the poem is contained in the *Mahābhārata*, *q.v.*; the complete version probably predates this. There have been many adaptations, including the medieval *Rāmacaritamānas* of Tulsīdās, *q.v.*, and in the epic poetry of Kālidāsa, *q.v.*

PUBLICATIONS

Rāmāyaṇa. As *The Ramayunu*, edited by K. Bass (Bengali recension by KrHivāsa), 1802; first Sanskrit edition, edited by G. Corresio, 10 vols., 1843–58; also edited by K. Pandurang Parab, 1888, T.R. Krishnacharya (southern recension), 2 vols., 1905, Krishnacharya

and T.R. Vyasacharya, 1911–14, G. Śrīkṛṣṇadāsa, 1935, G.H. Bhatt, P.L. Vaidya, and others (critical edition), 7 vols., 1960–75, and Amita Talwar, 3 vols., 1988; facsimile of earliest manuscript (1076), 1982; as *Ramayana* (bilingual edition), translated by William Carey and Joshua Marshman, 4 vols., 1806–10; also translated by R.T.H. Griffith (in verse), 5 vols., 1870–74; Manmutha Nath Dutt, 7 vols., 1889–91; Hari Prasad Shastri, 3 vols., 1952–59; Robert P. Goldman and Sheldon I. Pollock, 3 vols., 1984–91; abridged versions as either *Ramayan* or *Ramayana*, translated by Romesh C. Dutt, 1899; Wallace Gandy, 1914; M. Shiva Rau (bilingual edition), 1918; Dhan Gopal Mukerji, 1931; Aubrey Menen, 1954; R.K. Narayan, 1972; William Buck, 1976; P. Lal, 1981; Swami Topasyananda, 1983; P. and S. Nath, 1987; Swami Venkatesananda, 1988; Arshia Sattar, 1996; H.V. Hande, 1996; adapted by Pratima Mitchell, 1996; Shanti Lal Nagar, 2000; Krishna Dharma, 2000; selections in: *The Light of India; or, Sita*, translated by Narayana Hemchandra, 1896(?); *The Divine Archer*, translated by F.J. Gould, 1911; *The Indian Heritage*, translated by V. Raghavan, 1956; *The Bhagavan-Mahima: Hindu Scriptures*, translated by Angrirasa Muni, 1999.

*

Bibliography: *Ramayana and Ramakatha: An International Litera- ture Survey* by Gauri Shankar Singh, 1989.

Critical Studies: *The Riddle of the Rāmāyaṇa*, 1906, and *Epic India; or, India as Described in the Mahābhārata and the Rāmāyṇa*, 1907, both by Chintāmani Vināyaka Vaidya; *Valmeeki and His Epic* by D.A. Narasimham, 1923; *Beowulf and the Rāmāyaṇa: A Study in Epic Poetry* by I.S. Peter, 1934; *Studies in the Ramayana* by K.S. Ramaswami Sastri, 1948; *Lectures on the Ramayana* by V.S.S. Sastri, 1952; *Evolution of Morals in the Epics Mahābhārata and Rāmāyaṇa* by D.P. Vora, 1959; *The Society of the Rāmāyaṇa* by Ananda Guruge, 1960; *The Rāma Saga in Malaysia: Its Origin and Development* by Alexander Ziessniss, translated by P.W. Burch, 1963; *The Concept of Dharma in Valmiki's Ramayana* by B. Khan, 1964; *The Ramayana: A Linguistic Study* by S. Vrat, 1964; *India in the Ramayana Age* by S.N. Vyas, 1967; *The Ramayana in Greater India* by V. Raghavan, 1975, *Ramayana Tradition in Asia* (conference proceedings) edited by Raghavan, 1980, and *The Ramayana in Classical Sanskrit and Prakrit Mahakavya Literature* by Raghavan, 1985; *Character-Portrayals in the Ramayana of Valmiki: A Systematic Representation* by Alois Wurm, 1976; *The Ramayana in South East Asia* edited by Sachchidanand Sahai, 1981; *The Ramayana in Historical Perspective* by Hasmukh Dhirajlal Sankalia, 1982; *The Ramayana in Eastern India* (conference proceedings), edited by Asit K. Banerjee, 1983; *The Ramayana: The Story and Significance of Valmiki's Epic* by S.L.N. Simha, 1984; *Ramayana Traditions in Eastern India: Assam, Bengal, Orissa* by W.L. Smith, 1988; *Mystic Symbolism in Ramayan, Mahabharat, and the Pilgrim's Progress* by M.G. Gupta, 1993; *The Iliad and the Ramayana: A Comparative Study* by Vijaya Guttal, 1994; *The Iliad, the Rāmāyaṇa, and the Work of Religion: Failed Persuasion and Religious Mystification* by Gregory D. Alles, 1994; *The Legend of Rama: Artistic Visions*, edited by Vidya Dehejia, 1994; *The Rāmāyaṇa, Its Origins and Growth: A Statistical Study* by M.R. Yardi, 1994; *The Ramayana: Global View*, edited by Lallan Prasad Vyas, 1995; *Ramayanas of Kampan and Eluttacchan* by P. Padmanabhan Thampi, 1996; *Ramayana: A Journey* by Ranchor

Prime, 1997; *Ramayana: Around the World*, edited by Lallan Prasad Vyas, 1997; *Ramayana and Modernity* by D.M. Sinha, 1998; *History Revealed by the Rāmāyaṇa Astronomy* by Puspendu Chaudhuri, 1998; *Ramayana: International Perspecitve*, edited by Lallan Prasad Vyas, 1998; *The Ramayana of Valmiki: A Reading* by Madhusudan Pati, 1999; *The Scientific Dating of the Ramayana and the Vedas* by P.V. Vartak, 1999.

* * *

The version of the *Rāmāyaṇa* that is best known internationally is the Sanskrit one of Vālmīki, of the 1st or 2nd century. But the ones popular in India are those of Tulsīdās (Hindi, Avadhi dialect) in the north, the Kamban (Tamil) in the south, and the Krittibāsa Rāmāyaṇa (Bengali) in the east. All of them are based on the story of Rāma.

Rāma, son of Daśrath, King of Ayodhya (in northern India), is banished because of the intrigue of his stepmother, Kaikeyī. The kingdom goes to Bharata his half-brother. Along with his brother Lakṣmaṇa, and his wife Sītā, who insists on accompanying him, Rāma roams the forest. Rāvaṇa, the demon king of Laṅkā, carries away his wife in his absence, and so he has to fight a war to get her back. Recovering Sītā, he returns to Ayodhya in triumph, after his 14-year exile, and takes over the kingdom from Bharata who has held it in trusteeship for him.

According to Sir William Jones, the *Rāmāyaṇa* was composed in the year 2029 BC. Tradition has it that it was inspired when Vālmīki heard the anguished cry of a bird whose mate had been shot by a hunter. The epic has seven books (24,000 stanzas or 96,000 lines). The seventh book is believed to be a later addition. The metre used is largely the *anuṣṭup*, a tetrastich containing four feet. The fifth syllable of each line is short, the sixth long, the seventh alternately long and short, while the first four syllables and the eighth follow an arbitrary pattern.

The Rāmāyaṇa excels in rich imagery, expressive descriptions, and brilliant characterization. After his night of debauchery, Rāvaṇa, decked in all his jewels, lying spent on his couch, is like a huge thundercloud streaked with flashes of lightning. The sleeping women of his harem resemble lotuses in a pond, flowers in a garland, or stars fallen from Heaven. When Sītā is by Rāma's side, the forest seems to him lovely in the rains. The breeze is cool as camphor. The grassy slopes gleam and peacocks dance with glee. But after her abduction the sky looks like one that is wounded and the clouds stained red with the dim glow of the setting sun. The golden thongs of lightning appear to whip the clouds so that they thunder out their agony. ''It seems,'' says Rāma, ''that the lightning leaping from the clouds is like Sātā struggling in Rāvaṇa's hold.'' When Sītā is away from Rāma, the south wind seems to waft to him her caress. The lovely scarlet flowers of the Pampa lake set his heart afire. The gleaming sandy banks of the river, exposed as the water in it gradually recedes, are like the alabaster thighs of shy girls, bared as they move up their dress when prevailed upon to make love. When the erotic-minded Rāvaṇa camps on the Narmada bank, the river seems to him like a timid girl, the foaming waves her dress, the flowering trees by the riverside her diadem, the lotuses her eyes, the pair of ruddy geese her breasts, the gleaming sandbanks her thighs and the swans flying in the air her shining girdle.

Vālmīki's characters are exemplary in their conduct, but they are also human in their shortcomings. Rāma is the embodiment of calm and serenity; but at times he can be wrathful or maudlin. He threatens the ocean god for not getting his army across the ocean, and when Sītā has been abducted by Rāvaṇa he goes about piteously asking the trees where she has gone. The sagacious Janaka breaks down with grief when his daughter, Sītā, leaves for her husband's home. Lakṣmaṇa, Rāma's brother, is by nature impetuous and excitable, but he doesn't say a word when he learns of Rāma's banishment. The self-controlled and restrained Bharat cannot hold himself back when he learns his mother had asked for Rāma's exile and reviles not only her, but also his dead father. There are touches of humour, too, as when Rāma, assisting Sītā to get dressed in bark for going to the forest, has trouble putting the pieces in place, and between the two of them they make a clumsy job of it.

The *Rāmāyaṇa* is known throughout the world, and has been translated not only into Hindi and Indian regional languages, like Bengali, Tamil, Kannada, Kashmiri, Telugu, and Malayalam, but also into English, Latin, French, and Italian, making it a universal classic.

—K.P. Bahadur

THE RAPE OF PROSERPINE (De raptu Proserpine)
Poem by Claudian, c. AD 400

The Rape of Proserpine is the longest surviving version of the myth of the abduction of Ceres' daughter Proserpine by Pluto, the lord of the Underworld. Composed by Claudian at the end of the 4th century, it draws heavily upon the Latin poetic tradition, especially the epics of Virgil, Luean, and Statius. There are also reminiscences of the account of Persephone in Book V of Ovid's *Metamorphoses*. Claudian may have been influenced by Alexandrian and Orphic treatments of the myth too: there is no doubt that it was a popular theme among the poets for many centuries. It deals with the primordial conflict between the matriarchal earth-goddess and the patriarchal sky-god who supplanted her. The poem is written in hexameters, and the versification is basically classical, but with much less use of elision, which makes for a consistently smooth rhythm.

The Preface of *The Rape of Proserpine* compares the poet to the first sailor, with the implication that the work which follows is the culmination of Claudian's poetic journey. Book I begins with standard introductory devices and then moves to the Underworld, where Pluto is preparing to release the Titans and make war on Jupiter, because he has no wife, Then Fates intervene and Pluto is mollified by the promise of Proserpine, whom Jupiter had apparently always intended him to have. Venus is ordered to prepare the girl, so that Pluto will desire her. As the book ends, Pluto's horses are straining at the bit, ready to break out of Hades. Book II is preceded by another Preface in which Claudian's return to poetic composition at the behest of Florentinus is likened to Orpheus' singing of the deeds of Hercules after he had rescued his native land Thrace from Diomedes. The action resumes with a description of Proserpine wandering in the meadows of Sicily, attended by goddesses and nymphs. Only Venus knows what awaits Ceres' daughter on this particular morning. The idyllic scene is shattered by the terrifying arrival of Pluto in his chariot and Proserpine is carried off. Diana, goddess of virginity, and Pallas Athene try to stop the abduction, but are deterred by Jupiter. Proserpine calls to her mother in heart-rending tones so that even Pluto is moved: he tries to comfort her by listing all the powers she will gain as his wife. When they arrive in Hades, there is universal celebration, and the punishments of the wicked souls are temporarily suspended. Book III opens with a council of the gods, at which Jupiter notes that Nature has criticized his harsh treatment of humans. He declares that he has taken pity on this suffering race and that Ceres will provide them with the blessings of the grain when she has found her daughter. He stipulates, however, that nobody is to assist her in her search. Ceres, meanwhile, has a distressing dream about Proserpine and, upon returning to Sicily, attempts vainly to get information from the nurse Electra and from Venus. In the end, she resolves to search the entire world for her daughter. She makes two torches from trees in a grove sacred to Jupiter, lights them in Etna, and begins her tearful search.

The plot is a simple and well-worn one, embellished by two devices typical of later epic poetry: speeches and lengthy descriptions, In Book I, for example, Pluto makes a lengthy and well-structured speech to Mercury listing his grievances, and there is a substantial digression on the geography of Sicily and the wonders of Mount Etna. There is also a detailed account of the tapestry which Proserpine is stitching: it depicts the creation of the world out of chaos, the five zones of the earth, and the homes of Jupiter and Pluto. The descriptive passages have received much praise, not so much for their originality as for their beauty and economy of expression. The following lines are part of the digression on Etna:

> Now it vomits clouds of its own smoke and it darkens the day
> loaded with pitch-black vapour, now it threatens the stars
> with its huge boulders, and feeds the fires with its own
>   destruction.
> But although it boils and bubbles over with such heat,
> it knows how to keep faith with both the snow and the ash:
> the ice hardens securely amid such steam,
> protected by the hidden frost, and the harmless flames
> lick the nearby snows with undamaging smoke.

This passage also illustrates the scope for symbolic or allegorical interpretations of *The Rape of Proserpine*. The poem is much concerned with the struggle of polarities within the universe and the possibility of their peaceful co-existence. Just as the snows and the flames "keep faith" with each other on Etna, so the whole universe is created from chaos by the harmonization of opposites. At the beginning of the poem, Pluto threatens to plunge the world into disorder by attacking Jupiter. This is averted by the Fates, but only at the cost of setting up a conflict between Ceres and Pluto. None the less, it is clear that eventually an accommodation will be reached between the two: Proserpine will spend half the year with her husband, and half the year with her mother. When she has her daughter with her, Ceres will be happy and will provide crops for men.

The poem ends *in medias res*, perhaps because Claudian died before completing it. If Claudian intended to follow the mythological tradition, the agreement of Ceres and Pluto to share Proserpine would have been presented as a vindication of the rule of Jupiter: his just counsels preserve the universe from chaotic violence. As the text now stands, however, the hope of such a resolution is a distant one, only to be achieved after much suffering and effort on the part of Ceres. She, in fact, receives as much attention from the poet as Jupiter, in a poem which lacks a central figure. The torches she carries symbolize the revelation she brings to humans through knowledge of the growth of the grain. The strong mother-daughter bond between Ceres and Proserpine is a statement of female solidarity in the face of patriarchal control and sexual violence. Thus the main elements of the story—Pluto's "need" for a wife, Jupiter's decision to "give" him Proserpine,

and Venus' callous betrayal of the girl—are seen to raise highly problematic issues.

—David H.J. Larmour

RED CAVALRY (Konarmiia)
Story cycle by Isaak Babel, 1926

In the acute clarity of its descriptive detail and in its psychological realism, Isaak Babel's story cycle *Red Cavalry* bears many similarities to other works by Soviet writers about the Russian Civil War of 1918–21, including Dmitri Furmanov's *Chapaev*, Aleksandr Fadeev's *Razgrom* (*The Rout*), and the short stories of Vsevolod Ivanov. Its experimentalism is in some ways related to that of the Serapionovii brat'ia (Serapion Brothers) and its pictorial vividness has a counterpart in Sholokhov's *Tikhii Don* (*Quiet Flows the Don*). The principal differences between Babel's cycle and those other novels is that Babel's work is that of a Russian-Jewish writer, not a Russian one.

Red Cavalry marks the pinnacle of Babel's literary achievement—it is the work that demonstrates the duality of his nature most forcefully and vividly, and in it his personality splits in two. Without it being immediately obvious, the stories have two narrators: one is the Jewish war correspondent, Kirill Vasil'ievich Liutov, bespectacled, bookish, and sensitive, and the other is the person whom Liutov would like to become, and constantly strives to be—a true revolutionary and Bolshevik soldier with no fear of blood and killing. This dichotomy accounts for the extreme physical violence that is manifested in many of the stories; it is as though Babel were trying to overcome his own horror at what he has seen and witnessed, and to turn it into a kind of violent, surreal poetry. At the opposite end of the spectrum is the character of the Jew Gedali, who believes in "the International of good men" and with whom Liutov vainly remonstrates, more than half-convinced that the old man is right:

> "... The International, *panie* comrade, one does not know
> what to eat it with..."
> "One eats it with gunpowder," I replied to the old man.
> "And seasons it with the finest blood..."

The conflict is also sharply delineated in the character of the Red army soldier Bratslavskii, the son of the Zhitomir Rebbe Motale Bratslavskii, in the story "The Rebbe's Son," The chaos of Bratslavskii's life as he dies of typhoid on the floor of the train is reflected in the contents of his trunk:

> Here everything had been dumped together—the warrants
> of the agitator and the commemorative booklets of the Jewish
> poet. Portraits of Lenin and Maimonides lay side by side.
> Lenin's nodulous skull and the tarnished silk of the portraits of
> Maimonides. A strand of female hair had been placed in a book
> of the resolutions of the Sixth Party Congress, and in the
> margins of communist leaflets swarmed crooked lines of
> Ancient Hebrew verse. In a sad and meagre rain they fell on
> me—pages of the Song of Songs, and revolver cartridges.

Bratslavskii is in a sense Liutov's double, manifesting in an extreme form the latter's uncertainty about his personal, social, and historical identity. To the theme, common enough in "revolutionary" literature, of the wavering intellectual, detached from the "masses," Babel adds the new theme of the intellectual Jew, unable to reconcile himself to the brutality and slaughter involved in the creation of the "radiant future." The story "My First Goose" is the most famous example of this dilemma, with its attendant sense of helplessness and despair, in Babel's writings. But there are others, such as the scene depicted in "Beresteczko," of a group of Bolshevik-led Cossacks executing an aged Jew:

> Directly under my window several Cossacks were shooting an old Jew with a silvery beard for espionage. The old man was screaming and trying to tear himself free. Then Kudria from the machine-gun detachment took the old man's head and put it under his arm. The Jew calmed down and stood with his legs apart. With his right hand Kudrya pulled out his dagger and carefully cut the old man's throat, without splashing any blood on himself. Then he knocked on the closed-up window-frame.
>
> "If anyone's interested," he said, "they can come and get him. He's all yours. . . ."

These scenes, with their intense concrete and sensuous actuality, suggest nothing so much as scenes from a motion picture, and indeed this cinematic aspect of Babel's storytelling art is strongly pronounced in the cycle. It is as though Babel conveys Liutov's fear and squeamishness to the reader by putting him in Liutov's place, by making him see things through Liutov's eyes. From the depiction of the ravaged beehives of Volhynia ("The Way to Brody"), of Dolgushov's slow and agonizing death, his stomach torn out and exposed ("The Death of Dolgushov"), and of Matvei Pavlichenko's sadistic murder of his "master" ("The Life-Story of Pavlichenko, Matvei Rodionych"), to the unnervingly lifelike descriptions of fighting (in "Chesniki" and "After the Battle"), Babel seems intent on making us *see*—and this is reinforced by his use of colour imagery, which recurs throughout the stories. Seldom, however, does the author attempt to interpose himself between the reader and the events described. Indeed, the suspension of moral judgement is perhaps the feature of the cycle that a new reader will find most shocking and disturbing; for it is as if the author were reliving an experience in which no morality exists, and in which human life is no longer of any more account than the life of an animal.

—David McDuff

REMEMBRANCE OF THINGS PAST (À la recherche du temps perdu)
Novel by Marcel Proust, 1913–27

Remembrance of Things Past—in the phrase borrowed from Shakespeare's sonnet No. 30 by C.K. Scott Moncrieff for his English translation—is one of those titles that seems to have the quality of inevitability about them, as Marcel Proust's title *À la recherche du temps perdu* has likewise for French readers. Yet is was only after trial and error that Proust arrived at a formula that was both evocative and all-encompassing. He was not satisfied with the emphasis chosen by Scott Moncrieff, which ignored what he called the deliberate

parallelisms he had set up between *temps perdu* (time lost or wasted) at the beginning of he work and *temps retrouvé* (time regained) at the end. Proust always insisted that his work was planned and purposeful from the first word to the last, indeed it is his method in *Remembrance of Things Past* that gives the quest its backbone. This novel is remarkable among all novels for its sustained, meticulously detailed analyses and is far indeed from the popular misconception of rambling reminiscence. Its foremost quality lies not in lyrical effusion, emotional recollection, or the observation of social habits so much as in the exploitation of these elements for psychological enquiry. Proust examines from the point of view of an anonymous middle-aged narrator, later identified by the name Marcel, how this fictional creation—who is not to be considered coextensive with Proust—has come to value the past not as an escape from the present but as the integration of what has been with the potential creation of a work of art. This will be a fiction which, though fabricated from ephemeral moments of time, will succeed, through the faculty of imagination, in uniting past and present in an affirmation that nothing is ever lost. The resulting euphoric sense of totality regained will, like a feeling of religious salvation, withstand the threat of time as bringer of oblivion in an aesthetic victory, leaving words living when the heart is still, it is an essential part of the narrator's conclusion that his past life has been "an invisible vocation" leading to the realization that his sensibility from childhood to middle-age is the raw material for an aesthetic justification of his existence. By extension, since Proust constantly extrapolates from the particular to the general, this is the meaning the reader is to find likewise. It is the firmest wish of the narrator to invite the reader to become the reader of himself, thereby accepting the principle that a value must be granted to that inward investigation of our perceptions that may allow us to transcend for a span the fear of mortality and of being part of the contingent world.

The first part of the novel, *Swann's Way* (*Du côté de chez Swann*), when published in 1913 led to a reaction as much of bewilderment as of admiration. Certainly Proust's broad intention was hard to appreciate. Because of the war further publication was held up but the delay allowed Proust to elaborate his basic plan so that in 1919, when publication was resumed, the whole concept of moving from *le temps perdu* to *le temps retrouvé* had grown to encompass a great many more of Proust's themes, not least sexual deviance, which he had always wanted as a ground-theme but feared would be misunderstood. With hindsight all Proust's themes can be detected in his first volume, which begins with an evocation of that ambiguous area of consciousness between sleep and waking and goes on to consider memory first as a cerebral and only partly satisfying harking back, then as an involuntary state magically summoned up for the narrator by the dipping of the madeleine cake into his cup of tea, an experience that overwhelmingly brings a sensation of the fullness of past and present triumphantly fused together. Out of his cup of tea, as it were, comes the whole of his childhood. Here in the evocation of Comray are the first adumbrations of a sensibility that is rarely satisfied with its immediate pleasures but strives to find an idealized justification for the experience. The phrase: "tâcher de voir plus clair dans mon ravissement" ("seeking a clearer understanding of what delighted me"), evoking the balance of the intellectual and the impressionistic, is the key to the comprehension and appreciation of Proust's art. It reveals him poised between the French tradition of psychological analysis and the emerging modernism of ambiguous sensation.

Also in this first part we meet characters obsessed with their image and their petty snobbish concern with self-definition by means of exclusivity. Here also is the narrator's first minor success in triumphing over contingency by literary composition and even a suggestion of ambivalent sexuality that eventually becomes such a dominant feature. The novel is narrated in the first person throughout except for one section, "Swann in Love" ("Un amour de Swann"), written as an analytical study in the third person of a character who is intended as a foil to the narrator. Swann is a dilettante supposedly working on a study of Vermeer, which is never completed, thus counterpointing the narrator's successful quest. Furthermore, Swann's love affair with Odette examines the basic question of personal interactions and comes to the sorry conclusion—again prefiguring the narrator's experience—that love can only breed jealousy and as a mutually shared phenomenon is a myth. We are all condemned to be isolated individuals. The real triumph will be not in the field of personal relationships so much as in the compensatory act of artistic creation. A fundamental note of pessimism is sounded in the first part of the novel to be transformed for the narrator by the saving grace of art.

The second phase of the work, *Within a Budding Grove* (*À l'ombre des jeunes filles en fleurs*) followed in 1919 and was awarded the prestigious Goncourt prize, which boosted Proust's worldwide reputation. In this part the narrator examines the area of adolescence, in particular his encounter with Albertine, which will run parallel to the Swann-Odette story. Here too the narrator meets the painter, Elstir, whose work illuminates for him the potential of metaphor and its ability to condense contradictory observations. This discovery will be a key lesson for the narrator, among other aesthetic insights learnt from Bergotte, the writer, the Vinteuil, the composer, when he comes to the decision to create his novel.

The Guermantes Way (*Le Côté de Guermantes*) emphasizes the cut-throat world of high society and upper bourgeoisie that is Proust's main object of satirical observation.

The whole novel, in fact, is as deeply concerned with social analysis as it is with metaphysical, philosophical, and aesthetic matters, and comfortably rivals Balzac for its sociological comment on its period.

Sodom and Gomorrah (*Sodome et Gomorrhe*) is the part most frankly concerned with homosexuality which, after memory, is Proust's most important obsession and not only treated as an account of deviancy but also metaphorically used to evoke the themes of secrecy, hypocrisy, and social inadequacy. It contributes to the picture of society as a pessimistic charade from which the narrator—assumed throughout to be heterosexual—will stand apart.

In *The Captive* (*La Prisonnière*) and *The Fugitive* (*Albertine disparue*) Proust presents those more intimate aspects of personal relationships which reflect the narrator's conclusion, having lived with and lost Albertine, that the world is inadequate to our feelings since we are incapable of mutual exchange, let alone love. We are bounded by a self-centred and isolated existence, at best parallel to, but never integrating with another individual.

The narrator's experience of the world is so totally inward and separate that, represented yet again in *Time Regained* (*Le Temps retrouvé*) with the people he has known now grown old, weary, and decrepit, he must joyfully conclude, as he receives by sheer chance a whole series of involuntary memories, that the only way to make sense of his past essential self and his present existential dilemma is to use this raw material in a work of imagination. It is not clear whether that work is in fact the novel we have just read or else something in that vein. Either way this creation will have the sovereign virtue of challenging the threat of oblivion that is the final image of the novel as

the narrator sees his whole aesthetic adventure in the perspective opening before him of Time itself.

—Leighton Hodson

RENÉ
Prose by Vicomte de Chateaubriand, 1802

René was first published, together with a companion piece, *Atala*, as a fictional episode or literary illustration contained within a much longer non-fictional work of Christian apologetics, *Le Génie du christianisme* (*The Genius of Christianity*). Following the huge success of the two narratives, Vicomte de Chateaubriand excerpted them from the larger work and published them on their own. It is in this form that they have normally appeared since then. *René*, in particular, has come to be seen as embodying many of the aspects of French Romantic sensibility, with the eponymous hero-narrator suffering from storms of passion that he can never define fully ("le vague des passions") and carrying a contemporary moral and psychological sickness ("le mal du siècle"), whose roots are hinted at but never made explicit.

The work is short, barely 30 to 40 pages long in most editions, and takes the form of a brief prologue and epilogue framing a narrative by René of episodes of his life. The prologue offers a stylized, picturesque evocation of the banks of the Mississippi and the Louisiana countryside. Within this exotic landscape, two companions, Chactas, an aged, blind Indian who is the adoptive father of René, together with *père* Souël, a French missionary, press René to explain how an aristocratic young Frenchman came to bury himself in exile in the "deserts" of Louisiana and why he is so melancholic.

René's narrative, effectively a sort of confession, begins hesitantly and with a sense of shame to speak of self-inflicted grief and torment. He evokes a sad childhood and adolescence, dominated by the deaths of his parents and a sense of solitude. His only consolation lies in the tender love of his elder sister Amélie, with whom he shares the mournful pleasures of wandering the autumn countryside. As a result of his meditations on nature, death, and eternity, he is tempted by the idea of seeking in monastic retreat a refuge from the world, but then, typically, decides instead to travel, Neither the poetic ruins of the ancient world of Greece and Rome, nor modern London, nor even the Ossian-inspired songs of the last bard in Caledonia succeed in comforting his unquiet soul. His state of mind is symbolized by the image René offers of himself seated weeping on the summit of Mount Etna, contemplating the distant dwellings of the plain and the volcanic abyss at his side. René's narrative repeatedly proposes this mix of seething passion combined with a sense of alienation from other human beings.

After this unusual variant on the Grand Tour, René returns to Paris where he experiences a renewed feeling of isolation. Paris for him as a vast human desert. His restlessness draws him back to the country, where the absolute sense of solitude and the spectacle of nature give rise to lyrical evocations of ecstatic torment. Late-adolescent idealized erotic reveries are deflated by a sense of the purposelessness of existence. He writes to his sister to announce his intention to commit suicide. Amélie rushes to him and falls into his arms. The drama of incest which follows is only hinted at. René gives the impression he does not understand why his sister appears to be keeping a secret from him, in spite of the fact that at the time of narrating the events he knows the reason for the secret. This narratorial complication raises for the reader the question of whether René's narrative is a full confession of his emotions or an obscure attempt to disculpate himself from a shared forbidden passion. Amélie attempts to resolve the situation by withdrawing to a convent, committing herself to God and good works. René, after a final visit to the now abandoned family château, arrives at the convent for a last exchange with Amélie only to be asked to assist at her taking the veil. In a climactic scene of religious emotion, combined with images of death, sexual excitement, and scandal, the brother and sister are separated, and René takes the decision to go into what he sees as exile. René's last days before departing are given over to extracting some satisfaction from his excess of grief and from meditations on the peace within the convent walls and the storms and uncertainties outside.

The epilogue offers two contrasting comments on René's story. Chactas expresses pity and sympathy for those who suffer such emotional trials and, in an echo of the prologue, conjures up an image of the proud Mississippi regretting the natural simplicity of its source. Père Souël, however, severely catechizes René for self-indulgent morbidity and calls on him to think of his duties towards fellow human beings and of the harm he has caused. The cast of the tale are rapidly extinguished: Amélie dies of a disease caught from fellow nuns she was nursing; Chactas, père Souël, and René are killed in the wars between the French and the Natchez Indians.

In *René* the convention of the 18th-century novel of sensibility and a vocabulary of emotional religiosity are aimed by Chateaubriand at offering a demonstration of the superiority of Christian-inspired literature over that of pagan antiquity or what he saw as the godless literature of the 18th century. No simple moral conclusions are offered, however. René does not turn to religion to solve his mysterious dilemmas. In practice, attention has focused on the hero as the tragic, modern figure of the young, isolated individual alienated from society. His lyrical rêveries and melancholic wanderings charmed all the French Romantics at the same stage. A more specifically sociopolitical reading sees René as an aristocrat caught in the upheavals following the French revolution. Psychologically, the text offers meditations on the links between desire, death, and the family, with the breaking of the incest taboo as a pathological attempt to return to paradise lost. Put in more abstract terms, *René* explores the contradictions between human aspirations and an intimate conviction of the pointlessness of everything.

—C. Smethurst

THE REPUBLIC
Prose by Plato, 5th/4th century BC

The Republic is a philosophical treatise in the form of a dialogue between Socrates and a number of his questioners. The figure of Socrates, however, can be understood to be representing Plato's own views.

While *The Republic* has at its heart the question of definition of justice, the work covers other subjects: most notably Plato's account of the ideal city state, ruled by the ideal men—an aristocratic elite, trained and tempered by their education, who rule for the common good. The term "philosophy," in its modern academic sense, is too restricted to do justice to the scope of *The Republic*'s debate. Its discussion covers areas we would now assign to disciplines as diverse as politics, mathematics, aesthetics, sociology, theology, and psychology.

At the core of *The Republic* are four key ideas: (1) human nature is composed of different elements—the sensual appetites, pride, and reason; (2) the world perceived by the senses is composed of imperfect imitations of a divine world of perfect forms; (3) this ideal or divine world may, by proper education, be perceived by the faculty of pure reason, which is a property of the immortal soul, and should, properly, govern all the parts of a man's nature; (4) the innate superiority over other arts of philosophy, whose function it is to apprehend this truth. Ideas are not abstractions "upwards" from mundane objects; rather they are reflections "downward" from a divine world of higher truth. The world of the mathematician is therefore more "real" than that of the furniture maker, for the former has to do with pure thought, which is more akin to eternal truth.

These ideas emerge slowly and are at each stage advanced by cautious, step-by-step logic. In order to approach the disposition of a just man, Plato projects these problems onto the wider canvas of a whole society. He does this by drawing up his plan for a perfect city. Plato's account of his ideal city-state (the "Republic" of the title) is a project wherein ideal virtue is instilled by pragmatic means: Plato relies on the proven effects of gymnastics and the arts to inculcate manliness and sensitivity, while he will foster his rulers' (the guardians) capacity for pure reason by a study of the sciences closest to the world of the perfect forms—mathematics, geometry, and astronomy. The play may be utopian, its means of implementation are not. Plato's thought is marked by an iron grip of psychology and political reality. His guardians' bravery in war will be encouraged by the renouncing of any soldier who is capture alive; those who display bravery will be crowned by the whole army, and will be free to embrace any woman they choose. The city's children will be taken to the battlefield to learn the arts of war, but will be mounted on swift horses so that they may escape a defeat. All those—chiefly the poets—who expound principles contrary to those of the Republic will be censored or expelled. Plato recognizes the power of a society's myths to shape the sense of identity of its people. He proposes the manipulation of that power by deliberately creating the myths that will inspire the best conduct in his "guardians." Perhaps the greatest proof of Plato's pragmatism is that no sooner has he established his theoretical Republic than he describes the stages by which it will slide from its ideal state into tyranny.

Plato's account of justice is likewise a pragmatic one, based not on a prescriptive moral code, but on subtle psychological analysis. Proceeding by a sort of biology of man's moral nature, he isolates its different elements and concludes that man is happiest and most blessed when acting according to reason.

The use of a dialogue form aids the communication of Plato's ideas in a number of ways. Firstly, by its very structure, it breaks up into manageable segments what would otherwise be a huge and intractable weight of philosophical writing in prose. Secondly, the interplay of the different personalities engaged in the debate serves as a source of interest and entertainment. Plato's speech is courteous, diplomatic, and unfailingly modest. Thrasymachus, who bursts angrily into the conversation, is swiftly assuaged, and with Glaucon as Socrates' chief interlocutor, the debate proceeds from a battle of wits into a patient and methodical search for truth. Thirdly, Plato exploits the flexibility of a conversation in order to ease his reader through the difficulties of presenting what is occasionally a highly complex and abstracted argument. At times Socrates will go back over a point, or explain in particular detail an issue in depth until Glaucon can follow him.

One of the most contentious issues in *The Republic* is that of the status of art. As the objects of this world are but imperfect imitations of the world of divine forms, Plato attacks art for producing only ''imitations of imitations'' twice removed from eternal truth. Plato also criticizes poetry on the grounds that the emotions it excites are harmful to the severe self-control to be practised by his guardians.

Yet the poetic qualities of *The Republic* might lead us to question the seriousness with which Plato intends his banishment of poets and artists from the city—an act he compares to the renunciation of a beautiful but politically unacceptable choice of bride. The dialogue seems convincingly to demonstrate the importance of poetry to Plato's own thought. His argument is constantly illustrated with references to the poets. He himself retells stories such as that of Gyges and the ring of invisibility. His argument is illustrated by vivid images drawn from myth, for example, the comparison of the soul to Glaucos who was transformed from a fisherman into a sea god.

The fable of the prisoners in the cave demonstrates both Plato's capacity for myth-making, and his skill in rhetorical persuasion. Having accepted his account of the prisoners who (like the mass of ignorant humanity) see only shadows, mistaking them for reality, we are introduced to a single one who escapes and, after a difficult struggle, reaches the sunlight (true enlightenment). It is only natural that we should identify with that prisoner, and, having become involved with Plato's fable at an imaginative level, it is the harder to reject it at an intellectual one.

—Edmund Cusick

REQUIEM (Rekviem)
Poem by Anna Akhmatova, 1963 (written 1939–40)

The *Requiem* cycle describes the suffering of the women of Russia during Stalin's Terror, when it was, as Anna Akhmatova writes here, no longer clear who was an animal and who was still a person. It is ''a map of a journey leading through hell into the light'' (Amanda Haight, *Anna Akhmatova: A Poetic Pilgrimage*, 1976).

The kernel of the cycle was a poem written in 1935 when Akhmatova's son Lev Gumilev and her third husband N.N. Punin were arrested. As was usually the case, there was no legal or rational reason for the arrest. Lev's fault, for example, was simply that he was the son of Gumilev, executed for alleged counter-revolutionary activity, and of Akhmatova, also in disfavour (she had been barred from publishing by the Communist Party since the mid-1920s). Both victims were soon released, but Lev Gumilev was arrested again in 1937, exiled, called up to the army, and did not return until 1945. Both Punin and Lev Gumilev were re-arrested in 1949; the former died in a camp and the latter was finally disgorged from the Gulag only in 1956. Most of the cycle (ten poems with preamble and epilogues) was written in 1939–40 but the horrors it describes continued in Akhmatova's life and those of the nation for long after.

''Instead of a Preface'' records the urge behind the cycle: to give voice to suffering that turned its victims numb and dumb. Akhmatova's

cycle constitutes solidarity which the terror otherwise made impossible. In it she describes the psychological path travelled by Russian women after the arrest of husbands and sons: the immediate pain, the surprise that it can be borne, the urge to black out what has happened, the inability to grasp what is going on, fear for their survival, preparing to hear the sentence of death. When it comes the women are barely sensate but condemned to carry on living. Suffering has brought them to the edge of sanity and their own death would be welcome, but it does not come.

At the harrowing moment when the death sentence is carried out Akhmatova turns to Biblical imagery: Mary stands at the foot of the cross where her son is crucified. The figure of Mary symbolizes the impossibility of running away even from extreme suffering, and the epigraph likewise points to Akhmatova's decision not to emigrate and to go through whatever might befall Russia with her fellow citizens. *Requiem* is one of the many poems in which Akhmatova singles out images of women from history and literature whose fate in some way mirrored her own (Dido, Joan of Arc, Cleopatra, Phaedra, and others).

Critics differ about the significance of religion to the poem. Anatoli Naiman feels that its tragedy is balanced by its basic Christian feeling (in Judith Hemschemeyer's translation of *The Complete Poems*, 1990). Iosif Brodskii writes: ''The degree of compassion with which the various voices of *Requiem* are rendered can be explained only by the author's Orthodox faith; the degree of understanding and forgiveness which account for this work's piercing, almost unbearable lyricism only by the uniqueness of her heart, her self, and this self's sense of time'' (*Less than One*, 1986). Others do not conclude that religious language and Biblical quotation imply that Mary's endurance is the result of her faith. Basker finds that her strength is ''built on inconsolable loss and pitilessly searing detachment from the broken and now redundant ordinary self.''

Instead of moving on to resurrection the cycle ends with a defiant and retributive epilogue. Akhmatova declares the cycle an act of remembrance for the hundreds of women who stood for months in queues outside the prisons with her, hoping to find out the whereabouts of their loved ones, or to hand in a parcel, She insists on erecting a (verbal) monument to commemorate what has happened, on making public what the system conspired to conceal.

Foreseeing the possibility that ''they gag my exhausted mouth / Through which a hundred million scream,'' Akhmatova took precautions: the seditious poems were not written down but memorized by trusted friends. One or two of the poems were published as separate lyrics and the cycle eventually became widely known as a result of *samizdat*. It was published without Akhmatova's permission in Munich in 1963 but had to await *glasnost'* before it could be published in the Soviet Union (1987).

Although the cycle claims to be woven from words overheard in the prison queues and appears to be as simple as *Poem Without a Hero* is complex, it has an elaborate, symmetrical structure (see A.L. Crone, in *The Speech of Unknown Eyes*, 1990) and also uses intertextual allusion to extend its reference to the heroines of Euripides, whose suffering on account of the loss of their children also brings them to the verge of death; the wives of the 17th-century musketeers massacred by Peter the Great for rebellion; and the wives of the Decembrists punished for the 1825 insurrection. The poem thus puts the immediate situation into a long perspective of Russian history.

—Wendy Rosslyn

THE REVERIES OF A SOLITARY (Les Rêveries du promeneur solitaire)
Prose by Jean-Jacques Rousseau, 1782

Jean-Jacques Rousseau wrote *The Confessions* as an act of purification and atonement. He wrote *The Reveries of a Solitary* as an act of isolation. Begun in 1776, but not published until 1782, some four years after his death, *The Reveries* contains a series of meditations devoted to self isolation, both in the sense that Rousseau sought to isolate himself from human society, and in the sense that he sought to isolate his ''self,'' to discover the residual being when he was placed in solitude. Conceived as a sort of sequel or appendix to *The Confessions*, *The Reveries* presents ten short essays ostensibly representing the fruit of his random thoughts and daydreams as he wandered alone in the country or the outskirts of Paris. ''These pages will be,'' Rousseau suggested, ''no more than a formless record of my reveries . . . I shall say what I have thought just as it came to me, with as little connection as the thoughts of this morning have with those of last night.'' *The Reveries* emerged from Rousseau's rejection of the pleasures of and identity with society, a painful and recurrent perception that he was the systematic victim of various plots and persecutions, real or imaginary. Rousseau found the prototypes for his project in Descartes's *Meditationes de prima philosophia* (*Meditations on the First Philosophy*) and Montaigne's *Essays*. Like Descartes, Rousseau was concerned with the isolation and discovery of an irreducible self, though he eschewed the claims of Cartesian method. Like Montaigne, Rousseau equated the self with his essays, though he insisted that he wrote for himself alone. Indeed, for Rousseau, the act of writing is both the method of self discovery and the self itself.

Each of the *Reveries*, like the self, embraces irony and paradox, some deliberate, some not. Rousseau insisted that he was indifferent to public opinion, but laboured hard to set the record straight as he understood it. He sought self-sufficiency, but longed for society, constantly reiterating his abiding love for a humanity that he found deceitful and threatening. He perceived himself as truly innocent, but suffered terrible pangs of guilt and despair. He disclaimed books and learning, but drew on a vast erudition, writing on the irrelevance of books and writing. He rejected artifice, but did so with consummate artistry, articulating the random flow of his thoughts with carefully cadenced prose and choreographed essays. He proclaimed himself a man of powerful and sincere feelings, but constantly punctured his pretensions and presumptions.

The fifth *Reverie*, a miniature masterpiece, is indicative both of Rousseau's methods and of the work's themes as a whole. The essay revolves around the account of a brief period of happiness that Rousseau enjoyed on the Island of Saint-Pierre, a self-sufficient retreat in the middle of Lake Bienne, northwest of Berne. Here he was isolated from society aside from that of his companion Thérèse Le Vasseur and the island's caretakers. Without his books or writing materials, and thrown back upon his own resources, Rousseau passed his time by dividing the island into squares and examining the plants systematically. ''I did not want to leave even one blade of grass or atom of vegetation without a full and detailed description.'' Thus, blending ironically the themes of Robinson Crusoe on his island and Adam in the Garden of Eden, he begins a botanical inventory, for in his analysis of nature, he separates and isolates himself from it. His rational appropriation of nature undercuts an intuitive and spontaneous relationship.

The greatest moment of happiness occurred one day as he sat by the edge of the lake. ''The ebb and flow of the water, its continuous yet undulating noise, kept lapping against my ears and my eyes, taking the place of all and inward movements which my reverie had calmed within me, and it was enough to make me pleasurably aware of my existence, without troubling myself with thought.'' In this state he became aware of the insubstantial nature of the world, and his desire to dissolve into its flow. At the same time he also became aware that it was his own existence that separated him from reality, underlining the fundamental realization that it was himself that stood in the way of any final happiness.

The world is in a constant state of flux. Because of this, our desires and affections ''recall a past which is gone or anticipate a future which may never come into being: there is nothing solid there for the heart to attach himself to. Thus our earthly joys are almost without exception the creatures of the moment.'' Because of this Rousseau conceived the self as a disposition toward past and future, a double longing that looks back nostalgically to a lost past and forward anxiously to a promise in the future. Together these double longings circumscribe an empty present, a fallen state marked by a sense of estrangement at the centre of being. Anticipating Faust's wager with the devil in Goethe's *Faust*, Rousseau sighed, ''Even in our keenest pleasures there is scarcely a single moment of which the heart could truthfully say: 'Would that this moment could last for ever!''' a theme that he repeated in the incomplete tenth *Reverie*, recollecting his beloved Madame de Warens.

Anticipating many of the central themes of Romanticism, the essays that compose *The Reveries* trace Rousseau's search for himself and the foundation of happiness. Isolating himself from the world, be described the struggle for self-discovery, learning through this process that this self was a form constituted by irony and paradox, and that, through the act of writing and laying bare these ironies and paradoxes, he isolated himself. Rousseau became his reveries.

—Thomas L. Cooksey

RGVEDA
See THE VEDAS

RHINOCEROS (Rhinocéros)
Play by Eugene Ionesco, 1959

Writing about the Nazis in a 1940 diary, Eugene Ionesco told himself he was the only man left among the rhinoceroses. Watching his friends, formerly anti-fascists, become infected by the ideology, Ionesco felt at if he were watching a physical transformation. The skin seemed to harden and thicken. ''A horn grows on his forehead, he becomes fierce, he charges furiously. He no longer knows how to talk. He is becoming a rhinoceros.'' (*Present past, Past Present* [*Présent passé, passé présent*].)

The play, which was written in 1958 and premièred in 1959, is based on the story ''Rhinoceros,'' which was published in 1957, but when writing the story and the play Ionesco had no memory of using the word ''rhinoceros'' to describe the Nazis. It was only much later, rediscovering the old diary, that he realized the analogy must have remained intact in his unconscious, though when he wrote the story he was remembering how Nazification could metamorphose a community. But as he said in 1961, the success of his play throughout the world made him wonder whether he had hit on:

> a new plague of modern times, a strange disease that thrives in different forms but is in principle the same. Automatic systematized thinking, the idolization of ideologies, screens the mind from reality, perverts our understanding and makes us blind. Ideologies too raise the barricades, dehumanize men and make it impossible for them to be friends notwithstanding: they get in the way of what we call coexistence, for a rhinoceros can come to terms only with one of his kind, a sectarian with a member of his particular sect.

The resultant play is as relevant to left-wing totalitarianism and conformism as to fascism.

It cannot have been easy to solve the problems of staging an action in which the characters, one after another, turn into rhinoceroses. In the first scene an offstage rhinoceros is heard stampeding through the streets: the point is made through sound effects, reports of what has happened and stylized reactions. Everyone says "Oh, a rhinoceros," and then "Well, of all things."

Some of the comedy is reminiscent of Ionesco's earlier manner, as when the Logician proves syllogistically that a dog and Socrates are both cats, but of the five plays Ionesco based on his own stories this is the first with no thriller element, no policemen, no corpses. The first act closes quietly with a ludicrous cortège of mourners for the cat that has been trampled to death by the rhinoceros. People declare that they are not going to put up with the rhinoceros situation.

The second act opens in an office which serves as a microcosm to represent the social reaction to what is going on. An ex-schoolmaster refuses to believe in the rhinoceroses, but one of the employees has failed to turn up, and his wife rushes in to say that she has been chased by a rhinoceros now trying to climb the staircase, which is soon heard to collapse. We hear anguished trumpeting and the stage fills with dust, and when they all see the rhinoceros outside, the wife recognizes it as her husband. She jumps out of the window, and he gallops off with her on his back. The action parallels a passage in the diaries about jumping onto the broad back of the Nazi juggernaut.

Throughout the scene Ionesco demonstrates his skill in the realization of offstage events. When the others telephone the fire station to ask for ladders to be brought, they hear that other incidents have occurred. Seven rhinoceroses had been reported in the morning; now the number is up to 17.

Concentrated on an individual mutation—that of Bérenger's friend Jean—the second scene of Act II presents different problems. Since Jean cannot change physically on stage, Ionesco makes him keep rushing into the bathroom to check his appearance in the mirror from the moment Bérenger tells him that a bump has appeared on his forehead. This enables the actor to adjust his make-up on each exit. His skin turns progressively greener, while the bump grows into a horn, and the difficulty of showing him when the transformation is complete is side-stepped by making Bérenger shut him into the bathroom. A rhinoceros horn pierces through the door.

The analogy at the heart of the play is explored both visually and verbally. Denying the superiority of humanity, Jean claims to be sick of moral standards. Nature has its own laws, he argues, and they should build life on new foundations, going back to primeval integrity. When Bérenger defends the values civilization has evolved, Jean contends that we shall be better off without them.

Alone, Bérenger is in danger. He wishes he could grow a horn: a forehead without one has come to seem ugly. Starting to hate his white hairless body, he tries to imitate the trumpeting he hears outside, but the play has an upbeat ending. If necessary he will take on the whole lot of them. He will not give in.

—Ronald Hayman

RICE (Mi)
Novel by Su Tong, 1991

Published in China in 1991 and in an English translation by Howard Goldblatt in 1995, *Rice* is the first full-length novel by Su Tong, a writer who has emerged as one of the leading literary voices of the post-Mao era in China. Set in the 1930s, a decade when China was experiencing severe famine, internal strife, and invasion from abroad, *Rice* is a stark, realistic work that focuses on life in a single, hapless village as a prism of both personal and communal corruption. This novel and his other writings has earned Su Tong a comparison with the 19th-century French writers Honoré de Balzac and Emile Zola for his penetrating analysis of human characters made more depraved by the oppressive social conditions in which they must act.

Only a child during the massive disruptions caused by Mao Zedong's Cultural Revolution in the 1960s, Su Tong began publishing short stories and novellas in the 1980s, when Chinese writers were able to express themselves in forms that could adhere less rigidly to Maoist orthodoxy. Reviewing *Rice* in *World Literature Today*, Jeffrey C. Kinkley cites David Derwei Wang's characterization of Su Tong's oeuvre as "family melodrama with a gothic touch; looming behind the facade of domestic tales are decadent motives and unspeakable desires." This is in stark contrast to the ideals of the preceding generation of writers, who were often expected to extol the nobility of the peasantry and their stalwart, even cheerful, triumph over adversity through hard work and ideological purity.

Rice, the novel, can be seen as a grim moral parable that exposes the dark underbelly of the human spirit. The book's central character is a shady figure named Five Dragons, a greedy grifter who contrives to take personal advantage of the chaotic social landscape in which he finds himself. Lusting for sex and power, he is introduced as a boxcar-riding tramp who arrives in a town far from his own to plunder both its wealth and its self-respect. As others starve, he is portrayed as a glutton who devours several bowls of rice at a sitting or who chews raw kernels gleaned from dwindling shipments on the wharves ("Rice, it didn't matter whether he crunched it, chewed it, or slurped it, so long as it filled his belly.").

Covetous hunger is thus the central metaphor in *Rice*, a novel that derives its title from the staple food of the Chinese people and, by extension, rice's symbolism of a unified Chinese culture and the currency of mutual social interaction. Su Tong's choice of the famine-ridden 1930s as the setting for the novel underscores the author's determination to offer a critique of Chinese society at variance with the party line of the previous half century. Published just two years after the abortive Tiananmen Square uprising in 1989, *Rice* struck a chord with a new generation of readers in China and abroad who sought a more realistic appraisal of the country's situation in its contemporary literature.

Despite Su Tong's insistence on holding up a mirror to certain aspects of China's past (and present), *Rice* is more than slice-of-life journalism. Throughout the novel, rice is artfully used as a symbol both to characterize and deepen the action and emotional intensity. When Five Dragons voraciously eats rice, it becomes a sign of his greed; when, despite his exhaustion, he industriously carries sack of sack of it on his back, it becomes a proof of his determination to dominate his situation; when he sexually assaults a woman in a rice storehouse, forcing grains into her private parts, it becomes brutal evidence of his abusive nature and his misogyny. Su Tong makes it clear that the sins of the fathers are visited on the children, as when Five Dragon's ten-year-old son, Rice Boy, suffocates his younger sister, Little Bowl, by pouring a mound of rice over her. In the novel's epilogue, the dying and emaciated Five Dragons leaves town as he had come, in a boxcar, this time overflowing with new rice. As he draws his last breath amidst the abundance, another son, Kindling Boy, maliciously flings handfuls of rice into the face of a man finally described as no more than ''an uprooted rice plant, or a solitary puff of raw cotton.''

Reviewing the English-language translation for the *New York Times*, Richard Bernstein paid tribute to its ''grim, satirical power'' and to characters that were ''mean and treacherous, but also full of a redeeming vitality.'' Author Rick Moody pointed out the uniquely Chinese identity of the novel in cover blurb that termed *Rice* ''a cruel, heartrending, and enormously passionate assault on the traditions of the Western novel. There's no love here; there's no redemption; there's no triumph of the individual.''

—Edward Moran

RICKSHAW BOY (Luo tuo Xiangzi)
Novel by Lao She, 1937

Lao She's eighth novel was a monumental turning point in his career as a writer. By September 1936 when he started to serialize the novel *Rickshaw Boy* in a literary journal, Lao She had exhausted the caricatures of hapless intellectuals and petty bureaucrats he had used in earlier works. He needed new inspiration, which he found in a rickshaw puller. Representing the poor and the wretched had been at the center of the New Literature's mission since its inception in the 1910s and was now accepted as an urgent necessity by most progressive and left-wing writers. Lao She was never associated with their movement and there was no evidence that he ever believed in the Marxist ideology that had swept many young writers off their feet. His interest in a rickshaw puller's life may have had more to do with his emulating Charles Dickens's attention to the underprivileged (Lao She started his life-long love affairs with Dickens while teaching Chinese in London in the late 1920s) than with answering the call for proletarian literature. Either way, as the first full-length novel that has a laborer as its protagonist, *Rickshaw Boy* appealed to hungry critics and to the curious reading public who made the novel an instant classic.

As an accessible symbol of the laboring class, rickshaw men had appeared in New Literature multiple times before but no previous writer had given the subject the same degree of vibrancy and exactitude as Lao She did in *Rickshaw Boy*. The novel's photographic depiction of the deplorable living and working conditions of rickshaw pullers in Beijing in the 1930s (known as Beiping then) matches a number of contemporary sociological studies by Western scholars. The difference is that Lao She gives this anonymous mass of people a face and a voice in the protagonist Xiangzi, who has an

engrossing story to tell about hope and despair, ambition and defeat, a story that is terribly tragic and marvelously humane.

A migrant from the impoverished countryside, Xiangzi (meaning ''good omen'') comes to Beijing to seek a change of fortune. His muscle is a perfect match to pulling a rickshaw. Xiangzi, however, is not an ordinary rickshaw man. While others spend their meager earnings on drink, gambling and prostitutes, Xiangzi painstakingly saves his money for a grand purpose: to own a rickshaw and if luck permits, maybe to own a few of them to rent out for others to pull. Luck turns out to be what Xiangzi does not have: three times his ''Chinese dream'' is pricked by forces larger than himself—bandit-soldiers, corrupted policemen, and the untimely death of his wife in childbirth. In the wake of his broken dream lies Xiangzi's broken spirit. Having lost his honesty, pride, and work ethic, Xiangzi by the end of the novel has become a living dead man, surviving on swindling and handouts.

While the novel's embedded message about the incongruity of capitalist drive in pre-revolution China excites Marxist critics, Xiangzi's downward moral journey requires a more nuanced reading. With the ''diseased society'' working against him at every turn, Xiangzi's character flaws are given an equal if not greater share of blame. His nickname Luo tuo or camel suggests his pigheadedness, which causes him to make dubious choices on several occasions. In fact, his dream of owning a rickshaw originates with questionable economic benefits and progresses into an obsession that renders him incapable of leading a normal social life. As this dream becomes increasingly unattainable, it is his own selfishness rather than external adversity that causes his ultimate downfall. Almost all the characters who play a role in Xiangzi's life, such as Hu Niu (Tiger girl), a wiseacre who ruthlessly manipulates Xiangzi into a loveless marriage, Professor Cao, a leftist intellectual who first rescues Xiangzi then leaves him in limbo and Yuan Ming, a student radical who tastes his own medicine when Xiangzi heartlessly betrays him, are sympathetic but flawed people. There is no innocent victim in this diseased society.

Rickshaw Boy's popularity can be equally attributed to Lao She's unique style of storytelling, a style of eloquence and humor that is spiced up with the lively cadence and vibrant idioms of the Beijing dialect. In syntax and vocabulary, Lao She has created a new literary colloquialism that stands in sharp contrast to various unsatisfactory experiments in combining classical Chinese and translat-ese from European languages by many contemporaneous vernacular fiction writers. *Rickshaw Boy* cemented Lao She's reputation as the ''Master of Language,'' which he richly deserves.

—Dian Li

RIG-VEDA

See THE VEDAS

ROCK CRYSTAL (Bergkristall)
Story by Adalbert Stifter, 1853

''Rock Crystal'' is one of Adalbert Stifter's most popular tales from his collection *Bunte Steine* [Coloured Stones]. Bibliographies st 126 separate editions, with translations into many languages including Hebrew and Nepali. The tale is of utmost simplicity: two children, Conrad and Sanna, become lost on Christmas Eve as they walk back from their grandparents to their mountain valley. The following morning they are rescued. That is all that happens. There are no protagonists aside from nature itself. Some critics call the tale devoid of all action, while others see the children experiencing the cosmic glory of the Holy Night. For 24 hours we are with a trained meteorologist, observing with him every minute change in the weather of the winter day and night. The meteorologist is, at the same time, a painter who portrays realistically with blues, whites, greys, and blacks the ever-changing moods, the shifting gradations of light, and the children's sensations during each wintery hour.

In Stifter's typical manner, the opening section of "Rock Crystal" embodies one-third of the tale. This opening narrative focuses on the landscape and mindscape of the isolated community of Gschaid: the celebration of Christmas, the mentality of the inhabitants, the relationship between Gschaid and the nearest village of Millsdorf, home of the children's grandparents. In Gschaid a spirit of narrow clannishness has developed and outsiders are looked upon with suspicion. The cobbler's wife and the mother of the children, and even the children themselves are considered outsiders. This intolerance is matched, however, by the arrogance of the children's grandfather, the Millsdorf tanner, who has not visited Gschaid since the wedding of his daughter. Between the two valleys stands the mountain, their mountain, their source of wood, water, protection from landslides, their calendar from which they calculate the seasonal history. Stifter describes the mountain, its paths, its remoteness, its inscrutable otherness, six times within the narrative. The reader knows the geological and topographical detail of the path to the top of the icy mountain long before the children start their walk. The portrayal of the mountain gives powerful weight and priority to nature.

The snowfall that overtakes the children is first seen through their eyes: joy over the first flurries, the ground covered as if with a dusting of flour. As it snows more heavily, the going gets harder and their enthusiasm fades. Weariness sets in and lastly they become afraid. The reader follows a psychologically accurate description of the reaction of the two children, who keep going because they cannot see the danger that surrounds them and do not consider the limitation of their endurance. Conrad acts precisely as a child of the mountains would; there are no mature considerations or hesitations. He never utters his doubts. His sister is his responsibility; she trusts him implicitly.

Opinions differ in the analysis of the night on the mountain. Traditional interpretations, inspired by the original title and the explicit and implicit symbols and ciphers of Christmas, lead one to accept this tale as an affirmation of Stifter's Christian belief. Stifter shows us the parallelism of the village celebrating Christmas with the mountain-top experience of the children. One cannot help but be struck by the primitiveness and paucity of man's attempt to duplicate the grandeur of this night: candles versus stars and Northern Lights, bells and the organ versus the cracking of the ice. Stifter's repeated use of the number three and the shepherds finding and rescuing the children is surely not coincidental. "This is truly Christmas," says the shepherd. Sanna tells her mother: "Last night on the mountain I saw the Holy Christ," responding to the Northern Lights as a transcendent phenomenon. The mystery of Christmas reveals itself in the hour of Christ's birth, but only to the child. The mother and even

Conrad have outgrown this magic realm. The ending of the story, the coming together of father and mother, of the two villages, the father's recognition that he needs other people, the children's acceptance into the village community, the moral transformation of the villagers, and all of them kneeling in the snow to thank God for the rescue/salvation (*Rettung*) gives credence to this interpretation.

Wildbolz (*Adalbert Stifter*, 1976) claims, however, that the faith expressed here is the faith of the villagers and the faith of Sanna, but it is not, or is no longer, Stifter's faith. He bases his analysis on the changes that took place between the two versions of the story, changes not only in the title but in the essence of the tale. The Christian tendency of the original version is replaced with nature in all its power. Nature threatens, saves, or destroys. Destruction and salvation have the same origin. Stifter does not speak of divine nature as such, but he also does not prevent any reader from seeing the hand of God in the rescue.

Anti-Christian critics emphasize that the same cracking of the ice that contributes to the rescue could also bring about the children's destruction. The same heaven that shows them the spectacular movement of light is the source of the snow that robs them of all orientation and lets them wander into the deadly ice cave. The rescue is thus a combination of human strength and natural phenomena. The reader and the villagers are shown the meaninglessness of considering man to be the central point of reference. The villagers are self-centred and believe that they have assimilated the mountain into their world, but the children experience the opposite. They are not the centre of the world; they are not even able to determine the direction in which they are to go. They are tiny objects driven by impassionate nature.

The changes made between the two versions cannot be overlooked. The Biblical connotations of the images describing the light in the sky of the original version are countermanded by narrative reflections on other possible interpretations of these phenomena in the present version. The reader could ideally wish to fuse scientific fact and religious meaning, creating a sort of pantheistic unity of both. Stifter explicitly allows us to entertain an interpretation that goes beyond the purely natural, and takes pains to make the miraculous coincidence as plausible as possible. The reader must confront the Beyond, which the children see solely as a spacial realm, in its metaphysical implications. This confrontation with the Beyond acquires an existential implication in respect to the nature of man and his place within the natural order of things.

It is interesting to note that after years of secular interpretations, the latest critical voices tend to see again the inseparability of science and religious belief.

—Ingeborg M. Goessl

ROLAND, The Song of

See THE SONG OF ROLAND

LE ROMAN DE LA ROSE

See THE ROMANCE OF THE ROSE

THE ROMANCE OF THE ROSE (Le Roman de la rose)
Romance by Guillaume de Lorris and Jean de Meung

First 4,000 lines written by Guillaume de Lords, c. 1225–37; remaining 18,000 lines written by Jean de Meung, in the 1270s. *Guillaume de Lorris:* **Born:** c. 1200 in Lorris, near Orléans. Brother of a canon of the church in Orléans; possibly educated as a cleric. **Died:** c. 1237. *Jean (Clopinel or Chopinel) de Meung:* **Born:** in Meung-sur-Loire, c. 1260. **Education:** Educated as a cleric, possibly in Paris; closely associated with the court; translated works by Vegetius, Boethius, Aelred of Rievaulx, and Giraldus Cambrensis, and the letters of Abelard and Heloise. **Died:** c. 1315.

PUBLICATIONS

Le Roman de la rose (verse), edited by E. Langlois. 5 vols., 1914–24; also edited by Félix Lecoy, 3 vols., 1965–70; as *The Romaunt of the Rose*, by Chaucer, in *Works*, 1532, translation edited by R. Sutherland, 1967; as *The Romance of the Rose*, translated by F.S. Ellis, 3 vols., 1900; also translated by H.W. Robbins, 1962; Charles Dahlberg, 1971.

*

Critical Studies: *The Allegory of Love* by C.S. Lewis, 1936; *The Mirror of Love: A Reinterpretation of The Romance of the Rose* by Alan M.F. Gunn, 1952; *The Roman de la rose: A Study in Allegory and Iconography*, 1969, and *Reason and the Lover*, 1984, both by John V. Fleming; *Self-fulfilling Prophecies: Readership and Authority in the First Roman de la rose* by David V. Hult, 1986; *Latin Poetic Irony in the Roman de la rose* by Marc M. Pelen, 1987; *Rethinking the Romance of the Rose: Text, Image, Reception* edited by Kevin Brownlee and Sylvia Huot, 1992; *The "Romance of the Rose" and its Medieval Readers: Interpretation, Reception, Manuscript Transmission* by Sylvia Huot, 1993.

*   *   *

The Romance of the Rose was without doubt the most important work of the late Middle Ages in France; until a shift of sensibility occurred in the middle of the 16th century which robbed it of an audience which shared its cultural points of reference it was read and re-read by generation after generation. A vast work of some 22,000 lines, it is by two different authors, and the two parts of the poem have little in common but the bare bones of their subject matter.

The first part (4,028 lines in length) was written around 1230 by Guillaume de Lorris. As the author himself makes clear, it is an "art of love" in which the difficulties facing a would-be lover and the strategies he must adopt if he is to overcome them are set out. The object of the hero's affections is portrayed as a rose growing in a Garden of Love. This search for sexual gratification is, however, couched in metaphorical language. The young man's state of mind, the hurdles he must surmount, and the lady's feelings are expressed by means of allegorical personifications such as Jealousy, Danger, Shame, etc. It is shown how they help or hinder him in his quest. On the other hand, this first part of the romance is a guide to seduction in

the manner of Ovid, on the other a manual for the perfect courtier. A considerable leap of the imagination is required if a modern reader is to grasp the psychological and metaphysical refinements of this intellectually and emotionally subtle work, and one is made constantly aware of the fact that it is the product of a society which deliberately blurred the distinction between dream and reality, fact and fiction.

Jean de Meung, unlike Guillaume de Lorris, was no admirer of the code of chivalry. Taking up the unfinished work some 40 years after it first appeared, he consciously subverts his predecessor's values and assumptions. His "continuation" is in fact more than four times the length of the original and is a vehicle for the author's caustic wit at the expense of particular targets such as monks and women and the more general ones of hypocrisy and falsehood. Against the artificiality of "society," Jean de Meung extols the virtues of "nature," using the allegorical figure of Genius for a plea for honesty and simplicity, loyalty, and compassion. Jean de Meung was a moralist steeped in classical and clerical culture, a reader of Boethius and Plato, who saw the life of the courts as a world of illusion and *fin amour* as a game of dalliance in which ladies were flattered only to be seduced and who was unconcerned by the sweet sufferings of courtly lovers. His literary style is of a piece with his views. The extraordinary figure of the Old Woman is symptomatic of the difference between the two authors. In a bitter, cynical speech, she describes the reality of sexual love, and throughout the work of Jean de Meung makes love subservient to Nature and to Reason. The significance of this debunking of courtly behaviour was not lost upon Jean de Meung's critics such as Jean Gerson and Christine de Pizan who were quick to realize and rebut the consequences of his attack upon court etiquette and the role it gave women.

But more than a mere misogynistic tract, Jean de Meung's *The Romance of the Rose* is a "summa" in which his rationalism is brought to bear on a variety of social, theological, and philosophical questions. Indeed, his influence as a thinker remained so great that no understanding of French literature of the 14th and 15th centuries can be had without a knowledge of *The Romance of the Rose*, and especially of his contribution to it.

—Michael Freeman

THE ROMAUNT OF THE ROSE

See THE ROMANCE OF THE ROSE

LA RONDE (Reigen)
Play by Arthur Schnitzler, 1900

La Ronde is a work about people who make love without being in love. It consists of ten scenes or dialogues in which two characters of different social standing engage in a conversation before and after the sexual union, which is indicated by dashes in the text. In each of these scenes, one of the partners is a lover from the previous encounter: the prostitute and the soldier, the soldier and the housemaid, the housemaid and the young gentleman, the young gentleman and the married woman, the married woman and her husband, the husband and the little miss, the little miss and the poet, the poet and the actress, and the actress and the count. In the tenth scene, the circle becomes complete with the meeting of the two characters representing the lowest and the highest social standing: the prostitute and the count.

Arthur Schnitzler wrote *Liebesreigen* (*Circle of Love*) in the short period of three months during the winter 1896–97. He changed the title in 1899 to *Reigen* (*Hands Around; La Ronde*) because its central theme was the sexual act and not love. Schnitzler had *Hands Around* printed at his own expense; in the preface of this private edition he expressed his concern that the publication of this work was not opportune.

Schnitzler was right in his pessimism. The premiere of three scenes by a student theatre group in Munich in 1903 led to a scandal and a dissolution of the theatre group, with the students being expelled from the university. Various readings between 1905 and 1909 were accompanied by minor scandals. The play caused major scandals in Berlin and Vienna in 1921, with the producers and performers of the play in Berlin subsequently put on trial. Objections to *La Ronde* were also voiced by the Society for the Suppression of Vice and the Lord's Day Alliance in 1923 when it was read in New York City and was performed on 23 October 1926 at the Triangle Theatre there. The only country where the work was appreciated and accepted at this time was France where it had very successful runs in Parisian theatres.

The reasons for these scandals, especially in Germany and Vienna, were twofold: first, the subject matter of *La Ronde* was taboo, and second its author was Jewish. In this work Schnitzler shows language in the service of the Id and lays bare the pretensions and apparent ideals of men and women. The rising nationalism in the 1920s and strong anti-semitism in Austria and Germany did not promote a better understanding and reception of this play. Because of the many scandals caused by the performance of *La Ronde* and the many personal attacks against Schnitzler as its author, he withdrew permission to have the play performed anywhere except in France.

The copyright restriction Schnitzler imposed on *La Ronde* would have expired in 2001 (70 years after his death) in the Federal Republic of Germany and Austria. Because in other European countries, including the former German Democratic Republic, the copyright laws apply for only 50 years, Heinrich Schnitzler, Arthur Schnitzler's son, decided to lift the ban on 1 January 1982. Since then it has been performed in almost every major city in Europe and abroad. It was transformed into a musical in 1980, into an opera in 1982, and into a ballet in 1985. Between 1920 and 1985 seven films were based on the work, most notably Max Ophuls's *La Ronde*. In addition, numerous parodies have been written, including the successful *Reigen '51* by Kehlmann, Merz, and Qualtinger.

La Ronde is no longer a controversial piece because of more liberal attitudes towards sexual behaviour. This play, however, still has some contemporary relevance. It shows that permanent union through sex is impossible. All that is achieved is temporary relief from loneliness, which is then covered up with another affair. The end of these affairs is also predictable, although the beginning varies according to the special status of the partners. Each episode in *La Ronde* starts with great expectations and each one ends in disillusionment, similar to Erich Fromm's comment in the *Art of Loving* (1957):

If the desire of physical love is not stimulated by love, if erotic love is not also brotherly love, it never leads to union in

more than an orgiastic, transitory sense. Sexual attraction creates, for the moment, the illusion of union, yet without love this "union" leaves strangers as far apart as they were before.

With the added threat of contracting AIDS, La Ronde, which is a dance of love, can once again become a dance of death, as it was considered by previous generations.

—Gerd K. Schneider

ROSE GARDEN (Gulistān)
Prose and verse by Shaikh Muslih-al-Din Sa'di, 1258

Rose Garden, a classic masterpiece of Persian literature, was written by Shaikh Muslih-al-Din Sa'di in 1258. This didactic book is a mixture of prose and verse: the story is usually told in prose and the moral point is expressed in verse. The verses are mostly in Persian, though they include a few Arabic poems as well. There are eight chapters: 1) On the Manners of Kings; 2) On the Ethics of Dervishes; 3) On the Excellence of Contentment; 4) On the Advantages of Silence; 5) On Love and Youth; 6) On Weakness and Old Age; 7) On the Effects of Education; 8) On Proper Conduct in Life. Besides its literary value, *Rose Garden* is also a valuable source for the study of Sa'di's time and society.

All types of characters can be seen in this work, but Sa'di pays special attention to two groups of people, kings and dervishes, one representing worldly power and the other spiritual power. One will safeguard the country from external enemies, while the other will safeguard the society from corruption and moral decay. On the other hand, corrupt religious men can be more harmful than cruel kings. Therefore, Sa'di assumes the responsibility of advising both kings and dervishes, and devotes two chapters, which constitute almost half of his book, to these two groups.

In the first chapter of *Rose Garden* Sa'di addresses monarchs and admonishes them. At a time when kings had absolute control over the life and wealth of people, he bluntly warns them against injustice. He reminds them that they derive their power directly from the people; a king who is not loved by his subjects is doomed. He refers to the transitory power of kings and reminds them that only good fame will outlive their inevitable death. He narrates a story in which King Anushiravān receives the news of his enemy's death with sadness since it reminds him of his own death. In another anecdote he tells us about a cruel king who asks a dervish to say a prayer for him. The man asks God to take the king's life immediately. When the king asks what kind of prayer that was, the man says it was for the king's own good and for the good of other Muslims. Sa'di offers examples for kings to follow. In one of these, during a hunting trip King Anushiravān sends a soldier to a nearby village to get some salt, and makes sure that it is paid for. The soldier cannot understand what damage can possibly be done to the villagers if he gets the salt for free. The king's answer shows his wisdom and justice: if a king picks an apple from his subject's apple tree, his soldiers will uproot the whole garden. In this chapter Sa'di reminds kings of their duties to God, and gives them practical advice on how to treat friends, enemies, and subjects, and on how to appoint qualified officials to high positions.

In the second chapter Sa'di deals with dervishes and their manners. He offers examples for them, too. He tells the story of a pious man who throws his only rug in the way of a thief so that he would not go back empty-handed. Material attachment will block spiritual growth and will take away the freedom of thinking. He also narrates anecdotes about hypocrisy and corruption among religious men. Sa'di admonishes dervishes in the same way that he admonishes kings. He narrates a story about a hypocrite who eats less but prays more than usual in front of the king. When he goes home, he asks for food. When his smart son asks him why he did not eat enough at the king's court, he says that it was necessary to show his piety to the king by eating less. His son suggests that he might as well say his prayers again. In another anecdote a king asks a pious man if he ever thinks of the king. The pious man says that he does so only when he forgets God.

In Chapter 3 Sa'di discusses the virtues of contentment, and gives examples of men who are content with what they have without giving up individual effort. There are anecdotes about men who prefer to tolerate difficulties rather than stretch their hands out to greedy and selfish rich men. A poor man starves to death, but refuses to ask a rich man for help. A brave soldier who is wounded in battle risks his life, but does not go to the greedy merchant to ask for an antidote. In another story a poor man who is complaining about not having shoes calms down when he sees a man without legs. There is no end to man's desire; therefore, he must cease to desire. To this effect Sa'di narrates the story of a merchant who wishes to make one last trip before retiring from worldly affairs. But it turns out that the single trip he has in mind involves several long trips to far-away lands. On the other hand, a fisherman is not unhappy when he loses his day's catch because it has not been allotted to him.

Chapter 4 deals with the benefits of silence. There are occasions where silence is better than speech. A man can hide his ignorance behind silence. A man's wisdom and ignorance can only be known through his speech. A young and educated man keeps silent in his meeting with other scholars because he is afraid they might ask him something he does not know.

Chapter 5 deals with youth and passionate love, while Chapter 6 deals with the problems of old age and physical weakness.

Chapter 7 deals with education. Sa'di emphasizes the usefulness of learning a science or a skill over accumulating wealth. As an educator Sa'di stresses both worldly and religious education. He pays close attention to the role of teachers and parents in nurturing moral values in children. Teachers must be patient and encouraging and endowed with moral virtues.

The last chapter advises man on how to conduct his life. This is the only chapter with no anecdotes, and is mostly a collection of Sa'di's maxims and sayings. He blames men who work hard to gather money but never enjoy it, and those who learn science but never teach it to others. He also talks about the importance of choosing good friends and compromising with one's enemies. In general he recommends moderation in all aspects of life.

There are a few cases in *Rose Garden* where anecdotes are thematically placed in the wrong chapter, or there are contradictory anecdotes, or anecdotes which might seem to contradict Sa'di's humanitarian philosophy. However, it must be remembered that Sa'di's *Rose Garden*, unlike *Bustan*, does not depict the ideal world but the real world as it is, and the real world is full of contradictions. At any rate, Sa'di's overall philosophy is that of a humanist whose main mission is to tie the bonds of humanity together.

At the end of *Rose Garden* Sa'di once again refers to the fact that his ultimate goal was admonishment, and that he has tried to mix the bitter medicine of moralizing with the honey of story-telling so that it would be interesting. He has fulfilled his responsibility as a messenger, and has delivered his message. It is up to the reader to absorb it.

—Alireza Anushiravani

ROSE, THE ROMANCE OF THE

See THE ROMANCE OF THE ROSE

THE RUBAIYAT (Rubā'iyāt)
Poems by Omar Khayyam, 11/12th century

Rubā'iyāt (plural of *rubā'i*) are examples of a genre of Persian poetry known for its shortness and conciseness, consisting of four lines (quatrain). The first, the second, and the fourth lines rhyme, but the third line does not rhyme with the rest (AABA). Omar Khayyam, a Persian philosopher, mathematician, astronomer, and physician, is known to have composed 178 quatrains (although the exact number is disputed among scholars). His fame in the West came with Edward Fitzgerald's translation of his *Rubaiyat*, and since then the poems have been translated into several other languages.

Each *rubā'i* is self-contained and expresses a complete unit of thought. However, there are certain basic issues which run through all the quatrains and thus connect them thematically. The first two lines of a *rubā'i* make a statement; the third line brings it to its climax, and the fourth line sums up the main thought, as in the following (no. 8):

> He began creation with constraint,
> By giving me life he added only confusion;
> We depart reluctantly still not knowing
> The aim of birth, existence, departure.

The style of *The Rubaiyat* combines eloquence, beauty, and simplicity. Omar Khayyam is mainly interested in the conceptualization of his feelings as a philosopher and a scientist. In a sense there is nothing new in *The Rubaiyat*; they contain questions which have haunted man's mind for many ages. Omar Khayyam's innovation lies in pouring these universal questions into the simple and concise language of *rubā'i*.

Omar Khayyam does not talk of courtly love. He is not praising his beloved's face or hair, or bemoaning her separation as was the custom. Although some have claimed that Omar Khayyam is a mystical poet, he is not concerned with metaphysics or the Divine Reality. He is no moralist. He sees the beauty of life, and wants to enjoy it, although this beauty is doomed to annihilation. Why this is so is an unfathomable question that torments Omar Khayyam and casts him into confusion, so that nothing can console him.

The language of *The Rubaiyat* illustrates these two opposite aspects of life. Some images convey the idea of liveliness and pleasure: the flower, the nightingale, grass, spring, gardens, wine, and light; others evoke annihilation and death: darkness, the corpse, dust, the veil, departure, deception, dream, winter, chaos, and grief. The images of the potter (Creator), the pot (man), and the clay (matter, annihilation) sum up this polarity in a beautiful and tragic language (no. 43):

> It is a bowl the Creative Reason casts,
> Pressing in tenderness a hundred kisses on its brim;
> This cosmic potter makes such a rare bowl,
> Then throws it back again to the ground.

Once the Creator destroys his creatures, he uses their clay to create new creatures (transmigration of matter). The whole world is the master's toy shop, as if he takes pleasure in turning his beautiful creatures into dust (no. 71):

> I watched a potter in his work-place,
> Saw the master, his foot on the wheel's treadle;
> Unabashed, he was making a jug's lid and handle
> From a king's head and a beggar's hand.

Omar Khayyam's turbulent mind is looking for an answer which, to his dismay, he cannot find. Deeply frustrated by unanswerable questions, he finally resorts to drinking wine and seizing the day (*carpe diem*). But this must not be confused with the hedonism with which Omar Khayyam has usually been associated. His final resort to alcohol is the solution of a pessimistic philosopher, not an epicurean. As a rational philosopher he is concerned with the brevity and meaninglessness of human life rather than with the simplistic pleasure of drinking wine. In reading his *Rubaiyat*, one must remember that these quatrains were composed by a genius who wrote his treatise on algebra in his twenties, and whose revised astronomical calendar was more accurate than the Gregorian calendar (introduced by Pope Gregory XIII in 1582, almost 400 years after Omar Khayyam). Omar Khayyam questions the basic ideological tenets which were traditionally taken for granted as the absolute truth. His invitation to drink wine is only an indication of a mind frustrated by the temporality of life and the meaninglessness of death. *The Rubaiyat* tells the story of a nonconformist's struggle to solve the mysteries of life.

The following quatrains highlight the basic trends of Omar Khayyamic philosophy:

1) There is no plan behind man's creation, and his life is of no significance (no. 41):

> There was a water-drop, it joined the sea,
> A speck of dust, it was fused with earth;
> What of your entering and leaving this world?
> A fly appeared, and disappeared.

2) Man's knowledge and rational effort in solving the problems of life are in vain (no. 8):

> This ocean of being has come from the Obscure,
> No one has pierced this jewel of reality;
> Each has spoken according to his humour,
> No one can define the face of things.

3) Death is the only inevitable result of life, and there is no evidence of life after death (no. 46):

> Of all who went on this long road,
> Where is the one who has returned to tell us the secret?
> Take care to leave nothing for your needs on this two-
>   ended way,
> You will not be coming back.

4) Man has no control over his fate. He is merely an impotent victim (no. 50):

> We are the puppets and the firmament is the puppetmaster,
> In actual fact and not as a metaphor;
> For a time we acted on this stage,
> We went back one by one into the box of oblivion.

5) Life is transitory (no. 35):

> Alas, the book of youth is finished,
> The fresh spring of life has become winter;
> That state which they call youth,
> It is not perceptible when it began and when it closed.

6) In the short span of life available to man, all he can do is to drink wine and enjoy the time allotted to him (no. 112):

> Since nobody has a lien on tomorrow
> Gladden the sad heart now:
> Drink wine in moonlight, my dear,
> Because the moon will revolve a long time and not find us.

(translations by Peter Avery and John Heath-Stubbs)

—Alireza Anushiravani

THE RUBAIYAT OF OMAR KHAYAM

See THE RUBAIYAT

R.U.R.
Play by Karel Čapek, 1920

The enigmatic title of the Czechoslovakian writer Karel Čapek's play refers to its setting and subject matter, the factory and products of "Rossum's Universal Robots." Written in 1920, during his country's brief period of independence between the two World Wars, *R.U.R.* brought its dramatist international recognition and introduced the word "robot" (from Czech *robotit*, to drudge) into the English language.

The play is set sometime in the future. Its plot concerns the construction, in a factory located on a remote island, of what we would now describe as androids—machines outwardly resembling human beings—which are intended, in the factory manager Domain's idealistic words, to free humanity "from the degradation of labour." In order to achieve maximum occupational efficiency the robots have been constructed as simplified versions of the human worker, so that "mechanically they are more perfect than we are, they have enormously developed intelligence, but they have no soul."

Into this situation is introduced the figure of Helena, a representative of the Humanity League, whose aim is to bring civil rights to the robots. It is through her that we are gradually introduced to the ethical conflicts which the ability to create a worker population has produced. The project itself, we learn, was the outcome, not of idealism but of megalomania. Old Rossum, a physiologist who initiated the experimental programme aimed at reproducing human beings that culminated in the production of the robots was, according to Domain, was a madman who "wanted to become a sort of scientific substitute for God." Rossum's work has been simplified and perfected by his son, an engineer. It was he who, while continuing to construct machines with the outward appearance of human beings, in the cause of greater labour efficiency created them devoid of human sensations and emotions. Dr. Gall, the head of the factory's physiological department, has however modified the robots by installing a limited nervous system in order to introduce suffering and thereby avoid the corporeally damaging results of industrial accidents arising from the robot's inability to feel pain. It is these two elements, established in a traditionally discursive manner in an exposition involving Domain and Helena, that generate the action of the play and produce its climax. The human appearance of the robots causes Helena, and to some extent the audience, to view the machines as repressed human beings. This appears to be further supported by the fact that they occasionally experience "Robot's Cramp" during which they cease to operate and gnash their teeth.

Thus, by the end of Act I, in the manner of the well-made play, the audience is introduced to the issues and complications of the play. Also following the pattern of the well-made play the second act brings a further complication in the form of a rebellion of the world's robots. It is five years later and Helena is married to Domain. The robots have been used by many nations as soldiers but have turned their guns against those who employ them. Humanity now feels superfluous and is losing the will to reproduce itself. By the end of the second act the island's robots have become aggressive and appear poised to attack their human creators.

The final act brings the play to its climax. Under pressure from Helen, Dr. Gall has given the robots various human responses which amount to a kind of "soul." This has caused them to view humanity as redundant and to hate their own subjection, They rise in rebellion, destroying all human beings except one, Alquist, who, as the Clerk of Works of the factory and a builder, they consider to be subservient like themselves. The third act closes with the victory of the robots.

While illustrating humanity's failings, its violence, and its lust for power, Čapek is unwilling to conclude the play on a note of pessimism and so introduces a typical dénouement in the form of an Epilogue. Using a traditional, melodramatic plot-device, he reveals here that, unfortunately for the robots, old Rossum's manuscript containing the formula crucial to their construction has earlier been burnt by Helena. Alquist does not possess the knowledge to rediscover the formula, the human race has died out, and the robots, with their limited working life and inability to reproduce, will likewise be extinct in 20 years' time. The end of the world is indeed nigh, but is averted by the sexual awakening of two recently constructed robots, one named Helena after Domain's wife and the other aptly called Primus. Tested by Alquist, they reveal that they care for each other, indeed are willing to die for each other, and are sent out into the world by Alquist as the second Adam and Eve who will "be fruitful and multiply and replenish the earth . . ."

Although the plot itself follows the pattern of the well-made play, *R.U.R.* also reflects the influence of German expressionism. The apocalyptic vision of a future society in which industry appears to have become the master rather than the servant of mankind bears similarities to such plays as Georg Kaiser's *The Coral* (*Die Koratle*, 1917) and *Gas, I* and *II* (1918 and 1920). The groupings of characters in terms of their social roles—the scientists and engineers who run the factory and speak almost chorally, the robot-workers and the idealistic, enquiring young intruder, Helena—are all reminiscent of the generic characterization of expressionism. Finally, the optimism of the play's Epilogue, in which the new Adam and Eve are about to re-establish humanity after the apocalypse, can be seen as a clear parallel to the mood of early German expressionism.

—D. Keith Peacock

S

THE SACRED WAY (Iera Odos)
Poem by Angelos Sikelianos, 1935

"The Sacred Way," probably the best known of Angelos Sikelianos's poems, dates from February 1935 and marks the end of an apparent artistic block for the poet and the beginning of a new period of creativity. For most of the preceding decade Sikelianos had been preoccupied with his "Delphic Idea," and his usually prolific poetic output had been drastically reduced. The "Delphic Idea" was the poet's dream of founding an international spiritual and intellectual centre at Delphi, a doomed project which, however, gave rise to the two Delphic Festivals of 1927 and 1930, masterminded by the poet's American wife, Eva Palmer. The festivals won international acclaim with their revivals of ancient drama, games, and handicrafts, but ended in financial disaster for the Sikelianos couple. In 1933, Eva Palmer returned permanently to America, where she was joined by the couple's only son.

Greece at this time was experiencing economic depression and the political unrest that was to culminate in the unsuccessful *putsch* of March 1935 and the 1936 military coup that established the Metaxas dictatorship. 1935 was for Sikelianos also an artistic turning-point and a painful personal anniversary: 30 years earlier, in 1905, he had met Eva Palmer through her friendship with Raymond and Isadora Duncan. The poet's sister was married to Raymond Duncan. In the same year, Raymond and Isadora danced the full length of the Sacred Way, from Athens to Eleusis, taking four days to do so. By 1935, both Isadora Duncan and the poet's beloved sister, Penelope, were dead, and Eva Palmer had left Greece. (In the last months of 1935 Sikelianos retraced a part of Raymond and Isadora's dance on foot and delivered a series of four talks, the first in the middle of the Sacred Way and the remaining three on different days at the sanctuary of Eleusis.) The opening words of the poem:

> Through the new wound that fate had opened in me
> I felt the setting sun flood my heart
> with a force like that of water when it pours
> through a hole in a sinking ship

may thus be taken to refer both to the poet's unhappy personal circumstances and to the sorry state of Greek internal affairs. The poem's speaker describes himself in the following line as "like one long sick."

"The Sacred Way" belongs to a cycle of eight poems called *Orphica*, which offer interpretations of ancient myths and modern events based on Orphic beliefs. Fundamental to these poems is the central tenet of Orphism, rebirth, and the cycle deals with spiritual and artistic regeneration. The poems incorporate cyclical recurrence into their structure, by means of ring composition; thus the opening words of "The Sacred Way" recur towards the end. The cycle traces an Orphic journey of initiation, each poem marking a particular stage. "The Sacred Way" can be read as a microcosm of the whole collection: it recounts the solitary journey of an initiate along the Sacred Way, where the Orphic mysteries were celebrated.

Midway along the road, the poet pauses to rest and reflect, and is accosted by a gypsy with two cruelly chained dancing bears. This spectacle reveals to the poet that mankind's soul is still unredeemed and that even he, the self-styled initiate, is a "slave to the world," because he participates in the bears' torture by throwing the gypsy a coin. He draws a parallel between the grief of the mother bear over her cub's sufferings and Demeter's grief over Persephone. (Demeter and Persephone were central figures of Orphism and had a cult at Eleusis.) He also parallels Alcmene grieving over Heracles and the Virgin Mary over Christ, thereby underlining what he believed to be the recurrence of divine events (such as crucifixion). The bear is a timeless "testifying symbol of all primeval suffering."

The journey along the Sacred Way begins at sunset, but ends in darkness:

> night fell
> and again through the wound that fate had opened in me
> I felt the darkness flood my heart as water
> pours through a hole in a sinking ship.

Nevertheless, the poem closes with a glimmer of hope, as the initiate is comforted by a murmur telling him that the day will eventually come when all souls will rejoice together. In addition to this explicit reference to Orphic beliefs, the poem is further marked as "Orphic" by its metre, the iambic hendecasyllables invariably used by Sikelianos for his Orphic poetry.

The year 1935 and the poem "The Sacred Way" can be seen as turning-points in Sikelianos's poetic career. In the midst of personal unhappiness and disillusion, he appears to have experienced a new, if subdued, hope for artistic regeneration. In the muted tone and controlled lyricism, which depart drastically from earlier lyrical exuberance, Sikelianos found his mature voice.

—Sarah Ekdawi

SÆMUNDAR EDDA
See THE POETIC EDDA

THE SAGA OF KING ÓLÁF THE SAINT (Óláfs saga ins helga)
Prose by Snorri Sturluson, 12–13th century

The Saga of King Óláf the Saint survives both separately and as the central part of Snorri Sturluson's *Heimskringla*, his encyclopedic history of the kings of Norway. The two versions differ only slightly; the separate saga, for instance, includes an account of Óláf's birth, which in *Heimskringla* takes place not in *Óláfs saga* itself, but in the saga preceding it in the sequence. It is now accepted that the separate saga was written first, and later adapted to fit *Heimskringla* when the latter was written. In addition to numerous scaldic verses, many of them actually quoted in the saga and some composed by eye-witnesses to the events it describes, and various prose works, including the sagas of the Orkney and Faroe islanders, Snorri's chief source seems to have been his contemporary Styrmir Kárason's *Life of St. Óláf*, now preserved only fragmentarily and deriving from the anonymous *Oldest Saga* of St. Óláf, itself only partly preserved and dating from the turn of the 12th to the 13th century.

Snorri greatly reduces Styrmir's emphasis on Óláf's sanctity, clearly wishing to present Óláf as an earthly as well as a saintly king. He attributes miracles to him only near the end of his career and after his death, concentrating in the greater part of the saga, after a prefatory account of Óláf's youth as a Viking, on his attempts to subdue the Norwegian local rulers, often with aggressive missionary zeal. All goes well for him until he clashes with two powerful chieftains, Erling Skjálgsson and Thórir Hound, both uncles of a certain Ásbjörn Sigurdarson, whose story, told in the central chapters of the saga, constitutes a turning-point in Óláf's career.

Ásbjörn travels southwards from Hálogaland, in northern Norway, to buy grain, but is told by Seal-Thórir, the King's steward, that King Óláf has banned the sale of grain to northerners. He applies to his mother's brother, Erling Skjálgsson, a chieftain in the southwest, who arranges for his thralls to sell Ásbjörn the grain, as they are exempt from the King's ban. On his return northwards, however, Ásbjörn is stopped by Seal-Thórir, who outnumbers him and confiscates the grain. Next year Ásbjörn returns south, catches Seal-Thórir in the act of bragging about this to King Óláf, and kills him in the King's presence. The King orders his imprisonment and death, but the execution is delayed by a series of legal tricks, thanks to the influence of Erling, who meanwhile assembles a large force and finally sets Ásbjörn free, confronting the King with an offer of reconciliation and freedom to determine compensation for Seal-Thórir's death, in exchange for Ásbjörn's life. The King responds by giving Ásbjörn Seal-Thórir's job, which, however, Ásbjörn fails to take up when the humiliation of doing so is pointed out to him by his father's brother Thórir Hound, a chieftain in northern Norway. Ásbjörn is subsequently slain by one of the King's lackeys, but his brother passes on the spear used in the slaying to Thórir Hound, who himself uses it to kill another of the King's followers who had been present at Ásbjörn's slaying. After Thórir Hound and Erling have joined the Danish King Cnut and the latter has subdued Norway, King Óláf defeats Erling in battle but is forced to flee the country when Erling is murdered and his sons seek vengeance. When he attempts to reconquer Norway, he is defeated and slain at the battle of Stiklestad, at which Thórir Hound is one of his chief opponents.

Óláf's last battle is another turning-point; up to this point, the structure of the saga resembles an Icelandic Family Saga, with a lengthy introduction covering Óláf's rise to power, and a situation of conflict beginning in earnest with the story of Ásbjörn, reaching a climax with the murder of Erling, and leading to the revenge taken on Óláf at Stiklestad. From the accounts of miracles given shortly before Óláf's death onwards, however, the saga seems to take on the structure of a saint's legend, with a *passio* and *miracula* following on from a relatively secular *vita*; Thórir Hound is, indeed, the first of Óláf's opponents to acknowledge Óláf's sanctity when the blood of the slain king heals his wounded hand. By thus combining two types of narrative, Snorri creates a balanced picture of Óláf as an earthly monarch, with human virtues and failings, and a patron saint who will protect Norway forever. Important aspects of the overall structure of

this long saga (of some 250 chapters) include the two dreams Óláf has while abroad, first as a Viking and later as a fugitive, encouraging him to return to Norway, and his vision and dream before the battle of Stiklestad, in the first of which he sees the world and in the second a ladder leading to heaven. Also important in this respect are the activities of the Danish King Cnut, which for literary as much as historical reasons occur at significant moments in Snorri's account of Óláf's career and prepare the way for the brief rule in Norway, after Óláf's death, of Cnut's son Svein, whose harsh measures confirm many of Óláf's former Norwegian opponents in their recognition of his sanctity. Significant too is the changing stance of Einar Thambarskelfir, the archer who had fought loyally beside Óláf's predecessor and namesake, Óláf (Tryggvason), and who at first resists the young Óláf, is later reconciled with him, then swears loyalty to King Cnut when the latter's subjugation of Norway gives him hope of becoming its overlord under Cnut's auspices; but later still, faced with Cnut's ambitions for his son Svein, he proclaims Óláf's sanctity in Norway after avoiding taking part in the battle of Stiklestad, and in defiance of Cnut and Svein assists in offering the Norwegian throne to Óláf's son Magnús. Taken together with others of their kind, these examples illustrate Snorri's masterly handling of multi-stranded narrative, a technique he probably learned from his compatriot Karl Jónsson, who had used it in his *Sverris saga*, written near the end of the 12th century.

—Rory McTurk

ŚAKUNTALĀ
Play by Kālidāsa, 5th century AD

Kālidāsa wrote his most popular drama, the *Śakuntalā*, at the height of his poetic career, and it was to have a profound influence on Western literature, being admired by Goethe, among others.

The setting of the *Śakuntalā* is the mythical world of the *Mahābhārata*. King Duṣyanta, while chasing after a deer in the forest, happens to arrive at the hermitage of the sage Kaṇva; he falls immediately in love with his daughter, Śakuntalā. She reciprocates his love, and they marry according to the *gandharva* rite; that is, with only the mutual consent of both parties. While the king is away, Śakuntalā, distracted by her passion, neglects her duty to a visiting sage, Durvāsa, who curses her. As a result of this curse, Śakuntalā loses the ring of recognition which the king had given her. As a consequence, the king later forgets her and does not accept her when she goes to his palace. She is then taken by her mother, the nymph Menakā, to Heaven. But there is never a sad ending in Indian drama, and the ring is miraculously found by a fisherman, with the subsequent happy reunion of the two lovers.

Kālidāsa draws upon the Indian epics for the subject matter of this drama, but here the dramatist transforms the original story, characterized by its harshness, turning it into a play in which love is the predominant element and emphasizing the tension between love and public duty. However, Kālidāsa's intelligent handling of the incidents resolves this conflict between desire (*kāma*) and duty (*dharma*). He introduces the motif of the curse, which provokes the king's forgetfulness, justifying the monarch's apparent negligence of duty. The central role that the concept of *dharma* and the figure of the king play in Kālidāsa's drama suggest the author's connection with the court;

several allusions scattered throughout his dramas imply that he worked under the patronage of the Gupta monarch Candragupta II.

The hierarchical nature of traditional Indian society is evident in the characters and the plot, which Kālidāsa has borrowed from the idealized epic. It is also evident in the juxtaposition of these elements with those from popular literature and everyday life. This fact explains the importance given to the figure of the *vidūṣaka*, the buffoon, who is a friend and confidant of the king rather than his jester. Moreover, the king, his counsellors, and other members of the upper classes speak Sanskrit, traditionally considered the sacred language of the Brahmanic caste, while women, the buffoon, and minor characters speak different Prakrit dialects, which were commonly used by the uneducated masses.

Attempts have been made to compare Indian drama with Greek, but differences seem to dominate over the apparent affinities. An example of the difference between the two traditions is the total absence of tragedy in Indian drama: all plays end happily, and nothing indecorous appears on the stage. In addition, Indian drama is characterized by the interpolation of lyrical stanzas with prose dialogues: in the *Śakuntalā* the lyrical passages constitute one half of the whole play. Moreover, the concept of fate, central to the Greek tragedy, is absent from Kālidāsa's works, in which chance predominates. However, both traditions share a conception of drama as a source of entertainment leading to catharsis.

The *Śakuntalā* is written in a highly refined language, evidence of the poet's mastery of Sanskrit according to traditional Indian formalism. But language is not the only aspect of the play, that has attracted the attention of later poets: Kālidāsa's *Śakuntalā* fits perfectly into the principles codified in the *Nātyaśāstra* of Bharata, the earliest Indian work on dramatic theory. The play opens with a prelude and is then divided into seven acts. It is full of sentiments (*rasas*): the predominant sentiment is the erotic, but the heroic and the comic are also present. These elements make the *Śakuntalā* a masterpiece of its genre. However, despite its numerous merits, Kālidāsa's play is considered defective as a stage-play. The action takes place over seven years, and therefore does not respect the unity of time. Śakuntalā is supposedly taken away to Heaven in front of the audience. This fact does not deter some critics from affirming that "the supernatural is reduced to modest dimensions" in this play.

Characters in the *Śakuntalā* are the embodiments of social roles. Therefore, the conflict between individual and society never arises. The close interrelation between individuals and their social roles sustains the order in a society that is highly hierarchical. Nature—a dynamic force, which contributes to the cosmic unity in which people belong—also plays a central role in Kālidāsa's play. It has been said by several critics that the heroine of the drama, Śakuntalā, personifies the procreative energies of nature. It is therefore not surprising, to find that powerful images of nature dominate Kālidāsa's drama, particularly in the fourth act.

The hero and the heroine of Kālidāsa's play symbolize skilfully the conflict between desire and duty. It is ultimately this representation of a universal conflict that has made Kālidāsa so highly regarded over the centuries.

—Ana M. Ranero

SĀMA-VEDA

See THE VEDAS

THE SATIN SLIPPER (Le Soulier de satin)
Play by Paul Claudel, 1928–29

Paul Claudel started writing *The Satin Slipper* just after World War I and struggled with it during five of his busiest years at the French Foreign Office. Composition was delayed when part of the manuscript disappeared in the terrible September 1923 earthquake in Japan, but the play was eventually completed there in 1924.

The play has not been performed often, but has consistently challenged France's leading stage directors. The names of Jean-Louis Barrault and Antoine Vitez remain linked to *The Satin Slipper*. The former staged a pioneering shorter version, while credit goes to the latter for a memorable production of the whole text at the Avignon drama festival. A filmed version lasting nearly seven hours was shot in 1985 by the Portuguese director Manoel de Oliveira. Both in length and in scope the play indeed occupies a special place in French literature.

The Satin Slipper can arguably be called the most successful historical play in the French language. With the debatable exception of Victor Hugo, few French playwrights have excelled at this genre. Unlike Shakespeare and Strindberg, Claudel does not look for inspiration in his homeland's history. The play is subtitled "Action espagnole en quatre journées" and most, but not all, historical events or characters in the play relate to Spanish history. In a poem written as an introduction to the English translation, Claudel pays homage to Lope de Vega and the author of *Henry VI*. In the best Shakespearean tradition, Claudel distorts facts to suit his creative and ideological purposes. Columbus, Luther, the Invincible Armada are some of the landmarks he welds together in the four symbolic days of his play. Beyond the history of a nation, Claudel aims at illustrating the history of the Catholic faith and how it was spread to the confines of the earth. What Claudel never attempts is to draw detailed portraits of well-known historical figures. For instance he insists that the King of Spain at the end of the play should look like the King of Spades. Claudel has no desire to plumb the psychological motives behind the resolutions taken by such and such a king. Instead he undertakes to show Grace Abounding to the actors of history. The word "actor" is essential here. Claudel is very modern in that he presents his characters as first and foremost actors. The most obvious example is the character called "The Actress" who plays a major part in the last section of the play.

"L'Irrépressible" ("The Irrepressible One") is another character whose function is to highlight the theatricality of the play. This character embodies the most fiery part of the author's imagination, the part which is central to the act of creation but is nevertheless curbed by the author's reason. Through this character Claudel comments on his own methods and temptations while writing. This character represents unchecked spontaneity, a quality Claudel may have felt he was losing as he progressed slowly towards completion of his play.

Other episodic characters (different ones in each section) are used to bring in more straightforward comic relief. These characters belong squarely to the level of farce. They are one-dimensional characters with no inner life and delightfully strange names. However, their actions often are elaborate parodies of what takes place in the most serious scenes. For instance the tug-of-war between the Bidince Team and the Hinnulus Team (Fourth Day, scene V) echoes mockingly the scene between Dona Prouhèze and her Guardian Angel (Third Day, scene VII). In the latter scene the Angel describes himself as a fisherman patiently trying to catch the struggling soul of Prouhèze. In the other scene the two mock-professors are also fishing.

Through such characters Claudel introduces a grotesque kind of humour into the play. This is another aspect of the play's broad scope: Claudel mixes genres and tones in a challenging effort to cover the whole range of emotions from the ludicrous to the lyrical.

In many lucid texts—most notably in the volume *Ways and Crossways* (*Positions et Propositions*)—Claudel stressed the link he perceived between his strong religious convictions and his creative work. For him, Christianity offers the only challenge worthy of man. Contradiction, opposition, struggle are some of the words the poet and playwright repeatedly used to describe his faith. Religion gives man the opportunity to struggle between his craving for immediate individual happiness and higher desires. It forces man to make choices and as a result it makes drama possible, indeed, inevitable. Therefore Catholic theology is not exterior to Claudel the writer. On the contrary, the laws and mysteries of his religion furnished him with a paradigm of dramatic conflict that gives *The Satin Slipper* both its main plot line and its main theme. Claudel is not interested in the social dimension of the obstacle that separates Rodrigue from Prouhèze, but exclusively in its deeper religious significance.

—Pascale Voilley

SATIRE 10
Poem by Juvenal, 1st/2nd century AD

From the patchy knowledge we have of Juvenal's life, it is clear that Satire 10 is one of Juvenal's relatively late poetic productions. Both personally and in terms of his satire, Juvenal seems to have settled a little by the time of the writing of Satire 10 and to have discarded some of the rampant fury which characterizes, for example, Book I (Satires 1–5). In many ways it is the maturing process that has gone on over the period between Satire 1 and Satire 10 which makes this work of such value in Juvenal's output; Satire 10 builds upon the assumptions about society which have been worked through in its predecessors, and starts, if hesitantly, to put forward a social and personal ethic, alternative to those which Juvenal sees and abhors around him and which he attempts to demolish in his satires.

Satire 10 signals the breadth of its targets and its ambition in the great geographical sweep with which it opens, encompassing all known humanity (''from Cadiz to the dawn-streaked shores / of Ganges''; translation here and following from Peter Green). The concerns of this satire are to be wide-ranging and ''universal,'' in contrast to previous satires which concentrated specifically on such issues as homosexuality, femininity, hypocrisy, and ignorance (all in a Roman context). The early themes tackled here are wealth, glory, and complacency: wealth for the dangers, greed, and self-destruction it brings, complacency in the populus who follow current events only to stay on the winning side and who are willing, quite literally, to put the boot into the corpse of one who was their hero only yesterday.

Watching over Satire 10 is the presence of two philosophers of whom Juvenal says they ''had a point'': Democritus and Heraclitus, one ''helpless with laughter,'' the other ''weeping a fountain.'' In citing these two polarities Juvenal has found the perfect expression of the philosophy embodied in the cut of his satire: laughing at the ludicrousness of humanity while at the same time lamenting its folly. When Juvenal talks of the downfall of Sejanus it is with humour at the irreverent treatment meted out to a great statesman and the fickleness

of those who quickly say they ''never / Cared for the fellow,'' but it is also with a sadness at the recognition that such things happen.

There is, however, little of this ambiguity of reception when it comes to one of Juvenal's favourite targets, Hannibal, who rather than making Juvenal weep and laugh, engenders only anger and mocking contempt. For Juvenal, Hannibal is the supreme example of one who placed glory above virtue. In an echo of the opening line (Cadiz to Ganges), Juvenal notes that, for Hannibal, Africa, Spain, the Pyrenees, and Italy were all too small; Hannibal's final goal was Rome, and his defeat and subsequent fate as a ''humble hanger-on'' are a delight to Juvenal, who revels in the fact that Hannibal is now only a fit subject ''to thrill young schoolboys / And supply a theme for speech-day recitations!''

This Hannibal-like hunt for glory at the expense of virtue becomes central to the second half of the satire, as Juvenal works towards establishing a positive ethical basis for his criticism of contemporary society. Glory, while it is most often achieved only with death, is prayed for by those who want it in this life. And here Juvenal turns his satire to the subject of death, as that which ''alone reveals the puny dimensions / of our human frame,'' in the hope of revealing to humanity the folly of its belief in (temporal) glory. Juvenal is too subtle to dwell at length on the horrors of death. Instead, to emphasize the futility of the desire for ''glory'' and temporal (as opposed to universal) virtues, he turns, in great detail, to the horrors of old age, the implicit rhetorical question being, what is the use of glory (or anything) achieved in this life when at the end of it we are faced with the decline that senility brings? For Juvenal, himself very likely approaching his later years when he wrote this satire, old age consists of many, mostly physical, symptoms of decline: wrinkles, toothlessness, lameness, dripping nose, trembling voice, impotence, deafness, blindness, sciatica, loss of appetite, and ''diseases of every type.'' Even if one were to survive reasonably intact bodily and mentally, Juvenal points out, the aged are left with the ordeal of burying both their own generation and their sons and daughters; here he produces examples of unhappy old men, such as Nestor, Peleus, and Paris.

Having constructed such a diabolical picture of what old age holds for humanity, Juvenal then flushes out those who might seek comfort in youthful looks or intelligence. In his inimitable way he produces a string of examples of those whose wit and eloquence have been their downfall, while he counters the attraction of young physicality by noting how apparently inevitably the young become sexually corrupted and embroiled in adulterous relationships.

Finally, and as the logical outcome of the disillusioning of what he sees as human presumptions, Juvenal asks, ''Is there nothing worth praying for, then?'' For Juvenal, prayer itself is a pointless exercise. ''Fortune,'' he says, ''has no divinity,'' and it is humanity alone which creates such a divinity. What we must live by, according to Juvenal, is ''virtue.'' While Juvenal never goes to any lengths to establish what his concept of virtue entails, we are very sure by the end of Satire 10 what ''virtue'' is not and what it is opposed to. This in itself, coupled with the wedding of the dichotomous Democritus and Heraclitus, is a step closer towards the establishment of a positive social and personal ethos in Juvenal than many commentators allow. And it is this reversion to a positive ethos which makes Satire 10 the most central and crucial of works in Juvenal's *oeuvre*.

—Colin Graham

SAUL
Play by Vittorio Alfieri, 1785 (written 1782)

Vittorio Alfieri's tragedy, *Saul*, is considered to be one of the dramatist's masterpieces, along with the equally famous work, *Mirra*. Respectful of the Aristotelian three unities of space, time, and action, the play is a testament to the author's concept of liberty. For Alfieri, liberty is more than a political ideal. It is the desire to give value and meaning to his life beyond the confines of death and destiny. Thus the individual affirms the personal dignity of his own spirit. The tragic hero, Saul, is the embodiment of these ideals. *Saul* is the only one of Alfieri's dramas to be drawn from biblical material. Enthusiastic after reading the Old Testament for the first time, the dramatist felt compelled to evoke the figure of the noble hero. Saul was forsaken even by God, but was not content to allow himself to be rendered impotent. His struggle in the face of great adversity rendered him fascinating to the poet. The biblical account on which Alfieri based his plot is contained in the *First Book of Samuel*, 9–31 and the *First Book of the Chronicles*, 10. The details of the story, of Saul are made more linear by the poet in order to underscore the psychological study of the protagonist. In a burst of creativity, the frenetic composition of *Saul* took place between April and September of 1782.

Saul, a great warrior of humble origin, has been anointed king by the high priest Samuel, and, as leader of the Israelite army, has achieved numerous victories on the battlefield. As his capacity as a leader increases, Saul gradually detaches himself from his ties of obedience to the priestly caste, revoking the ire of God. Samuel is ordered secretly to anoint as king a humble shepherd, David. The new king becomes the closest friend of Saul's son, Jonathan, and marries Saul's daughter, Michol. Although, initially, Saul loves David as another son, he soon becomes jealous of the young hero and begins to hate him. He persecutes David until the young man is forced into hiding in the enemy camp of the Philistine army. The tragedy takes place at Gelboa where Saul and the Israelite forces are encamped ready to affront an enemy attack. David attempts to reach the Israelite forces in order to help his people in the imminent battle. Alfieri's drama presents an astute psychological study of Saul's final day which ends in a military defeat and the protagonist's suicide. The tragedy takes place entirely in the Israelite camp at Gelboa.

Central to the tragedy is the powerful figure of Saul, who easily overshadows the three supporting characters of his children, Jonathan and Michol, and his enemy, David. Saul, the play's hero, is profoundly alone and, indeed, his only antagonist lies within himself. The spiritual complexity of the protagonist is the key to understanding the drama. The king is torn apart by an intense interior struggle between conflicting passions: his paternal love for Jonathan and Michol, his tyrannical desire for political and military power, the realization of his decadence, and a desperate desire to recover his youthful grandeur. He is overcome by remorse and disgust with the squalid nature of his old age. This explains his ambivalence towards David. Saul's hatred of David is provoked by envy, yet he loves the young hero as a son because he recognizes in David the grandeur of his own lost youth.

Saul is at once a tyrant and a hero: tyrant because he desires total control of every situation and a hero because, in the final scene, he finds the courage to overcome the errors of his past and recuperate once more his own human and royal dignity in death. In the final act of the tragedy, Saul's world disintegrates. Abner announces the enemy's victory and the death of the king's sons before fleeing himself. In

choosing suicide, Saul dies a hero. His death represents an act of protest and is a courageous affirmation of his own heroic desire for freedom. Saul's final words: ''Empia Filiste, / me troverai, ma almen da re, qui . . . morto'' V.v. (Vile Philistine, me thou shalt find, but at least a king.. . here . . . dead) show that in his choice of death he becomes master of his own fate. He dies in regal splendour, ''like a king.'' The play closes with Saul's moral victory, not only over the tangible, Philistine enemy, but also over the personal demons which torment him: in death, he recovers his dignity. Alfieri is known as a poet of vast emotions (''forte sentire'') and the struggles depicted in his portrait of Saul are among the most moving moments of his entire dramatic corpus.

—Jordan Lancaster

SCARLET AND BLACK (Le Rouge et le Noir)
Novel by Stendhal, 1830

Stendhal's first important novel, *Scarlet and Black*, was written in 1830, but ever cautious because of the tense political atmosphere, he disavowed any connection between the events of the revolution of that same year and the contents of his novel, which he realized some would see as subversive.

Although *Scarlet and Black* is based on the newspaper account of a young man who had been executed for shooting his estranged mistress, Stendhal retained only the bare outline of the anecdote for his novel.

Julien, the youngest child in a family of woodcutters, is despised and mistreated. He decides to pursue a career in the priesthood since his ideal, a military life in Napoleon's army, is no longer possible. So he studies Latin with a priest and memorizes the entire New Testament, which leads the mayor to hire him to tutor his children. Julien is glad to leave his family but soon concocts a hypocritical scheme to seduce the mayor's wife. Madame de Rênal is carried away by the handsome and passionate young tutor and abandons herself to a reckless affair that awakens deep emotions in her for the first time. When suspicions are aroused against him, Julien leaves for a seminary to which he has been recommended, but this life proves too confining for a person of such talent and ambition, so he leaves to become the personal secretary to a marquis. It is not long before Julien seduces the marquis's flamboyant daughter, and then to his dismay finds that she is pregnant. After great misgivings, the marquis consents to let Julien marry his daughter and obtains a lieutenant's commission for him, but he receives a letter from Madame de Rênal accusing Julien of depravity. In a final fit of passion, Julien returns to his hometown where he finds Madame de Rênal in church. He fires his pistol at her, sending her wounded to the floor. Although she does not die, Julien is executed for his crime.

Stendhal half-seriously claimed to have used the Napoleonic Code as a model for his writing style. He attempted to create a dry, objective style that would set him apart from the sentimental and rhetorical exuberance of Romantic writers like Chateaubriand. In *Scarlet and Black*, Stendhal's narrator regularly intrudes into the narrative to banter with the reader. He mocks Julien's naive outlook and makes fun of his failure to assess correctly the situations in which he becomes embroiled. In many ways, the narrator assumes the stance of a man of wisdom and experience who sits in sardonic judgement on a foolish youth. Furthermore, the flow of the narrative is so filled with interaction between various characters and with psychological insight into their feelings and motivation that we do not have to huff and puff, as one critic puts it, through a long narrative in anticipation of a distant conclusion.

Although Stendhal's writing is outside the Romantic school, Julien nevertheless is a sensitive and passionate young man of genius. He is handsome to a fault, persecuted and misunderstood by his peers, and seemingly carried away by a precipitous series of events over which he appears to exercise little control. These are characteristics of a Romantic hero, but Julien's conscious use of hypocrisy to advance his socially ambitious agenda moves him toward the model of a newer type of protagonist, one that is cynical and worldly in his efforts to exploit the weaknesses of a society that itself has grown hypocritical because of its overwhelmingly materialistic aspirations.

Stendhal's realism is obvious. His characters live in the easily recognizable world of Restoration France. The daring and excitement of the Empire are gone and its concept of glory has been replaced by a bourgeoisie bogged down in petty materialism. The year *Scarlet and Black* was published saw Louis-Philippe come to power as the oxymoronic "bourgeois king" whom Stendhal referred to as the most knavish of kings. This bridging of the gap between romanticism and realism has led to the comment that *Scarlet and Black* is a hyphen mark in the history of the French novel.

As he did with other novels, Stendhal ended *Scarlet and Black* with a dedication to his readers possibly taken from Shakespeare, "To the Happy Few." The phrase is an invitation to us to become one of his intimates, to share in those uncommon qualities of the human spirit that allow us to see beyond the petty concerns of society and to understand the elusive nature of genius. Just as Julien finally realizes how wrong he has been, we too, in solidarity with Stendhal and Julien, can glimpse the profound workings of the human heart and thereby become one of the "Happy Few."

—Gary M. Godfrey

A SCHOOL FOR FOOLS (Shkola dlia durakov)
Novel by Sasha Sokolov, 1976

A School for Fools is one of the most poetic, subtle, and intriguing Russian novels to be written in the second half of the 20th century. Published first in America, it appeared in English a year later and has now been translated into many languages.

The hero/narrator is a schizophrenic youth of 20 recalling his life some two years earlier at a school for backward children in a small settlement near Moscow. We follow his thoughts and aspirations via a rambling stream of consciousness, which frequently takes the form of a dialogue with his *alter ego*, moves imperceptibly between past and present, and switches equally imperceptibly to intercourse with shadowy, characters who may be either dead or otherwise completely inaccessible. Though a "fool," the narrator has a subtle and sensitive mind that frequently reflects on the elusive boundary between sanity and madness, and on the inconstant nature of time (the latter a theme throughout Sasha Sokolov's *oeuvre*). Memory is, as might be expected, highly selective, but the youth displays the normal adolescent craving for individual identity, status, and sex. Monolinear chronology is suspended in the novel, making it, like the blurring of distinctions between life and death (also a characteristic Sokolovian

theme), not only a theme but also part of the novel's structure, radically affecting the reader's understanding of what is going on and demanding the sort of close attention more usually accorded to poetry.

Sokolov describes himself as a "formalist," with a particular aversion to dialogue, and, indeed, conventional dialogue does play a minimal role in this novel. But from the very beginning there is frequent interplay between the two sides of the narrator's character as well as—in reported, often simply imaginary, form—intercourse with a variety of shadowy and changing figures, of whom the most important are an eccentric but inspiring geography teacher, Pavel (also known as Savl) Petrovich Norvegov, who conducts informal tutorials in sex and other life skills, and an elusive and idealized girl, Vetka Akatova, also seen as a station prostitute, of whose love the youth dreams constantly. On the other hand there are various symbols of repression, including his father who works as a public prosecutor, the petty headmaster of the school Perillo, his crippled witch-like assistant Sheina Solomonovna Trakhtenberg (aka Tinbergen), and the psychiatrist Dr. Zauze who seeks to make the hero's two voices one, promising "rest and freedom" but in fact seeming to threaten that freedom which only madness can confer.

Though the atmosphere of the novel is poetic, there is little description of appearances or surroundings as such: the novel's principal landscape is of the mind, a mind, moreover, whose claim to sanity is that the world is crazy. The narrative is discursive, impressionistic, and unamenable to objective analysis, though frequent hints and repetitions tempt one to seek a key, as does the high frequency of references, both intertextual and to other aspects of Russian literature, art, history, and, indeed, Soviet reality. Alongside non-linear time, madness is the novel's main theme, and the hero's schizophrenia is reflected in many forms, such as the recurrent mirror imagery and, most obviously, in the (often semi-anagrammatic) dual character names; the same phenomenon appears, less remarkably, in frequent punning and word play. Although the narrator's freedom is at one level a limitation, it is on the whole celebrated in this novel, which is dedicated to a mythical Vitia Pliaskin (Vitia Dance). In *A School for Fool*'s system of interrelated imagery, freedom is linked with whiteness, transparency, the wind, and, by extension, flight and escape, personified by Norvegov who is associated with the wind, or by Mikheev the wildly cycling postman.

The book is written in punctuationless, often alliterative rhythmical prose recalling such early Modernists as Joyce and Woolf or, perhaps, Faulkner. Sounds merge and echo in a hallucinatory manner not entirely unlike certain Russian folk cadences. Sokolov creates characters who are principally byproducts of the narrative structure rather than individual psychological entities. The novel's construction is unusual, with the second of its five chapters making a complete break in the narrative, such as it is, which resumes in chapter three. The second chapter, containing a series of miniature stories, may be seen as a kind of draft of the rest of the book's contents. Whether or not this structure is justified, it must be emphasized that Sokolov's first novel is a highly literary product, with three epigraphs, countless allusions to world literature, and the theme of writing and creativity running throughout; indeed, the opening words are a schizoid monologue on literary techniques, or at least on how to describe the settlement in which the school is located. There is nothing predictable or standard about *A School for Fools*, a truly original work by a leading Russian expatriate writer.

—Arnold McMillin

THE SEAGULL (Chaika)
Play by Anton Cheknov, 1896

The Seagull provided the occasion for the greatest trauma of Anton Chekhov's life, and for his greatest triumph. The premiere of the play, in St. Petersburg on 17 October 1896, caused his greatest trauma because the audience did not understand his dramatic innovations, and booed. Although subsequent performances went well, Chekhov withdrew the play and swore that he would never write for the theatre again. Fortunately for us, however, Vladimir Nemirovich-Danchenko, an experienced drama coach, persuaded him to let a new theatrical venture in Moscow stage the play. Nemirovich-Danchenko collaborated with Konstantin Stanislavskii to form the Moscow Art Theatre. Its production of Chekhov's play, which opened on 17 December 1898, proved a great success, and has become legendary. Its meticulous attention to detail, naturalistic acting, and ensemble work created an extremely influential theatrical style that continues to affect the performing arts today.

The series of interrelationships between and among two pairs of characters provides a key to understanding *The Seagull*. One of these pairs consists of a well-known actress, Irina Arkadina, and her lover, Boris Trigorin, an established writer. The other consists of two young people: Konstantin Treplev, Arkadina's son, an aspiring writer, and Nina Zarechnaia, an aspiring actress. A subtle interplay of tensions soon develops that involves all four characters. When Treplev hopes to gain some recognition from his mother by putting on an avant-garde play in which Zarechnaia has the only role, his mother feels threatened, and makes fun of the attempt. Treplev brings down the curtain, and stomps off in disgust. He later shoots a gull, and lays it at Zarechnaia's feet, stating that he will shoot himself in the same way. Zarechnaia, however, has attracted Trigorin's attention. He says that he wishes to get to know her, since he believes that he depicts young girls poorly in his stories. Arkadina quickly senses the attraction between the two of them.

Thus, emotions swirl among these characters in what Stanislavskii called "underground currents." They all seek fulfilment through love and art. Yet Chekhov has created the situation so cleverly that these professional and personal concerns merge for each of them. Thus Arkadina's vanity as an actress prevents her from giving her son the recognition (and money) that he needs. Trigorin's professional success and his role as Arkadina's lover make Treplev jealous. Trigorin's status as a celebrity initially attracts Zarechnaia to him, but then she falls in love with him.

Characteristically, Chekhov leaves these tensions unresolved. Between Acts III and IV, Trigorin and Zarechnaia have a love affair. He abandons her when she becomes pregnant. She has the child, who dies soon afterward. She then succeeds in finding work as an actress in a provincial theatre. These events, which Treplev summarizes at the beginning of Act IV, prepare us for he crucial final scene between Treplev and Zarechnaia. She returns briefly, just to be near Trigorin, whom she still loves. She advises Treplev, "Believe, and bear your cross." But this is just what he cannot do. Convinced that he has no talent (although he has started to publish short stories), unloved by his mother, and abandoned by the woman he loves, he shoots himself offstage. While Treplev has experienced actual death, Zarechnaia has experienced a metaphorical death. The giddy, naive part of her has died, and has been resurrected as a mature woman. In Zarechnaia, Chekhov thus presents a secular version of one of the great themes in Russian culture: death and resurrection.

An awareness of the relationship between *The Seagull* and *Hamlet* deepens our understanding of Chekhov's play. (Both works feature a play within the play; the characters in *The Seagull* also quote from *Hamlet* on several occasions.) Thus, Treplev corresponds to Hamlet, Zarechnaia to Ophelia, Trigorin to Claudius, and Arkadina to Gertrude. In each case, however, the outcomes are reversed. Hamlet does not commit suicide, but Treplev does; Ophelia commits suicide, but Zarechnaia does not. Claudius is a usurper and a murderer, but Trigorin is an authentic creator. Gertrude is implicated in Claudius' crime, but Arkadina is guilty of nothing more than vanity. Such intertextuality, or a relationship between texts that the audience needs to understand as part of the meaning of the work, appears very frequently in modern art, but no major playwright had ever used it before to create characters. In its blend of psychological subtleties and sophisticated intertextuality, *The Seagull* is that rare work—a play whose greatness was recognized in its time and that continues to hold the stage today.

—Jim Curtis

SEAMARKS (Amers)
Poem by Saint-John Perse, 1957

Seamarks is a long poem written in celebration of the sea, and, like all Saint-John Perse's poems, a song of praise. Its French title, *Amers*, denotes coastal landmarks which act as aids to navigation, and seems to combine the words *mer* (sea) and *amour* (love). The adjective *amer* (bitter) is also suggested, perhaps evoking man's thirst, his dissatisfaction with human limits. Throughout the poem, the sea is not only an immense and physical presence but also a reflection of the human soul striving for fulfilment. In a letter explaining the poem's theme (*Oeuvres complètes*), Saint-John Perse wrote: "I chose a march towards the Sea as an illustration of that wandering quest of the modern spirit, forever drawn on by the appeal of its own rebelliousness."

It is fitting that the high point of Saint-John Perse's work should come with a major poem in praise of the sea, a constant inspiration throughout his poetry, and the source of his unique metrical form. "Poetry for me," he said, "is, above all, of the Sea." Of all the great elemental forces that fill his work like great pagan deities, none can compare with the power, grandeur, and movement of the sea.

In its structure the poem imitates the form of the choral ode in classical Greek drama. The first part, the "Invocation," is a prologue addressed to the sea, in which the poet prepares himself for the task of mediating between the divine sea and earthbound humanity. Acknowledging the sea's power and majesty and "its reign in the heart of man," he extols its capacity for giving man's spirit access to a higher dimension and welcomes the sea itself as it comes to participate in the act of creation.

There follows the longest part of the poem, entitled the "Strophe," the word being taken in its etymological sense of "the movement of the chorus around the altar." It is here that the "drama" of the poem unfolds: the confrontation on the shoreline of mankind with the sea—a confrontation that will become a marriage alliance, consummated in the final section of the "Strophe." The scene recalls the Greek amphitheatre, with a semicircle of coastal towns facing the sea: "Tall Cities," impatient to seal an alliance with the sea, and "Low-lying Cities," effete and corrupt, still prisoners of the earth ("the ancient Sorceress"), yet not beyond the reach of the sea's appeal—"You made your way, laughter of the sea, as far as these haunts of the landsman.'' One by one, eight human representatives descend to the shore, as Perse puts it in his explanatory letter, ''for questioning, entreaty, imprecation, initiation, appeal, or celebration.'' First, the Navigator, an *alter ego* of the poet, whose role is ''to dream for you this dream of the real,'' beckons his followers to the ''Threshold of knowledge.'' Then come the Tragédiennes, who long to rediscover their essential femininity and whose rhythmic advance is accompanied by a ritual casting off of all their worn-out trappings of the drama and by a call for new works in ''a lofty style . . . which will come to us from the sea and farther than the sea.'' Next the Patrician Women appear, disillusioned by their aristocratic lives, to honour the sea and submit to its empire. They are followed by the Poetess (perhaps reminiscent of Sappho), a Prophetess, and a group of adolescent gifts, impatient for womanhood; all, in their different ways, speak of the promise of love, or the anticipation of fulfilment, the young girls concluding with the cry: ''And the man of the sea is in our dreams. Best of men, come and take! . . . .'' Their call is answered by the arrival of a Stranger who has been sailing close to the shore, his desire gently awoken in the calm of evening.

The long final section of the ''Strophe,'' entitled ''Narrow are the vessels,'' recounts, in the form of a dialogue, or antiphon, between two Lovers, a night of love: a ritual union between mankind and the sea. This magnificent, frank, and subtle celebration of the act of love has frequently been compared to the Song of Songs. It is a summer night and the Lovers are in a narrow boat, which becomes a metaphor for their marriage couch and the woman's body. The sea is not here the traditional female principle, for it embraces both man and woman, as does the image of the ship; they are married, as it were, to the very movement of the waters, to the movement of universal Being. However, once beyond their shared experience of transcendence, as the woman delights in her security beside him (''Laid at your side, like the car in the bottom of the boat: rolled at your side, like the sail with the yard''), the man becomes restless for departure and reassures her they will sail off together: ''Love and sea of the same bed, love and sea in the same bed . . . .'' A final canto finds them in winter, at home on the shore, protected in their love by the enduring presence of the sea.

''The third part, or 'Chorus','' Saint-John Perse wrote, ''brings together in a single movement and a single collective voice all this human exaltation in honour of the Sea.'' Man is now fully integrated with the sea, which is identified with the Absolute. Here the poem assumes its most incantatory, ritualistic form to embrace the sea in all its infinite diversity. The Poet, as Leader of the Chorus, celebrates the ultimate alliance, that of language and sea, which takes up to the heart of Perse's poetics: the supreme interpenetration of poet, text, and subject as in a ritual of transubstantiation. The poem closes with a brief ''Dedication,'' which acclaims the triumph of the creative enterprise.

Seamarks is a massive and challenging poem. With its rich profusion of polyvalent images, dense and elliptical, with its wealth of internal harmonies, its multiple patterns of rhymes, assonances, and alliterations, with its exalted tone, combining lyricism and litany, it is one of the most beautiful and rewarding poems in French literature. However such qualities make it extremely difficult to translate successfully and the English reader would be well advised to read the French original alongside Wallace Fowlie's English version.

—C.E.J. Dolamore

THE SECOND SEX (Le Deuxième Sexe)
Prose by Simone de Beauvoir, 1949

First published in 1949, Simone de Beauvoir's path-finding study of women's position in society has played a significant role in the founding of modern feminist studies. Attacked in its day by the Right (and blacklisted by the Pope) for its attacks on marriage and motherhood, her study has also attracted criticism for its unwitting sexism, as well as its underrating of the unconscious, from later feminist writers. *The Second Sex*, completed in less than three years and covering over 1,000 pages, is divided into two volumes, and synthesizes its author's extensive, interdisciplinary reading. As Elias Canetti does in an equally eclectic and expansive study *Crowds and Power*, de Beauvoir incorporates historical, social, anthropological, psychoanalytic, and literary studies.

The first volume, *A History of Sex* (*Les Fairs et les mythes*), deals with the ways that women have been prevented from seizing independent identities and destinies for themselves distinct from men's. In the same way that Canetti orders his diverse material around a central unifying argument, de Beauvoir argues throughout her work that woman's oppression lies with the apprehension of herself as Other to men. Her experience is not authentic in its own fight, always measured as it is against male achievements. In existentialist terminology, woman is constantly in a state of immanence (or, worse still, stagnation), as long as social organizations privilege man's experience, allowing him to find transcendence (positive vindication of being) in his actions. Throughout the work, de Beauvoir's arguments allow for a two-fold appraisal of women's consciousness, as they explain woman's position as inferior yet also look to possibilities of her liberating herself from such a fixed identity.

De Beauvoir sees this unequal state of affairs as not being predetermined. Sex may be fixed, but the manufacture of gender is fluid, for as she states in what became a rallying slogan—''One is not born, but rather becomes, a woman.'' To prove this point, de Beauvoir looks at three explanations of sexual difference, finding in them evidence for her contentions but also seeing each theory as not providing a complete answer. Looking at physiological views of women's behaviour, de Beauvoir shows that, although the female species is more tied to her biological functions than the male, this dependence on the body does not account for her secondary status throughout history. It was when hunting cultures developed and when male prowess in war and hunting was valorized that the child-bearing, home-based female began to be denied transcendence.

De Beauvoir then examines psychoanalytic ideas, and, although discovering much to explain how gender is perceived and formed, she is wary of adopting Freud's theories on female motivation, as they seem to be a modified version of male psychology. She further rejects the notion that sexuality is the main determining factor in behaviour. The last part of this section is devoted to historical materialism, with de Beauvoir arguing that people inhabit a historical reality in which a metaphysical idea of transcendence becomes material. While espousing this Marxist Existentialism (and supporting self-determination in a Marxist sense), de Beauvoir finds Engels' unwillingness to speculate upon how communal ownership changed to private property a serious failing. Having analysed these positions, de Beauvoir embarks on a succinct historical survey, providing a history of woman's Otherness (and her complicity in her subjection) from the Nomads to contemporary France, and showing how economic and legal institutions have fixed female aspirations.

With its weight of evidence, the final part of this first volume, that deals with how men have enshrined and vilified women in their myth-making, is much more impressionistic. De Beauvoir's evaluation of the images of women in five male authors (Breton, Claudel, Lawrence, Montherlant, and Stendhal) anticipates much work in literary studies almost a quarter of a century later, of which Kate Millett's *Sexual Politics* is one of the best known examples.

Nature of the Second Sex (*L'Expérience vécue*), which forms part two of *The Second Sex*, is a more personal appraisal of the social institutions that shape and limit female experience. De Beauvoir provides a very sensitive account of girls' development through childhood and adolescence, that looks forward to her own testament of youth, *Memoirs of a Dutiful Daughter*. She adds to her picture of female maturation by sketching in the various roles that women are coerced to adopt in adulthood. In particular, the so-called "natural" identities of mother and wife are sharply attacked for thwarting female liberation. In contrast, de Beauvoir reinstates lesbianism as "natural," arguing that women in their original attachment to their mothers are homosexual. De Beauvoir's account of female development moves finally to a typology of fixed identities, such as The Woman in Love, The Narcissist, and The Independent Woman. In her description of the last type, de Beauvoir speculates on women's liberation and challenges existing notions of "natural" behaviour, arguing forcefully that women must have control over production and reproduction, and that men and women must one day recognize each other as subjects, "yet remain for the other an *other*." To reiterate her plea for self-fulfilment, de Beauvoir includes in the French edition a description (missing from Parshley's English translation) of 50 remarkable French women, reclaiming them for history. Such an excavation of female achievement can also be seen in later feminist works such as Elaine Showalter's critical survey, *A Literature of Their Own* and Caryl Churchill's play, *Top Girls.*

While de Beauvoir's novels are characterized by an elegant, precise, and detached style, such as might be expected from a trained philosopher, it is a surprise that her major philosophical work is composed in a rather turgid and overembellished way. Many of the points that she makes in *The Second Sex* are further illustrated in her fiction, where she provides a practical demonstration of her philosophical conclusions, and shows how women's personalities and capabilities are diminished by the circumstances of their lives.

—Anna-Marie Taylor

A SENTENCE FOR TYRANNY (Egy mondat a zsarnokságról)
Poem by Gyula Illyés, 1956 (written 1950)

"A Sentence for Tyranny" was written in 1950, but was first published only in the "revolutionary" last number of *Irodalmi Újság* (2 November 1956). Its author, a poet with strong left-wing sympathies and a constant critic of the pre-war regime, acquired the status of an esteemed "fellow traveller" in postwar Communist-controlled Hungary. His plays and poems were by then published in mass editions, so Gyula Illyés's personal interests would have dictated loyalty rather than defiance to the Communist regime. On the other hand, the programme of rapid and costly industrialization, combined with the forced collectivization of agriculture and the Socialist Realist regimentation in the arts, created a situation in which the great

majority of the people came to resent the rule of the party-state. Illyés, who had often written poems on major social or national issues, now reacted to the loss of freedom of the individual with a forceful poem which illustrated the state's encroachment upon elementary human rights.

The poem was probably modelled on Paul Éluard's famous poem "Liberté" written during the French resistance to German occupation. It is, in fact, an extended sentence which through 49 rhyming stanzas describes the all-embracing nature of tyranny. It opens with a negative assertion:

> Where seek out tyranny?
> There seek out tyranny,
> Not just in barrels of guns,
> Not just in prisons. . .

These "not justs" and "not onlys" continue over a number of lines until we reach the statement that it is everywhere: "There, omnipresent, not / Less than your ancient God." Illyés proceeds to assert that tyranny penetrates all domains of life; it even enters love-making, for "you regard beautiful only that / that it has once possessed." Tyranny takes over the imagination too: one feels like an inmate in a huge concentration camp, in which the Milky Way represents a minefield and the stars spy-holes. Like Aleksandr Solzhenitsyn, Illyés sees the victims of totalitarianism as both "prisoners and jailers," so the conclusion, "Of tyranny's stench you are not free / You yourself are tyranny," is quite logical. The poem ends on a deeply pessimistic note: Illyés, having described all the characteristics of tyranny and of those tyrannized, now states that one is helpless in the uneven struggle with this monster—all is in vain:

> because it is standing
> From the very first at your grave,
> Your own biography branding,
> And even your ashes are his slave

> (translations by Vernon Watkins)

The poem, although ostensibly a denunciation of Stalinist Communism, was not reprinted in Hungary in Illyés's lifetime. It was, however, translated into most languages and is often referred to as one of Illyés's most memorable and emblematic poems.

—George Gömöri

SENTIMENTAL EDUCATION (L'Éducation sentimentale)
Novel by Gustave Flaubert, 1869

Gustave Flaubert's third published novel, the *Sentimental Education*, like *Madame Bovary*, is set in 19th-century France and, like the preceding *Salammbô*, may be considered a historical novel, covering in this case mainly the events between 1840 and 1851. The reign of Louis-Philippe, France's monarch since 1830, had become unpopular, and he was forced to abdicate by the revolution of February 1848. However, the revolutionaries found themselves in the minority after the elections of April, and when their four-day uprising in June in

Paris was defeated many of the democratic liberties granted by the constitution were suspended. The conflict between various liberal and conservative groups was inevitable. The succeeding Second Republic lasted officially until December 1852 but was shaken by the coup d'état of December 1851, when Louis Napoleon (Napoleon III, nephew of Napoleon I), who had been elected president in December 1848, was given the power to remake the constitution after an armed insurrection was violently suppressed by the military. In December of 1852 Napoleon was elected emperor and remained in power until 1870, the beginning of the Franco-Prussian War, a debacle, Flaubert claimed, the French would have avoided had they read carefully the *Sentimental Education.*

As usual, Flaubert studied this historical background extensively in preparing the composition of his novel, which required six years of writing from 1863 to 1869. But he also drew from personal experience, notably his youthful encounter in 1836 with a Madame Schlesinger, for whom he nurtured a romantic passion for years and whom he met briefly again in 1867. The *Sentimental Education*, then, serves the double purpose of a political and an emotional initiation novel or, rather, the parody of one, for during the course of the action Frédéric Moreau, the book's anti-hero and to a certain extent Flaubert's alter ego, is too immersed in his own social and amorous ambitions to understand the significance of the political events taking place and too timid, indecisive, and shallow to develop a lasting love relationship. Uncommitted in the end to either a woman or a political stand, Frédéric meets again, by chance, Madame Arnoux, for whom he had maintained an idealized romantic attachment from the beginning of the novel, but again fails to consummate the love affair and in the final episode, reminiscing with his friend Deslauriers in 1867 about an equally unsuccessful visit to a brothel in 1837, decides that this event of his adolescence constituted perhaps the best time in his life.

Thus, the action of the novel is divided between Frédéric's emotional adventures with several women and the larger political events, in which he is relatively uninvolved but which parody and are parodied by his own social ambitions. The novel begins, in a parody of the typical Balzacian plot, in which the hero leaves the provinces of Paris to seek his fortunes, by depicting Frédéric's departure from Paris for his provincial home in Nogent by river boat, which is also carrying Madame Arnoux. After languishing in the provinces, where some hope for his advancement is invested in the patronage of a Monsieur Roque (whose daughter will become one of Frédéric's romantic attachments) and in the possible inheritance from an uncle, Frédéric returns to Paris supposedly to study law but instead attempts and abandons in turn various vocations: writer, painter, orator, and politician. He introduces himself into the Arnoux household and becomes friends with Madame Arnoux's husband. He also meets the wealthy Monsieur and Madame Dambreuse, who offer respectively worldly advancement and romantic intrigue. But nothing develops, and Frédéric returns to Nogent to stimulate inadvertently the love of the young Louise Roque. Part One ends with the sudden announcement of Frédéric's inheritance and his departure again for Paris.

In Part Two Jacques Arnoux introduces Frédéric to the *demi-monde* of Paris and to Rosanette, who eventually becomes Frédéric's mistress while she is also conducting an affair with Arnoux. The famous scene of the masked ball initiates Frédéric into the pleasures of the capital's night world, but he soon appears with Rosanette in public even during the day and unfortunately is seen with her at the horse races by Madame Arnoux. Nevertheless, Frédéric and Madame Arnoux's platonic relationship continues until Madame Arnoux fails

to come to a prearranged meeting with Frédéric (because of the illness of her child). Frédéric returns once more to Rosanette, with whom he spends several days at Fontainebleau during the Paris uprising of June 1848.

In Part Three Frédéric establishes a liaison with Madame Dambreuse, the woman of high-class Parisian society, to satisfy his pride and ambition, but her imperious ways and her revengeful jealousy exhibited at the auction of the Arnoux household goods repulse Frédéric, who convinces himself that he sacrifices a fortune in leaving Madame Dambreuse for the sake of his devotion to Madame Arnoux. Rosanette is a partial cause of this rupture between Frédéric and Madame Dambreuse but seems to be the principal one in a previous misunderstanding between Frédéric and Madame Arnoux, who is insulted in her very home by Rosanette with Frédéric present. To console himself Frédéric returns to Nogent thinking of Louise Roque, only to arrive at her wedding with Deslauriers.

In setting this series of love affairs ending with the loss of Frédéric's illusions against a background of failed revolution and frustrated hope for democracy, Flaubert evidently wished to dramatize lives of emotional and political disillusion. Frédéric's indecision and shifts in amorous allegiances are paralleled by the many turns in the political stances and fortunes of the minor characters: Deslauriers criticizes all forms of government; Sénécal is anti-royalist but a supporter of an autocratic democracy; Regimbart rejects all general political principles: a revolution for change is followed by fear of change and repression of liberties. Just as Frédéric's love ideal, Madame Arnoux, appears in the end as a grey-haired old woman, or just as the epitome of sexual attraction, Rosanette, is glimpsed as a fat widow with a child, so other's dreams are lost or compromised for the realities of living: the bohemian Hussonet obtains a government job controlling the theatres and the press; Pellerin, the painter, becomes a photographer, for Flaubert a distinctly inferior sort of artist.

The *Sentimental Education*'s method of detached realism and its implied criticism of artistic and political romanticism and contemporary ineptitude perhaps account for the initial hostile reactions of the critics, but the later generation of naturalists admired it, perhaps too uncritically, and imitated it, albeit often unsuccessfully. For 20th-century writers like Joseph Conrad and Ford Madox Ford—who were sympathetic to Flaubert's methods of the impassive author, limitation of point of view, and irony, and to the concept of the anti-hero—*The Sentimental Education* was a model of style and structure.

—Nicole Mosher

SES PURS ONGLES TRÈS HAUT DÉDIANT LEUR ONYX
Poem by Stéphane Mallarmé, 1887 (written 1868)

Stéphane Mallarmé wrote, or began to write "Ses purs ongles très haut dédiant leur onyx" ("Dedicating aloft the onyx of her pure nails") under the title "Sonnet allégorique de lui-même" ("Allegorical Sonnet about Himself"), in 1868, when he was 26 and still trying to find his way as a poet. He finally published it, without a title and with a number of revisions of a relatively minor nature, almost 20 years later, in 1887, when he was at the height of his powers. In it Mallarmé defines, in oblique and symbolic fashion, the nature of the creative task he has set himself. A reading lamp in the form of an onyx statuette of a woman holding the candle between her uplifted fingers symbolizes, in its quasi-religious pose, the anguish of the poet, a Phoenix among men who, in the darkness at midnight, has burned in the candle flame the manuscripts of his unsuccessful attempts at writing poetry. There is no urn on the sideboard in the empty room to collect the ashes of these unfulfilled dreams, not even a sea-shell, for this trivial empty object in which the sound of the sea can be heard has been removed by the master of the room who has sorrowfully decided to end his life as a poet. Near to the window open to the north stands a gilt-framed mirror whose carved unicorns, in the flickering light of the candle, seem to be charging a water-nymph whose naked body has sunk beneath the lake-like surface of the glass. And in the emptiness of this mirror enclosed by its frame rise up the reflections of the seven stars of the constellation of the Great Bear.

The poem could be taken as being merely descriptive, but its original title, "Allegorical Sonnet about Himself," must be borne in mind as well as the kind of ideas Mallarmé is known to have had at the time he began to write it. He shared the dissatisfaction with reality felt by other Symbolist poets such as his immediate predecessor, Baudelaire, and his near contemporary, Rimbaud, but his approach to the problem was a much more rational and philosophical one. He conceded that beyond reality there lies an apparently empty void, but sustained by his conviction that an ideal word must exist and helped perhaps by being introduced to the work of the German philosopher Hegel, he concluded that the ideal world lies hidden in the empty void, that "l'infini (the infinite)" is contained within "le néant (nothingness)," to use two words that stand in opposition to each other in French much better than do their equivalents in English. The poet's task is to cut himself off from all contact with reality, to create a kind of void within himself into which the ideal forms of the infinite world concealed within the apparent emptiness beyond reality can then flow. In the light of these ideas there is no doubt that the empty room of "Ses purs ongles" is symbolic of the poet's mind, emptied further of that symbol of emptiness in that the lamp is used for a destructive purpose and the mirror reflects and redoubles the emptiness around it. Throughout the first 13 lines of the sonnet Mallarmé thus emphasizes and re-emphasizes the notion of a total void. Then, in the very last line, there is a sudden and magical change as, in the blank surface of the mirror, rises the symbol of the infinite, the huge constellation that dominates the northern sky beyond the room. Into the poet's mind therefore, emptied of all reality, the ideal world has flowed or, as Mallarmé had put it more prosaically in a letter written in 1867: "Je suis maintenant une aptitude qu'a l'univers spirituel à se voir et à se développer à travers ce qui fut moi" ("I am now a means whereby the spiritual universe can become visible and can develop through what was once me").

In this key poem Mallarmé also gives some indication of the lines along which he was working in order to create what he called elsewhere "l'absente de tous bouquets" ("the ideal flower absent from any real bouquet"). For example, the constellation of the Great Bear is never actually named, nor is even the word "star" ever used, so in a sense it is not the seven stars of the Great Bear that appear at the end of the poem but seven sparkling points of light created by Mallarmé; seven ideal stars, one might say, absent from any real sky. Furthermore, not only does he offer the visual image of a constellation mysteriously appearing in an empty room, but he conveys a similar impression by auditive means in that the rhyme scheme is based exclusively on the two rhymes "ix" and "or," the one being the phonetic transcription in French of the letter "x," the generally accepted symbol of the unknown, and the other having as its primary

meaning "gold," the generally accepted symbol of the ideal world. Nor is this constant alternation between "ix" and "or" the only antithesis between "le néant" and "l'infini" in the poem. The flame of the reading lamp can destroy but it can also help to create; the term "Phoenix" suggests someone ultimately rising victorious from the ashes of his own destruction, as Mallarmé was indeed to do; an empty sea-shell contains within it the sound of the infinite sea. So throughout the poem the reader is insistently persuaded from all angles, semantically, auditively, and through a range of images, that "l'infini" is contained within "le néant."

To use all the resources of language in this extraordinarily involved way, not for the banal purpose of describing an already existent reality, but in order to conjure up nonexistent ideal forms, to be truly creative, was clearly a daunting task which Mallarmé, not surprisingly, was never to complete. But in the course of his long and patient struggle to do so he produced a number of poems which rank not only among the most ambitious and most complex in French literature but also among its finest achievements.

—C. Chadwick

THE SEVEN AGAINST THEBES (Septem contra Thebas)
Play by Aeschylus, 467 BC

The Seven Against Thebes is the first known treatment on the Greek stage of the Oedipus story and its aftermath. It formed the last part of Aeschylus' Theban trilogy. Of the first two plays, *Laius* and *Oedipus*, almost nothing survives.

The play is set in time of war and its atmosphere is martial. Aristophanes in *The Frogs* (*Batrachoi*) describes it as "a drama full of Ares." Thebes is under siege. Polynices, seeking to oust his brother Eteocles, the king of Thebes, is leading an army of select champions recruited in Argos against his native city. The two brothers are under a curse invoked by their dead father, Oedipus.

For most of the first three-quarters of the play Eteocles occupies and dominates the stage. He is there at the start as commander-in-chief, addressing his people and giving battle orders. A scout arrives and describes the enemy's forces, how they have assembled outside Thebes and how the seven champions have sworn a great oath either to take the city or die in the process. Eteocles chastises and calms the panic-stricken Theban women who form the chorus.

At the play's core is a sequence of seven pairs of speeches delivered by the scout and Eteocles. In his speeches the scout reports the presence of an enemy champion at each of Thebes' seven gates, giving extensive descriptions in epic style of the warrior and of his shield. Eteocles replies and in each instance allocates a Theban to defend the gate. Of the seven attackers, only the seer Amphiaraus is god-fearing and modest. He is there against his will and only with reluctance lifts an embargo on the continuation of the enterprise, reporting Apollo's oracle prophesying its failure. The others are boastful and overbearing in their behaviour. The emblems on their shields reflect their characters and intentions.

The staging of this scene remains a matter of controversy. It is not clear whether the Theban champions are present on stage and despatched at the end of each of the first pairs of speeches, or whether we are to suppose that they have already been assigned to their posts. In his seventh and final speech the scout reveals the identity of the attacker at the seventh gate. It is Eteocles' own brother, Polynices. At this point Eteocles recalls the curse upon the family and sees its fulfilment in the horror that awaits him. He ignores the chorus's pleas not to fight his brother and leaves the stage prepared to face him in mortal combat. There follows a memorable ode in which the chorus reflects on Oedipus' curse and on the troubles of the three generations of the family of Laius, introducing in the second stanza the memorable and characteristically Aeschylean image of Iron, ''the stranger from the Chalybes,'' as a kind of legal figure, dividing up the legacy of Oedipus and leaving the brothers just enough space to be buried in. A messenger arrives with the news that Thebes is safe and the invaders have been defeated. The good news is tempered with bad. The two brothers have killed each other. Their bodies are brought on and the chorus divides to deliver a song of ritual mourning for each.

At this late stage of the play as we have it a new theme is introduced. A herald announces a ban on the burial of the traitor brother Polynices. An altercation breaks out and the play ends with dissension and a threat of trouble to come. It is generally agreed that the topics of the refusal of burial to Polynices and the threat to defy the ban have been introduced by a later writer or producer anxious to incorporate material from Sophocles' *Antigone* and Euripides' *Phoenissae*. There is room for disagreement about the extent of the interpolator's activity in the last quarter of the play. It is very likely, however, that Aeschylus' play ended at line 961 with the conclusion of the ritual lament of the divided chorus. The manuscripts and some scholars introduce Oedipus' daughters Antigone and Ismene into the last scenes of the play. This was certainly not Aeschylus' intention and probably not the intention of the man who composed the new ending.

The Seven Against Thebes is an impressive and densely poetic play. The interpreter is hampered by the loss of the two opening components of the trilogy to which it belonged: analogy with *The Furies* warns us how many echoes and cross-references we are likely to miss. We would undoubtedly have a clearer understanding of the development and resolution of themes within the trilogy if we possessed even a little of the first two plays. The exact details of Oedipus' curse on his sons cannot be reconstructed from this play alone. One aspect of the play as it stands does emerge clearly enough, although critics have been slow to recognize it: Eteocles is one of the most striking personalities in Greek tragedy, and the manner in which he confronts his fate is truly tragic.

—David M. Bain

SEVENTH DUINO ELEGY (Duineser Elegien, VII)
Poem by Rainer Maria Rilke, 1923 (written 1922)

The seventh of Rainer Maria Rilke's ten famous *Duino Elegies* represents a critical turning point for Rilke's vision of the poet. In it Rilke realizes that he has been seeking the wrong objective in pursuing the transcendent realm. The poet's function is, Rilke comes to understand, not transcendence but transformation (*Verwanglung*). Rilke arrives at this epiphany by a somewhat circuitous route spanning the ten years (1912–22) of the *Elegies*'s poetic composition.

Rilke explores the angelic and human realms in the *Elegies*, moving in the ten poems from an early focus on the divine realm and its powers through a series of reflections and models until he arrives,

finally, back in the realm of the humanly possible. Rilke constantly backtracks to issues he cannot settle as long as his eyes are focused on the other-worldly realm. For Rilke this interior journey becomes an exploration not only of his own individual role, but of the poet's role in general. His ruminations in the *Duino Elegies* dramatize the construction of a poetics as well as an ontology.

In the first elegy, Rilke sets himself the problem of how to approach the transcendent realm represented by the angels. How can man, limited by his self-conscious state, attain the angels' realm of all encompassing super-consciousness? Rilke proposes several models for escaping the self-conscious state. First, he contemplates children and those who die young, who are not yet trapped in self-consciousness; second, the hero, who bypasses paralysing self-consciousness to move directly into action; and finally, lovers, particularly unrequited lovers, who have moved beyond isolated consciousness toward a larger unity with another consciousness (the beloved) or with consciousness at large if the love is unrequited.

Each of these categories, however, falls short of the ultimate goal of transcendence. Children grow up. Heroes are too unique to represent a general strategy for those who are already burdened with self-consciousness. Lovers frequently have the misfortune of being loved in return or the distraction of sexual urgency (explored in Elegy III) or the constant distraction of longing for the beloved, of future expectation.

After spending the majority of the first six elegies exploring the limits of these various categories of possible access to the transcendent realm, Rilke turns in the seventh elegy to an entirely different perception. He comes to understand that it is not the grand gesture of hero or lover that ameliorates self-consciousness, but rather the small, familiar interaction of our isolated consciousness with objects in the world. The event that takes place between consciousness and object, the duration created for the physical by means of consciousness, is what we can use to call to the angels. Children already know this secret but forget it. The poet must relearn the lesson in the course of the first six elegies so that he may realign his perceptions in the seventh.

In the seventh elegy, the speaker reverses the entire direction of his activity. What had been an attempt to call the angels in the opening lines, what had been summons or wooing becomes, by the end of the seventh elegy, a demonstration and celebration of the human condition, a rejoicing that praises the world of man to the angels. The speaker stops yearning for and pursuing transcendence and turns rather to the process of transforming the physical world within his consciousness. The poet discovers in the seventh elegy that one can escape solipsism by participating in the physical world, by transforming the physical world, by passing it through his own consciousness.

Once the poet recognizes that he has the power of rescuing objects from time and decay by transforming them within, his task becomes one of praise and accomplishment of such transformations. The poet can now show the world to the angel. He can reveal to the angel something that the angelic realm cannot perceive because of the physical world's discrete divisions and boundaries, which the all-encompassing consciousness of the angels does not recognize. The poet ceases his attempt to join the angels and accomplishes, because of his limits, something they could not.

In Elegy VII the poet discovers his task to be one of transformation, not transcendence. He discovers he can sing the living, the physical and limited world, that ''Hiersein ist herrlich'' (''Being here [in this physical world] is magnificent''). Human culture, architecture, religion, music and art, and the transformation of the physical world by human consciousness, has always had the power to create a kind of human transcendence. The finite world becomes the task of the poet and his gift to the angels. Now the angel is asked to praise human beings rather than the other way around: "O du Grosser, erzähls, dass wir solches vermochten, mein Atem / reicht für die Rühmung nicht aus" ("O you great one, tell of it, that we are capable of such things, my breath is not adequate to the praise").

In Elegy VII, Rilke sees as futile what took to be his poetic task as the *Duino Elegies* began, that is, the reaching of the transcendent realm. He has acknowledged that the isolated self-consciousness can never attain transcendence. In the course of this elegy, however, he has discovered how to proceed beyond that isolated self; he has discovered the ability to transform consciousness and world by having them interact in the poetic image. Thus the poetic task is the creation of an aesthetic space in which the image takes on meaning far beyond what the self alone can provide. The poetic image, like the cry of the bird uttered in the opening lines of this poem, is taken up by a larger forces of existence.

The angel will always remain "Unfasslicher" ("the ungraspable one"). But the poet can attract the angel's attention by revealing to it the transformed images of a newly created poetic space. In this elegy Rilke substitutes a realizable and fruitful poetic project for a futile one. He can now turn to the angel to verify his powers of transformation rather than looking at the angel for some sort of personal salvation.

Elegy VII represents an epiphany for the poet; he realizes that a pure poetic voice will grow beyond the personal and therefore will outgrow wooing the angel. He realizes that interaction with the world of objects and physicality, and not flight or pleading, will produce protection from solipsism. The poet radically shifts his focus from the transcendent realm to the earthly realm, to "Hiersein." Rilke decisively changes his poetic aim from that of transcendence to that of transformation of and within the physical world. He steps away from the realm of the angels and back to the realm of man. This enables him to affirm human existence even to the angels and moves him much closer to a geocentric and anthropocentric poetics. The final three elegies reaffirm this epiphany.

—Kathleen L. Komar

SHI NAIAN

See WATER MARGIN

THE SHIP OF FOOLS (Das Narrenschiff)
Poem by Sebastian Brant, 1494

Sebastian Brant's *The Ship of Fools* is a didactic-satirical work, originally written in German verse and was first published in Basle in 1494. It consists of a prologue and 112 short chapters, almost all of which deal with a particular kind of fool or manifestation of folly considered by Brant to be prevalent in the society of his day. His gallery of fools is extraordinarily varied: some merely display a tendency towards unwise or immoderate conduct (such as those who follow ostentatious fashions in dress [chapter 4], or who devote themselves to unprofitable study [chapter 27]); whereas others are unequivocally sinners (each of the medieval Seven Deadly Sins is for

example cast by Brant as a form of folly). What all of Brant's fools have in common, however, is a lack of accurate self-knowledge, combined with a failure to take account of the fact that they will die and be judged. For him, folly is at root a misguided attitude, but one which must inevitably lead to improper and ultimately sinful behaviour. Nevertheless, except in the case of certain irredeemable fools (such as heathen, heretics, and suicides, discussed in chapter 98), it can be overcome: if a fool attains self-knowledge and begins to live in the light of his own immortality, he can in time become wise and, eventually, inherit eternal life. It is precisely this process that *The Ship of Fools* seeks to initiate. As Brant states in both his prologue and his last chapter, he intends that his work should act as a mirror, into which a fool may look and, in so doing, recognize his folly and reform his behaviour accordingly.

Such a concept of folly owes much to medieval perceptions, most notably in the close parallel Brant draws between a fool and a sinner; but his proposed solution, with its implication that an individual can redeem himself without the intervention of the Church, or indeed even of Christ, is strikingly unmedieval. Like several other aspects of the work, it reveals the unmistakable influence of Renaissance humanism.

Brant does not present his fools to the reader in any obvious order; and this, along with his failure to exploit the narrative and structural possibilities of the notion of a ship of fools, has led certain critics to charge his work with lacking an overall plan. Nevertheless it is given a degree of unity not only by the all-embracing theme of folly, but also by the fact that, as a general rule, the layout of the individual chapters is consistent. In the original edition (and in some subsequent reprintings), the first page of each chapter, generally a verso, contains its title along with three or four-line motto and a substantial woodcut; and the remaining text of the chapter is printed on the facing recto. Furthermore the argument within chapters is often developed along similar lines: the initial motto tends to be followed by a brief definition or discussion of the folly involved, and then by a series of quotations or exempla, drawn primarily from Biblical or classical sources.

The woodcuts, which are reproduced in the English translations of both Edwin H. Zeydel and William Gillis, are of great interest. Their quality is for the most part remarkably high (it is generally accepted that as many as two-thirds of them were executed by no less a figure than Albrecht Dürer), and they are clearly viewed by Brant as an integral part of the work. Indeed, his prologue expresses the wish that those who are unable or unwilling to read his text might none the less be able to recognize and amend their folly simply by looking at the pictures. Given that numerous woodcuts do not obviously depict the folly that forms the subject of the accompanying chapter (several for example illustrate proverbs or exempla referred to in passing in the text), and indeed that some six woodcuts are used twice to illustrate quite different follies, this is surely an unrealistic hope; nevertheless the woodcuts do in most cases confirm, and in some cases indeed add to, Brant's didactic message. Moreover, the arrestingly humorous touches many of them display form a welcome complement to the somewhat relentless moralizing of much of the text.

Although it has been regarded by several modern critics as a work of only mediocre quality, *The Ship of Fools* enjoyed quite extraordinary popularity among Brant's contemporaries, and throughout the 16th century. It was not only enthusiastically lauded by his fellow humanists, but was clearly also read by an exceptionally wide range of people: no fewer than 16 German editions were published between

1494 and 1519, and already by 1500 it had been translated into Latin, French, and Dutch. Furthermore it was referred to, quoted from, and preached on by an enormous number of late 15th- and 16th-century authors.

There were no doubt many reasons for its success. Intellectual humanists were presumably attracted to its extensive use of quotations from classical literature and of Ciceronian rhetorical techniques, as well as to features such as Brant's comments on contemporary politics (notably in chapter 99) and his consistent, if often only implicit anti-clericalism. At the same time, the work's generally simple language, its widespread use of well-known proverbs, its largely traditional (medieval) rhyme scheme and metre, and above all its woodcuts, plainly made it palatable to a wider audience. Above all, however, Brant's concept of folly must have struck a chord with many who, perhaps like the author himself, felt confused or threatened by the complexity and instability of an age in which the medieval and early modern worlds converged. An approachable vernacular work that described countless contemporary follies, but reduced these to a readily comprehensible common denominator and prescribed for them an apparently straightforward remedy, must have seemed like the answer to many prayers.

—Nigel Harris

SHUIHU ZHUAN

See WATER MARGIN

SIDDHARTHA
Novel by Hermann Hesse, 1922

Siddhartha is set in India, but the background is not described in any detail, the plot is minimal, characterization is restricted, and no date is given for the action. The eponymous hero, whose (Sanskrit) name means "he who has achieved his aim," is portrayed in a lifelong quest for the ultimate meaning of existence, and for a way of living which will provide self-realization. An Indian atmosphere is created by means of an "oriental" pastiche, a complex and consistent attempt to render the feel of Sanskrit in German through formalized, liturgical structures and full exploitation of the lyrical possibilities of prose rhythm. The many influences outside those from India include Chinese thinkers, the German Romantics, and Carl Jung, who analyzed the author in the course of the novel's composition.

The novel is short, and consists of two separate parts—although the underlying structure, like so much else in this work, is triadic. The first part (four chapters) describes the background of Siddhartha as the son of a Brahman, his breakaway from the religious inadequacies of home, and his wanderings in the forests with an ascetic sect. Failing to find his goal, he visits Gotama, the Buddha, but is disappointed by the Great One's teachings and so resolves instead to discover his innermost self. Awakening for the first time to the beauty of the world, Siddhartha now embarks (in Part II) on a completely different lifestyle: for the next four chapters we see him experiencing the world of the senses through a long relationship with a beautiful courtesan; tasting growing professional success and power as the assistant of a

wealthy merchant; learning to gamble recklessly; and finally experiencing self-disgust as a result of excess. Recognizing this life as an elaborate form of game, the disillusioned hero returns (for the final four chapters) to visit the ferryman who had earlier brought him across the river to this world of "childlike adults." He stays with the ferryman, learns from him, and finally takes over his work in a humble capacity of service to his fellow men. Towards the end he is visited by his former mistress and their son; the former dies and the latter scorns his simple ways and gentle teaching, preferring to run back to life in the city. Siddhartha follows him, but then realizes that his son must find his own way to fulfilment, just as he himself had done in his own repudiation of the world of his father. His final visitor is a form of "shadow," an old friend from his youth, who has been on a comparable lifelong search and who has chosen to follow the teachings of Buddha. Govinda has failed to discover his goal within the confines of traditional religious striving, but recognizes that Siddhartha has done so in his simple life of service at the river.

That river itself serves an important symbolic function. Siddhartha, as ferryman, helps people to cross the water which separates the city, the outer world of extroversion, superficial excitement, and wild pleasures, from the introverted, lonely, and ascetic world of forests and mountains. Siddhartha has himself crossed that river twice in the course of his search, and he has managed to reconcile those two worlds and attitudes which the water divides. He goes on learning how to consolidate this insight by observing the old ferryman's life, by listening to the river, and by discovering a different attitude towards time. In his final dialogue with Govinda, he enumerates some of the insights he has gained. These include the idea that for each truth the opposite is equally true; that excessive searching—as practised by Govinda—is self-defeating and that to "find" is, paradoxically, "to be free, to be open, to have no goal." One must simply love and enjoy the world in all its aspects, and Govinda's final vision of Siddhartha's face is in fact an experience of universal metamorphosis, of a streaming river of faces of all time and all emotions, all the manifestations of life which Siddhartha has managed to accept. Govinda leaves him seated in the perfect position of the contemplative, which suggests serene universal insight into the whole of creation, immersion in life, and mystical identity with it. Nevertheless, although Siddhartha may have reached the highest state of wisdom, he is unable to communicate its essence to Govinda. For another of his realizations is that although knowledge may be communicable, wisdom is not.

Of all Hermann Hesse's novels, this is the work in which it is clearest that form is a part of meaning. The novel is borne along on a strong rhythmic current, on what seems an undertone of chant. All harsh sounds are avoided, while there is much alliteration and assonance. We find frequent use of parallelism in clause structure; repetition of individual words; anaphora; constant apposition. There is regular omission of the definite article, and sentences often open adverbially or adjectivally. The threefold repetitions, corresponding to the tripartite structure of the work, may create a liturgical aspect which is reminiscent of the Bible, but the language is not really Biblical but rather that of Pali, the language used in the canonical books of the Buddhists. At points this language can achieve something of an incantatory effect but for the most part it reflects the serene, balanced attitude of meditation, the object of which was described by Hesse as "a shifting of the state of consciousness, a technique having as its highest aim the achievement of pure harmony, a simultaneous and uniform functioning together of logical and intuitive thinking.'' Hesse regarded the speeches of Buddha as a model in this respect, and it is these he is emulating in *Siddhartha*. His success in this respect may in part be judged by the remarkable sales of the novel in India, where it has been translated into eight different languages.

—Peter Hutchinson

SILENCE (Chinmoku)
Novel by Endō Shūsaku, 1966

The novel *Silence* by Endō Shūsaku has been subject to a barrage of interpretations by a variety of critics. Most seek to account for the perceived illogicality of a self-confessed Catholic author selecting as the ostensible focal point of his novel the act of apostasy performed by his protagonist, the Portuguese missionary Rodrigues. Having insisted on entering the country in deliberate violation of the anti-Christian edicts that were being so ruthlessly enforced in Japan at the time (the early 17th century), Rodrigues's decision, following his inevitable capture, to renounce his God and all that his life to date has stood for has been widely condemned in the Japanese Christian community as an act of heresy. How, it is asked, could such a writer justify depiction of his protagonist succumbing to the repeated demands of the shogunate authorities to place his foot on the image of Christ attached to a crucifix (the *fumie* that was traditionally employed by shogunate officials as a means of rounding up those who clung to the outlawed faith)? Similarly, there have been those who have viewed Rodrigues's increasing despair at the apparent ''silence'' of God towards those who clung tenaciously to their faith in the face of the cruellest torture and death as evidence of a fundamental absence of faith within Rodrigues from the outset. Finally, from the ''traditionalist'' camp has emerged the suggestion that at the core of the novel lies the belief, expressed in the work by Rodrigues's mentor Ferreira (a man whose reported apostasy had seemed so improbable to his former students that they had determined to travel to Japan to investigate the truth of these rumours), that Japan was a ''swamp'' in which the roots of the ''sapling of Christianity'' were destined to ''rot, the leaves to grow yellow and wither.'' To such critics, *Silence* is a novel concerned primarily with the irreconcilable gap, both spiritual and cultural, between the East and West.

All such interpretations appear to be amply supported by an analysis of the first eight chapters of the novel. Significantly, however, the novel does not finish with Rodrigues's act of renunciation. The protagonist may emulate Ferreira in accepting a Japanese name, a wife, and a residence in Nagasaki, courtesy of the very authorities who have driven him to apostatize; however, Endō is at pains to stress in the brief concluding section that, for all his outward capitulation, inwardly Rodrigues is ultimately possessed of a faith more real and more profound than that which has inspired him to risk all in embarking on his mission to Japan in the first place. The distinction between Rodrigues before and after his decision to trample on the *fumie* is therefore significant. The early Rodrigues is fired by an impressive enthusiasm to rescue the abandoned believers in Japan and possessed of the vision of an omnipotent and omniscient God that appears sufficient to equip him with the resilience required to defy all the physical pain his fellow man can inflict upon him. Concomitant with his increasing concern at the perceived silence of God, however,

is the development of an inner hope that, paradoxically, he can acknowledge only at the moment of greatest despair. As he stands confronted by the image of Christ on the *fumie*, and as he recognizes there not the powerful image of beauty of European tradition, but the face of a man ''who quietly shares our suffering,'' so there is born within him a faith of a new dimension, a recognition that God, far from being silent, had spoken through His silence. From a theological standpoint, therefore, there can be no justification for the Christ on the *fumie* to break his silence to the despairing Rodrigues with the words, ''Trample! I more than anyone know the pain in your foot . . . It was to be trampled on by men that I was born into this world.'' From a literary perspective, however, this is the moment of catharsis. Endō's depiction of the scene is reminiscent of Rembrandt's ability to portray a shaft of light shining through the darkness. Thus, although Rodrigues's assertion in the immediate aftermath of his outward apostasy that ''Lord, you alone know that I did not renounce my faith'' may appear unconvincing at the time, by the end of the novel Endō is able to depict his protagonist agreeing to hear the confession of Kichijirō, the very man who has betrayed him, Judas-like, to the authorities, confident in the knowledge that ''even if he was betraying his fellow priests [for hearing a confession as an apostate priest], he was not betraying his Lord. He loved him now in a different way from before.''

With this one dramatic image—and with his protagonist's ultimate recognition that ''Our Lord was not silent; even if he had been silent, my life until this day would have spoken of him''—the focus switches from the physical act of apostasy to the psychological process that underlies this decision. At the same time, however, in highlighting the erosion of the distinction between Rodrigues, initially established as symbol of a ''powerful,'' ''Western'' faith, and the sly and ''weak-willed'' Kichijirō, this denouement represents a challenge to the received wisdom of the ''strong'' martyr and the ''weak'' apostate. To Kichijirō, the dilemma has always been acute, for as he argues, ''One who has trodden on the sacred image has his say, too. Do you think I trampled on it willingly? My feet ached with pain. God asks me to imitate the story, even though He made me weak. Isn't this unreasonable?''

But it is only at the very end that Rodrigues comes to recognize that whereas the ''strong'' martyrs suffer physical pain, the ''weak'' apostates are condemned to a life of psychological pain. The concept represents a constant refrain in Endō's corpus, and it is thus significant that the choice confronting Rodrigues in *Silence* is not simply that between martyrdom and apostasy: throughout the novel, the only torture to which the protagonist is subjected is psychological —the cruel threat that refusal to trample on the *fumie* will result, not merely in Rodrigues's martyrdom (an eventuality to which he has long since sought to reconcile himself), but in that of the Japanese peasants who, despite their own personal apostasies, are still subjected to torture in the ''pit,'' their destiny entirely in Rodrigues's hands. Again, the notion that, under the circumstances, the act of martyrdom can be seen as more selfish than agreeing to bear the pain of apostasy for oneself is heresy to the theologian. As author, however, Endō is not assessing the validity of either option: rather, by suggesting that, in the face of torture, both represent two opposing images of life, each involving equal anguish, he succeeds paradoxically in merging these two opposites into alternative expressions of the same concept—that of human love.

The novel *Silence* can thus be read as an attempt at demarcation of the proper terrain for the author of fiction. Inspired to write the novel by the chance discovery that historical records concerning the mission work of Giuseppe Chiara (the model for Rodrigues) cease abruptly in 1632, and interpreting this as evidence of Rodrigues's apostasy (and consequent rejection by the mission), Endō proceeds to reconstruct various "facts" about Rodrigues in an attempt to highlight a more profound "truth" behind these facts. In so doing, and in placing the emphasis firmly on the inner growth occasioned in his protagonist as a result of his gradual renunciation of his earlier pride and heroism, Endō here succeeds not only in plumbing ever deeper into human psychology, but also in hinting at the possibility of reconciliation of seeming incompatibilities that remains the hallmark of his subsequent literature.

—Mark Williams

A SIMPLE HEART (Un coeur simple)
Story by Gustave Flaubert, 1877

"A Simple Heart" is one of the three short stories that constitute the last work published by Gustave Flaubert, *Three Tales*. The tales have been criticized as a reworking of previously published material. "A Simple Heart" demonstrates a kinship with *Madame Bovary* in style and setting, while "The Legend of Saint Julian the Hospitaller" ("La Légende de Saint Julien l'hospitalier") and "Herodias" echo *The Temptation of Saint Anthony* and *Salammbô* respectively. However, upon its publication, *Three Tales* was immediately and unanimously acclaimed as Flaubert's latest masterpiece. The literary establishment at large may have been making up for its previous misjudgement of other, more important works of Flaubert's by loudly endorsing this new volume by the ageing master.

Three Tales has survived the test of time thanks in great part to the stylistic mastery displayed by Flaubert. These short stories are now widely recognized as representative of his entire literary production. None of the three is more marked by Flaubert's personal life and acute sensitivity than "A Simple Heart."

This is how Flaubert himself described the tale: "Just the account of an obscure life, that of a poor country girl, pious but fervent, discreetly loyal, and tender as new-baked bread. She loves one after the other a man, her mistress's children, a nephew of hers, an old man whom she nurses and her parrot. When the parrot dies she has it stuffed, and when she herself comes to die she confuses the parrot with the Holy Ghost. This is not all ironical as you may suppose, but on the contrary very serious and very sad. I want to move tender hearts to pity and tears, for I am tender-hearted myself." Flaubert's goal has certainly been achieved, for the portrait of that "simple heart" may well be the best expression of his sensitivity.

"A Simple Heart" is the story of Félicité, a servant whose destiny it is to be sacrificed. A country girl whose fiancé finally married a rich old woman, Félicité finds employment in Pont-l'Évêque, in the house of Madame Aubain, where she spends the rest of her life. Up at the crack of dawn, she is in charge of everything in the house, especially the two children, Paul and Virginie. Once, she even protects her mistress and the children from a charging bull, barely escaping a fatal goring. Her devotion to her work and others knows no limits. She also takes care of Victor, her nephew who happens to live nearby and whose family exploits Félicité's kindness. He becomes a sailor, and she, unable to understand maps, can only imagine the exotic places he visits, while she spends months waiting for news. One day, she is told abruptly of his death. Soon thereafter, little Virginie, always a weak

child, dies of pneumonia, and Félicité spends two nights at the side of the dead young girl. Félicité, whose "heart [grows] softer as time [goes] by," continues to tend the sick: people with cholera, Polish refugees, finally a lonesome dying man. With Paul now living in Paris, the house is a sad and mournful place, and the two ladies, mistress and servant, age side by side.

Afflicted by deafness, Félicité devotes herself to Loulou, a parrot Madame Aubain received as a gift. When the animal dies, Félicité follows her mistress's advice and has it stuffed. Upon Madame Aubain's death, Félicité remains alone in the run-down house with the parrot. Confusedly identifying the bird with religious symbols, she sees in the stuffed Loulou a representation of the Holy Ghost, and "[contracts] the idolatrous habit of kneeling in front of the parrot to say her prayers." As Félicité finally dies, the Corpus Christi procession passes below her windows. At her request, Loulou, now broken-winged, partially rotten, and eaten by worms, has been placed on the top of the procession's altar. The conclusion of "A Simple Heart" describes her final vision: "And as she breathed her last, she thought she could see, in the opening heavens, a gigantic parrot hovering above her head."

It is true that in the simple, provincial atmosphere of "A Simple Heart" one finds reminders of *Madame Bovary*. But in this story, Flaubert's restrained style, painstaking attention to detail, finesse of psychology, and emotional tact combine to create a touching portrait of a character who by traditional standards would be deemed insignificant. Flaubert projected into his tale much of his experience and feelings, and scenes of his beloved Normandy.

Beyond Flaubert's emotional goal of "moving tender hearts to pity and tears," the reader should not overlook the social critique implied in the callousness and selfishness of Madame Aubain's bourgeois society, a concern reminiscent of the *Sentimental Education*, and of Emma Bovary's own self-centred life. For instance, upon receiving the news of Victor's death, even Félicité is moved to criticize: "It doesn't matter a bit, not to them it doesn't." In an attempt to comfort Madame Aubain, who has been expecting news of her daughter for four days, Félicité states that she has not heard from Victor for six months. Not only does Madame Aubain show total ignorance of her servant's beloved nephew, but, adding insult to injury, she exclaims: "Oh, your nephew," with a shrug "that [seems] to say: 'Who cares about a young, good-for-nothing cabin-boy?'"

Félicité's ironic name foregrounds Flaubert's depiction of suffering and misery. Happiness, or at least one way to it, lies with the creation of one's personal myth. While some critics have looked for irony in the final confusion between parrot and Holy Ghost, it is in this apparent identification that Félicité attains her blessed and blissful status, as an admirable saint wholly devoted to others, despite their selfishness, greed, or other defects, and regardless of her own acknowledged stupidity. (Often her mistress would say: "Heavens, how stupid you are!" and she would reply: "Yes Madame.") This lay sainthood creates a link with the second tale, "Saint Julian the Hospitaller," which shares with "Herodias" a longing for less materialistic and more mythical times. In this respect, the three tales are united, and present a composite picture of Flaubert's own literary myths.

"A Simple Heart" is the most stylistically sophisticated of the *Three Tales*. It also serves as a poignant and effective introduction to Flaubert's creation.

—Pierre J. Lapaire

SIRENS (Sirene)
Poem by Giuseppe Ungaretti, 1933 (written 1923)

''Sirens'' is a short poem written in 1923, which is part of Giuseppe Ungaretti's second major volume of poetry, *Sentimento del tempo*. In its cultural and intellectual concerns, the poem marks a clear break with Ungaretti's earlier verse, which focused primarily on his experiences of World War I. Nevertheless, Ungaretti's tendency to deal with the abstract and the inner man in his early work (indeed throughout his poetry in general) is also clearly a bridging point.

The theme of ''Sirens'' is poetry itself, or rather, the process and the meaning of writing poetry. This is not evident immediately, either from its title or from a first reading of the text, and in this we see the first signs of Ungaretti's hermeticism as well as his abstractness (which underlies descriptions of physical objects and landscapes too). A note provided by the poet himself in which he defines the addressee of the poem, the ''Funesto spirito'' (Deadly spirit) of the opening, serves as an indispensable tool in interpreting the verses: ''E' l'ispirazione . . . è la musa sotto forma di sirena'' (It is inspiration . . . it is the Muse in the form of a siren). Perhaps the fact that the poem gains in meaning from the clarification of a note represents a weakness; however, it underscores the dependence of Ungaretti's poetry on symbolism and allusion.

In ''Sirens'' the poet is an ambivalent victim of his Muse. In this context, the poet becomes a Ulysses figure drawn along by the song of his own words. The poem itself, in its arrangement on the white sea of the page, assumes the significance of the ''isola fatale'' (fatal island) on which the Greek hero-poet might flounder, seduced by the sound-appearance of what the island-poem seems to be. The dialectic terms of ''Sirens'' are based on combinations of opposites such as the love, or excitement, which the Muse both inspires in the poet but which also causes him concern, or the impression he has of reaching his Ithaca of final meaning or reconciliation (that island) which only proves, however, to be a mirage. The seafarer-poet travels on a metaphorical sea of thoughts that both reveal and disguise the teasing presence of his island-home, that home being the resting place for all his restless, dissatisfied thinking.

The writing of the poem coincided with Ungaretti's move in 1921 from Paris to Rome. The baroque qualities of Rome, its intricate architectural splendour and its religious, spiritual aura, both aroused and baffled him. It set him thinking along the lines of contrasts and dualities, particularly with reference to the notion of death as represented in Michelangelo's works that incorporated the thematic contradiction, as Ungaretti saw it, of terrible justice (seen in the Sistine Chapel's Last Judgement), but also of great compassion (seen in the Pietà's sacrificial figure of Jesus). These two (Christian) aspects of death are present, by implication at least, in the final lines of ''Sirens'' in which Ungaretti seems to speak of death not only as the inevitable, or imposed, cessation of all passionate exploring, all restless thinking, but also as the moment of completion or fulfilment, almost of homecoming, leading to some ultimate revelation. In other words, if there is a terrible, objective justice that terminates legitimate human anxiety (the search for meaning), there is also, for believers, the chance of being cured (finding the Answer). Thus, ''Sirens'' is a poem that carries religious implications, without being a religious poem in any orthodox sense of the term.

For Ungaretti poetry was always a search for the religious. This is implied only abstrusely in ''Sirens'' but stated explicitly in his retrospective notes to the volume *Sentimento del tempo*:

Occorre considerate . . . l'uomo in preda, nel medesimo tempo, all'esaltazione della propria infallibilità fantastica di facitore, e al sentimento della precarietà della propria condizione . . . due aspetti . . . della vita, che è creazione e distruzione, vita e morte. Che cosa poteva essere la poesia se non la ricerca inesausta e mai approdata a soluzione del motivo di tutto ciò?

(It is necessary to consider . . . man as contemporaneously a victim of his own glorified and fantastic sense of infallibility and a victim of the sense of his own precariousness . . . two aspects . . . of life, which is creation and destruction, life and death. What else could poetry be if not the endless search for the unknowable answer to all of this?)

''Sirens'' is a poem about the inner struggle to know.

—Walter Musolino

SIX CHARACTERS IN SEARCH OF AN AUTHOR (Sei personaggi in cerca d'autore)
Play by Luigi Pirandello, 1921

The first performance of this epoch-making play took place in Rome on 10 May 1921 and caused a furore. Audience, actors, and critics fought on stage (those who had not left before the end). When the play was performed in Milan only months later, anger and condemnation were replaced by wild enthusiasm, and throughout the 1920s it gained the support of audiences and critics and was translated into many languages, conquering the theatrical ''capitals''—London and New York in 1922, Paris (in the famous Pitöeff production) in 1923, and (in Max Reinhardt's sophisticated production) Berlin in 1924. *Six Characters* had changed the course of theatre history.

The play, set in a theatre, critically examines and dissects an audience's assumptions about what theatre is. It relates the reality of life to the artifice of art form. It discusses illusion and reality, the tragedy of modern man's failure to communicate; it calls into question our sense of identity or of self, and dramatizes the subconscious.

Six stage characters—a father, mother, son, stepdaughter, and two small children, a boy and a girl—erupt on to a stage and interrupt rehearsals to impose their urgent, vibrant, and intensely-felt story upon a theatre company. The director (producer, in Luigi Pirandello's day) and actors are bowled over by the force of the characters' passionate need to relive their tragic story and to communicate what their author had been unable to finish. The father had forced his wife to live with another man (for reasons that are obscure—he merely claims that they were better suited). His son was brought up in the country, while his mother longed for him. When the mother's lover died, she returned from abroad with the children of her second liaison, and the father met the mother's daughter in a brothel and recognized her. They were then discovered by the mother. Predictably, the reconstitution of the original family causes problems of guilt and confusion, culminating in the death of the children, the withdrawal of the son into an implacable silence, and the stepdaughter's hatred. This compellingly tragic story is all the more tragic because unactable: the actors can never project the intensity of lived emotion felt by the characters and the characters complain ceaselessly that they do not do so. The referee (the producer) descends into the pathos of uncomprehending slogans, the refuge of non-comprehension, since the business of theatre is not life: ''One can't have this sort of thing on the stage. . . .''

Pirandello throws the two realities—the ghosts of real-life family tragedy and pathos, and the fiction of actors impersonating roles—on to the stage at the same time. The characters wear masks (appropriate to their fixed and unchanging roles): they confront the artifice of the theatre and clash with it. The planes of reality so created overlap and merge (as when the leading actor flirts with the stepdaughter), and the traditional spatial distinctions of theatre become blurred (characters enter from the auditorium). There is no curtain: a stagehand with a hammer begins the ''action,'' and there is a constant contrast between life relived in all its formless chaotic intensity and the ''worn-out apparatus of theatre, with its mechanisms, tricks, and routines, and its members—the actors and the director.''

This formula produces an ironic parody of naturalism in the insistence of the characters on the literal accuracy of every movement, gesture, and intonation of the actors—they strive for life itself (not theatre) until, at their insistence, life itself is born on stage: Mme. Pace is ''called into being'' by the urgent necessity of the father and the stepdaughter to re-enact the seduction scene. It is as if the tragedy is so moving that it produces the figure of Mme. Pace herself from the accurate reconstruction of her setting in her shop, complete with the hats and coats of her trade. Just as dreams and hallucinations have solid reality for those affected, so the fiction of the stage gives birth to a very three-dimensional reality, and Pirandello's play makes the imaginative leap towards the absurd, towards Ionesco and the theatre of the later 20th century: ''which actress will be able to present Mme. Pace like this?'' asks the Father. ''This here *is* Mme. Pace,'' is the reply.

In the end the dichotomy between theatre and life is intractable. Pirandello's *Six Characters in Search of an Author* meditates on a whole range of very modern 20th-century preoccupations: on identity and self, on communication, on the artificiality of everything we do that is ''theatrical''—and not least on the theatre itself, on impersonation, on the masks we all wear in different contexts, and on the deep-seated problems of the human psyche, our conscious and unconscious minds, as well as contemporary feelings about the family unit. No other modern play, perhaps, has opened so many doors on the modern consciousness.

—Christopher Cairns

THE SLEEPWALKERS (Die Schlafwandler)
Novels by Hermann Broch, 1931–32

Hermann Broch wrote his trilogy, *The Sleepwalkers*, between 1928 and 1932. It is an experimental work of extraordinary intensity both in its thematic concerns and in its stylistic complexity. Its central metaphor refers to an essential state of profound disarray: traditional values prove ever more ineffective in the search for individual orientation and in sustaining the established institutions, and no values have yet been found to satisfy the different needs of a new social order. Man's quest for self-assurance within communal bonds is therefore guided by spurious precept and deceptive promise, his irrational mind incapable of genuine experiences and thus groping to find spiritual security in various compensatory obsessions. Broch, in

essence, sees the cause of all modern catastrophes in the disintegration of a premodern hierarchy of religious verities. His trilogy portrays what he considers to be the final phase of an accelerating decline into chaos, which he seeks to illustrate through a variety of emblematic situations.

Three years (1888, 1903, and 1918), which occur during the reign of the last German emperor (Wilhelm II), are exemplified in the life stories of three main characters (the Junker Joachim von Pasenow, the petty bourgeois accountant August Esch, and the upstart businessman Wilhelm Huguenau), who represent three distinct patterns of psychosocial behaviour with its value system and sense of existential identity (romanticism, anarchy, realism). These concepts, somewhat at variance with their accepted definitions, signify attempts to control the perplexities of life in three different ways: through recourse to anachronistic conventions, in aggressive outbursts of sexual and religious sensuality, and with unscrupulous egotism.

Broch's fictional programme includes an astounding variety of narrative devices. They range from the speculative abstractness of a ten-part excursus on historical cognition and the disintegration of values to a form of Platonic dialogue, from parabolic tales to hymnic poetry, and from realistic descriptions to phantasmagoric inventions. This stylistic diversity supports an ever-expanding constellation of symbols and motifs, of carefully orchestrated variations, cross-references, reprises, and allusions. Especially in the second half of book III, this fictional technique reveals a compulsive tendency to construct systematic order, if not harmonious closure. The novel's structure thus anticipates, surely not inadvertently, that ''mystery of unity'' toward which its principal characters can only grope with unfulfilled longing.

Broch's narrational attitude, while often opting for the immediacy of homiletic appeals and a rhetoric of ecstatic enchantment, alternates between didactic satire, resigned irony, and analytical naturalism. What epistemological persuasiveness it loses through its fixation on a monocausal theory of history, it regains in the subtle elaboration of psychological insights. This suggests that the figure of Eduard von Bertrand, a successful cotton broker and entrepreneur with a lucidly critical mind, refined sensibilities, and a profound aversion to any social doctrine, is the pivotal character of the trilogy, even though he does not directly appear in its third part. His self-conscious nihilism with its graceful rejection of all intellectual and emotional illusions can only end in suicide after Esch, the fanatical agitator for social justice, had inveighed, in a scene of surrealistic intensity, against his effete withdrawal from the responsibilities of life. But his death also exemplifies the novel's implicit argument that such a reduction to nothingness must precede the spiritual renascence to come, which makes Bertrand also a precursor of the next historical era.

None of the other characters share his freedom from obsessions. Joachim von Pasenow, after a clumsy though liberating affair with a bar dancer, clings to the strictures of feudal convention when his brother's death in a duel ''for their family's honour'' necessitates his return to the ancestral estate. He must now marry a woman of his own class, Elisabeth Baddensen, who loves Bertrand, while he is still emotionally attached to the ''exotic'' foreigner Ruzena. As he turns his wife into an icon of purity, he himself becomes an ever more rigid paragon of patriotic provincialism. By contrast, the unemployed accountant Esch, a person of ''impetuous attitudes,'' tries to bring order into a life of erratic upheavals and to rectify the universal ''bookkeeping error'' created by industrial capitalism. His milieu is the workers' quarters along the Rhine between Mannheim and

Cologne with their stolid propriety and with their tawdry amusements. He carries his outrage at the many small injustices perpetrated against the underclass (e.g. the shabby treatment accorded the vaudeville artist Ilona and the harassment of the union organizer Martin Geyring) with missionary zeal but he succumbs more and more to the irrational conviction that all the world's ills result from the irresponsible practices of industrialists like Bertrand. Inevitably, his various efforts to promote freedom from abuse fail, and his goal of spiritual redemption recedes into a haze of hallucinations. Both his plan to emigrate to America and his hope of experiencing a mystical transformation through marriage (to a middle-aged tavern keeper, Mother Hentjen) are disappointed. As Esch slides back into obscurity, the deserter Huguenau assumes paradigmatic relevance. He imposes his control over a small town in the Mosel valley where a senile Pasenow serves as garrison commander and Esch owns the local newspaper. Driven by egocentric compulsions and free of moral restraints, the footloose Huguenau is a ruthless opportunist, a rapist and murderer, and the only one to profit from the impending revolutionary destruction of the old order. But the story of his career is only one section within a kaleidoscopic sequence of similarly parabolic tales, e.g. that of the young lieutenant Jaretzki, an alcoholic amputee, or that of Hannah Wendling, the case study of a genteel woman with social ambitions who ends in suicidal loneliness, or that of the bricklayer Gödicke who rebuilds his life after having been buried alive in a trench, and, perhaps most significantly, the improbable love story of the Salvation Army girl Marie in Berlin and the Talmudic scholar Nuchem.

The Sleepwalkers is a work of high intellectual ambition. Its complex fictional structure, the rigour of its moral concerns, and its psychological acuity make it one of the last outstanding examples of expressionist prose. It is also a major document of that cultural pessimism that was prevalent among liberal-conservative intellectuals during the 1920s. Exacting and of emphatic precision as Broch's philosophical temperament was in chronicling the decline of German (and Austrian) bourgeois culture and society, he had at best an uncertain vision of the future. In response to the competing ideological programmes that had gained currency after 1900, the conclusion of his trilogy projects no more than the utopian potential of Platonic idealism and of Paulinian spirituality. This reveals a deeply ambivalent disposition that is both driven by the dynamic of progressive modernism and tempered by the need for retrospective assurances.

—Michael Winkler

SLOVO O POLKU IGOREVE

See THE TALE OF THE CAMPAIGN OF IGOR

SNOW COUNTRY (Yukiguni)
Novel by Kawabata Yasunari, 1937, complete edition, 1948

Snow Country is not a long novel. It comes close to falling into the inconvenient range of the novella, hardly long enough to be a book and too long to be a magazine piece. Yet it was some 13 years in the writing. Between 1935 and 1937 Kawabata Yasunari published several related fragments in several magazines. None carried the title

Snow Country, which was assigned when, in 1937, with some revision, the fragments were brought together in book form.

There was no indication that the work was not finished. Then in 1940 Kawabata added another chapter. In 1946 and 1947 he attempted conclusions, and in 1948 the work was finally published as we have it. The ending could hardly be called conclusive. One of the three principal characters is caught in a warehouse fire, and we do not know at the close of the action whether she is alive or not. That was the way Kawabata worked. The list of clearly incomplete Kawabata works is impressive, and one could seldom be sure that an apparently completed work was in fact that.

Kawabata was a good literary critic, and good at characterizing his own work. The scenes and situations that interested him, he said, were ''islands in a distant sea.'' The first island was the Izu Peninsula, a mountain chain extending into the ocean some 60 or 70 miles southwest of Tokyo. Then came the Asakusa district of Tokyo itself, the chief entertainment district of the city between the two world wars. For Kawabata it was a place of homelessness. Then came the ''snow country,'' the districts west of the central mountain range of the main Japanese island, a place of dark winters closed off by storms from Siberia, and of hot-spring geishas who came close to being social outcasts.

The heroine of the novel, Komako, an ardent, passionate woman, is a geisha at a hot spring in the snow country. The hero, Shimamura, is a Tokyo dilettante who does not seem committed to much of anything at all. He is drawn to Komako, but knows that, after one of the sporadic visits that are the occasions for the action of the novel, he will leave and not return. So it is about a love that cannot be fulfilled.

The third major character, she who gets caught in the fire, is a strange, distant, beautiful girl who seems to hover on the edge of insanity, and for whom, even if she survives the fire, it is as difficult to expect real happiness as it is for Komako. Shimamura will probably make his last departure for Tokyo unblemished and unchanged. That is because he is incapable of love from the outset.

Loneliness, coldness, and the impossibility of love are at the heart of Kawabata's writing. In Japan and the West they are both old and modern themes. The sad circumstances of Kawabata's childhood make them intensely personal: he lost his parents and only sister in early childhood, and the grandfather who reared him, insofar as he was reared at all, when he was 14. From adolescence Kawabata was alone.

The lyricism of Kawabata's writing is so strong as to approach poetry. Much is ambiguous, much is left unsaid, much is said in a peculiar fashion. The opening lines of the book version of *Snow Country* are probably the most famous in modern Japanese literature. A train emerges from a long tunnel into the snow country, and ''the bottom of the night'' turns white. Many a reader of the translated text has had trouble with a simile likening Komako's lips to a pair of leeches; but that is what the original says, and the simile is every bit as eccentric in Japanese as in translation.

—Edward Seidensticker

THE SNOW QUEEN
Story by Hans Christian Andersen, 1845

''The Snow Queen'' is one of the most striking and original, and the longest, of Hans Christian Andersen's fairytales. It is though, in some ways, atypical. This is most obvious in its peculiar structure, consisting of one long story formed by seven shorter tales. As the individual stories would make little sense on their own, these divisions seem at first to be entirely arbitrary. Closer study reveals that they serve to divide the action, like a dream (and like many traditional fairytales), into a series of "moves." Each move offers a new narrative and a new scene to deal with previously established themes and symbols.

In terms of plot, "The Snow Queen" is the story of the search by a little girl, Gerda, for her friend Kay, who has been seduced from his home by the Snow Queen. Through this outward task Gerda is launched on what becomes an inner quest to strength and maturity. At the climax of her journey, her kiss redeems little Kay from the Snow Queen's physical and spiritual imprisonment, symbolized by a lump of ice in his heart. Both may then return to the known world they have left behind, whereon they find they have reached adulthood.

In thematic terms, "The Snow Queen" is generated by the opposition of two principles. The story plays continually with the interaction of these two principles, and of the symbols that represent them. The first is the summer principle of joy and sacrificial love, symbolized by the rose, by tears, and by the colour red. The second is the winter principle of evil, cold calculation, and spiritual death. It is symbolized by the Snow Queen, by snow and ice, and by the colour white. The polarization between these two forces, and the moral values they carry, is made apparent early on in the tale when we are told that in summer the rose bushes formed a bridge between the children, but in the winter the snow divided them. Shortly after, Kay issues a challenge to the Snow Queen: "Only let her come . . . I'll set her on the stove and then she'll melt." The Snow Queen does come but, far from conquering her, Kay is drawn captive into her queendom, first inwardly, then outwardly.

Searching to find Kay again, Gerda is at first drawn away from him into the heart of the opposing queendom, symbolized by the colour red. Throughout the tale, the clothing and nakedness of Gerda's hands and feet take on unusual prominence: on her departure from the Princess's bedchamber she has acquired "not only boots but also a muff," and it is her red shoes which lead her to the red house. There she falls under the benign spell of a good witch, is fed with cherries, and sleeps in a bed "with red silk pillows embroidered with coloured violets, and she dreamed as pleasantly as a Queen on her wedding day."

The witch's garden is stocked with beautiful flowers. Gerda converses with seven of the flowers, and subtle symbolism threads through their apparent nonsense. While Gerda learns nothing about little Kay from them, each flower's tale contains a hint or glimpse of her own destiny. The narcissus tells of a girl half undressed, discovering herself; the convolvulus of a maiden waiting for her knight; the hyacinth of three sisters, the last clad in white, who, while beautiful, are dead; the tiger-lily of a Hindu woman, clad in red, burning herself for love; the buttercup of a holy kiss which turns everything to gold; and the snowdrop, of a burst bubble. The flowers themselves, and their tales, each reflect an aspect of the climactic scene of Kay's redemption. When Gerda has listened to each of their tales she is inwardly prepared. At once she finds the summer has gone and she must seek Kay in the winter world of the Snow Queen.

The world she enters is a bare, fantastic landscape of castles and wastes of snow. Like a dream the tale shows an almost infinite capacity for creativity within its established symbols. Rose and snow undergo the magical transformation of their form into another substance, creating strange and beautiful harmonies. Beneath Kay's magnifying glass snowflakes appear as roses of ice; in the Princess's

Palace the flowers appear inwrought into the furnishings: "Over the centre of the floor two beds, each resembling a lily, hung from a step of gold. One, in which the princess lay, was white, the other was red."

That Andersen is interested in the unconscious mind is demonstrated even within the story. In the palace Gerda finds herself mysteriously transposed in "inner," psychic, space where the shadowy forms of the sleepers' dreams throng around her.

This magical world that at once represents the worlds "within and without" has a profoundly different atmosphere from the enchanted but familiar feel of most of Andersen's other tales. It is a truly fantastic realm, embodying elements of psychic experience in symbolic form. It is a spiritual landscape, conveyed at times in ecstatic prose: "Over them flew the black screaming crows and above all shone the moon, clear and bright—and so Kay passed through the long winter's night, and by day he slept at the feet of the Snow Queen."

Gerda's journey has the same unearthly quality, lit by the quivering red fires of the Aurora Borealis. The apocalyptic landscape has a mythic quality far exceeding the normal writ of fairytale. Like the confused letters of ice which at last spell the word "eternity," and like the glittering immensity of the Ice Palace itself, it seems to stem from a visionary realm. In this realm, the things of the spirit, like the Princess's dreams, take on a visible form. As Gerda prays, her breath freezes in the cold air, and her words take on living shapes, turning into angels.

The harmony between the worlds within and without is maintained, unbroken, to the tale's ending. As they make their escape from the domain of the Snow Queen it becomes summer and Kay and Gerda, having been tried, tested, and saved, can take on adulthood.

—Edmund Cusick

THE SOCIAL CONTRACT (Du Contrat social)
Prose by Jean-Jacques Rousseau, 1762

Jean-Jacques Rousseau is often considered to be the father of the modern state. Written in 1762, *The Social Contract* is his principal treatise on the political foundations of the modern state and is possibly the most significant of his writings. Taken frequently by critics to contradict the thought of Rousseau's other political treatise *Emile*, they are nevertheless complementary in that both deal with the problems of freedom.

The Social Contract begins with the now famous statement, "Man is born free; and everywhere he is in chains. One thinks himself the master of others, and still remains a greater slave than they" (I, i), a conception of human nature that was a central tenet of Romanticism. Rousseau was convinced that humans are social beings by nature and that they have sympathy towards others: and yet without institutions of government, social life appeared to lead to oppression and slavery. Rousseau recognized that in human development from a state of nature there comes a time when it is necessary for individuals to join and to form a society. He sought to answer the central problem of how to combine the certain advantages of the state of nature with those of the social state, to balance individual rights with the general good:

> The problem is to find a form of association which will defend and protect with the whole common force the person and goods of each associate, and in which each, while uniting

himself with all, may still obey himself alone, and remain as free as before. (I, vi)

His solution lay in perceiving the need for the concept of the social contract.

Through the social contract, the individual subject submerges itself within a larger structure: in fact, it demands "total alienation of each associate, with all its rights, from the whole community" (I, vi). Rousseau summarizes the social contract in the following manner:

> Each of us puts his person and all his power in common under the supreme direction of the general will, and, in our corporate capacity, we receive each member as an indivisible part of the whole. (I, vi)

It is only through such an abrogation of individual rights that universal rule can emerge. The essential basis for Rousseau's political doctrine in *The Social Contract*, is that the only "legitimate rule of administration" is expressed in the inalienable, indivisible, and absolute rule of the popular will.

Rousseau attempted to free politics from egotistical desires and impulses, to give free reign to the general will. The general will ("volonté générale") is the linchpin and the most disputed part of Rousseau's theory. He argued that people need to distinguish between their individual will and the general will in order to attain the common good. Thus, paradoxically, people ought to surrender their rights and freedoms to the sovereign (which might be the people themselves), in order that they may become freer than previously. Political institutions exist to achieve the common good, and participating via the social contract people will share in the common good, so becoming freer. In other words, theoretically the greater structure expresses what the people want. In place of "natural rights," one receives "civil rights," since all rights must rest on convention and consent. Majority rule appears as the prevailing order and "whoever refuses to obey the general will shall be compelled to do so by the whole body" (I, vii), to the extent that "This means nothing less than that he will be forced to be free" (I, vii).

The result of the contract is the establishment of the "sovereign" when "active," and the "state" when "passive," whose life is entirely the manifestation of the agglomeration of its members. The sovereign power is indivisible and inalienable, and officers of the state have a conditional conferral of power from the general will to which they must remain responsible. Thus, renouncing one's liberty and deferring to the sovereign is an act of self-transformation, the creation of a new political subject, in which "each man, in giving himself to all, gives himself to nobody" (I, vi). This eradicates the possibilities for injustice and inequality, and liberates the individual from the restrictions of his or her individual being, to find a truly social experience in collective equality with subjects who accept the same ideal.

The law, as the expression of sovereignty and as the act of the general will, is of vital importance to the destiny of the status. For this reason, the legislator has a significant role within *The Social Contract*, invested with a remarkable, near-divine quality. For it is from the legislator that the subject "receives his life and being" (II, vii), experiencing a true transformation of his life, forsaking the "physical and independent existence nature has conferred on us all" (II, vii) for a moral existence as a social being.

Rousseau was no liberal though, since he clearly did not separate the individual from the state. To protect the establishment of the social contract, at the end of the final draft of *The Social Contract*, Rousseau proposes an even more powerful sanction to ensure total political stability: he introduces a form of civil religion of "civil profession of faith" (IV, viii), to which all subjects must acquiesce upon punishment of death.

All these ideas are what Rousseau proposes as the ideal political state. However, the doctrine has its dangers. One of the principal problems quickly becomes how to define the common good and the general will. Critics, like Bertrand Russell, have been quick to point out that it invites an identification of the general will with some individual's conception of it, and there lies the road to totalitarianism. However, *The Social Contract* remains one of the most important documents of political and social theory, despite the ambiguous fact that it inspired both the liberal Kant and the conservative Hegel, and in addition, formulated the principles by which the despots of the French Revolution reigned in terror.

—Tim Woods

SOME PREFER NETTLES (Tade kuu mushi)
Novel by Tanizaki Jun'ichiro, 1928

Some Prefer Nettles, like a great deal of modern Japanese fiction, is autobiographical. But unlike much modern Japanese literature, which is so thinly disguised as fiction that it scarcely seems fiction at all, at least to the alien reader, in *Some Prefer Nettles* the characters are skilfully and forcefully drawn, and independent of the author.

The central crises clearly derive from Tanizaki Jun'ichiro's own experience. They concern opposing cultural pulls and a marriage that has no reason to continue but does so all the same, neither party having the strength of will to dissolve it. Tanizaki was over 40 when he wrote and published it in 1928. A native of Tokyo, he moved to the Osaka-Kobe region after the great earthquake of 1923; the principal characters are also natives of Tokyo who have taken up residence near Osaka. The husband, Kaname, has been drawn strongly to things Western and keeps company with a Eurasian prostitute, Louise, who plies her trade in the cosmopolitan city of Kobe. The mercantile culture of Osaka, meanwhile, is awakening him to the beauties and comforts of old Japan. While Louise pulls Kaname vigorously in the direction of the new and cosmopolitan, the slight, vaguely unhealthy Kyoto beauty who is the mistress of his father-in-law pulls even more strongly in the opposite direction.

Neither Kaname nor his wife is able to act with resolve. They make the happiness of their only son their excuse for doing nothing. A cousin comes visiting in the course of the novel, and even as Kaname seems inclined to imitate his father-in-law in a somewhat dilettantish pursuit of the traditional, he can see quite different possibilities in his cousin, a businessman from Shanghai who wastes no time getting things done. Having decided that he no longer needed his wife, the cousin merely told her to depart.

Kaname spends much of his time (when not at the puppet theatre or with Louise) lolling around with a volume of *The Arabian Nights*, looking for erotic passages. On the novel's last page, however, he is about to take up an old travel guide that few modern Japanese would be able to read, much less enjoy. We are seldom bothered with abstractions, and never for long.

The conflict between tradition and progress, and between East and West, was a strong element in Tanizaki's own life, and the parallels between his life and the novel are notable. He probably exaggerated the contrast between Westernizing Tokyo and traditional, conservative Osaka, but there could be no doubt that for him the Osaka merchant had stronger roots than the Tokyo intellectual. He was bringing to a close his youthful affair with the West.

In 1930 Tanizaki, his wife, and another novelist made a joint announcement that husband and wife were separating and the wife was moving on to the second novelist. *Some Prefer Nettles* was written two years before this event. There is thus a correspondence between the forces pulling at the novelist and those working upon his principal characters. If these were merely abstractions the result could well be trite, for there is nothing unique to Tanizaki or to Japan about the tension between home and the world, past and present, tradition and innovation. The strength of the work is in the fact that scene and character invoke them with great persuasiveness.

Some Prefer Nettles ends on an uncertain note. Nothing is resolved, yet the implications are strong. Even as Tanizaki was soon to divorce, so will Kaname, although he is unlikely to give up Louise. The movement back into the Japanese past, associated by Kaname with the advent of old age, will continue.

An early infatuation with the West followed by a return to the traditional has been called "the Tanizaki syndrome." It is still to be observed, so that the characters and situations of *Some Prefer Nettles* continue to be richly symbolic.

—Edward Seidensticker

THE SONG OF ROLAND (La Chanson de Roland)

Epic poem based on an historical event of 778, written c. 1100, possibly by Turoldus; of the many surviving manuscripts, that in the Bodleian Library, Oxford, is considered the oldest and best.

PUBLICATIONS

The Song of Roland: An Analytical Edition, edited and translated by Gerard J. Brault. 2 vols., 1978; also translated by Dorothy L. Sayers, 1957; W.S. Merwin, in *Medieval Epics*, 1963; Robert Harrison, 1970; D.D.R. Owen, 1972; Howard S. Robertson, 1972; C.H. Sisson, 1983; Glyn Burgess, 1990; Janet Shirley, 1996; Leonard Bacon, 2002.

*

Bibliography: *A Guide to Studies on the "Chanson de Roland"* by Joseph John Duggan, 1976.

Critical Studies: see the above editions; also: *La Chanson de Roland commentée* by Joseph Bédier, 1927; *The Ethos of the Song of Roland* by George Fenwick Jones, 1963; *The Chanson de Roland* by Pierre Le Gentil, 1969; *Reading the Song of Roland* by Eugene Vance, 1970; *Literary Technique in the Chanson de Roland* by Roger Pensom, 1982; *The Song of Roland: A Generative Study of the Formulaic Language in the Single Combat* by Genette Ashby-Beach, 1985; *The Sense of the Song of Roland* by Robert Francis Cook, 1987; *Ganelon, Treason, and the Chanson de Roland* by Emanuel J. Mickel, 1990; *The Subject of Violence: The Song of Roland and the Birth of the State* by Peter Haidu, 1993; *La chanson de Roland* by Wolfgang van Emden, 1995; *The Song of Roland: On Absolute and Relative Values* by Marianne J. Ailes, 2002.

* * *

About the year 1100, an anonymous French author recreated an event that had occurred more than three centuries earlier. The poem not only recalls the exploits of the legendary hero Roland but also provides a wealth of information about contemporary society.

The Song of Roland is based on an incident that took place on 15 August 778. After a short and indecisive campaign in Muslim-held Spain, Charlemagne sustained a crushing defeat in the Pyrenees while returning to his capital at Aachen. Basque (or Gascon) marauders ambushed and destroyed the army's rearguard, looted the baggage train, and dispersed before the Franks could retaliate. Only sketchy information is available but one chronicler, Einhard (d. 840), mentions Roland, prefect of the Breton march, as having been among the fallen. Roncesvalles (Roncevaux, in French) is first identified at the end of the 11th century as the pass where the action happened but the exact site of the battle remains uncertain.

In the poem, Saracens led by King Marsile of Saragossa are responsible for the attack upon the rearguard and the traitor Ganelon, who hates his stepson Roland, plans secretly the ambush with the enemy. At Roncevaux, Roland, who heads the rearguard, refuses to sound the oliphant to call Charlemagne to the rescue, this despite the urgent entreaty of his companion-in-arms Oliver. The Emperor avenges Roland's heroic death by defeating the remnants of Marsile's army, then another vast Saracen force led by the Emir Baligant. Later, at Aix, Ganelon admits that he caused Roland's death but denies that he committed treason. A judicial combat determines that this defence has no validity and the traitor is executed.

One of the earliest works in French literature, this epic is believed to portray in fairly accurate fashion the behaviour and mores of the aristocratic warrior class in France at the time of the First Crusade. Members of the upper nobility valued courage, strength, ability to give sound advice, and loyalty based on family and feudal ties. *The Song of Roland* is a profoundly Christian poem that exalts righteousness and martyrdom but also depicts violent individuals at times motivated by bloodthirstiness, greed, racial prejudice, and revenge. A war-like prelate, Archbishop Turpin, fights by the hero's side. Many details are provided about armour, weapons, and tactics but a good deal of epic exaggeration is also apparent in battle scenes.

The poem has some of the characteristics of the formulaic style of oral tradition but also other features usually associated with written literature. The author was familiar with the Bible; it is not clear that he was influenced by the classics. The entire work is constructed on a series of oppositions and parallels, and effective use is made of such narrative devices as foreshadowing, irony, repetition, and understatement. Gestures and symbols play an important role. Charlemagne is an idealized monarch but, though forewarned by dreams, is powerless to stay the course of events. Roland is surpassingly brave, loyal, and strong; however, some scholars believe the poet may have suggested that one can carry these virtues too far.

The oldest and best version of the poem, written in Anglo-Norman dialect, is found in a 12th-century manuscript preserved in the Bodleian Library at Oxford. When emended, this text has 4,002 decasyllabic verses arranged in assonanced strophes of varying length called *laisses*. A rhymed French version appeared in the 13th century. The poem was translated into several languages during the Middle

Ages and a 12th-century Latin prose adaptation, the *Pseudo-Turpin Chronicle*, had a great influence on the literature and art of the period.

—Gerard J. Brault

SONNET 90
Poem by Petrarch, 1470 (written before 1356)

The 90th poem from Petrarch's *Rerum vulgarium fragmenta* is emblematic of his strategy throughout the collection of raising vernacular love poetry in Italian onto a more serious footing, engaging in implicit rivalry with classical Latin verse. The sonnet represents a happy synthesis of personal innovation and traditional elements from both medieval and ancient poetry.

Petrarch's sonnets in translation have never exercised the fascination achieved by translations of Dante's *Commedia* (*The Divine Comedy*) or Boccaccio's *The Decameron*. This is largely because his poems lack the sheer narrative drive of the other two works, but also because he was a meticulous stylist in Italian, rewriting the poems several times, making both minor changes (of phrases, words, even syllables), and major alterations (of whole stanzas and the order of the poems), few of which can be conveyed in translation.

This sonnet is an evocation of Petrarch's first sight of the woman he loved, Laura, on whose name he plays in the first line of this, as of many other, poems: the line means both "Her blonde hair was spread out to the breeze," and "Laura's hair was spread out." That description of the hair has as subtexts the meeting of Venus with Aeneas in Virgil's *Aeneid* (Book I), and the flight of Daphne from Apollo in Ovid, *Metamorphoses* (Book I), so Petrarch endows Laura with qualities of divine, mythical beauty, and enriches the standard description of the woman, starting with the hair and eyes, with classical echoes. Lines 9–11 echo another description of Venus from *Aeneid* (Book I), yet there are by now a number of intimations of Laura's mortality which provide the central divine/human tension around which the poem revolves: in line four the poet hints that her eyes have lost some of their fire, line six also comes into the present and questions whether she did pity him; and this tension is resolved, as always in a Petrarch sonnet, in the final tercet: even if she no longer retains the beauty of a goddess, the wound in his heart is still as raw, despite the slackening of the bow of love.

The sonnet works round that central tension of divinity/humanity a further dichotomy between past and present. Indeed, there are three different tenses in the poem: the descriptive imperfect (1, 2, 3, 6, 7, 9, 11), the instantaneous past (8, 13), and the present (4, 6, 13, 14). Petrarch's innovation within both the classical and medieval traditions of female descriptions is to introduce his great obsession, the effect of time passing on the beloved. Venus and Daphne, of course, do not age; and although Beatrice's death is narrated in Dante's *La vita nuova* (*The New Life*), the ageing process is nowhere alluded to in Dante or any other of Petrarch's predecessors. Sonnet 90 is part of the whole collection's concern with human time: it consists of 366 poems in all (an introductory sonnet, plus one for every day of the year), several are anniversary poems, and a number mention the exact date (6 April 1327) of his first sighting of Laura and of her death (6 April 1348).

Apart from innovations of content, Petrarch made several improvements to the sonnet form. In terms of vocabulary, he eliminated his predecessors' technical-philosophical language which described the physiological and psychological effects of love, and the more vulgar expressions which belonged to early Italian realistic poetry. Instead he cultivates a middle elegance of extraordinary harmony and euphony, as here in the positive adjectives ("dolci," "vago," "begli," etc.). The imagery, also achieves appropriate consistency: the gold of Laura's hair, and the fire of her eyes, causing the tinder of love to flare up, and reaching a climax in the definition of her as "a heavenly spirit, a living sun."

The other major adjustment incorporated by Petrarch was an improvement in the structure of the sonnet: instead of 14 lines, in which occasionally the order of the quatrains or the tercets could be reversed without damaging the sense, Petrarch's sonnets have a logical flow which brooks no transposition and reaches satisfying closure in the final tercet. Each section of the sonnet has its own thematics and syntax. The first quatrain's third-person description shifts to first-person reaction; then, as often in Petrarch, this pattern is repeated in the tercets, resuming the matter and syntax of the first quatrain (third-person description), while the second tercet echoes the second quatrain (the subjective reaction). Lines 12–14 bring together all the strands of the poem: not only does line 12 bring to a climax the imagery of fire, but the adjectives "heavenly" and "living" crystallize the main human/divine tension in the sonnet, and even the noun "spirit" echoes the opening mention of the breeze; the past definite "saw" recalls the only other non-descriptive past tense "blazed"; and the parenthesis "though she may not *now* be quite the same" picks up the opening inset clause "her eyes, which are *now* so dimmed." The final line, as often in Petrarch, is not just a logical and satisfying conclusion, but has a proverbial quality, enhanced in the original by the stark assonance of the seven "a" vowels in the 11-syllable line. If the first half of the poem ended with a rhetorical question, exploiting the image of a love as fire, the second half concludes with a gnomic response, which recalls the classical picture of Cupid with his bow, and indeed returns to the opening echoes of Venus, Cupid's mother, appearing to Aeneas as a huntress.

By endowing vernacular love poetry with morally elevated themes like the passing of time, and the vanity of human pleasures, and by imitating classical poetry in its attention to structure and formal properties, Petrarch projected the Italian lyric towards a new status of seriousness which would exercise a profound influence on the future of European love poetry.

—Martin L. McLaughlin

SONNETS TO ORPHEUS (Die Sonette an Orpheus)
Poems by Rainer Maria Rilke, 1923

The *Sonnets to Orpheus* were written in February 1922 at Rainer Maria Rilke's retreat in the tower of Muzot, Switzerland: the first series of 26 poems between 2nd and 5th February, the second series of 29 between 15th and 23rd. In between these dates Rilke wrote the fifth, seventh, and eighth *Duino Elegies* and parts of the sixth, ninth, and tenth. Another seven or eight sonnets were written in the same month but not included in the *Sonnets to Orpheus*. After this excess of inspiration he was never to produce a coherent set or collection of original poems again.

Among the riches of sonnets in the western tradition that played a part in the making of this collection, the reader may well think particularly of the works of Baudelaire, August Platen (*Sonnets from*

Venice), C.F. Meyer, Mallarmé, Valéry, and Rilke's own earlier groups of sonnets; and among work which Rilke did not know, Gerard Manley Hopkins. Rilke's earlier sonnets in the two collections of *New Poems* anticipate themes and forms of the present cycle, but remain largely descriptive, their metaphysical content only implicit. The distinctive contribution in thematic terms of the present cycle is expressed in the title. Orpheus, as the archetype of the poet, is the addressee of the poems, which celebrate in abstract terms the life of the poet, its ecstasies and sorrows, rewards and dangers. In accordance with the primacy of poetry, all contents of human life are explicitly treated as the matter of metaphor: either metaphysical truths are hinted at by the metaphorical invocation of an aspect of reality, or the sensual world is itself interpreted and raised to metaphysical significance by its association with something numinous.

The celebrated first sonnet, making no concessions to the reader, leads straight to the heart of the procedure. If, according to legend, Orpheus made trees bow down when he sang, for Rilke the very song is a tree, growing in the auditor's ear, the matter of a temple: "There rose a tree. O pure transcendent climbing! / O Orpheus sings! O tree, high in their ear!. . ." (Sonnet I, 1). In the second sonnet it is a girl, in bed in the ear and "sleeping the world." Further sonnets insist that emotion is not a sufficient basis for poetry, or that Orpheus is reborn in every singer, that he partakes of the realms of life and of death, that he is called to praise human life and to transform it, as the grape is transformed into wine, into something of metaphysical significance (an alternative metaphor to that of the angel which runs through the Elegies):

Praising, that's it! One appointed for praising,
The was produced like the ore from the stone's
silence. His heart, O a transient winepress
of inexhaustible wine for mankind.

(Sonnet I, 7)

Only in the context of praising, an attitude which overcomes death, is sorrow allowed.

Another group of sonnets takes as its theme archetypal patterns of existence and aspects and accompaniments of life: the rider as one being in two; the rhythms of nature bringing fruit and fulfilment; the dance (the whole cycle is dedicated to the memory of Wera Ouckama Knoop, a young dancer); a dog (follower of his master as the poet is a follower of Orpheus), and so forth. Only the machine is refused a place in the constellation of life transformed into poetry: it can only serve, not be worthy of praise. The first part culminates in the hymn to Orpheus and statement of the necessity of his cruel end to create poetic speech and hearing, to give nature a mouth:

Lastly they beat you to bits, at revenge's behest,
whilst still your notes in the rocks and the lions re-echoed
and in the trees and the birds. To this day you sing there.

(Sonnet I, 26)

The second part opens with the praise of breathing, of the mirror and of the unicorn: the rhythmic, the mimetic, and the imaginative elements of the poetic universe. Flowers and gardens, especially the rose from which Rilke repeatedly pressed poetic significance, are the subject of a number of poems. The shallowness of modern attitudes, from the confusion of humanitarianism with mercifulness to the cult of the machine, is attacked: "All our attainments risk the machine's

crushing threat: it, / boasting its place in the soul, not in obedience, rebels" (Sonnet II, 10). The power of death, destruction, parting, and decay to produce wisdom, happiness, and constancy is invoked: a balance of rising and falling, wounding and healing, movement and stillness is needed to produce the totality of life, and a mystical awareness of the whole—even when one is bound up with a perhaps painful part of human experience—is not only a way to overcome suffering but the path to deeper meaning in general:

Where, in what timeless old gardens so blessedly watered, on which
trees, from which now tenderly leafless-made blossom's calyx
ripen strange species of fruits—consolations?

(Sonnet II, 17)

Poet and reader together can order that small fraction of reality which can be experienced, aware that our transience is only a part of a constant whole, but a necessary part:

Gods we are planning as yet in emboldened new sketches,
which peevish fate once again will destroy downright.
And yet they are the immortals: behold, we're allowed to
build in our harking him who will hear us at last.

(Sonnet II, 24)

Building on his previous work in sonnet form, Rilke varies it by introducing short-line sonnets, sonnets with some short lines, and different schemes of metre and rhyme. Frequent enjambment also contributes to rhythmic variation. The vocabulary is exact and full of daring new compound words, the syntax often elliptical. Rilke, with his leaning to spiritualism, felt these poems were dictated to him rather than written by him. It is not surprising that the precision of the writing does not prevent the meaning from remaining obscure in many cases, but the all-pervading metaphors create their own meaning aside from the logical one the reader would like to construct. The things of this life are rendered unfamiliar by Rilke's search for distinctions within what we usually think of as one, and for unities between what we conceive of as two.

With this work Rilke created the most pregnant, even laconic assertion of the primacy of art and poetry in particular, as bearer of the metaphysical significance of the world. Mysticism, freed from religious content, finds its echo here in a pattern of thought halfway between romanticism and existentialism.

—Alfred D. White

SPLEEN
Poems by Charles Baudelaire, 1861 (written 1845–51)

"Spleen" is the title of four poems in *The Flowers of Evil* that are usually grouped together. It would not have been a wholly inappropriate heading for some of the neighbouring pieces, but Charles Baudelaire also employed this anglicism as one of the two opposed elements in the most substantial section, "Spleen and Ideal," of that volume. Moreover, *Le Spleen de Paris* is the alternative title for his *Little Poems in Prose*.

The first "Spleen" poem is a sonnet beginning with a personification of "Pluviôse," the rainy fifth month of the Republican calendar, corresponding more or less in time to Aquarius, from the latter part of January to the latter part of February. Its opening quatrain is very atmospheric and could be seen equally in terms of a "tableau parisien" (Parisian scene), but the introduction of the poet's cat in the second quatrain establishes a *correspondance* between it and Baudelaire himself:

Mon chat sur le carreau cherchant une litière
Agite sans repos son corps maigre et galeux;
L'âme d'un vieux poète erre dans la gouttière
Avec la triste voix d'un fantôme frileux.

(The tiles afford no comfort to my cat
that cannot keep its mangy body still;
the soul of some old poet haunts the drains
and howls as if a ghost could hate the cold.)

The poem loses some of its intensity, however, as the spotlight switches to "the dapper Knave of Hearts and the Queen of Spades," figures from a pack of cards rather than real people, despite their symbolism.

The second poem, of 24 lines, beginning "J'ai plus de souvenirs que si j'avais mille ans" ("Souvenirs? / More than if I had lived a thousand years!"), evokes very well the poet's host of memories, but they are recollections redolent of death and decay rather than sweet souvenirs. Some of the images, however, are very striking: "Je suis un cimetière abhorré de la lune" ("I am a graveyard that the moon abhors"), "Je suis un vieux boudoir plein de roses fanées" ("I am an old boudoir where a rack of gowns, / perfumed by withered roses, rots to dust"); and in the final section of the poem the portrait of the artist as an old Sphinx forgotten and ignored. Here Baudelaire spells out the slow pace of time and makes explicit mention of "ennui" (boredom), the synonym of "spleen," "fruit de la morne incuriosité / Prend les proportions de l'immortalité" ("the fruit of glum indifference which gains the dimension of eternity").

The third poem, one dense block of 18 alexandrines, depicts the poet as the king of a rainy realm, rich but impotent, young and yet very old. Most of all he is *bored*. Nothing can distract him, his hounds, his hawk, his fool, the ladies of the court. His appetites are dulled, sex has lost its appeal, "the bed of state becomes a stately tomb." His malady has transformed him into a paradoxical young skeleton or a dazed corpse in whose veins the green waters of Lethe have taken the place of blood. If the identity of the king remains unclear, the message of the poem is plain for all to see.

The last of the quartet commences—"Quand le ciel bas et lourd pèse comme un couvercle" ("When skies are low and heavy as a lid"). The first three of the five quatrains are subordinate clauses beginning with an anaphoric "when." They create a claustrophobic feeling of darkness, depression, and confinement. In the eyes of the poet, the whole planet has become a damp dungeon and the falling rain resembles prison-bars. In this context the best image that Baudelaire can find for hope is a bat beating the walls of the cell with its wings and banging its head against the rotting ceiling.

In the main clause, held back until stanza 4, the "action" is in the form of a sudden peal of bells, whose din is interpreted by the poet as a frightful howl of fury. After this unexpected outburst of noisy protest, the imagery of the last stanza is more reminiscent in its tonality of that of lines 1–12: in a nightmarish vision of silence in his soul a line of hearses files slowly by, hope now defeated can but weep, and the earlier "ennuis" are replaced by a more acute despotic *Angst*,

dramatically planting its black flag (historically the emblem of all-out war, or popular fury, and of anarchy) on the poet's bowed skull.

Yet there is an incantatory musicality in the lines, created in part by repetition, alliteration, and onomatopoeia, in part by rhythm and rhyme, as is exemplified by the third quatrain:

Quand la pluie étalant ses immenses traînées
D'un vaste prison imite les barreaux,
Et qu'un peuple muet d'infâmes araignées
Vient tendre ses filets au fond de nos cerveaux

(When rain falls straight from unrelenting clouds,
forging the bars of some enormous jail,
and silent hordes of obscene spiders spin
their webs across the basements of our brains)

The word "spleen" was perhaps first used in French in 1745. For Chateaubriand, it was already a "physical sadness," a "veritable malady." In Baudelaire's case, it would probably be futile to speculate at length on the extent to which it may have had its source in a innate melancholic disposition, physical or psychological in its nature, or in the "atony" to which he sometimes referred, or in hashish, or in the syphilis he contracted at the age of 19. What is really important is the fact that he was able to transmute the negative experience into positive expression: viewed in this way, the "spleen" may stand for all the forms of evil that Baudelaire transformed into the flowers of his poems.

—Keith Aspley

SPRING AWAKENING (Frühlings Erwachen)
Play by Frank Wedekind, 1891

Spring Awakening, Frank Wedekind's first play of note, was written in the winter months of 1890–91 and was first published at his own expense in 1891. The illustration for this edition, a view of a spring meadow, with flowers and trees in bloom, and swallows, is ironical. It contains everything that is lacking in the lives of the characters in the play.

The title is deliberately misleading and ironic, as is the subtitle, *A Children's Tragedy*. The main characters are, in fact, adolescents, and this is one of the first plays to treat the relationship of adolescents to the adult world. In the first act Wedekind presents groups of adolescents. The collective, utter ignorance of the girls regarding sex is conveyed, not without humour, as is the pressure of schoolwork on the boys, to the exclusion of all else. However, the work as a whole concentrates on the experiences of three individuals in its exposure of the adults' artificiality and hypocrisy, and their indifference towards the needs of adolescents.

Frau Bergmann tries to keep her daughter Wendla in a state of suspended childhood. She responds with pathetic evasion to all of Wendla's requests for enlightenment. Moritz Stiefel is under unbearable pressure to avoid the ignominy of having to repeat a year at school, and is plagued with feelings of guilt at the onset of puberty. Melchior Gabor appears to be confident and independent, but he is also deeply disturbed. He is depressed at the thought that the morality extolled by adults is just a façade that enables them to indulge their instincts. Events do nothing to dispel this fear. At no point do any adults help Wendla, Mortiz, or Melchoir.

Although the contents of the first act, with its allusions to sex and child beating, outraged the reading public (there was no prospect at the time that the play would be performed), most of the scenes are of realistic dialogue. It is from about the second act onwards that the style that one associates with Wedekind dominates the play. It emerges that Moritz has been subject to cruel pressure; he is convinced his mother will go mad and his father will have a heart attack if he does not live up to their expectations. Moritz commits suicide almost to atone for not finishing his homework. Frau Bergmann says she would deserve to be sent to prison if she were to tell Wendla how babies come into the world, but later has no hesitation in having a backstreet abortion performed on her daughter after she becomes pregnant as a result of the ignorance in which she is kept. Wedekind constantly exploits the grotesque in his merciless exposure of the perverted realm of bourgeois values.

The grotesque is combined with caricature at the beginning of Act III where the schoolteachers debate Moritz's suicide in a scene of considerable inanity. They have ridiculous names such as Headmaster Sunstroke, Professors Flyswatter and Bonebreaker. The impression conveyed by this, that they are totally devoid of humanity, is reinforced by their unnatural diction. Sunstroke's information to his colleagues that schools have been closed where the rate of suicides has reached 25 per cent (and so they might lose their jobs) is an illustration of Wedekind's penchant for sick humour. Melchior is made the scapegoat for the suicide. The father has found among Moritz's belongings Melchior's essay which was intended to enlighten Moritz about sex; clearly his essay caused Mauritz's death!

Wedekind satirizes the entire bourgeois establishment. The vicar conducting Moritz's travesty of a funeral condemns him to eternal death. A doctor demonstrates either his collusion in the abortion or his incompetence when he diagnoses Wendla's state as anaemia and prescribes a lucrative brand of pills. Melchior's father, a lawyer, lectures on morality but congratulates himself on having retained Melchior's letter to Wendla, admitting responsibility for getting her pregnant. He has his son committed to a corrective institution where, he assures his wife, Melchior will learn Christian values. Immediately following is a scene in the institution where the inmates play a masturbation game.

Some minor characters are variations on Wedekind's exposure of society's grotesque values and how they infect the adolescents. Hänschen Rilow flushes down the toilet reproductions of titillating paintings, one of which is from a secret drawer in his father's desk. He and Ernst Röbel enter into a homosexual relationship, certain that this will be condoned when they have respectable positions, one as a millionaire, the other as a vicar.

When Wendla dies, Melchior is plagued by guilt. He is on the point of accepting Mortiz's invitation to join him in death when a mysterious masked man (this role was played by Wedekind himself when the play was eventually performed) appears in a macabre graveyard scene. He convinces Melchior of the folly of suicide, pointing out that he is being brainwashed by the distorting morality of society. He emphasizes that the abortion killed Wendla, not the pregnancy. This final scene debunks the traditional German tragedy in which the hero atones for his faults though a noble death.

A censored version of the play was performed in 1906. The authorities sometimes justified granting permission for performances by claiming that the play represented a serious plea for reform.

However, Wedekind is so venomous in his condemnation of conformist society in this work that one suspects he considered it beyond redemption. Society's response to situations is so automatic that the possibility of change seems negligible, and the adolescents who survive do so by adapting to its perverted values. When the teachers comfort Moritz's father at the funeral by saying that he would not have passed his examinations anyway, one is tempted to think that they meant this sincerely and that the father did find their words a consolation. Although the style of *Spring Awakening*, which exploits satire and the grotesque to uncover the concealed truth, is anti-Naturalist, there is nowhere to be found in it the belief in a spiritual reawakening that characterizes the works of Expressionist dramatists, who, paradoxically, came to admire Wedekind.

—D.J. Andrews

STEPPENWOLF (Der Steppenwolf)
Novel by Hermann Hesse, 1927

Steppenwolf is set in an unnamed Swiss town at some point in the early 1920s. It attempts to reflect the contemporary and widespread feeling of ''sickness of the age'' within a single character, and its disrupted presentation of events in part reflects the disjointed mind of a figure who views himself as an incurably split personality, an irreconcilable amalgam of man and wolf. But the novel is also one of several major works by early 20th-century German writers which employ an unsettling structure to reflect the disintegration of traditional modes of living which World War I had brought with it. Partial inspiration for this approach may actually be detected in the German Romantics' attitude to form, for the Romantics (several of whom feature by name in the text) were among Hermann Hesse's favourite writers. There is, however, also considerable influence of modern psychoanalytic theory in form and in content. Just as Hesse himself had been healed by Jungian analysis, the split in his hero's mind is painfully reconciled through a range of therapies: not just probing of the unconscious, but practical sex-therapy which awakens his dormant sensual powers, dance therapy, music, and even drug-induced psychedelic experience. There are two principal lessons in the novel: first, that personality is manifold, layered, and complex, not simply dualistic; and second, that liberation of the self consists of far more than simply an insight into and understanding of that self—the hero has in fact an abundance of self-knowledge from his constant self-analysis, but what he needs is to engage in life properly, to incorporate and synthesize experiences, and sometimes to stand back from existence in order to achieve equilibrium.

The hero, Harry Haller, bears the same initials as his creator, an obvious invitation to establish parallels between the two (and a considerable amount of the detail and psychological analysis is indeed drawn from Hesse's own experiences around this period). The fiction is that Harry has disappeared, leaving behind a manuscript for his landlady's nephew. The latter, in a plain and pedantic introduction, relates the circumstances of Harry's life from an outsider's point of view. We then have the beginnings of Harry's first-person account of the life of a 48-year-old man who is suffering from physical pains and headaches, who torments himself with constant analysis of his split personality, who is both attracted to the bourgeois existence and repelled by it, who has a propensity for the bottle, and who has resolved to take his own life on his 50th birthday. A sort of interlude now follows, a ''Tract of the Steppenwolf'' which Harry is mysteriously handed as he walks the night streets. (In early editions of the novel, this ''tract'' was actually printed on a different, cheap sort of paper and in different typography.) The tract provides a third-person analysis of Harry's personality, in clear, bold, and sometimes ironic language which approximates to that of psychoanalytic diagnosis. It views Harry as typical of the artistic and European types, and as consisting not of two separate natures, but of thousands. It also denounces, in language reminiscent of Nietzsche, the cosy existence of the modern bourgeois.

The next major event (in a novel which contains little narrative) is the encounter with an old acquaintance—a professor who emerges as an arch representative of the bourgeois and their self-satisfied yet militaristic mentality. Unable to suppress the wolf-like side of his personality, Harry expresses his inner feelings about bourgeois attitudes at the dinner party to which he has been kindly invited, and he then storms out to roam the streets. On entering a disreputable-looking bar, he meets a call-girl, Hermine (note again the key initial), whose psyche, in Jungian terms, clearly corresponds to Harry's ''anima''; the confrontation with this, the feminine side of his unconscious, is an important aspect of the healing process. Hermine comforts him and takes him under her wing in an almost motherly manner, later teaching him to dance, to take life less seriously, and to enjoy physical love with Maria, a beautiful prostitute friend of hers. He is also introduced to a jazz saxophonist, Pablo, a man without repressions, in whom he sees another, completely different, unreflective attitude towards music and life. Hermine, Maria, and Pablo are sometimes associated with mirrors, and they may all be seen as reflections or projections of aspects of Harry's personality.

The penultimate event of the novel is an extended masked ball in which Hermine is, significantly, disguised as a young man and in which Harry finally engages in a mystical experience of intense pleasure and self-abandon. When the ball is over, Pablo invites Harry to join him and Hermine in experiencing his ''Magic Theatre,'' which turns out to be a drug-induced working out of various aspects of Harry's personality, including a wild attack on motor cars, the observation of a scene which reveals the deep savagery within him, the re-experiencing, more positively, of all his former love encounters, and finally the act of murdering Hermine as she lies asleep after having made love with Pablo—an act which Hermine had predicted he would carry out, but which seems motivated by a type of bourgeois jealousy Harry has obviously not yet overcome. Harry's behaviour in murdering Hermine is condemned, and he is sentenced to ''eternal life'' both for lacking a sense of humour and for confusing imagination with reality. The novel concludes positively, with Harry accepting that he must learn to follow the example of such ''Immortals'' as Mozart and Goethe (who both feature in dreams/hallucinations); that is, that he must learn to ''laugh'' as they do, and thus create distance between themselves and life. He also recognizes that he must continue to play this painful but therapeutic self-revealing ''game.''

The tone of this work is constantly changing, and there are even two poems included within it. Hesse's prose brings out, above all, the unhappiness of his hero's restless mind, with its obsessive, rhetorical analysis; but the author is also able to communicate the occasionally elated and even lyrical mood of a sensitive intellectual who has rediscovered ''living.''

—Peter Hutchinson

THE STORM (La bufera)
Poem by Eugenio Montale, 1941

''The Storm'' first appeared in the Milanese weekly *Tempo* (6–13 February 1941); it was then reprinted in *Finisterre* (*poesie del '40-'42*) in Lugano in 1943 (reissued in Florence in 1945); and again as the opening poem of the first section of *La bufera e altro* (entitled ''Finisterre''), first published in 1956 and reprinted in 1957. The first publication of the poem was prefaced by an unidentified hendecasyllable in Spanish (''Porque sabes que siempre te he querido. . . ''), which was then replaced by two lines from the 16th-century French poet, Agrippa D'Aubigné (''Les princes n'ont point d'yeux pour voir ces grand's merveilles, / Leurs mains ne servent plus qu'à nous persécuter. . .'' *A' Dieu*). This latter quotation at once contextualized the poem, which is in essence a love poem, within a broader historical and ''theological'' framework, as Eugenio Montale pointed out in a letter to Silvio Guarnieri (29 November 1965): ''The Storm (the opening poem) is the war, in particular *that* war after *that* dictatorship (see the epigraph); but it is also cosmic war, everlasting and involving everybody.''

The poem's 23 lines are divided into four strophes of 3, 6, 6, and 8 lines respectively (the second enclosed entirely within parentheses) whose metre consists substantially of traditional hendecasyllables (20 out of 23 lines, two shorter seven-syllable lines [3 and 10], and a five-syllable one [9]), which, like another memorable poem in the volume, ''L'anguilla'' [The Eel], is made up of a single grammatical sentence sustained by a regular series of enjambments.

The opening stanza of the poem describes the advent of the March storm with its prolonged thunderbolts and hail, and this description continues briefly in the lightening with which the third stanza opens; but the quick shift from the external world to the internal in the poem's parenthetical second stanza with its admixture of vocal and visual details (the sound of crystal, the gold fading on mahogany on the spines of bound volumes) and above all, its sense of intimacy (it is defined as a ''nido,'' a nest), of a vibrant feminine presence, clearly hints that the thrust of the poem is not so much physical as metaphysical.

This feminine presence which is at the heart of the poem (just as it is at the heart of Montale's mature poetry, the poems of *The Occasions*, and *La bufera e altro* itself, which it would not be an exaggeration to define as a modern Petrarchan experience) is manifest, as in his medieval predecessors, through the light burning in the woman's eyes (but by means of an imaginative periphrasis which is wholly modern: ''brucia ancora / una grana di zucchero nel guscio / delle tue palpebre'' [there still burns a grain of sugar in the shell / of your eyelids]), a light which has osmotically internalized the lightning with which stanza three opens.

This stanza constitutes almost literally the moment of illumination with its attendant oxymora, paradoxes, and heightened use of language. The lightning, like a flashbulb—the fourth section of the volume is in fact subtitled ''Flashes' e dediche'' [Flashes and Dedications]—blanches and freezes trees and walls, catching them in that forever of an instant (''li sorprende in quella / eternità d'istante''), but in a tragic, sacrificial entelechy incorporating Goethe (''every entelechy is a fragment of eternity'') and Mallarmé (''Tel qu'en Lui même enfin l'éternité le change'': the opening line of his sonnet on the tomb of Edgar Allan Poe). The real Christ-like light of the world belongs to the woman, apostrophized as ''strana sorella'' [strange sister], and bound to the poet almost by a surfeit of love—''piú che l'amore'' [more than love]—but, as Montale stressed in the Guarnieri letter, it was not intended to be reductive), a love which is both ''manna / e distruzione'' [manna / and destruction] and which she bears within her, cross-like, as her damnation (''ch'entro te scolpita / porti per tua condanna'' [that carved inside / you are condemned to bear]).

In the fourth and final strophe lightning gives way to ''lo schianto rude,'' the hard crack of thunder, but in its turn that is immediately replaced by a series of sounds of musical instruments rich in reverberations: ''sistri'' or rattles (used in the worship of the Egyptian Isis, but rendered by Arrowsmith as ''castanets,'' perhaps in anticipation of the Andalusian dance or fandango, normally accompanied by castanets and guitars, mentioned in the following line) and ''tamburelli'' or tambourines. But there is nothing here of the ''dance, and Provençal song, and sunburnt mirth'' of which Keats spoke. It would be more appropriate to speak (as Montale later did in ''La Primavera hitleriana'' [Hitler Spring]) of a ''tregenda'' [Witches' Sabbath]. Indeed, the orchestra pit or Hell-mouth (''golfo mistico'') of the later poem, is already present here in the ''fossa fuia'' (thieving ditch) of the final stanza, heightened through alliteration with both ''fremere'' (to shake) in the preceding line and ''fandango'' in the following, and redolent with overtones from both Dante (''fuia'' as adjective occurs in *Inferno* XII) and D'Annunzio (''La nave'' [The Ship]). And two of the strophe's verbs underline this Hellishness: ''scalpicciare'' (to stamp) with its implications of to crush underfoot as of horses in battle (a hapax in Montale's poetry), and the no less rare ''annaspare'' (to flounder, as if, for example, while drowning), the latter highlighted through both metrical stress (on the line's sixth syllable) and the dots immediately following. Against this background there emerges the figure of the woman who turns to wave to the poet before going into the darkness. But the literal darkness (''buio'') with which the poem concludes is memorably attenuated by literary and iconographic echoes. The salutation of the woman, standard in Dante, Petrarch, and the poets of the *dolce stil nuovo*, here takes on a sombre hue, echoing as it does the conclusion of Leopardi's ''A Silvia'' (''To Silvia''); and that literary reminiscence is complicated by visual images of Piero della Francesca and Mantegna inextricably bound up in the poet's image of his beloved.

—Tom O'Neill

THE STORY OF BURNT NJAL

See NJÁLS SAGA

THE STORY OF JUST CASPAR AND FAIR ANNIE
(Geschichte vom braven Kasperl und dem schönen Annerl)
Novella by Clemens Bretano, 1817

The Story of Just Caspar and Fair Annie had an interesting genesis. Written at a time when Clemens Brentano was seeking to return to the Roman Catholic faith in which he had been brought up, it is basically an amalgam of two stories, supposedly derived from real-life incidents narrated by him to a friend. The first story, that of Caspar, is based on an account of the suicide of a young soldier, who feels he has been dishonoured; the second, which centres on the fate of the fair Annie, relates to a case of infanticide said to have happened in Silesia and which may also contain elements taken from a well-known German folksong. Another source is thought to be the memoirs of the

public executioner of Nuremberg, which had appeared in 1801, and which would undoubtedly have appealed to Brentano's enthusiasm for popular traditions.

The English title as it stands is somewhat misleading, ''Just'' suggests someone concerned with equity in the administration of the law, whereas in the German original Caspar is ''bray''—that is, honest, upright, decent, law-abiding. Anxious above all about his ''honour,'' his reputation in the eyes of the world, he has the misfortune to discover that his father and stepbrother are horse thieves and, unable to bear the disgrace, shoots himself over his mother's grave in the cemetery. Meanwhile, his fiancée Annie has left their native village to take up a better position as a maidservant in an aristocratic household. Here she is seduced, and in a sequence reminiscent of the Gretchen tragedy in Goethe's *Faust* murders her illegitimate child and is herself executed.

Although the story is usually regarded as an important example of the German novella, the narrative techniques adopted by Brentano are by no means straightforward. There are two main narrators. The first of these, thought by some critics to reflect Brentano's own personality, is a man of some education and leisure who is nevertheless plagued by doubts and insecurity as to his purpose and mission in life. The second, Caspar's grandmother Anna Magaret, is a formidable old lady, a woman of the people, firm in her religious faith and confident that God knows what is best for us. After hearing her version of the events that have befallen Caspar and Annie, the first narrator intervenes in the action and is able to restore their lest honour by ensuring that both will have a decent Christian burial. Interspersed throughout the text, however, are several much shorter narratives. There is a story about a French lieutenant who shoots himself after being ordered to do something dishonourable; there is the story of the huntsman Jürge, whom Anna Margaret persuades to ask for forgiveness on the eve of his execution; and there is the story of Annie's childhood where an encounter with the public executioner seems to foreshadow her destiny. Although these different strands are woven together with consummate mastery, it is undoubtedly the case that there are several separate foci. The German literary historian Benno von Weise thus considers the work to have a seminal character. It is the starting-point, he claims, for the development in 19th-century German literature of both the detective story and the novella of village life, while at the same time—through the commentary of the first narrator—it explores the late Romantic interest in the psychology of the creative personality.

There is certainly general agreement that *The Story of Just Caspar and Fair Annie* is an outstanding achievement of German Romanticism. The most obvious Romantic element is the supernatural fate-motif; the executioner's sword rattles in its case when Annie passes it as a child and she is subsequently bitten by the severed head of the huntsman. Beyond this, however, is Brentano's conscious adoption of the language of the people in Anna Margaret's narration. The tone is colloquial, and at times ungrammatical; the syntax is simple, and often illogical, the main events being recounted in a series of ''leaps and bounds'' that Brentano—and Herder before him—held to be typical of the genuine folksong and ballad. Above all, the characterization of Anna Margaret herself represents Brentano's tribute to the wisdom and simple piety of unspoilt ordinary people. Believing as he did that such people have much to teach the so-called better and more sophisticated classes, she becomes his medium for a religious outlook on life to which he aspired but which he himself felt unable to attain. For her, striving for honour in the eyes of the world, as both Caspar and Annie try to do, is presumption. God alone is the judge of honourable conduct, and what is dishonourable in terms of worldly reputation may yet be honourable in His sight. If Caspar had hurried home and not been so attentive to what people were saying about his treatment of his horse, he would have forestalled his father and step-brother and prevented them from committing their crime; if Annie had borne her illegitimate child, her village would have tried to help and support her.

Brentano is sometimes accused of inconsistency, but his message is perfectly clear. Wherever worldly honour comes first, there is disaster; when worldly honour is thrown to the winds, the outcome is propitious. This is demonstrated when the first narrator refuses to be intimidated by ceremonial etiquette and audaciously demands an interview with the Duke which leads to the posthumous pardon for both Caspar and Annie. In addition, the Duke's mistress, on discovering that her brother, Annie's seducer, is being attacked by an angry crowd, casts off her disguise and thus invites public scandal. The Duke, however, is shamed into marrying her, and the story ends with the unveiling of an allegorical statue depicting both justice and mercy. Felt by many critics to be a little too contrived for modern tastes, this represents Brentano's conviction that, beyond all the incongruities and cruelties of this transient life, there is an eternal order in which all paradoxes are reconciled.

—Margaret C. Ives

DIE STRUDLHOFSTIEGE
Novel by Heimito von Doderer, 1951

Scope and structure of Heimito von Doderer's approximately 900-page novel *Die Strudlhofstiege* and its somewhat more voluminous sequel, *Die Dämonen* (*The Demons*) suggest epic universality. Doderer took the Austrian painter and novelist Albert Paris Gütersloh as a model, appropriating the latter's concept of the "total novel." A closer look reveals that Doderer's seemingly boundless literary universe is subdivided into partially overlapping plot lines and character clusters which provide continuity. *Die Strudlhofstiege*, Doderer's first major success, is paradigmatic of his organically evolving creativity. The episodes and characters of his works are drawn from a meta-framework, his personal creative reference system which, as Roswitha Fischer showed, is composed of observations, factual news, results of studies and imaginary persons and events. Albeit only in passing, figures such as Julius Zihal from his earlier book *Die erleuchteten Fenster* recur in *Die Strudlhofstiege*.

The novel evolves around two different dates. The narrative present, between 1923 and 1925, is shaped by events which occurred during 1910 and 1911. This bi-levelled structure enables the narrator to make cross-references between two formative decades in Austrian history, suggesting a continuity between the Austro-Hungarian empire and the Social Democratic republic. Furthermore, Doderer's technique keeps the reader's interest alive throughout the text and allows for detailed accounts and digressions, Doderer's favourite devices. The final merging of the disparate elements signifies that nothing in this world is accidental. Some loose ends, created, for example, by the youthful perplexity of René Stangeler (one of Doderer's pseudonyms assigned to a character who mirrors the author as a young man), connect *Die Strudlhofstiege* with *The Demons*. Both are educational novels, Bildungsroman, set in Vienna, and presuppose a fair knowledge of the city, because Doderer uses locations as symbols. The title of *Die Strudlhofstiege* alludes to a famous art deco

structure, the Strudlhof staircase, which connects two distinct neighbourhoods of Vienna's 9th district. University institutes, clinics, and municipal buildings are located above the *Alsergrund*. The latter, located close to the Danube Canal, is the site of the Liechtensteinpark, after 1938 a haven for persecuted Jews, an ancient Jewish cemetery, and the police prison. Portentous encounters are staged on the Strudlhofstiege, most importantly, the novel's baroque central scene which severs obsolete bonds establishing more valid allegiances among the protagonists.

Doderer's pre-occupation with history is apparent throughout—his dissertation dealt with 15th-century historiography. Yet *Die Strudlhofstiege* is a profoundly subjective text rather than a historical novel suggesting that the individual must assert him/herself against the collective. Like Elias Canetti, Hermann Broch, and Bertolt Brecht, Doderer recognized 20th-century mass culture as a qualitatively new phenomenon. With its multitude of characters, *Die Strudlhofstiege* tries to represent a metropolitan mass society. However, despite the crowds he depicts, the author insists on the autonomy of the individual. His rejection of ideologies is decidedly bourgeois. Mistrust of politics was common in postwar Germany and Austria. Moreover, Doderer's attitude reflects his background, that of a World War I veteran and prisoner of war in Siberia who in 1933 joined the National Socialist Party at the time it was outlawed in Austria only to change his mind after the Nazi invasion in 1938, to convert to Catholicism and then to fight as an airforce major in World War II, who was taken prisoner by the British, and returned to Vienna in 1946.

By its structure, *Die Strudlhofstiege* is a belated example of the German realist novel, but more precisely, it is an attempt on the part of Doderer to come to terms with his times, his controversial life and work, and his bewilderment as a writer and a private person. A number of characters, through their interaction, intellectual development, political careers, and their personal and professional relationships mirror aspects of Doderer's own experience. Thus the most burning issues of the Austro-Fascist era and the post-war years, ethnic strife and the Holocaust, are suppressed. Rather, *Die Strudlhofstiege* vacillates between modernism and reaction. So does its author, an old-fashioned story-teller at heart, who nonetheless championed the experimental Wiener Gruppe in the 1950s. Like his creator, Doderer's protagonist Melzer is thrown into the chaos of World War I and left traumatized. However, the alienation of veterans, their inability to function in a democratic society and to cope with friends and the opposite sex, but most of all, civilian life, represent important social issues with which critics of the following generation such as Klaus Theweleit continue to wrestle. Doderer's solutions are personal and private: in 1925 Melzer redeems himself by saving the life of Mary K., a Jewish woman who never comes to terms with the fact that he does not marry her. Assisting her prepares the way for Melzer's most meaningful relationship: he is united with his soul mate Thea Rokitzer. His ability to establish this ultimate bond is proof that he has been healed.

As a myriad of plot lines illustrate, all of Doderer's characters suffer from distorted perceptions. Everyone is in search of self-realization. The assumption that everyone possesses a "real" self, an inalienable, but buried identity, remains unquestioned. Those who find themselves have the chance of becoming "simple" persons like Melzer, and eventually of finding their seemingly pre-ordained significant other (of the opposite sex). Those who fail to overcome their "false" realities, like Etelka Grauermann, end up in disaster or death—Mary K. is lucky to lose only a leg in a traffic accident. Hers is only one example of how a brush with death can bring about a spiritual transformation. She survives, and her handicap liberates her from her conventional life, but most of all, from her illusions. A feeling of well-being accompanies such changes indicating that the character has embarked on the journey toward self-realization. On this path even the minutest object, every coincidence, is significant and as if arranged by a higher power to guide the individual. Doderer's rhetorical devices—puns, irony, symbols, and leitmotifs—underscore the relevance of each detail. The climax of this literary firework of attraction and repulsion, trial and error, is the Melzer's engagement party, an idyll reminiscent of Goethe's *Wilhelm Meister* novels and Stifter's *Der Nachsommer* (*Indian Summer*).

Doderer himself appears to have felt dissatisfaction about the fact that his grandiose epic leads to little more than conventional couplings and private bliss—at least this is what the ending seems to imply. As the plot lines merge, the ostensibly air-tight universe is undermined by reflections about the novel as a literary genre.

—Dagmar C.G. Lorenz

ŚŪDRAKA

See THE LITTLE CLAY CART

THE SUFFERINGS OF YOUNG WERTHER (Die Leiden des jungen Werthers)
Novel by Johann Wolfgang von Goethe, 1774

At a time when, in Germany at least, the novel was still struggling to establish itself as a serious literary form, and had little to show but cumbersome copies of foreign originals, Johann Wolfgang von Goethe succeeded in producing a work which was not only original, but also short, swift, and of undeniable emotional intensity. The literary expression of such highly-charged passion, and its destructive consequences, had hitherto been confined to high tragedy. Its presentation in prose narrative, coupled with a powerful sense of everyday reality suggested by Werther's individually dated letters to his friend Wilhelm which form the bulk of the work, moreover mirroring events of which many readers would have been aware, represented a unique innovation in Germany.

Although not, strictly speaking, autobiographical, the novel unites two strands of experience from Goethe's immediate past; his love for Charlotte Buff, who was later to marry Christian Kestner, with whom Goethe was on friendly terms, and the fate of Karl Wilhelm Jerusalem, a friend of Kestner's who had recently committed suicide out of unrequited love for a married woman, using pistols he had borrowed from Kestner. Kestner in turn wrote a detailed account of the circumstances of Jerusalem's death to which Goethe had access while composing the novel.

The story is simple. A sensitive young man, who shares a birthday with Goethe, is sent by his mother to a small town to settle the matter of a legacy. He responds rapturously to the beauty of the spring landscape—it is the month of May. He meets and quickly falls in love with Lotte, who is "as good as engaged" to Albert, who is temporarily absent. Lotte values the friendship of a kindred spirit—they share an enthusiasm for the rhapsodic poetry of Klopstock—but quite clearly has no intention of responding to Werther's passion. Werther

remains in the town from May to September 1771, then forces himself to leave and take up employment with a legation in a nearby city. He outstays his welcome at a social gathering restricted to members of the aristocracy, is asked to leave, feels outraged, and resigns. He returns to the town there Lotte and Albert, now husband and wife, are living. His passion for Lotte becomes all-consuming and he gradually loses his already tenuous grip on everyday reality. He finally shoots himself, with a pistol borrowed from Albert, just before Christmas 1772. The entire story is told in the form of letters by Werther to his friend Wilhelm (whose replies we never see) collected after his death by a fictitious editor who takes up the narration towards the end when the balance of Werther's mind is obviously becoming disturbed. But perhaps Goethe's own account of the story, in a letter to Schönborn of June 1774, goes closer to the heart of the matter. He calls the novel a story "... in which I portray a young man who, endowed with profound, pure feeling and true penetration of mind, loses himself in rhapsodic dreams, undermines himself by speculation until he finally, ravaged by the additional effect of unhappy passion and in particular by an infinite love, shoots himself in the head." Werther's love for Lotte is, therefore, not the central, motive force in the novel, not the reason for the tragedy, but merely its occasion.

Werther is the tragedy of an individual sensibility which cannot be accommodated by the society in which it finds itself, nor, perhaps, ultimately, by the limitations of human existence. From the outset, before he has even met Lotte, we see Werther lamenting that human existence is a "prison"—the image recurs obsessively—and we sense the potential danger which lies in his "solution" to this dilemma: "I withdraw into my inner self and there discover a world—a world, it is true, rather of vague perceptions and dim desires than of creative power and vital force. And then everything swims before my senses, and I go on smiling at the outer world like someone in a dream" (May 22, Book 1). This surrender to radical solipsism results in Werther's progressive disability to come to terms with external reality, which is manifest before he meets Lotte. In the second letter we see him "enjoying" the natural scene—it is spring—and proclaiming: "I could not draw now, not a line, and yet have never been a greater painter than in these moments" (10 May, Book 1). This is a profound delusion. Either he is not an artist—and there is relatively little evidence in the novel that he is—or he is going through a particularly barren period. The letter continues with an ecstatic evocation of the beauty of nature, through which Werther senses the powerful presence of the divinity as an all-pervading, loving presence, only to end with the despairing realization, "But this experience is more than I can bear. I succumb to the power and glory of these visions." Werther has indeed the artist's capacity for intense experience, to which his epistolary evocations of nature still bear convincing witness; what he lacks, and lacks totally, is the critical distance, self-control, the power to shape experience into art. His frustrated artistic ambitions, like his frustrated erotic passion, are expressions of a more general incapacity, indeed unwillingness, to come to terms with life in general, to establish a viable balance between outer and inner worlds, between self and other. At times this seems the result of instinctive reaction, but on occasion we can see Werther making a conscious choice. Shortly after leaving his employment at the legation we witness him musing about the character of his temporary host: "Moreover he values my mind and my talents more than my heart, which alone is my only source of everything, all the strength, all the blessedness, all the misery of my existence. Ah, anyone can know what I know. My heart alone is my own" (9 May, Book 2). In opting for the glory of individual authenticity, with all its emotional heights and depths, Werther rejects the culture of shared, commonsense rationality according to which society in general lives. Romanticism—almost a generation before its time—declares war on Rationalism. That the outcome of this battle is inevitable tragedy does not, however, destroy the dignity of Werther. (His name is derived from the German *Wert*, signifying value or worth.) And it is a battle which, while firmly anchored in late 18th-century sensibility and society, may have much wider complications. Reviewing the best-selling novel of his youth after an interval of 50 years, Goethe suggests that the story of Werther can be seen as the story of a young man with a desire for freedom who has to come to terms with a set of old-fashioned social norms. Werther's frustrations may thus lay claim to a degree of universality and, Goethe concludes, "... it would be pretty bad if everybody did not have a period in his life when *Werther* strikes him as though it had been written exclusively for him" (*Conversations with Eckermann*, 2 January 1824).

Although the initial success of the novel was probably due to what many readers, including the self-appointed guardians of public morality, saw as its scandalous nature—its apparent advocacy of adulterous passion and allegedly positive portrayal of suicide—its continued popularity to the present day indicates that Goethe's claim for the universality of the novel was correct. This is nowhere better illustrated than in the furore which greeted Ulrich Plenzdorf's *The New Sorrows of Young W.* (1972), which appeared in the capital of the former German Democratic Republic, and, taking Goethe's novel as its point of departure, again raises the question of the rival claims of personal authenticity and social integration which Goethe had so convincingly addressed 200 years earlier.

—Bruce Watson

SUN STONE (Piedra de sol)
Poem by Octavio Paz, 1957

Octavio Paz wrote this long, ambitious poem during a crucial moment in his life. He had returned to Mexico in 1953 after 11 years abroad including five years as Mexican cultural attaché in Paris. His return to Mexico was controversial, for he had become a radical poet and critic, reviewing the Mexican cultural tradition along the surrealist lines he had part adopted from Paris. *Sun Stone* can be seen as summarizing his experiences as a Mexican poet nourished by a European tradition. He has not altered it from its first edition of 300 copies in 1957; there are at least six different punished translations of the poem in English.

The title alludes to the Aztec calendar stone that stands in the Museum of Anthropology and History in Mexico City. The poem is composed of 584 hendecasyllables, with the first six repeated at the end to make the poem appear to close like a circle. There are no full stops, so the poem is meant to flow like the passing of time itself, or like history, which is one of its themes, where a series of epiphanies is undermined by the nightmares of recorded history. The number 584 is deliberately related to a Mayan system and the cycle of the planet Venus around the sun. Venus in the Mexican cosmology was the plumed serpent Quetzalcoatl, a man god who disappeared to journey through the underworld, and, it was prophesied, would return from the East. The ancient Mexicans linked the ending of the 584-day cycle

of Venus/Quetzalcoatl with the ending of an epoch and the beginning of another, a rebirth which is also one of the themes of the poem.

Two verbs structure the flow of the lines: "voy" ("I go") and "buscar" ("to seek") and suggest that this is a quest poem. Anecdotally the poem can be seen as being about the poet awake at night while his love or muse lies next to him asleep. Through erotic empathy with the woman he journeys into her mind, into the past, into history, as the night turns into dawn and hope. Given the learned associations with the title, and Paz's dense allusive lines, the poem might appear to need notes, which Paz did not supply, though the first edition carried a prologue which Paz suppressed until his 1979 complete poems.

Paz sees life as split between two colliding forces which he calls notationally history and poetry. By history he means all that confines an individual's liberty, from laws and taboos of society to authoritarian politics and dehumanizing work. By poetry Paz means the freedom to express oneself fully, to break out of the prison house of life through love and art. *Sun Stone* is structured on a spiral which moves alternately in and out of the alienation of history via sudden moments—Paz called them "poetic instants"—of liberation. There are many allusions and references to the trap or nightmare of history imprisoning the poet. We see the poet lost in a labyrinth, forgetting his name, his purpose, asking questions about his past with references to Berkeley, Paris, India, Mexico, and Spain. He lists in a litany form all that divides man from his freedom: "the bars of the banks and prisons/the bars of paper, barbed-wire fences, / bells, barbs, and spikes, / the monochord sermon of arms / the cloying scorpion with hat / the tiger with top hat, president / of the Vegetarian Club and Red Cross." Rather than resign to societal values and be a victim, Paz proposes surrealist values, suggests not giving into the laws, like Abelard, and being castrated, "better crime, / suicidal lovers, incest." There is yet another angry list that deals with history's famous victims, some personally important to Paz's own intellectual formation, like Montezuma (betrayed by Cortés), Trotskii (betrayed by Stalin and murdered in Mexico) and Madero (betrayed by the Mexican revolution).

Opposed to these elements of "history" Paz offers a combative view of love as able to change the world. There is a reference to the Spanish Civil War, and the bombing of Madrid in 1937, when the poet and his lover make love as a way of opposing the evil of fascism by reaching an area of moral purity outside time and corrupt politics, a paradise recovered via erotic and sexual love as the couple copulate: "There is no you nor I, tomorrow, yesterday or names, / truth of two in one body and soul / oh total being." Lovers become the true revolutionaries, "if two kiss / the world changes." For the male poet it is woman who embodies the other that redeems him from alienation, and she is given many names in the poem, from Venus to Isabel, Laura, Maria, etc., often taking the identity of the muses of famous poets (Petrarch, Garcilaso), and especially that of Melusine, half woman, half serpent, a water nymph who is spied upon during her Saturday transformation back to her mythic self and is thus betrayed by the male's gaze. Melusine's role in the poem is an act of homage to the surrealist André Breton who refers to her in his works *Nadja*, 1928, and *Arcane 17*, 1944. Woman then is all women, an archetype that goes back to Kali, Aphrodite, Ishtar; she is "door to being." Some of the best lines in the poem form part of Paz's celebration of woman.

What happens when two lovers dissolve the barriers that keep people trapped in their solitary, anguished egos is that life itself becomes more alive, "true life," "the forgotten astonishment of feeling alive.'' This is the poetic message for the ideologically rigid Mexico of the late 1950s. Paz argued that the world can be changed, but not the Mexican Revolutionary way.

—Jason Wilson

THE SUPPLIANT MAIDENS (Supplices)
Play by Aeschylus, c. 463 BC

Aeschylus' *The Suppliant Maidens* is our first extant example of a type of play in which a city is begged to come to the aid of an individual or group often under pressure or constraint from another party: the ''suppliant'' play. Later instances are provided by Euripides' own *Suppliant Women* (*Supplices*) and *Children of Heracles* (*Heracleidae*) and Sophocles' *Oedipus at Colonus* (*Oedipus Coloneus*). In this case the suppliants are the Egyptian monarch Danaus and his 50 daughters. The city is their ancestral home, Argos, whose spokesman is the Argive king Pelasgus. Their supplication is for refuge at Argos and protection from their pursuers, the 50 sons of Aegyptus to whom, for reasons not clearly given in the play, they refuse to be given in marriage.

The play starts with the arrival on the Argive coast of the suppliant girls and their father. After a long choral introduction setting the scene, Danaus instructs his daughters on how to conduct their supplication. The arrival (long heralded by Danaus) of the Argive king leads once more to dialogue between actor and chorus in which the Danaids explain their kinship and the reasons for their supplication. In alternating choral lyric and spoken dialogue a great scene of formal supplication develops, culminating in the supreme gesture of the suppliants, the threat to commit suicide by hanging themselves if they are not accepted. The dilemma of the Argive king is great. He can hardly resist such pressure, yet he does not wish to bring about the bloodshed of his subjects in a costly war. He takes Danaus with him to attempt to convince an assembly of Argives to accept the suppliants. This proves successful, and Danaus returns and informs his daughters. Presently Danaus observes the arrival of the Egyptian vessel. The girls flee in terror to altars whence the newly disembarked Egyptian herald seeks to move them. Pelasgus arrives and in a verbal battle drives off the herald, making it clear that Argos will fight to defend its suppliants. The grateful suppliants leave the stage and make for the city, uncertain of the outcome of the impending battle.

Until fairly recently *The Suppliant Maidens* was regarded as our earliest Greek tragedy. However, the publication in 1952 of a scrap of papyrus (P. Oxy. 2256. 3) giving information about one of the tragic competitions at the Dionysia has changed that supposition. In all probability *The Suppliant Maidens* was the first play of a trilogy concerned with the fate of the Danaids (it certainly gives the impression of being the opening of a trilogy). We know also of a play entitled *Aigyptioi*. The papyrus fragment reports a competition in which Aeschylus defeated Sophocles with a trilogy, the final play of which was entitled *Daughters of Danaus*. The titles of the first two plays have yet to be supplied. The most natural assumption is that these were *The Suppliant Maidens* and *Aigyptioi*. If so, *The Suppliant Maidens* is in fact a relatively late play since Sophocles' dramatic career began no earlier than 470 BC. The most likely date for the *Danaid* trilogy is 464–63 BC.

It is not easy to assess critically what is essentially the first act of a drama, the final two acts of which are lost to us. If we had the whole,

no doubt much of the thematic material would be seen to have further resonances. Even so, *The Suppliant Maidens* is an impressive and exciting piece, pitching us into a conflict of which it is tantalizing not to know the outcome.

Although the revelation of P. Oxy. 2256. 3 is a salutary warning to those who believe plays can be firmly dated on stylistic grounds, one cannot really blame those who saw in the play an indication of the characteristics of the very earliest tragedy. Certain features have an undoubtedly archaic appearance, most notably the general air of simplicity and grandeur, the role of chorus as actor (in this case the protagonist), and the extreme economy of dramatis personae. Apart from the chorus only three personages appear on stage, namely Danaus, Pelasgus, and the Egyptian herald (it is still a matter of dispute whether a subsidiary chorus of handmaidens features in the conclusion of the play).

The massive choral contributions to the play contain some of Aeschylus' most impressive poetry (some of which is difficult to interpret). The passage on the inscrutability of Zeus' purpose foreshadows the famous Zeus-hymn in *Agamemnon*: ''shaggy and bushy are the devices of his wits and where they stretch is difficult to perceive.''

—David M. Bain

ŚVETĀŚVATARA

See UPANISHADS

THE SYMPOSIUM
Prose by Plato, 4th century BC

A symposium in ancient Greece was a drinking party, literally ''drinking together.'' The songs, conversations, and other merriments that often accompanied such gatherings became the basis for a loose-knit literary genre concerned with the play of conviviality, wit, and occasionally wisdom. Ancient Greek and Roman literature offers a number of examples, including Plutarch's *Symposiaca*, Macrobius' *Saturnalia*, and even *Dinner at Trimalchio's* (*Cena Trimalchionis*) in Petronius' *Satyricon*. It was also a favourite literary vehicle in the Middle Ages and Renaissance, including the *Convivio* of Dante, the *Heptaplomeres* of Jean Bodin, and the many gargantuan banquets of Rabelais. The greatest of this genre, and certainly the model for many of the later incarnations, is *The Symposium* of Plato, a work scholars generally attribute to Plato's middle period, somewhere between 385 and 378 BC. Indeed, *The Symposium* is arguably Plato's masterpiece, exceeded only by *The Republic* in its influence.

Ostensibly Plato's *Symposium* offers the account of a drinking party celebrating the victory of the dramatic poet Agathon, during the Lenaian Festival at Athens in 416 BC. During the course of the party, seven guests, including the comic playwright Aristophanes, Socrates, and later Alcibiades, deliver extemporaneous speeches praising love. While Plato labours to construct an elaborate series of narrative frames to explain the origins of his account, it is clear upon close examination that the work is intricately choreographed, that its very structure embodies Plato's doctrine of love while presenting a parody of a tragedy with its accompanying satyr play.

The Symposium begins with a multilayered narrative frame, three steps removed from the actual events of the party. Plato dramatizes an account of the party given to a friend by Apollodoros, who in turn had heard it from Aristodemos, who had actually been present. In this account, Aristodemos offers his recollection of the speeches delivered by Phaedros, Pausanias, Eryximachus, Aristophanes, Agathon, Socrates, and later Alcibiades. Each speaker delivers a speech praising love. Thus Phaedros speaks of the power of physical love and beauty to inspire great actions. Pausanias develops that theme, but distinguishes heavenly from earthly love. The physician Eryximachus sees love as the harmonious balance of opposites rather than something physical. Aristophanes the comic poet, on the one hand, weaves a moving fable of early humans hunting for their lost opposites. Agathon the tragic poet, on the other hand, tells a tale of love as the youngest of the gods, the source of virtue. The centrepiece of *The Symposium* is Socrates' speech. After questioning Agathon, he proceeds to recount what he had been taught about love by a wise woman named Diatima.

As the speech of each of the six speakers took as its starting point some aspect of the previous speaker while purporting to advance, correct, or clarify it, so Diatima leads Socrates through six stages of love from the physical to an apprehension of love itself, stages that in fact echo the earlier speeches. "One goes always upwards for the sake of this Beauty, starting out from beautiful things and using them like rising stairs," Diatima declares. This image of the ladder or stair of love became a favourite in Renaissance iconography. Continuing, she explains:

> from one body to two and from two to all beautiful bodies, then from beautiful bodies to beautiful customs, and from customs to learning beautiful things, and from these lessons he arrives in the end at this lesson, which is learning of this very

Beauty, so that in the end he comes to know just what it is to be beautiful.

The six steps of Diatima's stairs point to a spiritual development that recapitulates the development through the six speeches. In turn, it points to the six steps that the reader must pass over to get at the Beautiful through the accounts of Diatima, Socrates, Aristodemos, Apollodorus, his friend, and finally Plato, the narrative layers echoing the spiritual levels.

Socrates' remarks are interrupted by the drunken arrival of Alcibiades, who himself decides to deliver a speech. If the first six speeches may be taken as a single unit, presenting a serious celebration of love and beauty, the speech of Alcibiades stands in comic relief (in effect, the satyr play that conventionally accompanied the tragedy). This association is reinforced when Alcibiades compares Socrates to Silenus, a special statue of the satyr king which, while ugly on the outside, contained something wholesome and beautiful on the inside. This comparison reflects ironically on the drunken and lecherous Alcibiades himself, who while beautiful on the outside, is ugly and corrupt on the inside. He is at the bottom of the Platonic stairs, a point borne out not only by his own comic account of his unsuccessful attempt to seduce Socrates, but by Plato's own knowledge of Alcibiades' subsequent history.

Plato's *Symposium* is one of the masterpieces of Attic Greek prose, if not world literature in general. While commemorating the victory of Agathon as a tragic playwright, it does so by creating a complete dramatic cycle in itself. Its celebration of love and the Beautiful is itself an intricate, elegant, and eloquent work of art with the textual richness and density of poetry, a work that exercised a profound influence on Western thought and iconography from the Renaissance to the present, a profound reminder of the driving force of the erotic beneath the rational being.

—Thomas L. Cooksey

T

TAITTIRĪYA

See UPANISHADS

THE TALE OF THE CAMPAIGN OF IGOR (Slovo o polku Igoreve)

Anonymous medieval heroic poem in Old Russian, concerning the campaign of Prince Igor of Novgorod-Severesk against the nomadic Polovtsian tribes. Composed between 1185 (date of the events described) and 1 October 1187 (before the death of the Prince of Galich, cited as still living). The manuscript was preserved in a single copy, probably from the early 16th century. It was acquired by Count A. Musin-Pushkin between 1788 and 1792, and published by him in 1800. The original manuscript was destroyed in the Moscow Fire, 1812, although a copy from 1795 survives.

PUBLICATIONS

[Selections], translated by D. Ward, in *Forum for Modern Languages*, 2. 1966.

*

Bibliography: *The Igor Tale: An Annotated Bibliography of Non-Soviet Scholarship on the Slovo o polku Igoreve* by N. Cooper, 1978.

Critical Studies: *History of Early Russian Literature* by N.K. Gudzy, translated by Susan Wilbur Jones, 1949; ''The Puzzles of the Igor Tale on the 150th Anniversary of Its First Edition'' by Roman Jakobson, in *Speculum*, 27, 1952; *History of Russian Literature from the Eleventh Century to the End of the Baroque* by D. Cizevskij, 1962; ''The Authenticity of the Slovo o polku Igoreve,'' in *Oxford Slavonic Papers*, 23, 1967, *Slovo o polku Igoreve i kul'tura ego vremeni*, 1978, and *Lay of the Warfare Waged by Igor*, 1981, all by D.S. Likhachev; *Slovo o polku Igoreve i ego sovremenniki* by B.A. Rybakov, 1971; *Early Russian Literature* by John Fennell and Anthony Stokes, 1974; *Poetika ''Slova o polku Igoreve''* by Boris Gasparov, 1984; *Lances Sing: A Study of the Igor Tale* by Robert Mann, 1990.

* * *

The Tale of the Campaign of Igor is both the greatest and the most controversial work of medieval Russian and Ukrainian literature. In highly poetic language it depicts the unsuccessful campaign undertaken in 1185 by a minor prince of Rus', Igor Sviatoslavich, from the principality of Novgorod-Seversk against the steppe nomad people known as the Polovtsians or Cumans. It is controversial for two reasons, firstly because the only manuscript that contained the text of the work was destroyed in the Fire of Moscow of 1812, and secondly because there is nothing comparable among extant literary works of the 11th to 14th centuries. As a result, theories about its origin, author, and literary context must remain supposition.

The manuscript was acquired by Count A. Musin-Pushkin, a well-known collector of antiquities, some time between 1788 and 1792, and was published in 1800 to enormous acclaim. The discovery that the Ossian texts were forgeries together with the unfortunate loss of the sole manuscript in 1812 led to doubts about the work's authenticity—it is still questioned by a minority of scholars to this day. While it is certain that, failing the miraculous appearance of another copy, these doubts can never be laid to rest entirely, it is also obvious that the dense poetic and bold epic qualities of the work ensure that the tale fits even less well with the neoclassicism and pre-Romanticism of the 18th century than it does with what is known of the culture of Kievan Rus' at the end of the 12th century. The onus must therefore be on those who deny its medieval provenance to prove their case.

The tale is rich in historical references, since it seeks to set Igor and his foolhardy campaign in the context of historical explanation and contrast. The anonymous author, writing—it would appear—between 1185 and 1187, expresses his admiration of Igor and his brother, Vsevolod, accompanied by their sons, who ventured deep into hostile steppe territory to fight and lose a battle against overwhelming odds. At the same time, he laments Igor's breaking of the recent agreement between the two main princely clans to coordinate efforts against the Polovtsians. The results of the 1185 campaign were internal feuding and unopposed Polovtsian raids, and the author appeals in the tale to the powerful princes of the west and north east whose lands did not border the steppe to come to the aid of the land of Rus', an appeal destined, as the despairing tone suggests, to be ignored. He looks back nostalgically at the 11th century, the zenith of Kievan power, and at the birth of the tradition of princely feuding at the end of that century. Patriotic attachment to the land of Rus' overweighs loyalty to Igor as the author sorrowfully condemns Igor's ancestor Oleg of Chernigov, the first of that branch of the family to ally with the Polovtsians against his brother princes, thereby forging a tradition of discord that weakened Rus' through the 12th century: and so it was in the days of Oleg son of Sorrow that civil wars were sown and grew, and in them perished the patrimony of the sons of Dazhbog.

There is thus a strong political message embedded in this epic poem, as well as a lyrical strain, created partly by the pervasive use of nature imagery. Not only are the heroes compared to falcons or wild animals and the enemy to ravens, but nature itself takes part in the action, warning against the campaign with an eclipse of the sun (here transferred on poetic grounds from a point part way through the campaign), while beasts howl and night groans. As the main Polovtsian force moves up to crush the Russian army, a blood-red sky heralds the dawn and black clouds come from the sea to cover the four Suns (the four Russian princes who were attacked from the south, the direction of the sea). When the Russian banners fall, the grass and trees bow down in sorrow, and when Igor escapes birds show the way to the river Donets and safety.

Much of the lyrical tone stems from the use of phrases drawn from folksong and wedding laments together with the ironic use of imagery: death is depicted in terms of a feast, battles in terms of the peaceful activities of ploughing, sowing, and harvesting. The author's own feeling of sadness is also expressed through the figure of Iaroslavna, Igor's wife, who laments on the ramparts of Putivl

1527

invoking the wind, river, and sun in turn, reproaching them and asking them to return Igor to her, a plea that is soon answered.

With its vivid and often symbolic use of colour (for the Russians, the colours scarlet, gold, and silver are reminiscent of icons), the tale possesses an emotional intensity unique in early Russian or Ukrainian literature. It is clearly the product of a court environment, composed by an author with a sophisticated knowledge of history and local flora and fauna. Given the combination of admiration of Igor's valour and criticism and of his foolhardiness, he was probably attached not to Igor's own court but to that of one of the more senior princes of his clan, perhaps Sviatoslav of Kiev, since at the conclusion of the work Igor is seen (contrary to historical fact) riding to Kiev to pay his respects to Sviatoslav as the sun shines and the Russian land rejoices. Though obviously possessing strong connections with oral tradition, especially an undocumented folk epic tradition, some stylistic links with literary works point to the tale being a literary composition, probably sung. Though firm answers to questions of authorship, genesis, and style are lacking, the work's rich poetic texture repays the scrutiny of the modern reader.

—Faith Wigzell

TALES FROM THE VIENNA WOODS (Geschichten aus dem Wienerwald)
Play by Ödön von Horváth, 1931

The title, *Tales from the Vienna Woods*, offers the prospect of an evening's nostalgia, when Vienna was Vienna, the Danube was blue, and the air was filled with the reassuring tones of Johann Strauss. The additional reassurance of the "Volksstück," the traditional folk-play with its simple tale simply told suggests comedy, intrigue, a love story and, of course, a happy end. Indeed the curtain rises on a romantic vista: Danube, ruined castle, and the air, as the stage direction notes, alive with the sound of music—"as if in the background someone is playing Johann Strauss's 'Tales from the Vienna Woods'."

Viennese waltz music is heard frequently throughout the play, but all too often as an uncomfortable counterpoint and disturbance to the action on stage. Ödön von Horváth sets his play in the present, not the past, and is writing "against the grain." The audience's expectations are roused and the illusion then shattered with the disturbing revelation that characters who profess morality and traditional values are driven by a more self-centred animal amorality.

Women are the prey in Horváth's world, and in *Tales from the Vienna Woods* the sacrificial victim is Marianne, a naive young girl who has seen more romantic films than is good for her. Reality is life with her father, the Zauberkönig, who runs a toy shop in a quiet street in the middle-class eighth district of Vienna. He has seen the advantages of an alliance in the street and is pushing her to marry their next-door neighbour Oskar, a butcher. Marianne is trapped and can see a lifetime's drudgery caring for both her new husband and her father. She is easily swept off her feet with the arrival of Alfred, a feckless, out of work gambler with an affectation of style and a vocabulary spiced with clichés, which Marianne, in thrall to her screen heroes, misinterprets as love.

Love, in Horváth's Vienna, is a smoke-screen for ruthless exploitation. Marianne leaves home, is disowned by her father, has a child by Alfred, and loses her pride by being obliged to appear in a nude revue, her liberty when caught stealing in a pitiful attempt to survive, and, finally, her child, who dies precisely as a carefully contrived family reconciliation and return to family values has been arranged. The happy end to this play is a hollow mockery. Oskar gains his bride, but it is he and the Zauberkönig who will live happily ever after.

Marianne's fate is not tragic but pathetic. She and her companions in this play successfully illustrate the motto Horváth gave to the work: "Nothing is so infinite as the human capacity for stupidity." Horváth presents this travesty of true love conquering all by ensuring that the audience recognizes the shallowness of his characters. They should speak, he said, in educated German, but we must always sense that their normal idiom is dialect and that it is their "telephone voices" that we hear. The image they create is challenged by means of a recurrent stage direction *Stille* (Silence). The play is full of telling moments as the action stops in mid-sentence, catching the audience unawares and reminding them of the true implications of what has just been said and done.

As the play progresses, Marianne finds she has exchanged a life of finding her father's lost suspenders in the eighth district for a life in the 18th district with Alfred finding his. Such repetitions and moments of harsh humour combine with a dialogue that is deliberately rich in cliché, as the hypocrisy of the middle class is stripped away to reveal its true confusion and lack of moral base. Marianne's appearance in the cabaret at Maxim's encapsulates Horváth's technique of montage and contrast and his analysis of middle-class attitudes.

The floor show at Maxim's offers, to quote the master of ceremonies, three "sensational *tableaux vivants*, created by the most talented artists to the highest aesthetic standards." The first is "Danube Water Sprites" performed to the "Blue Danube." The water sprites have tail fins covering their legs but are otherwise naked. Tableau Two is "Our Zeppelin" and, to the tunes of a popular military march, three naked girls are displayed. The first holds a propeller, the second a globe, and the third a little Zeppelin. The audience, says the stage direction, "roars its approval, rising to its feet and breaking spontaneously into the first verse of "Deutschland, Deutschland, über alles" before resuming its seats." Tableau Three, to the accompaniment of Schumann's wistful "Träumerei," is entitled "In Pursuit of Happiness." The girls, naked, struggle to be the first to reach a golden orb on which stands happiness, equally naked. It is a beautifully sentimental *son et lumière*.

The cabaret turns allow Horváth to combine sex (the girls), power and aggression (the Zeppelin), and tradition (the music) to show the truly instinctive and unthinking base supporting the façade of middle-class respectability. The Zauberkönig's loud approval of naked girls in cabaret turns to outrage when he recognizes that "happiness" is in this instance "his" Marianne, who has been forced to humiliate herself to provide for her child. Unforgiving in its hypocrisy, Horváth's Vienna exacts a fearful price from its victims in the name of respectability.

Written in the 1930s as an attack on communal blindness and hypocrisy, *Tales from the Vienna Woods* is as relevant now as it was then. To those who wish to pretend that society has changed since the Nazi era, Horváth's play is an uncomfortable reminder that the middle-class capacity for self-deceit is as infinite as its capacity for stupidity.

—Alan Best

TARTUFFE
Play by Molière, 1664

Tartuffe was Molière's most controversial comedy. A three-act version was privately performed at court in 1664 but denounced by churchmen. A five-act version had one public performance in 1667 and was immediately banned. In 1669, thanks to King Louis XIV's protection, an amended version of the five-act play had a highly successful run in Paris. It has continued to excite controversy ever since.

Tartuffe is a director of conscience in the household of Orgon. A director of conscience in 17th-century France was supposed to be a man of piety who would advise on how to live a good Christian life. Molière's Tartuffe, however, is a criminal whose exaggerated pretence of piety has duped Orgon into complete subservience to him. The comedy therefore has two centres of interest: Tartuffe's hypocrisy and Orgon's gullibility, both of which are represented by a wide range of theatrical devices, in particular visual effects derived from farce.

Acts I and II are devoted to showing the gullible Orgon in a ridiculous light. Before he comes on stage a servant gives a verbal portrait of his outrageous infatuation with Tartuffe: "Orgon loves him a hundred times more than mother, son, daughter, or wife." Having whetted our appetite by this description, Molière next shows Orgon in action. He neglects news of his wife's illness to ask repeatedly after Tartuffe's health and then relates Tartuffe's caricatural displays of piety as if they were the mark of a saint.

He is ridiculed further as he tries to force his daughter to agree to marry Tartuffe, for he is constantly interrupted by Dorine, a servant, and finally goaded into striking her. His blow miscarries and he retreats in anger from the stage.

Tartuffe's entrance is delayed until Act III. Each scene in which he appears represents visually or verbally some aspect of religious fraud. He makes his entrance with a celebrated piece of stage business, pretending to be scandalized by Dorine's low-cut dress. He takes a kerchief from his pocket and orders the servant to cover her breasts. But Tartuffe's underlying lust is displayed during an interview with Elmire, Orgon's wife, who has come to beg him to withdraw from his betrothal to Orgon's daughter. During their conversation Tartuffe squeezes Elmire's fingers, puts his hand on her knee, moves his chair closer as she recoils, and makes to touch her neck. Having visibly betrayed his lasciviousness, he professes his love for his employer's wife, using the elevated language of religious devotion. However, Orgon's son, Damis, has been spying on the interview, and just as Tartuffe is assuring Elmire that his position as director of conscience will enable him to cover up any affair between them, Damis bursts in and reveals that he has heard all. A moment later Orgon arrives and Damis denounces Tartuffe to his father.

Tartuffe wriggles out of this compromising situation by feigning repentance for unspecified misdeeds and kneeling to beg forgiveness. Orgon, blind to the reality of the situation, is perversely determined to infuriate his family by favouring Tartuffe. He accuses his son of lying and drives him out with a stick. Further to show his contempt for everybody he decides to disinherit his son and hand over his entire property to Tartuffe.

The family unite in Act IV trying to undo the evil effects of Orgon's perverse behaviour. Cléante appeals to Tartuffe to reconcile father and son; without success. Mariane pleads with her father to be released from marrying Tartuffe, but he insists that a repugnant marriage would be a profitable mortification for her. At this crisis Elmire offers to prove to her husband that Tartuffe really did try to seduce her, and a trap is laid for the imposter.

Elmire makes Orgon hide under the table while Tartuffe is fetched to see her. She obliquely implies that she is favourably disposed to Tartuffe's advances: he responds by urging her to give him some physical proof of her affection. The more he presses her, the more desperate Elmire becomes for her husband to come out of hiding. Finally she sends Tartuffe from the room and Orgon at last emerges from beneath the table. Tartuffe returns hoping to embrace Elmire but finds himself confronting the irate Orgon, who at last sees Tartuffe for the criminal he is and orders him out. However, Tartuffe is now the legal owner of the house and he threatens Orgon with eviction, as always "in the interests of religion."

Tension mounts in Act V as further details of Tartuffe's hold over Orgon intensify the family's consternation. A legal agent representing Tartuffe arrives to evict the family. Their collective anger drives them near to beating him. Worse follows. Valère brings news that Tartuffe has denounced Orgon to the King for a political offence and is on his way to have him arrested. Valère loyally offers to help Orgon escape but is prevented by Tartuffe's arrival with an officer to arrest Orgon. In a final twist the soldier arrests Tartuffe instead, explaining that the King has seen through Tartuffe's imposture and has pardoned Orgon.

The comedy was doubly offensive to churchmen. Firstly for making fun of the church's task of giving spiritual advice and secondly for satirizing a religious hypocrite in such a way that genuinely pious Christians were exposed to ridicule as well. Molière defended himself as a comic dramatist, saying he was entitled to attack dishonest spiritual advisers. He also maintained that he had clearly distinguished between Tartuffe's gross hypocrisy and true Christian piety, which is described in the play by Cléante. Whatever Molière's intentions, his vivid portrayal of a lecherous and dishonest spiritual adviser was bound to raise awkward questions about the conduct of any person giving spiritual advice and, while Cléante's descriptions of true piety are persuasive and apparently well founded, they have been judged inadequate to counterbalance the disturbing implications of Tartuffe's hypocrisy.

Molière's mastery of theatrical technique, especially his blend of farcical situations with high comedy, has ensured *Tartuffe's* enduring popularity on the stage, and his play continues to generate debate by its provocative treatment of religion.

—David Maskell

TENTATIVA DEL HOMBRE INFINITO (The Infinite Man's Attempt)
Poem by Pablo Neruda, 1926

One of the tensions behind the astounding popular appeal of Pablo Neruda's second collection of poems, *Twenty Love Poems and a Song of Despair*, was the poet's drive to be modern. The Romantic notion of the poet as a bohemian outsider, as a seer, was combined with an avant-garde pull towards capturing actuality, the present moment, through the senses. In his successful love poems written in Santiago, Chile's capital, but drawing on two love affairs from his Temuco days, Neruda had tried out some daring images. He was aware of the direction modern poetry had been taking in its need to be outrageous and radical, because one of the path-finders leading the way was also Chilean, the millionaire avant-garde poet Vicente Huidobro (1893–1948).

The result of Neruda's experimentation with the then latest and most daring ways of writing was *Tentativa del hombre infinito*, printed in December 1925 but actually published in 1926. The most striking element was the absence of punctuation and capital letters. Taking liberties with the conventions of typography had begun with Guillaume Apollinaire's cubist poem "Zone" in 1913. Apollinaire also invented pictorial typography for what he called *calligrammes*, where a poem about rain took the verbal form of lines of words "raining" down the page, that is, where the object represented by words was evoked by the design of words on a page. Huidobro, who had arrived in Paris in 1916, was indebted to Apollinaire and the cubists, and participated in the Parisian avant-garde (cubism, dadaism), eliminating punctuation, rhyme, metre, and most of the other conventions associated with traditional lyric. Neruda followed suit in distant Chile. But his long poem is not derivative, and Neruda himself saw it as one of the "nucleos" (nuclei) of his work.

The second area of influence that helps a reader penetrate Neruda's long poem is surrealism, and the surrealist practice of automatic writing. The idea that a poem was a psychic document revealing in irrational images the true inner meaning of life, a liberation of the repressed unconscious, appealed to many Latin American poets unable to participate in Parisian surrealism. The surrealist stress on experiment before artistic and aesthetic ordering allowed poets to defy immediate understanding in the hope of breaking through to deeper levels. It is true that *Tentativa* is difficult, but it is only superficially surrealist. Neruda himself called it "extraordinarily personal," and counted it as a kind of failure, in his own words, "a frustrated experience of a cyclical poem that shows a development through darkness, an approximation towards things with great problems of defining them." Here the title reveals the intention, the experiment: "tentativa," an attempt, not a conclusion. It is a process poem, reaching towards a meaning never quite given in the actual lines. The second part of the title, "of an infinite man" suggests that man contains "the infinite" inside him, in his psyche, but does not quite know how to express this "infinite."

The poem does tell a kind of story in journey form. There is a first person, the poet's speaking voice, in conflict with the dark forces of the night and self, alone in his room, hoping that imagination can take him away from his existential anguish. The poet wishes to depart, and sees himself as a sailor, a fisherman, a captain. *Twenty Love Poems and a Song of Despair* ends with the idea that "it is time to leave" while Neruda sought all sorts of ways of broadening his horizon, finally leaving Chile for five years in 1926. The story is also about a poet looking for inspiration, as if inspiration comes after writing, not before. There are key lines referring to the act of writing itself: "oh soledad quiero cantar" ("Oh solitude I want to write"), where the stress is on the will to write, or "no sé hacer el canto de los días" ("I don't know how to make the song of days"), where it is the poet's incapacity to write poems that motivates this poem. The poetics emerges in the line "yo no cuento yo digo en palabras desgraciadas" ("I do not tell I say it in wretched words").

The starting point of this journey is the poet's sadness—"mi corazón está triste" ("my heart is sad"), he is a "centinela" (sentry), a "sonámbulo" (sleepwalker), and feels stuck in his room, alone. There are many references to wanting to break out, to feeling trapped in "un cuadrado de tiempo completamente inmóvil" ("a block of completely immobile time"). The poet defines this entrapment: "Estoy solo en una pieza sin ventanas / sin tener que hacer con los

itinerarios extraviados" ("I'm alone in a room without windows / with nothing to do with erring itineraries") which could be decoded as: the poet does not know how to live a more poetic life. This feeling of not being a true adventuring poet is repeated: "querias cantar sentado en tu habitación ese día / pero el aire estaba frio en tu corazón. . ." ("you wanted to sing sitting in your bedroom that day / but the air was cold in your heart . . ."). He is an "inmóvil navío" ("immobile ship"). Within this state of alienation the poet looks for some self-image of survival, and the poem ends with a sense of dawn and hope with the poet awake on his feet like a sea-captain, learning how to write with "ternura" ("tenderness"). He is the "labriego salvaje" ("wild peasant") of *Twenty Love Poems and a Song of Despair*, the innocent child about to steal fruit. He evokes himself: "ya lo comienzo a celebrar entusiasta sencillo / yo tengo la alegria de los panaderos contentos. . ." ("now I begin to celebrate, simple enthusiast / I have the joy of a contented baker. . ."). The last word is the preposition "todavía" (still), a temporal adverb that implies hope. The story then is of a poet who suffers a sense of claustrophobia, and projects an adventurous escape from a boring, meaningless life through his imagination.

In his prologue to his only short story *El habitante y su esperanza* [The Inhabitant and His Hope], 1926, Neruda defined himself as having a dramatic and Romantic view of life—"what does not reach me deeply through my sensibility does not count." At the core of *Tentativa* is a sense of frustration and suffering, a Romantic sincerity concealing some biographical check in the poet's life, allowing this poem to be read as a conjuring trick with words to change his life into something more meaningful.

—Jason Wilson

THE TEST OF VIRTUE (Le Fils naturel)
Play by Denis Diderot, 1757

There is no denying the influence of Denis Diderot's reflections on drama and theatre. However, his fame in this field rests on a handful of texts only. More surprisingly, in spite of his abiding interest in the problems of the stage, Diderot devoted a very short part of his life to his theatrical experiments. The year 1757–58 saw most of his writings on drama, including *The Test of Virtue*. In those days plays were normally produced before they were printed, but *The Test of Virtue* was published long before it was performed. In addition to the play the volume contained several key-texts on drama and was a great success with three reprints in 1757 alone. Over the years the book also went into several reprints in German, Russian, Italian, and Dutch. Yet *The Test of Virtue* also occasioned many gibes and misunderstandings. In his *Letter to d'Alembert* Rousseau reacted violently to statements in the play that he interpreted as vicious personal attacks. There had already been many unpleasant episodes between the two close friends, and this time the rift was inevitable. *The Test of Virtue* preaches fraternity and asserts Diderot's faith in the society of his time. Rousseau could not share Diderot's optimism and felt keenly that his need to be alone was misconstrued by his friend.

The Test of Virtue is a landmark in the history of French drama because Diderot meant it to launch a new genre. He thought that between the two well-charted genres, tragedy and comedy, there was ample room for at least one new genre. Diderot hesitated a lot about the name for the new genre or even genres to be developed in this unexplored territory between tragedy and comedy. "Tragédie domestique," "tragédie bourgeoise," "drame" were some of the names he considered before opting for "genre sérieux." In his eyes, the old tragicomedy could not be viewed as a forerunner of the "genre sérieux." There was too much contrast in the old tragicomedy. The aim of the new "genre sérieux" on the contrary was to combine elements taken from tragedy and comedy.

Diderot's poetics for the "genre sérieux" prescribed many rules: the subject matter must be worthy of interest, the plot simple, realistic, and relevant to bourgeois families. Finally Diderot decided prose was a more suitable medium than verse for the new genre.

Another key-word in Diderot's poetics is "tableau." Painting was as dear to Diderot's heart as drama and his texts on drama give evidence of his knowledge of the expressive means at the disposal of painters. For him a tableau means a moment in a play when the attitudes of the cast outlined on the stage set give the spectator the illusion that he is in front of a painting. Ideally, tableaux should make dialogue redundant. Their emotional impact should be such as to convey the point of a scene effectively and economically while fostering a feeling of communion in the audience. In the name of verisimilitude Diderot disapproved of reversals of fortune so common in 17th-century plays. Tableaux were for him a much more natural way of heightening tension.

The weaknesses of the play derived partly from Diderot's failure to achieve the desired result with his tableaux. His verbose and sentimental dialogues all too often destroy the genuine pathos his tableaux could hope to generate. The play violates a second principle extolled by Diderot: the plot is neither simple nor believable. The hero's virtue is indeed put to too many tests: Dorval saves his friend's life, secretly gives away his fortune to the woman he loves, and agrees to marry a woman he does not love. Finally Diderot relies for his conclusion on the hackneyed trick of the long-lost brother. On the whole, the play is not nearly as revolutionary as it could have been if Diderot had applied his own principles more strictly. What the play did bring was a new tone as well as a new token of legitimacy for the bourgeoisie. Furthermore, the dialogues that follow the play contain a truly dazzling reflection on fiction and reality. The hero Dorval is presented at the same time as the protagonist of a real adventure, the author of the play *The Test of Virtue* which tells this same adventure, the actor interpreting the part of Dorval in the play, and the critic who explains and passes judgement on the play. Diderot himself plays the part of a mere witness and pretends to serve as a foil to Dorval's genius. Diderot examines with great insight the borderline between reality and fiction so that as a whole the volume stands out as a forerunner of Pirandello's work.

—Pascale Voilley

THE THEATRE AND ITS DOUBLE (Le Théâtre et son double)
Prose by Antonin Artaud, 1938

In February 1938 Antonin Artaud's revolutionary ideas on the theatre, and in particular theatrical production, were grouped together in one volume entitled *The Theatre and Its Double*. This collection of miscellaneous essays and letters comprises a statement on the dramatic arts, equalled only in its influence over the development of 20th-century theatre in the west by the vision of Brecht. Seminal

extracts, including his essay on Balinese theatre (first published in the *Nouvelle Revue Française* issue of October 1931), the lectures at the Sorbonne—"a Mise en scène et la métaphysique" ("The Metaphysics of Theatre Production") in December 1931 and "Le Théâtre et la peste" ("The Theatre and the Plague") in April 1933, and the Duchamp-inspired "Le Théâtre alchimique" ("The Alchemical Theatre") initially conceived in 1932, convey the essence of a concept which has since become synonymous with the name of Artaud, the theatre of cruelty.

Artaud's original manifesto for the theatre of cruelty heralded the inception of a new metaphysics, to be fashioned out of words, experiences, and gestures, but based on cosmic notions involving Creation, Becoming, and Chaos, which would save contemporary theatre from the moribund psychologizing to which it had fallen prey. The word "cruelty" is mentioned only perfunctorily. From the second and even the third manifestos it is still unclear what this new "theatre" actually is. Quite what Artaud envisaged is only tangible when *The Theatre and Its Double* is considered as a whole.

The cruelty is that which is inflicted through the medium of an Artaudian theatrical production on the haplessly passive spectator, whose emotional and physical turmoil will first replicate (double) and then rejoin the spectacle, thereby authenticating what should be, as Artaud saw it, the unitary experience of theatre. His aim was to involve the audience deeply in the performance, and in a direct way that would be entirely beyond the scope of other artistic media. In a sense this involves the reorientation—back to its classical roots—of theatre, which should concentrate all its forces on its own unique status, as a live (and therefore perishable) form of communication. However, *The Theatre and Its Double* proposes radical manoeuvres by which this goal may be attained. Artaud wrote:

> We abolish the stage and the auditorium and replace them by a single site, without partition or barrier of any kind, which will become the theatre of the action. A direct communication will be re-established between the spectator and the spectacle.

He conceived a kind of frontal assault on the spectator, a total theatre in which all available means of expression would be brought to bear. Thus, *The Theatre and Its Double* redefines the language of theatre as consisting:

> of everything that occupies the stage, everything that can be manifested and expressed materially on a stage and that is addressed first of all to the senses instead of being addressed primarily to the mind as in the language of words . . . such as music, dance, plastic art, pantomime, mimicry, gesticulation, intonation, architecture, lighting, and scenery . . . .

Artaudian theatre is, then, anti-bourgeois and intensely visceral. But it need not necessarily be a temporary, hell of blood and fear; the theatre of cruelty, as is made clear in *The Theatre and Its Double,* stakes claim to a fundamental truth of human existence, it is, above all, an "ontological cruelty," linked to the suffering of existence, and to the "poverty of the human body."

In "Le Théâtre alchimique" Artaud wrote that the theatre:

> must be considered as the Double not of everyday, ubiquitous reality, of which it has gradually become the inert copy, as vain as it is watered down, but of another, dangerous type of

reality, in which the Principles like dolphins poke their heads out of the water before returning in haste to the darkest depths of the ocean.

What impressed him about the Balinese troupe he saw in action (in July 1931 at the Colonial Exhibition in the Bois de Vincennes) was the extent to which their performance expressed these mysterious Principles. Their stylized movement, syncopated vocal delivery, elaborate costume, pantomimist gestures, and attention to rhythm in music and dance were a revelation. These "animated hieroglyphs" realized a new physical language, based on the sign rather than the word. In bypassing the intervention of the verbal, the textual, the Balinese captured, with the utmost rigour, Artaud's idea of "pure theatre." He interpreted their "symbolic sketch" as a triumphant valorization of the role of the theatre producer, whose creative power "eliminates the words."

Like Artaud, Brecht capitalized on the immediacy and intimacy of the theatrical performance, but he moved in the opposite direction. Employing a technique he labelled *Verfremdungseffekt* ("alienation effect") Brecht sought to break the implicit social tie between actor and audience, so as to recreate their relationship in terms of a dialectic. In Artaud's case, technical innovation in the theatre stemmed from absolute need. Throughout his life, consciousness usually involved some form of physical or mental pain. A dreadful stammer prevented him from ever producing a conventional acting performance, though everything he did on stage (and on film) was virtuoso. Drugs, especially opium, provided anaesthesia and the possibility of creation (rarely achieved) through the perception of a Rimbaldian *dére; aglement,* disturbance or unjumbling (depending on one's point of view), of the senses. But, even in a drug-induced state, Artaud was acutely conscious of the limits alternately prescribed and transgressed by his own physical condition. The image is that of a tormented physical presence, stacked with creative energy waiting to be released. It is perhaps ironic that the theories of someone who is primarily considered an abstract theorist, who so rarely put his theories into practice, should be so corporeally centred.

But this fact is crucial to the appreciation of Artaud's work. As Jacques Derrida puts it, he "knew that each word, once it falls from the body, offering to be understood or received, exhibiting itself, becomes a stolen word." The Double in Artaud's theatre is thus an illusion. The plague is not the image of the theatre; it *is* the theatre. Similarly, the theatre *is* metaphysical, just as it *is* alchemical. The relation between the theatre and its double (the spectacle and the spectator) is, therefore, one of the exact identity, born of a dynamic interaction of the senses in which all traces of convention have been systematically effaced.

—David Platten

THE THEATRICAL ILLUSION (L'Illusion comique)
Play by Pierre Corneille, 1635–36

Pierre Corneille admitted that *The Theatrical Illusion* was a "strange monster." His previous comedies had shown characters from contemporary French life. *The Theatrical Illusion* is a disconcerting mixture of fantasy and reality, of caricature and realism.

Pridamant, in search of his long lost son, Clindor, consults a magician, Alcandre, who offers to conjure up visions of events in Clindor's life (Act I). Ensconced in the magician's cave, Pridamant sees his son serving as valet to the ridiculous braggart soldier, Matamore. Three men, Clindor, Matamore, and Adraste, are all suitors of Isabelle, but she prefers Clindor to the other two (Act II). Isabelle's servant, Lise, who is also in love with Clindor, out of jealousy arranges for Adraste to ambush Clindor, but in the scuffle Clindor kills Adraste (Act III). Sentenced to death for murder Clindor awaits execution in prison. Lise, however, repents of her plot and arranges his escape with the help of her lover, the jailer. At the end of Act IV the magician tells Pridamant that he will next see that his son has risen in the world. True enough, Act V shows Clindor richly dressed as the favourite of Prince Florilame, but, to Pridamant's horror and despair, he sees his son first unfaithful to Isabelle and then killed for seducing the Prince's wife. Then Alcandre discloses that this tragic incident is an illusion. Clindor and his friends have become actors and they are revealed behind a curtain counting the takings after the performance of the little tragedy just witnessed by Pridamant. Alcandre assures Pridamant that the theatre is an admired profession and the comedy ends as a celebration of the "theatrical illusion."

The play is a strange monster because, as Corneille himself pointed out, it defies classification by genre, and it also breaks many of the dramatic conventions of its period. The first act is a prologue. Acts II and IV seem to be a comedy by virtue of the status of the characters and the style of speech, but the tone verges on tragedy when Adraste is killed and Clindor is in danger of execution. Act V contains a miniature tragedy whose bloody ending is in fact an illusion. Unity of place is observed only in the sense that Alcandre and Pridamant are present throughout the action in the magician's cave in Touraine, but other elements of scenery, show us in turn Géronte's house, Clindor's prison, Florilame's garden, and the stage of a Parisian theatre. The duration of the action is nominally that of its representation, so in theory observes the rule that the represented action should not exceed 24 hours. But at the same time there is a lapse of four days between Acts III and IV and two years pass between Acts IV and V. All this ambiguity is appropriate in a play whose French title, *L'Illusion comique,* contains a pun: "comique" can mean "comic" or "theatrical." So the comedy plays constantly with the concept of theatrical illusion.

The chief interest of the play lies not in the plot but in the self-conscious exploitation of theatrical conventions. This extends to the characters, especially Matamore, whose speech is grotesquely boastful, while his actions show that he is a coward. This is cleverly represented by reference both to the décor and to the duration of the action, further examples of Corneille's playful handling of theatrical illusion. No sooner has Géronte threatened Matamore that his valets will come out of his house to thrash him, than Géronte's door becomes a focus of Matamore's fear. As soon as he sees Géronte's door opening he flees, and later, on seeing Clindor and Isabelle emerge through the door, he mistakes them for the valets and is stricken with terror (Act III, scenes 3–4, 7–8). When Adraste attacks Clindor, Matamore flees into Géronte's house, where he remains concealed in the attic for four days between Acts III and IV. This long passage of time between the acts, technically an infringement of the unity of time, in fact generates comedy when Matamore reappears. He is taunted with being driven down by hunger and invents fantastic reasons to account for his long period of hiding. At the end of the scene he makes his final exit, again to escape the imaginary valets (Act IV, scene 4).

The framing scenes, in which Alcandre and Pridamant in the magician's cave watch events from Clindor's life, are an image of spectators watching a play in the theatre. Alcandre enjoins Pridamant not to step beyond the limits of the cave, yet the visions conjured up involve Pridamant's emotions to such an extent that finally the father interrupts the dialogue "on stage," begging Alcandre to save his son from death. Then Alcandre dissipates the illusion by showing the actors counting their takings and explains that the characters whom Pridamant thought real were only actors. So the magician Alcandre, described as an emaciated centenarian with astonishing strength and agility, is offered by Corneille as a symbol of the paradoxical powers of the dramatist, who magically engages the emotions of the spectator in the illusion of reality. Composed at the very moment that French theorists were insisting on the need for drama to obey certain conventions in order to convey a plausible illusion of reality, Corneille's comedy ironically subverts these conventions while at the same time celebrating the indefinable and magical power of the theatre.

—David Maskell

THÉRÈSE (Thérèse Desqueyroux)
Novel by François Mauriac, 1927

François Mauriac's most successful novel, *Thérèse*, was published when he was 42. It is better constructed than its principal rival, *Knot of Vipers* (*Le Noeud de vipères*), with fewer loose ends and a less obvious Catholic apologetic purpose. It is also, unlike Mauriac's other studies of the Catholic, landowning bourgeoisie of the Bordeaux area of south-western France, a book which deals with one of the major themes of European 19th-century and 20th-century literature, that of the unhappy woman whose discontent stems from the fact that she is superior to the environment in which she has to live and especially to the men with whom she has to spend her life.

Thérèse, like Flaubert's Emma Bovary, Tolstoi's Anna Karenina, Galsworthy's Irene Forsyte, and D.H. Lawrence's Constance Chatterley is married to a worthy but extremely dull man, Bernard, who can satisfy neither her emotional, her intellectual, nor her sexual needs. During the disaster of her honeymoon with the brutal and rather hypocritical Bernard, she has glimpses of what sexual pleasure might be "as a traveller, seeing a landscape shrouded in rain, imagines what it could be like if the sun were shining." But, unlike Emma, Anna, Irene, or Constance, Thérèse does not turn to adultery. The narrow, provincial society in which she lives offers no suitable man and she would, in any case, quickly be found out. Indeed, so fully has Bernard put her off sex that she never even considers the possibility, in spite of some disturbing discussions with her sister-in-law, Anne, for whom she seems at one stage to entertain feelings beyond those of mere friendship. Instead, she tries to poison her husband, initially almost without realizing what she is doing, later more deliberately. Suspicions grow that Bernard's stomach pains are not due to natural illness and when they disappear on his being removed from Thérèse's care, she is interviewed by the examining magistrate. However, the evidence against her is now sufficient to bring her to trial and she benefits from what is known in French law as a "non-lieu." This is a decision that an examining magistrate can take and which leaves the possibility open, if further evidence is forthcoming, for a formal charge to be made. The novel is told in flashback, with the announcement of the "non-lieu" and consequent avoidance of a public scandal on the very first page. But the reader, like Thérèse, knows that in the pocket of an old raincoat there is a small bottle of poison which, if discovered, could lead to an open trial and, if she is convicted, to a long period of imprisonment.

This never happens and the interest of the novel lies less in the question of whether Thérèse will be found out than in what led her to try to poison her husband in the first place. Mauriac, a Catholic novelist whose "second conversion" in 1930 did not improve the quality of his work, suggests at one point that this might be some sort of metaphysical evil which is constantly prowling around the human soul and seeking to ensnare it. For the modern reader, her sensitivity heightened by the ideas developed by the women's movement, there is less mystery about why Thérèse behaved as she did. Adultery, even if Thérèse had been interested, would not have enabled her to escape from the male-dominated society which oppresses her. She had, in fact, no way out except through an act which defied all the rules of any society, and that was her tragedy.

Thérèse, in this respect, is one of the most intriguing examples of a book that goes beyond the conscious intentions of its author without ever contradicting them. Enlightened though Mauriac was in many of his social and political attitudes, especially for a French Catholic, he can have had little knowledge of the women's movement when he wrote the novel and gave little sign of sympathy for it in his later life. Biographical evidence suggests that he felt as imprisoned in society as Thérèse did and the dominant image in the novel is that of claustrophobia. After her release by the examining magistrate, Thérèse is kept a virtual prisoner in the house by Bernard, being allowed out only for long walks in the rain and attendance at Mass. When, eventually, he agrees to let her go and live in Paris, she is cast into useless and sterile exile. There is nothing she can do and she has enough money not to need to work. Physically, she feels at home only in the Landes area near Bordeaux, but the society that has grown up there is one that can find no place for her.

—Philip Thody

THE THOUSAND AND ONE NIGHTS

Collection of stories by an unknown author. Some of the stories have Arab origin, but many are from Persia, India, and other Eastern civilizations. Based on 9th-century Persian text, *Hazār Afsāneh* [Thousand Stories] (translated into Arabic not later than the 10th century), with other stories added. Standard edition appeared in the 15th century. Written in simple (rather than classical) Arabic, with traces of Egyptian.

PUBLICATIONS

Sung to Shahryar: Poems from the Book of the Thousand Nights and One Night, edited by E.P. Mathers, translated by J.C. Mardrus. 1925.

*

Critical Studies: *The Minstrelsy of "The Arabian Nights": A Study of Music and Musicians in the Arabic "Alf Laila wa Laila"* by Henry George Farmer, 1945; *Thèmes et motifs des Mille et Une Nuits: Essai* *de classification* by Nikita Elisséeff, 1949; *The Art of Story-Telling: A Literary Study of the Thousand and One Nights* by Mia I. Gerhardt, 1963; *Arabian Nights' Entertainments* edited by Andrew Lung, 1969; *Scheherazade in England: A Study of Nineteenth-Century English Criticism of the Arabian Nights* by Muhsin Sassim Ali, 1981; *Arabian Nights' Entertainments: The Thousand and One Nights* edited by G.F. Townsend, translated by J. Scott, 1985; *The Arabian Nights in English Literature: Studies in the Reception of The Thousand and One Nights into British Culture* edited by Peter L. Caracciolo, 1988; *Arabesques: Narrative Structure and the Aesthetics of Repetition in One Thousand and One Nights* by Sandra Naddatt, 1991; *The Arabian Nights: A Companion* by Robert Irwin, 1994; *Nocturnal Politics: The Arabian Nights in Comparative Context* by Ferial J. Ghazoul, 1996; *The Thousand and One Nights in Arabic Literature and Society*, edited by Richard C. Hovannisian and Georges Sabagh, 1997; *Sheherazade Through the Looking Glass: The Metamorphosis of The Thousand and One Nights* by Eva Sallis, 1999.

* * *

The Thousand and One Nights, also known as the *Arabian Nights' Entertainments* or simply *The Arabian Nights*, is an Arabic text which dates, in its written form at least, from the 9th century AD (when it is referred to as a book of fairytales called *Hazār Afsāneh*). What happened to the text after this date and until it appeared in the form we now have it is unclear; what can be discerned is that the geographical and cultural compass of the text broadened considerably; the most recent version of *The Thousand and One Nights* contains tales from, and of, Arab, Indian, Persian, and possibly Chinese origin. While there was a written version of the text made by an Egyptian redactor towards the end of the 18th century, it was the translation of the text into French (*Mille et Une Nuits*) by Antoine Galland over the period 1704–17 which brought *The Thousand and One Nights* to prominence. Galland's version was by no means complete; he omitted the explicit sexual references in the text and played upon the already preexisting Western conceptions of the Orient by emphasizing the fantastical elements of the stories.

Indeed, the fate of *The Arabian Nights* since Galland's popular version has been almost exclusively to shore up the West's most unconsidered notions of "the East." Perhaps the fact that the predominant oriental cultures (in the West's view) are represented in the text of *The Thousand and One Nights* has added to this tendency. In the anonymous 1798 English translation, which was taken from the French of Galland, the work is described as "containing a better account of the customs, manners, and religion of the Eastern nations, the Tartars, Persians, and Indians, than is met with in any author hitherto published." The cultural, political, and, of course, colonial value of the text is thus recognized by the English publisher, whose readers would have had very concrete reasons for wanting to "know" about "the East," and whose preconceptions of the Orient are confirmed and enhanced through their particular reading of the text. Later Victorian English versions by E.W. Lane, John Payne, and most notably Sir Richard Burton testify to the continuing need of the colonists to "know" the East in the way they presumed *The Thousand and One Nights* allowed them to: seeing in *The Arabian Nights* a mixture of exoticism and fantasy, and the opportunity to show both disgust and excitement at the thrill of explicit sexuality and "heathenism." And it may be because of the popularity of *The Thousand and One Nights* in the West (where it has become the stuff of children's stories and pantomime) that Eastern scholars have continued, as their predecessors did, to consider it a minor text in Arab literature. (Some Western commentators would argue that it is the secular nature of the *The Thousand and One Nights* that makes it unpopular in the Arab world).

The Thousand and One Nights works within a complicated framework. The "Prologue" sets up the nature of the work's narratives: put briefly, King Shahryar, finding his wife has betrayed him, begins a custom whereby he sleeps with a virgin every night and has her executed the next morning. When all the virgins have been killed or have fled, the only one the king's Vizier can find is his own daughter, Scheherezade. To delay her fate, she begins telling the tales that make up *The Thousand and One Nights* (and together last that long); and so a succession of tales within tales begins.

The eclectic nature of the stories, which have been gathered at different times and from different cultures, means that the range of themes and of types of subject covered is one of the joys of *The Thousand and One Nights*. Even from a comparison of the best-known stories (in the West), such as "Sinbad the Sailor," "Aladdin," and "Ali Baba and the Forty Thieves," the variety contained within the text is obvious. (The tale of "Ali Baba and the Forty Thieves" does not, incidentally, figure in any manuscript of *The Thousand and One Nights*. It first appears in Galland's translation, but the source for it is not obvious). But the fact that these three tales have become best known in the West out of the immensity of the work is revealing about how the West has read *The Arabian Nights*; all three of these tales involve the magical and fantastical, playing on the exotic and colourful, and have become "classic" children's stories.

Yet this is not the nature of the whole text, which contains many more facets and many more types of tales. One aspect of the work that this very selective version entirely excludes is the humour of many of the stories within *The Thousand and One Nights*. "The Ass," which is a short and pithy joke on the charming simplicity and duping of a fool, is a useful example, as is "The Tale of the Hunchback," a farcical comedy of a tailor, a broker, a steward, and a doctor all successively lumbered with disposal of the same corpse (which later turns out not to be a corpse at all). Indicative too of the intricacy of many of the stories are the six tales of the barber's brothers (which are contained within "The Hunchback"), all of which build up their main character to a fall from grace. The fifth brother, for example, goes through an extended reverie in which he considers the fortune he will make from the inheritance of glassware he has been given by his father. In his imagination he accumulates great wealth, slaves, and influence; it is only when he imagines how, by pushing her away with his foot, he will spurn the advances of the beautiful wife he will marry that he is brought back to reality as he kicks over the basket of glass and makes himself penniless again.

The Thousand and One Nights is a work that should be recognized for many of the features that have always been associated with it: fantastical stories, gigantic birds, mythical figures, jinnees, and sumptuous and exotic settings. But it should also be recognized that this impression is a selective one, fostered by a Western sense of what the East is and should be. *The Thousand and One Nights* is the source of diverse strands of diverse cultures; it contains anecdotes, social satires, and sexual comedies which should all be read as integral to the work. Read thus, its cultural variety, its seriousness and humour, and its narrative skills are its strengths.

—Colin Graham

THE THREE MUSKETEERS (Les Trois Mousquetaires)
Novel by Alexandre Dumas *père*, 1844

The Three Musketeers is Alexandre Dumas *père*'s most important venture in the art of the historical novel and in melodrama. Set in that golden age of French history, the 17th century, it covers the period from 1625 to 1628, when Richelieu was beginning to consolidate his power.

Young D'Artagnan comes to Paris to seek his fortune. Hardly has he arrived in the capital than he is involved in duels with the three musketeers Athos, Porthos, and Aramis, who nevertheless soon become his friends. The four musketeers (for so they become when D'Artagnan joins them in chapter 47) have many adventures, chief of which is to bring back some diamonds from England and so shield the Queen of France from Richelieu's intrigues. All are involved in adventures and escapades during this dash to Windsor and London, but D'Artagnan manages to make contact with the Duke of Buckingham, to whom Anne of Austria had given the jewels as a love-token. And so the Queen can wear the diamonds at the ball which Richelieu had planned as her downfall.

The evil genius of the novel is Lady de Winter, a spy in the Cardinal's service—rich, beautiful, mysterious, and malevolent—who does evil for evil's sake. She poisons D'Artagnan's mistress Constance Bonacieux; through her influence Buckingham is assassinated by John Felton. After many narrow escapes, Lady de Winter is finally cornered by the musketeers and sentenced to death. Loosely based on a minor volume of 17th-century memoirs, Gatien de Courtilz de Sandras's *Mémoires de M. d'Artagnan* (1700), *The Three Musketeers* purports, until chapter 6, to be the transcript of a 17th-century chronicle (by the Comte de la Fère, alias Athos) which Dumas has mysteriously brought to light. In fact, however, it displays many of the qualities of Romanticism and is a supreme example both of the adventure story and of the historical novel.

Like Vigny but unlike Balzac, Dumas places prominent historical figures—Louis XIII, Anne of Austria, Richelieu, Buckingham, the Duchess de Chevreuse, Tréville, Cavois—in the foreground of *The Three Musketeers*, firmly believing that these should not be overshadowed by minor characters of his own invention. Even D'Artagnan and the other three musketeers are minor historical figures, though each is about ten years older than his prototype.

In so far as Dumas has refashioned Richelieu and Buckingham according to his imagination, there is a gulf between history and historical fiction. But there is a gulf between official history and secret history likewise. The fact that *The Three Musketeers* is said to be a transcript of a contemporary chronicle is significant: the novel pretends to the status of authentic history, but history that has been overlooked; its events, through improbable, are historically true. (Its major anachronisms, few in number, are at the religious level.) Milady is unrecorded in the pages of history precisely because her missions were so successful, and because she was a spy: she is even condemned by a sort of *Vehmgericht*, or secret tribunal. Thus Dumas intermeshes all things, great and small: such is the nature of the secret history of the world. In the struggle of Richelieu and Buckingham he also, in true Romantic fashion, over-emphasizes the influence of personality upon historical events.

But Lady de Winter is gratuitously wicked, embodying the evil of melodrama and therefore set apart from the historical nexus of cause and effect. In the starkest and most simplistic terms *The Three Musketeers* is a contest of good versus evil, of simple but strong characters, of bluff, even noble, male comradeship and unfeeling feminine guile: Lady de Winter's seduction of Felton is one of the high points of the book. Moreover, it is a contest in which good eventually triumphs; a contest full of seemingly improbable turns of events (in the tradition of the Gothic novel), as when it turns out that Lady de Winter was once Athos's wife; full, too, of fine coincidences, as when D'Artagnan recovers the diamonds in the nick of time or Lord de Winter arrives just too late to prevent Buckingham's assassination.

Dumas *père* is a master of racy, challenging dialogue and the supreme master of narrative tempo, especially the tempo of split-second success or failure. There can be no doubt that he would nowadays have made a name for himself as a scriptwriter in films and television, yet in his *Three Musketeers* and other popular masterpieces he favours a *dramatic* presentation of his story, with carefully laid settings (as in Victor Hugo's Romantic dramas) and well rounded scenes. This technique is quite unlike Balzac's more cinematic approach in *A Harlot High and Low* (*Splendeurs et misères des courtisanes*). At the same time Dumas's scenes, although dramatic, are like tableaux: they often resemble history paintings by Delaroche.

In Delaroche's manner Dumas *père* presents a clear pristine world, as when, in chapter 59 of *The Three Musketeers*, Felton stands looking out to sea as Lady de Winter sets sail from Portsmouth to France. Here are no shades of grey, but the unequivocal expression of what is vividly beautiful: as the Romantics—and especially Hugo—held, there is a beauty in ugliness. But there is a Shakespearean dimension too, the sense of a cosmic clash between good and evil, and, at the end of the work, the beginning of a restoration of the moral order. Simplistic perhaps (because melodramatic), but dramatic in every sense.

The Three Musketeers is written with immense verve and panache. Its energetic style mirrors the cult of energy that it exemplifies (in this respect Dumas shares Stendhal's outlook). Nothing detracts from the onward movement of its plot: how different this is from Balzac's didacticism! Its unflagging momentum has every appearance of being effortlessly maintained; and this appearance seems indeed to have been the reality of the matter, since the novel first appeared in daily serial form (each chapter roughly corresponding to one newspaper instalment) and Dumas *père* was limited in the extent to which he could revise in retrospect. This greatest of all "blood-and-thunder" novels goes far beyond Eugène Sue's achievement in *The Mysteries of Paris*, or what Balzac had achieved by way of melodrama in *The Black Sheep*.

—Donald Adamson

THREE POEMS: 2, 63, AND 76
Poems by Catullus, mid-1st century BC

Catullus' poems are normally divided into three groups: the polymetricals (Poems 1–60), the long poems (61–68), and the elegies (69–116). Each group is sometimes considered a collection unto itself, with its own principles of order and thematic coherency. The issue of the collection aside, there can be no denying that Catullus' poems divide themselves as to metre and topic. The polymetricals deal centrally with the affair Catullus apparently carried on with his lover, whom he calls Lesbia and who is usually identified historically as Clodia Metelli. They also give shape to a variety of circumstances quite apart from the affair with Lesbia, evoking the full range of human emotion. The long poems deal mostly with topics that centre around nature, convention, or myth. They demonstrate that this superbly accomplished lyricist was also able to write on larger topics with equal authority. The elegies, on the other hand, while also treating the affair with Lesbia, give shape to a panoply of encounters, emotions, and thoughts, now complementing, now expanding on the topics raised in the polymetricals. The elegies are perhaps noteworthy also for the tremendous emotional swings depicted in them (particularly poems 76 and 85) and for their obscenity.

Many of the polymetricals are exemplary of their group, but none perhaps more than poem 2, which introduces Catullus' readers to his ''girl'' *(puella)* and her sparrow *(passer)*. As there is no critical consensus about the symbolical value of the sparrow, readers make of the bird what they will. It is perhaps most useful to see the bird in its Greek context, where it takes pride of place in the fragments of Sappho as Aphrodite's special bird. More specifically, the sparrow is depicted in Sappho's fragments (and elsewhere) as the bird that conveys Aphrodite physically from her home with the other gods to earth. The sparrow can be understood to mediate, in this way, the movement from ideal to real space.

Given this, we might see the sparrow of Poem 2 as symbolic of Lesbia's love psychology. This poem bemoans the fact that Lesbia is somehow assuaged by the bird's activity, while Catullus can only pine away at the poem's end, wishing he might feel the better for its devotion. Since the sparrow mediates, in its Greek context, the gulf between ideal and real space, we might see its symbolical resonance in Poem 2 as portending Lesbia's own flight from a more idealized repose, in which she contemplates love from afar, to a more active response on her part toward Catullus' advances. The death of the sparrow in Poem 3 announces just such a movement on her part in its celebration of Lesbia's submission to Catullus. Poems 5 and 7, in quick succession, give fuller shape to the ways in which the affair proceeds, before it suddenly ends, for whatever reasons, in Poem 8. It is a strategic reminiscence in Poem 8 when Catullus asks Lesbia rhetorically ''whose lips will you now bite.'' Initially, the sparrow danced about Lesbia's body, erotically nibbling her fingertips and flittering about her breast and lap. In recalling those nibbles at the end of the affair, Catullus brings the opening poems of the Lesbia cycle, of which Poem 2 is the crux, full circle, confirming the importance of this sparrow, possibly the most famous bird in all of Western writing.

If the polymetricals are laden with the emotions of love won and love lost, the long poems are no less emotionally charged, but in the less personal manner befitting their subject matter. These poems abound in stunning moments of raw emotion and pure vision, but there is nothing in Western writing quite like Poem 63. The poem's story, given here somewhat roughly for the sake of brevity, considers the figure of Attis, who was conceived from the castrated genitals of the androgynous Cybele and the daughter of the river Sangarios. Attis grew into a beautiful man, and Cybele later fell in love with him. In order to prevent him from marrying and belonging to someone else, Cybele made Attis go mad, and in his rage, castrate himself.

Poem 63 commences *in medias res,* on the night in which Attis disfigures himself. Central to the poem's drama is Attis' transformation from male to female, for it renders to the poem's situation a tension that is broken only at its conclusion, when Attis realizes the permanence and the dimension of what he/she has wrought. A night of frenzied celebration precedes that moment of truth, however, and Catullus articulates the full force of the ritual dancing, drum beating, and singing, played in honour of Cybele. Eventually, having worked

him/herself into a fever pitch of devotion, Attis sleeps a drunken sleep. When he/she is awakened the next morning by the bright light of the sun and recognizes what has transpired he/she pines for a restoration of who he/she was and a return to Attica, whence he/she came to Phrygia, the setting for the poem's drama. There can be no escape, however, from the devotion demanded by Cybele, a fact not lost on Catullus, who prays at the poem's end for the goddess to avert his house from the grip exerted on her worshippers.

Part of tile virtuosity of the poem lies outside of the story it tells in the skills of prosody that Catullus brings to bear in its construction, Always in Catullus, but especially in the long poems, sound, in Alexander Pope's phrase, is equal to sense. Repetition is one strategy deployed to ensure this equilibrium, as in vv. 63–71, where the personal pronoun ''I'' *(ego)* is repeated ten times by Attis, almost as a mantra to reclaim his/her lost sense of identity. Consistent alliteration also helps to stress certain points, as, for example, at the poem's conclusion, where the determination of the poet's prayer to avert the fury of Cybele is confirmed in the repetition of labial and dental sounds (*b* and *d*). Catullus' poem also excites its reader's attention on the grounds of its individuality, for there is much that is original in Catullus' treatment of Attis. Also unique, though in a different way, is the prayer at the poem's end, which renders to what had been seemingly a detached version of an old story a personal resonance. Nor is the force of that prayer wasted in the context of the larger collection of poems. It helps to link this bizarre story of sexual extremism, shifting identities, and blurred genders, to the other poems of Catullus' collection, where love is often conceived (especially where Lesbia is concerned) as both madness and slavery.

The themes of madness and slavery also converge in the elegiac Poem 76 where the affair with Lesbia has gone sour many times over and the poet is reduced to pleading to the gods, in whom he never seemed to believe, to cure him of his illness. Now Catullus can no longer bear the emotional or spiritual dependencies and can no longer muster the mental energy required to forbear. He does the only thing left for him to do, which is to look to a higher power for relief. The pure energy of love's emotion, captured with such acumen in preceding poems, confirms the seriousness of Catullus' situation in this poem and the difficulty of his task in the absence of divine intervention. One wonders if Catullus did, in fact, recover the wholeness of his heart. If the collection as we have it is any indication of the chronology of the affair and the emotional life of its author, then the vague musings, the soft pornography, the sometimes harsh obscenities of some of the later elegies, may be a witness to the faltering emotions of a heart that is not whole.

—Joseph Pucci

THE THREE SISTERS (Tri sestry)
Play by Anton Chekhov, 1901

The third of Anton Chekhov's great plays, *The Three Sisters* was written specifically for the Moscow Art Theatre, where it was first produced on 31 January 1901 with Stanislavskii in the role of Vershinin and Chekhov's wife Olga Knipper as Masha. The play received a lukewarm reception from the critics, but soon became a favourite of audiences, turning into the longest running play in Russia. Knowing that he was writing for a particular company sympathetic to his dramatic innovations, Chekhov was able to create this play as more of an ensemble piece than had been possible with either *The Seagull* or *Uncle Vanya*. It is not so much individual characters as a provincial world of hopeless dreams and nostalgia that is evoked by the three educated Muscovite sisters, Olga, Masha, and Irina, who with their brother Andrei have been stranded in a provincial backwater by the death of their father a year before the action opens. The plot is minimal, depicting merely the changes in this environment over three and a half years during which Andrei marries the vulgar, self-seeking Natasha and the sisters lose the opportunity and the hope of leaving the town as their friends the artillery officers do in the end. In this respect it is a supreme example of Chekhov's ability to strip away the artificial elements of traditional dramatic plotting, focusing the audience's attention instead on the human situations presented. As Beverley Hahn remarks, "the drama conveys both the provisional, chaotic, and unpredictable nature of each moment of life and yet the peculiar consistency with which these moments add up to a given fate."

In essence the characters and situation are comic: the three sisters, passive and hampered by cultural pretensions and dreams of the metropolis, see their goal receding. Natasha in her bourgeois vulgarity is obviously a butt while Masha's husband Kulygin is simply a joke of a Latin teacher, and yet this play is not a comedy. Whereas Chekhov deliberately entitled *The Seagull* and *The Cherry Orchard* comedies, this one he called a drama. Following his views that drama should imitate real life albeit with elements of poetry, Chekhov weaves into his play elements of lyricism and of everyday banality. The manner in which the predatory Natasha, all demure smiles when she is being courted by Andrei, proceeds to turn her husband from a potential scholar into a fat drunken slob and make herself the mistress of the house is far too sinister to be simply funny.

The lyricism and elegiac mood of *The Three Sisters* are a more complex matter, created partly through technical devices such as disjointed conversations where characters pursue their own thoughts behind a mask of conventional exchanges, or silences which indicate the importance of what is not being said, or else auditory devices like Masha's endless singing of a snatch of song emphasizing the dull repetitiveness of life. The sisters themselves, with their poetic search for meaning expressed in images of snow or birds, lift their predicament out of either the comic or the merely depressing. Most effective of all in creating a lyrical mood, however, is the use of different time planes: all three sisters live partly in the future which is represented by the idea of a return to Moscow, city of opportunity and real life. With masterly effectiveness Chekhov uses the opening moments of Act I not only in traditional manner to present to us information about Olga, Masha, and Irina's background but also to reveal the depth of their nostalgic attachment to the past and hence to the dream of the future. As the play progresses Olga becomes a headmistress—clearly she is destined to remain there for ever. Masha is forced by the departure of her lover to return to her boring provincial husband and Irina's attempts to escape through marriage are also doomed when her fiancé Tuzenbakh is shot by the malicious Solenyi in a futile duel. Dreams fade and the sisters are forced into the present, where, unlike Natasha, Kulygin, and Natasha's lover Protopov, they have never made any attempt to belong. In the other great Chekhov plays there is always one character at least who, albeit absurdly, expresses an unbounded optimism in the future, however remote, but in *The Three Sisters* it seems at best half-hearted. As the regiment that had brought colour and hope into their lives moves away to the rousing strains of a military march, Olga feels that maybe if we wait a little longer, we shall find out why we live and suffer, and only Masha, following the

now dead Tuzenbakh, can be more optimistic." . . . we must just go on working . . . It's autumn now, winter will soon be here, and the snow will cover everything . . . but I'll go on working and working! . . . ," while Olga, who has the concluding line, underscores the frustration and desperation of that optimism with her sigh: "if only we knew, if only we knew!"

It is not only the lyricism of the play but also the tension between values, spiritual versus practical, and the themes of betrayal and disillusion versus hope and a search for a meaning in life that give the play its depth. Comic elements there certainly are (one need only think of Natasha boring everyone by talking about her baby while Solenyi has the courage to suggest the child should be boiled in oil) but these merely serve to keep the play from sliding too much into gloom. While it is conventional to remark that Chekhov's characters belong to the dying era of tsarism, it is also true that the evocation of lost chances and frustrated ideals is one with an almost universal relevance.

—Faith Wigzell

THE THREEPENNY OPERA (Die Dreigroschenoper)
Play by Bertolt Brecht, 1928

Bertolt Brecht's reworking of John Gay's *The Beggar's Opera*—translations by Elisabeth Hauptmann and music by Kurt Weill—opened on 31 August 1928 at the Schiffsbauerdamm Theatre in Berlin. Its enormous popular success provided one of the theatrical sensations of the decade. Brecht retained considerable elements of Gay's original story unchanged. In particular he preserved the "alienating" equation between the bourgeoisie and a gang of criminals on which Gay's work was based, as well as the element of the parody of conventional art-forms. In Gay's play the forms and attitudes of Handelian opera are the target, in Brecht's case various aspects of bourgeois theatre (the happy end, identification with the hero/ine) and (reinforced by Weill's score) the sentimentality general within bourgeois culture. Brecht transposed the action into early Victorian London and enriched the story with songs in cabaret style, using a number of disparate sources, among them François Villon and Rudyard Kipling—so much so that he was rather unfairly (and not for the last time) accused of plagiarism. Of the songs, "Mack the Knife" has become a popular standard.

Macheath, leader of a violent London gang, marries Polly, the daughter of Peachum, "the beggars' king," leader of a rival gang devoted to exploiting the poor and monopolizing the crime of the city. Peachum's intrigues to bring Macheath to justice eventually succeed—despite Macheath's close friendship with chief police Brown—but the play finishes with a happy end, a mock-heroic liberation scene parodying Beethoven's *Fidelio* in which Macheath receives a royal pardon and is elevated to the ranks of the hereditary peerage.

In the combination of popular and classical musical traditions, its unique evocation of a seedy yet glitzy underworld, its brilliant dialogue and humour, Brecht's *Threepenny Opera* is a typically ambiguous product of the "Golden Twenties": socially critical and radical in its attitudes, but by no means unenjoyable to its supposed target, the bourgeoisie. Like all Brecht's early work it illustrates certain of his theories of the epic theatre, which Brecht began to formulate systematically in his *Notes on "Mahagonny"* in 1930. His use of the 18th-century source shows clearly Brecht's fascination with those traditional forms of theatre that do not conform to the conventions of the ''theatre of illusion'' perfected by the late 19th-century dramatists and producers. The play is neatly poised between the anarchy and cynicism of the early plays (*Baal, Drums in the Night*, and *In the Jungle of Cities*) and the more didactic tone of the works of the early 1930s.

The success of the stage show led to a film version, in the course of which Brecht was involved in (unsuccessful) litigation when he tried to have the story-line changed for greater political effect, among other things expanding Macheath's business into the world of banking. His own *Threepenny Novel* (1934) is an attempt to rework elements of the material into a more hard-hitting political statement. But the dispute with the film company enabled Brecht to explore the particular theory of culture distinctive to the film, and to reflect on the consequences for his own subsequent writing of the *Threepenny Opera*'s extraordinary mixture of glamorous and popular success with political satire and social criticism. While the play remains—with *Happy End* and *The Rise and Fall of the City of Mahagonny*—a work highly evocative of the 1920s, it has a significant place in the evolution of Brecht's mature style.

—Hugh Ridley

THUS SPOKE ZARATHUSTRA (Also sprach Zarathustra)
Prose by Friedrich Nietzsche, 1883–85 (complete edition 1892)

''I have with this book given mankind the greatest gift that it has ever been given . . . it is not only the most exalted book that exists . . . it is the most profound.'' Not all readers will necessarily agree with Friedrich Nietzsche's hyperbolic assessment of his central work, although few will deny his assertion that ''this work stands alone.'' If ever a book deserved to be labelled *sui generis*, this is it. It has few obvious sources, apart from the Bible, and although profoundly influential, did not give rise to imitations.

The first two parts were written (in 1883) in two fortnight-long bursts of creative fever which Nietzsche, although a convinced atheist, could only describe as ''inspiration and revelation''; he felt himself to be the medium of ''overwhelming forces.'' The fever abated, however, and the third and fourth parts came much more slowly (in 1884 and 1885), while the planned continuation never materialized at all.

Nietzsche chose the name of Zarathustra to link his fictional character with Zoroaster, the 8th-century BC Persian sage and founder of the Parsi religion. Nietzsche believed that Zoroaster was the first propagator of the idea that the struggle between good and evil is objectively rooted in existence, that these values are ''given'' in the cosmos and hence capable of discovery. Nietzsche's Zarathustra, by contrast, is conceived as the first great ''immoralist,'' who teaches that there is no moral world-order of this kind, but that the business of evaluation and the construction of moral systems is fundamental to human existence.

Structurally the work consists of a lengthy prologue, followed by four parts, each a series of discourses by Zarathustra on various named subjects: *Of the Despisers of the Body, Of War and Warriors, Of Marriage and Children*, for example. This pattern starts to dissolve in the third part, which is largely devoted to Zarathustra's agonized acceptance of the doctrine of the Eternal Recurrence and gives way, in part four, to a loose narrative about the various ''Higher Men'' with whom Zarathustra has now decided to consort, but who are ultimately rejected as worthy recipients for his message.

Zarathustra's discourses consist, typically, of short paragraphs, often of only one or two sentences and characterized by rhetorical tension derived from pseudo-Biblical repetition or antithesis. Metaphor abounds and the text is rich in parody and puns, many of which cannot be rendered in translation. In contrast to Nietzsche's other books, it is not a work of analysis or argument, but of ''prophetic'' utterance interspersed with chapters which hover between heightened prose and lyric poetry. Nietzsche himself claimed that the work belongs primarily to the realm of music and it is perhaps not entirely fanciful to think of it as a prose symphony with recurrent leitmotifs—the Death of God, the *Übermensch*, the Ultimate Man, Self-Overcoming, the Will to Power and the Eternal Recurrence.

Although the Death of God is the basic premise of Zarathustra's message, no explanation is to be found in the work and we must look to Nietzsche's other writings, principally *The Gay Science* (*Die fröhliche Wissenschaft*). Nietzsche's atheism is presented as a self-evident cultural fact, yet one that mankind would prefer to deny for fear of its terrible consequences. The belief in God has simply become redundant as a result of modern science, which Nietzsche sees as the end product of a long tradition of intellectual analysis which has its origins in Christianity itself. Nietzsche believed that his historical self-subversion of Christianity had little in common with ''traditional'' atheism. He claimed to be observing and diagnosing, rather than polemicising, when he spoke of ''honest, scientific atheism.'' The Death of God can be experienced as a catastrophe, or as a challenge, depending on the individual, and it is the *response* to the challenge that is the main concern of Nietzsche/Zarathustra.

Mankind is now at a fateful crossroads, Zarathustra proclaims in the prologue. It can regress down the path towards the Ultimate Man, or progress upwards towards *Übermensch*. (There is a translation problem here which is still to be overcome: Superman is comical, Overman lacks positive suggestive power, Beyond-Man or Ultra-Man, while appropriately stressing the notion of transcendence, are infelicitous). The Death of God is fateful for uncreative conformists who need allegiance to absolute value systems, but liberating for the few who joyfully embrace the possibility of self-transcendence and the attainment of personal authenticity, unlimited by any divine authority. The crowd to which Zarathustra proclaims the beauty of the *Übermensch* responds indifferently, so he shows them his vision of the Ultimate Man, a diminutive and contemptible being, devoted to the pursuit of undemanding happiness, denying the creative longing for self-transcendence that marks all higher men, a willing slave to comfort and convention, barely distinguishable from the animals. The crowd's enthusiastic response to this image and their rejection of the *Übermensch* persuade Zarathustra that their fate is already sealed and that he should rather lack ''living companions who follow me because they follow themselves.''

The majority of the chapters of the first two parts of the work are devoted, often obliquely, to the upward development of man on the path marked *Übermensch*. The new relationship between man and the world is celebrated in ''Of the Afterworldsmen'' where, by a neat pun, Zarathustra identifies believers in a world beyond this world, i.e. traditional metaphysicians, with ''backwoodsmen,'' primitive and limited men, unable to come to terms with life, who take the ''death-leap'' into an ''inhuman, dehumanized world which is a heavenly nothing.'' Instead, Zarathustra enjoins his audience ''no longer to bury their heads in the sands of heavenly things, but to carry it freely, an earthly head which creates meaning for the earth,'' and to listen to the voice of the healthy body, ''perfect and square built.'' This joyful acceptance of embodied, physical existence on this earth, the only world of which we can have certain knowledge, is seen as a fundamental precondition for upward human development (''Of the Despisers of the Body'').

Zarathustra seeks to rehabilitate the world and the flesh, urging us to reclaim and re-evaluate human territory which has been denied, downgraded, and demonized by two millennia of ''otherworldly'' belief systems. The earth takes on a new innocence; it is no longer seen as ''merely'' this world (in contrast to a ''better'' world in a now fictitious ''beyond''), but as the *only* world, and it must be re-evaluated positively by creators who freely accept the task of living joyfully in it. The icon for this ecstatic affirmation of human existence is *Übermensch*. The concept is not Darwinistic: it will not simply come about, by natural selection and mutation, but must be *willed*; it describes a process rather than a state, a quality of being, characterized by ceaseless self-perfecting. It represents the beautiful process of the sublimated Will to Power in a strong individual. The writings of Nietzsche's middle period show a progress towards a monistic stance, culminating in the provisional view that the will to achieve, and to increase, power might be seen as the basis of all human activity. Power is not necessarily outwardly directed or exerted on other people. The most remarkable example of this process, it is argued, is when a genius applies his rational, creative power, not to works of art, but to *himself as a work of art*, forming, shaping, directing, fulfilling his potential by the development of innate powers and the assimilation of appropriate experience, and by so doing continually both transcending and—paradoxically—realizing himself and producing true human (Zarathustra will say *Super*-human) beauty.

Yet it is not the elusive beauty of the *Übermensch* that is the main idea of the work, Nietzsche argues; it is mysterious Eternal Recurrence, the thought that everything may recur, down to the smallest, trivial detail, eternally. Nietzsche claimed that this thought came to him like a mystic revelation, but there is good internal evidence that it is a construct, with a clear function. In a contemporary jotting Nietzsche wrote: ''We created the most difficult thought—*now let us create the being* for whom it is light and blessed.'' The *Übermensch* is such a being whose joy in the success of his own existence craves eternity, *wills* that his own life be repeated because he sees the Eternal Recurrence as ''the highest formula of affirmation'' of his life.

The idea becomes a touchstone for Nietzsche, his personal categorical imperative. To the weak and unsuccessful, who suffer from life and wish it to end, the thought is horrific, but to those who affirm life to the full, it is a blissful, self-validating prospect. Its symbolic function is not unconvincing. Doubts arise, however, when we realize that Nietzsche apparently thought that is was a *scientifically* valid proposition (he claims that the Law of Conservation of Energy ''demands the Eternal Recurrence'') and when we bear in mind that he lacked the necessary scientific training to pursue this view. Nevertheless it remains central to Zarathustra's gradual process of self-realization and was to have been the subject of the final book in Nietzsche's magnum opus, *The Revaluation of All Values* of which in the end only the first book, *The Anti-Christ* (*Der Antichrist*), was ever written.

Although *Thus Spoke Zarathustra* is, strictly speaking, an incomplete book, few readers will fail to experience a sense of elation, triumph, and liberation, as Zarathustra, in the last words of the Fourth Book, leaves his cave, with renewed determination to follow the strenuous creative path towards authentic selfhood, ''glowing and strong, like a morning sun emerging from behind dark mountains.''

—Bruce Watson

THYESTES
Play by Seneca, c. 48 BC

Seneca's *Thyestes* is this Stoic philosopher's most gruesome and influential drama. Earlier Greek and Roman playwrights had written dramas based upon the Thyestes myth, but none of these has survived. In many ways, this material deals with family tragedy and betrayal at its bloodiest. The House of Pelops is accursed. The grandfather, Tantalus, has been condemned to the Underworld for shocking shamelessness and inhospitality. Attempting to trick the gods who had honoured him, Tantalus slew, dismembered, and cooked his son Pelops, and sought to serve to the gods this monstrous cannibal feast. They detected the cheat, restored Pelops to life, and eternally punished the ungrateful Tantalus. His famous punishment entailed being immersed in a pool of water and surrounded by fruit trees. Whenever Tantalus made the least attempt to eat or to drink, water and food receded beyond his grasp—thus the poignant origin of the word ''tantalize.'' Thereafter, a curse lay upon his entire family line. Seneca's drama describes how the third generation, the brothers Atreus and Thyestes, fare badly indeed.

After the death of Pelops, Atreus had reigned, but his brother, Thyestes, by means of foul play, had sought to seize the throne, failed and was banished by King Atreus. Since then, Atreus has long meditated some enormous means of revenge, for he suspects that Thyestes had seduced his wife, Aërope, perhaps even calling the authenticity and legitimacy of his offspring into question.

The play opens with the arrival of the Ghost of Tantalus. A Fury has coerced him to rise from the Underworld to inspire the present generation with new feats of crime and vice. The ghost is reluctant, but the Fury forces him to cast a dreadful spell upon the present generation; then Tantalus is permitted to return to his punishment in the lower regions.

In the play, Atreus the King has become a half-crazed tyrant from long meditating upon retribution. He feigns brotherly love and induces a timid and fearful Thyestes to return from exile with his sons. Atreus claims that there has been a reconciliation, and that now he and Thyestes will rule together, sharing the throne. Once his naive brother has returned, however, Atreus secretly slaughters Thyestes' three sons in a sacrilegious rite, cooks their headless carcasses, and, unbeknownst to the innocent, frightened, and slightly intoxicated brother, feeds the dismembered pieces to Thyestes in an unholy banquet. As the befuddled Thyestes, racked by premonitions and self-doubts, dines alone upon his children at centre stage, Atreus the director, orchestrator, and engineer of this terrible scene lurks downstage, unseen on the side, observing and exulting in triumph. Atreus is almost at the pinnacle of success, feverish with joy at so successfully managing this reprisal. He boasts and gloats aloud; his evil prayers have been answered; he has no further need of the gods. Indeed, he feels himself to be a god, his spirit elevated amongst the stars, his head knocking at heaven's gate. Yet even this extremity of requital is not enough: he must reveal all to his brother and brag to him openly of his achievements. Happily, he displays the three heads to his brother.

When Thyestes knows all, he is almost speechless with self-recrimination. Surprisingly, the fiendish Atreus, too, is equally unappeased: he aspired to arrange some heinous, unthinkable vendetta that would exceed possibility, and he therefore feels cheated and unsated. His crazed lust for revenge exceeds all natural bounds, and his suspicion of his own wife and children is entirely unassuaged. Thyestes dumbly appeals to the gods for some sort of requital and justice, and the two in tandem helplessly exchange words of challenge and recrimination.

Here is exemplified an almost pure "revenger's tragedy." Subsequently, it exerted considerable influence upon Elizabethan and Jacobean drama, where violent vengeance, at the hands of characters like Marlowe's Jew of Malta and Shakespeare's Iago, is dazzlingly played out on centre stage. Here, too, are a number of other features congenial to Renaissance dramatists: brooding meditations and soliloquies; ghosts and supernatural (and unnatural) sights, omens, and sounds; and wavering, and braggart egos ultimately unable to cope.

Clearly, Senecan tragedy, as we might expect after 500 years, deviates considerably from classic Greek paradigms. His scenes are more isolated, staccato, and disjointed; his choruses more remote from the drama, his characters more brooding, passionate, rhetorical, and hysterical. He is closest to Ovid and Euripides among his predecessors; but his theatre more savage and melodramatic than that of the earlier masters. However, his plays, featuring, as they do, insecurity, explosive vice, and irrationality, say something pertinent and profound to our own vicious, unstable, and seemingly godless century. Assuredly, on his stage the age of heroes is long past, and his modern characters are nervous, agitated, and rash. Across the centuries, they speak to us in words we can understand.

Moreover, the Senecan characters are above all pitifully ironic figures; they rant and strut, but somehow fail completely to achieve anything like heroism. Indeed, in *Thyestes* both brothers are victims not only of the general curse of Pelops, but also of Tantalus' disease and punishment: both seek fulfilment and repose, but neither ever realizes the least satisfaction. Thyestes is ever uncertain, gloomy, guilt-ridden, and inept; while Atreus, ever the mad ranter and irate revenger, is never fully sated. Both live almost in the kind of hell portrayed in Jean-Paul Sartre's *No Exit* (*Huis Clos*): they torment one another interminably, without solace or release. Seneca has thus drawn for us a perceptive psychological portrayal of sadistic dictatorship and of little men caught in a web of their own weaving, which constitutes the essence of their permanently tormented lives. Senecan drama was frequently underrated in the 19th century, but it is increasingly regaining status and respect. *Thyestes* is one of Seneca's most intense and remarkable accomplishments.

—Anna Lydia Motto & John R. Clark

TIGER AT THE GATES (La Guerre de Troie n'aura pas lieu)
Play by Jean Giraudoux, 1935

In the mid 1930s, Jean Giraudoux was an extremely successful playwright whose fanciful mind and innovative use of language had captivated a wide public. In plays like *Amphitryon 38* and *Intermezzo*, he had found his audience with his stylistic artistry and his search for the ideal world, going beyond ordinary reality. When *Tiger at the Gates* was first performed in 1935, Giraudoux's reputation took on new dimensions. It was now unmistakably clear that he was an important dramatist, capable of addressing a major theme and writing a work of serious dimensions.

The playwright took as his theme the question of war and peace, seeking to demythologize war and to make its destructive effects plain to all. The source of the play was clearly his growing concern about Germany and its increasingly warlike stance in Europe. Conflict was beginning to seem inevitable to everyone at that time and Giraudoux wanted to call attention to what was happening.

Although the work had its source in the actuality of the day, the dramatist, as was his custom, did not present his theme directly in a modern setting—he turned, instead, to legend and literature. His immediate source is *The Iliad*. In the legend, Helen, wife of Menelaus, King of Sparta, is carried off by Paris, the Trojan prince, son of Priam and Hecuba. Infuriated by this action, the Greeks wage war against the Trojans who are destroyed. Hector, the main Trojan warrior, is killed, and his wife, Andromache, is taken away into slavery.

Giraudoux begins his play at the moment when the Trojans are waiting for an emissary from the Greeks who is going to ask for the return of Helen. Hector, having just returned from war, is desperately hoping for peace, but conflict seems inevitable. As he says, war is part of mankind's nature: "If every mother cut off her son's right-hand index finger, the armies of the world would fight without index fingers. And if they cut off their sons' right legs, the armies would be one-legged." He notes with despair that there are many people in his own ranks who are hoping for war, either as a means of justifying disappointing existences or as a way of scorning life.

At first, Hector does succeed in avoiding the ineluctable forces of war. He manages to convince some of his people that war is not beautiful; he allows himself to be humiliated by one of the Greek representatives, who slaps him and whom he refuses to fight; he thinks that he has even managed to persuade Helen of the dangers of trifling with war. Helen, the reason for the conflict, is only toying with the question of love—she does not love Paris, she loves men.

In the second act, Ulysses and his Greek followers arrive, determined to begin the conflict unless Helen is released. Yet Hector convinces Ulysses, an intelligent man held in high esteem, of the folly of war and the two of them make an arrangement to return Helen to Greece. The agreement is based, however, on the assumption that Helen has not been touched by Paris. The Trojans cannot accept what they see as an attack on their masculinity and they explain in some detail how Paris took Helen. With the agreement seemingly in ruins, Ulysses is nevertheless willing to give peace another try, although he is realistic enough to realize that it is virtually impossible to halt the hand of fate. Yet he will join with Hector in attempting to deceive fate and he makes plans to leave with Helen. Although Hector thinks that peace is finally at hand, the inevitability of war becomes even clearer. Before Ulysses can make his departure with Helen, Ajax, a drunken Greek soldier, makes advances toward Andromache. Hector contains himself and Ajax eventually plans to depart, leaving one to assume that again peace is near. Just at that time, however, Demokos, one of the most war-like of the Trojans, makes an attempt to encourage the Greeks to fight. Trying to put an end to this once and for all, Hector stabs Demokos, exclaiming, as the curtain begins to fall, that "the Trojan war will not take place" (the actual French title of the play). Yet the dying Demokos manages to maintain that Ajax, not Hector, has killed him. The Trojan war will take place and the curtain rises once again, symbolizing the beginning of conflict.

These final moments of the work underscore the irony of the situation. Hector, the man of peace, has inadvertently brought about the Greek-Trojan war. Had he not stabbed Demokos, it is unlikely that Demokos would have been able to arouse the Trojans to battle. And Hector probably would not have stabbed Demokos had he not been angered by Ajax's attempts to embrace Andromache. Thus, the couple of peace end up triggering this major conflict. And the ultimate irony of the play is presented when, at the end, Helen is seen embracing a young man, suggesting that the forthcoming destruction will have been fought for a person for whom love is nothing but a plaything. Even more importantly, there is the suggestion that Helen was simply a pretext for the battle that humankind always seeks out.

The normal interpretation of this play is that mankind is at the mercy of destiny—the tiger at the gates. In spite of everything one may try to do, the sleeping tiger will awake and the war will begin. It is possible, however, to look upon the play as an example of a different path taken by the playwright. Giraudoux was trying to explore to what extent mankind itself could take some of the control of its future away from fate. In that respect, the dramatist seems to be stating that mankind has to bear some of the responsibility for the seeming inevitability of war. He was making this point at the very moment when war with Germany was looming on the horizon and he was asking people to take on the burden of doing what they could to prevent this conflict.

—John H. Reilly

THE TIME OF INDIFFERENCE (Gli indifferenti)
Novel by Alberto Moravia, 1929

Alberto Moravia's first novel, written in his early twenties, was hailed as marking a rebirth of the genre in Italy. *The Time of Indifference*, with the amorality of its characters' motives and its explicit examination of lust, owed some of its impact to its status as a *succès de scandale*. Although it can be read as a tale of corruption of bourgeois mores under Fascist rule, *The Time of Indifference* has many psychological themes in common with his later work. Moravia's characters in his first novel grapple with sexual and existential alienation, family tensions that bear a distinct Freudian imprint, and an inability to communicate and grasp the reality of the world beyond the social norms.

The Time of Indifference is, on one level, a grotesque parody of the drama of the high bourgeoisie: money and the preservation of status are arguably the strongest motives of its characters. Mariagrazia, a widowed mother, faces having to sell her house because of her debts to Leo Merumeci, the parvenu who has been her lover for some 15 years. Leo, who now has nothing but a thinly veiled disdain for his mistress, has not only engineered the financial crisis and disguised the true value of the house, but also covertly lusts after Mariagrazia's daughter, Carla. The "indifferent ones" of the novel's Italian title are Carla and her brother Michele. Carla feels hemmed in by the objects and rituals of her world, but her craving to break out into a "new life" becomes no more than a self-destructive inclination to comply with Leo's quasi-incestuous designs on her, while Michele is portrayed as struggling vainly against his indifference in an attempt to create a life of real emotion.

The Time of Indifference revolves around the grim inevitability of Leo's seduction of Carla, and Michele's increasingly violent but humiliatingly inadequate attempts to shock himself out of his psychological slough by attacking Leo. Michele's alienation also dominates his relationship with Lisa, an old flame of Leo's. When Michele first visits Lisa, he is indifferent to her hamfisted amorous advances, but still tries to play the role of lover. Mariagrazia fails to notice the sexual undertones of Leo's attitude to her daughter, but mistakenly suspects that Lisa and Leo are renewing their affair, and becomes increasingly jealous.

At a lunch arranged for Carla's 24th birthday, Michele tries to slap Leo. Their hollow reconciliation only worsens Michele's frustration at his inability to act with conviction. Leo encourages Carla to drink too much, but his move to take advantage of her ends in failure when she vomits. Leo tries to assuage his frustrated libido by visiting Lisa, who, convinced that she is loved by Michele, refuses his advances. Michele arrives and catches the two in a compromising embrace and, while aware of what is really happening, decides to use the incident as a pretext to rid himself of Lisa's tiresome attentions. Outside Lisa's house, Leo offers Michele a taxi-ride home, during which he advises him to take on Lisa as a cheap and convenient lover. When, that evening, Michele finds Lisa at the family home, the darkness of a power-cut is enough to undermine his attempts to fend her off, Leo once more begins pawing Carla, and, unknown to either of them, Lisa sees them in an embrace, After dinner, Michele's renewed attempts to stoke up some hatred for Leo end in his hurling an ashtray which misses its intended target and strikes his mother on the shoulder. Leo leaves, but not before slipping a note to Carla with instructions for their meeting that night. Carla subsequently attends her tryst with no enthusiasm and only a fragile hope that it will bring about the radical change for which she yearns.

Wandering through the city streets the next day, Michele imagines the routes his life might take. He fantasizes either escaping into a world of greater sincerity, or adapting to his current situation in a form of moral self-abnegation which involves offering his sister to Leo in return for money. Momentarily convincing himself that a single sincere act of love can trigger off a moral recovery, he goes to Lisa. She is only too willing to receive him, until his failing efforts to be honest to her turn into an attempt to humiliate her. She retaliates by revealing that Leo and Carla are lovers. To spite both Lisa's scepticism and his own invincible indifference to this news, Michele promises to kill Leo. But the would-be murder turns to bathos, when, after elaborately fantasizing about the killing and his subsequent trial, Michele forgets to load his revolver and is easily disarmed. Carla, who had been in bed with Leo at the time of Michele's arrival, enters the room. In the ensuing argument, Michele intuits the similarity of their existential predicaments. But, lacking in conviction as usual, he fails to persuade her that a new life is possible. Michele's proposal to auction the house threatens Leo's financial scheming, so he responds by offering marriage to Carla and work to Michele. Although she is at first disgusted by the thought, Carla's inclination is changed when Michele pleads with her to refuse: ironically enough, Michele's only wholehearted utterance of the book has the opposite effect to that intended. On the way home, Carla tells her brother that she will marry Leo, despite Michele's horror that this will mean the fulfilment of his earlier fantasies of an arrangement with Leo based on an exchange of Carla for money.

Some formal aspects of the novel may seem unconvincing, such as its laborious theme of light and dark, and the repetitiveness with which the character's failure to communicate is rendered by phrases such as "he would have liked to reply" or "she would have liked to shout." The most successful scenes are those in which Moravia conveys the squalor of unreciprocated lust and the claustrophobia of family gatherings where tense relationships are acted out through teeth-gritted commonplaces.

The Time of Indifference can be read as an undercutting of the Bildungsroman model of a journey from youthful idealism, via chastening experience, to social success. Neither of the siblings undertakes any kind of existential journey at all. Michele's experiences are a series of non-events. His persistent idealism, which too often takes the form of visions of perfect women or self-aggrandizing day-dreams, is a symptom of his continuing indifference rather than a spur to overcoming that indifference. Carla's bleak aspirations come true, but they fail totally to signal a major change in her life. As the novel closes, Carla leaves for a ball and seems nonchalantly to have adapted to her situation. Michele resigns himself to an affair with Lisa, still locked into his spleenful inactivity.

—John Dickie

THE TIN DRUM (Die Blechtrommel)
Novel by Günter Grass, 1959

The Tin Drum, Günter Grass's first novel, attracted immediate attention upon publication in 1959. Praised as a new, daring voice in post-war German fiction by some and attacked as blasphemous and obscene by others, the novel has stood the test of time and is generally considered Grass's most important work. Intent on breaking with the prevailing mode of prose fiction in the 1950s that offered "timeless and placeless parables," Grass chose as a primary geographical setting his native city of Danzig (now Polish Gdansk) and the first half of the 20th century as the specific time period for his—albeit highly unorthodox—literary analysis of Nazism.

The inmate of a mental institution, Oskar Matzerath, writes down the story of his life during his two-year confinement, from 1952 until his thirtieth birthday in September 1954. Oskar's first-person narrative begins before his birth, in October 1899 when his mother, Agnes, is conceived by his grandmother, Anna Bronski. Oskar, whose stories can lay claim to only limited believability, visualizes the past by means of the Matzerath family photo album and evokes it by playing his tin drum. The writing/narrating process forms one narrative level that is both separate from and parallel to Oskar's fictitious autobiography, which he narrates in chronological order.

The first of the novel's three books treats the period from around 1900 to the infamous *Kristallnacht*, the organized assault on Jewish businesses and synagogues on 8 November 1938. In September 1924 Oskar is born; his intellectual faculties are fully developed at birth—hence the prospect of taking over his parents' grocery store does not particularly excite him. But the successful severing of the umbilical cord makes his return to his mother's womb impossible. On his third birthday he is given a tin drum; he also stages a fall as a means of cloaking his decision to stunt his growth and his refusal to join the adult world.

Since Oskar's intellectual abilities do not require any further formal training, he sabotages his admission to school by using his destructive ability to shatter glass with his voice. But Oskar derives contrasting educational experiences from the classical, harmonious author Goethe on the one hand and the demonic monk Rasputin on the other. Oskar, a keen observer of the Danzig petty bourgeois milieu, implies that actions originating in the private sphere have a bearing on contemporary history.

For example, Jan Bronski, Agnes's cousin, is angry when she marries Alfred Matzerath, a German national from Rhineland. In 1920, Bronski becomes a Polish citizen and a clerk at the Free City of Danzig's Polish post office. Because Agnes continues her relationship with her cousin even after her marriage—hence Oskar claims two "putative" fathers—Matzerath attends the regular Sunday rallies of the Nazi party and becomes a member of a movement embarked on a disastrous political course.

In contrast to Matzerath, Oskar sees beyond the trappings of political manipulation; with his drumming he turns the martial music at a Nazi rally into the Charleston and ruins the assembly. In a different vein, Oskar plays the role of a tempter who entices people to steal and, in the process, to probe their consciences. On Good Friday in 1936, upon seeing eels—both signs of death and phallic symbols—at the beach, Agnes feels pangs of conscience because of her adulterous relationship. A few months later she dies from intentionally induced fish poisoning. Oskar loses his tin drum supplier, a Jewish toy merchant, to suicide during the *Kristallnacht*.

The second book deals with the time spanning World War II. Oskar is instrumental in arranging the unheroic deaths of his two putative fathers. Bronski (in 1939) and Matzerath (in 1945) die as a consequence of the political decisions they have made. But family life goes on: Oskar seduces Maria Truczinski with the help of fizz powder, and Matzerath marries Maria. In 1942, Maria gives birth to son Kurth, whom Oskar believes himself to have fathered. In 1943–44, Oskar is with his friend and master, Lilliputian Bebra, on the front in France providing entertainment for the German troops. After his return to Danzig, he appears as the imitator of Christ and the new Jesus, and he becomes leader of the gang of young Dusters. But the group is betrayed, and its members are arrested.

At Matzerath's funeral, Oskar, now 21 years old, decides to resume his interrupted growth and become a responsible adult. He falls into Matzerath's grave when he is hit by a stone thrown by Kurth. His tin drum, the instrument of an ethically indifferent artist, remains in the grave. Although Oskar arises, he turns into a hunchback below average height and remains a conspicuous outsider.

The post-war scene of the third book changes from Danzig to Düsseldorf, where the Matzerath family settles. Oskar's efforts to become a useful member of society go awry when Maria rejects his marriage proposal. Oskar again devotes himself to art, first as a nude model, then as a drummer in a jazz band. The band performs in the Onion Cellar, a restaurant where prosperous guests, who are oblivious to the horrors of their Nazi past, are given onions and weep profusely. Oskar's art in the service of mourning turns into art in the service of commerce when he goes on lucrative concert tours arranged by his agent Bebra.

Oskar's predilection for nurses, with their radiance of eroticism and death, leads him to the failed attempt to seduce Sister Dorothea. As a prime suspect of her murder when her ring finger is found in his possession, Oskar flees to Paris but cannot avoid arrest. These events mark the end of his fictitious autobiography. Since the suspicion of murder proves to be unfounded, Oskar is faced with the long-dreaded release from the mental institution and departure from his protective metal bed. Oskar's frightening vision of the black cook—the opposite of his grandmother and her sheltering skirts—stems from his feelings of guilt. Although he possessed superior insight, Oskar initially refused—and later on only partially retracted his refusal—to participate actively in the life of family and society. As a kind of atonement Oskar composes his autobiography, a work which does not let the past sink into oblivion by challenging the reader to confront it.

The Tin Drum received the prize of influential Gruppe 47 in 1958, when the novel had not yet been completed. It is now generally recognized as the most important German post-war novel and one of the significant modern novels of the western world, and has sold millions of copies in an impressive number of languages. Although its complexity and linguistic ingenuity resist any interpretation on a single level, the novel's political thrust remains its most persuasive characteristic.

—Siegfried Mews

TITUREL
Poetic fragment by Wolfram von Eschenbach, written c. 1210–20

Wolfram von Eschenbach's *Titurel* consists of two fragments (131 and 39 four-line strophes) of a narrative work probably written either after or concurrently with his other unfinished work *Willehalm*. The modern recognition of the fragment as a literary form with its own aesthetic validity has encouraged some critics to argue that the two fragments are in themselves a finished work. References to the work's beauty and unique magic owe much, if indirectly, to this view of the fragment. This is, however, so foreign to medieval aesthetic concepts that most critics accept the two fragments as self-contained drafts of episodes that could subsequently have been incorporated into a longer whole: evidence of Wolfram von Eschenbach's ''loose-leaf'' (A.T. Hatto, 1980) compositional technique.

The subject matter of the first fragment is the love of the children Sigune and Schionatulander (six syllables pronounced to the same rhythm as ''shout a little louder''!). Separated after Sigune insists that Schionatulander must prove worthy of her love by serving her on the field of knightly combat, the two lovers suffer the effects of love as they are traditionally described in medieval literature and eventually reveal the existence of their love to Gahmuret and Harzeloyde, Parzival's parents, at whose court they have been brought up. The first part of this fragment establishes Sigune as a member of the family of the keepers of the Grail. The second fragment is set in a wood: Schionatulander catches a hunting dog, whose leash and collar bear an inscription concerning the love relationship of former owners. Anxious to read the inscription, Sigune unties the leash, the dog escapes, and she insists that a slightly reluctant Schionatulander leaves to catch it again. This second fragment, especially, is laden with the narrator's prophecies of doom. We know the outcome of Schionatulander's search from Wolfram von Eschenbach's earlier *Parzival*: on four hauntingly described occasions the hero comes across Sigune self-reproachfully mourning her dead lover.

Wolfram von Eschenbach is generally believed to have developed the story of Sigune and Schionatulander from nothing more than a short episode in Chrétien de Troyes's *Conte du Graal* (*Perceval*), in which Percival meets (once only) an unnamed lady mourning a dead knight. On the other hand, if the one-line comment in *Parzival* that Schionatulander died on account of a ''setter's leash'' was not to be completely incomprehensible to his audience, Wolfram von Eschenbach must either have previously acquainted them with the story or possibly have had some written source, now lost, also known to his audience.

The interpretation of this fragmentary work, which its author may in any case have decided not to complete, is fraught with conjecture and contradiction, although there is agreement that the key to the work appears to lie in the interpretation of Schionatulander's search for the leash and the apparently programmatic name of the dog: ''Gardevîaz'' (Keep to the path).

In view of the sense of guilt and self-reproach displayed by Sigune in *Parzival*, some critics see in *Titurel* a pendant to *Parzival*: the development from innocence through the tragic guilt of the heroine to her mature, though belated, understanding of the true relationship between love and chivalry. Though a lady may demand unquestioning obedience from a knight as the price of her love, if, in exploiting this, she frivolously imposes unjustifiably dangerous and pointless tasks on him, she may be observing the letter of the chivalric ethos but is ignoring its spirit and original purpose. As such the work is seen as a questioning of the entire code of feudal chivalry.

Schionatulander's search has also been likened to the quest for the Grail and given an allegorical dimension. It is possible that the inscription, for knowledge of which Sigune would exchange a kingdom, is a prophetic anticipation of the fate of the lovers. Sigune's wish to read the end of her own story then ceases to be an immature exercise of power, and her sense of guilt becomes more complicated. The search becomes one for the knowledge of true love (Ohly), of the transience of happiness and youthful beauty (Wolf), or that suffering and death are part of the experience of love (Haug).

Wolfram von Eschenbach's use of a strophic form, unusual in courtly romances, can be attributed either to the lyrical atmosphere of the fragments or to their strongly tragic sense. This brings them closer to heroic epic, for which composition in strophes is the norm. It is clear that Wolfram von Eschenbach derived the complicated structure of his four-line strophe from a structure used in contemporary heroic poetry.

During the 1260s Wolfram von Eschenbach's *Titurel* fragments were incorporated by Albrecht von Scharpfenberg into a longer *Jüngerer Titurel*, a massive compendium of Grail stories. Albrecht's pretence that the work was produced by Wolfram von Eschenbach for Hermann of Thuringia was believed throughout the Middle Ages, but it is doubtful whether any further fragments by Wolfram von Eschenbach are embedded in the work.

—Alan Deighton

TO HIMSELF (A se stesso)
Poem by Giacomo Leopardi, 1835 (written 1833)

''To Himself'' is undoubtedly one of Giacomo Leopardi's most intensely mournful poems and probably also his most bitterly judgemental and dismissive. It is nevertheless a poem of great passion. Dealing with the theme of love scorned or betrayed, its cause is attributed to the end of the poet's relationship with a Florentine lady, Fanny Targioni-Tozzetti, who had befriended him during the last of his stays in Florence in 1830. It was a relationship apparently in which Leopardi blindly and unrealistically pursued his desire for romance with a woman who was interested in him as a quaint, literary celebrity rather than as a man. Critical consensus gives the poem's year of composition as 1833 and its date of publication as 1835, thus placing it among the poems composed in the last four years of Leopardi's short life.

Although Leopardi the poet was characterized by his generally pessimistic outlook, his darkness of spirit in this poem has nothing to do with philosophy, notwithstanding references to the world, life, and destiny. As the title declares, the poem is obsessively introverted. Its structure of 16 compact lines, mostly composed of short, epigram- matically terse sentences, channels the emotional, at times vitriolic, tone in such a way as to create a narrowness of focus which thematically centres on a dialogue between the poet and his heart, that is, his feelings.

Right from the poem's opening, Leopardi's determination to protect himself against the need for love, and so against the possibili- ties of future disillusionment, is expressed through the use of verbs in the imperative or quasi-imperative mode (the first verb is a future in the original), as he invokes variously stillness, rest, and quiet for his damaged, ingenuous heart: "Now be forever still / Weary my heart," "Rest still forever," "Lie quiet now. Despair / for the last time." The last imperative is not at all cajoling though, being directed towards nature—a word summarizing for Leopardi the state of things—as the poet delivers a sarcastic denunciation of life and the illusions it provides like love. This is interesting because in so poignantly and powerfully personal a poem, the cause of the poet's pain is not seen in private, that is in anecdotal or biographical terms (no woman is identified or accused), but is interpreted from an ontological view- point as the poet relates his condition to the general fate of all human beings. In so doing, of course, he proves its inescapability and, by implication, his own victimization:

> And now you may despise
> Yourself, nature, the brute
> Power which, hidden, ordains the common doom,
> And all the immeasurable emptiness of things.

> (translated by John Heath-Stubbs)

This tendency towards philosophical generalization is typically Leopardian: and here, as in many of his poems, Leopardi again instinctively assumes the role of Everyman. For some famous critics such as Benedetto Croce and Luigi Russo neither the emotion nor the short, philosophical aphorisms succeed in sustaining the poem's lack of "poetic vision." Leaving aside the ideological or aesthetic preju- dices of any critic and the subjectivity implied finally in any assess- ment of what constitutes "poetry," most others have seen the poem's success lying in its perfect fusion of sentiment and rhetoric. Still others have pointed out how the poem approximates a madrigal, a judgement which captures perfectly the poem's contrapuntal move- ments of thought as it darts between considerations on the strengths and weaknesses of desire, on the futility of optimism but the drive to hope, on the unfeelingness of the world towards the individual but also on that individual's battling heroics to survive indifference, albeit with anger and reprobation.

It can also be argued in support of the poem that the sparseness of imagery is consistent with the desolate clarity of the theme. Perhaps a more plausible criticism might be that the poem inevitably leads critics beyond it to explain its circumstances and its meaning fully. To understand the poem to be about love lost is to know the crucial meaning of love for Leopardi and how consistently he pursues it through his other poetry. Taken self-referentially, however, there is no need to see love as *the* issue in the poem but, at best, as one of several possible issues that could inspire such despair in a person, such loss of faith in the emotions. The poet who seems arbitrarily to reduce life to the twin negatives of "boredom and bitterness," who condemns the world as "dirt," is a man trying desperately to protect himself. In so far as anyone can be love-stricken and love traditionally

strikes through the heart, then we must assert that "To Himself," is a poem about a love-stricken heart, even at the moment that it claims its independence from such enslaving feelings.

This, however, is the paradox of Leopardi's poem. In it, the poet feels as intensely as he ever has, in some ways even more so. The vengeful and distressed lament of "To Himself" transcends the strictures of its own would-be impositions for if everything is immeasurably empty, the human cry is still there to fill the vacuum with its own life.

—Walter Musolino

TO THE READER (Au Lecteur)
Poem by Charles Baudelaire, 1855

This poem, the opening text of *The Flowers of Evil*, appeared in print for the first time in June 1855 in the *Revue des Deux Mondes* in a selection of 18 Charles Baudelaire poems. In both contexts it operates as an introduction or prologue. In *The Flowers of Evil* it also constitutes a second dedicatory text, to the reader, after the first one, "to the impeccable poet / to the perfect magician of French letters / to my beloved and revered master and friend / Théophile Gautier / with a sense of the deepest humility / I dedicate these sickly flowers." As the famous final line of "To the Reader" destined to be incorporated by T.S. Eliot into *The Waste Land*, reveals, Baudelaire associates himself with his reader, the "hypocrite lecteur,—mon semblable,—mon frère!" ("hypocrite reader, my alias,—my twin!").

In the ten quatrains of alexandrines Baudelaire paints a sorry portrait of the human condition, as the opening four lines amply demonstrate:

> La sottise, l'erreur, le péché, la lésine,
> Occupent nos esprits et travaillent nos corps,
> Et nous alimentons nos aimables remords,
> Comme les mendiants nourrissent leur vermine.

> (Stupidity, delusion, selfishness and lust
> torment our bodies and possess our minds,
> and we sustain our affable remorse
> the way a beggar nourishes his lice.)

The poet and his reader are shown to be weak, cowardly, and sinful.

Right from this liminal text Baudelaire issues a series of reminders of the evil he chose to couple with the flowers in the title of the collection. The devil and demons are living forces at work in his universe and present in this poem, but in the third stanza Satan is rendered more God-like by the epithet Trismegistus that Baudelaire transfers to him from Hermes. As is the case elsewhere in *The Flowers of Evil*, Satan, for Baudelaire, is an ambiguous figure, not lacking in attraction, and in "To the Reader" God is conspicuous by his absence.

Baudelaire was very aware, from bitter-sweet experience, of a whole series of dualities—God and the devil, good and evil, heaven and hell, "Spleen and Ideal," man and woman. Aspects of the battle between body and soul are suggested in lines 7 and 8: "Et nous rentrons gaiement dans le chemin bourbeux, / Croyant par de vils pleurs laver toutes nos taches" ("How cheerfully we crawl back to the mire: / a few cheap tears will wash our stains away!"). The full carnality of the weakness of the flesh is conveyed by the fifth stanza:

Ainsi qu'un débauché pauvre qui baise et mange
Le sein martyrisé d'une antique catin,
Nous volons au passage un plaisir clandestin
Que nous pressons bien fort comme une vieille orange.

(Like a poor profligate who sucks and bites
the withered breast of some well-seasoned trull,
we snatch in passing at clandestine joys
and squeeze the oldest orange harder yet.)

The feeling that animal passions are rampant is reinforced by references to jackals, panthers, female hounds, monkeys, scorpions, vultures, and snakes, and by the enumeration of adjectival present participles to describe the monsters—yapping, howling, grunting, crawling.

Baudelaire wallows in self-pity to some extent, giving the impression that his will is weak, but in the poem he writes of ''the precious metal of *our* will'': indeed the first person plural is employed throughout, at least until the direct address in the last two lines to the reader.

There is a baroque quality in some of Baudelaire's images, in the band of demons revelling in our brains, in the play of antithesis, in the general fascination with death. At the same time he seems very original, whether it be in the inventiveness of the rhyming of ''helminthes (helminths, intestinal worms) with ''plaintes'' (complaints or moans),'' or of ''houka'' (hookah) with ''délicat'' (delicate), or in the concentration on ''l'Ennui'' which comes across as an updated version of the Romantics' *mal du siècle.*

The poem builds to a climax as Baudelaire holds back until the start of the tenth stanza that noun, the key-word probably of the whole volume, presented as a monster whose introduction occupies the whole of the previous stanza:

Il en est un plus laid, plus méchant, plus immonde!
Quoiqu'il ne pousse ni grands gestes ni grands cris,
Il ferait volontiers de la terre un débris
Et dans un bâillement avalerait le monde;
C'est l'Ennui!—l'oeil chargé d'un pleur involontaire,
Il rêve d'échafauds en fumant son houka.

(He is even uglier and fouler than the rest
although the least flamboyant of the lot;
this beast would gladly undermine the earth
and swallow all creation in a yawn;
I speak of Boredom which with ready tears
dreams of hangings as it puffs its pipe.)

Boredom, or ''spleen'' or ''ennui,'' is depicted as an insidious vice and a squeamish monster, not manifesting itself in grand gestures or loud cries, but none the less laying waste to the earth and engulfing its inhabitants with a yawn.

It has been claimed that ''To the Reader'' changes the emphasis from physical to moral evil. Man sins through insecurity, and insecurity, unfulfilment, is the very condition of life. (A.E. Carter, *Charles Baudelaire*, 1977). Moreover, there is a ruthlessness and a realism about Baudelaire's dissection of mankind: he observes our delight in stolen pleasures, he lays bare our all too human frailties, he is aware of our inability to resist sin and temptation. The poem becomes a panorama of life and, as such, a microcosm of a significant part of *The Flowers of Evil*. The address to, and identification with, the reader at the end, act perhaps as a warning as well as a reminder, before the reader proceeds to the remainder of the volume, where at least in the texts that are illustrations of the ''ideal,'' the other side of the coin, some of man's more noble, more positive aspirations, could be revealed.

—Keith Aspley

TORQUATO TASSO
Play by Johann Wolfgang von Goethe, 1790

In 1780, when Johann Wolfgang von Goethe first conceived the idea of writing a play about the 16th-century Italian poet Torquato Tasso, it sprang, as he later wrote to his patron Duke Carl August, from his ''innermost nature'' (Rome, 28 March 1788). In Tasso's sufferings as an artist at court Goethe evidently identified a medium in which to explore and express his own problems and experience, which he, the *Sturm und Drang* genius, author of *The Sufferings of Young Werther*, had yet to resolve after barely four years striving for acceptance in Weimar. He completed two, no longer extant, acts in poetic prose by 1781, but, perhaps because he was so closely involved with the subject matter that he might have produced another *Werther*, he laid the project aside, resuming work on it only in Italy in 1787. By now his art had acquired a new orientation, a drive to objectivity, which enabled him to complete the play, while maintaining the function of the first two acts essentially unchanged. It was completed in Weimar in 1789, cast in blank verse and published in 1790 as volume six of the Göschen edition of his collected works, the last of the eight volumes to appear. Though the play remained ''bone of my bone and flesh of my flesh'' (Eckermann, 6 May 1827), the greater detachment he had achieved meant that *Torquato Tasso*, like the edition itself, would serve as a reckoning with his past life and work. Its first performance was in Weimar in 1807.

The historical Tasso was highly revered in the 18th century and Goethe was familiar with factual and apocryphal accounts of his strained relations with the court of Ferrara, his house-arrest following infringements of courtly *mores*, his love for the Princess Leonore, his subsequent imprisonment and banishment, and above all, his pathological melancholia and persecution mania. This is the raw material that Goethe fuses with his own experience: he too knew the pressures and restrictions that court life imposed on the natural poet, whose work was not truly appreciated, he suffered as his love for Frau von Stein grew, but remained remote from fulfilment, while on the deepest level he sensed the threat of derangement occasioned by the discrepancies between an intensely subjective perception of the world and the hard realities of life and social convention. This does not mean, however, that the configuration of characters and relationships in *Torquato Tasso* merely mirrors Goethe's position in relation to the Weimar court. There is much of Goethe not only in Tasso himself, but in all the characters, not least in his antagonist—and complement—Antonio.

The action of the drama is notoriously slight: we witness the agony of Tasso's life at court, exacerbated by his oversensitivity and impetuosity, which feed on his paranoia to culminate in madness and banishment. From the start he is portrayed as inhabiting his own subjective world of the imagination, a fault which needs a ''cure.'' An instrument of this cure is to be Antonio, the courtier-diplomat, who on his arrival finds Tasso crowned with a laurel wreath, taken from the bust of Virgil, as a token of the court's esteem for the epic *Gerusalemme liberata* (*Jerusalem Delivered*), which he has just presented to the

Duke. Antonio's disdain provokes a confrontation in which Tasso draws his sword, for which he is placed under house-arrest. Humiliated, he suspects betrayal and conspiracy, even by his beloved Princess, whose reciprocation remains platonic; he determines to leave the court and we follow his progressive disorientation and descent into madness. In a final encounter with the Princess, Tasso mistakes her muted and distressed expression of a desire to help as a declaration of love, and embraces her, thereby ensuring his irrevocable banishment. The play might well have ended here, but in the final scene Tasso's ravings are met by Antonio's assurance that he will not abandon him; he forces Tasso to take a grip on himself and to recognize what he is: a poet. Painfully aware of all that he has lost, Tasso affirms the validity of his creative powers:

> One thing remains—
> That Nature gave us tears and cries of pain
> When man can bear his sufferings no more.
> She gave that to you all. To me she gave
> The added gift of melody and speech
> To vent my sorrows fully. Where the rest
> Are silent in their sorrows, some kind God
> Decreed that I should speak.

As Tasso acknowledges this truth, Antonio takes his hand, and the curtain falls as Tasso compares himself to a shipwrecked mariner clinging for safety to the rock which threatened his destruction.

The ending has provoked debate as to whether the catastrophe of Tasso's loss is thereby mitigated and the possibility of salvation left open. The weight of opinion inclines towards viewing the play as depicting the "tragedy of the artist," occasioned by the apparent incompatibility of Tasso's poetic vocation and real life in society, what Goethe called "the disproportion between talent and life" (Caroline Herder in a letter to her husband, 20 March 1789). Tasso's failure is complete, and the power to articulate his suffering will not restore his loss. If Tasso is at fault, so too is the court, and it is the distinctive feature of Goethe's attitude to his subject that he displays both criticism and understanding. In his poetic vision of the Golden Age (II, 1) Tasso evokes a time when spontaneous desire and fulfilment were synonymous, only to be reminded by the Princess that such times are past and convention must modify behaviour. Tasso's subjectivism is criticized as inadequate and dangerous, while simultaneously being acknowledged as the source from which his poetry springs. While recognizing his intimate kinship with Tasso, Goethe is distancing himself from that potential self-destructiveness which makes Tasso "an intensified Werther" (Eckermann, 3 May 1827). There is no salvation for Tasso, but through the discipline of art and the realization that poetic expression can transfigure suffering, Goethe himself is able to advance in a positive spirit.

—David Bell

THE TOWER (Der Turm)
Play by Hugo von Hofmannsthal, 1925

Hugo von Hofmannsthal's preoccupation with the material that provided the plot for his last major drama goes back to October 1901, when he began a "very free" verse translation of Calderón's *La vida es sueño* (*Life Is a Dream*). He put this work aside in spring 1902

without, however, abandoning the project altogether. In the summer of that year he turned to it again, now opting at first for a prose adaptation to be titled *The Tower*, which was to be part of a cycle of Calderón transcriptions for Vienna's Burgtheater. The play that had begun as a poetic "descent into the cavernous kingdom of the self" had by now assumed a strong socio-political dimension, the result of the author's profound disorientation at the end of World War I. Through the revival of the allegorical baroque *Trauerspiel* (literally, mourning play), this testimonial tragedy explores the conflicting forces that shape history. In its final form, though, it shows the destruction of spiritual culture at the hands of ruthless power, and it points toward a future of dictatorial oppression in which the interplay of multifarious rights, interests, and justifications have been obliterated and the world is totally out of balance.

The Tower exists in two distinct versions, each with extensive variants and showing significant changes in style, dramatic density, and thematic development. The first version was finished in November 1924 and published in 1925; the second was completed and published, after extensive consultations with the director Max Reinhardt and other friends, in autumn 1927. The drama was first performed on 4 February 1928, concurrently at the Prinzregententheater in Munich and at the Hamburg Schauspielhaus.

The action of the play is situated in a kingdom of Poland whose "atmosphere is more legendary than historical" and resembles that of the 16th century. Its protagonist is Sigismund, King Basilius' only son, who was abandoned after birth and has been kept in solitary confinement in a remote tower for the last six years. Unaware of his noble lineage, the young prince has found a protector in Julian who plans to use him for his own advancement to high office and against a monarch who, frightened by a prophecy that his heir will depose him, clings to his claim of absolute power with frantic determination. When a war he ill-advisedly started is lost, and widespread misery leads to uprisings, Julian seeks the official recognition of his charge by arranging a meeting between the royal father and his son. But their encounter fails to bring about a reconciliation when Basilius, insisting on his divine right to demand unquestioning obedience, tests Sigismund's profession of loyalty by ordering him to kill Julian whom he accuses of treason. Outraged by this wanton offence against elementary humanity, the hitherto passive youth takes impetuous action. With Julian's help he subdues the king and wrests from him the insignia of his authority. Both rebels are soon overpowered by the courtiers, however, and a disillusioned Sigismund is returned to his prison. Even the offer to lead a seditious army cannot rouse him from his dejection. Once again, all reality is for him but a dream and the "tower" of his inwardness is the only true world he acknowledges. To be sure, he does not dissuade a people in revolt from liberating him and proclaiming him their king, but he finds it impossible to break out of his self-absorbed seclusion. Thus Julian, who had secretly fanned the rebellion, seizes power, but only for a short time. For he is shot as the soldier Olivier, the "red Satan," takes control of the rabble. A master of demagogy and diabolical in the use of force, this populist usurper tries to coerce Sigismund into joining his cause, thus creating not an alliance of equals but a military dictatorship with the appearance of historical legitimacy. But his power depends entirely on the strength of his plundering troops. When a force of peasant patriots vanquishes his army, his death goes almost unnoticed, as a new figure enters the political arena. He is an orphan and the leader of homeless children who, as a pacific messiah, will inaugurate a new secular order based on modesty and devotion to justice and peace. He takes the place of the "fraternal" Sigismund who dies after Olivier's mistress, a gypsy with the gift of conjuring forth the buried bones of the departed, cuts him with a poisonous dagger. His last words are the plea: ''Bear witness: I was there. Even though nobody recognized me.''

Hofmannsthal cut much of the ''atmospheric'' dialogue and some merely ''colourful'' figures (e.g. the gypsy) from the ''new version'' of 1927. He also changed the last act drastically, above all replacing its utopian vagueness with an ending of stark pessimism. Now a coup d'état of the high nobility forces an ignoble Basilius to abdicate in Sigismund's favour. But the new king dismisses their council and retains only Julian as his adviser, without acting, however, on his pragmatic policies. This renders him powerless against Olivier who has quickly risen to dictatorial power by eliminating all of his opponents. In the end, the king is murdered in an ambush when he refuses to serve a brutal regime as a legitimating puppet.

Unable to envision a society shaped by democratic compromises and disenchanted with the idea of a populist restoration of a reformed aristocracy, Hofmannsthal's spiritual conservatism could foresee only the nihilism of mob rule. Consequently, he refused to recognize any power, even the transcendent one of a judging God, as justifiable authority. Instead he came to fear that all institutions of public life are corrupt and fated to destruction (''in der Hand der Fatalität'') when a crisis of universal dimensions has severed the natural familial bonds of spirit and might. He saw secular authority either as driven by blind ambition toward self-aggrandizement or as destroyed by profound depression and haughty self-isolation. Worldly power can therefore be expressed only in absolute dichotomies: on the one hand there is rebellious anarchy, which defines the momentum of policies, and on the other, chiliastic utopianism which offers refuge for an autonomous but disinherited mind. It is this irreconcilable polarity that signifies the present inability of history to rejuvenate itself.

The search for an ever more elusive synthesis of spirit and ''life'' defines both the play's extraordinary ambition and its artistic failure. Its subtle network of suggestive nuances is forced to support an inordinate weight of allegorical abstractness, and its genteel antiquarian language often strains at sustaining the sombre tone of meaningful statements. Its structure and the complexity of its theme rather than the dramatic potential inherent in its characters have made *The Tower* more a reading drama than a part of the German theatrical repertoire.

—Michael Winkler

THE TOY CART

See THE LITTLE CLAY CART

THE TRIAL (Der Prozess)
Novel by Franz Kafka, 1925 (written 1914–15)

The Trial begins with the arrest of Josef K. and ends with his execution. But this is no ordinary arrest, Josef K.'s trial is no ordinary trial, and the court which exercises jurisdiction over him is no ordinary court. His arrest is largely nominal as after being informed of it, Josef K. is allowed to go about his normal business as a senior clerk in a bank. No formal charge is laid against him. The questions which insistently force themselves on the reader are: why has Josef K. been arrested? what has he done wrong? No explicit answer is ever provided.

The emissaries of the court take Josef K. by surprise in his lodgings early in the morning, but they are only menial employees who have no knowledge of the reasons for his being accused. Greedy and corrupt, they eat his breakfast and try to trick him into allowing them to go off with his clothes. The impression they make is consistent with the impression made by the court throughout the novel. The supreme judges are totally inaccessible and such information as Josef K. is able to learn about them indicates that they are vain and capricious. The law books he manages to see are obscene. The principles underlying the law he is assumed to have transgressed are not revealed. One persuasive reading of the novel is to see it as the story of an ordinary man persecuted and destroyed by a powerful bureaucratic tyranny, a prophetic image of the totalitarian systems which were to arise in central Europe after the author's death.

The very first sentence of the novel seems to state Josef K.'s innocence: ''Someone must have been telling lies about Josef K., for without having done anything wrong he was arrested one fine morning.'' However, it soon becomes apparent that the events of the story are presented primarily from the perspective of the central character. In other words, this opening assertion reflects Josef K.'s perception of things and is not necessarily that of an objective narrator. Appreciation of the narrative technique is vitally important to a proper appreciation of the work. We see things from Josef K.'s point of view but the story is narrated in the third person. There is, then, a narrator at work in the text who does sometimes provide information which is independent of Josef K.'s consciousness, such as the summary of the way Josef K. has been in the habit of spending his evenings. This narrator performs the essential function of shaping the pattern of the story, including the rounding-off of an ending, which makes for narrative coherence and economy. In terms of the conventions of narrative fiction, there is no reason to doubt that it is a guarantee of the accuracy of the outward contours which are described and, in particular, of the central facts of Josef K.'s arrest, trial, and execution. And yet, given the extraordinary nature of the events which take place, this narrator is remarkably reticent. He has no privileged insight into why these things happen: he passes no direct judgements. The reader is left to draw his own conclusions. The organization of the story, together with Josef K.'s behaviour, gradually raises doubts in the reader's mind about the reliability of Josef K.'s conviction that he is blameless. When he is arrested he insists that he does not know the law under which he is accused and yet, at the same time, asserts that he is not guilty. From this point on he repeatedly protests his innocence to almost everyone he meets. When he considers writing a deposition in his defence he rejects totally any possibility of guilt: ''Above all, if he were to achieve anything, it was essential that he should eliminate from his mind the idea of possible guilt. There was no such guilt.''

Despite these avowals, Josef K.'s actions betray a recognition on his part that the court does have a claim upon him. He is summoned to a preliminary hearing before a magistrate on a Sunday in order that his trial should not interfere with his job, denounces the proceedings, and expresses his contempt for the court. Although he has not been summoned, the following Sunday he returns to the court-room of his own volition, only to find it empty. His trial now becomes a matter of overwhelming concern to him. Although he initially resolves that he will not seek any outside help, he begins to solicit help from anyone he thinks might be of assistance. Everyone he meets seems either to have some connection with the court or at least to know as much about his case as he does himself: his uncle, the lawyer, the lawyer's maid, the court painter, his business clients, and the prison chaplain. The physical presence of the court begins to spill over and spread out everywhere. It proliferates through the attics of various buildings; it invades the bank, the painter's studio, and the cathedral. Every step he takes seems to bring him into contact with his trial. This obsessive awareness is not the mark of a clear conscience. Whatever his words may indicate, his behaviour is that of a man who feels guilty.

Josef K's series of encounters with people from whom he seeks advice culminates in his meeting with the prison chaplain in the solemnity of the cathedral. There is a significant difference between this meeting and his earlier ones. It is the priest who takes the initiative and who addresses him. He tells him Josef K. is wrong to seek outside help and, in the parable of the man from the country and the gatekeeper, warns him against the danger of deceiving himself about the Law. Josef K. learns nothing from this advice. In the final chapter two executioners call for him, take him out to a deserted quarry, and thrust a knife in his heart. He dies, in his own words, ''like a dog!''

Josef K.'s sense of guilt cannot be attributed to any one specific action; nor can it be characterized as universal human guilt. There are other accused men in the story but, equally, there are many who do not stand accused by the court. Josef K.'s failing may be found in his lack of humility and self-understanding, in his aggressive impatience and stubbornness. Paradoxically, his guilt lies in his blind refusal to countenance even the possibility that he may in some sense be guilty, in which case the court is justified in its measures, however cruel and corrupt it may seem to be. It is impossible to define its essence in precise terms. Certainly it would be a gross oversimplification to describe it as the agent of divine justice, although some religious, transcendental quality is implied. It represents, despite appearances, a realm of transcendental values which Josef K. is incapable of understanding.

Ultimately it is impossible to ascribe any one single meaning to *The Trial*. It presents a double image: an innocent man destroyed by a despotic authority and a guilty man rightly condemned. We are not forced to chose between these possibilities; they co-exist and inter-penetrate each other. Franz Kafka's novel constantly challenges the reader to supply his own interpretation of its elusive substance.

—B. Ashbrook

THE TRICKSTER OF SEVILLE (El burlador de Sevilla)
Play by Tirso de Molina, 1625

The action of *The Trickster of Seville* is built around the elements of disguise, seduction, and flight. The term *burlador* (and its related forms, *burlar* and *burla*) designates deceits or ''tricks'' of different types. The first are the disguises Don Juan adopts in order to carry out his seductions; second are the seductions or sexual ''deceits'' themselves; finally there are the moral deceits insofar as Don Juan believes he will not be called to account for his actions. Don Juan seduces four women in Tirso de Molina's play, and each seduction occurs in a different place. Two of the women (the Duchess Isabela and Doña Ana) are nobles, two (Tisbea and Aminta) are from the common ranks of society.

The principal themes of the work are introduced in Act I, with the seduction of the Duchess Isabela in the palace in Naples. Isabela is deceived in part because Don Juan has artfully disguised himself as the Duke Octavio, but also because she has committed herself to a pre-arranged nocturnal encounter with the Duke. After Don Juan is recognized as an impostor, he flees to Spain, where he and his aide, Catalinón, land on the coast of Tarragona; there Don Juan attempts to seduce a fisherwoman, Tisbea. Unlike the other women in the play, Tisbea claims to be strong enough to resist his advances, yet she too falls eventually.

In Act II Don Juan disguises himself as the Marqués de la Mota, and in an attempt to seduce a cousin of the Marqués, the noblewoman Ana de Ulloa, he kills her father, Don Gonzalo de Ulloa, in a duel. In Act III Don Juan interrupts the wedding celebration of the peasant couple, Aminta and Batricio, and steals the bride away. At the close of Act III Don Gonzalo returns from the dead and as the ''Stone Guest'' challenges Don Juan to accept a dinner invitation. Once Don Juan is dragged down into Hell by the Stone Guest the other couples in the play are married off happily.

The Trickster of Seville thus has what may be regarded as two conclusions—or a conclusion in two parts. The first, where Don Juan meets the Stone Guest, is tragic in tone. The second allows for the reconciliation of those members of society who have been dishonoured by Don Juan, and is comic in the dramatic sense. The first conclusion enacts the near sacrificial elimination of the tyrant of seduction in the form of a banquet; this ritual elimination in turn permits accession to civil society or social life.

The action of *The Trickster of Seville* is set within a larger, theological framework that demands (and produces) divine retribution for Don Juan's actions. Throughout the play his aide Catalinón advises him to mend his ways and repent, but Don Juan refuses, always insisting that he has plenty of time to repent (''¡Qué largo me lo fiáis!''). At one level, Catalinón is simply cowardly and Don Juan defiant; Don Juan has heroic aspirations, however misguided his actions may be. But on another level, Tirso de Molina's play is a late example of the drama of the Counter-Reformation in Spain; the insistent moral overtones of the work serve as a warning of the powers of divine justice and retribution regulating earthly life.

It has been said that the artistry of Tirso de Molina's play ties in its internal pace, its dramatic rhythm, and its language, rather than in its detailed psychological characterizations. *The Trickster of Seville* is, to be sure, a formulaic work; yet is has, built into its formulae, a greater degree of psychological complexity than often is recognized. On the one hand Tirso de Molina seems to have understood the psychology of the seducer, and to have recognized the mobile sense of selfhood required to sustain a life of disguise and deceit. Such mobility demands of the trickster the ability to imagine himself in the role of others and also the negative capability for the absorption of alien roles as his own. As a result of this process, Don Juan has a vacillating, almost vacant identity; indeed, he defines himself from the beginning of the play as ''A man with no name'' (''Un hombre sin nombre''). On the other hand, Tirso de Molina seems to have comprehended the psychology of those who exhibit the desire *for* seduction. This is where the distinctiveness of the play is to be found. Don Juan seduces women of all social ranks, and has a social-levelling effect; as a result, the motives of the different strata of society are reduced to their common denominator in desire.

Linguistically and thematically, *The Trickster of Seville* has been seen as an example of Mannerism or of the Baroque in Spain, and may be compared to the art of El Greco. In its rapid movement, violent changes of scene, its poetic use of visual perspectives, its elaborately constructed metaphors and figures of speech, and in its consciousness of time and space the play is, indeed, baroque. On the one hand, Don Juan is acutely aware of time: time is, for him, the intensity of the moment; yet on the other hand Tirso de Molina reminds his audience of the pressures of theological time—the time for justice, when Don Juan will be forced to account for his actions.

When viewed in social terms, *The Trickster of Seville* represents a moment of the decline of the nobility in Spain. As Aminta says, ''La desvergüenza en España / Se ha hecho caballería'' (''Shame itself has become the knighthood of Spain''). Don Juan is the anti-type of the typical hero of the Spanish Golden-Age theatre, on whom the values of honour are so often staked. Whereas the prototypical hero upholds the standards of society by remaining faithful to the values of honour, Don Juan seeks, by transgressing social norms, to undermine the order of society itself. If the typical heroes of the theatre of Golden-Age Spain are characteristically the proponents of a conservative ideology, then Don Juan is both socially subversive and threateningly modern.

The figure of the ''trickster'' derives in part from legend, in part from Spanish ballads, and partly from the seducing courtier or *galán* of the Spanish theatre, with his real-life counterpart in the degenerate nobility. Tirso de Molina's play is none the less the first full-blown example of the Don Juan legend in literature and art, and has served as the source for countless works since, including, most prominently, Molière's *Dom Juan*, Mozart and da Ponte's *Don Giovanni*, Zorilla's *Don Juan Tenorio*, Kierkegaard's *Either/Or* (in the figure of the Seducer), and Shaw's *Man and Superman*.

—Anthony J. Cascardi

THE TROJAN WOMEN (Troades)
Play by Euripides, 416 BC

Euripides' drama of the defeated Trojans and their experience with Greek brutality and inhumanity followed the infamous siege of the neutral island of Melos in 416 BC and immediately preceded the departure of the Athenian expeditionary force against Syracuse, a campaign that ended disastrously for the Athenians in 413 BC. Thucydides' account of the parley between the Athenian commanders and Melian representatives and the subsequent siege is marked by opportunism, arrogance (*hubris*), and rejection of the claims of justice (Thucydides 5, 84–116). The Athenian victory resulted in the slaughter of the Melian men, and the enslavement of the women and children. Thucydides (and Euripides) saw the campaign as critical; the glory of the event was eclipsed by the suffering of the vanquished.

Euripides' *The Trojan Women* was part of a lost, probably connected, trilogy, *Alexander* (= Paris), *Palamedes,* and *The Trojan Women;* the satyr play was *Sisyphus.* The plays, in succession, treated the tragic error that attached to Priam's compassion and ultimate tragic error in the rescue and nurture of Paris (*Alexander*); the political intrigue against the high-minded Palamedes which had dire consequences for the Greek perpetrators (*Palamedes*); vignettes of cruelty and suffering after defeat (*The Trojan Women*); in all likelihood, the satyr play dealt with deceit and destruction. The coherence seems somewhat strained because the plots are still uncertain.

The theme of *The Trojan Women* is the debasement of human nature and the sorrow war brings for its victors as well as the defeated. The persistent tone is sorrow rather than bitterness. The play opens with Poseidon's renunciation of Troy to escape the pollution of death. Athena, properly the patroness of the Greeks, regards them as sinners bound for personal disaster in their return to Greece. As sackers of cities, temples, and tombs, nemesis is inescapable. Hecuba, the former queen reduced to rags and misery, expresses hatred for Helen, and observes that even the victorious Greeks have made their wives widows and their virgins husbandless. Talthybius, the Greek herald, forthright, unimaginative, but basically sympathetic, reports the assignment of the Trojan women to the respective lords and captors: Cassandra to Agamemnon; Polyxena, as it finally emerges, to be sacrificial victim to dead Achilles: Andromache, Hector's widow, to Neoptolemus, Achilles' son; and Hecuba to the detested Odysseus. Cassandra is introduced carrying a bridal torch and dressed in her prophetic robes; consecrated to Apollo, and to virginity, truthful but never believed, her words and fire-dance accent Greek insensitivity and forecast the ultimate holocaust. The chorus of women performs a solemn dance recalling the entry of the Trojan Horse into the city.

Brilliant spectacle ensues with the arrival of a chariot carrying Andromache and Astyanax, Hector's son. Talthybius reports, with some reluctance, that by order of Odysseus Astyanax must die. The separation of mother and child is deeply poignant. The chorus sings of an earlier siege of Troy, involving Telamon of Salamis and Heracles when, because of the Trojan king Laomedon's deceit, the gods had once before abandoned Troy. Menelaus, pompous, arrogant, conceited, and an incompetent commander, indicates that he endorses Helen's execution. Hecuba responds with a measure of urgency, composes a pun on Helen's name (''destroyer'') and criticizes Helen's still elegant attire.

A debate, technically an *agon*, a contest or legalistic argument, ensues between Helen and Hecuba. Helen offers a cool, rational defence of her past actions, and seeks to exonerate herself from personal guilt by alleging that she is the victim of others and of divine powers, of Hecuba and Priam (who raised Paris), of Aphrodite (who captivates mortals and awarded her to Paris), of Paris (by reason of his physical beauty and sexual appetite), and of Menelaus (who was foolish enough to leave Helen and Paris alone in his palace). Hecuba's hatred knows no bounds: she rejects the Judgement of Paris as fiction, argues that Aphrodite equates with Aphrosyne (lewdness, folly, or mindlessness), that Helen was intrigued from the outset by eastern luxury and exotically designed clothes (which she still wears in contrast to Hecuba's rags). Hecuba's is a speech of deep-seated hatred and contempt, fired by prejudice. Her ''courtroom'' rhetoric is more persuasive; but Helen's beauty is invincible. The chorus responds with a prayer for the destruction of the Greeks. Talthybius reappears with the corpse of Astyanax resting on Hector's massive shield but only after he has bathed the child's battered body, thrown from the walls of Troy, in the Scamander river. Hecuba arranges the burial of the child and pronounces an impressive, agonized lament over her grandson. The chorus responds with unrestrained lamentation over the exodus of the Trojan captives and the ultimate devastation of the city.

Throughout, Euripides lays emphasis on suffering and maltreatment and plays down the heroism of men on the battlefield. The heroic focus of the *Iliad* has shifted to the fate of the losers. The concentration on women as the objects of men's aggression and brutality underscores the harshness of the drama. Perhaps the most impressive moments in the play are Cassandra's sophistic outburst in her ''mad'' scene when she argues that the Greeks have won a hollow victory, for they have destroyed the possibilities of the continuing life of their native land, her prophecy that her forced marriage to Agamemnon will be prelude to his destruction, and her forecast that the sly, unpleasant Odysseus will be a wanderer for years to come. Finally, the play offers a timeless litany of the suffering that war brings to victors and victims alike.

—Alexander G. McKay

TROPISMS (Tropismes)
Prose by Nathalie Sarraute, 1939

Tropisms cannot be called a novel; indeed, it is in many ways an anti-novel, for it consists of 24 discontinuous fragments rarely longer than two pages, with changing, unnamed characters set against shifting, unconnected backgrounds, and no overall plot. Published in 1939 after a lengthy period of gestation (the first pieces were written in 1932), it was Nathalie Sarraute's first book, and was to be hailed after the war as one of the founding texts of the *Nouveau Roman* movement. In it, Sarraute brings about a radical shift in the centre of interest of narrative fiction, reacting implicitly—as she was later to do explicitly in the essays of *L'Ère du soupçon* (*The Age of Suspicion*)—against all the enabling conventions of the realist novel as it had developed and been perfected throughout the 19th century. The surface realism of objects and situation (description), the moral algebra of human nature and motivation (character analysis), and the linear plot constructed as a sequence of significant events linked by cause and effect (narrative), are all rejected as inauthentic, and replaced by a more modest, yet fundamental, investigation of deep-seated psychological states which Sarraute called "tropisms."

Tropism (from the Greek *tropos*), was originally a biological term designating the ability of certain organisms to orient themselves automatically according to some external physical influence (heliotropes turn to face the sun, moths fly photo-tropically towards a candle). In the 1920s, Valéry used it to define the "obscure forces" that made people respond to events or words in certain predetermined, largely unconscious ways, and Sarraute extends this metaphorical sense, though retaining the connotations of an involuntary, quasibiological reflex, to form the basis of her new approach to psychological writing. Rejecting the traditional broad labels of human behaviour (love, jealousy, greed, anger, etc.) as both too crude and too abstract to account for real interactions between people, she sets out to locate and transcribe the "subtle, scarcely-perceptible" (*The Age of Suspicion*) influences that actually condition the things we say and do. The decision to centre the narrative interest of *Tropisms* on the "innumerable swarm of sensations, images, feelings, memories, impulses, and tiny, half-performed actions.. . that jostle on the threshold of consciousness" (*The Age of Suspicion*) experienced by her anonymous characters has a number of significant consequences for the way the book is written.

In the first place, this kind of micro-psychological writing, aiming to recreate deep-seated, often unexplored states of mind, can by definition have recourse to no pre-existing descriptive language. Sarraute therefore relies heavily on metaphor, and on our ability to intuit what is really going on at a deep level from the often banal and ambiguous evidence of surface exchanges. This constant interplay between surface and depths places considerable demands on the reader, and requires far greater involvement in the process of making sense of the book than would be the case with a traditional novel. The problem (though in fact Sarraute regards the destabilization of our

comfortable expectations of familiarity as a good thing) is compounded by the fragmentary narrative form: there are no big, significant events or motives from which the thread of a conventional plot might be woven, and we have scarcely begun to grasp the dynamics of one situation before it is over, thrusting us unceremoniously into a different one. Nor can we build up any satisfying relationship with the characters, who are referred to only as "he," "she," "they," and are in any case constantly changing; we generally perceive what is going on from the perspective of one of the participants, but the analysis of their state of mind is not done for us by a conventional narrator. Instead, we must balance their often obsessive thoughts about themselves against what we hear and see, through their eyes and ears, of the other people with whom they are locked in generally antagonistic relationships, and try to decide who is right, who is being unreasonable, etc. It is only by understanding the relationship as a whole that we can acquire knowledge of the individuals, and it is one of the profoundly original aspects of Sarraute's writing to have introduced this relational approach to character-drawing, in contrast to our normal view of characters in novels (and people in the real world) as discrete psychological "islands," with their own independent characteristics, desires, values, and so on.

Both the relationship between characters and the underlying, often banal situation (a couple having breakfast, a child being led across the road by his grandfather, women out shopping), are often conveyed initially through dialogue, which tends to be equally banal, even cliché-ridden (in contrast to the highly intellectualized language customary in character-analysis). This overt dialogue conceals a stream of half-formed, semi-coherent thoughts to which we are also given access through an inner monologue, or "subconversation" (*The Age of Suspicion*), revealing in detail the gap between words and intentions, the "innumerable petty crimes" (*The Age of Suspicion*) hidden behind what we say. On an even deeper level, Sarraute manages to hint at the pressures and urges underlying even these semi-conscious thoughts, often by metaphorical means (fragment XVII, for instance, uses the extended metaphor of a picnic in a suburban wood to convey the constricted, half-alive circumstances from which a family is unable to escape, while the home-seeking couple in fragment III lead a grey existence "like the waiting-room of a deserted suburban station"). The situations evoked contain a pronounced element of criticism, both existential (men and women who are unable to break free from the tyranny of a domineering partner or family member) and social (the emptiness and conventionality of bourgeois respectability, and its absurd hold over those who aspire to attain it). In the context of pre-war French conformism, this consistent implication that both social and individual relationships are rooted in the abuse of power made *Tropisms* a quietly revolutionary book as much in terms of values as of technique.

—Andrew Rothwell

THE TUTOR (Der Hofmeister)
Play by Jakob Michael Reinhold Lenz, 1774

The subtitle of *The Tutor, The Benefits of Private Education*, seems at first to be a sarcastic comment on the thesis around which the play is built, for the opening scenes focus on questions of education and contrast the enlightened views of the privy councillor, who sends his son Fritz to a public school, with the authoritarian and fundamentally anti-educational views of his blustering brother, the major, who is in the process of hiring a private tutor. The arguments of the privy councillor are given special credence by Jakob Michael Reinhold Lenz's detailing of the network of bad motives that sustain private education, as Läuffer, the tutor, is forced by his position into servile obedience to the whims of the major and his conceited wife, both of whom are more concerned with themselves than with the interests of their children, Leopold and Gustchen. At the beginning of the second act the privy councillor lectures Läuffer's father on the evils of being a private tutor, especially the requirement to deny oneself freedom and therefore the possibility of self-realization, and more generally on the way that the acceptance of tutoring positions by members of the middle classes contributes to the moral decay of society.

Läuffer's father, however, subverts this level of argument by introducing the idea that the enlightened and humanitarian gestures of the privy councillor do not represent universal truths but are rather a function of his privileged position and that his moralizing injunctions fail to take into account the real economic circumstances of the middle classes. Thus the characters, who seemed initially to have been set up as vehicles for discussing a thesis, take on a life of their own, and Lenz's interest in the individuality of the experience of each of them leads to a certain fragmentation of the plot. The isolation and inauthenticity of life in the major's household draws Läuffer and Gustchen into a romantic affair, and when this is discovered and they flee, the action of the play follows their individual fates. Gustchen and the resultant baby lodge with an old lady until Gustchen's concern for her father makes her leave and try to find him, but before being able to do so she throws herself into a pond in a state of exhaustion and despair. Although Läuffer finds refuge with an eccentric schoolmaster, his remorse eventually drives him to castrate himself. Interspersed with these scenes is the story of the distress suffered by the major. The privy councillor, too, is estranged from his son Fritz, for in another branch of the action which portrays student life in Halle, Fritz accepts imprisonment on behalf of his indebted friend Pätus but this noble act is maliciously misrepresented to his father by another student.

The complicated plot is held together less by a discussion of educational principles than by the coherence of the author's vision and the emergence of a number of typical situations. One of these is the estrangement of parents from their children, and the pain this causes both. Despite the initial contrast between the major and the privy councillor, we become more aware of the parallels between these two fathers, who both feel that they have been deserted by their children, and this motif is developed further in the breach between Pätus and his father—and beyond, in the gulf between Pätus's father and the father's mother. There is also the motif of enforced renunciation, which applies not only to fathers who have to endure the loss of their children but also and especially to a range of characters leading up to the castrated Läuffer who have to forego loving sexual relationships. Even the brief affair between Läuffer and Gustchen is an example of this in as much as Lenz portrays the two as relating to each other only through pre-formed literary models.

It is this vision that at the deepest level holds the play together, a vision of human beings as unfree. At one level, what is innovatory about Lenz's writing is his ability to show the mechanisms by which social power translates itself through specific circumstances into the unfreedom of the individual, and in *The Tutor* it is primarily the power of class and age (parenthood) that prevents the individual from developing an identity and a life of his own. In this respect and in the range of social types who appear on stage Lenz looks forward to the realism of the 19th century, but perhaps most particularly in the way that he shows his characters internalizing these structures of compulsion so that they take on a form and a necessity independent of their original source. At the same time there is much that is grotesque and laughable about characters who submit to such necessity. Lenz's uncertainty whether to call *The Tutor* a comedy or a tragedy reflects the tension between this absurd rigidity of character, which Lenz in his *Anmerkungen übers Theater* [Notes on the Theatre] defined as the essence of comedy, and the pessimistic vision of the world, the awareness of constraint and suffering, that lies behind it.

It is therefore appropriate that, having taken us to the point where the only logical conclusion can be social and moral collapse and pain, Lenz superimposes a self-mocking conciliatory ending: mere chance determines that the major is on hand to rescue Gustchen as she throws herself into the pond, that the financial entanglements are resolved by Pätus winning a lottery, or that the old woman to whom Gustchen entrusted the baby turns out to have been Pätus's grandmother. Even Läuffer seems able to look forward to a happily married future with the dimwitted peasant girl Lise, who is more interested in feeding her poultry than in having children. The final scene of the play has a series of reconciliations, primarily that between Gustchen and Fritz, who adopts her baby and declares in his concluding speech that he will definitely not allow it to be educated by a private tutor. This last reference simply serves to show how far *The Tutor* has moved beyond its initial pedagogic thesis, and indeed how far Lenz has moved beyond that tradition of Enlightenment writing for which there was an ordered framework to existence within which individual problems could be answered by specific proposals for reform.

—David Hill

THE TWELVE (Dvenadtsat')
Poem by Aleksandr Blok, 1918

Written in January 1918, *The Twelve* is Aleksandr Blok's poetic response to the Bolshevik Revolution and is acknowledged as the greatest poetic work inspired by this climactic event in Russian history. It is at once a celebration and a highly personal interpretation of the Revolution, and it marks the culmination of Blok's development as a poet.

For all its ostensible realism and sustained sense of immediacy, *The Twelve* is a work of Symbolist art inseparably related by its imagery and by the ideas which underlie it to the three volumes of Blok's lyric poetry. It is not, therefore, primarily a political poem. It is an immensely complex work conceived in a very real sense as a parallel to the revolution that it depicts, for the Revolution was seen by Blok as an explosion of the same creative energy that is experienced by the artist in the act of poetic creation. His term for this creative force was ''the Spirit of Music,'' and from 1908 onwards it became increasingly associated in his thought with the Russian masses. ''Art is born,'' he wrote, ''of the eternal interaction between two kinds of music—the music of the creative individual and the music which sounds in the depths of the popular soul, the soul of the masses.'' The 12 sections, therefore, into which the poem is divided may be characterized as the movements of an essentially musical composition designed to evoke a process of cultural transformation that was itself conceived in musical terms, as a process in which destruction and creation were apprehended as dissonance and harmony. This ''musical'' conception is reflected in the use of metre, rhyme, assonance, and alliteration, in the repetition of images (especially colour symbols), in the snatches of folk songs, revolutionary songs, and romances that interrupt the narrative, and in the stylistic discords produced by the juxtapositions of obscenities, slang, and contemporary political slogans with literary allusions and religious imagery.

The central figures of the poem embody "the music which sounds in the depths of the popular soul." They are the 12 Red guards patrolling the streets of revolutionary Petrograd to whom the title refers and who are transformed in the course of the work from an undisciplined, vengeful, and destructive rabble into a cohesive force capable of building the future and led by Christ. Together with the number 12, the appearance of Christ in the last line of the work has been taken to suggest that a parallel to the 12 apostles was intended. The hypothesis is strengthened by the names given to the two named members of the Twelve—Pet'ka/Petrukha and Andriukha (diminutives of Petr [Peter] and Andrei [Andrew])—and by statements in Blok's diary and notebooks of the period. The portrayal of the Twelve, however, cannot easily be reconciled with this view, and sceptics have pointed also in this connection to Blok's professed discontent with his Christ image. The reasons for his dissatisfaction and the meaning of the image are among the major subjects of debate provoked by the poem. As a symbol of salvation, of Russia's rebirth and redemption through blood and torment, it was clearly an appropriate image. In addition, it may have been intended to express the belief, bequeathed by Gogol' and, most notably, Dostoevskii, that the Russian people were destined to restore Christ to a world which had lost Him. Yet the Revolution was seen by Blok as giving birth to a new era unlike any that had been known in human experience. To the extent that it failed to express this idea, the Christ image may be said to have fallen short of his requirements, and herein, perhaps, lies the main reason for his reservations about it.

Less contentiously the Twelve have also been interpreted as embodying one of the pivotal "pagan" concepts in Blok's thought and poetry—the concept of "the elemental" (*stikhiia*) which ultimately merged in his thinking with that of "the Spirit of Music" and which developed under the influence of the Platonic ideas that he absorbed at the beginning of his career. It was his term for the concept of matter derived from Plato as a chaotic, inert force which forms the raw material of life and art and is ever resistant to the Good that would change it. Such inertia and resistance to change are indeed the dominant features of the Twelve in the first ten sections, and the plot of the poem, modelled on the *commedia dell'arte* plot that Blok had employed previously in his play *The Puppet Show*, is a dramatization of their release from these restraining attributes. Its symbolic expression is the accidental shooting by Petrukha of their seductive embodiment, his former girlfriend Kat'ka, the eventual effect of which is the new sense of purpose reflected towards the end in the "sovereign tread" of their march and in the increasingly disciplined verse that evokes it. In section 12 the tortuous transition is finally completed from the mixed metres, variable line-lengths, and changing rhyme-schemes of section one to regular quatrains of trochaic tetrameters culminating in a nine-line stanza in the same metre in which the conflicting elements of the poem are integrated in a final harmonious chord.

Pointing to the future, this sense of harmony produced by the poem's conclusion implies also a comment on Russia's past. It expresses Blok's hopes for the restoration of a harmonious, unified Russian nation, for a nation no longer split by the religious reforms of the 17th century which had alienated the Old Believers or by the

legacy of Peter the Great's westernizing policies which had antagonized both the Old Believers and much of the peasantry. As Blok's notebooks confirm, the Revolution was closely associated in his thought and imagination with the great peasant rebellions of the 17th and 18th centuries. He saw it as an expression of the same anger, as a reawakening of the same alienated masses, and with his Old Believer spelling of the name "Jesus" in the poem's last line he reaffirmed his faith in their historical destiny as at once the creators of a new civilization and the healers of ancient national wounds.

—James B. Woodward

TWENTY-SIX MEN AND A GIRL (Dvadstat' shest' i odna') Story by Maksim Gor'kii, 1899

Maksim Gor'kii first achieved renown through his stories of the 1890s, among which "Twenty-Six Men and a Girl" is widely regarded as his most impressive achievement. The tightly structured narrative, highly evocative setting, and striking imagery richly support the subtly stated and perhaps surprising theme—the relationship of the individual to the group. It is the first of these characteristics that is perhaps most responsible for the artistic quality of "Twenty-Six Men and a Girl"; similar narrative structures appear elsewhere in Gor'kii, and the work's theme, while rarely stated quite so effectively, is also not unique to this story. However, in most of his shorter tales, as in his novels, Gor'kii's descriptive abilities rather than the narrative thrust serve to hold the reader's interest; the juxtaposition of scenes is more important than plot. Here the storyline, while simple, none the less contains several surprising elements which effectively highlight the ideas that Gor'kii is attempting to convey.

The title in Russian is more concise: "Twenty-Six and One," with the feminine ending of the last word conveying the point that the "One" is female. The story is set in Kazan', where Gor'kii himself lived and worked in the mid-1880s, during the latter part of his teenage years. Gor'kii was to document his Kazan' years in several stories as well as in *My Universities,* the third part of his autobiographical trilogy—indeed, the first-person narrative also imparts an autobiographical cast to "Twenty-Six Men and a Girl." His continued interest in this period is understandable, for it was then that he first became associated with revolutionary circles and held his first adult jobs, experiencing directly the life of those at the bottom of society.

It is this latter aspect of his experience that dominates the opening pages of the story and imparts to the work as a whole a sense of genuineness and immediacy. The locale of the story is a pretzel bakery in which Gor'kii himself worked, and in a few detailed paragraphs he manages to convey the dreary and oppressive nature of the toil. Although the working day begins at six in the morning and does not end until ten at night, the long hours are less burdensome than the conditions in which the 26 find themselves. The bakery occupies one room in a stuffy yet damp basement; a bit of light (but no sun) filters in through grated windows that look out onto slime-covered bricks. The air is thick with dust, the walls covered with dirt and mould.

The story deals with Tania, a 16-year-old maidservant who works in a shop located on the second floor of the building. Each morning she stops by the bakery, bringing a bit of joy to the men's lives with her mere presence. One day a new worker, an ex-soldier who thinks himself especially attractive to women, arrives to work in the next-door bakery; it is owned by the same person, but just four people work there in much better conditions baking rolls. The former soldier, in talking to the pretzel makers, describes how the women who work upstairs literally fight over him. One of the 26 confronts him, claiming that their Tania would not be so easy to attract. The newcomer accepts the challenge, and promises that he will win Tania over within two weeks. The men nervously observe Tania each morning, fearful of what will happen. As it turns out, Tania succumbs, and the men surround her when she leaves for her rendezvous with the new worker. They are angry with her for betraying the faith they had in her; for her part, she contemptuously shouts back at them and walks off, never to return.

Complementing the powerful descriptions and the spare story line is the effective use of imagery. Critics have noted that the enormous oven dominating the pretzel bakery bears traits of a cruel pagan deity; Tania herself could be seen as an idol to whom the ''worshippers'' bring tribute. Although most of the story takes place within the bakery, Gor'kii manages to make effective use of the world ''inside'' and that ''outside,'' where the 26 seem to be on alien territory. Equally telling is the contrast between the world above, that of Tania, and the world below, where the men dwell. Even when she comes for her visits, she remains above the men, staying at the threshold several steps above the basement floor. Her world is both higher and unattainable.

That Tania should not live up to the men's expectations is perhaps less surprising than the way in which Gor'kii uses the plot to introduce an unexpected theme. For ultimately the story reveals both Gor'kii's revolutionary sympathies as well as his belief that people need to have faith in themselves, and not in others. The anonymous first-person narrator uses ''we'' and does not single himself out among the ''26''; strength is to be found in the collective and not in the individual. The story turns out to be less about Tania's downfall than the men's (temporary) worship of an idol and failure to see the inner strength that they in fact possess. They give her free pretzels and even do small chores for her, but when one of them dares to ask her to repair his only shirt, she contemptuously turns him down. She is simply an ordinary, somewhat self-centred 16-year-old, basking in the attention of others; her fall may startle her admirers, but it is only the logical outcome of the test to which they put the false idol in which they have come to believe. Gor'kii's point is that their interest in Tania has turned the men away from themselves and from the inner strength that they do possess. Early in the story he describes their singing: ''All 26 would sing; the loud, well-rehearsed voices would fill the shop, which was too small for the song. It would strike against the stone walls, moan, cry, and revive our hearts with a gentle, tingling ache, re-opening old wounds and awakening longings.'' The spirit of the song, in which the ''26'' become one, gives them the fortitude to get through each day and to retain their sense of humanity. Thus, Gor'kii implies, the true ideal resides in oneself and within the group to which the individual belongs; seeking salvation in others will only lead people astray.

—Barry P. Scherr

U

UBU REX (Ubu Roi)
Play by Alfred Jarry, 1896

In this five-act satirical farce, Alfred Jarry adapts the serious story of seizure of power to the comic aims of ridicule and relief. Mère Ubu, playing upon her husband's bestial instincts, urges him to overthrow Wenceslas, King of Poland. After enlisting Bordure's assistance, Ubu usurps the throne in the second act, murdering the ruler and two of his sons. Bourgelas, another son, escapes with his mother. Meanwhile, in order to placate the Poles and satisfy his greed, Ubu offers the people gold that he reclaims through taxation. In the third act, Ubu assumes authority, liquidating the nobility and magistrates, and confiscating national wealth. He also condemns Bordure who, taking refuge in Russia, requests Czar Alexis to help restore order and justice. Alexis attacks, and Mère convinces Ubu of the necessary recourse to war.

In Act IV, while Ubu battles against the Russians, his wife plunders the treasures of Poland. Ubu kills Bordure, but the decimation of his army compels him and his two Palotins to retreat. In fending off a rapacious bear, the Palotins perceive their leader's cowardice and abandon him. In the final act, Ubu's wife flees Bourgelas's avenging army, arriving at the cave where Ubu is sleeping. Darkness enables her to impersonate the angel Gabriel which, in turn, impels him to confess his wrongdoings. The light of day, though, reveals her identity, and Ubu reverts to his former ways. Bourgelas attacks, and the Ubus, along with the Palotins who return, sail home full of nostalgia for Poland.

Ubu's grotesqueness evokes caricature and disbelief. His rotund body and pear-shaped head seem ludicrous and fantastical, and the opening trite insults between him and his wife suggest a slapstick show or a puppet-play. Like the closing scenes in farce, a comic resolution dispels danger as husband and wife return home, physically secure and morally unchanged. Lack of development of character excludes introspection: throughout the play, Ubu remains stupid, indolent, and totally egocentric; his wife stays avaricious, complaining, and domineering. Through incongruities and inversions, Jarry employs irony to elicit surprise and induce absurdity. Besides his ridiculous appearance, Ubu swears meaningless oaths ("by my green candle," "shittr"), exaggerates the ordinary (his feast becomes a two-day orgy), and misconstrues reality (a bear is a "little bow-wow"). By exploiting the unexpected, Jarry has this Falstaff-like personage debunk the solemn and dignify the preposterous: his stepping on Wenceslas's toe incites revolution; unlike the agile Czar, he jumps over a trench; and, seated safely on a rock, he recites a *paternoster* during the Palotins' struggle with the bear. Jarry also uses dramatic parody: like Macbeth urged to depose Duncan, Ubu yields to his wife's goadings, but his clumsiness, moral blindness, and inanities turn potential pathos into rollicking burlesque. Disparities of language and action heighten the ridiculous. During deliberations and battles, Ubu blends religious and literary references with nonsensical statements, thereby reducing the serious and dignified to the trivial and foolish. In the dream-sequence that recalls epic conventions, medieval allegories, and Renaissance romances, mère Ubu convinces her husband that her ugliness is comparable to Aphrodite's beauty and her depravities to saintly accomplishments.

The deceptions and distortions, though, present a superficial enjoyment that obscures the horrors of human bestiality and bourgeois shallowness. Ubu's self-absorption and obsession with material wealth and sensual gratification explain his callous disregard and vicious abuse of others: and, prodded by his unbridled instincts, he acts irrationally and erratically. In depicting this primal nature devoid of reason and discipline, Jarry converts innocuous horseplay into actions provoking appalling disgust. For example, Ubu's attack on his guests with bison-ribs provokes amusement; but his subsequent serving of human excrement at table replaces laughter with repugnance. His wife's duplicity punctures pleasure. By injecting false courage into Ubu's cowardly character, she yields to her insatiable greed for wealth and power, manipulating her husband to commit pillage and genocide.

As caricatures, they resemble cartoon animations; but their self-interest, insensitivity, and indignities reflect the values and evils in bourgeois society. Exemplifying the ethos of this post-Darwinian era, Ubu disregards spiritual values; religion lacks belief, and Ubu facilely recites prayers to escape danger and death. He is a survivor whose instincts endure, and whose bestial superiorities destroy the weak and unfortunate. If Ubu is Everyman, he is also, paradoxically, Nobody, with his prosperity encasing a spiritual void. Instead, Ubu's obesity suggests a material gluttony that assures an aggression necessary for success and stature.

In neglecting the unities of time, place, and action, Jarry constructs a series of scenes resembling a montage of inconsistent happenings and absurd characterizations. Ubu's ludicrous appearance, irrational behaviour, and vile words demonstrate a rejection of the established principles of versimilitude and decorum. At the first performance, the audience, expecting entertaining farce, was stunned and outraged. But by shattering the illusions that often, paradoxically, define reality, Jarry reveals the potential evils inherent in the subconscious. Through the humour, resulting from fantasy and foolishness, Jarry attacks the materialism, ego-centricism, and superficialities, which, embodied by Ubu, reflect bourgeois aims and attitudes. Ubu's jokes are meaningless, insensitive utterances, and his unscrupulous deeds become unconscionable crimes. Satire, moreover, evolves into a probing of the dynamics of human impulses. Time and place dissolve, and Ubu emerges as an emblem of man's primal nature. Futility and absurdity characterize Ubu's endeavours: his actions end at the beginning; his speech is claptrap; his uncontrolled affections and merciless, unrelenting aggressions destroy order and civilization. Jarry goes beyond a renunciation of conventional dramatic practice and accepted social standards. By creating a drama that suggests the later theories and plays of Artaud, Beckett, Genet, and Ionesco, he forces the spectator to confront, through Ubu, the savagery, isolation, and pain of human existence.

—Donald Gilman

UNCLE VANYA (Diadia Vania)
Play by Anton Chekhov, 1897

"*Uncle Vanya* is an unforgettably good play . . . It is a real tragedy. It has in it the flatness and poignancy of life itself. There is no depth of reflection upon humanity at which it were inappropriate to discuss this play if one were master of obedient words." Desmond MacCarthy's thoughts (in *The New Statesman*, 16 May 1914), prompted by the London premiere at the Aldwych Theatre, remain equally valid today.

To the superficial eye, Anton Chekhov's "scenes from country life" may appear singularly unexciting, a tedious demonstration of the dramatist's advice (quoted by I.Y. Gurliand in *Teatr i iskusstvo* [*Theatre and Art*], 11 July 1904) that "everything on stage should be just as complex and also just as simple as in life. . . . People eat their dinner, just eat their dinner, yet at the same time their happiness is taking shape and their lives are being smashed . . . ." Against a background of rural torpor, one high summer in the 1890s, a tightly knit group of characters dream and yearn, rage and pine, as happiness eludes them.

There are eight leading roles—an old, retired professor (Serebriakov) and his young second wife Elena); the doting mother of his first wife (Mme. Voinitskaia) and his estate-manager, brother of his late first wife (Ivan Voinitskii, known as Uncle Vanya); the Professor's unmarried daughter by his first wife (Sonia); a doctor (Astrov); an old nurse (Marina); and an impoverished landowner (Telegin). Tensions mount during the disruptive visit of Serebriakov and Elena to the provincial estate that once was owned by the Professor's first wife.

On one level, *Uncle Vanya* illustrates a typically Chekhovian theme, the inexorable passage of time. For six years, unnoticed, Sonia has loved Astrov; for 25 years, unvalued, Vanya has slaved for his idol, Serebriakov. Ten years ago, Vanya might have proposed to Elena, but did not; during those ten years, Doctor Astrov has become overworked, cynical, unloving.

For the past 50 years, Vanya's mother has scribbled pointless notes in pointless pamphlets; if we are to believe Vanya, for 25 years Professor Serebriakov has delivered worthless lectures and concocted worthless books. Astrov's maps chronicle the degeneration of the flora and fauna over the past half- or quarter-century.

Time's corrosiveness eats also into the future. Elena, aged 27, declares that she too will be old five or six years hence, and she wonders how they will live through the long Russian winter; Vanya, aged 47, ponders how to fill the next 13 years, should he survive till 60.

More than any other Chekhov play, *Uncle Vanya* is weighted towards old age and autumn. Its first act has no equivalent of Nina (*The Seagull*), Irina (*Three Sisters*), or Anya (*The Cherry Orchard*), young women greeting the springtime of life with innocent hopes and dreams. Of its principal characters, four are old and emotionally sterile—Serebriakov (unloved by his young wife), Voinitskaia (unloving towards her son), Telegin (abandoned the day after his wedding), and Marina (preoccupied with noodles and knitting). The "younger" quartet, caught in a web of emotional—sexual non-fulfilment, lacks all youthful buoyancy. Vanya and Astrov hurtle towards loveless middle-age; Elena drifts lethargically, purposeless and beautiful; Sonia works unceasingly, stoical and plain.

Uncle Vanya is perhaps Chekhov's saddest play. Like Astrov's maps, it seems to chart man's foolish flight from happiness and harmony. The "demon of destruction" to which Elena refers lies deep in everyone, despoiling the planet and producing endless human waste. Caught in the isolation of unrequited love or idiotic self-love, the leading characters are frozen in frustration.

Confronted by this spectacle of loneliness, lethargy, and non-achievement, a deflated audience might easily echo Vanya's bitter remark: "Lovely day to hang yourself . . . ." One of the first Russian reviewers of the play described it as "mood (*nastroenie*) in four acts" (N. Rok [N.O. Rakshanin], in *Novosti i Birzhevaia gazeta*, 6 November 1899). But this "mood" is not one of sorrow unconfined. Like all Chekhov's major plays, *Uncle Vanya* abounds in comic touches. Characters laugh at themselves and at each other, while sensitive audiences respond with a smile or shiver of self-recognition.

After the London premiere in May 1914, Desmond MacCarthy wisely observed that "we have no right to label this atmosphere 'ussian,'" and regard it with complacent curiosity . . . If Tchekov's intellectuals are half dead, the other half of them is very much, painfully much, alive. They suffer more consciously; there is intensity in their lassitude . . . ." MacCarthy subsequently added (in *The New Statesman and Nation*, 13 February 1937): "If you regard *Uncle Vanya* as a study in Russian character you will miss its point, and worse, you will not be touched . . . Though the atmosphere of it is Russian, the human nature in it is universal. That is what makes it moving."

Chekhov's play also offers an element of muted optimism and faith. No one dies, and life continues (as in Beckett). Numerous characters complain of their "unbearable" sufferings (Serebriakov, Elena, Astrov, Vanya), yet suffering must be borne, as Sonia advocates. Hope and hopelessness are held in fine balance; endurance may be the closest we can come to happiness.

A successful production of *Uncle Vanya* should be poignant but never ponderous, comic but never cold. The Act III map-scene between Astrov and Elena fuses serio-comic eroticism with ecological earnestness, while Vanya's bungled attempt to shoot Serebriakov combines tragic desperation and absurd farce. Chekhov's depiction of stunted lives contains a tantalizing dream of life as it could or should be.

Significantly, Chekhov himself detested an earlier version of *Uncle Vanya*, a rudimentary farce-melodrama known as *The Wood Demon* (*Leshii*), 1889. Although the two works have many characters, speeches, and situations in common, their essence is radically different. *Uncle Vanya* (written at some unknown point between 1890 and 1896, probably in 1896 itself) represents a condensation and distillation of its ungainly predecessor. Whereas *The Wood Demon* resolves life's problems much too neatly (a bullet for Voinitskii, a husband for Sonia, reconciliation for Elena with Serebriakov), *Uncle Vanya* displays wondrous insight into perpetual frustration, waste, and grief.

When the curtain finally falls, with Sonia seeking to console her inconsolable uncle, wry smiles and kindly laughter cannot conceal the aching desolation.

—Gordon McVay

UNDER FIRE: THE STORY OF A SQUAD (Le Feu: Journal d'une escouade)
Novel by Henri Barbusse, 1916

Under Fire: The Story of a Squad was actually written partly in the front-line trenches of World War I, partly in hospital after Henri Barbusse had been wounded. His works have always tended to be a less than easy compromise between narrative and message, in which the propaganda element tends to stand constantly in the way of the relating of a tale. Add to this a strong measure of fiery emotionalism and it is not surprising that much of his writings could be encompassed in Brian Rhys's description of one of Barbusse's non-fiction works as "inspiring and exasperating by turns."

Under Fire is not immune from these deficiencies, even though it is drawn from direct experience of war-time fighting in the trenches. It begins with a strange section marked "Vision," in which those remote beings at the seat of power determine that war shall break out, while the millions who fight and suffer as a result of that edict are depicted as slaves who are driven by the horrors of the military conflict to experience the will to rise up, like some military proletariat, and create a new internationalist world.

Like its frankly far superior German counterpart, *All Quiet on the Western Front*, the novel is written in the first person and the historic present, which clearly lend it immediacy and directness of impact, although it is drawn from such close quarters that there is little sense of a positively structured literary whole. It is more a collection of episodes than a coherent narrative strand.

The common soldiers who are depicted in *Under Fire* are largely working class in origin, very diverse in their backgrounds yet very much on common ground in that they have been forced by the brutal and brutalizing conditions of war to revert to a primeval, semi-animalistic state. Life is reduced to the basics of eating, drinking, sleeping, and fighting. They become very much creatures who are close to the earth. They share a sense of class solidarity and of contempt for their social superiors, as one incident illustrates. A couple of journalists dressed up to the nines appear on a visit of inspection, to be condemned by one of the *poilus* as "trench tourists." These visitors speak of the common soldiery as if they were an alien race. It is almost as if the journalists were enjoying a trip to the zoo, observing the animals and their antics behind bars.

As in *All Quiet on the Western Front*, the events in the life of the ordinary private soldier are seen in terms of setting off, joining battle, and returning—but unlike the Crusades, these episodes are seen as fundamentally meaningless: chance, not fate, determines who lives and who dies. In depicting this constant struggle against the odds to survive, dialogue, for the most part taut and well-written, predominates. But there are also telling moments of descriptive writing, notably when the soldiers go with one of their number to visit his native village, which has been retaken, only to find that the village has been totally obliterated in the fighting. There is a powerful evocation of the senselessness of a victory that destroys what it purports to be defending.

In the end, though, the descriptions of battle, all uniformly harrowing, tend to desensitize the reader with their routine awfulness:

> I recall that I strode over a smouldering corpse, quite black, with a rivulet of red blood shrivelling on him . . . In the ground there are several layers of the dead . . . There are no bodies. But worse than that, a solitary arm protrudes bare and white as stone, from a hole which shows faintly on the other side of the water. . .

It is almost as if language itself is giving up the unequal struggle to express that which cannot adequately be conveyed by mere words.

During one advance, an officer leads the soldiers under his command astray, and in order to proceed further they are faced with the choice of exposing themselves to the withering fire in the open or

picking their way through a latrine trench. The debasement that they are forced to confront if they are to stand a chance of survival epitomizes both the way in which war has crushed every last drop of civilized humanity out of them and also the total inability of those who have been set in authority above them to rise to the challenges of leadership.

At the end of the novel, the soldiers discuss the meaninglessness of the conflict. As one of them puts it: "Two armies fighting each other—it's just like one huge army committing suicide!" The only possible meaning to come out of the war would be that its sheer awfulness would ensure there would be no more war, and that the common people should be instrumental in bringing reality to this resolve: "All the masses should agree together . . . . All men should be equal."

The political message then emerges fully into the light of day. Of the triumvirate of abstractions on which the French revolution was founded, only one has any validity: "Equality is for ever unchanging. Liberty and fraternity are just words, whilst equality is a fact." The novel ends on a note of half-optimism: "Between two masses of gloomy cloud a tranquil gleam emerges, and that sliver of light, so edged in black, proves none the less that the sun is there."

—Rex Last

UPANISHADS

Final sections of the four Hindu *Vedas, q.v.*, dating from c. 800–500 BC, which describe the personal significance of the Hindu religion and speculate on the relationship between man and the universe. 108 of them are traditionally identified as classical Upanishads (although as few as 14 have been suggested as properly belonging to the group). The texts form the basis of much Indian philosophy, and many of the ideas are also reflected in Buddhist teachings. Fifty Upanishads were published in a Persian translation (1656–57) by Prince Muhammed Dara Shikoh, and then in a Latin version (as *Oupeknhat*, 1801–02) by Anquetil Duperron, before Sanskrit and English editions were published.

PUBLICATIONS

The Upaninsads, translation and introduction by Valerie J. Roebuck. 2000.

*

Critical Studies: *The Philosophy of the Upanishads and Ancient Indian Metaphysics* by Archibald E. Gough, 1882–84; *Philosophy of the Upanishads* by Paul Deussen, 1906; *The Religion and Philosophy of the Vedas and the Upanishads* by A.B. Keith, 1925; *A Constructive Survey of the Upanishadic Philosophy* by R.D. Ranade, 1926; *The Katha Upanishad: An Introductory Study in the Hindu Doctrine of God and of Human Destiny* by Joseph Nadin Rawson, 1934; *Upanishad Drama* by Sivananda Sarasvati, 1947; *Upanishadic Teaching and Western Philosophy* by Betty Heimann, 1949; *Upanishads, Gita, and the Bible: A Comparative Study of Hindu and Christian Scriptures* by Geoffrey Parrinder, 1962; *Katha Upanishad: Sāṁkhya Point of View* by Anima Sen Gupta, 1967; *The Message of the Upanishads* by Swāmī Ranganathananda, 1968; *The Further Shore: Two Essays* by Swāmī Abhishiktananda, 1975; *The Vision of Self in Early Vedānta* by William Beidler, 1975; *The Supreme Doctrine: Discourses on the*

Kenopanishad edited by Swāmī Prem Chinmaya and Ma Ananda Prem, 1977; *Bliss and the Upanishads: An Analytical Study of the Origin and Growth of the Vedic Concept of Ananda* by G. Gispert-Sauch, 1977; *A Study of Nominal Sentences in the Oldest Upanishads* by Gunilla Gren-Eklund, edited by Neil Tompkinson, 1978; *Upanishad Vahini* by Sathya Sai Baba, translated by N. Kasturi, 4th revised edition, 1980; *The Philosophy of the Upanishads* by Balbir Singh, 1983; *Yoga of the Rishis: the Upanishadic Approach to Death and Immortality* by V. Madhusudan Reddy, 1985; *Life in the Upanishads* by Shubhra Sharma, 1985; *Encyclopaedia of the Upanishads* by N.S. Subrahmanian, 1985; *The Upanisads and Modern Thought* by Vetury Ramakrishna Rao, 1986; *Journey of the Upanishads to the West* by Purna Chandra Mukhopadhyay, 1987; *Sakara's Interpretation of the Upanishads* by G.R. Pandey, 1988; *Humanistic Trends in Some Principal Upanishads* by Namita Kar, 1989; *An Essay on the Upanishads: A Critical Study* by V.R. Narla, 1989; *Geographical Knowledge in Upanisads* by B.G. Tamaskar, 1989; *The Supreme Knowledge: Revealed Through Vidyas in the Upanishads* by Swāmī Brahmananda, 1990; *In Search of Meaning: A Phenomenological Reading of the Upanishads* by Antonio F.X. Rodrigues, 1990; *The Upanishads and Early Buddhism* by Sanjay Govind Deodikar, 1992; *Women Education and Upanishadic System of Education* by K.N. Misra, 1993; *The Upanisads: A Socio-religious Appraisal* by Jose Thachil, 1993; *Finger Pointing to the Moon: Discourses on the Adhyatma Upanishad* by Osho, 1994; *The Upanisadic Etymologies* by Maan Singh, 1994; *God's Love in Upanishad Philosophies* by Pritam Sen, 1995; *A Critical Study of the Later Upanishads* by S.G. Desai, 1996; *Reality and Mysticism: Perspectives in the Upanisads* by R. Puligandla, 1997; *The Supreme Wisdom of the Upanisads: An Introduction* by Klaus G. Witz, 1998; *Pearls from Upanisads* by R.B. Sharma, 1998; *Philosophy of Upanishads* by Chakravarti Ananthacharya, 1999; *Studies in the Upanisads* by Govindagopal Mukhopadhyaya, 1999; *A Study of Taittirīya Upanisad* by Meena P. Pathak, 1999.

* * *

The word "Upanishad" is from *upa* (near), *ni* (down), and *sad* (to sit). It means literally "sitting down near." The pupils who wished to know about the *Upanishads* sat by their teachers and learnt it from them. Going back to 800 BC, the books are, by tradition, believed to be of divine origin, and revealed by god to inspired sages. Though some put the number of the *Upanishads* at 150, the genuine ones are believed to be 108. Of these the classical ones on which Śanākarāchārya commented are 11 in number: *Chhāndogya, Bṛhadāraṇyaka, Kena, Aitareya, Māṇḍūkya, Īśa, Kaṭha, Muṇḍaka, Taittiriya, Śvetāśvatara,*

and *Praśna*. Most of the *Upanishads* are in Sanskrit prose (with occasional verse), but five of them are in verse alone.

The spiritual wisdom contained in the *Upanishads* is, as Paul Deussen has commented, "unequalled in India or perhaps anywhere else in the world." The soul, they maintain, is of the same nature as the Cosmic Absolute known as Brahman. It is changeless and eternal, and transmigrates from a body at death into another body, the circumstances being determined by the individual's actions in his previous life or lives. The soul is only apparently associated with the body it dwells in, like the "redness" of transparent glass when placed over red cloth. The concept that it is the soul which acts and suffers is one stemming from ignorance. When this ignorance is removed, Brahman, which is the only truth, is realized; and this can happen in one's lifetime itself. Then actions become desireless and, like burnt seed, will not sprout into results. The circle of births and rebirths is broken for such a man, and he has achieved emancipation.

Although there is a great deal of repetition, prolixity, and sometimes even obscurity in the *Upanishads*, and the Sanskrit is often terse, abundant compensation is given in their vivid comparisons and rich imagery. The nature of Brahman is described as "without limit, as when we drop a lump of salt in water the whole solution is salty from wherever you might taste it." The soul and Brahman are like "two birds sitting on the same tree. One eats the fruits of the tree with relish, the other looks on without eating." The soul taking a new body is like "a caterpillar leaving one blade of grass and grasping another," or as though "a goldsmith may take a piece of gold and fashion it into a lovelier form." In a beautiful verse the sage Yajñavalkya compares man to a mighty tree. The simile of the chariot is used to explain the nature of the soul: "The soul is the rider, the body the chariot, the intellect the charioteer, the mind the reins. The senses are the horses, their objects the roads." The path of emancipation is "sharp as a razor's edge." There is the lighter side too, as when the hypocrisy of priests is exposed: "The priests who move along chanting a hymn, are like dogs going together, and what they say is 'may the gods bring us more food; let us eat and drink!'"

The *Upanishads* do not take a gloomy view of life. They are in favour of hard work and a full existence. "Man should live a hundred years," one of them says, "and carry out the tasks allotted him." If one is patient with the *Upanishads*, one will be rewarded as the man "seeking goodly pearls, who, when he had found one pearl of good price, went and sold all that he had and bought it." Schopenhauer had the *Upanishads* on his table and read through passages daily before going to bed. "They are the products of the highest wisdom," he said, "destined sooner or later to become the faith of the people."

—K.P. Bahadur

V

VĀLMĪKI

See RĀMĀYANUA

THE VEDAS

The most ancient Hindu writings, reputedly compiled by Vyāsa, and believed to have been composed between 3000 and 500 BC. They contain songs, poems, prose, and speeches, and form the principal sacred texts of Hinduism. Of the four *Vedas*—*Rig-Veda* [Wisdom of Hymn], *Sāma-Veda* [Wisdom of Chants/Melodies], *Yarjur-Veda* [Wisdom of Sacrifice], and *Atharva-Veda* [Wisdom of Atharvan]—the *Rig-Veda* (sometimes referred to simply as "the *Veda*"), which comprises 1,028 hymns to deities, is believed to be the oldest, and is considered the most important; the *Atharva-Veda* is the youngest. Each *Veda* is generally considered to have three sections or strata—*samhitā* (hymns and chants), *brāmana* (details of sacrifice), and the *Upanishads, q.v.* (speculative, philosophical texts). The oldest existing text is of the *Atharva-Veda*, dating from AD 800–1,000, and texts for the other *Vedas* date from after c. 1500.

PUBLICATIONS

Yajur-Veda, as *Kapiṣṭhala-Kaṭha-Saṁhita* (individual *Veda*), edited by Raghu Vira. 1932; selection edited as *The Vedic Truth Vindicated* (bilingual edition), 1891; as *The Yajurveda*, translated by Devi Chand, 3rd revised edition, 1971; selections as: as *The Texts of the White Yajurveda*, translated by R.T.H. Griffith, 1899; *The Veda of the Black Yajus School*, translated by Arthur Berriedale Keith, 2 vols., 1914; *Agnimitra of the Kaṭha Śākhā*, translated by P.D. Navathe, 1980.

*

Bibliography: *Vedic Bibliography* by R.N. Dandekar, vol. 1 (1930–45), 1946; vol. 2 (1946–60), 1961; vol. 3 (1961–72), 1973; vol. 4 (1972–83), 1985.

Critical Studies: *Vedic Culture* by M. Giri, 1921; *Religion in Vedic Literature* by P.S. Deshmukh, 1933; *Vedic Religion and Philosophy* by Swāmī Prabhavananda, 1940; *Savitar or Aurora Borealis; A Study in the Rig Veda* by Y. Venkataramiah, 1941; *Rigvedic India* by A.C. Das, 1947; *The Heart of the Rigveda* by M.R. Gopalacharya, 1971; *Positive Sciences in the Vedas* by D.D. Mehta, 1974; *Women in Rgveda* by Bhagwat Saran Upadhyaya, 1974; *In the Image of Fire: Vedic Experiences of Heat* by David M. Knipe, 1975; *The Vedas: Essays in Translation and Exegesis* by Ananda Kentish Coomaraswamy, 1976; *The Civilized Demons: The Harappans in Rgveda* by Malati J Shendge, 1977; *Verbal Forms in the Rgveda* by Gajānana Bālakrsna Palasule, 1978; *Sexual Symbolism from the Vedic Ritual* by Sadashiv Ambadas Dange, 1979; *Poetry and Speculation of the Rig Veda* by Willard Johnson, 1980; *Rig Veda: A Scientific and Intellectual Analysis of the Hymns* (includes text and translations), 1981, and *Sciences and the Veda*, 1981, both edited by

J.K. Trikha; *Philosophy of the Vedas* by Kanayalal M. Talreja, 1982; *Vedic Mythopoeia: An Approach to Religion, Myth and Poetry* by Usha Choudhuri, 1983; *The History and Principles of Vedic Interpretation* by Ram Gopal, 1983; *Function and Form in the "-áya-" Formations of the Rig Veda and Atharva Veda* by Stephanie W. Jamison, 1983; *The Vision of Cosmic Order in the Vedas* by Jeanine Miller, 1985; *Modern Commentators of Veda* by A.K. Pateria, 1985; *Heat and Sacrifice in the Veda* by Uma Marina Vesci, 1985; *Rgveda as the Key to Folklore: An Imagery Experiment* by Carsten Bregenhøj, 1986; *Axiological Approach to the Veda* by Sahebrao Genu Nigal, 1986; *Political Legacy of the Rigveda* by C. Ashokvardhan, 1987; *Materialism in the Vedas* by Uma Gupta, 1987; *Some Women's Rites and Rights in the Veda* by Hanns-Peter Schmidt, 1987; *Rgvedic Aesthetics* by P.S. Sastri, 1988; *Glimpses of Veda and Vyakarana: Reflections on Some Less Familiar Topics* edited by G.V. Devasthali, 1989; *A Vedic Concordance* by Maurice Bloomfield, 1990; *Veda and Indian Culture: An Introductory Essay* by Kireet Joshi, 1991; *Accomplishing the Accomplished: Vedas as a Source of Valid Knowledge in Sankara* by Anantanano Rambachan, 1991; *The Essence of the Vedas and Allied Scriptures* by Basdeo Bissoondoyal, 1993; *Divine Hymns and Ancient Thought* by Sadashiv A. Dange, 1992–95; *Srauta Sacrifice in the Atharva-Veda* by B.S. Mehra, 1994; *The Khila-Suktas of the Rgveda: A Study* by Usha R. Bhise, 1995.

* * *

The word "Veda," from *vid* (to know), means "sacred knowledge." The *Vedas* are four in number—*Rig, Yajur, Sāma*, and *Atharva*—and are traditionally believed to have been revealed by divine agency to the *rishis* (sages) whose names they bear. According to popular belief the *Rig-Veda* was compiled by Vyāsa and addressed to various gods, chiefly to Agni the god of fire, and Indra the god of the firmament. The *Vedas* are revered as *apauruṣeya*—"not of human origin." The *Rig-Veda* is the oldest and most widely known. Its origins date back probably to 3000 BC. The *Atharva-Veda* is comparatively recent. Except for Egyptian and Mesopotamian literature, that of the Vedas is the oldest in the world.

The *Rig-Veda* (*rik* meaning "a verse") has 11,000 hymns spread over ten books. The stanzas have four lines, each having usually 8, 11, or 12 syllables; but sometimes they have only five or four. The metre is not uniform, and there is no rhyme. The Vedic poets were expert craftsmen, and their Sanskrit is simple, spontaneous, and rich in figures of speech, particularly comparisons. For example, the bow pressed close to a warrior's ear is compared to a loved woman held in his embrace, and the twang of the bowstring to the secrets she whispers to him.

The *Vedas* did not advocate asceticism. They prefer a full life of learning, domestic bliss, and finally renunciation. Lopamudra, a sage, says "one does not break his penance if he has children." They are a mirror of their age. The acts of generous kings, legends of heroes, social manners and customs like marriage and funeral ceremonies, drinking and gambling, black magic spells and incantations, and village life are all vividly described in them. A lover casts a spell on a girl to make her "desire my body, my feet, love my eyes and lips, and hasten to lie on my bosom." A man who lost his fortune gambling complains, ''My mother-in-law hates me, and no one pities me. They all say they find no more use in a gambler than in an aged horse that's for sale!'' Nonetheless, the emphasis is on character. The goddess of learning tells a teacher not to bring her one who is envious of others, crooked, discontented, and licentious, but the one who is pure, attentive, intelligent, and chaste. Hard work on the fields is the way to prosperity, and a farmer says: ''The land I plough with my sharp-pointed smooth-handled plough, making neat furrows, enables me to possess a sheep, a horse to draw my cart, and a plump lass!''

The *Sāma-Veda* and the *Yajur-Veda* use the hymns of the *Rig-Veda*, merely rearranging them for purposes of ritual. The *Atharva-Veda* has neither the sanctity nor the importance of the *Rig-Veda*: the old Buddhist texts omit it altogether.

The *Vedas* advocated ideals which were to become the basis of Hindu culture. They have survived the war-filled, strife-torn centuries, and one may still hear them chanted in deep voices by Hindu priests in temples or by devout Hindu worshippers in their homes. To today's world they have a particular message—that of friendly co-existence. There should be unity not only in the country, they say, but throughout the world. The *Atharva-Veda* goes even further: ''Varuṇa belongs not to our land only,'' it declares, ''but to foreign lands too.'' The cooperation that the United Nations is supposed to represent in our time was conceived of in the *Vedas* more than 3,000 years before Christ.

—K.P. Bahadur

LA VIDA DE LAZARILLO DE TORMES

See LAZARILLO DE TORMES

THE VILLAGE NOTARY (A falu jegyzője)
Novel by Baron József Eötvös, 1845

The exposure in this novel of social evils has earned Baron József Eötvös the title of the ''Hungarian Dickens.'' Already an active politician, he had published pamphlets on prison reform (*Vélemény a fogházjavítás ügyében*) and on the ''emancipation'' of the Jews (*Die Emanzipation der Juden*), advocating their admission to full citizen rights. In literature, he had declared himself a disciple of Victor Hugo in an essay (1837) arguing that the writer must promote justice, but must also give pleasure. So the reader would begin *The Village Notary* knowing what to expect.

The novel describes a year in an imaginary village, beginning just before local elections. The village notary is Tengelyi, who has repeatedly championed the oppressed and repeatedly suffered for it; his integrity has made him enemies. He is ''noble,'' one of the five per cent of the population exempt from taxation and military service, and having the vote. He owes his present job to an old student friend, Réty, the number two in the county administration.

Réty's formidable second wife is plotting with the family lawyer Macskaházy to steal some papers belonging to Pastor Vándory which are now at Tengelyi's house, with the notary's own papers. These papers certify the holder's nobility, and hence his right to vote.

When Tengelyi goes home, his loving 16-year-old daughter Vilma makes him promise not to be angry about something she has done behind his back. He laughs, but is horrified when she tells him she has taken the wife, Zsuzsi, and children of the outlaw Viola into the family home. Tengelyi praises her, but Viola's devotion to his family is a byword, and he will certainly try to visit them; he might be caught in the notary's house. Moreover, Vilma is in love with Ákos, Réty's son by his first wife, but there is strong parental opposition to their marriage.

These threads converge at Tengelyi's house the evening before polling-day. The papers are stolen, but Viola is there, catches the thief, seizes the papers, and goes into hiding again. So Tengelyi cannot produce his papers when challenged at the polling-station by Macskaházy and the chief justice, Nyúzó, as obviously a brute as Macskaházy is a sneak. Nyúzó first caused Viola's troubles; annoyed at Zsuzsi for repelling his advances (she and Viola were already married), he required Viola, then a farmer, to provide in person a relay of horses when Zsuzsi was in labour. Viola was seized and beaten; then he broke loose and picked up an axe, killing a man with it. He has been on the run ever since.

Viola's hideout is betrayed; Macskaházy and Nyúzó set fire to it. Viola is caught, and Macskaházy grabs the papers. Viola's trial before a summary court (*statárium*) brilliantly portrays the infinite variety of human nature. The central figure is a lawyer, Völgyesy, the court's notary. He objects that the case should not come before a *statárium*, challenges Nyúzó's right to sit on the bench, as a personal enemy of the accused, and—worst of all—encourages Viola to testify. So Viola tells the whole story of the plot to steal Tengelyi's papers, but a majority votes against minuting his evidence. He is sentenced to death but is rescued in a thrilling episode with a slapstick interlude—just the relief needed after the trial.

Viola visits Macskaházy by night, and demands the papers. A fight ensues; Viola kills Macskaházy and flees with the papers. Nyúzó then tries to frame Tengelyi for the murder; thus Tengelyi cannot be saved unless Viola comes forward. When he does, he is intercepted and killed by a gendarme—the same man whom Macskaházy had earlier employed to steal Tengelyi's papers. But before dying Viola just manages to give the papers to Ákos and confess that he killed Macskaházy, which clears the notary.

Ákos duly marries Vilma; his sister Etelka also makes a happy marriage. These young couples personify hope for the future; the novel is ultimately optimistic. There are no spectacular reforms but the situation is certainly better than a year earlier when the novel opened. The main evildoers have disappeared: Mrs. Réty poisons herself when her plot to steal the papers is exposed; her weak husband resigns his office, to which he had inevitably been re-elected; Macskaházy is dead. Nyúzó, the only survivor, is quietly dismissed after a scandal over improvements to his house. The tragedy is the life and death of Viola—''a man richly gifted by nature''—and the death of his family through illness—something much more common then than now.

Although complicated, the plot is a superb unity, without detachable sub-plots. Eötvös portrays a society in which everybody in widely differing degrees commits, condones, or suffers evil. The novel was compared to a medical textbook; Eötvös brings in all the evils of his day, but does not invent them. His style may be dated, but it is pointed, not verbose. There are digressions, including answers to critics; the novel appeared serially. There is comic relief when it is most needed. Still, what makes *The Village Notary* a masterpiece—perhaps the first Hungarian novel deserving the title—is its humanity.

—D. Mervyn Jones

THE VISIT (Der Besuch der alten Dame)
Play by Friedrich Dürrenmatt, 1956

Friedrich Dürrenmatt's three-act tragicomedy *The Visit* was written in 1956 and had its premiere the same year in Zurich. The plot is set in the run-down city of Güllen, somewhere in Europe, whose inhabitants await eagerly the return of their "native," the billionairess Claire Zachanassian. She represents their only hope of getting out of their economic malaise. Upon her arrival, she demands the murder of her former lover Alfred Ill as the condition for providing financial assistance. 45 years earlier, she had been forced to leave the town in disgrace, because Ill, who had made her pregnant, denied his fatherhood. She worked her way first through bordellos, then through several marriages, amassing a huge fortune of which she will give the inhabitants a part if Ill is murdered. The mayor and the city first reject Claire's offer, but Claire waits because she knows that the people will eventually agree to it. Slowly, the support for Ill weakens. Ill, who had hopes of becoming the mayor of Güllen, sees himself deserted by everyone and also realizes that fleeing the city would not save his life from the all-powerful Claire, the "Goddess of Fate," whose life has only one purpose: to seek vengeance for the terrible wrong that has been done her. Ill, who at first denies his guilt, finally accepts it. At a town meeting, Ill's murder is agreed upon by the inhabitants, and Ill accepts his death sentence. This is done through such masterful use of multilayered language that even the attending reporters and the rest of the world do not realize the inhumanity committed in their presence. Ill is murdered not by one person, but symbolically by the group so that the guilt is borne by all. The play concludes in a perverse manner with a Sophoclean chorus praising the greatness of man.

Since its publication and premiere this play, considered by many to be Dürrenmatt's finest, has been translated into numerous languages and interpreted in conflicting ways. Some critics consider *The Visit* a religious play, because Ill, after some inner struggle, accepts his guilt and makes peace with God and himself. Others emphasize the political aspect, seeing in the corruption by money and material goods a situation similar to that after World War II where the Marshall Plan was created to rebuild the German economy. Critics have connected *The Visit* with many literary traditions and writers. Some interpret *The Visit* as a parody of Greek tragedy or the classical German drama, and see a relationship to Mark Twain's story "The Man that Corrupted Hadleyburg," Ödön von Horváth's *Judgement Day*, Curt Goetz's *The House in Montevideo*, Max Frisch's *Andorra*, or some of Franz Kafka's works. Claire is sometimes associated with Medea, Venus, or Mao's widow Qiang Qing. The variety of interpretations and associations with other works led Murray B. Peppard to the conclusion: "Even the most exhaustive critique cannot raise all the possibilities of interpretation or explore all the lines of suggestibility contained in the play, and the lengthiest commentary cannot provide adequate compensation for the pleasure of new discoveries that can be made by every new reading of the text" (*Friedrich Dürrenmatt*, 1969). The comprehensive nature of this play was noted by E. Speidel: "In short, when all these interpretations are added up, one cannot help but conclude that Dürrenmatt's play must embody, in three short acts, the whole tradition of drama from Sophocles to Brecht."

The Visit is indeed a complex play. It encompasses three sub-plots: Claire's return to Güllen in order to buy justice for a crime she cannot forget; the relationship between Ill and the inhabitants of Güllen; and finally the change in Ill himself. Dürrenmatt handles the language in such a way that all sub-plots are associated. Furthermore, language

reveals, by contrasting words and deeds, the real intent of the Gülleners. In reality, they negate the values they seem to affirm. An example is the scene in which Ill, fearing for his life, gets seeming moral support from the inhabitants who buy goods from him on credit:

> Man One: We'll stick by you. We'll stick by *our* Ill. Come what may.
> The Two Women (munching chocolate): Come what may, Mr. Ill, come what may.
> Man Two: Remember, you're the town's most popular personality.
> Man One: Our most important personality.
> Man Two: You'll be elected Mayor in spring.
> Man One: It's dead certain.
> The Two Women (munching chocolate): Dead certain, Mr. Ill, dead certain.
> Man Two: Brandy.

(translated by Patrick Bowles)

Through the repetition of certain words or phrases having more than one referent, the hollowness of the word, or language, becomes evident. With the exception of Claire, the characters use language not as a means of honest communication but to conceal thoughts; the Apollonian surface becomes transparent and the Dionysian element in man is laid bare.

Dürrenmatt's message seems to be that salvation lies not with the collective or the accumulation of wealth at the expense of moral values but with the soul-searching of the individual who accepts moral responsibility for his deeds. Justice, one of the key words and elements in this play, has a different meaning for everyone: for Claire it is personal vengeance, for the people of Güllen it means accumulation of wealth, for Ill it is a just atonement for a crime which he committed not only against Claire but against humanity.

—Gerd K. Schneider

THE VOICE OF THINGS (Le Parti pris des choses)
Poems by Francis Ponge, 1942

As Martin Sorrell suggests in his critical study (1981), *The Voice of Things* is a title that signifies at once the siding with things and the side things take. Francis Ponge attempts, in effect, a dissection of things through linguistic play in order to lend structure and purpose to those stark and intractable faces of matter so frequently intolerable to consciousness in recent literature.

Each prose poem proposes, or rather performs, a decisive investigation that often involves an opening of the object always with flourishing language. "The Orange" progresses from the elasticity of the peel to the relative firmness of the pip. "The Oyster" is the unlocking of "an obstinately closed world" whose palatable reality, like that of the orange, is pursued to the precious centre. "Bread" organizes the venture from resistant crust to yielding inner dough, as does "Snails" from the inert enclosing shell to the emerging and trailing slime. In all cases, there is an effort to grasp the indisputable pithiness of things that assail the senses, at times almost riotously ("the sensational explosion" in "The Orange," "an amorphous mass in the act of eructating" in "Bread"), while delivering itself through language as "expression"—literally, as that which has been squeezed out and collected in the closed and compacted form of the poem. The object functions anew as unfettered sensation rather than systematized idea, its logic of effect spawning a logic of text that embraces simultaneously the joy of language in its own right. Linguistic manipulation would seem to posit the kneadable thickness of things as Ponge releases through language a host of associations and variations that account for the lasting appeal of mute yet penetrable form. Indeed, taking the side of things through linguistic intervention, Ponge seeks nothing less than to sway things over to his side, in a gathering that knows no refusal.

The presentation of the object remains inseparable from the rigourous verbal network each prose poem encompasses. As the object reveals itself, so do the complexities and intrigues of language, spinning out multiple layers and crisscrossings of meaning the poet must organize into an ordered and harmonious whole. In the final poem of the work, ''The Pebble,'' Ponge passes judgement on himself while concluding: ''Having undertaken to write a description of stone, he became entangled.'' There is less criticism here than a subdued and congratulatory mirth, for through writing Ponge has not only succeeded in overcoming the recalcitrant nature of the pebble (multiplied as shingle, it forms ''a bed as unyielding to the foot as to the mind'') but in engaging himself with his chosen object to the point of complete and enraptured immersion in the language that describes it.

The intensified relation with the object is accompanied by an ever-extended and exacting discovery of language that imposes its own detours and solutions. The quest for renewed and vital contact with the surrounding world requires indeed linguistic entanglement that ensures at once a greater accessibility to things and a heightened sensibility of words. Thus, while the object is expressed, it is also assigned a model of expression in some way equivalent to it, yet functioning distinctively in terms of language as a polished and, in part, self-referential artefact. Rhetorical device is flaunted through the frequent use of conceits and an insistent punning, as Ponge calls attention to the workings of language rather than furthering a seamless figurative construct. The object cannot be pondered without similar investigation of the words that disclose its relations with self and other objects. Blackberries are explored by way of ''typographical bushes'' bearing verbal fruit of their own. The orange is prized as much for the pronunciation of its name as for the appeal of its juice, sound and substance blending in their identical effect on the larynx. At the centre of the oyster, ''a formula pearls,'' and so the poem itself is delivered as part definition/description, part rhetorical ornament. In truth, the whole work acts as a kind of diverse streaming forth of inner silent effort observed by the poet in things (ripening, budding, hatching, secretion) and twinned with his own personal task of expression, so that he might prolong and champion each natural outburst as linguistic offering.

If Ponge readily subscribes to the differential factor of words and things that allows a tensional, sometimes even tenuous interplay of verbal wit and referential concern, he steadfastly examines the difference between things so that analogy, is frequently qualified by opposition. The thing exists less in itself as a containable and hermetic whole than in relation to other things and to what it is not. Admitting that the pebble ''is not an easy thing to define well,'' the poet endeavours to situate it between what it has been part of and is no longer, and what it will be but is not yet. In the temporal progression from massive and unbroken rock to the infinite division of sand, the pebble serves as a middle point, an intersection that is at once inimitable yet impossible to isolate, and so can literally be thought through in a process of tireless unravelling that measures present

solidity and resistance in relation to past rupture and future disintegration. Elsewhere, the orange is compared to, and contrasted with, the sponge, as is the oyster with a medium pebble, the butterfly with a match, water with an armoire, and the shrimp with surrounding, more tangible, aquatic life.

Uniformity is negated as the diversity of all things triumphs endlessly through the study of any one thing, and in this diversity upheld by language, enhanced by the bold relief language further provides, the poet uncovers the binding mechanism of his own thought and art while incorporating the lesson of things—of their ceaseless and often thwarted aspiration, which only he can fully realize as proportionate and exultant expression.

—Michael Brophy

VOICES IN THE EVENING (Le voci della sera)
Novel by Natalia Ginzburg, 1961

The narrator of *Voices in the Evening* is Elsa, a 27-year-old woman who, having finished her studies at the local university, spends most of her time listening to the mindless chatter of her oppressive mother, and occasionally going to town to return books to the library. The plot revolves around the De Francisci family, owners of the only factory in the village. The head of the family, Balotta, is a self-made man who, in spite of having become a rich employer in the pre-war period, has kept faith with the socialist principles of his youth, and is never happier than when he is in his own factory where he can talk to and share his ideas with his workers. As Alan Bullock says, Balotta is ''totally unreceptive to anything outside the narrow sphere of his business interests'' (*Natalia Ginzburg: Human Relationships in a Changing World*); thus, he cannot understand his children, nor their way of life when they grow up.

The novel is written in the deliberately sparse style typical of Natalia Ginzburg. The dialogue is full of, for example, repetitions of the phrases ''she said'' and ''he said,'' which are used to great effect to emphasize the tedium of everyday existence. There are two very distinct parts to the novel. In the first half, the plot is fragmented into flashback episodes which depict past incidents in the lives of the members of the De Francisci family and a few other characters who gravitate around them. The character of Gemmina, Balotta's eldest daughter, who early in the novel is portrayed as an egoistic spinster involved in sterile charity work, is revealed more fully in the light of her previous disappointing experience with Nebbia, whom she loved and who married another woman. The most crucial moments in Gemmina's life are quickly sketched: first, the unforgettable night in which she got lost on the mountains with Nebbia, a friend of her brothers who, for his part, only admired her masculine stamina; and then the evening in which she shyly confessed her feelings to him, leaving the young man completely astonished, but rejecting firmly any kind of emotional link with her.

All Balotta's children seem destined to be unhappy in love; they are not able to establish lasting relationships with anybody. Vincenzino is a prime example. Elsa presents him, in his later years, as a fairly successful writer. His personal life, however, is in tatters: he first became involved with a Brazilian girl, of whom he tired very quickly, and then married Cate, whom he never loved, although she was approved of by his father. Incapable of communicating with each other, and without any interests in common, these two endure a marriage that is a complete disaster. Cate tries to fill her existential vacuum first with children, and then with numerous fleeting love affairs, which leave her and Vincenzino even more bitter towards one another and discontented with their lives. The marriage ends in separation, with Cate realizing that they are both to blame (''Why have we spoilt everything?'') and that her previous uneventful existence with her husband represented, in fact, some kind of happiness.

The only couple in the novel who seem to have a satisfying marriage are Mario, the third of Balotta's sons, and Xenia, a Russian refugee, who, feeling no need to communicate with anybody, never learns to speak Italian. After his marriage, Mario seems to enjoy a lifestyle different from the one he was used to, and appreciates the sophistication to which his wife has introduced him. Xenia, who continues to pursue her artistic career after her marriage, seems to bring a calming influence to bear on Mario's nervous disposition. Later, however, the narrator manages to sow a strong suspicion (although one never confirmed) that Xenia might, in some way, be responsible for her husband's death, especially after her remarriage to the Swiss doctor she had employed to treat Mario for a stomach complaint.

In the background to the main plot are also depicted Balotta's brother and sister, an old and almost senile pair who at times irritate the energetic Balotta with their uncritical approval of everything and everybody. Slightly more prominent, however, are the youngest of the De Francisci children, Raffaella, who during the war casts aside her passive female role in order to become a Communist partisan, and Purillo, Balotta's nephew. Purillo is a survivor, always ready to conform to the political reality in which he finds himself. Thus, he is a supporter of Mussolini during the Fascist period, which fortunately allows him to save Balotta's life, and, at the end of the war, he manages to fit perfectly into the local community. He marries Raffaella who, disappointed with post-war politics, devotes all her boundless energy to their only child, Pepé, thus becoming an obsessive mother.

In the second part of the novel, Ginzburg focuses sharply on the slightly banal love affair between the narrator of the story, Elsa, and the youngest son of Balotta, Tommasino. In the earlier section of *Voices in the Evening*, however, the author's treatment of other such relationships has made it clear that romantic attachments are, by nature, ill-fated. The love affair between Elsa and Tommasino startles the reader. The lovers meet in town once a week, in a rented room, where they can forget the past and nurture their precarious love. Tommasino is portrayed as possessing both the qualities and the faults of his elder brothers: he is artistic like Vincenzino, and as ineffectual as Mario. Elsa tries in vain to convince Tommasino of the depth of her feelings for him. Yet it is Tommasino's apathy that makes him eventually accept the engagement that Elsa's suffocating mother imposes upon them. However, once he comes into contact with the shallowness of his fiancée's home life and the trivial chatter of her ever-present mother, who takes over their lives, he becomes increasingly withdrawn. Elsa, realizing that the fragile equilibrium they had constructed in their rented room has been shattered, breaks off their engagement in an act of unexpected courage, thereby saving at least the memory of her lost love.

The second part of the novel is stylistically weaker, since the characters Tommasino and Elsa never really come to life, and remain totally immersed within the petty preoccupations of their narrow and futile existence. The end of *Voices in the Evening* is but a recurrence of Elsa's mother's initial monologue, with only one difference: the past tense employed by the author at the beginning of the book is replaced by the use of the present, as if Elsa's life has become an endless litany of the same phrases and the same gestures as her mother's, in an unending routine that will never change.

—Vanna Motta

VOYAGES TO THE MOON AND THE SUN (Voyage dans la lune and L'Histoire des états et empires du soleil)
Novels by Savinien Cyrano de Bergerac, 1657–62

The *Voyages* are made up of two completely separate works. In the first, the fictional Cyrano lands on the moon, more by luck than judgement, and encounters a manifestly better world, where his own precise identity causes puzzlement: is he a man? There is widespread scepticism about his claim to humanity (for a while he is thought to be a featherless parrot, to be kept in a cage) but eventually he is given the benefit of the doubt and released. Cyrano goes on to discover an advanced state of technology, including prefigurations of mobile homes, electric light, and record-players. On the moon we find philosophers who argue the infinity of the universe in time and space. Cyrano's profession of Christian faith is ridiculed: miracles are the consequence of ignorance, resurrection is a foolish myth, God does not exist. But our hero returns to the earth quite unaffected by these arguments, still foolishly defending divine Providence as though he had learned nothing from his trip through space.

The *Sun* continues Cyrano's imaginary career. He is now an outcast and put in jail but manages to build a machine that allows him to escape skyward. The sun turns out to contain a land of brilliant, weightless luminosity. In magical landscapes, trees turn into little men who then collectively form one perfect young man. There is a bird-heaven, where Cyrano is again arrested, this time as a member of the cruel human race that arrogates to itself total dominion to destroy at will the animal and plant worlds. He is himself condemned to a lingering death by stings and bites, but fortunately the birds accept a plea of mercy and let him go. He comes upon the Talking Trees, which possess both speech and reason, and finally the philosopher Campanella, who has telepathic powers and takes him to the superior province of philosophers, where Cyrano meets Descartes. The *Sun*, unfinished, stops at this point.

Savinien Cyrano de Bergerac's obvious claim to fame as a narrator lies in the brilliance of his imagination. But this virtuosity is not simply gratuitous. It relates to the author's joy in acquiring knowledge and thereby penetrating a world of infinitely rich possibilities. But to achieve this, independent critical enquiry is essential; religious authority and the Scriptures must be called into question. The *Voyages* are studded with sceptical comments: on the Flood, on the Tree of Knowledge and the serpent in the Garden of Eden, and on miracles generally. The human propensity for believing in supernatural marvels springs from mental laziness but also from man's arrogance in thinking that he has been accorded a special place in Creation. By contrast, Cyrano de Bergerac conveyed the sense of a limitless cosmos, where the earth revolves around the sun (a bold endorsement in the middle of the 17th century of the Copernican theory) and mankind occupies a merely contingent position. There is no place here for the notion of a benevolent, omniscient Christian God creating the world. Matter contains an inherent dynamism. Our belief in our preeminence and in our immortal soul is based on self-delusion. Indeed, it is not at all clear *what* man is. The human race has degenerated since the ancient Greeks; men have even sunk below the animals.

Only if human beings recover a proper sense of humility can the race exploit the full potential, as yet barely suspected, of our enigmatic universe. Superior beings like Socrates' demon live on the moon in a community of intellectual equality and independent reasoning. On the sun one can find an even more marvellous way of life, where people speak the perfect language of nature, and philosophers, even better, have no need of speech at all to communicate their transparently open thoughts. Learning at the highest level links up with pure moral integrity. All this is set in a world of infinite plasticity, where a great force blindly pulsates, endlessly renewing nature. This universe with its endless plurality of worlds liberates the mind, teaching us to reject all forms of dogmatism. There are no certain answers; man must depend upon his imagination and capacity for knowledge.

These are the attitudes that prevail. But Cyrano de Bergerac does not present them in a simply didactic form. The use of philosophical dialogue, particularly in the *Moon*, precludes a definitive view. Cyrano is himself an unreliable narrator, as his final remarks about God's providence in the *Moon* make clear. But no single character is to be trusted implicitly; even the most noble, like Socrates' demon, reveal their limitations. The mode throughout both *Voyages* is ironic. Sometimes, sun and moon are direct reversals of the earth. Lunar creatures walk on all fours and are foolishly proud of it as human beings are of their bipedalism; the solar birds assume their immortality with as little justification as the natives of Earth. The simple antithesis of cherished assumptions is an effective means of deflating human pomposity.

But Cyrano de Bergerac is not just an ironic satirist. Mankind may disappoint or appal; the world remains none the less a source of wonderful inspiration. The author can see in the phenomenon of magnetism not just a physical interaction but a passion and animism that relate it to human love. Above all, the dream of flight pervades these works. In the *Moon*, initial terror at being airborne gives way to "an uncommon joy." In the *Sun*, the four months' flight are passed exempt from all cold, hunger, melancholy, in an archetypal fantasy of freedom. Reason and dream interpenetrate in the *Voyages* to give them their unique flavour.

—Haydn Mason

THE VOYEUR (Le Voyeur)
Novel by Alain Robbe-Grillet, 1955

The Voyeur occupies a key place in Alain Robbe-Grillet's career. It was his third novel, but as he had failed to find a publisher for the first one—the title of which, *Un régicide*, already introduces the theme of murder central to writer's entire oeuvre—it was in fact his second published book. Robbe-Grillet's early offerings found a perceptive champion in Roland Barthes, whose sensitivity to the author's original way of describing objects ironically proved almost too influential. Barthes unwittingly contributed to the creation of an anti-humanist, highbrow image Robbe-Grillet has allegedly found it difficult to live with. Robbe-Grillet's own essays *For a New Novel* (*Pour un nouveau roman*) give a cunningly simple picture of his views on such issues as commitment, characterization, plot, and time. Persistently accused of

lacking interest in man, Robbe-Grillet claimed that his novels achieve total subjectivity: unlike Balzac's novels, his stories are always told from the limited point of view of an ordinary man living half in the real world and half in his own fantasy world. This ambition indeed comes close to being realized in *The Voyeur*: the events that take place on the unnamed island are largely, but not exclusively, presented to the reader through the eyes of the disturbed and disturbing Mathias.

Mathias is a salesman who travels back to his native island for the first time in many years in the hope of doing good business in the dwindling community of fishermen to whom his name might still be familiar. He constantly refers to the Mareks as his old friends and pretends to have known a Jean Robin. To be able to stay in business, Mathias has made up his mind that he must sell virtually all his watches in one afternoon, his deadline being the 4.15 p.m. ferry. The strict schedule we see him prepare mentally during his outward journey could hint at a morbid obsession with time, but could equally plausibly be interpreted as the understandable result of stress on an efficient salesman momentarily down on his luck, up to the end of Part I, the behaviour of Mathias thus remains mysterious for the reader. The narrative is deliberately slowed down by flashbacks, anticipations, transposed memories and hallucinations which yield frightening but ambiguous insights into the inner life of the "traveller," as Mathias is often called. *The Traveller* was Robbe-Grillet's working title, and Maurice Blanchot commented on the similarity between the words "voyeur" and "voyageur" (traveller).

At the beginning of Part III, the body of a 13-year-old girl is found in the sea, and gradually all doubts are dispelled about the circumstances of her death and Mathias's part in it. His clumsy attempts to work out a solid alibi and destroy evidence of his crime (candy wrappers, cigarette butts, the girl's pullover) would probably lead to his arrest if the whole population of the island were not convinced that only local boys involved with the girl could have wanted to kill her. But in fact few people (with the exception of Robert Marek and Jean Robin's girlfriend) make any real effort to find out whether the girl was actually murdered and by whom. Robert's son Julien, who saw Mathias rape and kill Jacqueline, lets the traveller know the crime had a witness, and Mathias resigns himself, or perhaps aspires, to being denounced. But Julien keeps their secret and Mathias leaves the island a free man.

The stylization of Robbe-Grillet's writing draws attention to itself. The structure of the novel has been compared to the images of the contemporary Dutch artist M.C. Escher. Escher's most stunning works are constructed like frames in a film where each successive image is gradually transformed into a slightly different one until the process is reversed leading us back to the original. Likewise the narrative of *The Voyeur* is built around a pattern of slightly different frozen sequences starting and ending on the ferry. The centre of the narrative is the rape scene which is constantly alluded to but never actually described. The same visions obsess Mathias before and after, thus blurring the linearity of the chain of events. Some details recur with unmissable frequency. Mathias is attracted by all objects that have the shape of an eight: knots on doors, spectacles, pieces of string or rope, handcuffs, etc. But Robbe-Grillet thwarts any attempt by the reader to settle on any definitive version of the causal relationship between his character's sexual perversion and these objects. Robbe-Grillet's style is remarkable for the originality of the expression of causality. A major influence fully acknowledged by Robbe-Grillet is that of Camus's *The Outsider* (*L'Étranger*). Like Meursault, another famous murderer whose name begins with an "M," Mathias is a killer without a motive. But in Robbe-Grillet's view, clearly stated in the 1958 article "Nature, Humanism, Tragedy," the end of Camus's novel restores moral significance and anthropomorphism. The aim of Robbe-Grillet in *The Voyeur* is to take the refusal of mystical correspondences between man and the world to its logical conclusion and therefore devise a style that does not tacitly re-establish these denounced magical correlations. The discrepancies that can easily be found between Robbe-Grillet's theory and his practice should not be used to fuel any polemics, but rather to read his novels more carefully in order to tease out the real secret of his baffling matt style.

—Pascale Voilley

VYĀSA

See BHAGAVADGĪTĀ and THE VEDAS

WAITING FOR THE BARBARIANS (Perimenontas tous Barbarous)
Poem by C. P. Cavafy, 1904 (written 1898)

"Waiting for the Barbarians" was written in 1898 and printed in 1904, as a self-contained pamphlet for private distribution, in accordance with C. P. Cavafy's idiosyncratic publishing practices. Although it is not among the poems the poet disowned (in the year he regarded as a watershed in his artistic development, 1911), "Waiting for the Barbarians" was not included by the poet in later collections of his work. It does, however, form the subject of a lengthy self-commentary note found among Cavafy's papers and thus it would appear that the poet acknowledged its position among the works of his maturity. It is generally regarded by critics as an example of his best work.

Cavafy distinguished three broad categories into which his poetic *oeuvre* could be divided: historical, erotic, and philosophical. Critics have sometimes relabelled the third category "didactic," but this term sits uneasily with what Cavafy himself called the "light irony" characteristic of his work. Boundaries between the three categories remain, in any case, highly unstable, since eroticism and history frequently coincide in the poems and the term "philosophical" could be loosely applied to almost all of them. Most of the poems are in some sense historical, since there is a marked tendency to return to the past, and it is, perhaps, this category that the poet regarded as his most characteristic, in view of his own designation of himself as a "historian-poet."

"Waiting for the Barbarians" is ostensibly a historical poem set in Rome: it refers to an emperor, praetors, consuls, and senators. The scenario is, however, imaginary and the poem takes the form of a pseudo-historical dialogue. It is not clear whether there is actually more than one speaker or whether a single voice is both posing and answering questions. Further, in spite of period detail (such as the embroidered togas worn by the consuls and praetors), the poem presents not facts, but speculation about what will happen when the barbarians arrive—barbarians who turn out, in the end, to be nonexistent.

The poem falls into two unequal parts: the dialogue of lines 1–33 and the closing couplet (lines 34–5). It is metrically stricter than the Cavafian norm, which is unrhymed iambic lines of varying lengths. Here, Cavafy elects to use 15-syllable lines (the standard line of Modern Greek poetry, deriving from the folk tradition) for questions, and 12- or 13-syllable lines (a non-standard line-length) for answers. The final couplet is in 13-syllable lines, and the poem does not make use of rhyme. One reason for the use of the 15-syllable line may be to subvert the reader's expectations by expressing doubt in what is normally the discourse of authority. Cavafy may also be consciously alluding to a common device of Greek folk poetry known as "questions that miss their target."

The main body of the poem consists of a series of questions, beginning in the opening line: "What are we waiting for, assembled in the forum?" The questioner goes on to ask why the senators have stopped legislating, the emperor and dignitaries are in ceremonial garb, and the orators are conspicuous by their absence. The invariable response is: "Because the barbarians are coming today." The last of these questions is:

Why this sudden bewilderment, this confusion?
(How serious people's faces have become)
Why are the streets and squares emptying so rapidly, everyone going home lost in thought?

The answer is that the barbarians have not come and are not coming: "There are no barbarians any longer." The couplet that closes the poem also takes the form of a question and a response; this time, the response explains the question without answering it: "Now what's going to happen to us without barbarians? / Those people were a kind of solution."

"Waiting for the Barbarians" is open to a variety of conflicting readings and thus exemplifies the obliqueness and understated irony characteristic of the mature Cavafy. Some critics have read it as an allegory of Cavafy's own time and place (Alexandria at the turn of the century), identifying the Romans as the Egyptians and the barbarians as the English forces of occupation. Others have suggested that the poem refers to a predicament in the poet's personal life. Others again have seen the poem as a timeless and universal symbol of the human condition. It has also been read as an allegory of writing.

Cavafy's own note on the poem remains, in many ways, the most instructive reading available, although it shares some of the elusiveness of the poem itself. The poet hints at a parallel with modern history, but says that both Romans and barbarians are symbolic and do not represent anyone in particular. He suggests that the poem concerns people who wish they did not have knowledge and long to lead the simple life of the uneducated for whom nothing is jaded. In other words, at one level, "Waiting for the Barbarians" is about the desire to abdicate responsibility and set aside the trappings of civilization. The barbarians are the noble savages of civilized man's imagination.

"Waiting for the Barbarians" defies reduction to any single reading, since its implied terms of reference encompass Roman history, modern Egyptian politics, the poet's personal circumstances, and mankind's dilemma. Its teasing ambiguity and multiplicity of levels are characteristic of Cavafy's mature work.

—Sarah Ekdawi

WAITING FOR GODOT (En attendant Godot)
Play by Samuel Beckett, 1952

Waiting for Godot is now a classic of the modern theatre. When it was first performed in Paris in January 1953 and in its subsequent productions around the world, however, the situation was entirely different. Most spectators were confused and many left before the performance had ended. Those who stayed had difficulty understanding what this new type of theatre was about. The normal dramatic structure had totally changed. The language very often did not have a sequential rational pattern; communication among the characters was difficult and they frequently resorted to incomplete, childish sentences in order to make themselves understood. At times, the visual actions spoke more directly than words. The set was composed only of a mound of dirt and a bare tree. Finally, there seemed to be no plot, nothing appeared to be happening.

In the first act, we are introduced to two elderly men, Vladimir and Estragon, who could be tramps. They are awaiting the arrival of a Mr. Godot, who is going to save them. Pozzo and Lucky pass by and, eventually, a young boy appears and says that Mr. Godot will not arrive today, but will surely come tomorrow. Following this broad outline, the second act is a duplication of the first.

The play contains no progression of plot, no development of characterization, no climax. This complete reversal of the traditional theatre techniques announced a major change in modern drama. Samuel Beckett happened to be writing at the same time as a number of other dramatists, all independently transforming the shape of theatre, writing plays that would later be classified under the rubric of the theatre of the absurd, the new theatre or the anti-theatre. All of these new playwrights were expressing the absurdity and the hopelessness of the human condition and they were to have a lasting effect on the direction of drama, perhaps none more so than Beckett and *Waiting for Godot*.

In the play, Vladimir mentions that one of the two thieves crucified with Christ was saved and the other was damned. He is preoccupied, however, with the fact that only one of the four Evangelists provides this account, thus making the odds for salvation even less promising. This concern with salvation—at best one out of two will be saved—is the kernel of the play and all of the characters are presented in pairs: Vladimir and Estragon, Pozzo and Lucky, the boy in the first act and the boy in the second.

The two main couples of the play (Vladimir and Estragon, Pozzo and Lucky) are different but, at the same time, they complement each other. Vladimir, called Didi, is the more philosophical of his pairing, while Estragon, called Gogo, is the more active. Didi is the one who remembers that they are waiting for Godot, while Gogo is uncertain as to what he has seen or heard or why he is there. Pozzo and Lucky represent master and slave, since Lucky is tied to Pozzo and is often whipped by him. When Pozzo orders Lucky to speak, Lucky appears to utter gibberish, although he is really expressing his sense of the absurdity of the human condition. In the final analysis, all four of the characters are caught in the void of existence.

Their only hope for salvation from this nothingness is the arrival of Godot, who will provide the sense of coherence and purpose that they lack. While waiting for Godot, the characters are forced to go through their lives suffering but hoping for salvation. One of the ways that Didi and Gogo get through their suffering is by following a series of habitual routines that allow them to "pass the time" without thinking too much.

Yet, in spite of their many activities, nothing really changes and they have moments when they are agonizingly aware of this. All they can do is to wait for the salvation that they hope Godot will bring. At the same time, their lives sometimes assume an arbitrary brutality. Gogo goes off-stage at one point and says that he was beaten by unknown people. Although Godot is supposed to represent salvation, Gogo is afraid of him and he thinks that the vicious Pozzo, who beats Lucky, may be Godot. In addition, there is the fear that the two tramps may be "tied" to Godot in the same way that Lucky is tied to Pozzo.

At one point, Didi recites a piece of doggerel about a dog who stole a crust of bread in which the story repeats itself endlessly, exactly like the life the two tramps are leading. Beckett once said that he did not need to write a third act to the play, since he had already pointed out the stagnant repetitiveness of life by the end of the second act. The two men are still waiting and they are still uncertain about the past or

the future. This sense of uncertainty leads to the feeling of hopelessness and the frequent repetition of the phrase, "I can't go on."

The one element that does seem certain is the passage of time and its fleeting quality. Didi sums up the state in which he and Gogo find themselves:

> Was I sleeping while the others suffered? Am I sleeping now? Tomorrow, when I wake, or think I do, what shall I say of to-day? That with Estragon my friend, at this place, until the fall of night, I waited for Godot? That Pozzo passed, with his carrier, and that he spoke to us? Probably. But in all that what truth will there be? . . . He [Estragon]'ll know nothing. He'll tell me about the blows he received, and I'll give him a carrot. (Pause.) Astride of a grave and a difficult birth. Down in the hole, lingeringly, the grave-digger puts on the forceps. We have time to grow old. The air is full of our cries.

The main image of the hopelessness and despair of the situation is brought forth compellingly at the end of each act. At the end of Act I, Estragon says, "Well? Shall we go?" Vladimir replies, "Yes, let's go." The stage direction says: "They do not move." The end of Act II is exactly the same, with the exception that the two characters exchange their parts in the dialogue. At the final point of each act, the actions of the two men speak more directly than their words. It is clear that they cannot go, they must wait for Godot. It is also clear that Godot will not arrive.

—John H. Reilly

WALLENSTEIN
Plays by Friedrich von Schiller, 1798–99

Widely regarded as the greatest German tragedy, *Wallenstein* depicts the last four days in the life of Albrecht Wenzel Eusebius Wallenstein, Duke of Friedland (1583–1634), one of the most prominent and enigmatic figures during the first half of the Thirty Years War (1618–48).

Soon after Friedrich von Schiller began work on the project he realized that the vastness of material could not be compressed into one drama. To provide the audience with the information essential to understand Wallenstein's tragedy, it was necessary to give a picture of the political and religious situation in the 17th century, the atmosphere of the times, the course of the war up until the action begins, and finally the attitude of the army which was the basis of the duke's power and the instrument for achieving his goals. The resulting trilogy enabled the author not only to accommodate these requirements but also to introduce several sub-plots and to develop a great number of other characters. Thus, *Wallenstein's Camp* and a large portion of *The Piccolomini* are in effect the exposition to *Wallenstein's Death*.

Wallenstein's Camp was completed in 1798 and premiered at the opening of the renovated Weimar Hoftheater on 12 October 1798. Having no plot, it provides a picture of the army, the historical setting, and a description of Wallenstein, the soldier's idol. Written in irregular rhymed quadrameters, it consists of short scenes interspersed with music, songs, and dance which depict the different kinds of soldiers and camp followers gathered at the duke's winter quarters at Pilsen 1633–34.

In December 1798 *The Piccolomini* was completed and premiered 30 January 1799 in Weimar. Completing the exposition, this part of the trilogy details the elaborate precautions Wallenstein has taken to protect his position as the all-powerful commander-in-chief of the imperial forces battling the Protestants. He has neither forgotten nor forgiven Emperor Ferdinand II of Austria for removing him from command in 1630. This had thwarted his plan not only to bring the war to a close but also fulfil his ambition to establish a new dynasty as King of Bohemia. Having been recalled in 1632 to deal with the threat posed by King Gustavus Adolphus of Sweden, he is determined to avoid a second humiliating dismissal. Essential to his plan is to win the allegiance of the army and the officer corps away from the emperor. Two examples illuminate his character and clarify some of the reasons for his downfall: first, he encourages Colonel Buttler to apply to the court for promotion to general and for a patent of nobility. To win Buttler's loyalty, the duke secretly advises the court to write the colonel an insulting letter of rejection. Again in a cynical effort to ensnare the loyalty of Max Piccolomini, who is almost a son to him, he sends the young warrior to escort his daughter, Thekla, to Pilsen rightly suspecting the two will fall in love during the long journey. Similar to Sophocles' *Odepius*, all of Wallenstein's efforts to achieve his goal have precisely the opposite effect of that intended.

The long exposition which paints Wallenstein as a decisive and enigmatic leader is contradicted when he finally appears. We see that he is unsure of himself, indecisive, and reluctant to move ahead. Several times he says that he regards his manipulations and negotiations with the Protestants primarily as insurance against another dismissal rather than a decided fact. Now he learns from his wife, who has just returned from court, and from other sources, not only that has he lost control of events but more seriously that he is suspected of treason. He realizes that he is about to be caught in the very net he wove to protect himself, and that he is himself primarily to blame for this new turn of events. The way he sees it, his enemies are leaving him no choice, that by their very suspicions they are forcing him into a course of action which he might not wish to take. What he does not know is that the emperor has already taken steps to neutralize his commander. He has issued secret orders to General Octavio Piccolomini, whom Wallenstein mistakenly regards as his closest friend and ally, appointing him commander-in-chief. Another secret decree declares the duke an outlaw wanted dead or alive, but Octavio is to activate the orders only if Wallenstein rebels openly. Meanwhile, he manoeuvres secretly to win back the loyalty of the officer corps. *The Piccolomini* ends on an ominous note.

Schiller completed *Wallenstein's Death* in early spring. It was first performed on 20 April 1799 in Weimar and received excellent reviews. All the conflicting forces that have been building up reach the climax and are resolved in Wallenstein's assassination. In Act I, scene 2, the duke learns that his envoy to the Swedes, Sesina, has been captured by troops loyal to the emperor, together with documents which testify to his double dealing. The peripeteia occurs when he decides to come out in open rebellion. As Schiller himself remarked, Wallenstein did not fall because he rebelled, he rebelled because he fell. The public break with Ferdinand is the signal for Octavio to activate his orders. All but a few regiments declare for the emperor. At this point the duke undergoes a change of personality. As the reports of defection and betrayal arrive one after another, his true nature as a man and leader emerges. While those remaining with him succumb to panic, he is the picture of composure and self-control. He knows that there is little hope for either his cause or himself, but he perseveres with increasing determination. His resolution in the face of adversity

gains our admiration and sympathy, even as Buttler and his assassins are breaking down the door. His fall and death outrage our sense of justice and produce the feelings of waste which have been essential ingredients of tragedy since classical antiquity.

In the final analysis, Wallenstein's tragic flaw was his ambition and love of power which made him fatally self-centred. He saw himself as the measure of all things, the man of destiny beyond good and evil. To him, individuals were unimportant in their own right, serving only as a means for attaining his goals. Such egoism clouded his ability to assess his situation accurately and disabled his power to judge character. Hence, he was easily deceived by Octavio; he underestimated the depth of Max's moral convictions, and it never occurred to him to take Buttler's pride and sense of honour into account should he ever find out about the secret letter, as he did. Finally, he egregiously misjudged the depth of the army's commitment to its oath of loyalty to the emperor.

—John D. Simons

THE WANDERER (Le Grand Meaulnes)
Novel by Alain-Fournier, 1913

The Wanderer is a story of youthful idealism and adventure which grew out of Alain-Fournier's obsession with a young woman he met briefly at the age of 19 and his subsequent preoccupation with the search for pure, idealized love associated with lost childhood. Narrated by François Seurel, the timid son of a schoolmaster, who is both observer and participant in events, the novel reveals a complex web of emotions and relationships. The quest of François's schoolfriend, Augustin Meaulnes, for the unknown, beautiful young woman glimpsed during a fantastical wedding party (the *"fête étrange"*) in an old château where he finds himself by chance becomes the great adventure of their adolescence, then François's hero-worship of Meaulnes and identification with his quest gives the quiet, serious boy a vicarious excitement and becomes the focal point of his existence.

The air of mystery that surrounds the "lost domain" and the young woman (Yvonne de Galais) is sustained by the narrator's use of fairytale devices (Meaulnes falls asleep on a cart journey and the home, wandering from the path, brings him to the old château), dreamlike events (the wedding party run at the whim of children in fancy dress) and initially unexplained happenings (Meaulnes's moodiness; the melodramatic behaviour and reappearances of the flamboyant Frantz de Galais who becomes Meaulnes's hero in turn).

François's eagerness to take over the quest when Meaulnes, discouraged, leaves for Paris, reveals that he shares—even exceeds—Meaulnes's idealism and romanticism. In fact, Meaulnes disappears from the reader's view for large stretches of the book and is then only seen through his letters and diary. François's position as sole narrator privileges his viewpoint, which is deeply subjective, the alluring gloss he puts on people and events seducing the reader into sharing his assumptions and expectations. His presentation of Meaulnes as romantic hero is, however, subtly undermined by Meaulnes's actual behaviour when viewed objectively, though the reader is rarely allowed direct access to his thought-processes. Meaulnes's "adventure" comes about initially by chance and although he does indeed become a "wanderer" he seems driven by anguish, indecision, and despair rather than by a dynamic heroism. Similarly, the view of Yvonne as the idealized princess on a pedestal ("la princesse lointaine") is countered by her fragile health and down to earth common-sense when she is allowed to speak in her own voice.

The marriage of Yvonne and Meaulnes, brought about by François in his desire to create a traditional fairytale ending to the great adventure, ends in tragedy when Meaulnes, consumed by an obscure and unexplained remorse, adheres to an adolescent pact with Yvonne's self-absorbed and self-dramatizing brother Frantz and leaves Yvonne after their wedding night to search for Frantz's missing fiancée. Although multiple explanations for his behaviour are offered—François's speculations that Meaulnes cannot reconcile his ideal with reality and is driven to destroy his happiness once it has been achieved are characteristically romantic—the real reason, revealed in the rather clumsy device of a diary written by Meaulnes, is more mundane and has significant implications for Alain-Fournier's views on love. Meaulnes's guilt over his relationship in Paris with a young seam-stress, Valentine, to whom he turned in despair and whom he rejected when he discovered she was Frantz's lost bride, and his subsequent remorse are the secret burdens which, unknown to François, doom his marriage before it takes place and precipitate his abrupt departure.

Implicit in this tale is the destructive power of obsessive idealism which seeks to impose a false role on other people: both Yvonne and Valentine are victims of this tendency in the men who ''love'' them. Valentine tried to evade the stereotype of ''princess'' Frantz sought to impose on her by running away, only to find herself cast, by Meaulnes, in another role—that of substitute lover and instrument of his betrayal both of his friend Frantz and of his own concept of pure, innocent love. The idealization of love relationships is also severely undermined by the tragic fate of Yvonne. Doomed to unhappiness by her loyalty to her brother and to Meaulnes, she is abandoned by her new husband and dies a painful and unromantic death after bearing his child. In effect, both female characters are cast by the author in sexually stereotypical roles—the pure beauty (her sexuality mani-fested only in her motherhood) and the ''fallen woman''—a division disturbingly exacerbated by social class.

The novel can be seen as a ''rites of passage'' narrative, charting the painful transition from adolescence to adulthood. However, there is certainly no fairytale happy-ever-after ending and it is debatable whether the characters really do grow up. François, assuming respon-sibility for Yvonne and her baby, appears to confront and accept reality, and his rejection of the petulant, self-centred behaviour of Frantz suggests that he perceives the pernicious nature of misplaced idealism, but the closing lines, after Meaulnes's return, intimate that François continues to romanticize his friend, for he anticipates Meaulnes's further departure, his little daughter wrapped in a cloak, in search of new adventures. The ending is deeply melancholic. François senses the loss of the only thing left to him of the ''great adventure'' in which he has invested all of his energies, emotions, and hope. Even the image of ''the happy couple,'' Frantz and Valentine, reunited by Meaulnes, is rendered problematic, for their domestic felicity is played out in the context of Frantz's childhood miniature cottage in the woods.

Alain-Fournier wrote of his desire to evoke ''the end of youth'' (''la fin de la jeunesse''). The atmosphere of nostalgia and regret and the association of pure, ideal love with the landscape of childhood suggest that the narrative reflects the blighting of youthful ideals by reality. It is equally possible to argue, however, that the tragedy of this novel is that it is real-life happiness that is blighted.

—Penny Brown

THE WANDERING SCHOLAR IN PARADISE (Der Fahrende Schüller ins Paradies)
Play by Hans Sachs, written 1550

In the 15th and 16th centuries Nuremberg experienced an extraor-dinarily lush flowering of literary life which was, however, more remarkable for its quantity than its quality. The prominent poets were craftsmen practising one trade or another, and their products too were artisan rather than artistic in nature. Thanks not least to Richard Wagner's *The Mastersingers of Nuremberg*, the best known of these poets today is Hans Sachs who, with more than 6,000 poems and plays to his credit, must rank as one of the most prolific writers of all time. Among this vast output the *Fastnachtspiele* (shrovetide plays) rank as his finest work. According to his own catalogue of his writings he composed 85 of these plays, 81 of which have survived. Regarded as classic examples of the genre, they are characterized by rich humour and wit, and Sachs reveals acute powers of observation and a feeling for theatrical effectiveness. For his subject matter Sachs drew heavily on Boccaccio's *Decameron*, the *Gesta Romanorum*, and works like Hermann Bote's *Till Eulenspiegel* and Johannes Pauli's *Schimpf und Ernst* [Levity and Seriousness], but for about a third of the plays no specific source has been identified.

Pauli's collection of anecdotes provided the source for Sachs's *The Wandering Scholar in Paradise*, written on 8 October 1550. Running to 322 lines of rhyming couplets, it has three characters, statistics which are indications of the artistic economy typical of his best *Fastnachtspiele*. The brevity of these plays underlines the fact that they were intended merely as brief contributions to the shrovetide festivities in an inn or private home.

The play opens with a peasant woman contrasting the happiness she enjoyed with her first husband with her present lot, married unhappily to a miser. An itinerant student enters and asks her, in rather high-flown courtly language, for a gift of money, mentioning that he is just back from Paris (one of the leading universities of the day). The woman understands him to say he is just back from Paradise and asks whether he has seen her late husband there. The student immediately realizes her stupidity and plays her along, asking her to describe her husband. He pretends he does remember him and claims the man is living on charity, wearing only the cap and shroud in which he was buried. When the woman asks whether the student will return to Paradise he assures her that he will and would be delighted to take a present from her back with him. She fetches 12 gold guilders and a complete set of clothes which the student says it will be a pleasure to deliver. He says it will be some time before he can return with news of her late husband, but the woman says that meanwhile she will scrape together more money for him and gives the student a small sum for his trouble. The student departs, leaving the woman singing happily. Her new husband hears her and asks the reason. She relates what has happened and he affects to believe that she should have given the student even more money and declares he will ride after him to give him another ten guilders. The woman is overjoyed, but the man (in an aside) curses her stupidity and gullibility and declares that he will catch and thrash the student before returning to beat his wife. The student meanwhile is congratulating himself on his luck, but then he sees the woman's husband coming and hides the bag of clothes in a bush. The student tells the peasant he has seen which way the man he wants went and agrees to look after his horse while he pursues the culprit. The student rides off on the horse, leaving the peasant to realize that he has been even more stupid than his wife. He tells his wife the student agreed to take the additional money to her first husband and that he had given him the horse to expedite his return to Paradise. The woman is delighted and reveals that she has already told the whole village about the affair. She believes that their laughter meant that they rejoiced with her, but her husband tells her they were laughing at her. Sachs enshrines the moral in the peasant's concluding speech: it is a misfortune for a man to have such a gullible wife for she might squander all his wealth, but because she is well-meaning it will be easier to endure. But men too can make stupid mistakes. So one should be prepared to forgive one's partner so that harmony may reign in a marriage.

Though the story is borrowed from Pauli, the wily student, the stupid peasant woman, the miserly peasant are all stock figures of Sachs's plays, but they have elements of individual characterization. Here they are such more subtly presented than in Pauli. Whereas Pauli says at the outset that the woman is ''not quite wise,'' Sachs reveals her stupidity gradually in the course of conversation with the student. His portrayal of the husband is also more subtle: instead of reacting angrily, he is depicted as more calculating.

No account of the content can convey an impression of the simplicity of the language and of the humour and charm that lie in the modes of expression. The woman's description of her first husband as ''einfeltig und frumb'' (''honest and upright'') is a recurrent motif, reminding the audience of the contrast she had painted at the beginning between him and her second husband. The wheedling approach of the student and the woman's naive questions reveal Sachs's sensitivity and delicate touch. The student's notion of joy in paradise as consisting in drinking a glass of wine on a feast day and playing cards, and the woman's assertion that she will behave in exactly the same way when her new husband dies are just two examples of the delightful touches of humour that pervade the play.

Sachs's Fastnachtspiele are primarily intended to entertain and amuse but many of them, like this one, conclude with a moral, a development associated with the fact that whereas in the 15th century shrovetide plays had served as safety-valves for human urges that were normally repressed, especially during Lent, after the Reformation they came to offer entertainment tempered with a modicum of didacticism. Only rarely does Sachs sacrifice plot to the elaboration of a moral precept.

—John L. Flood

WAR AND PEACE (Voina i mir)
Novel by Lev Tolstoi, 1863–69

When Lev Tolstoi first thought of writing *War and Peace* he gave it the title *Three Eras*, referring to the years 1856 (when the hero returns home from exile after the death of Tsar Nicholas I and the Crimean War), 1825 (the year of the Decembrist Revolt and the reason for the hero's exile and ''the period of [his] delusions and misfortunes''), and 1812 (the Battle of Borodino and Russia's defeat of Napoleon). His moral integrity then forced him to consider Russia's ''failures and shame'' and start earlier, in 1807 (Treaty of Tilsit) and then 1805 (Battle of Austerlitz). In effect he ended up with only the last three and when the first 38 chapters were published in *The Russian Messenger* in 1865 the editors entitled them *1805*. In 1866 it was to be called *All's Well That Ends Well* and only in the following year was its final title decided. The novel was completed in 1869. Tolstoi, however, refused to call it a novel, or even a historical chronicle. It was ''what the author wished and was able to express in the form in which it is expressed'' and he justified this unsatisfactory definition by stating that all Russian literature which rose above the mediocre did not fit into any of the conventional categories of novel, story, or poem, citing Pushkin's *Eugene Onegin* (*Evgenii Onegin*), Lermontov's *A Hero of Our Times* (*Geroi nashego vremeni*), Gogol's *Dead Souls* (*Mertvye dushi*) and others, including his own *Childhood*.

Leaving to one side whether or not it is a novel, more particularly a historical novel, it is clearly anti-historical in intent. The vast, panoramic canvas includes ''real'' historical characters—Tsar Aleksandr I, Napoleon, the Austrian emperor, generals, diplomats, politicians, and so on—but it also presents a philosophy of history. ''History would be a fine thing,'' he wrote, ''if only it were true.'' He studied relevant documents, books, archives, and personal recollections of the period, and distrusted them all. History to Tolstoi was the sum total of what individuals thought and did; the ''great men'' of history had little or no influence over events, the changes and evolutions noted by historians were illusions, and there was no such thing as progress or historical advancement. At the Battle of Borodino Pierre Bezukhov sees only a succession of incomprehensible acts: Napoleon deludes himself in thinking his orders are carried out or that there is such a thing as a grand strategy; Kutuzov, as much idealized as Napoleon is satirized, knows all this, sleeps through councils of war, and lets things take their inevitable course; and the outcome depends basically on the morale of the troops. And here the book's title is significant in a way other than epitomizing one of the most obvious features of Tolstoi's style—the use of contrast. It is as if he wants to point up the fact that all those great events and important people that have always been thought to be the stuff of history are quite irrelevant. What is crucial are the lives of the thousands of ordinary people, their personal joys and disappointments, their births and their deaths, their loves and hates, their feelings, thoughts, shortcomings, and ambitions. That is reality and everything else is a harmful illusion.

Nevertheless it is in his characterization, not in his philosophizing or beating the reader over the head with his own idiosyncratic though stimulating ideas, that Tolstoi's greatness as a writer really lies. If they had the choice most readers might choose to forget the ''war'' and cherish and admire the ''peace.'' The reader lives with Tolstoi's characters as with those of no other writer. All the 900 or so are sharply individualized and stand out clearly when they appear (even the dogs are differentiated). Albeit with a vast historical backcloth, *War and Peace* is based on the stories of three families: the Bolkonskiis—the old aristocratic Prince, a crusty ''Voltairean,'' his daughter Maria, and son Andrei; the Moscow gentry Rostovs—the gentle, conservative Count, the motherly countess, and their children Nikolai and the utterly charming and delightful Natasha; and the wealthy Bezukhovs, especially the Tolstoian ''seeker of the truth'' Pierre. There are also their numerous relations and friends. The lives of these families are shown in all their variety, at dinner parties and in conversation at home, at grand balls at the Imperial Court, at entertainments with mummers at Christmas, on country estates, at hunting parties, in intrigues, social climbing, drunken escapades of army officers, their births, marriages, and deaths, love affairs, financial matters and the endless complications, joys, and heartbreaks of everyday life.

The world Tolstoi creates is bright, healthy, and happy. There are none of the grotesques of Gogol' or the abnormalities of Dostoevskii. His characters are generally likeable and even the horrors of war are treated with such an epic sweep and magisterial overview that death, injury, and even the futility of it all are lessened. The mood of *War and Peace* is largely serene. Tolstoi, although historically fatalistic, is optimistic about the human condition. His love of life shines through even its darkest pages and his praise of the value of family life is unstinting and unsurpassed. His acceptance of life in all its vicissitudes is contagious, yet it is accompanied by a search for meanings and his searing psychological analysis exposes everything false. His prejudices, however, are not disguised. He prefers the country to the town, Russia to the West, the submissive personality to the ambitious or pretentious, and ultimately peace to war. On finishing the book the reader, as an early admirer of Tolstoi put it, should have experienced not a work of fiction, but life itself.

—A.V. Knowles

WATER MARGIN (Shuihu zhuan)

Chinese novel deriving from oral tales based on incidents of the 12th century. Earliest manuscript, dated 1370, was probably written largely by Shi Naian, and augmented, revised, and/or edited by Luo Guanzhong; but later editions vary in content, and in length from 71 chapters to more than 120.

PUBLICATIONS

Shuihu zhuan. 1550 (after the 1370 manuscript); revised edition, 1590–95; as *Zhongyi shuihu quanzhuna* [The Complete History from the Riverbank of Loyalty and Righteousness] (120 chapters), edited by Li Zhi, 1614; 71-chapter edition, 1644; modern editions: 4 vols., 1920; *Yibai ershi hui de Shuihu*, preface by Hu Shi (120 chapters), 20 vols., 1929; *Jin Shengtan qishiyi hui ben Shuihu zhuan* (71 chapters), 24 vols., 1934; *Shuihu quan zhuan*, edited by Zhong Zhenduo, Wang Liqi, and others, 4 vols., 1954; as *All Men Are Brothers*, translated by Pearl S. Buck, 2 vols., 1933; as *Water Margin*, translated by J.H. Jackson, 2 vols., 1937; as *Outlaws of the Marsh*, translated by Sidney Shapiro, 3 vols., 1980, abridged edition, 1986; as *The Broken Seals: Part One of the Marshes of Mount Liang*, translated by John Dent-Young and Alex Dent-Young, 1994; as *The Gathering Company: Part Three of the Marshes of Mount Liang*, translated by John Dent-Young and Alex Dent-Young, 2001.

*

Bibliography: ''A Survey of English-Language Criticism of *Shui-hu chuan*'' by C.J. Alber, in *Tsing Hua Journal of Chinese Studies*, 2, 1969.

Critical Studies: *The Evolution of a Chinese Novel: Shui-hu-chuan* by Richard G. Irwin, 1953; *The Classic Chinese Novel* by C.T. Hsia, 1968; ''The Modern Relevance of *Shui-hu chuan*'' by J. Chesneaux, in *Papers on Far Eastern History*, 1971; ''The Seditious Art of the *Water Margin*: Misogynists or Desperadoes?'' by P.S.Y. Sun, in *Renditions*, 1, 1973; ''Narrative Patterns in *San-kuo* and *Shui-hu*'' by P. Li, in *Chinese Narrative: Critical and Theoretical Essays*, edited by Andrew H. Plaks, 1977, and ''*Shui-hu chuan* and the Sixteenth-Century Novel Form: An Interpretive Analysis,'' in *Chinese Literature*, 2(1), 1980, and *The Four Musketeers of the Ming Novel*, 1987, both by Plaks; *The Margins of Utopia: Shui-hu hou-zhuan and the Literature of Ming Loyalty* by E. Widmer, 1987; *The Story of the Stone: Intertextuality, Ancient Chinese Stone Lore, and the Stone Symbolism in Dream of the Red Chamber, Water Margin, and The Journey to the West* by Jing Wang, 1992; *Out of the Margins: The Rise of Chinese Vernacular Fiction* by Liangyan Ge, 2001.

* * *

The novel *Shuihu zhuan* (variously translated as *Water Margin, All Men Are Brothers*, or *Outlaws of the Marsh*) has been popular with Chinese readers for almost four centuries. Its authorship is traditionally assigned to a 14th-century writer of fiction and drama, Luo Guanzhong (c. 1330–1400), and also jointly to him and a more obscure figure named Shi Naian. The novel as it is read now is almost certainly a later redaction, perhaps dating from the early to mid-16th century, and has been published in editions of different lengths, from 71 (the most popular), to 100, 110, 115, and 124 chapters.

The story derives its source material from oral tales which originated in historical fact. The central legend is about a 12th-century band of outlaw-rebels who, according to the legends, occupied a mountain in northern China, eventually made peace with the Song dynasty Emperor, and helped him conquer another rebel group in the South. The novel tells of the gradual gathering and dissolution of the band: in the early days one *haohan* (''good fellow'' or ''stalwart,'' as they are generally called) after another is forced by unjust circumstances to seek refuge from the law and to join with others as bandits who live off the land. Soon the numbers grow, a hierarchy develops, and the outlaws reach an apogee of strength and prosperity. However, the leader, Song Jiang, has always wanted to serve the Emperor in a legitimate way, and finally achieves his wish, though he thus puts an end to the life of the rebel utopia. In the service of the Emperor the band wins great honour but steadily loses members in battle until only a handful remain. In the end Song Jiang commits suicide along with his closest companion, Li Kui.

The novel divides into units consisting of either a single hero's evolution from common citizen to outlaw or of some valiant mission in which many participate. These units are sometimes interspersed with unrelated sub-plots, but all weave together to lead into and out of the central scene of action in the text, the mountain fortress which is home to the bandits.

Early on, the novelist presents character types and themes that reappear throughout. These types include the coarse, swarthy men who combine naive heartiness with a tendency to cold-bloodedness (Li Kui, Lu Da, and Wu Song); the clean-shaven and valiant heroes who embody the values of honesty and civility (Lin Chong, Lu Junyi); and the magicians and masterminds who advise on strategy (Wu Yong, Gongsun Sheng). Thematic issues include such things as the requital of official injustice, the definition of true leadership, and the mutual recognition of what it takes to be a *haohan*.

Perhaps not surprisingly, one of the singular undercurrents of the book is misogyny. Women frequently appear as adulteresses who must be ruthlessly exterminated, few of the major heroes are married, and lustful behaviour is frowned upon. Song Jiang, for example, who is ''not very interested in women,'' marries but neglects his wife and drives her to adultery. When she threatens to reveal his connections with outlaws, he murders her. He is led to such an act neither because of her mockery of his sexual inadequacy (in one of the most humorous scenes of the novel) nor her adultery itself, but because of the threat of breaking the code of honour with his fellow *haohan*.

It is significant that in the latter half of the novel, when Song Jiang's band is already declining, a figure enters who subtly eclipses the other male heroes. He is Yan Qing, a handsome and physically adept young man who is at the same time more socially versatile. He symbolizes the eclipse of the band most pointedly when he shoots at a flock of geese in the sky: this is interpreted as an ill omen since he thus disturbs the integrity of a naturally formed group.

At first reading, *Water Margin* will perhaps seem episodic and unorganized, a situation that is partly owing to the nature of the source material and partly to the lengthy evolution of the text as we have it now. However, like *Golden Lotus*, though to a lesser extent, *Water Margin* achieves cohesiveness by means of what may be called correlative patterning, that is, multiple levels of textual or figural recurrence. From minute to large scale, such repetition at times merely provides a sense of linkage, at others it creates an ironic contrast between parallel elements. These patterns of meaning have been celebrated in a famous commentary on the novel by Jin Shengtan of the 17th century.

In general *Water Margin* is written in an extremely lively, colloquial style, and is filled with proverbs, folk idioms, and comic obscenity. Unfortunately, putting this flavour into English has proved difficult so that at times the reader must bear with somewhat wooden and naive-sounding translations.

—Keith McMahon

THE WAVES OF SEA AND LOVE (Des Meeres und der Liebe Wellen)
Play by Franz Grillparzer, 1831

The subject matter of Franz Grillparzer's tragedy of Hero and Leander derives from the epic poem by Musaeus, while other literary stimuli came to him from the German folksong "Edelkönigskinder" and the poems Ovid, Marlowe, and Schiller had devoted to the fabled lovers. Shakespeare's *Romeo and Juliet* provided a further model through its sensitive romantic treatment of youthful eroticism. Grillparzer avoided the established conventions of Weimar classicism and instead of adopting an anachronistic form, wrote a modern psychological verse play in a style which gave full scope to the complexities of conscious and unconscious motivation in the exploration of first love. The result is an essentially realistic contemporary drama in an antique setting. Grillparzer's faithful adherence to the fundamental principles of living theatre—a tangible action, clear motivation, vivid characterization, close commerce between image and gesture, word and image—was a tribute of his esteem for the Spanish baroque theatre of Calderón and Lope de Vega. These qualities were matched in him by that psychological acumen and perspicacity which mark out the forerunner of modern drama, especially as it was to develop in *fin de siècle* Vienna, the cradle of psychoanalysis.

The Waves of Sea and Love portrays the awakening of erotic love in all its impetuosity in a young woman who has come to the island sanctuary of Sestos to dedicate her life as virgin priestess to the goddess Aphrodite. It is clear from the expository first act that family pressures and close connections with the temple (the priest is Hero's uncle) have supplanted freedom of choice in determining her vocation. Hero, the untried novice, is under the illusion that she knows her own heart and mind, that she is fully alive to the implications of

complete surrender to the religious life, and that she can find fulfilment in serene contemplation and dutiful service. Her tragedy consists in the loss of self, the defeat of the will in face of a primal impulse for which she is not prepared. The tragedy portrays the human will and its resolve as fallible, as unequal to the surge of passions. The elemental power of love and desire, which first announces itself with discreet subtlety, unfolds as an irresistible moving force, no less potent than the ever-changing sea. This poetic metaphor is woven into the fabric of the play's language, as is the imagery of light and darkness, twin indicators of the theme of the conscious and unconscious life of the emotions. At the initiation ceremony in act one, where Hero must abjure marriage, her eye lights on the handsome, shy figure of Leander and the fateful spark is kindled. Characteristically, Grillparzer chooses to illuminate the inner dimension of subliminal and semi-conscious experience through attitude and gesture, as the stage directions indicate. In performing the sacred rites of self-dedication to the priesthood, Hero's trembling hand, her lapse of memory, and confused ritual acts, betray an untimely loss of that equilibrium and self-possession (*Sammlung*) which is the ideal and goal of the contemplative life. On hastily concluding the ceremony, she pretends to attend to her shoe, thereby stealing a furtive parting glance at Leander: this signals her nascent captivation.

If the opening act merely hints at Hero's latent erotic susceptibility, the second confirms and substantiates the growing bond of feeling. Leander's friend Naukleros recalls the tell-tale detail of the preceding temple scene, Hero's revealing glance ("Observing you, she stood in hesitation / For one, two, three brief, eternal moments"). He also interprets the meaning of that glance ("The pity of it!" and "Him I might well have liked!"). Leander cannot hide his tears of agony or the agony of desire, while Hero betrays her latent feelings by singing a song of Leda and the swan, a barely repressed sublimation of her womanly desires. When the lovesick Leander craves a drink of water from Hero's pitcher in the forbidden grove, this innocent gesture stands in symbolic anticipation of the bond that is to join the lovers in defiance of a hostile law. Though the priest's suspicions are early aroused as to his charge's inner feelings, he continues to play an ambiguous role as spiritual counsellor, caring relative, and unsparing moral judge. The audacious Leander gains access to Hero's chamber by scaling the walls of her tower, and in the course of the lovers' meeting it becomes clear that she has neither the resolution nor the will to resist. Hero's desperate question, put largely to herself, formulates the crucial issue of the tragedy: "What is it that so darkens Man's mind and so estranges him from his very Self, compelling service to an alien Self?" The resourceful priest, aware that Hero's lamp had been burning all night, ensures that the following day's duties make her physically exhausted and unable to watch for her lover another night. (Hero's lamp is more than just a tangible instrument of the action: it is developed into a complex symbol of the love relationship, being overlaid with connotations of the rational and irrational elements of the mind.) In his stern cross-examination of her, he meets with a degree of evasive cunning which betokens a new, maturer woman who is prepared to defend her love to the last. The net of tragedy inevitability closes in upon the lovers in the final act, as the lamp which was to guide Leander across the Hellespont is extinguished by the priest, who overtly acts as an instrument of the gods. This salving of the private conscience in a man of religion has about it a peculiarly modern polemic; as a figure of compromise, he has much of the compliant functionary about him. The dramatist's own experience of stiff authoritarianism, external respectability, and bigotry in the age of Metternich's Vienna, gives the play a remarkably authentic groundswell of social realism.

The last act shows Hero rising to the height of her tragic stature in her grief over the drowned Leander. All dissimulation is cast off as she gives utterance to the full burden of emotion and the torment of the heart. Her profession of undying love rises to a pitch of elevated eloquence that recalls the memorial paean to the dead Anthony by Shakespeare's Cleopatra:

> Come, he was all there is! What still remains
> Is but a shadow; it fades, a nothingness.
> His breath was purest air, his eye the sun,
> His body like the power of budding nature;
> His life was life itself, both yours and mine,
> The universal life.

Hero's death is depicted as another *Liebstod* such as we may find in Kleist's *Penthesilea* or, later, in Wagner's *Tristan und Isolde*, yet lacking that ecstatic, transcendental quality which was foreign to the Austrian poet. Grillparzer pays minute attention to the symptoms of physiological change (clouded vision, double heartbeat, coldness, numbed posture, various signs of debility) in portraying the final stages of ebbing life. The poetic and the prosaic are frequently in contention in Grillparzer, yet when they harmonize, as they do in this play, the result is convincing and masterly.

—Alexander Stillmark

WE (My)
Novel by Evgenii Zamiatin, in English 1924; in Russian, 1952 (written 1920)

Written in 1920 but banned in the Soviet Union until 1988, *We* is a dystopian fantasy, one of the first novels of the 20th century to satirize a scientific, collectivist society of the future.

This new world, the product of a revolution 1,000 years before the narrative commences, is presented in diary form by a high-ranking mathematician, D-503, for whom its laws represent a near-perfect logical and rational ideal, almost a ''paradise on earth.'' The basic principle of the One State is that of enforced happiness, whereby the inhabitants are compelled to repress individual and irrational impulses in favour of a precisely regulated, machine-like harmony. Their lives are governed by strict rules, known as the ''Tables of Daily Commandment,'' which control virtually every aspect of daily existence, including procreation. They are identified by state-allotted letters and numbers, dress in identical blue uniforms, and march to work in fours accompanied by military music. They are housed in transparent glass apartments, permitting easy surveillance, and are confined to a symmetrically-built glass city, beyond whose walls they are forbidden to travel in case of ideological infection. The only concession to privacy is the Personal Hour, during which the blinds of the apartments may be lowered and guests entertained.

The element of coercion in the One State is supplied by a god-like dictator, the Benefactor, who has an efficient and ruthless secret police at his command to expose and punish dissent, as well as an army of devoted artists to sing his praises. If D-503 is to be believed, however, a perfect balance has been achieved between compulsion and consensus. Deviation from the norm is rare: his fellow-citizens prefer the security of their mechanical existence to the complexities of individual freedom, and express their support unanimously at election-time. In the eyes of its scientific chronicler, this world is normal, stable, and vastly superior to the chaotic, savage, inefficient system of the ''ancients.'' In contrast, the One State is a well-oiled, efficient machine in which the members happily fulfil their duties as acquiescent cogs.

Yet this order is revealed to be inherently unstable in the course of the narrative, with D-503 ironically among its first casualties. Initially, the diary is planned as an enthusiastic ode to the Benefactor that will accompany a special rocket mission to subjugate other planets to the ''beneficent yoke of reason.'' D-503 is employed as an important engineer on this project, called the Integral. Soon, however, his record begins to falter, detailing instead his mental breakdown as the result of an erotic encounter with a mysterious and attractive woman, I-330. A disciplined and dedicated revolutionary, I-330 leads a secret conspiracy of rebels, the Mephi (taken from the Greek word for the devil, Mephistopheles), who are seeking to overthrow the state. The love-affair itself arouses passionate, powerful, hitherto unencountered emotions in D-503, which his logical mind is unable to comprehend, let alone control. He dreams for the first time and starts to experience the yearnings of a soul. Moreover, I-330's intellectual critique of the status quo, which extols the virtues of permanent rebellion with a mathematical logic he is powerless to resist, begins to undermine his blind faith in the system. His anxieties are further compounded when he realizes that the dissident element is well-organized and in fact reaches into the heart of the Establishment itself, including friends whose political loyalties he had thought total.

The novel reaches a climax when the Benefactor, made aware of the growing disorder, makes compulsory a surgical brain operation which will remove the last area of mental activity not already under state control: dream, fantasy, and subconscious desire. With the Mephi rebellion under way, D-503 experiences divided loyalties. He is finally persuaded that I-330 is exploiting him in order to hijack the Integral for her own purposes, and freely volunteers for the operation. Cured of his psychological trauma, his last diary entry records in the glacial and detached language of an automaton I-330's execution at the hands of the Benefactor. Rebellious elements are still at large in the city, but D-503 concludes by expressing his hope and conviction that rationalism will triumph.

At the time of writing *We* Evgenii Zamiatin was greatly influenced by H.G. Wells, whose novels he viewed as a new literary genre which looked less towards the utopian future than towards the perceived ills of modern capitalism; in his own words, they were ''socio-fantasies,'' social pamphlets which masqueraded as science fiction. *We* is similarly a fantasy that distorts and exaggerates certain aspects of modernity, both Western and Russian. Zamiatin belonged to a long tradition of Russian writers—most importantly Dostoevskii—who were critical of rational and utilitarian thought. Much of his concern with dehumanization was anticipated in two earlier stories about suburban Britain, ''The Islanders'' and ''Fishers of Men,'' the products of a two-year stay during World War I. His glass city is arguably modelled on London's Crystal Palace, a symbol of enlightenment and progress, while several other images could have derived from his impressions of the shipyards in Newcastle-upon-Tyne, where he worked as a naval architect designing ice-breakers for the Entente.

Yet much of the satire is targeted specifically at political and artistic developments in the Soviet Union just after the Bolshevik Revolution. The Benefactor and his secret police are thinly-disguised portraits of Lenin and the Cheka. The banal verse of the One State poets and D-503's paeans to ''man as machine'' are parodies of the Russian Proletarian poets, whose factory-based poetry workshops enjoyed official patronage at the time. The Integral itself is arguably modelled on Vladimir Tatlin's projected Monument to the Third International, while the physical geography of the city resembles St. Petersburg and may have been influenced by early Russian Constructivist and Futurist architectural designs. Clearly, Zamiatin feared the consequences of an egalitarian political system which believed blindly in the benefits of scientific progress and demanded total ideological compliance. His novel undoubtedly owes part of its classic status to the accuracy with which it predicted the Stalinist era.

While distrusting modernity, however, Zamiatin was fascinated by speed and mechanization. This central ambiguity expresses itself often in his work. He believed, for example, that literary language should reflect modern consciousness. Thus, the prose style of *We* is compressed, high-voltage, and elliptical. While this is designed partly to reflect D-503's way of thinking and seeing (scientific imagery is employed consistently throughout the novel), it has a quality which is recognizably Zamiatin's own. This aspect of his art, along with his highly inventive use of metaphor and elaborate imagistic systems, is possibly his greatest contribution to Russian literature.

—Philip Cavendish

THE WEAVERS (Die Weber)
Play by Gerhart Hauptmann, 1892

One of the most powerful social dramas in German literature, *The Weavers*, is also the first German play to attempt a realistic representation of an entire community of working-class people on stage. Written at a time when the young Gerhart Hauptmann was influenced by naturalism and its scientific interpretation of the world, the work portrays the Silesian weavers as victims of socio-economic circumstances. The dramatic incidents mirror problems associated with the Industrial Revolution, such as the unemployment caused by the introduction of power looms, and the exploitation of labour by capitalist entrepreneurs. Hauptmann shows how a mass of people are driven to violent reaction when their misery becomes unbearable.

Based on actual events which took place in the Eulengebirge in 1844 as the Industrial Revolution reached eastern Germany, the play became the most controversial of its time when it was finally presented to the general public in Berlin in 1893. This ''symphony in five movements with one grim, leading motive—hunger'' (Huneker) received thunderous applause from the audience, but was regarded by the authorities as inflammatory.

The play is without a conventional plot. Its action is ''realistic,'' presenting the weavers in their wretched situation from various angles—Hauptmann gives dramatic shape to the social and economic forces which condition an entire class. The first act shows the starving weavers en masse, visiting the premises of their employer in order to sell their cloth. Tractable and docile, they are exploited by the manufacturer whose magnanimous gesture in taking on an extra two hundred unemployed weavers is exposed as humbug—the new rates of pay will be even lower than the current starvation wages. The second act focuses on the sufferings of a small group of weavers in the cramped room which they call home. The third act is set in a public bar and gives the audience a cross-section of the local community as weavers come into contact with the views of others from outside the weavers' narrow social sphere: some (the smith, the rag-and-bone man) are sympathetic but most (the policeman, the commercial traveller, the innkeeper, the joiner-employer) are impervious to their plight. The fourth act is set in the sumptuous home of the employer, whose guest is the local parson. The arrival of a mob of weavers outside the house is condemned by the clergyman who regards any threat to the prevailing social order as a transgression against the laws of God. The superintendent of police is called to deal with the rioting weavers, but the employer and his family are forced to leave before the weavers take possession of the house and set about destroying it. The fifth act follows the weavers' revolt to another village: the action is set in the home of a pious old weaver, Old Hilse, who refuses to jeopardize his hopes for salvation in the life to come by joining his ''poor brothers'' in their continued destruction of employers' houses and factories. The weavers are led by Jäger, an unruly soldier who has recently returned and, appalled at their wretched situation, has stirred the weavers to defiance. At the end of the play, shots are heard as the weavers begin fighting the soldiers who have been sent to put down the riot. Old Hilse, stubbornly staying at his loom near a window, is fatally wounded by a stray bullet.

The impact which *The Weavers* has on audiences is produced by its frequently innovative dramatic qualities: its unusual yet authentic dramatic theme—the revolt of the entire social body of the weavers, springing from their hunger and poverty; the absence of a conventional single ''hero'' (only one minor character appears throughout all the acts of the play) and the creation of a ''collective hero,'' the mass of weavers in their moment of revolt against long-endured, unbearable suffering; the technically brilliant way in which Hauptmann handles a multiplicity of events and characters, producing intense thematic concentration which gives the play the effect of ''harmonious and unified construction'' (Lawson); the avoidance of sentimentality through the employment of a chronicle framework which presents events ''naturalistically,'' in an objective, documentary fashion, while still evoking sympathy—''the moving power is the event, the action, the class articulate in revolt'' (Raymond Williams).

Hauptmann employs several techniques in order to articulate an entire class on the stage: first, he focuses on small representative groups in their familiar environments in order to illustrate the effects of their crushing poverty (Acts Two and Five). Second, he employs a ''choral method'' to create a sense of individuals belonging to the same class, shaped by the same social forces, but with the less typical figures giving dramatic life to the whole through their interaction with the others: in the first act, for instance, the weavers are presented as a *whole*, with individual weavers speaking in the patterns of speech of the whole group. Hauptmann creates the illusion of real speech by having the weavers speak in Silesian dialect, with unfinished sentences, interjections, single words, short phrases, and people talking across each other. Third, the inflammatory marching song recited on several occasions by Jäger, telling of the weavers' oppression, functions not only as a leitmotif throughout the play, but also as a dramatic lever—by expressing the weavers' unspoken emotions, the song enables the weavers to understand their situation clearly for the first time, and resignation and despair gradually give way to hatred and violence. All these techniques have the effect of translating economic fact into dramatic, emotional experience.

Critics have praised the play as a naturalistic ''milieudrama''— much of its dramatic effect depends on the creation of a loosely connected sequence of detailed pictures of the environment (the stage directions are given in the minutest detail and, in the original edition, the dramatis personae of each of the five acts was printed before that act, suggesting a series of separate tableaux). Yet the acts are not static pictures; Hauptmann established a dynamic relationship between setting and action in so far as milieu is shown to be a force which shapes the human characters involved and so actually determines the dramatic action. Each of the five acts of the play has an increasingly dramatic conclusion, illustrating how a mass of individually passive weavers gradually, as the social and economic pressure on them intensifies, form into a destructive, disorganized mob.

—David Rock

THE WHITE GUARD (Belaia gvardiia)
Novel by Mikhail Bulgakov, 1927–29, (written 1924–29)

The White Guard is Mikhail Bulgakov's first novel, dating from 1922, although he had been working on related themes since at least a year earlier. The initial manuscript was completed in 1924, and two of the book's three parts were published the following year in the literary journal *Rossiia*, which, however, was closed down before the final part could appear. Publication details are complicated by the fact that Bulgakov was then invited by the Moscow Art Theatre to turn the book into a play, which for many years was far better known in the Soviet Union than the novel. The premiere of *The Days of the Turbins*, as it was called, was a major theatrical event of the decade: a *succès de scandale*, in that it was seen as an apologia for the old regime—a criticism which was also applied to the book. (Banned in March 1929, it was restaged in February 1932 with Stalin's approval, remaining in the repertoire until 1941.) The play differed considerably from the original novel, however, both for valid theatrical reasons and for political ones. With an increased interest in the book, the first two parts were republished in Riga (Latvia) in 1927, but with the addition of a fraudulent third part based not on Bulgakov's manuscript but on an early version of the play. The novel was first published in its entirety in Paris (1927–29), in a version authorized by Bulgakov after he had rewritten its final part. (See for this Lesley Milne's account in her *Mikhail Bulgakov: A Critical Biography*, 1990.) The complete version did not appear in the Soviet Union until 1966, 26 years after the author's death, in a volume of his selected prose.

Essentially, *The White Guard* is a historical novel based on Bulgakov's own experiences in his native Kiev during 1918–19. With the end of World War I, the German occupying armies are forced to leave the Ukraine, taking with them the "Hetman" Skoropadskii, the leader of the puppet government set up by them. Kiev is then occupied temporarily by the Ukrainian nationalists under Semen Petliura, until they are driven out by the Red army. (The later reoccupation of the city by the Whites is outside the scope of the novel.) Seen as a historical account the book may not be objective, but as a novel it gives a vivid depiction of events from the perspective of the Russian intelligentsia in the city, isolated from "the real Ukraine, a country of tens of millions of people." Emotionally attached to the old regime, the "White Guard" consider themselves duty-bound to defend the Hetman, who for all his government's inadequacies comes closest to representing their own values. Preparing to go into battle, however, they learn that he has fled and there is no one left to defend. To them Petliura's forces seem little more than barbarians, and there is thus no choice but to welcome the Bolsheviks when they defeat Petliura 47 days later.

There is perhaps something of a Tolstoian flavour in Bulgakov's portrayal of a clash of peoples, represented by numerous characters, from the commanding officers to the ordinary people in the street—whether they support the Hetman, Petliura, or the "third force" of the Bolsheviks. The main protagonists, however, are based on members of the author's own family. Alexei Turbin (like Bulgakov at that time) is the conscientious doctor, enlisting with the forces to defend the city; Nikolka, his brother, the young, enthusiastic cadet. Their sister Elena takes over the role of their recently deceased mother, but is herself abandoned by her husband, Talberg, a White officer who leaves with the Hetman for Berlin. Surrounding them are their friends (also army officers) and their young, lovingly clumsy cousin, Lariosik. With their traditions of order, decency, and honour, they stand in sharp contrast to the many who act out of cowardice or their own self-interest, including their landlord, the comical Vasilisa, who lives in the downstairs apartment with his avaricious wife Wanda.

The house, in fact, is recognizably the one actually occupied by the Bulgakovs in Kiev (opened in 1991 as the Bulgakov Museum), symbolized by its stove with tiles showing scenes from the life of Peter I, by its clocks, its chocolate-coloured books and cream-coloured blinds. The importance of family is a major theme: "For this . . . [man] goes to war, which, if the truth be known, is the only cause for which anyone ought to fight." But the family members cannot escape outside events, as symbolized in the conflict between Mars and Venus, in the "snowstorm from the north" and apocalyptic visions from the Book of Revelations.

There are many scenes of brutality, but also of tenderness and humour, and an awareness of life's continuity, against the background of the eternal and rather mysterious city of Kiev. Alexei, trying to return home, is wounded and pursued, but is rescued by a mysterious woman who visits him after he has miraculously recovered from near-death. A major theme throughout is that of a deep but undogmatic religious belief, and of death and resurrection—for Alexei is said actually to have died and is saved only as a result of Elena's prayers to the Virgin Mary. (Previously he had dreamt of Paradise, into which all are admitted regardless of their beliefs: a passage inadvertently omitted from Glenny's English translation, but included as an appendix in Milne's book referred to above.) The final paragraph, one of the most beautiful in Russian literature, uses the symbol of the stars to conjure up a vision of eternity:

> But the sword is not fearful. Everything passes away—suffering, pain, blood, hunger and pestilence. The sword will pass away too, but the stars will still remain when the shadows of our presence and our deeds have vanished from the earth. There is no man who does not know that. Why, then, will we not turn our eyes toward the stars? Why?

—A. Colin Wright

THE WHITE HORSEMAN (Der Schimmelreiter)
Novella by Theodor Storm, 1888

The White Horseman, which exists in 41 translations and 171 editions, has often been claimed as Theodor Storm's crowning achievement. It concerns the conflict of a progressive man, a strong, self-reliant individual with the regressive force of popular superstition, with stupid masses and with the malevolent powers of nature.

The reader follows Hauke Haien from his boyhood to his death through an elaborate triple framework technique. Already as a child he shows the willpower, determination, defiance, obstinacy, and temper that drives him as a man to build his life's work, a dike, a project that will cause his ultimate demise. Haien becomes the architect of his own downfall, driven by pride and ambition. Hermand calls him the enlightened man, a figure typical of the imperialistic age of Bismarck. Silz sees a similarity between Hauke and the older Faust, in that both take up the battle with the sea to win land for their fellowmen, and both, so it seems, are helped by the devil. However, for Hauke there is no redemption. When he stops striving, his fate is sealed, his destruction inevitable. The character traits of the genial rationalist are developed first: his mathematical mind, his eternal striving to attain his goal, his absolute determination to rise in society, to marry Elke, to become dikemaster, to prove to his society his ability and skills. His critical superior intellect, his inborn talent allow him to overcome his greatest obstacle, his poverty. Parallel to these characteristics grow his negative trends: excessive ambition, lack of control over his temper, disdain and later hatred for others, and egomania culminating in hubris of mythic porportions.

Hauke's first opponent in his rise to the top are the laws of society which concern themselves less with his talent and ambition and more with his possession. The dikemaster has to be the wealthiest man in the community. When he achieves this goal through his marriage, his inheritance and hard work, the number of his enemies, led by Ole Peters, grows steadily. The construction of the new dike with its modern profile should prove his capability and bring about his triumph over their mediocrity. However, Hauke becomes unfaithful to himself. The dike planned for his fellows and built with them, becomes an instrument against them. He fights against superstition and in so doing strengthens the rumour of his alliance with the devil. More and more, he fits the role of Nietzsche's superman: hard, domineering, lonely, and extremely energetic. In monomaniac fashion the dike becomes *his* dike; thus it cannot bring about a reconciliation with society.

One of the highpoints of the novella is Hauke's controversial prayer at the bed of his wife after the birth of their child. Hauke sees God from his own rational perspective, a God that is bound by his own rational laws. Thus Hawke has created for himself a God according to his own image, i.e. he has reversed the creative act. He and God are equal. Wittmann and Hermand consider this prayer blasphemous, whereas Silz and Blankenagel call it unconventional but deeply religious. While his pride had kept him from praying up to this point, we now find him on his knees at the cradle of his child "as if it were the place of eternal salvation." Wife and child and thus he himself become his deities. Hauke sees therefore no reason for submission. The reader, however, realizes that rationality has failed Hauke, that God/nemesis/fate has already spoken: Hauke's only child is feeble-minded. The irrational child calls Hauke the omnipotent father. Through Wienke, Storm shows that there is a power higher than man, and we see the parallelism between the feeble-mindedness of the child and the egocentrism of the father.

After the completion of his dike, Hauke is for the first time without a definite goal and thus vulnerable. The sickness of the marshes, as Storm calls it, befalls him. One can consider this illness and the physical manifestation of his emotional collapse. He becomes defenseless against the pressures of society and of the sea and repeatedly is unable to find the site of deterioration at the point of contact between the old and the new dike (i.e. between tradition and progress). The vigorous, healthy Hauke could not be held back by either man or nature. The weakened Hauke is beguiled by the deceptive play of nature and the fallacious advice of the villagers.

Hauke's death in the floodwaters led to various interpretations: suicide, despair after the loss of his family, sacrifice for his guilt, titanic will to act, titanic negation of faith are just a few. It is not the power of nature that destroys him, but the death of his wife and child. Now Hauke understands God does not want his work, the reconstruction of the dike, but God demands his sacrifice. Silz sees the death as total extinction (*völliges Ausgelöschtwerden*), Martini as fate that destroys no matter how strong the fight to prevent it. Schuster sees the suicide as an external sign for an internal happening. Through his hubris Hauke caused the death of his family, his only bond to his community. They alone believed in him and kept his spark of humanity alive. His life has now become meaningless, but his death can be meaningful. "Lord, God, take me—spare the others!" he utters. Hauke atones for his previous guilt and weakness.

Some critics call the sacrificial death an act of superstition, whereby the enlightened Hauke is recreated as a phantom double, outliving the end he thought to find by his plunge into the abyss. It is ironic that Hauke who spent his whole life furthering technological progress and enlightened thinking should be remembered not as a genial inventor by as the spectre of doom. Martini defines Hauke's guilt not as a sin of commission or omission, but rather as an existential guilt with the basis in the absoluteness of the will.

The complexity of *The White Horseman* which goes way beyond the narrow confines of the novella affirms Thomas Mann's opinion that Storm is a master and will remain one.

—Ingeborg M. Goessl

THE WILD DUCK (Vildanden)
Play by Henrik Ibsen, 1884

As Henrik Ibsen himself admitted, *The Wild Duck*, written in 1884 and produced in Bergen in the following year, was somewhat different from the group of realistic plays, including *A Doll's House* and *Ghosts*, which preceeded it. With this play Ibsen's drama was to move into a new, symbolic phase which initially failed to impress contemporary critics who, for the most part, saw only pretentiousness and obscurantism and were unsympathetic to the play's humble setting and characters. Only gradually was Ibsen's play recognized as a painful, but at times ironically comic, comment upon humanity's need for the protection of illusion.

Dramatically, the most innovative feature of *The Wild Duck* lies in Ibsen's weakening of the well-made plot structure of explication, complication, climax, and dénouement which had dominated his earlier realistic plays. Now situation becomes more important than event, and the symbolism, which Ibsen had earlier grafted onto the realism of his plays in order to widen their implication from the particular to the general, becomes, on one level, a fully integrated feature of the play and, on another, a means by which the characters themselves attempt to imbue their ordinary lives and actions with deeper significance. From the former arise most of the tragic elements of the play, while from the latter stem ironic comedy and pathos.

As the title suggests, at the centre of the play is the image of the wild duck which, when shot, dives to the bottom of the lake to die but which, in this case, has been rescued by a clever hunting dog and now resides, injured, in the Ekdals' attic. It is in relation to this image that the majority of the play's characters are viewed and, as the play progresses, we gradually penetrate deeper and deeper into their past and present lives.

The symbolism of the wild duck is primarily associated with the Ekdal family, all of whom have in some manner been injured by old Werle, a rich merchant and owner of the Hoidal works. Significantly it was he who shot the wild duck. Werle's first victim was Ekdal senior who was, in the past, his business partner but was left by Werle to take sole responsibility and suffer imprisonment for illegal tree-felling. In consequence Ekdal has lost his status in society and is now supported partially by clerical work provided by Werle. Ekdal spends much of his spare time hunting rabbits in the fantasy forest which he and his son Hjalmar have created in their attic. Hjalmar and his wife Gina have also been injured by Old Werle. As the play progresses we learn that Gina had an affair with Old Werle which resulted in the birth of Hedvig, who is now 14 years old. To mitigate the consequences of his actions Old Werle encouraged Gina to marry Hjalmar and set the couple up in a small photography business. Even Hedvig suffers from association with her natural father in that she has inherited from him a disease which will gradually lead to blindness.

Whereas Old Werle has at least attempted to provide recompense for the injuries caused, his son Gregers, who has returned from a sojourn in the cold north bringing with him an equally cold logic, attempts to reveal the truth to his father's victims. He is unshakeably certain that, as a result, his father will be forced to face his guilt and that the Ekdals will be happier for being relieved of the delusions under which they live.

As Ibsen himself employs the symbolism of the wild duck to reveal the nature of the relationship that exists between the Ekdals and the Werles, so also do a number of the characters themselves attempt to infuse their lives with significance, and define a pattern to their mundane existence by describing themselves and their actions in terms of Romantic and at times sentimental imagery. Chief of these is Gregers Werle who has decided that his over-riding "task in life" is to unburden others of their illusions. From his arrival in the Ekdal household, to the incomprehension of Hjalmar, Gina, and Hedvig, he weaves his own symbolism around the wild duck. He compares himself firstly to the duck itself and then to the clever dog who retrieved the duck from the bottom of the lake. The prosaic responses of Hjalmar and Hedvig provide a touch of comic irony intended by Ibsen to reveal Gregers's pretentiousness. By employing such ironic undercutting Ibsen allows this phoniness to appear at first comic but gradually, through the interaction between Gregers, Hjalmar, and Hedvig, he begins to reveal how it can also inhibit and even destroy relationships with others. Hedvig has already been emotionally crippled by being confined, on account of her partial blindness, to the apartment in which Hjalmar and his father live out their lives in self-delusion. Indeed, she is portrayed as behaving like one much younger than her actual age. She is in consequence highly susceptible to emotional pressure and it is under such pressure, exerted by Gregers, that she adopts his suggested "spirit of sacrifice," and attempts to prove her love for her father by killing not her beloved wild duck, as suggested by Gregers, but herself.

Having cruelly rejected Hedvig when it is revealed by Gregers that she may not be his child, Hjalmar's self-dramatization keeps him ignorant of the real reason for her death. He is unable to understand her need to prove her love for him and, as the pragmatic realist Doctor Relling points out, "Before the year is out little Hedvig will be nothing more to him than a fine subject to declaim on." It is Relling, with his insistence that the average man needs his "saving lie" in

order to be happy, who is placed by Ibsen in opposition to Gregers with his fanatical "claim of the ideal." At the close of the play Hedvig is dead but Hjalmar and Gregers remain the same as they always were. The ironic comedy gives way to the sombre conclusion that idealism may not be the virtue that it may superficially appear.

—D. Keith Peacock

WILHELM MEISTER'S APPRENTICESHIP (Wilhelm Meisters Lehrjahre)
Novel by Johann Wolfgang von Goethe, 1795–96

Johann Wolfgang von Goethe's novel, first published in 1795–96, is generally considered the epitome of the German Bildungsroman, although Goethe did not consciously write such a novel. The term *Bildungsroman* was coined later in 1817 by Karl (von) Morgenstern and popularized by Wilhelm Dilthey in 1870, but one strand of the divided reception shows a reading of the novel in terms of Bildung, the successful self-cultivation of the protagonist, already between 1796–1800, although the term Bildungsroman was not yet available. This reading was to become the dominant interpretation of *Wilhelm Meister's Apprenticeship* for the next two centuries to come. There was, however, from the beginning also a reading which questioned the protagonist's development into a mature and well-balanced human being in the sense of the humanist ideology of the 18th century, with its emphasis on the ideal of harmony.

The original version of the novel, entitled *Wilhelm Meister's Theatralische Sendung* [Wilhelm Meister's Theatrical Mission], was written between 1777 and 1785, but remained a fragment. The original manuscript is lost, but a contemporary copy was discovered in 1909 and published in 1911. This novel, divided into six books, corresponds to the first four books of *Wilhelm Meister's Apprenticeship*, although the emphasis is on the theatre as a positive experience rather than a transition to other types of educational experience. If the title of the original version is not considered ironic, the *Theatralische Sendung* is to be interpreted as an artist novel (*Künstlerroman*).

The story of Wilhelm Meister, the son of a middle-class merchant, is set in the world of late 18th-century Germany. Wilhelm is not interested in entering his father's business, but in becoming a poet, playwright, and actor, if not the founder of a national German theatre. Falling in love with a young actress, he uses his business trips on behalf of the family firm to acquaint himself with a travelling theatre company. When the latter goes bankrupt, Wilhelm rescues it by advancing funds from his father's business. His financial involvement makes him not only a business partner in the theatre company, but also affords him an opportunity to write, act, and direct. After a brief engagement of the company at a nobleman's castle, where Wilhelm endears himself to the nobility as a well-educated member of the bourgeoisie, he is invited to direct a production of Shakespeare's *Hamlet*. This production reflects the development of professionalism among actors and the founding of a national theatre in Germany during the 18th century. Playing the title role, Wilhelm is a success as actor and director, but soon actors and audience become tired of the demands of literary drama on the stage, preferring opera and slapstick farce. Frustrated in his ambitions on the stage, Wilhelm turns his interests toward the nobility, hoping to find his educational goals realized within the circles of the aristocracy. Reform-minded representatives of the nobility welcome Wilhelm as a member of the bourgeoisie and acquaint him with their multinational enterprise of emigration to America and acquisition of land abroad to avoid loss of property due to revolutionary upheaval in Europe. This union of the reform-minded aristocracy and the progressive bourgeoisie is Goethe's response to the French Revolution. Favouring the American Revolution, Goethe has Count Lothario, who distinguished himself in the service of the revolutionary army, exclaim: "Here [in Germany], or nowhere, is America" (Book VII, Chapter 3). At the end of the novel, Wilhelm marries a countess and inherits not only his share of his father's business, but also the estate of an Italian orphan of noble birth (Mignon). The end of the novel reflects the pervasive irony of the work: instead of being cultivated, Wilhelm becomes married and rich. The irony of the ending is encapsulated in a quotation from the Bible: the protagonist feels "like Saul, the son of Kish, who went in search of his father's asses and found a kingdom" (Book VIII, Chapter 10).

Among the characters of the novel that need to be mentioned are Felix, Wilhelm's illegitimate son from his first love affair with an actress, as well as Mignon and the Harper as tragically Romantic figures who accompany Wilhelm on his travels. Mignon, an immature child-woman, representing the spirit of poetry, is an androgynous genius figure, while the Harper is the prototype of the oral poet of the heroic past. Mignon turns out to be the daughter of the Harper by incest. Secretly in love with Wilhelm, Mignon dies when his impending marriage is announced. The Harper kills himself, when his life story and transgression are revealed. Finally, there is the life story of a pietist woman, entitled "Bekenntnisse einer schönen Seele" ("Confessions of a Beautiful Soul"), a kind of female Bildungsroman. The "Confessions" are inserted between Books V and VII to introduce the reader to the aristocratic circles Wilhelm is about to enter after his departure from the theatre.

Wilhelm and the reform-minded aristocrats are guided by a secret society, the "Gesellschaft vom Turm" ("Society of the Tower"), which is modelled after the Masonic societies of the 18th century. The "Gesellschaft vom Turm" pronounces Wilhelm's apprenticeship completed, when he has acknowledged his illegitimate son. Functioning as a "machinery of fate," as Schiller called it, the "Gesellschaft vom Turm" is, however, neither omniscient nor omnipotent. Wilhelm is successful in protesting against its guidance in his marriage to the countess, yet he is obedient when he is sent on the road again for further travel. It is part of the irony of the novel that chance and coincidence constantly interfere with the rational planning of the "Gesellschaft vom Turm."

Wilhelm Meister's Apprenticeship had a great influence on the Romantics and the history of the German novel. It provided, so to speak, the blueprint for all subsequent German novels from the 19th to the 20th century. Among the first commentaries on the novel are the correspondence between Friedrich Schiller and Goethe, the letters by Wilhelm von Humboldt and Christian Gottfried Körner, and Friedrich Schlegel's essay "Über Goethes Meister" ("On Goethe's Meister") of 1798. Goethe's novel became the prime model for Romantic irony. It was translated into English by Thomas Carlyle in 1824.

Goethe's sequel to Wilhelm Meister's Apprenticeship was Wilhelm Meister's Travels, published in 1821 and in a revised version in 1829. This novel marks the transition from Bildungsroman to archival novel, a modernist prose narrative that functions as a fictional archive for a multitude of narrative texts. The narrator serves as editor who presents the various texts stored in the archive of the novel to the reader. The basic structure consists of a loose collection of novellas, aphorisms, and factual documents connected by a frame narrative with its own plot. This rudimentary plot shows Wilhelm Meister depositing his son Felix at a boarding school, while he himself is trained as a surgeon. Wilhelm's application to this skill pays dividends as he is able to save his son's life. At the end of the novel, Wilhelm Meister is ready to depart from Europe to follow his wife and the rest of the "Gesellschaft vom Turm" to North America. In his essay "James Joyce und die Gegenwert" [James Joyce and the Present] of 1936, the Austrian novelist Hermann Broch identified Wilhelm Meister's Travels as the prototype of the modernist novel in German literature. Without doubt, Goethe's last novel is, in the words of Jane K. Brown, "an experiment in narrative form" whose achievements could only be appreciated in retrospect of Joyce's Ulysses.

—Ehrhard Bahr

WILLEHALM
Unfinished poem by Wolfram von Eschenbach, written c. 1210–12

Willehalm is an epic poem of almost 14,000 lines written by Wolfram von Eschenbach probably during the second decade of the 13th century, Wolfram von Eschenbach tells us that he acquired a copy of his source from the Landgrave Hermann of Thuringia, to whose death in 1217 he appears to refer towards the end of his work.

Though structural analyses suggest that the work is substantially complete, most critics agree that Wolfram von Eschenbach failed to finish it. Although Wolfram von Eschenbach's source is known to have been a version of a French "chanson de geste," La Bataille d'Aliscans, though not one identical with any extant text, it is nonetheless obvious that Wolfram von Eschenbach treated his source with such liberty that it provides only an unreliable guide to the contents of his intended conclusion. This lack of a final ending, coupled with the fact that the work does not fit comfortably into any recognized medieval genre, hampers attempts to interpret the work, though there is general agreement on a number of themes.

A realistic work with a clear topical relevance, Wolfram von Eschenbach himself claimed that Willehalm, unlike Parzival or Titurel, is true. Though the events it describes are essentially fictitious, its hero can be identified with a cousin of Charlemagne, Count William of Toulouse, who after a military career spent fighting the Arabs in southwest France and Catalonia, founded and withdrew to the monastery of Saint Guilhelm-du-Désert in the valley of Gellone. He was canonized in 1066. The work, written at a time of almost constant war in the Holy Land, owes its topical relevance to its discussion of the Holy Wars and the relationship between Christians and Muslims.

The central question of the work is how to distinguish right and wrong when they are interwoven: how is one to act when traditionally unquestionably virtuous modes of behaviour have clearly evil consequences? This is the quandary in which the hero of the work and his wife find themselves. Willehalm is married to Gyburc, the now baptized former wife of Tibatt, a heathen, and daughter of Terramer, the heathen emperor. In the work what begins as a private feud between two families over a woman, very soon, owing to the religious difference, acquires the public aspect of a crusade. This becomes especially clear when, having suffered initial defeat, Willehalm is forced to seek the support of the emperor to ensure final victory. It is nonetheless a victory that brings little joy since it has to be gained at the expense of Gyburc's family and of a military culture which, in all respects other than religion, is the ethical equal of Christian knighthood.

Wolfram von Eschenbach is undoubtedly an orthodox Christian but, in contrast to his source in which there is rejoicing at the death of every heathen, he clearly questions the justification for the religious slaughter that he describes. The centre of this questioning is the discussions on religion between Gyburc and her father and her speech to the assembled nobles before the final battle. To her father Gyburc accounts for her decision to be baptized, insisting on the essential identity of human and divine love, and asserts her loyalty to the principles of this, in her view, superior religion. To the nobles, however, while not denying this superiority, Gyburc argues from the principle that all men are ''the creatures of God's hand.'' All, even Christians, begin life theoretically as heathens: indeed, some heathens (Elijah, Enoch, Noah, etc.) are saved even without baptism. Unlike the fallen angels, fallen Man has been given the chance of salvation through God's grace, and Gyburc appeals to the assembled Christians to show in victory the same mercy towards the heathen. This is, of course, far from religious toleration, though Wolfram von Eschenbach appears to move somewhat closer to this in Willehalm's magnanimous treatment of the heathen king Matribleiz at the end of the work and his reaction on his chance discovery of the tent in which the fallen heathen kings are laid out. Willehalm, regretting his intrusion, is moved by the observance of alien rites sincerely believed to place the tent under his protection and to ask Matribleiz to arrange the burial of the heathen dead according to their own religion at his own (Willehalm's) expense.

The confrontation between the Christian and Muslim worlds is also presented within one figure in *Willehalm*, that of Rennewart, whom the readers know to be the abducted brother of Gyburc. Angry that his heathen family apparently abandoned him, he nonetheless refuses baptism, arguing that it is not appropriate to him. Even so he is nevertheless a keen supporter of Willehalm's cause and instrumental in ensuring the final victory of the Christians. He is also the knight servitor of Willehalm's niece, Alyze. The French source ends optimistically with the baptism and marriage of Rennewart to Alyze, but Wolfram von Eschenbach presents us with no such ready solution. Rennewart disappears from the unfinished work, and Wolfram von Eschenbach leaves his readers to piece his fate together as best they may.

In view of Wolfram von Eschenbach's evaluation of the heathen world in this work, it is difficult to see how he could have solved the dilemma of Rennewart with a conversion, as he had with the figure of Feirefiz in *Parzival*. It is also notable that even the clearly approaching victory of the Christians at the end of the work does not alleviate its extremely bleak atmosphere of death and mourning. Wolfram von Eschenbach seems to be implying that while there are limited solutions to the problems of individuals, the general problem of the religious war is beyond solution. It is this implication that has led some critics to argue that Wolfram von Eschenbach, unable to find a convincing moral and aesthetic solution to his conundrum, abandoned the work, providing it merely with a laconic temporary or emergency ending.

Willehalm was one of the most popular works of vernacular literature in Germany during the Middle Ages. It was provided in the 1240s with a long continuation by Ulrich von Türheim, which may have started as a separate work on Rennewart, and in the 1260s with

an introduction by Ulrich von dem Türlin describing the events leading up to Wolfram von Eschenbach's work.

—Alan Deighton

WILLIAM TELL (Wilhelm Tell)
Play by Friedrich von Schiller, 1804

''Tell is the kind of folk play you want. The cursed subject matter, with its historical elements thrown together so as to confound poetry, almost drives me to distraction, but the theatrically effective and the popular are present in a high degree,'' Friedrich von Schiller wrote to the dramatist and actor-manager August Wilhelm Iffland (letter of 5 August 1803) as he was about to begin drafting *William Tell*. Eight months later he reported to Christian Gottfried Körner about the first performance, directed by Goethe, who had taken place in Weimar on 17 March 1804: ''Tell makes a greater impact on stage than my other plays . . . I feel that I am gradually gaining control of the theatre'' (letter of 12 April 1804). Ironically, it was to be the last play he completed before his early death.

At one level *William Tell* is an obviously political work. Set in 1291 but written during the Napoleonic occupation of Europe, it celebrates the Swiss yeoman Tell who kills the Austrian governor Gessler, and the farmers of Uri, Schwyz, and Unterwalden who, vowing eternal alliance on the renowned Rütli meadow, set up the Swiss Confederation before ejecting the Austrian usurpers from their land. Using Aegidius Tschudi's *Chronicon Helveticum* and Johannes Müller's *Geschichten Schweizerischer Eidgenossenschaft* as his chief sources, inspired by the arguments of Jean Jacques Rousseau and the aims of the recent French and American revolutions, Schiller champions national unity and democratic freedom. In Switzerland Tell—a figure of international legend rather than an historical personality—soon became the supreme symbol of patriotism. In Germany the play was similarly employed in support of national aspirations from the Wars of Liberation to the aftermath of the Versailles Treaty, although during World War II it was banned from school syllabuses by Hitler. The conservative establishment has sometimes voiced objections to *William Tell*. Goethe, for his Weimar production, deleted the whole episode about the assassination of Emperor Albrecht I by his nephew ''Parricida.'' Iffland made Schiller tone down the more subversive-sounding statements for the first and extremely successful Berlin performance of 4 July 1804, although they were reinstated in the book edition of the same year. Otto von Bismarck condemned Tell as a ''rebel and murderer.'' However, there have also been criticisms from the left. Ludwig Börne, for example, dismissed Tell as a ''philistine'' and ''petty bourgeois,'' while Max Frisch reinterpreted the confederates as provincial bigots and Tell as a terrorist resorting to ''the methods of *El-Fatah*.''

At another level *William Tell* is a philosophical work, dramatizing the ethical and metaphysical notions Schiller developed, under the influence of Immanuel Kant, primarily in his treatises *On the Aesthetic Education of Man* and *On the Naive and Sentimental in Literature*. The original peaceful existence of the Swiss, recalling that of the ancient Greeks, embodied a ''beautiful'' and ''naive'' harmony between duty and inclination, matter and mind, nature and humanity. The Austrian rule destroys this happy condition, which thus becomes a ''sentimental'' (i.e. speculative) ideal. The successful revolt of the Swiss ends in an ''idyll,'' portraying the ideal as once more present in reality. The interaction between Tell and his fellow countrymen reflects a "classical" balance between the individual and the social or between the particular and the general.

Throughout the play the Swiss emphasize that they are fighting only to restore the old patriarchal rights of which the Austrians have deprived them, and that they are applying only the necessary amount of force against a tyranny which has become intolerable. Although a conservative might describe their behaviour as seditious and a radical as reactionary, Schiller himself commends it as revealing a wise moderation which he, like many of his German contemporaries, felt had been abandoned in France as the Revolution turned into the Terror. Tell's innocence is underlined by Gessler's gratuitous acts of provocation, as well as by his own lengthy plea of self-defence and by the contrast with Parricida's self-seeking crime, all of which is designed to demonstrate what Schiller calls "the necessity and legitimacy of self-help in a strictly circumscribed case" (note to Iffland, spring 1804). Nevertheless, Tell's killing of Gessler in an ambush remains morally dubious and Schiller's attempts at justifying it prove dramatically unconvincing.

Translated into numerous foreign languages, a regular standby of the German repertoire for over a century and a half, and a rich quarry of catch-phrases, *William Tell* is less popular today. Combining a large cast, an abundance of violent events, and plenty of pomp and circumstance, culminating, of course, in Tell's shooting the apple off his young son's head, it offers a lively spectacle but is blighted by staginess. The precise geographical references provide some solid foundations, but the blank verse and lyrics are stilted, the characters mere representatives of ideas or communities, and the sets and special effects—noble mountains, grim fortresses, storms, night, rainbow, sunrise—calculatedly allegorical. Swiss virtue is juxtaposed with Austrian villainy in black-and-white fashion. The disjunction of the two main plots, which concentrate alternately on the progress of Tell and on that of the Confederation, creates a sense of epic breadth but tends to dissipate the suspense. Although Ludwig Tieck, for one, paid homage to "a master, a virtuoso, who is no longer baffled by even the most difficult task," Joseph von Eichendorff rightly noted that "the abstract idea of freedom has by no means been transformed into live figures; it is a reflected nature, a rhetoric translated into the rustic with noticeable condescension." For all its theatrical power, *William Tell* is flawed by wooden characterization, sententious dialogue and, above all, a romantic utopianism which glosses over the problems implied in its topic. In his one play with a happy ending, Schiller denies his own tragic insight into the incompatibility of the ideal and the real for the sake of wishful thinking.

—Ladislaus Löb

WINDOWS (Les Fenêtres)
Poem by Charles Baudelaire, 1863

Charles Baudelaire's problematic collection, *Le Spleen de Paris* (*Paris Spleen* or *The Parisian Prowler*), is also known as *Little Poems in Prose*. The author died before its publication and never settled on a definitive title for the collection. Indeed, although the poems' published order was set according to a plan that Baudelaire had drawn up, there is no certainty as to the author's ultimate intentions concerning them. Since they were written for the most part during the final period of his life, after the publication of *The Flowers of Evil*—Claude

Pichois calls the prose poems Baudelaire's "*Fleurs du banal*" ("Flowers of Banality")—at a time when the poet's illness and general deterioration precluded careful editorial attention, there is no saying whether he would ultimately even have published them as a volume. Although Baudelaire oversaw the printing of 20 of them as *Little Poems in Prose* in three issues of *La Presse* (August-September 1862), and publication of six more was planned in a fourth issue (they were rejected, apparently on moral grounds), he himself pointed out in his dedication the fragmentary, unstructured nature of the volume, comparing it to the severed vertebrae of a snake, which can be reassembled in any order desired. Even more than his other works, the poems in *Paris Spleen* can be judged as "provocative" in every sense of the term, perhaps the extreme example of that transmutation of "muck" into "gold" he claimed as the goal of his poetry in the unpublished epilogue to the 1861 edition of *The Flowers of Evil*. In a letter to Sainte-Beuve, Baudelaire spoke of a "disagreeable moral" that typically characterized or defined his prose poems. They can also, however, be seen as a valid response to Rimbaud's later accusation that Baudelaire's "vaunted form [in the verse poems] is shoddy (*mesquin*)": as his quintessential poetic vision freed from the shackles of French classical prosody. As such they were very influential on subsequent French poets, starting with Rimbaud himself in his *Illuminations* and *Une saison en enfer* (*A Season in Hell*).

"Vision" is indeed what "Windows" is primarily about, as the poem's title suggests. Typically, in a collection of works that generally eschew narration, rhythm, and rhyme, though not "music" (as the poet points out in his dedication), this poem is a brief text, almost an essay, in five unequal paragraphs describing a characteristic Parisian situation reminiscent of the one in the poem "Parisian Landscape" ("Paysage") of *The Flowers of Evil*. The speaker looks out of his window, across a "wave of roofs," at another, dark window through which he sees an old woman, and he "remakes [her] story," which he "sometimes recounts to himself, weeping." It could just as well be an old man, the poet says. What matters is not the reality he is looking at, but how he perceives it: the most important thing is that it "helps [him] to live, to feel that [he] is, and what [he] is."

The poem's longest paragraph is the first: a disquisition on windows. To the poet, the darker they are the better; candle illumination from the inside is even more satisfactory: "There is no object more profound, more mysterious, more fruitful, more shadowy, more dazzling than a window illuminated by a candle." Like many of Baudelaire's most important poems, this one is both visionary and *about* poetic vision, both creative and critical. His poet is a "voyant" a seer, as in Rimbaud's celebrated formulation, but he is also, like many residents of the city, a "voyeur." What he is looking at is at the same time matter for penetration and food for creative imagination. As such is both essential, on the one hand, and dispensable or interchangeable, on the other. It is this dichotomy that permitted Baudelaire to write "traditional" poetry on what he considered new—read urban—subjects, as epitomized in the "Parisian scenes" of *The Flowers of Evil*, and helped him to become what he called in his well-known essay on Constantin Guys "the painter of modern life."

Dichotomy, polarity, and paradox, so characteristic of this poem, are the true stuff of Baudelaire's poetics. The "two simultaneous postulations, one toward God, the other toward Satan," of which he speaks in his private diary, "Mort coeur mis à nu" ("My Heart Laid Bare"), inform his thinking and his creation. It is thus we find the hyperbolic series of contradictory adjectives cited above, applied to the windows that compose the poem's subject, contradictorily described somewhat later as a "black or shining hole," as well as the polarity between the poet and the old woman at whom he is looking (and not looking, and who could as well be an old man), whose "history, or rather her legend," he has recast. Liberated from the constraints of traditional form in his final creative period, Baudelaire was enabled here, even more than in his verse poems, to discover and to sing the mystery of the modern city, the poetry of the everyday, the transcendence of the commonplace.

—David Sices

WOES OF WIT (Gore ot uma)
Play by Aleksandr Griboedov, 1825

A satirical verse drama, *Woes of Wit*, is Aleksandr Griboedov's greatest literary achievement. First conceived probably in 1812, it was completed in 1824, and refused publication, but was circulated widely in manuscript. A censored version of the play was published in 1833 in order, according to Alexander Herzen, to remove the attraction of forbidden fruit.

The four decades between the end of the Napoleonic campaign and the Crimean War began in Russia with Tsar Aleksandr I's mystical fantasies of a Holy Alliance of European powers inspired and led by Russia and was succeeded by the repressive and generally stagnant reign of Nicholas I. It was a time also when certain sections of the intelligentsia began to question many of Russia's institutions, her history, and her place in Europe and, more particularly, to attempt to define a specific Russian identity. This was especially true in the arts, notably in literature. While the philosopher Chaadaev was claiming that Russia did not belong to any of the families of Europe, and lived outside the times, the critic Belinskii complained that Russia had no literature at all that it could call its own, or which expressed the distinctive spirit of the Russian people. One way of trying to be "national" would be to free literature from the severe limitations imposed upon it by an almost complete dependence on western literary genres. The onset of Romanticism, when it reached Russia in the 1820s, certainly allowed writers a far greater freedom than was permitted by the traditions of French neo-classicism that had governed Russian literature for almost 50 years.

Woes of Wit is the first successful manifestation of this new mood, both in form but more particularly in content. This is not to say, however, that it does not in many respects conform to much in the French neo-classical comedy of manners; its antecedents, in Molière particularly, are indisputable. It largely observes the three unities of time (24 hours), place (Famusov's house), and action (there are no sub-plots, for example). There is the central love story, albeit unhappy; the plot is based on misunderstandings; and the action is propelled by coincidences. The main characters include certain stock types: Sof'ia, the spoilt young heroine dreaming of finding ideal love; Famusov, the father planning a successful marriage for his daughter; and Liza, the maid with admirable common sense, looking after her charge and fully aware of the faults and pretensions of her superiors. Certain of the names of the characters denoting aspects of their personalities and the aphoristic title of the play all conform to traditions. Yet there are also notable innovations that ensured the play's popularity and its lasting success. There is no fifth act and consequently none of the traditional summing-up of what has happened, nor any authorial moralizing. There is no concentration on the depiction of one particular human vice that the comedy of manners

was expected to portray. The numerous characters are representatives, in the main, of Moscow high society, which gives the play a rather more obvious social realism. The form of the verse freed itself from the dictates of neo-classical traditions. Its basic iambic structure has variable and innovative rhythms, the line length and rhyming schemes are unconventional, and the idiomatic, contemporary, and colloquial language is so striking that it led Pushkin correctly to predict that many of its lines would become proverbial.

In spite of all its unexpectedness in form, versification, and notably in language, it is however the actual content of the play that ensured its popularity and established it as a forerunner of much of what was to follow when Russian literature proved itself the equal of any. There is the familiar background where much of the discussion and many of the characters would be immediately recognizable to contemporaries. All the topical references locate it firmly in Moscow high society—the rebuilding of Moscow after the visitation of Napoleon, the aristocratic English Club, the predominance of French fashions. The characters typify much of post-Napoleonic Russian society: the petty and malicious gossip, the hypocrisy and conservatism where birth, background, rank, wealth, and social connections count for everything and advancement depends solely on sycophancy and nepotism. For Griboedov that society is a philistine and spiritually empty one. More importantly he also suggests an element of growing dissatisfaction among a small section of society. This is memorably represented by Chatskii. The leading protagonist and motivator of what little action there is, he finds everything about the society tedious, conceited, and complacent and wonders why he returned to it. He fearlessly and indignantly inveighs against its manifold shortcomings—this is partly an expression of the revolt of the young against their reactionary elders but it also has a political significance. He is suspected of being a freemason (and might even become a Decembrist) and is condemned as a free-thinker, a dangerous (and mad) man preaching liberty and a deep suspicion of all authority. He soon realizes that there is no place for him there and is forced to run away. Chatskii is also the first in a succession of characters in Russian literature known as "superfluous men" after the term given currency by Turgenev in a short story of 1850. The dissatisfied, upper-class intellectual who is (or regards himself as) superior to the society from which he sprang or in which he finds himself, he can find no appropriate outlet for his talents. He has no roots and no place he can consider home and is condemned to a futile existence and in many cases a pointless death. Chatskii was succeeded by Pushkin's Eugene Onegin, Lermontov's Pechorin, Turgenev's Rudin and many others, but remains in some ways different from them. He is honest and has a capacity for love; his sharp tongue is directed at people fully deserving of his criticisms; he has no cynicism nor professed or real boredom and is notably superior to the society he so despises. And his role on the stage is as challenging to Russian actors as is Hamlet's to English-speaking ones.

—A.V. Knowles

THE WOMAN IN THE DUNES (Suna no onna)
Novel by Abe Kōbō, 1962

The Woman in the Dunes is undoubtedly Abe Kōbō's most important work. Not only is it his best known work, but it also marks a significant development in Japanese fiction. With its combination of documentary realism and a sense of the unreal, this novel is rightly regarded as Abe's first mature work. It succeeded in popularizing a fantastic realism in tune with the Japan of its time, and then in finding an overseas audience.

A man has been declared legally dead, failing to reappear seven years after being reported missing in 1955. This was before the welfare boom under way in the ''present'' of 1962, but at a time when Japan was becoming socially and economically stable. After the first chapter, the narrative joins the man and records his story. He is a teacher and amateur entomologist, visiting a sandy coastal spot half a day's train ride from Tokyo to look for a new species of beetle. He misses the last bus back to the station (or so the locals tell him), and spends the night in a former fishing village inundated by shifting sand dunes. The house where he stays, owned by a young widow, is located in a trough between the dunes, and is reached via a rope ladder. In the morning, the rope ladder is gone and the man realizes he is trapped. As one escape plan after another fails, he gradually becomes familiar with the woman. At the end of the story, she is pregnant by him and has been taken to hospital because of complications. As they take her away, the villagers leave the rope ladder hanging, but the man no longer wants to escape, having become more intimately involved in his new life than he had been in his old one.

The sand metaphor can be read many ways. The title, strictly translated as ''The Sand Woman,'' also leaves open whether ''woman'' means the character in the novel, or a gendered personification of nature as that which flows and needs stabilizing by (male) civilization. As for the man, he describes his obsession with sand in existential terms: ''. . . I rather think the world is like sand. The fundamental nature of sand is very difficult to grasp when you think of it in its stationary state. Sand not only flows, but this very flow is the sand.'' However, he also realizes that he has sought and found the opposite of motion: ''Yes, he remembered, when everything was in ruins some ten years ago, everybody was madly rushing around looking for a liberty where they could stop walking. Should he conclude, then, that this liberty was now giving them indigestion? . . . [H]adn't he himself been drawn to these dunes because he was tired of playing blind man's buff with a phantom? . . . Sand . . . 1/8 mm endlessly flowing . . . it was a reverse self-portrait on negative film of himself, as he clung to a liberty where he could stop walking'' (quoted from English version.)

The Woman in the Dunes combines realism with techniques modeled on the allegories of Kafka and ''inferior'' literary forms such as mysteries, with their emphasis on tension, or science fiction with its striking inventions. Abe leaves behind Leninist concepts of the masses and the didactic approach of even his best 1950s work. Emerging from a cultural movement rooted in proletarianism and trade unions, he now positively espouses the idea of a market-based readership. The sand image had, in fact, been recently used in journalism to attack an alleged capitalist strategy of divide and rule, breaking up the solidarity of the masses and reducing them to individual consumers, like grains of sand.

Certainly, the many possible readings of Abe's imagery can be traced to his goal of writing literature that the reader must interpret in the context of his or her own world, a goal which had been present in Abe's work, for all its dogmatic aspects, almost from the beginning. This characteristic also gave the novel an enormous potential for reception in other cultures. After the success of Teshigawara Hiroshi's impressive film in Cannes (1964), The Woman in the Dunes was published the same year in English, next in Czech, and before 1970 in some twenty languages on both sides of the iron curtain. Abe had

mixed feelings about being identified with a classic work in his own lifetime, but he produced his best fiction in the decade and a half that followed.

—Thomas Schnellbächer

WOMEN OF TRACHIS (Trachiniae)
Play by Sophocles, c. 430–420 BC

Women of Trachis is set in the northern Greek city of Trachis in the district of Mails. It takes its title from the chorus, a group of young women from that town.

The date of the first production of the play is uncertain. Some scholars have placed it very early in Sophocles' career, others very late. Present critical opinion tends towards a relatively late date. The play's theme is not derived from major epic, although some of the material was undoubtedly obtained from Creophylus' lost epic The Capture of Oechalia.

At the start of the play, Deianeira, the wife of Heracles, is full of foreboding about her husband's long absence. When Heracles killed Iphitus, the son of the king of Oechalia in Euboea, the family of Heracles was exiled to Trachis. During the first part of the play it emerges that the period of Heracles' absence is crucial to his ultimate destiny. When he departed, Heracles left with Deianeira information about oracular utterances which stated that he was doomed either to die or to capture Oechalia and win a happy existence. (Later Deianeira reveals a prophecy to the effect that 15 months after his departure from Trachis Heracles will die or else achieve repose.) Hyllus, Heracles' eldest son, arrives with the news that Heracles is campaigning against Oechalia and presently a messenger arrives with good news: Heracles has taken Oechalia and is on his way home, preceded by his herald Lichas. Lichas enters, escorting a group of captive girls among whom is one of striking appearance and demeanour. This is Iole, the daughter of the king of Oechalia, Heracles' personal prize. This acquisition is the true object of his campaign. In his narrative of the events leading to the capture of Oechalia, Lichas conceals this from Deianeira, but the messenger reveals the truth and, under pressure, Lichas is forced to confess. In order to recover Heracles' love, Deianeira resorts to magic means: she sends via Lichas a celebratory gift to Heracles, a robe smeared with blood of the centaur Nessus who, as he died, had assured her that his blood combined with the venom from the Hydra would regain Heracles' affections should he ever lose interest in her.

After the departure of Lichas, Deianeira returns in a state of great anxiety, having seen the destructive powers of the centaur's blood. It has destroyed the rag which she had used when anointing Heracles' robe. Her misgivings are justified. Hyllus arrives with news of the disastrous effects of her gift: the robe clings to Heracles like glue and eats away his flesh. Deianeira retires in silence to the palace accompanied by her son's curse. Shortly after this her nurse reports her suicide. In the final scene of the play we witness Heracles' agonies and hear him beg for release through death. When Hyllus reveals to him that it is the blood of Nessus that has brought about his downfall, he knows that his time has come: he has been informed by an oracle that he would die at the hands of someone already dead. Two things remain: he must be taken to Mount Oeta and cremated alive on a funeral pyre and Hyllus must marry Iole. Hyllus reluctantly agrees to his father's first order (refusing, however, to set light to the pyre), but rejects with horror the proposed marriage. Eventually his father's will prevails and Heracles is carried from the stage to fulfil his destiny.

The ending of the play presents a major and perhaps unresolvable problem of interpretation. As it stands the audience is confronted with unrelieved gloom: Deianeira dead, Hyllus ruthlessly forced into a marriage which is repugnant to him, and Heracles about to die on his pyre. Will the audience, however, supply a happier ending? Will they be aware that the pyre was not the end for Heracles and that it led to his apotheosis? Will they also realize that Hyllus' enforced marriage is part of a divine plan? The story of Heracles' apotheosis on the pyre was almost certainly current at the time when the play was first produced and it might be considered unlikely that the first audience could totally suppress the recollection of it. On the other hand, it might be argued that, given the bleak atmosphere of the end of the play, it is inappropriate that such optimistic thoughts be allowed to intrude. Overall the critical reception of the play has been far from favourable. This may be a reflection of modern critical prejudice: the Greek idea of unity in literature differs from the modern and it is doubtful whether the Greek reader or the Greek audience would have felt, as modern critics have, that the play splits into two halves (the word ''diptych'' has often been used in this connection). In any case a basic unifying factor is Zeus' (inscrutable) purpose: the chorus' words ''and there is nothing of this which is not Zeus'' (i.e. ''Zeus is present in all this'') provide a final motto for the play. There has been a tendency to regard Heracles' behaviour at the end of the play as excessively brutal. Here, perhaps, critics have been seduced into sentimentality by Sophocles' wonderfully sympathetic portrayal of Deianeira.

—David M. Bain

WOYZCEK
Play by Georg Büchner, 1879 (written 1835–37)

Georg Büchner was one of Germany's leading avant-garde drama-tists of the 19th century and his reputation is based largely on the strength of the drama *Woyzeck*. His other avant-garde drama is *Danton's Death* of 1835, dealing with the French Revolution. Büchner himself was involved in German revolutionary events, caused by the July revolution of 1830 in Paris. Because of his authorship of the politically radical pamphlet *Der Hessische Landbote (The Hessian Courier)* of July 1834, Büchner was forced to flee to Strasbourg in March 1835. He finally settled as a political refugee in Switzerland. After completion of his medical studies, Büchner was appointed lecturer of comparative anatomy at the University of Zurich, where he died of typhoid in 1837.

The problem with the text of *Woyzeck* is the fact that there is no authorized version. Written between 1835 and 1837, the collection of manuscripts was first deciphered by Karl Emil Franzos and published in 1878 and 1879 under the title *Wozzek*. All subsequent versions in print are reconstructions on the basis of this manuscript, which comprises some 27 scenes (some editions are divided into 24 or 29 scenes) with no act divisions, and whose sequence cannot be clearly established. For all practical purposes, however, there is a commonly adopted sequence of scenes which serves as both a reading and an acting text. The reader or audience, however, must be aware that there is no final version authorized by Büchner. Even the ending of the play is not fully ascertained. The work was first performed on 8 November 1913 at the Residenztheater in Munich and had a great influence on German naturalist and expressionist drama and a particular influence on Bertolt Brecht and Antonin Artaud. Alban Berg based his opera *Wozzeck* (1921) on the text edited by Karl Emil Franzos in 1878 and 1879. His opera ends with Marie's son being told of his mother's death while continuing to ride his hobbyhorse, uncomprehending. A film version was directed and produced by Werner Herzog in 1979.

Based on an actual murder, committed by a Johann Christian Woyzeck, and the subsequent discussion of his presumed insanity in the forensic medical literature of the 1820s, Büchner's play deals with the murderer as a victim of political and social conditions rather than as a criminal. Franz Woyzeck is a common soldier, barely making a living to support his common-law wife Marie and his son born out of wedlock. Although criticized for his immoral life by his captain and used for medical experiments by a doctor, Woyzeck manages to survive in his working-class environment. His world collapses, however, when he begins to suspect Marie of betraying him with the drum major. Marie and the child have been the centre of Woyzeck's life, and the loss of both lover and child drives him to murder and suicide (unless one of the final scenes is read to suggest a trial and perhaps execution). Woyzeck kills Marie in a fit of jealousy, but this jealousy is based on an ontological tragedy which he understands, even though he cannot articulate it. Woyzeck's world has become uncentred, and he asserts his identity through this violent act, before he is destroyed himself. Superficially a ''working-class tragedy,'' in the words of Victor Price, *Woyzeck* is a drama of metaphysical nihilism. There is no hope of divine intervention or justice, only the awareness of tremendous forces driving man to his self-destruction. Woyzeck cannot control these forces, only grasp their enormity.

—Ehrhard Bahr

Y-Z

YAJUR-VEDA

See THE VEDAS

YERMA
Play by Federico García Lorca, 1934

Yerma, the second play of Federico García Lorca's trilogy of rural Andalusian tragedies, was first performed on 29 December 1934. The author repeatedly termed *Yerma* a work without a plot, the "tragedy of the sterile woman," a concept echoed by the title. Although García Lorca called his heroine Yerma, this is not a woman's name but an adjective normally applied to barren land. Because of García Lorca's numerous affirmations and because Yerma's name foretells her destiny, Spanish critics have deemed the play a tragedy of sterility. The only lack of consensus concerns how general or specific its scope may be: is García Lorca portraying the tragic plight of a sterile individual, or of all sterile women? Or is *Yerma* a political critique, an allegory of national or cultural sterility?

Before completing *Yerma*, García Lorca stated that the play would have four major characters and choruses, "as classical tragedies should," but the four main characters are not easily identifiable. The heroine overshadows all others, so that the most precise description might be "dramatic monologue with supporting cast." Besides the chorus of laundresses and groups of girls and women whose functions are essentially choric, there are anonymous crowds at the *romería* (pilgrimage), the nameless male and female masks, Juan's unnamed spinster sisters, and several men at the shrine who function as anonymous vehicles of fertilization. Only a handful of characters have names: Juan, Yerma's husband; Víctor, the shepherd representing pure, innocent, adolescent love; Yerma's friend, María; and Dolores, a lusty village woman practising white witchcraft. Juan and Víctor, given their importance in Yerma's life, qualify as major characters, although neither spends much time on stage, and Yerma's girlhood companion, María, functions largely as a contrasting portrait of contented maternity, intensifying Yerma's unfulfilled longing.

If *Yerma* is compared to *Blood Wedding*, significant similarities emerge: the marriage of convenience, arranged between families for economic reasons; the triangle of two men and a woman, in which the husband's concern is his honour, while the wife (although caring little for her husband) remains faithful, sacrificing her possible happiness to an empty patriarchal code of marital fidelity. Wifely loyalty, denying the longings of the heart, is a major factor in both tragedies which, without the triumph of duty over desire, might be merely dramas of adultery.

The play ignores the unity of time customary for classical tragedy. When the action begins, Yerma and Juan have been married for two years. In the second *cuadro* (each of the three acts comprises two *cuadros*), Yerma's marriage is three years old. By the second act, it has lasted for more than five years, and an unspecified additional time elapses between the second and third acts, sufficient for Yerma's desperation for a child to drive her to attempt extreme measures (e.g. spells in the cemetery at midnight; a pilgrimage later) in her quest for pregnancy. The play's total duration is some eight to ten years, but the unity and intensity of emotion are undiminished. On the contrary, Yerma's growing frustration builds to a rising crescendo, which peaks with her violent, homicidal outburst in the climactic final scene.

Critics who see *Yerma* simply as a tragedy of sterility (and perhaps even the poet himself) are overlooking two exceptionally significant details that bear upon interpretation. First, Yerma's husband does not want children, and has consciously opted against paternity (there are repeated references to his onanism, and Juan proclaims unmistakably that he does not want children). Second, *vox populi* (represented by groups with choric functions) and individual characters indicate clearly that Yerma is not infertile but unfertilized. Her drama is thus not one of sterility but of thwarted maternal instinct. Yerma's barrenness results not from her own biological incapability but from Juan's refusal to permit her productivity, which has profound hermeneutical implications: Yerma is a victim of patriarchally-imposed restrictions. *Yerma* abounds in imagery or enclosure, and Juan repeatedly confines his wife to the house, bringing his spinster sisters to prevent her sallies. Feminist readings, therefore, might well see *Yerma* as expressing male fears of feminine creative potential.

Unquestionably, García Lorca intended to create a cosmic, mythic dimension, as evinced by his use of music. The song of the washerwoman in Act II is a pagan paean to cosmic force or the god of fertility, a condensation of all that surrounds and frustrates Yerma in the daily lives of others. And like the song of the laundresses, that of the pilgrims (using the religious procession as a cynical veil for the search for new lovers) is used to create effects approaching the orgiastic, which contrast with Yerma's outer restraint and inner conflict. The play also contains Yerma's tender lullaby to her imaginary child, setting the mood for the opening scene, and Víctor's song, asking why the shepherd should sleep alone, which achieves great dramatic effect as it makes almost tangible the remedy to Yerma's barrenness—a solution which her honour prohibits.

Although part of the tragedy results from Juan's masculine fear of feminine weakness and facile corruptibility (notwithstanding Yerma's proud proclamations of her honour and integrity), the heroine is also a product of her patriarchal culture and paternalistic upbringing, the morality of García Lorca's day which decreed that "decent women" should not enjoy sexual relations but accede only for the sake of procreation. Yerma's tacit acceptance of the ancient code making familial honour dependent upon feminine virtue and her obsession with motherhood as the prime purpose for her existence directly reflect women's education in Hispanic countries generally, and Yerma's scrupulous internalization of these cultural imperatives destroys her when the two are brought into conflict by her husband's rejection of fatherhood. Maternity is an option for Yerma only at the price of her honour and she chooses honour at the expense of her own happiness. But Juan is not only quite content with the childlessness that so anguishes Yerma, he imposes yet another conflict upon her, demanding that she accept his sexual advances immediately after hearing that she must forget children forever. Raised to consider sexuality as justified exclusively for procreation, Yerma reacts in violent defence of her honour, killing the man who intended to use her solely for his pleasure. Her final proclamation, "I have killed my child," reveals her awareness of the full consequences of her crime, which has placed motherhood forever beyond her grasp. Clearly, Yerma's tragedy transcends the individual; her plight is that of women not only in Hispanic countries but also in the Arabic world (whose culture was still alive in Andalusia) and all areas where women's productive potential is stifled.

—Janet Pérez

YOU THE ONLY ONE ("Décalques")
Poem by Paul Éluard, 1928

You the only one and I hear the grasses of your laugh
You it is your head which removes you
And from the height of mortal danger
Upon the blurred globes of rain from the valleys
Beneath the heavy light beneath the sky of earth
You bring forth the fall.
The birds are no longer a sufficient refuge
Nor sloth nor fatigue
The recollection of the woods and the fragile streams
In the morning of caprices
In the morning of visible caresses
In the early morning of absence the fall.
The barques of your eyes lose their way
In the lace of disappearances
The chasm is unveiled it is for others to extinguish it
The shadows which you create are not entitled to the night.

"You the only one" was first published in April 1928 in *Cahiers du Sud* as "Décalques" ["Tracings"] and was also included in the poem-sequence "Firstly" in *L'Amour la poésie* [Love Poetry] in 1929. It is typical of Paul Éluard's surrealist love poems, combining simple diction with powerful and bewildering imagery aimed at disrupting perception.

An initial explosive image—"the grasses of your laugh"—immediately grasps the reader's attention but threatens to drown the rest of the poem. Since the subsequent lines continue to provoke disarray, it is tempting to detect a blueprint, commonsense image "behind," so to speak, the cluster of surrealist ones. A naturalistic picture can be reconstructed—a woman standing on a rainy, windswept hilltop. However, finding naturalistic solutions implies that the poem is a mere puzzle, whereas the commonsense image has no more preeminence than the shifting movements of objects. The "real" is only part of the picture.

The combination of "grasses" and "laugh" sets in motion a play of substitution between two elements associated with woman, the principle of identity in Éluard's love poetry. The missing term is "ripple": the grasses ripple like her laughter, or her laughter causes the grasses to ripple. A "feminine landscape" is intimated, and the sentiment is one of traditional Petrarchism yet transformed by the extraordinary linguistic compression of the image, an economy maintained in line 2, where an absent, unspecified hat may have blown from the woman's head. The dislocation of "your head which removes you" suggests that she has "laughed her head off" in the wind.

The Surrealist revolution in perception was concentrated on ordinary objects. Perhaps more than any other Surrealist, Éluard experimented with a simple diction. In "You the only one" this comprises

the familiar ingredients of daily life (birds, grasses, light, woods, eyes, rain), words with pastoral, even Edenic associations that prevail in other non-concrete words (absence, the fall, disappearances). One critic (Jean-Charles Gateau) "explains" the poems by citing direct pictorial influences (e.g. Max Ernst, Giorgio de Chirico, Yves Tanguy). However, this conflation of the visual with the literary is inadequate. Éluard is not a narrowly mimetic poet, even if imitative gestures can be found in his language. Surrealist paintings frequently play with scale or position, and in "You the only one" each raindrop is a world, with "sky or earth" a stunning reversal where each is filled with the other. The "of" phrase here, as with "grasses of your laugh," establishes a confusion as to agency, launching infinite oscillations and interpretations. The woman is a Surrealist Eve figure, a morally unindicted vessel for the Fall. The marvellous (a surrealisation of the notion of grace) enters with the converging worlds of dream and reality.

Jean Paulhan argues in *Les Fleurs de Tarbes (The Flowers of Tarbes)* that writers live in fear of cliches, and best outwit them when they engage with them directly. "Fragile streams" is a fine example of Éluard practising this. By avoiding a word like "tinkling," "fragile" works by association, substituting cause for effect, and transforming sound into touch. The same procedure applies in the "lace of disappearances" where the Romantic cliché of lace for foam is both used and avoided, for the sea is not mentioned, and extinguishing a chasm introduces another absent notion, fire.

Much critical attention has been rightly devoted to the elaborate myth of seeing in Éluard's work. Line 11 is only partly voyeuristic. The image is of light made up of touching particles, tangibility rendered visible and unifying the senses. "The barques of your eyes" is another peculiar image. Perhaps there is a similarity between the curve of hulls and that of eyes; or maybe the boats are reflected in the eyes. The world for Éluard takes place inside the eyes: external reality is not strangely "out there," but mystically imbricated within the sensory apparatus of human beings.

In the final elusive proposition a strange logic pertains: Woman/Light creates shadows; these shadows are privileged, "caused" by the Woman and do not therefore belong in the world of night (there can be no shadows where there is darkness/Woman's absence).

A number of other features contribute to the sense of universal predication in the poem. Éluard used punctuation increasingly rarely, and the near absence of it in "You the only one" strengthens the syntactic ambiguity both at the line-end and within the line: the valleys are or are not beneath the light and the Woman or the Light, or both, are beneath the sky/earth. This procedure in Éluard is a stylistic analogue for the continuity and fluidity of sensory experience. The dismantling of perceptions is further compounded by the use of prepositions ("upon" and "beneath"). There are no—or there are only—transitional states in this poetry of immediacy. The syntactic structures of the poem may be viewed as an egalitarian attitude directed on to language itself and sweeping aside the hierarchical meaning of clauses and subclauses. A similar attitude can be witnessed in Éluard's reliance on the sonorities of assonance, consonance, alliteration, internal, sometimes vertical rhyme, and often verbatim repetition (see ll. 10 and 11), all exploited to produce a sense of full interconnectedness. Lastly enumeration, with each object simultaneously distinct and subsumed by the next one, rehearses Éluard's dictum that "Everything is comparable to everything else." This poem attests eloquently to that conviction.

—Roll Venner

YOUNG TÖRLESS (Die Verwirrungen des Zöglings Törless)
Novel by Robert Musil, 1906

Young Törless was a pioneering work of German modernism, often considered as one of the earliest examples of literary expressionism. It was fashionable in its subject matter, dealing with young people, and contains many of the ingredients of turn-of-the-century ''decadent'' Vienna: an emphasis on sensuality, the release of suppressed sexual energies, the crisis of identity, a concern with problems of perception generally and, in particular, with the failure of language as a means of expression and communication, and a playing off of the aesthetic against the moral individual. Formally it foreshadows later developments in its tendency to form a hybrid between narrative and essay in intellectualizing the novel form. This presents the reader with a certain difficulty, as his/her intention will inevitably be split between the interest in the realistic plot and the intellectual perspectives linked to it.

The story deals with the eroticism of adolescent love between boys in a military boarding school on the periphery of the Austro-Hungarian empire. Young Törless, Robert Musil's protagonist, is drawn into the events surrounding a fellow pupil, Basini, who is of an almost feminine beauty and, in a way similar to Tadzio in Thomas Mann's *Death in Venice*, represents a temptation towards self-dissolution. Having committed a small offence, the morally weak Basini finds himself at the mercy of his fellow pupils who exploit the situation. They use him as the guinea-pig in their experiments, exploring the limits to which manipulation and torture of a fellow human being can be taken, all under the pretext of punishing and reforming him. This aspect of the novel has been taken to be prophetic of later historical events in Germany, and looking back from the 1930s, Musil himself declared that it depicted ''today's dictators in nucleo.''

Törless himself seeks in vain to maintain the distance of an observer who is merely concerned with finding an answer to his burning question: what happens in Basini? How can his rational and moral self cope with such moral debasement, how can it maintain its identity under the onslaught of the irrational? The confusions at this level are specific to the state of adolescence. Musil pinpoints that terrifying sense of exposure to the unknown forces of sexuality, which are a deep threat to the adolescent's existence. While Törless falls under the spell of Basini's sensuality, he realizes what his observations of Basini had already made evident: that the uncanny is indeed a matter of perspective, and that what looks threatening when seen from a distance loses its terror when entering into the closer sphere of our experience. The homoeroticism of Basini's sensuality, so Musil maintains, is merely accidental, connected with the material that happened to be at hand, and which obviously had an autobiographical basis. Models for the fictional characters have been painstakingly identified by his biographer.

The dangers inherent in adolescence are summed up in images of doors and bridges. While Basini appears to have fallen through a trapdoor, Törless in the end emerges with painfully acquired knowledge, morally still totally uncommitted but with the wisdom of the aesthete whose sense of life has been deepened and enriched by the experience. The developmental differential is measured in Törless's relationship to his mother. Typical for an initiation story, it starts with his separation from her. For him she is an untouchable figure, belonging to an impeccable formal society, while in contrast the local prostitute, Božena, is the embodiment of crude sexuality, an uncanny and destructive temptation. At the end Törless is taken home by his mother, and it is made clear that he has found a bridge over the gulf that separated the only two female figures in the novel.

The other main focus of the novel is an epistemological one, a complex of ideas reflecting the crisis of sensibility at the turn of the century. Musil burdens his adolescent hero with intellectual perspectives such as the rejection of a system of perception and categorization of the world, and a deep language scepticism, ideas which around the same time were also formulated by Musil's contemporaries Rilke and Hofmannsthal. The experiences which lead Törless into his musings are centred around ''epiphanies'' (to use Joyce's term) which leave him trembling and yet triumphant. His ''confusions'' on this level are concerned with the recognition that concepts like ''the infinite'' have two faces: a rational one, producing results in mathematical calculations, and an irrational one, if one is unguardedly exposed to their unmitigated force, e.g. when staring straight into the infinite blueness of the sky.

Törless finds that he can enter into a more intimate communication with the world of objects. His ''secret'' knowledge gives him a sense of superiority over his friends and teachers. The theme of the ''other'' way of approaching the world, the contemplative, mystical way as opposed to the purely rational, aggressive, and scientific one, will remain the dominant preoccupation throughout Musil's work.

Where this novel is concerned the reader will have to decide whether he can credit the young artist Törless with the weight of these reflections or whether they have to be attributed to the (at times) intrusive older narrator. The reader may also wonder whether the author himself did not fall prey to the organic fallacy when he attempted to link this epistemological superstructure as it were naturally to the more realistic psychology of his adolescents, and pretended to solve both at one stroke at the end of the book.

—Lothar Huber

ZADIG
Novella by Voltaire, 1748

Although not the first tale by Voltaire to be written, *Zadig* was the first to appear in print, in 1748. It inaugurated his career as a *conteur*, for which he is now best known, and it remains one of his finest stories. As its full title *Zadig; ou, la Destinée* makes clear, it is concerned with the theme of Fate, as befits a work with an ''Asian'' setting (actually, Babylon). But in a letter of the time Voltaire makes clear that by Fate he had meant Providence; and Providence is bound up with personal happiness. More specifically, does one guarantee being happy by being virtuous? Our hero Zadig thinks so at first: ''Zadig, having great wealth and therefore friends, possessed of good health, a pleasing face, a just and moderate mind, a heart both loyal and noble, thought that he could be happy.'' The story is made up of a series of episodes in which he is regularly thwarted in this desire. He comes to realize that mankind is more frequently disposed to evil than to good. On his way through life he is beset by judicial corruption, sectarian dogmatism, envy, jealousy, deceit. In particular, the Court at Babylon is full of vile, fickle creatures who indulge in endless backbiting; Voltaire pays off old scores from the humiliations he had recently suffered at Louis XV's court in Versailles.

Things get steadily worse, until Zadig is forced to flee for his life from Babylon. By now he is in love with Queen Astarté and loved by her, but her jealous husband Moabdar has decided to exact his revenge. Alone at night under the stars, he feels despair at the human condition: ''men as they really are, insects devouring each other on a tiny atom of mud.'' But the rest of the universe is magnificent: ''vast globes of light'' pursuing their course in an ''inimitable order.'' Zadig oscillates between contemplation of the sublime and the pain of his present situation. Such is the duality of perspective that will remain right through to the end of the *conte*.

Zadig's fortunes change and he is reunited temporarily with Astarté, but only to lose her forever, as he thinks, to the deceit of his rival Itobad. He begins to question Providence and to wonder whether ''everything was ruled by a cruel fate that oppressed the good and aided the green knights [i.e. the Itobads].'' The story opens out onto a broader philosophical terrain. Enter the hermit Jesrad, a sage figure who offers to console Zadig in his misfortunes. As they travel along, Jesrad performs a series of increasingly mystifying actions. They stay at four different houses. The first host is generous; Jesrad steals a magnificent golden bowl from him. The second is a miser; Jesrad gives him the bowl. The third is a civilized and courteous man; Jesrad burns his house down. Finally they stay with a widow, kindly and virtuous, who sends her 14-year-old nephew the next day to accompany them safely over a dangerous bridge; Jesrad seizes the boy and drowns him in the river beneath. To Zadig's protestations of mounting bewilderment, the hermit responds with some semblance of persuasiveness, at least for the first three (the first and second were moral lessons to correct respectively the sins of vanity and avarice; the third host was to learn that a vast fortune lay concealed beneath his house). But Zadig finds the murder quite unacceptable and condemns Jesrad for his wickedness. Jesrad invokes a version of Leibnizian Optimism. Zadig is judging from imperfect knowledge. The world necessarily contains a proportion of evil, but everything has a purpose. Besides, the universe proclaims the wisdom, the infinite variety and the power of God and his creation. Zadig is counselled to give up arguing against that which must be adored. He replies: ''But . . .''; at which point Jesrad, who has already changed from a hermit into a majestic angel, takes wing for the farthest heavens, with the parting injunction to Zadig to head for Babylon. Zadig follows this advice, which is crowned with total success. He marries Astarté, becomes king, and inaugurates an era of sweetness and light.

To what extent, then, is one to take Jesrad at face value? Can anything justify the murder of a child? Yet we live in a majestic universe, awesomely rich and beautiful. Voltaire is confronting the problem that will never cease to haunt him: evil undoubtedly exists, but so does God with equal incontrovertibility, as the cosmic harmony demonstrates. Whatever Zadig's doubts, his final attitude towards Jesrad is one of submission on his knees; and Jesrad's final message reads the future correctly, permitting Zadig to fulfil his destiny as a philosopher-ruler. Ultimately, it seems, human freedom has some meaning, human wisdom can lead to happiness. Jesrad may be incomprehensible, but he is not a mere figure of fun as Pangloss will be in *Candide*. Zadig becomes a champion of truth, like his great forbear Zoroaster. We shall however continue to live in a world of misfortune and misanthropy. The *conte* bears ample witness to the complexity of Voltaire's ironic stance about the human predicament.

But *Zadig* is not just a story of ideas. It is also a delightful fantasy, though this is often overlooked in favour of the philosophical aspects. The work is a succession of brief tales, told with pungent gusto and in an air of parody-heroic romance which gives the *conte* its particular flavour. Set in the marvellous kingdom of Arabia, it ironically

undercuts the fabulous in order to convey moral and philosophical truths about the real world that we actually inhabit.

—Haydn Mason

ZAZIE (Zazie dans le métro)
Novel by Raymond Queneau, 1959

Zazie, to François Mauriac's loudly voiced indignation, was Raymond Queneau's biggest commercial success, elicited the most flattering review from Roland Barthes, and has been enjoying ever growing critical recognition in recent years. The unforgettable central character is a brat who knows how to get her own way, yet fails to fulfil her most cherished ambition, which is to ride on the Paris underground. Yet, like all Queneau's books, *Zazie* is above all about the adventures of language.

Queneau started work on the novel in 1945, and right from the start the underground played a major part in it. A Norman by birth, Queneau was soon conquered by Paris and the capital in many ways fuelled his imagination. Abandoned plans for the novel included having the 12-year-old a pickpocket living underground with her tough granny. In the published version, Zazie's discovery of life takes place above ground and not within the bowels of the city. And the grandmother is replaced by Uncle Gabriel, whose sexuality, not surprisingly, fascinates Zazie. Gabriel, who is first introduced as a man with the physique of a bouncer and fastidious tastes for the dainty things of life, is a marginal. He works as a performer in a gay nightclub and lives with the ethereal and soft-spoken Marceline. The end of the book makes a point very dear to Queneau's heart, as appearances are shown to be unreliable and deceptive.

Other characters in the book have an unsettled identity. The strangest of them all is probably Pédro-Surplus, who reappears under the guise in turn of Trouscaillon, Bertin Poirée, and finally Aroun Arachide. Unclassifiable and perhaps demonic, Pédro-Surplus could be interpreted as Queneau's modern version of Proteus, a being whose essence is metamorphosis.

Zazie herself is somewhat androgynous and at all levels ambivalent. A very believable teenager with her handful of imperious obsessions and appetites, she is unlike any child figure to be found in earlier literature, To be sure there are precious few memorable portrayals of female children in Western literature, but Queneau does not win by default. Zazie comes to life because of her passion for blue jeans, her lies, her sharp instinct to call everybody's bluff, and her sadistic ''Lolitishness.'' Zazie became a type in the French literary landscape of the 1960s. In the middle of the decade Françoise Sagan encouraged fashion designer Yves Saint-Laurent to publish his delightful illustrated story of *La Vilaine Lulu* [Nasty Lulu], which tells of the more than impish practical jokes the ugly and outspoken ten-year-old of the title is fond of playing on smaller children and their helpless mothers. It is not after all a coincidence that Queneau finally brought out *Zazie* at the outset of a decade that discovered, or rediscovered, the very young.

Zazie is never afraid to let people have a piece of her mind, and ''mon cul'' (my arse) is her most common way of finishing a sentence. Queneau displays great flair in his use of offensive slang. His characters call each other names throughout the novel, but the effect is more than realism and local colour. He delights in the robust inventiveness to be found in the terms of abuse created by streetwise characters.

Another character whose language is unforgettable is Turandot's parrot Laverdure. If on the one hand uneducated people can come up with gutsy verbal creations worthy of a Céline, on the other hand they sometimes repeat each other in the most ludicrous ways. Laverdure is a yardstick by which Queneau measures human verbal behaviour. Queneau playfully asks, is human language after all so much less mechanical than Laverdure's?

Phonetic spelling is another trademark of Queneau's output. In this particular novel, it cleverly reinforces the theme of disguise: words that have been run together acquire a puzzling appearance on the page, indeed they become as mysterious as Gabriel and Marceline. Queneau likes to play on the gender as well as on the national origin of words. In his interviews Queneau always insisted on the spontaneous, unsystematic origin of his zaniest verbal creations. Phonetic distortions, or rather restitutions, are not consistent but only sprinkled to highlight a situation, speed up a comic scene to a climactic ending, or camouflage a more serious reflection upon contemporary vernacular French as a literary medium.

Queneau's puns may be less famous than Jacques Lacan's, but they stem from the same belief in the deepest layers of meaning in word-games. Queneau underwent several years of psychoanalysis during his difficult years as a peripherally Surrealist maths-buff, and his thorough knowledge of Freud's writings may have influenced his use of puns in his fiction and poetry. When he indulges in what reads like gratuitous punning, it is only as an extra tease for the expert reader.

Queneau's style does not ape popular speech. It is richly rhetorical and draws on all the resources of the French language. *Zazie* ranks as one of Queneau's major achievements because childhood and language were the two things his sensitivity captured best.

—Pascale Voilley

ZONE
Poem by Guillaume Apollinaire, 1913

"Zone" is the threshold poem that leads the reader into *Alcools*. The term "alcools" suggests both "intoxication" and "distillation," and the volume encompasses all the passions of a volatile man, while each poem tries to express the quintessence of a moment. Every such moment speaks true, engaging the poet's whole being until it evaporates, and is replaced by another equally true and equally transient. Guillaume Apollinaire remarked in 1913 that each of his poems commemorates an event in his life "and generally with sadness." Certainly the dominant mood in "Zone" is melancholy, and the joyous moments are all irretrievably past. There is also little of the wry humour that can be found elsewhere in *Alcools*. But "Zone" is rich in something that Apollinaire considered to be both the source and the most effective expression of creativity: surprise. Surprise is generated by unexpected juxtapositions; it forces us to took at the world with new eyes. Like the Surrealists, Apollinaire dislocates the everyday world, offering us dreamlike images, sometimes sinister, sometimes comic, always moving and mysterious. He is at his most resonant when he is melancholy, but he had an appetite for life and a deep curiosity that show themselves in his use of rare or invented words, his delight in obscure legends, his experiments with form and

metre, his interest in modern art, and his love of both the natural world and the city. He is an eminently receptive creature. Particularly clear in "Zone" is his compassion for the lost souls on the margins of society. His own experience of hopeless love and of stateless and rootless wandering taught him sympathy for the city's outcasts, and for all those displaced persons who trailed across the map of Europe in the years before World War I, bearing with them, as he says in "Zone," their faith, their hopes, and their "unreal" crimson eiderdowns, as he carries with him his own burden, which seems equally unreal: his heart, his dreams, and his words.

"Zone" is written in free verse, rhythmical rather than metrical, but modulating occasionally into regular metre: lines 60–70, which describe the formal procession of the birds of the air, are appropriately written in classical alexandrines. The poem is organized by its rhyming couplets, rather than by stanzas, with the rhyme sometimes replaced by assonance. The method is apt: the poem is a long meditation which follows the poet's wanderings in Paris, from early morning to the following dawn. The sections are irregular, their length and shape determined by the shifts in the poet's attention, the movement of his thought, and the strength of his feeling. There is no punctuation in *Alcools*. Apollinaire believed that the rhythm and the lay-out of the text should shape our reading. If at times we hesitate over the placing of a pause, that is part of the poet's intention, for it opens up possibilities, where punctuation would fix and limit meaning, and it encourages us to read with closer attention.

"Zone" begins tentatively with a sequence of three single lines. In the first and third of these, the poet speaks of himself in the familiar second person: "tu es las de ce monde ancien. . . ,'' "Tu en as assez. . .'' ("you are tired of this ancient world," "You have had enough"), while the second line conjures up a familiar landmark in a startling image: "Shepherdess, O Eiffel Tower, the flocks on the bridges are bleating this morning." The power of that line depends on a paradox: it brings the modernity of the city into the poem, but does so with an image drawn from the pastoral tradition, turning the stream of traffic into a flock of sheep; later, the poet's solitude is emphasized by the "herds of lowing buses" driving past him. A group of three lines next introduces the theme of religion, which seems to the poet more modern than the city, because it is timeless. Yet all the poet's love of Paris appears in his picture of a sunlit street, and all his feelings for people whose lives are ruled by the factory siren that groans and the "rabid clock" that "barks." Apollinaire here transmutes the everyday—shop-signs, posters, newspaper headlines—into a world that hovers between vision and nightmare. The movement gathers pace as he recalls his childhood and the role of religion in his life. A lyrical passage links the modern and the ancient, imagining the risen Christ as an aviator, flying high, followed by an aeroplane, escorted by figures from Greek legend and Jewish and Christian tradition who ascended the heavens, greeted by all the birds of nature and of poetry, real or imaginary, the larks and the phoenix. Back on earth, the poet is alone in the crowd, grieving for lost love, regretting the innocent faith of former centuries which was also the faith of his childhood, and mocking his inability to seek consolation in religion. He is a child of his century, doomed to ironic self-awareness and inhibition. The poem begins to fragment as the poet, again addressing himself in the second person, recalls images from his past ("You're in the garden," "Here you are in Rome"), moving restlessly from the south of France to Prague, from Rome to Amsterdam. Summing up his life, he links past and present, second person and first, in six anguished lines:

> Tu as fait de douloureux et de joyeux voyages
> Avant de t'apercevoir du mensonge et de l'âge
> Tu as souffert de l'amour à vingt et à trente ans
> J'ai vécu comme un fou et j'ai perdu mon temps
> Tu n'oses plus regarder tes mains et à tous moments je
>   voudrais sangloter
> Sur toi sur celle que j'aime sur tout ce qui t'a épouvanté.

> (You made both painful and happy journeys
> Till you learned of the existence of lies and of age
> You suffered in love at twenty and at thirty
> I have lived like a madman and wasted my time
> You no longer dare to look at your hands and at every
>   moment I want to weep
> For you for the woman I love for everything that has
>   appalled you.)

But at this point the poet's eye turns outwards again, and he speaks "with tears in your eyes" of the emigrants in transit whom he has seen in the Gare Saint-Lazare, exhausted Jews on their way across the Atlantic; and of those who decide to stay in Paris, where they live like exiles in dark hovels. The image recalls the description, a few lines earlier, of the poet himself in the Jewish quarter of Prague, "like Lazarus terrified of the daylight": resurrection and rescue are painful, profoundly disturbing experiences. Sitting in the garden of an inn near Prague, he observes "instead of writing your story in prose / The beetle that sleeps in the heart of the rose." Prague is the setting of his tale of the Wandering Jew, "Le Passant de Prague" ("The Passer-by of Prague," in *L'Hérésiarque et Cie*). Images of alienation and exile, of being doomed to wander and unable to die, come together in "Zone" and make of the poet a modern Wandering Jew.

Now the poem becomes increasingly fragmented, a sequence of single lines offering snapshots, in the present tense, of bars, cafés, and brothels where the poet has felt both his own humiliation and the pitiable humanity of the poor and the degraded. As dawn approaches he is still alone, listening to the milk-churns clanking in the street, gulping down a last raw drink ("Cet alcool brûlant") as he has swallowed the painful events of his life, which like alcohol both stimulate and destroy. The poem ends as he turns towards home, to sleep among his collection of native fetishes and masks (like his friend Picasso, he was fascinated by African artefacts). They are, he says, the Christs of another, lesser religion, but powerful symbols of hope none the less. They take us back to the poem's beginning, yearning again for religion's power to console. But the poet is no longer a child, and he is lost in a relativist limbo: the word "zone" once denoted the area around the walls of Paris that was neither city nor countryside. He desperately needs to believe in what his intellect cannot accept; love eludes him, memory mocks him, and he is afraid of the very renewal that he desires. In the final lines of the poem, the sun rises in a blood-red sky, evoking a dead body with its throat cut: "Soleil cou coupé." It would be an unbearable desolation were it not that the poem makes a persuasive harmony out of its discords. Free verse alternates with traditional metre to mirror the problematical coexistence of past and present, and the poem achieves a balance that softens its final despair.

The last poem in *Alcools*, "Vendémiaire" (the name of the harvest month in the Revolutionary calendar), describes another walk through Paris, from evening to dawn; it lacks the magic of "Zone" because it explicitly claims a victory that in "Zone" is slowly and painfully achieved, so that the reader lives through it: the dawning awareness that the poem's creation is the one consolation that endures.

—Norma Rinsler

NOTES ON ADVISERS AND CONTRIBUTORS

ADAMSON, Donald. Visiting fellow, Wolfson College, Cambridge. Formerly chairman of the Board of French Examiners, University of London; fellow of the Royal Society of Literature; fellow of the Institute of Linguists. Author of *The Genesis of "Le Cousin Pons,"* 1966, and *Illusions Perdues*, 1981. **Essays:** "L'Abandonée"; *Cousin Bette*; *Eugénie Grandet*; Théophile Gautier; Edmond and Jules Goncourt; *Lost Illusions*; "The Necklace"; Blaise Pascal; *Three Musketeers*.

AHMED, Ali (deceased). Writer of novels, short stories, plays, and poetry. Author of the novels *Twilight in Delhi*, 1940, *Ocean of Night*, 1964, and *Rats and Diplomats*, 1985, and of *Ghālib: Two Essays* (with Alessandro Bausani), 1969, and *The Golden Tradition: An Anthology of Urdu Poetry*, 1973. Translator of the poetry of Ghālib and others. **Essay:** Asadullah Khan Ghālib.

AINSWORTH, Peter F. Senior lecturer in French, University of Manchester; general editor, with D.J. Adams, of *Manchester French Monographs*. Author of *Jean Froissart and the Fabric of History*, 1990, and Froissart's *Chronicles* (with others) for *Lettres Gothiques* series (Livre de Poche). **Essay:** Jean Froissart.

AIZLEWOOD, Robin. Instructor, School of Slavonic and East European Studies, University of London. **Essays:** "About This"; *A Hero of Our Time*; "Incantation by Laughter".

ALEXANDRONI, Margareta. Lecturer in Norwegian, University College, London. Freelance teacher of Norwegian and translator; teacher of translation skills at University of Surrey. Author of 42 short stories, published in magazines throughout Scandinavia. **Essay:** *Kristin Lavransdatter*.

ALLEN, Roger. Professor of Arabic language and literature in the Department of Asian and Middle Eastern Studies at the University of Pennsylvania; Chair of the language advisory committee of the School of Arts and Sciences; co-director of the International Studies Program at the Wharton School and the School of Arts & Sciences.

ANDERSEN, Hans Christian. Lector in Danish, University of Newcastle upon Tyne. **Essay:** Hans Christian Andersen.

ANDERSON, J.K. Professor of classical archaeology, University of California, Berkeley. Author of *Ancient Greek Horsemanship*, 1961, *Military Theory and Practice in the Age of Xenophon*, 1970, and *Xenophon*, 1974. **Essay:** Xenophon.

ANDREWS, D.J. Lecturer in German, University of Glasgow. Co-editor of *The French Revolution: German Responses* (special issue of *Strathclyde Modern Language Studies*), 1991. **Essays:** *Michael Kohlhaas*; August Wilhelm and Friedrich von Schlegel; *Spring Awakening*.

ANUSHIRAVANI, Alireza. Assistant professor of comparative and English literature, Shiraz University, Iran. Formerly assistant director, Center for Renaissance Studies, Newberry Library, Chicago; visiting lecturer, University of Illinois, Urbana-Champaign; instructor, Parkland College; instructor, Shiraz University. Author of *Conversation with Modern Persian Poets: Farrokhzād, Shāmlū, Akhavān-i Sālis* (with Professor Girdhari Tikku), and articles in *Literature: Afro-Asian Perspectives*, *Middle East Studies Association Bulletin*, and *Turkish Studies Association Bulletin*. **Essays:** Farid al-Din Attār; *The Conference of Birds*; *The Rose Garden*; *The Rubaiyat*; Muslih-al-Din Sa'di.

ARCHIBALD, Brigitte Edith Zapp. Associate professor, North Carolina Agricultural and Technical State University. Author of *Women Writers of the Renaissance and Reformation*, 1987, *Women Writers of the Seventeenth Century*, 1989, and *An Encyclopedia of Continental Women Writers*, 1991. **Essays:** Annette von Droste-Hülshoff; Jeremias Gotthelf; Eduard Mörike; Johann Nepomuk Nestroy; Christoph Martin Wieland.

ARNOLD, A. James. Professor of French, University of Virginia, Charlottesville. Author of *Paul Valéry and His Critics: A Bibliography*, 1970, *"Les Mots" de Sartre*, 1973, *Modernism and Negritude: The Poetry and Poetics of Aimé Césaire*, 1981, and Valéry entry in *A Critical Bibliography of French Literature*, vi, 2, 1980. Editor of *Caligula (1941)* by Camus, 1984. **Essays:** Albert Camus; Jean-Paul Sartre.

ARROWSMITH, William. Former professor of classics at: University of Texas, Austin; Boston University; Yale University, New Haven, Connecticut; Johns Hopkins University, Baltimore; New York University; and Emory University, Atlanta. General editor of *The Greek Tragedy in New Translation*. Translator of works by Petronius, Euripides, Aristophanes, and Cesare Pavese. Editor of *Image of Italy*, 1961, *The Craft and Context of Translation* (with Roger Shattuck), 1962, and *Five Modern Italian Novels*, 1964.

ASHBROOK, B. Instructor, department of German, University of Glasgow. **Essays:** *The Castle*; *The Physicists*; *The Trial*.

ASPLEY, Keith. Senior lecturer in French, University of Edinburgh; member of the editorial board of *Aura*. Author of *Myth and Legend in French Literature*, 1982, *André Breton the Poet* (with Peter France), 1989, and *Poetry in France* (with David Bellor and Peter Sharratt), 1992. **Essays:** "Alchimie du verbe"; *Free Union*; *The Infernal Machine*; Alphonse de Lamartine; *Mad Love*; *Ode to Charles Fourier*; "Spleen".

ATKINS, Stuart. Emeritus professor of German, University of California, Santa Barbara; president of the Modern Language Association of America, 1972. Author of *The Testament of Werther in Poetry and Drama*, 1949, *Goethe's Faust: A Literary Analysis*, 1958, and *The Age of Goethe*, 1969. Editor and translator of *Goethe: Faust I and II*. Editor of *The German Quarterly*, 1952–57, and *Heinrich Heine Werke*, 1973–78. **Essay:** *Faust*.

ATKINSON, Howard. **Essay:** Friedrich de la Motte Fouqué.

AVERY, Peter. University lecturer, Cambridge University; director of the Cambridge Faculty of Oriental Studies Middle East Centre.

Author of *Modern Iran*, 1965. Translator, with John Heath-Stubbs, of *Thirty Poems of Hafiz of Shiraz*, 1952, and *The Rubaiyat of Omar Khayyam*, 1979. **Essays:** Omar Khayyam; Jalalu'd-Din Rumi.

AVELING, Harry. Associate professor of Indonesian/Malay, La Trobe University, Melbourne, and adjunct professor of Southeast Asian Literature, Ohio University. Critic and translator of Indonesian and Malay literatures: most recent works include *Secrets Need Words: Indonesian Poetry 1966–1998* (2001), and *Shahnon Ahmad: Islam, Gender and Power* (2000). Awarded Anugerah Perkembangan Sastera Esso-Gapena by the Federation of Malay Writers' Associations in 1991 for contributions to the international recognition of Malay and Indonesian literatures. **Essays:** Chairil Anwar; *The Fugitive*; Dorothea Rosa Herliany; Pramoedya Ananta Toer.

BAHADUR, K.P. Administrator with the Uttar Pradesh Government, India. Author of more than 50 books including works on philosophy, sociology, and history, and novels, books for children, and translations. **Essays:** *Bhagavadgītā*; *Mahābhārata*; *Rāmāyana*; *Upanishads*; *The Vedas*.

BAHR, Ehrhard. Instructor, department of Germanic languages, University of California. **Essays:** Nelly Sachs; *Wilhelm Meister*; *Woyzeck*.

BAILEY, Alison. University of London.

BAILEY, D.R. Shackleton. Pope professor of Latin language and literature, Harvard University, Cambridge, Massachusetts; editor of *Harvard Studies in Classical Philology*. Author of *Propertiana*, 1956, *Cicero*, 1971, *Two Studies in Roman Nomenclature*, 1976, and *Profile of Horace*, 1982. Editor/translator of several volumes of Cicero's correspondence. **Essay:** Cicero.

BAIN, David M. Reader in Greek, University of Manchester. Author of *Actors and Audience*, 1977 (revised 1987), and *Masters, Servants, and Orders in Greek Tragedy*, 1982. Editor and translator of *Samia* by Menander, 1983. **Essays:** *Amphitryo*; *Antigone* (Sophocles); *The Brothers*; *The Clouds*; *Medea*; *The Seven Against Thebes*; Sophocles; *The Suppliant Maidens*; *Women of Trachis*.

BALDWIN, Barry. Professor of classics, University of Calgary, Alberta. Author of *Studies in Lucian*, 1973, *Studies in Aulus Gellius*, 1975, *The Roman Emperors*, 1980, *Suetonius*, 1983, and many chapters, monographs, articles, and reviews of Greek, Roman, and Byzantine history, language, and literature. Translator (with commentary) of *Philogelos*, 1983, and *Timarion*, 1984. **Essay:** Lucian.

BAMIA, Aida A. Professor of Arabic, University of Florida. Field of expertise: modern Arabic literature and Maghribi and Francophone literatures. **Essays:** Assia Djebar; *Fantasia: An Algerian Cavalcade*.

BANCE, Alan. Professor and head of the Department of German, University of Keele, Staffordshire. Author of *The German Novel 1945[–]1960*, 1980, and *Theodor Fontane: The Major Novels*, 1982. Editor of *Die Kapuzinergruft* by Joseph Roth, 1972, *Weimar Germany: Writers and Politics*, 1982, and co-editor and contributor, *The Second World War in Fiction*, 1984. Translator of *Art of the Nineteenth Century* by A.M. Vogt, 1973. **Essays:** Theodor Fontane; Thomas Mann; Arthur Schnitzler.

BARFOOT, Gabrielle. Lecturer in Italian, Queen's University, Belfast. Author of "Dante in T.S. Eliot's Criticism," in *English Miscellany*, 1973, and "The Theme of Usury in Dante and Pound," in *Rivista di Letterature Moderne e Comparate*, 1977. **Essays:** Grazia Deledda; Vasco Pratolini; Italo Svevo.

BARSBY, John. Professor of classics, University of Otago, New Zealand. Author of *Ovid*, 1978. Translator (with commentary) of *Amores, Book One* by Ovid, 1973, and *Bacchides* by Plautus, 1984. **Essays:** Ovid; *The Brothers Menaechmus*; *The Eunuch*; *Phormio*; *The Pot of Gold*.

BARTA, Peter I. Instructor, department of linguistic and international Studies, University of Surrey. **Essays:** *The Bronze Horseman*; Ferenc Molnár; Iurii Olesha.

BASSNETT, Susan. Instructor, Graduate School of Comparative Literary Theory and Literary Translation University of Warwick. **Essays:** Vittoria Colonna; "The Flame"; Gabriela Mistral; "Rain in the Pine Forest"; St. John of the Cross; Gaspara Stampa.

BATLEY, Edward M. Instructor, Department of German, Goldsmiths' College. **Essay:** *Don Carlos*.

BEATON, Roderick. Lecturer in modern Greek language and literature, King's College, University of London. Author of *Folk Poetry of Modern Greece*, 1980, and articles on modern and medieval Greek literature, oral poetry, and traditional music. **Essays:** Constantine Petrou Cavafy; Yannis Ritsos; George Seferis; Angelo Sikelianos.

BEICHMAN, Janine. Professor, department of Japanese literature, Daitō Bunka University. Author of *Masaoka Shiki: His Life and Works* (1982; reissued 2002), *Embracing the Firebird: Yosano Akiko and the Birth of the Female Voice in Modern Japanese Poetry* (2002). Translator, *Oriori no uta/Poems for All Seasons by Ôoka Makoto* (2002). **Essays:** Rin Ishigaki; Masaoka Shiki; Akiko Yosano.

BELL, David. Lecturer in German, University of Manchester. Author of *Spinoza in Germany from 1670 to the Age of Goethe*, 1984. **Essay:** Torquato Tasso.

BELL, Ian A. **Essays:** *The Art of Poetry*; *Candide*; *Cloud in Trousers*; *The Game of Love and Chance*; *Jacques the Fatalist*; *Lazarillo de Tormes*; *One Hundred Years of Solitude*.

BERGIN, Thomas G. Sterling professor of romance languages Emeritus, Yale University, New Haven, Connecticut. Author of many books, including *Giovanni Verga*, 1931, *Dante*, 1965 (as *An Approach to Dante*, 1965), *A Diversity of Dante*, 1969, *Petrarch*, 1970, and *Boccaccio*, 1981. Editor or translator of works by Dante, Petrarch, Vico, Shakespeare, William of Poitou, Quasimodo, and editor of collections of Italian and French literature. **Essays:** Dante Alighieri; Giovanni Boccaccio; Petrarch.

BEST, Alan. Instructor, department of German, University of Hull. **Essays:** Fritz Hochwälder; *Tales from the Vienna Woods*.

BINGHONG LU. Professor, Beijing Language Institute; member of the Beijing Writers' Association. Formerly associate professor and department director, Peking Languages Institute. Author of *Stylized*

Intonation in English and Chinese, 1982, *A Concise Chinese[-]English Dictionary* (with others), 1982, and *Reader for Language Teaching and Studies*. Translator of the Chinese stories *Kite Streamers*, 1983, and *The Fascinating Sea*, 1984, *The Lure of the Sea*, Armand Hammer's autobiography and O. Henry's stories. **Essays:** Bai Juyi; Du Fu; Li Bai.

BLANE, Sandra. Instructor, School of European Languages, University of London. **Essay:** *Bérénice*.

BOBRICK, Elizabeth. Instructor, Department of Classics, Wesleyan University. **Essay:** *Characters*.

BOOTH, Joan. Instructor, Department of Classics and Ancient History, University College of Swansea, Wales. **Essays:** *Loves*; Poem 85; Sextus Propertius; Tibullus.

BORGESON, Paul W., Jr. Associate professor of Spanish, University of Illinois, Urbana-Champaign. Author of *Hacia el hombre nueve: Poesía y pensamiento de Ernesto Cardenal*, 1984, and *El poder de Sueño, La lucha continua: Arte y sociedad en "La Espiga Amotinada."* Editor of *Los talleres del tiempo: versos escogidos*, 1992, *Carlos Germán Belli: Obra poética*. **Essays:** "Death and the Compass"; "Considerando en frio"; "The Eternal Dice"; Juan Rulfo.

BRADY, Patrick. Shumway Chair of Excellence, Romance Languages, University of Tennessee, Knoxville. Formerly Favrot professor of French, Rice University, Houston, Texas. Author of two books in French on Zola, and *Marcel Proust*, 1977, *Structuralist Perspectives in Criticism of Fiction*, 1978, *Rococo Style Versus Enlightenment Novel*, 1984, and *Rococo Poetry in English, French, German, Italian: An Introduction*, 1992. **Essay:** Émile Zola.

BRAULT, Gerard J. Professor of French, Pennsylvania State University, University Park. Author of *Early Blazon: Heraldic Terminology in the Twelfth and Thirteenth Centuries*, 1972, and *Eight Thirteenth-Century Rolls of Arms in French and Anglo-Norman Blazon*, 1973. Editor of *Celestine: . . . the First French Translation (1527) of the Spanish Classic La Celestina*, 1963, and editor and translator of *The Song of Roland*, 2 vols., 1978. **Essays:** Chrétien de Troyes; *The Song of Roland*.

BRAUND, S.H. Lecturer in classics, University of Exeter, Devon. Author of *Beyond Anger: A Study of Juvenal's Third Book of Satires*, 1988, and articles on Juvenal. Translator of Lucan, 1992, and of *The Greece and Rome New Survey*, 1992. **Essays:** Juvenal; Lucan; Martial.

BROPHY, Michael. Assistant professor of French, University of North Carolina, Wilmington. Author of a book on Eugène Guillevic, and articles in *Initiales, Australian Journal of French Studies, Forum for Modern Language Studies, ALFA (Actes de langue française et de linguistique), LittéRéalité, Europe, Dalhousie French Studies,* and *The French Review*. Editor, with Rodopi, of *Chiasma* (series), forthcoming. **Essays:** René Char; *The Voice of Things*.

BROSMAN, Catherine Savage. Catherine B. Gore professor of French, Tulane University, New Orleans; member of the editorial boards of *French Review* and *Claudel Studies*. Author of *André Gide: L'évolution de sa pensée religieuse*, 1962, *Malraux, Sartre, and Aragon as Political Novelists*, 1965, *Roger Martin du Gard*, 1968, *Jean Paul Sartre*, 1983, *Art as Testimony: The Work of Jules Roy*, 1989, *French Novelists 1900–1930* (Dictionary of Literary Biography series), 1988, *French Novelists 1930–1960* (Dictionary of Literary Biography series),1988, *French Novelists Since 1960* (Dictionary of Literary Biography series), 1989, *An Annotated Bibliography of Criticism on André Gide, 1973–1978*, 1990, *Simone de Beauvoir Revisited*, 1991, *Nineteenth Century French Fiction Writers, 1800–1860* (Dictionary of Literary Biography series), 1992, *Nineteenth Century French Fiction Writers, 1860–1900* (Dictionary of Literary Biography series), 1992, other critical studies, and three collections of poetry. **Essays:** *The Age of Reason*; *The Counterfeiters*; *Man's Fate*; Roger Martin du Gard; *Nausea*.

BROTHERSTON, Gordon. Professor of literature, University of Essex, Wivenhoe. Author of *Manuel Machado: A Revaluation*, 1968, *Latin American Poetry: Origins and Presence*, 1975, *The Emergence of the Latin American Novel*, 1977, and *Image of the New World*, 1979. Editor or co-editor of *Selected Poems* by César Vallejo, 1976, *Ficciones* by Jorge Luis Borges, 1976, and collections of Spanish American fiction and poetry. **Essay:** Rubén Darío.

BROWN, Jennifer L. Instructor, department of French and Italian, Tulane University. **Essays:** *Chéri*; "Moses."

BROWN, Penny. Lecturer in comparative literary studies, University of Manchester; member of the National Executive Committee of British Comparative Literature Association. Author of *The Poison at the Source; The Female Novel of Self-Development in the Early Twentieth Century*, 1992, *The Captured World: The Child and Childhood in English Women's Fiction*, 1993, and an article on George Sands in *Comparative Literary Studies*, 1989. **Essays:** *Lélia*; *The Wanderer*.

BRYSON, Dorothy. Instructor, Department of French, University of Glasgow. **Essay:** *In the Labyrinth*.

BULLOCH, A.W. Associate professor of classics, University of California, Berkeley. Author of *Callimachus: The Fifth Hymn*, 1984, and the chapter on Hellenistic poetry in *Cambridge History of Classical Literature I: Greek Literature*, 1984. **Essays:** Apollonius; Callimachus.

BULLOCK, Alan. Reader in Italian Literature, University of Leeds. Author of *Domenico Torde e il carteggio colonnese della Biblioteca Nazionale di Firenze*, 1986, *Il Fondo Tordi della Biblioteca Nazionale de Firenze: Catalogo delle Appendici*, 1991, and *Natalia Ginzburg: Human Relationships in a Changing World*, 1991. **Essay:** Natalia Ginzburg.

BURNS, B. Lecturer in German, University of Strathclyde. **Essay:** Theodor Storm.

BUSCALL, J.M. Currently writing a study of post-modernist literature. Formerly NAVF research scholar at the University of Trondheim, Norway (1993–94). **Essay:** *Peasant Tales*.

CAIRNS, Christopher. Reader in Italian Drama, Vew Aberystwyth; commissioning editor for Edwin Mellen Press ("Studies in the Italian Theatre"). Author of *Domenico Bollani, Bishop of Bresina . . .*

Nieuwkoop, 1975, *Italian Literature, the Dominant Themes*, 1977, and *Pietro Aretino and the Republic of Venice*, 1985. **Essays:** Pietro Aretino; Pietro Bembo; Tommaso Campanella; Baldassarre Castiglione; Bernardo Dovizi da Bibbiena; *Henry IV*; *The Mistress of the Inn*; Ruzzante; *Six Characters in Search of an Author*.

CANCIAN, Alessandro. Researcher of religious anthropology, department of philosophy and social science, University of Siena, Italy. Author of essays and articles on various aspects of Iran's religious history and on literature of Islamic countries. **Essays:** Tahar Ben Jelloun; Qurratulain Hyder; *Plagued by the West*.

CARENAS, Francisco. Professor of Spanish. Author of *Poetas españoles en Estados Unidos*, 1969, *La Sociedad Española en la Novela de la Postguerra*, 1971, *Juan Goytisolo* (with others), 1975, *La figura del sacerdote en la moderna narrativa española*, 1975, and *La vuelta de los cerebros*, 1976. **Essay:** *Pascual Duarte's Family*.

CARLSON, Marvin. Essays: Jean Anouilh; Bjørnstjerne Bjørnson; Alexandre Dumas *fils*; Georges Feydeau; Kālidāsa; *Little Clay Cart*.

CARTER, Steven D. Professor of Japanese, University of California, Irvine. Author of *Unforgotten Dreams: Poems by the Zen Monk Shōtetsu* and other books and articles. **Essay:** Saigyō.

CATANI, Remo. Instructor, Department of Italian, University of Wales. **Essay:** Giosuè Carducci.

CAVENDISH, Philip. Essay: *We*.

CAWS, Mary Ann. Distinguished professor of English, French and comparative literature; co-director of the Henri Peyre Institute for the Humanities, City University of New York Graduate Center. Author of many books, including *Surrealism and the Literary Imagination*, 1966, *The Poetry of Dada and Surrealism*, 1970, *The Inner Theatre of Recent French Poetry*, 1972, *The Eye in the Text*, 1981, *A Metapoetics of the Passage*, 1981, *Yves Bonnefoy*, 1984, two books on André Breton, two books on René Char, and books on Robert Desnos and Pierre Reverdy. Editor or translator of works by Tristan Tzara, Char, Reverdy, Mallarmé, Breton, and Saint-John Perse, and editor of critical collections on French writing. Senior editor of HarperCollins World Recorder. **Essay:** André Breton.

CERVI, Andrea C. Research student, Newnham College, Cambridge. **Essays:** Paul Celan; Rainer Maria Rilke.

CHADWICK, C. Emeritus professor of French, University of Aberdeen. Author of *Études sur Rimbaud*, 1959, *Mallarmé, sa pensée dans sa poésie*, 1962, *Symbolism*, 1971, *Verlaine*, 1973, and *Rimbaud*, 1979. Editor of *Sagesse* by Verlaine, 1973. **Essays:** "Art poétique"; "Le Bateau ivre"; "Le Cimetière marin"; *Un Coup de dés jamais n'abolira le hasard*; "Fleurs"; Arthur Rimbaud; "Ses purs ongles très haut dédiant leur onyx"; Paul Verlaine.

CHAMPAGNE, Roland A. Professor of French, University of Missouri, St. Louis. Author of *Beyond the Structuralist Myth of Ecriture*, 1977, *Literary History in the Wake of Roland Barthes*, 1984, *Claude Levi-Strauss*, 1987, *French Structuralism*, 1990, and *The Vernant Group of Contextualist Analysis*, 1992. **Essay:** Marguerite Duras.

CHANCE, Linda H. Associate professor of Japanese, University of Pennsylvania. Author of *Formless in Form: Kenkō, Tsurezuregusa, and the Rhetoric of Japanese Fragmentary Prose* (1997). **Essay:** Kenkō.

CHEESMAN, Tom. Lecturer in German, University College Swansea, Wales. Author of *Shocking Ballads*, 1993. Editor of *Recent Ballad Research*, 1990. **Essay:** Jacob and Wilhelm Grimm.

CHLEBEK, Diana. Associate professor of bibliography, The University of Akron. Author of numerous articles and essays on contemporary and nineteenth-century literature and women writers. **Essay:** Luisa Valenzuela.

CHRISTENSEN, Erik C. Teacher of English, French, and world literature, Seattle, Washington. Ph.D. in comparative literature from University of Washington. Author of articles on Johannes V. Jensen in Scandinavian Studies (1998, 2000) and on Johannes V. Jensen and Jorge Luis Borges in Edda (1998). **Essay:** Johannes V. Jensen.

CICIONI, Mirna. Senior Lecturer, La Trobe University, Melbourne, Victoria. Co-editor of *Women in Italian Culture*, 1993. **Essays:** Giorgio Bassani; Primo Levi; *The Periodic Table*.

CLARK, John R. Professor of English, University of South Florida, Tampa. Author of *Form and Frenzy in Swift's "Tale of a Tub,"* 1970, *Senecan Tragedy*, 1988, *The Modern Satiric Grotesque*, 1991, *Seneca: A Critical Bibliography, 1900–1980*, 1989, *Essays on Seneca*, 1992, also many articles in scholarly journals. Editor of *Satire—That Blasted Art*, 1988. **Essays:** (with Anna Lydia Motto) *Epigrams*; *Lysistrata*; *Oedipus*; *Thyestes*.

CLARK, Stephen J. Assistant professor of Spanish, Northern Arizona University. Author of *Autobiografa y revolución en Cuba* (1999) and articles in literary journals. Editor and translator of *Belated Declaration of Love to Séraphine Louis: A Bilingual, Critical Edition of Denzil Romero's Short Stories* (2000). **Essays:** Reinaldo Arenas; Antonio Skármeta.

CLARKE, Shirley. Part-time lecturer, University of Birmingham. Author of "Valle-Inclán's Translations of Three Novels of Eça de Queiróz," in *Hispanic Studies in Honour of Joseph Manson*, edited by D.M. Atkinson and A.H. Clarke, 1972. Co-editor (with A.H. Clarke) of *Industrias y andanzas de Alfanhu* by Rafael Sánchez-Ferlosio, 1968. Currently translating Gil Vicente's trilogy, *Auto da Barca do Inferno, Auto da Barca do Purgatório*, and *Auto da Barca da Glória*. **Essay:** José Maria de Eça de Queirós.

COAD, David. Essays: *Aminta*; *The Immoralist*; St. Jerome.

COHN, Ruby. Professor of comparative drama, University of California, Davis. Author of *Samuel Beckett: The Comic Gamut*, 1962, *Currents in Contemporary Drama*, 1969, *Edward Albee*, 1969, *Dialogue in American Drama*, 1971, *Back to Beckett*, 1974, *Modern Shakespeare Offshoots*, 1976, *Just Play: Beckett's Theatre*, 1980, *Pocket Theatre of Postwar Paris*, 1987, *Retreats from Realism in Recent English Drama*, 1990, and *New American Dramatists 1960[–]1990*, 1991. **Essay:** Antonin Artaud.

COLLIE, Michael. Professor of English, York University, Downsview, Ontario. Author of two books on Jules Laforgue, *George*

Gissing: A Biography, 1977, *The Alien Art: A Critical Study of George Gissing's Novels*, 1979, a bibliography of Gissing, and *George Borrow, Eccentric*, 1982. Editor of *Les Derniers Vers* (with J.M. L'Heureux), 1965, and *Les Complaintes*, 1977, both by Laforgue. **Essay:** Jules Laforgue.

CONACHER, Desmond J. Professor emeritus of classics, Trinity College, University of Toronto. Author of *Euripidean Drama: Myth, Theme and Structure*, 1967, *Aeschylus: Prometheus Bound: A Literary Commentary*, 1980, *Aeschylus' Oresteia: A Literary Commentary*, 1987 and 1989, and articles in *Sources of Dramatic Theory*, vol. 1, 1991. Editor of *Euripides*, 1988, and *Alcestis*, 1988. **Essays:** Aeschylus; Euripides.

CONSTANTINE, David. Lecturer in German, Queen's College, Oxford. Author of *The Significance of Locality in the Poetry of Friedrich Hölderlin*, 1979. Editor of *German Short Stories*, 1976. **Essays:** Hans Jakob Christoffel von Grimmelshausen; Friedrich Hölderlin.

COOKE, Ray. Author of "Image and Symbol in Khlebnikov's *Night Search*, in *Russian Triquarterly 12*, 1975, and "Magic in the Poetry of Velimir Khlebnikov," in *Essays in Poetics 5*, 1980. **Essay:** Velimir Khlebnikov.

COOKSEY, Thomas L. Associate professor of English and Philosophy, Armstrong State College, Savannah, Georgia. Author of articles in *Essays in Literature*, 1987, *Studies in Medievalism*, 1992, *Edinburgh Review* and *Quarterly Review*. Editor of *Romantic Prose Writers* (Dictionary of Literary Biography series), 1991. **Essays:** *The City of God*; *Cupid and Psyche*; Lucretius; *Philosophical Dictionary*; *The Praise of Folly*; Pythian Odes Four and Five; *Reveries of a Solitary*; *The Symposium*.

CORNWELL, Neil. Senior lecturer in Russian Studies, University of Bristol. Formerly lecturer in Slavonic studies, Queen's University, Belfast. Founding editor, *Irish Slavonic Studies*. Author of books on V.F. Odoyevsky and Pasternak, *The Literary Fantastic, James Joyce and the Russians*, and of articles, reviews, and translations of 19th- and 20th-century Russian literature. Translator of Odoyevsky and Daniil Kharms. **Essays:** Isaak Babel; Evgenii Zamiatin.

COSTA, C.D.N. Professor of classics, University of Birmingham. Editor of *Medea* by Seneca, 1973, *Lucretius V*, 1984, *Seneca 17 Letters*, 1988, and of the collections *Horace*, 1973, and *Seneca*, 1974. **Essay:** Seneca.

(CROFT), Sally McMullen. Ph.D. student, Cambridge University. **Essays:** Hugo von Hofmannsthal; Stéphane Mallarmé.

CROSS, Carmen. Ph.D. candidate, Georgetown University. Field bibliographer for the Modern Language Association, reviewer for the *Middle East Studies Association Bulletin* and *Journal of Arabic Literature*. **Essay:** Imru' al-Qays.

CUBBIN, G.P. Lecturer in German, Cambridge University. Author of numerous articles on German literature. **Essays:** *Nibelungenlied*; Wolfram von Eschenbach.

ČULÍK, Jan. Lecturer in Czech studies, University of Glasgow, United Kingdom. Author of *Knihy za ohradou: Česká literatura v exilových nakladatelstvích 1971–1989 (Books behind the Fence: Czech Literature in Emigré Publishing Houses 1971–1989)*, 1991; *. . . jak Češi myslí (. . . The Way Czechs Think)*, 1999; *. . . jak Češi jednají (. . . The Way Czechs Act)*, 2000; *V hlavních zprávách: Televize (On the Main News: Television)*, with Tomáš Pecina, 2001; editor, author, and co-author of entries on Czech twentieth-century writers in *Dictionary of Literary Biography*, vol. 215, 1999, and vol. 232, 2001, editor of the Czech-language internet cultural and political daily *Britské listy*. **Essays:** Miroslav Holub; Milan Kundera.

CURTIS, James M. Professor of Russian, University of Missouri. Author of *Culture as Polyphony*, 1978, and *Solzhenitsyn's Traditional Imagination*, 1989. **Essays:** *The Cherry Orchard*; *The Lady with a Dog*; *The Seagull*.

CUSHING, G.F. Emeritus professor of Hungarian language and literature, University of London. Author of *Hungarian Prose and Verse*, joint editor, with G.A. Hosking, *Perspectives on Literature and Society in Eastern and Western Europe*. **Essay:** Baron József Eötvös.

CUSICK, Edmund. Lecturer in English, Liverpool John Moores University. Formerly lecturer in English literature, St. David's University College, Lampeter, Dyfed; assistant editor, Oxford English Dictionaries, Oxford. **Essays:** *The Bible*; *Justine*; *The Last Temptation*; *Metamorphoses*; *The Republic*; "The Snow Queen".

CZAYKOWSKI, Bogdan. Poet, critic and professor emeritus, University of British Columbia. His recent publications include *Antologia poezji polskiej na obczyźnie*, 2002. **Essay:** Tadeusz Borowski.

CZERNIAWSKI, Adam. Polish poet and critic. His recent publications include a bilingual *Selected Poems* (2000) and a memoir *Scenes from a disturbed childhood* (2002). **Essay:** Cyprian Kamil Norwid.

CZIGÁNY, Lóránt. Visiting professor, University of Budapest. Author of *The Reception of Hungarian Literature in Victorian England*, 1976, and *The Oxford History of Hungarian Literature*, 1984. **Essay:** Sándor Petőfi.

DAVIDSON, James N. Junior research fellow, Trinity College, Oxford. Formerly graduate scholar, St. Hugh's College, Oxford. Author of articles in *Journal of Roman Studies*, 1991, and *Historia*, 1990. **Essays:** Demosthenes; Theophrastus.

DAVIES, Catherine. Lecturer in Hispanic Studies, University of London. Author of a forthcoming book on Cuban literature. **Essay:** José Lezama Lima.

DAYDI-TOLSON, Santiago. Assistant professor of Spanish, University of Virginia, Charlottesville. Author of *The Post-Civil War Spanish Social Poets*, 1983, and articles on Gabriela Mistral, José Angel Valente, and other writers. Editor of *Vicente Aleixandre: A Critical Appraisal*, 1981, and *Five Poets of Aztlán* (forthcoming). **Essay:** César Vallejo.

de COSTA, René. Professor of Romance languages and director of the Center for Latin American Studies, University of Chicago, Illinois. Author of *The Poetry of Pablo Neruda*, 1979, *En pos de Huidobro*, 1980, *Vicente Huidobro, Huidobro: The Careers of a Poet*, 1984, and many articles on Pablo Neruda, Jorge Luis Borges, and other writers. Editor of works by Huidobro and Pedro Prado, and of a collection of articles on Huidobro. **Essay:** Pablo Neruda.

DEIGHTON, Alan. Lecturer in German, University of Hull. Author of articles in academic journals on medieval German literature. Editor of *New German Studies*. **Essays:** *Parzival*; *Titurel*; *Willehalm*.

DICKIE, John. Instructor, Department of Italian, University of Wales. **Essays:** *Bread and Wine* (Silone); *Francesca da Rimini*; *The Time of Indifference*.

DICKSON, Sheila J. Lecturer in German, University of Strathclyde. **Essay:** Clemens Brentano.

DIGGLE, James. Director of studies in classics, Queen's College, Cambridge.

DOLAMORE, C.E.J. Instructor, Department of French, University of Leeds. **Essays:** Eugène Ionesco; *Seamarks*.

DOWDEN, Ken. Lecturer in classics, University College, Cardiff. Author of articles on Greek religion and on Apuleius, including "Psyche on the Rock," in *Latomus 41*, 1982, and "Apuleius and the Art of Narration," in *Classical Quarterly 32*, 1982. **Essay:** Apuleius.

DRIVER, Sam. Professor and chairman of the department of Slavic languages, Brown University, Providence, Rhode Island. Author of *Anna Akhmatova*, 1972. **Essay:** Anna Akhmatova.

DUNKLEY, John. Lecturer in French, University of Aberdeen. Author of *Gambling: A Social and Moral Problem in France 1685–1792* (forthcoming), *Beaumarchais; Le Barbier de Séville*, 1991. Co-author/editor of *Culture and Revolution*, 1990, and *Voices in the Air; French dramatists and the Resources of Language* (forthcoming). Editor of *Amusements Sérieux et comiques*, 1976, *Electre*, 1980, *Le Joueur*, 1986, and *Le philosophe sans le savoir* (forthcoming). **Essays:** *The Barber of Seville*; Denis Diderot; Jean-Jacques Rousseau.

DURRANI, Osman. Senior lecturer in German, University of Durham. Author of *Faust and the Bible*, 1977, *German Poetry of the Romantic Era*, 1986, and numerous articles in *Modern Language Review* and *German Life and Letters*. **Essays:** Adelbert von Chamisso; Alfred Döblin; *The Glass Bead Game*.

EILE, Stanislaw. Senior lecturer in Polish, University of London. Formerly associate professor, University of Cracow; visiting professor, University of Michigan. Author of the following books in Polish: a biography of Stefan Zeromski, 1961, *The Legend of Zeromski*, 1965, and *The Semantics of the Novel*, 1973, articles in English on Polish drama and literature for journals including *The Adolescent Hero*, 1984, *Intellectuals and the Future in the Habesburg Monarchy 1890–1914*, 1988, *New Literary History, Soviet Jewish Affairs, Perspectives on Literature and Society in Eastern and Western Europe*, 1989, and articles in English on Polish drama and literature

for books including *World Authors*, 1991, *The Everyman Companion to East European Literature*, 1993. **Essays:** Jerzy Andrzejewski; *Ashes and Diamonds*; Bolesław Prus; *Pan Tadeusz*; Stanisław Wyspiański.

EKDAWI, Sarah. Post-doctoral research student. Author of a number of articles on Greek poetry, individually and with Elli Philokyprou. **Essays:** Fragment 1 ["Address to Aphrodite"]; Fragment 31 ["Declaration of Love for a Young Girl"]; "The Sacred Way"; "Waiting for the Barbarians."

ELSIE, Robert. Ph.D., University of Bonn. Specialist in Albanian affairs. Author of *Anthology of Modern Albanian Poetry* (1993); *History of Albanian Literature* (1995); *Studies in Modern Albanian Literature and Culture* (1996); *Kosovo: In the Heart of the Powder Keg* (1997); *Dictionary of Albanian Religion, Mythology and Folk Culture* (2001); and *Introduction to Albanian Literature* (forthcoming). **Essay:** Ismail Kadare.

ERMOLAEV, Herman. Professor of Russian Literature, Princeton University, New Jersey. Author of *Soviet Literary Theories 1917[–]1934: The Genesis of Socialist Realism*, 1963, and *Mikhail Sholokhov and His Art*, 1982. Editor and translator of *Untimely Thoughts* by Maksim Gor'kii, 1968. **Essay:** Aleksandr Solzhenitsyn.

EVANS, Jo. Instructor, Department of Hispanic Studies, University of Edinburgh. **Essay:** Jorge Guillén.

FALCHIKOV, Michael. Senior lecturer in Russian, University of Edinburgh. Author of "Rerouting the Train of Time," in *Modern Language Review*, 1, 1980, and other articles on Boris Pil'niak and Russian literature, translator of *Postscripts* (stories by Viktor Nekrasov), 1991, and other translations from Russian literature. **Essay:** Boris Pil'niak.

FEHSENFELD, Nancy Kanach. Director of studies and lecturer, Princeton University, New Jersey. **Essays:** Aleksandr Pushkin; Ivan Turgenev.

FENOULHET, Jane. Senior lecturer in Dutch, University College London. Author of *Basisproza 1930–1990* (1993) and of articles on Dutch and Flemish literature in literary journals; editor, *Dutch Crossing. A Journal of Low Countries Studies*. **Essays:** Cees Nooteboom; Simon Vestdijk.

FERNÁNDEZ-BRAVO, Alvaro. Assistant professor of literature, Universidad de San Andrés, Argentina. Author of *Literatura y frontera: procesos de territorialización en las culturas argentina y chilena del siglo XIX* (1999) and articles on Latin American Literature in academic journals. **Essays:** René Depestre; Umberto Eco; *The Name of the Rose*; Juan José Saer.

FERRARO, Bruno. Head of Italian section, Department of Romance Languages, University of Auckland. **Essays:** Giordano Bruno; "The Infinite."

FLETCHER, John. Professor of comparative literature, University of East Anglia, Norwich. Author of *The Novels of Samuel Beckett*, 1964, *Samuel Beckett's Art*, 1967, *New Directions in Literature*, 1968, *Claude Simon and Fiction Now*, 1975, *Novel and Reader*, 1980, and *Alain Robbe-Grillet*, 1983. **Essays:** Colette; Madame de Lafayette; André Malraux; Molière; Alain Robbe-Grillet; Marquis de Sade.

FLOOD, John L. Institute of Germanic Studies, University of London. **Essays:** Sebastian Brant; *The Wandering Scholar from Paradise.*

FOSTER, David William. Director, Spanish Graduate Studies, Arizona State University. **Essay:** Leopoldo Marechal.

FOULKES, A.P. Professor of German, University College, Cardiff. Author of *The Reluctant Pessimist: A Study of Franz Kafka*, 1967, *The Search for Literary Meaning*, 1975, and *Literature and Propaganda*, 1983. Editor of *Das deutsche Drama von Kleist bis Hauptmann* (with others), 1973, and *The Uses of Criticism*, 1976. **Essays:** Gerhart Hauptmann; Franz Kafka; Gottfried Keller.

FOWLIE, Wallace. Professor emeritus of French, Duke University, Durham, North Carolina. Author of many books, including poetry, a novel, studies of François Villon, Stéphane Mallarmé, Arthur Rimbaud, Paul Claudel, Marcel Proust, André Gide, Jean Cocteau, Stendhal, and the Comte de Lautréamont, general books on French literature, and autobiographical works. Editor or translator of works by Maurice Scève, Honoré de Balzac, Saint-John Perse, Cocteau, Claudel, Charles Baudelaire, Molière, François Mauriac, Rimbaud, and of several anthologies. **Essays:** Guillaume Apollinaire; Paul Claudel; Jean Cocteau; Jean Genet; André Gide; Marcel Proust; Saint-John Perse; Paul Valéry.

FREEMAN, Michael. Professor of French language and literature, University of Leicester. Formerly lecturer in French, University of Leicester. Author of articles on Pierre de Larivey, Guillaume Coquillart, François Villon, Etienne Jodelle, the comic theatre, and many articles on Portuguese subjects, notably Fernando Pessoa. Editor of *Oeuvres* by Coquillart, 1975, *Les Esprits* by Larrivey, 1979, and *L'Eugène* by Jodelle, 1987. Co-editor of a collection of conference papers on Villon, 1992. **Essays:** "Apology for Raymond Sebond"; "Ballade des dames du temps jadis"; "Ballade des Pendus" Jaochim Du Bellay; *Gargantua and Pantagruel*; "Heuruex qui, comme Ulysee, a fait un beau voyage"; "Hymn to Autumn"; *The Lusiads*; Guillaume de Machaut; Michel de Montaigne; "On the Power of the Imagination"; François Rabelais; *Romance of the Rose*; Pierre de Ronsard; François Villon.

FROST, Frank J. Professor of Greek history, University of California, Santa Barbara; associate editor, *American Journal of Ancient History*. Author of *Greek Society*, 2nd edition, 1980, *Plutarch's Themistocles*, 1980, and many articles on Greek history and archaeology. **Essay:** Plutarch.

FULKS, Barbara P. Visiting professor, North Carolina Central University. Author of articles in *Monographic Review*, 1988, and *La Corónica*, 1989. **Essays:** *Kiss of the Spider Woman*; Manuel Puig.

FULLER, Michael A. Associate professor of Chinese, University of California at Irvine. Author of *The Road to East Slope: The Development of Su Shi's Poetic Voice*, 1990. **Essay:** Su Shi.

GARTON, Janet. Senior lecturer in Scandinavian Studies, University of East Anglia, Norwich; editor, *Scandinavica*, director and secretary,

Norvik Press. Author of *Writers and Politics in Modern Scandinavia*, 1978, *Jens Bjørneboe: Prophet without Honor*, 1985, and several articles on modern Scandinavian literature. Editor of *Facets of European Modernism*, 1985, and *New Norwegian Plays*, 1989. Translator of *An Aquarium of Women* by Bjørg Vik, and *The Sleeping Prince* by Knut Faldbakken, 1988. **Essays:** Knut Hamsun; Henrik Ibsen; Snorri Sturluson; Sigrid Undset.

GASCOYNE, David. Ex-poet, translator, and critic. Author of *A Short Survey of Surrealism*, 1935, *Hölderlin's Madness*, 1938, *Thomas Carlyle*, 1952, *Novalis (Hymns to the Night)*, 1989, and *Collected Journals 1936–1942*, 1991. **Essay:** Francis Ponge.

GATT-RUTTER, John. Vaccari professor of Italian Studies, La Trobe University, Melbourne, Victoria. Author of *Writers and Politics in Modern Italy*, 1978, *Italo Svevo—A Double Life*, 1988, and *Alias Italo Svevo—Vita di Ettore Schmutz Scrittore Triestino*, 1991. **Essays:** *The Betrothed*; *Confessions of Zeno*; *The Good Soldier Švejk and His Fortunes in the World War*; *If on a Winter's Night a Traveller*; *The Prince*.

GIANOULIS, Tina. Freelance writer, editor, and researcher. Contributing writer for www.glbtq.com, an online gay, lesbian, bisexual, transgendered, and queer encyclopedia (2002), *World War I Reference Library* (2001–02), *Constitutional Amendments: From Freedom of Speech to Flag Burning* (2001), *International Dictionary of Films and Filmmakers* (2000), *St. James Encyclopedia of Popular Culture* (1999), and *Gay and Lesbian Literature* (1997–98). **Essays:** Nicole Brossard; Francesca Duranti.

GIBSON, Margaret. Reader in medieval history, University of Liverpool. Author of *Lanfranc of Bec*, 1978. Editor of *The Letters of Lanfranc*, 1980, and *Boethius: His Life, Thought and Influence*, 1981. **Essay:** Boethius.

GIBSON, Robert. Professor of French, University of Kent at Canterbury. Author of *The Land Without a Name*, 1978, and *Modern French Poets on Poetry*, 1979. Editor of *Studies in French Fiction*, 1988, and *Annals of Ashdon*, 1988. Translator of *Le Grand Meaulnes*, 1968. **Essays:** Alain-Fournier; *Night Flight*; Antoine de Saint-Exupéry.

GILES, Mary E. Instructor, Department of Humanities, California State University. **Essay:** Emilia Pardo Bazán.

GILMAN, Donald. Instructor, Department of Modern Languages and classics, Ball State University. **Essays:** *Aucassin and Nicolette*; *The Holy Terrors*; "Ode to Michel de l'Hospital."

GLATZER, Nahum N. University professor of Judaica, Boston University; Chief Editorial Adviser, Schocken Books, New York. Author of books in German on the Talmud and Leopold Zunz, and of *Franz Rosenzweig: His Life and Thought*, 1953, and *Essays in Jewish Thought*, 1978. Editor of *The Complete Stories* by Franz Kafka, 1971, *Twenty-One Stories* by S.Y. Agnon, 1970, and, with others, *Schriften, Tageböcher, Briefe* by Kafka, from 1983. **Essay:** S.Y. Agnon.

GLEDSON, J. Instructor, Department of Hispanic Studies, University of Liverpool. **Essays:** *Dom Casmurro*; *Posthumous Memoirs of Braz Cubas*.

GODFREY, Gary. Instructor, Department of Foreign Languages, Weber State University. **Essays:** *No Exit*; *Pierre and Jean*; *Scarlet and Black*.

GOESLL, Ingeborg M. Instructor, Department of Foreign Languages and Literatures, University of Missouri-St. Louis. **Essays:** *Rock Crystal*; *The White Horseman*.

GOETZ-STANKIEWICZ, Marketa. Professor emerita of Germanic studies and comparative literature at the University of British Columbia. She is the author of *The Silenced Theatre: Czech Playwrights Without a Stage* (1979) and editor, among others, of *The Vaněk Plays: Four Authors, One Character* (1987), *Good-Bye, Samizdat: Twenty Years of Czechoslovak Underground Writing* (1992) and *Critical Essays on Václav Havel* (1999). **Essays:** Václav Havel; Ivan Klíma.

GOLD, Janet N. Associate professor of Latin American literature, University of New Hampshire. Author of *Clementina Suarez: Her Life and Poetry* (1995) and essays in literary journals. **Essays:** Gioconda Belli.

GOLDBERG, Sander M. Professor of classics, University of California, Los Angeles. Formerly assistant professor of classics, University of Colorado, Boulder. Author of *The Making of Menander's Comedy*, 1980, "Scholarship on Terence and the Fragments of Roman Comedy," in *Classical World 75*, 1981, *Understanding Terence*, 1986, *Ruined Choirs of Roman Epic Verse*, 1993, and many other articles and reviews. **Essays:** *The Grouch*; Menander; Terence.

GOLDBLATT, Howard. Research professor, The University of Notre Dame. Author, editor and translator of more than forty books on or from China and Taiwan. **Essay:** Xiao Hong.

GÖMÖRI, George. Lecturer in Slavonic Studies, Cambridge University. Author of *Polish and Hungarian Poetry 1945 to 1956*, 1966, and *Cyprian Norwid*, 1974. Editor, with others, of *Love of the Scorching Wind* by László Nagy, 1973, and *Forced March* by Miklós Radnóti, 1979. **Essays:** Witold Gombrowicz; *Ferdydurke*; Zygmunt Krasiński; Czesław Miłosz; Miklós Radnóti; "A Sentence for Tyranny"; Mihály Vörösmarty; Sándor Weöres; Stanisław Witkiewicz.

GOONETILLEKE, D.C.R.A. Professor and chairman, Department of English, University of Kelaniya, Sri Lanka. Author of *Developing Countries in British Fiction*, 1977, *Images of the Raj: South Asia in the Literature of Empire*, 1988, *Joseph Conrad: Beyond Culture and Background*, 1990, and numerous articles in international journals. Editor of *The Penguin New Writing in Sri Lanka*, 1992, and several anthologies of Sri Lankan literature. **Essay:** *A Doll's House*.

GRAHAM, Colin. Researcher, University of Bristol. Editor of *Selected Poetry of Samuel Ferguson*, 1992, and *Selected Prose of Samuel Ferguson* (forthcoming). **Essays:** *The Art of Love*; *The Mabinogion*; *Malloy, Mallone Dies, The Unnamable*; *Satire 10*; *The Thousand and One Nights*.

GRAVES, Peter J. Head of Department of German, University of Leicester. Author of *Three Contemporary German Poets*, 1985 and numerous articles and reviews on German literature. **Essays:** "Death Fugue"; *The Investigation*; *The Lost Honour of Katharina Blum*.

GREEN, Roger. Modern Greek librarian, Taylor Institution, Oxford. Author of *Notes from Overground* (as *Tiresias*), 1984. **Essay:** Nikos Kazantzakis.

GREEN, R.P.H. Senior lecturer in Latin, University of St. Andrews, Fife. Formerly advisory editor to Respublica Litterarum; Secretary of the International Association for Neo-Latin Studies. Author of *Seven Versions of Carolingian Pastoral*, 1980, and *The Works of Ausonius*, 1991. **Essays:** Ausonius; *Confessions*, Book I; *The Mosella*.

GRUZELIER, Claire E. D.Phil. research student, Balliol College, Oxford. **Essays:** St. Augustine; Aurelius.

GURGANUS, Albert E. Assistant professor of modern languages, The Citadel, Charleston, South Carolina. Author of *The Art of Revolution: Kurt Eisner's Agitprop*, 1986. **Essays:** *The Causcasian Chalk Circle*; *The German Lesson*.

HAAC, Oscar A. Professor of French, State University of New York, Stony Brook. Author of *Les Principes Inspirateurs de Michelet*, 1951, *Marivaux*, 1973, and *Jules Michelet*, 1982. Editor of works by Michelet. **Essays:** Marivaux.

HABERLY, David T. Associate professor of Portuguese, University of Virginia, Charlottesville. Author of *Three Sad Races: Racial Identity and National Consciousness in Brazilian Literature*, 1983, and numerous articles on Brazilian, Portuguese, Spanish American, and comparative literature. **Essays:** Joaquim Maria Machado de Assis; Fernando Pessoa.

HAINES, Brigid. Lecturer in German, University College of Swansea, Wales. Author of *Dialogue and Narrative Design in the Works of Adalbert Stifter*, 1991. **Essay:** *The Jews' Beech Tree*.

HÁJEK, Igor. Lecturer in Slavonic languages and literatures, University of Glasgow. Author of numerous articles and reviews. Coeditor and contributor, *Modern Slavic Literatures 2*, 1976, and *Dictionary of Czech Writers 1948–1979*, 1982.

HALPERIN, David M. Associate professor of literature, Massachusetts Institute of Technology, Cambridge. Author of *Before Pastoral: Theocritus and the Ancient Tradition of Bucolic Poetry*, 1983, "Solzhenitsyn, Epicurus, and the Ethics of Stalinism," in *Critical Inquiry 7*, 1980, "The Forebears of Daphnis," in *Transactions of the American Philological Association 113*, 1983, "Plato and Erotic Reciprocity," in *Journal of the History of Ideas 45*, 1983, "Platonic Erôs and What Men Call Love," in *Ancient Philosophy 5*, 1985, and *One Hundred Years of Homosexuality and Other Essays on Greek Love*, 1990. **Essay:** Theocritus.

HARRIES, P.T. Fellow in Japanese, Queen's College, Oxford. Formerly lecturer in Japanese, School of Oriental and African Studies, University of London; editor of *Bulletin of the European Association for Japanese Studies*. Author of *The Poetic Memoirs of Lady Daibu*, 1980, "Personal Poetry Collections," in *Monumenta Nipponica 36*, 1980, and "Arthur Waley," in *Britain and Japan 1859–1991: Themes and Personalities*, 1991. **Essay:** Bashō.

HARRIS, Nigel. Instructor, Department of German Studies, University of Birmingham. **Essay:** *The Ship of Fools*.

HARRY, Patricia. Lecturer in French, Royal Holloway, University of London. **Essay:** Paul Scarron.

HART, John. Senior classics master, Malvern College, Worcestershire. Author of *Herodotus and Greek History*, 1982. Winner of BBC Television's "Mastermind" competition, 1975. **Essays:** Herodotus; *Lives of Lysander and Sulla*.

HART, Thomas R. Professor emeritus of comparative literature and romance languages, University of Oregon, Eugene; editor of *Comparative Literature*. Author of *Gil Vicente: Casandra and Don Duardos*, 1981, *Cervantes and Ariosto: Renewing Fiction*, 1989, and many articles on Spanish and Portuguese literature. Editor of *Obras dramticasÆ castellanas*, 1962, and *Farces and Festival Plays*, 1972, both by Gil Vicente. **Essay:** Luís de Camões.

HAWKESWORTH, E.C. Lecturer in Serbo-Croat, University of London. Author of *Ivo Andrić: A Bridge Between East and West*, 1984. **Essay:** Ivo Andrić.

HAYMAN, Ronald. Essays: *Against Sainte-Beuve*; *The Balcony*; *Endgame*; *The Flies*; *The Maids*; *Rhinoceros*.

HEENAN, Patrick. Freelance writer and researcher. Formerly English teacher, book editor, lecturer in history and politics. **Essay:** Akutagawa Ryūnosuke.

HERMANS, Theo. Professor of Dutch and comparative literature, University College London. Author of *The Structure of Modernist Poetry* (1982), *Translation in Systems* (1999), editor of *The Manipulation of Literature* (1985), *The Flemish Movement* (1992), *Crosscultural Transgressions* (2002), and other titles. **Essay:** Hugo Claus.

HIBBERD, John. Reader in German, University of Bristol. Author of *Salomon Gessner*, 1976, *Kafka*, 1975, and *Kafka: Die Verwandlung*, 1985. Editor of *Texte, Motive und Gestalten Der Goethezeit* (with H.B. Nisbet), 1989. **Essays:** *Doctor Faustus*; *The Lulu Plays*; *The Metamorphosis*; *Nathan the Wise*.

HIGGINS, James. Professor of Latin American literature, University of Liverpool, Liverpool. Formerly honorary professor of University of San Marcos, Lima, Peru. Author of *A History of Peruvian Literature*, 1987. **Essays:** José María Arguedas; *Deep Rivers*.

HILL, David. Instructor, Department of German Studies, University of Biringham. **Essay:** *The Tutor*.

HILLEN, Sabine. Instructor, Department of French and Italian, Tulane University. **Essay:** *Memoirs of Hadrian*.

HILTON, Ian. Instructor, School of Modern Languages, University College of North Wales. **Essays:** *The Blue Angel*; Günter Eich; Siegfried Lenz; Heinrich Mann; "Palau".

HIRATA, Hosea. Associate professor of Japanese, Tufts University. Author of *The Poetry and Poetics of Nishiwaki Junzaburo: Modernism in Translation* (Princeton University Press, 1993) and *Discourses of Seduction: History, Evil, Desire, and Modern Japanese Literature* (Harvard University Press, forthcoming). **Essay:** Nishiwaki Junzaburō.

HITCHINS, Keith. Professor of history, University of Illinois, Urbana-Champaign. Author of articles on Azerbaijani, Kazakh, Kurdish, Romanian, and Tajik literatures and of *Rumania, 1866–1947* (1994). **Essays:** Mircea Eliade; Abdulla Goran.

HODSON, Leighton. Instructor, Department of French, The University, Glasgow. **Essays:** *The Bald Prima Donna*; *Remembrance of Things Past*.

HOMERIN, Th. Emil. Professor of religion, University of Rochester. Author of *Umar Ibn al-Farid: Sufi Verse, Saintly Life; From Arab Poet to Muslim Saint: Ibn al-Farid, His Verse, and His Shrine*, and essays in journals of literature, religion, and Middle Eastern Studies; associate editor, *Muslim World*. **Essay:** 'Umar Ibn al-Fârid.

HOOD, Edward Waters. Associate professor of Spanish, Northern Arizona University. Author of *La ficción de Gabriel García Márquez* (1993); translator and critic of contemporary Central American literature. **Essay:** Manlio Argueta.

HOPKINS, Louise. Teacher of English and Drama. Author of a forthcoming book on Angela Carter. **Essay:** Marcel Pagnol.

HUBBARD, Thomas K. Assistant professor of classics, University of Texas at Austin. Author of *The Pindaric Mind*, 1985, and *The Mask of Comedy*, 1991. **Essays:** *Georgics*; *Idyll* I; *Idyll* IV; Olympian One.

HUBER, Lothar. Lecturer, Birkbeck College, London. Editor of *Musil in Focus* (with J.J. White), 1982, and *Franz Werfel: An Austrian Writer Reassessed*, 1989. **Essays:** *The Man Without Qualities*; Franz Werfel; *Young Törless*.

HUTCHINSON, Peter. Fellow of Selwyn College, Cambridge. Author of *Literary Presentations of Divided Germany*, 1977, and *Games Authors Play*, 1983. **Essays:** *Siddhartha*; *Steppenwolf*.

HYSLOP, Lois Boe. Professor emerita of romance languages, Pennsylvania State University, University Park. Author of *Henry Becque*, 1972, and *Baudelaire, Man of His Time*, 1980. Editor, with F.E. Hyslop, of *Baudelaire on Poe*, 1952, *Baudelaire: A Self-Portrait*, 1957, *Baudelaire as a Literary Critic*, 1964, and *Baudelaire as a Love Poet and Other Essays*, 1969. **Essay:** Charles Baudelaire.

IVES, Margaret C. Senior lecturer in German studies, University of Lancaster. Author of *Brecht's Galileo—An Introduction and Commentary*, 1967, *The Analogue of Harmony: A Reexamination of Schiller's Concept of Harmony with Particular Reference to His Theory of Personality*, 1970, *Enlightenment and National Revival*, 1979, and articles in *Theology, Comparison, Journal for 18th-Century Studies, European Studies Review*, and other journals. Editor of *Women Writers of the Age of Goethe*, 1988. **Essay:** *The Story of Just Caspar and Fair Annie*.

JACKSON, David. Instructor, School of European Studies, University of Wales. **Essays:** *Maria Magdalena*; Conrad Ferdinand Meyer.

JAMES, Tony. Senior lecturer in French, University of Manchester. Formerly general editor of Vinaver Studies in French. Author of "Berlioz the Poet," in *Hector Berlioz: Les Troyens*, edited by I. Kemp, 1989, *Dream, Madness and Creativity in Nineteenth-Century France* (forthcoming), and numerous articles on the history of psychiatry and 19th-century French literature. **Essay:** *The Hunchback of Notre-Dame.*

JANES, Regina. Professor, Department of English, Skidmore College, Saragoga Springs, New York. Author of articles on Carlos Fuentes and Mary Wollstonecraft in *Journal of the History of Ideas*, 1978, and on Edmund Burke in *Bulletin of Research in the Humanities*, 1979, interviews with Guillermo Cabrera Infante and Carlos Fuentes in *Salmagundi*, 1978 and 1981, *Gabriel Garcia Marquez: Revolutions in Wonderland*, 1981, *"One Hundred Years of Solitude": Modes of Reading*, 1991, and "Beheadings," in *Representations*, 1991. **Essays:** Alejo Carpentier; Gabriel García Márquez.

JENKINSON, D.E. Instructor, Department of European Languages, Goldsmith's College, University of London. **Essay:** *Andreas.*

JILLINGS, Lewis. Visiting associate professor, Department of Germanic Languages, UCLA, Los Angeles. Formerly senior lecturer in German, University of Stirling, Stirling, Scotland. Author of *"Diu Crone" of Heinrich von dem Türlein: The Attempted Emancipation of Secular Lyric*, 1980, and *Martin Luther Selections* (with Brian Murdoch), 1977. **Essays:** "Ein feste Burg"; Gottfried von Strassburg; Hartmann von Aue; Martin Luther; Walther von der Vogelweide.

JOHNSON, Jeffrey. Associate professor of Japanese, University of Utah. Editor of *Bakhtinian Theory in Japan Studies* (2001), "Saikaku and the Narrative Turnabout" in *Journal of Japanese Studies* and "El haiku en la obra de Federico García Lorca" in *Letras Peninsulares*. **Essay:** Ihara Saikaku.

JONES, D. Mervyn. Retired member of H.M. Diplomatic Service. Formerly fellow of Trinity College, Cambridge, Exeter, and St. Antony's College, Oxford. Author of *Five Hungarian Writers*, 1966. **Essays:** *The Village Notary*; Count Miklós Zrínyi.

JONES, Roger. Lecturer in German, Keele University, Staffordshire; member of editorial board of Manchester New German Texts. Translator of *The Broken Jug* by Heinrich von Kleist. **Essay:** *The Devil's Elixirs.*

JONES, W. Glyn. Essays: William Heinesen; Halldór Laxness.

KARWOWSKA, Bożena. Senior instructor of Russian and Polish languages and literatures, department of Central, Eastern, and Northern European studies, University of British Columbia. **Essay:** Wisława Szymborska.

KEITH-SMITH, Brian. Instructor, Department of German, Bristol University. **Essays:** Johannes Bobrowski; *Confessions of Felix Krull, Confidence Man; The Gas Trilogy*; Ernst Toller.

KILANY, Hanaa. Arabic language lecturer, Emory University, Atlanta. **Essays:** Al-Khansa'; Yusuf Idris.

KILLICK, Rachel. Instructor, Department of French, University of Leeds. **Essays:** *Hérodiade*; "La Jeune Parque" *The Last Poems.*

KING, Jonathan. Lecturer in French, University of Aberdeen. Editor of *Albert Camus: Selected Political Writing*, 1987. **Essay:** *Le Crève-coeur.*

KING, Peter. Emeritus professor of Dutch. Author of *Dawn Poetry in the Low Countries*, 1971; Word indexes to Vondel's *Bespielingen van Godt en Godtsdienst* and *Lucifer*, 1973; concordances of the works of Joost van den Vondel: *Maria Stuart of Gemartelde, Majesteit, Leeuwendalers*, 1982; Multatuli's *Max Havelaar: Fact or Fiction?*, 1987. **Essays:** Constantijn Huygens; Martinus Nijhoff.

KIRTON, W.J.S. Lecturer in French, University of Aberdeen. Author of plays for radio and stage. **Essay:** Victor Hugo.

KLOPP, Charles. Associate professor of romance languages, Ohio State University, Columbus. Author of "'Peregrino' and 'Errante' in the *Gerusalemme liberata*," in *Modern Language Notes*, 1979, the entry on Giosuè Carducci in *European Writers: The Romantic Century* (forthcoming), and articles on Italian literature. **Essays:** Eugenio Montale; Torquato Tasso.

KNOWLES, A.V. University of Liverpool. **Essays:** *First Love*; Denis Fonvizin; *A Month in the Country; The Minor; Oblomov; War and Peace; Woes of Wit.*

KOEPKE, Wulf. Distinguished professor of German. Author of *Erfolglosigkeit*, 1977, *Lion Feuchtwanger*, 1983, *Johann Gottfried Herder*, 1987, and *Max Frisch*, 1991. Editor of *J.G. Herder— Innovator Through the Ages*, 1982. Co-editor of *Deutschsprachige Exilliteratur in Kontext der Epoche*, 1984, *Deutsche Exilliteratur*, 1989, *German and International Perspectives on the Spanish Civil War*, 1992, *Exilforschung*, and *Herder Yearbook*. **Essay:** *Berlin Alexanderplatz.*

KOLBERT, Jack. Professor emeritus of French literature, Susquehanna University. Author of *The Worlds of Elie Wiesel: An Overview of His Career and His Major Themes* (2001), *The Worlds of André Maurois* (1985), *L'Art de Michel Butor* (1970) (with Claude Book-Senninger), Introduction to *The Distant Friend by Claude Roy* (1987) (*L'Ami lointain*), translated by High Harter), and hundreds of articles, essays, and reviews in literary journals and newspapers; reviewer in *The French Review*. **Essays:** Gabrielle Roy; Elie Wiesel.

KOMAR, Kathleen L. Instructor, Department of Germanic Languages, University of California. **Essay:** *Seventh Duino Elegy.*

KONRAD, Linn Bratteteig. Assistant professor of French, Rice University, Houston. Author of "Modern Hieratic Ideas on Theatre: Maurice Maeterlinck and Antonin Artaud," in *Modern Drama 22*, 1979, "Symbolic Action in Modern Drama: Maurice Maeterlinck," in *Themes in Drama 4*, 1982, and "Maurice Maeterlinck in the Pharmaceutical Tradition," in *Romanic Review 73*, 1982. **Essay:** Maurice Maeterlinck.

KONSTAN, David. Jane A. Seney professor of Greek, Wesleyan University, Middletown, Connecticut. Author of *Some Aspects of Epicurean Psychology*, 1973, *Catullus' Indictment of Rome: The Meaning of Catullus 64*, 1977, *Roman Comedy*, 1983, and a commentary on *Dyskolos* by Menander, 1983. **Essays:** *Daphnis and Chloe*; Plautus.

KONSTANATAKOS, Myrto. Instructor, Department of French, Royal Holloway and Bedford New College. **Essay:** *Les Misérables.*

KWONG, Charles. Assistant professor of Chinese and director of the Chinese Programme at Tufts University. Author of *Tao Qian and the Chinese Poetic Tradition: The Quest for Cultural Identity*, associate editor, *Anthology of Chinese Women Poets: From Ancient Times to 1911* (forthcoming), and articles in *Chinese Literature: Essays, Articles, Reviews*. **Essay:** Tao Qian.

LAMPORT, F.J. Fellow of Worcester College, Oxford. Author of *A Student's Guide to Goethe*, 1971, *Lessing and the Drama*, 1981, and *German Classical Drama*, 1990. Translator of *Five German Tragedies*, 1969, and *The Robbers* and *Wallenstein* by Friedrich von Schiller, 1979. **Essays:** Johann Wolfgang von Goethe; Gotthold Ephraim Lessing; Friedrich von Schiller.

LANCASTER, Jordan. Visiting professor of Italian, University of Calgary, Canada. Author of "Autobiography in Eighteenth-Century Italy" (dissertation), 1992. **Essays:** *Conversation in Sicily*; Carlo Levi; *Master Don Gesualdo*; *Orlando Furioso*; Jacopo Sannazaro; *Saul*.

LAPAIRE, Pierre J. Associate professor of French, University of North Carolina at Wilmington. Author of *Montherlant et la parole: étude d'un langage dramatique* (forthcoming), "La loi de couplaison de Saussure et *La Cloche fêlée* de Baudelaire," in *Language and Style*, 1987, "Valeurs et fonctions du silence dans *Le Cardinal d'Espagne*," in *French Review*, 1989, "Pouvoir politique et antithéâtre chez Camus, Montherlant et Sartre," in *Romance Quarterly*, 1989, and other articles on Marguerite Yourcenar, Albert Camus, and 20th-century French drama. **Essays:** *The Cid*; *Le Père Goriot*; *Phaedra*; *The Plague*; "A Simple Heart".

LARMOUR, David H.J. Essays: Anacreon; *Odes* Book I, Poem 5; *Odes* Book IV, Poem 7; *On the Commonwealth*; *Prometheus Bound*; *The Rape of Proserpine*.

LAST, Rex W. Essays: Henri Barbusse; *Before the Storm*; *The Conceited Young Ladies*; Georg Kaiser; Erich Maria Remarque; *Under Fire*.

LATIMER, Dan. Professor of English and comparative literature, Auburn University, Alabama; co-editor of *Southern Humanities Review*. Author of *Contemporary Critical Theory*, 1989, "Real Culture and Unreal Nature: Wordsworth's Kingdom of Dissimilitude," in *New Orleans Review* 14, 1987, "Sex in Paradise Lost: Neurosis in the Blissful Bower," in *Literature and Psychology 30*, 1980. "Anxieties of Reading: Paul de Man and the Purloined Ribbon," in *Comparative Poetics*, "Erotic Susceptibility and Tuberculosis: Literary Images of a Pathology," in *Modern Language Notes 105*, 1990, and "Against Post Modernism. A Marxist Critique," in *Textual Practice 6*, 1992. **Essays:** *The Birth of Tragedy*; *The Magic Mountain*; *The Radetzky March*.

LATIMER, Renate. Associate professor of German, Auburn University, Alabama. Translator of *Farewell to Love and other Misunderstandings* by Hubert Eisenreich (forthcoming), and other German and Austrian short stories. **Essays:** *Elective Affinities*; *Indian Summer*.

LEE, John. Essays: *Oedipus at Colonus*; On the Sublime.

LEE, Mabel. Honorary associate professor of Chinese, University of Sydney. Author of writings on modern and contemporary Chinese intellectual history and literature; co-editor of the *University of Sydney East Asian Series* and the *University of Sydney World Literature Series*; translator from the Chinese of the novels *Soul Mountain* (2000) and *One Man's Bible* (2002) by 2000 Nobel Laureate Gao Xingjian, and also of three books of poetry *Masks and Crocodile* (1990), *The Dead in Exile* (1990) and *Yi* (2002) by Yang Lian, the 1999 winner of the Flaiano International Literature Prize for Poetry. **Essay:** Gao Xingjian.

LEFEVERE, André. Instructor, Germanic Languages, University of Texas at Austin, Texas. Author of *Translation, Rewriting and the Manipulation of Literary Fame*, 1992, and *Teaching Translation: A Little Primer*, 1992. **Essays:** Willem Bilderdijk; Gerbrand Bredero; Guido Gezelle; Pieter Corneliszoon Hooft; Joost van den Vondel.

LEVIN, Harry. Irving Babbitt professor of comparative literature, Harvard University, Cambridge, Massachusetts. Author of many critical books, the most recent being *The Myth of the Golden Age in the Renaissance, Grounds for Comparison, Shakespeare and the Revolution of the Times*, and *Memories of the Moderns*. Editor of works by Ben Jonson, Earl of Rochester, James Joyce, Shakespeare, and Nathaniel Hawthorne, and of anthologies.

LEVY, Silvano. Lecturer in French, University of Keele, Staffordshire. Author of "The Early Works of René Magritte" (thesis), 1981, and articles in *Artscribe International, The Linguist, Journal of Literary Semantics, Modern Language Review, Times Higher Education Supplement, Circa*, and *Apollo*. **Essays:** *Antigone* (Anouilh); *The Fall*; *The Outsider*.

LEWIS, Virginia L. Assistant professor of German, Drake University, Des Moines, Iowa. Author of *Flames of Passion/Flames of Greed: Acts of Arson in German Prose Fiction, 1850–1900*, 1991, and "Work and Freedom in the Minority Community: Ferdinand von Saar's Die Troglodytin," in *The German Mosaic: Cultural and Linguistic Diversity in Society*, 1992. **Essay:** *Effi Briest*.

LI, Dian. Assistant professor of East Asian studies, University of Arizona. Contributor of essays and translations to journals including *Jintian* (Today), *Modern Chinese Literature and Culture*, Babel (Europe), *The Kenyon Review, The Green Mountains Review, Journal of Modern Literature in Chinese, Tamkang Review* (Taipei), *Translation Quarterly* (Hong Kong). **Essays:** Bei Dao; *Rickshaw Boy*.

LICASTRO, Emanuele. Professor of Italian, State University of New York. Author of *Luigi Pirandello: dalle novelle alle commedie*, 1974, and *Ugo Betti: An Introduction*, 1985. **Essays:** *Christ Stopped at Eboli*; Eduardo De Filippo; *Filumena Marturano*; *The House by the Medlar Tree*; The Ninth Tale of the Fifth Day of *The Decameron*.

LIN, Sylvia Li-chun. Assistant professor, The University of Notre Dame. Co-translator of Chu T'ien-wen, *Notes of a Desolate Man*, and Alai, *Red Poppies*. **Essay:** Li Ang.

LISBOA, Maria Manuel. Assistant lecturer in Portuguese, Cambridge University. Formerly held lectureship in Portuguese and Brazilian literature, University of Newcastle, 1988–93. Author of many articles including "Manuel Bandeira: sexualidade e subversão," in *Colóquio Letras*, May-August 1990, and "Madwomen, Whores and Torga: Desecrating the Canon?," in *Portuguese Studies*, 7, 1991, also introduction (in Portuguese) to an edition of José Régio's *Histórias de mulheres*, 1993, and translation of two chapters of *Three Persons on One: A Centenary Tribute to Fernando Pessoa*, edited by Bernard McGuirk, 1989. **Essay:** Clarice Lispector.

LLOYD, Heather. Instructor, Department of French, University of Glasgow. **Essay:** *Guigemar*.

LLOYD, Rosemary. Professor, Department of French and Italian, Indiana University, Indiana. Formerly lecturer, Cambridge University. Editor of *Baudelaire et Hoffmann*, 1979, *Baudelaire's Literary Criticism*, 1981, *Mallarmé: Poésies*, 1984, and *Madame Bovary*, 1990. **Essays:** *L'Après-midi d'un faune*; *Madame Bovary*.

LÖB, Ladislaus. Reader in German, University of Sussex, Brighton. Author of *Mensch und Gesellschaft bei J.B. Priestley*, 1962, *From Lessing to Hauptmann: Studies in German Drama*, 1974, *Der arme Millionär: A Radio Course in German* (with E.R. Baer), a textbook on German, and articles on German drama for journals and anthologies. Editor of *Grabbe über seine Werke*, 1991. **Essays:** Friedrich Hebbel; Heinrich von Kleist; Frank Wedekind.

LONG, Jacqueline. Instructor, Department of Classics, University of Texas at Austin. **Essay:** Claudian.

LORENZ, Dagmar. Instructor, Department of German, Ohio State University. **Essays:** Heimito von Döderer; *Professor Bernhardi*; Joseph Roth; *Die Strudlhofstiege*.

LOSELLE, Andrea. Instructor, Department of French, University of California. **Essay:** *Journey to the End of the Night*.

LUCENTE, Gregory L. Associate professor of romance languages, Johns Hopkins University, Baltimore. Author of *The Narrative of Realism and Myth: Verga, Lawrence, Faulkner, Pavese*, 1981, and articles on D'Annunzio, Joyce, Silone, and *verismo*. **Essays:** Luigi Pirandello; Giovanni Verga.

LUFT, David S. Associate professor of history, University of California at San Diego, La Jolla. Author of *Robert Musil and the Crisis of European Culture 1880–1942*, 1980, "Schopenhauer, Austria, and the Generation of 1905," in *Central European History*, March 1983, and a forthcoming essay on Otto Weininger. **Essay:** Robert Musil.

LUNDELL, Torborg. Instructor, Department of German and Slavic Languages, University of California. **Essays:** "The Emperor's New Clothes"; *Gosta Berling's Saga*; Ivar Lo-Johansson; *Miss Julie*.

LUPKE, Christopher. Assistant professor of Chinese language and culture, Washington State University. Editor of *The Magnitude of Ming: Command, Allotment and Fate in Chinese Culture*, forthcoming, and many essays and translations; associate editor, *Journal of Modern Literature in Chinese*, 2002–. **Essay:** Huang Chunming.

MARFANY, J.F. Instructor, Department of Hispanic Studies, University of Liverpool. **Essay:** Camilo José Cela.

MARRONE, Gaetana. Associate professor of Italian, Princeton University, New Jersey; editorial consultant for Novecento Editrice,

Princeton University Press, Cambridge University Press, Hartcourt, Prentice Hall. Author of *La Drammatica di Ugo Betti. Tematiche e Arche Tipi*, 1988, *The Cinema of Liliana Cavani. The Gaze and the Labyrinth* (forthcoming), and many articles on modern Italian literature and cinema. **Essays:** Ugo Betti; Elsa Morante.

MASKELL, David. Lecturer in French, University of Oxford. Author of *The Historical Epic in France*, 1973, *A Descriptive Bibliography of Montaigne's Essays*, 1983, and *Racine: A Theatrical Reading*, 1991. **Essays:** "On Vanity"; Quintilian; *Tartuffe*; *The Theatrical Illusion*.

MASON, Eve. Formerly fellow in German, Newham College, Cambridge; affiliated lecturer, German Department, Cambridge University. Author of *Stifter, Bunte Steine* (Critical Guides to German Texts series), 1987, "Stifter and the Enlightenment," in *The Austrian Enlightenment and its Aftermath, Austrian Studies II* edited by R. Robertson and E. Timms, 1991, "Two Views on Bürgerlichkeit in Gottfried Keller's *Die Leute von Seldwyla*," in *Gottfried Keller 1819–1890* edited by J.L. Flood and M. Swales, and numerous articles in *German Life and Letters, Modern Language Review, Cambridge Quarterly, Adalbert Stifter Heute*, and *Germanistik*. **Essay:** *Family Strife in Hapsburg*.

MASON, Haydn T. Professor of French, University of Bristol. Author of *Pierre Bayle and Voltaire*, 1963, *Voltaire*, 1975, *Voltaire: A Biography*, 1981, *French Writers and Their Society 1715–1800*, 1982, and *Cyrano de Bergerac: L'Autre Monde*, 1984. Co-author of *Voltaire and his World*, 1985, *Myth and its Making in the French Theatre*, 1988, *The Tempest of the French Revolution*, 1989. Editor of *Les Fausses Confidences* by Marivaux, 1964, *The Leibniz-Arnauld Correspondence*, 1967, and *Zadig and Other Stories* by Voltaire, 1971. **Essays:** *Poem on the Disaster of Lisbon*; Voltaire; *Voyages to the Moon and the Sun*; *Zadig*.

MAUS, Derek. Assistant professor of English and communication, SUNY College at Potsdam; editor of several collections of essays on Dostoyevsky, Camus, the Cold War, and postmodernism; contributor of scholarly essays on American and Russian literature to such publications as *Southern Quarterly, Papers in Language and Literature*, and *The Journal of Literary Studies*. **Essays:** Peter Høeg; Masuji Ibuse.

MAY, Gita. Professor and chairman of the department of French and romance philology, Columbia University, New York. Author of *Diderot et Baudelaire, critiques d'art*, 1957 (3rd edition, 1973), *De Jean-Jacques Rousseau à Madame Roland*, 1964 (2nd edition, 1974), *Madame Roland and the Age of Revolution*, 1970, *Stendhal and the Age of Napoleon*, essays on Diderot and George Sand in *European Writers*, 1984/1985, and many articles and reviews. Editor, with Otis Fellows, of *Diderot Studies III*, 1961, and of works for Diderot's *Oeuvres complètes*. **Essays:** Madame de Staël; Stendhal.

McADOO, Jane. Instructor, Department of European Languages, Goldsmith's College. **Essays:** *The Devil in the Flesh*; Jean Giono; *The Hussar on the Roof*; *The New Life*; Raymond Radiguet.

McCOBB, E.A. Lecturer, German Department, University of Hull. Author of *Georger Eliot's German Background*, 1982. **Essay:** Andreas Gryphius.

McCARTHY, Patrick. Member of the department of French, Haverford College, Pennsylvania. Author of *Céline*, 1975, and *Camus: A Critical Study of His Life and Work*, 1982. **Essay:** Louis-Ferdinand Céline; Pier Paolo Pasolini.

McDERMOTT, A. Instructor, Department of Hispanic and Latin American Studies, University of Bristol. **Essay:** José Hernández.

MCDUFF, David. Writer and translator. Formerly editor at Stand Magazine, and Anvil Press. Translator of *The House of the Dead*, 1985, and *Crime and Punishment*, 1991, both by Fedor Dostoevskii, and *Complete Poems of Edith Södergran*, 1984 and 1992. **Essays:** *Crime and Punishment*; *Red Cavalry*; Edith Södergran.

McGREGOR, R.S. Professor, Faculty of Oriental Studies, University of Cambridge.

McGREGOR, Richard J.A. Social Sciences & Humanities Research Council of Canada Post-doctoral fellow, Institut Français d'Archéologie Orientale du Caire. Author of *Sanctity and Mysticism in Medieval Egypt: the Wafaʿ Sufi Order and the Legacy of Ibn ʿArabi* forthcoming from the State University of New York Press and "New Sources for the Study of Sufism in Mamluk Egypt," *Bulletin of the School of Oriental and African Studies* vol. 65, no. 2 (2002). **Essay:** Muhyi al-Din Ibn al-Arabi.

MCLAUGHLIN, Martin L. Instructor, Christ Church College, Oxford. **Essays:** Dino Buzzati; Italo Calvino; *Fontamara*; *Jerusalem Delivered*; *The Moon and the Bonfires*; "Sonnet 90".

MCKAY, Alexander G. Instructor, Department of Classics, McMaster University. **Essays:** *The Aeneid*; *Ajax*; *Electra* (Sophocles); *In Defence of Marcus Caelius Rufus*; *The Oresteia*; *Orestes*; *The Persians*; *The Trojan Women*.

McMAHON, Keith. Associate professor, University of Kansas, Lawrence, Kansas. Formerly member of the faculty, Princeton University, New Jersey. **Essays:** *Golden Lotus*; Lu Xun; *Water Margin*.

MCMILLIN, Arnold. Professor of Russian literature, University of London; member of the editorial boards of *Birmingham Slavonic Monographs, Slavonic and East European Review*, and *Studies in Russian and German*. Formerly Slavonic editor of the *Modern Language Review*. Author of *A History of Byelorussian Literature*, 1977, *Aspects of Modern Russian and Czech Literature*, 1989, *From Pushkin to "Palisandriia,"* 1990, *Under Eastern Eyes*, 1991, and *Symbolism and After*, 1992. **Essays:** *The Brothers Karamazov*; Vasil Bykaw; *Cancer Ward*; *Eugene Onegin*; Aleksandr Griboedov; *The Idiot*; *Kreutzer Sonata*; *Notes from Underground*; *One Day in the Life of Ivan Denisovich*; *The Ordeal*; *A School for Fools*; Sasha Sokolov.

MCTURK, Rory. Instructor, School of English, University of Leeds. **Essays:** *Egils saga*; *Njls*Æ *saga*; The Poetic *Edda*; The Prose *Edda*; *The Saga of King Óláf the Saint*.

MCVAY, Gordon. Reader in Russian, University of Bristol. Author of *Esenin: A Life*, 1976, *Isadora and Esenin*, 1980, articles on Russian literature, especially Sergei Esenin, the peasant poets, the Imaginists, and Anton Chekhov, in scholarly journals in Britain, the United

States, Canada, and France, and articles and reviews in *Plays and Players*. **Essays:** *The Bedbug*; *Fathers and Sons*; *Uncle Vanya*.

MEECH, A.J. Instructor, Department of Drama, University of Hull. **Essays:** *The Life of Galileo*; *Minna von Barnhelm*.

MEWS, Siegfried. Professor of German at the University of North Carolina and chairman of the department. Formerly editor, University of North Carolina Studies in the Germanic Languages and Literatures; executive director, South Atlantic Modern Language Association; editor, *South Atlantic Review*; president, South Atlantic Modern Language Association. Author of *Ulrich Plenzdorf*, 1984. Editor, with Herbert Knust, of *Essays on Brecht: Theater and Politics*, 1974, and *Carl Zuckmayer*, 1981. Editor of *The Fisherman and His Wife: Günter Grass's The Flounder in Critical Perspective*, 1983, and *Critical Essays on Bertolt Brecht*, 1989. **Essays:** *The Tin Drum*; Carl Zuckmayer.

MIHAILOVICH, Vasa D. Professor emeritus of Slavic literature, University of North Carolina, Chapel Hill. Editor of *Serbian Poetry from the Beginnings to the Present* (1988), *Songs of the Serbian People* (1997), 2 volumes of *Dictionary of Literary Biography* (1994, 1997). Contributor of numerous articles and reviews to reference books and scholarly magazines. **Essays:** *Envy*; Milorad Pavić; Miodrag Pavlović; Mikhail Mikhailovich Zoshchenko.

MIKÓS, Michael J., Professor of Slavic languages, University of Wisconsin-Milwaukee. Author of *Medieval Literature of Poland* (1992), *W pogoni za Sienkiewiczem* (1994), *Polish Renaissance Literature* (1995), *Jan Kochanowski: Laments* (1995, 1998), *Polish Baroque and Enlightenment Literature* (1996), *Adam Mickiewicz: The Sun of Liberty* (1998), *Polish Literature from the Middle Ages to the End of the Eighteenth Century* (1999), *Juliusz Slowacki: This Fateful Power* (1999), *Polish Romantic Literature* (2002), and numerous articles. **Essay:** Juliusz Słowacki.

MILES, Gary B. Associate professor of history, University of California, Santa Cruz. Author of *Virgil's Georgics*, 1980, and of articles on Virgil, Theocritus, the Bible, Roman Imperialism, and other subjects in *American Journal of Philology, Shakespeare Quarterly, Harvard Theological Review, Comparative Studies in Society and History*, and other journals. **Essay:** Virgil.

MILLER, Paul Allen. Instructor, Department of Classical and Modern Languages and Literatures. Texas Tech University. **Essay:** Persius.

MILNOR, Kristina. **Essay:** Petronius.

MINER, Earl. Townsend Martin professor of English and comparative literature, Princeton University, New Jersey. Author of *Dryden's Poetry*, 1967, *An Introduction to Japanese Court Poetry*, 1968, *The Metaphysical Mode from Donne to Cowley*, 1969, *The Cavalier Mode from Jonson to Cotton*, 1971, *Seventeenth-Century Imagery*, 1971, *The Restoration Mode from Milton to Dryden*, 1974, *Literary Uses of Typology*, 1977, and *Japanese Linked Poetry*, 1979. Translator, with Hiroko Odagiri, of *The Monkey's Straw Raincoat and Other Poetry of the Basho School*, 1981. Editor of *A History of Japanese Literature* by Jin'ichi Konishi, from 1984.

MIYOSHI, Masao. Professor of English, University of California, Berkeley. Author of *The Divided Self: A Perspective on the Literature of the Victorians*, 1969, *Accomplices of Silence: The Modern Japanese Novel*, 1974, and *As We Saw Them: The First Japanese Embassy to the United States (1860)*, 1979. **Essays:** Kawabata Yasunari; Natsume Sōseki.

MIZENKO, Matthew. Assistant professor of Asian languages and literatures, Amherst College, Massachusetts. **Essay:** Dazai Osamu.

MORAN, Edward. Writer and literary researcher. Associate editor of *World Authors 1900–1950* (H. W. Wilson, 1996); contributing writer to *World Authors 1990–1995* (H. W. Wilson, 2000) and *Current Biography* magazine. Co-author (with W. Patrick Coyne) of *Clarence S. Day: A Bibliography* (2002). **Essays:** *The Peony Pavilion*; *Rice*; Su Tong; Tang Xianzu.

MOSHER, Nicole. Assistant professor of French. Formerly associate editor of *Style*. Author of *La Poésie visuelle; Le Calligramme de l'époque Alexandrine a l'époque Cubiste*, and several articles. **Essays:** *Against Nature*; *Sentimental Education*.

MOTTE, Warren. Professor of French and comparative literature, University of Colorado. Author of *Small Worlds: Minimalism in Contemporary French Literature* (1999), *Playtexts: Ludics in Contemporary Literature* (1995), *Questioning Edmond Jabès* (1990), and *The Poetics of Experiment: A Study of Georges Perec* (1984). **Essays:** *Life A User's Manual*; Georges Perec.

MOTTO, Anna Lydia. Professor of classics, University of South Florida, Tampa. Author of *Seneca Sourcebook: Guide to the Thought of Lucius Annaeus Seneca*, 1970, *Seneca* (Twayne's World Authors series), 1973, *Senecan Tragedy*, 1988, *Seneca; A Critical Bibliography, 1900–1980, Essays on Seneca* (forthcoming), and some 90 articles in scholarly journals. Editor of *Satire—That Blasted Art*, 1973, and *Seneca: Selected Moral Epistles*, 1985. **Essays:** (with John R. Clark) *Epigrams*; *Lysistrata*; *Oedipus*; *Thyestes*.

MOTTA, Vanna. Instructor, School of European Studies, Department of Italian, University of Wales. **Essays:** *House of Liars*; *Voices in the Evening*.

MUIR, Kenneth. Formerly King Alfred professor of English literature at University of Liverpool; vice-president of the International Shakespeare Association: F.B.A.; F.R.S.L. Author of many books, including *Shakespeare's Tragic Sequence*, 1972, *Shakespeare the Professional*, 1973, *The Singularity of Shakespeare*, 1977, *The Sources of Shakespeare's Plays*, 1977, *Shakespeare's Comic Sequence*, 1979, and studies of Milton, Elizabethan literature, and the comedy of manners. Editor of five plays by Shakespeare, and works by Thomas Wyatt, Keats, and Middleton, and of anthologies. Translator of *Five Plays* by Racine, 1960, and *Four Comedies* by Calderón, 1980. **Essay:** Pedro Calderón de la Barca.

MURDOCH, Brian. Senior lecturer in German, University of Stirling, Fife. Author of *Remarque, Im Westen nichts Neues*, 1984, *Fighting Songs and Warring Words*, 1989, *The Recapitulated Fall*, 1974, *Hans Folz and the Adam Legends*, 1976, *Old High German*, 1983, and numerous books and articles on medieval German and Celtic literature. Translator of *Kudrun*, 1987. **Essay:** *All Quiet on the Western Front*.

MURK-JANSEN, S.M. Instructor, Robinson College, Cambridge. **Essay:** Hadewijch.

MURPHY, Brian. Professor emeritus, University of Ulster, Coleraine, Londonderry. Formerly senior lecturer, Royal Military Academy, Sandhurst; lecturer in Russian, University College, Swansea. Introduction and notes to: *Svad'ba* by A.P. Chekov, 1963, *Chetyre rasskaza* by I. Babel, 1964, and *Rasskazy dvatsatykh godov* by M. Zoshchenko, 1969. Author of *60 Russian Proses*, 1960, *Key to 60 Russian Proses*, 1960, "The Style of Isaak Babel," in *Slavonic and East European Review*, 1966, "Aspectual Usage of the Present Tense in Serbo-Croat," in *Proceedings of the Royal Irish Academy*, 1974, "Sholokhov and Lukomsky," in *Journal of Russian Studies*, 1978, "Academic Life in Recent Soviet Fiction," in *Soviet Studies*, 1979, *Mikhail Zoshchenko: A Literary Profile*, 1981, "Turgenev and Flaubert—a Contrast in Styles," in *New Zealand Slavonic Journal*, 1983, "An Introduction to the Stories of Isaak Babel," in *Journal of Russian Studies*, 1984, "The Don after the White Retreat: Extracts from Verkhne-Donskaia Pravda," in *Revolutionary Russia*, 1989, "Introduction and Commentary to Sholokhov's Tikhii Don," in *New Zealand Slavonic Journal*, 1975–1990, and "The Don Rebellion March-June 1919," in *Revolutionary Russia*, 1993. **Essay:** Mikhail Sholokhov.

MUSOLINO, Walter. Instructor, Department of Italian Studies, La Trobe University, Bundoora Campus, Victoria. **Essays:** "The Broom"; *Cuttlefish Bones*; "To Himself"; "Sirens."

NAFF, William E. Professor emeritus of Japanese, University of Massachusetts. Founding chairman of the department of Asian languages at University of Massachusetts; also taught at University of California-Los Angeles, Stanford University, and University of Oregon. **Essay:** Shimazaki Haruki.

NAPIER, Susan. Assistant professor of Japanese, University of Texas, Austin. Author of *Escape from the Waste: Romanticism and Realism in the Fiction of Mishima Yukio and Ōe Kenzaburō*, 1991. **Essay:** Ōe Kenzaburō.

NISETICH, Frank J. Associate professor of classics, University of Massachusetts, Boston. Translator of *Victory Songs* by Pindar, 1980. **Essays:** Pindar; Sappho.

NORLEN, Paul. Author of *"Textens villkor": A Study of Willy Kyrklund's Prose Fiction* (1997) and articles on twentieth-century Swedish, Danish and Norwegian writers. **Essay:** Tarjei Vesaas.

OAKLEY, Bob. Instructor, Department of Hispanic Studies, University of Birmingham. **Essays:** Carlos Drummond Andrade; Mário de Andrade; João Guimarães Rosa.

O'CONNELL, David. Instructor, Department of Modern and Classical Languages, Georgia State University. **Essays:** Marcel Aymé; Robert Brasillach.

ODBER de BAUBETA, P.A. Director of Portuguese studies, Department of Hispanic Studies, University of Birmingham. **Essays:** Barcas Trilogy; *Farsa de Inês Pereira*.

OJALA, Jeanne A. Professor of history, University of Utah, Salt Lake City. Formerly President of the Western Society for French History (USA/Canada). Author of *Auguste de Clobert . . . 1793–1809*, 1979, "Marshal Suchet," in *Napoleon's Marshals*, 1987, *Madame de Sevigne* (with William T. Ojala), 1990, and "Prostitution in Paris, 1789–1793," in *Viewing the Heritage of Women in Western Tradition*, 1990. **Essays:** François La Rochefoucauld; Marguerite de Navarre.

O'NEILL, Tom. Instructor, Department of Italian, Melbourne University. **Essays:** Giuseppe Tomasi di Lampedusa; Leonardo Sciascia; "The Storm".

OSCHERWITZ, Dayna. Assistant professor of French, Southern Methodist University. Author of articles on Patrick Chamoiseau, Gisèle Pineau, Calixthe Beyala, and Paul Smäil, among others. **Essays:** Patrick Chamoiseau; Edouard Glissant.

PADDON, Seija. Assistant professor of English, Concordia University, Montréal, Québec. Formerly a member of the editorial board of *EXILE*. Translator of *Not You, Not the Rain* by Sirkka Turkka, 1991, *Fragments* by Pentti Saaritsa, 1991, and *Boy Devil* by Kirsti Simonsuuri, 1992. **Essay:** *Kalevala*.

PARROTT, (Sir) Cecil. Professor emeritus in central and southeastern European studies, University of Lancaster; British Ambassador to Czechoslovakia, 1960–66. Author of *Czechoslovakia: Its Heritage and Future*, 1968, two volumes of memoirs: *The Tightrope*, 1975, and *The Serpent and the Nightingale*, 1977; also *The Bad Bohemian: The Life of Jaroslav Hašek*, 1978, and *Jaroslav Hašek: A Study of Svejk and the Short Stories*, 1982. Translator of *The Good Soldier Svejk* (complete version), 1973, and *The Red Commissar and Other Stories*, 1981, both by Haek. **Essays:** Karel Čapek; Jaroslav Hašek.

PATERSON, Alan K.G. Professor of Spanish, St. Andrews University, Fife, Scotland. Author of numerous articles on Spanish Golden Age poetry and drama, including "The Traffic of the Stage in Calderón's *La vida es sueño*," in *Renaissance Drama 4*, 1971, and "The Alchemical Marriage in Calderón's *El médico de su honra*," in *Romanistisches Jahrbuch 30*, 1979. Editor of *La venganza de Tamar* by Tirso de Molina, 1969. **Essay:** Lope de Vega Carpio.

PAUL, Georgina. Instructor, Department of German Studies, University of Warwick. **Essay:** Christa Wolf.

PEACOCK, D. Keith. Lecturer in drama. Author of *Radical Stages: Alternative History in Modern British Drama*, 1991. **Essays:** *Brand*; *The Ghost Sonata*; *The Insect Play*; *Peer Gynt*; *R.U.R.*; *The Wild Duck*.

PEACOCK, Noel A. Instructor, Department of French, The University, Glasgow. **Essay:** *Don Juan*.

PEARSON, Roger. Queen's College, Oxford. **Essay:** *The Charter House of Parma*.

PEREZ, Janet. Instructor, Department of Spanish, Texas Tech University. **Essays:** Rafael Alberti; Vicente Aleixandre; *Blood Wedding*; *The Christ of Velazquez*; Antonio Machado; *Mist*; Ramón Pérez de Ayala; Ramón J. Sender; Ramón del Valle-Inclán; *Yerma*.

PETERKIEWICZ, Jerzy. Author of many books, including novels (*Future to Let, Isolation, Green Flows the Bile*), plays (*The Third Adam*), verse, and critical books (*The Other Side of Silence: The Poet at the Limits of Language*, 1975). Editor and translator of *Polish Prose and Verse*, 1956, *Five Centuries of Polish Poetry 1450–1970* (with Burns Singer), 1970, and *Easter Vigil and Other Poems*, 1979, and *Collected Poems*, 1982, both by Karol Wojtyla (Pope John Paul II). Formerly professor of Polish language and literature, University of London.

PHILOKYPROU, Elli. Post-doctoral research student. Author of a number of articles on Greek poetry, individually and with Sarah Ekdawi. **Essays:** Odysseus Elytis; *Mythistorima*; Kostes Palamas.

PIKE, Christopher R. Lecturer in Russian studies, University of Keele, Staffordshire; editor of the journal *Essays in Poetics*. Author of "Formalist and Structuralist Approaches to Dostoevsky," in *New Essays on Dostoevsky* edited by Malcolm V. Jones and Garth M. Terry, 1983. Editor of *The Futurists, The Formalists and the Marxist Critique*, 1980. **Essays:** Anton Chekov; Fedor Dostoevskii; Leo Tolstoi.

PIRIE, Donald Peter Alexander. Writer and teacher. **Essays:** Jan Kochanowski; Adam Mickiewicz; Bruno Schulz.

PLATTON, David. Instructor, Department of French, University of Leeds. **Essay:** *The Theatre and Its Double*.

POCOCK, Gordon. Author of *Corneille and Racine: Problems of Tragic Form*, 1973, and *Boileau and the Nature of Neo-Classicism*, 1980. **Essays:** Nicolas Boileau; Pierre Corneille.

POLLACK, Beth. Associate professor of Spanish and head of the department of languages and linguistics, New Mexico State University. Recent publications in the area of translation include, with Ricardo Aguilar Melantzon, Ron Aria's novel *El Camino a Tamazunchale* and Denise Chavez's novel *Por el amor de Pedro Infante*; translated into English Ricardo Aguilar's book of personal essays *Windward* (*Puerto del Sol*, 2002). Contributor of interviews and articles on Latin American Jewish Writers. **Essays:** Isabel Allende; Demetrio Aguilera Malta; *The House of the Spirits*.

POLUKHINA, Valentina. Senior lecturer in Russian, University of Keele, Staffordshire. Author of *Joseph Brodsky: A Poet for our Time*, 1989 and articles on Russian and Soviet writers for *The Fontana Biographical Companion to Modern Thought*, 1982. Editor of *Brodsky's Poetics and Aesthetics* (with L. Loseff), 1990, and *Brodsky Through the Eyes of his Contemporaries*, 1992. **Essays:** Andrei Belyi; Aleksandr Blok; Iosif Brodskii; Vladimir Maiakovskii; Osip Mandel'shtam; *A Part of Speech*; Boris Pasternak; Marina Tsvetaeva.

PORTER, Charles A. Professor of French, Yale University, New Haven, Connecticut. Author of *Restif's Novels; or, An Autobiography in Search of an Author*, 1967, and *Chateaubriand: Composition, Imagination, and Poetry*, 1978. **Essay:** Chateaubriand.

PREBLE-NIEMI, Oralia. **Essays:** Miguel Ángel Asturias; Rosario Castellanos; Nicolás Guillén; José Marti.

PREDMORE, Michael P. Instructor, Department of Spanish and Portuguese, Stanford University. **Essay:** *Platero and I.*

PRUNSTER, Nicole. Instructor, Department of Italian Studies, La Trobe University, Bundoora Campus, Victoria. **Essays:** *The Comic Theatre*; *La cortigiana*; *The Mandrake*; Pietro Metastasio.

PUCCI, Joseph. Assistant professor of classics and of medieval studies, Brown University. Author of various articles and book reviews in *Classical Philology, Classical World, Ramus, Classica et Mediaevalia, Arethusa,* and *Latomus.* **Essays:** *Consolation of Philosophy*; Aurelius Clemens Prudentius; Three Poems: 2, 63, 76.

PURVER, Judith. Instructor, Department of German, University of Manchester. **Essays:** Bettina von Arnim; Joseph von Eichendorff; *Memoirs of a Good-for-Nothing*; Caroline de la Motte-Fouqué.

PUVACIC, Dušan. Lecturer in Yugoslav studies, University of Lancaster. Contributor to Yugoslav literary journals. Editor of *Kritički radovi Branka Lazarevića*, 1975, and translator into Serbo-Croat of many works of English and American literature. **Essay:** Miroslav Krleža.

RAGUSA, Olga. Da Ponte professor and chairman of the department of Italian, Columbia University, New York; editor of the journal *Italica.* Author of *Mallarmé in Italy: A Study in Literary Influence and Critical Response*, 1957, *Verga's Milanese Tales*, 1964, *Narrative and Drama: Essays in Modern Italian Literature from Verga to Pasolini*, 1976, *Luigi Pirandello: An Approach to His Theatre*, 1980, and an essay in *"Romantic" and Its Cognates: The European History of a Word* edited by H. Eichner, 1972. **Essays:** Vittorio Alfieri; Alessandro Manzoni.

RANERO, Ana M. Ph.D. candidate in the department of Sanskrit and Indian studies at Harvard University. Formerly teaching assistant in the department of comparative literature at the University of Illinois at Urbana-Champaign, Urbana, Illinois. **Essays:** Kabīr; *Śakuntalā* ; Tulsīdās.

RATHI, Girdar. Instructor, Sahitya Akademi, New Delhi.

RAWSON, Judy. Senior lecturer and chairman of the department of Italian, University of Warwick, Coventry. Editor of *Fontamara* by Ignazio Silone, 1972. **Essays:** Cesare Pavese; Ignazio Silone; Elio Vittorini.

REID, J.H. Senior lecturer in German, University of Nottingham. Author of *Critical Strategies: German Fiction in the Twentieth Century* (with E. Boa), 1972, *Heinrich Böll: Withdrawal and Re-Emergence*, 1973, and articles in *Modern Language Review, German Life and Letters, Renaissance and Modern Studies, Forum for Modern Language Studies,* and other periodicals. **Essay:** Heinrich Böll.

REID, Robert. Lecturer in Slavonic studies, Queen's University, Belfast. Author of articles on Lermontov in *New Zealand Slavonic Journal 1, The Slavonic and East European Review 60*, 1982, and *Essays in Poetics 7*, 1982. Editor and contributor, *Problems of Russian Romanticism* (forthcoming). **Essays:** Ivan Goncharov; Mikhail Lermontov.

REILLY, John H. Professor of French, Queens College, City University of New York. Author of *Arthur Adamov*, 1974, and *Jean Giraudoux*, 1978. Editor of *Intermezzo* by Giraudoux, 1967. **Essays:** Arthur Adamov; Jean Giraudoux; *The Mad Woman of Chaillot*; *Tiger at the Gates*; *Waiting for Godot.*

REYNOLDS, Barbara. Reader in Italian, University of Nottingham, now retired; general editor of the *Cambridge Italian Dictionary.* Author of *The Linguistic Writings of Manzoni*, 1950, *The Passionate Intellect: Dorothy L. Sayers' Encounter with Dante*, 1989, and *Dorothy L. Sayers: A Biography*, 1993. Translator with Dorothy L. Sayers, of *Paradise* by Dante, 1962, and of *Vita Nuova* by Dante, 1969, and *The Frenzy of Orlando* by Ariosto, 2 vols., 1975. **Essays:** Ludovico Ariosto; Niccolò Machiavelli.

RIDLEY, Hugh. Instructor, Department of German, University College Dublin. **Essays:** Gottfried Benn; *Buddenbrooks*; *Death in Venice*; *The Threepenny Opera.*

RINSLER, Norma. Professor of French language and literature and vice principal, King's College, University of London. Author of *Gérard de Nerval*, 1973, and of many articles on Nerval, Victor Hugo, *Les Chimères* by Nerval, 1973. **Essays:** "L'Angoisse"; Gérard de Nerval; "Il pleure dans mon coeur . . ."; "Zone."

RIORDAN, Colin. Instructor, Department of German, University College of Swansea, Wales. **Essay:** Uwe Johnson.

ROBINSON, Michael. Professor, University of East Anglia. Formerly professor in the department of drama and theatre arts at the University of Birmingham; lecturer in the department of English and drama, Loughborough University, Leicestershire. Author of *The Long Sonata of the Dead: A Study of Samuel Beckett*, 1969, *Sven Delblanc: Åminne*, 1981, *Strindberg and Autobiography*, 1986, and essays on Ibsen, Strindberg, and Beckett. Translator and editor of *Strindberg's Letters*, 1992. **Essay:** August Strindberg.

ROBINSON, Philip E.J. Instructor, Department of French, Keynes College, University of Canterbury. **Essays:** *Emile*; *The False Confessions*; *Les Liaisons Dangereuses*; *Manon Lescaut.*

ROCK, David. Lecturer in German, Department of Modern Languages, University of Keele, Staffordshire. **Essays:** *Immensée*; *The Weavers.*

RODGERS, Eamonn. Professor of Spanish and Latin American studies, University of Strathclyde. Formerly senior lecturer in Spanish, Trinity College, Dublin. Author of *From Enlightenment to Realism: The Novels of Gladós 1870–1887*, 1987, and articles in *Bulletin of Hispanic Studies, Forum for Modern Language Studies, Anales Galdosianos,* and *Cuadernos Hispano-americanos.* Editor of *Tormento* by Pérez Galdós, 1977. **Essay:** Benito Pérez Galdós.

ROGISTER, Margaret. Instructor, Department of German, University of Durham. **Essay:** Ivan Goll.

RONNICK, Michele Valerie. Assistant professor of classics at Wayne State University, Detroit, Michigan. Author of *Cicero's Paradoxa Stoicorum: A Commentary, an Interpretation, and a Study of Its Influence (Studien zür klassischen Philologie* series), 1991, *Cicero on Self-Realization and Self-Fulfillment*, 1991, *Bibliography* on *Cato the Elder* and *Cato the Younger* (forthcoming), and articles in numerous journals including *Ceres, Classical Outlook, American Classical League Newsletter, Rivista di Cultura Classica e Medioevale*. **Essay:** *On Old Age*.

RORRISON, Hugh. Lecturer in German, University of Leeds, Yorkshire. Author of essays in the collections *Modern Austrian Writing*, 1980, and *Brecht in Perspective*, 1982, and of "Kroetz Checklist," in *Theatrefacts 3*, 1976. Editor of *Erwin Piscator: The Political Theatre* (also translator), 1978, and *Mother Courage* by Brecht, 1983; adviser on German theatre for *Oxford Companion to the Theatre*, 1983. **Essays:** Georg Büchner; Franz Grillparzer.

ROSSEL, Sven H. Professor of Scandinavian and comparative literature, University of Vienna; affiliate professor, University of Washington, Seattle. Author and editor of 35 books, 100 articles and 300 reviews. Member of the Royal Danish Academy of Science and Letters.

ROSSLYN, Wendy. Reader in Russian literature, University of Nottingham. Formerly lecturer in Slavonic studies, University of Nottingham. Author of *The Prince, the Fool and the Nunnery: the Religious Theme in the Early Poetry of Anna Akhmatova*, 1984. Editor of *The Speech of Unknown Eyes: Akhmatova's Readers on her Poetry*, 1990. Editor and translator of *Remembering Anna Akhmatova* by Anatoly Mayman, 1991. **Essays:** *Poem Without a Hero*; *Requiem*.

ROTHENBERG, John. Instructor, Department of French, University of Leeds. **Essays:** Samuel Beckett; Nathalie Sarraute.

ROTHWELL, Andrew. Instructor, Department of French, University of Leeds. **Essays:** "Art"; *Tropisms*.

RUCH, Lisa M. Doctoral student, Department of Comparative Literature, Pennsylvania State University. Author of "The Legendary Story of Albina and Her Sisters: Its Role in the Medieval Chronicle Tradition," in *Medieval Myths: Rulers, Saints and Heroes* (forthcoming). **Essays:** *Erec and Énide*; *Lancelot*; Georges Simenon.

RUTHERFORD, R.B. Instructor, Christ Church College, Oxford. **Essays:** *Meditations*; *On the Crown*; *Phaedrus*; Sallust.

SALE, William Merritt, III. Professor of classics and comparative literature, Washington University, St. Louis. Author of *Existentialism and Euripides*, 1977. Editor and translator of *Electra* by Sophocles, 1973. **Essays:** Hesiod; Homer; *The Iliad*; *The Odyssey*.

SALUMETS, Thomas. Ph.D., Princeton University (1985). Fellow of the Alexander von Humboldt Foundation, president-elect of the Association for the Advancement of Baltic Studies, and co-editor (with Sander Gilman) of the novels of F. M. Klinger; former chair of University of British Columbia's Comparative Literature Program (1995–1998), editor of the *Journal of Baltic Studies* (1998–2001), and acting head of UBC's department of Germanic studies (2000–01). Areas of special interest are eighteenth-century German literature, colonial and postcolonial Estonian literature, literary didactics, and figurational sociology (Norbert Elias). Life course research is among his present central concerns; he is currently working on a biography of the contemporary poet and essayist Jaan Kaplinski. **Essays:** Jaan Kaplinski; Jaan Kross.

SANDOMIRSKY, L. Natalie. PhD., Yale University. Professor emerita of foreign languages, Southern Connecticut State University, New Haven. **Essay:** Ahmadou Kourouma.

SAMMONS, Jeffrey L. Leavenworth professor of German, Yale University, New Haven, Connecticut. Author of *The Nacht-wachen von Bonaventura: A Structural Interpretation*, 1965, *Angelus Silesius*, 1967, *Heinrich Heine, The Elusive Poet*, 1969, *Six Essays on the Young German Novel*, 1972, *Literary Sociology and Practical Criticism: An Inquiry*, 1977, *Heinrich Heine: A Modern Biography*, 1979, *Heinrich Heine: A Critical Bibliography of the Secondary Literature 1956–1980*, 1982, *Raabe: Pfisters Mühle*, 1988, *Wilhelm Raabe: The Fiction of the Alternative Community*, 1989, *Heinrich Heine*, 1991, and *The Shifting Fortunes of Wilhelm Raabe: A History of Criticism as a Cautionary Tale*, 1992. **Essays:** *Danton's Death*; Heinrich Heine; Ludwig Tieck.

SANDARS, N.K. Author of *Prehistoric Art in Europe*, 1967 (revised edition, 1984), and *The Sea-Peoples, Warriors of the Ancient Mediterranean 1250–1150 B.C.*, 1978. Translator of *The Epic of Gilgamesh*, 1960 (revised edition, 1972), and *Poems of Heaven and Hell from Ancient Mesopotamia*, 1971. **Essay:** *Epic of Gilgamesh*.

SANFORD, Gerlinde Ulm. Associate professor of German, Syracuse University. **Essay:** *Abdias*.

SANKO, Hélène N. Associate professor, Department of Classical and Modern Languages and Cultures, John Carroll University, Cleveland, Ohio. Author of "French in Cleveland," in *Encyclopedia of Cleveland History*, 1987, "The Heroic Odyssey of the First French Woman on the American Continent," in *Proceedings of Foreign Language Teaching*, 1991, "Authentic Materials for Classroom Use: The Illustrations of Denis Diderot's *Encyclopedia*," in *Proceedings of Foreign Language Teaching*, 1991, and "L'Abbé Jean-Baptiste Dubos et la presse," in *Bulletin de la Société Américaine de Philosophie de Langue française*, 1992.

SATO, Kumiko. Assistant professor of Japan studies and Asian literature, Earlham College, Indiana; fields of expertise: Japanese women's writings, science fiction, and popular culture and literature. **Essay:** Tsushima Yuko.

SAUNDERS, Barbara. Social worker. Author of *Contemporary German Autobiography: Literary Approaches to the Problem of Identity* (forthcoming), "Christa Wolf's *Kindheitsmuster*: An East German Experiment in Political Autobiography" (with Neil Jackson), in *German Life and Letters*, July 1980, and an article on Max Frisch in *Forum for Modern Language Studies 18*, 1982. **Essay:** Elias Canetti.

SCHERR, Barry P. Professor of Russian, Dartmouth College, Hanover, New Hampshire. Author of *Notes on Literary Life in Petrograd, 1918–1922: A Tale of Three Houses*, 1977, "Gor'kij's *Childhood*: The Autobiography as Fiction," 1979, "Russian and English Versification: Similarities, Differences, Analysis," 1980, *Russian Poetry: Meter, Rhythm, and Rhyme*, 1986, *Maxim Gorky*, 1988, "Beginning at the end: Rhyme and Enjambment in Brodsky's Poetry," 1990, "Pasternak, Hegel, and Christianity: Religion in *Doctor Zhivago*," 1991. Co-editor of "Russian Verse Theory since 1974: A Commentary and Bibliography," 1980. Co-editor of *Russian Verse Theory: Proceedings of the 1987 Conference at UCLA*, 1989.

Essays: *The Bridge on the Drina*; *Doctor Zhivago*; Maksim Gor'kii; *The Lower Depths*; Iurri Trifono; *Twenty-Six Men and a Girl*.

SCHNEIDER, Gerd. Instructor, Department of Foreign Languages, Syracuse University. **Essays:** *La Ronde*; *The Visit*.

SCHNELLBÄCHER, Thomas. Ph.D., Berlin Free University. Author of a Ph.D. dissertation about Abe Kōbō's programmatic essays, 2001. **Essays:** Abe Kōbō; *The Woman in the Dunes*.

SCOBBIE, Irene. Formerly reader in Scandinavian studies, University of Edinburgh. Author of *Pär Lagerkvist: An Introduction*, 1963, *Sweden: Nation of the Modern World*, 1972, *Pär Lagerkvist's Gäst hos verkligheten*, 1974, and articles on Lagerkvist, Strindberg, P.O. Sundman, Stig Claesson, and other writers. Editor and contributor, *Essays on Swedish Literature from 1880 to the Present Day*, 1978. Editor of *Aspects of Swedish Literature*, 1988. **Essays:** Pär Lagerkvistl; Selma Lagerlöf.

SCOTT, Mary. Assistant professor of Asian studies, University of Puget Sound, Tacoma, Washington. **Essay:** *The Dream of the Red Chamber*.

SEIDENSTICKER, Edward. Professor emeritus of Japanese, Columbia University, New York. Author of *Kafu the Scribbler*, 1965, *Low City, High City*, 1983, and *Tokyo Rising*, 1990. Translator of *The Tale of Genji* by Murasaki Shikibu, 1976, and works by Tanizaki Jun'ichirō, Kawabata Yasunari, Mishima Yukio, and other modern and classical Japanese writers. **Essays:** Murasaki Shikibu; *Some Prefer Nettles*; *Snow Country*.

SERAFIN, Steven. General editor, *Encyclopedia of World Literature in the 20th Century*, 4 vols. (1999); editor, *Twentieth-Century Eastern European Writers*, 3 vols. (1999–2001); with Alfred Bendixen, *The Continuum Encyclopedia of American Literature* (1999); with Valerie Grosvenor Myer, *The Continuum Encyclopedia of British Literature* (2002).

SEVERIN, Dorothy S. Instructor, Department of Hispanic Studies, University of Liverpool. **Essay:** Fernando de Rojas.

SHARLET, Jocelyn. Assistant professor of comparative literature at the University of California at Davis. Co-translator with Kamran Talattof of the Persian novella *Women Without Men* by Shahrnush Parsipur. **Essays:** al-Qasim ibn 'Ali Abu Muhammad al-Basri al-Hariri; Ahmad ibn al-Husayn Abu al-Tayyib al-Ju'fi al-Kindi Al-Mutanabbi; Ibrahim ibn Abi al-Fath Abu Ishaq Ibn Khafajah.

SHARMAN, Ruth. Freelance translator and writer. Formerly press officer, Fontana Paperbacks, London. Author of an article on Giraut de Borneil in *Medium Aevum*, 1982, reviews in *French Studies* and *Romance Philology*, and prize-winning poems in the Arvon International Poetry Competition and the National Poetry Competition, 1990. Editor of *The Poems of Giraut de Borneil*, 1984. **Essay:** François Mauriac.

SHAW, Barnett. Playwright and actor. Chevalier dans l'ordre des arts et des lettres (France). Translator of several plays by Feydeau, Labiche, and Dumas *père*. **Essay:** Alexandre Dumas *père*.

SHAW, David. Instructor, Department of French, University of Leeds. **Essays:** *Fables*; *Maxims*; Honoré d'Urfé.

SHEREEN, Faiza W. Director of the Center for International Programs and associate professor of English, University of Dayton, Ohio. Author of the play, *The Country Within* (1991), translator of Abdelkebir Khatibi's *Civilisation de l'imtersigne* (1996), and contributor of numerous essays in literary theory and postcolonial literature to literary periodicals. **Essay:** Abdelkebir Khatibi.

SHIMOKAWA, Emi. Ph.D. candidate, Harvard University. **Essay:** Sakutarō Hagiwara.

SHOICHI SAEKI. Professor at Chuo University, Tokyo. Author of *In Search of the Japanese Self*, 1974, *Japanese Autobiographies*, 1974, and *Mishima Yukio: A Critical Biography*, 1978 (all in Japanese). Editor, with Donald Keene, of *Zenshu* [Collected Works] by Mishima, 36 vols., 1973–76. **Essays:** Mishima Yukio; Tanizaki Jun'ichiro.

SICES, David. Professor of French and Italian, Dartmouth College, Hanover, New Hampshire. Author of *Harmony of Contrasts: Music and the Musician in Jean-Christophe*, 1968, *Theatre of Solitude: The Drama of Alfred de Musset*, 1974, *2001 French Idioms*, 1982, the Musset entry in *European Writers*, 1984, *The Comedies of Machiavelli*, 1985, and *French Idioms*, 1991. **Essays:** *Camille*; *Chatterton*; *Lorenzaccio*; Alfred de Mussett; Romain Rolland; "Windows."

SIMOES DA SILVA, Tony. Lecturer in English, University of Exeter, UK; research interests in Postcolonial Anglophone and Lusophone writing, 20th century writing, cultural and social theories. Author of *The Luxury of Nationalist Despair: The Fiction of George Lamming* (2000). **Essays:** José Craveirinha.

SIMONS, John D. Professor of German, Florida State University. Author of *Friedrich Schiller*, 1981, "In Erratos Veritas: Schiller and Freud on Slips," in *German Quarterly*, 1983, "Hamartia and Até in Schiller's Dramas," in *Colloquia Germanica*, 1986, and numerous articles on 18th- and 20th-century German figures, and German-Russian literary relations. **Essay:** *Wallenstein*.

SINGH, G. Retired professor of Italian, Queen's University, Belfast. Author of *Leopardi and the Theory of Poetry*, 1964, *Leopardi e l'Inghilterra*, 1968, *Montale: A Critical Study of His Poetry, Prose and Criticism*, 1973, and *Ezra Pound*, 1979, *T.S. Eliot: poeta, drammaaturgo e critico*, 1985. Editor of *Da Swift a Pound: Saggi critici di F.R. Leavis*, 1973, *F.R. Leavis: the Critic as Anti Philosopher*, 1982, *F.R. Leavis: Valuation in Criticism*, 1986, and *Collected Essays of Q.D. Leavis*, vol. I, 1983, vol. II, 1985, vol. III, 1989. Translator of *Poesie de Kabir* (with Ezra Pound), 1966, *Poesie di Thomas Hardy*, 1968, *New Poems by Montale*, 1976, *Nearche un minuto* (Poems), 1986, *Olga e Pound* (Poems), 1987, and *Leopardi e i poeti inglesi*, 1990. **Essays:** Guido Cavalcanti; Gabriele D'Annunzio; *The Divine Comedy*; Giacomo Leopardi; Mīrā Bāī; Alberto Moravia; Salvatore Quasimodo; Umberto Saba; Sūrdās; Rabindranath Tagore; Giuseppe Ungaretti.

SKRINE, Peter. Professor of German and head of department, University of Bristol. Formerly senior lecturer in German, University of Manchester. Author of *The Baroque*, 1978, and *Hauptmann*,

Wedeking and Schnitler, 1989. Co-editor of *Bristol German Publications*. **Essays:** *The Bluebird*; *The Intruder*; *Peter Schlemihl*.

SMETHURST, Colin. Instructor, Department of French, University of Glasgow. **Essay:** *René*.

SMITH, C.N. Senior lecturer, School of Modern Languages and European History, University of East Anglia, Norwich; editor of *Seventeenth-Century French Studies*. Author of many articles and of reviews of the performing arts. Editor of works by Antoine de Montchrestien, Jacques de la Taille, and Pierre Matthieu. **Essays:** Louis Aragon; *Around the World in Eighty Days*; Honoré de Balzac; Julius Caesar; Blaise Cendrars; *The Colloquies*; *Cyrano de Bergerac*; Savinien Cyrano de Bergerac; *Don Quixote*; *Hedda Gabler*; Prosper Mérimée; *Military Servitude and Grandeur*; Jacques Prévert; Edmond Rostand; Eugène Scribe; Suetonius; Honoré d'Urfé; Jules Verne.

SMITH, Natalie. Instructor of Russian, University of Texas at Austin. She is currently writing a book on Russian-language literature and journalism of the Soviet Third-wave emigration. **Essays:** Péter Esterházy; Albert Memmi; Tatyana Tolstaya; *The Pillar of Salt*.

SMITH, Sarah Cox. Instructor of Japanese, Brigham Young University. Author of "Translation in the Age of Mechanical Reproduction: Writing In(to) Japanese," *PAJLS*, vol. 2 (summer 2001). **Essays:** Ōgai Mori.

SMYTH, David. Lecturer in Thai, SOAS, University of London. Author of *Thai: an essential grammar* (2002), translator of several Thai novels and short stories and contributor to major reference works. **Essay:** Siburapha.

SOWARDS, J. Kelly. Distinguished professor of humanities and history, Wichita State University, Kansas. Co-author of *The Julius exclusus of Erasmus*, 1968, and author of *Desiderius Erasmus*, 1975. Member of the editorial board of *The Collected Works of Erasmus*, and editor of vols. 25 and 26, 1984. **Essay:** Desiderius Erasmus.

SPEIRS, Ronald. Professor of German, University of Birmingham. Author of *Brecht's Early Plays*, 1982, *Bertolt Brecht*, 1987, *Thomas Mann: Mario und der Zauberer*, 1990. **Essays:** *Baal*; *Mother Courage and Her Children*.

STAMM, James Russell. Associate professor of Spanish and Portuguese, New York University. Author of *A Short History of Spanish Literature*, 1966 (revised edition, 1979), and numerous articles on the early Spanish novel and theatre. Editor, with Herbert E. Isar, of *Dos novelas cortas: Miguel de Unamuno*, 1967. **Essays:** Miguel de Cervantes; Miguel de Unamuno.

STARRS, Roy. Head of Japanese and Asian studies, University of Otago, Dunedin, New Zealand. Author of *Soundings in Time: The Fictive Art of Kawabata Yasunari* (1998), *An Artless Art: The Zen Aesthetic of Shiga Naoya* (1998), and *Deadly Dialectics: Sex, Violence and Nihilism in the World of Yukio Mishima* (1994); editor of *Nations Under Siege: Globalization and Nationalism in Asia* (2002) and *Asian Nationalism in an Age of Globalization* (2001); coeditor of *Japan and Korea: Contemporary Studies* (1997) and *Cultural Encounters: China, Japan and the West* (1995); review editor of the *New Zealand Journal of Asian Studies*. **Essay:** Shiga Naoya.

STATHATOS, C.C. Professor of Spanish, University of Wisconsin-Parkside, Kenosha. Author of *A Gil Vicente Bibliography (1940–1975)*, 1980 (supplement, 1982). Editor of *Floresta de enganos* by Gil Vicente, 1972. **Essay:** Gil Vicente.

STEIN, Susan Isabel. Instructor, Department of Classical and Modern Languages and Literatures, Texas Tech University. **Essays:** *The Kingdom of this World*; *The Lost Steps*; *Mr. President*.

STEINER, Carl. Professor of German, George Washington University, Washington DC. Author of "Ernst Jünger," in *German Fiction Writers, 1914–1945* (Dictionary of Literary Biography series), "Heinar Kipphardt, Robert Oppenheimer and Bruder Eichmann: Two Plays in Search of a Political Answer," in *Amerika! New Images in German Literature*, 1989, *Karl Emil Franzos, 1848–1904. Emancipator and Assimilationist*, 1990, and "Deutscher und Jude; das Leben und Werk des Karl Emil Franzos (1848–1904)," in *Autoren damals und heute*, 1991. **Essay:** Ernst Jünger.

STEPHENSON, R.H. Instructor, Department of German, University of Glasgow. **Essays:** *Goetz of Berlichingen with the Iron Hand*; *Ode to Joy*.

STERLING, Eric. Distinguished research professor of English, Auburn University Montgomery, Alabama. Ph.D. Indiana University; author of *The Movement Towards Subversion: The English History Play from Skelton to Shakespeare* (1996), two books on the Holocaust, and many articles on Jewish literature. **Essay:** *Mr. Mani*; Amos Oz; A.B. Yehoshua.

STEWART, Mary E. Fellow and lecturer in German, Robinson College, Cambridge. Author of numerous articles on the German novel since 1880 and modern Swiss literature in *Modern Language Review*, *German Life and Letters*, *Journal of European Studies*, and other periodicals. **Essays:** *The Fire Raisers*; Max Frisch; Hermann Hesse; *I'm Not Stiller*.

STILLMARK, Alexander. Lecturer in German, University College, London. Author of "Stifter's Symbolism of Beauty," in *Oxford German Studies*, 1971, "Stifter's Early Portraits of the Artist," in *Forum for Modern Language Studies*, 1975, and "The Poet and His Public: Hofmannsthal's "idealer Zuhörer," in *London German Studies 1*, 1980. Joint editor of and contributor to *Adalbert Stifter Heute*, 1985, *Deutsche Romantik und das 20. Jahrhundert*, 1986, *Grillparzer und die Europäische Tradition*, 1987, *Erbe und Umbruch in der neueren deutschsprachigen Komödoe*, 1990, *Between Time and Eternity. Nine Essays on W. B. Yeats and his Contemporaries Hormannsthal and Blok*, 1992, and *Lenau zwischen Ost und West*, 1992. **Essays:** *The Difficult Man*; Ödön von Horváth; Novalis; Adalbert Stifter; *The Waves of Sea and Love*.

STOPP, Elisabeth C. **Essay:** *Hymns to the Night*.

STOREY, Ian C. Professor and chairman of classics department, Trent University, Peterborough, Ontario; editor of the *Journal of the Canadian Church Historical Society*. Author of several journal articles, including "The Symposium at Wasps 1299ff," in *Phoenix 39*, 1985, "Dating and Re-dating Eupolis," in *Phoenix 44*, 1990. **Essays:** Aristophanes; *The Birds*; *The Frogs*; *Hippolytus*; *Philoctetes*.

STRECHER, Matthew Carl. Associate professor of English and Japanese literature, Tōyō University, Japan. Author of *Dances With Sheep: The Quest for Identity in the Fiction of Murakami Haruki* (2002), *Haruki Murakami's* The Wind-Up Bird Chronicle: *A Reader's Guide* (2002), and essays in scholarly journals. **Essay:** Murakami Shikibu.

STRONG, Sarah M.. Associate professor of Japanese language and literature, Bates College. Translator of *Miyazawa Kenji's* Night of the Milky Way Railway: *A Translation and Guide* (1991) and essays in literary journals; literature editor, *Journal of Japanese Language and Literature*, from 2002. **Essay:** Miyazawa Kenji.

STUBBS, J.R. University of Manchester. **Essays:** Joris-Karl Huysmans; Max Jacob; Comte de Lautréamont.

SUBIOTTO, Arrigo V. Emeritus professor of German and honorary fellow, Institute for Advanced Research in the Humanities, University of Birmingham. Author of *Bertolt Brecht's Adaptations for the Berliner Ensemble*, 1975, and of numerous articles on Brecht, Grass Hochhuth, Dürrenmatt, Frisch, Müller, Braun and other writers. Editor of *Hans Magnus Enzensberger: Poems*, 1985. **Essays:** Bertolt Brecht; Günter Grass.

SUGAR, Mary. Editor of Gale Group online databases. Editor and author of *Worldmark* encyclopedias. Editor of *American Intervention in Yugoslavia: A Diplomatic History since 1991*, by Dr. R. H. Whealey (2001). **Essay:** Evelyne Accad.

SULLIVAN, Henry W. Professor of Spanish and chairman of the department of modern languages and literatures, University of Ottawa. Author of *Tirso de Molina and the Drama of the Counter Reformation*, 1976, *Juan del Encina*, 1976, *Calderón in the German Lands and the Low Countries: His Reception and Influence 1654–1780*, 1983, and many articles on Spanish Golden Age drama and the theory of tragedy. **Essay:** Tirso de Molina.

SZÉPE, Helena. Freelance writer; author of many articles on German literature. Formerly associate professor of German, Roosevelt University, Chicago. **Essay:** Hermann Broch.

TAILBY, John E. Lecturer in German, University of Leeds. Author of "Peasant Figures in Fifteenth-century *Fastnachtspiele* from Nuremberg," in *Daphnis 4*, 1975, and articles on medieval German drama in *The Oxford Companion to the Theatre*, 1983, and *Cambridge Guide to World Theatre*, 1988. Editor of *Der Reimpaardichter Peter Schmieher*, 1978, and *The Staging of Religious Drama in Europe in the Later Middle Ages* (with Peter Meredith), 1989. **Essay:** Hans Sachs.

TAYLOR, Myron. Associate professor of English, State University of New York, Albany. Author of articles on Shakespeare in *The Christian Scholar, Studies in English*, and *Shakespeare Quarterly*. **Essay:** Plato.

TAYLOR, Anna-Marie. Instructor, Department of Drama, University College of Wales. **Essays:** Simone de Beauvoir; *Ghosts; Love in the Time of Cholera; The Mandarins; The Master Builder; The Second Sex*; Georg Trakl.

THODY, Philip. Professor of French literature, University of Leeds, Yorkshire. Author of two books on Camus and two books on Sartre, books on Genet, Anouilh, Laclos, Aldous Huxley, and Barthes, and a novel, *Dog Days in Babel*, 1979. Editor of works by Camus and Sartre. **Essays:** *L'Assommoir; Athalie; Bajazet; The Earth; Germinal; The Gods Are Athirst; Memoirs; The Miser; Thérèse; Ubu Rex*.

THOMAS, David. Lecturer in drama, University of Bristol. Author of *Henrik Ibsen*, 1983. Editor of volume 8 (on the Restoration and 18th Century) of *Theatre in Europe: Sources and Documents* (forthcoming). **Essay:** Ludvig Holberg.

THURMAN, Judith. Author of *Isak Dinesen: The Life of a Storyteller*, 1982. **Essay:** Isak Dinesen.

TOORAWA, Shawkat M. Assistant professor of Arabic literature, Cornell University. Co-author of *Interpreting the Self: Autobiography in the Arabic Literary Tradition* (2001), and author of journal articles on Arabic literature, Arab-Islamic culture, and Mauritian literature. **Essays:** Adonis; Dev Virahsawmy.

TORRANCE, Robert M. Professor of comparative literature, University of California, Davis. Author of *The Comic Hero*, 1978. Translator of *The Women of Trachis* and *Philoctetes* by Sophocles, 1966.

TROJANOWSKA, Tamara. Associate professor in the department of Slavic languages and literatures at the University of Toronto. She has recently completed a manuscript: *Identity on Trial: Gombrowicz, Rozewicz, Mrozek and the Conflicts of Modernity*. **Essay:** Tadeusz Różewicz.

VANACKER, Sabine. Instructor, Modern Dutch Studies Department, University of Hull. **Essays:** Louis Couperus; Multatuli; Paul van Ostaijen.

VENNER, Rolf. Instructor, University of Kent, Canterbury. **Essays:** Paul Éluard; *Paris Peasant*; "You the Only One."

VERANI, Hugo J. Professor of Spanish-American literature, University of California, Davis. Author of *Narrativa contemporánea*, 1979, *Onetti: El ritual de la impostura*, 1981, and *Octavio Paz: Bibliografía crítica*, 1983. **Essays:** Jorge Luis Borges; Julio Cortazar; Octavio Paz.

VERTHUY, Maïr. Associate professor of French, and fellow of the Simone de Beauvoir Institute, Concordia University, Montréal; editor of *Canadian Women's Studies*. Author of articles on Hélène Parmelin, Christiane Rochefort, Roger Vailland, Michèle Mailhot, and other writers. Editor of *Femme*, 1984. **Essay:** Gabrielle Roy.

VILAIN, Robert. Lecturer in German, Royal Holloway, University of London. Author of "'Wer lügt, macht schlechte Metaphern': Hofmannsthal's 'Manche freilich' and Walter Pater," in *Deutsche Vierteljahrsschrift*, 1991. **Essay:** "Bread and Wine" (Hölderlin).

VOILLEY, Pascale. Ph.D. candidate, University of Aberdeen. Contributor to *Littérature Comparée* edited by Didier Soullier (forthcoming). **Essays:** Georges Bernanos; *The Blue Flowers; The Satin Slipper; The Test of Virtue*; Boris Vian; *The Voyeur; Zazie*.

WALBANK, Frank W. Emeritus professor of ancient history and classical archaeology, University of Liverpool; honorary fellow, Peterhouse, Cambridge. Author of *Aratos of Sicyon*, 1933, *Philip V of Macedon*, 1940, *A Historical Commentary on Polybius*, 3 vols., 1957, 1967, 1979, *The Awful Revolution*, 1969, *Polybius*, 1973, *The Hellenisitic World*, 1981, *Selected Papers*, 1985, and *History of Macedonia III: 336–167 B.C.*, 1986. Editor of *Cambridge Ancient History*, vols. VII.1, VII.2, VIII (ed. 2), 1976–1989. **Essays:** Quintus Ennius; Polybius.

WALLACE, Albert H. Professor of romance languages, University of Tennessee, Knoxville. Author of *Guy de Maupassant*, 1973, and articles on Maupassant and Flaubert. **Essay:** Guy de Maupassant.

WALKER, Bruce. Professor of English, University of Detroit Mercy, Detroit, Michigan; contributor of more than 100 reference book essays on philosophy, literature, film, music, religion; and historical figures; author of CliffsNotes on Ken Kesey's *One Flew Over the Cuckoo's Nest* and Lewis Carroll's *Alice's Adventures in Wonderland*; author of *These Simple Themes*, Ford Motor Company film for the Country Music Hall of Fame, Nashville, Tennessee; contributor of essays to periodicals, including the *Journal of Country Music*. **Essay:** Søren Kierkegaard.

WALSH, George. Publisher and freelance writer. **Essay:** Carlo Goldoni.

WALTON, J. Michael. Instructor, Department of Drama, University of Hull. **Essays:** Aristotle; *Electra* (Euripides); *Ion*; *Oedipus the King*.

WASIOLEK, Edward. Essays: *Anna Karenina*; *The Death of Ivan Ilyich*; *The Gentlemen from San Francisco*.

WATSON, Bruce. Programme director, European Studies, Royal Holloway, University of London. Author of essays and journal articles, including "Reception as Self-Definition: H.M. Enzensbergers Ed. of G. Büchners Der Hessische Landbote," in *G. Büchner, Tradition and Innovation*. **Essays:** *The Good Person of Szechwan*; Friedrich Nietzsche; *Sufferings of Young Werther*; *Thus Spoke Zarathustra*.

WEBB, Shawncey J. Instructor, Department of Modern Languages, Ball State University. **Essays:** *The Book of the City of Ladies*; Christine de Pizan; Alain-René Lesage; Marie de France.

WEISSBORT, Daniel. Professor of comparative literature, and director of the translation workshop, University of Iowa, Iowa City; Co-Founding Editor, with Ted Hughes, *Modern Poetry in Translation*. Author of three books of poetry, *The Leaseholder*, 1971, *In an Emergency*, 1972, and *Soundings*, 1977. Editor and translator of many books, including works by Gorbanevskaya, Vinokurov, Evtushenko, and Claude Simon, and of collections of Russian poetry. **Essay:** Vasko Popa.

WELSH, David. Professor emeritus, University of Michigan, Ann Arbor. Author of *Russian Comedy*, 1966, *Adam Mickiewicz*, 1966, *Ignacy Krasicki*, 1969, and *Jan Kochanowski*, 1974. **Essay:** Henryk Sienkiewicz.

WHITE, A.D. Instructor, Department of German, University of Wales. **Essays:** *Group Portrait with Lady*; *Andorra*; *Sonnets to Orpheus*.

WHITE-WALLIS, Sally A. Lecturer in French, University of Exeter. Author of an essay on Yourcenar in *Strathclyde Modern Language Studies*, vol. xi, 1991, and an essay on *Anna Soror* by Yourcenar, in *Actes du Colloque*, 1992. **Essay:** Marguerite Yourcenar.

WHITTON, Kenneth S. Chairman of the school of European studies, University of Bradford, Yorkshire. Author of *The Theatre of Friedrich Dürrenmatt: A Study in the Possibility of Freedom*, 1980, *Dietrich Fischer-Dieskau: Mastersinger*, 1981, *Lieder for the Layman: An Introduction to German Song*, 1984, several textbooks, and *Wir waren vier*, a series for British television. Translator of *Schubert's Songs* by Fischer-Dieskau, 1977. **Essays:** Friedrich Dürrenmatt; Peter Weiss.

WIGMORE, Juliet. Lecturer in German, University of Salford, Lancashire. Author of "Ingeborg Bachmann," in *The Modern German Novel* edited by K. Bullivant, 1987, "The Emergence of Women's Writing since 1945 in the German-speaking Area," in *European Insights* edited by A. and W. Brassloff, 1991, and "*Vergangenheitsbewältigung* in Austria: the Personal and the Political in Erika Mitterer's *Alle unsere Spiele* and Elisabeth Reichart's *Februarschatten*," *German Life and Letters 44*, 1991. **Essays:** Ingeborg Bachmann; *The Lime Works*.

WIGZELL, Faith. Instructor, School of Slavonic and East European Studies, Senate House, London. **Essays:** *The Bronze Horseman*; *Dead Souls*; *The Devils*; *The Diary of a Madman*; *The Government Inspector*; *The Tale of the Campaign of Igor*; *The Three Sisters*.

WILLIAMS, Mark. Lecturer in Japanese studies. Author of "Life after Death: The Literature of an Undeployed Kamikaze Squadron Leader," in *Japan Forum 4:1*, 1992. Translator of *Foreign Studies* by Endō Shūsaku, 1989. **Essays:** Endō Shūsaku; *Silence*.

WILLIAMS, Rhys. Instructor, Department of German, University College of Swansea, Wales. **Essays:** Carl Sternheim.

WILSON, Jason. Instructor, Department of Spanish and Latin American Studies, University College of London. **Essays:** "Arte poética"; Ernesto Cardenal; *Sun Stone*; *Tentativa del hombre infinito*.

WINFIELD, Jerry Phillips. Associate professor of modern foreign languages, Mercer University, Macon and Atlanta, Georgia. Author of *La primavera de la Muerte—The Poetry of Carlos Bousoño*, 1986, and *Dámaso Alonso*, 1992. Editor of *Twentieth-Century Spanish Poets* (forthcoming). **Essay:** Luis Cernuda.

WINKLER, Michael. Professor of German studies, Rice University, Houston, Texas. Author of *George-Kreis*, 1972, *Deutsche Literatur im Exil 1933 bis 1945. Texte und Dokumente*, 1977, and *Exilliteratur 1933–1945*, 1989. **Essays:** *Auto-da-Fé*; *The Death of Virgil*; *The Sleepwalkers*; *The Tower*.

WOODMAN, A.J. Professor of Latin, University of Durham. Formerly professor of Latin, University of Leeds, Yorkshire. Author of *Velleius Paterculus: The Tiberian Narrative*, 1977, *Valleius Paterculus: The*

Caesarian and Augustan Narrative, 1983, *Rhetoric in Classical Historiography*, 1988, and *Tacitus: Annals IV* (with R.H. Martin), 1974. Editor, with David West, of *Quality and Pleasure in Latin Poetry*, 1974, *Creative Imitation and Latin Literature*, 1979, *Poetry and Politics in the Age of Augustus*, 1984, *Past Perspectives: Studies in Greek and Roman Historical Writing*, 1986, *Author and Audience in Latin Literature*, 1992, and *Tacitus and the Tacitean Tradition*, 1993. **Essays:** *Annals*; Catullus; Horace; Livy; Tacitus; Thucydides.

WOODS, M.J. Lecturer in Spanish, King's College, University of London. Author of *The Poet and the Natural World in the Age of Gngora*, 1978, and "Pitfalls for the Moralizer in *Lazarillo de Tormes*," in *Modern Language Review 74*, 1979. **Essay:** Luis de Góngora.

WOODS, Tim. Lecturer in English, University College of Wales. Author of works on American modernist poetry, Paul Auster, and the postmodern novel. **Essays:** Thomas Bernhard; "La Chanson du mal-aimé"; Evgenii Evtushenko; *Petersburg*; *The Social Contract*.

WOODWARD, James B. Professor of Russian, University College, Swansea, Wales. Author of *Leonid Andreyev: A Study*, 1969, *Gogol's "Dead Souls,"* 1978, *Ivan Bunin: A Study of His Fiction*, 1980, *The Symbolic Art of Gogol: Essays on His Short Fiction*, 1982, and *Metaphysical Conflict: A Study of the Major Novels of Ivan Turgenev*, 1990. Editor of *Selected Poems* by Alexander Blok, 1968. **Essay:** Ivan Bunin; Nikolai Gogol; *The Twelve*.

WRIGHT, A. Colin. Professor of Russian, Queen's University, Kingston, Ontario; vice-president, International Bulgakov Society. Formerly president, Canadian Association of Slavists. Author of *Mikhail Bulgakov: Life and Interpretations*, 1978, and articles in various journals, including *Canadian-American Slavic Studies* and *Canadian Slavonic Papers*. Editor of *Rashel'*, 1972, and *Minin i Pozharski*, 1976, both by Bulgakov. **Essays:** Mikhail Bulgakov; *The Master and Marguerita*; *The White Guard*.

WRIGHT, Barbara. Freelance translator. Translator of works by Queneau, Robbe-Grillet, Sarraute, Pinget, and Tournier. Contributor to the *Times Literary Supplement*. **Essays:** Raymond Queneau.

WRIGHT, Elizabeth. Fellow in German, Girton College, Cambridge. Author of *Hoffmann and the Rhetoric of Terror*, 1978, *Psychoanalytic Criticism: Theory in Practice*, 1984, and *Postmodern Brecht; A Representation*, 1989. Editor of *Feminism and Psychoanalysis: A Critical Dictionary*, 1992. **Essay:** E.T.A. Hoffmann.

YANG, Xiaobin. Croft assistant professor of Chinese, University of Mississippi, author of *The Chinese Postmodern: Trauma and Irony in Chinese Avant-Garde Fiction* and other essays published in *positions, American Imago*, etc. **Essays:** Lao She; Mo Yan.

YOHANNAN, John D. Professor emeritus, City College of New York. Author of *A Treasury of Asian Literature*, 1956, *Joseph and Potiphar's Wife in World Literature*, 1968, and *Persian Poetry in England and America: A Two-Hundred Year History*, 1977. Editor, with Leo Hamalian, of *New Writing from the Middle East*, 1978. **Essay:** Shams al-Din Muhammad Hafiz.

YOUNG, Howard T. Professor of romance languages, Pomona College, Claremont, California. Author of *The Victorious Expression*, 1964, *Juan Ramón Jiménez*, 1967, and *The Line in the Margin: Jiménez and His Readings in Blake, Shelley, and Yeats*, 1980. **Essays:** Federico García Lorca; Juan Ramón Jiménez; Saint John of the Cross.

YOUNG, Robin. Lecturer in English and European literature, University of Wales, Aberystwyth. Author of an Ibsen study, *Time's Disinherited Children*, 1989, and translator of modern Scandinavian poetry. **Essay:** Hunger.

ZABOROWSKA, Magdalena J. Associate professor, program in American culture and center for Afroamerican and African studies, University of Michigan. Author of *How We Found America: Reading Gender through East European Immigrant Narratives* (1995) and essays in literary, cultural, and architectural journals; editor of *Other Americans, Other Americas: The Politics and Poetics of Multiculturalism* (1998) and co-editor of *The Puritan Origins of American Sex: Religion, Sexuality and National Identity in American Literature* (2000). **Essay:** Maria Kuncewicz.

ZANKER, G. Senior lecturer in classics. Author of "Callimachus' Hecale: A New Kind of Epic Hero?" in *Antichthon 11*, 1977, "Simichidas Walk in the Locality of Bourina in Theocritus, Id. 7," in *Classical Quarterly N.S. 30*, 1980, and "Current Trends in the Study of Hellenic Myth in Early Third-Century Alexandrian Poetry: The Case of Theocritus," in *Antike und Abendland 35*, 1989. **Essays:** *Aetia*; *Hecale*; *Idyll* VII.

ZARUCCHI, Jeanne Morgan. Associate professor of French, University of Missouri, St. Louis. Author of *Perrault's Morals for Moderns*, 1985, and articles on *Perrault in 17th Century French Studies, Studi Francesi, Dix-Septième Siècle*, and other journals. Co-editor of *French 17 Bibliography*. Editor and translator of *Memoirs of My Life* by Charles Perrault, 1989. **Essay:** Charles Perrault.

LANGUAGE INDEX

Albanian
Ismail Kadare

Arabic
Adonis
al-Qasim ibn 'Ali Abu Muhammad al-Basri Al-Hariri
Al-Khansa'
Ahmad ibn al-Husayn Abu al-Tayyib al-Ju'fi al-Kindi al-Mutanabbi
Imru' al-Qays
Muhyi al-Din Ibn al-Arabi
Ibrahim ibn Abi al-Fath Abu Ishaq ibn Khafajah

Belarusian
Vasil Bykaw

Bosnian
Ivo Andrić

Chinese
Bai Juyi
Bei Dao
Ding Ling
The Dream of the Red Chamber
Du Fu
Gao Xingjian
Golden Lotus
Huang Chunming
Journey to the West
Lao She
Li Ang
Li Bai
Lu Xun
Mo Yan
Su Shi
Su Tong
Tang Xianzu
Tao Qian
Water Margin
Xiao Hong

Croatian
Miroslav Krleža

Czech
Karel Čapek
Václav Havel
Jaroslav Hašek
Miroslav Holub
Ivan Klíma
Milan Kundera

Danish
Hans Christian Andersen
Isak Dinesen
William Heinesen
Peter Høeg

Ludvig Holberg
Johannes V. Jensen
Søren Kierkegaard

Dutch
Willem Bilderdijk
Gerbrandt Bredero
Hugo Claus
Louis Couperus
Desiderius Erasmus
Guido Gezelle
Hadewijch
Pieter Corneliszoon Hooft
Constantijn Huygens
Multatuli
Martinus Nijhoff
Cees Nooteboom
Paul van Ostaijen
Simon Vestdijk
Joost van den Vondel

Egyptian
'Umar Ibn al-Fârid
Yusuf Idris
Naguib Mahfouz
Tawfiq al-Hakim

Estonian
Jaan Kaplinski
Jaan Kross

Farsi
Jalâl Âl-e Ahmad

Finnish
Kalevala
Väinö Linna

French
Arthur Adamov
Alain-Fournier
Jean Anhouilh
Guillaume Apollinaire
Louis Aragon
Antonin Artaud
Aucassin and Nicolette
Marcel Aymé
Honoré de Balzac
Henri Barbusse
Charles Baudelaire
Beaumarchais
Simone de Beauvoir
Samuel Beckett
Tahar Ben Jelloun
Georges Bernanos
Nicolas Boileau

Robert Brasillach
André Breton
Nicole Brossard
Albert Camus
Louis-Ferdinand Céline
Blaise Cendrars
Patrick Chamoiseau
René Char
Chateaubriand
Chrétien de Troyes
Christine de Pizan
Paul Claudel
Jean Cocteau
Colette
Pierre Corneille
Savinien Cyrano de Bergerac
René Depestre
Denis Diderot
Assia Djebar
Joachim Du Bellay
Alexandre Dumas *père*
Alexandre Dumas *fils*
Marguerite Duras
Paul Éluard
Georges Feydeau
Gustave Flaubert
Anatole France
Jean Froissart
Gao Xingjian
Théophile Gautier
Jean Genet
André Gide
Jean Giono
Jean Giraudoux
Edouard Glissant
Edmond and Jules Goncourt
Guillaume de Machaut
Victor Hugo
Joris-Karl Huysmans
Eugène Ionesco
Max Jacob
Alfred Jarry
Abdelkebir Khatibi
Ahmadou Kourouma
Milan Kundera
Choderlos de Laclos
Madame de Lafayette
Jean de La Fontaine
Jules Laforgue
Alphonse de Larmartine
François La Rochefoucauld
Comte de Lautréamont
Alain-René Lesage
Maurice Maeterlinck
Stéphane Mallarmé
André Malraux
Marguerite de Navarre
Marie de France
Marivaux
Roger Martin du Gard

Guy de Maupassant
François Mauriac
Albert Memmi
Prosper Mérimée
Henri Michaux
Molière
Michel de Montaigne
Alfred de Musset
Gérard de Nerval
Marcel Pagnol
Blaise Pascal
Georges Perec
Charles Perrault
Francis Ponge
Jacques Prévert
Abbé Prévost
Marcel Proust
Raymond Queneau
François Rabelais
Jean Racine
Raymond Radiguet
Arthur Rimbaud
Alain Robbe-Grillet
Romain Rolland
The Romance of the Rose
Pierre de Ronsard
Edmond Rostand
Jean-Jacques Rousseau
Claude Roy
Gabrielle Roy
Marquis de Sade
Antoine de Saint-Exupéry
Saint-John Perse
George Sand
Nathalie Sarraute
Jean-Paul Sartre
Paul Scarron
Eugène Scribe
Georges Simenon
The Song of Roland
Madame de Staël
Stendhal
Honoré d'Urfé
Paul Valéry
Paul Verlaine
Jules Verne
Boris Vian
Alfred de Vigny
François Villon
Voltaire
Elie Wiesel
Marguerite Yourcenar
Émile Zola

German
Bettina von Arnim
Ingeborg Bachmann
Gottfried Benn
Thomas Bernhard
Johannes Bobrowski

Heinrich Böll
Sebastian Brant
Bertolt Brecht
Clemens Brentano
Hermann Broch
Georg Büchner
Elias Canetti
Paul Celan
Adelbert von Chamisso
Alfred Döblin
Heimito von Doderer
Annette von Droste-Hülshoff
Friedrich Dürrenmatt
G&uunl;nter Eich
Joseph von Eichendorff
Theodor Fontane
Caroline de la Motte Fouqué
Friedrich de la Motte Fouqué
Max Frisch
Johann Wolfgang von Goethe
Ivan Goll
Gottfried von Strassburg
Jeremias Gotthelf
Christian Dietrich Grabbe
Günter Grass
Franz Grillparzer
Jacob and Wilhelm Grimm
Hans Jakob Christoffel von Grimmelshausen
Andreas Gryphius
Hartmann von Aue
Gerhart Hauptmann
Friedrich Hebbel
Heinrich Heine
Hermann Hesse
Fritz Hochwälder
E.T.A. Hoffmann
Hugo von Hofmannsthal
Friedrich Hölderlin
Ödön von Horváth
Uwe Johnson
Ernst Jünger
Franz Kafka
Georg Kaiser
Gottfried Keller
Heinrich von Kleist
Friedrich Gottlieb Klopstock
Jakob Michael Reinhold Lenz
Siegfried Lenz
Gotthold Ephraim Lessing
Martin Luther
Heinrich Mann
Thomas Mann
Conrad Ferdinand Meyer
Eduard Mörike
Robert Musil
Johann Nepomuk Nestroy
Nibelungenlied
Friedrich Nietzsche
Novalis
Erich Maria Remarque

Rainer Maria Rilke
Joseph Roth
Hans Sachs
Nelly Sachs
Friedrich von Schiller
Friedrich and August Wilhelm von Schlegel
Arthur Schnitzler
Carl Sternheim
Adalbert Stifter
Theodor Storm
Ludwig Tieck
Ernst Toller
Georg Trakl
Walther von der Vogelweide
Frank Wedekind
Peter Weiss
Franz Werfel
Christoph Martin Wieland
Christa Wolf
Wolfram von Eschenbach
Carl Zuckmayer

Greek (Ancient)
Aeschylus
Anacreon
Apollonius
Aristophanes
Aristotle
Callimachus
Demosthenes
Euripides
Herodotus
Hesiod
Homer
Longus
Lucian
Menander
On the Sublime
Pindar
Plato
Plutarch
Polybius
Sappho
Sophocles
Theocritus
Theophrastus
Thucydides
Xenophon

Greek (Modern)
Constantijn Petrou Cavafy
Odysseus Elytis
Nikos Kazantzakis
Kostes Palamas
Yannis Ritsos
George Seferis
Angelo Sikelianos

Hebrew
S.Y. Agnon

The Bible
Amos Oz
A.B. Yehoshua

Hungarian
Baron Jószef Eötvös
Péter Esterházy
Gyula Illyés
Ferenc Molnár
Sándor Petöfi
Miklós Radnóti
Mihály Vörösmarty
Sándor Weöres
Count Miklós Zrínyi

Icelandic
Egils saga
Halldór Laxness
Njáls saga
Snorri Sturluson

Indian
Bhagavadgītā
Asadullāh Khān Ghālib
Qurratulain Hyder
Kabīr
Kālidāsa
The Little Clay Cart
Mahābhārata
Mīrā Bāī
Rāmāyana
Sūrdās
Rabindranath Tagore
Tulsīdās
Upanishads
Vedas

Italian
Vittorio Alfieri
Dante Alighieri
Pietro Aretino
Ludovico Ariosto
Giorgio Bassani
Pietro Bembo
Ugo Betti
Giovanni Boccaccio
Giordano Bruno
Dino Buzzati
Italo Calvino
Tommaso Campanella
Giosuè Carducci
Carlo Cassola
Baldassarre Castiglione
Guido Cavalcanti
Vittoria Colonna
Gabriele D'Annunzio
Eduardo De Filippo
Grazia Deledda
Bernardo Dovizi da Bibbiena

Francesca Duranti
Umberto Eco
Natalia Ginzburg
Carlo Goldoni
Giuseppe Tomasi di Lampedusa
Giacomo Leopardi
Carlo Levi
Primo Levi
Niccolò Machiavelli
Alessandro Manzoni
Pietro Metastasio
Eugenio Montale
Elsa Morante
Alberto Moravia
Pier Paolo Pasolini
Cesare Pavese
Petrarch
Luigi Pirandello
Vasco Pratolini
Salvatore Quasimodo
Ruzzante
Umberto Saba
Jacopo Sannazaro
Leonardo Sciascia
Ignazio Silone
Gaspara Stampa
Italo Svevo
Torquato Tasso
Giuseppe Ungaretti
Giovanni Verga
Elio Vittorini

Japanese
Abe Kōbō
Akutagawa Ryunosuke
Bashō
Chikamatsu Monzaemon
Dazai Osamu
Endō Shūsaku
Hagiwara Sakutarō
Ibuse Masuji
Ihara Saikaku
Ishigaki Rin
Kawabata Yasunari
Kenkō
Masaoka Shiki
Mishima Yukio
Miyazawa Kenji
Ōgai Mori
Murakami Haruki
Murasaki Shikibu
Natsume Sōseki
Nishiwaki Junzaburō
Saigyō
Shiga Noaya
Shimazaki Haruki
Tanizaki Jun'ichiro
Tsushima Yuko
Yosano Akiko
Zeami

Kreol
Dev Virahsawmy

Kurdish
Abdulla Goran

Latin
Apuleius
St. Augustine
Aurelius
Ausonius
Boethius
Caesar
Catullus
Cicero
Claudian
Ennius
Horace
St. Jerome
Juvenal
Livy
Lucan
Lucretius
Martial
Ovid
Persius
Petronius
Plautus
Propertius
Prudentius
Quintilian
Sallust
Seneca
Suetonius
Tacitus
Terence
Tibullus
Virgil

Norwegian
Bjørnstjerne Bjørnson
Knut Hamsun
Henrik Ibsen
August Strindberg
Sigrid Undset
Tarjei Vesaas

Old Norse
The Poetic *Edda*

Persian
Farid al-Din Attār
Abu'l Qāsim Ferdowsi
Shams al-Din Muhammad Hafiz
Omar Khayyam
Jalalu'd-Din Rumi
Muslih-al-Din Sa'di
The Thousand and One Nights

Polish
Jerzy Andrzejewski
Tadeusz Borowski
Witold Gombrowicz
Jan Kochanowski
Zygmunt Krasiński
Maria Kuncewicz
Adam Mickiewicz
Czesław Miłosz
Cyprian Kamil Norwid
Bolesław Prus
Tadeusz Różewicz
Bruno Schulz
Henryk Sienkiewicz
Juliusz Słowacki
Wisława Szymborska
Stanisław Witkiewicz
Stanisław Wyspiański

Portuguese
Jorge Amado
Mario de Andrade
Luís de Camões
José Craveirinha
José Maria de Eça de Queiroz
Gilberto Freyre
João Guimarães Rosa
Clarice Lispector
Joaquim Maria Machado de Assis
Fernando Pessoa
Rachel de Queiroz
Nélson Rodrigues
Miguel Torga
Gil Vicente

Romanian
Mircea Eliade

Russian
Andrei Belyi
Aleksandr Blok
Iosif Brodskii
Ivan Bunin
Anton Chekhov
Fedor Dostoevskii
Sergei Esenin
Evgenii Evtushenko
Denis Fonvizin
Ivan Goncharov
Maksim Gor'kii
Aleksandr Griboedov
Velimir Khlebnikov
Mikhail Lermontov
Vladimir Maiakovskii
Osip Mandel'shtam
Boris Pasternak
Boris Pil'niak
Aleksandr Pushkin
Mikhail Sholokhov
Sasha Sokolov

Aleksandr Solzhenitsyn
*Tale of the Campaign of Igo*r
Tatyana Tolstaya
Lev Tolstoi
Iurii Trifonov
Marina Tsvetaeva
Ivan Turgenev
Evgenii Zamiatin
Mikhail Mikhailovich Zoshchenko

Serbian
Danilo Kiš
Milorad Pavić
Miodrag Pavlović
Vasko Popa

Spanish
Demetrio Aguilera Malta
Rafael Alberti
Vicente Aleixandre
Isabel Allende
Reinaldo Arenas
Manlio Argueta
Gioconda Belli
Pedro Calderón de la Barca
Camilo José Cela
Luis Cernuda
Miguel de Cervantes
Federico García Lorca
José María Gironella
Luis de Góngora
Jorge Guillén
Juan Ramón Jiménez
St. John of the Cross
Lazarillo de Tormes
Antonio Machado
Emilia Pardo Bazán

Ramón Pérez de Ayala
Benito Pérez Galdós
Fernando de Rojas
Juan José Saer
Ramón J. Sender
Antonio Skármeta
Tirso de Molina
Miguel de Unamuno
Luisa Valenzuela
Ramón del Valle-Inclán
Lope de Vega Carpio

Sumerian
Epic of Gilgamesh

Swedish
Pär Lagerkvist
Selma Lagerlöf
Ivar Lo-Johansson
Edith Södergran

Thai
Siburapha

Ukrainian
Anna Akhmatova
Isaak Babel
Mikhail Bulgakov
Nikolai Gogol'
Iurii Olesha

Welsh
The Mabinogion

Yiddish
Elie Wiesel

TITLE INDEX

The index includes the titles of all works listed in the Fiction, Verse, and Play sections of the individual entries in the book; uncategorized titles for some entrants are also included. A few titles from other sections (Other, Prose, etc.) are included; in these cases, no abbreviation appears before the author's name. The following abbreviations, preceding the authors' names, are used:

f	fiction
p	play
v	verse
radio	radio play
scr	screenplay
tv	television play

The name(s) in parentheses after the title is meant to direct the reader to the appropriate entry, where full publication information is given.

Airman's Odyssey (f Saint-Exupéry)
Al-āʿish fī al-haqīqa (f Mahfouz)
Aisureba koso (p Tanizaki)
Aisuru hitotachi (f Kawabata)
Aita Tettauen (f Pérez Galdós)
L'aiuola bruciata (p Betti)
Ajas (p Wyspiański)
Ajax (p Sophocles)
Akanishi Kakita (f Shiga)
Akarumi e (f Yosano)
Akhenaten: Dweller in Truth (f Mahfouz)
Akiko Shihen Zenshū (v Yosano)
Akiko Shinshū (v Yosano)
Akritan Songs (v Sikelianos)
Akropolis (p Wyspiański)
Akt przerywany (p Różewicz)
Aktaion onder de sterren (f Vestdijk)
Akula: rasskazy (f Tolstoi)
Akuma (f Tanizaki)
Akuryō no gogo (f Endō)
Aladins Problem (f Jünger)
Alafroïkiotos (v Sikelianos)
Alain und Elise (p Kaiser)
Alarcos (p Schlegel)
El alarido de Yaurí (f Sender)
L'alba ai vetri: Poesie 1947–1950 (v Bassani)
El alba del alhelí (v Alberti)
Un albergo sul porto (p Betti)
Alberto Caeiro, Ricardo Reis, Alvaro de Campos, Fernando Pessoa (v Pessoa)
Albertus; ou, L'Âme et le péché (v Gautier)
Albine (f Dumas *père*)
Alboin der Langobardenkönig (p Fouqué)
Album de douze chansons (v Maeterlinck)
Álbum de familia (f Castellanos)
Álbum de família (p Rodrigues)
Album de vers anciens 1890–1900 (v Valéry)
Alcaic Poems (v Hölderlin)
El alcalde de Zalamea (p Calderón de la Barca)
Alceste (p Pérez Galdós)
Alceste (p Wieland)
Alcestis (p Euripides)
L'Alchimiste (p Nerval)
L'Alchimiste (p Dumas *père*)
Alcide al bivio (p Metastasio)
Alclasán: famtomina (p Asturias)
Alcools: Poèmes 1898–1913 (v Apollinaire)
Alcools: Poems (v Apollinaire)
La alegropeya (v Marechal)
Aleid. Twee fragmenten uit een onafgewerkt blyspel van Multatuli (p Multatuli)
El Aleph (f Borges)
Alessandro nelle Indie (p Metastasio)
Alexandre Chenevert, caissier (f Roy)
Alexandre le grand (p Racine)
Alexis; ou, Le Traité du vain combat (f Yourcenar)
Alguien que anda por ahí y otros relatos (f Cortázar)
Alguma poesia (v Andrade)
Algunas odas (v Neruda)
Alguns contos (f Lispector)

Alguns poemas ibéricos (v Torga)
El alhajadito (f Asturias)
Alì dagli occhi azzurri (f Pasolini)
Alibi (v Morante)
Aline et Valcour; ou, Le Roman philosophique (f Sade)
Alkestis (p Hofmannsthal)
All Strange Away (f Beckett)
All That Fall (radio Beckett)
All That Fall (p Beckett)
Alla-Moddin (p Tieck)
Alla periferia (f Cassola)
Alladine et Palomides (p Maeterlinck)
Allah n'est pas obligé (f Kourouma)
L'allegoria dell' autunno (v D'Annunzio)
Allégories (v Cocteau)
L'Allégresse (v Char)
Allegria di naufragi (v Ungaretti)
Alléluia pour une femme-jardin (f Depestre)
Allenda a verdad (f Pardo Bazán)
Aller retour (f Aymé)
Allerzielen (f Nooteboom)
Alles will den Propheten sehen (p Nestroy)
Les Alliés sont en Arménie: Poème (v Jacob)
All'uscita (p Pirandello)
Alma española (f Valle-Inclán)
Alma y vida (p Pérez Galdós)
Almansur (v Tieck)
Almas de violeta (v Jiménez)
Las almenas de toro (p Vega Carpio)
L'Alouette (p Anouilh)
Les Alouettes naïves: Roman (f Djebar)
Aloys und Imelde (p Brentano)
Alphabets (v Perec)
Al'piyskaya balada (f Bykaw)
Als vom Butt nur die Gräte geblieben war (v Grass)
Als der Krieg ausbrach, Als der Krieg zu Ende war (f Böll)
Als der Krieg zu Ende war (p Frisch)
Altaergeheimnissen (v Vondel)
Der Alte vom Berge, und die Gesellschaft auf dem Lande: zwei Novellen (f Tieck)
Alte Geschichten: Zwei Erzählungen (f Hesse)
Die alte Jungfer (p Lessing)
Der alte Mann mit der jungen Frau (p Nestroy)
Alte Meister: Komödie (f Bernhard)
Alto es el sur (v Asturias)
Un' altra libertà (v Bassani)
Altri versi e poesie disperse (v Montale)
L'altro figlio (p Pirandello)
Altsächsischer Bildersaal (f Fouqué)
Alves & ca (f Eça de Queirós)
Alwin (f Fouqué)
Alzir; ili, Amerikantsii (p Fonvizin)
Alzire; ou, Les Américains (p Voltaire)
Am Leben hin (f Rilke)
Am Weg (f Hesse)
Am Ziel (p Bernhard)
Amadeo I (f Pérez Galdós)
Amagaeru (f Shiga)
Amal; ou, La Lettre du roi (p Gide)
Amāma al'arsh (f Mahfouz)

Les amandiers sont morts de leurs blessures (v Ben Jelloun)
L'Amant (f Duras)
L'Amant complaisant (p Anouilh)
L'Amant de la Chine du Nord (f Duras)
L'Amant fantôme (f Simenon)
L'Amant sans nom (f Simenon)
L'Amante anglaise (f Duras)
L'Amante anglaise (p Duras)
La amante: Canciones (v Alberti)
L'amante di se medesimo (p Goldoni)
L'amante infelice (f Moravia)
L'amante militare (p Goldoni)
Amantes, Quinze (v Brossard)
Les Amants de la mansarde (f Simenon)
Les Amants de Verone (p Prévert)
Les Amants du malheur (f Simenon)
Les Amants jaloux (p Lesage)
Les Amants magnifiques (p Molière)
Amar ds aprende amando (v Andrade)
Amar después de la muerte (p Calderón de la Barca)
Amar y ser amado; divina Filotea (p Calderón de la Barca)
Amar sin saber a quién (p Vega Carpio)
Amar, verbo intransitivo (f Andrade)
Amaury (f Dumas *père*)
Ámbito (v Aleixandre)
Le ambizioni sbagliate (f Moravia)
L'Âme enchantée (f Rolland)
''Ame no ki'' o kiku onnatachi (f Ōe)
Amédée; ou, Comment s'en débarrasser (p Ionesco)
L'America libera: Odi (v Alfieri)
Americanas (v Machado de Assis)
Amerika (f Kafka)
Amerika (p Klíma)
Amers (v Saint-John Perse)
Les Âmes fortes (f Giono)
Les Âmes mortes (p Adamov)
L'ameto (p Boccaccio)
L'Ami d'enfance de Maigret (f Simenon)
L'Ami des femmes (p Dumas *fils*)
L'Ami lointain (f Roy)
L'amica delle mogli (p Pirandello)
Le amiche (f Pratolini)
Amicizia (p De Filippo)
L'Amie de Mne Maigret (f Simenon)
Les Amies (v Verlaine)
El amigo Manso (f Pérez Galdós)
Aminta (p Tasso)
Al-Amira al-Bayda aw Bayad al-Nahar (f Tawfiq Al-Hakim)
Amistad funesta (f Martí)
Amitié cachetée (v Char)
Amitié du prince (v Saint-John Perse)
Ammalet Beg (f Dumas *père*)
Ammonizione ed altre poesie (1900–1910) (v Saba)
Amor y ciencia (p Pérez Galdós)
Amor con amor se paga (p Martí)
O amor de Castro Alves (p Amado)
El amor de Don Perlimplín con Belisa en su jardín (p García Lorca)
El amor desatinado (p Vega Carpio)
El amor en los tiempos del cólera (f García Márquez)
El amor enamorado (p Vega Carpio)

Amor es más laberinto (p Juana Inés de la Cruz)
Amor mundo y otros cuentos (f Arguedas)
Amor mundo y todos los cuentos (f Arguedas)
L'amor paterno; o, La serva riconoscente (p Goldoni)
Amor y pedagogía (f Unamuno)
L'amor prigioniero (p Metastasio)
Amor und Psyche (p Hofmannsthal)
Amor vincit omnia (p Lenz)
Un amore (f Buzzati)
L'amore artigiano (p Goldoni)
L'amore coniugale e altri racconti (f Moravia)
L'amore di Galatea (p Quasimodo)
Amore regale (f Deledda)
L'amore tanto per fare (f Cassola)
Amores (v Ovid)
Amori fatali; La leggenda nera; Il ritratto (f Deledda)
Amori moderni (f Deledda)
Amori senza amore (f Pirandello)
L'amorosa spina (v Saba)
L'amorosa visione (v Boccaccio)
L'Amour (f Duras)
Amour (v Verlaine)
L'Amour à Montparnasse (f Simenon)
L'Amour absolu (f Jarry)
L'Amour africain (p Mérimée)
Amour d'Afrique (f Simenon)
Amour d'exilée (f Simenon)
L'Amour en visites (f Jarry)
L'Amour et la vérité (p Marivaux)
L'Amour et l'argent (f Simenon)
Amour et piano (p Feydeau)
L'Amour, la fantasia: Roman (f Djebar)
L'Amour la poésie (v Éluard)
L'Amour méconnu (f Simenon)
L'Amour médecin (p Molière)
Amours (v Cendrars)
Les Amours de Psyché et de Cupidon (f La Fontaine)
Amphion: Mélodrame (p Valéry)
Amphitryo (p Plautus)
Amphitryon (p Kleist)
Amphitryon (p Molière)
Amphitryon 38 (p Giraudoux)
Ample discours au roi (v Du Bellay)
Amras (f Bernhard)
Das Amulet (f Meyer)
Amy Robsart (p Hugo)
Amycus et Célestin (f France)
L'An 1964 (v Char)
Anabase (v Saint-John Perse)
Anacreon Done into English (v Anacreon)
The Anacreonta (v Anacreon)
Anak Semua Bangsa (f Toer)
Anakreon (v Mörike)
Anatol (p Schnitzler)
Anatomie jedné zdrženlivosti (p Havel)
L'anconitana (p Ruzzante)
Anděl strážný (p Havel)
Andor (f Molnár)
Andorra (p Frisch)
André (f Sand)

A Bird of Paper (v Aleixandre)
Birds, Lysistrata, Assembly-women, Wealth: A New Verse Translation with Introduction and Notes (p Aristophanes)
Bisaraha ghayr Mutlaqa (n Idris)
Bismarck (p Wedekind)
Bitni ljudi (f Pavlović)
Bitoku no yorimeki (f Mishima)
Bitterzoet (v Nooteboom)
Biyon no tsuma (f Dazai)
Bizancio (f Sender)
Las bizarrías de Belisa (p Vega Carpio)
Bjälbo-Jarlen (p Strindberg)
Bjørger (f Hamsun)
Black (f Dumas *père*)
The Black Monk and Other Stories (f Chekhov)
Le Blanc à lunettes (f Simenon)
Le Blanc de l'Algérie: Recit (f Djebar)
Blanche ou l'oubli (f Aragon)
Blanco (v Paz)
Les Blancs et les bleus (f Dumas *père*)
Les Blancs et les bleus (p Dumas *père*)
Eine blassblaue Frauenschrift (f Werfel)
Blaubart (f Frisch)
Blaubart und Miss Ilsebill (f Döblin)
Die blaue Blume (v Hauptmann)
Der blaue Tiger (f Döblin)
Blazhenstvo (Son inzhenera Reina v 4-kh deistviakh) (p Bulgakov)
Le Blé en herbe (f Colette)
Die Blechtrommel als Film (p Grass)
Bleikeplassen (f Vesaas)
Blencong (f Herliany)
Die Blendung (f Canetti)
Blessures des mots: journal de Tunisie (f Accad)
Der Blinde (p Dürrenmatt)
Die blinde Führerin (f Fouqué)
Die blinde Göttin (p Toller)
Der blinde Spiegel (f Roth)
Bliznets v tuchakh (v Pasternak)
Blokha (p Zamiatin)
Blood and Feathers: Selected Poems (v Prévert)
Blæsende gry (f Heinesen)
Blue Bamboo: Tales of Fantasy and Romance (f Dazai)
The Blue Eyed Lady (f Molnár)
Blues for a Black Cat and Other Stories (f Vian)
Blues Untuk Bonnie (v Rendra)
Blumenstrauss: Gewunden aus den neusten Romanen und Erzählungen (f Fouqué)
Der Blütenzweig: Eine Auswahl aus den Gedichten (v Hesse)
Bluzhdaiushchie zvezdy: Rasskaz dlia kino (f Babel)
Bō ni natta otoko (p Abe)
Bobette, mannequin (f Simenon)
Bobette et ses satyres (f Simenon)
Boca de ouro (p Rodrigues)
Boccaccio's First Fiction (f Boccaccio)
Bocksgesang (p Werfel)
La boda del poeta (f Skármeta)
Bodas de sangre (p García Lorca)
Bodas reales (f Pérez Galdós)
Bödeln (f Lagerkvist)
Bödeln (p Lagerkvist)

Bodo von Hohenried (f Fouqué)
Bodong (f Bei Dao)
Boertigh, amoreus, en aendachtig groot Lied-Boek (v Bredero)
Le Boeuf clandestin (f Aymé)
Der Bogen des Odysseus (p Hauptmann)
Boh (f Moravia)
Böhlendorff und andere: Erzählungen (f Bobrowski)
Böhlendorff: A Short Story and Seven Poems (f Bobrowski)
Le Bois sacré (p Rostand)
Boitempo; A falta que ama (v Andrade)
Bolesław Śmiały (p Wyspiański)
Bolhabál (p Illyés)
Bolívar (v Asturias)
Bol'shim detiam skazki (f Zamiatin)
Bonheur (v Verlaine)
Le Bonheur de Lili (f Simenon)
Bonheur d'occasion (f Roy)
Le Bonheur fou (f Giono)
El bonito crimen del carabinero y otras invenciones (f Cela)
Bonjour, Monsieur Prassinos (v Queneau)
La Bonne Chanson (v Verlaine)
Les Bonnes (p Genet)
Boodschap van de vogels en andere opgezette dieren (v Gezelle)
A Book That Was Lost and Other Stories (f Agnon)
Boquitas pintadas (f Puig)
Boquitas Pintadas (scr Puig)
Borghesia (f Ginzburg)
Bori notesz (v Radnóti)
Boris Godunov (p Pushkin)
Børn av tiden (f Hamsun)
Der böse Geist Lumpazivagabundus; oder, Das liederliche Kleeblatt (p Nestroy)
Der böse Rauch (p Sachs)
Die Bösen (f Mann)
Die bösen Köche (p Grass)
Bosszú (p Eötvös)
A boszorkány (p Molnár)
Botchan (f Natsume)
Bötjer Basch (f Storm)
Botschaften des Regens (v Eich)
La bottega del caffè (p Goldoni)
Botteghe oscure (f Morante)
Les Bouches inutiles (p Beauvoir)
Le Boulanger, la boulangère, et le petit mitron (p Anouilh)
La Boule noire (f Simenon)
Le Bourgeois de Gand; ou, Le Secrétaire du Duc d'Albe (p Dumas *père*)
Le Bourgeois Gentilhomme (p Molière)
Le Bourgeon (p Feydeau)
Le Bourgmestre de Furnes (f Simenon)
Le Bourgmestre de Stilmonde (p Maeterlinck)
Le Bourru bienfaisant (p Goldoni)
Bourses de voyage (f Verne)
Le Bout de la route (p Giono)
Les Boutades du capitaine Matamore et ses comédies (p Scarron)
La boutique del mistero (f Buzzati)
Le Bouton de Rose (p Zola)
Bouvard et Pécuchet (f Flaubert)
Boží muka (f Čapek)
Brabach (p Mann)
Bramy Raju (f Andrzejewski)

Il colpevole (v Montale)
Un colpo di pistola (scr Moravia)
Combabus (f Wieland)
Combat avec l'ange (f Giraudoux)
Come prima, meglio di prima (p Pirandello)
Come tu mi vuoi (p Pirandello)
Comedia de Calisto y Melibea (p Rojas)
Comédia de Rubena (p Vicente)
Comedia del diantre y otras dos (p Sender)
Comédia do viúvo (p Vicente)
Comedia sin título (p García Lorca)
Comédia sobre a divisa da cidade de Coimbra (p Vicente)
La Comédie de celui qui épousa une femme muette (p France)
La Comédie de la mort (v Gautier)
Comédie de la nativité de Jésus-Christ (p Marguerite de Navarre)
La Comédie des Tuileries (p Corneille)
Comédie Française (p Diderot)
Comédie jouée à Mont-de-Marsan en 1547 (p Marguerite de Navarre)
Comedy of Vanity and Life-Terms (p Canetti)
Comme l'eau qui coule (f Yourcenar)
Comme nous avons été (p Adamov)
Comme le temps passe (f Brasillach)
Commedie del Cinquecento 2 (p Ruzzante [or Ruzante])
Comment les Blancs sont d'anciens Noirs (f Cendrars)
Comment c'est (f Beckett)
Comment la trouves-tu? (p Dumas *fils*)
La Commère (p Marivaux)
Commune présence (v Char)
Il commune senso delle proporzioni: piccolo thriller da viaggio (f Duranti)
Les Communistes (f Aragon)
Como elas são todas (p Machado de Assis)
Como en la Guerra (f Valenzuela)
Como quien espera el alba (v Cernuda)
Comodhia (p Kazantzakis)
Las compañías convenientes y otros fingimientos y cegueras (f Cela)
Il compagno (f Pavese)
Le Compagnon du tour de France (f Sand)
Les Compagnons de Jéhu (f Dumas *père*)
Les Compagnons de la Marjolaine (p Verne)
Les Compagnons duns le jardin (v Char)
Company (f Beckett)
Complainte du pauvr' propriétaire (p Feydeau)
Les Complaintes (v Laforgue)
The Complete Justine, Philosophy in the Bedroom, and Other Writings (f Sade)
Complete Maigret Short Stories (f Simenon)
The Complete Perfectionist: A Poetics of Work (v Jiménez)
Complete Poetical Works (v Quasimodo)
Les Complices (f Simenon)
La composición (f Skármeta)
Le Comte de Beuzeval; (f Dumas *père*)
Le Comte de Monte-Cristo (f Dumas *père*)
Le Comte de Morcerf; Villefort (p Dumas *père*)
Le Comte de Moret (f Dumas *père*)
Le Comte Hermann (p Dumas *père*)
Le Comte Morin, député (f France)
Le Comte Ory (p Scribe)
La Comtesse de Charny (f Dumas *père*)
La Comtesse de Rudolstadt (f Sand)

La Comtesse de Saint-Géran; (f Dumas *père*)
La Comtesse de Salisbury (f Dumas *père*)
La Comtesse de Tende (f Lafayette)
La Comtesse d'Escarbagnas (p Molière)
La Comtesse Romani (p Dumas *fils*)
Le Con d'Irène (f Aragon)
Con il piede straniero sopra al cuore (v Quasimodo)
Concierto barroco (f Carpentier)
Le Concile féerique (v Laforgue)
La Condamnée (v Char)
O conde de Abranhos; A Catastrophe (f Eça de Queirós)
El condenado por desconfiado (p Tirso de Molina)
El condenado por desconfiado (p Machado)
Las condenados (p Pérez Galdós)
Condenados a vivir (f Gironella)
La Condition humaine (f Malraux)
Le Condor et le morpion (v Apollinaire)
The Condor (f Stifter)
La Confession de Claude (f Zola)
La Confession d'un enfant du siècle (f Musset)
La Confession d'une jeune fille (f Sand)
Le Confessionnel (f Simenon)
Les Confessions de Dan Yack (f Cendrars)
Confessions of a Hooligan: Fifty Poems (v Esenin)
Confidence africaine (f Martin Du Gard)
Une Confidence de Maigret (f Simenon)
Les Confidences (f Lamartine)
Configurations (v Paz)
Il conformista (f Moravia)
Le Confort d'ami (v Guillaume de Machaut)
El congreso (f Borges)
La Conjuration (p Char)
Connaissance du temps (v Claudel)
Le Connétable de Bourbon; ou, L'Italie au seizième siècle (p Dumas *père*)
La Conquérante (f Brasillach)
Les Conquérants (f Malraux)
The Conqueror in Constantinople (v Pavlović)
La Conquête de la toison d'or (p Corneille)
La consagración de la primavera (f Carpentier)
La Conscience (p Dumas *père*)
Conscience l'innocent (f Dumas *père*)
Il consiglio d'Egitto (f Sciascia)
Consignas (v Alberti)
The Conspirators: A Play (p Mérimée)
Constance Verrier (f Sand)
Constancia, y otras novelas para vírgenes (f Fuentes)
Constellations (v Breton)
Consuelo (f Sand)
Cont escolhidos (f Lispector)
Un conte à votre façon (f Queneau)
Conte bleu; Le Premier Soir; Maléfice (f Yourcenar)
Un conte de fées (p Dumas *père*)
Il conte di Carmagnola (p Manzoni)
Le Conte du Graal (v Chrétien de Troyes)
Les Contemplations (v Hugo)
Contemporary Arab Women Writers and Poets (f Accad)
La contesa de' Numi (p Metastasio)
Il contesto (f Sciascia)
Contos de aprendiz (f Andrade)

Contos fluminenses (f Machado de Assis)
Contos novos (f Andrade)
Les Contrabandiers de l'alcool (f Simenon)
Contradictions (v Ritsos)
Il contrattempo; o, Il chiaccherione imprudente (p Goldoni)
Il contratto (p De Filippo)
Contre une maison sèche (v Char)
Contre la peine de mort (v Lamartine)
La Convention Belzébir (p Aymé)
Conversación en La Catedral (f Vargas Llosa)
Conversations with Eternity: The Forgotten Masterpiece of Victor Hugo (f Hugo)
Conversazione in Sicilia (f Vittorini)
Los convidados de agosto (f Castellanos)
Los convidados de plata (f Carpentier)
Convivencia (v Guillén)
Coplas de Juan Descalzo (v Guillén)
Coplas de Juan Panadero (Libro I) (v Alberti)
Coplas de Juan Panadero 1949–1977; Vida bilingüe de un refugiado español en Francia 1939–1940 (v Alberti)
Coquelicot du massacre (f Accad)
El corazón amarillo (v Neruda)
El corazón con que vivo (v Guillén)
Corinne; ou, L'Italie (f Staël)
Coriolan (p Brecht)
Il cormorano (p Ginzburg)
Le Cornet à dés: Poèmes en prose (v Jacob)
Corona benignitatis anni dei (v Claudel)
La corona de Hungría (p Vega Carpio)
Corona: Ein Rittergedicht in drei Büchern (v Fouqué)
La corona merecida (p Vega Carpio)
Corona trágica: Vida y muerte de la Serenísima Reina de Escocia María Estuarda (v Vega Carpio)
El coronel no tiene quien le escriba (f García Márquez)
Corpo (v Andrade)
Corpo de baile: sete novelas (f Guimarães Rosa)
Corps mémorable (v Éluard)
Corruzione al palazzo di giustizia (p Betti)
Corte de amor (f Valle-Inclán)
La Corte de Carlos IV (f Pérez Galdós)
La Corte de los Milagros (f Valle-Inclán)
Le Cortège priapique (v Apollinaire)
Côrtes de Júpiter (p Vicente)
La cortigiana (p Aretino)
Cortigiana stanca (f Moravia)
Corto viaggio sentimentale e altri racconti inediti (f Svevo)
La coscienza di Zeno (f Svevo)
Cose leggere e vaganti (v Saba)
Così è (si vi pare) (p Pirandello)
Cosima (f Deledda)
Cosima (p Sand)
Le cosmicomiche (f Calvino)
Cossack Tales (f Gogol')
La costanza della ragione (f Pratolini)
Costetick mal (v Huygens)
La Côte: Recueil de chants celtiques inédits (v Jacob)
Couleur du temps (p Apollinaire)
Couleurs (v Prévert)
Un coup de dés jamais n'abolira le hasard (v Mallarmé)
Le Coup de grâce (f Yourcenar)

Le Coup de lune (f Simenon)
Un Coup de tête (p Feydeau)
Couplets from Kabir (v Kabīr)
Cour d'assises (f Simenon)
Courir les rues (v Queneau)
La Couronne de vulcain (f Jacob)
Courrier-sud (f Saint-Exupéry)
Courrier-sud (scr Saint-Exupéry)
Cours naturel (v Éluard)
Courte-Queue (f Roy)
Crackling Mountain and Other Stories (f Dazai)
The Crackling Sun: Selected Poems (v Aleixandre)
Crainquebille (p France)
La Création du monde (p Cendrars)
Création et rédemption: Le Docteur mystérieux, La Fille du marquis (f Dumas *père*)
Creatures That Once Were Men (f Gor'kii)
Crepusculario (v Neruda)
Le Crepuscule au loin (f Wiesel)
The Crescent Moon: Child-Poems (v Tagore)
Crésus (p Giono)
Le Crève-coeur (v Aragon)
Le Crève-coeur et Les Yeux d'Elsa (v Aragon)
La Crevette dans tous ses états (v Ponge)
Cri écrit (v Cocteau)
A criação do mundo: Os dois primeiros dias (f Torga)
Las criaturas saturnianas (f Sender)
The Cricket beneath the Waterfall and Other Stories (f Krleža)
Crickets and Frogs: A Fable (v Mistral)
Le Crime de M. Lange/Les Ports de la nuit (p Prévert)
Le Crime de Sylvestre Bonnard, membre de l'Institut (f France)
O crime do Padre Amaro (f Eça de Queirós)
Un crime en Hollande (f Simenon)
Crime impuni (f Simenon)
Un crime (f Bernanos)
Les Crimes célèbres (f Dumas *père*)
Les Crimes de l'amour: Nouvelles héroïques et tragiques (f Sade)
The Crimes of Love (f Sade)
Crispin, rival de son maître (p Lesage)
El Cristo de Velázquez (v Unamuno)
Cristo versus Arizona (f Cela)
Cristóbal nonato (f Fuentes)
A Critical Edition of the Circumstantial Verse of Joachim Du Bellay (v Du Bellay)
La Critique de L'École des femmes (p Molière)
Croazia segreta (v Ungaretti)
La crociata degli innocenti (scr D'Annunzio)
La Croix de Berny (f Gautier)
Il crollo della Baliverna (f Buzzati)
Cromwell (p Hugo)
Cromwell et Charles Ier (p Dumas *père*)
Cronaca familiare (f Pratolini)
Cronache di poveri amanti (f Pratolini)
Crónica de una muerte anunciada (f García Márquez)
Crónica del alba (f Sender)
Crónicas de Bustos Domecq (f Borges)
Cronus y la señora con rabo (f Sender)
La Cruche cassée (p Adamov)
La Crucifixion (v Cocteau)
A császár (p Molnár)

David mit Batseba (p Sachs)
Davor (p Grass)
A Day in the Country and Other Stories (f Maupassant)
Dažhyts' da svitannya (f Bykaw)
De alleenheersching (v Bilderdijk)
De amor y de sombra (f Allende)
De aquí en adelante (v Argueta)
De arme Heinrich (f Vestdijk)
De Batavische gebroeders (p Vondel)
De berg van licht (f Couperus)
De besegrade (v Weiss)
De boeken der kleine zielen (f Couperus)
La de Bringas (f Pérez Galdós)
De bruid daarboven (p Multatuli)
De bruine vriend (f Vestdijk)
De Cartago a Sagunto (f Pérez Galdós)
De dans van de reiger (p Claus)
De derde october (v Bilderdijk)
De doden zoeken een huis (v Nooteboom)
De dokter en het lichte meisje (f Vestdijk)
De dood betrapt (f Vestdijk)
De echt (v Bilderdijk)
De eieren van de kaaiman (p Claus)
De fantasia en andere verhalen (f Vestdijk)
De filmheld en het gidsmeisje (f Vestdijk)
De filosoof en de sluipmoordenaar (f Vestdijk)
De fortabte spillemænd (f Heinesen)
De Fuerteventura a París (v Unamuno)
De geestenwereld (v Bilderdijk)
De geruchten (f Claus)
De geschiedenis van Woutertje Pieterse (f Multatuli)
De grenslijnen uitgewist (f Vestdijk)
De Heerlijkheit der Kercke (v Vondel)
De held van Temesa (f Vestdijk)
De hondsdagen (f Claus)
De hotelier doet niet meer mee (f Vestdijk)
De imaginum, signorum, et idearum compositione (v Bruno)
De innumerabilibus, immenso et infigurabilii seu de universo et mundis (v Bruno)
De kellner en de levenden (f Vestdijk)
De kloke jomfruer (f Undset)
De Klucht van Symen sonder soeticheyt (p Bredero)
De koele minnaar (f Claus)
De komedianten (p Claus)
De komedianten (f Couperus)
De koperen tuin (f Vestdijk)
De la costilla de Eva (v Belli)
De la rue au bonheur (f Simenon)
De la terre á la lune (f Verne)
De la vigilia estéril (v Castellanos)
De leeuw en zijn huid (f Vestdijk)
De Leydsche Weezen aan de burgery (v Bilderdijk)
La de los tristes destinos (f Pérez Galdós)
De måske egnede (f Høeg)
De mensen hiernaast (f Claus)
De Metsiers (f Claus)
De moment en moment (v Char)
De monade, numero et figura libea consequens quinque de minimo magno. Menura (v Bruno)
De muis en kikvorschkrijg (v Bilderdijk)

De nadagen van Pilatus (f Vestdijk)
De nieuwe zee-straet van 's Gravenhage op Scheveningen (v Huygens)
De nygifte (p Bjørnson)
De ode (f Couperus)
De Oñate a La Granja (f Pérez Galdós)
De ondergang der eerste waereld (v Bilderdijk)
De ongelukkige (f Couperus)
De onmogelijke moord (f Vestdijk)
De oubliette (f Vestdijk)
De overnachting (f Vestdijk)
De partu virginis (v Sannazaro)
De persconferentie (f Vestdijk)
De Pretore Vincenzo (p De Filippo)
De redding van Fré Bolderhey (f Vestdijk)
De rerum natura (v Lucretius)
De ridder is gestorven (f Nooteboom)
La de San Quintín (p Pérez Galdós)
De schandalen (f Vestdijk)
De Spaanschen Brabander Ierolimo (p Bredero)
De Ster van Bethlehem (v Nijhoff)
De stille kracht (f Couperus)
De stomme ridder (p Bredero)
De to baronesser (f Andersen)
De triplici minimo et mensura ad trium speculativarum scientiarum et multarum activarum artium principia (v Bruno)
De un cancionero apócrifo (v Machado)
De un momento a otro (p Alberti)
De unges forbund (p Ibsen)
De usynlige (p Holberg)
De uytlandighe herder (v Huygens)
De verdwenen horlogemaker (f Vestdijk)
De verliefde ezel (f Couperus)
De verlossing (p Claus)
De verminkte Apollo (f Vestdijk)
De vervoering van Grol (v Vondel)
De verwondering (f Claus)
De verzoeking (f Claus)
De verzoeking (p Claus)
De vijf roeiers (f Vestdijk)
De vliegende Hollander (v Nijhoff)
De vliegende hollander (v Vestdijk)
De voet in 't graf (v Bilderdijk)
De vuuraanbidders (f Vestdijk)
De wandelaar (v Nijhoff)
De ziekte der geleerden (v Bilderdijk)
De ziener (f Vestdijk)
De zwaardvis (f Claus)
De zwaluwen neer gestreken (f Couperus)
De zwarte keizer (f Claus)
De zwarte ruiter (f Vestdijk)
Dearest Father: Stories and Other Writings (f Kafka)
Death in Midsummer and Other Stories (f Mishima)
Death in Venice and Other Stories (f Mann)
Death of an Inquisitor and Other Stories (f Sciascia)
The Death Penalty (f Torga)
Der Besuch aus dem Elysium (p Werfel)
Debet ock kredit (p Strindberg)
Debut (v Brodskii)
Un début dans la vie (f Balzac)
Decameron (f Boccaccio)

A Dove in Santiago (v Evtushenko)
Il dovere del medico (p Pirandello)
Le Doyen de Killerine: Histoire morale composée sur les mémoires d'une illustre famille d'Irlande (f Prévost)
Dózsa György (p Illyés)
Dr. Renault's Fristelser (f Jensen)
Le Drac (p Sand)
A Draft of Shadows and Other Poems (v Paz)
The Dragon: Fifteen Stories (f Zamiatin)
La Dragonne (f Jarry)
La Dragontea (v Vega Carpio)
Dragoon; suivi de Olympe (f Giono)
Drámák (p Illyés)
The Dramatic Works (p Fonvizin)
Dramatik (p Lagerkvist)
Dramatische Dichtungen für Deutsche (p Fouqué)
Dramatische Dichtungen (p Grabbe)
Dramatische Entwürfe aus dem Nachlass (p Hofmannsthal)
Dramatische Spiele (p Fouqué)
Un drame au Pôle Sud (f Simenon)
Un drame dans les airs (f Verne)
Un drame dans les prisons (f Balzac)
Un drame en Livonie (f Verne)
Les Drames galants, La Marquise d'Escoman (f Dumas *père*)
Drammatica fine di un noto musicista (p Buzzati)
Drammi intimi (f Verga)
The Dream below the Sun: Selected Poems (v Machado)
Dream of Fair to Middling Women (f Beckett)
The Dreams of Chang and Other Stories (f Bunin)
Drei Akte: Der Tyrann; Die Unschuldige; Variété (p Mann)
Drei Erzählungen (f Bobrowski)
Die drei Erzählungen (f Sternheim)
Drei Frauen (f Musil)
Drei Märchen (f Arnim)
Drei Märchen (f Fouqué)
Drei Märchen (f Storm)
Drei Novellen (f Storm)
Die drei Nüsse (f Brentano)
Die drei Sprünge des Wang-lun (f Döblin)
Drei Stücke (p Lenz)
Die dreifache Warning: Novellen (f Schnitzler)
Die Dreigroschenoper (p Brecht)
Der Dreigroschenroman (f Brecht)
Driemaal XXXIII Kleengedichtjes (v Gezelle)
Das dritte Buch über Achim (f Johnson)
Drogi nieuniknione (f Andrzejewski)
Le Droit du seigneur (p Voltaire)
Un drôle de Coco (f Simenon)
Drôle de drame (p Prévert)
Dromen met open ogen (v Huygens)
Dronning Tamara (p Hamsun)
Dronningen paa 16 aar (p Andersen)
Dropadi: Teks pu en trazi-komedi mizikal baze lor Mahabharata (p Virahsawmy)
Drottningar i Kungahälla jämte andra berättelser (f Lagerlöf)
Drugaia zhizn' (f Trifonov)
Druhý sešit směšných lásek (f Kundera)
Drunken Boat (v Rimbaud)
Der Dschin (f Werfel)
Du Bellay (v Du Bellay)

Du fährst zu oft nach Heidelberg und andere Erzählungen (f Böll)
Du monde entier au coeur du monde (v Cendrars)
Du Wanxiang (f Ding Ling)
Dubrovskii (f Pushkin)
Le Duc de Foix (p Voltaire)
La Duchesse de Langeais (scr Giraudoux)
La Duchesse des Folies-Bergères (p Feydeau)
La duda inquietante (f Gironella)
Due cortigiane; Serata di Don Giovanni (f Moravia)
Due dialoghi di Ruzante in lingua rustica (p Ruzzante [or Ruzante])
I due gemelli veneziani (p Goldoni)
Le due maschere (f Pirandello)
Due novelle (f Bassani)
Due poemetti (v Buzzati)
Duel (f Chekhov)
The Duel (p Ionesco)
The Duel and Other Stories (f Chekhov)
Duell mit dem Schatten (f Lenz)
Duellen (f Weiss)
Los duendes de la camarilla (f Pérez Galdós)
Dúfnaveislan (p Laxness)
Dui Bon (f Tagore)
Duihua yu fanjie (p Gao)
Duineser Elegien (v Rilke)
Dulce dueño (f Pardo Bazán)
Dulce patria (v Neruda)
D'un château à l'autre (f Céline)
D'une sérénité crispée (v Char)
Dunungen (p Lagerlöf)
Dunyâ Allah (f Mahfouz)
Al-Dunyâ Riwaya Hazaliya (p Tawfiq Al-Hakim)
Duo (f Colette)
Duo d'Amour: Poèmes d'amour 1920–1950 (v Goll)
Duo yu (p Gao)
El duque de Viseo (p Vega Carpio)
La duquesa de Benamejí (p Machado)
La duquesa de Benamejí, La prima Fernanda y Juan de Mañara (p Machado)
Le Dur Désir de durer (v Éluard)
Durcheinanderthal (f Dürrenmatt)
Dürrenmatt: His Five Novels (f Dürrenmatt)
Dursli, der Brannteweinsäufer; oder, der Heilige Weihnachtsabend (f Gotthelf)
Duše se kupaju poslednji put (v Pavić)
Dusze w niewoli (f Prus)
Dva goroda (v Evtushenko)
Dva gusara—Metel' (f Tolstoi)
Dva tovarishcha (f Tolstoi)
Dvärgen (f Lagerkvist)
Dvenadtsat' (v Blok)
Dvoinik (f Dostoevskii)
Dvoiniki (f Pil'niak)
Dvorianskoe gnezdo (f Turgenev)
Dvukhmuzhniaia (f Sholokhov)
A Dwelling Place of My People: Sixteen Stories of the Chassidim (f Agnon)
Dye liubimykh (v Evtushenko)
Dye pary lyzh (v Evtushenko)
Dym (f Turgenev)
Dyskolos (p Menander)

Die Frau des Falkensteins (f Fouqué)
Die Frau des Richters (f Schnitzler)
Die Frau des Weisen: Novelletten (f Schnitzler)
Die Frau im Fenster (p Hofmannsthal)
Frau Jenny Treibel (f Fontane)
Die Frau ohne Schatten (p Hofmannsthal)
Die Frau ohne Schatten (f Hofmannsthal)
Frauen vor Flusslandschaft: Roman in Dialogen und Selbstgesprächen (f Böll)
Frauen-Liebe und Leben: Ein Lieder-Cyklus (v Chamisso)
Frauenliebe (f Fouqué)
Das Frauenopfer (p Kaiser)
Fräulein Else (f Schnitzler)
Fräulein Julie (p Weiss)
Die Freier (p Eichendorff)
Der Freigeist (p Lessing)
Freiheit in Krähwinkel (p Nestroy)
Freiwild (p Schnitzler)
Das fremde Mädchen (p Hofmannsthal)
French Kiss: Etreinte/exploration (f Brossard)
Les Frères corses (f Dumas *père*)
Les Frères corses (p Dumas *père*)
Les Frères Kip (f Verne)
Les Frères Rico (f Simenon)
Les Frères Zemganno (f Goncourt)
Freuden und Trauer-Spiele, auch oden und Sonnette sampt Herr Peter Squentz (p Gryphius)
Der Freund (f Mann)
Freunde: Erzählungen (f Hesse)
Die Freunde machen den Philosophen (p Lenz)
Das Friedenfest (p Hauptmann)
Friedrich und Anna (p Kaiser)
Friedrich, Prinz von Korsika (p Nestroy)
The Friend of the Family and The Gambler (f Dostoevskii)
Die Frist (p Dürrenmatt)
Fritiofs saga (p Lagerlöf)
Der fröhliche Weinberg (p Zuckmayer)
Fröken Julie (p Strindberg)
Frøken Smillas fornemmelse for sne (f Høeg)
From an Abandoned Work (f Beckett)
From Desire to Desire (v Evtushenko)
From Lorca's Theatre: Five Plays (p García Lorca)
From Marriage to Divorce (p Feydeau)
From Nicaragua with Love: Poems, 1976–1986 (v Cardenal)
From the Poems of Giosuè Carducci (v Carducci)
From the Rivers (v Bobrowski)
Front Rouge (v Aragon)
La frontera de cristal: Una novela en nueve cuentos (f Fuentes)
La Frontière de Savoie (p Scribe)
Frost (f Bernhard)
Fru Inger til Østråt (p Ibsen)
Fru Marta Oulie (f Undset)
Fruen fra havet (p Ibsen)
Die frühen Gräber (v Klopstock)
Frühere Verhältnisse (p Nestroy)
Die früheste Geschichte der Welt: Ein Geschenk für Kinder (f Fouqué)
Frühlings Erwachen (p Wedekind)
Fruit from Saturn (v Goll)
Fruit-Gathering (v Tagore)
Les Fruits d'or (f Sarraute)

Frygten for flertallet (f Bjørnson)
Ftesë në studio (f Kadare)
O Ftochoulis tou Theou (f Kazantzakis)
Il fu Mattia Pascal (f Pirandello)
Fuenteovejuna (p Vega Carpio)
La fuga in Egitto (f Deledda)
La fuggitiva (p Betti)
Függő (f Esterházy)
The Fugitive (p Tagore)
The Fugitive and Other Poems (v Tagore)
El fugitivo (f Sender)
Fuglane (f Vesaas)
Fuglen i pæretræet (p Andersen)
Fuharosok (f Esterházy)
Fuhrmann Henschel (p Hauptmann)
La Fuite de M. Monde (f Simenon)
Fukai kawa (f Endō)
Fukuzatsuma kare (f Mishima)
Fulgor y muerte de Joaquín Murieta (p Neruda)
Fumizukai (f Mori)
Der Fundevogel: Ein Märlein (f Grimm)
The Funeral of Bobo (v Brodskii)
Los funerales de la Mamá Grande (f García Márquez)
Fünf Gesänge (v Rilke)
Fünfzehn Hörspiele (p Eich)
Der Funke Leben (f Remarque)
Il fuoco (f D'Annunzio)
Fuoco grande (f Pavese)
Fuori di chiave (v Pirandello)
Furcht und Elend des Dritten Reiches (p Brecht)
Fureur et mystère (v Char)
Las furias y las penas (v Neruda)
Fürsorgliche Belagerung (f Böll)
Furstarna: en krönika från Gustav Vasa till Karl XII (f Lo-Johansson)
Die Fürstin Russalka (f Wedekind)
The Further Confessions of Zeno (f Svevo)
Fushigi na kagami (f Mori)
Fushinchū (f Mori)
Fustigada luz (1972–1978) (v Alberti)
Fusuma (f Shiga)
Futago no hoshi (f Miyazawa)
Fūten rojin nikki (f Tanizaki)
Fuyo no Tsuyu Ouchi Jikki (p Mishima)
Gabriel Lambert (f Dumas *père*)
Gabriel Lambert (p Dumas *père*)
Gabriel Schillings Flucht (p Hauptmann)
Gabriel (p Sand)
Gabriela, cravo e canela (f Amado)
Gabriella (p Machado de Assis)
Gadis Pantai (f Toer)
Gaido bukku (p Abe)
El galán de la Membrilla (p Vega Carpio)
Las galas del difunto (p Valle-Inclán)
Galatea (p Metastasio)
La Galatea (f Cervantes)
La Galère (v Genet)
La Galerie du Palais; ou, L'Amie rivale (p Corneille)
Das Galgenmännlein (f Fouqué)
Galib: The Man and His Couplets (v Ghālib)
A Galician Girl's Romance (f Pardo Bazán)

Der geprüfte Abraham (v Wieland)
O gerente (f Andrade)
Der gerettete Alkibiades (p Kaiser)
Das gerettete Venedig (p Hofmannsthal)
Der Gerichtstag (p Werfel)
The German Lieutenant, and Other Stories (f Strindberg)
Germinal (p Zola)
Germinie Lacerteux (f Goncourt)
Geroi nashego vremeni (f Lermontov)
Geron, der Adelich (f Wieland)
Gerona (f Pérez Galdós)
Gerona (p Pérez Galdós)
Ho gerontas me tous chartaitous (v Ritsos)
Hoi gerontisses kai thalassa (v Ritsos)
Gerpla (f Laxness)
Gerska æfintýri (f Laxness)
Gertrud (f Hesse)
Gerusalemme conquistata (v Tasso)
Gerusalemme liberata (v Tasso)
Gerushim me'uharim (n Yehoshua)
Gesaku zammai (f Akutagawa)
Gesammelte Gedichte 1912–1956 (v Benn)
Gesammelte Hörspiele (p Dürrenmatt)
Gesammelte Romane und Novellen (f Mann)
Gesammelte Schriften (f Schnitzler)
Gesammelte Schriften (f Storm)
Die gesammelten Gedichte (v Hofmannsthal)
Die gesammelten Schriften (f Benn)
Der Gesang im Feuerofen (p Zuckmayer)
Gesang vom lusitanischen Popanz (p Weiss)
Gesänge aus den drei Reichen (v Werfel)
Ein Geschäft mit Träumen (radio Bachmann)
Die Geschäfte des Herrn Julius Cäsar (f Brecht)
Die Geschichte des Agathon (f Wieland)
Die Geschichte des Prinzen Biribinkers (f Wieland)
Geschichte vom braven Kasperl und dem schönen Annerl (f Brentano)
Die Geschichte von der 1002. Nacht (f Roth)
Geschichten (f Grass)
Geschichten aus dem Wienerwald (p Horváth)
Geschichten aus vierzig Jahren (f Zuckmayer)
Geschichten aus zwölf Jahren (f Böll)
Geschichten ut Bollerup (f Lenz)
Die Geschwister (p Goethe)
Die Geschwister von Neapel (f Werfel)
Die Gesellschaft auf dem Lande (f Tieck)
Das Gesetz: Erzählung (f Mann)
Das Gesicht: Komödie (p Lenz)
Die Gesichte der Simone Machard (p Brecht)
Gesloten gedichten (v Nooteboom)
Das Gespräch der drei Gehenden (f Weiss)
Gespräch Sanct Peters mit den Landsknechten (v Sachs)
Gestelsche liederen (v Vestdijk)
Gestern (p Hofmannsthal)
Les Gestes et opinions du docteur Faustroll, Pataphysicien (f Jarry)
Der gestiefelte Kater (p Tieck)
Das gestohlene Dokument und andere Novellen (f Mann)
Die gestundete Zeit (v Bachmann)
Gestures and Other Poems 1968–1970 (v Ritsos)
Der geteilte Himmel (f Wolf)
Gethsémani (v Lamartine)

Gethsemani, Ky (v Cardenal)
Die getreu Fürstin Alcestis (p Sachs)
Geuse-vesper (v Vondel)
Die Gewehre der Frau Carrar (p Brecht)
Das Gewürzkrämerkleeblatt; oder, Die unschuldig Schuldigen (p Nestroy)
Het gezicht van het oog (v Nooteboom)
Ghālib Urdu kalamka intikhab (v Ghālib)
Ghare-Baire (f Tagore)
Ghazals of Ghalib (v Ghālib)
Ghost Trio (p Beckett)
Ghosts; A Public Enemy; When We Dead Wake (p Ibsen)
Ghosts; An Enemy of the People; Wild Duck; Hedda Gabler (p Ibsen)
Giaffah (f Deledda)
Giambi ed Epodi (v Carducci)
La giara (p Pirandello)
Gibeoniter; oder, die sieben Bruder (p Gryphius)
Gibier de potence (p Feydeau)
Giftas (f Strindberg)
Il gigante orripilante (f Calvino)
I giganti della montagna (p Pirandello)
Gigi (p Colette)
Gigi et autres nouvelles (f Colette)
Gignesthai (v Ritsos)
Gikyoku zenshū (p Mishima)
Un Gil-Blas en Californie (f Dumas *père*)
Gilberto poeta: algumas confissões (v Freyre)
Gildet på Solhaug (p Ibsen)
Gilles! (p Claus)
Gilles en de nacht (f Claus)
Gilles und Jeanne (p Kaiser)
Gillets hemlighet (p Strindberg)
Gillette; or, the Unknown Masterpiece (f Balzac)
Ginga tetsudō no yoru (f Miyazawa)
Gioas re di Giuda (p Metastasio)
Il giocatore (p Betti)
Il gioco segreto (f Morante)
La Gioconda (p D'Annunzio)
La giornata d'uno scrutatore (f Calvino)
Il giorno della civetta (f Sciascia)
Giorno dopo giorno (v Quasimodo)
Giovanni Episcopo (f D'Annunzio)
Giralda; ou, La Nouvelle Psyché (p Scribe)
Girigbukarna (f Lo-Johansson)
Le Gisant mis en lumière (v Char)
Gisella (f Cassola)
Giselle (p Gautier)
Gītānjali (v Tagore)
Giulietta (f Ginzburg)
Il giuocatore (p Goldoni)
I giuochi della vita (f Deledda)
Il giuoco delle parti (p Pirandello)
Giuseppe riconosciuto (p Metastasio)
Giuseppe Ungaretti: Selected Poems (v Ungaretti)
Giv'at haChol (f Agnon)
Gjakftohtësia—novela (f Kadare)
Gjenerali i ushtrisë së vdekur—roman (f Kadare)
Gläserne Bienen (f Jünger)
Das Glasperlenspiel (f Hesse)
Glaube, Liebe, Hoffnung (p Horváth)

Der grosse Traum (v Hauptmann)
Die grosse Wut des Philipp Hotz (p Frisch)
Der grossmüthige Rechtsgelehrte; oder, Der Sterbende Ämilius Paulus Papinianus (p Gryphius)
La Grotte (p Anouilh)
Die grüine Flöte (p Hofmannsthal)
Die Gründung Prags (p Brentano)
Der grüne Heinrich (f Keller)
Der grüne Kakadu, Paracelsus, Die Gefährtin (p Schnitzler)
Ein grünes Blatt (f Storm)
Grupa Laokoona (p Różewicz)
Gruppenbild mit Dame (f Böll)
Grzechy dzieciństwa (f Prus)
Guárdate del agua mansa (p Calderón de la Barca)
Guatemala (v Martí)
Gubijinso (f Natsume)
Gucio zaczarowany (v Miłosz)
Gudrun (f Jensen)
Guds bustader. Spel i tre skrift (p Vesaas)
Les Guèbres; ou, La Tolérance (p Voltaire)
Guelfes et Gibelins (f Dumas *père*)
La guerra (p Goldoni)
La guerra (v Machado)
La guerra carlista (f Valle-Inclán)
La guerra del fin del mundo (f Vargas Llosa)
Guerra del tiempo: Tres relatos y una novela: El Camino de Santiago, Viaje a la semilla, Semejante a la noche, y El acoso (f Carpentier)
La Guerre (v Ungaretti)
La Guerre au Luxembourg (v Cendrars)
La Guerre civile de Genève (v Voltaire)
La Guerre de Troie n'aura pas lieu (p Giraudoux)
La Guerre des femmes (f Dumas *père*)
La Guerre des femmes (p Dumas *père*)
Guðsgjafaþula (f Laxness)
Guest of Reality (f Lagerkvist)
Guest of Reality and Other Stories (f Lagerkvist)
Le Guetteur mélancolique (v Apollinaire)
La Gueule de pierre (f Queneau)
Guignol's Band (f Céline)
Guilai de moshengren (v Bei Dao)
La Guinguette à deux sous (f Simenon)
Guiqulai xi (p Lao)
Guirnalda civil (v Guillén)
Gulat di Jakarta (f Toer)
Guli Hiwênawi (p Goran)
Gulistān (v Sa'di)
Die Günderode (f Arnim)
Guojia zhishang (p Lao)
Gushi xinbian (f Lu Xun)
Gushu yiren (f Lao)
Gustalin (f Aymé)
Gustav Adolf (p Strindberg)
Gustav Adolfs Page (f Meyer)
Gustav III (p Strindberg)
Gustav Vasa (p Strindberg)
Gustave III; ou, Le Bal masqué (p Scribe)
Gustos y disgustos son no más que imaginación (p Calderón de la Barca)
Gusuko Budori no denki (f Miyazawa)
Gūtara mandanshū (f Endō)

Der gute Gott von Manhattan (p Bachmann)
Der gute Mensch von Sezuan (p Brecht)
Der gutmütige Teufel; oder, Die Geschichte vom Bauer und der Bäuerin (p Nestroy)
La Guzla (v Mérimée)
Gvozdena zavesa (f Pavić)
Gyges und sein Ring (p Hebbel)
Gymnadenia (f Undset)
Gymnopedia (v Seferis)
Gysbreght van Aemstel (p Vondel)
Gyubal Wahazar; czyli, Na przełęczach absurdu (p Witkiewicz)
Gyümölcskosár (v Weöres)
Ha estallado la paz (f Gironella)
Ha llegado el invierno y tú no estás aquí (v Gironella)
Há uma gota de sangue em cada poema (v Andrade)
L'Habit vert (p Musset)
El habitante y su esperanza (f Neruda)
El hablador (f Vargas Llosa)
El hacedor (v Borges)
Hadīth al sabāh wa-al-masā' (f Mahfouz)
Hadrat al-muhtaram (f Mahfouz)
Hadriana dans tous mes rêves (f Depestre)
Der Hafen ist voller Geheimnisse: Ein Feature in Erzählungen und zwei masurische Geschichten (f Lenz)
Der Hagelstolz (f Stifter)
Hagi no hana (f Tanizaki)
Haha no shi to atarashii haha (f Shiga)
Hahn-Hahn grofno pillantása (f Esterházy)
Hai-iro no tsuki (f Shiga)
Haïr à force d'aimer (f Simenon)
Hakai (f Shimazaki)
Hakata kojorō namimakura (p Chikamatsu)
Hakhnasath Kallah (f Agnon)
Hako otoko (f Abe)
Hakobune Sakuramaru (f Abe)
Hakuōshū (v Yosano)
Halewijn (v Nijhoff)
Halifax (p Dumas *père*)
A hallgatás tornya (v Weöres)
Halma (f Pérez Galdós)
Halte-Hulda (p Bjørnson)
Ham Kalām, Fārsī rubā'iyāt-i Ghālib kā tarjamah, &sunddot; Akbārabādī (v Ghālib)
Hamilkar Schass aus Suleyken (f Lenz)
Haminas (v Craveirinha)
Al-Hamir (p Tawfiq Al-Hakim)
Hamlet (p Dumas *père*)
Hamlet (p Gide)
Hamlet 2 (p Virahsawmy)
Hamlet in Wittenberg (p Hauptmann)
Hamlet; oder, die lange Nacht nimmt ein Ende (f Döblin)
Hams al-junūn (f Mahfouz)
Han d'Islande (f Hugo)
Han er ikke født (p Andersen)
Han no hanzai (f Shiga)
Han som fick leva om sitt liv (p Lagerkvist)
Han-teijo daigaku (f Mishima)
Hana (f Akutagawa)
Hana no machi (f Ibuse)
Hana no warutsu (f Kawabata)

Kovets sipurim (f Agnon)
Kozō no kamisama (f Shiga)
Kozō wa shinda (p Abe)
Közügy (v Illyés)
Kōzui wa waga tamashii ni oyobi (f Ōe)
Krakatit (f Čapek)
Krakonošova zahrada (f Čapek)
Kraljevo (p Krleža)
Der Krämmerskorb (p Sachs)
Der Kranichtanz (p Zuckmayer)
Kranji Bekasi Jatuh (f Toer)
Krapp's Last Tape (p Beckett)
Krapp's Last Tape and Other Dramatic Pieces (p Beckett)
Krasnoe derevo (f Pil'niak)
Krasnogvardeitsy (f Sholokhov)
Krates und Hipparchia (f Wieland)
Kratskrog (f Hamsun)
Kreitserova sonata (f Tolstoi)
Krekelzangen (v Bilderdijk)
Kreshchenyi kitaets (f Belyi)
Kreuzweg (p Zuckmayer)
Krevet za tri osobe (p Pavić)
Krieg den Philistern! (p Eichendorff)
Ein Kriegsende (f Lenz)
Krijgsdans (v Bilderdijk)
Krinagoras (v Elytis)
Krishna (p Virahsawmy)
Kristin Lavransdatter (f Undset)
Kristina (p Strindberg)
Kristnihald undir Jökli (f Laxness)
Kristofor Kolumbo (p Krleža)
Kristuslegender (f Lagerlöf)
Król-Duch (v Słowacki)
Król Kazimierz Jagiellonczyk (p Wyspiański)
Król Popiel i inne wiersze (v Miłosz)
Królowa polskiej korony (p Wyspiański)
Kronbruden (p Strindberg)
Kronikë në gur—roman (f Kadare)
Kroniki (v Miłosz)
V kruge pervom (f Solzhenitsyn)
Kruglyi god: Stikhotvoreniia dlia detei (v Blok)
Kruhlyansky most (f Bykaw)
Krushqit janë të ngrirë (f Kadare)
Krzyżacy (f Sienkiewicz)
He ksanatonismene musike (v Palamas)
Ksiadz Marek (p Słowacki)
Księżniczka Magdalena; cyzli, Natrętny książe (p Witkiewicz)
Kto brat, kto sestra; ili, Obman za obmanom (p Griboedov)
Kuangye de huhan (f Xiao)
Kuć nasred druma (v Popa)
Kuchibue o fuku toki (f Endō)
Kufsah shehorah (f Oz)
Kühle Wampe (scr Brecht)
Kühle Wampe: Protokoll des Films und Materialien (p Brecht)
Kula i druge pripovetke (f Andrić)
Kulka, Hilpert, Elefanten (f Eich)
Kulliyāt (v Sa'di)
Külön világban (v Illyés)
Különc (p Illyés)
Különös testamentum (v Illyés)

Der Kulterer (f Bernhard)
Kumārasambhava (v Kālidāsa)
Kumo no Iroiro (f Yosano)
Kumo no ito (f Akutagawa)
Kumo to namekuji to tanuki (f Miyazawa)
Kun en Spillemand (f Andersen)
K'ung I-chi (f Lu Xun)
Kungsgatan (f Lo-Johansson)
Kuniko (f Shiga)
Kunstens dannevirke (p Andersen)
Die Kunstradfahrer und andere Geschichten (f Lenz)
Kur mod onde ånder (f Heinesen)
Kuriyama daizen (f Mori)
Kurka wodna (p Witkiewicz)
Kurōdiasu no nikki (f Shiga)
Kuroi ame (f Ibuse)
Kurotokage (p Mishima)
Kusa no fushido (f Tsushima)
Kusa no Yume (v Yosano)
Kusamakura (f Natsume)
Kusamura (f Tsushima)
Kush e solli Doruntinën (f Kadare)
Kushū (v Akutagawa)
Kútbanézőb (v Weöres)
Kvaeðakver (v Laxness)
Kvinden og aben (f Høeg)
Kvinnor ropar heim (f Vesaas)
Kwan-hasshu tsunagi (p Chikamatsu)
Ho kyklos ton tetrastichon (v Palamas)
Kyoko no ie (f Mishima)
He kyra ton Ambelion (v Ritsos)
Kys': roman (f Tolstaya)
Le là (v Breton)
Là-bas (f Huysmans)
La-da'at ishah (f Oz)
La-ga'at ba-mayim, la-ga'at ba-ruah (f Oz)
Het laatste bed (f Claus)
Laatste verzen (v Gezelle)
Lábadozó szél (v Radnóti)
La'bat al-Mawt (p Tawfiq Al-Hakim)
Laberinto (v Jiménez)
Laberinto de amor (v Marechal)
Le Laboratoire central (v Jacob)
Laboremus (p Bjørnson)
Labyrinthe des sentiments (f Ben Jelloun)
Le Lac d'angoisse (f Simenon)
Laços de família (f Lispector)
La Lacune (p Ionesco)
Ład Serca (f Andrzejewski)
Ladera este (1962–1968) (v Paz)
El ladrón de niños (p Alberti)
Lady Inger of Ostraat; Love's Comedy; The League of Youth (p Ibsen)
Lady Johanna Gray (p Wieland)
Lady und Schneider (p Nestroy)
The Lady with Lapdog and Other Stories (f Chekhov)
Lae pai khang na (f Siburapha)
Lagar (v Mistral)
Lagar II (v Mistral)
Al-Lahza al-hariga (p Idris)
Le Laird de Dumbicky (p Dumas *père*)

Lenz (f Büchner)
Leo Armenius (p Gryphius)
Léo Burckart (p Dumas *père*)
Léo Burckart (p Nerval)
Léocadia (p Anouilh)
Léocadie (p Scribe)
Leonarda (p Bjørnson)
Leonce und Lena (p Büchner)
Léone (v Cocteau)
Leone Leoni (f Sand)
Les Léonides (p Rolland)
Léonie est en avance; ou, Le Mal joli (p Feydeau)
Léonie et les siens (f Roy)
Leopardi's Canti (v Leopardi)
Leopold Wagner, Verfasser des Schauspiels von neuen Monaten im Walfischbauch; oder, Eine Matinee (p Lenz)
Leopoldo Marechal (v Marechal)
Leprosorio (v Arenas)
Leshii (p Chekhov)
Lessico famigliare (f Ginzburg)
Lessico famigliare No. 2: Il cocchio d'oro (f Ginzburg)
Lessico famigliare No. 2: La luna pallidassi (f Ginzburg)
Let Us Follow Him, and Other Stories (f Sienkiewicz)
Leto (f Gor'kii)
Lettera amorosa (v Char)
Letters from the Underworld and Other Stories (f Dostoevskii)
Lettre à mon juge (f Simenon)
Lettre à un otage (f Saint-Exupéry)
La Lettre I du dictionnaire (v Char)
Lettres à Guillaume Apollinaire, 1904–1918 (f Apollinaire)
Lettres à Marcie (f Sand)
Les Lettres d'Amabed (f Voltaire)
Lettres galantes d'Aristénète (f Lesage)
Das letzte Abenteuer (f Doderer)
Der letzte Akt (scr Remarque)
Letzte Gaben (v Droste-Hülshoff)
Der letzte Held von Marienburg (p Eichendorff)
Die letzte Station (p Remarque)
Die letzte Station (radio Remarque)
Die Letzten (f Rilke)
Die letzten Erzählungen (f Hoffmann)
Die Leute von Seldwyla (f Keller)
Leutnant Gustl (f Schnitzler)
Leutnant Welzeck (f Kaiser)
Het leven en de werken van Leopold II (p Claus)
Der Leviathan (f Roth)
Leviia gravia (v Carducci)
Levins Mühle (f Bobrowski)
Leyenda (v Jiménez)
Lezama Lima (f Lezama Lima)
La Lézarde (f Glissant)
Li (p Virahsawmy)
Les Liaisons dangereuses (f Laclos)
Liangge youqijiang (f Huang)
Liasse: Vingt-et-un textes suivis d'une bibliographie (v Ponge)
Libertação (v Torga)
Libertad bajo palabra (v Paz)
Libertad bajo palabra: Obra poética 1935–1958 (v Paz)
Libertas und ihr Freier (f Eichendorff)
Liberté d'Action (v Michaux)

Liberty Bar (f Simenon)
Liblikas ja peegel (p Kaplinski)
Libro armilar de poesía y memorias bisiestas (v Sender)
El libro de arena (f Borges)
El libro de las décimas (v Guillén)
Libro de las preguntas (v Neruda)
Libro de Manuel (f Cortázar)
Libro de poemas (v García Lorca)
Libro del mar (v Alberti)
Il libro delle vergine (f D'Annunzio)
Libro que no muerde (f Valenzuela)
Libussa (p Grillparzer)
Libussa, des Kaisers Leibross (f Sternheim)
Lição de coisas (v Andrade)
Lichnaia zhizn' (f Zoshchenko)
Lichtzwang (v Celan)
Liden Kirsten (p Andersen)
Lidice (f Mann)
Liebe geprüft (v Grass)
Liebe in Florenz; oder, Die unziemliche Neugier (p Hochwälder)
Liebelei (p Schnitzler)
Eine Liebesgeschichte (f Mann)
Eine Liebesgeschichte (f Zuckmayer)
Liebesgeschichten und Heiratssachen (p Nestroy)
Liebesrache (p Fouqué)
Der Liebestrank (p Wedekind)
Het lied van de moordenaar (p Claus)
Lied vom Weltende (v Miłosz)
Das Lied von Bernadette (f Werfel)
Die Lieder (v Walther von der Vogelweide)
Lieder Gedichte Chöre (v Brecht)
Liederbuch dreier Freunde (v Storm)
Liederen, eerdichten et reliqua (v Gezelle)
Lieto fine (f Duranti)
Le Lieutenant-Colonel de Maumort (f Martin Du Gard)
Life and Death and Other Legends and Stories (f Sienkiewicz)
Life and Opinions of the Tomcat Murr: Together With a Fragmentary Biography of Kapellmeister Johannes Kreisler on Random Sheets of Waste Paper (f Hoffmann)
Life by the Fells and Fjords (f Bjørnson)
Life of a Man (v Ungaretti)
Ligazón (p Valle-Inclán)

Light Breathing and Other Stories (f Bunin)
Light Upon Light: Inspirations from Rumi (v Rumi)
The Lighting of the Christmas Tree (p Lagerlöf)
Ligostevoun hoi eroteseis (v Ritsos)
La Ligue; ou, Henri le Grand: Poème epique (v Voltaire)
Lihun (f Lao)
Lika (f Bunin)
Lila (p Goethe)
Lili-sourire (f Simenon)
Lili Tristesse (f Simenon)
Liliane und Paul (f Mann)
The Lilies, Twardowski's Wife, and Religious Poems (v Mickiewicz)
Liliom (p Molnár)
Lilít e altri raconti (f Levi)
Liljecronas hem (f Lagerlöf)
Lilla Weneda (p Słowacki)
Lille Eyolf (p Ibsen)

La Lozana andaluza (p Alberti)
Lu curaggio de nu pumpiere napulitano (p De Filippo)
Lucelle (p Bredero)
Luces de Bohemia (p Valle-Inclán)
Luchana (f Pérez Galdós)
Lucía Jerez y otras narraciones (f Martí)
Lucidor (p Hofmannsthal)
Lucie (p Sand)
Lucie Gelmeroth (f Mörike)
Lucien Leuwen (f Stendhal)
Lucienne et le boucher (p Aymé)
Lucifer (p Vondel)
Lucifer vieillissant (f Goll)
Lucinde (f Schlegel)
Lucius (v Eichendorff)
Lucky Peter's Travels and Other Plays (p Strindberg)
Lucrèce Borgia (p Hugo)
Lucretia (p Sachs)
Lucrezia (f Couperus)
Lucrezia Floriani (f Sand)
Lugar de Lázaro (v Guillén)
El lugar del hombre (f Sender)
Luis Cernuda para niños (v Cernuda)
Luis Pérez el gallego (p Calderón de la Barca)
Luiz e Maria (f Queiroz)
Luk i lira (v Evtushenko)
Luk phuchai (f Siburapha)
Lukas, sanftmütiger Knecht (f Lenz)
Lulet e ftohta të Marsit—roman (f Kadare)
Lulu (p Wedekind)
Lumie di Sicilia (p Pirandello)
Lumières d'hommes (v Prévert)
Lumina ce se stinge (f Eliade)
Luna de enfrente (v Borges)
La luna de los perros (f Sender)
Luna de miel, luna de hiel; Los trabajos de Urbano y Simona (f Pérez de Ayala)
La luna e i faló (f Pavese)
Luna silvestre (v Paz)
La Lune de miel (f Balzac)
Lunes en papier (f Malraux)
Lung phrahm haeng ko loi (f Siburapha)
Lungo viaggio di Natale (p Pratolini)
Luo (f Huang)
Luotuo Xiangzi (f Lao)
La lupa; In portineria (p Verga)
Les Lurettes fourrées (f Vian)
Os Lusíadas (v Camões)
Lusitania (p Döblin)
Lust and Liberty (v Machiavelli)
Die lustigen Musikanten (p Brentano)
O lustre (f Lispector)
Lustspiele (p Lessing)
Lustspiele nach dem Plautus (p Lenz)
Le Lutrin (v Boileau)
Lux in Tenebris (p Brecht)
Luzbel desconcertado (v Guillén)
La Lycéenne (p Feydeau)
Lyckan (f Lo-Johansson)
Lyckklaght ann het vrouekoor, over het verlies van mijn ega (v Vondel)

Lycko-Pers resa (p Strindberg)
Lydia and Mäxchen: Tiefe Verbeugung in Einem Akt (p Döblin)
Lykka for ferdesmenn (v Vesaas)
Lykke-Peer (f Andersen)
Lykkens blomst (p Andersen)
The Lyric Poems of Jean Froissart (v Froissart)
Lyric Poetry (v Alighieri)
Lyricorum libellus (v Kochanowski)
Lyrics in the Original Greek with Translations (v Sappho)
Die Lyrik (v Wolfram von Eschenbach)
Lyrik: Auswahl letzter Hand (v Benn)
Le Lys dans la vallée (f Balzac)
Le Lys rouge (f France)
Le Lys rouge (p France)
Lyset (p Bjørnson)
Lysistrate (p Aristophanes)
Lyubka the Cossack and Other Stories (f Babel)
O lyubvi, poezii i gosudarstvennoi sluzhbe (p Blok)
Ma Bole (f Xiao)
Ma non è una cosa seria (p Pirandello)
Ma soeur Jeanne (f Sand)
Má veselá jitra (f Klíma)
Má zlatá řemesla (f Klíma)
Ma'aseh rabi Gadi'el haTinok (f Agnon)
A maçã no escuro (f Lispector)
Macbeth (radio Brecht)
Macbeth (p Maeterlinck)
Macbeth (p Schiller)
Macbett (p Ionesco)
Die Maccabäer (p Sachs)
La Machine à écrire (p Cocteau)
La Machine infernale (p Cocteau)
Die Macht der Gewohnheit (p Bernhard)
Maciej Korbowa i Bellatrix (p Witkiewicz)
Macunaíma (f Andrade)
The Mad Dog: Stories (f Böll)
Madame Bovary (f Flaubert)
Madame de. . . (p Anouilh)
Madame de Chamblay (f Dumas père)
Madame de Chamblay (p Dumas père)
Madame d'Ora (f Jensen)
Madame Dorthea (f Undset)
Madame Gervaisais (f Goncourt)
Madame Legros (p Mann)
Madame Sganarelle (p Feydeau)
Madame Sourdis (f Zola)
Mädchen (f Sternheim)
Madeleine (p Zola)
Madeleine Férat (f Zola)
Mademoiselle Daphné (f Gautier)
Mademoiselle de Belle-Isle (p Dumas père)
Mademoiselle de Maupin (f Gautier)
Mademoiselle du Vissard (f Balzac)
Mademoiselle Fifi (f Maupassant)
Mademoiselle Fifi and Other Stories (f Maupassant)
Mademoiselle Merquem (f Sand)
Mademoiselle Million (f Simenon)
Mademoiselle la Quintinie (f Sand)
Mademoiselle X (f Simenon)

Mal giocondo (v Pirandello)
Mal vu mat dit (f Beckett)
La mala hora (f García Márquez)
Le Malade imaginaire (p Molière)
La Maladie de la mort (f Duras)
Maladrón: Epopeya de los Andes verdes (f Asturias)
Malancha (f Tagore)
Mālavikāgnimitra (p Kālidāsa)
I malcontenti (p Goldoni)
Maldición eterna a quien lea estas páginas (f Puig)
El maleficio de la mariposa (p García Lorca)
Malemort (f Glissant)
Malempin (f Simenon)
Le Malentendu (p Camus)
Maler Nolten (f Mörike)
Eine Malerarbeit (f Storm)
Das malerische und romantische Westfalen (v Droste-Hülshoff)
Malgrétout (f Sand)
Malhamat at harāfīsh (f Mahfouz)
Le Malheur d'aimer (f Roy)
Le Malheur passe (p Maeterlinck)
Les Malheurs des immortels (v Éluard)
Malik il-qutn (p Idris)
Al-Malik Udib (p Tawfiq Al-Hakim)
Malina (f Bachmann)
Malini (p Tagore)
Mallarmé in English Verse (v Mallarmé)
Malom a Séden (p Illyés)
Malone meurt (f Beckett)
Mama, kijk, zonder handen! (p Claus)
Mama i neitronaiia bomba i drugie poemy (v Evtushenko)
Mamai (f Zamiatin)
Les Mamelles de Tirésias (p Apollinaire)
Mamzel Zann (p Virahsawmy)
A Man Is Not a Flea (f Zoshchenko)
Man manut (f Siburapha)
Måna är död (f Lo-Johansson)
Mañanas de abril y mayo (p Calderón de la Barca)
Manas: Epische Dichtung (v Döblin)
Mānasi (v Tagore)
Manatsu no shi (f Mishima)
El mancebo y los héroes (f Sender)
O mandarim (f Eça de Queirós)
The Mandarin and Other Stories (f Eça de Queirós)
La Mandarine (p Anouilh)
Les Mandarins (f Beauvoir)
Mandorin wo hiko otoko (p Tanizaki)
La mandragola (p Machiavelli)
Mandragora (f Fouqué)
Man'en gannen no futtobōru (f Ōe)
Manette Salomon (f Goncourt)
Mangeront-ils? (p Hugo)
Mangir (f Toer)
A Mania for Solitude: Selected Poems 1930–1950 (v Pavese)
La Manivelle/The Old Tune (p Beckett)
Manji (f Tanizaki)
Man-Making Words: Selected Poems (v Guillén)
Manman Dio contre la Fée Carabosse (f Chamoiseau)
Der Mann im Strom (f Lenz)
Mann ist Mann (p Brecht)

Der Mann mit den Messern (f Böll)
Der Mann mit den Messern: Erzählungen (f Böll)
Der Mann ohne Eigenschaften (f Musil)
Il mannello di Natascia (1930–1936) (v Pratolini)
Il mannello di Natascia e altre cronache in versi e in prosa (1930–1980) (v Pratolini)
Mannen utan själ (p Lagerkvist)
Le Mannequin d'osier (p France)
Männer und Helden (v Fontane)
Människor (f Lagerkvist)
Manon Lescaut (p Sternheim)
Mansarda; Psalam 44 (f Kiš)
Mantatoforos (v Ritsos)
Il mantello (p Buzzati)
Manteq al-Tayr (v Attār)
The Mantle and Other Stories (f Gogol')
Mao Bole (f Xiao)
A mão e a luva (f Machado de Assis)
Maocheng ji (f Lao)
Maoshi huicui (f Mo)
Die Mappe meines Urgrossvaters (f Stifter)
Al-Maqamat (f al-Hariri)
Mar (p Torga)
Mar Mani (n Yehoshua)
Mar morto (f Amado)
El mar y las campanas (v Neruda)
Marat/Sade; The Investigation; and The Shadow of the Coachman's Body (p Weiss)
La Marâtre (p Balzac)
Al-marāya (f Mahfouz)
Le Marbrier (p Dumas *père*)
Le Marchand de Venise (p Vigny)
Le Marchand d'oiseaux (f Brasillach)
Das Märchen (p Schnitzler)
Das Märchen der 672 Nacht und andere Erzählungen (f Hofmannsthal)
Das Märchen von dem Baron von Hüpfenstich (f Brentano)
Das Märchen (f Hauptmann)
Marco Spada (p Scribe)
Marcovaldo; ovvero, Le stagioni in città (f Calvino)
La Mare au diable (f Sand)
Il mare colore del vino (f Sciascia)
La marea (f Gironella)
La Maréchale d'Ancre (p Vigny)
Maremoto (v Neruda)
Il marescalco (p Aretino)
Il maresciallo (f Ginzburg)
Marfisa (v Aretino)
Al margen (v Guillén)
O marginal Clorindo gato e a visita (v Andrade)
Marguerite (f France)
Les Marguerites de la Marguerite des princesses (v Marguerite de Navarre)
Le Mari de la veuve (p Dumas *père*)
Maria (v Craveirinha)
María Carmen Portela (v Alberti)
A María el corazón (p Calderón de la Barca)
Maria Magdalena (p Hebbel)
Maria Nefeli (v Elytis)
Maria Sabina (p Cela)
Maria Stuart i Skotland (p Bjørnson)

Matsu no ha (v Miyazawa)
Les Maudits du Pacifique (f Simenon)
Maudits soupirs pour une autre fois (f Céline)
Maulwürfe (f Eich)
Mauprat (p Sand)
Mauprat (f Sand)
Maurerpigen (p Andersen)
A Mauriac Reader (f Mauriac)
Maurice (f Scribe)
Mäusefest und andere Erzählungen (f Bobrowski)
Un mauvais rêve (f Bernanos)
Mauve (v Brossard)
Ho mavros hagios (v Ritsos)
Max Ernst: Peintures pour Paul Éluard (v Éluard)
Max Havelaar (f Multatuli)
Les Maxibules (p Aymé)
Mayakovsky (v Maiakovskii)
Mayapán (v Cardenal)
La Mayor (f Saer)
El mayor encanto amor (p Calderón de la Barca)
El mayor monstruo los celos (p Calderón de la Barca)
Mazepa (p Słowacki)
Mazurca para dos muertos (f Cela)
À me de jeune fille (f Simenon)
Me'Az ume'Atah (f Agnon)
Mecanique jongleuse (v Brossard)
Mecanique jongleuse; Masculin grammaticale (v Brossard)
MeChamat haMetsik (f Agnon)
El mechudo y la Llorona (f Sender)
Medea: A Modern Retelling (f Wolf)
Medea and Other Plays (p Euripides)
Medea (p Euripides)
Medea (p Pasolini)
Medea (p Seneca)
Le Médecin de campagne (f Balzac)
Le Médecin de Java (f Dumas *père*)
Le Médecin malgré lui (p Molière)
Le Médecin volant (p Molière)
Médée (p Anouilh)
Médée (p Corneille)
Medicamina faciei femineae (v Ovid)
El médico de su honra (p Calderón de la Barca)
Il medico dei pazzi (p De Filippo)
Il medico olandese (p Goldoni)
Meditación en el umbral: Antologiá poética (v Castellanos)
Méditations (v Lamartine)
Méditations poétiques (v Lamartine)
Mediterranee (v Saba)
Medlennyi den' (v Mandel'shtam)
Medúza (v Weöres)
Medved' (p Chekhov)
Meer end perler og guld (p Andersen)
Eine Meerfahrt (f Eichendorff)
Das Meerwunder (f Hauptmann)
Megáfon; o, La guerra (f Marechal)
Meghadūta (v Kālidāsa)
La meglio gioventù: Poesia friulane (v Pasolini)
Die mehreren Wehmüller und ungarischen Nationalgesichter (f Brentano)
Meian (f Natsume)

Meido no Hikyaku (p Chikamatsu)
Meier Helmbrecht (p Hochwälder)
Meierbeths Glack und Ende (p Eichendorff)
Meijin (f Kawabata)
Mein Freund (p Nestroy)
Mein Name sei Gantenbein (f Frisch)
Mein trauriges Gesicht: Erzählungen (f Böll)
Meine neunzehn Lebensläufe und neun andere Geschichten (f Doderer)
Meissonier (f Barbusse)
Meister Floh (f Hoffmann)
Meistererzählungen (f Lenz)
Meisterzählungen (f Bachmann)
El mejor alcalde, el rey (p Vega Carpio)
Le mejor de Octavio Paz: El fuego de cada día (v Paz)
Mejor está que estaba (p Calderón de la Barca)
El mejor mozo de España (p Vega Carpio)
Mejores cuentos (f Pardo Bazán)
Los mejores poemas (v Mistral)
Los mejores versos (v Guillén)
Melampe (p Holberg)
El melanclico (p Tirso de Molina)
Melancolía (v Jiménez)
Mélange (v Valéry)
Mélanges (v Ronsard)
Mélanges et Chansons (v Ronsard)
Meleager (p Wyspiański)
Meli (f Lagerlöf)
Méliador (f Froissart)
Mélicerte (p Molière)
Los melindres de Belisa (p Vega Carpio)
Melissa (p Kazantzakis)
Mélite; ou, Les Fausses Lettres (p Corneille)
Mellem slagene (p Bjørnson)
Melusina (p Grillparzer)
Melusine (p Goll)
La mémoire tatouée (f Khatibi)
Memoiren einer Ungenannten (f Fouqué)
Mémoires de deux jeunes mariées (f Balzac)
Les Mémoires de Maigret (f Simenon)
Mémoires d'Hadrien (f Yourcenar)
Mémoires d'un honnête homme (f Prévost)
Mémoires d'un maître d'armes (f Dumas *père*)
Mémoires d'un médecin: Joseph Balsamo (f Dumas *père*)
Les Mémoires d'un prostitué (f Simenon)
Mémoires d'un vieux suiveur (f Simenon)
Mémoires d' un volontaire (f France)
Mémoires et aventures d'un homme de qualité qui s'est retiré du monde (f Prévost)
Mémoires pour servir à l'histoire de la révolution française (f Balzac)
Mémoires pour servir à l'histoire de Malte; ou, Histoire de la jeunesse du commandeur de *** (f Prévost)
La memoria del mondo e altre storie cosmicomiche (f Calvino)
Memorial de Ayres (f Machado de Assis)
Memorial de Isla Negra (v Neruda)
Memorias de un cortesano de 1815 (f Pérez Galdós)
Memórias póstumas de Bráz Cubas (f Machado de Assis)
Memushiri kouchi (f Õe)
Men livet lever (f Hamsun)
Menaechmi (p Plautus)
Menander und Glycerion (f Wieland)

Monné: outrages et defies (f Kourouma)
El mono gramático (v Paz)
Monochorda (v Ritsos)
Monology (v Kundera)
La Monomachie de David et de Goliath (v Du Bellay)
Monseigneur Gaston Phoebus (f Dumas *père*)
Monsieur Alphonse (p Dumas *fils*)
Monsieur Barnett (p Anouilh)
Monsieur Chasse (p Feydeau)
Monsieur de Chimpanzé (p Verne)
Monsieur de Pourceaugnac (p Molière)
M. Gallet décédé (f Simenon)
Monsieur La Souris (f Simenon)
M. Le Modéré (p Adamov)
Un monsieur libidineux (f Simenon)
Monsieur Nounou (p Feydeau)
Monsieur Ouine (f Bernanos)
Monsieur Parent (f Maupassant)
Un monsieur qui est condamné à mort (p Feydeau)
Un monsieur qui n'aime pas les monologues (p Feydeau)
Monsieur Ripois (scr Queneau)
Monsieur Sylvestre (f Sand)
Monsieur Vincent (p Anouilh)
Le Monstre blanc de la terre de feu (f Simenon)
Les Monstres sacrés (p Cocteau)
Mont de piété (v Breton)
La Montagne secrète (f Roy)
Montanha: Contos (f Torga)
Montauk (f Frisch)
Monte Mario (f Cassola)
Monte-Cristo (p Dumas *père*)
La Montée de la nuit (v Char)
Les Monténégrins (p Nerval)
Montes de Oca (f Pérez Galdós)
La Montespan (p Rolland)
Montjoye (p Machado de Assis)
Mont-Oriol (f Maupassant)
Mont-Revêche (f Sand)
Il monumento (p De Filippo)
Het Moortje (p Bredero)
Moppels Abenteuer im Viertel unter Wiener Wald, in Neu-Seeland und Marokko (p Nestroy)
La morale del branco (f Cassola)
Morale élégmentaire (v Queneau)
Moralités légendaires (f Laforgue)
Moravagine (f Cendrars)
Le morbinose (p Goldoni)
Morceaux choisis (v Cocteau)
Ein Mord, den jeder begeht (f Doderer)
Der Mörder (f Schnitzler)
Die mörderisch Königin Klitemnestra (p Sachs)
Mordre en sa chair (v Brossard)
More (v Evtushenko)
Le More de Venise (p Vigny)
More Pricks Than Kicks (f Beckett)
More Stories from Tagore (f Tagore)
Die Morgenlandfahrt (f Hesse)
Morgonvinden (p Vesaas)
Morgue und andere Gedichte (v Benn)
Morriña (f Pardo Bazán)

Mors porträtt och andra berättelser (f Lagerlöf)
Mort à crédit (f Céline)
La Mort conduit l'attelage (f Yourcenar)
La Mort d'Agrippine (p Cyrano de Bergerac)
La Mort d'Auguste (f Simenon)
La Mort de Belle (f Simenon)
La Mort de César (p Voltaire)
La Mort de Danton (p Adamov)
La Mort de Pompée (p Corneille)
La Mort de Socrate (v Lamartine)
La Mort de Tintagiles (p Maeterlinck)
Mort d'un personnage (f Giono)
La Mort heureuse (f Camus)
Morte delle stagioni (v Ungaretti)
Morte dell'inquisitore (f Sciascia)
La morte di Abele (p Metastasio)
I morti non fanno paura (p De Filippo)
Mortiz Gottlieb Saphir und Berlin (p Fouqué)
Les Morts ont tous la même peau (f Vian)
Morts sans sépulture (p Sartre)
Mosaïque (f Mérimée)
La moscheta (p Ruzzante [or Ruzante])
The Moscow Notebooks (v Mandel'shtam)
Mosella (v Ausonius)
Mosén Millán (f Sender)
Moskauer Novelle (f Wolf)
Moskovskie povesti (f Trifonov)
Moskva (f Belyi)
Moskva kabatskaia (v Esenin)
Mōsō (f Mori)
Most bez obala (f Pavlović)
Mostellaria (p Plautus)
Mother Earth and Other Stories (f Pil'niak)
The Mother's Prayer (p Tagore)
Motiv (v Lagerkvist)
Motivos de San Francisco (v Mistral)
Motivos de son (v Guillén)
Motivsuche (f Lenz)
Motsart i Sal'eri (p Pushkin)
Mottetti (v Montale)
Motýl na anténě (p Havel)
La Mouche bleue (p Aymé)
Les Mouches (p Sartre)
Le Mouchoir (p Feydeau)
Le Moulin de la Sourdine (f Aymé)
Le Moulin de Pologne (f Giono)
The Mountain Giants and Other Plays (p Pirandello)
Mourir de ne pas mourir (v Éluard)
Les Mousquetaires (p Dumas *père*)
Le Moutardier du page (p Jarry)
Le Mouvement perpétual (v Aragon)
Mouvements (v Michaux)
La moza de cántaro (p Vega Carpio)
Mozart auf der Reise nach Prag (f Mörike)
Mozart and Salieri: The Little Tragedies (p Pushkin)
Mramor (p Brodskii)
MS Amroha Verses (v Ghālib)
Mtsyri (v Lermontov)
Mtwa; czyli, Hyrkaniczny światopogld (p Witkiewicz)
Mudan Ting (p Tang)

Prantik (v Tagore)
Pranto de Maria Parda (v Vicente)
Prap phayot (f Siburapha)
Der Präsident (p Bernhard)
Der Präsident (p Kaiser)
Praxéde (f Dumas *père*)
Pre-morning: A New Book of Poetry in English and Russian (v Evtushenko)
Les Précieuses ridicules (p Molière)
Précis de l'Ecclésiaste en vers (v Voltaire)
Predeo slikan čajem (f Pavić)
Predlozhenie (p Chekhov)
Predsedatel' Revvoensoveta Respubliki (f Sholokhov)
Predvaritel'nye itogi (f Trifonov)
Préface à un livre futur (v Lautréamont)
The Pregnant Pause; or, Love's Labor Lost (p Feydeau)
Le Préjugé vaincu (p Marivaux)
Preludio e canzonette (v Saba)
Preludio e fughe (v Saba)
Le premier amour est toujours le dernier (f Ben Jelloun)
Premier Amour (f Beckett)
Le Premier Homme (f Camus)
Le Premier Livre des amours, le Cinquième des Odes (v Ronsard)
Premier livre des antiquités de Rome (v Du Bellay)
Première amoureuse (f Goncourt)
La première Éducation sentimentale (f Flaubert)
La Première Enquête de Maigret, 1913 (f Simenon)
Premières alluvions (v Char)
Premières et nouvelles méditations poétiques (v Lamartine)
Premières méditations poétiques (v Lamartine)
Premières poésies 1830–1845 (v Gautier)
Premières poésies, Poésies nouvelles (v Musset)
Premières proses et premiers poèmes (v Giono)
Premiers poèmes (v Éluard)
Los premios (f Cortázar)
Preobrazhenie (v Esenin)
La presa di Granata (p Sannazaro)
Préséances (f Mauriac)
Presencia (v Cortázar)
Presencias (v Aleixandre)
Presentación al templo: Poemas (Madrid, 1951) (v Castellanos)
Présentation de Pan (f Giono)
Le Président (f Simenon)
Prestuplenie i nakazanie (f Dostoevskii)
The Pretenders; The Pillars of Society; Rosmersholm (p Ibsen)
La Prêtresse des vaudoux (f Simenon)
Prévert vous parle: 18 poèmes (v Prévert)
Priča o kmetu Simanu (f Andrić)
Priča o vezirovom slonu (f Andrić)
La Priére de l'absent (f Ben Jelloun)
Prière mutilée (v Cocteau)
I prigioni (v Saba)
Prijsvaerzen (v Bilderdijk)
Prilli i thyer (f Kadare)
Prim (f Pérez Galdós)
Prima Ballerina (p Hofmannsthal)
Prima che il gallo canti (f Pavese)
Prima che tu dica ''Pronto '' (f Calvino)
La prima Fernanda (p Machado)
Primater' (p Blok)

Primavera ed altri racconti (f Verga)
Primavere elleniche (v Carducci)
Primechaniia paporotnika (v Brodskii)
Primeiras estórias (f Guimarães Rosa)
Primeiro andar (f Andrade)
Primer romancero gitano (v García Lorca)
La primera República (f Pérez Galdós)
Primeras canciones (v García Lorca)
Primeros poemas (v Aleixandre)
Los primeros versos de amor (v Neruda)
O primo Basílio (f Eça de Queirós)
Primo vere (v D'Annunzio)
Le Prince corsaire (p Scarron)
Le Prince des Sots (f Nerval)
Le Prince frivole (v Cocteau)
Le Prince travesti; ou, L'Illustre Aventurier (p Marivaux)
La Princesse de Babylone (f Voltaire)
La Princesse de Bagdad (p Dumas *fils*)
La Princesse de Clèves (f Lafayette)
La Princesse de Montpensier (f Lafayette)
La Princesse de Navarre (p Voltaire)
La Princesse d'Élide (p Molière)
La Princesse Flora (f Dumas *père*)
La Princesse Georges (p Dumas *fils*)
La Princesse Isabelle (p Maeterlinck)
La Princesse lointaine (p Rostand)
La Princesse Maleine (p Maeterlinck)
El príncipe constante (p Calderón de la Barca)
El príncipe despeñado (p Vega Carpio)
Le Printemps 71 (p Adamov)
Prinz Eugen der edle Ritter (f Hofmannsthal)
Prinz Friedrich von Homburg (p Kleist)
Der Prinz von Homburg (p Bachmann)
Prinz Zerbino; oder, Die Reise nach dem guten Geschmack (p Tieck)
Prinzessin Brambilla (f Hoffmann)
Die Prinzessin von Chimay (p Hochwälder)
Pripovetke (f Andrić)
Prise d'Alexandrie (v Guillaume de Machaut)
Prisiaga prostoru: stikhi (v Evtushenko)
La Prison (f Simenon)
La Prison amoureuse (v Froissart)
Prison Poems: The Moonlight Sonata: The Prison Tree and the Women: Farewell (v Ritsos)
Le Prisonnier de la Bastille: Fin des Mousquetaires (p Dumas *père*)
Les Prisons (v Marguerite de Navarre)
Pritvornaia nevernost' (p Griboedov)
Privar contra su gusto (p Tirso de Molina)
Prjónastofan Sólin (p Laxness)
Pro eto (v Maiakovskii)
Proba intermedy (p Griboedov)
Procedura penale (p Buzzati)
Le Procès (p Gide)
Le Proces de Shamgorod (tel qu'il se deroula le 25 fevrier 1649) (p Wiesel)
Het proces van meester Eckhart (f Vestdijk)
Proclama del conquistador (v Cardenal)
Il prodigo (p Goldoni)
Proêmes (v Ponge)
Proeve eener navolging van Ovidius' gedaanterverwisselingen (v Bilderdijk)

Profesèr Madli (p Virahsawmy)

Le Professeur Taranne (p Adamov)

Professor Bernhardi (p Schnitzler)

Der Herr Professor Kant (v Lenz)

Professor Unrat; oder, das Ende eines Tyrannen (f Mann)

Progetto Burlamacchi (f Duranti)

Progrès (p Céline)

Lo prohibido (f Pérez Galdós)

Proino astro (v Ritsos)

Projet pour une révolution à New York (f Robbe-Grillet)

Prokleta avlija (f Andrić)

Prologos sti zoi (v Sikelianos)

I promessi sposi (f Manzoni)

Prometeo; Luz de domingo; La caída de los Limones (f Pérez de Ayala)

Prometheas (p Kazantzakis)

Le Prométhée mal enchaîné (f Gide)

Prometheus (p Andrzejewski)

Prometheus Vinctus (p Aeschylus)

Promethidenlos (v Hauptmann)

The Promised Land and Other Poems: An Anthology of Four Contemporary Poets (v Ungaretti)

Le Prophète (p Scribe)

Le prophète voile (p Khatibi)

Prosanatolismi (v Elytis)

Prosas bárbaras (f Eça de Queirós)

Prosas Encontradas (f Alberti)

Prosas profanas y otros poemas (v Darío)

La Prose du Transsibérien et de la petite Jehanne de France (v Cendrars)

The Prose Poems and La Fanfarlo (v Baudelaire)

The Prose-Poetry of Su Tung-p'o (v Su Shi)

Proseka (v Evtushenko)

Prosto serdtse (v Tsvetaeva)

Prostoe kak mychanie (v Maiakovskii)

Der Protagonist (p Kaiser)

Protée (p Claudel)

Protesilas i Laodamia (p Wyspiański)

Protest (p Havel)

O protocolo (p Machado de Assis)

O Protomastoras (p Kazantzakis)

La Provence, point Oméga (v Char)

The Proverb and Other Stories (f Aymé)

Proverbio de la muerte (f Sender)

Provinces: Poems 1987–1991 (v Miłosz)

Le Provincial à Paris (f Balzac)

Provinciales (f Giraudoux)

Il provino (p Moravia)

Provintsialka (p Turgenev)

Provisional Conclusions: A Selection of the Poetry of Montale 1920–1970 (v Montale)

Proza i publitsistika o voine (f Sholokhov)

Der Prozess (f Kafka)

Der Prozess der Jeanne d'Arc zu Rouen 1431 (p Brecht)

Der Prozess um des Esels Schatten (p Dürrenmatt)

Der Prozess um des Esels Schatten (radio Dürrenmatt)

Der Prozess (p Weiss)

La Prude; ou, La Gardeuse de cassette (p Voltaire)

La prudencia en la mujer (p Tirso de Molina)

La prueba (f Pardo Bazán)

La prueba de los amigos (p Vega Carpio)

Prusskie nochi: Poema napisannaia v lagere v 1950 (v Solzhenitsyn)

Průvodčí cizincŭ a jiné satiry (f Hašek)

První parta (f Čapek)

Przedświt (v Krasiński)

Przyrost naturalny Biografia sztuku teatralnej (p Różewicz)

Psalle et sile (v Calderón de la Barca)

Psalm (v Bernhard)

Psalm dobrej woli (v Krasiński)

Psalm żalu (v Krasiński)

Psalmy przyszłości (v Krasiński)

Psałterz Dawidów (v Kochanowski)

Pseudolus (p Plautus)

Psikheia (v Tsvetaeva)

Psyché: Egy hajdani költőnő írásai (v Weöres)

Psyché (p Corneille)

Psyche (f Couperus)

Psyché (p Molière)

Psyche (f Storm)

An Psyche (v Wieland)

The Psychiatrist and Other Stories (f Machado de Assis)

Psychologia balnearia; oder, Glossen eines Badener Kurgastes (f Hesse)

Ptaki (f Schulz)

P'tit Bonhomme (f Verne)

Pu sa man (f Su)

La pubblica felicità per la restaurata salute dell'Imperatrice Regina nel 1767 (v Metastasio)

Pubis angelical (f Puig)

The Public Prosecutor and Other Plays (p Hochwälder)

El público (p García Lorca)

El público y Comedia sin título: Dos obras teatrales póstumas (p García Lorca)

La Puce à l'oreille (p Feydeau)

La Pucelle de Benouville (f Simenon)

La Pucelle d'Orléans (v Voltaire)

Pugachov (v Esenin)

I pugnalatori (f Sciascia)

La Puissance des morts (p Maeterlinck)

La Puissance du souvenir (f Simenon)

Le Puits aux images (f Aymé)

Le Puits de sainte Claire (f France)

Pułapka (p Różewicz)

Pulchérie (p Corneille)

I puntigli domestici (p Goldoni)

El purgatorio de san Patricio (p Calderón de la Barca)

Puriteinen en piraten (f Vestdijk)

Purumura (p Mori)

Pushkin Threefold: Narrative, Lyric, Polemic, and Ribald Verse (v Pushkin)

Pushkin's Fairy Tales (f Pushkin)

Puszták népe (f Illyés)

Put u raj (p Krleža)

La Putain respectueuse (p Sartre)

La putta onorata (p Goldoni)

Pygmalion (p Kaiser)

Pygmalion (p Rousseau)

Pygmalion (p Tawfiq Al-Hakim)

He pyle (v Ritsos)

Pyramides (v Ritsos)

Ritter, Dene, Voss (p Bernhard)
Rituelen (f Nooteboom)
Rivage (v Jacob)
Rivalen (p Zuckmayer)
Les Rivalités en province (f Balzac)
Riviera (p Molnár)
La Rivière sans repos (f Roy)
La rivolta dei poveri (p Buzzati)
The Road to the City: Two Novelettes (f Ginzburg)
La Robe prétexte (f Mauriac)
Robert der Teufel (p Nestroy)
Robert Guiskard (p Kleist)
Robert Motherwell, el Negro (v Alberti)
Robert und Guiscard (v Eichendorff)
Robert-le-diable (p Scribe)
Robert: Supplément à L'École des femmes (p Gide)
Robespierre (p Rolland)
Robur le Conquérant (f Verne)
Rockaby (p Beckett)
Rockaby and Other Short Pieces (p Beckett)
Röda rummet (f Strindberg)
Rodinka (f Sholokhov)
Rodinný večer (p Havel)
Rodogune, Princesse des Parthes (p Corneille)
Rodrich (f Fouqué)
Rodzina Połanieckich (f Sienkiewicz)
Le Roi Candaule (p Gide)
Le Roi de Boétie: nouvelles (f Jacob)
Le Roi des glaces (f Simenon)
Le Roi du Pacifique (f Simenon)
Le Roi s'amuse (p Hugo)
Un roi sans divertissement (f Giono)
Le Roi se meurt (p Ionesco)
Rokovye iaitsa (f Bulgakov)
Rokumeikan (p Mishima)
Rollende stenen, getijde (v Nooteboom)
Rolls Royce and Other Poems (v Bassani)
Rom (v Schlegel)
I Rom (p Strindberg)
Roma 1950: Diario (v Pasolini)
Roma, peligro para caminantes 1964–1967 (v Alberti)
Romagem de agravados (p Vicente)
Le Roman comique (f Scarron)
Le Roman de la momie (f Gautier)
Le Roman d'Elvire (p Dumas *père*)
Le Roman d'une dactylo (f Simenon)
Le Roman d'une femme (f Dumas *fils*)
Le Roman inachevé (v Aragon)
Roman Nights and Other Stories (f Pasolini)
Roman Poems (v Pasolini)
La romana (f Moravia)
Romance de ''Angélica y Medoro'' (v Góngora)
Romance de lobos (p Valle-Inclán)
Romancero del destierro (v Unamuno)
Romancero espiritual (v Vega Carpio)
Romances (v Góngora)
The Romances (f Gautier)
Romances de Coral Gables (v Jiménez)
Romances sans paroles (v Verlaine)
Romane, Erzählungen, Aufsätze (f Roth)

Les Romanesques (p Rostand)
Romantic Comedies (p Molnár)
Romantische Dichtungen (v Fouqué)
Romantische Dichtungen (f Tieck)
Romantische Lieder (v Hesse)
Romany (f Pil'niak)
Romanzen und Bilder (v Meyer)
Romanzen vom Rosenkranz (v Brentano)
Romanzen vom Thale Ronceval (v Fouqué)
Romanzero (v Heine)
Romanzi e novelle (f Deledda)
Romanzi e racconti (f Buzzati)
Romanzi Sardi (f Deledda)
Il romanzo della ruffiana (f Aretino)
Il romanzo di Ferrara (f Bassani)
Romeo and Juliet (p Neruda)
Roméo et Jeannette (p Anouilh)
Roméo et Juliette (p Cocteau)
Romeo und Juliet (p Goethe)
Romiossini and Other Poems (v Ritsos)
He Romiosyne (v Ritsos)
Römische Elegien (v Goethe)
Rommelpot van 't Hanekot (v Vondel)
Romolo ed Ersilia (p Metastasio)
Romulus (p Dumas *père*)
Romulus der Grosse (p Dürrenmatt)
Rondedans (v Bilderdijk)
Rondon-Tō (f Natsume)
Rōnen (f Akutagawa)
The Rope and Other Plays (p Plautus)
Rosa (f Hamsun)
La rosa de papel (p Valle-Inclán)
A rosa do povo (v Andrade)
La rosa en la balanza (v Marechal)
La rosa profunda (v Borges)
La rosa separada (v Neruda)
Rosamunde Floris (p Kaiser)
Rosario de sonetos líricos (v Unamuno)
Rosarium ex floribus vitae passionisque domini nostri Jesu Christi consertum (v Brant)
Las rosas andinas: Rimas y contra-rimas (v Darío)
The Rose and the Windows (v Rilke)
Rose Bernd (p Hauptmann)
Rose caduche (p Verga)
La Rose de François (v Cocteau)
Rose et Blanche (f Sand)
Le Rose et le vert; Mina de Vanghel (f Stendhal)
Le Rose et le vert, Mina de Vanghel, et autres nouvelles (f Stendhal)
La Rose publique (v Éluard)
Die Rosen der Einöde: Fünf Sätze für Ballet, Stimmen und Orchester (p Bernhard)
Rosenaltaret (v Södergran)
Der Rosenkavalier (p Hofmannsthal)
Le Rosier de Madame Husson (f Maupassant)
Roskam (v Vondel)
Rosmersholm (p Ibsen)
Rosmonda (p Goldoni)
Der Rossdieb zu Fünsing (p Sachs)
Rosshalde (f Hesse)
Der rote Hahn (p Hauptmann)

Unveiling (p Havel)
Unverhofft (p Nestroy)
Unwiederbringlich (f Fontane)
Der unzusammenhängende Zusammenhang (p Nestroy)
Uomini e no (f Vittorini)
L'uomo, la bestia, e la virtù (p Pirandello)
L'uomo che andrà in America (p Buzzati)
L'uomo che guarda (f Moravia)
L'uomo dal fiore in bocca (p Pirandello)
Uomo e donna (v Betti)
Uomo e galantuomo (p De Filippo)
L'uomo e il cane (f Cassola)
L'uomo prudente (p Goldoni)
Un uomo solo (f Cassola)
Ur klyvnadens tid (v Lo-Johansson)
Ura me tri harqe: triptik me një intermexo (f Kadare)
Uraniia (v Brodskii)
Uranus (f Aymé)
Urbain Grandier (p Dumas *père*)
Urfaust (p Dürrenmatt)
Úridivat (p Molnár)
Urna (v Belyi)
Ursule Mirouët (f Balzac)
Das Urteil (f Kafka)
Urzijn en Valentijn (v Bilderdijk)
L'Usage de la parole (f Sarraute)
L'Uscoque (f Sand)
'Usfur min al-Sharq (f Tawfiq Al-Hakim)
L'usignolo della chiesa cattolica (v Pasolini)
Uspravna zemlja (v Popa)
Uta nikki (v Mori)
Utage no ato (f Mishima)
Utakata no ki (f Mori)
Utolenie zhazhady (p Trifonov)
Utolenie zhazhdy (f Trifonov)
Utrennii narod: novaia kniga stikhov (v Evtushenko)
Utro delovogo cheloveka (p Gogol')
Utsukushi hoshi (f Mishima)
Utsukushii tabi (f Kawabata)
Utsukushisa to kanashimi to (f Kawabata)
Utwory poetyckie (v Miłosz)
Het uur u (v Nijhoff)
Het uur u gevolgd door een idylle (v Nijhoff)
Las uvas y el viento (v Neruda)
Uvazhaemye grazhdane (f Zoshchenko)
Uzurakago (f Natsume)
Va et vient: Dramaticule (p Beckett)
Vaaren (f Undset)
Les Vacances de Maigret (f Simenon)
La vaccaria (p Ruzzante [or Ruzante])
A vacsora (p Molnár)
Vaderlandsche oranjezucht (v Bilderdijk)
Vadim (f Lermontov)
Vagabondaggio (f Verga)
La Vagabonde (f Colette)
La Vagabonde (p Colette)
La Vagabonde (scr Colette)
Les Vaincus (p Rolland)
Valaki (p Molnár)
Valčík na rozloučenou (f Kundera)

Valda dikter (v Lagerkvist)
Valentine (f Sand)
Valentino (f Ginzburg)
Valerie, Die Sinnesänderung, und Der Weihnachtsbaum (f Fouqué)
La Valise trouvée (f Lesage)
Válka s mloky (f Čapek)
El valle de las hamacas (f Argueta)
Vällustingarna (f Lo-Johansson)
Vālmīki Pratibha (p Tagore)
Válogatott versei (v Illyés)
Válogatott versek (v Illyés)
Válogatott versek 1930–1940 (v Radnóti)
A valsa n.6 (p Rodrigues)
La Valse des toréadors (p Anouilh)
Valuable Nail: Selected Poems (v Eich)
Valvèdre (f Sand)
Le Vampire (p Dumas *père*)
Van een huys-man en een barbier (p Bredero)
Van en over alles en iedereen (f Couperus)
Van en over mijzelf en anderen (f Couperus)
Van oude menschen, de dingen die voorbijgaan (f Couperus)
Il Vangelo Secondo Matteo (p Pasolini)
Varia carmina (v Brant)
Várias histórias (f Machado de Assis)
Variété (p Mann)
Vårnatt (f Vesaas)
La Vase (p Ionesco)
Vassa Geleznova (p Adamov)
Vassa Zheleznova (p Gor'kii)
Vaste est la prison: Roman (f Djebar)
Der Vater (p Weiss)
Die Väter; oder, Knock Out (p Sternheim)
Vaterländische Schauspiele (p Fouqué)
Das Vaterunser, ein Psalm (v Klopstock)
À vau-l'eau (f Huysmans)
Le Vaurien (f Aymé)
Vautrin (p Balzac)
Věc Makropulos (p Čapek)
I vecchi compagni (f Cassola)
I vecchi e i giovani (f Pirandello)
Il vecchio bizzarro (p Goldoni)
Il vecchio della montagna (f Deledda)
Il vecchio e i fanciulli (f Deledda)
Vecher (v Akhmatova)
Vecher v Sorrente (p Turgenev)
Vechera na khutore bliz Dikan'ki (f Gogol')
Vechernii al'bom (v Tsvetaeva)
Vechnye temy (f Trifonov)
Vechnyi muzh (f Dostoevskii)
Ved rigets port (p Hamsun)
La vedova scaltra (p Goldoni)
La vedova spiritosa (p Goldoni)
Vefarinn mikli frá Kasmír (f Laxness)
Vegetation (v Ponge)
Il vegliando (f Svevo)
VeHayah he'Akov leMishor (f Agnon)
Veil of Shame: The Role of Women in the Modern Fiction of North Africa and the Arab World (f Accad)
La Veillée Allemande (p Dumas *père*)